THE OXFORD COMPANION TO IRISH HISTORY

SECOND EDITION

EDITED BY S. J. CONNOLLY

OXFORD
UNIVERSITY PRESS

Great Clarendon Street, Oxford OX2 6DP

Oxford University Press is a department of the University of Oxford.
It furthers the University's objective of excellence in research, scholarship,
and education by publishing worldwide in

Oxford New York

Auckland Cape Town Dar es Salaam Hong Kong Karachi
Kuala Lumpur Madrid Melbourne Mexico City Nairobi
New Delhi Shanghai Taipei Toronto

With offices in

Argentina Austria Brazil Chile Czech Republic France Greece
Guatemala Hungary Italy Japan Poland Portugal Singapore
South Korea Switzerland Thailand Turkey Ukraine Vietnam

Oxford is a registered trade mark of Oxford University Press
in the UK and in certain other countries

Published in the United States
by Oxford University Press Inc., New York

First edition published 1998
Second edition published 2002
Published as an Oxford University Press paperback 2004
Published as an Oxford Paperback Reference paperback 2007

British Library Cataloguing in Publication Data
Data available

Library of Congress Cataloging in Publication Data
Data available

Typeset by SPI Publisher Services, Pondicherry, India
Printed in Great Britain
on acid-free paper by
Ashford Colour Press Limited, Gosport, Hampshire

ISBN 978-0-19-923483-7

1 3 5 7 9 10 8 6 4 2

Contents

List of Maps

Preface

THE appearance of a second edition provides the opportunity for a variety of additions and improvements. Two areas in particular which were inadequately covered in the first edition are now given fuller treatment. These are the visual arts and Irish prehistory. I have also expanded the coverage of literary figures, while avoiding any attempt to duplicate the universal coverage of this area offered in the *Oxford Companion to Irish Literature*. Entries dealing with the recent past have been revised to take account of events since 1997; this includes biographical entries on two important political figures no longer alive. In addition other entries have been revised to take account of more recent research, update bibliographical references, and correct errors pointed out, with varying degrees of kindness, by reviewers, colleagues, and correspondents.

S. J. CONNOLLY

February 2001

Preface to the First Edition

'THIS volume will serve its purpose if it proves a useful companion to ordinary everyday readers of English literature.' In these modest terms Sir Paul Harvey introduced the first and most celebrated of the Oxford Companions. Six decades later, as the range of the series expands to include Irish history, the notion of 'the ordinary everyday reader' is rather more problematic than it was in 1932. Yet the central conception behind the present volume remains essentially the same: that anyone with a question to ask about a significant individual, event, or institution in the Irish past should be able to search here with a reasonable prospect of finding at least the beginnings of an answer. There is also the hope that, as with Sir Paul's original, the network of cross-references and allusion built into the design will prove to have its own momentum: that for some at least one query will lead on to another, so that the Companion becomes a book to explore rather than merely consult. The nature of the volume requires that the majority of entries should be on fairly predictable subjects. But there are also topics that have not previously figured in standard histories, and that even specialists may find new and revealing. With more conventional subjects, too, there is at least the possibility that a different arrangement, cutting across conventional boundaries of sub-discipline and chronology, will suggest new perspectives. Even the necessarily rigid constraints of space, all too often requiring contributors to attempt what one aptly described as the equivalent of a *haiku*, may perhaps encourage a clarity of definition less easily achieved in more extended treatments.

To take on a project of this kind means embracing the unavoidable limitations as well as the possibilities. Any feasible one-volume compendium must involve selection and compression. There are thus no prizes for detecting regrettable omissions in what follows; the real test is whether, on a significant scale, what has been included is self-evidently of lesser importance than what has been left out. In particular it was necessary to accept from an early stage that the *Companion* could not be a dictionary of Irish biography. The original list of individuals seeming to require an entry would by itself have accounted for well over half the projected volume. The revised selection attempts to combine two aims: to include those figures about whom users of the volume are most likely to want to enquire, and to maintain some sort of balance between the different areas of life—political, cultural, intellectual, religious, economic—with which the volume tries to deal. A substantial number of individuals not covered in their own right are identified, with brief biographical details, in entries where their names occur. There are also entries on leading families, both Gaelic and Anglo-Irish, picking out both members important in their own right and the principal links in the chain of succession.

The selection of entries has also been significantly influenced by the existence of a separate *Oxford Companion to Irish Literature*, edited by Professor R. J. Welch and published in 1996. There seemed little point in attempting what would inevitably be a more superficial general coverage of the field of literary history. Instead, the topic is approached in two specialist entries: Dr Patrick Maume's mini-essay on the interaction between literature and history, and Dr Nicholas Williams's survey of the main developments in literature in Irish from the early middle ages to the present. Coverage of individual authors is confined to those, such as Swift and Yeats, whose influence and activities extended beyond the purely literary, along with a few others, such as Carleton and Somerville and Ross, chosen because of the frequency with which historians have turned to them as observers of the society in which they lived.

Where chronology is concerned, brief entries on the earliest period of human settlement are followed by fuller treatments of the early medieval, medieval, early modern, and modern periods, with the density of coverage increasing gradually as one moves forward in time. There is no fixed terminal date. Entries on major themes, movements, and institutions take the analysis up to the time of writing. On the other hand, there are no entries on living persons, and the latest specific event to be given an entry of its own is the Anglo-Irish agreement of 1985. The aim is a volume that does not duck the challenge of writing about the recent past, but that does not pretend to pass judgement on events and individuals whose history is still unfolding.

The Irish past, whether recent or more distant, is a peculiarly contentious one. To long-standing attempts to redefine its lineaments in the service of one or other of the island's political traditions has been added a more recent debate (see the entry for 'history and historians', below) on the extent to which the pursuit of a neutral, value-free history may have introduced its own distortions and evasions. The purpose of this *Companion* is to open doors, not to close them. Contributors dealing with contested areas have been asked to ensure that differences in interpretation are fully and fairly represented. They have not been discouraged from making their own views explicit, and alert readers will thus discover what should in this context be taken as reassuring variations in emphasis and evaluation. It should also be noted that the inclusion of a headword does not necessarily commit either editor or contributor to an endorsement of its validity as a term of analysis. On the contrary, authors dealing with labels such as 'gaelicization' or 'constructive unionism' have been as concerned to point up their limitations as to explain what they are taken to mean. The inclusion of such entries is further recognition of the extent to which all interpretations are products of a particular context, requiring constant reassessment and revision—the continuing dialogue between past and present that keeps history alive.

S. J. Connolly

April 1997

Acknowledgements

The preparation of the first edition of the *Companion* was aided by grants from a number of sources. A scheme financed by the European Structural Fund enabled me, at an early stage in the research, to draw on the assistance of Mr Caoimhín Ó Murchadha in extracting from the *Dictionary of National Biography* a classified list of possible subjects for biographical entries. The University of Ulster agreed to use funds from the bequest of the late T. K. Daniel to employ Dr Hiram Morgan as a research officer in the School of Modern History. During the time he was associated with the project, Dr Morgan assisted in the last stages of the compilation of the headword list and undertook much of the paperwork associated with commissioning entries from contributors. He also wrote a substantial proportion of the entries relating to the early modern period. I should also like to acknowledge gratefully a personal research grant towards the costs of travel and research awarded by the British Academy.

Most of the work on the *Companion* was done while I was a member of the Department of History at the University of Ulster. I am grateful to my colleagues there for the mixture of good will and bracing sarcasm with which they monitored the project's ups and downs. In particular I must mention Professor T. G. Fraser, a head of department without equal in his commitment to upholding values of scholarship, humanity, and the promotion of learning at a time when all three had become increasingly easy to lose sight of within our system of higher education. The work was finished following my move to the School of Modern History at The Queen's University of Belfast, to whose members I am grateful for their forbearance towards what in the last few months was an increasingly distracted new colleague.

At Oxford University Press I should like to thank Michael Cox, who invited me to undertake the project; Pam Coote, who maintained remarkable calm as an agreed timetable slipped to the very edge of the acceptable; Wendy Tuckey, who coped with good-humoured efficiency with the tangled process of commissioning and monitoring contributors; and Alison Jones, who took over the last stages of the volume's production. Edwin and Jackie Pritchard, as copy editors, devoted scrupulous care to a manuscript submitted in what must have been an irritatingly piecemeal fashion. In relation to the second edition, I must thank Edwin and Jackie Pritchard, who once again gave expert attention to the text, and Rebecca Collins, who steered us through the process of revision from start to finish.

The compilation of a *Companion* covering the whole field of Irish history took me far, at times alarmingly far, beyond the bounds of my own expertise. I am most grateful to my editorial advisers, Professor R. V. Comerford, Dr M. T. Flanagan, Professor Robin Frame, and Dr Katharine Simms, for their advice and assistance at every stage, from the first version of the headword list to the scrutiny of draft entries submitted. I am also grateful to the individual contributors for undertaking what were often heroic feats of survey, condensation, or both, and in many cases for completing these in the face of numerous other commitments. Closer to home I must thank Mavis Bracegirdle, for sharing four years with yet another historical project, and Helen Connolly, for her assistance in preparing part of the final manuscript.

Editorial Advisers

Early Medieval Ireland Marie Therese Flanagan, Queen's University, Belfast

Gaelic Ireland Katharine Simms, Trinity College, Dublin

Medieval Ireland R. F. Frame, University of Durham

Modern Ireland Richard Vincent Comerford, National University of Ireland, Maynooth

Contributors

DHA	D. H. Akenson, Professor of History, Queen's University, Kingston, Ontario
JHA	J. H. Andrews, formerly Associate Professor of Geography, Trinity College, Dublin
MA	Martyn Anglesea, Keeper of Fine Art, Museums and Galleries of Northern Ireland
JA	Joost Augusteijn, Lecturer in European History, Leiden University
TB	Terry Barry, Senior Lecturer in Medieval History, Trinity College, Dublin
JB	Jonathan Bell, Head Curator, Ulster Folk and Transport Museum
EB	Edel Bhreathnach, Post-doctoral Research Fellow, National University of Ireland, Galway
AB	Andrew Bielenberg, Lecturer in History, University College, Cork
EEB	Eileen Black, Curator of Fine Art, Ulster Museum, Belfast
CB	Cormac Bourke, Curator of Medieval Antiquities, Ulster Museum, Belfast
JBr	John Bradley, Lecturer in Late Medieval Irish History, National University of Ireland, Maynooth
PAB	Paul Brand, All Souls College, Oxford
BMSC	Bruce Campbell, Professor of Medieval Economic History, Queen's University, Belfast
JPC	John Price Carey, Lecturer in Early and Medieval Irish, University College, Cork
TMC-E	Thomas M. Charles-Edwards, Professor of Celtic and Fellow of Jesus College, University of Oxford
BNC	Bronagh Ní Chonaill, research student, Dept. of Medieval History, Trinity College, Dublin
CC	Caitriona Clear, Lecturer in History, National University of Ireland, Galway
JC	John Coakley, Lecturer in Politics, University College, Dublin
PC	Peter Collins, St Mary's University College, Belfast
RVC	Richard Vincent Comerford, Professor of Modern History, National University of Ireland, Maynooth
PhC	Philomena Connolly, Archivist, National Archives, Dublin
SC	S. J. Connolly, Professor of Irish History, Queen's University, Belfast
EMC	E. Margaret Crawford, Senior Research Fellow, Centre for Social Research, Queen's University, Belfast
VC	Virginia Crossman, Lecturer in History, University of Staffordshire
BC	Bernadette Cunningham, Deputy Librarian, Royal Irish Academy, Dublin
MED	Mary Daly, Associate Professor of History, University College, Dublin
DD	David Dickson, Senior Lecturer in Modern History, Trinity College, Dublin
TPD	Terence Dolan, Professor in Old and Middle English, University College, Dublin
SD	Seán Duffy, Lecturer in Medieval History, Trinity College, Dublin
MD	Mairead Dunlevy, Keeper, Art and Industrial Division, The National Museum of Ireland, Collins Barracks

Contributors

SGE	Steven Ellis, Associate Professor of History, National University of Ireland, Galway
CAE	Revd Canon C. A. Empey, St Anne's Vicarage, Dublin
CE	Colmán Etchingham, Lecturer in Medieval Irish History and Old Irish, National University of Ireland, Maynooth
PF	Paul Ferguson, Map Librarian, Trinity College Library, Dublin
FF	Fiona Fitzsimons, Eneclann Ltd, Trinity College, Dublin
MTF	Marie Therese Flanagan, Senior Lecturer in History, Queen's University, Belfast
AF	Alan Ford, Professor of Theology, Nottingham University
RFF	Robin Frame, Professor of History, University of Durham
TGF	T. G. Fraser, Professor of History, University of Ulster
RAG	R. A. Gailey, formerly Director, Ulster Folk and Transport Museum
NG	Neal Garnham, Senior Research Fellow, University of Ulster
FG	Frank Geary, Senior Lecturer in Economics, University of Ulster
RG	Raymond Gillespie, Senior Lecturer in Modern History, National University of Ireland, Maynooth
PHG	Peter Gray, Lecturer in History, University of Southampton
DNH	David Hempton, Professor of History, Boston University
ACH	A. C. Hepburn, Professor of Modern Irish History, University of Sunderland
RJH	Robert Heslip, Curator in History, Ulster Museum, Belfast
RFGH	Very Revd Professor R. F. G. Holmes, Union Theological College, Belfast
SJSI	S. J. S. Ickringill, Senior Lecturer in History, University of Ulster
AJ	Alvin Jackson, Professor of Modern Irish History, Queen's University, Belfast
KJ	Keith Jeffery, Professor of Modern History, University of Ulster
DJ	David Johnson, Senior Lecturer in Economic and Social History, Queen's University, Belfast
WJ	Walford Johnson, Senior Lecturer in Economics, University of Ulster
DBJ	Dorothy Johnston, Keeper of Manuscripts, University of Nottingham
HK	Hugh Kearney, Amundson Professor of History, University of Pittsburgh
FK	Fergus Kelly, School of Celtic Studies, Dublin Institute for Advanced Studies
JK	James Kelly, Lecturer in History, St Patrick's College, Drumcondra, Dublin
LK	Liam Kennedy, Professor of Economic and Social History, Queen's University, Belfast
SBK	S. B. Kennedy, Head of Fine and Applied Art, Ulster Museum, Belfast
VK	Vincent Kinane, Librarian, Dept. of Early Printed Books, Trinity College, Dublin
M-LL	Marie-Louise Legg, Honorary Teaching Fellow in History, Birkbeck College, London
JnL	John Logan, Lecturer in History, University of Limerick
JL	James Loughlin, Reader in History, University of Ulster
SMcC	Sinéad McCartan, Curator of Prehistoric Antiquities, Ulster Museum, Belfast
DMcM	Deirdre McMahon, Lecturer in History, Mary Immaculate College, Limerick
GMacN	Gearóid MacNiocaill, Professor of History, University College, Galway
NMacQ	Norrie MacQueen, Senior Lecturer in Political Science, University of Dundee
ELM	Elizabeth Malcolm, Professor of Irish Studies, University of Melbourne

JPM	J. P. Mallory, Reader in Archaeology, Queen's University, Belfast
EAM	Dr Elizabeth Matthew, Honorary Research Fellow, University of Reading
PM	Patrick Maume, Research Fellow, Dept. of Politics, Queen's University, Belfast
KMa	Kim Mawhinney, Curator of Applied Art, Ulster Museum, Belfast
BM	Bernard Meehan, Keeper of Manuscripts, Trinity College, Dublin
MNíM	Máire Ní Mhaonaigh, University Lecturer in the Dept. of Anglo-Saxon, Norse and Celtic and Fellow of St John's College, Cambridge
KM	Kenneth Milne, formerly Principal, Church of Ireland College of Education, and historiographer for the Church of Ireland
HM	Hiram Morgan, Lecturer in History, University College, Cork
RM	Rachel Moss, Lecturer, Dept. of History of Art, Trinity College, Dublin
CNOC	Colmán N. Ó Clabaigh, OSB, Glenstal Abbey, Co. Limerick, and St Benet's Hall, Oxford
TO'C	Thomas O'Connor, Lecturer in Modern History, National University of Ireland, Maynooth
EO'H	Eunan O'Halpin, Professor of Contemporary Irish History, Trinity College, Dublin
PO	Philip Ollerenshaw, Principal Lecturer in British Economic and Business History, University of the West of England
TO'L	Thomas O'Loughlin, Senior Lecturer in Theology, University of Wales, Lampeter
MO	Michael Open, Administrator, Queen's Film Theatre, Belfast
VP	Vivienne Pollock, Curator in History, Ulster Museum, Belfast
LJP	Lindsay Proudfoot, Reader in Geography, Queen's University, Belfast
ABS	A. B. Scott, Emeritus Professor of Latin, Queen's University, Belfast
RS	Richard Sharpe, Reader in Diplomatic, Wadham College, University of Oxford
KS	Katharine Simms, Senior Lecturer in Medieval History, Trinity College, Dublin
BGCS	Brendan Smith, Lecturer in Medieval History, University of Bristol
JS	J. P. Smyth, Lecturer in Sociology and Social Policy, Queen's University, Belfast
DJS	David Sturdy, Professor of History, University of Ulster
CS	Catherine Swift, Lecturer in Medieval History and Old Irish, National University of Ireland, Maynooth
JT	John Turpin, Professor of the History of Art, National College of Art and Design, Dublin
RW	Richard Warner, Keeper of Archaeology and Ethnography and Head of Human History, Ulster Museum, Belfast
HW	Harry White, Professor of Music, University College, Dublin
NJAW	Nicholas Williams, Lecturer in Irish, University College, Dublin

Note to the Reader

The organizing principle of the volume is an alphabetical listing of headwords. These include personal and family names, events, institutions and movements, titles of books or other literary works, contemporary slogans and catch phrases, as well as modern terms that reflect the preoccupations and debates of historians. The Subject Index offers an analytical guide to the volume, in the form of a list of the most important headwords, grouped by category. Readers who would like to orient themselves with a brief chronological narrative may wish to turn to Professor Kearney's entry on 'England'—a suggestion that itself is testimony to some of the contradictions built into Ireland's history.

Cross-referencing, indicated by an asterisk (*), has been guided as far as possible by common sense. This means that in some cases asterisks have been added to what are in fact slight variants of the actual headword (e.g. '*Celtic' where the headword is 'Celts'). It also means that cross-references have been inserted where they seem most likely to assist the reader, rather than mechanically wherever a headword occurs in the text. Thus, for example, we have not asterisked every reference to Dublin, to the army, or to women.

Irish personal names (see 'surnames') have a complex history, which has presented a number of problems in terms of the arrangement of entries. Readers should note the following:

(i) Names in 'Mc' and 'Mac' are ordered as if spelled 'Mac' and grouped together before other headwords beginning with 'M'.

(ii) However, it should be noted that surnames began to be used only in the eleventh century. Before then 'A mac B' (distinguished by lower-case 'mac') meant that A was literally the son of B. Biographical entries from this period are grouped under Christian name: thus Áedán mac Gabráin appears under 'A', not 'Mac'.

(iii) For similar reasons early English (or 'Norman', though see the entry on this label) names are written with lower-case 'f' for 'fitz'. But these are nevertheless, following the usual convention, listed under 'F'.

(iv) Names beginning with 'de' are ordered according to the main part of the name, for example de Lacy under 'L', de Valera under 'V'.

For the period up to 1169 personal names are given in the Irish form, with anglicized versions in brackets. Thereafter they are given in the anglicized form, with Gaelic versions, where necessary, in brackets. Those whose careers straddle that borderline have had to be allocated to one side or the other: thus 'Diarmait Mac Murchada (Dermot MacMurrough)', but 'Rory O'Connor (Ruaidrí Ua Conchobair)'.

Place names have been given in their contemporary form, with modern equivalents supplied where appropriate, for example 'King's Country (Offaly)'. Following a commonly adopted compromise, we refer to the city of Derry and the county of Londonderry.

The bibliographies attached to longer entries are necessarily selective. Preference has been given to works that offer an accessible overall introduction, or provide guidance on further reading.

Entries are signed with initials, which can be identified from the list of contributors (p. xv). Unsigned entries are the work of the general editor. Where he has contributed to composite entries, this is indicated by the initials 'SC'.

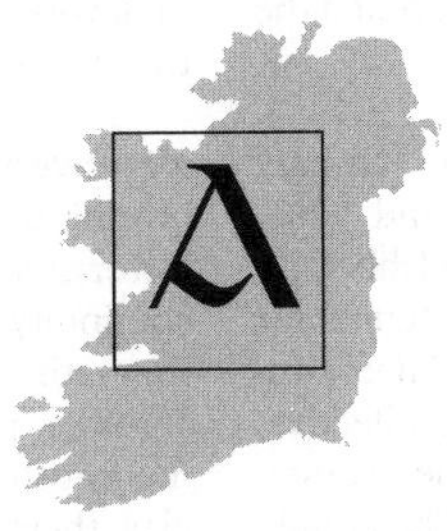

Abbey theatre, Dublin, created in 1904 as a successor to the Irish Literary theatre founded in Dublin 1899 by littérateurs (including *Yeats, Lady *Gregory, and Edward Martyn (1859–1923)) and amateur actors wishing to produce an Irish national drama in opposition to commercial theatre. Initially envisaged as a poetic theatre, the Abbey became dominated by easily stereotyped forms of 'realism'. Much of its history has been dominated by conflict between its rival inspirations, patriotism (often linked to puritanism) and artistic excellence. This was exacerbated by a need for financial support due to its non-commercial nature. Two of the Abbey's most generous private patrons, Edward Martyn and Annie Horniman, were alienated by political and religious disagreements, and the theatre survived on a shoestring until the new *Irish Free State government in 1924 made it the first state-subsidized theatre in the English-speaking world. This brought fresh constraints, at first limited by the reputation of Yeats. The founding directors also displayed a certain unresponsiveness to new forms of stylistic experimentation; Sean O'Casey was defended against nationalist protests over *The Plough and the Stars* (1926), but alienated by the turning down of his Expressionist-influenced play *The Silver Tassie* (1928).

O'Casey's departure is seen in retrospect as a major landmark in a process of artistic decline exacerbated by the demise of the founders and seen as reaching its nadir in the 1940s and 1950s under the direction of Ernest *Blythe. Since the late 1960s Abbey standards have improved but it is still frequently criticized as unadventurous. PM

abduction of heiresses became a major concern during the 18th century. Although some such episodes were collusive, intended to circumvent parental opposition, most were genuine kidnappings, intended to force the victim into an immediate wedding ceremony or to compromise her so thoroughly that marriage to the perpetrator became her only option. *Froude's allegations that abduction was an 'act of war' by Catholics against the Protestant landed class were rejected by *Lecky in a celebrated controversy. Modern accounts support Lecky in attributing abduction primarily to economic motives. By the end of the 18th century the spread of new standards of civility had largely ended abduction among the gentry. But the carrying off of well-dowried farmers' daughters by smallholders and labourers remained common in the first half of the 19th century.

Abercorn (Hamilton). The family's Irish history began when **James Hamilton** of Linlithgow (d. 1618), created 1st earl of Abercorn in the Scottish peerage in 1606, was granted lands in Co. Tyrone. His son **James Hamilton**, the 2nd earl, was created Baron Strabane in 1616, but in 1633 passed this title, along with the Irish estate, to his brother **Claude Hamilton** (d. 1638). Claude's grandson **Claude Hamilton** (d. 1690) succeeded to the Abercorn title as 4th earl around 1680. A Catholic, he supported *James II and was killed in action during the *Williamite War. Although the estates and title were thus forfeited, Claude's Protestant brother **Charles Hamilton** (d. 1701) obtained a reversal of the attainder and succeeded as 5th earl in 1692. **John James Hamilton** (1756–1818), the 9th earl, created marquis of Abercorn in 1790, built up a following of active and capable members in the House of Commons during the 1790s, and had aspirations to be lord lieutenant. **James Hamilton** (1811–85), the 2nd marquis, became duke of Abercorn in 1868.

Abercromby, Sir Ralph (1734–1801), a highly regarded Scottish soldier, appointed commander-in-chief of the Irish army in October 1797. Horrified by what he found he issued a controversial general order (26 Feb. 1798) denouncing the indiscipline of the government forces. He was also attacked for his cautious approach to the disarming of the *United Irish movement in Leinster and resigned in March, opening the way for the unrestrained military repression that preceded the *insurrection of 1798.

Aberdeen, John Campbell Gordon, 7th earl of (1847–1934), *lord lieutenant of Ireland, 1886, 1905–15. Strongly influenced by his wife Ishbel, he sought to make the viceregal palace a centre for reconciliation and economic progress. Their contributions varied between the modestly effective, the harmless, and the risible. Not in the cabinet, Aberdeen was given no political role. The couple retired, reluctantly but to the delight of *Birrell, in February 1915. They published two volumes of memoirs, *We Twa* (1925) and *More Cracks with 'We Twa'* (1929). ACH

abjuration, oaths of. The first such oath was a formula abjuring the supremacy of the pope and other Catholic doctrines imposed by the *Cromwellian regime in 1657. The second, introduced in England in 1702, declared Queen Anne to be rightful sovereign and denied the title of James II's heirs (see REVOLUTION OF 1688). It was imposed on Irish office holders, teachers, and lawyers, and on clergy of the established church, from 1703, and on Irish voters from 1704. From 1709 it could be demanded from any adult male by magistrates, and was also to be taken by priests registered under the act of 1704 (see PENAL LAWS). The determined refusal to comply of all but a handful of priests made this last requirement impossible to enforce. The oath was likewise resisted by some Presbyterian ministers, on the grounds that it endorsed a prelatical church establishment.

abortion, outlawed in Ireland under the Offences against the Person Act (1861), has become a significant political issue only in recent years. In 1983 a 'pro-life' group campaigned successfully for a referendum that added to the *constitution a clause asserting the mother's and the foetus's equal right to life. In 1985 the Society for the Protection of the Unborn Child took legal action against two Dublin clinics which counselled women and sometimes referred them to Great Britain for abortions. In 1986 these clinics were ordered to cease counselling. In 1992 the Supreme Court overturned a High Court decision to prevent a 14-year-old girl pregnant as a result of rape from leaving the country to get an abortion. A constitutional amendment recognizing the right to travel and the right to information was carried by a referendum later that year. In Northern Ireland, where the British Abortion Act of 1967 was never enacted, the united opposition of the churches deterred government from trying to clarify the legal position following the suspension of devolved government, and patients are referred to clinics elsewhere in the United Kingdom. CC

absentees. Concern over the failure of Irish proprietors to reside in the country has a long history, somewhat misleading in its apparent continuity. In the medieval period, particularly in the 14th century, Irish parliaments denounced absentee proprietors for taking resources out of the lordship, neglecting their lands, and failing to play their part in defence. In 1360 a council at Kilkenny complained to Edward III that 'five sixths of the land and more' were in absentee hands. This was an exaggeration, but a pardonable one: the greatest absentee, Edward's son *Lionel of Clarence, was by marriage earl of Ulster and lord of Connacht, and had further lands in Kilkenny and Munster. Between 1297 and 1380 a series of royal ordinances threatened absentees with sequestration of anything from a proportion of their revenues to the lands themselves if these were not defended. Such measures were patchily applied, for many absentees had influence at court. This produced added friction.

The ill repute of absentee landlords in later times has given these medieval criticisms resonance. They need careful handling. From 1171 some of those who acquired Irish lordships—such as the *Marshals, *Lacys, and *Verdons—already had extensive lands in England and Wales, and even Normandy. Like all medieval magnates, they were peripatetic, and hence absent from most of their estates most of the time. This was taken for granted; possession of widespread centres of influence was a mark of status, and one of the ways in which regional societies were tied to the court. Many lesser proprietors, both lay and ecclesiastical, also held lands on both sides of the Irish Sea. Consciousness of absenteeism as a problem appeared later, in particular circumstances. From the 1240s English law, which in the absence of a male heir divided lands equally between heiresses, led to repeated partitions. The Marshal heiresses, for instance, carried diminishing fragments of Leinster to other English noble families, to whom they might be of limited significance. A clearer distinction emerged between lords who were normally resident and those who were usually absent; the former resented the latter and used them as scapegoats when explaining the condition of Ireland to the king. This happened at a time when frontiers were contracting, revenues declining, and defence costs rising. Absentee lordship became a problem as much for absentees as for their critics. Economic and political pressures in the later 14th century led many, including the Despensers who sold Kilkenny Castle to the

Butlers, to liquidate their assets. The *Mortimers, whose vast Irish lordships retained their interest, were the major exception.

The supposed ill effects of absentee landlordism reappeared as a major cause of concern in the 18th century. Absentee *landlords, generally assumed to be resident in England, were pilloried as a parasitic class who neglected their estates and drained the country of capital. Estimates of the sums remitted annually in rents to absentees rose from £325,000 in 1729, when Thomas Prior's *A List of the Absentees of Ireland, and the Yearly Value of their Estates and Incomes Spent Abroad* first appeared, to Arthur *Young's 1779 estimate of £730,000. Yet this latter figure was still less than 14 per cent of the total annual rental of over £5.3 million. Absenteeism was also a prominent part of the more radical assault on landlordism mounted in the mid- and late 19th century. Yet a return of 1872 showed that 46 per cent of estates had resident landlords, while the owners of another 25 per cent lived elsewhere in Ireland.

Absenteeism was in any case a complex phenomenon. Owners of more than one property had no choice but to be absentees somewhere, while others were called away by the demands of politics or office. Many landlords who were absentees from their main Irish estates remained either seasonally or permanently resident elsewhere in Ireland. Most important of all, absenteeism was not synonymous with bad estate management: levels of landlord investment depended on personal attitudes, not residence.

Frame, R., *English Lordship in Ireland 1318–1361* (1982)
Vaughan, W. E., *Landlords and Tenants in Mid-Victorian Ireland* (1994)

RFF/LJP

absolutism, a political ideology which gave the crown supreme power by divine right, was developing in all western European monarchies in the 16th and 17th centuries. Its practice by the Tudors and Stuarts is often referred to as 'arbitrary government', since it was never constitutionally sanctioned. Masked in England by the importance of parliament and traditions of the common law, the growth and abuse of royal power was more evident in Ireland.

Immensely powerful *lords deputy had a standing *army and regularly resorted to commissions of *martial law despite their stated intention to establish the common law. They abused the royal right to household purveyance to maintain the garrison and under the pretext of reform attempted to establish a permanent taxation (*composition) which would have obviated the need to call *parliament. Parliaments, constrained as they were by *Poynings's Law, became infrequent after 1534 and extensive use was made of *privy council proclamations. In 1605 proclamations were used to extend English legislation on *recusancy to Ireland and the resulting *mandates were upheld by Sir John *Davies and the law officers—one of several rulings which overturned the liberties and rights of both Gaelic Irish and *Old English. The apotheosis of this approach was *Wentworth's policy of 'thorough' in the 1630s. HM

accountancy. The term accountant was first used in Ireland in 1761; the first accountancy partnership was formed in the 1790s. In 1888 the Institute of Chartered Accountants in Ireland was founded by the leading accountants from Dublin, Belfast, and Cork. Unlike the Institute of Chartered Accountants of England and Wales, whose members could only practise their profession in those two countries, members of the Irish institute, who were automatically admitted when they had passed the institute's examination, were free to practise throughout the world. Although the institute attempted to gain overall control of the profession in Ireland it failed to achieve this. The Society of Incorporated Accountants in Ireland, founded in 1901, and the Association of Certified and Corporate Accountants both operated as Irish branches of British organizations. MED

acre, a unit of territorial measurement that, in Ireland as elsewhere, could have varying meanings. In different contexts an 'acre' could refer to a parcel of land physically marked out on the landscape, a notional subdivision of a larger unit such as a ploughland or *ballyboe, or a measured area of standard size. Of the several different measured acres in use, that based on a perch of 21 feet (1 acre=160 square perches) was used in the plantation of *Ulster, and became established as the 'Irish' or 'plantation' acre, equal to 1.62 statute acres. The Cunningham acre, of Scottish origin and used in Ulster, was equal to 1.29 statute acres.

Adair, Patrick (d. 1694), *Presbyterian minister and historian. He was the son of the Revd William Adair of Ayr, who had administered the *Solemn League and Covenant in Ulster, and nephew and son-in-law of Sir Robert Adair, a major Scottish landowner in mid-Antrim. He was ordained and installed in Cairncastle, Co. Antrim, in 1646 by the Army Presbytery. Deposed for nonconformity in 1661, he spent three months under house arrest in Lord *Massereene's home in Dublin following *Blood's plot. In 1674 he was called to the Rosemary Street congregation in Belfast. He frequently represented Irish Presbyterians in negotiations with governments. He travelled to London to greet *William III in 1689 and welcomed him to Ireland in 1690. He was one of the original trustees of the *regium donum. His invaluable *True Narrative of the Rise and Progress of the Presbyterian Church in Ireland* covers only the period 1640–70. The manuscript was lost but was discovered and published in 1866, edited by W. D. Killen. Adair presented the Scottish settlements and Munro's army as the means used by God to bring true religion and increased happiness to the poor, feckless, idolatrous Irish. RFGH

admiralty court, established in Dublin in the 1570s as a subordinate jurisdiction of the English high court of admiralty which was anxious to assert authority in Ireland where *pirates were selling stolen goods without interference.

Ambrose Forth (d. 1610) was appointed judge but had to compete with other maritime jurisdictions claimed by *chancery, by the *lord deputy, by the *provincial presidents, and by various coastal towns and landowners. Furthermore London retained the lucrative right to issue letters of marque to privateers who were authorized to sell their prizes only in English ports.

Adam *Loftus, Forth's successor from 1612, benefited from the Irish statute against pirates and received the assistance of a marshal and registrar of the court. Unfortunately London was now appointing and running vice-admirals and vice-admiralty courts round the Irish coast without reference to his court. However, all admiralty courts gained from a series of judicial rulings against ports and landlords claiming admiralty rights.

In the 1640s the *Confederate Catholics demanded an independent Irish admiralty court. After the court was revived by the Commonwealth in 1656, the jurisdictional inconsistencies continued with the vice-admiralty of Munster vying with Dublin as late as 1745. The Dublin court eventually achieved independence from London following *legislative independence, but stagnated during Sir Jonah *Barrington's long absences in the 1810s and 1820s and by the 1860s was barely judging a dozen cases a year. The Admiralty Court (Ireland) Act (1867) overhauled its procedures and provided a properly salaried staff. HM

Adomnán (**Eunan;** Latin **Adamnanus**) (*c.*628–704), from the same Donegal family as *Colum Cille, was *Iona's ninth abbot (679). Adomnán is best remembered for his *Vita Columbae* (Life of Colum Cille) which, despite hagiographical commonplaces, is a major source for the history of Iona and insular *monasticism. Its account of royal anointing influenced the development of kingship in Europe. His other book, *On the Holy Places*, deals with places mentioned in the Bible. Posing as the account of a pilgrim 'gallic bishop, Arculf', it is a complex manual for solving exegetical problems using geographical knowledge. His medieval reputation as a scholar, one of the few Irish writers who was labelled 'illustrious', rested on this work. It was one of the first early Irish works in print. His diplomatic and legal interests took him to Northumbria on behalf of Irish captives, and to the Synod of Birr (697) which produced the *Lex innocentium*, his **cáin*, protecting women, children, and non-combatants. He compiled a series of *Canones*, and is the latest-named authority in some recensions of the *Collectio canonum Hibernensis* (which he may have helped formulate). He is praised by *Bede for accepting the Roman calculation of Easter. TO'L

adoption. Legal adoption was introduced in England and Wales in 1926 and in Northern Ireland in 1929. In independent Ireland legislation was delayed by the strength of traditional attitudes to the family, deference to Catholic teaching on the rights of natural parents, and fears that Protestant couples might obtain control of Catholic children. An act of 1952 permitted the adoption of orphan and illegitimate children by couples of the same religious denomination. The latter restriction was removed in 1974, having been ruled unconstitutional in excluding adoptive parents of mixed religion, but the ban on adopting legitimate children remains.

adventurers, see CROMWELLIAN LAND SETTLEMENT.

Adventurers, Act for, passed by the English parliament in February 1642, in a notable assertion of its claim to legislate for Ireland, in order to finance the suppression of the *rising of 1641. Investors, known as adventurers, were to subscribe towards the cost of the reconquest, their subscriptions to be converted into parcels of Irish land out of 2.5 million acres to be confiscated in equal amounts from each province. Despite huge propaganda, only a third of the projected £1 million was ever raised. This act, which by its nature prejudiced the possibility of a negotiated resolution of the Irish war, was the basis of the *Cromwellian land settlement. HM

Áedán mac Gabráin (d. *c.*606), king of Dál Riata, is the earliest Irish ruler in Scotland to be more than a name. Iona entries in the *Annals of*

Ulster record his fighting for the succession after the death of Conall mac Comgaill in 574, and his battles against the Picts in Orkney and in eastern Scotland, the Britons in Manaw Gododdin, and the English of Northumbria, battles in which he was not always successful but which indicate the range of his interests and ambitions. Áedán is closely associated with St *Colum Cille at the meeting of kings at *Druim Cett and in the story recounted by *Adomnán of how the saint 'ordained' him as king of Dál Riata. RS

Aer Lingus, a 'semi-state' body (see STATE ENTERPRISE), opened its first route in 1936, from Dublin to Bristol, extending to London later that year. Additional seasonal services, to the Isle of Man and Liverpool, completed the schedule until the outbreak of the *Second World War. In wartime, Aer Lingus operated only the Liverpool service plus occasional flights to Manchester. By 1948 the airline was flying, complete with hostesses, to London, Liverpool, Glasgow, Manchester, the Isle of Man, Paris, and Amsterdam. From 1965, jets flew on the European routes. In 1958 the New York and Boston routes were inaugurated. In 1971 Boeing 747s were introduced to the transatlantic services. PC

aes dána meant literally, 'people of gift', 'skill' or 'craft', especially the poetic craft. Besides free landowners, early Irish law recognized those whose freedom was purchased by their skill. Within this class poets whose father and grandfather had also been poets (**fili*) enjoyed a hereditary nobility, only lost after two generations of the family had failed to produce a versifier. Other crafts or skills such as medicine, law, history, music, masonry, carpentry, and metalworking originally purchased nobility only for the practitioner himself, while the status at law of lesser artists such as jesters, jugglers, pipers, and drummers depended on the status of their employers. KS

Affane, battle of (*c*.8 Feb. 1565), the last private battle between noblemen in Ireland. It arose when Gerald FitzGerald, earl of *Desmond, attempted to levy traditional dues in the *Decies in Co. Waterford. Black Tom Butler, earl of *Ormond, intervened with a larger force and paraded his defeated rival through the streets of Waterford. Although both earls were summoned to London and bound over to keep the peace on bonds of £20,000, only Desmond ended up in the Tower. HM

agrarian protest was a distinctive feature of Irish rural society from the appearance of the *Whiteboys in Co. Tipperary in 1761 to the *Famine. Secrecy was protected by the administration of oaths and the use of disguise. Protestors stated their demands in public proclamations and letters to individuals, often issued in the name of a mythical leader ('Captain Right', 'Captain Rock'), and borrowing the language of official or legal documents. Failure to obey was punished by destruction of property or livestock, or by the beating, mutilation, or killing of offenders. Early protest movements made relatively sparing use of violence; assassination and serious injury became more common following the bloody events of the 1790s.

The main agrarian movements of the 18th century were the *Houghers, the Whiteboys, the *Oakboys, the *Hearts of Steel, and the *Rightboys. In 1821–4 the Rockites (followers of 'Captain Rock') were active in much of Munster. Other names used in the early 19th century included Threshers, Carders, Whitefeet, Terry Alts, Lady Clares, and Molly Maguires. The nature of the organizations concealed behind these names remains obscure. There is occasional evidence of communication and joint action between districts. But in other cases it is likely that local groups drew independently on an increasingly familiar repertoire of methods, ritual, and symbolism.

Agrarian protest was traditionally seen as reflecting the alienation of a Catholic Gaelic peasantry from an Anglicized, Protestant *landlord class imposed by conquest. Modern accounts emphasize instead the conservative and defensive nature of most protest. The major outbreaks of the late 18th century arose in response to new developments, such as the *enclosure of common land, the farming out of *tithe collection, or increasing levels of county *cess. The great peaks of agrarian disturbance in the first half of the 19th century (1813–16, 1819–23, 1831–4) likewise coincided with periods of depression and falling prices. The defensive nature of agrarian crime is also evident in its concentration in the relatively affluent counties of the south and east, where the pressure for innovation in land use and estate management was most marked, and in a gradual westward shift, reflecting an advancing frontier of commercialization, in the location of the most acute disturbances. Recent studies also emphasize the extent to which much protest was directed, not by tenants against landlords, but against tenant farmers by the *agricultural labourers and *cottiers who were their employees and subtenants.

Agrarian crime declined after the Famine, as population pressure eased and living standards rose. Threats, assaults, and property damage all increased sharply with the return of agrarian depression from the late 1870s; but this was in the context of a movement (see LAND WAR) quite different, in its level of organization, ideology, and social composition, from the agrarian secret societies of earlier decades.

Clark, S., and Donnelly, J. S. (eds.), *Irish Peasants: Violence and Political Unrest 1780–1914* (1983)

agricultural labourers first became a significant element in rural society during the 18th century, as commercialization and population growth hastened the stratification of a hitherto largely undifferentiated peasant population. Pure wage earners, hired by the day or for a longer period and using the cash they earned to purchase food and other necessities, were mainly to be found in the monetized north and east. Elsewhere labourers paid in cash more commonly purchased *conacre, while many were *cottiers, exchanging labour directly for potato ground. Male and female *servants, unmarried and generally young, lived in the houses of landlords and farmers and performed both indoor and outdoor work. Migrant workers (spalpeens—see SEASONAL MIGRATION) from poorer regions provided extra hands at times of peak demand. This complex hierarchy, in which farmer, smallholder, and labourer shaded imperceptibly into one another, makes *census statistics difficult to interpret. But recent estimates suggest that by 1841 the agricultural workforce consisted of 400,000 farmers, defined as persons living primarily off their own landholdings, 1 million labourers and cottiers, and 300,000 smallholders partly dependent on employment as hired labour.

After 1845 the labouring population fell sharply. Heavy *Famine mortality and displacement of population was reinforced by continued heavy emigration as post-Famine adjustment, substituting livestock for tillage, reduced the demand for labour. The census of 1901 classified only 333,000 males as agricultural labourers, while by 1912 only one in three persons working in agriculture was a hired labourer, as opposed to a farmer or assisting relative.

Conflict between farmers and labourers over wages, conacre rents, and related issues contributed substantially to pre-Famine *agrarian violence. Continued tension after 1850 reflected the limited extent to which labourers, despite falling numbers, shared in the general prosperity of the post-Famine decades. The English National Agricultural Labourers' Union sought to establish itself in Ireland during the 1870s, and there were also several local labourers' organizations. During the *Land War the labourers were successfully co-opted into the general anti-landlord alliance. The Labourers Act (1883), allowing boards of guardians (from 1898 rural district councils) to provide cottages for rural labourers, and to prosecute employers who provided inadequate housing, took some account of their needs, but the wider hopes awakened by the slogan 'the land for the people' remained unfulfilled. The discontent of labourers, many now organized by the *Irish Transport and General Workers' Union, once again contributed substantially to social unrest during the *Anglo-Irish War and *Civil War. In independent Ireland the muted disaffection of farm labourers was reflected in the significant rural base, up to the late 1960s, of the *Labour Party.

agriculture

Medieval and Early Modern Agriculture

Agriculture in the pre-Norman period was typically mixed. It is worth stressing, because of later statements about the semi-nomadic life of the Irish, that early Irish agriculture was not fundamentally different from agriculture in the rest of north-western Europe. To judge by the laws, a normal farm had at least a share in a plough-team and clients owed annual payments of grain and grain products to their lords. **Críth Gablach*, of the early 8th century, pictures its lowest-ranking normal free commoner, the *ócaire*, as possessing one plough ox, while the most prosperous, the *bó-aire* or *mruigfher*, has a complete plough-team. Excavations and pollen analysis have confirmed the mixed character of farming but have produced varying figures for the proportions of animal bones belonging to different species. Usually *cattle were the most important element in an early Irish farmer's livestock, but in heavily wooded areas the relative importance of *pigs would have increased. A commoner's livestock came to him mainly from a grant from his lord. Co-operative farming was normal in both the arable and livestock components of the farm: the most important example was probably joint-ploughing, practised by all but the most prosperous commoners, but co-operation was normal at harvest (in the *methel*, 'reaping-party'), while joint-herding was also significant enough to merit a legal text to itself. Farming also brought together men and women in different stages of production: the man did most of the work caring for sheep and harvesting flax, but the woman was then responsible for working it up into finished material.

Críth Gablach and other texts give a good idea of the tools and buildings used in farming; progress is being made in identifying the artefacts and foods referred to by early Irish terms. The biggest normal investment appears to have been in a watermill, of the horizontal type, which was usually owned by a consortium of neighbours and worked on a rota. The distribution of early mills is unknown, but, again, they were important enough to merit a separate legal tract (of the 7th century). Another legal tract, of the same date and probably by the same author, proposed a legal regime for bee-keeping. This element in farming was then much more significant than it is today, since, in the absence of sugar, honey was the normal sweetener. The tract on bees is also revealing in that it assumes that relations between neighbouring farmers were subject to a particular set of laws, known as *comaithches*, 'neighbourhood'.

The main legal tract on 'neighbourhood' is a little later, of the 8th century. It presupposes a landscape of scattered farms. Its preoccupation is with trespass by livestock when they are being pastured in enclosed fields. It assumes that neighbours' pasture will be separated by fences (described in some detail) and that trespass by animals will usually involve leaping over or breaking through such fences. The text is not concerned, therefore, with all pasture; in particular unenclosed common land, used especially between 1 May and 1 November, raised few specific legal problems. The most valuable land was pasture kept ungrazed until the winter. Hay was not cut, but the grass was left to be grazed. This was the most important difference in farming technique between Ireland and England or Francia in the same period. The tract is not concerned with trespass onto arable fields; possibly arable was included together with 'preserved pasture', kept for the winter; alternatively arable may typically have been unenclosed and thus subject to a different legal regime. There are hints that open-field strips were common.

*Anglo-Norman conquest and settlement transformed the institutional and socio-economic contexts of agriculture in the areas affected. The Anglo-Normans introduced *feudal property law and established the *manorial system with its tripartite tenurial division between the demesne lands of the lord, freeholdings held for mostly fixed rents by free tenants and leaseholders, and customary holdings held for rents and services by unfree tenants (**betaghs*). English lords and colonists, bringing with them their dietary preferences for wheaten bread and ale, expanded and developed arable production along established English lines. They also promoted a more commercialized and monetized economy by founding *fairs, markets, and *boroughs, minting a coinage, and demanding that rents mostly be paid in cash. Substantial *immigration added impetus to population growth and the pollen record indicates that more land was brought into agricultural production and that existing land was exploited more intensively. Technology also advanced in a range of small but significant ways, of which one of the most notable was the introduction of the windmill. Whether the Anglo-Normans introduced the English three-field system now seems unlikely, but they were responsible for introducing the rabbit, hedgehog, pheasants, dovecotes, fallow deer, pike, carp, and possibly bream, perch, and gudgeon, thereby altering Ireland's native fauna for good.

By west European standards Irish seigniorial agriculture was wholly unexceptional in its methods and results and hardly amounted to the 'agricultural revolution' that has sometimes been claimed. Labour was in relatively limited supply, partly because customary tenants owed comparatively light labour rents but more particularly because there seems to have been none of the rural congestion so manifest in parts of England and continental Europe. Capital, too, was scarce and expensive; hence crops and livestock were mostly produced by relatively land-extensive methods. Husbandry was typically mixed, since animals were essential for draught power and manure, and were themselves dependent upon the arable for fodder and forage. Nationally, oats were the main arable crop but on Leinster manors wheat and oats were grown in roughly equal quantities in three-course rotations, along with small quantities of barley, peas, and beans. Regular fallowing and fallow grazing were the principal means by which soil fertility was maintained, although near the coast (as in south-west England) there are some well-documented cases of land being dressed with sea-sand. Yields, as recorded by manorial accounts, were much the same as those reported by *Gerald of Wales in the late 12th century, i.e. rarely more than four or five times the seed sown and, in the case of oats, frequently less. For draught power greater use was made of the grass-fed ox than the grain-fed *horse.

Encouraged by the need for manure and a buoyant international demand for *wool, sheep farming expanded and in Leinster sheep-corn husbandry became the dominant mixed-farming type. The growth in sheep farming was especially important on the estates of *Cistercian monasteries, many of which made forward sales of wool to Italian merchants. An agrarian economy thus evolved producing grain for mostly local, small-scale, and internal markets and wool, woolfells, skins, and hides for export. Notwithstanding that Irish wool was relatively coarse and low in value, almost 1 million sheep were producing wool for export at the close of the 13th century, the bulk of them in the hands of relatively small flockmasters. Most of this wool was shipped out through the Leinster ports and it was through these same ports that significant quantities of provisions—grain and legumes—were sent to the armies of Edward I in Wales, Gascony, and Scotland. Internal demand, in contrast, was more dispersed than concentrated and even the largest Irish towns could be provisioned from relatively restricted hinterlands. Incentives to innovate, intensify, and specialize were consequently comparatively weak and the agrarian economy always remained fragmented into a medley of local and regional economies.

Beyond the Anglo-Norman territories, in the western and north-western third of the country, the pre-existing Gaelic agricultural economy survived relatively unaltered. Irish property law determined tenurial relations and production and distribution were based upon principles of reciprocity and redistribution rather than market exchange. Outside the western coastal ports money was rarely used and within the countryside cows and cattle remained the principal measures of wealth and status. Production was here primarily for consumption and pastoralism, for institutional as well as economic and environmental reasons, retained its former prominence.

From the late 13th century the agricultural economy ceased to expand. Then, from the beginning of the 14th century, output began to contract as law and order broke down, freak weather conditions precipitated widespread famine (1315–22), a Scottish invasion in 1315 (see BRUCE, EDWARD) inflicted lasting damage on the lands of the English Lordship, murrain devastated sheep flocks, and plague (see BLACK DEATH) triggered a major mortality crisis. As labour became scarcer and security deteriorated, agriculture became even more land extensive. There was also much decay and destruction of fixed capital stock. Pastoral husbandry, with its more limited labour requirements, therefore expanded at the expense of arable husbandry and in the least populous parts of the north and west assumed a semi-nomadic form. Pastoral products continued to dominate Irish exports although, as the agricultural economy became less specialized and commercialized, the volume of Irish exports contracted significantly.

In the 16th century low *population and a limited market structure meant that every region continued to be, to some extent, self-sufficient. Thus the pattern of agriculture was little differentiated throughout the country. Evidence of extensive destruction of grain during the *Nine Years War, for example, suggests that this was grown throughout the country. However, the climate and landscape dictated that livestock was to be particularly important and the most valued animals, cattle, were used as measures of wealth. Live cattle were rarely exported, although skins were.

Growth in labour supply in the early 17th century, due to rising population, prompted a rise in agricultural output. The structure of this output, however, remained much the same as in the late 16th century, reflecting the organic way in which agriculture had evolved to suit the ecology of Ireland. Some native Irish agricultural practices, such as ploughing by tail (in which the horse's tail was attached directly to the plough without using harness), were adopted by settlers. In Munster the *sheep sector expanded to provide wool for south-west England, and in Ulster grain, mainly oats, was grown more extensively. The most significant innovation was the growth of live cattle exports from almost none in 1600 to about 15,000 beasts a year in the 1630s. This reflected the beginnings of commercialization in the agricultural economy.

Agricultural output continued to expand throughout the early seventeenth century, despite harvest crises in 1622–4, 1628–32, and 1639–41. The *Confederate War had a traumatic effect. Trade collapsed, instability retarded arable cultivation, and the number of livestock fell as animals were slaughtered for food, hides being exported. In the 1650s livestock were imported.

In the late 1650s the agricultural structure began to shift from dependence on live cattle to processed goods such as salt beef, butter, and cheese, although grain continued to be locally important in Munster. This shift was speeded up by the *Cattle Acts and by the development of transatlantic markets. Ideas of agricultural improvement were promoted in specialist works and in popular form by almanacs. The absence of major harvest crises, especially during the European crises of the 1690s, assisted the transformation. The development of a more complex internal marketing structure resulted in the emergence of specialized agricultural regions. East Connacht and the midlands became established as fattening regions for cattle. Commercial *dairying developed in the hinterlands of the major ports in Ulster and south-east Ireland, along with Kerry, Cork, and Limerick. Land of more marginal quality, in Roscommon, Clare, and

Westmeath, saw an expansion of sheep rearing. This basic structure was to persist until the re-orientation of Irish agriculture, in response to changes in market conditions, in the last decades of the 18th century.

Agriculture in Modern Ireland

The development of Irish agriculture since the late 18th century has been governed by five elements. Two of them, soil and climate and the system of land tenure, were more or less fixed during this period. The others, price movements, government policy, and technological change, can be considered as variables.

In Ireland the high levels of rainfall, the mild winters and cool summers coupled with a large proportion of gley and peaty soils, have meant that Irish agriculture's natural advantage has been in the production of pastoral rather than arable crops. Consequently, over the period 1700–1900, as subsistence production for household needs diminished, and as output for the market place increased, the long-term tendency was for Irish agriculture to specialize in livestock and livestock produce. From time to time though, particularly between 1780 and the 1830s, market forces diverted agriculture into cereal production, where its comparative advantage was less.

The second and less important of the fixed factors was the system of *land tenure. The basic structure remained virtually unchanged throughout the period. It consisted of a tripartite division, similar in theory to that in Britain. At the top were the *landlords, nearly all Anglo-Protestant. The middle tier consisted of tenant farmers, increasingly, except in the north-east, Catholic-Irish. At the bottom were the *agricultural labourers. Sometimes these were paid by money wages, sometimes by small acreages of land in lieu or by a combination of the two. This variety in modes of payment led to a confusion of nomenclature, and holders of these plots have been described as *'cottiers' or 'small farmers'. This configuration was often untidy. First, as it developed in the late 18th century, a bewildering array of *middlemen and subtenants came into being which obscured the basic relationship. Secondly, particularly after the *Great Famine, the farm labouring class greatly diminished in importance so that by 1900 one-half of Irish farms were worked exclusively by the farmer and his family.

The system of land tenure, as it operated in practice, has been much criticized. First it was said that, unlike their English counterparts, Irish landlords simply exploited rather than developed their estates. This criticism may have some justification, particularly for the early part of the period. However, it must be pointed out that the land hunger that existed in Ireland from the 1780s to 1900 greatly limited the freedom of action of any landlord intending improvements. For example, a landlord wishing to consolidate scattered or subdivided holdings as a precondition to investment would have to disturb or evict existing tenants. This was fiercely resisted (see AGRARIAN PROTEST). The second criticism, that many tenants, particularly in the 19th century, had short leases, or none at all, and were therefore constrained in the improvement of their farms by insecurity of tenure, probably has less justification. Essentially, whatever the legal theory, for most of the period tenants who paid their rent were secure in their tenure.

In so far as the nature of the landed system did create a problem for agriculture, it was mainly a result of the small average size of farms in Ireland. The *Land Acts of 1881–1903, which effectively abolished landlordism and created a nation of peasant proprietors, did nothing to alter this fundamental problem.

The product mix of Irish agriculture has been highly responsive to movement in the relative prices of cereal and pastoral products. During most of the 18th and 19th centuries the relationship favoured pastoral production, a trend which fitted in well with Ireland's natural advantage. Thus in the period up to 1780 price considerations encouraged the export of animal products, notably beef, butter, and pork. At this stage the only important arable product indirectly exported was *flax, which was embodied in the export of *linen goods. However, from 1780 this changed. Growing population in both Britain and Ireland increased the demand for basic foodstuffs like *bread and *potatoes. During the *revolutionary and Napoleonic wars this was intensified as foreign supplies on the British market were interrupted causing grain prices to rise rapidly. Under these twin pressures, acreage under crops rose markedly, as did exports. Grain exports rose over twelvefold between 1780–4 and 1815–19 while the volume of pasture-based products rose by less than 80 per cent, which was simply in line with the growth of population. This trend was reversed in the 19th century. Over the period from the end of the Napoleonic wars to the *First World War all agricultural prices fell. But cereal prices fell much more than livestock prices, a half compared to a seventh. The pattern of Irish production responded accordingly.

In general government policies during this period tended to reinforce production trends dictated by price movements. In the late 18th and early 19th centuries, when cereal prices were high, government policy encouraged arable production through bounties and tariffs. From 1846 the introduction of free trade favoured the already pre-existing trend towards pastoral production, as overseas competition was less of a problem in this area than it was in cereals. Only for the period between c.1820 and 1846 might it be said that government policy, which still offered arable protection, ran counter to trends dictated by world price movements.

Technological change, resulting in increased productivity from both land and labour, was perceptible in Ireland from the late 18th century with the spread of crop rotation and manuring, and improved breeds of livestock. The major development of the late 19th century was the replacement of human by horse power, a consequence, in part, of declining rural population and the rise in wages it entailed. By 1900 machinery was becoming more prevalent, and there was a renewed interest in livestock breeding, a movement fostered, though not initiated, by the Department of *Agriculture and Technical Instruction. Co-operative and private creameries were spreading, converting butter-making from a farm- to a factory-based industry. Nevertheless, despite these undoubted and sometimes underestimated improvements, technological change in Irish agriculture was slower than that of its major economic competitors.

By the early 20th century the patterns of commercial Irish agricultural production and exports were not wildly different from what they had been three centuries earlier. In 1908 86 per cent of output and no less than 94 per cent of agricultural exports consisted of livestock and livestock products.

When the 20th century opened rural Ireland was still a society of landlords and tenant farmers. In this it was no different from England and many other regions of Europe. But this picture of stability and continuity in social structure was already undergoing change. A series of Land Acts from the 1880s onwards, culminating in the Wyndham Act of 1903, effectively abolished the landlord class in Ireland. By the early 1920s, the majority of farmers owned the land they worked. The thoroughness of this social revolution is evidenced by the fact that today the Irish Republic has the largest proportion of owner-occupiers of any rural society within the *European Union.

Despite the change in tenure system, the fundamentals of Irish agriculture did not change. The natural resource endowments of soil and climate, and the pressure of international market forces, continued to shape agricultural production. In practice this meant that Irish agriculture was geared increasingly towards a low-intensity livestock production, with prices determined by the British and world markets. The winds of technical change swept the countryside, gently prior to the 1950s when horse technology predominated, more insistently thereafter as mechanization, rural electrification, and the use of chemical inputs took hold. The big break with the past, however, was in relation to government policy. This was minimal in the late 19th century, that is, until tenure reform forced its way onto the political agenda. Subsequently state interventions spread to the technical and economic aspects of farming, with the government acquiring increasing responsibilities for the state of agriculture. In large part this was due to a chronic oversupply of agricultural commodities on world markets, and hence weak prices, over much of the century.

The beginnings of institutionalized intervention may be traced to the Department of Agriculture and Technical Instruction, founded in 1899. Its aim was to increase farm productivity and hence living standards. The methods were largely indirect and persuasive: disseminating technical information and seeking to raise the quality of farm produce for export. In these efforts it was complemented by the voluntary activities of the *Irish Agricultural Organization Society, founded in 1894 to promote agricultural co-operative societies. By 1914 there were 350 dairy co-operative societies on the island, and these were to constitute the seedbed for the eventual emergence of Irish-owned multinational food corporations during the last quarter of the 20th century.

State intervention in agriculture took a more determined form under the crisis conditions of the First World War. Attempts were made to fix prices—a harbinger of policies to come—but these were not particularly successful in Ireland. Prices soared during the period 1914–20 and farmers' incomes reached levels which were not surpassed until the years following the *Second World War. The fortunes of Irish agriculture during the inter-war period were adversely affected by falling prices on the international market. This problem was intensified for southern (but not Northern) Irish farmers by the United Kingdom's resort to agricultural protectionism after 1931, exacerbated by the *'Economic War'. The *Fianna Fáil government of the period embarked on the most ambitious range of agricultural policies yet attempted, in an effort to remould Irish agriculture. The interests of the cattle industry were downgraded, even penalized, and selected tillage crops such as wheat and sugar beet were heavily subsidized. This curious episode served to reveal the limitations of state intervention. Farmers' incomes continued to suffer. The policy of 'speeding the plough' failed to reverse the long-run tendency towards pastoral farming. Rural depopulation, the most conspicuous feature of social change in the countryside throughout the century, continued apace.

The artificial market conditions of the 1940s, occasioned by war and post-war adjustment, signalled a recovery in prices and incomes. But there was no price bonanza as during the First World War. The downward pressure on agricultural prices on the world market resumed during the following two decades. In response, the farming lobby agitated for larger subsidies and grants, and looked enviously towards Europe and the heavily protected position of continental farmers under the Common Agricultural Policy.

The entry of the Irish Republic into the (then) European Economic Community in January 1973 finally relieved Irish taxpayers of the increasingly onerous task of subsidizing agriculture, while serving to defuse emerging urban–rural tensions. Henceforth 'farming' Brussels was the order of the day. The benefits to Northern Irish farmers were more muted, as they had already enjoyed a good measure of protection and price support by virtue of membership of the United Kingdom. Even the European Community could not shelter farmers indefinitely from trends in international markets. Overproduction within the Community and the large divergence between EC and world market prices gave rise to pressures for reform. Price supports were progressively, if gradually, reduced. They remained substantial none the less: in a typical year in the 1990s some 40 per cent of Irish farmers' income was said to be derived from grants and subsidies. But the spectre of reform remained to haunt Irish farmers.

The privileged status of agriculture over much of the century, in the sense of being the net beneficiary of transfers of resources from other sectors of the economy, did not solve some of its more intractable problems. It is true the number of farms declined over time, farm household size was pared back, and farm labourers disappeared in most parts of the countryside. Yet a majority of farms remained below the threshold of economic viability, average incomes were less than in industry, and underemployment persisted. These generalizations applied with ever greater force to the west of Ireland, where structural problems were compounded by demographic weaknesses, in particular an aged labour force and a high proportion of non-family households. On the positive side, farmers shared in the rising prosperity of Irish society, especially after the 1950s. Although the numbers engaged in agriculture declined progressively—in 1911 just over half the male labour force in Ireland was engaged in agriculture, by 1991 the corresponding share was under 15 per cent—agricultural output and agricultural exports continued to rise. This was a reflection of productivity gains, based in large part on the greater use of new or improved capital inputs (from machinery to plants and animals), more intense specialization, and more skilled farm management.

In the early 20th century agriculture and the farming population dominated the rural economy. As the century closed, not only had the practice of farming been transformed by massive technical change, farming itself had become only one among a range of economic activities located in the countryside. Rural industrialization, the development of *tourism and service-type activities, and the rise of commuter belts constituted the dynamic areas of growth. Thus, not only had the significance of agriculture in the overall economy declined: the typical rural dweller no longer worked the land.

Crotty, R. D., *Irish Agricultural Production: Its Volume and Structure* (1966)

Gillespie, Raymond, *The Transformation of the Irish Economy* (1991)

Ó Gráda, Cormac, *Ireland: A New Economic History* (1994)

TMC-E/BMSC/RG/LK/DJ

Agriculture and Technical Instruction, Department of (DATI), created in 1899, in response to the report of Horace *Plunkett's *Recess Committee, to improve Irish *agriculture through education and the encouragement of local co-operation and initiative. To this end it incorporated a popular element in the form of advisory bodies (the Council of Agriculture, the Agricultural Board, and the Board of Technical Instruction), the majority of whose members were nominated by local authorities. As part of its educational and developmental brief, DATI took over a variety of powers and functions, such as the promotion and inspection of *fisheries and the collection of agricultural statistics, previously entrusted to other departments. It was, in fact if not in name, a ministry of agriculture and, in a new departure in Irish administration, its head was expected to represent the department in parliament. The department's work, which included training *national schoolteachers in rural science and domestic economy, and improving plant and livestock breeds, was hampered both by conflict with other departments, particularly the *Congested Districts Board, and by the suspicion with which it was viewed by nationalists who saw it as an attempt to undermine aspirations to self-government by improving living standards. After 1922 it was absorbed into the Department of Lands and Agriculture. VC

Aífe (*c*.1152–*c*.1189), daughter of Diarmait *Mac Murchada by Mór, daughter of Ua Tuathail, king of Uí Muiredaig. According to *Gerald of Wales Diarmait, in 1166, offered *Strongbow her hand in marriage, along with succession to the kingship of Leinster after his death. Their marriage was celebrated at Waterford on 23 August 1170. Aífe bore Strongbow a son, Gilbert, and a daughter, Isabella. Gilbert was still alive in 1185, but had died by 1189 when Isabella was married to William *Marshal, who thereby succeeded to the lordship of Leinster. MTF

Aiken, Frank (1898–1983). An *IRA commander during the *Anglo-Irish War, Aiken was one of the more politically minded opponents of the *Anglo-Irish treaty. After succeeding Liam Lynch as IRA chief of staff (Apr. 1923) he took immediate steps to end the *Civil War. A founder member of *Fianna Fáil, he became minister of defence (1932–9) and then minister for co-ordination of defensive measures (1939–45), giving him a key position in the management of wartime *neutrality.

Aiken was minister for external affairs 1951–4 and 1957–69. In the latter period he developed Ireland's notably activist *foreign policy at the *United Nations. His approach confirmed a distinct Fianna Fáil 'style' in foreign policy, echoing de *Valera's assertion of 'small power' rights and responsibilities at the *League of Nations in the 1930s. NMacQ

Aikenhead, Mary (1787–1858). Born in Cork, to a Protestant doctor and his Catholic wife, and received into the Catholic church in 1802, Aikenhead became active in philanthropic activities in Dublin city in the first decade of the 19th century. On the advice of Archbishop *Murray, she set up the Irish Sisters of Charity in 1815. CC

Ailech, see GRIANÁN OF AILECH.

air corps, a subordinate arm of the *army since 1922, based at Baldonnell outside Dublin. Until the 1970s its operational role was never properly defined: its own commanding officer said it 'was not an effective combat unit ... during the Emergency' of 1939–45. The acquisition of modern helicopters in the early 1960s, and its expanded fisheries protection role since Ireland joined the *European Union, gave it a new lease of life. It is now reasonably well equipped for its main activities: security patrols, air ambulance duties, search and rescue tasks and other work in aid of the civil power, fisheries protection flights, and close co-operation duties with ground forces. EO'H

Airgialla, meaning perhaps 'the hostage-givers', is the name of a kingdom (or, more accurately, a federation of subkingdoms, independent of each other but conceding nominal suzerainty to an overking) traditionally said to have been established by three brothers known as the three Collas. In its earliest state it ran from Coleraine to Newry, and westwards to the Foyle, where it was bounded from the 5th century on by the lands of the northern *Uí Néill. It included, therefore, all of the modern counties of Derry, Tyrone, and Monaghan, Armagh west of the Bann, parts of Fermanagh and Louth, and perhaps a small corner of Meath. Over the centuries it was gradually pushed southwards by the advance of the northern Uí Néill, and by the 12th century the kingship of Airgialla and that of Fernmag in modern Co. Monaghan seem to have become synonymous. The Ua Cerbaill rulers of Fernmag also now ruled Co. Louth but this was lost as a result of the Anglo-Norman invasion, and became known as Uriel. Monaghan, known as Oirghialla, survived as long as the Gaelic order prevailed, ruled over by a branch of the Uí Cerbaill who had adopted the surname Mac Mathghamhna (*MacMahon). SD

air travel in Ireland began in 1909–10, with Harry Ferguson's first powered flight, in Co. Down. In April 1912, Kilkenny man Denys Corbett Wilson made the first crossing of the Irish Sea, landing near Enniscorthy. Alcock and Brown landed near Clifden on 15 June 1919, after the first transatlantic crossing, from Newfoundland. Midland Scottish Air Ferries began the first cross-channel passenger service in May 1933, between Renfrew and Belfast. Before the *Second World War, a number of small air services linked Belfast, Scotland, Liverpool, and the Isle of Man. The first passenger service from southern Ireland was inaugurated by *Aer Lingus, between Dublin and Bristol, in May 1936. In 1940 Dublin airport opened, destined to become a major international centre of air travel.

After the war, Aer Lingus began services to Britain and Europe. In 1946, as the result of a bilateral agreement between the Irish and British governments, Aer Lingus ceased to be the sole carrier from Dublin to Britain. In 1947 a customs-free airport was opened at Shannon to attract the transatlantic trade. In 1948 an abortive attempt was made by Aerlinte, sister airline of Aer Lingus, to establish a transatlantic service. This finally came in 1958, with services to New York and Boston. The introduction of Boeing 747s opened up routes to other US centres. In 1965 jet aircraft were put on the European routes. In 1946 British European Airways took over scheduled services from Belfast to Britain. Aldergrove, later renamed Belfast International, replaced the nearby Nutts Corner as Northern Ireland's main airport in 1963. In 1967 BEA began the first regular Belfast to London jet service. In 1965 British Midland became the other main airline flying out of Belfast. Since 1971 the Harbour airport, now called Belfast City airport, has been the base for smaller airlines flying to other provincial centres. In addition to the main airports in Dublin, Shannon, and Belfast, there are regional airports at Cork, Galway, *Knock, and Derry. In addition to the major carriers, many other smaller airlines have come and gone. Since the 1960s, increased prosperity has enabled millions to fly to package holiday destinations.

Nowlan, Kevin B. (ed.), *Travel and Transport in Ireland* (2nd edn., 1993)

PC

aisling, see LITERATURE IN IRISH.

Alen, John (1476–1534), archbishop of Dublin 1529–34, an experienced lawyer and aggressive administrator. He was a close ally of Henry VIII's lord chancellor, Cardinal Thomas Wolsey, who secured his provision in September 1529 to Dublin, where he was consecrated on 13 March 1530. Using his dual position as lord chancellor and archbishop, Alen tried to reassert the authority and jurisdiction of the see of Dublin, compiling for this purpose a register of see records dating back to the *Anglo-Norman conquest. But the fall of Wolsey early in his episcopate fatally undermined him, and left him exposed when Henry VIII imposed a large fine on him for infringing royal jurisdiction. Desperate to increase his income, Alen clashed with the influential *FitzGerald family. When the *Kildare rebellion broke out, Alen sought to flee to England, but his ship ran aground at Clontarf and he was seized by Thomas FitzGerald, who 'brained and hacked him in gobbets'. AF

Alen, Sir John (d. 1561), appointed master of the rolls in 1533 as part of Thomas Cromwell's bureaucratic drive against *Kildare hegemony; by 1538 he was lord chancellor, heading the commission for the *dissolution of the monasteries. In 1546 he highlighted *St Leger's squandering of monastic revenues, but was jailed for having benefited illicitly himself. Reinstated as chancellor between 1548 and 1550, Alen saw off St Leger, retrieved his monastic leases, and advised on the *Laois-Offaly plantation. HM

All for Ireland League, see O'BRIEN, WILLIAM.

Alliance Party of Northern Ireland, a centrist political party established in April 1970, mainly by people not previously involved in politics. It has sought to develop a political middle ground for Catholics and Protestants in Northern Ireland, on a platform of reconciliation within the United Kingdom. Its strongest support has been in the middle-class suburban areas, although paradoxically its modest success has played a major part in putting the *Northern Ireland Labour Party out of business. It has made relatively little impact in the west of the province and in rural areas generally.

The party's initial rationale was that a strong body of support for conciliation existed, but was masked by the first-past-the-post electoral system which operated in the province prior to 1973. The reintroduction of *proportional representation poured some cold water on this: the party has never obtained more than about 13 per cent of the vote in local council elections and 10 per cent in regional elections; since the early 1980s levels of support have been slightly lower. Far from encouraging the emergence of a strong centre, PR actually facilitated the emergence of more extreme parties within each ethnic camp. Although Alliance has retained a strong core of committed Catholic and Protestant supporters, its electoral successes have been in situations where this core has been enhanced by a local minority which is too small to sustain its own ethnic parties, such as the Catholic minority in East Belfast and North Down. ACH

American Civil War (1861–5), fought between the federal government of the United States and eleven southern confederate states, who asserted their right to leave the Union in response to growing demands for the abolition of slavery. Irishmen fought on both sides, but in far greater numbers (perhaps in excess of 140,000) for the Union, whose armies included several Irish units. This was probably due less to ideology than to the concentration of Irish settlement in the northern states that formed the Union heartland. While many distinguished themselves in battle, it should be noted that Irishmen as a national group were actually under-represented among the combatants. They were also prominent in agitation against conscription, and were often hostile to black Americans, whom they saw as their rivals for employment. In the short term, Irish involvement in the war gave rise to the *Fenian raids into Canada (1866), and provided military experience for some who subsequently returned to Ireland. Later it would be used to bolster the image of Irish-Americans as belligerent defenders of freedom. NG

American Revolution. The military struggle associated with this term lasted from 1775 to 1781 on the American mainland, although the formal peace was not signed until 1783. More generously defined, the origins of the Revolution are commonly found in the period after the end of the Seven Years War in 1763, and a possible conclusion can be seen in 1789 when George Washington was inaugurated as the first president of the United States under the constitution which had been constructed in the Philadelphia Convention of 1787. As a result of the successful revolutionary war the United States emerged as an independent country, and so the 'first' British empire ended.

Among the important writings associated with the Revolution are some which resonated outside North America as well as within it. Most obviously there is the Declaration of Independence itself, essentially the work of Thomas Jefferson, written and published in 1776, the same year as Tom Paine's *Common Sense*. The United States constitution received its best-known defence in the *Federalist Papers*, written by Alexander Hamilton, James Madison, and John Jay. The first ten amendments to the constitution, 1789, usually known as the Bill of Rights, have also had an important domestic and international role in the history of civil liberties.

The evidence suggests that a majority of those in the colonies from an Irish background supported the revolutionary, patriot cause. These included such prominent figures, among many others, as John Dunlop (born in Co. Tyrone), the printer of the Declaration of Independence, Charles Thomson (born in Co. Londonderry), the leader of the radical movement in Philadelphia and then secretary to the Continental Congress, and Aedanus Burke (born in Co. Galway) of South Carolina, who was a particularly prominent opponent of the federal constitution at the time of its ratification, 1787–8. The state in which immigrants from Ireland were in sufficient numbers to achieve effective political mobilization as a group was Pennsylvania. Here, in Philadelphia but more importantly in some of the then western counties of the state, there is evidence of a distinctively radical position on a number of issues. These include strong commitment to the Revolution in a state where there was particularly significant support for the loyalist cause, support for the state constitution of 1776 with its unicameral legislature and generous franchise, and in 1787 hostility to the new United States constitution. It has been argued that the predominantly Presbyterian settlers from Ireland were politically allied to Calvinists from other backgrounds in the state.

As the American crisis developed during the 1760s and 1770s, many on both sides of the Atlantic saw parallels between the grievances of the colonists and those of Ireland. The withdrawal of regular troops for service in North America, along with the threat of French or Spanish invasion, provided the occasion for the formation of the *Volunteers, whose extra-parliamentary pressure was crucial to the achievement of *free trade and *legislative independence. Moderate Irish *patriots became less sympathetic as the colonists progressed from demands for representation to republicanism and the pursuit of independence, although in radical circles, particularly in Presbyterian Ulster, support for the American cause remained significant throughout.

Doyle, D. N., *Ireland, Irishmen and Revolutionary America 1760–1820* (1981)

SJSI

Ancient Order of Hibernians (AOH), the largest Irish-American benevolent society, established in New York in 1836. Much of its inspiration, though few of its activities, probably came from the Irish secret society tradition. By 1900 it had 100,000 members. In Ireland and Great Britain it was small until after 1900, when the power and influence of a reunited American order stimulated the appearance of rival constitutional and revolutionary strands. Catholic and broadly nationalist, it shared with the *Christian Brothers the slogan 'Faith and Fatherland'. The Belfast Nationalist leader Joseph *Devlin, national president of the order (1905–34), turned its mainstream, known as the 'Board of Erin', into a political machine for the *Nationalist Party, and during the years 1903–6 and 1910–14 the American parent body followed this lead. Under Devlin the AOH in Ireland and Britain supported the *United Irish League and in some areas virtually supplanted it: membership grew from 10,000 in 1905 to 60,000 in 1909, preponderantly in Ulster and neighbouring counties, and in Dublin. It was attractive to businessmen for its *freemason-style activities, to workers for its benevolent activities, and to young Ulster Catholics as a rival to the *Orange Order. It benefited greatly from its role as an 'approved society' under the National Insurance Act of 1911. Known disparagingly by independent nationalist,

Labour, and *Sinn Féin opponents as 'the Molly Maguires' (after the secret society which operated covertly within the AOH in the Pennsylvania coalfield in the 1870s), it was regarded as synonymous with jobbery, machine politics, and sectarianism. In Ireland it acquired a 'green Tory' image after 1921, whereas its divisions in British cities delivered the former 'Irish vote' to the Labour Party. In *Northern Ireland it was closely associated with the old *Nationalist Party, but since the early 1970s it has contracted drastically.

For Devlin the AOH had three attractions: it provided a direct link to Irish-American influence and money; it harnessed the Catholic content of Irish nationalism to lay leadership; and it provided new dynamism to replace the fading issue of land tenure. For a while this worked, but the AOH ethos was really one of simple emigrant nostalgia, little suited to the nationalist heartlands of Ireland. There it was soon supplanted by a Gaelic movement which, though scarcely less Catholic in membership, offered a more dynamic sense of Irish identity. ACH

Anderson, John (*c*.1760–1820), entrepreneur. Arriving in Cork from his native Scotland in 1780, Anderson quickly established himself as a merchant in the city. A £500 investment multiplied quickly and by 1789 he could successfully bid for, and establish, the first Irish mail coach service. This proved both reliable and profitable. In 1791, borrowing £40,000, Anderson purchased a large Co. Cork estate, including the town of Fermoy. The town, which Anderson largely rebuilt, became the centre of his mail coach organization. In 1800 Anderson opened the Fermoy Bank. Later he reputedly declined a baronetcy, though the title was subsequently bestowed on his son. In 1807 he purchased, in partnership, the nearby Barry estates. However, this investment ultimately proved disastrous. The property was heavily mortgaged, and land values fell. In 1816 the Fermoy Bank closed and its proprietor was bankrupted. Anderson's attempts to revive his fortunes failed, and he died in reduced circumstances in 1820. NG

Andrews, John Millar (1871–1956), prime minister of Northern Ireland (1940–3). Andrews, the proprietor of a linen spinning mill, was typical of the gentrified businessmen who dominated Ulster *Unionism after the Edwardian era. He served as minister of labour 1921–37, and minister of finance 1937–40. He succeeded *Craig as prime minister in November 1940, but lacked the flair necessary for wartime leadership, and was excessively loyal to undeserving and superannuated members of his cabinet. Having refused to yield to backbench pressure for a major overhaul of the government, he resigned in April 1943. AJ

Anglo-Irish agreement (15 Nov. 1985), signed at Hillsborough, Co. Down, by the British prime minister, Margaret Thatcher, and the Irish *taoiseach, Garret FitzGerald. It was agreed that the British and Irish governments would consult regularly and formally on major aspects of Northern Ireland policy, and a small secretariat of British and Irish civil servants was established at Maryfield, near Stormont. The agreement reflected a long-term move on the part of the British government away from possible internal solutions to the *Northern Ireland conflict and towards the negotiation of a new all-Ireland constitutional relationship. The alarming rise in *Sinn Féin's electoral fortunes, at the expense of the constitutionalist *Social Democratic and Labour Party, in the wake of the *hunger strikes of 1981 added urgency to the quest for political progress. A widespread campaign of protest produced the relatively novel spectacle of unionists in violent confrontations with the police, but failed to repeat the success of the *Ulster Workers' Council in overturning the *Sunningdale agreement. SC/ACH

Anglo-Irish agreements (1938), concluding the *Economic War. There were three agreements: defence, finance, and trade. Despite pressure from de *Valera, no progress was made on *partition. The defence agreement abrogated articles 6 and 7 of the *Anglo-Irish treaty and returned the *treaty ports. In the finance agreement, the Irish government paid a lump sum of £10 million as a final settlement of all financial claims under the treaty and subsequent agreements, although it continued the £250,000 annuity for damage to property during 1919–21. Both governments repealed penal duties on imports. The trade agreement, which caused dissension in the British cabinet, restored Commonwealth preference to Irish goods with free entry to the British market. A tariff commission was to review Irish protective duties and restrictions; preferences were given to certain classes of British goods, including coal.

The agreements, particularly defence, were bitterly attacked by Winston Churchill in the House of Commons. In the *Dáil James *Larkin was the only opponent. DMcM

Anglo-Irish free trade agreement. Concluded in 1965, this provided for a phased dismantling of the tariff barriers which had existed between Britain and Ireland since the 1930s (see PROTECTIONISM). Free trade was to be achieved by 1975. The agreement reflected the continuing ties between the two economies and a joint interest in joining the European Economic Community (see EUROPEAN UNION). Despite the agreement, the proportion of Irish exports destined for the British market fell sharply from 75 per cent in 1960 to 43 per cent by 1980, though Britain continued to provide approximately one-half of Irish imports throughout this period. MED

Anglo-Irish treaty (1921), concluding the *Anglo-Irish War. Tortuous preliminary negotiations between de *Valera and the prime minister, David *Lloyd George, concluded with agreement on a conference in London 'to ascertain how the association of Ireland with the community of nations known as the British Empire might best be reconciled with Irish national aspirations': a formula already incompatible with traditional republican goals. The Irish delegation, headed (following de Valera's contentious decision to remain at home) by *Griffith and *Collins, was instructed to press for *external association, and to ensure that any breakdown came on the question of *partition. On 2 November, however, Griffith agreed to accept continued Irish association with crown and *Commonwealth in exchange for a promise of 'essential unity'. When *Craig firmly rejected proposals for an all-Ireland parliament, Lloyd George offered what the Irish delegates allowed themselves to be persuaded was the alternative solution of a *boundary commission. The negotiations reached a dramatic climax on 5 December when Lloyd George, offering the threat of a resumption of war balanced by the last minute concession of fiscal autonomy for the new Irish state, demanded immediate agreement on a settlement within the empire. On 6 December the delegates signed a treaty establishing the *Irish Free State as a self-governing dominion within the British Commonwealth.

Back in Ireland, Griffith and Collins defended the treaty as the best settlement that could be obtained under the circumstances. However, it was immediately rejected by de Valera and other *Sinn Féin leaders. The main issues of contention were Ireland's continued subordination to the British crown, as represented in the *oath of allegiance and the office of *governor-general. Northern Ireland, due mainly to the hopes vested in the Boundary Commission, played little part in the controversy; nor, more surprisingly, did the defence facilities that Britain was to continue to enjoy (see TREATY PORTS). After bitterly divisive debates the *Dáil voted on 7 January 1922 to ratify the treaty by a small majority of 64 votes to 57. The refusal of a large section of Sinn Féin and the *IRA to accept the settlement laid the foundations for the *Civil War that followed six months later. In Britain, despite opposition from Conservative diehards, the treaty was ratified by act of parliament on 31 March 1922. However, Conservative dissatisfaction with the treaty contributed to the downfall of Lloyd George's coalition in October 1922.

Pakenham, Frank, *Peace by Ordeal* (5th edn., 1992)

DMcM

Anglo-Irish War, the campaign against government forces mounted by the *Irish Volunteers, now increasingly known as the *Irish Republican Army (IRA). Conventionally dated from 21 January 1919, when nine Volunteers, including Dan *Breen and Sean *Treacy, killed two policemen in an ambush at Soloheadbeg, Co. Tipperary, it continued until a truce on 11 July 1921 opened the way for the negotiation of the *Anglo-Irish treaty.

The development of a highly effective form of guerrilla warfare, wholly different from the tactics of the *rising of 1916 or earlier insurrections, represented a gradual adaptation to practical necessity, dependent more on local initiative than on central planning. IRA activity during 1919 consisted mainly of arms seizures and attacks on individual policemen. A successful attack on the police barracks at Carrigtwohill, Co. Cork, on 2 January 1920, marked the commencement of more ambitious raids and ambushes. By June the IRA had killed 55 police. Sixteen occupied barracks had been destroyed in attacks, and hundreds of others abandoned as indefensible. In Dublin members of a squad directed by Michael *Collins had begun systematically killing off detectives from the political division of the *Dublin Metropolitan Police.

In response to this challenge the government deployed regular troops and created two new forces, the *Black and Tans and *Auxiliaries, to reinforce the *Royal Irish Constabulary. The *Restoration of Order in Ireland Act continued and extended the emergency powers created by the wartime *Defence of the Realm Acts. But draconian security policy alienated the civilian population without suppressing IRA activity. The events of late 1920, notably *'Bloody Sunday' (21 Nov.) and the killing of fifteen Auxiliaries in an ambush at Kilmichael, Co. Cork (28 Nov.), marked a sharp escalation in violence. The same period saw the appearance of 'flying columns', bodies of IRA men permanently under arms of the kind led by Tom *Barry in Co. Cork and responsible for the Kilmichael ambush. Continued violence in the first half of 1921 brought the total death toll for the period to 405 police, 150 military, and an estimated 750 IRA and civilians.

The term 'Anglo-Irish War', like the older 'War of Independence', raises complex issues. IRA activists and leadership determinedly employed the vocabulary of conventional warfare to assert their status as combatants in a national conflict. In doing so they glossed over the sporadic, hit-and-run character of most operations, the limited scale of the violence prior to late 1920, and the predominance among the early victims of the IRA of the locally recruited, and predominantly Catholic, RIC. The government was equally determined to deny the 'murder gang' the legitimacy of belligerent status. It condoned reprisals, including the widespread destruction of property in such incidents as the Black and Tan raid on Balbriggan, Co. Dublin, on 20 September 1920, and the 'sack' of Cork city by Auxiliaries and Black and Tans on 11–12 December 1920. It also ignored the assassination, clearly by security force members, of several republican activists (see MACCURTAIN, THOMAS). But *Lloyd George's insistence that 'you do not declare war on rebels' meant that the military never got a really free hand, and that authority remained confusingly divided between police and army.

Assessment of the IRA's claim to represent the popular will is also difficult. Modern historians, reacting against an earlier tradition of uncritical glorification, have emphasized the extent to which violence was deliberately employed by a militant minority to block any possibility of a compromise settlement, and the ruthless action, shading into a more general intimidation, against 'informers' and 'collaborators'. IRA activity was geographically uneven, high levels of activity in the western counties of Munster and part of the midlands contrasting sharply with relative tranquillity elsewhere. Although the *Dáil had declared as early as January 1919 that a state of war existed between Britain and Ireland, a section of *Sinn Féin was known to be unhappy with the bloodshed. IRA activists for their part demonstrated a reluctance to submit to the authority either of Volunteer GHQ or of the 'politicians' of Dáil Éireann. These divisions were later to contribute to the *Civil War of 1922–3. But for the moment what was remarkable was the success with which differences were concealed in the face of a common enemy.

Augusteijn, Joost, *From Public Defiance to Guerilla Warfare* (1996)

Fitzpatrick, David, *Politics and Irish Life 1913–21: Provincial Experience of War and Revolution* (1977)

Hart, Peter, *The I.R.A. and its Enemies—Violence and Community in Cork, 1916–1923* (1998)

Townshend, Charles, *The British Campaign in Ireland 1919–21* (1975)

Anglo-Norman colonization and settlement, a process which occurred mainly between *c*.1170 and *c*.1270, directed by the new *feudal aristocracy. It should be distinguished from the conquest (see ANGLO-NORMAN INVASION) as such: not all conquered territories were settled by significant numbers of Anglo-Norman tenants or town dwellers (*burgesses), but where this did occur, primarily in Leinster, Meath, and Munster, the demographic, social, and economic consequences proved to be abiding. Ireland was never again to be Gaelic in the sense that it had been before the conquest. Seen in its European context, the colonization of Ireland was part of a wider demographic movement, ranging from the settlement of wetlands and forests to accommodate an expanding population in north-western Europe to the penetration of the emerging Baltic and central European states by large numbers of German and Flemish colonists. Most villages and towns in the Anglo-Norman areas of Ireland, as in northern and central Europe generally, owe their origin to an immensely significant demographic shift that may without risk of exaggeration be compared to the changes wrought by the industrial revolution. Thus the Anglo-Norman conquest was the occasion rather than the cause of large-scale settlement. Had it occurred a century earlier or later, its impact on Ireland would have been greatly diminished.

The growth of historical interest in settlement originated in a pioneering article by A. J. Otway-Ruthven in 1965. Her challenge was quickly taken up by a rising generation of historians, historical geographers, and archaeologists, and shows no sign of slackening pace. As a measure of the new-found interest in settlement, Robin Frame dedicated a chapter to the subject in his book *Colonial Ireland, 1169–1369* (1981).

Unlike the carefully devised schemes that characterized the Irish *plantations of the 16th and 17th centuries, Anglo-Norman settlement patterns were more individualistic, not to say hit and miss, with a high incidence of misses. Feudal lords, whether they ruled great lordships or humble fiefs, were not obliged to fulfil plantation quotas like their Elizabethan and Jacobean successors. Neither were they medieval real estate agents. Their objective was the exploitation of their feudal and seigniorial prerogatives to the utmost. Where such considerations coincided with the location of their castles at points that were equally well placed for the exploitation of trade routes—like Kilkenny or Carlow—well and good. But as often as not their seats of power were selected for administrative or military considerations, for example Shanid, Nenagh, Dunkerrin, Knockgraffon, which never developed in the medieval period as significant centres of commerce. *Trim was the administrative axis of the great lordship of Meath, but it was *Drogheda that emerged as the engine of regional commerce. Nevertheless, within these constraints, the great lords undoubtedly sought to maximize their revenues by endowing their demesne manors and towns with considerable investments in the form of prime arable land. In spite of the turbulent circumstances of the initial conquest, the structures of the great lordships were carefully planned by their founding lords. The Butler lordship (see ORMOND (BUTLER)), comprising some 750,000 statute acres, was divided into seven *cantreds or baronies, each administered from a seigniorial centre or *caput*: Arklow, Tullow, and Gowran in Leinster, and Nenagh, Caherconlish, Dunkerrin, and Thurles in Munster. Each *caput* had its castle, demesne lands, seigniorial court, and town, with a dependent population of military tenants, free tenants, burgesses, tenants-at-will, cottiers, farmers, and, usually, servile tenants of the *betagh class.

The newly imported institution of the *manor was the vehicle of colonization. Having first taken care of the military needs of a conquered territory by building castles and organizing military fiefs, the lord sought to profit from the remainder by developing his demesne lands and founding a town as a focus for trade and as a school for essential crafts within his lordship. The skills for the latter, like the technology, had to be imported. Hence it was necessary to encourage immigration by demanding lighter labour services than were customary elsewhere in the Angevin world and by granting autonomy to the towns.

That a numerically significant assortment of landless English and Welsh labourers, serfs fleeing oppressive labour services, or medieval carpetbaggers seeking their fortune in the new colonial towns settled in Ireland seems undeniable, if we are to judge from the evidence of later manorial records, of the Dublin Guild Merchant Roll *c.*1190–1265, and of archaeological work on densely concentrated moated sites. Some settlements were highly successful. At the beginning of the 14th century there were about 200 small tenants on the demesne lands in Gowran. More problematical is the question of the population of the manorial town, which was composed of 515 burgages. Unfortunately, it is impossible to deduce from this how many burgesses actually rented them. Nor is it possible to estimate how many cottiers occupied dwellings in the lanes and backstreets, though they may have been as numerous as the burgesses. The total immigrant population, together with the knights and free tenants and their humbler dependants on the outlying manors (which accounted for 86 per cent of the entire area of the cantred), was probably well in excess of 1,000 households in an area of some 44,000 acres. Compared to the painfully slow progress of later plantations, such an achievement was remarkable.

But there were failures too, and not just near the thinly populated frontier. Even in the densely settled regions of Co. Kilkenny, we know of at least five towns that did not endure: the Newtown of Jerpoint, Coolaghmore, Danesfort, Odagh, and Tullaherin, and perhaps two others. In 1303 we hear of two towns called Kukomor and Clonetheran, near Thurles, which clearly survived only in the form of burgage tenures. This seems to have been all that remained of urban foundations that never got off the seigniorial drawing board. Nevertheless, the Anglo-Norman settlement reinforced a partial conquest to such a degree that it struck deeper social and cultural roots in strategic areas of Ireland than did a more comprehensive but exclusively aristocratic conquest of England a century earlier.

Barry, T. B., *The Archaeology of Medieval Ireland* (1987)
Empey, C. A., 'Conquest and Settlement: Patterns of Anglo-Norman Settlement in North Munster and South Leinster', *Irish Economic and Social History*, 13 (1986)
Otway-Ruthven, A. J., 'The Character of Norman Settlement in Ireland', *Historical Studies*, 5 (1965)

CAE

Anglo-Norman invasion (1169–72). Although 1169 has traditionally been considered as marking the beginning of the Anglo-Norman invasion of Ireland, the first overseas mercenaries actually arrived around August 1167 in the returning party of Diarmait *Mac Murchada, exiled king of Leinster, who, with their military help, recovered his patrimonial kingdom of *Uí Chennselaig. They were augmented in May 1169 by the arrival of Robert *fitz Stephen with 390 fighting men, and of Maurice fitz Gerald with about 140 soldiers, by *Raymond le Gros around May 1170, and by Richard fitz Gilbert, alias *Strongbow, in August 1170. It is the exaggerated role attributed by *Gerald of Wales to his uncles, Robert fitz Stephen and Maurice fitz Gerald, that has resulted in 1169 being regarded as the beginning of Anglo-Norman intervention.

Following Strongbow's arrival, Diarmait's position strengthened considerably; he not only consolidated his hold on the kingdom of Leinster, and the cities of Waterford and Dublin, but embarked on aggressive incursions into the bordering kingdom of Meath and on a bid to challenge Ruaidrí Ua Conchobair (see O'CONNOR, RORY) for the high kingship of Ireland. After Diarmait's death in spring 1171, Ruaidrí attempted, but failed, to assert control over the Anglo-Normans, now under the leadership of Strongbow, and, in particular, to capture the city of Dublin. The concern of King *Henry II that Strongbow, a prominent dissident tenant-in-chief, was now a lordless man in Ireland with potential capacity to attempt a forcible recovery of his lost earldom of Pembroke occasioned the English king's personal intervention in Ireland in September 1171. Henry not only successfully asserted lordship over those of his subjects who had gone to Ireland, but also received the submission of a significant number of Irish kings. This transformed the nature of Anglo-Norman intervention in Ireland: from mercenary activities undertaken initially in support of Diarmait Mac Murchada, and subsequently in pursuit of individual personal territorial aggrandizement, what was to become an enduring link was now forged between the English crown and Ireland.

Although the term 'Anglo-Norman invasion' enjoys wide currency, there is no scholarly consensus about how the incomers should be described: Norman, Cambro-Norman, Anglo-Norman, Anglo-French have all been used. Contemporary Irish sources invariably described them as *Saxain*, that is English; this usage is supported also by the two principal contemporary Anglo-Norman sources, Gerald of Wales and the so-called *Song of Dermot and the Earl*.

(See also NORMANS; ORPEN, GODDARD HENRY.)

MTF

Anglo-Scottish wars. These wars, which were relatively intensive from 1296 to 1346 and continued episodically during the rest of the medieval period, had a deep impact on Ireland. The proximity of north-east Ireland to south-west Scotland and the Isles meant that Ulster was almost as much a frontier as the Anglo-Scottish borders themselves. In the early stages of the war Edward I drew heavily on Ireland. Irish expeditionary forces sailed to Scotland in 1296, 1301, and 1303; supplies were shipped from the eastern and southern ports to Skinburness near Carlisle; and a large part of the Irish revenues was devoted to the war. As in England, government demands disturbed the economic and social stability of the areas affected. During the *Bruce invasion (1315–18), which damaged every province and weakened the earldom of *Ulster permanently, Ireland was a major sub-theatre of the wider conflict.

Although further Irish expeditions sailed to Scotland in 1322, 1333, and 1335 (when war taxation was granted in a parliament at Kilkenny), the military and political context had begun to change. After the death of Robert Bruce in 1329, Scottish royal power declined in the west, where the MacDonald lordship of the Isles emerged. Especially after the murder of William de *Burgh in 1333, English authority retreated from Ulster, where the vacuum was filled by the *O'Neills and from *c.*1400 by a branch of the *MacDonnells. The weakening of the Scottish monarchy, and the shift of the English military focus to France, also meant that hostilities became more spasmodic, and were mostly confined to the land frontier between the two kingdoms. The north of Ireland was thus once more part of a largely autonomous Gaelic world around the North Channel, where the Scottish and English kings competed for diplomatic influence.

Frame, R., *English Lordship in Ireland 1318–1361* (1982)
Lydon, J. F., 'Edward I, Ireland and the War in Scotland, 1303–1304', in id. (ed.), *England and Ireland in the Later Middle Ages* (1981)
—— *The Lordship of Ireland in the Middle Ages* (1972)

RFF

annals, chronologically arranged records of significant events, are the most significant body of evidence available for earlier periods of Irish history, and remain an important source, for Gaelic Ireland in particular, up to the 16th century. Most Irish annals survive in relatively recent manuscripts, of which the earliest is that of the *Annals of Inisfallen*, from the end of the 11th century; the remainder are found in manuscripts ranging from the late 14th down to the 17th century, and are combinations of several earlier texts. Most annalistic texts are of monastic origin: the earliest set, the *Iona Chronicle*, of the 8th century, survives incorporated into later annals. Perhaps the most important surviving text is the *Annals of Ulster*, in two manuscripts of the 15th–16th centuries, but transmitted faithfully as far as early medieval linguistic forms are concerned. A substantial part of the Ulster text for this period reappears, sometimes abridged, in the so-called *Clonmacnoise group: the *Chronicum Scotorum*, the *Annals of Tigernach*, and the *Annals of Clonmacnoise*, an English translation by Conell Mageoghegan in 1627 of a lost original; this group, from the 10th century onwards, is independent of the *Annals of Ulster*. A further text, the *Annals of Roscrea*, seems to be connected with the Clonmacnoise group.

Annals also survive from the south, e.g. the *Annals of Inisfallen*, in which much of the pre-10th-century material was probably taken from a member of the Clonmacnoise group, and compressed and garbled in the process. The first part of this was compiled in the monastery of Emly towards the end of the 10th century, and continued at Toomgraney in Co. Clare; thence transcribed in the monastery of Killaloe after the mid-11th century; and the manuscript transferred to Lismore about 1119, where it was continued; from the later 12th century the text was in the monastery of Inisfallen. Some of the 13th-century material in Inisfallen recurs in a rather later set of annals, the so-called MacCarthaigh Book, a compilation drawing on various sources in Munster and the south Ulster area, and even *Gerald of Wales. In the same way, Munster material has been incorporated in the *Annals of Tigernach*, as also central Leinster material of the 11th century; in the *Chronicum Scotorum* material from Munster and Leinster has been added for the later 11th century.

From the beginning of the 11th century the *Annals of Ulster* has a substantial core of material from Armagh down to 1189, as has the first part of the *Annals of Loch Cé*, and then annals from Derry for 1190–1220; in *Loch Cé*, this is matched by material from north Connacht, found also in the so-called *Cottonian Annals*, which down to 1228 were probably compiled in the *Cistercian abbey of Boyle; thereafter they were continued in the *Premonstratensian abbey of Loch Cé. This latter, and the *Annals of Connacht*, are the two chief Connacht sets of annals; both derive from a text compiled by a member of the Ó Maolchonaire family probably in the mid-15th century, and in the 16th century further processed by a member of the Ó Duibhgeannáin family. The ultimate compilation is the *Annals of the *Four Masters*, produced in the 17th century.

Anglo-Irish annals follow a similar pattern, though with more attention to English events, with early sets of annals incorporated into texts such as the *Annals of St Mary's*, Dublin; the *Annals of Multyfarnham* (down to 1274), compiled by Stephen Dexter, OFM; the *Kilkenny Chronicle*, also a Franciscan compilation, and the *Annals of* *Clyn, going down to the Great Plague of 1348–9; Pembridge's annals continue accounts down to 1370, and this is bridged to 1421 by Henry of Marleburgh's chronicle. A number of 15th-century compilations by Philip Flattesburg, surviving in several manuscripts, have yet to be critically edited.

Grabowski, K., and Dumville, D., *Chronicles and Annals of Mediaeval Ireland and Wales* (1984)

MacNiocaill, G., *The Medieval Irish Annals* (1975)

GMacN

Annesley, Francis, see MOUNTNORRIS, FRANCIS ANNESLEY, LORD.

anniversaries. The formal commemoration of important events has been a feature of Irish political culture since the 17th century, though often a contentious one. Guy Fawkes's day, 5 November, was first established by the *Cromwellian regime in 1656. It was confirmed in the 1666 Act of *Uniformity, along with 30 January (the execution of Charles I) and 29 May (the *Restoration). These last two, as celebrations of monarchy, had a particular appeal to royalists and later *Tories. In 1662 the Irish parliament had also ordered the annual commemoration of 23 October as a day of thanksgiving for deliverance from the *rising of 1641. This remained the main Protestant festival in Ireland for most of the 18th century.

Commemoration of *William III continued sporadically through the 18th century. From the 1790s, and especially after the establishment of the *Orange Order, celebration of the military victories at the *Boyne and *Aughrim took over from the commemoration of William's birthday (4 Nov.), and the theme of the defence of civil and religious freedom, which had made the Williamite tradition attractive to *patriots and radicals, gave way to the exaltation of Protestant supremacy. From the 1820s 12 July was joined in the Protestant festive calendar by the *Apprentice Boys' celebrations of 18 December and 12 August.

Official support for 23 October and 4 November was withdrawn by the short-lived Whig administration of 1806. Thereafter successive governments promoted St Patrick's Day (17 Mar.) as a non-party national festival. It became a bank holiday in 1903, and remains independent Ireland's principal national holiday. In Northern Ireland, though still a bank holiday, it was celebrated more enthusiastically by Catholics, and was marked by parades of the *Ancient Order of Hibernians. AOH parades were also held on 15 August, the Catholic festival of the Assumption of the Virgin Mary. Easter commemorations of the *rising of 1916 regularly brought republicans in Northern Ireland into confrontation with the security forces. In the south official commemoration of the rising was suspended from 1972, in response to the growing violence of the *Northern Ireland conflict, but the occasion is kept up by republicans, as is an annual commemoration at the grave of Wolfe *Tone at Bodenstown, Co. Kildare.

The continued sensitivity of political anniversaries in a divided society is also evident in the status of Armistice Day (11 Nov.), replaced from 1945 by Remembrance Sunday. Initially intended to commemorate the dead of the *First World War, it was largely co-opted in Northern Ireland into the *unionist political calendar. In 1987 an *IRA bomb killed eleven participants in the ceremony at Enniskillen, Co. Fermanagh. In independent Ireland what were initially significant Armistice Day ceremonies were marginalized by public hostility and government indifference. A war memorial park at Islandbridge outside Dublin, constructed 1931–8, lay largely derelict until refurbished and formally opened in 1994.

Walker, Brian, *Dancing to History's Tune: History, Myth, and Politics in Ireland* (1996)

Anti-Partition League, founded by Nationalists in *Northern Ireland in November 1945, following the election of a Labour government at Westminster, with the twin aims of developing an effective parliamentary protest movement to replace the desultory abstentionism of the previous decade, and of providing an effective constituency organization. It succeeded in neither: its base remained effectively rural, conservative, and clerical, leaving Catholic Belfast to a variety of labour groups; it also failed to develop effectively as a regular constituency organization, so that once the going got rough after 1949 it was unable to resist the revival of the trend (part republican inspired, part demoralization) to elect abstentionist candidates. Developments in the south, where de *Valera began a 'worldwide' anti-partition campaign after losing power in 1948 through the intervention of the neo-republican *Clann na Poblachta, and the *interparty government took Ireland out of the *Commonwealth, appeared to be helpful to the league, but in practice repolarized Ulster politics and split the *Northern Ireland Labour Party. The league's conservatism and traditional nationalism ultimately drove a wedge between it and its British allies, the *Friends of Ireland. The league organization in Britain continued throughout the 1950s, but in Northern Ireland it was moribund after 1951. ACH

anti-Semitism, see JEWS.

anti-slavery societies, initially dominated by Quakers and Unitarians, were active in Ireland from the 1780s. The issue was given political prominence by its association with *O'Connell, who took a leading part in parliamentary debates on abolition in the British empire in the 1830s, and in 1841–2 promoted the abolitionist 'Address of the People of Ireland to their Countrymen and Countrywomen in America', which attracted 70,000 signatures. O'Connell clashed with the *Young Irelanders in 1843–5 over his refusal to accept donations from Irish-American bodies which would not condemn slavery. PHG

Antrim, Randal MacDonnell, 2nd earl and 1st marquis of (1609–83). Antrim was a remarkable Gaelic Catholic survivor of the mid-17th-century civil wars. Gaining political prominence as a courtier in 1635 on marrying Katherine Manners, widow of the duke of Buckingham, he suggested that Charles I create a new army in Ireland to deal with the Scots Covenanters; when this saw no action he allegedly plotted with the king to use it against the English parliament.

After the *rising of 1641, Antrim was a royalist intermediary with the *Confederate Catholics, thereby securing the dispatch of Alastair Colla MacDonnell to support the king in Scotland (with the private subplot of regaining ancestral lands there). In the mayhem, he kept creditors at bay by building up a squadron of privateers and raising Irish mercenaries for foreign service. As the king's cause flagged, Antrim gravitated into confederate politics, becoming president of the supreme council and a chief opponent of peace with *Ormond, whose lord lieutenancy he was said to covet. After failing to succeed Owen Roe *O'Neill as general of the Ulster army, he saved himself by defecting to parliament. Despite his collaboration with both the confederates and Cromwellians, he regained his estates following the *Restoration, as a result of court connection and creditor pressure. HM

Apprentice Boys, a Protestant political society, named after the thirteen apprentices who on 7 December 1688 shut the gates of Derry against Catholic troops under Lord Antrim. Their motive was fear of an impending massacre of Protestants, aroused by the recent circulation of an inflammatory forgery (the 'Comber letter'), rather than allegiance to *William III; on 21 December the citizens agreed to accept a Protestant but nominally Jacobite garrison under Robert *Lundy. In retrospect, however, the closing of the gates initiated Derry's resistance to *James II.

The brotherhood of the Apprentice Boys of Derry, founded in 1814, has branches throughout Northern Ireland, in Britain, and in North America. Its members celebrate the shutting of the gates on 18 December and the lifting of the siege of *Derry on 12 August. (In both cases, as with the battle of the *Boyne, the gap between the old and new *calendar has been mistakenly taken as eleven days rather than ten.) Violence following the celebration of 12 August 1969 was an important stage in the development of the *Northern Ireland conflict.

Aran Islands, limestone outcrops dominating the sea lanes and *fisheries of Galway Bay. At the beginning of the Christian period great stone *cashels, most notably Dún Aonghasa, were built; later St Enda's monastery attracted scholars and ascetics from all over western Europe. Because of their strategic importance they were fought over by the O'Flahertys and O'Briens in the Middle Ages and by the *Confederate Catholics and parliamentarians in the early 1650s. In the 19th century Aran attracted archaeological, ethnographic, and philological interest. The *Board of Works 'restored' the ruined cashels; writers such as J. M. Synge found inspiration there; and in 1932 Robert Flaherty made his famously contrived documentary film *Man of Aran*. Economically and socially this *Gaeltacht area has suffered similar difficulties to other western parts, but now enjoys a thriving tourist trade on the back of a massive process of mythologization. HM

archers. Short bows, which were probably known in Ireland before the *Anglo-Norman intervention, were a main weapon of foot soldiers of both Gaelic and settler origin from the 12th century to the 16th. *Gerald of Wales emphasized the value of the archers, some mounted, who accompanied the invaders from south Wales. By the 14th century the accounts of army paymasters distinguished between ordinary infantry raised in Ireland and the more expensive longbowmen (*sagittarii*), who were mostly in the retinues that governors brought from England. The Statute of *Kilkenny (1366) enjoined archery practice on the settler population, but 'English bows' remained scarce even in the eastern counties. RFF

architecture. The majority of the architectural monuments surviving from the *neolithic and *Bronze ages are funerary or ritual, with few known habitation sites remaining. The most impressive structures from this period are court tombs such as Clady Halliday, Co. Tyrone, and passage tombs such as Newgrange. Both are constructed using megaliths covered by a large cairn of stones and earth. Some, like Newgrange, retain corbel-vaulted chambers. Other monuments from the period include dolmens, stone alignments, and wedge tombs.

The earliest *hillforts, such as Rathgall, Co. Wicklow, probably date from the last millennium BC. Typically they are constructed of one to four defensive ramparts following the contours of a hilltop; some, known as promontory forts, make use of naturally sheer gradients to minimize the amount of defensive construction. *Raths, circular or near circular enclosures with one or more earthen banks, are common countrywide, as are their stone equivalents, *cashels. These structures probably contained small dwellings and provided protection for livestock. Chronology is uncertain, although it is thought that the earliest date to the beginning of the early Christian period (*c.*400–*c.*500), and the latest to well after the *Anglo-Norman invasion. Artificial lake islands, known as *crannogs, were used as dwellings from the late Bronze Age to the 17th century, although most date to the early Christian era.

The introduction of *monasticism saw the development of small proto-urban settlements. Buildings, except in the most exposed of areas such as *Sceilig Mhichíl, were constructed from organic materials. Stone construction probably became more common during the 10th century. By the 9th or 10th century monastic sites were often characterized by several small oratories, a *round tower, a *high cross or crosses, and wooden dwellings, all contained within a roughly circular enclosure. Early stone oratories were skeuomorphs of their wooden predecessors; for example, the restored church on St Macdara's Island, Co. Galway, is small and rectangular in plan with a steeply pitched, corbelled stone roof. The walls have an inward lean and project at the east and west ends, mimicking wooden barge board supports; the gable finials are petrified copies of the crossed ends of gable rafters.

During the 12th century, while the rest of Europe witnessed the erection of large, architecturally complex Romanesque buildings, Irish building design remained conservative. Although the highly elaborate *Cormac's chapel was probably responsible for the introduction of elements of the style to Ireland, it is not typical of Irish Romanesque. Irish churches remained simple in plan, enlarged only by the addition of a chancel to the traditional single cell structure. The round-arched doors, chancel arches, and windows were emphasized by the application of low-relief sculpture, using a combination of indigenous and continentally inspired motifs, as at the Nuns' church, *Clonmacnoise (*c.*1167).

The advent of the Anglo-Normans and the *12th-century reform brought Irish architecture more in line with European trends. The religious orders, such as the *Cistercians at *Mellifont, built larger cruciform churches and combined them with cloisters and domestic buildings in a coherent and consistent manner. New Gothic cathedrals were erected in the larger towns under the influence of the Anglo-Normans, with several, such as *Christ Church in Dublin, showing close affinity to contemporary buildings in Britain. The Anglo-Normans initially built wooden fortifications on artificial earthen mounds (*mottes), sometimes with a raised enclosure at its base (bailey). From *c.*1190 to *c.*1310 larger stone fortresses of various design were erected, such as *Trim Castle, Co. Meath. After a 14th-century hiatus in building activity, the 15th century saw the foundation of many new friaries, particularly in the west of Ireland, and the renovation of several 13th-century religious houses. The *tower house, a new type of fortified residence, emerged at the beginning of the century; generally rectangular in plan, some tower houses are up to six storeys high and incorporate a number of defensive features; popular throughout the country, they continued to be built up to the 1650s. A development of the tower house was the semi-fortified house, typified by Burntcourt, Co. Tipperary (*c.*1641). These houses combined defence with a more formal symmetrical layout along the lines of Renaissance planning.

Completely unfortified residences did not become commonplace until the late 17th century with the appearance of mansions such as Beaulieu, Co. Louth (1660s). The architecture of this period was essentially Anglo-Dutch inspired. The Royal hospital, at Kilmainham outside Dublin (1680–84), by Sir William Robinson is the earliest public building to survive from this time. Towards the second quarter of the 18th century a new trend emerged, inspired principally by Italian architect Andrea Palladio's interpretation of classical Roman and Renaissance architecture. Many of the larger country houses of the period, such as *Castletown, and Richard *Castle's Russborough in Co. Wicklow (1742), reflect the style. Its most important protagonist was Edward Lovett *Pearce, whose *Parliament House (1729) was one of the first public Palladian buildings. The second half of the 18th century saw a new interest in town planning, particularly in the cities of Dublin, Cork, and Limerick, with the creation of wide streets and residential squares. Elegant town houses were erected, many decorated with fanlights over their doorways and fine *plasterwork interiors. Many smaller estate towns were also formally laid out. Towards the end of the 18th century Palladianism gave way to neoclassicism, looking directly to ancient Rome for inspiration. One of the earliest buildings in the style was Thomas Cooley's *Royal Exchange (1769). The most important architect during the last quarter of the century was James *Gandon, responsible for the *Four Courts and *Custom House in Dublin.

After the 1800s the emphasis of building activity shifted. At provincial level government-financed buildings such as jails, courthouses, and barracks were erected. Neoclassicism remained popular into the 1850s, particularly in public buildings such as the General Post Office in Dublin (1815) by Francis *Johnston and Galway courthouse (1812) by Sir Richard Morrison, but also in churches of all denominations, for example St Francis Xavier, Gardiner Street, Dublin (begun 1829), by J. B. Keane. In the early part of the century, funded by the Board of the *First Fruits, the *Church of Ireland erected many small Gothic revival churches. Following *Catholic emancipation (1829), the Roman Catholic church augmented its church-building campaign, predominantly, although not exclusively, favouring the neo-Gothic style.

Increased trade and industrialization led to a demand for new types of building. *Banks adopted the classical-Italianate idiom in both city and regional branches; industry required a more utilitarian approach and adhered less to any particular 'style'. Towards the turn of the century new *suburbs, built of red brick, and laid out on a grid system, were created to cater for the growing workforce.

During the 1920s and 1930s the 'modern movement' began to manifest itself in small-scale domestic buildings. The first major building to show the influence of the style was the terminal building, Dublin airport (1943), by Desmond FitzGerald. An increasing confidence in the use of steel and reinforced concrete led to greater areas of glass and to greater building heights, demonstrated by Michael Scott's Busáras (Central Bus Station) (1953) in Dublin. During the 1950s and 1960s the hitherto traditional approach to church building yielded to innovative design seen, for example, in the work of Liam McCormack at the church of St Aonghus, Burt, Co. Donegal.

Craig, Maurice, *The Architecture of Ireland* (1982)

RM

Ardnacrusha, the hydroelectric electricity generation plant constructed on the river Shannon 1925–9, was the first major public investment undertaken by the government of the *Irish Free State, and a symbol of the new state's optimism in the aftermath of the *Irish Civil War. The project—the brainchild of an Irish engineer, Thomas McLoughlin—was opposed by established businessmen, many of them unionists, who favoured a rival scheme on the river Liffey. The fact that the contract for the generating station was awarded to the German firm of Siemens added to the controversy. An unsuccessful strike by construction workers, who were demanding higher wages, became a test of the government's will to control labour costs. The scheme was completed in 1929. Responsibility for its management passed to the *Electricity Supply Board. MED

Ardnaree, battle of (23 Sept. 1586), fought on the banks of the river Moy in Co. Mayo, where Sir Richard *Bingham, the provincial governor, surprised a force of up to 2,000 *redshanks that had been invited into Connacht by the Mayo Burkes, killing about 1,000 mercenaries and an equal number of camp followers. HM

Arianism, a Christian heresy involving the denial of the full divinity of Christ, taking its name from its 4th-century originator, Arius of Alexandria. Arian opinions led to the imprisonment in 1702 of Thomas *Emlyn. From 1813 their public expression ceased to be a crime, and some leading Irish Presbyterian ministers acknowledged their Arianism, plunging the *Synod of Ulster into the bitter controversy that led to the *Remonstrant schism of 1830. RFGH

aristocracy. Parallel with the formation between the mid-16th and the early 18th centuries of an *ancien régime* landed elite, Ireland acquired a titled aristocracy. The kingdom possessed a peerage of medieval origin, but natural wastage and infrequent creations ensured that this had become a small and somewhat antiquated order. The Tudor monarchy began its rehabilitation, but this did not commence in earnest until the 17th century. Between them James I (1603–25) and Charles I (1625–49) conferred 116 peerages on 85 individuals, 50 of whom were Englishmen. Creations on this scale excited a predictably adverse reaction among existing peers, while there were also English objections to the presence of Irish peers in royal funeral processions.

The main beneficiaries of these creations were *New English landowners, ensuring that by 1688 Protestant peers greatly outnumbered Catholics. Five Protestant lay peers and four bishops attended the *patriot parliament, indicating that religiously based animosities were less entrenched among the aristocracy than among commoners; but those absent, in a total peerage of about 130, nevertheless outnumbered those present by two to one. *James II sought to rectify this by promoting loyal *Jacobites, but these peerages were not recognized by the Williamites. In the 18th century death and forfeiture, along with conversions, ensured that the Irish aristocracy became emphatically Protestant.

The financial difficulties of many Irish landowners in the early 18th century discouraged some from accepting peerages and contributed to the decision of 60 per cent of peers not to attend parliament. As a result, control of the House of *Lords passed to the bishops and a small number of active peers. These circumstances helped ensure that the Irish peerage continued to be regarded in England as an inferior order, though Englishmen constituted a high proportion of those who were admitted to its ranks between 1690 and 1760. This practice was encouraged by the fact that an Irish peerage did not disbar one from sitting in the House of Commons at *Westminster, and no fewer than 22 of the 24 men ennobled between 1715 and 1727 were or became MPs there.

As the economy grew in the second half of the 18th century, the number of Irish landowners and politicians admitted to the peerage increased markedly. Thirty-four of the 50 new peerages created between 1761 and 1785 went to Irishmen, and by 1799 two-thirds of the richest landowners in the country were ennobled. Some families, like the *Conollys, showed no interest in the peerage, but they were very much the exception.

There were 163 lay members of the Irish peerage in 1786, of whom 100 or so were resident and 70 were politically active. The continuing higher status of the English peerage encouraged Irish politicians, like the second Lord Shannon (see BOYLE), to seek English titles. Yet *patriot peers like Lord *Charlemont and the earl of *Kildare were nevertheless sufficiently confident to assert, and to secure, separate recognition for the Irish peerage. The status of the Irish aristocracy was, however, dealt a severe blow by the Act of *Union, when Irish peers lost the automatic right to membership of an upper house. Instead seats in the House of Lords of the united parliament were allocated to 28 lay lords, who were elected for life, and four spiritual lords.

G.E.C., *The Complete Peerage* (13 vols., 1910–59)

JK

'aristocratic home rule', a term popularized by *Curtis to refer to the period of relatively weak royal government which coincided with the *Wars of the Roses, when the lordship of Ireland was left increasingly to its own devices. Curtis thought he detected the emergence among the English of Ireland during this period of a home rule party, akin to the 19th-century movement.

Allegedly this reflected the growth of a separate sense of identity and spirit of self-reliance among the lordship's political community, in reaction to ill-considered initiatives from London; and it was epitomized by the *declaration of 1460 proclaiming that Ireland was 'corporate of itself'. Although historians remain divided about the contemporary significance of all this, such sentiments were undoubtedly important for the future when, in Elizabethan Ireland, they sharpened into a separate sense of *Old English identity.

Nevertheless, the hallmark of English local administration in the late Middle Ages, in Ireland as in England, was 'self-government at the king's command'. Traditionally, the king (or in Ireland his deputy) appointed the leading landowners (the nobles and 'county gentry') to important but unpaid office in each shire as *sheriff, *keepers/ justices of the peace, *escheators, and *coroners, and these ruled the shire under the supervision of the king's *council, the central *courts of law, and itinerant justices. Frequently too, provincial magnates co-ordinated the rule and defence of particular regions for the crown. Thus 'aristocratic home rule' was actually a normal part of English administration. Its differing interpretation in Ireland and England largely reflects separate historiographical traditions—the focus in Ireland on tension and confrontation between crown and community, and the stress in England on the peaceful extension of metropolitan values to the provinces.

In Ireland, a full but subordinate central administration, headed by a governor and usually based in Dublin, was interposed between the normal central and local tiers of government, so that the lordship's everyday administration was mostly discharged without reference to the king and council in England. The king, however, appointed the leading officers of his Irish administration and all important matters were referred to him. At times, the king might take a close interest in Irish affairs, intervening extensively in government, and he usually ensured that his leading ministers were partly recruited in England and not simply from the English of Ireland. Not surprisingly, this sometimes led to tensions between locals and outsiders, notably in 1341–2 (see RESUMPTION, ACTS OF), and, since there was no clear delimitation of functions between Dublin and Westminster, also between the two administrations.

Ellis, S. G., *Reform and Revival: English Government in Ireland 1470–1534* (1986)

Lydon, J. F., *The Lordship of Ireland in the Middle Ages* (1972)

SGE

Armagh, conventionally regarded as the most important Patrician (see PATRICK) site and thereafter as the ecclesiastical capital of Ireland. A large monastic complex had certainly evolved by the 8th century, and this is known to have developed secular urban trappings—craftsmen's quarters and streets—by the 11th century at the latest. But with modern archaeological confirmation of the antiquity of the Christian site (probably a pre-Christian hillfort converted to ecclesiastical functions in the 5th or 6th century), and given the successful consolidation of its power and status over several centuries as the premier ecclesiastical centre (helped along by its own Patrician propaganda), it is quite possible that social and commercial functions were in evidence at Armagh before 1000. Little beyond a few treasures from its workshops survive (notably the Book of *Armagh) and St Patrick's bell shrine (*c.*1100), and much remains to be understood of Armagh's early morphology.

Armagh's premier status in the new diocesan arrangements created as part of the *12th-century reform was disputed by Dublin until the 17th century (see PRIMATIAL CONTROVERSY), and it failed to develop (compared for example with Downpatrick) in the Anglo-Norman period. The cathedral was substantially enlarged in the mid-13th century, but lying outside effective English influence the town failed to develop further. Its mainly non-Gaelic medieval archbishops never resided.

Late 16th- and early 17th-century sources emphasized, perhaps exaggerated, Armagh's devastated state. As churchland property it lay outside the *Ulster plantation but several *Church of Ireland archbishops attempted to revive its fortunes at a time when much of the town's hinterland to the north was undergoing intensive colonization and economic transformation. It seems new streets to the east of the cathedral were planned in the 1620s, but no dramatic change occurred until the long archiepiscopate of Richard *Robinson (1765–94). The town's layout continued to reflect its origins—a street pattern which radiated outwards from the cathedral on the hill.

Robinson's programme, directing and encouraging civic and ecclesiastical reconstruction, acted as a catalyst for Armagh's emergence as a distinctive urban society. The fine classical architecture, institutional and domestic, reflects both the strength of this process and the skills of the two architects locally patronized, William Cooley and the Armagh-born Francis *Johnston. From fewer than 2,000 inhabitants in 1770 the town peaked at over 10,000 inhabitants in the 1840s. Thereafter it entered a gentle decline and, as the neighbouring towns to the north became mainly industrial, Armagh remained as educational, cultural, and service centre for much of south Ulster.

The town was never a predominantly Anglican enclave; the three main denominations were well represented with Catholics always the strongest numerically. The relative invisibility of Catholic Armagh was transformed with the construction of a twin-spired cathedral between 1840 and 1873, the scale and height of which more than rivalled the old cathedral (which itself had recently been reconstructed). The sharpness of Armagh's communal divisions in more recent times has been intensified by the contrasting religious make-up of its hinterland to the north and the south.

Clarkson, Leslie, 'Armagh 1770: Portrait of an Urban Community', in David Harkness and Mary O'Dowd (eds.), *The Town in Ireland* (1981)

DD

Armagh, Book of, a copy of the New Testament made for Abbot Torbach (d. 808) of Armagh in 807 by the master-scribe Ferdomnach (d. 846) and two assistants. Its small format suggests that it was originally intended for the abbot's personal use, but in the course of time it came to be regarded as one of the insignia of the *coarb of St *Patrick. As such it was used to record the offering made to Armagh by *Brian Bóruma in 1002. Until the late 17th century it was kept as a relic by its hereditary stewards before passing into private hands and eventually into the library of *Trinity College, Dublin. What has given this biblical manuscript its special interest for historians is that it also contains at the front a collection of 7th-century texts about St Patrick and at the back a copy of the 4th-century Life of St Martin of Tours. The Lives of St Patrick thus collected have sometimes been treated as though they were associated with the later reliquary status of the book. RS

Armagh outrages, the name commonly given to a concerted campaign of Protestant attacks on Catholic households in Armagh and adjoining counties, commencing after the battle of the *Diamond and continuing into 1796. Large numbers of Catholics, estimated at up to 7,000, fled the region, many settling in north Connacht, where some were later involved in the rising that followed *Humbert's landing. The newly formed *Orange Order, though disclaiming responsibility, was widely blamed for the violence. Although a meeting of magistrates chaired by Lord Gosford (28 Dec. 1795) strongly condemned the attacks, it was clear that many local officials and landowners tolerated or even encouraged the reassertion of Protestant supremacy. News of the Armagh expulsions, widely publicized by the *United Irishmen, contributed substantially to the growing sectarian bitterness of the years before the *insurrection of 1798.

Armagh Registers, seven volumes preserved in the *Public Record Office of Northern Ireland. They date from the middle of the 14th to the middle of the 16th century and are associated by name with the following archbishops: Milo Sweteman (1361–80), Nicholas Fleming (1404–16), John Swayne (1418–39), John Prene (1439–43), John Mey (1443–56), Octavian de Palatio (1478–1513), and George Cromer (1521–43). They contain a wide range of documents including accounts of visitations of the dioceses within the province of Armagh, correspondence with Rome, summonses to attend parliament, grants of rents and office, and records of the proceedings of the archbishop's court. They constitute one of the most important and underused sources for medieval Irish history. An edition of only one register, that of John Mey, has yet been published, although there are plans to publish the others. None of the archbishops for whose archiepiscopates a register survives was Irish and they normally resided among the English of Co. Louth, only rarely visiting the city of Armagh itself. Their dealings with the bishops and lay rulers of the parts of the province *inter Hibernicos*, which were often difficult, constitute a particularly fascinating and well-documented feature of the registers. BGCS

Armour, James Brown (1841–1928), leading Presbyterian clergyman and *home ruler. Born in Lisboy, Ballymoney, in the heartland of the northern liberal tradition, he was a Liberal Unionist between 1886 and 1892. His conversion to home rule owed less to national sentiment than to disenchantment with Anglican dominance inside the Unionist alliance. In addition Armour, like many Ulster liberals, was disappointed by the apparently limited extent of Conservative land reform. He achieved political prominence through a bold home rule declaration, delivered to a special meeting of the Presbyterian General Assembly on 15 March 1893. Armour helped to reorganize Ulster Liberalism in 1895, but withdrew from active politics until 1912–14. He supported home rule at the General Assembly of 1913, and in October 1913 helped to organize an important meeting of Protestant home rulers in Ballymoney town hall. Thereafter ill health and old age brought further marginalization: he remained blind to the appeal of *Sinn Féin, and regarded *partition with abhorrence. His last speech to the General Assembly, delivered in June 1924, revived his long-standing complaints concerning Presbyterian under-representation in public office. At the end he was what he had always been: a critic of the Anglican establishment in the style of the early 19th century. AJ

arms crisis (1970). This became public on 6 May 1970, when two *Fianna Fáil ministers, Neil Blaney (agriculture and fisheries) and Charles Haughey (finance), were dismissed by the *taoiseach, Jack *Lynch, for allegedly using government money to import arms for the *Irish Republican Army. This involvement in arms trafficking was an expression of the concern in the more *republican wing of Fianna Fáil over the development of a new *Northern Ireland conflict. Lynch may have been genuinely unaware of what was going on, but it was noted that he acted only after Liam Cosgrave, leader of the opposition party *Fine Gael, had informed him of the affair. Blaney and Haughey were subsequently charged, along with three others, with conspiring to import arms. However, the charges against Blaney were dropped in July and Haughey and the others were acquitted in October.

The issue was influenced by tensions within the government. Both Haughey and Blaney had leadership ambitions and they attempted to bring Lynch down by showing he was weak on one of the founding principles of Fianna Fáil. However, Lynch easily survived their challenge by calling upon party unity and loyalty to the leader. Blaney was expelled from the party in 1972. Haughey remained on the back benches and was eventually rehabilitated, becoming party leader in 1979. Kevin Boland, who had resigned as minister for local government in sympathy with Blaney and Haughey, left Fianna Fáil and set up a new party, Aontacht Éireann, with negligible electoral impact. JA

army. The medieval lordship of Ireland was never at peace behind stable borders. Its governors had frequently to summon forces to deal with local challenges, which became more common in the later Middle Ages as the colony stood increasingly on the defensive (see GAELIC RECOVERY). From time to time they might also be required to raise troops to participate in the king's wars in France or (particularly in the period 1296–1335) in the *Anglo-Scottish wars: in 1296, for instance, John de *Wogan led a paid force of 3,157 men to Edward I's first Scottish campaign.

Since frontier conditions prevailed in much of Ireland, a well of experienced manpower existed in the country. Direct tenants of the crown owed *knight service within Ireland in respect of their lands; they were periodically expected to fulfil their obligations either in person or (more often) by paying scutage. In addition, all able-bodied males aged between 16 and 60 were expected to possess arms and horses in proportion to their wealth, graded according to a schedule definitively set out in the Statute of Winchester (1285), which was extended to Ireland in 1308. Their personal service could be called upon in an emergency, though this general levy too might take the form of taxation, designed to hire substitutes. It is likely that unpaid levies formed an occasional supplement to paid forces.

Exchequer records surviving from the late 13th and 14th centuries show that *justiciars mustered paid armies almost every year. Such armies included some 'men-at-arms' (knights and other heavily armed cavalry), but consisted mostly of *hobelars and infantry. Apart from the justiciar's own household (based around 20 men-at-arms whom he was obliged to retain from his annual fee of £500), they were made up primarily of contingents led by settler nobles and gentry; but they might also include Gaelic chiefs who took the king's wages and semi-professional captains of *kerns or (mostly in the 15th century) *gallowglasses. Many of the elements in royal armies were thus little different from the forces to which they were opposed. Armies rarely stayed in the field for more than a few weeks or contained more than 1,000 men, reflecting the spasmodic, small-scale character of warfare in Ireland.

Medieval states rarely maintained standing armies. Before the mid-14th century virtually the only forces in that category in Ireland were the small garrisons kept in certain royal castles. The sense of crisis in the late Middle Ages, however, sometimes led the king to provide governors, especially those coming from England, with retinues of English men-at-arms and *archers which would be kept in pay for a fixed term of months or years; from 1361 their wages tended to be paid by the English exchequer. In 1361 *Lionel of Clarence brought around 800 English troops to Ireland, but such retinues were commonly less than half that size. As well as forming a core for armies raised locally, they might serve in 'wards' or garrisons at key points in Leinster and Munster. From the 1420s English help was available only occasionally. Anglo-Irish governors adopted various expedients in order to keep some standing forces. In 1474 the 7th earl of Kildare inaugurated a brotherhood of 13 lords, who were to supply 40 horse and 120 archers to be maintained from the customs revenues (see BROTHERHOOD OF ST GEORGE). But usually such troops were supported through a combination of parliamentary subsidies and the unpopular measure of imposing *coyne and livery on the *Pale counties. Despite these standing forces, most military activity continued to depend on a governor's ability to raise armies from scratch for particular objectives.

After the *Kildare rebellion, the royal army became a permanent force of English troops, although gallowglasses and kerns continued as auxiliaries for some time, and loyal subjects were occasionally called up to 'hostings'. For the remainder of Henry VIII's reign a minimum garrison of 500 was required and for the rest of the century at least 1,500. Numbers rose to peaks of 3,000 to fight Shane *O'Neill, 6,000 during the second *Desmond War, and possibly 20,000 in 1601–2. Costs escalated accordingly, putting an increasing burden on English taxpayers. Delayed arrival of treasure meant Dublin officials had to use their own funds or raise short-term loans to prevent mutinies by unpaid soldiers.

Most recruits were from the west country, Wales, and northern England, levied on a county basis after commissions were sent down by the privy council. Enlistment, theoretically voluntary, became particularly unpopular during the *Nine Years War. The county provided 'coat money' and the state 'conduct money' covering expenses to the ports of departure, usually Chester, Bristol, or Holyhead. Importing victuals from England became a necessary alternative to *cess when large numbers of troops were deployed during wartime, but 'contrary winds' on the Irish Sea often delayed delivery. Housing conditions were generally poor for men who were themselves often poorly shod and clothed. Training was limited and weapons—increasingly *firearms—were sometimes unserviceable. The army was a far more motley crew than that depicted in John *Derrick's *Image of Ireland*.

Diseases such as dysentery, typhus, and *Irish ague were rampant, killing up to a third of servicemen. At the height of the Nine Years War there were only six surgeons, even though each company was supposed to have one. Hospitals were eventually established at Derry, Dublin, and Cork. Desertion was rife and captains willingly took Irish replacements on less pay. Cavalrymen, assisted by their horseboys, fared better than infantrymen.

The lord deputy was the commander-in-chief, the Irish treasurer doubling as the treasurer-at-wars. The marshal headed the army on a day-to-day basis. During the *Tudor conquest this office became a sinecure for the *Bagenals, with other posts showing similar tendencies towards nepotism, corruption, and inefficiency. The captains, in charge of the companies (usually 100 strong), were responsible for paying, feeding, and clothing their men. They commonly cheated the state, the cess-payers, and their own companies, even though they already had the benefit of ten 'dead pays'.

Under James I numbers fell to 1,000 foot and 300 horse until the outbreak of war with Spain and France in the late 1620s. In 1640 *Wentworth, anticipating conflict between king and parliament in England, created a mostly Catholic Irish army of 8,000 foot and 1,000 horse, which was disbanded after his fall.

The subsequent *Confederate War, involving upwards of 60,000 combatants, replicated the problems of the Tudor conquest on a vast scale. With finance short, all parties resorted to demanding contributions on a county basis. Problems of billeting, feeding, and pay made mutinies commonplace. Only Oliver *Cromwell's army was well supplied and financed, though it met the familiar problems of disease.

After the *Restoration Charles II's government reduced the army to just below 7,000 men, less than half its size in 1655 but still well above pre-1641 peacetime numbers. As a safeguard against the political and religious radicalism of the force inherited from Cromwell, the new establishment included a Royal Regiment of Footguards, consisting of 1,200 men freshly raised in England. Later, following *Blood's plot, there were further dismissals throughout the army, the resulting vacancies being filled by new recruits. Army organization improved with the establishment by 1683 of a regimental structure, and the opening in 1684 of the Royal hospital at Kilmainham to provide for veterans. But government continued to be unwilling or unable to provide adequate funding, and arrears of pay led to a serious mutiny at Carrickfergus, Co. Antrim, in May 1666.

Following the accession of *James II the character of the Irish army was transformed, first by the introduction of Catholic officers like Justin *MacCarthy, then by a series of purges designed to replace Protestants with Catholics at all levels. After the *Williamite War the army regained its exclusively Protestant character, but in other respects there were radical changes. Irish Protestants as well as Catholics were now excluded, on the grounds that recruitment might weaken the Protestant interest within the kingdom. Instead the Irish army, though paid for out of Irish revenues and with senior appointments in the gift of the lord lieutenant, was in practice a part of the

English regular army, with regiments serving tours of duty in Ireland on a rotating basis. An English act of 1699 fixed the Irish peacetime military establishment at 12,000 men (as compared to 7,000 in England). In practice a section of this force was always deployed outside the kingdom: Ireland, in other words, became the base for a proportion of Britain's strategic reserves, and bore a share of the overall cost of imperial defence. In 1769 the Irish establishment was increased to 15,000, the 'augmentation' that provided the occasion for *Townshend's confrontation with the *undertakers.

The part of the establishment stationed in Ireland was expected to repel invasion and prevent insurrection. It also frequently acted in support of the civil powers in enforcing the law. However, the Irish military establishment quickly became notorious for its incompetence, corruption, and indiscipline, while service abroad, absenteeism, desertion, and the large number of pensioners and invalids included on the establishment ensured that its effective strength probably never exceeded 6,000 men. By mid-century the army's role was more clearly one of national defence, while also providing a strategic reserve of troops. Further changes were to follow. The enlisting of Irish Protestants began in 1745, while the surreptitious recruiting of Catholics was apparently commonplace by the 1780s. The *Catholic Relief Act of 1793 officially permitted Catholics to be enlisted in the ranks and to hold commissions.

The Act of *Union amalgamated the Irish and British military establishments. However, assimilation was not complete until 1822 when the Irish barrack boards were finally abolished. Prior to this a number of other difficulties had arisen, not least the status of Irish Catholic officers, who held their commissions under the Irish act of 1793 and had to wait for the Army Indemnity Act (1817) to confirm that these could legally be exercised in Great Britain.

The availability of barracks and cheap land led to the maintenance during the 19th century of an Irish garrison force of around 26,000 troops, about 14 per cent of total army strength. These troops continued to be employed as a strategic reserve for the empire, while being used both for internal security duties and for national defence. Throughout the century soldiers were used in aid of the civil power, though their role was not always a suppressive one. Soldiers were employed both in the *Ordnance Survey and in organizing poor relief during the *Great Famine. In garrison towns, such as Fermoy, as well as in Dublin, the army became important in economic and social life. However, relations between the army and the resident population were not always cordial, and local conflicts did occur.

An estimated 130,000 Irishmen served during the Napoleonic wars, and throughout the 19th century a sizeable proportion of the British army was Irish. In 1830 the figure exceeded 40 per cent, and although this steadily fell away to 13 per cent in 1899, it was still more than the Irish share of the United Kingdom population (9 per cent). Although the Irish gained a reputation for military fervour, there is little evidence that in fighting terms Irishmen were actually very different from Scottish, Welsh, or English troops. Lack of alternative employment opportunities at home contributed more to the high levels of Irish enlistments than any alleged fighting spirit.

Within the army tensions also arose between Catholic and Protestant soldiers, while in the 1860s attempts were made by *Fenian agitators to recruit serving soldiers. These proved to be passing threats, and the army in Ireland continued to be loyal to the crown. There is some evidence that the rising tide of Irish nationalism in the early 20th century depressed recruitment. Yet during the *First World War more Irishmen than ever before or since—over 200,000—served in the British army. Most of the British army units initially deployed during the *rising of 1916 were composed of Irishmen. Many Irishmen also served in the crown forces during what is somewhat misleadingly called the *Anglo-Irish War, though it was decided in 1919 not to station Irish infantry battalions in Ireland. There is evidence of nationalist feeling in some of the British army's Irish units during these years, and there was an actual mutiny in the 1st Battalion *Connaught Rangers in India in June 1920. For the regular army in Ireland the strains of 'counter-insurgency warfare' were considerable, and the commander-in-chief in Ireland, General Sir Nevil Macready, reported in the early summer of 1921 that the great bulk of his forces would need to be relieved by the end of the year. There were problems, too, of co-ordination with the increasingly militarized *Royal Irish Constabulary and its explicitly paramilitary *Auxiliary Division.

After *partition, when six of the eight Irish infantry regiments were disbanded, Irish enlistments fell off sharply, although significant numbers from both north and south joined up during the *Second World War. In the years since 1945 *Northern Ireland has proved proportionately to be a good recruiting area, and even in the late 1980s up to 20 per cent of Irish recruits for the British army still came from independent Ireland.

After the establishment of Northern Ireland the regular British army garrison in the province quickly fell away to no more than five battalions (including by the 1930s Irish regiments). For much of the province's history, up to the late 1960s, the army played no active part in maintaining the security of the state, which was left to the *Royal Ulster Constabulary (RUC) and the *Ulster Special Constabulary. The only time soldiers were used for riot control duties between 1922 and 1969 was for eleven days in July 1935 when sectarian violence broke out in Belfast. In the 1950s, however, army barracks provided targets for *IRA attacks and arms raids.

Regular soldiers were deployed in Northern Ireland 'in aid of the civil power' in August 1969, when the police proved unable to contain rioting in Belfast and Derry. Although the British government viewed this move merely as a temporary measure, for some five years the army effectively took the leading security role in the province. At the end of 1969 there were some 8,000 troops in Northern Ireland. Numbers reached a peak of 21,800 in July 1972 for 'Operation Motorman', when the security forces entered nationalist no-go areas. After this the numbers of regular troops fell back to below 10,000. A political consequence of army deployment was that control of security policy gradually shifted from Belfast to London, culminating in 1972 with *'direct rule' from London. In the mid-1970s, however, a policy of 'Ulsterization' was adopted, by which the leading role in security policy passed back to the civilian RUC, albeit with the army continuing in a supporting role, and supplemented by the *Ulster Defence Regiment (later subsumed within the Royal Irish Regiment).

In independent Ireland, by contrast, the army had from the start an important though anomalous role in national affairs. Formally constituted and organized for external defence, its main military function has always been an internal security one.

The army was established in January 1922, and was soon involved in *civil war against anti-treaty forces. By 1923 its strength stood at over 50,000 men. Victory, the need for economy, and civilian unease at its disruptive potential saw its rapid reduction. At the time of the officers' demobilization crisis or *army mutiny in March 1924, it had fewer than 20,000 men. By 1932 it had under 6,000, and virtually no fighting equipment other than rifles. There was also no worthwhile system of reserves. The army was allowed no say in defence policy, which consisted simply of statements that Ireland would abjure military alliances and would stay out of any war unless attacked. It was obliged to maintain large numbers of former British barracks and posts for purely internal security purposes, and government habitually used it both to assist in all manner of civil emergencies, and to act as both judge and jailer of persons charged with crimes against the state. (See INTERNMENT; SPECIAL COURTS.)

In 1934 a 'volunteer force' was set up. Intended largely to siphon off potential recruits from the IRA, it proved the mainstay of expansion in 1939/40, when the army found itself in a desperate position as it reorganized into two mobile divisions to defend Irish *neutrality. Entirely reliant on Britain for equipment and supplies, it had no worthwhile air or sea defences, and was incapable of land operations above company strength. Its operational capacity gradually grew, while *military intelligence performed vital counter-espionage and security tasks. After the war the army, cut to under 10,000 men, reverted initially to its dispiriting pre-war condition, confirmed by Ireland's refusal to join the North Atlantic Treaty Organization. In 1958, however, Ireland made its first military contribution to *United Nations operations. These became a mainstay of army life: at any one time up to 10 per cent of strength may be serving abroad on peacekeeping, observer, and humanitarian duties. After 1969 the *Northern Ireland conflict caused a revitalization. Numbers doubled to about 14,000, and modern infantry equipment and patrol vehicles were provided for border security. Other signs of modernization include the enlistment of women, and the recognition of representative associations for officers and men. External defence policy, however, remains rooted in neutralist rhetoric. Political exigencies make it unlikely that the army will ever be able to close many of the barracks it needlessly occupies, or to eschew the debilitating secondary tasks routinely thrust upon it by government. Despite the commitment and professionalism of its members, the army in independent Ireland remains what it always has been, an under-equipped infantry force just large enough to meet any likely internal security threat and to perpetuate the public illusion that the state is seriously committed to independent external defence.

See also FOREIGN ARMIES, IRISH IN; MILITIA; WARFARE; YEOMANRY.

Bartlett, Thomas, and Jeffery, Keith (eds.), *A Military History of Ireland* (1996)

Falls, Cyril, *Elizabeth's Irish Wars* (1950)

RFF/HM/SC/NG/KJ/EO'H

Army Comrades' Association, see BLUESHIRTS.

army mutiny (1924), a confrontation initiated by *IRA veterans within the Free State army, who on 6 March presented a memorandum to government demanding the suspension of post-*Civil War demobilization, and discussions on progress beyond the *Anglo-Irish treaty to a republic. *Cosgrave insisted on submission to military discipline, but promised an inquiry. On the night of 18–19 March troops arrested dissident officers gathered in a Dublin pub. The cabinet demanded the resignation of the adjutant general and two other senior officers, and accepted that of Richard *Mulcahy as minister of defence, on the grounds that this action had not been properly authorized. Ministers also condemned Mulcahy and his staff for encouraging the continued existence within the army of the *IRB, whose supposed clandestine influence had been another source of discontent. Although government claimed to have vindicated the supremacy of civilian over military authority, the peaceful resolution of the crisis depended heavily on the willingness of those who had confronted the 'mutineers' to be offered as sacrifices. Meanwhile the departure of Mulcahy and of Joseph McGrath, minister of industry and commerce, who had resigned in sympathy with the dissident officers, left the conservative wing of *Cumann na nGaedheal, headed by *O'Higgins, in undisputed control.

art schools. In the early 18th century drawing masters advertised classes in Dublin. The most important establishment was that of Robert West, whose drawing school was supported by the *Royal Dublin Society from 1746. It added further schools or classes in ornamental drawing in 1756, architectural drawing in 1764, and modelling in 1811. Drawing alone was taught, based on copying engravings of the old masters and casts of the antique. The society was in receipt of state funding and managed the schools successfully, making a major contribution to the development of Irish art, especially landscape painting. The best students went on to study in Rome or London. Many became craftsmen who played a decisive role in the building and furnishing of Georgian Ireland. In Cork the beginning of art education can be traced to the arrival in 1818 of a collection of plaster casts of Vatican marbles—made under Canova's direction—and given to Cork by *George IV, but the school fell into abeyance in the 1830s. From 1829 Irish fine art education took place principally in the antique and life schools of the *Royal Hibernian Academy. These schools, which continued until 1940, were subvented by the state and the Academy students went on to study on the Continent.

During the 19th century the Board of Trade, and from 1854 the Department of Science and Art, promoted the establishment of schools of design in the United Kingdom. Under these auspices the Royal Dublin Society schools of drawing became a school of design in 1849. In 1877 this was nationalized and renamed the Dublin Metropolitan School of Art. A Cork School of Design was established in 1850, funded municipally from 1856, and in 1884 it was provided with purpose-built studios by the brewer W. H. Crawford. Schools of design were also established in Waterford in 1852 and in Limerick in 1854. The Belfast School of Design, oriented to the linen industry, opened in 1850 but, due to disagreements with the state, it ceased to function and was closed in 1855. In 1870 it was re-established, and municipalized in 1901. In Derry a school of design was set up in 1874 and was, like the others, absorbed municipally following the passing of the Technical Instruction Act of 1899. By the late 19th century, schools of design had become general art schools where women were a substantial part of the student body. Mainly they taught still life and drawing of ornament, rather than fine art figure drawing. From the early 20th century the arts and crafts were also important.

In 1900 the Department of *Agriculture and Technical Instruction, Dublin, took over supervision of art schools. After *partition and the *Anglo-Irish treaty, the Departments of Education in Northern Ireland and the Free State took control. In 1930 the Vocational Education Act restructured all the technical colleges, including art departments, in the Free State but the institutions did not develop much in the period 1930–60. Major changes came in the 1960s. First the Belfast School of Art, which moved into a modern building in 1968, became part of the Ulster Polytechnic and later of the University of Ulster. In the Irish Republic the National College of Art, as the Dublin Metropolitan School of Art had become in 1936, was reconstituted by statute, following serious student disturbances, as the National College of Art and Design (1971). From 1969 the Regional Technical Colleges (later Institutes) were established, incorporating the old technical school art departments, as in Cork, Waterford, Limerick, Galway, Sligo, and Athlone. The Dun Laoghaire School of Art, Co. Dublin, emerged in the 1960s from a technical college and specialized in film and the new media, becoming an Institute of Technology. The College of Marketing and Design, Dublin, became a school of the Dublin Institute of Technology with a particular strength in interior design. The National College of Art and Design, which had moved from its historic site in Kildare Street to new buildings in Thomas Street in 1980, had the widest range of specialisms and was the first institution in the state from 1980 to introduce degrees in art and design at undergraduate and later at postgraduate levels. It became a recognized college of the *National University of Ireland in 1996.

Strickland, Walter, *A Dictionary of Irish Artists* (1913)
Turpin, John, *A School of Art in Dublin since the Eighteenth Century: A History of the National College of Art and Design* (1995)

JT

Asquith, Herbert Henry (1852–1928), politician and barrister. As a Liberal, Asquith served as British home secretary (1892–5), chancellor of the exchequer (1905–8), and prime minister (1908–17). His interest in Irish affairs began whilst at Oxford. Speaking against *coercion soon after entering parliament in 1886, he came to prominence as junior counsel for *Parnell at the special commission (see 'PARNELLISM AND CRIME'). In 1912 he introduced the third *home rule bill. Visiting Ireland after the *rising of 1916, he unsuccessfully advocated the immediate implementation of home rule. From 1920 he concentrated solely on Irish affairs in parliament, opposing *partition and seeking dominion status for all Ireland. Asquith was in every way the natural political heir to *Gladstone. NG

assize, a form of civil legal remedy available in the courts of the medieval lordship whose distinctive characteristic was that of allowing a jury to give a verdict on the merits of a claim in the defendant's absence from court. The two main types of assize were *novel disseisin*, where the claimant asserted he had been unjustly dispossessed of land, and *mort d'ancestor*, where he asserted that a close relative had died in possession of land and he was the rightful heir. A less common form (*darrein presentment*) allowed a patron to assert his right to present a rector to a church at a vacancy. All three types of assize had been created by *Henry II and his advisers for use by litigants in England between 1166 and 1179. *Novel disseisin* and *mort d'ancestor* were in use in Ireland before the end of the 12th century, *darrein presentment* a little later. 'Assize' also refers to the jury giving the verdict in such cases; *assizes came to mean the regular county sessions of royal justices held from the last quarter of the 13th century onwards to hear assizes and try prisoners in custody in local gaols. PAB

assizes of counties, and towns and cities accorded county status, were the primary local courts of criminal trial in Ireland for around 300 years. The assize system consisted of justices of assize, empowered by royal commissions, travelling the country to try both civil and criminal cases. Its origins in Ireland may be traced back to the eyre courts of the 13th and 14th centuries (see COURTS OF LAW). However, the holding of comprehensive courts of assize was always dependent upon military control, and it was not until after the *Flight of the Earls that the goal of regular assizes across the country could be realized. Even then several areas existed as independent *liberties under private patronage. By 1614 five assize circuits had been established. The judges of the superior courts were required to travel these circuits as justices of assize, holding an assize for each county jurisdiction subject to the crown. The 17th century saw the circuits consolidated. By 1695 every county was visited twice yearly, in spring and summer. The final provincial *palatinate jurisdiction was abolished in 1716, leaving only Co. Dublin outside the system, with its own autonomous courts.

The assizes now formed a regular and comprehensive system of criminal and civil equity across Ireland. In 1796 a sixth circuit was established to reduce the pressure on the courts' staff. As well as their legal functions assizes also fulfilled social, economic, and political roles, for example providing the focus for balls and fairs. Court business was accompanied by a great deal of the work of *local government, managed by county *grand juries. A number of changes occurred during the 19th century. By 1850 much of the existing civil business of the assizes had been delegated to the quarter sessions (see COURTS OF LAW). From 1877 a single 'winter assize' was held for each province, at a central venue, solely to deal with criminal business. In 1885 the system returned to a five-circuit structure.

From 1919 the *Anglo-Irish War disrupted all the royal courts. Rival *Dáil courts were established, and in many areas the assizes ceased to function. Following *partition, the *Irish Free State replaced the assizes with essentially similar circuit courts. In *Northern Ireland the restructured courts of assize were finally abolished in 1978, and their powers transferred to the new crown courts.

McCavitt, J., 'Good Planets in their Several Spheares: The Establishment of the Assize Circuits in Early Seventeenth-Century Ireland', *Irish Jurist*, NS (1989)
McDowell, R. B., *The Irish Administration 1801–1914* (1964)

NG

Athenry, battle of (10 Aug. 1316), one of the bloodiest battles in later medieval Ireland. It was fought at Athenry, Co. Galway, between the Anglo-Irish of Connacht led by William Liath de Burgh, cousin of Richard de *Burgh, the Red Earl, and a vast army of the Irish of Connacht and elsewhere, under Felim O'Connor (Fedlimid Ua Conchobair). The latter was killed amid a great slaughter and the *O'Connors never regained their former power. SD

Aughrim, battle of (12 July 1691), in the *Williamite War. The Williamites had crossed the Shannon at Athlone on 30 June. The marquis de Saint-Ruth, *Jacobite commander, made a stand at Kilcommodon or Aughrim Hill, 16 miles to the south west, in Co. Galway. His army was strongly placed behind a marsh, but was outflanked when Williamite cavalry crossed a causeway to its left, Saint-Ruth being decapitated by a cannon ball before he could order a response. The slaughter of the fleeing Jacobites, bringing their total losses to over 7,000, makes this the bloodiest battle fought in Ireland.

Augustinian canons. St *Malachy was the chief promoter of the Augustinian canons. His first contacts were with the canons of Guisborough in Yorkshire and these may have influenced some of the foundations made before 1140.

His visit to the Augustinians of Arrouaise in France in 1140 occurred at a time when the community was making new foundations. The Arroasians had adopted many of the *Cistercian observances (including the annual general chapter) and Malachy introduced their observance into a number of monasteries in the north of Ireland. They were promoted by Laurence *O'Toole (Lorcán Ua Tuathail) in the province of Dublin and established in some Munster monasteries at the beginning of the 13th century. They received widespread support from Gaelic and Anglo-Norman patrons but were isolated from the rest of the order by 1200. By the late 13th century most houses had dropped the Arroasian observances and conventual life had collapsed in many houses in Gaelic areas by the 15th century.

The Augustinian canons of the congregation of St Victor also had a number of houses in Ireland, the most important of which was the abbey of St Thomas the Martyr in Dublin (founded 1177). CNÓC

Augustinian friars (the order of Hermits of St Augustine), a religious order that established eleven houses in Ireland between 1282 and 1341. Founded from England, they initially gravitated towards Anglo-Norman settlements. At first they were directly governed by the English provincial as one of the five 'limits' of the English province, but from 1394, following agitation by the Anglo-Irish friars, they were granted increasing powers of self-government.

A second phase of expansion saw nine new friaries (eight in Connacht) founded between *c.*1380 and 1500. In 1457 the Connacht houses were given autonomy by the prior-general, who allowed the appointment of a rector with the same powers as the vicar provincial. The *Observant reform movement within the order emerged at Banada, Co. Sligo, in 1423 and eventually spread to seven other houses. In 1479 Callan, Co. Kilkenny, was made the head of an Observant congregation which was directly subject to the prior general of the order.

Government of the Irish limit had passed to the Gaelic friars by 1518 with the appointment of Richard Nangle as vicar provincial. He held the post again in 1539 but accepted the *Reformation and became, on account of his skill at preaching in Irish, the first Anglican bishop of Clonfert. The twelve houses in the *Pale, Munster, and Leinster were suppressed by 1539–40, but the houses in Gaelic areas survived into the reign of Elizabeth. A revival of the friars began in 1613 and continued throughout the 17th and 18th centuries. In 1750 there were 128 friars in Ireland but, like the other mendicants, the Augustinians went into decline with the closure of their Irish novitiates by *Propaganda Fide in 1751 (see RELIGIOUS ORDERS). CNÓC

Australia received only about 5 per cent of the emigrants who left Ireland during the 19th century. These, however, made up nearly a quarter of all immigrants during that period. A proportion of Irish arrivals came by *transportation, many of them being joined subsequently by wives and children. Of the remainder, a majority received some form of government assistance towards the cost of a long and expensive journey. The largest groups of emigrants came from a group of south-midland counties (Kilkenny, Tipperary, Limerick, Clare) and from south and central Ulster (Cavan, Fermanagh, Tyrone). Irish immigration peaked during the gold rush of the 1850s and fell off sharply after the 1880s.

Reliance on assisted passage meant that settlement in Australia was determined less by pressures in Ireland than by the needs of the colony: there was, in particular, no great surge of migrants during the *Great Famine. Closer official regulation may also help to explain why Irish settlers in Australia were more evenly distributed, both geographically and in terms of occupation and social status, than was initially the case in the *United States and elsewhere. In addition their status as the second largest ethnic group (after the English) made them less vulnerable to discrimination.

The legend of the bushranger Ned Kelly (1854–80), along with overemphasis on transportation as a route to Australia, has encouraged a stereotype of outcast rebelliousness. Mid-19th-century statistics reveal that Irishmen were indeed over-represented among convicted criminals, but also within the police force. Most of the Irish born who achieved prominence in the early decades of Australian history were from the Protestant middle and upper classes, like Sir Richard Bourke, governor of New South Wales 1831–8. However, Michael *Dwyer, Gavan *Duffy, and Daniel *Mannix, in their different ways, provided examples of what was to become an increasingly well-established pattern of pragmatic assimilation. In politics, the Irish of Australia strongly supported *home rule for Ireland, but showed less enthusiasm for the separatist *republicanism that later displaced it.

Auxiliaries, the Auxiliary Division of the *Royal Irish Constabulary (RIC), raised from among demobilized officers of the British army in response to the escalation of the *Anglo-Irish War. Recruitment began in July 1920 and by November 1921 some 1,900 men had joined. While nominally under RIC command, outside Dublin the Auxiliaries in fact operated independently. Divided into companies of about 100 men, they were heavily armed and highly mobile. By mid-1921 fifteen companies were scattered through what were considered the ten most disturbed counties, mainly in the south and west. Recruited hurriedly and with insufficient planning as to their role, the Auxiliaries soon gained a well-deserved reputation for drunkenness and brutality. Unable to discipline them, their commander, Brig. Gen. Frank Crozier, a former *Ulster Volunteer Force officer, resigned in February 1921. The sobriquet *Black and Tans was often applied to the Auxiliaries, as well as to British-born RIC constables, although the two groups were distinctly different. Disbanded in 1922, many Auxiliaries subsequently joined the Palestine police force. ELM

Averell, Adam (1754–1847), *Methodist minister. Born in Co. Tyrone and educated at *Trinity College, Dublin, Averell was ordained into the *Church of Ireland in 1777. However, he did not take up clerical office until 1789, and the intervening years were spent as a private tutor and schoolmaster. Slowly Averell became more *evangelical in his views, and in October 1792 he preached for the first time to a Methodist congregation. Four years later he became a member of the Dublin Methodist Conference, and began a long career as a Methodist preacher and administrator. In 1818 the Methodist movement in Ireland split, and Averell emerged as the leader of the minority Primitive Wesleyan Methodist Conference. This group, whose presidency he retained until his retirement in 1841, regarded itself less as an independent church than as a religious society within the established church. In 1878, after *disestablishment, the two Methodist factions reunited, leaving Averell's influence to be seen as perhaps ultimately divisive. NG

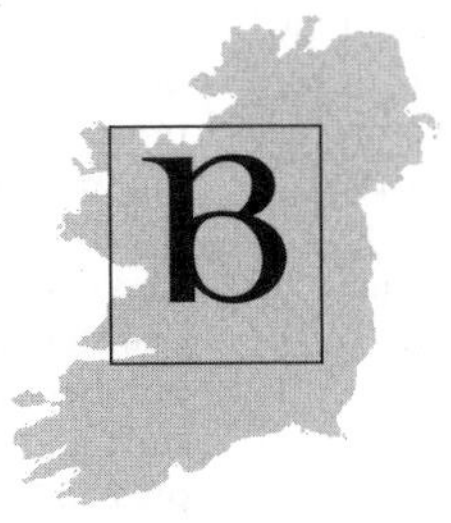

Bagenal, Nicholas (1508–91), from the English midlands, made marshal of the army and granted Newry with the lordships of Mourne and Carlingford in 1548. He built up Newry as a mainly Gaelic town. In 1577 *Sidney made him chief commissioner of Ulster, in the hope of eventually erecting a *provincial presidency. Bagenal helped contain the *O'Neills, first Turlough and then Hugh, but his authority never extended beyond south-east Ulster. The marshal disliked the interference of other English colonists and administrators, especially *Perrot, with whom he quarrelled violently in 1587. His son **Henry Bagenal** succeeded him as marshal and was killed at the battle of the *Yellow Ford. HM

Baginbun is immortalized in the rhyme 'At the creek of Baginbun | Ireland was lost and won', first attested in Meredith Hanmer's *Chronicle of Ireland* (1571), where it was applied to the landing place of Robert *fitz Stephen in 1169. Baginbun, in fact, has been identified as Dún Domnaill, the landing place in 1170 of *Raymond le Gros, who erected a fortification there, repulsed an attack by the men of Waterford, and thereby secured a foothold in Leinster. MTF

Bagwell, Richard (1840–1918), gentleman-historian, born in Clonmel, Co. Tipperary, educated at Harrow and Oxford. The son of John Bagwell, *Liberal MP for Clonmel 1857–74, Bagwell wrote a number of anti-*home rule articles in the *Dublin University Magazine*. His life's work was *Ireland under the Tudors* (3 vols., 1885–90) and *Ireland under the Stuarts and during the Interregnum* (3 vols., 1909–16). His scholarship, based largely on printed sources, was solid and balanced if somewhat uncritical. Standish O'Grady in his populist *Red Hugh's Captivity* (1889) asked: 'Has the reader ever rambled through *Ireland under the Tudors* on a holiday? Does he desire another pleasure trip of the sort?' HM

baile biataigh, see BALLYBOE.

baking, see BREAD.

Bale, John (1495–1563), a pugnacious English reformer who served as bishop of Ossory 1552–3. A Carmelite friar, Bale was born at Dunwich in Suffolk and educated at Cambridge University. He converted to Protestantism in the 1530s, and in 1540 had to flee to the Continent. There he began his broad-ranging scholarly career, as a bibliographer, Protestant dramatist, and highly influential commentator on the Book of Revelation. On Edward VI's succession in 1547 Bale returned to England, but, disappointed of advancement, he accepted the bishopric of Ossory in 1552. His appointment was an attempt by the English authorities to impose a firmly Protestant prelate on a strategically important diocese. Bale's entertaining account (in his *Vocacyon*) of his brief time as bishop provides a unique insight into the impact of English Protestantism in an Irish context. Though a few people may have responded positively, local reaction to the new religion was hostile and even, after the news of Edward's death and the accession of the Catholic Mary, violent. Fearing for his life, Bale fled from Ireland, never to return. AF

Balfour, Arthur (1848–1930), 1st earl of Balfour. Balfour succeeded his uncle Lord Salisbury as Conservative prime minister 1902–5. As *chief secretary for Ireland 1887–91 he influenced Conservative Irish policy for a generation. Intellectual, sceptical, and uninspiring, he was a ruthless administrator. He became known as 'Bloody Balfour' after the 'Mitchelstown massacre' in 1887, when police fired on an angry crowd, and his tenure in Ireland was dominated by resolute efforts to resist the *Plan of Campaign. He introduced 'perpetual' *coercion legislation in 1887. But he was also associated with what came to be called *'constructive unionism', establishing the *Congested Districts Board, 1891, and supporting proposals for a Catholic university. Intellectually he despised nationalism; he probably despised Ulster *Unionism too, but gave it pragmatic respect, especially after the *devolution crisis. He expected Irish independence to come, and as an elder statesman in cabinet supported *Lloyd George's abortive *home rule proposals in 1916 and the *Anglo-Irish treaty of 1921. His brother **Gerald Balfour** (1853–1945), who also served as chief secretary for Ireland (1895–1900), gave a greater boost to nationalism than perhaps he intended with his *Local Government Act of 1898. ACH

ballads. The ballad tradition in Ireland extends back at least to the closing decade of the 16th century, but its history in modern Ireland is more commonly associated with the widespread publication of ballad sheets and chapbooks from the middle of the 18th century onwards. In the period 1780–1900, many of these publications were directly related to political developments, and street ballads in particular can be regarded as a running commentary on Irish political life. By the late 1790s, collections of ballad texts were commonplace, most of them explicitly associated with revolution and nationalist or patriotic sentiment. The events of 1798 were to become a standard trope in the ballad repertory. *Emmet, *Tone, *O'Connell, and *Parnell were frequently eulogized. In the 19th century, the ballads of *Young Ireland (published in the **Nation* and separately as *The Spirit of the Nation* (1843, 1845)) not only enshrined the doctrinaire nationalism of *Davis and his peers: they also demonstrably fomented Irish political opinion. The appropriation of the ballad tradition by political movements led to a more literary strain of text, in which Ireland's personification as a young or old woman emulated the conventions of bardic poetry. A more violent strain of balladry was fostered by the *United Irishman* (1848–) and by the songs published in the *Fenian weekly, the *Irish People* (1863–5). From the middle of the 19th century onwards, a proliferation of ballad collections, some with music, was published in Ireland and the United States.

Although many ballads were set to newly composed airs, the provenance of the music for the most part is obscure. Thomas Moore's *Irish Melodies* (1808–34) were adapted on occasion, as were songs taken from opera.

The extent to which contemporary political ballads inspired by the *Northern Ireland conflict were proscribed by the British and Irish media awaits research.

Shields, Hugh, *Narrative Singing in Ireland* (1993)
Zimmerman, Georges-Denis, *Songs of Irish Rebellion* (1967)

HW

Ballinasloe, Co. Galway, the site of Ireland's best known *fair. While patents were granted for fairs on this site in the 17th century, they did not prosper until the early 18th century. There were a number of fairs in the town by the 1750s, each of which performed a different economic function. The *wool fairs, for instance, attracted the Leinster and Munster wool combers in large numbers to purchase raw wool. Even in years, such as the 1770s, when the wool trade was depressed the sales at Ballinasloe continued to rise. More famous than the wool fair was the autumn horse fair which attracted purchasers from as far away as France as well as the quartermasters of the British army seeking horses. The Ballinasloe fairs were victims of the early 19th-century trade depression and by the middle of the century had shrunk considerably in size before finally ceasing in the early 1900s. The horse fair was revived in the 1950s as part of a local festival. RG

ballot. The secret ballot, ending the system whereby a voter's choice was publicly declared and entered beside his name, was introduced throughout the United Kingdom from 1872. Its impact on Irish politics was relatively minor. Already before 1874 *O'Donovan Rossa's election for Tipperary, and a series of subsequent by-election victories for *home rulers, had demonstrated that voters were prepared to defy pressure from *landlords (and in some cases priests) in order to support popular nationalist candidates. The act did, however, make it easier for Ulster Protestant voters to back the cause of land reform, contributing to the significant electoral advance of Ulster *Liberalism before and during the *Land War.

ballybetach, see BALLYBOE.

ballyboe (ballybetach) (Ir. *baile biataigh*, 'residence of a food provider'), a medieval territorial unit, a subdivision of the *cantred, of varying extent, depending on the quality of the soil and the nature of the terrain. GMacN

Ballymote, Book of, a large manuscript anthology of genealogical, legal, historical, and literary material compiled *c.*1383–7 (with two main assistant scribes) by Maghnus Ó Duibhgeannáin, a hereditary *seanchaidh*, or historian, from a family with branches in Leitrim and Roscommon. Unlike the Book of Uí Mhaine, which was written for a patron, Bishop (later Archbishop) Muircheartach Ó Ceallaigh, the Book of Ballymote was apparently intended as a source-book for the compiler's professional needs. It contains texts from 11th- and 12th-century manuscripts, including the Book of *Leinster, together with some borrowings from European literature, a tract on the *ogam alphabet with many innovative variations, retold sagas, and aristocratic *genealogies updated to the 1390s. Handwriting and illuminations recall 12th-century *decorated manuscripts. KS

Balscot, Alexander de (d. 1400), also known as 'Petit', a key figure in the Irish administration from the 1370s to 1400. From Oxfordshire, he became a canon of Ossory and then bishop of Ossory (1371) and of Meath (1386). His range of experience within the lordship's administration was very extensive. He served both as treasurer (1376–84) and as chancellor (1385–6, 1395–7, and 1399–1400). His experience prompted appointment on four occasions as *justiciar (1379, 1387–9, 1391–2, and 1400). He was thus deeply involved in the military and financial crises facing the lordship in the 1370s and 1380s, a key local adviser during *Richard II's Irish expeditions, and partly responsible for the implementation of Richard's settlement after 1395. DBJ

Baltinglass rebellion (1580–1). James Eustace, Viscount Baltinglass, led this Catholic revolt in the *Pale with support from his family's traditional enemy, Feagh MacHugh *O'Byrne, who defeated Lord Deputy Grey at *Glenmalure. Fearing widespread conspiracy, Grey overreacted and arrested Kildare and Delvin, who had earlier refused Baltinglass support. A secondary revolt by William Nugent, Delvin's brother, encouraged the sort of conspiracy which Grey had originally feared. Fifteen Palesmen, including the uninvolved Nicholas Nugent, were executed. Rebel lands were given to Grey's servants, cronies, and army captains; Baltinglass and Nugent fled to the Continent. HM

Bandon, the largest and in economic terms most successful new town of the *Munster plantation. Originally laid out as two towns on opposite banks of the river Bandon by minor players in the plantation, it was united under its second owner, Richard *Boyle, 1st earl of Cork, and expanded greatly under his patronage to become the anchor and bastion of the New English colony in early 17th-century west Cork. The town was walled and strongly fortified by 1618 (with Irish tenants and the unskilled clustered outside the walls). It remained under Protestant control throughout the Confederate War, but briefly passed into Jacobite control in 1689 (see WILLIAMITE WAR), at which time the walls were comprehensively razed.

The distinctive feature of Bandon's urban economy for more than 200 years was high-quality textile manufacturing, and the distinguishing characteristic of urban society for an even longer period was its strongly Protestant composition. *Woollen and *linen weaving in town and hinterland gave ground to *cotton in the early 19th century, but the mill-based prosperity of Bandon's cotton industry was short-lived: employment collapsed in the 1820s, and the development of *brewing and *distilling in the town failed to halt the exceptional decline of the urban population. Its former role as a military town was also threatened after the end of the *revolutionary and Napoleonic wars. Population peaked at around 10,000 in the early 1820s, then fell by a third in the following 30 years, by a further 42 per cent in the next three decades, and by an additional 22 per cent by 1911. Catholics may have been in a majority in the town by 1800, but even in decline the strongly Protestant reputation of the town and its inner hinterland remained.

Simms, Anngret, and Andrews, J. H. (eds.), *Irish Country Towns* (1994)

DD

Bangor, founded as a monastery on the south shore of Belfast Lough by St Comgall in the middle of the 6th century and presided over by him for 50 years. Among his monks were two who established a name for themselves elsewhere, St Moluag of Lismore, prominent in the west of Scotland, and the more famous *Columbanus of Bobbio, whose Life by Jonas is the earliest source of information on Comgall. Among its early abbots was Mosinu moccu Min, author of a short computistical tract that survives. From the late 7th century there survives the *Antiphonary of Bangor*, an important witness to the hymns of the early Irish church, which includes a poem on the abbots of Bangor. Parallels between one text of the difficult Latin verse known as the *Hisperica famina* and passages in the *Antiphonary* have led to the suggestion that Bangor was one of the schools where this exotic Latin culture flourished. Until the mid-8th century the *Annals of Ulster* take a considerable interest in the leaders of the religious community at Bangor, giving rise to the inference that early collections of annals were assembled at Bangor to form the major collection that underlies the *Annals of Ulster* and other extant collections (see ANNALS) for the period down to that date. RS

banking. During the 17th and 18th centuries financial intermediaries developed in response to a growing demand, especially from *landlords, for cash remittance between provincial Ireland and

Dublin and between Dublin and Britain. The demand for small-denomination currency, for safe deposit facilities for cash, and for the discount of bills of exchange also led to specialization of function and to the emergence of formal banking facilities. At the same time, financial transactions such as lending on mortgage were undertaken by a range of individuals, especially attorneys, through whose hands a great deal of money might pass. Banks were often established as an adjunct to other business activities, and the first bank in Ireland appears to have been that of Edward and Joseph Hoare, established in 1680 in Cork. The Hoare brothers were merchants extensively involved in overseas trade and foreign exchange, and theirs was the first of many banks that were mercantile in origin. Another early example was the highly successful bank established by David Digues *La Touche, a *Huguenot whose textile business from the early 1690s brought him into contact with a substantial number of businessmen in both Dublin and provincial Ireland, and who developed an extensive correspondent network in Ireland, Britain, and Holland. Underpinned by the growth of trade, formal banking facilities appeared in several towns and cities during the 18th century, though bank failures in the 1750s led to more state intervention. In order to distinguish bankers and merchants more clearly and prevent abuse of credit facilities, one of the clauses in an act of 1756 specifically prohibited bankers from carrying on 'trade or traffick as merchants in goods or merchandises imported or exported'. By the later 1790s Dublin was the most important banking centre in Ireland, followed by Cork, and then by Clonmel, Limerick, Waterford, and Belfast.

Although there was intermittent pressure for the establishment of a national bank, most notably in 1695 (the year after the formation of the Bank of England and the same year that the Bank of Scotland was established), and again in 1719, this aim was not achieved until 1783 when the Bank of Ireland was established in Dublin by royal charter, with a capital of £600,000. Managed by a governor (the first was David La Touche), deputy governor, and court of directors (on which Catholics and, initially, even *Quakers were prohibited from serving) the bank became government banker and also performed a range of public and commercial banking duties. Despite its resources, the Bank of Ireland did not establish branches either within or outside Dublin. Consequently the country continued to rely on a small but growing number of private banks. These were subject to a range of restrictions, including unlimited liability and a maximum of six partners. A major weakness of this structure was its vulnerability to abrupt downturns in economic activity; this was demonstrated most clearly in the bank failures that accompanied post-war deflation and depression after 1815. Indeed, by 1820 the number of private banks had declined to 20, about half the number operating in 1804.

In an effort to promote financial stability, the law was changed to allow banks to have more than six partners, though still with unlimited liability. Two clusters of joint-stock bank promotion followed: the first saw the creation of the Northern (1824), the Provincial and the Hibernian (1825), and the Belfast (1827); in the second, the most significant new creations were the Agricultural and Commercial (1834), the National (1835), the Ulster and the Royal (1836), and the Tipperary Joint Stock (1838). Banks established at this time, together with the Bank of Ireland, dominated the system until well into the 20th century. After the 1820s, bank failure was relatively rare in Ireland and the system evolved into a remarkably stable one irrespective of economic climate. Of the few failures, two stand out: the grossly mismanaged Agricultural and Commercial in 1840, and the Munster Bank Ltd. (set up in 1864 and which had taken over La Touche's Bank in 1870) in 1885. Out of the wreckage of the latter, however, came the enduring Munster and Leinster Bank Ltd., with its head office in Cork. In times of financial crisis, the Bank of Ireland sometimes stepped in to help support the system and limit the damage, thereby acting in this respect as a central bank. Three major banks (Northern, Belfast, Ulster) had head offices in Belfast, three (Bank of Ireland, Royal, Hibernian) in Dublin, and two (National and Provincial) in London. Banks became limited liability concerns in the 1880s. Apart from the Bank of Ireland, no bank based within a 50-mile radius of Dublin was permitted to issue its own notes, but all others did, and the restriction was lifted in 1845. To overcome an initial staff shortage, especially at more senior levels, banks recruited from England and Scotland, both of which had more established banking traditions.

Banks offered a range of credit facilities (overdrafts or 'cash credits' which might be renewable, fixed period loans, and discounts for bills of exchange), and both current and deposit accounts. Through the development of branch networks from the 1820s, they also played a major role in providing country districts with metallic and paper currency in appropriate denominations. Moreover, by allowing banks to spread their business over a wider geographical area, branch systems improved the stability of the system, but were never a sufficient guarantee against failure.

From fewer than 200 branches in 1850 the system developed quickly, if unevenly, to reach over 850 by 1913. An increasingly noticeable feature from mid-century was the opening of sub-branches on a part-time basis, often on market days or *fair days, and such offices accounted for about 40 per cent of the total in 1913. In addition to the joint-stock banks, there were Trustee Savings Banks dating from 1817, aimed specifically at the 'small' saver, and Post Office Savings Banks from 1861. The former were hit hard by the *Great Famine, while the latter rapidly became the more important, and by 1920 had accumulated deposits of £14.1 million, four times the £3.5 million in the Trustee Savings Banks. But even the combined total of deposits in both systems was less than 10 per cent of the £183 million in the joint-stock banks at this date.

To a large extent, banking business in Ireland remained subject to regular seasonal patterns, reflecting the agricultural base of the country and the fact that important industries such as *distilling, *brewing, and *linen were related to agriculture. The linen boom of the 1860s had a profound impact on the profitability of those banks heavily involved in the north-east, leading to dividends of up to 30 per cent, while agricultural depression, in the early 1860s, late 1870s/1880s, or early 1920s, led to tight credit restrictions in rural Ireland.

The last years of the Union were prosperous ones for Irish agriculture and for the banks. This was a key factor leading to the affiliation of two of them, the Belfast with London, City and Midland, and the Ulster with London, County and Westminster, in 1917. This move, coming as it did during a long period of rising tension in Anglo-Irish relations, provoked considerable controversy, though in keeping with their well-established policy the banks wherever possible refrained from public comment on political questions. *Partition inevitably led to changes in the banking system, though all banks which had branches in each of the now separate states continued to operate them, the exception being the Belfast Bank, which sold its Free State branches to the Royal Bank in 1923.

Unlike several new states founded after the *First World War, the government of the *Irish Free State inherited a banking system in which there was complete trust and which enjoyed enduring stability, assisted by the reputation gained over the decades before partition and the huge increase in deposits that had characterized the years before 1921. In the 1920s and 1930s the Bank of Ireland retained its status as the Free State's premier bank, and its governor normally chaired the standing committee of Irish banks, originally assembled as an ad hoc committee to deal with the problem of labour unrest in 1919, but now a permanent body. A major banking commission in 1926, followed the next year by a Currency Act (which created a currency commission and a separate Saorstát pound tied to *sterling) and in 1938 by a banking commission, were the financial landmarks of the first decades of independence. Among the most important net results of these were that individual banks in the Free State (unlike those in Northern Ireland) lost their power to issue their own notes, and also that informed opinion in the Free State moved increasingly in favour of a fully-fledged central bank. The creation of the latter was hastened by the increase in financial pressures occasioned by the outbreak of war in 1939 and following the Central Bank Act of 1942 it came into existence in 1943. Since that time its functions have been periodically widened: it became responsible for supervising banks in 1971 and *building societies in 1989.

Another major development in both the Republic and Northern Ireland since the Second World War was amalgamation on an unprecedented scale. Thus, the Bank of Ireland took over the Hibernian in 1958 and the National Bank in 1966. In the latter year Allied Irish Banks came into existence with the merger of the Munster and Leinster, the Provincial, and the Royal Banks, while four years later the Northern Bank absorbed the Belfast Bank but was itself sold by Midland to National Australia Bank in 1987—a reminder of the global nature of the banking system by the late 20th century.

Barrow, G. L., *The Emergence of the Irish Banking System 1820–1845* (1974)

Hall, F. G., *The Bank of Ireland 1783–1846* (1949)

McGowan, Padraig, *Money and Banking in Ireland* (1990)

Ollerenshaw, Philip, *Banking in Nineteenth-Century Ireland* (1987)

PO

Baptists, one of the most important of the sects that appeared during the English civil wars, established themselves in a number of towns during the 1650s. They were regarded as a potential threat to order both by the *Cromwellian regime and by the *Restoration government. In the 18th century they survived as a numerically insignificant minority: in 1800 there were five congregations, all in the south or south-east, with roughly 500 members, mainly from the urban lower middle classes. During the 19th century numbers rose rapidly, to over 4,000 by 1861 and 7,000 by 1901. This growth was mainly in Ulster, and the new recruits, mainly converts from other Protestant denominations, were drawn predominantly from small farming or industrial working-class backgrounds. However, there was also a middle-class element, particularly following the *revival of 1859, while Dublin, with a membership drawn from the affluent southern suburbs, remained both the largest and most influential Baptist congregation.

bardic poetry in its most general sense refers to verse composed by the professional poetic class found in all Celtic societies, the bards, who earned rich rewards for singing poems in praise of their patrons, or satires against their patrons' enemies. However, surviving verse compositions in Irish from before *c.*1200 are religious or historical in character, the product of the learned **fili*, rather than straightforward eulogies to the aristocracy such as the bards composed orally. It is not until the amalgamation of these two classes in the course of the 12th century to produce hereditary, literate professional praise-poets, the *filidh* or *fir dhána* of the later Middle Ages, that a substantial body of praise-poems begins to survive in written form. As part of this development, by 1200 the poets had forged a new standard literary language, Classical Early Modern Irish, and evolved strict rules of metre and rhyme to be rigidly observed in their most prized mode of composition, *dán díreach*, or 'straight poetry'. The less demanding mode, *brúilingeacht*, used by less educated poets, or by hereditary Irish historians, lawyers, or clerics when composing in verse, observed the same rules of metre, but used imperfect rhymes, while a third, even easier mode, *óglachas*, used by amateurs and comic poets, employed much simplified versions of the metres and imperfect rhymes.

The majority of such poems are formally addressed to lay patrons, Irish chieftains, Anglo-Irish barons, and their respective relatives. These consist of eulogies to be recited at banquets hosted by the patrons, elegies to grace their funerals or commemorative feasts, epithalamiums for weddings, poems to celebrate newly built palaces or churches, and occasionally inauguration poems or incitements to battle. A further 20 per cent or so are poems on religious subjects, though composed by the same professional bards who were responsible for the secular eulogies. The remaining compositions consist of Tudor and Jacobean poems of courtly love, in the style of contemporary English verse though in bardic metres, political exhortations, poetic contentions, and miscellaneous personal pieces. Works of 16th- and early 17th-century poets like Tadhg Dall Ó hUiginn, Eochaidh Ó hEodhasa, and Fearghal Óg Mac an Bhaird are best preserved, because at that date a literate reading public collected their work in anthologies based on artistic merit. Surviving medieval manuscript collections normally contain poems addressed to a particular ruling family, for example the 14th-century Book of Magauran, or composed by a particular poet or family of poets such as the lost *duanaire* or poem-book of Muireadhach Albanach Ó Dálaigh (*fl.* 1213), or the Ó hUiginn poems in the so-called 'Yellow Book of *Lecan'.

The value of these texts for a historian lies partly in their factual information: it was a poet's duty to immortalize a list of his patron's victories, and when he extolled a subject's relatives he included wives, mothers, and grandmothers, who are normally unrecorded in formal *genealogies. But they are most interesting as testimony to the public image a patron wished to have propagated. When the subject is urged to make war or peace with the English, for example, the poet is unlikely to be offering unwelcome advice, as his payment depended on the patron's satisfaction with his poem. An unwarlike man, however, like Cúchonnacht Maguire (Mág Uidhir) (d. 1589), could be praised as dashing and aggressive, if he paid well enough.

Bergin, O., *Irish Bardic Poetry*, ed. D. Greene and F. Kelly (1970)
Knott, E., *Irish Classical Poetry* (1960)
Simms, K., 'Bardic Poetry as a Historical Source', in T. Dunne (ed.), *The Writer as Witness* (1987)

KS

bardic schools. Texts concerning the education of pre-Norman poets, jurists, and historians, such as the *brehon *law tracts, Middle Irish tracts on versification edited by Thurneysen, and the *Auraicept na nÉces* or 'Poets' Primer', appear to emanate from church schools or clerically educated authors, some recorded in the *annals as holding high ecclesiastical office. However these tracts also mention oral bards, who learned by ear to compose in the new Latin-style syllabic metres, and it is possible that this class had a secular education involving apprenticeship to a master-poet. Middle Irish (AD 900–1200) glosses on an Old Irish tract concerning poetic inspiration, *Coire Goiriath*, show glimpses of a system of education and examination administered by the poets themselves, using the term *oide* or 'foster-father' for the teacher, and calling the pupil *felmac*, a word also used of the pupil in Latin schools, and of the apprentices of a blacksmith. Similarly a tract on the maintenance owed by a **tuath*, or petty kingdom, to its local judge included provision for his apprentice lawyers.

Annals in the Middle Irish period increasingly note scholars in Irish history, law, and poetry as well as Latin subjects, perhaps reflecting an increase in laymen holding hereditary church office. Concurrently oral bards gradually merged with literate, church-trained *fili, or learned poets, to produce a unified literate class of *fir dhána* or 'men of [poetic] skill', the court praise-poets to the later medieval chieftains, who used from *c.*1200 to the mid-17th century a new standard literary language (Classical Early Modern Irish).

The new diocesan structures and continental monastic orders of the *12th-century church reform ended the pursuit of Irish secular studies in church schools. Something of a hiatus is found in the written record of Irish legal, genealogical, and annalistic material during the 13th century, though poetry continued to flourish, perhaps because poets' training was already independent of the church. By the 14th century Irish annals, now compiled by lay historians, unequivocally refer to lay schools, each run by an *ollamh or 'master' of the relevant branch of Irish learning, such as poetry (*dán*), customary or 'brehon' law (*féineachas*), traditional history (*seanchas*), music (*ceol*), or medicine (*leigheas*). The relationship between master and pupils was that of *fosterage, a contract involving mutual obligations and the payment of a fee. The art of *filidheacht*, or versification, was taught to students in each of the various disciplines, all of whom used books in their schools as well as oral instruction, and basic doctrine for each profession is found encapsulated in verse compositions, as well as prose tracts. The legal, poetic, and historical schools, while not oblivious to later *canon law, or the newer Romance literature, based their teaching on their heritage of pre-Norman learning, but the medical schools used standard medical texts translated into Irish from contemporary English and continental sources.

Ó Cuív, B. (ed.), *Seven Centuries of Irish Learning* (1961)
Simms, K., 'The Brehons of Later Medieval Ireland', in D. Hogan and W. N. Osborough (eds.), *Brehons, Serjeants and Attorneys* (1990)

KS

Barnewall, Sir Patrick (d. 1622), the leading Catholic opponent of Sir Arthur *Chichester's regime. He rallied the *Palesmen to the cause of Dublin's *recusants in the *mandates crisis of 1605, with a petition complaining about the use of the court of *Castle Chamber to enforce penal legislation. Sent for interrogation in England and placed in the Tower, Barnewall merely gained the opportunity to negotiate, funded by money collected throughout Ireland. He returned a hero when the policy was suspended. A well-timed summons to England prevented him from standing for the 1613 parliament after he objected to the government's creation of new boroughs.

HM

Baronial Constabulary. Constables were first appointed in the baronies and parishes of Ireland during the 14th century. Their duties were extensive, being military and civil as well as criminal. Constables in particular acted for magistrates, who often appointed them.

In 1787 the government, dissatisfied with the ineffectiveness of these local constables, established a new constabulary force, which could be dispatched to disturbed counties. But magistrates and *grand juries resented this usurpation of their traditional powers and the force was deployed in only four counties. In 1792 the Irish parliament reaffirmed the right of grand juries to appoint eight constables in baronies where the 1787 act was not in operation. But all such constables had to be Protestants; most were poorly paid, unarmed, and lacked uniforms; and many seem to have worked only on a part-time basis. This Baronial Constabulary, known as the 'Barnies', remained the main agent of law enforcement in rural Ireland until 1822 when it was replaced by the new centrally controlled Irish Constabulary (see POLICE). ELM

barony, a territorial division of a *county composed of a number of *townlands. There are about 270 baronies in Ireland. The origins of both the term and the divisions are obscure, though the name was in use in the 16th century, while by the 19th baronies were reckoned to relate to former Gaelic lordships. As administrative units they served as bases for taxation, law enforcement, and general administration until the *local government reforms of the mid-19th century made them largely redundant. The 1891 *census was the last to be taken on a barony basis. NG

Barrington, Sir Jonah (1760–1834), a lawyer of impecunious landed background, MP for Tuam 1792–8 and Bannagher 1799–1800. Appointed an admiralty court judge in 1798 and knighted in 1807, he was removed from office for embezzlement in 1830, by which time he had long retreated to France to escape his creditors. *Personal Sketches of his Own Times* (1827–32) offered highly coloured accounts of Protestant elite society and politics. *The Rise and Fall of the Irish Nation* (1833) gave a vivid account of the bribery supposedly used to secure the passage of the *Union. But there are suggestions that Barrington himself had been a go-between in some of these transactions, and now went into print after failing to blackmail the government.

Barry, Gerald de, see GERALD OF WALES.

Barry, James (1741–1806), the finest of all Irish painters in the 'grand manner', left his native Cork, for Dublin, in his early twenties. There he met Edmund *Burke, who arranged for him to go to London to further his career. He arrived there in 1764. The following year, financed by Burke, he embarked upon a continental tour, with Rome as the final destination. So impressed was he by the works of antiquity and the old masters that he determined to specialize in history painting in the 'grand manner', that is, to paint historical subjects derived from Greek and Roman mythology and history. Thereafter, he never waivered from his commitment to this, the most exalted of the artistic genres. On returning to London in 1771, he met with considerable success and became a member of the Royal Academy. The high point of his career was his mural series of 1777–83 at the Royal Society of Arts—*The Progress of Human Culture*—possibly the most important cycle of history paintings in the British Isles. However, lack of support for history painting on a grand scale eventually led him into penury and despair, a situation made worse by his unstable and aggressive personality. In 1799 he was expelled from the Royal Academy for verbal attacks on its members and operations, the first and only artist ever to suffer such a fate. He died a lonely recluse, a martyr to his obsession with the promotion of history painting above all else. EEB

Barry, Kevin (1902–20), the first *IRA man to be executed in the *Anglo-Irish War. Barry was caught while taking part in a raid on a military lorry collecting bread in Church Street, Dublin. His court martial and death sentence caused a great amount of public indignation, particularly due to his tender age. Despite many pleas to have his sentence commuted, he was hanged on 1 November 1920. His tragic end made him a frequent topic of ballads. JA

Barry, Tom (1897–1980), legendary leader of the West Cork Flying Column during the *Anglo-Irish War. Barry served in the British army during the *First World War, and joined the *Irish Republican Army after demobilization. His column is particularly known for its ambush at Kilmichael, Co. Cork, on 28 November 1920, in which fifteen *Auxiliaries were killed. Opposing the *Anglo-Irish treaty, Barry continued in the IRA after the *Civil War, briefly becoming chief of staff in 1937. JA

bastard feudalism, the name given by late Victorian historians to forms of lordship and clientship, increasingly recorded in written contracts, typical of English, and Irish, society in the later Middle Ages. These relationships—involving military, household, or administrative service in return for annuities and other types of patronage—were blamed for *faction, disorder, and abuse of the legal system. Disapproval is strongly marked in the writings of Irish scholars, who have regarded such ties as less reputable than those, based on land tenure, associated with earlier *feudalism. Recent work on England and Scotland suggests that the purely feudal age is a mirage, and that relationships akin to bastard feudalism have a long history; their spread was a response to the complexity of government and society in the later medieval period, one feature of which was the literacy and archival consciousness that has ensured the survival of the evidence. The Irish material includes contracts of varying types made from the late 13th century between magnates and lesser Anglo-Irish and Gaelic lords, preserved in collections such as the *Ormond deeds and the Red Book of the earls of Kildare. It awaits fuller study in the light of less hostile interpretations of medieval lordship. RFF

Bates, Sir Richard Dawson (1876–1949), *Unionist apparatchik and government minister. Bates was a solicitor who, in 1905, accepted the post of secretary to the new *Ulster Unionist Council. He assisted James *Craig in 1912–14, an unsung but unquestionably effective manager of resistance to the third *home rule bill. In 1921 he was appointed minister of home affairs in the new government of *Northern Ireland. Trained in the front line of party politics, Bates proved to be a vigorously loyalist minister, successfully defending the *partition settlement from the *IRA onslaught of 1921–2: he was a keen proponent of the Civil Authorities (*Special Powers) Act (1922). He was awarded a baronetcy in 1937, but clung to office until 1943. An unpopular and inefficient wartime minister, Bates retained the enervated style of the Craig administration; he survived a parliamentary vote of censure in July 1942, but was increasingly regarded as a political liability. He remained vigorously suspicious of Catholic influence to the end. AJ

bawn, the fortified enclosure surrounding a castle or *tower house, from Irish *badhún*, meaning a cattle fort. Square or rectangular with corner towers and protected gateways, bawns were a regular feature throughout medieval Ireland. They are also associated with the *Ulster plantation, where their construction was a minimum requirement for grantees, native and British. Between 1610 and 1622, 152 were built. Brackfield, Co. Londonderry, is a good surviving example of a plantation bawn. HM

Bealtaine (1 May), the first day of summer and one of the four traditional 'quarter days', important in the calendar customs of Goidelic-speaking areas up to the twentieth century. The name's derivation is uncertain: *-taine* has been taken to mean 'fire', and to refer to the ancient custom of purifying cattle on the eve of Bealtaine by driving them between two bonfires. Many medieval tales open with a supernatural being's appearance on Bealtaine, just before sunrise; the day shares these otherworld associations with *Samhain. JPC

Bede (673–735) was a monk of Jarrow in Co. Durham, a scholar whose biblical commentaries and school books were very widely read, but who is now best known for his *Lives of St Cuthbert* and his *Ecclesiastical History of the English People*. Bede's *History* is a source of the first importance concerning those Irish clergy from *Iona and elsewhere who worked to convert the English, including not only St Áedán of Lindisfarne but many less familiar names; and also for the larger number of English and even Frankish religious who came to Ireland to study in the 7th century. He is the principal source for the close Irish connections of the Northumbrian kings Oswald, Oswiu, and Aldfrith, all of them baptized and educated among the Irish. Bede was a passionate believer in the Roman position in the *paschal controversy. He provides an important witness to the spread of the Roman paschal calculation in southern Ireland, its eventual adoption in the north of Ireland, and its final acceptance by the community of St *Colum Cille. In spite of his own clear opinion, and his openness on the subject of the Roman position of many Irish churches, Bede's text was the subject of a Protestant reading in the 19th century that emphasized the anti-Roman views of the 'Celtic' churches, treating especially Iona and its missionaries in Northumbria as early Protestants, opposed to the authoritarian orthodoxy represented by the Roman mission in southern England. RS

Bedell, William (1571–1642), a reforming provost of *Trinity College, Dublin, and bishop of Kilmore. Born at Black Notley in Essex in 1570, Bedell was educated at the *puritan Emmanuel College, Cambridge (MA 1592, fellow 1593, BD 1599). After ministry in Essex he served 1607–10 as chaplain to the British ambassador to Venice, where his intellectual and cultural horizons, and his acquaintance with Roman Catholicism, were considerably widened. He returned to an Essex parish, and was plucked from relative obscurity in 1627 to serve as provost of Trinity College. There he found an ill-governed and chaotic university and determinedly set about reforming it, drawing up a set of statutes and introducing teaching in Irish to enable clerical graduates to minister to the native population in its own language. In 1629 he was appointed bishop of Kilmore and Ardagh (resigning Ardagh in 1633). Here again Bedell demonstrated his interest in Irish culture, overseeing the translation of the Old Testament into Irish and seeking to redefine the objectives of the church away from an exclusive mission to the English and Scots colonists to the creation of an indigenous Protestantism. He also devoted himself to curbing abuses amongst his clergy and improving their income. Though his success was limited, he was, unlike many other Protestant ministers, left unmolested in the *rising of 1641. The account of his death, from natural causes, in 1642, written by his son, records the stirring tribute paid to him at his graveside by the local Irish chieftain. The hostility that Bedell aroused amongst his fellow Protestants was largely a product of his implicit rejection of the essentially Anglicizing assumptions of the Protestant *Reformation in Ireland. AF

Beere, Dr Thekla (1901–91), secretary of the Department of Transport and Power (1959–66), the first woman to head a department in the civil service of independent Ireland. A woman with a wide variety of interests, she was a founder member of the youth organization An Oige, served on the boards of the **Irish Times* and the *Rotunda hospital, and chaired the Commission for the Status of Women in 1970. CC

Belfast (Ir. *Béal Feirste*, 'the mouth of the sandbank, or ford'), the main centre of the industrial revolution in Ireland and, since 1921, the capital of *Northern Ireland. Although the site of a 13th-century castle, Belfast was not a place of any importance before the *Flight of the Earls. Founded for English and Scots settlers by Sir Arthur *Chichester in 1603, the infant town was incorporated by the crown as a *close borough as early as 1613, in order to provide two loyal MPs to the Irish *parliament. Belfast's role as the bastion of loyalty in Ireland, so pronounced from the 19th century onwards, thus goes back to its very origins. Its ethos, however, was commercial rather than aristocratic, and for much of the 18th century the small town manifested a radical and democratic outlook, beginning with the mass emigration of disaffected Presbyterians to *colonial America, and culminating in the *United Irish movement. This long aberration ended in bourgeois recoil from the horrors of the *insurrection of 1798, and growing enthusiasm for the Act of *Union.

Although the Chichester/*Donegall family owned the town until 1844, their belated conferment of long leases on the larger tenants after 1750, notwithstanding the *Steelboys' protests, ended a major constraint on growth. At the end of the 18th century the town had a thriving *linen trade and an infant *cotton industry. By 1830 linen manufacture had supplanted cotton, and Belfast became the world's leading producer; the establishment of a *railway network during the 1840s boosted its regional role; and growing confidence in the city's economy generated sufficient capital to transform its shallow river approaches into a major port. Employment in textiles and clothing continued to expand thereafter, together with industries such as *shipbuilding, *engineering, rope manufacture, whiskey *distilling, and tobacco products. It was a classic example of 'take-off', as one economic development provided stimulus for the next.

Economic growth transformed Belfast from a small, Presbyterian commercial town into a large and ethnically mixed industrial centre. A population of 1,000 in the late 17th century grew slowly to about 8,000 in 1759 and 25,000 in 1808. The industrial explosion took it from 70,447 in 1841 to 349,180 in 1901, across which period it was the fastest growing centre in the United Kingdom. It was designated a city in 1888. There were boundary extensions in 1841, 1853, and 1896, and *suburban authorities were separately incorporated in 1973. The city proper declined from a peak of 443,671 in 1951, but the Belfast Urban Area contained 475,967 people in 1991, plus a further 250,000 within daily commuting range.

Population growth brought the native–settler rivalries of rural Ulster into the town. By 1850 *Church of Ireland/Presbyterian differences were merging into an essentially political 'Protestant' consciousness articulated by the *Orange Order, but owing much to the Conservative Presbyterian theology of Henry *Cooke. The Catholic minority, in contrast, retained a distinct identity of its own: it shifted and evolved during the 19th century, but the main elements included a shared religious practice, growing residential segregation, a relatively constrained occupational structure, and, with increasing coherence after 1885, a political identification with the nationalist programme of the rest of Ireland.

Ethnic division manifested itself in the waves of Catholic/Protestant rioting which became endemic in the main working-class neighbourhoods, beginning with a 12 July clash in 1813 and continuing with polling day battles in 1832, 1835, and 1841. Flare-ups in 1843 and 1852 were rather more serious, and 1857 was the first of a series of outbreaks of massive and uncontrollable rioting, lasting over days or weeks, that continued in 1864, 1872, 1886, 1912, 1920–2, 1935, and 1969–71. So great was the scale of conflict that changes in policing, from the Orange-influenced Town Police to the mainly Catholic *Royal Irish Constabulary (1865–1921), and then to the *Royal Ulster Constabulary, made little difference.

The undercurrent of fear generated by recurrent violence produced total residential segregation in most working-class neighbourhoods. This was paralleled in the workplace by high levels of segregation within linen mills and other large places of employment; the virtual absence of Catholic workers from the modern, skilled industrial sector; and periodic expulsions of Catholics and their perceived sympathizers from workplaces, most notably in 1920–2, when up to 10,000 were shut out. The continued pattern of rioting, given a political dimension by *home rule and by *partition, meant that segregation did not wither with the passage of generations and the decline in immigration: it increased, and reinforced the city's distinct sectoral pattern of ethnic development. The south-western sector remained Catholic as it expanded, while the rest of the city's development was strongly Protestant, closing off other Catholic inner-city neighbourhoods from further growth after about 1860. It is probably no coincidence that from this date the Catholics' faster growth rate, which took them from 8 per cent of the urban population in 1784 to 34 per cent in 1861, was reversed: Catholics fell to 23 per cent by 1926, before beginning to rise again, to 43 per cent of the city proper (34 per cent of the Belfast Urban Area) in 1991.

Belfast's politics have been shaped by its ethnic division. Prior to male household suffrage (see FRANCHISE) they approximated to British political culture: established church *Tories, supported by most plebeian Presbyterians, opposed and usually defeated elite Presbyterian *Liberals supported by Catholics. After William Johnston's electoral success (see PARTY PROCESSIONS ACT) in 1868 this structure collapsed: Irish and British political cultures diverged, as traditional Conservatism embraced Orangeism to become *Unionism, nationalism won the support of the Catholic community, and Liberalism died. The Unionist–nationalist dichotomy has continued to predominate, throwing off non-sectarian challenges from the *Northern Ireland Labour Party and various other socialist groupings rather more easily than it has the extreme ethnic challenges from the popular Protestantism of the *Democratic Unionist Party and the republicanism of *Sinn Féin that were permitted by the reintroduction of *proportional representation after 1973.

Bardon, Jonathan, *Belfast: An Illustrated History* (1982)

ACH

Belfast Academical Institution, later Royal Belfast Academical Institution, opened in 1814 as a non-denominational college of higher education, though in practice drawing most of its students from the *Presbyterian population. The government, despite the involvement of *Drennan and other prominent radicals, initially granted funding, but withdrew this for a period (1817–29) when the *Synod of Ulster insisted on allowing ministers to take their degrees there, rather than studying for a period outside Ireland as the government wished. The alleged *Arianism of teaching staff was the immediate cause of the second *subscription controversy. Collegiate education ceased with the opening of the *Queen's College in Belfast, and 'Inst' went on to become a leading boys' grammar school.

Belfast boycott. Originally ordered by the *Dáil cabinet in August 1920 as a boycott of Belfast-based banks and insurance companies, this rapidly expanded into a wider campaign to exclude *Northern Irish goods from the nationalist-dominated south. In some border counties Protestant-owned businesses were also proscribed. The lifting of the boycott was included in the *Craig–Collins pacts but it continued, enforced by anti-treaty forces and tolerated by the new *Irish Free State government, up to the outbreak of the *Civil War. Although the immediate impetus came from recent attacks on Catholics in Belfast (to nationalists 'the Belfast pogrom'), which had included mass expulsions from shipyards and engineering works, it was also hoped to demonstrate to Ulster *Unionists the economic cost of *partition. The actual result was to make partition more of a reality, by significantly weakening banking and commercial links across the newly established frontier between north and south.

Belfast Harp Festival (11–14 July 1792), a crucial event in the revival of Gaelic *musical culture. A committee of judges heard some ten harpers (including Denis Hempson, Arthur O'Neill, and Charles Byrne), six of whom were blind. The purpose of the festival, at which premiums were paid to the players according to their prowess and their command of hitherto unknown melodies, was to redeem the last surviving fragments of a generally lost tradition ('all that remains of the music, poetry and oral traditions of Ireland'). Edward Bunting (1773–1843) was one of three musicians appointed to transcribe the harp melodies: it was this experience which stimulated his lifelong devotion to the collection of Irish music.

A Belfast Harp Society was formed in 1808, but perhaps the most immediate result of the festival was the publication of Bunting's *General Collection of the Ancient Irish Music* (1797). HW

Belfast Natural History and Philosophical Society (Belfast Society), founded 1821 by the physician James Lawson Drummond (1783–1853) and seven friends. Membership expanded, drawing mostly on the commercial, industrial, medical, professional, and academic communities. In 1831 the society opened a museum and library in College Square. At meetings, members read papers on scientific subjects, history, and antiquities; papers were published in the society's *Proceedings*. In 1910 the society transferred its collections to the developing municipal museum, but retained ownership of the building, now the Old Museum Arts Centre. The Belfast Society (its present title) holds lectures, gives financial support to research and publications, and has about 140 members.

DJS

Belfast News-Letter, founded in 1737 by Francis *Joy, a Belfast papermaker. It was the first *newspaper in Ulster and is still the oldest daily paper in Ireland. Initially issued bi-weekly, it became a daily in 1855. It began as a *patriot journal, supporting *free trade and the repeal of *Poynings's Law. Francis Joy's grandson Henry Joy, proprietor from 1782, was a *Volunteer. From 1795, under the new owner George Gordon, the paper became more conservative, compensating for falling readership by accepting a government subsidy. In the 19th and 20th centuries the *News-Letter* remained a Protestant/unionist paper. In 1845 it was acquired by the Henderson family of the *Newry Telegraph*. It is now owned by Century Newspapers. M-LL

Bell, a Dublin-based monthly magazine of literature and social comment (1940–54), a seminal influence on its generation of intellectuals. It was notable, particularly under the editorship of *O'Faolain, as an outspoken liberal voice at a time of political and intellectual stagnation, fiercely critical of censorship, Gaelic revivalist ideology, clericalism, and general parochialism. Under Peadar *O'Donnell (1946–54), the *Bell* became more left-wing in content and irregular in frequency of publication but continued to produce material of high quality. It was also notable as an outlet for new writers such as Michael MacLaverty and James Plunkett. PM

Bellahoe, battle of (Aug. 1539). *Geraldine League leaders Conn *O'Neill and Manus *O'Donnell raided the northern *Pale with an army of *redshanks and Gaelic clansmen, burning Ardee and Navan and carrying off a large booty of goods and cattle. Lord Deputy *Grey, with half his garrison and a levy of Palesmen, caught up with the raiders at a river ford on the Meath–Monaghan border and won an overwhelming victory, removing threats of national insurrection and Scottish invasion. HM

Bellew, a leading *Old English family. **John Bellew** (d. 1693) was restored to the family lands in Cos. Louth and Meath at the *Restoration and created Baron Bellew of Duleek in 1686. He was wounded and taken prisoner at the battle of *Aughrim, as was his son **Sir Walter Bellew**, who died in 1694, soon after his release. Walter's brother **Richard Bellew** (d. 1715) also supported *James II. In 1697, after he had *conformed to the Church of Ireland, his outlawry was reversed and he was allowed to return to Ireland. He later contested seats in the British parliament (1709, 1712) as a *Whig. The peerage became extinct in 1770, on the death of Richard's son, the 4th baron.

Another branch of the family was descended from **Patrick Bellew**, who also obtained lands in Louth, as well as in Co. Galway, at the Restoration and was created a baronet in 1688. **Sir Edward Bellew**, the 4th baronet (*c.*1760–1827), was a leader of the conservative, pro-*veto faction in Catholic politics in the early 19th century. **Sir Patrick Bellew**, the 5th baronet (1798–1866), Whig MP for Co. Louth 1831–2, 1834–7, was created Baron Bellew of Barmeath in 1848. In 1883 the family owned 4,300 acres in Cos. Louth and Meath.

Bellings, Richard (d. 1677), secretary of the supreme council of the Catholic *Confederation and an ambassador to France and Italy. In the 1650s he was a pro-*Ormond pamphleteer in recriminations between the exiled confederate factions. After the *Restoration Bellings regained part of his lands in the *Pale and subscribed to the loyal Catholic *Remonstrance of 1666. His *History of the Irish Confederation and the War in Ireland*, published by J. T. *Gilbert in seven volumes (1882–91), gives the Catholic politicking of 1641–9 a simplistic ethnic coloration, but uses many confederate records destroyed by fire in 1711. HM

Benburb, battle of (5 June 1646), the largest engagement of the *Confederate War, between the 6,000 strong armies of Owen Roe *O'Neill and the Scottish commander Robert Munroe. Munroe's Scots, intending a rendezvous with the Laggan and Coleraine armies, encountered the Irish near Benburb, Co. Tyrone. After O'Neill's cavalry returned from defeating the Coleraine force, his pike advanced down Drumflugh hill. Munroe was forced back towards the Blackwater river, losing 2,000 to 3,000 men. O'Neill chased off the Laggan army but otherwise did not follow up the only pitched battle the Gaelic Irish ever won. HM

Benedictines. A Benedictine community existed at Christ Church, Dublin, from 1085 until 1096. This is the earliest reliable reference to the black monks in Ireland. In 1076 Muireadhach Mac Robhartaigh (Marianus Scotus II, d. 1088) and companions settled in Regensburg and in 1090 founded the monastery of St James which became the mother house of a congregation of ten Irish Benedictine monasteries (*Schottenklöster*) in German-speaking territories. Priories at Cashel (*c.*1134) and Ross Carbery (*c.*1134) recruited novices for these foundations. The congregation declined in the 14th and 15th centuries and St James, Regensburg, passed to Scottish monks in 1515.

Savigniac houses at Erenagh (founded 1127), St Mary's, Dublin (founded 1139), and six other Benedictine communities became *Cistercian in the 12th century. The Cluniacs and the order of Tiron each had one house in Ireland. Five monasteries were established by the Anglo-Normans and there were approximately eighteen foundations in Ireland in the 13th century. A number of these failed and at the *dissolution of the monasteries only Fore (Co. Westmeath), Downpatrick (Co. Down), and Ross Carbery (Co. Cork) appear to have had communities.

A monastery was established at Glenstal, Co. Limerick, in 1927. CNÓC

Bennett, Louie (1870–1956), general secretary of the *Irish Women Workers' Union from 1917 to 1955. Born in Dublin into a prosperous merchant family, Bennett co-founded the Irish Women's Suffrage Federation in 1911. Bennett's belief in vocationalism as an alternative to socialism and capitalism led her to membership of the *Commission on Vocational Organization 1939–43. In the IWWU she displayed a matriarchal style of leadership. She consistently opposed limits on women's right to work, refusing to sign the report of the Commission on Youth Unemployment in 1951 for this reason. CC

Beresford, a leading political dynasty of the late 18th and early 19th centuries. **Tristram Beresford** (b. 1574) came to Ireland as manager for the *Irish Society of the Londonderry Plantation. The family settled in Coleraine. His son **Sir Tristram Beresford** (d. 1673), knighted in 1665, sat in the Irish parliaments of 1634 and 1661–5. **Sir Marcus Beresford** (1694–1763) married the daughter and only heir of the 3rd earl of Tyrone and was permitted to perpetuate the title by becoming viscount and then earl of Tyrone. **George de la Poer Beresford** (1735–1800) was created marquis of Waterford in 1789. However it was George's younger brother **John Beresford** (1738–1805) who attained national eminence. In the late 1780s and 1790s Beresford formed part of a powerful trio of Irish ministers who directed the government of Ireland under successive lords lieutenant. His position as chief commissioner of the revenue from 1780 brought control of extensive patronage, and his unobtrusive style may have given him more influence with the British prime minister, William Pitt, than either of the other two leading Irish office holders, John *Foster and John *Fitzgibbon.

The continuing political eminence of the Beresford clan in the early 19th century confirmed the status of the Waterford election of 1826, when a freeholders' revolt co-ordinated by local *Catholic Association activists allowed Henry Villiers Stuart to defeat Lord George Beresford by a large margin, as a landmark in the campaign for *Catholic emancipation, and in the rise of popular politics.

Beresford, Lord John George (1773–1862), *Church of Ireland archbishop of Armagh 1822–62, having previously held the sees of Cork, Raphoe, Clogher, and Dublin. Younger son of the 1st marquis of Waterford and member of the powerful *Beresford family, he was a conservative in matters of both church and state, and viewed tractarians with some suspicion. He opposed the granting of *Catholic emancipation, seeing *'Protestant ascendancy' as intrinsic to the constitution. As archbishop of Armagh, when the *Tithe War was at its fiercest, he drew heavily on his personal resources to aid clergy whose incomes were withheld.

Initially Beresford, in contrast with *Whately, strongly opposed the *national schools, and was president of and munificent contributor to the rival *Church Education Society. He was to experience intense abuse when, in the light of reality, he later tolerated the national system.

The cost of the restoration of Armagh cathedral was borne by him and as chancellor of Dublin University (*Trinity College) he gave generously to the library and towards the foundation of the chair of ecclesiastical history. He also provided Trinity with what is, perhaps, its (undeservedly) most popular architectural feature, the campanile. KM

Berkeley, George (1685–1753), *Church of Ireland clergyman and philosopher. The son of a revenue official, Berkeley was fellow of *Trinity College, Dublin 1707–24, and dean of Derry 1724–34. He spent 1729–31 in Rhode Island, pursuing plans for a college (originally planned for Bermuda) to educate both native Americans and the sons of planters. He became bishop of Cloyne in 1734. Berkeley's philosophical works have been misunderstood as denying the existence of the material world; in fact their concern was to refute the theoretical construct of a material stratum separate from our sense impressions. The three sermons published as *Passive Obedience* (1712) exposed Berkeley to allegations of *Jacobitism, though in 1715 and 1745 he wrote against Stuart claims. The *Querist* (1735–7) argued that Ireland should seek prosperity through the internal exchange of its own produce, facilitated by paper money. This rejection of the contemporary preoccupation with the accumulation of gold and silver through foreign trade is seen in retrospect as a major theoretical advance, though Berkeley's thinking here was largely a specific response to the limitations that English commercial restrictions (see FREE TRADE AGITATION) imposed on Ireland's economic prospects.

Bermingham, a family particularly prominent in the early 14th century. **Robert de Bermingham,** probably from the English west midlands, had been granted by *Strongbow lands in Offaly, where the Berminghams held Tethmoy and Carbury on the Meath border. They participated in the conquest of Connacht, and by the late 13th century had divided into Athenry and Tethmoy branches. **William de Bermingham** was archbishop of Tuam from 1289 to 1312, and **Richard de Bermingham**, lord of Athenry (d. 1322), won a great victory there against the Irish in 1316 during the *Bruce invasion. Their kinsman **Peter de Bermingham** of Tethmoy (d. 1308) murdered the *O'Connors of Offaly in 1305. This deed was celebrated in one of the Middle English *Kildare Poems, but was denounced in the 1317 *Remonstrance. His son *John (d. 1329) was made earl of Louth in 1319. **William**, John's brother, an associate of the 1st earl of *Desmond, was executed by the *justiciar in 1332. His son *Walter became justiciar of Ireland in 1346. Although under English law Walter's lands passed to heiresses after

1361, male cadet lines resisted their claims and retained Tethmoy and Carbury. Both branches of the family, considerably *Gaelicized, remained locally significant into the 16th century. RFF

Bermingham, John de (d. 1329), earl of Louth. Bermingham commanded the force that defeated and killed Edward *Bruce at the battle of *Faughart in 1318. This exploit led Edward II to grant him the earldom and *liberty of Louth in 1319. He was son of Peter de Bermingham (d. 1308), who had murdered many of the *O'Connors of Offaly in 1305. The earl formed a link with the king's favourite Hugh Despenser, and was *justiciar of Ireland in 1321–4. He seized the Irish lands of the Despensers' enemy Roger *Mortimer, and brought troops from Ireland to the Scottish campaign of 1322. After the fall of Edward II and the Despensers in 1326, his star waned. His rule was unwelcome to the gentry of Louth; in June 1329 they assassinated him and many of his followers, and rapidly obtained pardons from the Mortimer government in England. RFF

Bermingham, Walter de (d. 1350), son of William de Bermingham, who was executed by the *justiciar in 1332. Walter was quickly rehabilitated by Edward III, for whom he fought in Scotland in 1335. He supported Ralph *Ufford against the 1st earl of *Desmond in 1345, and in 1346 was appointed to succeed Ufford as justiciar. He took inquisitions against Desmond at Clonmel and Tralee, and was one of the few 14th-century governors to visit Connacht. RFF

Bernard, John Henry (1860–1927), *Church of Ireland clergyman. Bernard was concurrently dean of *St Patrick's cathedral and lecturer in divinity at *Trinity College, Dublin, then bishop of Ossory (1911–15) and archbishop of Dublin (1915–19), before returning to Trinity as provost 1919–27. He contributed energetically to the deliberations of the *Irish Convention of 1917, and was statesmanlike in his attitude to the newly created Free State. A noted administrator and scholar, his writings on philosophy and theology attracted international attention, and his *Commentary on the Gospel According to St John*, published posthumously, is still discussed by scripture scholars. KM

betagh, from the Irish *biatach*, a food-rendering *client, seen by the *Anglo-Normans as a servile tenant, synonymous with a *'serf'. Judging from the fact that betaghs lived in communities called 'betaghries', it seems that Anglo-Normans inherited them from their former Gaelic lords. In theory they were bound to do labour service on the demesnes at the will of the lord, but in practice precedent hardened into immutable manorial custom, with the result that services were limited to a few days' seasonal work. By 1300 betagh services were generally commuted to rent, which may explain why the betaghs disappear as an identifiable group in the 15th century. CAE

Bianconi system, started by Charles (Carlo) Bianconi (1786–1875), an Italian immigrant who came to Ireland in 1802 as a pedlar of prints. On his journeys he saw the need for a regular and inexpensive system of transport. In 1815 he started his first service, a one-horse, two-wheeled car to carry passengers, goods, and mail on the 8-mile Clonmel–Cahir route in Co. Tipperary. This was such a success that many other routes followed. Bianconi was able to purchase high-class horses and cars, due to the low price of horses following the *revolutionary and Napoleonic wars, and a carriage tax which led many to sell off their jaunting cars cheaply. His open-topped cars, unlike the *stage coaches whose routes radiated from Dublin, ran mainly between provincial towns. By the 1840s his cars, affectionately known as 'Bians', were working daily over 3,000 miles of road. His larger cars, known as 'Finn McCools' and 'Massey Dawsons' (the latter after a popular landlord), could carry up to 20 passengers. This veritable transport revolution made most of rural Ireland more readily accessible, greatly furthered trade, and reduced the price of many goods. Many 'Bians' were to continue on Irish roads until their replacement by *railways and later motor buses. PC

biblical exegesis, from the mid-5th century, can be seen in terms of a scholastic repetition where original works are systematic guides to the inherited tradition. Irish exegesis has to be interpreted in this way, as it is paralleled in content and quality by work from the rest of the Latin world. However, it does have some qualities of its own. The productivity of Europe between 500 and 800 is meagre when compared with the 9th century, but in this period the work of Irish scholars is significant disproportionally to the country's size or background. Another peculiarity of Irish exegesis is the extent to which it is anonymous: we possess few names, and it is modern research that attributes works to Irish scholars. This raises the question of an Irish school of exegesis, and the search for tell-tale Irish symptoms in such works. While there are prominent features of Irish works (e.g. interest in grammar and computistics in the midst of exegesis), these cannot settle the question as they are not exclusively Irish.

O'Loughlin, T. (ed.), *The Scriptures and Early Medieval Ireland* (1999)

TO'L

bicycle riding became popular in Ireland because the roads were and are comparatively less crowded. Though John Boyd Dunlop invented the pneumatic tyre in Belfast in 1889, he was not a good businessman and his company passed to an English concern. The Dunlop Pneumatic Tyre Company, which had manufactured tyres in Belfast and Dublin, soon relocated to the English midlands, the centre of the bicycle industry. Early Irish bicycles were manufactured by Pierce Company of Wexford, Lucania Cycles in Dublin, and Gordon Brothers of Hillsborough, Co. Down, who manufactured about 700 racing bikes a year. The larger English manufacturers soon swamped the Irish market. In the 1930s Raleigh of England, responding to the *protectionist policy of *Fianna Fáil, began production in Ireland. They produced 50,000 bikes a year in Dublin, with tyres made in Cork. The bicycle was for long the only affordable means of transport for a high proportion of the Irish people. Since the 1960s, with increasing prosperity, the cycle has declined while the car has multiplied. Nevertheless, with the continuing popularity of cycling for leisure and sport, Ireland continues to produce world-beating cyclists of the calibre of Sean Kelly and Stephen Roche. PC

Biggar, Joseph Gillis (1828–90), nationalist politician and MP for Cavan 1874–90. A prosperous provision merchant, Biggar was drawn to the *home rule movement, joined the *IRB in 1875, and was a member of the supreme council (transacting its business on House of Commons notepaper) until expelled for refusing to quit parliament (1877). He pioneered the tactics of obstructing parliamentary business which he and *Parnell perfected. He was a treasurer of the *Land League. A Presbyterian by upbringing, he became a Catholic in 1877. RVC

'big wind', the storm which ravaged Ireland, particularly the west, north, and midlands, on the night of Sunday, 6 January 1839. High winds uprooted trees, destroyed buildings, killed livestock, and, in built-up areas, spread fires. Although one newspaper put total deaths at 300 or more, a survey of contemporary reports has found about 90 documented fatalities, 37 of them at sea. When old-age pensions were introduced in 1909 memories of the storm were one of the tests used to identify persons over 70.

Bingham, Sir Richard (1528–99), *provincial president of Connacht 1584–96. Bingham disliked *Perrot's *composition of Connacht but eventually became its most ardent supporter. It brought him into conflict with the Mayo *Burkes in 1586. He reduced their castles, hanged their leaders, and defeated their *redshanks at *Ardnaree. In 1589 Bingham, with his kinsmen and clients, began a systematic reduction of north Connacht. War was renewed with the Burkes, O'Flaherty forced into revolt, and *O'Rourke's lordship overrun. Bingham now began demanding the right to follow traitors into Tirconnell and Fermanagh. An attack by *Maguire (May 1593) against the Binghams was one of the earliest actions of the *Nine Years War. Bingham's government collapsed after the fall of Sligo in January 1595. By August only Galway and Clare were free of revolt. The deteriorating situation in Connacht was blamed on Bingham's arbitrary government. Leaving in 1596 to defend himself in England, he was imprisoned in the Fleet for abuse of martial law. Rehabilitated in 1598 as marshal of Ireland, he died on arrival in Dublin. HM

Birr, Synod of, see ADOMNÁN.

Birrell, Augustine (1850–1933), Liberal politician and Ireland's longest-serving *chief secretary (Jan. 1907–May 1916). A London barrister and wit, he gave the name 'birrelling' to light essay-writing. A cabinet career characterized by legislative failure—the 1906 education bill (England) rejected by the Lords, the *Irish council bill rejected by the *Nationalist Party, the *Home Rule Act (1914) stifled by the Ulster *Unionists—ended in disaster at Easter 1916. After 1910 Irish policy was directed by *Asquith and *Lloyd George, Birrell's wife's terminal illness being part of the explanation. His achievements were the Universities Act of 1908, which provided colleges acceptable to Catholics, and the 1909 *Land Act which revised *Wyndham's 1903 act in the tenants' favour. Strongly pragmatic, he saw off the formidable *MacDonnell. The key to his approach was a strong Liberal–Nationalist alliance; the confrontational policies of his successors were no more effective. He commended and, with *Things Past Redress* (1937), practised posthumous autobiography.

ACH

Black and Tans. The failure of the *Royal Irish Constabulary to combat *IRA raids in 1919 convinced the government that the police needed to be reinforced. From January 1920 British ex-soldiers and sailors were recruited and, by November 1921, some 9,500 such men had joined the RIC. A shortage of RIC uniforms meant that recruits were issued with khaki military trousers and dark green police tunics. Although full RIC uniforms were soon substituted, this mixed dress gave rise to the new policemen's distinctive sobriquet, the Black and Tans.

Hurriedly and inadequately trained, recruits were posted to RIC barracks, mainly in Munster, west Connacht, and Dublin. Thus strengthened, the RIC from mid-1920 was encouraged to pursue the IRA more vigorously. The government, at first tacitly and then openly, condoned reprisals by the police (see ANGLO-IRISH WAR). The leading role of the Black and Tans in some of these incidents may have been exaggerated, as British-born and Irish-born policemen were difficult, when in full uniform, to tell apart. Nevertheless, the Black and Tans gained a fearsome reputation for brutality, which only helped alienate the population from the RIC as a whole. Of policemen recruited in 1920–1 over one-third died, were dismissed or discharged, or resigned: a very high wastage rate indeed, attesting both to the difficulties of service and to the inadequacies of recruits. But 63 per cent went on to secure government pensions when the RIC was disbanded in 1922. ELM

Black Death, the name given to an epidemic of bubonic and pneumonic plague that spread rapidly from Asia to Europe in the 1340s, arriving in the British Isles in the summer of 1348 and causing huge loss of life and massive social disorder. Our main source for its arrival in Ireland is the chronicle of the Kilkenny-based Franciscan friar John *Clyn. He claims that the plague first hit the ports of Drogheda and Howth (or Dalkey). Dublin and Drogheda are said to have been almost wasted of inhabitants, so that in Dublin alone, by Christmas 1348, 14,000 had died (a figure that is no doubt exaggerated), along with many of the Franciscans in the friaries of Dublin and Drogheda. Clyn's account, noting that there was hardly a house in which only one had died, with whole families being carried off, and describing how bishops, prelates, nobles, and others came in their thousands on pilgrimage to St Mullins, Co. Carlow, captures something of the prevailing sense of horror and crisis.

As the risk of infection was increased by social contact, townspeople suffered more severely than rural communities. It was reported, for instance, in 1351 that the greater part of the citizens of Cork had died. For this reason it is usual to suppose that the native Irish were less severely affected, as was bluntly stated in a petition sent by the Anglo-Irish to the king in 1360, though the Irish annals do report its devastating effect on Moylurg, Co. Roscommon, in 1349. We have no accurate way of estimating the mortality figures. The archbishop of Armagh, Richard *Fitzralph, preaching before the pope in August 1349, claimed that the plague had killed two-thirds of the English population but had not affected the Irish and Scots to the same extent. Modern estimates range between a third and a half of the population. The Black Death hastened an economic decline which had been under way already for several decades, producing a prolonged agricultural depression. As a result, lands formerly held by the Anglo-Irish colonists were abandoned, and manors, villages, and some of the smaller rural boroughs were deserted. There was also, as in England, a movement away from demesne farming, whereby lords ceased direct management of outlying estates and instead leased them out to others. The plague periodically recurred after the initial outbreak in 1348–9.

Butler, Richard (ed.), *The Annals of Ireland by Friar John Clyn and Thady Dowling* (1849)

Gwynn, Aubrey, 'The Black Death in Ireland', *Studies*, 24 (1935)

SD

Black Oath, the popular name for the sworn abjuration of the Scots *Presbyterian covenant. Scottish royalist settlers, orchestrated by *Wentworth, requested that an oath be introduced for their countrymen as an expression of loyalty. The Irish privy council issued an order in May 1639 for all adult Scots in Ireland over 16 to reject the *Solemn League and Covenant. With the army presence in Ulster, most Scots conformed though many others took flight. HM

Black Pig's Dyke, otherwise the 'Worm Ditch', the popular name given to a series of linear earthworks—banks, ditches, and timber palisades—situated on the southern border of Ulster. This system may also include the Dorsey, a double line of defensive features in south Armagh. The 'Dyke' dates to the *Iron Age *c.*500–50 BC and is commonly interpreted as an interrupted defensive system to impede cattle-raiding from the south. The name derives from a tale relating how a schoolmaster-magician was tricked into transforming himself into a pig and driven across Ireland, rooting up the landscape as he went.

JPM

black rent, the name that came to be given to the protection money exacted, mostly by Gaelic lords, from local communities and even from the Dublin government. Art *MacMurrough levied it in Leinster from the 1370s. In the 15th and early 16th centuries it became so widespread and regular as to constitute a form of unofficial taxation. It has parallels elsewhere, for example in the 'blackmail' collected by the lineages of the Anglo-Scottish borders. RFF

Blood's plot, a plan by disaffected Protestants to seize *Dublin Castle and stage provincial risings, discovered in March 1663 but subsequently renewed, with further arrests in May and June. Seven members were expelled from the House of Commons for complicity in the plot; an eighth, Col. Alexander Jephson, MP for Trim, was hanged. Their involvement reflects the hostility, extending well beyond irreconcilable opponents of monarchy and episcopacy, created among Irish Protestants by the Act of *Settlement.

The conspiracy took its name from **Thomas Blood** (*c.*1618–80), a former parliamentary soldier born in Co. Meath. In 1670, acting ostensibly for private reasons but possibly as the agent of a rival courtier, he tried to murder *Ormond in London. Arrested the following May while attempting to steal the English crown jewels, he was pardoned and granted Irish lands worth £500 a year, returning to the radical underground as a government spy, a role he may have already played in the 1660s.

blood sports have taken various forms in Ireland, including *bull baiting, *cock fighting, and *fox hunting. They have, at various times, been enjoyed by spectators and participants from all classes and creeds. Concern at the cruelty of some sports began to be voiced from the middle of the 18th century, but when some events were finally suppressed in the 1790s it was more for public order reasons than out of concern for animal welfare. United Kingdom legislation to control cruel sports was enacted in 1835, and animal baiting, dog fighting, and cock fighting became illegal. This legislation, with some relatively minor later amendments, remains in force in both Irish states. Societies concerned with the welfare of animals, and opposed to some blood sports, began to be formed in Ireland from 1864, some years later than similar organizations in England. (However, it should be noted that Richard Martin (1754–1834), acknowledged as the founder of the Royal Society for the Protection of Animals in England, was a Co. Galway landlord.) Despite their prohibition, clandestine animal baiting and fighting continue across Ireland, with little effective opposition. Other blood sports, such as hare coursing and fox hunting, have not been legislated against and continue to be popular. Occasional protests are staged, but serious parliamentary opposition remains limited. NG

'Bloody Sunday'. The original 'Bloody Sunday' was a massacre of Russian protesters on 9 January 1905. Its first Irish namesake was 21 November 1920, when *IRA men in Dublin killed thirteen men and injured six others, most, though not all, of whom were British intelligence agents. Later two arrested IRA leaders, Peadar Clancy and Richard McKee, were killed, along with another prisoner, supposedly while trying to escape. The same afternoon *Auxiliaries dispatched to search for wanted men at a crowded Gaelic football match in Croke Park opened fire, possibly after coming under attack, killing twelve people. More recently the name has been applied to 30 January 1972, when paratroopers sent to make arrests following a banned *civil rights march in Derry shot dead fourteen civilians. The rapid escalation of violence that followed helped precipitate *direct rule in Northern Ireland.

Blow, James (d. 1759), *printer and bookseller in *Belfast. Blow specialized in religious publications, including editions of the Bible, and was succeeded by his son Daniel (*fl.* 1747–78). VK

Blueshirts, popular name for the Army Comrades' Association, a political movement formed by ex-servicemen from the Free State army in February 1932. In reaction to the unexpected victory of de *Valera in the general election, supporters of *Cumann na nGaedheal flocked to its ranks, and it soon included members who had no previous military connections. Following de Valera's more decisive electoral victory in January 1933, the movement's political nature was reinforced, and it began to adopt the trappings of continental European fascist movements, including the wearing of distinctive shirts (in this case blue ones, which gave the movement its popular name).

In July 1933 Eoin *O'Duffy, Garda commissioner until his dismissal by de Valera, took over as leader of the movement, whose formal name was now altered to National Guard. The Blueshirts engaged in a significant trial of strength with the government in August 1933, when a successful ban on a major march demoralized the movement. Shortly thereafter, however, the National Guard merged with Cumann na nGaedheal and the *Centre Party to form *Fine Gael, of which O'Duffy became first leader.

Although O'Duffy's political inexperience and tendency towards extremism caused his tenure of the leadership of the new party to be short-lived (he was forced to resign on 21 Sept. 1934), the Blueshirts continued in existence under new names—first as the Young Ireland Association and later as the League of Youth—before fading away following further tensions between O'Duffy and his former Fine Gael colleagues. They last came to significant public attention when O'Duffy and some of his followers left Ireland in 1936 to fight on Franco's side in the *Spanish Civil War.

Ideologically, and in terms of its rituals, the Blueshirt movement had much in common with continental European fascism: it was suspicious of party politics, sympathetic towards the notion of a strong leader, antipathetic towards communism, and nationalist in orientation. Its ideologues provided an intellectual justification for this package, especially by reference to corporate social theory. But, as in the case of other fascist-type movements, these ideas were disseminated imperfectly among members of the movement, many of whom were motivated more by hostility to *Fianna Fáil's radical economic policies and its continued links with the *IRA.

Manning, Maurice, *The Blueshirts* (1971)

JC

Blythe, Ernest (1889–1975), a rare example, by the early 20th century, of an Ulster Protestant embracing cultural and political nationalism. Born in Co. Antrim, he joined the *Gaelic League and *Irish Republican Brotherhood while a clerk in Dublin, and was imprisoned during the *rising of 1916. As *Cumann na nGaedheal minister for finance (1922–31) he won lasting notoriety by reducing old-age pensions, but also initiated the state subsidy to the *Abbey theatre. He was managing director of the Abbey 1941–67, where he insisted that only Irish-speaking actors could be employed. As Earnán de Blaghd he published poetry and memoirs.

bó-aire, a term used in the early Irish *law tracts for a prosperous farmer of commoner rank. He is normally the client of a lord from whom he receives a fief of stock or land. In return he pays an annual food-rent consisting of a milch-cow (*bó*): this probably explains the term *bó-aire* (lit. 'cow-freeman'). In addition, he must provide fixed quantities of bread, malt, bacon, and other foodstuffs. He must also prepare a feast for his lord during the winter months, as well as providing a spell of manual labour at sowing-time and harvest. A *bó-aire* is permitted to receive fiefs from three lords at the same time. The **Críth Gablach* provides an idealized account of the possessions of a prosperous *bó-aire*. These include 20 cows, 20 pigs, 20 sheep, and 2 bulls. He also has 6 oxen and full ploughing equipment. At public assemblies he is entitled to be accompanied by two retainers.

FK

Board of Green Cloth, an organization of woollen workers in early 19th-century Dublin. Many employers in the 1820s believed that the board co-ordinated unions in sometimes violent action against them. The British trade union historians Sidney and Beatrice Webb compounded what was probably an overblown view of the board's influence when they wrote that it was a joint committee of the Dublin trades 'whose dictates became the terror of the employers'.

PC

Board of Works (Office of Public Works), established in 1831, reflecting the anxiety of British politicians to promote the economic improvement of Ireland and thus to reduce poverty and disorder. Consisting of three salaried commissioners, plus staff, the board took over duties previously performed by a number of different bodies, including the directors-general of inland navigation, the Dublin Board of Works, and the commissioners of civil buildings. In addition to being responsible for expenditure of public money on projects such as the completion of *Kingstown (Dun Laoghaire) and Dunmore harbours, the board was empowered to make loans, not exceeding £500,000 in total, for works initiated either by local authorities or by private individuals. A further £50,000 was made available for distribution as free grants for the construction of roads and bridges in poor districts.

Over the following decades the board's functions were extended to encompass *fisheries, drainage, and *railways. Its lending powers were also increased. Loans were made available for a variety of purposes from drainage and sanitary improvements to the erection of labourers' cottages. The number of public buildings in the board's charge grew to include the *Queen's Colleges and all buildings connected with the *Royal Irish Constabulary, the *post office, and the *national school system. In 1882 it was made responsible for the preservation of national monuments. Between 1831 and 1914 the board paid out £49 million in grants and loans. Not all of this money was well spent. Despite the substantial sums invested in inland navigation, for example, Irish waterways failed to become profitable concerns.

The greatest challenge faced by the board, and to which, ultimately, it proved unequal, came during the *Famine, when for a two-year period (1845–7) it was the primary body responsible for relief. Required to adhere to strict rules concerning the type of public works undertaken and the wages paid, the board was criticized by landlords for sponsoring useless works, and by tenants for the inadequacy of the relief thus provided.

The Board of Works was transferred to the *Irish Free State in 1922 and placed under the control of the Department of *Finance. Its responsibilities are now largely confined to the construction and maintenance of public buildings.

Griffiths, Tony, *The Irish Board of Works 1831–78* (1987)
Lohan, Rena, *Guide to the Archives of the Office of Public Works* (1994)

VC

Boate, Gerard (1604–50), Dutch author of *Ireland's Natural History* (1652) who died soon after his arrival in Ireland as physician with Oliver *Cromwell's army. In 1645 this London-based *adventurer wrote a description of Ireland and how it might be further improved by consolidation of the English Protestant interest. He synthesized information on geography, environment, and resources from his brother Arnold (physician-general to the English army in Ireland till 1644), refugee English planters, and earlier accounts, to set new standards of accuracy. Samuel Hartlib, another 'common scientist', had Boate's description published posthumously with the express purpose of encouraging replantation by continental Protestants as well as English adventurers. HM

Boer War, the name by which the South African or second Anglo-Boer War of 1899–1902 is popularly known. Many Irish nationalists, including Arthur *Griffith who spent some time in the Transvaal during the late 1890s, drew a parallel between the plight of the Boers—white, Christian nationalists—and the Irish, each resisting the might of the British empire. Two Transvaal Irish brigades were formed to support the Boer cause. One was led by an Irish-American adventurer, Col. John Blake, along with Maj. John *MacBride, while the other was commanded by Arthur Lynch. Although a few recruits joined from Ireland and the USA, essentially these units were drawn from the existing Irish community in *South Africa. Together they never numbered more than about 400 men, a striking contrast to the 28,000 or so Irishmen who served against them in the British army. In Ireland, an 'Irish-Transvaal Committee', including Griffith, James *Connolly, W. B. *Yeats, and Maud *Gonne, was formed to support the Boer republics and dissuade young Irishmen from joining up to fight on the British side. Although this effort had only a slight impact, the anti-war campaign as a whole greatly invigorated the Irish nationalist movement at a time when it was still suffering from the effects of the Parnellite split in 1890. KJ

bogs, regionally widespread and locally extensive deposits of peat of varying but, in geological terms, recent post-glacial origin. Bogs are estimated to have covered up to 3 million acres, or approximately one-seventh of Ireland's land area in the past. They have acted, variously, as a major constraint on the human exploitation of the Irish environment during later prehistoric and early historic times and, in more recent centuries, as a reservoir of colonizable land and as a source of fuel.

Irish bogs have been classified in various ways according to the environmental conditions in which they originated and the relative importance of the climatic and other factors which promoted their development. The most commonly used classification distinguishes between *raised bogs* and *blanket bogs*. Raised bogs occur widely in lowland areas in the Irish midlands, east of the Shannon and Suck rivers, and in the north. They first began to develop between 10,000 and 7,000 years BP (before present), and are termed 'raised' because of their manner of growth. As existing lakes are colonized by fens and marshes, so deep layers of fen peat build up, eventually creating base-deficient conditions which permit invasion by more acidic plants such as sphagnum moss. These mosses grow into small hummocks, which dry out and are colonized by heathers. The pools created between these hummocks attract further sphagnum colonization, and the process is repeated, progressively raising the bog's surface. Continued growth depends on adequate rainfall and vegetable debris, but once begun is self-perpetuating.

Blanket bogs first developed rather later during the prehistoric period, from *c.*5,500 years BP, and in the specific context of early woodland clearance and agricultural land use in upland areas at a time when Ireland's climate may have been becoming wetter. The modern distribution of blanket bog is much less extensive than it originally was, but still runs in a discontinuous arc from the Sperrin mountains in Co. Londonderry, south through the coastal uplands of western Connacht, to west Cork and Kerry in the far south-west. Elsewhere it is confined to mountain ranges such as the Mournes, Wicklows, and Knockmealdowns.

The development of blanket bogs depended on the existence of podzol soils, which were characterized by an impervious iron pan. This impeded drainage within the soil and led to waterlogging and the growth of rushes. Eventually, these rushes built up a mineral-deficient layer of peat liable, as in raised bogs, to invasion by sphagnum moss. With continued waterlogging the rushes spread and the ground finally became buried under a blanket of acidic peat.

The discovery in the west of Ireland of numerous *neolithic and *Bronze Age field walls, tombs, and scratch-plough ridges beneath these blanket bogs, for example at Belderg and Bunnyconnellon, both in Co. Mayo, demonstrates the extent to which their growth curtailed early agriculture. Throughout the early Christian and medieval periods they remained beyond exploitation by contemporary agricultural technology. Only with the rise in population since the early modern period, and improvements in drainage, have bogs come to be regarded as land to be reclaimed rather than wasteland to be avoided. During the immediate pre-*Famine period, many bogs on the margins of cultivation in the west of Ireland were colonized by smallholders and squatters, driven there by the locally extreme pressure of population on relatively limited land resources. Subsequently, with the collapse of Ireland's population after the Famine, these areas were abandoned.

Turbary rights represent an equally historic form of exploitation. Traditionally, the right to dig peat or 'turf' for fuel constituted an important element in leasehold agreements between landlords and tenants. Yet turf was never widely exploited as an industrial fuel, manufacturers in Dublin, Cork, and Belfast preferring to import coal. Various reasons have been adduced for this. Although cheaper than coal, turf had only half its calorific value and was as bulky to transport, while its production could be halted by wet weather. In the present day, by contrast, domestic rights of turbary survive, but exist alongside the commercial exploitation of bogs in Co. Mayo and the midlands for both horticulture and fuel. Experiments to generate electricity from peat followed the rise in demand for native fuels during the First World War, and peat production was nationalized in 1946 (see BORD NA MÓNA). By 1970, 135,000 acres of bog were yielding 4 million tons of peat per annum, and turf-generated *electricity amounted to 20 per cent of demand.

Mitchell, F., *Shell Guide to Reading the Irish Landscape* (2nd edn., 1986)

LJP

Boland, Gerald (1885–1973). Born in Manchester, Boland fought in the *rising of 1916 and later, with *Lemass, provided the organizational brains behind the successful launch of *Fianna Fáil. As minister for justice he directed the firm suppression of the *Irish Republican Army during the *Second World War. In May 1970 his son **Kevin Boland**, minister for local government, resigned from the cabinet in sympathy with Haughey and Blaney (see ARMS CRISIS). He later (1971) set up a rival republican party, Aontacht Éireann, which achieved negligible impact.

bombing campaigns in Great Britain have been resorted to by militant Irish nationalists on a number of occasions since the 1880s. Based on the perception that Britain's presence in Ireland is primarily one of self-interest, they have been intended to make the government believe that the cost of staying in Ireland is too high. This strategy has, however, never been successful. In particular the human casualties which have been the inevitable result have in general only strengthened British resolve and led to a clampdown on the separatists.

The first time the tactic was used was during the dynamite campaign of 1883 to 1885, initiated by *Clan Na Gael. (An earlier explosion, at Clerkenwell, London, on 13 Dec. 1867, which had killed fifteen persons, was part of a bungled attempt to release a *Fenian prisoner, rather than terrorism by bomb.) During the *Anglo-Irish War *IRA units in England and Scotland attacked economic targets with firebombs. A bombing campaign in Britain, under the direction of Sean *Russell, became the main strategy of the IRA in 1939, but this soon petered out. In the renewed *Northern Ireland conflict since 1969 bombs in Great Britain were once again part of IRA strategy, causing enormous damage that increased the pressure to find a political solution, but came no nearer than earlier campaigns to forcing a unilateral British withdrawal. JA

Bonaght of Ulster (see BUANNACHT). This was the prerogative exercised by the de Burgh (*Burke) earls of billeting fixed quotas of mercenary retainers or 'satellites' on each of the Ulster chieftains 'for the defence and peace of those parts'. Successive members of the MacQuillin family held the post of 'constable of the bonaght' and in 1323 Sir Henry de Mandeville was granted command over 'all satellites of our bonhaght in Ulster', a circumstance leading Edmund *Curtis to suppose erroneously that the de Mandeville and MacQuillin families were related. The exaction became unenforceable after the murder of William de *Burgh, last resident earl, in 1333.

KS

Bonar Law, Andrew (1858–1923), British Conservative leader and, from October 1922 to May 1923, prime minister. Son of an Ulster Presbyterian minister, Bonar Law was born in New Brunswick but brought up near Glasgow where he entered

Conservative politics. In 1911 he became party leader. Having kept up his Ulster family connections, Bonar Law threw the Conservatives wholeheartedly behind the *Unionist campaign against the third *home rule bill. At a rally at Blenheim Palace on 29 June 1912 he proclaimed that there was 'no length of resistance to which Ulster can go in which I would not be prepared to support them'. His support for the Unionist position was equally critical in the election of November 1918 and during the negotiation of the *Anglo-Irish treaty. TGF

Book of Rights, see *LEBOR NA CERT.*

border campaign, an *Irish Republican Army campaign in Northern Ireland 1956–62, also known as Operation Harvest, which was the code name for the original somewhat over-ambitious battle plan. Operations started on 11 December 1956 when three IRA flying columns infiltrated Northern Ireland from the Republic. Their targets consisted of British army depots and centres of administration. Hopes that their actions would be taken up by local Volunteers were never fully realized. The enthusiasm which had been generated by the IRA's arms raids in 1954–5 had given its leadership the false impression that their use of force was widely supported. This was confirmed by the response to their first few operations. A public outburst of sympathy in the Republic followed the death of three southern Volunteers in operations in the north. The public imagination was particularly captured by Sean South, killed in an attack on the *Royal Ulster Constabulary barracks at Brookeborough, Co. Fermanagh, on New Year's Day 1957. His funeral in Limerick attracted tens of thousands of mourners. This enthusiasm resulted in some good electoral results for *Sinn Féin in 1957, but the IRA soon found out that support for the use of force among the nationalist community north and south was limited, and that hostility amongst unionists was far larger than they had anticipated.

Most operations were concentrated in the first couple of years. The campaign then fizzled out as a result of the harsh measures, including *internment, taken by both Irish governments. In 1957 there were 341 recorded incidents, but by 1959 this was reduced to 27. The campaign was officially called off in February 1962 due to a lack of public support. The emphasis on material targets is reflected in the fairly low casualty figures. In the entire period six RUC, eight IRA men, two republican civilians, and two members of a rival republican organization were killed, while 32 members of the crown forces were injured. JA

Bord na Móna ('The Turf Board'), founded in 1946 as a state-owned company with a statutory responsibility to produce fuel from Irish peat *bogs. It succeeded another state company, the Turf Development Board, which had been formed in 1935 as part of the policy of developing indigenous resources in order to achieve self-sufficiency. Turf was an important source of domestic fuel, given the dearth of Irish *coal supplies. Bord na Móna used modern machinery in place of traditional methods of harvesting turf and the company became a major employer throughout the midlands, where it built a number of planned villages. A substantial proportion of the company's output was sold to the *Electricity Supply Board for generation purposes. MED

borough, an area of settlement endowed with certain privileges and the right of local self-government, usually confirmed by royal charter. The origins of the practice are Norman French. More than 170 boroughs were established in medieval Ireland. By 1615, 81 returned members to the Irish *parliament; the incorporation in 1683 of Dunleer, Co. Louth, the last parliamentary borough to be created, brought the number to 117. These were far from homogeneous: some had become bustling cities, while others were almost totally depopulated. Voting qualifications varied (see FRANCHISE) but most were effectively controlled by one or two 'patrons'. The de facto exclusion of Catholics from borough corporations began with the *Restoration, and was confirmed by law in 1691. Between 1704 and 1780 Protestant dissenters were excluded by the *sacramental test. Even after the *Catholic Relief Act of 1793 borough government remained in practice a Protestant monopoly, only gradually eroded by a combination of electoral reform and increasing Catholic prosperity and political awareness. Meanwhile the powers of the boroughs themselves were declining, while under the Act of *Union only 33 retained the right to send members to parliament. After *partition there was further delegation of borough powers to county councils in the *Irish Free State. In Northern Ireland local government reorganization in 1972 redefined most boroughs, and deprived all of the majority of their powers. NG

borstal. In 1901 a prison for male offenders aged 16 to 23 was established at Borstal in Kent. A similar institution was opened in Ireland, at Clonmel, Co. Tipperary, in 1906. In Northern Ireland after 1920 male offenders were initially sent to a borstal in England, but in 1927 part of the reformatory at Malone in Belfast was converted into a borstal. In 1956 this borstal was transferred to Millisle, Co. Down, and a second borstal was opened in Armagh jail in 1963. A borstal for girls existed in Armagh between 1954 and 1961; thereafter girls were sent to a Scottish borstal. In the south the Clonmel borstal continued to operate until 1956 when it was replaced by St Patrick's Institution at Mountjoy jail in Dublin. This was supplemented by open young offenders' institutions in Co. Dublin (1968) and Co. Cavan (1972). No female borstal was established in the Republic. ELM

bothach, a semi-free dependant occasionally mentioned in the early Irish *law tracts. He is housed in a *both* 'hut' by his lord in return for his labour. He is on the same social level as a **fuidir*. FK

Boulogne expedition (1544). In the conciliatory atmosphere of *surrender and regrant 600 Irish *kerns commanded by *Old English officers fought for Henry VIII in France. The expedition, which confirmed the Irish reputation for ferocity, was a high point for the Old English. Edward Walshe, a company commander, wrote a patriotic tract entitled *The Office and Duety of Fightyng for our Country* (1545), while Richard *Stanihurst celebrated it in his contribution to Holinshed's *Chronicles* (1577). HM

Boulter, Hugh (1671–1742), political prelate. Born in London, Boulter was bishop of Bristol from 1719 before becoming *Church of Ireland archbishop of Armagh in 1724. His appointment, immediately following the *Wood's Halfpence dispute, reflected the government's concern to tighten control of Irish affairs. Over the next two decades Boulter was a key figure in the management of the kingdom, working closely with a succession of *lords lieutenant and serving regularly as *lord justice in their absence. Throughout he remained committed to upholding what he considered the English interest in Ireland, pressing for the appointment of English-born office holders in both church and state and warning against what he saw as the national pretensions of Irish Protestants. He was at the same time a conscientious churchman, who promoted the reform of the church's finances and the raising of pastoral standards, and gave active support to the *charter schools and other improving ventures. He contributed generously to famine relief in 1740–1, and left most of his fortune for the purchase of glebes and the augmentation of small benefices. His letters, edited in 1769–70 by his secretary Ambrose Philips, remain a much cited source.

Boundary Commission, set up under the *Anglo-Irish treaty of 1921 to delineate the boundary of *Northern Ireland. During discussions with the cabinet in December 1919, James *Craig had suggested a commission to hold a vote along the six-county border, but the idea did not form part of the subsequent *government of Ireland bill. At a critical point in the treaty negotiations *Griffith accepted a formula for a boundary commission to 'make the Boundary conform as closely as possible to the wishes of the population'. Griffith and *Collins maintained that this would transfer significant territory, including Co. Fermanagh, Co. Tyrone, and Derry city, to the new *Irish Free State. But in the final draft of the treaty the wording stipulated that the wishes of the inhabitants had to be compatible with economic and geographical considerations. The commission did not begin work until late 1924, chaired by the South African jurist Richard Feetham, with Eoin *MacNeill and J. R. Fisher representing the Free State and Northern Ireland. Arguing that the terms of the treaty prevented him from reconstituting Northern Ireland *de novo*, Feetham refused to transfer Fermanagh and Tyrone. The economic clause of the treaty also meant the retention of Derry and Newry. When these recommendations were leaked to the *Morning Post* in November 1925 MacNeill resigned in protest. The commission was abandoned in favour of a tripartite agreement confirming the existing border while releasing the Free State (and Northern Ireland) from certain financial obligations arising from the treaty. TGF

boxing as a professional sport has its origins in 18th-century prize fighting, a fashion encouraged by London society. The English Broughton rules (1743) were printed in Ireland and probably adhered to. The sport was popularized by fighters such as Dan *Donnelly and Jack Langan. Irish gentlemen followed the example of the prince regent and took instruction from prize fighters. However, excessive *gambling on fights, and consequent malpractice, led to a decline in interest and esteem. At the end of the 19th century the success of Irish-American fighters John L. Sullivan (1858–1918) and James J. Corbett (1866–1933) in the professional ring rekindled interest in the sport, but professional boxing has only occasionally attained a high profile in Ireland.

The Irish Amateur Boxing Association (IABA) was formed in Dublin in 1911, though individual clubs had existed for some years. The sport was encouraged by both the police and the army, and in *Trinity College. Despite the murder of the IABA chairman, a policeman, in 1920, there was great continuity in amateur boxing after *partition. The IABA continued as an all-Ireland body, and the *Gárda Síochána and Free State army emerged as the sport's main sponsors. The National Boxing Stadium, a major international venue, was built in Dublin by the IABA in 1939. In Northern Ireland individual clubs came to be associated with certain industrial employers or the Catholic church. There is still a high level of amateur participation in Ireland, with 7,000 active boxers being affiliated to the IABA in 1980.

NG

Boycott, Capt. Charles Cunningham (1832–97). An English-born former soldier appointed agent for Lord Erne's Co. Mayo estates in 1873, Boycott came into conflict with the *Land League at Lough Mask in 1880 and was the first prominent victim of Parnell's policy of consigning those who broke the league's code of conduct into 'moral coventry'. He responded by drafting in Ulster *Orangemen to assist in farm work, but 1,000 troops were needed to protect them. The conflict made his name a synonym for social ostracism.

JL

Boyle, one of the most important political dynasties of the 17th and 18th centuries. The founder of the family's fortune was Richard *Boyle, 1st earl of Cork, whose material success and meteoric social ascent was the platform for the achievements of his equally remarkable offspring. He sent his five sons to university and on the Grand Tour but provided no formal education for his seven daughters (see WOMEN). Most importantly he invested heavily in negotiating advantageous marriages for his offspring. The sons married into the English peerage and the daughters into the Irish, the exceptions being the unmarried Robert *Boyle and Mary, countess of Warwick, who ignored her father's wishes after falling in love with Charles Rich, then an impoverished younger son. In these transactions the large fortune at Boyle's disposal made up for his own lowly social origins. Boyle also promoted the ecclesiastical careers of his cousins: Michael Boyle (bishop of Waterford and Lismore 1619–35) and Richard Boyle (bishop of Cork, Cloyne, and Ross 1620–38 and archbishop of Tuam 1638–41). Thus Boyle spun webs of connections across Ireland and further afield.

The 1st earl was succeeded by his eldest surviving son Richard (d. 1699), who had cultivated *Wentworth and was an active royalist, unlike his collaborationist brother Roger, earl of *Orrery. He had the benefit of Roger's assistance during the Protectorate and was created earl of Burlington after lending Charles II large sums of money at the *Restoration. He opposed the *cattle bill in the English Lords saying that it was the unhappiest day for Ireland since the rising of 1641. Yet this senior line was now effectively an English aristocratic family backed by Irish rents. Burlington, gaining the largest part of the founder's estate and buying more confiscated lands, enjoyed a rental of £20,000 at his death.

Orrery's inheritance from the 1st earl consisted of lands at Charleville, to which he added further property in Imokilly and Limerick, giving him a rental of £4,000. To rival the duke of *Ormond at Kilkenny and add prestige to his lord presidency, he spent £23,000 (mostly borrowed) on building a mansion at Charleville and on remodelling Castlemartyr. His grandson Charles, 4th earl of Orrery (1674–1731), was imprisoned for suspected *Jacobite activities 1722–3. His son John, the 5th earl (1707–62), also allegedly a leading Jacobite, was prominent in literary circles and wrote a controversial early biography of *Swift. He gained the additional title of earl of Cork on the death of the 3rd earl of Burlington in 1753.

The most politically eminent member of the Boyle family in the 18th century was Henry *Boyle, the great *undertaker. His father was a younger son of the 1st earl of Orrery, killed in action in Flanders in 1693. Boyle inherited the house and lands at Castlemartyr, but the initial basis of his political power was his role as land agent for Richard, 4th earl of Cork and 3rd earl of Burlington (d. 1753) and controller of his Munster parliamentary seats. Later Boyle acquired Clonakilty from Burlington, who was forced to sell most of his Irish estate after engaging his architectural passions in two hugely expensive Palladian houses at Piccadilly and Chiswick. In 1748 William Cavendish, the 4th duke of Devonshire, married Burlington's heiress, thereby obtaining his remaining Irish estates and interests. The problem was that the *Ponsonbys, the Boyles' rivals, who had bought up some of Burlington's Munster lands, were already connected with the Cavendishes in a double marriage alliance dating from the 3rd duke's lord lieutenancy (1737–44). This provides part of the background to the *money bill dispute of 1753–5.

Boyle's son Richard, 2nd earl of Shannon (1728–1807), though a less formidable political figure than his father, was a major borough proprietor, controlling the return of up to nine MPs in the Irish parliament. He was briefly in opposition (1789–93) following the *regency crisis, but otherwise generally supported government and held a variety of offices.

Canny, N. P., *The Upstart Earl* (1982)

Hewitt, Esther (ed.), *Lord Shannon's Letters to his Son* (1982)

HM

Boyle, Henry (1684–1764), the greatest of the *undertakers. A grandson of the 1st earl of *Orrery, he inherited an estate at Castlemartyr, Co. Cork, and entered parliament in 1707 as a protégé of Alan *Brodrick. On Brodrick's death Boyle became leader of his Munster-based following, by then in opposition. In 1733 the government accepted his election as *speaker, and after some initial friction he established himself as principal undertaker. When his dominance was challenged by the *Ponsonby family and Archbishop *Stone, he initiated the *money bill dispute. Opinions differ as to how far Boyle cynically manipulated popular *patriotism, and how far events, and more enthusiastic allies, carried him beyond his initial carefully calculated show of strength. Either way his acceptance in 1756 of a pension of £30,000 a year for 31 years, and the title of earl of Shannon, in exchange for resigning the speakership, caused bitter public disillusion among those who had come to see him as a champion of the Irish interest. Though now sharing power with the Ponsonbys, Shannon remained until his death the head of a leading political interest.

Boyle, Richard (1566–1643), 1st earl of Cork, the most successful of the *New English. A Kentish younger son who became deputy *escheator of crown lands after achieving entry into official circles with forged introductions, Boyle built a substantial estate by coercing landholders and defrauding the state in the campaign against *concealed lands.

Marriage in 1603 to Catherine Fenton, daughter of the Irish council secretary, brought respectability. He bought *Raleigh's vast *Munster plantation grant for the knock-down price of £1,500—part of a strategy of acquiring land whereby he gained by the prior investment of others. Boyle was soon the richest man in Ireland with an annual rent-roll of £20,000.

His wealth brought him status and power—Irish privy counsellor (1612), lord (1616), earl (1620), lord high treasurer of Ireland (1631). Between 1629 and 1632 Boyle served as lord justice with Adam *Loftus, an ally of his *factional rival Lord *Mountnorris. *Wentworth, however, was determined to make an example of Boyle as the New Englishman who had most defrauded the crown. He forced the upstart to move an enormous family tomb erected in *St Patrick's cathedral, Dublin, to a side aisle. Acting on information from Mountnorris, he also fined Boyle £15,000 for his impropriation of Lismore diocese.

HM

Boyle, Robert (1627–91), scientist. Born at Lismore, the son of Richard *Boyle, 1st earl of Cork, he was educated privately and at Eton. After a European tour, 1638–44, he settled at the family manor house in Stalbridge, Dorset. He developed ties with the London scientific circle around the German refugee Samuel Hartlib, who advocated social and economic reform through applied science. Boyle visited Ireland 1652–4 and collaborated on dissections with William *Petty. From 1655 to 1668 he lived in Oxford, joining the scientific circle which included Wilkins, Hooke, and Ward. When the Royal Society was founded (1660), Boyle was among its leading figures. From 1668 he resided permanently in London.

As a scientist, Boyle's aim was to champion mechanistic as against scholastic explanations of natural phenomena. He upheld a corpuscular theory according to which the structure, motions, and interactions of matter are the product of the mechanical properties of elemental particles. He favoured the 'experimental learning' advocated by Francis Bacon, arguing that empirical evidence rather than pure speculation should be the foundation of scientific propositions. Boyle did extensive research in chemistry and pneumatics. His best-known book, *The Sceptical Chymist* (1661), was devoted to the discrediting of scholastic explanations. His study of pneumatics included his famous experiments, using an air pump, on the properties of a vacuum and on the functions and elasticity of air; in 1662 he formulated the law named after him.

Boyle was a deeply religious man who wrote numerous theological works; in the 1680s he was active in promoting the publication of Irish texts of the Old and New Testaments. He was concerned about the religious implications of his scientific studies, but saw the new science as complementing the revelations of Christianity by providing independent evidence for the work of a creator.

Hunter, M. (ed.), *Robert Boyle Reconsidered* (1994)
Maddison, R. E. W., *The Life of the Honourable Robert Boyle, F.R.S.* (1969)

DJS

Boyle, Roger, see ORRERY, ROGER BOYLE, 1ST EARL OF.

Boyne, battle of (1 July 1690), in the *Williamite War. The *Jacobites chose the river Boyne as the best barrier against *William III's progress south towards Dublin, garrisoning Drogheda and placing their main force (25,000 men) at the most likely crossing point, Oldbridge, 3 miles upstream. The Williamite army, 36,000 strong, camped opposite, on the north bank. However, *Schomberg's son Meinhard led a third of the Williamite force upriver, where they crossed the Boyne at Rosnaree after a half-hour engagement against 800 dragoons commanded by Sir Neil O'Neill. *James II, overestimating the threat, led two-thirds of his army to the left, but was unable to attack because of two intervening ditches. Meanwhile the main Williamite army crossed at Oldbridge, overwhelming the depleted Jacobite right, though the cavalry under *Tyrconnell made repeated counter-attacks. Threatened with encirclement, the main Jacobite force retreated. Since it had never engaged the enemy, overall losses were relatively light, about 1,000 Jacobites and 500 Williamites being killed.

Less strategically important than *Aughrim, the battle owed its subsequent fame primarily to the presence in person of both William, who remained in the centre of the fighting throughout, and James, whose precipitate flight from the battlefield aroused derision on both sides. Overshadowed for most of the 18th century by celebrations of King William's birthday (4 Nov.), its anniversary became the central festival of the *Orange society from the 1790s. The Order's decision to celebrate the main anniversary on 12 July seems to have derived from a misunderstanding of the 1752 *calendar reform. The battle was in fact fought on 11 July new style.

Boyse, Joseph (1660–1728), *Presbyterian minister and polemicist. Born in Leeds and educated at English dissenting academies, he was the countess of *Donegall's chaplain before accepting a call to join the Revd Daniel Williams in the pastorate of Wood Street congregation in Dublin. As well as attacking popery, he defended Presbyterianism against episcopalian critics like Archbishop *King, orthodox Christology against the *Arianism of Thomas *Emlyn, and Presbyterian political principles against William Tisdal, *Church of Ireland vicar of Belfast. He opposed *subscription to the Westminster Confession as a test of orthodoxy, urging liberty for ministers and ordinands to make their own declarations of faith, a proposal accepted by the *Synod of Ulster as its Pacific Act of 1720. RFGH

Brabazon, Sir William (d. 1551), vice-treasurer and three times lord justice, the prototype *New Englishman—a hard man with sticky fingers. He began the conquest of Gaelic Ireland by attacking the O'Mores and O'Connors while *St Leger was away in 1546. The *dissolution of the monasteries, in which he was prominent, presented an opportunity to overhaul government finances. However, Brabazon, St Leger, and other officials profited themselves by renting out confiscated lands at rates far below market values and leaving thousands of pounds of rent arrears uncollected. This massive fraud was not uncovered until three years after his death. HM

Bramhall, John (1594–1663), a dominant force amongst the *Church of Ireland bishops in the 1630s and again in the early 1660s. Born in Yorkshire, Bramhall was educated at Cambridge (BA 1612, MA 1616, BD 1623, DD 1630), was ordained, and came to the notice of Archbishop Laud, who recommended him to *Wentworth when the latter was appointed lord deputy in 1633. Appointed bishop of Derry in 1634, he was entrusted by Wentworth and Laud with the task of bringing the Church of Ireland into closer conformity with the Church of England, and gradually took over the day-to-day running of the Irish church. Bramhall helped secure the passage of the English Thirty-Nine Articles and a set of ecclesiastical canons in the Irish *convocation in 1634, and took a personal hand in driving out nonconformist *Presbyterian ministers from Down and Connor in 1634–6. He also devoted much energy to regaining from the laity much of the alienated property and endowments of the Irish church, creating considerable resentment amongst Protestant and Catholic landholders alike. The fall of Wentworth led in 1641 to Bramhall's imprisonment by the Irish parliament, but after the *rising of 1641 he fled to England. As a strong supporter of the king, he spent much of the 1640s and 1650s in exile on the Continent, returning briefly to Ireland in 1648–9. He devoted much of his time to writing, attacking Thomas Hobbes and defending the *high-church cause. Bramhall returned to Ireland after the *Restoration, and was appointed archbishop of Armagh in 1661. As primate he sought to ensure that the new church was properly endowed and that its clergy conformed strictly to its beliefs and canons. AF

Braose, William de (d. 1211). In 1177 *Henry II made a speculative grant of the kingdom of Limerick, alias the *O'Brien kingdom of Thomond, to Philip de Braose, a younger son, who failed to take possession, probably because of lack of resources; in 1200 his nephew William de Braose, a powerful landed magnate in England, Wales, and Normandy, purchased the kingdom of Limerick from King *John for 5,000 marks (£3,333 6*s*. 8*d*.), a sum he proved unable to pay. King John, who used monetary indebtedness as a mechanism for exerting control over powerful subjects, gave the recovery of this debt as the ostensible reason for his expedition to Ireland in 1210 and the confiscation of all de Braose's lands. De Braose died in exile in France. MTF

brass money, sometimes (though not in contemporary usage) gunmoney, the copper and copper alloy coinage, to an estimated value of over £1.5 million, issued in the name of *James II 1689–90. Initially widely accepted, its value was depressed by overproduction, by competition with the silver circulating among French soldiers, and by dwindling confidence in the Jacobite cause. Protestant rhetoric presented *William III as having delivered the kingdom from 'Popery, brass money and wooden shoes'.

bread making in Ireland goes back more than a thousand years. Wheat and barley cultivation dates from *neolithic times, oats and rye later. As climatic conditions changed to favour oats and barley cultivation breads of these grains dominated. Wheaten bread became a luxury consumed by chiefs and on festivals. At different periods various combinations of grains were used in bread. In the 17th century pea and bean meals were mixed with corn; in the 19th century *Indian meal with oatmeal was a popular mixture. *Potatoes too were mixed with flour to make a variety of breads—fadge, boxty, and potato apple.

Records and archaeological remains indicate that simple mills driven by wind or water were widespread in pre-*Norman times. Meal for bread making was further refined by sieving into flour. The baking process varied. Cooking was sometimes on a baking flag (heated flat stone) or metal griddle, hung over the fire or supported on a tripod. The loaf then cooled on a trivet. In contrast to continental Europe, communal ovens were uncommon in Ireland.

Most flat open-baked breads—oaten, wheaten, and potato farls—were unleavened. Leavens used were yeast, barm (liquid yeast), and, more commonly, sour dough. The sour dough method was a repetitive process of withholding a small portion of fermented dough for the next kneading. For soda bread making, raising agents were bicarbonate of soda or potassium bitartrate (cream of tartar). The former was used with buttermilk, the latter with fresh milk.

The role of bread in the Irish diet waxed, waned, and waxed again. During the 17th century bread was a common component of diet, particularly in the east. From the early 18th century, however, potatoes became the staple of the masses. After the *Great Famine the population lost confidence in potatoes, and bread, made with roller-milled white flour, regained its former importance. EMC

Breen, Dan (1894–1969), Tipperary Volunteer (see IRISH (NATIONAL) VOLUNTEERS) famous for his involvement in the Soloheadbeg ambush on 21 January 1919, which caused the death of the first policemen since 1916. This ambush is widely though incorrectly regarded as the start of the *Anglo-Irish War. His tempestuous nature made him the most wanted man in Tipperary, despite his subordinate position to Seamus Robinson and Sean *Treacy. Breen had a somewhat chequered career in republican politics during and after the Civil War, and was *Fianna Fáil TD (Dáil deputy) for Tipperary until 1965, but is best known for his somewhat self-indulgent autobiography *My Fight for Irish Freedom* (1924). JA

brehon law, from Irish *brethem*, 'a judge', the term used for the system of law in use in Gaelic Ireland. See LAW.

Bréifne, see O'ROURKE.

brewing. *Dublin emerged as the main centre of the industry in the 18th century; the city provided the largest market for beer, which was costly to transport. *Guinness (established in 1759) at this point competed with 60 other commercial brewers in the greater Dublin area. The competitiveness and quality of beer produced in Dublin and *Cork began to improve dramatically towards the end of the 18th century. The excise duty on beer had been abolished in 1795, reducing costs. The quality of Irish barley, malting techniques, and brewing methods were all improving, enabling Dublin and Cork brewers to eliminate British imports; they also began to extend their markets into rural areas. Beamish Crawford of Cork was the largest brewer in the country, producing 100,000 barrels in 1810; they were followed by Guinness in Dublin who produced 70,000. The output of most breweries outside the major cities was quite small; many of them were located in the major barley-growing counties of Cork, Offaly, Laois, Tipperary, Louth, and Kildare. Following the rapid expansion of the industry during the Napoleonic War output stabilized, but production became more concentrated in larger concerns, the number of licensed brewers falling from 319 in 1791 to 118 by 1846. Shortly after the turn of the century Ireland became a net exporter of beer, and a number of the Dublin breweries by the 1830s were building up an extensive trade with Britain, notably to Lancashire. Guinness exported half of its output of 80,000 barrels by 1840, a trade which expanded dramatically with the growth of the British railway network. The *railways also opened up the rural Irish market in the post-*Famine era, enabling the larger urban breweries to displace their smaller rural rivals. The *temperance movement in the 1840s, and higher duties on spirits in the 1850s, gave beer a more widespread appeal. Output grew in the second half of the 19th century and the industry became further centralized in the larger urban breweries. The number of breweries in Ireland fell from 118 in 1846 to 39 at the turn of the century, when Dublin produced about three-quarters of total output and 96 per cent of exports. Guinness was by this time one of the seven largest companies in the world, and its huge turnover made brewing by far the most important industry in the Irish Free State.

Bielenberg, A., 'The Irish brewing industry and the rise of Guinness 1790–1914', in R. G. Wilson and T. R. Gourvish, *The Dynamics of the International Brewing Industry since 1800* (1998)

Dennison, S. R., and MacDonagh, O., *Guinness 1886–1939* (1998)

AB

Brian Bóruma (Boru) (d. 1014) king of Munster, was among the most successful of all early Irish monarchs. Succeeding to the kingship of *Dál Cais on the death of his brother Mathgamain in 976, he managed in the course of a long reign, by a combination of military skill and political astuteness, to enforce his authority over much of the country. In so doing, he became the first ruler outside the *Uí Néill to make a bid for the overlordship of Ireland, thereby indicating that the *high kingship was in fact a prize to be won by the most powerful claimant. The pursuit of this prize was to occupy a large number of able rulers in the centuries following Brian's death.

However, the road to success chosen by Brian was not in itself new. On assuming power, he immediately set about consolidating his authority in his home base, Munster, by bringing those responsible for the slaying of Mathgamain to justice. To this end, he attacked the *Vikings of Limerick and the Uí Fhidgeinte, and subsequently engaged the *Eóganacht Raithlind in battle. Osraige was next to claim his attention and a series of punitive expeditions by Brian forced the submission of a number of that territory's kings. Rocked by internal dynastic struggles, the Leinstermen, against whom Brian next advanced, were similarly unable to halt his march. But his progress was checked somewhat by the opposition of *Máel Sechnaill II (Malachy), who was equally anxious to exert control over Leinster. Both rulers were also involved in a struggle for dominance over Connacht. They were eventually forced to come to terms in 997. Though Brian and Máel Sechnaill joined forces to defeat the Dublin Norse at the battle of Glenn Máma two years later, the truce agreed between them soon broke down. Brian remained in control, forcing Máel Sechnaill to submit, thereby conceding the title of high king, in 1002.

Brian's position in the southern half of the country being now relatively secure, he turned his attention northwards and engaged in a number of campaigns to bring the kingdoms of *Cenél nEógain, *Cenél Conaill, and *Ulaid into line. Despite giving hostages to Brian, the northern rulers maintained a certain independence and Flaithbertach Ua Néill, king of Cenél nEógain, attacked Brian's ally, Máel Sechnaill, in 1013. Around this time too the Leinstermen sought to throw off Munster dominance and gathered together Norse allies in preparation for battle against Brian. It was at the subsequent encounter in *Clontarf in 1014 that Brian was slain.

Annalistic records and the heroic biography in **Cogadh Gaedhel re Gallaibh* claim that the Munster king was buried with full pomp and ceremony at *Armagh. Although undoubtedly a tribute to Brian's stature, this is also indicative of his skill as a politician during his lifetime. Recognizing the importance of controlling the church, Brian intervened continuously in ecclesiastical affairs. He took care to dominate important churches in Munster and elected members of his own immediate family to high office in them. His brother Marcán, for example, was abbot of Killaloe, Holy Island, and Terryglass. Brian also cultivated close relations with Armagh, as the church which claimed primacy and one intimately associated with the dynasty of Uí Néill. In 1005, when journeying northwards, he bestowed 20 ounces of gold upon the clergy of Armagh, and in 1012 he granted complete immunity to Patrick's churches. Furthermore, he is given the title *imperator Scottorum* by his confessor, Máel Suthain, in the Book of *Armagh.

Brian's influence in ecclesiastical circles certainly contributed to his considerable success. The real key to that success, however, was his skill as a military strategist. From the beginning, he made extensive use of naval power, particularly in his campaigns against Connacht and *Mide. He also had recourse to Norse allies; the Vikings of Waterford, for example, were active against Máel Sechnaill on his behalf. Moreover, he engaged in the building of fortifications for defence purposes. Being so closely linked to his personal ability as a military commander and as a politician, his power to a large extent died with him. Nevertheless, his descendants continued for generations to bask in his glory.

Ó Corráin, Donncha, *Ireland before the Normans* (1972)

MNíM

Brigid, the saint of Kildare, is a figure of legend more than history. She was claimed by the Fothairt, a subordinate population in north Leinster, and a very early poem refers to her: 'Splendid the child, splendid the dignity that will come to you after a time from the lineages of your kindreds. She will be called on account of her virtues "Power of zeal", truly godly. She will be a second Mary, mother of the great Lord.' By the mid-7th century Kildare was a major church with a shrine to Brigid described in the Life of the saint by Cogitosus. It seems clear that neither he nor the other writers of her Lives had any clear historical information, and there is evidence already from the 10th century to suggest that the cult began from the Christianization of a pagan goddess. None the less devotion to St Brigid spread widely outside Ireland, so that already in the 9th century she was the most widely known Irish saint. RS

Brodrick (Midleton), Co. Cork landed family, established in Ireland from the 17th century and politically active into the 20th. Its Irish presence was established by two brothers. **Sir Alan Brodrick**, a royalist and supporter of *Ormond, was one of the judges in the court of claims (see SETTLEMENT, ACT OF) following the *Restoration, and amassed a fortune as farmer of the Irish estates of the future *James II, while his brother **Sir St John** was an associate of Ormond's enemy *Orrery. St John's son Alan *Brodrick was one of the leading *Whig politicians of the early 18th century, and became Viscount Midleton in 1717. His brother **Thomas Brodrick** (1654–1730) was a prominent backbench member of the British House of Commons, and headed the parliamentary inquiry into the financial scandal known as the South Sea Bubble. Later Viscounts Midleton lived primarily in England. **Charles Brodrick**, son of the 3rd viscount, returned to Ireland as Church of Ireland bishop of Clonfert and Kilmacduagh (1795–6) and Kilmore (1796–1802), and archbishop of Cashel 1802–22. **St John Brodrick** (1856–1942), 1st earl of Midleton, British secretary of state for India 1903–5, was chairman of the Irish Unionist Alliance and chief spokesman for the southern *unionists during and after the *Anglo-Irish War. He led the attempt to reach agreement with the constitutional nationalists on a form of self-government at the *Irish Convention of 1917.

Brodrick, Alan (*c.*1660–1728), created Viscount Midleton 1717. The second son of the Co. Cork landed family (see BRODRICK (MIDLETON)), Brodrick was prominent in the *sole right agitation and a leading *Whig in the fierce party rivalry of Queen Anne's reign (1702–14). Though appointed lord chancellor in 1714, he resented the favour shown to his former Whig ally William *Conolly, and encouraged his parliamentary followers, led by his son, **St John Brodrick** (*c.*1685–1728), sporadically to harass the administration over public finances, the *sacramental test, and other issues. In 1725 the British government finally chose between the rivals, confirming Conolly's position as chief *undertaker while Midleton resigned the chancellorship. The apparent link with his opposition to *Wood's Halfpence gave this departure some aura of *patriotism. But his sponsorship of patriot issues, from the sole right issue on, remains impossible to disentangle from the pursuit of party and personal advantage.

brokerage and clientelism, forms of behaviour in which public representatives explicitly or implicitly trade political favours for electoral support. Brokerage refers to the practice by which public figures offer their services in liaising with the authorities on behalf of those who believe that they do not themselves have effective access, as when a *Dáil deputy seeks to obtain redress for a constituent in respect of some grievance. Clientelism refers to a more permanent set of relations between relatively powerful 'patrons' who extract concessions from the public authorities on behalf of relatively powerless 'clients'; the latter reciprocate by offering personal support to their patrons, typically but not necessarily in the electoral arena.

Elements of brokerage and clientelism are to be seen in varying degrees in all societies. Analysts agree that the work of Irish politicians has been characterized to a marked extent by brokerage-type activities. There is, however, no consensus that these activities can be described as clientelist, since the capacity of politicians to deliver real (as opposed to imaginary) favours has been greatly reduced by the development of meritocratic procedures within the public sector, and there is little evidence of the existence of sustained, semi-institutionalized networks linking patrons with clients.

It may be true that the Irish electoral system, permitting or even encouraging intense intra-party competition within multi-seat constituencies, has placed Dáil deputies under pressure to give close attention to the needs of their constituents. But as Irish society has developed, and as the bureaucratic procedures of the modern state have replaced the personal linkages characteristic of more agrarian societies, the opportunities for brokerage and clientelism have in general diminished. JC

Bronze Age Ireland. 'Bronze Age' is a techno-cultural term denoting the time during which metal was first used in Ireland, beginning around 2500 BC. It is subdivided into an Early Bronze Age and a Late Bronze Age, each defined by mainly metalwork typologies. Comparatively little is understood about the transitory period—the Middle Bronze Age.

The earliest metal objects are mainly copper, and copper mines are known at Mount Gabriel, Co. Cork, and Ross Island, near Killarney, Co. Kerry. The occurrence of a distinctive pottery coinciding with the earliest metal objects led some archaeologists to the belief that 'Beaker folk' travelled across Europe spreading the knowledge of metalworking. Others believe, however, that beaker pots were prestige objects, appropriated and copied for their associated social value. Beaker pots are often associated with a range of distinctive objects (sometimes referred to as the 'Beaker Package'), including stone wrist-guards, tanged copper daggers, barbed and tanged arrowheads, and V-perforated buttons. The continuation of *Neolithic traits, such as the use of *megalithic tombs, indicates the important role of the indigenous population in the spread of metalworking throughout Ireland.

The Early Bronze Age proper is marked by the addition of tin (probably imported from Cornwall) to copper to make bronze at around 2000 BC. This period is best known from its burials, pottery, and bronze artefacts. The pottery is highly decorated and is found mainly in graves. The bronze tools were simple in form and include flat axes, daggers, and halberds that were cast in open stone moulds. Gold was the other primary metal utilized, mainly for personal ornaments, and includes 'sun discs', earrings, and the spectacular half-moon shaped necklaces known as lunula. The burial evidence shows that both inhumation and cremation were used to dispose of the dead and the fact that many graves contain the remains of only one individual indicates the increasing importance of the individual in society. Inhumations were often positioned on their side in a crouched position and placed in a stone-lined grave called a cist, or just a simple pit in the ground. Cremations were also placed in cists and pits, either in a flat unmarked grave or a visible burial mound. Collective cremation is also known and sometimes both disposal customs are represented in one grave. Cemeteries of burials exhibiting the range of burial practices have been discovered, and at Cloghskelt, Co. Down, 25 such graves have been excavated. Analysis of the human remains from Bronze Age graves indicates that adult males, females, and children were accorded the same treatment. Grave goods can also indicate status and the crouched burial of an adult male associated with pottery and a copper dagger decorated with gold wire from Topped Mountain, Co. Fermanagh, suggests this individual was of high social status. Settlement evidence for this period is scarce, but a new range of megalithic monuments appears which includes stone circles, stone rows, and standing stones.

The transitional period, or Middle Bronze Age, occurred between the 15th and 12th centuries BC. An enigmatic and extremely common monument of this period is the so-called *fulacht fiadh*, which is an outdoor cooking place comprising a trough and mound of burnt stones.

Metal technology in the later part of the Bronze Age became increasingly sophisticated with the use of multi-component clay moulds. Gold ornaments such as torcs, dress and sleeve fasteners, and collars, and metal weapons including spearheads, socketed axes, and swords, were produced. Both gold and bronze objects are often found in hoards. The deposition of many objects in lakes and rivers, and the construction of sacred ponds, suggests a ritual connected with what the pollen evidence suggests was a drastically deteriorating climate. The rise of a warrior aristocracy, and of social instability, is indicated by numerous weapons and the construction of *hillforts, which seem to have served as centres of power. Social stresses were probably exacerbated by the worsening climate and by population movement away from the increasingly waterlogged highlands.

By the end of the Bronze Age great technological advances had occurred, vast quantities of warlike objects had been produced, and habitation had become focused on hilltop enclosures. Strengthened contacts and communication with Britain and Europe are suggested by the importation of amber and the exportation of Irish metal ores and metalwork. For the four centuries from the 6th century until the inception of the *Iron Age in the 3rd century BC information about Irish society is almost totally lacking.

Cooney, G., and Grogan, E., *Irish Prehistory: A Social Perspective* (1994)

SMcC

Brooke, Sir Basil (1888–1973), Viscount Brookeborough, prime minister of Northern

Ireland 1943–63. A Fermanagh landowner, Brooke represented the socially conservative and trenchant *unionism of western Ulster. A distinguished veteran of the *First World War, he offered the Ulster Unionist leadership a potent combination of military talent and a ferocious loyalism. In November 1920 he was appointed to command the *Ulster Special Constabulary in Fermanagh, and swiftly emerged as an effective leader of the assault on the *IRA. He was elected to the Northern Ireland House of Commons in 1929, and was minister of agriculture between 1933 and 1941; he was promoted to the Ministry of Commerce by John *Andrews, whom he succeeded as prime minister in 1943. He held office until 1963, an achievement which reflected the comparative stability of Ulster Unionism after the Second World War, and his own relaxed and charming style of political management.

Although lacking the *evangelical convictions of other Unionist leaders, Brooke was, especially in his early ministerial career, overtly hostile to the northern Catholic challenge. He was uninterested in political reform, but oversaw the importation into Northern Ireland of the Attlee government's welfare legislation. He helped to win the most substantial Unionist constitutional victory of the post-war years, the *Ireland Act (1949), but proved unable to address the economic and labour problems which, in the last years of his administration, were helping to destabilize his party. He had a Palmerstonian flair: trenchantly patriotic, populist, insouciant. AJ

Brotherhood of St George. As betokened its status as the English lordship's administrative capital, Dublin was the centre for the cult of St George in Ireland. The city was open for the annual St George's Day pageant which included a dragon and was centred on St George's Chapel—richly decorated with cushions—in *St Patrick's cathedral and was organized by the master and wardens of St George's Guild. 'St George' was the rallying cry of English armies in Ireland, and by municipal act of 1448 the guild was entitled to one good cow from every prey taken by the city. Thus, when, in 1474, the Irish parliament authorized a standing force, the Brotherhood of Arms, to assist the governor in the lordship's defence, it seemed natural to dedicate it to St George. The Brotherhood of Arms of St George comprised thirteen magnates who elected annually on St George's Day a captain of the 120 archers and 40 horsemen at its disposal. It was financed by a new tax called poundage on the lordship's imports and exports. Although briefly disbanded and restored in 1479, the brotherhood survived into the 1490s to be formally abolished by Sir Edward *Poynings when poundage was consolidated into the king's customs revenue. SGE

Browne, see KENMARE.

Browne, George (d. 1556), archbishop of Dublin 1536–54, a somewhat equivocal promoter of the early *Reformation. An Oxford-educated English Augustinian friar, he came to the notice of Thomas Cromwell as a supporter of royal supremacy. His appointment to the see of Dublin was followed by the passing of the Irish Reformation legislation in the parliament of 1537, and his chief role subsequently was to enforce these religious and jurisdictional changes. Faced with indifference and opposition from his clergy, and finding exhortation and ecclesiastical discipline ineffective, he sought to gain the support of the civil arm to impose the reforms. However, frustrated by political infighting within the Dublin administration, and further spancelled by the fall of his patron Cromwell in 1540, Browne in his later career came to terms with his clerical colleagues' innate conservatism: he put aside his wife; showed little enthusiasm for Edwardian Protestantism; and, on being deprived of his see in 1554 after the return to Catholicism under Mary, was pardoned and made a prebendary of *St Patrick's cathedral. AF

Browne, Noel (1915–97), government minister and social reformer. Browne was trained as a medical doctor and was attracted into politics by the social radicalism of *Clann na Poblachta. He was elected as a TD for Dublin South East in 1948, and became minister for health in the first *interparty government. Using *Irish Hospitals sweepstake money, he was able to bypass the restrictions of the Department of Finance, and mount a successful campaign against the scourge of *tuberculosis. In pursuing his welfarist agenda, he became embroiled in the *Mother and Child controversy and was forced into resignation on 11 April 1951. His later political career, though extensive, was overshadowed by this débâcle: he sat in the Dáil as an Independent (1951–3 and 1957–8) and as a representative of the National Progressive Democratic Party (1958–63). He was a *Labour TD between 1969 and 1973, and a Labour Senator (1973–7): he then left the party, and was returned to the Dáil as an Independent Labour representative, though he later shifted his allegiance to the newly founded Socialist Labour Party. His controversial autobiography *Against the Tide* (1986) was aptly titled: Browne had travelled across the spectrum of Irish politics, and was ultimately impatient with the compromises and discipline of mainstream party membership. He had a passionate commitment to social justice, but ultimately lacked the political and personal skills to enact his ideals. AJ

Bruce, Edward (d. 1318), earl of Carrick, lord of Galloway, and self-styled king of Ireland, brother of Robert I, king of Scots. Bruce had a reputation as an ambitious knight and an energetic, if sometimes rash, military commander, who distinguished himself at Bannockburn (1314). He was appointed heir presumptive to the Scottish throne in April 1315, and then led an expedition to Ireland with the intention of conquering it and, perhaps, of launching from there an invasion of Wales. He landed at Larne on 25 May, and was proclaimed king of Ireland, having been joined by some of the Irish, most notably the king of *Cenél nEógain, Donal *O'Neill (Domhnall Ó Néill), who sent his famous *'Remonstrance' to the pope explaining his support. In his first campaign Bruce defeated the local Anglo-Irish colonists, and marched south where, on 29 June, he burned Dundalk, before being forced to retreat by an army led by the earl of Ulster, Richard de *Burgh. When the two armies met on 1 September at Connor, Co. Antrim, the earl was decisively defeated. Next, Bruce's army marched to Meath where, in early December, he defeated the lord of Trim, Roger *Mortimer, and was joined by the latter's tenants, the de *Lacys. The Anglo-Irish assembled a substantial army to oppose him but in a skirmish near Ardscull, Co. Kildare, on 26 January 1316, their quarrelling leaders failed to overcome him and he marched further south into Laois and Offaly. By now, though, Bruce's army was feeling the effects of the severe famine which coincided with his invasion, and he made a hasty retreat to Ulster. Here Bruce set up an administration and won some of the Anglo-Irish to his cause, though most continued to oppose him. He also set about the capture of *Carrickfergus Castle, which surrendered to him in September 1316. At this point Edward returned to Scotland and by Christmas was joined in Ireland by his brother Robert and an army of *gallowglasses. They marched south, forced the earl of Ulster to retreat from Ratoath, and by 21 February were at Castleknock, perhaps with the intention of taking Dublin. The citizens, however, refortified the town walls and burned the suburbs, and the Bruce brothers, unwilling no doubt to risk a lengthy siege, passed on south. By early April they were in north Munster, proposing to join forces with a faction of the *O'Briens, but chose not to risk a dangerous encounter with the government army. Instead they withdrew hurriedly to Ulster, and Robert himself to Scotland. Virtually nothing is heard of Edward for the next year and a half until, in the autumn of 1318, he again marched south, but was defeated and killed at the battle of *Faughart. The defeat of his planned overthrow of the English lordship of Ireland was one of the most notable achievements in the career of the hapless Edward II.

Duffy, Seán, 'The Bruce Brothers and the Irish Sea World, 1306–1329', *Cambridge Medieval Celtic Studies*, 21 (1991)

Frame, Robin, 'The Bruces in Ireland, 1315–18', *Irish Historical Studies*, 19 (1974–5)

Orpen, G. H., *Ireland under the Normans*, iv (1920)

SD

Brugha, Cathal (1874–1922), leading republican in the *Anglo-Irish War. After a long involvement in the *Gaelic League and the *Gaelic Athletic Association, he joined the *Irish Volunteers in 1913. He was crippled in the *rising of 1916, but subsequently became chief of staff of the Volunteers. He presided over the first meeting of *Dáil Éireann and became its first minister for defence. As such he proposed that Volunteers take an oath of allegiance to the Dáil in August 1919. He was one of the most militant opponents of the treaty and was killed at the start of the *Irish Civil War. JA

Brunswick clubs, militant Protestant societies launched in August 1828 to provide a replacement for the *Orange Order, which had been suppressed along with the *Catholic Association by the Unlawful Societies Act of 1825.

Bryce, James (1838–1922), 1st Viscount Bryce of Dechmount, Liberal politician and academic. Born in Belfast, of mixed Ulster Presbyterian and Scots parentage, Bryce became regius professor of civil law at Oxford before entering parliament in 1880. A distinguished constitutionalist whose many classic works included *The Holy Roman Empire* and *The American Commonwealth*, his political achievements were more modest; he served briefly in cabinet as president of the Board of Trade (1894–5) and chief secretary for Ireland (Dec. 1905–Jan. 1907). At *Dublin Castle he alienated the Nationalist leaders by adhering closely to the views of Sir Antony *MacDonnell on the proposed *Irish council bill, and was quickly translated to the dignity of the British embassy in Washington. ACH

buannacht (Eng. 'bonaght') signified from the 12th to the 16th centuries the billeting of mercenary soldiers on civilians, though by the 16th century it could also mean a land tax exacted in lieu of actual billeting, which was styled by the Anglo-Irish 'bonaght-beg' ('little bonaght'). It derived from *buanna* (pl. *buannadha*, *buannaighe*, 'bonies'), a word of uncertain etymology which is first found in Irish texts of the 11th and 12th centuries with the meaning 'hired soldier'. English writers in the Tudor period often use the abstract 'bonaght' to denote the mercenaries themselves, rather than the imposition. KS

building societies were established in the major Irish cities during the second half of the 19th century. In *Dublin the high cost of new housing and the relatively small size of the artisan class meant that there was only a limited demand for their services. In *Belfast, by comparison, housing costs were lower, the city was expanding rapidly, and the large number of skilled workers employed in the *shipbuilding and *engineering industries created a ready market for modest houses. By the 1880s there were a total of eight building societies lending money to Belfast builders. Several building societies were formed in the *Irish Free State during the late 1930s in order to meet growing demand for owner-occupied housing; however, their capital base remained weak. The 1942 Building Societies Act, which determined the financial basis under which they would conduct business, was in part prompted by demands that British building societies be permitted to operate in the Free State. However, the low level of personal savings meant that local authorities (and ultimately the exchequer) continued to provide the overwhelming majority of mortgages for private housing until the late 1960s. MED

bull baiting was probably introduced to Ireland from England, where it had been a popular pastime at least from the 13th century. Bulls, sometimes mutilated and invariably tethered, were baited by both men and dogs. Such displays were generally a precursor to the slaughter of bulls, and were often justified by a belief that baiting made the meat of an animal more tender. By the late 17th century bull baiting was less popular with Ireland's elite, whose sporting allegiances were to some extent transferred to *cock fighting. However bull baits as spectacles continued to draw large crowds from among the common people. In fact, in 1779 it was necessary to pass legislation to try to prevent the Dublin mob seizing bulls and staging impromptu baits in the city's streets. After the *insurrection of 1798 baits were discouraged by the authorities, who saw them as potentially dangerous gatherings. Legislation of 1835 finally made baiting illegal on grounds of cruelty, although it was not until 1837 that the traditional baiting by Kilkenny's butchers was successfully suppressed. NG

bureaucracy in independent Ireland reflects many of the strengths and weaknesses of British administrative culture. The key defining instruments are the *Ministers and Secretaries Act (1924) for central government, the *city and county management system for local administration, and the civil service and local authority appointments commissions, which ensure that public officials are selected on a meritocratic basis. Underpinning these is a set of assumptions about how officials should be recruited, and how they should behave. These have been remarkably successful in ensuring high standards of probity and political neutrality, and in preventing corruption and other abuses of power by officials. The obverse of this has, some critics say, been an unacceptable inflexibility in procedures and decision-making, coupled with a propensity to suppress initiative—although Ireland's economic transformation in the 1960s is generally credited to the ideas of a Department of Finance official, T. K. Whitaker. Until the 1970s senior administrative posts were held mostly by men who had entered public service as school leavers rather than as Oxbridge-style graduates, and to date very few women have achieved high office. Membership of the *European Union has provided major challenges and opportunities: senior officials of departments such as Agriculture now spend almost as much time in Brussels as in Dublin. The last two decades have seen the adoption of a more open attitude towards the public, reflected in developments in administrative law, in the work of the ombudsman, and in the National Archives Act 1986. They have also seen a shift towards a more managerial attitude towards public business, including highly competitive selection processes and fixed-term contracts for top officials. EO'H

burgess, a burgage tenant of a medieval borough. The burgess was distinguished from other inhabitants of the borough by burgage tenure, which entitled him to a plot fronting on a thoroughfare, usually the high street, and included an arable tenement outside the town. By virtue of their tenure, burgesses were entitled to the rights and liberties conferred on their borough by royal or seigniorial charter, in essence the protection of their trade, persons, and property from injurious interference by seigniorial officials. These included the right to have their own hundred court for all pleas arising within the borough, to buy and sell burgage lands at will, and to have a gild merchant (see GUILDS), freedom from toll and vexatious distraints for debts, licence to marry freely, and protection against external competi-

tors. Although burgesses were required to provide transportation for salt, iron, and wine at the behest of their lord, such privileges were sufficient to attract settlers in considerable numbers from Angevin lands to the numerous manorial towns created by Anglo-Norman lords in Ireland around the end of the 12th century. The scale of burgage land attached to the new boroughs is a measure of the importance their lords attached to them.
CAE

Burgh, Hubert de (d. 1243), earl of Kent, *justiciar of England 1215–32, and virtual ruler from 1219 during Henry III's minority. He was nominally also justiciar of Ireland for a few weeks in 1232, but his main importance in Irish history lies in the fact that he assiduously promoted the interests of his nephew Richard de *Burgh, justiciar of Ireland 1228–32, whose conquest of Connacht was launched during Hubert's rule.
RFF

Burgh, Richard de (d. 1243), known to historians as the 'conqueror of Connacht', one of the leading barons of Ireland from 1214 and *justiciar 1228–32. His father William de *Burgh (d. 1205) had received lands in Munster from King *John in 1185; he had also obtained a grant of Connacht *c.*1195, but despite vigorous campaigning had failed to realize it. Richard got a royal charter renewing the grant in 1215, but this was not activated until after the death in 1224 of the Irish king, Cathal *O'Connor (Cathal Crobderg Ua Conchobair). Richard's conquest, which was pursued from 1226–7, was facilitated by the backing of his uncle Hubert de *Burgh, the justiciar of England. He lost favour when Hubert fell in 1232, but soon recovered it; the conquest, in which many other settler families gained lands, proceeded again from 1235. Richard died while campaigning with Henry III in Gascony. RFF

Burgh, Richard de (*c.*1259–1326), earl of Ulster and lord of Connacht, known as the Red Earl, in his day the most powerful man in Ireland. He was the son of Walter de Burgh and Avelina, daughter of John fitz Geoffrey. He gained possession of his inheritance on 5 January 1281 and led violent campaigns in Connacht and Ulster in 1286 and 1288, on the latter occasion being opposed by his great Geraldine rival John fitz Thomas, later 1st earl of *Kildare. On 27 September 1286 Richard and Thomas de *Clare of Thomond formed the Turnberry 'band' with a group of Scottish nobles, whose aid they enlisted for a campaign in Ireland. Some time afterwards he seized the Isle of *Man and handed it over to King Edward in June 1290. His quarrel with fitz Thomas came to a head in 1294 when the latter imprisoned him, and the dispute was not finally resolved until a transfer of lands was agreed between them in 1298. He served on the Scottish campaign in 1296 and in 1303, and in 1302 his daughter married Robert Bruce. Richard opposed the invasion of Ireland by Edward *Bruce in 1315, and was defeated in battle, although the citizens of Dublin later imprisoned him, suspecting his loyalty, and he may have forfeited his earldom for a time. In 1326 he retired, due to ill health, to the priory of Athassal, Co. Tipperary, where, on 29 June, he died. He was succeeded by his grandson William de *Burgh.
SD

Burgh, William de (1312–33), earl of *Ulster, called 'the Brown Earl' by Gaelic annalists. His assassination near Carrickfergus by some of his own knights speeded the disintegration of the lordships of Ulster and Connacht. William was the grandson and heir of *Richard, the Red Earl; his mother was Elizabeth de *Clare, an heiress of the earl of Gloucester. After his marriage to Edward III's cousin Matilda of Lancaster, he came to Ireland in 1328 and was embroiled in conflicts with the 1st earl of *Desmond, the Mandevilles of Ulster, and his own kinsman Walter de Burgh, who dominated Connacht. While serving as king's lieutenant in 1331–2, he took strong action against his opponents, imprisoning Walter de Burgh in the castle of Northburgh, where he died. It was this that seems to have provoked the fatal conspiracy against him, as he was preparing to join Edward III on campaign in Scotland. RFF

Burke (de Burgh). The founder of this family in Ireland was William de Burgh (d. 1205), a brother to Hubert de *Burgh, earl of Kent, who received lands in southern Tipperary from Prince John, perhaps as early as the prince's first visit to Ireland in 1185. About 1192–3 William allied with Donal O'Brien (Domnall Mór Ua Briain), king of Thomond, against the *MacCarthys, and married O'Brien's daughter, by whom he had a son and heir, Richard de *Burgh (d. 1243). Richard obtained confirmation of a speculative grant of the kingdom of Connacht originally made to his father and in 1235, after a prolonged war of conquest, became lord of 25 cantreds of the province of Connacht, the five remaining cantreds near Athlone being reserved to the English king, who immediately leased them for an annual rent to King Felim O'Connor (Fedlimid Ó Conchobair) (d. 1265). Richard's eldest son Richard II having died in 1248, his second son Walter (d. 1271) became lord of Connacht and was further appointed earl of *Ulster in 1263, while a third son, William Óg (d. 1270), was to become ancestor of the MacWilliam Burkes, lords of Mayo. Earl Walter's son Richard de *Burgh III (d. 1326), known as the 'Red Earl' of Ulster, ruled almost half Ireland. He forced John fitz Thomas, successor to the FitzGerald lords of Sligo and later to become 1st earl of *Kildare, to exchange his holdings in north-east Connacht for lands elsewhere in Ireland. He also repeatedly dethroned the defiant Donal *O'Neill (Domnall Ó Néill) and replaced him with his own candidates for kingship of *Cenél nEógain, drawn from the Clandeboye *O'Neills. He played a prominent part in Edward I's war against Scotland, although his sister was married to James Stewart and his daughter Elizabeth to Robert Bruce. In 1315 his earldom of Ulster was invaded by Robert's brother Edward *Bruce, and the earl himself was defeated at the battle of Connor, where his cousin Sir William Liath (d. 1324), son of William Óg, was captured by the Scots. By 1317, however, the earl was imprisoned in Dublin, suspected of complicity with the invading Scots.

The defeat and death of Edward Bruce at *Faughart (1318) did not lead to a complete reinstatement of the earl's former power as his lands had been badly ravaged, and he was now growing too old to mount an effective military reconquest against the rebel Donal O'Neill. The 'Red Earl's' eldest son John had predeceased him, leaving a minor, William de *Burgh, 'the Brown Earl', to succeed on his grandfather's death in 1326. In 1328 Earl William entered Ireland to take over his inheritance and found that both Sir Walter de Burgh (d. 1332), son of William Liath and head of the Mayo Burkes, and Sir Henry de Mandeville (d. 1337), seneschal of Ulster, were accused of conspiring with his arch-enemy, Maurice fitz Thomas FitzGerald, the rebellious 1st earl of *Desmond. By driving de Mandeville out of Ulster and starving Walter Burke to death, Earl William set in train his own assassination (6 June 1333) which was followed by a rising of the de Mandevilles and their neighbours, the de Logans, in alliance with the Irish of Ulster. The earl left only a baby daughter Elizabeth as heiress. She later married Prince *Lionel of Clarence, and through their daughter Philippa the legal ownership of the earldom of Ulster and lordship of Connacht was transmitted to the *Mortimer family and ultimately to the English crown. However, while English officials retained a weak presence in the Ulster colony during a series of long minorities, the province of Connacht was beyond their control. At first it was torn by a feud between the Clanwilliam Burkes of Mayo, led by Edmond 'the Scot' (Éamonn Albanach, d. 1375), a younger brother of Walter MacWilliam, and their opponents, the Clanricard Burkes, the younger sons of Richard III, whose lands lay in the Galway area and who were led by the 'Red Earl's' second son Edmond the Bearded (Éamonn na Féasóige, d. 1338). Edmund the Scot won this war by drowning his opponent in 1338, and went on to dominate the whole province as MacWilliam ochtar, or 'the northern MacWilliam', while the defeated Clanricard Burkes of Galway were governed by his brother William, or Ulick 'an Fhíona' ('of the Wine', d. 1353), whose son Richard (Riocard Óg) founded an independent lordship over the Galway Burkes, using the title MacWilliam Uachtar, or 'the southern MacWilliam', otherwise 'MacWilliam of Clanricard'. Under the policy of *surrender and regrant, the Upper Macwilliams became earls of Clanricard from 1543. Meanwhile the descendants of Edmond the Bearded had become the Burkes of Clanwilliam, with a lordship on the boundaries of Cos. Limerick and Tipperary. KS

Burke, Edmund (1729–97), political writer. Born in Dublin, he was educated at *Trinity College and studied law in London. His early work *A Philosophical Enquiry into the Origin of our Ideas of the Sublime and the Beautiful* (1787) influenced a number of Irish artists (see PAINTING), and he was later to use his influence in England to promote the careers of several among them, notably James *Barry.

Burke was private secretary to the chief secretary for Ireland, William Gerard Hamilton, during 1761–4, and from 1765 private secretary to Lord Rockingham. Elected to the British parliament in 1765, he emerged as a leading orator and theorist of the new reformist *Whig Party. He attacked George III's personal government, called for conciliatory treatment of the American colonists, introduced an economical reform bill (1780) to reduce official corruption, and led the attack on Warren Hastings's abuse of power in *India. Following the *French Revolution, however, Burke became a defender of the existing order against what he saw as a destructive quest for abstract liberty, publishing *Reflections on the Revolution in France* (1790) and breaking with his Whig colleague Charles James Fox.

Burke's mother was a Catholic of the Co. Cork Nagle family, and he was shaken when Nagle relatives were caught up in the show trials of prominent Catholics provoked by the *Whiteboy movement. He was partly educated in a Catholic school in Co. Cork, his wife was an Irish Catholic, and his lawyer father may have been a convert. Yet opinion is divided between those who see this background as shaping his whole political outlook and those who see the mature Burke primarily as a metropolitan reformer. His open advocacy of *free trade for Ireland cost him his Bristol constituency in 1780. On the other hand he was cool towards *legislative independence, which he saw as strengthening an intolerant Protestant elite. In the 1790s, notably in his *Letter to Sir Hercules Langrishe* (1792), he advocated Catholic relief as the only means to prevent revolution in Ireland. His son **Richard Burke** (1758–94) was a somewhat ineffectual agent for the *Catholic Committee 1791–2, until replaced by *Tone.

Burke, Richard, see CLANRICARD, RICHARD BURKE, 4TH EARL OF.

Burke, Ulick, see CLANRICARD, ULICK BURKE, 1ST MARQUIS OF.

Butler, see ORMOND (BUTLER).

Butler, John (*c.*1731–1800), Catholic bishop of Cork from 1763 until 1787 when he resigned to marry a cousin, conforming a few months later to the *Church of Ireland. His desertion followed his unexpected inheritance of the family estates, and the title Lord Dunboyne, on the death of two brothers and a nephew. Butler returned to Catholicism just before his death, and left part of his estate to *Maynooth College.

Butler, Thomas, see ORMOND, 'BLACK TOM' BUTLER, 10TH EARL OF.

Butt, Isaac (1813–79), founder of the *home rule movement. Born in Co. Donegal, Butt was educated at *Trinity College, Dublin, where in 1833 he co-founded and edited the *Dublin University Magazine* (see 'ORANGE YOUNG IRELAND'), and became professor of political economy 1836–40. Conservative in politics, Butt opposed Daniel *O'Connell in the repeal debates held in Dublin corporation 1843, and served as Tory MP for Youghal 1853–65. After being called to the bar 1838, however, Butt developed professional links with nationalists, defending the *Young Irelanders William Smith *O'Brien and T. F. *Meagher in 1848 and various *Fenians in 1865–8. Thereafter he became involved in nationalist politics, becoming president of the Amnesty Association 1869, and founding the Home Government Association 1870. Butt represented Limerick and led the home rule party in parliament 1870–9.

As a political leader Butt had both significant achievements and failures. His most enduring political contribution was to cast the political demand of constitutional nationalism in the form it was to retain for over forty years, and to mobilize a party at Westminster committed, ostensibly, to achieving it. What was once seen as Butt's conversion to nationalism, however, is now more commonly viewed as part of a coherent strand of Protestant *patriotism going back to his days with *'Orange Young Ireland'. Certainly there was an underlying ideological continuity, a Conservative cast of mind and commitment to the British empire which inhibited his ability effectively to prosecute the home rule cause. Unlike Parnell, who accepted home rule as the best Westminster would deliver, Butt believed it was the most desirable solution to the Irish question and was prepared to wait until a reluctant parliament might concede it; and while the former organized a disciplined party to give effect to his efforts, Butt was too personally and ideologically opposed to parliamentary coercion to exert ruthless leadership.

Thornley, David, *Isaac Butt and Home Rule* (1964)

JL

butter, see DAIRY INDUSTRY.

Byrne, Edward, distiller, sugar baker, and merchant, generally regarded as the wealthiest Dublin merchant of his day, and active in the affairs of the *Catholic Committee in the 1790s.

Byrne, Miles (1780–1862), *United Irishman. The son of a Co. Wexford farmer and *middleman, whose family remained highly conscious of their status as displaced gentry, Byrne fought in the *insurrection of 1798 and took a prominent part in Robert *Emmet's conspiracy (1803). Escaping to France, he served in the *Irish Legion, lost favour after the fall of Napoleon, but was recalled in 1828, serving in support of the Greek revolt against Turkish rule. His vivid *Memoirs* appeared posthumously in 1863.

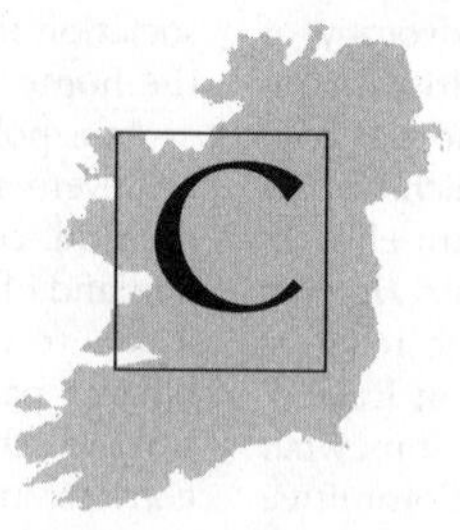

cáin (promulgated law) contrasted with *aurradus*, or customary law. Glossed by Latin *lex*, or Irish *riagal* (from Latin *regula*), it described particular *law tracts such as *Cáin Lánamna* (on marriage) or particular church decrees e.g. *Cáin Adomnáin* (*Adomnán's *Lex innocentium* AD 697). From a decree imposed by royal and/or church authority, *cáin* came to mean a tax or tribute, notably in the *'Book of Rights'. *Cáin* could also mean the fine for violating a ruler's ordinance. Complaints during the 15th and 16th centuries were made against Anglo-Irish lords who took 'canes' or fines from thieves instead of enforcing common *law. KS

calendar. By the late 16th century the Julian calendar, introduced by Julius Caesar in 45 BC, was seriously out of line with the solar year. Pope Gregory XIII introduced a reformed calendar in 1582, but this was not adopted in Ireland and Britain until 1752. The gap between the old style (Julian) and new style (Gregorian) calendars was ten days up to 28 February 1700 (old style), and eleven days thereafter.

calendar custom, the celebration of an annual cycle of festivals, was an important part of rural sociability. In Catholic popular culture the four main festivals of the Celtic year continued to be observed. *Imbolg, the start of the agricultural year, had become St Bridget's Day (1 Feb.), marked by weaving rush crosses that were hung in dwelling houses and agricultural buildings to provide protection for the coming season. *Bealtaine, the beginning of summer, continued as May Day, marked by local communities preparing a bush decorated with ribbons, often the cause of raids and fighting between the men of neighbouring districts, and by lighting bonfires. *Lughnasa, marking the beginning of harvest, continued in the form of late summer festive gatherings, often on hilltops, some of which (like those at *Croagh Patrick) had been converted into religious pilgrimages. *Samhain survived, in Ireland as elsewhere, as November Eve or Hallowe'en, when the spirits of the dead were released on earth. There was also St John's Eve (23 June), the midsummer festival, when bonfires provided the focus for energetic communal festivities. Two other festivals, St Patrick's Day (17 Mar.) and the Assumption (15 Aug.), had their roots more in the ecclesiastical calendar than in popular tradition, and increasingly took on the status of political *anniversaries. To these fixed festivals were added Christmas and Easter, as well as the *patterns celebrated on local saints' days.

The Protestant festive calendar was more limited and more secular in character. In Ulster, and also in some towns of Leinster and the midlands, May Day was celebrated by decorating, not a bush, but a maypole on the English model. St John's Eve was celebrated in some areas by processions of *freemasons. Other seasonal holidays were Christmas and Easter, with Easter Monday in particular being a major occasion for dancing, sports, and *cock fighting across much of Ulster. To these could be added political anniversaries (23 Oct., 12 July). For all denominations *fairs provided not just a commercial venue but a further important addition to the annual cycle of sociability and recreation.

Callan, battle of (1261). On 24 July, near Kenmare, Finghin 'of Ringrone' MacCarthy (Fíngen Reanna Róin Mac Carthaig, d. 1261), after destroying a number of Anglo-Norman castles, heavily defeated the *justiciar, William de Dene, the barons of *Desmond, and his cousin and rival Donal Rua Mac Carthy (Domnall Ruad MacCarthaig). John fitz Thomas and his son Maurice were killed, leaving only an infant heir over the Desmond branch of the Geraldines, which temporarily interrupted their expansion. KS

camogie, essentially a women's version of *hurling, was invented by female members of the *Gaelic League. It was first played publicly at Navan, Co. Meath, in 1904. Unlike other Gaelic sports camogie is not controlled by the *Gaelic Athletic Association, though camogie clubs rely on GAA facilities and funding. The game's appeal has always been limited, with most support coming from teams in Dublin, Cork, and Belfast. NG

Campbell, Agnes, 'the Lady of Kintyre', Scottish noblewoman. Her third marriage in 1569 connected her husband, Turlough Luineach *O'Neill, and her half-brother, the earl of Argyll, who controlled the flow of *redshanks into Ireland. Consequently it was through the agency of Agnes (and her daughter Finola *MacDonnell) that most Scots mercenaries were recruited. Nevertheless Agnes was regarded as a calming influence on Turlough, encouraging him to follow the example of Scottish magnates in conforming to the dictates of state policy. She established a small Scots settlement around O'Neill's chief castle at Strabane, Co. Tyrone. HM

Campion, Edmund (d. 1581), English scholar subsequently executed as a *Jesuit traitor, the guest of leading Dublin families in 1570–1. The result was *Histories of Ireland*—a typical example of *Renaissance historiography, with emphasis on moral exemplification, education, and reforming statesmanship. The account puffed up the *Old English role in Ireland and lionized the deputyship of *Sidney, even though his parliament then terminating had come close to disaster. Campion's *Histories* remained unpublished until 1633, but in the mean time they had been used by various scholars, especially Richard *Stanihurst in his contribution to Holinshed's *Chronicles* (1577). HM

Canada. Although Canada came into being officially only in 1867 (comprising at that time the provinces of Ontario, Quebec, New Brunswick, and Nova Scotia), 'Canada' in general usage refers to all of what was once British North America and New France, and which today spans the North American continent from *Newfoundland to British Columbia. Although the Irish in Canada (both immigrants and later generations) have never acted with the strident ethnic assertiveness characteristic of the Irish in the urban *United States, they have had a much greater impact upon the national and provincial polities than have the American Irish upon their respective jurisdiction. This is because the Irish in Canada were a 'charter group', one of the bands of earliest settlers, and thence operated from a position, not of disadvantage, but of relative privilege. Equally important, they were numerically consequential. In 1867, for example, the Irish were the largest ethnic group in the anglophone population, making up 40.1 per cent of persons of British Isles origin in the new Canadian confederation.

The Irish in Canada (meaning the multigenerational ethnic group) were roughly two-thirds Protestant in the 19th and 20th centuries.

The most obvious Irish impacts upon the Canadian polity were threefold. First, the Protestant Irish strongly enforced the loyalist tradition on which English-speaking Canada was founded. ('Loyalist', in Canadian usage, refers to those people who left the thirteen colonies at the time of the *American Revolution and, being loyal to the crown, moved northward to British North America.) Second, in the second half of the 19th century and the first half of the 20th, the *Orange Order was the largest voluntary organization in Canada. It was tightly tied to the provincial and national Tory parties, but was also influential among the Liberals outside the province of Quebec. Third, in Ontario, the Catholics of Irish extraction spearheaded a campaign to turn the non-denominational school system, created in 1846 and modelled on the Irish *national schools, into one wherein Catholic 'separate schools' received governmental funding.

In matters of residence, occupation, and social mobility, Irish persons in Canada, whether Protestant or Catholic, have not been ghettoized or heavily discriminated against. From the 1850s onward (when reliable data first become available), their socio-economic profiles have equalled, or exceeded, the national norms.

Akenson, D. H., *The Irish in Ontario: A Study in Rural History* (1984)

—— *Being Had: Historians, Evidence and the Irish in North America* (1985)

Houston, C. J., and Smyth, W. J., *Irish Emigration and Canadian Settlement: Partners, Links and Letters* (1990).

DHA

canals were greatly encouraged by the Irish parliament because overland transport was slow and expensive. Between 1730 and 1787 parliament provided upwards of £800,000 for canal construction. It was also hoped that canals would act as a spur to industrialization. The Newry navigation was the first, begun in 1731, connecting Carlingford Lough with the river Bann at Portadown. Its purpose was to bring the recently discovered *coal deposits in east Tyrone to Dublin. The inland section was completed in 1742, predating the Bridgewater canal at Manchester by 20 years. Newry ship canal, handling vessels up to 150 tons burden, was completed in 1769, making the town a major port. The entire navigation was 18 miles long, with fifteen locks. The Tyrone navigation, built between 1733 and 1787, linked Coalisland via a 4-mile cut to the river Blackwater which ran into Lough Neagh. An extension was built to the collieries at Drumglass. Because of inefficiency and neglect, the scheme never fulfilled its promise. The Lagan navigation, from Belfast to Lough Neagh, was completed in the 1780s. The marquis of *Abercorn initiated the building, between 1791 and 1796, of the 4-mile Strabane canal, linking that town with the river Foyle. Many progressive landowners engaged in canal building to stimulate industry and commerce. *Landlords were behind the construction of the 42-mile Ulster canal, connecting Belfast to Beleek, via Upper and Lower Lough Erne. Built between 1825 and 1842, it cost £250,000. An extension, through Leitrim, brought the canal to the headwaters of the Shannon in 1859. It was a commercial disaster, largely due to poor engineering.

By 1803 the Grand canal linked Dublin to Shannon harbour, 80 miles away, a journey of eighteen hours. It was later extended to Ballinasloe and Kilbeggan. A chain of hotels was built along the route. It was comparatively successful during its long existence. The Royal canal, linking Dublin to Mullingar, was completed in the early 1820s, with branches to Longford and Richmond harbour on the Shannon. The Royal went bankrupt before completion, and was taken over in 1814 by the Directors-General of Inland Navigation, a body formed in 1800. The Midland Great Western railway bought it in 1846. On both canals, boats drawn by towing horses carried around 80 passengers, on a usually pleasant cruise, with on-board catering. By 1906, the Royal carried only 22 regular boats compared to 140 on the Grand. The Royal and Grand canals eventually passed to *Coras Iompar Éireann, ultimately closing to traffic in 1961.

Between 1839 and 1850 extensive canalization, on the Shannon system, provided work for the destitute during the *Great Famine. However, it never carried much traffic. In 1830, there were only 487 miles of inland navigation in Ireland, compared to 4,534 in England. Irish canals were never as successful as British, because there was not the volume of coal, raw materials, manufactured goods, and passengers. Traffic in goods and passengers moved away from canals to coaches, railways, and ultimately motor vehicles. Recently many inland waterways have been reopened for tourism.

McCutcheon, W., 'The Transport Revolution: Canals and River Navigations', in Kevin B. Nowlan (ed.), *Travel and Transport in Ireland* (2nd edn., 1993)

PC

canon law in the Irish context is found in three forms. First, in the specifically insular form, the *penitentials; second, in synodal decrees, legislation presented as such (e.g. first Synod of *Patrick), or as a law promulgated at a synod (e.g. the *Cáin Adomnáin*); third, in *collectiones*, lawbooks for use in administration or the courts. From Ireland we have, comparatively, an embarrassment of riches in all three forms, and the earliest evidence for the interaction of Christian law with legal systems from outside the Graeco-Roman world. Thus early Irish law manifests the influences of canon law in its language and discussions, while canon law was adapted to Irish legal practices. One of the fruits of this interchange for canon law was the development of the penitentials. This need to integrate two legal corpora, native and canon, may be seen as the distinctive feature of Irish canon law. If the lawyers of both systems were not to be continually at loggerheads, they had to be able to systematize the contents of their respective laws and develop a jurisprudence for this process. We see this in the *Collectio canonum Hibernensis*, compiled in Ireland in the late 7th–early 8th centuries, one of the earliest systematic codes (i.e. laws arranged by topics) of Christian law in Latin. By presenting laws in an encyclopedic, and supposedly consistent, format the differences between conflicting laws were overcome. The collectors had searched their sources for materials, and by arranging them in a system suggested that these sources were in harmony—for every judgement had its place within their collection. The *Collectio* also casts light on Irish society, as it draws from Irish law (e.g. on inheritance, *marriage, rules of evidence, property). These links with native law made necessary a theory of the origins of both legal systems and their respective competencies. The result was the notion of a natural law functioning alongside a revealed law. Its systematic arrangement, combined with the possibility of integration with other systems, accounts for the popularity of the *Collectio*, both as a legal textbook and as a model of imitation and excerption, in continental Europe between the 8th and the 12th centuries.

Hughes, K., *Early Christian Ireland: Introduction to the Sources* (1972)

O'Loughlin, T., 'Marriage and Sexuality in the *Hibernensis*', *Peritia*, 11 (1997)

TO'L

Canterbury, the primatial see of the English church, played an important though at times contested role in Irish ecclesiastical affairs in the 11th and 12th centuries. Although it is possible that

Dúnán (Donatus), the first recorded bishop of Dublin, was consecrated at Canterbury *c.*1028, the first certain evidence of an Irish bishop being consecrated there relates to Gilla Pátraic (Patricius), bishop-elect of Dublin in 1074. His two successors, Donngus (Donatus) in 1085 and Samuel in 1096, were also consecrated at Canterbury, as also, in 1096, was the first known bishop of Waterford, Máel Isú (Malchus). The Synod of *Ráith Bressail (1111), which outlined a nationwide diocesan structure for the Irish church, envisaged that the pre-existing sees of Dublin and Waterford would, on the death of their incumbents, be incorporated into the new hierarchical constitution. However, a disputed episcopal election in the city of Dublin in 1121 ensured that recourse was once again made to Canterbury for the consecration of Gréne (Gregorius). In 1140, Patrick, a bishop-elect of Limerick, sought consecration at Canterbury, also probably in the context of a disputed election. At the Synod of *Kells (1152) presided over by the papal legate, Cardinal John Paparo, the diocesan constitution of the Irish church received papal endorsement, without acknowledgement of the fact that Canterbury had consecrated bishops for Dublin, Waterford, and Limerick. It was almost certainly Canterbury's response to this diminution of its perceived rights that occasioned the procural of the papal grant **Laudabiliter*. While Canterbury's interest in the Irish church has been interpreted as expansionist and imperialist in intention, it is more likely that it was always secondary to its precedent primatial claims over the see of York; professions of obedience from Irish bishops afforded useful supporting evidence for Canterbury's primacy within a British Isles context. MTF

Cantillon, Richard (d. 1735), economist and financier. Born in Co. Kerry, Cantillon began his career as a financial agent for the British army in Spain, then made a spectacular banking career in France, exploiting contacts with the *Jacobite court. He was murdered in mysterious circumstances at his London house. His *General Essay on Commerce*, published 1755, is regarded as a landmark in the understanding of economic processes.

cantred, a term akin to the Welsh *cantref*, imported by the *Anglo-Normans to describe a pre-conquest territorial unit, reflecting political divisions existing at the time of the invasion. Thus *Theobald Walter was granted five-and-a-half cantreds in Munster in 1185. He subsequently used them to determine the shape of his seigniorial manors. The cantreds also provided the framework for the divisions of the county, similar to the hundred in England. Because both the county and diocesan administrative systems were created concurrently, the cantred and rural deanery frequently encompassed the same area. Modern *baronies are sometimes derived from their medieval predecessor, the cantred. CAE

capital punishment. Although monetary payment could atone for almost any crime under native Irish law, an offender unable to pay was liable to slavery or the death penalty. The death penalty (normally hanging) was also the standard punishment under the common law of the medieval lordship for a range of serious offences, including homicide, arson, robbery, and theft, though ordained clerics were exempt from such punishments by virtue of benefit of clergy and many other offenders received pardons. A 1495 statute made premeditated murder into a form of treason. Down to 1791 convicted male murderers were therefore liable to drawing and quartering as well as hanging; female offenders were liable to burning.

The use of capital punishment was also affected by the distinction made under the common law of the medieval lordship of Ireland between those who lived under English law (not just those of English origin, but also those of Irish origin who had obtained the right to use English law) and the 'pure' Irish. It was only a felony to kill members of the first group; killing a 'pure' Irishman (even one normally resident within the lordship) was at most a civil offence, for which compensation was payable at a fixed rate. This went not to the family of the victim, but to his lord. The difference in treatment attracted contemporary as well as later criticism and from figures as different as Sir John *Davies and James *Connolly. It did not wholly disappear until the 16th century.

During the early modern period benefit of clergy became available to almost all first offenders (including women as from 1634), but as the death penalty was extended to a wider range of offences the more serious also generally ceased to be 'clergiable'. During the 18th century, it became common to commute many death sentences to *transportation; long terms of imprisonment became the norm for most offences only from the 1820s onwards. A series of statutes between 1832 and 1837, paralleling English reforms, abolished capital punishment for most offences other than treason and murder. Up to the late 1840s executions nevertheless remained significantly more common, in relation to population, than they were in England; from the 1860s, by contrast, they became somewhat less common. In both countries capital punishment ceased to be carried out in public in 1868.

Capital punishment was retained in both Irish states after *partition. In independent Ireland there were 24 executions between 1924 and 1954, in Northern Ireland thirteen between 1922 and 1961. In the Irish Republic the Criminal Justice Act (1964) abolished capital punishment for ordinary murders, while creating a new offence of capital murder, comprising the murder of a police officer or prison officer and certain specific cases of a political nature. The death penalty was abolished for these offences in 1990, and outlawed by a constitutional referendum in June 2001. In Northern Ireland capital punishment was abolished in 1966, except for the murder of a police officer or other crown servant, and murder as part of a seditious conspiracy. In 1973 the law in Northern Ireland was brought into line with that of the rest of the United Kingdom, where the death penalty had been abolished in 1969.

PAB/SC

Caravats and Shanavests, rival groups whose feuding caused considerable violence, particularly in Cos Tipperary, Waterford, Kilkenny, Limerick, and Cork, during 1806–11. The conflict, originally interpreted as an example of *faction fighting, in fact had a social basis. The Caravats were a movement of *agrarian protest. The Shanavests were prosperous farmers banded together to resist this challenge from the rural poor, although their movement was also linked to earlier *United Irish organization.

Carew, Sir George (1555–1629), created earl of Totnes (1626), *provincial president of Munster 1600–3. Carew arrived to assist his cousin Peter *Carew in the 1570s but afterwards entered government service, becoming master of the ordnance in 1588. Having left Ireland in 1592, he was reappointed after the *Nine Years War spread to Munster. He was a factional rival of the lord deputy—supporting Robert Cecil whereas *Mountjoy was a friend of *Essex. His mixture of brute force and skilful diplomacy quelled Munster within a year.

The Spanish landing at *Kinsale reignited war in Munster; Carew extinguished it by storming the O'Sullivan stronghold of Dunboy (June 1602). The early reduction of Munster enabled him to steal some of Mountjoy's thunder at court. As an acknowledged expert on Ireland, Carew inspected the *Ulster plantation (1610) and suggested new boroughs to create a Protestant majority in the 1613 parliament.

His considerable archive on Ireland (the Carew Manuscripts at Lambeth Palace) was exploited by his bastard son Thomas Stafford to write up the Munster campaign in *Pacata Hibernia* (1633).

HM

Carew, Sir Peter (1514–75), a Devonian courtier and soldier who pursued claims to lands granted to his ancestors by *Henry II. In 1568 the Irish privy council upheld his claims to the Carlow barony of Idrone. The 10th earl of *Ormond blamed this land-grabbing for his brother Edmund's involvement in the first *Desmond revolt, even though Carew enjoyed good relations with the Kavanaghs who actually occupied Idrone. Carew died en route to Co. Cork, pursuing further claims.

HM

Carleton, William (1794–1869). The son of a Co. Tyrone Catholic tenant farmer, Carleton was intended for the priesthood but converted to Protestantism after travelling as a 'poor scholar'. He drew on his knowledge of Irish life to write sketches for the *Christian Examiner*, an evangelical journal edited by the Revd Caesar Otway (1780–1842), and later for his *Traits and Stories of the Irish Peasantry* (1830–3), and for a series of novels, including *Valentine M'Clutchy* (1845) and *The Black Prophet: A Tale of Irish Famine* (1847). Despite widespread popularity, personal problems and failure to secure copyright left him chronically insecure; he wrote hastily and copiously for journals of different outlooks, and his post-*Famine work, except for his incomplete *Autobiography* (1870), is didactic and sentimental. He enjoys a lasting reputation as a witness of pre-Famine rural society from within.

PM

Carmelites or white friars are first mentioned in Ireland in 1271 when a letter of protection was issued in their favour. The earliest foundation was at Leighlinbridge, Co. Carlow, *c.*1272 and by 1356 23 friaries had been established. All the founders were Anglo-Irish but Gaelic patronage of the new foundations is probable. The Irish houses were governed by the English provincial until 1305 when an independent Irish province was established. An earlier attempt in 1294 to set up a Hiberno-Scottish province foundered in the face of English opposition. Racial tension was not as much an issue for the Carmelites as for the other orders of friars and a Gaelic friar, David O'Buge, was provincial between 1321 and 1327. As with the other mendicants, the Carmelites expanded into Gaelic Ireland in the 15th century, establishing four houses between 1400 and 1508.

All the friaries in territory controlled by the government were suppressed by 1540 (see DISSOLUTION OF THE MONASTERIES) but in 1575 there were still four or five houses in existence in

Gaelic territory. In 1625 the reformed or Discalced Carmelites arrived in Ireland and frequent disputes occurred with the unreformed or Calced friars over the occupation of sites. The decision of *Propaganda Fide in 1751 to close the Irish novitiates (see RELIGIOUS ORDERS) had a particularly severe effect on the Carmelites, who had no continental houses in which to train novices and clerics. CNÓC

Carrickfergus, Co. Antrim, the principal town of *Anglo-Norman Ulster, strategically located controlling Belfast Lough. The place name, meaning 'the rock of Fergus', is thought to preserve the memory of a *Dál Riata king, and the rock possibly functioned as a fortress in early historic times. A castle was commenced *c.*1178 by John de *Courcy and the town was laid out along High Street, stretching from the castle to the Franciscan friary (founded *c.*1232). Burgesses are first referred to in 1221. The town was captured by Edward *Bruce in 1315 but the castle held out for another year. During the later Middle Ages Carrickfergus became an isolated frontier post. It was burnt by the Scots in 1386 and again in 1402, and was forced to pay *'black rent' to the *O'Neills during the 15th and 16th centuries. Despite its detached position the town managed to retain links with Lecale and the *Pale by means of the sea.

In 1569 Carrickfergus received a new charter from Elizabeth I and it became a major base for government operations in Ulster during the late 16th century. Sir Arthur *Chichester remodelled the town. He rebuilt the parish church, erected a new town wall, and constructed a magnificent Renaissance-style residence for himself at Joymount on the site of the former Franciscan friary. The town retained its strategic importance throughout the 17th century but by 1700 it was overshadowed by the growth of Belfast. In 1760 the castle was captured and briefly held by the French commander *Thurot's expeditionary force. JBr

Carson, Revd Alexander (1776–1844), 'Carson of Tobermore'. Born in Co. Tyrone and educated at Glasgow, Carson was *Presbyterian minister at Tobermore, Co. Londonderry, until 1804, when he broke away to form his own independent congregation. In 1827 he joined the *Baptists, and became one of their most eminent preachers and controversialists.

Carson, Edward (1854–1935), Lord Carson of Duncairn, *Unionist leader. Carson was born in Dublin into a liberal, professional family. His success as a crown prosecutor during the *Plan of Campaign was rewarded in 1892 by his appointment as solicitor-general for Ireland and his election as Unionist MP for *Trinity College, Dublin. He transferred his legal practice to London in 1893, and swiftly built up a reputation in the courts and in the House of Commons: his speech on the second reading of the *home rule bill (1893) and his defence of the marquis of Queensberry in the first Oscar Wilde trial (1895) were widely acclaimed. His defence of Irish landlordism from the backbenches made him a critic of Lord Salisbury's Conservative government until he was silenced in 1900 through appointment as solicitor-general for England. The decisive Conservative and Unionist defeat sustained in January 1906 removed many of his ministerial rivals, leaving him free to emerge as one of the most prominent politicians in the United Kingdom.

Carson sacrificed something of this British pre-eminence in February 1910, when he accepted the leadership of the Irish Unionist Parliamentary Party. During the third home rule crisis (1912–14) Carson contributed a charismatic personality, inspired oratory, and skilful parliamentary leadership to the mass mobilization created by James *Craig. He encouraged popular belligerence, while privately seeking a constitutional agreement: like earlier Irish leaders, Carson sought to force a settlement through the threat of militancy. This strategy brought Ireland close to civil war by July 1914.

Although Carson remained leader of the Ulster Unionists until 1921, he was diverted into other areas after 1914. He served briefly as attorney-general in the first wartime coalition, resigning in October 1915 in order to lead backbench unrest: he was one of the architects of *Asquith's fall in December 1916. He served unsuccessfully as 1st lord of the admiralty between January and July 1917; from July 1917 until January 1918 he was a member of the war cabinet. He returned to his legal practice in 1919, and accepted a lordship of appeal in May 1921.

Carson was a paradoxical figure. By the end of his career he seemed the epitome of high Toryism, condemning the *Anglo-Irish treaty (1921), the proposed Alternative Prayer Book of the Church of England (1927), and trimming British government policy in India (1933). Yet he had begun his career as a radical. He was from middle-class origins, and represented the powerful bourgeois Unionism of Edwardian Ireland; yet he had a strong faith in the political importance of the landed gentry, and sought desperately to defend their waning position. He was strongly legalistic, yet had also subverted the British constitution.

The integrity and ambiguity of his thought reveal his Gladstonian origins.

Jackson, Alvin, *Sir Edward Carson* (1993)

AJ

cartography, see MAPS.

Casement, Sir Roger (1864–1916), British diplomat and Irish patriot. Casement joined the British colonial service in 1892 and gained an international reputation as a humanitarian for his reporting on the exploitation of native workers by European employers in Africa and South America. He received a knighthood in 1911 and retired from the service in 1913.

Casement's Irish nationalism had grown stronger over the years. He joined the *Gaelic League early on, and was involved in the foundation of the *Irish Volunteers. He believed passionately in the necessity of German aid for a successful uprising. To obtain this he made his way to Berlin in 1914. Although the German government agreed to send a shipload of arms to Ireland, this fell far short of his expectations. Realizing the inadequacy of German support he returned to Ireland to postpone the planned *rising of 1916 but was arrested after landing. His trial for treason attracted enormous attention, and there were many appeals on his behalf. To discredit him, the government circulated extracts from his diaries detailing homosexual activity. Long controversial, these became widely accepted as genuine, but the debate regarding their authenticity has been reopened in recent years. Casement was hanged in August 1916 after converting to Catholicism. In 1965 his remains were returned to Ireland, where they received a state funeral.

JA

Case of Ireland's being Bound by Acts of Parliament in England Stated, The (1698), published by William *Molyneux in response to the proposed *Woollen Act. In what must be seen as a series of fall-back positions rather than a single argument, Molyneux maintained that Ireland's 12th-century Gaelic rulers had not been conquered but had submitted voluntarily to English rule, that conquest did not confer unlimited rights, that the majority of the current inhabitants of Ireland (Catholic as well as Protestant) were descendants of settlers rather than of the aboriginal Irish population, and that all persons had in any case a natural right to live only under laws to which they had given their consent. The book was condemned by the English parliament (although the later claim, popularized by Charles *Lucas, that it was burned by the hangman is untrue). In Ireland, though at first condemned as unnecessarily provocative, it was reprinted and widely quoted during the controversies surrounding the *Declaratory Act (1719) and *Wood's Halfpence, and enjoyed a new vogue, initially inspired from colonial America, from the 1770s. By this time, however, Molyneux's historical argument was given less prominence than his appeal to natural rights, and his suggestion that a parliamentary union would be an equally satisfactory means of allowing Irishmen to give their consent to the laws that bound them was quietly ignored.

Cashel. From the 4th or 5th century Cashel was the royal seat of the *Eóganacht. In 978 *Brian Bóruma (Brian Boru) made himself king of Cashel and his descendants, the Uí Briain (*O'Brien), continued to style themselves as such. In 1101 a synod was held there, presided over by King Muirchertach *Ua Briain who donated the site to the church. Ten years later Cashel was formally constituted as the head of an archdiocese. The architectural remains all date from its ecclesiastical history, and consist of a *round tower, the 12th-century *Cormac's chapel, a 13th- or 14th-century cathedral, and 15th-century residential buildings.

RM

cashel, a term popularly used for a stone *ringfort. The Anglicized form of Irish *caiseal* ('stone fort'), it is frequently found as a place-name element.

RW

Cashel, Synod of (1101), the first occasion on which identifiable elements of the *12th-century reform of the Irish church were implemented. Presided over by Muirchertach *Ua Briain, king of Munster, and attended by numerous clerics and lay magnates, the synod is notable for Muirchertach's assigning the site of *Cashel to exclusively ecclesiastical use, but above all for its eight reforming decrees. These attempted to adapt the European reformers' objective (namely combating lay encroachment upon the church and its prerogatives) to specifically Irish conditions, and sought to outlaw some categories of *marriage within the forbidden degrees of kindred.

CE

Castle, Richard (*c.*1695–1751), one of Ireland's most prolific Palladian *architects. Of German origin, Castle spent some time in London where he probably became acquainted with the Palladian movement and its English exponents. He arrived in Ireland *c.*1728 and worked with Edward Lovett *Pearce on the designs for the *Parliament House and the Newry canal scheme. Following Pearce's death in 1733, Castle took over the practice and found particular success in country house design; amongst his most notable country houses are Westport House, Co. Mayo (1731), Powerscourt House, Co. Wicklow (1731–40), and Carton House, Co. Kildare (1739–45). In Dublin he designed the Printing House in *Trinity College (1734), the *Rotunda lying-in hospital (1750–7), and the Fishamble Street music hall (1740, no longer extant), together with a number of domestic buildings including *Leinster House (1745–51) and nos. 80 and 85 St Stephen's Green (1736–7, 1738). Apart from Pearce, Castle's work is principally influenced by the English architect Sir James Gibbs. RM

Castle boards, the term (see DUBLIN CASTLE) coined to characterize a distinctive feature of *government and administration in Ireland from the 18th century until independence. The poverty of the country, and the relatively undeveloped state of *local government, were widely believed to necessitate a greater degree of state intervention in Ireland than was required in England, with areas such as *schools and economic development meriting special attention. In addition to the grant-aiding of local authorities, a number of government-appointed boards were created in the 18th century to undertake specific tasks, an early example being the *Linen Board (1711). The drive for more efficient and more economical government in the early 19th century led to the abolition of some boards, many of which had become mere conduits for government patronage. At the same time new bodies, such as the *Board of Works and the Board of National Education, were created to advance the social and economic regeneration of the country. One advantage of appointed boards was that ministers were thereby enabled to bring sections of the community not normally represented on local government bodies into the administrative process. In 1914 there were thirteen boards in operation, including the *Land Commission and the *Congested Districts Board. VC

Castle Chamber. This prerogative court, modelled on the English Star Chamber, reflected an early modern concern for social control as well as the centralizing power of the state. An intention to separate the judicial and administrative functions of the Irish *privy council had been mooted as early as 1534 but the court came into operation only in 1571. It sat twice a week during legal term with the *lord deputy usually in attendance. Its normal penalties were fines and imprisonment, but pillory, loss of ears, whipping, and land confiscation also occurred.

Although a court of appeal and arbitration, it was essentially a rapid-action political tribunal. It tried riot and assault cases (affronts to the queen's peace) and also forgery of the lord deputy's signature, conspiracy, and treasonable words. Most significantly, it punished jurors whom the state construed as having perjured themselves by finding the wrong verdict—for instance the jury which in 1582 acquitted Morris FitzGerald for alleged involvement in the *Baltinglass rebellion. It also was used against the opponents of *cess.

During James I's reign *Palesmen complained that Castle Chamber was extending its jurisdiction into spiritual matters when it punished Catholics who disobeyed the *mandates and juries who had failed to return names of local *recusants. *Wentworth used the court against Richard *Boyle for impropriating church property, the Galway jury holding up his proposed plantation of Connacht, and Scots settlers refusing the *Black Oath. Wentworth's *absolutist use of Castle Chamber contributed not only to his own impeachment but also to the court's abolition. HM

Castlereagh, Viscount, courtesy title of **Robert Stewart** (1769–1822), of the Co. Down landed family, who in 1821 succeeded his father as 2nd marquis of *Londonderry. Elected MP for Co. Down in 1790, he was *chief secretary 1798–1801. Chiefly responsible for steering the Act of *Union through the Irish parliament, he seems at first to have underestimated opposition to the measure, but adroitly managed the bargaining and persuasion required to turn an initial parliamentary defeat into a safe majority for the proposal. During the *insurrection of 1798 he supported firm action against the immediate military threat but also joined in *Cornwallis's subsequent policy of conciliation. His contemporary reputation as the epitome of reaction owes more to his later career as British foreign secretary 1812–22, when he took a leading part in the reconstruction of Europe as a system of authoritarian monarchical states following the *revolutionary and Napoleonic wars, and was also associated with harsh repression in Great Britain.

castles. There is limited annalistic evidence to suggest that Gaelic Irish lords were building castles or *caisléin* in the late 12th century just prior to the *Anglo-Norman invasion. However, these military fortifications, which also served as administrative and judicial centres, were first constructed in large numbers by the Anglo-Normans in earth and wood, either as *motte and baileys or as ringwork castles, to overawe the island during their military campaign. The first stone structures appeared within a decade at *Carrickfergus, Co. Antrim, and Trim, Co. Meath, with strong rectangular keeps located in the centre of a ward delimited by curtain walls. Royal castles were also built at major population centres such as *Dublin and *Limerick at the start of the 13th century. A major variant in castle design was the circular keep at places like Dundrum, Co. Down. As the century progressed, the keep ceased to be separate and was incorporated into the curtain walls as an entrance gateway. This is best represented by Roscommon, constructed at the end of the 13th century against the Gaelic Irish of Connacht. But economic difficulties and the changing nature of warfare in the 14th century led to the start of the construction of up to 7,000 *tower houses, small single stone towers with a defended *bawn. A few large castles were built in the 15th century, such as Cahir, Co. Tipperary, by the *Ormonds. The era of castle construction ended in the 17th century with the increasingly efficient use of siege cannon. TB

Castletown House, Co. Kildare, one of the largest and most influential houses of 18th-century Ireland, was commissioned by William *Conolly as a symbol of his importance and *patriotism. The initial design for the Palladian mansion was by the Florentine architect Alessandro Galilei (1691–1737) *c.*1718; his work was continued (probably from *c.*1725) by Edward Lovett *Pearce. The construction and interior decoration were completed under the supervision of Speaker Conolly's great-nephew Tom Conolly and his wife Louisa Lennox (1743–1821). The staircase hall is decorated with particularly ornate *plasterwork (1759–60) by the Lafranchini brothers. RM

catechisms were produced by both Protestant and *Counter-Reformation reformers, to educate clergy and laity in Christian doctrine. The first Irish-language catechism was John Kearney's Protestant text published in 1571. Catholic catechisms were based on the Council of *Trent's 1566 catechism. Basically a priest's text, it functioned as a doctrinal and devotional source book for preaching and teaching, containing a survey of faith and morals, stressing church loyalty, appreciation of the mass, and devotion to Mary. Popular versions in Irish were produced by Irish Louvain Franciscans like Florence Conry (1593) and Bonaventure O'Hussey (1608). Domestic Irish-language versions included Archbishop Michael O'Reilly's 1739 catechism while Andrew Donlevy's version was published in Paris in 1742. English-language versions were available from 1687. Archbishop Butler's version appeared in 1777 and in 1829 Jeremiah Donovan translated the *Maynooth Catechism*, which was widely used in national and secondary schools and stressed the Christian life as obedience to concrete rules. This Tridentine tradition remained in place until *Vatican II. In the 1960s and 1970s various unsuccessful efforts were made to provide a modern catechism, the Dutch Catechism (1967) being a controversial but influential example. The publication of the *Catechism of the Catholic Church* in 1992, with an English translation in 1994, marked a return to a structured statement of the faith but the text awaits its popularizers. TO'C

Cathal mac Finguine (d. 742), of the *Eóganacht Glennamnach, king of *Cashel from 721, was notable for his challenge to the supremacy of the *Uí Néill kings. By attacking Leinster and raiding Brega (Co. Meath, north Co. Dublin, and part of Co. Louth) at intervals, he hoped to curb the ambitions of northern rulers who sought to extend their sway further south. His reign is celebrated in such literary works of a later period as the 12th-century satirical narrative *Aislinge Meic Conglinne*. MNíM

Catholic Association, established May 1823 to campaign for *Catholic emancipation. Initially composed of the same mixture of merchants, professional men, and landowners that had dominated previous such organizations, it was transformed by the *Catholic rent into a mass-based political movement of an unprecedented kind. It was suppressed in March 1825 under the recently introduced Unlawful Societies Act. A New Catholic Association launched in July remained within the letter of the law by confining its formal proceedings to issues of religion and public welfare, leaving the direct agitation of Catholic grievances to separate public meetings.

Catholic Bulletin, a Catholic and nationalist publication which appeared between 1911 and 1939. Like the *Catholic Pictorial* and the *Irish Rosary*, it was strongly hostile to *freemasonry. In its early years it catered for a fairly broad range of interests and was a forum for important articles on Catholic social teaching by *Maynooth professor Peter Coffey. It grew more strident in tone in the 1920s. Opposed to the *Anglo-Irish treaty, it objected to the *Irish Free State's pragmatic policies on *Northern Ireland. Later it campaigned for the passage of the *Censorship of Publications Act. Its political, cultural, and religious radicalism gradually isolated it. TO'C

Catholic Committee. The first body established to give formal representation to Catholic interests in the 18th century was a Catholic Association (1756) composed of Dublin business interests and mainly concerned with commercial privileges. In 1760 Charles *O'Conor and John *Curry established a more broadly based Catholic Committee, but prior to the 1790s this was only sporadically active. From 1791, however, a more militant group, headed by John *Keogh and Edward *Byrne, seized control of the committee, provoking the secession in December 1791 of a conservative faction headed by Lord *Kenmare. Several of the new leadership had links with the *United Irish movement, and in 1792 Edmund *Burke's son Richard was replaced as secretary by *Tone. The culmination of the new, more assertive strategy was the *Catholic Convention held in December 1792. The committee dissolved itself following the *Catholic Relief Act of 1793, reappearing briefly in 1795 when *Fitzwilliam's appointment seemed to hold out the promise of further gains. A new Catholic Committee (formally the General Committee of the Catholics of Ireland) was established in May 1809 to continue the campaign for *Catholic emancipation, but was suppressed in 1811 under the *Convention Act, after seeking to broaden its base by adding elected delegates to its membership.

Catholic Convention, a representative assembly organized by the *Catholic Committee, at Tailor's Hall, Dublin, on 3–8 December 1792 to prepare a petition for relief from the remaining *penal laws. The nationwide election of delegates, accompanied by the raising of subscriptions and the collection of signatures for a declaration of principles, was a landmark in the process of *politicization, anticipating tactics of mass agitation later developed by *O'Connell. The 231 delegates were mainly businessmen and country gentlemen. Forty-eight were also members of the Dublin Society of *United Irishmen, and United Irishmen like *Tone and Luke Teeling, a leading Co. Antrim linen merchant, were prominent in the proceedings. In a deliberate snub to the Irish executive, the convention's petition was not sent through the lord lieutenant, but presented directly to the king in London. The presumption of the 'Popish parliament' created resentment and alarm among Protestant conservatives. But the evidence of Catholic determination and organizational strength, and the implied threat of a Catholic–radical alliance, persuaded the government to grant a substantial *Catholic Relief Act in 1793.

Catholic emancipation, the admission of Catholics to the positions from which they were still excluded following the *Catholic Relief Acts of 1778, 1782, and 1793. Principally these were the right to hold senior government offices or be members of the *privy council, to be a judge, king's counsel, or sheriff of a county, or to sit in parliament. Petitions for the removal of these restrictions were rejected by large parliamentary majorities in 1805 and 1808. From 1812, however, Lord Liverpool's Tory ministry accepted that emancipation was an open question, which ministers could support or oppose. *Grattan's emancipation bill of 1819 failed by only two votes, and in 1821 an emancipation bill introduced by William Conyngham *Plunket passed through the Commons. The political argument had thus been won by 1821; but the hostility of the House of Lords, and of King *George IV, remained a formidable obstacle.

The establishment in 1823 of the *Catholic Association began a new phase in the campaign for emancipation. The introduction of the *Catholic rent transformed the association from a small Dublin-based caucus into a mass movement with branches throughout the country. The momentum thus created was maintained by public meetings, and by the skilful use of newspapers to disseminate news of the agitation. The Catholic clergy, ex-officio members of all branches, played a vital role as local organizers and channels of information. The rhetoric of the movement was broadened to include not just legal disabilities but grievances such as excessive demands for *tithes and the partisan administration of justice. The agitation suffered a setback in 1825, with the suppression of the Catholic Association and the disagreements caused by O'Connell's acquiescence in the *wings. In the general election of 1826, however, Catholic activists in several counties, despite O'Connell's initial scepticism, offered a dramatic demonstration of the power of the Catholic electorate. In Co. Waterford Villiers Stuart inflicted a dramatic defeat on Lord George Thomas Beresford, while in Cavan, Monaghan, Westmeath, and Louth large numbers of *40-shilling freeholders likewise defied their landlords to support pro-emancipation candidates. These successes provided the impetus for the formation in a number of counties of Liberal clubs to provide a permanent electoral organization. After another period of partial stasis during 1827 the final crisis came with O'Connell's bold decision to stand against Vesey FitzGerald in the Co. Clare by-election of 1828. His overwhelming victory confirmed the collapse of proprietorial control over Catholic voters, and convinced *Wellington and *Peel that emancipation could not be delayed. However, it took several months of behind the scenes negotiation, during which Ireland seemed to come close to explosion, before the last Catholic Relief Act became law on 13 April 1829.

O'Ferrall, Fergus, *Catholic Emancipation: Daniel O'Connell and the Birth of Irish Democracy* (1985)

Catholicism. The history of Irish Catholicism enters a new phase in the 17th century. The attachment to traditional forms, and the dislike of externally imposed innovation, so characteristic of *recusancy give way to a more positive commitment to the doctrines and practices of the *Counter-Reformation. Already before 1660 the abandonment of the *Cromwellian regime's initial schemes for transplantation and the forcible suppression of popery had confirmed that Catholicism was to remain the religion of the great majority. Yet warfare and repression had partially undone the administrative and pastoral reforms achieved in the fifty years before 1641, and popular religious practice retained a strong local flavour. The further gradual reshaping of Irish Catholicism along the lines laid down by the Council of *Trent was to be accompanied by efforts to establish sustainable relations with the succession of political jurisdictions within which the church found itself: the Irish Protestant state until 1801, the United Kingdom until 1922, and latterly the twin states born of *partition.

Pastoral and institutional reform

Tridentine reformers took advantage of the stability of the *Restoration period to renew efforts to establish administrative structures and to take on the most glaring excesses of the old Catholicism. Their work received a dramatic setback with the Stuart defeat in the *Williamite War. However, despite Catholic exclusion from the Irish Protestant state (see PENAL LAWS), pastoral and institutional modernization continued. Penal-era Catholicism bore the marks of poverty and political exclusion but was coloured too, thanks to its largely French-educated clergy and *Jacobite connections, by the Catholic *Enlightenment. It stayed in touch with continental developments in church organization, theology, and liturgy. Modest but real progress was made in setting up diocesan and parochial structures, providing education, and modernizing devotional practice. By the middle of the 18th century a church which was recognizably Tridentine was emerging, led by cautious bishops and gentry, served by a reasonably well-formed clergy, and including a prosperous merchant class which had, already, a mind of its own. Further down the social and economic ladder the old Catholicism remained strong.

After the political upheaval of the 1790s further progress in pushing back this old Catholicism was slow, hampered by rapid *population increase, massive impoverishment, clerical shortages, and the dogged persistence of the old ways. Change accelerated, however, as the century progressed. By the mid-19th century, a massive church-building programme was transforming the Irish landscape. The mesh of relationships which bound the Catholic community together was taking on the rigidity associated with more complex structures. Religious practice itself was being revamped from above to conform to continental models of popular piety, a phase in the so-called *devotional revolution. Catechesis, especially through parish *missions, was pivotally important here and, while it often lacked theological subtlety and emotional depth, it was imposing in its consistency and rigour. The newer institutional Catholicism satisfied the religious needs of the majority who were happy to belong to the more *ultramontanist church already emerging prior to the first *Vatican Council. It generally proved more than a match for Protestant proselytizing efforts and for the remains of the old Catholicism. Ongoing *emigration, which accelerated in the second half of the 19th century, ensured that Irish Tridentine Catholicism would become an international phenomenon.

By the late 19th century, the regulation of the land question consumed the energies of the Catholic community. Given that most priests were drawn from the ranks of the tenant farmers, it was hardly surprising that the institutional church swung in behind land reform. Success here completed the formation of a stable, peasant proprietor class which, along with the urban-based commercial and professional elites, had become the backbone of the Catholic church. By the century's end, even the very poorest Catholics were at least formally part of the Tridentine ecclesiastical structures. Overseen by a conservative episcopate, dutifully served by a plentiful clergy, composed of a theologically unsophisticated but sacramentally observant laity, the late 19th-century Irish Catholic church was integrated into a papally oriented international organization and the centre of a vast missionary network. It seemed to be a Tridentine success story which encouraged many Catholics to believe that maintenance of existing structures rather than continued reform was the order of the day. Their error was revealed from the 1960s onwards, when new wealth, increased mobility, and declining esteem for tradition and establishments weakened many Catholics' relationship with the highly institutionalized and clericalized church. These changes were coincidentally rather than causally related to Vatican II.

Church–state relations

The leaders of the Catholic community worked to establish sustainable and, if possible, advantageous relations with the state. Under the Stuarts this was a major challenge: the conflict between loyalty to monarch and to pope, dramatized in the *Remonstrance controversy, rendered Catholics second-class, suspect subjects. After 1691 the penal laws formalized the exclusion from the Protestant state of a Catholic community whose continued links with the Jacobite court seemed to confirm its inherent disloyalty. However, gradually developing a *modus vivendi* with the Protestant state, the Catholic community built up an impressive record of loyalty to the crown. The state, whether it liked it or not, found itself having to deal with the increasingly well-organized and influential clergy and laity, who were obedient but desirous of improved political status. Their task was eased by papal refusal to recognize the Jacobite succession in 1766. This freed the Catholic community from its awkward loyalty to an exiled monarch and his interference in ecclesiastical appointments. Episcopal independence was enhanced.

In the second half of the 18th century more relaxed attitudes among Irish Protestants, combined with the military needs of the British state, produced limited but significant measures of *Catholic relief. Catholic reaction to these measures was mixed. The bishops and gentry favoured gradual reform, leaving the initiative with the Irish parliament and the crown. Radical reformers pushed for more and, by 1792, Catholic opinion was sufficiently politicized to permit the election of a national *Catholic Convention which petitioned George III for the Catholic franchise. The 1798 *insurrection marked the collapse of the association of interests which had crossed denominational boundaries to demand political reform and Catholic relief. The Catholic bishops and gentry, more impressed by the existing measures of Catholic relief and the promise of full emancipation than by French-inspired political radicalism, joined with a shaken Protestant establishment in supporting the Act of *Union.

Despite the Union the *politicization of the Irish Catholic community proceeded. It had two aspects. At home, support for the *O'Connell-led *Catholic emancipation and *repeal campaigns was massive, forging the Catholic community into a significant force in domestic and British politics and setting the scene for the later growth of *nationalism. In the broader British context, as Irish Catholics re-entered political, economic, and cultural life, the Catholic community took on aspects of an establishment church, without, however, having legal ties with the state.

State-funded provision for primary education, the *national schools, was the first theatre of explicit church–state co-operation. There were teething difficulties, exacerbated by tensions between the churches over the vexed question of proselytism and by disagreement among Catholic bishops over relations with the state. Despite this, and further bitter disputes over the *Queen's Colleges and the *ecclesiastical titles bill, links between the Catholic church and the state deepened, *poor relief and health provision being relatively successful co-operative ventures.

However, as the church institutionalized itself and deepened its relationship with the state, it risked losing its capacity to adapt creatively to changing political and social conditions. The *Famine had left a deep scar, emigration was heavy, and nationalism was gaining the people's loyalties. In the post-Famine period, political initiative ebbed away from the clerical church as it had in the 1790s. Nationalism now took on a life of its own. Whether the clerical church desired it or not and despite the deep divisions left by the *Parnell affair, late 19th-century Catholicism found itself grafted onto Irish nationalism. Whatever the bishops may have thought of the *Sinn Féin victory of 1918, they were obliged to acquiesce in their people's political decision.

Partition divided the Catholic community between two jurisdictions, and *civil war split southern Catholic political opinion. While the 1922 Free State *constitution declared itself religiously neutral, the huge southern Catholic majority meant that the Irish Free State took on a Catholic identity. In any case, the new state needed the stability and recognition which a close relationship with the institutional Catholic church could help secure. While this arrangement of convenience suited both church and state, stability came with a heavy price. Northern Catholics languished in second-class citizenship while, for their southern counterparts, independence meant economic and cultural isolation.

By the late 1950s, when economic necessity obliged the government to jettison old nationalist certainties and open the country to free-market capitalism (see *ECONOMIC DEVELOPMENT*), the close church–state relationship in the *Republic was losing its attraction for the state. The clerical church, straitjacketed in old convictions and anxious to protect the status quo, was slow to adjust. The development of the *Northern Ireland conflict revealed a versatile, violent nationalism, capable of manipulating the institutional church but armed with its own agenda.

The erosion of church–state relations and the growth of spiritual individualism constitute a challenge for contemporary Irish Catholicism equal to that faced by the Tridentine reformers of three centuries ago.

Connolly, S. J., *Religion and Society in Nineteenth-Century Ireland* (1985)
Corish, Patrick, *The Irish Catholic Experience* (1984)
Rafferty, Oliver, *Catholicism in Ulster 1660–1970* (1994)

TO'C

Catholic Relief Acts (1774–93), a series of enactments partially dismantling the *penal laws. Historians disagree over how far Irish Protestant attitudes to Catholicism changed during the second half of the 18th century. The long period of peace since the *Williamite War undoubtedly encouraged greater confidence, and *Jacobitism quickly declined after 1745. Yet the execution of Nicholas *Sheehy revealed the continued strength of anti-Catholicism, and *patriots remained divided as to how far their rhetoric of liberty extended to the Catholic majority. Recent accounts stress the initiative taken by British government, concerned particularly to tap the large reserve of potential military manpower in Ireland. The revived *Catholic Committee further added to pressure for concessions.

Bishop *Hervey's act of 1774 introducing a new oath of allegiance prepared the way for change. The Relief Act of 1778, introduced by Luke *Gardiner but promoted by the government, enabled Catholics who had taken this oath to bequeath land to a single heir. However, MPS rejected Gardiner's proposal to allow the purchase of land. Instead the act permitted Catholics to take leases for up to 999 years, which conferred none of the political rights attached to freehold. Two further measures introduced by Gardiner in 1782 allowed Catholics to buy land, except in parliamentary boroughs, and removed most of the restrictions affecting Catholic education and the Catholic clergy.

Following the *French Revolution British government looked to further relief legislation to prevent any alliance between Catholics and radical *Presbyterians. Sir Hercules Langrishe's act of 1792 allowed Catholics to practise law. Following continued pressure from the Catholic Committee, an act of 1793, introduced by Chief Secretary Robert Hobart and forced through by government influence, gave Catholics the right to vote and to hold most civil and military offices. The violent anti-Catholic rhetoric of the bill's opponents, and the resentment of Protestants at this perceived betrayal by British government, contributed significantly to the growth of *religious conflict.

After 1793 Catholics were still barred from sitting in parliament, from the offices of *lord lieutenant, *chief secretary, and chancellor of the exchequer, and from other senior political positions. They could not be king's counsel, judges or governors, *sheriffs or sub-sheriffs, and could not hold higher military rank than colonel. Hopes for further relief were briefly raised under *Fitzwilliam, and again at the time of the Act of *Union. But it was not until 1829 that the last Catholic Relief Act (see CATHOLIC EMANCIPATION) removed these remaining disabilities.

Bartlett, Thomas, *The Fall and Rise of the Irish Nation* (1992)

Catholic rent. Subscriptions to the *Catholic Association, reflecting its narrow initial membership, were fixed at 1 guinea per year. In February 1824 *O'Connell proposed a new category of associate member, with a minimum subscription of 1 penny per month. The aim was to raise revenue, and to refute claims that the association spoke only for an unrepresentative elite. But at least as important, in practice, was the impetus that the implementation of the scheme provided for the creation of a nationwide network of local agents and committees. By March 1825, when the association was suppressed, about £17,000 had been collected, of which £7,000 came from Leinster and £6,500 from Munster. A 'New Catholic Rent', between 1826 and 1829, brought in another £35,000.

Catholic University, founded by the Irish bishops in 1854 with strong papal encouragement as a response to the 'godless' *Queen's Colleges. The founding rector was the distinguished English convert John Henry *Newman, whose *The Idea of a University* had its origins in lectures he delivered in Dublin, and whose appointments to the academic staff included Gerard Manley Hopkins and Eugene *O'Curry (as professor of archaeology and Irish history). Both temperamentally and philosophically Newman's relations with the hierarchy, and especially with *MacHale (who particularly resented *Cullen's predominant role), were at times uneasy. Furthermore, the institution, lacking a charter and state funding, struggled to survive, though its medical school in Cecilia Street, Dublin, achieved a considerable reputation. After five years as rector Newman resigned, despite efforts by the bishops and others to persuade him to remain. In 1882 the Catholic University was assigned one-half of the fellowships of the newly created *Royal University of Ireland, for whose degrees its students were eligible. In 1883, as University College, Dublin, it came under *Jesuit control, with Fr. William Delany as president. KM

cattle have been farmed in Ireland since the *neolithic period. Archaeologists, using the evidence of bone remains, identify several distinct types of early cattle, some possibly produced by selective breeding. Larger types of cattle may have been introduced to Ireland by *Vikings, *Anglo-Normans, and 17th-century settlers, but it was not until the later 18th century that systematic attempts to create breeds with fixed characteristics became widespread. The Kerry was recognized as a distinctive type by this period, but it was during the late 19th century that its characteristics became standardized to produce a hardy 'poor man's' cow, kept for both milk and meat. An Irish type of longhorn was also identified, particularly in midland counties, and the English agricultural improver Robert Bakewell may have used some of these in developing his famous breed. Other types of cattle, such as the Dexter and Irish Moil, were ascribed ancient antecedents, but were not developed as pedigree breeds until the early 20th century.

By the early historic period, *law tracts and literature clearly show the central importance of cattle in determining social status within Irish society. Large-scale cattle farming is suggested by early medieval texts, and by the late 18th century herds of over 1,000 cattle were recorded in rich grazing lands in Cos. Tipperary and Limerick. These have remained major centres of production ever since. At the other end of the farming scale, the ownership of a cow was also crucial, providing both manure, essential for the successful cultivation of potatoes on marginal land, and milk, which along with potatoes could provide a healthy if monotonous diet. In these areas, the management of cattle often involved a system of transhumance, known as *booleying*, when animals were moved to common hill grazing during summer.

Between 1850 and 1900 there was a 60 per cent increase in cattle numbers in Ireland, mostly of imported breeds such as Shorthorns, which by 1900 had become the most common cattle breed throughout northern Europe. The Department of *Agriculture and Technical Instruction for Ireland succeeded in establishing a national Dairy Shorthorn herd, and these remained dominant until the 1930s, although encouragement was also given for the purchase of other breeds, including Herefords, Aberdeen Angus, and Galloways. Friesian cattle became common in dairying districts during the 1950s, while in more recent decades breeds such as the Charolais and Polled Hereford have typified a movement towards greater diversity of breeds, mostly imported from mainland Europe.

Kelly, Fergus, *Early Irish Law* (1988)
Lucas, A. T., *Cattle in Ancient Ireland* (1987)
Wallace, R., *Farm Livestock of Great Britain* (1907)

JB

Cattle Acts (1663, 1671), English acts, the first imposing a prohibitive duty on cattle or sheep imported from Ireland during the main fattening season, the second a complete ban on imports of Irish livestock, beef, pork, and bacon. The ban expired in 1679, but was renewed in 1681 and extended to mutton, beef, and cheese. As with the *Woollen Act, the acts represented a surrender to English commercial interests rather than a deliberate attack on Irish prosperity. Their main impact was to encourage a transfer of Irish agricultural resources to the production of butter and salted beef, for export to continental Europe (especially France) and the colonies, and also of wool. The ban on meat imports was lifted in 1758, and that on live cattle in 1759, as demand in Great Britain began to outstrip domestic supply.

cattle driving, see RANCH WAR.

ceann comhairle. Referred to in the English-language text of the *constitution of Ireland as 'Chairman of Dáil Éireann', but invariably known by the Irish title of the office, the *ceann comhairle* (literally 'head of council') presides over sessions of the *Dáil and is automatically returned for the same constituency following a dissolution.

Céile Dé (Culdee), an ascetic of the 8th century and later. As *céile* (pl. *céili*) denoted the client or vassal of a lord, the Céile Dé ('Client of God') acknowledged only a celestial lord, in contrast to the *manaig* of the early Irish *church, who were often not true monks but legal and economic dependants closely resembling those of a secular lord. A notable Céile Dé was Máel Ruain (d. 792), founder (in 774) and abbot of Tallaght. The Tallaght documents describe his and his associates' regime, featuring prayer, vigils, the divine office, fasts, mortifications of the flesh, strict sabbatarianism, and care for the poor. They reflect differences of opinion: Máel Ruain's insistence on total abstinence from alcohol was rejected by Dublitter, abbot and bishop of Finglas (d. 796), who declared that his community would also attain heaven, despite their consumption of beer. How far the Céili Dé were a novel reformist movement is debatable, for their practices are consistent with the ascetic tendency found in Irish religious literature as early as the 7th century or even the 6th. Although they criticized the worldliness of the older churches, Céili Dé communities or individual anchorites (recluses) often lived in dependence on such churches and, for example, managed to overcome misgivings about the propriety of eating food produced by their degenerate brethren. They may be regarded simply as stricter observants within multifunctional communities. Even a Céili Dé foundation such as Tallaght was seemingly concerned with more than ascetic *monasticism. The Tallaght documents suggest a pastoral ministry was conducted, while the annals report Tallaght's involvement in high politics and in inter-church rivalry already in the first quarter of the 9th century. In the second quarter of that century *Fedelmid mac Crimthainn, king of Munster, combined church office and Céili Dé sympathies with a violent campaign against the leading ecclesiastical settlements of the midlands, which were associated with his *Uí Néill adversaries. Céili Dé are occasionally noticed at various churches after the 9th century and were perhaps the main if not the sole practitioners of monasticism in the strict sense. However, the headship of the Céile Dé at *Clonmacnoise, who cared for the destitute, was a hereditary office in the 11th and 12th centuries.

Etchingham, C., *Church Organization in Ireland* AD *650 to 1000* (1999)

Hughes, Kathleen, *The Church in Early Irish Society* (1966)

O'Dwyer, Peter, *Céli Dé* (2nd edn., 1981)

CE

céilsine, see CLIENTSHIP.

Celtic Ireland. A now discredited concept based on the premiss that large numbers of Celtic settlers from mainland Europe came to Ireland some time in the *Bronze Age or the *Iron Age. They are supposed to have brought with them the language that was to become Irish, and to have replaced a mixed and complex cultural and genetic history, at least 7,000 years in the making, with a new Celtic culture and Celtic ethnicity. The present, very widespread misuse of the term 'Celtic' to describe anything Irish has led to its virtual abandonment as a cultural descriptor by archaeologists, who now mostly subscribe to a minimalist model of small-scale incursions by Celtic warrior-adventurers during the Iron Age and perhaps proto-Celtic warriors late in the preceding Bronze Age. That there was indeed small-scale but high-impact inward movement by people who, if not strictly Celts, were linguistically and culturally their heirs, cannot be doubted. Such incursions brought, for instance, the elements that make up the Irish *La Tène Iron Age and the term 'Celtic' could, with some justification, be applied to artefacts and art styles that belong to that cultural milieu.

The most established scholastic use of the term 'Celtic' is to describe the group of languages, of which Irish is one, that appears to be derived from, or is closely allied to, the tongue spoken by the mid-European Celtic peoples in the centuries immediately before Christ (see IRISH LANGUAGE). However, given that the notion of a major incursion of Celts into Ireland is unsupportable (see IRON AGE), the mechanism by which the language of the Celts became the Irish language remains to be explained. In the oldest known document containing a significant number of Irish tribe- and place-names—the 2nd-century Cosmography of Ptolemy of Alexandria—many of the name-forms seem to be non-Celtic. It would appear, therefore, that the language of a small Celtic aristocracy ousted the indigenous language to become the sole Irish tongue by the 6th century.

There can be no doubt that some Celts reached Ireland during the later part of the Bronze Age or the Iron Age, and that they were responsible for what became the dominant language. To describe the Irish people or their culture as 'Celtic', however, is a nonsense that fails to take account of the influence of the many races and cultures that have contributed to their long and complex history. RW

Cenél Conaill were a dynasty within the *Uí Néill, based in modern Co. Donegal. Often at odds with their *Cenél nEógain cousins to the east, their other major enemy was the northern *Connachta. Prior to 765, a number of their kings were kings of Tara (see HIGH KINGSHIP), most notably Domnall mac Áedo (*fl.* 628–42), who defeated a *Cruthin-led alliance at Mag Rath (Moira, Co. Down) in 637, and Loingsech mac Óengusso (*fl.* 696–703). In alliance with his kinsman *Adomnán, Loingsech promulgated *Cáin Adomnáin* in 697 in favour of *Iona, the church founded by another member of the dynasty, *Colum Cille. CS

Cenél nEógain were the most powerful grouping within the northern *Uí Néill, claiming descent from Eógan, eldest son of *Niall Noígiallach. The fertile lands of Inishowen, Co. Donegal, are named after them but in time their territory extended over much of Cos. Londonderry and Tyrone; from the 11th century, *Tullaghoge in Co. Tyrone became their inauguration site. Between the 8th and 12th centuries, a number of their rulers were kings of Tara (see HIGH KINGSHIP). In the same period, they were overlords of *Armagh, a church which sought archiepiscopal primacy over Ireland. In the post-*Norman period, their descendants became known simply as *O'Neills. CS

Cennick, John (1718–55). A *Moravian evangelist with roots in Calvinistic Methodism, Cennick first arrived in Ireland in 1746 and made an initial impact on popular Protestantism in Dublin. His greatest influence, however, was in the north of Ireland, where he was instrumental in establishing some 200 Moravian societies in the period 1747–52. Cennick has left a remarkable journal of his early experiences in Ireland, now located in Moravian Church House in London. It offers a vivid account of noisy meetings, theological disputes, internecine arguments, prickly personality clashes, and immense evangelistic optimism. Cennick's career ended unhappily as ill health and strained relations with the Moravians sapped his energies, but there is no denying his significance in the early expansion of popular *evangelicalism in Ireland. DNH

censorship in Ireland has a long and complex history. Little is known of the situation prior to the 17th century, though *printing was under way in Ireland from 1551. From 1604 to 1732 a royal patent theoretically created a printing monopoly in Ireland, enabling state control, while potentially suspect imported books could be seized by customs officials. Catholic devotional literature and seditious pamphlets were the main targets of these measures. However, the king's printer's monopoly was challenged from 1660, and book smuggling is known to have taken place. The English Licensing Act (1662) did not apply in Ireland. Instead the press was controlled by prosecutions at common law for libel or blasphemy. The success of such trials hinged on the fact that, until 1793, it was the judge who determined whether or not a work constituted a libel, juries deciding only on the fact of publication. *Parliament also took summary proceedings against publishers who infringed its privileges. In the last quarter of the 18th century several acts were created to control the popular press. Stamp Acts of 1774, 1785, and 1798 imposed substantial duties on newspapers. Press Acts of 1784 and 1798 required publishers to register themselves with the stamp commissioners and provide large sureties against possible prosecution. The latter acts were inspired by growing political opposition in the press. Yet pamphlets were not so closely controlled, and political debate continued in this form.

These measures, supplemented by further legislation, continued as the effective means of censorship into the 19th century. By mid-century, however, the focus of censorship had shifted from the seditious to the obscene. Between 1842 and 1889 several acts specifically imposed censorship on printed material. The Obscene Publications and Customs Consolidation Acts (1857 and 1876) were the most important. Together they allowed obscene material to be destroyed, owners to be prosecuted, and, unofficially, the maintenance of a blacklist. The *First World War brought new priorities, and the censorship of news was surreptitiously undertaken. In the *Anglo-Irish War propaganda was perhaps more important than censorship.

After *partition the law in *Northern Ireland remained unamended. In the *Irish Free State however, the government established the Committee on Evil Literature in 1926, and in 1929 set up the Irish Censorship Board. The board was given statutory powers to ban books or periodicals it saw as indecent, encouraging crime, or promoting *contraception or *abortion. This development was largely due to the lobbying of religious organizations. A broad measure of public support was accompanied by some condemnation. Banning reached a peak in 1936 when 171 orders were issued. The board was always a focus for controversy. Some liberalization occurred in 1946 when appeals were allowed. From 1967 bans were limited to twelve years, though rebanning was permitted. In 1979 the clause on contraception, but not abortion, was withdrawn.

Other media, as well as print, have also been subject to censorship. While British acts requiring plays to be submitted to the lord chamberlain never applied in Ireland, and the Censorship Board's remit did not include drama, indirect attempts at censorship in the *theatre did take place. In 1909 the *lord lieutenant threatened to remove the *Abbey theatre's patent if it staged a George Bernard Shaw play which had previously been refused a licence in England, while in 1957 the producer of a play at Dublin's Pike theatre was arrested under the obscenity laws. Censorship of films in the Irish Free State was begun in 1923, while *cinema in Northern Ireland comes under the auspices of the British Board of Film Censors. The broadcast media were effectively controlled by the state ownership of broadcasting bodies. From 1971 a number of organizations linked to terrorism were explicitly prohibited from featuring in broadcasts in the Irish Republic. In 1988 a similar ban was implemented in the United Kingdom. Both were rescinded in 1994.

Adams, M., *Censorship: The Irish Experience* (1968)
Inglis, B., *The Freedom of the Press in Ireland 1784–1841* (1954)

Pollard, M., *Dublin's Trade in Books 1550–1800* (1989)

NG

census. In Ireland, as elsewhere, the first official enumeration of inhabitants came only in the 19th century. Earlier there had been privately organized local headcounts, including a large-scale survey of the diocese of Elphin (1749) initiated by the Church of Ireland bishop Edward Synge (1691–1762). But most estimates of national *population, by *Petty, *Dobbs, and others, were based on hearth tax returns. The so-called 'census' of 1659 relates to a special poll tax levied in the confused period preceding the *Restoration.

A projected census in 1813–15 collapsed when *grand juries failed to co-operate. The censuses of 1821 and 1831, conducted over a period of weeks by locally chosen enumerators, are valuable but flawed. That of 1841, conducted on a single day by the *Royal Irish Constabulary, with forms completed where possible by householders themselves, is both fuller and significantly more accurate. Further censuses were taken every ten years between 1851 and 1911. A census was taken in independent Ireland in 1926, 1936, and at five-yearly intervals from 1946. In Northern Ireland there were censuses in 1926, 1937, 1951, and every five years from 1961.

Religious affiliation was not noted on census forms until 1861, although the enumerators' records for the 1831 census were retrospectively amended in 1833 to provide the basis for an elaborate though approximate computation by the commissioners of public instruction. Data on Irish speakers were first collected in 1851, but become more reliable from 1881, when information was more prominently requested.

The manuscript returns of the censuses of 1821–51 were preserved in the Public Record Office, Dublin, but only fragments survived the office's destruction at the start of the *Civil War. The returns for 1861–91 were not preserved. Full records of the censuses of 1901 and 1911 survive and are open to inspection; the returns from later censuses remain closed.

Central Board, a scheme of Irish local government devised by the English Liberal Joseph Chamberlain in 1885 as a substitute for an Irish parliament. In its final form it combined an elected 'National Council' to deal administratively with education and communication, together with an overhaul of county government. Misled by Capt. William *O'Shea into thinking that Parnell approved of the scheme, Chamberlain was deeply affronted when he and his followers scornfully rejected it, and was later to be a formidable opponent of *Gladstone's home rule bills. JL

Centre Party (more correctly the National Centre Party), a political party whose formation, arising from a decision by the National Farmers' and Ratepayers' League (founded 6 Oct. 1932), was agreed on 4 January 1933. It overtook *Labour to become the third largest party after the 1933 general election (9.2 per cent of the vote, eleven seats), but on 8 September 1933 voted for a merger with *Cumann na nGaedheal and the National Guard (see BLUESHIRTS) to form *Fine Gael. The party was conservative and pro-treaty and appealed in particular to larger farmers. Its leader Frank MacDermot (1886–1975) and other prominent members had been associated with the *Nationalist Party. Apart from MacDermot, its most important representative was James *Dillon (1902–86), son of John *Dillon and later a leader of Fine Gael. JC

ceramics. Archaeology clearly documents the use of pottery in Ireland from the *Neolithic through to the medieval period. The arrival of oriental porcelain in Ireland during the early 18th century prompted the Irish to attempt to produce fine wares for the table. Delftware factories, making tin-glazed earthenware, were established in Belfast in 1698 and in Dublin about 1735. The Dublin pottery went through various hands before being taken over by Henry Delamain in 1752. It produced wares on a large scale until its closure in *c.*1767. Other delftware potteries were in existence for short periods in Rostrevor, Youghal, and possibly Limerick. In Belfast the Downshire Pottery (*c.*1790–1807) had been set up to make a refined earthenware for the table called creamware.

Although 18th-century attempts to create porcelain in Ireland were unsuccessful, retailers were able to satisfy demand through imports. Towards the end of the 18th century, the number of fine ceramic retailers grew. In Dublin Josiah Wedgwood and James Donovan had shops, furnished with kilns, which allowed them to decorate and personalize imported English porcelain.

Throughout the 19th century, many local potteries were established to produce domestic earthenware. These included nine around the Coalisland area, and others at Castle Espie, Youghal, and Larne. The pottery at Belleek, founded by David McBirney in 1863, also produced quantities of earthenware for the local domestic market, but is better known as the first pottery in Ireland to produce porcelain. Belleek's distinctive style of exceptionally fine parian porcelain has now become world famous and is still in production today.

The rise of art pottery in England and Europe only briefly touched Ireland. Frederick Vodrey (1845–97) produced art pottery in Dublin from around 1873 until 1897. His work was characterized by classical shapes decorated with either monochrome or streaked glazes. Around the turn of the century members of the Irish Decorative Arts Association decorated blank pottery with Celtic designs but it was not until 1929, when Kathleen Cox (1904–74) set up a studio in Dublin, that real art or studio pottery was produced in Ireland. During the 20th century new potteries were established to produce domestic and tourist wares. These included Carrigaline (1928–79), Arklow (1934–), and Wade (1946–90) in Armagh. In 1965 the Irish government established the Kilkenny Design Workshops and in 1970 the World Crafts Council Conference was held in Ireland. The following year saw the formation of the Crafts Council of Ireland. These bodies have helped to establish studio potteries and continue to support the many ceramic artists working in Ireland today producing both functional and sculptural ceramic work.

Archer, M., *Irish Pottery and Porcelain* (1979)
Dunlevy, M., *Ceramics in Ireland* (1988)
Francis, P., *Irish Delftware: An Illustrated History* (2000)

KMa

cereals have been grown in Ireland since at least 3800 BC. Oats have been the most important Irish cereal, as they are particularly suited to the mild, damp climate. During the historic period, most wheat cultivation has been carried on in the drier south-eastern counties of Leinster. The grain of wheat is valued for *bread, and its straw for thatch. Barley has also been cultivated for flour and straw but, especially in recent centuries, it has also been used extensively in *brewing and *distilling.

Exports of grain from Ireland to England were well established by the end of the 17th century. There was a general increase in this trade during the 18th century, and production and exports boomed during the *revolutionary and Napoleonic wars (1793–1815). A severe slump followed the return of peace, but by the 1820s Ireland was being described as 'the granary of Britain'. Production peaked around the mid-19th century, but since then there has been an almost continuous decline in grain cultivation. Between 1855 and 1901, the acreage of oats fell by 48 per cent, barley by 90 per cent, and wheat by 29 per cent. Production increased sharply in the 20th century during the *First and *Second World Wars, but by the 1990s only about 800,000 acres of land throughout Ireland were planted with cereals of any kind.

See also TILLAGE. JB

cess was the *Old English term for government exactions to maintain the vastly expanded garrison during the *Tudor conquest. In addition to the *lord deputy's normal household cess, which applied to the *Pale only, general cesses of grain and meat were placed on the Pale and neighbouring districts at equal rates per ploughland. Every autumn cessors appointed for each county took up supplies at low fixed rates. Transport demands and troop billeting exacerbated the problem. Bribery, extortion, and intimidation were rife, the food supply was diminished, the market distorted, and government repayment slow. The largest cesses were in 1558, 1559, 1560, and again in 1575.

Although some well-connected landowners had 'freedoms' from cess, Pale society united in 'the country cause' with tax strikes, petitions, and deputations of *'commonwealthmen' to court. In the late 1560s and early 1570s government attempts to import victuals from England using contractors failed. The Palesmen negotiated an end to cess at court in 1585, after *Perrot tried to railroad them into a permanent *composition.

A different type of cess, levied by *grand juries on counties and baronies for the upkeep of roads and bridges and for other public purposes, was introduced in 1634. HM

chambers of commerce first appeared in Ireland in the late 18th century. The *Belfast and *Dublin chambers were both founded in 1783, though the Dublin chamber succeeded a Committee of Merchants which had functioned from 1761. A Committee of Merchants was formed in *Cork in 1769 and similar committees existed in *Waterford and *Limerick by 1805. Many of the original members were either Catholics or dissenters. The formation of these committees reflects the expansion of the Irish merchant community during the 18th century, and its resentment at the fact that political power continued to rest with the landed community, which generally took little account of mercantile interests. MED

chancellor, the royal official who had custody of the Irish great seal and was responsible for issuing letters in the king's name sealed with it. The first Irish chancellor was Ralph Neville, bishop of Chichester and chancellor of England, who was granted the Irish *chancery for life in 1232. The office was subsequently held by bishops and priors of the Hospital of St John of Jerusalem in Ireland, as well as by administrators. The chancellor was the most senior member of the Irish *council, frequently travelling around the country with the *justiciar and taking part in military operations. He was paid an annual fee at the Irish exchequer and also received the money paid for the issue of letters under the great seal, out of which he had to maintain a staff of clerks. In 1395 this variable amount was replaced by an increase in his yearly fee.

With the growth of the court of chancery (see COURTS OF LAW) from the 16th century, the judicial functions of the chancellor (now generally referred to as lord chancellor) became more important. But the holder of the office remained a central figure in the Irish executive. He presided over the Irish *privy council when the chief governor was out of Dublin, and was frequently chosen as a *lord justice. Indeed chancellors, as long-term office holders, often had more experience in government than the chief governors. Furthermore they enjoyed considerable patronage in the courts and locally over *justices of the peace and *sheriffs, and hence over elections.

Following the Act of *Union the chancellor lost one important function, that of presiding over meetings of the House of *Lords. Thereafter the office became primarily a legal one, though holders left office on changes of government. In 1922 the functions of the lord chancellor passed to the chief justice of the Irish Free State.

PhC/HM

chancery, the secretariat of the Dublin government which issued letters and orders in the king's name, authenticated by the Irish great seal. The Irish chancery was established in 1232; before this, official documents had been authenticated by the *justiciar's personal seal. The chancery issued letters patent, which were notifications of appointments, grants, and other matters of general interest, and letters close, addressed to individuals or groups of people, and mostly containing orders and instructions. The two types of letter were differentiated by the manner in which the seal was attached, letters patent having a seal hanging from a cord or strip of parchment at the base of the document, while the seal on letters close was attached after the letter was rolled up and had to be broken before the document could be read. Copies of outgoing letters were kept in the *patent and close rolls. The chancery also kept files of warrants authorizing the issue of letters under the great seal, and *inquisitions and other documents sent in by officials in response to chancery orders.

In addition to the *chancellor, the officials of the chancery included the keeper of the rolls, responsible for the custody of the records, and the clerk of the hanaper, who received and accounted for fees paid for sealing documents with the great seal. There were frequent complaints about understaffing and the incompetence of the clerks. Several attempts at reform and reorganization were made but these met with little success. The lack of professionalism in the Irish chancery has been seen as one reason why it did not, like the English chancery, evolve as a court of equity in the 15th century. The chancery did not have any fixed location, but travelled around the country with the justiciar. An attempt in 1395 to provide a permanent base in Dublin was ineffective.

In 1534 chancery at length began an equity jurisdiction in line with its English counterpart. This proved popular. Not only were its procedures quicker than the Irish common law courts, where impartial verdicts were difficult to obtain from juries, but also its arbitration system suited *brehon law cases emanating from newly incorporated Gaelic lordships.

In the 18th century much chancery work concerned inheritance, especially trusts which were not recognized in common law. In the early 19th century it became increasingly involved in dealing with bankrupt landlords: by 1844 receivers appointed by chancery were having to administer 874 Irish estates. The *Encumbered Estates Act of 1849 empowered three commissioners of the court to order land sales.

In the 1850s the court was reformed and in 1878 it became one of the five divisions of the Supreme Court (see COURTS OF LAW). PhC/HM

Charitable Bequests Act (1844). Like the increased *Maynooth Grant, this was part of the programme of reforms by which *Peel's government hoped to detach moderate Catholics from *repeal. It sought to facilitate legacies for Catholic religious or charitable purposes, previously subject to control by an overwhelmingly Protestant board with sweeping powers. Three Catholic bishops, led by Daniel *Murray, accepted places on the new supervisory board. They came under attack from *MacHale and others, who objected to a continued prohibition of legacies to religious orders, to the invalidation of bequests made less than three months before death, and to what they claimed was potential interference in church discipline. *O'Connell, after some hesitation, supported MacHale. The dispute was a shorter-lived, though quite bitter, demonstration of the same division within the clergy, between an accommodationist minority, and a politically militant majority, that was revealed in the controversies over *national education and the *Queen's Colleges.

charity. Until the mid-18th century the provision of charity was largely restricted to private almsgiving. Increasingly, however, organized charity became more common, reaching its apogee in the 19th century when literally hundreds of charitable organizations were established, though many remained in existence for only a few years.

Charitable provision represented not simply an expression of compassion, but also the discharge of a religious obligation and, increasingly, an attempt to neutralize the perceived threat to society posed by rising levels of poverty and destitution. By preventing poor people from falling into destitution, and hence perhaps into criminality, society might be protected and law and order preserved. Individual charity was rarely indiscriminate, and organized charity never. A clear distinction was made between the deserving and undeserving poor: the former, such as the elderly, the long-term sick and disabled, and widows with children, were regarded as appropriate recipients of aid; the latter, those judged to be able but unwilling to work, required punishment rather than assistance. Some of the earliest charitable endeavours were the establishment of *hospitals for the sick poor, including Steevens hospital (1733), Mercer's hospital (1734), and the Lying-in hospital (1745), all in Dublin. Charities generally targeted particular groups, often those perceived as being most vulnerable, and most likely to benefit from assistance. Thus from the late 18th century a number of charities were established in the cities of Dublin and Cork to help young women, including unmarried mothers, who, it was feared, might otherwise turn to *prostitution.

Many, though not all, charities aimed to assist the adherents of a particular religion, with Catholic charities catering for Catholics, and Protestant charities for Protestants. Religious divisions sometimes prompted competition between charities, most notably in relation to the care of children. Women were particularly active in charity work, both on an individual and organizational level. During the 19th century a large number of charities were established and run by middle-class women to aid poor women and children. Charity was not simply a province of the rich. The generosity of the poorer classes towards each other caused frequent comment.

Irish people continue to give generously to charities, particularly those aimed at the Third World. This generosity has been linked to Ireland's experience of *famine. It must also be seen as reflecting the central place which the Catholic church still holds in Irish society.

See also POOR RELIEF.

Jordan, A., *Who Cared: Charity in Victorian and Edwardian Belfast* (c.1992)

Luddy, M., *Women and Philanthropy in Nineteenth-Century Ireland* (1994)

VC

charity schools on the English and Welsh model were a product of the movement for the reform of religion and manners that was a conspicuous feature of the *Church of Ireland in the late 17th and early 18th centuries. These small schools were sponsored by individual *landlords and philanthropists, by clergy, *parish vestries, and municipalities. Reports cite nineteen charity schools in 1712 and by the 1720s there were several hundred. A society to propagate them was founded, but never played the significant role of the SPCK (Society for the Promotion of Christian Knowledge) in Great Britain.

The schools gave priority to nurturing the children of the Protestant poor in church formularies and basic literacy, and sometimes (helped by donations of money and equipment from the *Linen Board) in aspects of linen production. A leading advocate was the Co. Sligo clergyman Edward Nicholson, who (1712) described charity schools as giving preference to orphans and 'after the poor children of Protestants are taken in we fill with poor children of Papists'.

A shift towards a policy of proselytization developed in the 1720s (culminating in the state-supported *charter schools) as both church and state became aware that despite the *penal laws popery survived and showed signs of resurgence. KM

Charlemont, James Caulfeild, 1st earl of (1728–99), *patriot leader. An ancestor, Captain Toby Caulfeild, came to Ireland with *Essex, and the title derived from a fort erected by *Mountjoy on the river Blackwater (Co. Armagh). The 1st earl was a connoisseur of the arts, overstretching his income to build Charlemont House on Rutland (now Parnell) Square, Dublin, and a 'Casino' in the grounds of his villa at Merino, north of the city. In politics he was a classic aristocratic *Whig, combining an inflexible commitment to public virtue and the defence of Ireland's constitutional rights with a concern for social hierarchy and a dread of popular disorder. He was elected commander-in-chief of the *Volunteers in July 1780, but once legislative independence was achieved sought to discourage radicalism within the movement, and in particular to curb the influence of Bishop *Hervey. He opposed the *Catholic Relief Acts of 1792 and 1793, but was apparently reconciled to emancipation before his death.

charter schools, so called from the charter of George II (6 Feb. 1734) by which the Incorporated Society in Dublin for Promoting English Protestant Schools in Ireland was established. It was specified that 'the children of the Popish and other poor natives' were to be instructed in the English tongue and the formularies of the established Church of Ireland. From the first the children of the Catholic poor had priority. Boys and girls from 6 years of age were boarded (usually in schools remote from their families) and prepared for work in farming, the linen trade, and domestic service, following which they were apprenticed to Protestant masters. Funding came from crown grants, parliamentary subsidies (totalling over £1 million by 1824), and a 'corresponding society' in England. The scheme was intended to attract landlords, who generally gave 2 acres in perpetuity, with further acreage at a favourable rent, and contributed to the cost of building. There were never more than 60 or so schools in existence at any one time, some of their pupils coming from three provincial nurseries and a nursery in Dublin. Masters and mistresses fed and clothed the children according to the society's rates. A per capita sum was levied from masters in respect of the children's work, which led to severe exploitation. A series of private and public inquiries, culminating in the disclosures of the Irish Education Inquiry of 1825, revealed extensive cruelty and neglect, and shortly afterwards state support was withdrawn. KM

Chartism, British working-class movement, named from the People's Charter (1838), a manifesto demanding universal suffrage, secret ballot, and other radical reforms. Following the rejection of reform petitions endorsed by Chartist conventions in 1839 and 1842, the movement revived with the recession of 1847, but lost momentum after a huge reform petition, backed by a mass rally on Kennington Common, London (11 Apr. 1848), had failed to overawe the government.

Individual Irishmen, notably Feargus *O'Connor and James Bronterre O'Brien (1804–64), a Longford-born political journalist, were prominent among the movement's leaders. Chartism was, however, strongly opposed both by *O'Connell and by the Catholic clergy. Patrick O'Higgins (1790–1854), a Dublin woollen merchant, established a Chartist association in Dublin (1839), and a more successful though still limited Irish Universal Suffrage Association (1841). In England there were occasional violent clashes between Chartists and Irish supporters of O'Connell, but recent studies insist that there was nevertheless significant rank and file support for Chartism among Irish immigrants to Great Britain.

*Young Ireland was initially cool towards Chartist radicalism. From March 1848, following the eruption of revolution throughout continental Europe and the conversion of *Lalor, *Mitchel, and others to progressive social policies, Chartists and *Irish Confederation members in Great Britain began to co-operate closely. After the rejection of the third Chartist petition and the transportation of Mitchel, militants in both movements laid plans for co-ordinated insurrectionary action. Government responded with troop deployments and widespread arrests, but in the event faced only sporadic rioting in some northern English centres.

chemical industry. The most significant concentration of chemical manufacturing activity in Ireland during the 18th and 19th centuries was oriented towards supplying the *linen industry with chemicals for finishing and bleaching. In *Cork the manufacture of gunpowder at Ballincollig from the late 18th century down to the early 1900s was an important industry. The manure and fertilizer industry was also important in both Cork and *Dublin. There were a number of soap factories in Dublin and *Belfast, and from the mid-1890s explosives were made in Arklow. AB

Chichester, Sir Arthur (1563–1625), created Lord Belfast 1613, founder of the *Donegall family. A younger son of a minor Devon landowner, Chichester came to Ireland as a professional soldier during the *Nine Years War. As governor of Carrickfergus, he implemented the scorched earth policy in a ferocious raid on east Tyrone in 1601. In 1603 he was granted Belfast Castle and surrounding lands. To this was later added further lands in Antrim and Down and the peninsula of Inishowen in Co. Donegal. As lord deputy (1605–15), Chichester declared the Ulster Irish free from their lords, promoted the common law with regular *assize circuits, and established freeholders. Cahir *O'Doherty's revolt meant that his original *Ulster plantation plan to consolidate the freeholders and reward the military servitors for their wartime services was overtaken by more radical schemes. Elsewhere Chichester experimented with transplantation, shifting the Grahams from the Scots borders to Roscommon and attempting to move the O'Mores from the midlands to Kerry.

Winning hearts and minds was more difficult. Chichester banished Catholic priests, launched the *mandates, and used the court of *Castle Chamber against recalcitrant leaders. He had the Book of *Common Prayer translated into Irish (1608). Bishop *O'Devany was executed as an example, but the intended showdown with Catholics in the 1613–15 parliament proved more of a stand-off. Chichester's imposing tomb in Carrickfergus church disguises a lifelong struggle with debt accumulated in public service and in the attempted development of his hastily acquired Irish estates. HM

chief secretary. The office of chief secretary originated in the 17th century when the holder acted as personal assistant to the lord lieutenant or lord deputy. By the 18th century it had developed into one of the principal offices of state in Ireland, and by the later part of the 19th century it carried far more political weight than that of lord lieutenant. The chief secretary acted as the main exponent of government policy in the Irish house of commons, and subsequently at Westminster, and also supervised the running of the chief secretary's office, the hub from which the spokes of government radiated. As government interventionism increased over the course of the 19th century so the responsibilities of the chief secretary grew. By the end of the century he was answerable to parliament for 29 government departments, some of which, such as the *Local Government Board and the *Congested Districts Board, were in practice autonomous. Generally filled from the junior ranks of English politicians, the office was a notoriously stressful one, combining a heavy workload and much travelling. But if some chief secretaries such as Thomas Pelham (1795–8) or Sir Michael Hicks Beach (1886–7) buckled under the strain, others, like Robert *Peel and Arthur *Balfour, emerged with their career prospects enhanced and their reputations firmly established. VC

childbirth. Until the 17th century childbirth was in the hands of female midwives, who had usually learned their skills informally. In Ireland the midwife was often a 'handy woman' (*bean chabhartha*). As well as attending births, such women also sometimes worked as healers, in which role they commanded considerable respect. But, with the invention of forceps in the 17th century, male surgeons, who had a monopoly of the use of surgical instruments, came to play a larger role in childbirth. By the late 18th century these male midwives had turned a traditional female craft into a male profession.

This transformation can be traced in some detail in Ireland. The first original work in English on midwifery was published in 1671 by James Wolveridge, a graduate of Trinity College, Dublin, then working in Cork. It was addressed to women. But when Sir Fielding Ould (1710–89), a leading Dublin male midwife, published another influential text in 1742, it was addressed to male surgeons and argued that surgeons should routinely attend births.

The Irish College of Physicians had been given the power, under its 1692 charter, to license midwives, but it was a power the college seldom exercised as physicians considered midwifery beneath them. So the initiative was taken by surgeons. The *Rotunda hospital was founded in 1745 by Bartholomew Mosse (1712–59), a surgeon, and in 1774 the master of the hospital began to give lectures for male medical students and female midwives. In 1785 the first chair of midwifery in Ireland was established by the new Irish College of Surgeons and in the same year *grand juries were empowered to pay for the training of female midwives at the Rotunda.

A maternity hospital was opened in Belfast in 1793, one in Cork in 1798, and two more in Dublin: the Coombe in 1829, and the National Maternity hospital, Holles Street, in 1894. After 1851, with the expansion of the dispensary system, county authorities sent midwives attached to dispensaries to Dublin for training at the Rotunda or Coombe hospitals.

Legislation in 1917 prohibited unqualified 'handy women' from practising as midwives and established a central board to regulate training. This system was further tightened in 1931 and by the mid-1930s it was claimed that only in Mayo did 'handy women' still flourish.

Campbell Ross, I. (ed.), *Public Virtue, Public Love: The Early Years of the Dublin Lying-in Hospital, the Rotunda* (1986)

Donnison, J., *Midwives and Medical Men: A History of the Struggle for the Control of Childbirth* (2nd edn., 1988)

Farmar, T., *Holles Street, 1894–1994: The National Maternity Hospital: A Centenary History* (1994)

ELM

Childers, Erskine (1870–1922), English-born writer and republican. Despite a career in the British civil service and armed forces, Childers became an Irish *home ruler in 1908. In aid of the home rule cause he used his yacht, the *Asgard*, to arm the *Irish Volunteers in the *Howth gun-running. He became increasingly republican and in 1919 he was appointed director of publicity for the *Irish Republican Army. He was elected to the *Dáil in 1921 and became its minister for propaganda. He was first secretary to the Irish delegation in the negotiations leading up to the *Anglo-Irish treaty, which he opposed. Thoroughly disliked by the Free State government he became one of the first republicans to be executed during the *Irish Civil War. JA

children. In Ireland the 19th and 20th centuries saw a growing perception of children as both a state resource and a group in need of legal protection. The Children Act of 1908 was the culmination of over three-quarters of a century's attempts to regulate the lives of children by gradually outlawing most full-time child labour, by sending young offenders (including vagrants, or homeless children) to *reformatories or industrial schools, by setting out conditions under which children could be removed from parents or guardians, by acts for the prevention of cruelty to children in the 1880s and 1890s, and by the enforcement of compulsory primary education on all children from 1892. These acts were strengthened by further legislation in the 20th century.

Children had a precarious grip on life, and infant mortality rates remained high until the middle of the 20th century, particularly in cities. The major childhood killer was diarrhoea, particularly in the first year of life. After that, the childhood diseases of diphtheria, scarlet fever, and whooping cough could be fatal, and poor nutrition could cause permanent disability. Children with rickets were a common sight in the poorer parts of towns and cities up to the post-war period, when the introduction of comprehensive new health care systems in both jurisdictions reduced infant and child mortality considerably. Universal family allowances, also called children's allowances (introduced in 1944 in independent Ireland, 1945 in Northern Ireland), eased the burden of subsistence for working-class parents.

'Illegitimate' children had, up to the 1950s, a much higher death rate than the 'legitimate'. Although their survival rates improved greatly with the early 19th-century development of orphanages and *workhouses to replace the lethal *foundling hospitals, their lives in institutional care were often grim, and developments in government-subsidized childcare were slow.

In the early 20th century there are signs that childhood was being thought of in a new way. Catholic bishops' pastorals in the 1920s and 1930s might have advised parents to chastise disobedient teenagers, but they also urged parents not to be 'austere' or 'aloof', and to tolerate the noise and disorder of their children's playing. Numerous accounts tell us that Santa Claus started coming to many (though not all) Irish children, urban and rural, middle class and working class, in places as far apart as the Blasket Islands and Dublin city, as early as the 1920s. His appearance, spontaneously adopted by parents themselves, was in sharp contrast to the massive commercialization of children's leisure that has occurred since the 1960s. CC

cholera, a disease spread via contaminated water or food, had been endemic in Bengal for centuries; it reached Europe in the 1820s due to improved transport and communication. Ireland experienced four major cholera epidemics: in 1832–3, 1848–50, 1853–4, and 1866–7. In the early 1830s cities and towns, many of which had poor water and sewage facilities, were most seriously affected. But the worst epidemic occurred during the *Great Famine, when a population already weakened by starvation and fever rapidly succumbed to this new disease. While around 25,000 died from cholera in 1832–3, perhaps as many as 35,000 died in 1848–50. Irish emigrants were also blamed for spreading cholera in both Britain and the United States.

Contagion (person-to-person) theories vied with miasma (airborne) theories to explain the spread of the disease and it was not until the work of John Snow in the 1850s and Robert Koch in the 1880s that the true mechanisms of dissemination were identified. This led to sanitary reforms which effectively eliminated cholera as a serious medical threat in Ireland before 1900. ELM

Christ Church cathedral, the cathedral church of the archdiocese of Dublin and *Glendalough. A cathedral has existed on this site since *c.*1028 when the Norse king of Dublin, Sitric Silkbeard, co-founded the cathedral of the Holy Trinity with Bishop Dúnán of Dublin. Shortly after the *Anglo-Norman invasion the construction of a new cathedral was commenced, building work starting at the east end with a new choir and transepts over a crypt. The nave was probably completed shortly after 1234. Detailing within the building exhibits parallels with contemporary buildings in the Severn valley in England, suggesting the involvement of masons from that area in the cathedral's construction. An *Augustinian priory was established at the cathedral in 1163 and domestic buildings belonging to the priory were erected to the south of the cathedral during the 13th century.

Various additions were made to the cathedral during the 14th century, including the extension of the choir and the addition of the chapel of Great St Mary. In 1562 the nave vaults collapsed, causing extensive damage to the south side of the building. Although repaired almost immediately, the fabric of the cathedral suffered from much neglect in ensuing centuries. The present building is largely Gothic revival work, dating from extensive 'restoration' carried out during 1871–8 by George Edmund Street.

As the principal church of the *Old English colony in Ireland Christ Church played an important role in the civic life of the city. Until the 16th century *lords deputy took their oath of office in the cathedral, and it was here that Lambert *Simnel was crowned in 1487. In 1608 law courts were established over the semi-ruined priory buildings to the south of the cathedral buildings. RM

Christian Brothers, the Irish Catholic lay teaching order founded by Edmund Rice (1762–1844), who opened a school for poor boys in Waterford in 1802, followed shortly by schools in other Irish towns. In 1820 his community was confirmed by papal brief as the 'Institute of the Brothers of the Christian Schools of Ireland', Rice being elected first superior-general, and its constitution owing much to that of the 17th-century De La Salle order. Eventually schools were founded in England, Australia, and elsewhere.

Curriculum and school routine were imbued with religious doctrine and observance, which inhibited the order from connection with the *national school system. At the instigation of Daniel *Murray, the politically moderate archbishop of Dublin, several schools entered the system for a few years, only to withdraw in 1836. Despite correspondence between government, the national commissioners, and the order over decades, the commissioners failed to find a way of modifying their rules to accommodate the ethos of the Christian Brothers' schools, which entered the system only after political independence.

The schools were strongly nationalist in tone (*Pearse was a pupil), and played a major part in the revival of the Irish language and in the education of many of the leaders of the independence movement and of post-independence Ireland. KM

Christianization. The conversion of the Irish to Christianity was a process and not an event. Christian communities already existed in 431 when their first bishop, *Palladius, was papally appointed. *Patrick worked apparently in a pagan environment later in the 5th century. His sphere of activity was Ireland's northern half; that of Palladius, it seems, was Leinster. Tradition asserts the pre-Patrician status of Ailbe, Déclán, Ciarán, and Ibar in Munster and south Leinster, but the chronology of these saints is obscure.

Patrick addressed himself to the whole spectrum of the social hierarchy, referring in his *Confession* to converts among slaves and among the sons and daughters of kings. But there is no evidence for evangelism other than in the person of Patrick. The early church did not actively evangelize, and the first phase of Christianization must be put down to the influence of immigrants from *Roman Britain and to the prestige of imperial institutions. There were numerous lines of communication: the presence of Irish colonists in south *Wales and Cornwall in the 5th and 6th centuries is attested by inscriptions in ogam (itself based on the Latin alphabet), and many are Christian in character. No doubt there were contacts with Gaul.

With the exception of Patrick's testimony the conversion of the Irish is unsupported by documentation. Carved crosses based on the *chi-rho* (the first letters of the Greek name for Christ) which occur in the south-west suggest 6th-century influence from Britain or Gaul. A small shrine from Clonmore, Co. Armagh, and that preserved at Bobbio in northern Italy are the oldest examples of native Christian metalwork; made *c.*680, they are classical in form but decorated with patterns of pre-Christian ancestry. Some Irish churches may have been deliberately sited close to pre-Christian centres, as Armagh and Baslick beside *Emain Macha and *Crúachain respectively. Some Irish saints—pre-eminently *Brigid—appear to be old deities euhemerized. *'Holy wells' throughout Ireland were dedicated to the saints but may have had a prior significance. Festivals and the feasts of the church exhibit, in the vernacular tradition, the assimilation of pre-Christian practices.

As early as the 6th century Christianity had been embraced by the Irish learned classes—the practitioners in the fields of genealogy, poetry, *senchas* (history), and law, and contemporary canons issued by the church are no longer thought to indicate the continued coexistence of paganism. Early Latin loanwords in Old Irish denote the institutions, personnel and material accoutrements of the Church. There is thus cumulative evidence to suggest that Christianity was adopted by the Irish with relative ease—bearing out a tradition (which is no more than that) that conversion was achieved without martyrdom.

Bieler, L., 'The Christianization of the Insular Celts during the Sub-Roman Period and its Repercussions on the Continent', *Celtica*, 8 (1968)

CB

Church Education Society, formed in 1839 by members of the *Church of Ireland as a preferred option to the *national schools. The church was bitterly divided on the issue, Archbishop *Whately being a national schools commissioner, while Archbishop *Beresford and eleven other bishops supported the society, largely through diocesan education societies. By 1849 the society claimed 1,868 schools and 111,877 pupils, and in 1855 took over the *Kildare Place *teacher-training institution. Following the disendowment and *disestablishment of the church in 1870 the society's fortunes steeply declined. KM

Churchill, Lord Randolph (1849–94). A leader of the 'Fourth Party' group of radical MPs within the British Tory Party, Churchill was secretary of state for India 1885–6, chancellor of the exchequer and leader of the House 1886. A volatile, brilliant populist whose career was shaped chiefly by personal and political opportunism, Churchill's Irish interests developed during the viceroyalty (1876–80) of his father, the 6th duke of Marlborough, and embraced both reaction and conciliation. Thus he opposed the compensation for disturbance bill 1880, but supported extension of the Irish franchise 1884, and was instrumental in effecting the short-lived Parnellite–Tory understanding of 1885. In 1886, however, he virulently opposed *home rule and recklessly encouraged Ulster *Orange extremism in support of the Union; a stance concisely expressed in his statement that against home rule 'Ulster will fight, and Ulster will be right.' JL

Churchill, Winston S. (1874–1965), British statesman, prime minister 1940–5 and 1951–5. Some of Churchill's earliest memories were of Dublin where his grandfather, the duke of Marlborough, was viceroy, with his father, Lord Randolph *Churchill, as private secretary. By the time of the third *home rule bill, Churchill was 1st lord of the admiralty in *Asquith's government. In 1912, perhaps prompted by his father's views in 1886, he joined *Lloyd George in advocating some kind of Ulster exclusion. Even so, his advocacy of home rule provoked strong unionist protests when he visited Belfast in February 1912. A speech at Bradford on 14 March 1914, in which he accused *Carson of engaging in a treasonable conspiracy, heightened tension just days before the *Curragh incident. As secretary of state for war in Lloyd George's government, he supported the formation of the *'Black and Tans' and the *Ulster Special Constabulary, arguing for strong measures against *Sinn Féin. He was a member of the British negotiating team during the negotiation of the *Anglo-Irish treaty, coming to respect Michael *Collins. He criticized the return of the *treaty ports in 1938 as part of the policy of appeasement. In June 1940 his government briefly flirted with the idea of enticing de *Valera to enter the *Second World War on the promise of unity, but he came to resent Ireland's *neutral stance. His radio broadcast of 13 May 1945, in which he extolled the loyalty and friendship of Northern Ireland while accusing de Valera's government of frolicking with the Germans and Japanese, was bitterly resented. TGF

church in medieval Ireland. In 431 the chronicler Prosper of Aquitaine recorded the papally backed mission of Bishop *Palladius to the 'Irish believing in Christ'. This was probably directed to a Christian community which had developed in the east and south-east of the country through slave and trading links with *Roman Britain and contact with Irish colonies in *Wales. Toponomy indicates the presence of other early missionaries at Dunshaughlin (*Domnach Sechnaill*, the church of Secundinus) and Kilashee (*Cell Ausaile*, the church of Auxilius) in Leinster.

The best known of these missionaries is the Roman-Briton *Patrick who operated among the pagan population around *Dún dá Lethglais* (Downpatrick) in the north-east in the mid-5th century (though earlier and later dates and locations cannot be ruled out). His cult, based on his *Confession* and *Letter to Coroticus*, was promoted by the Armagh church from the 7th century to promote its claims to primacy over the other Irish churches.

The spread of Christianity in 5th- and 6th-century Ireland was slow and sporadic but by the 7th century the church was well established and had adapted to its environment. A significant development was the transition from an organization based on territorial dioceses governed by bishops to one in which networks of monasteries (*paruchiae*) were the norm and in which abbots were the pre-eminent administrators. This unusual state of affairs was commented on by *Bede but there is considerable debate as to its extent. Early Irish *monasticism owed much to British influence and the earliest Irish founders received their initial formation in monasteries such as that of St Ninian at *Candida Casa* at Whitern (modern Scotland) or particularly that of St David at Menevia (Wales).

The high standard of learning, calligraphy, metalwork, and sculpture which characterized the Irish *monastic schools was much commented on by contemporaries. Irish monks in Ireland and on the Continent showed a command of *Latin composition, *biblical exegesis, and computing that had few parallels, even if their views sometimes clashed with contemporary continental scholarship. The practice of *peregrinatio* or exile for the sake of the gospel was another feature of this period; notable *peregrini* included *Columbanus (d. 615) in Gaul, Switzerland, and Italy, Killian (d. 689) in Germany, and Donatus (d. 876) in Italy, and these (and many others) disseminated Irish ideas and practice throughout Europe (see MONASTERIES, IRISH, IN CONTINENTAL EUROPE). A particularly important innovation were the *penitentials or confessors' manuals which were composed from the 6th century onwards and which greatly influenced the development of confession and spiritual direction in the church.

By the 8th century the Irish church was respected, powerful, and wealthy. As well as controlling church life, monasteries dominated the economy, played a prominent part in secular politics, and were the most important patrons of all branches of the arts. With this increase in prestige came a decline in fervour; contemporary evidence indicates that in many monasteries the abbacy and other major offices had become hereditary. Tension over rights and property sometimes erupted into pitched battles between communities. The *Céile Dé reform movement which emerged in the late 8th century was largely a reaction to this decadence. Its main centres were the monasteries of Finglas and Tallaght near Dublin.

In 795 the annals record the first *Viking attack on Ireland. Though the Vikings had an initially disruptive effect on church life their impact was not as devastating as monastic chroniclers or later historians have held and has undergone serious revision in recent historiography. From 841 they began to establish permanent bases in Ireland which developed into significant settlements at *Dublin, Wexford, *Waterford, *Cork, and *Limerick. Through trade links and intermarriage they gradually became Christian and by *c.*1028 a bishopric was established at Dublin. These Norse-Irish bishops had strong links with England and some of the first bishops of Dublin, Limerick, and Waterford were consecrated by the archbishop of *Canterbury and acknowledged his primacy. Other contacts with England and the Continent during the 11th and 12th centuries fostered a reform movement (see TWELFTH-CENTURY REFORM) which culminated in 1152 at the Synod of *Kells when metropolitan sees were erected at Armagh, Dublin, Tuam, and Cashel and suffragan dioceses were established. The movement, whose chief promoter was St *Malachy, also introduced the *Cistercian monks (1142) and Arroasian *Augustinian canons and attempted to reform marital and sexual mores.

The Anglo-Norman presence after 1169 led to an Anglicization of the episcopate and by the end of the 15th century ten of the wealthier sees were controlled by the Anglo-Irish, thirteen were normally held by Gaelic bishops, with the remaining nine fluctuating between the two groups or held by absentees. A similar process in the monasteries led to tension between the Gaelic and Anglo-Irish Cistercians (see MELLIFONT). In the 13th century the four orders of mendicant friars (*Franciscan, *Dominican, *Augustinian, and *Carmelite) were introduced and by 1340 had founded 86 friaries. These were also riven by racial tension and all four were controlled by English or Anglo-Irish superiors until the emergence of the *Observant movement among the Gaelic friars in the 15th century.

The Irish church in the century before the *Reformation has traditionally been seen as presenting a bleak picture: racial antipathy was rife, conventual life had collapsed in most Cistercian and Augustinian monasteries, and hereditary succession to church office was common in Gaelic areas. Other developments, however, suggest a more positive image. Between 1400 and 1508 90 new friaries were founded, mostly in Gaelic areas, and it was these friars, particularly the Observant Franciscans, who were recognized as the preachers, confessors, and ascetics of the period. In the *Pale, where the structure of diocesan synods and episcopal visitation was better organized, growing lay piety found expression in the establishment of chantries and guilds and in devotions like the Jesus mass. In Gaelic Ireland this need was met by the growth of the *Franciscan Third Order and the widespread translation of continental devotional texts into Irish.

Corish, P., *The Irish Catholic Experience: A Historical Survey* (1985)

Watt, J., *The Church in Medieval Ireland* (1972)

CNÓC

Church of Ireland, the largest Protestant church in Ireland. From 1537 to 1870 it was the established state church, governed by the English monarch. Since *disestablishment in 1870, it has been an independent self-governing church, a member of the worldwide Anglican communion.

In theory, the Act of *Supremacy of 1537 meant that the Church of Ireland 'took over' the pre-*Reformation church structure and subjected it to royal control. In practice the transition from pre-Reformation to reformed church was much more complicated, for two reasons. First, the authority of the king in the 16th century was limited to the *Pale and the Anglo-Irish areas of the country. In the Gaelic areas, far away from Dublin, the papal church continued for most of the 16th century uninterrupted. Second, even within the Church of Ireland, formal adherence to royal supremacy was, for many clergy and laity, perfectly compatible with thoroughly traditional Catholic religious practices and beliefs. Anglo-Irish Catholic 'survivalism', both within and outside the Church of Ireland, was a very powerful conservative religious force in the 16th century. Equally, the power of church and state to impose uniformity through civil and ecclesiastical discipline was limited by the ineffectiveness of legal structures and the unwillingness of the English authorities to sanction rigorous enforcement for fear of alienating the local population. Clear distinctions between the Church of Ireland and the Catholic church are as a result difficult to formulate. Even the Twelve Articles of 1567—the first formulation of the church's faith—were general and inclusive, much less detailed than the English Thirty-Nine Articles.

This confused identity of the Church of Ireland began to change in the reigns of Elizabeth (1558–1603) and James (1603–25). First there was the exodus of Anglo-Irish from the established church: increasingly in the 1570s and 1580s they opted for *recusancy, refusing to attend official services and instead identifying with the *Counter-Reformation Catholic church. At the same time English leaders of the Church of Ireland, most notably Archbishop Adam *Loftus of Dublin, sought to ensure that the church adopted a more firmly Protestant theological position. The fruits of this increasing confessionalization were evident in the early 17th century, when the Church of Ireland episcopate was extended to every diocese in Ireland, and its ministry transformed by the influx of committed Protestant clergy from England and Scotland, reinforced by ordinands trained in *Trinity College, Dublin. Thus in 1575, out of fifteen royally appointed bishops, three were English and the rest native Irish or Anglo-Irish; by 1603, six were English-born and ten Irish or Anglo-Irish; by 1625 there were fifteen English bishops, five Scots, and only three native Irish or Anglo-Irish. Two signs of the new self-awareness were the 104 articles of religion adopted by the Irish *convocation in 1615, which extended and amended the English Thirty-Nine Articles in a more distinctively Calvinist direction, and the historical work of James *Ussher, which sought to establish the non-Roman character of the *Celtic Irish church. The distinctive independent polity which the Church of Ireland created in the first three decades of the 17th century enabled it to employ *puritans from England and *Presbyterians from Scotland who could not be accommodated by their national churches.

The creation of a firmly Protestant Church of Ireland was not paralleled by the conversion of the Irish population. Its pastorate concentrated upon the English and Scottish settlers and officials, to the exclusion of native Irish and Anglo-Irish parishes and dioceses. The influx of English clergy confirmed this trend towards an Anglicized church. Only in exceptional cases, such as that of William *Bedell, did Church of Ireland ministers embrace the idea of preaching Protestantism to the Irish people in their own language. The church, however, did not abandon the goal of spreading Protestantism: the church leaders were firmly committed to the imposition of conformity throughout Ireland by the exercise of the Act of *Uniformity. The problem (as they saw it) was that the state repeatedly proved unwilling to use to the full the machinery of the civil law to force Catholic recusants to attend church.

From 1633, under the direction of Lord Deputy *Wentworth, Archbishop Laud of Canterbury, and Bishop *Bramhall of Derry, there was a dual shift of policy. First, attention shifted from penalizing recusants to reforming the church itself. Bramhall and Wentworth made the perfectly valid point that the church was severely handicapped by a shortage of resources: ministers were poorly trained, benefices impoverished, churches ruined, and church lands detained by laymen. Using the powers of the government and of the *High Commission to the full, they set about restoring the church's fortunes. Second, they sought to curb the tendency within the Church of Ireland towards independence: in convocation in 1634 the Irish church was made to adopt the Thirty-Nine Articles, together with stricter disciplinary canons, designed to exclude puritans and Presbyterians from its ministry. This was followed by a purge of nonconformist clergy in the Presbyterian strongholds in Ulster.

The fall of Wentworth in 1640–1, and the start of the *Confederate War, began a period of turmoil and uncertainty. English Protestant clergy were a particular target of the native Irish in the *rising of 1641: some were murdered, and many forced to flee. Following the victory of the English parliamentary forces, the Church of Ireland, though not legally disestablished, was deprived of the marks of establishment. The *Cromwellian regime prohibited the use of the Book of

*Common Prayer, substituting the more puritan Directory of Worship, and took control of the two Dublin cathedrals and Trinity College. While some clergy went into exile or retirement, many served in the rather ill-defined state church thus created. Time did not, however, allow for the fulfilment of ambitious, perhaps unrealistic, plans for educational development, nor for the pastoral revitalization that was intended to result from a wide-ranging survey of the church carried out during the Interregnum.

The *convention of 1660 included a substantial dissenting element, and a return to episcopacy was not initially to be taken for granted. However, the general mood of conservatism produced by the disorders of the preceding 20 years ensured majority support for the restoration of the pre-1641 establishment. On 27 January 1661 twelve bishops were consecrated to fill vacancies caused by death or deprivation.

Under the initial leadership of John Bramhall, archbishop of Armagh 1661–3, the convocation of 1661–6 addressed major tasks of reconstruction, including the disciplining or removal of dissenting ministers who had taken office in the church, particularly in the north, during the Commonwealth. The 1666 Act of *Uniformity strengthened the hands of disciplinary bishops. Absenteeism, plurality, ruined churches, and non-existent *glebes remained part of the picture. But there was also a renewed attention to pastoral care. The preaching and writing of Jeremy *Taylor, bishop of Down and Dromore 1661–7, contributed intellectual activity of the highest order, while others revived an interest in liturgical matters that was a marked feature of the Caroline period. There were daily services in many churches in Dublin and other towns, and eucharistic practice gained fresh emphasis.

Scarcely had the established church settled back into its role than it was to undergo a further period of turbulence as *James II made clear his intention to promote the interests of Catholicism. Having initially extended a wary welcome to him, the Church of Ireland quickly came to understand that its prerogatives were at risk. Although several bishops responded to his summons to attend the *'patriot parliament', the incidence of *non-jurors was negligible, as compared with the situation in England, and some of the church's leaders, including William *King, even envisaged a post-Revolution settlement that would come to terms with dissent.

Such theological compromise was not required, though the church felt anything but secure. The 18th century, commonly perceived as a period of unchallengeable Anglican hegemony, was by no means experienced as such by contemporary church leaders. Certainly, the dangers posed by a supposedly subversive *Toryism among the *high-church clergy had passed by 1714, the Catholics were contained by the *penal laws, and dissent (with its uncomfortably large number of adherents) was severely constrained by the *sacramental test. Furthermore, in prelates such as Hugh *Boulter and George *Stone the interests of church and state seemed finally to have coalesced. Yet throughout the century there were voices that were far from complacent. William King questioned not only the morality of the penal laws, but also their efficacy in promoting religious change. Others who sought more constructive means of strengthening Protestantism included John *Richardson, the advocate of evangelization through Irish, and Henry Maule, bishop of Dromore 1732–44, whose attempts to provide free schooling for the Catholic and Protestant poor laid the foundations for the *charter schools.

Archbishop King and, later in the century, Richard *Woodward, while strenuously defending the *raison d'être* of the established church, castigated those clergy who by their neglect of duty weakened its position, and the wealthy laity who resisted the imposition of *tithes. A century that began with an alarming House of Lords report on the *State of Popery* (1731) drew to a close with equally alarming Catholic pressure for concessions that government sought to assuage by a series of *Catholic Relief Acts.

By the Act of *Union, the churches of England and Ireland were united 'for ever' (in fact, 70 years). But the influence of the Irish episcopate in the British House of Lords was a shadow of what it had been in Dublin, and the diminishing power of the Church of Ireland to influence (and, in particular, to reverse) government policy soon became obvious.

Reform in the early 19th century came from more than one source. William Stuart, archbishop of Armagh 1800–22, and Charles Brodrick, archbishop of Cashel 1801–22, both deplored the inefficiencies that exposed the church to criticism of its privileges, both inside and outside parliament, and zealously sought to remove abuses that inhibited its pastoral mission. The early decades of the 19th century also saw a widespread *evangelical movement, not always espoused by the hierarchy, that sought by preaching and philanthropy to promote religious zeal. Where such commitment extended to the attempted conversion of the Catholic population (see SECOND REFORMATION), the result was to inflame sectarian animosities still further. Yet reform of the church from within was too little and too late to satisfy the demands of parliamentary and other critics. Though achievements were far from negligible, especially where the building of the ubiquitous *'first fruits' churches was concerned, it became increasingly difficult, in the political climate of the age, to defend the scale of the church's endowments when set against its de facto constituency (and, indeed, its performance). The radical policies of the *Whig government of the 1830s (the *Church Temporalities Act, reform of tithes, rejection of the church's demand for control of the new *national schools) initiated an erosion of status that culminated with *disestablishment in 1869.

A much slimmed-down institution emerged from the process, perhaps just in time to meet the challenges posed by the political upheavals that gave birth to the separate jurisdictions of *Northern Ireland and the *Irish Free State. Like other Irish churches since the *partitioning of the island, the Church of Ireland has maintained its pastoral and administrative unity. But while the Representative Church Body is based in Dublin, where also the General Synod usually meets, three-quarters of the church's members (in 1991 279,280 out of a total of 368,467) live in Northern Ireland. Numerical decline in the south and west, discernible long before partition, was hastened by several factors: emigration (or migration north for political reasons), disproportionate losses of young men in the *First World War, and the Roman Catholic church's rules governing the upbringing of the children of mixed marriages (see *NE TEMERE*).

Several generations have grown up in the transformed political, social, and religious environment created by partition. The northern members of the church have found themselves part of what has sometimes appeared to be a beleaguered *unionist majority. The southern members, after a difficult initial period in a Free State that clearly sought to identify itself with Catholic social teaching and Gaelic culture, showed increasing confidence as what is now the *Republic of Ireland became more pluralist.

Ford, A., McGuire, J. I., and Milne, K. (eds.), *As by Law Established: The Church of Ireland since the Reformation* (1995)

Murray, James, et al., 'The Church of Ireland: A Critical Bibliography 1536–1992', *Irish Historical Studies*, 28/112 (1993)

AF/KM

Church Temporalities (Ireland) Act (1833), a major reform imposed by the *Whig government on the *Church of Ireland. It reduced two of the four archbishoprics, Tuam and Cashel, to bishoprics, united 10 of the 20 existing bishoprics to adjacent sees, revoked the right of churchwardens to levy church *cess for the upkeep of ecclesiastical buildings, and permitted tenants on episcopal lands to purchase their holdings at a fixed annual rent. The purchase sums and reserved rents thus arising, along with the income from the suppressed sees, the proceeds of a tax on ecclesiastical livings, a substantial levy on the disproportionately wealthy dioceses of Armagh and Derry, and the income and functions of the Board of *First Fruits, were vested in ecclesiastical commissioners, who were to use them for the building, upkeep, and improvement of churches and other buildings. The act provided for a more efficient and rational allocation of the church's resources, but significantly eroded its status as a self-governing corporation.

cin comocuis, see KINCOGISH.

cinema has been an important part of popular culture in Ireland since the earliest screenings of the Lumière Cinématographe programmes promoted by theatrical entrepreneur Dan Lowrey in April 1896. The success of that first event at the Star of Erin theatre, Dublin, led to further screenings in Cork and Belfast later that year. The earliest Irish films were also shot at this time, including street scenes in Dublin and Belfast, a fire engine en route to a fire, and numerous shots from the train between the two cities. Cinema as curiosity, largely presented in *music halls, continued until the early years of the 20th century when, on 12 August 1908, St George's Hall, High Street, Belfast, became Ireland's first full-time cinema. The famous Volta Cinema in Dublin, with which James Joyce was initially associated, followed shortly after this, in 1909. From that time until the *First World War, the cinema industry expanded across the island, with cinemas being built and existing halls being adapted to show the new medium. By 1916 there were 149 cinemas and halls showing motion pictures. Meanwhile the first fiction films set in Ireland were released, largely through the Kalem Company. Among them was an early adaptation of *Willy Reilly & his Colleen Bawn*, (*c.*1909), a story that was remade by John MacDonagh for the Film Company of Ireland in 1919.

The cinema exhibition industry enjoyed a boom in the second and third decades of the century: by 1930 the number of cinemas, north and south, had risen to 265. However the film production industry remained weak. The number of films made was small and though these frequently had local success they rarely made significant impact on even the British market. With the making of *Man of Aran* by Robert Flaherty, Ireland as a location for 'serious' film-making was established. Set in the *Aran Islands in 1934, this documentary is the most memorable visual record of life on the west coast in that era. At that time there were also a few films made in Northern Ireland, notably by the director and actor Richard Hayward. However, the overriding image of Ireland portrayed in films was not created in Ireland, but in Hollywood, where John Ford won an Oscar for *The Informer* (1935), from Dudley Nichols's adaptation of Liam O'Flaherty's novel of the *Anglo-Irish War. Ford, who claimed Irish descent, included numerous remarkable Irish characters in his films, and was responsible for, arguably, the most famous film set in Ireland, *The Quiet Man* (1952). More insidious, perhaps, were the whimsical portrayals of Ireland in such films as Disney's *Darby O'Gill and the Little People* (1959).

By the time of the coming of sound to cinema in the late 1920s, American films had become the dominant influence on Irish film-goers and would-be film-makers alike. The often lurid view of life portrayed in films gave rise to the disapproval of the Catholic Church and from 1923 films in the Irish Free State were, in common with elsewhere, subject to *censorship. Moral concerns were later reinforced by political ones, when first Chaplin's *The Great Dictator* and then Michael Balcon's *San Demetrio, London* were banned until the end of the *Second World War, in the interests of preserving the country's *neutrality. During this time, British censorship applied to cinemas in Northern Ireland, with the result that films were sometimes freely available one side of the border but banned on the other.

The 1930s also saw a boom in the building of cinemas to profit from the huge popularity of sound films. Construction peaked in the late 1930s when it was clear that 'cinema exhibition' was an industry with a future and cinemas were built in all large and most small towns. Unlike Great Britain, where a duopoly of ownership dominated the industry, the ownership of Irish cinemas was less centralized, with most cinemas owned by local entrepreneurs as family businesses. Decline began in the 1960s, as audiences fell off with the spread of *television into growing numbers of Irish homes. Lack of confidence in the economic future of cinema exhibition discouraged investment. Instead faded picture palaces were closed and demolished, or converted into bingo halls or furniture stores.

It was the ambition of successive governments to encourage the use of Ireland as a location for big-budget films, supported by the film studios built in Ardmore, near Bray, Co. Wicklow, which opened in 1958. Two celebrated documentaries dealing with the Irish struggle for independence, *Mise Eire* (I am Ireland—1959) and *Saoirse?* (Freedom?—1961), both by George Morrison, created a greater awareness of the possibilities of Irish film-making. However, major investment in wholly Irish feature films never really materialized. After over a decade of uncertain financial results and changes of ownership, the studios were bought by Radio Telefis Éireann in 1973; then, after the involvement of John Boorman and substantial capital investment, they became the National Film Studios in 1975. However financial troubles forced them to close again in 1982.

Bob Quinn, a film-maker from the west coast, started making feature films in the mid-1970s—most notably two features in Irish, *Caoineadh Airt Ui Laoire* (1975) and *Poitin* (1977). In Dublin, Kieran Hickey made two influential short features, *Exposure* (1978) and *Criminal Conversation* (1980). With these and films by Cathal Black and Joe Comerford, it was clear that a new film-making movement was underway. This was nurtured by the establishment of Bord Scannan na hÉireann (the Irish Film Board) in 1980. However it was not until the emergence of Neil Jordan with *Angel* (1982), followed by Jim Sheridan with *My Left Foot* (1989), that Irish films made any significant popular impact outside the British Isles. Jordan has made important works in Ireland, Great Britain, and America, including his biopic of *Michael Collins* (1996), which broke Irish box office records. Each of Sheridan's first three films was nominated for Oscars.

Though a few of these new Irish films were widely released across the country, the majority found it difficult to break into a film exhibition industry that was increasingly dominated by the major American companies. This tendency was extended with the arrival of multiplex cinemas encompassing over a dozen screens in a single building. The cementing of the 'popcorn culture' attitude to cinema has been greatly at odds with the approach of most of the films by the new wave of Irish directors, who, largely, are committed to film culture and quasi-political film-making. As a result indigenous Irish films are less seen in their native land than the films of most other European nations.

Rockett, Kevin, *The Irish Filmography: Fiction Films 1896–1996* (1996)

MO

circus entertainment in its modern form came to Ireland in 1784 when Philip Astley, a former soldier and established London showman, opened a riding school and auditorium for equine displays in Dublin. However, performing animals and travelling exhibitions of exotic species had been known at least from the mid-17th century, while roving groups of performers such as acrobats have even older roots. Astley's success, perpetuated by his son, did not immediately lead to a succession of Irish imitators, and it was not until the middle of the 19th century that travelling circuses became popular and common forms of entertainment. Even then Ireland did not develop its own indigenous circuses, but was rather part of a circuit followed by British and foreign shows. In the British Isles as a whole, the star acts tended to be continental in origin. The short heyday of the circus came at the turn of the century. Shows were held not only in tents, but in *theatres and *music halls. A growth in the popularity of other entertainments, including spectator sports, the *cinema, and ultimately *television, has resulted in the decline of the circus. In recent years worries over animal welfare have given rise to some opposition to performances. NG

Cistercians, religious order founded at Cîteaux in 1098. The Cistercians were introduced to Ireland in 1142 by St *Malachy as part of his policy of church reform. From their first monastery at Mellifont in Co. Louth they expanded rapidly, establishing a further 26 houses by the end of the 12th century. This expansion, however, rested on an insecure base as Cistercian life was radically different from preceding forms of Irish *monasticism. Problems created by increasing isolation from the rest of the order, tension between Gaelic and Anglo-Irish monasteries, and lax observance in Gaelic houses culminated in the 'conspiracy of *Mellifont' (1216–28). The Mellifont filiation was broken up and its houses assigned to English, Welsh, and French houses. It was restored in 1274.

By 1228 there were 34 Cistercian monasteries of either Gaelic or Anglo-Irish foundation and the order had reached the peak of its expansion. Financial difficulties caused by speculation on wool prices and the gradual disappearance of the lay brother initiated a period of decline at the end of the 13th century. By the late 15th century, despite attempts at reform, conventual life had collapsed in many of the houses, with only Dublin and Mellifont having sizeable communities. A number of the monasteries were changed into secular colleges at the *Reformation but most were dissolved between 1538 and 1542. A short-lived attempt at restoration was made by Abbot Luke Archer of Holycross in the early 17th century. The order was re-established in Ireland in 1832 with the foundation of Mount Melleray, Co. Waterford. CNÓC

citizenship (in independent Ireland). The *Anglo-Irish treaty and the *constitution of the *Irish Free State linked citizenship and allegiance in the *oath of allegiance. Article 3 of the constitution declared a citizen anyone domiciled in the Free State who was born in Ireland, had one Irish-born parent, or had been resident in the Free State for seven years.

In 1930 a draft Irish nationality bill provided for reciprocal recognition of Irish, British, and *Commonwealth citizenship. The British government objected that this ignored the common British citizenship possessed by all Commonwealth citizens. This bill nevertheless formed the basis for two measures, the Nationality and Citizenship Act and the Aliens Act, passed by de *Valera in 1935. The Nationality Act defined natural-born citizens, nationality following after marriage, and the status in Ireland of citizens whose states accorded Irish citizens certain rights and privileges. Under the Aliens Act, entry and residence requirements did not apply to UK and Commonwealth citizens. This was continued after Ireland left the Commonwealth in 1948.

Article 9 of the 1937 constitution stated that nationality would be determined by law but emphasized that gender would not affect citizenship. It also declared that 'fidelity to the nation and loyalty to the state are fundamental political duties of all citizens'.

Two further Nationality Acts were passed in 1956 and 1986. The 1956 act extended Irish citizenship to those born in Northern Ireland after 1922. The 1986 act dealt with naturalization and citizenship after marriage to aliens. There were further amendments to the 1956 and 1986 acts in the Irish Nationality and Citizenship Act, 1994. DMcM

city and county management, based on the concept of a legal division of policy and executive powers between elected councillors and local bureaucracy, is perhaps the most distinctive innovation in Irish administration since independence. The system, inspired by developments in city management in the United States and first embodied in the Cork city management bill (1929), had its origins in the manifest failings of local government during the 1920s, when committees of elected councillors discharged public business in a notoriously partisan, inefficient, and corrupt manner. *Fianna Fáil initially condemned as profoundly undemocratic the removal of administrative power from local politicians, but once in office from 1932 it enthusiastically embraced the idea and gradually extended it to all cities and counties. EO'H

civil registration. The state began to keep registers of all marriages, except those of Catholics, from 1845. Compulsory official registration of all births, marriages, and deaths began in 1864. Statistical tests for internal consistency suggest that there was initially serious under-registration, largely eliminated by 1911. There was also, lasting longer, considerable over-registration, apparently due to the desire of local medical officers to increase their stipends.

civil rights movement, a grouping devoted to political and social reform in *Northern Ireland, led by the Northern Ireland Civil Rights Association. NICRA was founded in Belfast early in 1967 by a group which included liberals, trade unionists, communists, and republicans, but no active politicians. It drew inspiration from the success of Martin Luther King's movement in the USA and more practical guidance from the British-based National Council for Civil Liberties. Its aims were to achieve universal suffrage and the abolition of multiple business voting in local government elections; the abolition of the *Special Powers Act and of the *Ulster Special Constabulary; an end to religious discrimination in public employment and housing allocation; and an end to the manipulation of electoral boundaries ('gerrymandering').

NICRA made little progress until it was sparked into life by an especially glaring case of housing misallocation at Caledon, Co. Tyrone, in June 1968. Civil rights protest marches followed, first at Dungannon and then in *Derry on 5 October 1968, where unjustifiably violent police suppression of the banned march was exposed on the world's television screens. By this time NICRA's activities had secured the support of various *Nationalist and *Northern Ireland Labour Party politicians. Its activities, and British government pressure, forced the Northern Ireland government to make some concessions, which in turn sparked a unionist backlash. After December 1968 NICRA was increasingly influenced by the *People's Democracy. It became more militant, and many of its original committee withdrew from public life during 1969; others who first entered politics through civil rights activities later became founders of the *Social Democratic and Labour Party (SDLP). By 1971 NICRA was strongly influenced by the official republican movement. Its civil liberties focus had less appeal in the context of massive rioting and growing paramilitary activity. It was revived somewhat by its opposition to *internment after August 1971, and it was once more in the spotlight as a result of *Bloody Sunday in 1972, but its style of street protest had been overtaken by events, while its libertarian concerns were more effectively articulated, in such a bitterly divided society, through different means. ACH

Civil Survey. Together with the earlier Gross Survey and the later *Down Survey, the Civil Survey (1654–6) was one of the inquiries into Irish land and land ownership that were intended as preliminaries to the *Cromwellian confiscation. It covered property belonging to forfeiting persons, the church, and the state in every county except Clare, Galway, Mayo, Roscommon, and Sligo. It also inquired into all lands claimed by English and Protestants, and was therefore more comprehensive than the Down Survey, which was concerned only with forfeited land. Commissioners were appointed in each county who, with the aid of local juries, collected a great mass of information relating to the boundaries, acreage, value, and ownership of baronies, parishes, and townlands, and the endowment of these areas in woods, buildings, mills, minerals, fisheries, and other resources. It was a survey by inquisition, not by mapped measurement, and was available only in tabular form.

During the period after the *Restoration the Civil Survey was one of the principal records of land tenure. It was used in addition to the Down Survey for the compilation of the books of *Survey and Distribution. The records survive for all or part of fourteen counties and were published in nine volumes (1931–53) under the editorship of R. C. Simington. PF

Civil War, see IRISH CIVIL WAR; CONFEDERATE WAR.

Claidheamh Soluis, An (Sword of Light), established in 1899 as the newspaper of the *Gaelic League. It was edited by Eoin *MacNeill (1899–1901) and Patrick *Pearse (1903–9). It continued under the names *Fáinne an Lae* (1918–19, 1922–30) and *Misneach* (1919–22), reverting briefly to *An Claidheamh Soluis* in 1930–1.

clan. The Irish word *clann* is a borrowing from the Latin *planta*, meaning a plant, an offshoot, offspring, a single child or children, by extension race or descendants. The Children of Israel, for instance, are translated as *Clann Israhél*; the *O'Donnell (Ó Domhnaill) family were poetically known as Clann Dálaigh, from a remote ancestor called Dálach. Clann was used in the later Middle Ages both to provide a plural for surnames beginning with 'Mac' or 'Son of' (e.g.

Clann Charthaigh, Clann Suibhne for the men of the *MacCarthy and *MacSweeny families) and also to denote a subgroup within a wider surname, the descendants of a recent common ancestor, e.g. the Clann Aodha Buidhe or *O'Neills of Clandeboy, whose ancestor Aodh Buidhe died in 1283. Such a 'clan', if sufficiently closely related, could have common interests in landownership, but any political power wielded by their head was territorially based, included unrelated tenants and subjects, and did not include relatives who had gone to live under another jurisdiction. Walter Scott's vision of the blood tie as an all-embracing claim on the loyalty of a Scottish clan to their chief did not apply. KS

Clancarty, earldom held by the *MacCarthys of Muskerry. **Donough MacCarthy** (1594–1665), Viscount Muskerry, combined Gaelic descent with *Old English politics, supporting *Ormond (his brother-in-law) in the *Confederation of Kilkenny and opposing *Rinuccini. Created earl of Clancarty in 1658, he regained his estate at the *Restoration. He was predeceased by his eldest son **Cormac**, killed serving alongside the future *James II at the naval battle of Lowestoft (1665) and interred at Westminster abbey. When Cormac's son Charles, the 2nd earl, died in 1666, Donough's second son **Callaghan** (d. 1676) abandoned a career in a French monastery to become 3rd earl and, for a time, a Protestant. **Donough** (1668–1734), the 4th earl, fought for James II in the *Williamite War and fled to the *Jacobite court after escaping from the Tower of London in 1694. In 1698 he returned to England to strengthen his position by consummating his marriage with Elizabeth, daughter of the earl of Sunderland, whom he had married in 1684 through the agency of his uncle Justin *MacCarthy. He was arrested but subsequently allowed to live abroad on a pension. **Robert** (1685–1769), styled 5th earl despite his father's attainder, served as a naval officer and governor of Newfoundland 1733–5, and was a close associate of Sarah, duchess of Marlborough. He caused an outcry by petitioning in 1735 for the restoration of the family estates, before going to France around 1741 to join the Jacobite court.

clandestine marriages performed without licence or the publication of banns had an obvious appeal to couples anxious to marry in secret, to escape family disapproval, or simply to avoid the trouble and expense of the legal formalities. They were most commonly performed by suspended or unemployed clergy known as 'couple beggars'. An act of 1726 made it a capital offence for any priest or suspended Protestant clergyman to perform a marriage in which one or both parties was a Protestant, and declared all such unions invalid. The Council of *Trent declared invalid marriages not performed by the parish priest of one of the parties, or a clergyman authorized by him. This, however, took effect only when the decree had been formally published in each diocese, something not achieved in all parts of Ireland until 1827.

Clan Na Gael, an Irish-American revolutionary organization formed to pursue Irish independence after the defeat of the *Fenian rising of 1867. Founded by a journalist, Jerome J. Collins, its most important leaders were William Carroll, a Philadelphia doctor, and John *Devoy. Within ten years it had around 10,000 members and in the late 1870s became formally linked with the *Irish Republican Brotherhood in Ireland through a joint revolutionary directory. Having initially hoped to organize an Irish insurrection when England became involved in international conflict, Devoy was led by lack of opportunity and a concern to maximize fully the forces of Irish nationalism into the *'New Departure'. The result, however, was a strengthening of constitutional nationalism while the *Parnell connection was partly responsible for a Clan split in the 1880s. The organization was reborn in 1900 on the basis of a firm commitment to military struggle. It opposed, as a poor substitute for independence, the *Land Act of 1903, and played an important supporting role for republican militants in Ireland, especially in the acquiring of German arms for the *Irish Volunteers in 1914. JL

Clann Colmáin were one of two major southern *Uí Néill dynasties, based in Mide (centred on modern Co. Westmeath). Their eponym, Colmán Már, was reputedly a great-great-grandson of *Niall Noígiallach. An early centre of Clann Colmáin power is said to have been Loch Drethin (north of Mullingar), but their 10th- and 11th-century descendants, the Uí Máelsechlainn, were located at Lough Ennell. The Clann Colmáin provided a number of 8th- and 9th-century kings of Tara (see HIGH KINGSHIP). They subsequently conquered lands of the *Síl nÁedo Sláine in Meath, but their power declined after *Máel Sechnaill mac Domnaill (d. 1022) submitted to *Brian Bóruma. CS

Clann na Poblachta ('party of the republic'), political party founded on 6 July 1946. Made up largely of *republican activists and led by Sean *MacBride, the party managed quickly to establish a nationwide network of branches and members and to win significant victories at by-elections. It won 13.2 per cent of the vote (ten seats) in the 1948 general election, and joined the first *interparty government. Internal disagreements between the party leader and one of his ministers, Noel *Browne, over the latter's *'Mother and Child' scheme resulted in a split within the party and seriously damaged its credibility as a radical movement.

The party never recovered from this blow; it was reduced to two seats at the general election of 1951 and, although it continued to contest elections until 1965, its position was always that of a marginal force. Its policies were left-leaning and nationalist, and its tone was moralistic on the matter of ethics in public life. JC

Clann na Talmhan ('party of the land'), political party founded on 29 June 1939. Initially confined to the west of Ireland, it later extended its organization in the east and south. The party polled well at a by-election in 1940, but its major victory came at the general election of 1943, when it won 10.3 per cent of the votes (thirteen seats). It improved slightly on this electoral performance in 1944 (10.8 per cent), but its number of seats fell back to eleven. Although its support dropped to 5.6 per cent (seven seats) in 1948, it entered the first *interparty government in that year. Its support continued to decline subsequently, but it was nevertheless able to join the second interparty government in 1954. It continued to contest elections until 1961 but disappeared in 1965, much of its support transferring to *Fine Gael.

Its programme was that of a populist, agrarian party, appealing in particular to the interests of smaller farmers. Its most prominent figures, including its eventual leader Michael Donnellan, were farmers from the west of Ireland. JC

Clann Sínaich (Uí Sínaich), a branch of the Uí Echdach of *Airgialla, supplied abbots of *Armagh from the late 8th century, and held the abbacy by hereditary succession from at least 965 until 1134, usually as married laymen, a practice prohibited by the Synod of *Cashel in 1101. Cellach, an unmarried member of the family, succeeded in 1105, received orders on his election, and was consecrated bishop in the following year, thereby reuniting the two offices. An attempt to return to the old order after Cellach's death in 1129 was eventually prevented by the efforts of his successor, St *Malachy. SD

Clanricard, Richard Burke, 4th earl of (1572–1635), knighted in the field for his bravery in the cavalry charge which won the battle of *Kinsale. The only Irish Catholic trusted in an administrative capacity, Clanricard was made *provincial president of Connacht in 1604. Married to an English heiress, he was mostly absent from his magnificent Jacobean mansion at Portumna. To pay for his courtier lifestyle, he leased lands to improving tenants, including English Protestants. His court connections (he became earl of St Albans from 1628) and immunity from *recusancy fines made him a tough opponent of *Wentworth's attempt to colonize Connacht. HM

Clanricard, Ulick Burke, 1st marquis of (1604–57). Clanricard died on his estates in Cromwellian England after an eventful career combining Catholicism and loyalty to the crown. He succeeded in the struggle, already joined by his father Richard, the 4th earl, to exempt his patrimony from *Wentworth's proposed colonization of Connacht. When his relatives and tenantry joined the *Confederate Catholics, he became a valuable intermediary between the king and the Confederation. *Ormond made him royalist commander in Connacht in 1645 but he had no army, mounting debts, and controlled only his own lands and a few castles. In 1648 he earned the opprobrium of the Catholic clergy by allying with *Inchiquin and besieging Galway.

After Ormond left him in Ireland as lord deputy in 1650, Clanricard took £20,000 from Charles of Lorraine but rejected his pretensions to a protectorate. He proved unable to prevent the parliamentarian advance across the Shannon, but carried out his instructions of fighting as long as possible, eventually submitting in 1652 after a rearguard action on the Connacht–Ulster border. Parliament allowed him life and estate for kindnesses to Protestant refugees in 1641. Clanricard's letter-books, covering 1641–53, are an important source on wartime conditions as well as high politics. HM

Clanricard Burke, see BURKE (DE BURGH).

Clanwilliam Burke, see BURKE (DE BURGH).

Clare, one of the greatest medieval baronial houses, with large estates in England, Wales, and (until 1204) Normandy; its members were involved in Ireland from 1170 to the mid-14th century. The most famous was Richard de Clare, or *Strongbow (d. 1176), lord of Striguil (Chepstow) and claimant to the earldom of Pembroke, who became lord of Leinster. His only son died young, and his lands passed to his son-in-law William *Marshal. When the male line of the Marshals died out in 1245, the co-heirs included the head of the senior branch of the Clares, Richard, earl of

Gloucester (d. 1262), who received Kilkenny as his portion. He and his eldest son Earl Gilbert (d. 1295) paid visits to Ireland. His second son Thomas de *Clare (d. 1287) was granted *Thomond in 1276, and this cadet line remained active in Munster until 1318. After the death at Bannockburn in 1314 of Earl Gilbert II, Kilkenny was partitioned between his three sisters. The youngest, Elizabeth, lady of Clare (d. 1360), also had extensive lands in Ulster, Connacht, Munster, and Meath through her marriages to John de Burgh (d. 1313), son of Richard de *Burgh, earl of Ulster, and to Theobald de *Verdon (d. 1316). She was mother of William, the last de *Burgh earl of Ulster (d. 1333), and influential at court. Important records of the administration of her Irish lands survive. On her death, her estates passed to Edward III's son *Lionel, later duke of Clarence, who had married her granddaughter Elizabeth de Burgh, the Ulster heiress. RFF

Clare, Richard de, see STRONGBOW.

Clare, Thomas de (d. 1287), granted *Thomond by Edward I in 1276, and perhaps the last of the medieval conquistadors. A younger brother of the earl of Gloucester, he was a confidant of the king, whom he accompanied on crusade in 1270–2. He went to Ireland in 1274, participated in campaigns in Wicklow, and married a daughter of the Geraldine lord, Maurice fitz Maurice. His later years were dominated by the attempt to conquer Thomond. He built castles at Bunratty and Quin, and exploited the quarrels of the *O'Briens. His execution in 1277 of Brian Rua O'Brien (Brian Ruad Ó Briain), with whom he had allied, was denounced in the Gaelic history *Caithréim Thoirdhealbhaigh*, and in the 1317 *Remonstrance. From 1309 his son Richard showed equal vigour; but after Richard's death at the battle of *Dysert O'Dea in 1318, and the partition of his lands between heiresses, English power in Thomond waned. RFF

Clark, Sir George Smith (1861–1935), *Belfast *shipbuilder. Apprenticed at *Harland & Wolff, in 1880 Clark entered into a partnership with Francis Workman to form *Workman Clark & Company. In 1917 Clark received a baronetcy for his wartime services to the shipbuilding industry. In 1920 he resigned from the board of directors, apparently in protest at the financial dealings which were to lead to the company's temporary liquidation seven years later.

Drawn into politics by the issue of home rule, Clark was a committed *Unionist. From 1907 to 1910 he was MP for North Belfast. FG/WJ

Clarke, Adam (*c.*1760–1832), Wesleyan *Methodist preacher, theologian, and linguist, the most distinguished scholar thrown up by the Methodist movement in Britain or in Ireland. Born in Co. Londonderry of humble parents, Clarke was converted under Methodist influence in 1778, was stationed in England in 1782, and settled in London in 1795. He somehow combined a dedicated career as a Methodist preacher, including three stints, in 1806, 1814, and 1822, as the president of the Wesleyan Conference, with a prolific scholarly output. His miscellaneous works were published in a thirteen-volume edition in 1836. Although primarily interested in theology, biblical studies, the natural sciences, and history, Clarke's special forte was a quite remarkable facility with languages. This interest extended to the Irish language, the use of which Clarke enthusiastically supported, not solely on grounds of missionary expediency. In the early 1820s he helped persuade the British and Foreign Bible Society to print and circulate copies of the scriptures in Irish. DNH

Clarke, Thomas (1857–1916), lifelong republican and first signatory of the 1916 Proclamation. Clarke grew up in South Africa before settling in Dungannon, Co. Tyrone. At the age of 21 he emigrated to the United States, where he became involved in *Clan Na Gael. He went to England in 1883 on a bombing mission (see BOMBING CAMPAIGNS IN GREAT BRITAIN), but was arrested and sentenced to penal servitude for life. Upon his release in 1898 he returned to the USA. In 1907 he came to Dublin and bought a newsagent's which became a centre of *IRB activity. With Sean MacDermott he was responsible for the publication of the radical newspaper *Irish Freedom*. In protest against the visit of George V to Ireland he organized the first commemoration of Wolfe *Tone at Bodenstown in 1912. As one of the founders of the IRB military council, which organized the *rising of 1916, he was responsible for inviting Pearse to become their front man. He fought in the General Post Office, and was executed after the rising. JA

class. The class structure of modern Ireland has been moulded by a number of factors, both external and internal. The colonial and imperial relationship with Britain led to a situation where the various collectivities within the island tended not to relate to each other directly, but mediated their relationships through the British link. The internal dynamic of conflict in the 19th century came to focus on the question of *nationalism versus *unionism rather than on the ownership and control of the means of production. In objective terms, 19th-century Ireland had a clear class structure where various groups (tenants, labourers, *landlords, industrial workers, bourgeoisie) often came into conflict over the allocation, control, and ownership of resources. *Agrarian agitation and the *Land War provide one example of this.

What was absent from the Irish situation, in contrast to other European countries, was the emergence of a class *for itself*, the construction of a distinct class-consciousness which welded people together around common concerns and actions. The formation of the European socialist parties were an index of this process in Europe. In Ireland, questions of religion, nation, and ethnicity caused cleavages which continually disrupted any movement towards class politics.

Attempts were made to raise the class question, or to merge it with the national cause. James *Connolly championed a socialist republic, and James *Larkin's trade union agitation had a distinct class flavour. However, class politics was subordinated to the national question and de *Valera's comment that 'labour must wait' aptly encapsulated the situation. *Partition reinforced the subordination of class to nation as well as ensuring that the southern economy would be dominated by the agricultural sectors until the 1960s.

Significant changes to the class structure did not begin to occur until the 1960s. In the Republic, the ending of economic *protectionism in 1958 and entry into the *European Union in 1972 led to a decline in small-scale local industry and agriculture and a shift towards more service-based occupations. More jobs became knowledge based, leading to an expansion in higher education, and the traditional classes of *agricultural labourers and industrial workers (both skilled and unskilled) entered a period of rapid contraction. Women began to enter the workforce in greater numbers. In Northern Ireland, the collapse of traditional male-dominated heavy industry and the rapid decline of the textile industry—mainly staffed by low-paid female labour—brought about a broadly similar pattern of change, which was reinforced by the rapid expansion of the state sector in the 1970s. In both parts of Ireland the most significant changes to the class structure were the increased involvement of women in the workforce, the expansion of the state and service sector, and the spread of knowledge-based occupations.

The last two decades in the Republic have seen a change in this pattern where politics were dominated by the divisions of the *Civil War. Politics have assumed a new volatility as the class basis of traditional politics changed and the class structure assumed a form similar to other western European countries. Loyalty to a particular party has declined and significant sectors of the new class and occupational structure have no political allegiances or display a shifting and opportunist attitude. The political effects of changes in the class structure are less visible in Northern Ireland. Although the changes have, if anything, been more far reaching, effects on traditional political allegiances have been slight. There is little evidence that the pattern of ethnic allegiances in politics and voting preferences has undergone any significant change.

Hutton, S., and Stewart, P., *Ireland's Histories: Aspects of State, Society and Ideology* (1991)

JS

clientship (*céilsine*) in early Irish law was the relationship between a lord (*flaith*) and a client (*céile*). It took two principal forms, called 'free clientship' and 'base clientship' after the Irish terms *sóerchéilsine* and *dóerchéilsine*. In free clientship both the client and the lord could end the relationship at will and without penalties; base clientship did not bind the client permanently to the lord, but it did include penalties which were incurred if one party ended the relationship early against the will of the other.

Base clientship was the more important of the two varieties. First, the status of being noble depended upon being the lord of base rather than of free clients; and, secondly, base clientship was firmly associated with, though perhaps not necessary to, the status of a free commoner. For **Críth Gablach* the lowest grade of noble consisted of lords of five base clients, the next grade consisted of lords of ten clients, and so on. Similarly, a normal word for the commoner, both inside and outside the legal texts, was *aithech*, literally '(food-) render-payer'. Base clientship was, therefore, one of the principal determinants of the shape of early Irish society. It was the subject of a tract within the 8th-century law-book the *Senchas Már, Cáin Aicillne*; most of this text is preserved intact, whereas we only have fragments of its companion tract, *Cáin Sóerraith*, dealing with free clientship.

For *Cáin Aicillne*, base clientship normally endured for the lifetime of the lord. It was initiated by a grant or gift from the lord to the client, usually of cattle. Together with this grant came a further payment, 'the chattels of submission', equivalent in value to the client's honour price (see *enech*) and marking the personal subordination of a freeman to a lord. The lord, therefore, began the relationship by making one-off payments to the client. The latter, by contrast, made fixed annual payments throughout the term of the relationship. The lord created a debt by the initial grant, which the client, the recipient of the grant, took a lifetime of renders to discharge. The client's fixed annual payments took the form of food renders, including both livestock products and grain. Whereas the lord's grant was normally in the form of cattle, the client's render came from both his livestock and arable farming.

Sometimes at least a free client also received a grant from his lord and gave food renders in return. The grant, however, appears to have been much less in value than in base clientship. The renders were proportionately much more valuable, probably amounting to the entire returns from the livestock given. The point may have been that free clientship was not intended to provide the client with further economic resources; since the grant was small, the renders were absolutely of minor significance though proportionately to the grant they were valuable. TMC-E

Cloncurry, Valentine Lawless, 2nd Baron (1773–1853), radical turned *Whig. Although his *Personal Recollections* (1849) minimized his role in the *United Irish conspiracy, Lawless was in fact prominent in the movement's militant faction, and chief organizer of its underground activities in England. Imprisoned in 1798 and 1799–1801, he travelled abroad 1802–5, then returned to Ireland to become a reforming landlord and a magistrate. He supported *Catholic emancipation, *repeal, and the *Tithe War, but was close to the marquis of Anglesey, lord lieutenant 1830–4, under whom he became an English peer and a privy counsellor.

Clonmacnoise was during its heyday one of the largest and most important *monastic centres in Ireland. Situated at the crossroads of two important medieval routes, the Shannon and the *Eiscir Riata, the monastery was founded in the mid-6th century by St Ciarán. By the 8th century it had expanded to become a thriving centre of art and learning.

The 11th-century *Annals of Tigernach* and the 12th-century *Lebor na hUidre* (Book of the *Dun Cow) were produced in the Clonmacnoise scriptorium. The remaining *high crosses and over 600 complete and fragmented memorial slabs indicate the presence of important stone workshops; a strong tradition of fine *metal-working is also associated with the site.

The wealth and accessibility of the monastery made it an obvious target for attack. Between 834 and 1163 it was plundered or burned 35 times by both native and *Viking foes. When the monastery was raided by *Anglo-Norman forces in 1179, 105 houses were burned, an indication of the size of the settlement at that time. Clonmacnoise was finally destroyed as an active religious centre in 1552 by an English garrison stationed at Athlone. The remnants of the settlement include eight churches, two *round towers, and an impressive Anglo-Norman fortification. RM

Clontarf, battle of (1014). This most famous of all Irish battles was fought near *Dublin between *Brian Bóruma (Boru) at the head of a predominantly Munster army on the one side, and an alliance of Leinster and *Viking forces on the other. While a significant encounter at the time, its fame grew even more in the telling, and tracts such as **Cogadh Gáedhel re Gallaibh* and the Old Norse *Brennu-Njáls Saga* present us with a considerably embellished version of events. In such literary accounts, the battle is portrayed as a struggle for the sovereignty of Ireland with the victory of Brian's forces signalling, according to Irish scribes, the final defeat of a foreign oppressor. Annalistic records, generally of a more sober nature, suggest that the battle should instead be viewed as an attempt by the Leinstermen, with the help of their Norse allies, to assert their independence against their dominant Munster neighbour. Moreover, despite being defeated, the Leinstermen did in fact gain respite following the encounter, since Brian's death in the battle marked the beginning of a temporary decline in *Dál Cais power. MNíM

Clontibret, battle of (27 May 1595), Hugh *O'Neill's first victory over crown forces. Sir Henry Bagenal's army was sharply encountered in an eight-hour fight at Clontibret after resupplying the Monaghan garrison. The English were astonished at O'Neill's generalship and the expertise of the Irish troops. Only a cavalry charge on O'Neill himself prevented complete disaster. Bagenal's official losses were 31 killed and 109 wounded. O'Neill was proclaimed a traitor the following month. HM

'close' and 'open' boroughs, contemporary terms distinguishing between those parliamentary boroughs that were under the control of a single patron and those—the eight county boroughs along with Derry and Swords, Co. Dublin—in which large electorates ensured that a genuine contest was at least possible. See FRANCHISE.

Clotworthy, Sir John (d. 1665), a *puritan opponent of *Wentworth and leading anti-Catholic politician with estates in Antrim and Londonderry. Clotworthy received a seat in the English Long Parliament in 1640 and appeared as a witness at Wentworth's trial. Rumours about his activities aroused Catholic fears prior to the *rising of 1641. He reported the subsequent massacres to the Commons and became an *adventurer. His wish to accelerate the reconquest made him an unpopular supporter of peace with the king in 1645–8. Charles II created him Viscount Massereene (1660) when he returned to England to represent adventurer and soldier interests.

See also MASSEREENE. HM

Clyn, John, Franciscan friar and chronicler. Clyn was guardian of the friary at Carrick-on-Suir, Co. Tipperary, in 1336, but by his own account wrote his Latin chronicle in the Kilkenny friary. This begins with the birth of Christ, is sketchy and derivative until around 1264, but thereafter becomes a full and largely original account. It ends with the plague outbreak of 1348–9 (see BLACK DEATH). Clyn's concluding statement that he has left parchment 'for the continuation of the work . . . if any of the sons of Adam manages to avoid this pestilence' suggests that he may himself have succumbed to the plague. Perhaps because he was writing at the centre of the Butler lordship, he is more informative about events in Gaelic Ireland than other contemporary chroniclers. ABS

coach building. *Dublin was the main centre of this industry; by the end of the 18th century there were over 40 coach factories in the city employing up to 2,000 men, some of whom were among the best craftsmen in the city. Coach works were also to be found in *Cork, *Belfast, and some of the other larger provincial towns. By 1885 the number of firms in Dublin had been reduced to ten, employing 200 hands. A number of coach makers diversified into the construction of *railway carriages from the mid-19th century, and by the early 20th century some of the best firms (like Johnson & Perrott in Cork and Huttons in Dublin) had moved into the *motor car trade. AB

coalition, see INTERPARTY GOVERNMENT.

coal mining in Ireland has never matched that of Great Britain. The various periods of folding and faulting during the geological formation of Ireland greatly denuded its original coal deposits. Also, Ireland's easy access to cheap supplies in Britain and the absence of concerted industrialization, outside the north-east, greatly reduced the impetus towards mining. In 1900 Ireland produced only 125,000 tons, compared to Scotland's 30 million tons annually. Sporadic mining of anthracite deposits at Crataloe, west Clare, Kanturk, Co. Cork, Coalbrook and Castlecomer, Co. Kilkenny, Co. Carlow, and the Slieve Ardagh hills in Tipperary has now ceased. In Leitrim, Arigna's bituminous coal, originally mined for local iron furnaces, supplied the nearby power station, until closure in 1990. Mining was carried on at Coalisland, Co. Tyrone, from the 18th century. Between July 1924 and December 1926, 36,000 tons were raised, by Sir Samuel Kelly & Co., with heavy government subsidies and miners imported from Scotland and Cumberland. However, it proved an uneconomic proposition and was closed in 1926. Further unsuccessful mining was carried on in Coalisland in the 1950s. Poor quality 'limestone coal', found at Ballycastle, Co. Antrim, is no longer mined. Although the *Second World War gave a boost to Irish mining, in peacetime competition from abroad and other power sources, as well as modern environmental pressures, have all but done away with Irish coal mining. PC

coarb (O.Ir. *comarbae*, 'heir', 'successor'), a distinctive office of the later medieval *church among the Gaelic Irish. In this period coarb appears interchangeable with *erenach, denoting the episcopally nominated lay guardian of a parish church and headman of the family in hereditary occupation of church lands. The coarb, however, often had charge of a church which had held comparatively high rank in pre-Norman Ireland, or one still possessed of relatively extensive **termon* lands. *Comarbae*, often coupled with a saint's name (e.g. *Comarbae Pátraic*, successor of *Patrick, i.e. head of *Armagh) in the *annals from the 10th century, denoted the administrator of a (usually eminent) church who was not necessarily either in major orders or a monastic abbot. However, he and his church derived their legal status from the clerical grade (priestly or episcopal) associated with that church. The vernacular title and its Latin equivalent *heres* in law and *hagiography of the 7th and 8th centuries seem, like erenach, to bespeak not secularized degeneration but recognition from the outset of the temporal dimension of ecclesiastical authority, which might be envisaged as an inheritance (*orbae*, whence *comarbae*). The pope was sometimes referred to as *Comarbae Petair* (Peter's heir). CE

cock fighting was probably introduced to Ireland by British settlers, though domestic origins are also possible. Whatever the practice's precise roots, by the 17th century cocks were being bred and trained for fighting, and metal spurs began to be fitted to birds. Despite suppression during *Cromwell's rule, cock fighting remained a popular urban and rural spectacle, and a focus for *gambling, throughout the 18th century. A heyday was reached around 1750, by which time permanent cockpits had been constructed in many towns and teams of cocks were organized to represent Irish counties. From the end of the century, however, attitudes amongst some of the elite moved against *blood sports and cock fighting was made illegal in 1837. Despite this prohibition, cock fighting is still practised illegally in isolated areas, notably along the Irish border. The complexity of the law ensures that successful prosecutions are few. NG

Coercion Acts, general term for a series of measures commencing with the Suppression of Disturbances Act (1833). Like the earlier *Insurrection Act, this empowered the *lord lieutenant to proclaim a district as disturbed, permitting the imposition of a curfew and other restrictions, as well as detention without trial for up to three months. It differed from the Insurrection Act in providing for trial by military courts rather than magistrates in special session. The Crime and Outrage Act (1847) once again imposed curfew and other restrictions on proclaimed districts, as well as authorizing the dispatch to such districts of extra police, to be paid for by the inhabitants. The act, modified in 1856, was regularly renewed up to 1875. A different approach, targeting individuals rather than districts, appeared in the suspension, in 1871 and 1881, of *habeas corpus. The Prevention of Crime Act, in force for three years from 1882, permitted trial for specific offences by a panel of three judges and created a legal offence of intimidation. Arthur *Balfour's Criminal Law and Procedure Act (1887) once again defined intimidation and conspiracy, gave resident magistrates in districts proclaimed under the act powers of investigation and summary jurisdiction, and empowered the lord lieutenant to suppress subversive organizations. This was a permanent measure, still relied on in the early stages of the *Anglo-Irish War.

See MARTIAL LAW; SPECIAL COURTS.

Cogadh Gaedhel re Gallaibh is a Middle Irish text which describes the various Viking invasions of Ireland in the 9th and 10th centuries and more especially the resistance to them provided by the *Dál Cais under the leadership of Mathgamain mac Cennétig and of his brother *Brian Bóruma (Boru), culminating in the victory of Brian's forces at the battle of *Clontarf. Though based in part on annalistic and other sources, the text is not in fact contemporary with any of the events it relates, but was written at the behest of Brian Bóruma's great-grandson Muirchertach *Ua Briain, at the height of that king's power in the early years of the 12th century. Hence, the *Cogadh* is in effect a skilful piece of Uí Briain dynastic political propaganda. MNíM

Cogan, Miles de (d. 1182), Anglo-Norman adventurer who arrived in Ireland with *Strongbow in 1170 and played a pivotal role in the capture of Dublin. He left Ireland in the entourage of *Henry II in 1172, but returned in 1177 when Henry gave a speculative grant of the kingdom of *Desmond to him jointly with Robert *fitz Stephen. He was killed in 1182 near Lismore by Ua Meic Thíre, king of Uí Meic Caille. MTF

Coigley (O'Coigley, Quigley), James (1761–98), Catholic priest, arrested at Margate with Arthur *O'Connor on 28 February 1798 and executed on 7 June. Although he denied to the end the charge of treasonable contact with the French Directory, Coigley is now seen as a key figure in the conspiratorial network linking *United Irishmen, English radicals, and revolutionary France, and has also been speculatively identified as a crucial go-between in the construction of a United Irish–*Defender alliance in the early 1790s.

coinage, see MONEY.

Collins, Michael (1890–1922), republican and statesman. Born in Clonakilty, Co. Cork, Collins moved to London in 1906 where he worked as a clerk in the Post Office and later for a firm of stockbrokers. While in London he became involved with the *Irish Republican Brotherhood. He returned to Ireland in 1915 and fought in the General Post Office during the *rising of 1916. On his release he became increasingly influential in *Sinn Féin and the *Irish Volunteers. He was elected to the first *Dáil for South Cork and for Tyrone, first becoming minister for home affairs and from April 1919 minister for finance. In the latter function he organized the Dáil Loan which financed the republicans' alternative government. As director of organization and intelligence for the *IRA he played a leading part in the co-ordination of the military campaign in the *Anglo-Irish War. His intelligence network in Dublin was renowned, and he was responsible for the 'Squad' which eliminated government intelligence. His success and determination to get things done brought him into conflict with some other leaders such as de *Valera and Cathal *Brugha.

Collins was a reluctant delegate to the negotiations that produced the *Anglo-Irish treaty, but accepted their outcome and was appointed chairman and minister for finance of the *Provisional Government responsible for the establishment of the new Irish state. He regarded the treaty only as a means towards obtaining a 32-county republic. His conspiratorial nature came to the fore in his secret arrangement with the anti-treatyites to attack Northern Ireland while officially recognizing it. He became commander-in-chief of the Free State army when the *Irish Civil War broke out, and was killed on 22 August 1922 at Beal na Blath, Co. Cork, during an inspection tour of the south.

Generally seen as a man of action, he commanded great respect, admiration, and loyalty among those around him. He has been much idealized since his death, often described as the man who single-handedly defeated the British forces. This view has been challenged in more recent writing. The widespread admiration for him has, nevertheless, fuelled much speculation about what Ireland would have been like if he had lived. Such speculation emphasizes his view of the treaty as a stepping-stone, his progressive social views, and his potential to reunite a divided republican movement.

Coogan, Tim Pat, *Michael Collins: A Biography* (1990)

Hart, Peter, *Mick: The Real Michael Collins* (2005) JA

colonial and post-colonial models. Ireland has been described as England's oldest colony. While the colonial *origins* of the connection between England and Ireland are not in doubt, the extent to which colonial models illuminate the historical relationships between the two is more contentious.

Broadly speaking, one can distinguish three types of models. First, there are those of an implicit kind: loose allusions to the political subordination of Ireland to England and the economic exploitation of the former by the latter. These tend to lack a basis in social theory of any kind and are commonly found in Irish nationalist writings of the last two centuries. Images of colonial domination also find limited expression in some Irish unionist writings, particularly in relation to the 18th century, but interestingly not with reference to time periods after the Act of *Union. In these writings the colonial notion is put more to descriptive than to analytical use.

Then there are those models which deal explicitly with notions of colonialism. These are grounded, to varying degrees, in theory and accord colonial relationships substantial weight within their explanatory schemes. Here one can distinguish two subtypes. There are those whose explanatory scope is clearly limited in space and time. Some of the best examples belong to studies of 17th-century Ireland, where processes of colonization in Munster and Ulster (see PLANTATION), and in the New World, are effectively linked and explicated. Others, not many in fact, adopt a more ambitious time frame, seeking to encompass centuries of Irish history within a framework of colonial assumptions. A good example is Hechter's model of internal colonialism. In terms of this model, social groups within the core region (in this case England) dominated the peoples of peripheral regions politically and exploited them materially. As interactions between the English core and the Irish, Scottish, and Welsh peripheries multiplied over time, conflict and underdevelopment ensued. The predicted result for Ireland, as well as other areas of the Celtic fringe, was weak industrialization, low levels of income, and political alienation and mobilization along ethnic lines.

Finally, there are theories of post-colonialism. These are of recent origin and emanate from the unlikely context of literary and cultural criticism. Though developed initially in relation to colonial societies outside Europe, including the white dominions of the British empire, they have found an application in the Irish context. From the perspective of post-colonial theorizing, Ireland is a formerly colonial society with an experience little different from that of India, Algeria, or Ghana. In other words, Ireland should be modelled historically in much the same way as a Third World country in thrall to an imperial power. Within these writings there is a heavy emphasis on cultural subordination and resistance: the imposition of metropolitan, that is English, values, culture, and language on the indigenous peoples of Ireland, and the native reaction to this. Moreover, even after the achievement of political independence, the heritage of colonialism is still held to exert a baleful influence on Irish culture and society.

Does the post-colonial cap fit? Ironically, in view of the emerging hegemony of theory in cultural studies, the model suffers from theoretical underdevelopment. Relationships between variables are poorly specified and their dynamic loosely sketched. More often than not, the depth of historical scholarship bears little relation to the extent of theoretical speculation. In particular the economic processes which are held to underpin colonialism are relatively neglected. More generally, one might remark that while good model building, even grand theorizing, remains a legitimate goal, it is proving an elusive one. This despite the length of the Irish–English connection and a wealth of historical materials.

Hechter, M., *Internal Colonialism: The Celtic Fringe in British National Development, 1536–1966* (1976)

LK

colonial nationalism, a term originally coined in 1902 to describe movements for autonomy in

Britain's overseas dominions, and subsequently applied by J. G. Simms to the *patriotism of 18th-century Irish Protestants.

colonial North America. The 'thirteen mainland' colonies which eventually formed the *United States of America had distinctive individual histories. However, by the mid-18th century, they were part of recognizable regional or sectional groupings. Massachusetts, New Hampshire, Connecticut, and Rhode Island formed the most easily identified section, New England. New York, New Jersey, Delaware, and Pennsylvania were usually termed the Middle Colonies. Maryland, North and South Carolina, and Georgia formed, with the addition of the biggest colony both in terms of size and population, Virginia, the South. Virginia also had the longest continuous history of any of the thirteen colonies, tracing its origins back to the settlement at Jamestown in 1607. Georgia was the youngest colony, having been granted its charter in 1732. The colonies were established under a variety of royal charters, but in their provincial government they all had a representative element, as well as a royal governor. Representation was underpinned by a broad franchise based on white male property ownership variously defined.

The religious variety in the colonies was great, without parallel in any European country at the time. Although New England was predominantly Calvinist and Congregational, in the Middle Colonies no group dominated. Presbyterians, Anglicans, Quakers, Dutch Reformed, Moravian, Mennonites, and Lutherans were all present, as were others. In the South, the Anglican church was the dominant and, characteristically, established church. However, by the middle years of the 18th century, Methodists and Baptists as well as Presbyterians were rapidly growing minorities. The South was also the major area of primary production, notably tobacco in Maryland and Virginia, and had a plantation economy, focused on sugar, cotton, and indigo in South Carolina and Georgia, based on the institution of chattel slavery. Both New England and the Middle Colonies had more varied economies, but overall some 90 per cent of the population derived their livelihood from the land.

There is much evidence to show that it was the availability of land in the mainland colonies that was a major attraction to emigrants from Ireland, as it was to those who left from England, Scotland, and Wales as well as from other parts of Europe. Seventeenth-century movement of population seems to have had a New England orientation, but by early next century the focus had changed. Although such distinctively Irish settlements as Londonderry, New Hampshire, remained, for the most part New England Calvinism and Scottish and Irish Calvinism had an uneasy relationship. More and more emigrants from Ireland entered the colonies through Philadelphia and its outports such as New Castle, Delaware, and then moved to the then western counties of Pennsylvania as well as the growing city of Philadelphia. Of course, entry through this port reflected connections with Ireland relating to the trade in flax seed and other products. Once in western Pennsylvania, where the *Quaker-dominated colony tended to prefer the often belligerent Irish settlers to be, some moved on into the valley of Virginia and then to the back country of the Carolinas. Some entered the Carolinas directly without the detour through Pennsylvania and Virginia. Inevitably, even more overwhelmingly than other settlers, these migrants were involved in agriculture, however rough and ready their methods.

Most of the 17th- and 18th-century migrants came from a Presbyterian background, although recent scholarship suggests that Roman Catholics and Anglicans were a larger minority than had once been thought likely. It is now clear, for instance, that among the indentured servants who crossed the Atlantic there were many from a Catholic background who found the practice of their religion impossible in the colonies. It is also worth noting that Irish Quakers emigrated. Indeed, one of the most striking careers of any Irish migrant in the colonial period is that of James Logan, William Penn's most important lieutenant, born in Lurgan, Co. Armagh, of Scottish parents.

Irish emigrants had a more significant role in the early growth of the Presbyterian church in America than those who came directly from Scotland. Francis Makemie, born in Ramelton, Co. Donegal, in 1658, helped establish the Synod of Philadelphia in 1706. William Tennant, born in Ireland 1673 and a graduate of Edinburgh University, founded the 'Log College' at Neshaminy, Pennsylvania, as a pioneering Presbyterian seminary. He and his sons were profoundly involved in 18th-century doctrinal controversy. William himself also helped found the Synod of New York in 1746.

Estimates of the numbers who left Ireland for the colonies in this period are understandably problematic. Between 1717 and 1760, it is thought that 100,000 people from Ireland settled in America. Overall throughout the period 1607–1776 as many as 250,000 people may have arrived.

Jones, M. A., 'The Scotch-Irish in British America', in B. Bailyn and P. D. Morgan, *Strangers within the Realm* (1991)

Middleton, R., *Colonial America* (1992)

SJSI

Columbanus (d. 615), born in Leinster, the most famous of the medieval Irish *peregrini* on the Continent, upon whose exploits the notion of the Irish reconverting Europe is chiefly based. He studied at *Bangor, and became learned in *Latin and the scriptures. This is borne out in his writings which, in fine Latin, show his acquaintance with the theological currents of his time. Around 590 he went to Gaul, and established several monasteries (e.g. Luxeuil) in the Vosges. In 603 Columbanus came into conflict with the local bishops, refused to recognize their authority, and appealed directly to Rome. His letter to the pope reveals a perception of Europe as a Christian cultural unit focused on Rome. Later Columbanus was expelled from Gaul over his refusal to bless King Theuderic's illegitimate sons. Columbanus and other monks, including Gall, travelled in what is now eastern France and Switzerland. On this journey he quarrelled with Gall, who left him and became a hermit. Finally, Columbanus arrived at Bobbio in northern Italy and established another monastery (*c.*612).

Columbanus is the first Irish writer who has left a body of writings, but its extent is debated: of the 34 attributed texts, doubts have been raised about 27. There is agreement that eight of these are not genuine, and six are doubtful (or Columbanus plus accretions), and only recently has a consensus emerged that the thirteen *Instructiones* are his. Thus there are 20 works that can be used to establish his thought. Our information about him comes from what we can glean from his writings, a life by Jonas of Bobbio, and later lives of St Gall. Hence the details and dates of his life are matters of controversy.

Stancliffe, C., 'The Thirteen Sermons Attributed to Columbanus and the Question of their Authorship', in M. Lapidge (ed.), *Columbanus: Studies in the Latin Writings* (1997)

TO'L

Colum Cille (*c.*521–597), founder of the monasteries of *Iona, Derry, and *Durrow, born into the Northern *Uí Néill lineage of *Cenél Conaill. The defining act of his life was his leaving Ireland to be a pilgrim of Christ in Britain, where he established himself with twelve followers at Iona in the territory of Scottish *Dál Riata. By the 10th century stories were in circulation that he did this to expiate his role in the battle of Cúl Drebene in 561; it has been seen as a penance imposed by a synod held at Teltown in 562, but these explanations may have been spun out of allusive remarks in *Adomnán's Life of the saint. While later poetic tradition portrayed Colum Cille as a permanent exile from Ireland, Adomnán shows that this was not so. Colum Cille was never cut off from Irish contacts, founding churches in Ireland after 563 and visiting his foundations on more than one occasion. His close kinship with the northern Uí Néill high king Áed mac Ainmerech may have helped Colum Cille at the meeting of the kings at *Druim Cett, and he appears to have been closely connected also with *Áedán mac Gabráin, king of Dál Riata. From his death he was immediately regarded as a saint and efforts were made in the 7th century to collect stories of him while memories remained. These served as one of the sources for Adomnán's Life of the saint, written in 697. An Irish poem in his praise, *Amra Coluimb Chille*, is thought to date from soon after his death and was studied in church schools in the 10th and 11th centuries. By this date Colum Cille was seen not only as an exile from his homeland but as specially a patron of Irish poets, and an abundant literature sprang up in verse about him or composed in his name. In the mid-12th century a new Life was composed in Irish in the form of a homily at Derry, by that date the principal church in the Columban community. In the early 16th century Manus *O'Donnell had Adomnán's Life translated into Irish, fusing this with a modern paraphrase of the Middle Irish homily and many other anecdotes and poems about the saint, to produce the fullest version of his legendary history.

RS

comarbae, see COARB.

Combination Acts. Legislation prohibiting *trade union activity under heavy penalties was passed by the Irish parliament in 1729 and 1743, and reinforced by subsequent enactments. Since Ireland was not covered by the British Combination Acts of 1799–1800, a specifically Irish act was passed by the United Kingdom parliament in 1803. The whole body of anti-combination legislation was repealed in 1824.

combinations, see TRADE UNIONISM.

Commercial Propositions, negotiated 1784–5, an attempt to rationalize the laws governing trade between Great Britain and Ireland by reducing or eliminating tariffs. In addition to removing anomalies left by the settlement of 1782, the prime minister, William Pitt, hoped to reinforce the connection between the two kingdoms by having Ireland contribute to the cost of imperial defence. Irish *patriot opinion, however, saw this requirement, and an accompanying proposal that the Irish parliament should be bound to replicate British legislation relating to shipping, as infringements of *legislative independence. There was also resentment that Ireland was still excluded from the East India Company's lucrative monopoly, and that points already agreed had been revised to meet objections from English interests. The commercial bill was abandoned after passing its first reading (15 Aug. 1785) by an unacceptably low majority. Its failure, confirming Pitt's concern at the instability of the Anglo-Irish connection, helped prepare the way for the Act of *Union.

Commission on Vocational Organization, appointed by the *Fianna Fáil government in 1939 to report on the practicability of developing vocational organization in Ireland; the means of achieving this; the rights and powers that should be conferred on vocational bodies; and the relationship between vocational bodies and the government and legislature. Irish interest in vocational organization was a response to the publication in 1931 of the papal encyclical *Quadragesimo anno*, which discussed the 'Reconstruction of the Social Order'. It was also in part a reaction against the substantial increase in intervention by government in the economy since the Fianna Fáil government had come to power in 1932. Support for the concept was much stronger within *Fine Gael, the main opposition party, than in government ranks. The commission recommended the establishment of a national vocational organization, which would act as the final arbiter in disputes between various interest groups and would play a major role in negotiating collective wage and price agreements. When the report was published in 1943 it was largely ignored, though it influenced the structure of the *Labour Court which was established in 1946.
MED

Common Prayer, Book of, the authoritative text for the liturgy of the *Church of Ireland, containing services for morning and evening prayer, holy communion, baptism, confirmation, marriage, burial, and ordination, together with (usually) the Thirty-Nine Articles. It was first used in the reign of Edward VI, when Cranmer's English Prayer Books of 1549 and 1552 were imposed on Ireland by royal authority, but it was not till 1560 that the Irish Act of *Uniformity established the revised Elizabethan English Prayer Book as the statutory norm. An Irish translation by William Daniel was printed in Dublin in 1608. The Irish Act of Uniformity of 1666 adopted the changes made to the English Prayer Book in 1662. With *disestablishment in 1870 responsibility for the liturgy of the Church of Ireland passed to the General Synod, which in 1878 authorized a revised Book of Common Prayer. Further revisions were published in 1926 and 1933. In 1984 a completely new liturgy was issued—the Alternative Prayer Book—which has since become standard in the Church of Ireland.
AF

commons, an area of waste land over which members of specified communities enjoyed customary rights such as estover (collection of wood or other necessaries), pasture, and turbary (see BOGS). These rights of *public* commons were usually of medieval origin, and unlike similar rights of *private* commons, which might be granted by a *landlord to his tenant for a determinable period over part of his estate, could not be extinguished by the proprietor of the land. By 1800, public commons remained as a significant feature of the agrarian landscape in those parts of eastern Ireland which had been heavily *manorialized by the *Anglo-Normans. Most public commons had originally been granted to a particular manor or borough, and remained in their titular ownership if not their discretionary control. Others were owned by the crown or were shared by the residents of contiguous districts or the owners of estates there. By the early 19th century, the surviving commons appeared increasingly anachronistic in an age of farm improvement, and were subject to some 40 parliamentary acts of *enclosure between 1800 and 1840. By this time public commons were in any case being increasingly overrun by squatters, as population pressure increased. Many of these squatters were eventually, through undisturbed possession, to gain freehold rights of land ownership.
LJP

Commonwealth. The transition from British empire to British Commonwealth, which had begun before 1914, accelerated during the *First World War. The South African statesman Smuts was influential in formulating the idea of a British Commonwealth of Nations, united by ties of history and tradition rather than close constitutional bonds. The term 'empire' continued to be used by the British government, though not by the dominions.

In 1921 dominion concern at the *Anglo-Irish War was expressed at the imperial conference taking place in London and Smuts favoured dominion status as a solution. The treaty was welcomed by the dominions, although the consequences of including in the Commonwealth a country with different history and traditions were not foreseen.

The Irish played little part in the 1923 imperial conference but after that, with Canada and South Africa, were determined to extend dominion status by removing inequalities. In the imperial conferences of 1926 and 1930, and the Operation of Dominion Legislation conference in 1929, the Irish played a leading role in the drafting of the Balfour declaration and the Statute of *Westminster, which gave the dominions constitutional independence. The Balfour declaration stated that the dominions were 'autonomous communities ... equal in status, in no way subordinate ... in any aspect of their domestic or external affairs though united by a common allegiance to the Crown and freely associated as a member of the British Commonwealth'. Equality of status was 'the root principle'. However, the Irish contribution to these constitutional landmarks in the Commonwealth lacked electoral appeal at home.

In 1932, when de *Valera abolished the *oath of allegiance, the British government mobilized the dominions to protest but this backfired. It stiffened de Valera's distrust of the Commonwealth and he rejected Commonwealth arbitration on the *land annuities. His vigorous response made Canada and South Africa reluctant to intervene again as the dispute intensified. However, an Irish delegation (excluding de Valera) attended the imperial economic conference at Ottawa, and Irish officials continued to attend Commonwealth meetings at the *League of Nations.

The *External Relations Act and the 1937 *constitution implemented de Valera's policy of *external association. They were discussed at the 1937 imperial conference, when British and Commonwealth delegates accepted that they did not affect the Free State's position as a member of the Commonwealth.

When war broke out in 1939, Ireland was the only neutral dominion. Churchill tried to enlist dominion support over the *treaty ports but was unsuccessful. The dominions, particularly Canada, helped to mitigate the tension between Ireland, Britain, and America over *neutrality. After the war, although he considered secession, de Valera maintained the uneasy Irish relationship with the Commonwealth.

When the *interparty government took office in 1948, it decided not to attend the Commonwealth prime ministers' conference in October 1948 but before this, in circumstances still controversial, Taoiseach John A. *Costello suddenly announced the repeal of the External Relations Act while on a visit to Canada. After pressure from Commonwealth prime ministers, the British government agreed to recognize 'the specially close relationship between Eire and the Commonwealth' and not to treat Ireland as a foreign country for purposes of trade and citizenship. These principles were incorporated in the *Ireland Act 1949.

Mansergh, Nicholas, *The Unresolved Question* (1991)

DMcM

Commonwealth Labour Party, a pro-British breakaway from the *Northern Ireland Labour Party founded in December 1942 by Harry *Midgley. It contested six seats at the 1945 Northern Ireland general election, winning 8 per cent of the vote, but only Midgley was elected. The party proved to be little more than a stepping stone in Midgley's political odyssey, and faded out soon after he left to join the *Ulster Unionist Party in 1947. ACH

commonwealthmen, also 'true Whigs' or 'real Whigs', a minority tradition in political writing and activism emphasizing the radical element in *Whig ideology. Though influenced by 17th-century *republican writers like James Harrington and Algernon Sidney, commonwealthmen generally advocated a mixed constitution of monarchy, aristocracy, and parliament. They showed some interest in *parliamentary reform, strictly confined to securing the better representation of property owners. But their main concern was with parliamentary control of the executive, combined with civic virtue, as the only barriers against corruption and despotism. Their writings form one strand in the origin of late 18th-century American, British, and Irish radicalism. The best-known Irish commonwealthmen were *Toland, *Hutcheson, and the circle round *Molesworth, though *Swift, as he made clear in the fifth **Drapier's Letter*, could in some respects claim to be part of the same tradition.

Communist Party. The first Communist Party of Ireland was formed in October 1921, when members of the Socialist Party of Ireland, formed in 1917 and led by Roddy Connolly (son of James *Connolly), affiliated to the third *International. It dissolved in 1924, when James *Larkin's Irish Workers' League took over both the membership and the role of Comintern affiliate. Re-established in 1933, it dissolved following the Nazi invasion of Russia in 1941. It was revived in 1948 as the Irish Workers' League, and once again became the Communist Party of Ireland in 1970. In none of these guises has it attracted significant electoral or popular support.

composition, an agreement compounded between various parties, refers to the commutation of *coyne and livery (for the upkeep of *bastard feudal armies) and *cess (for the upkeep of government troops) into permanent taxes in the last quarter of the 16th century. The idea of universal commutation was devised by Edmund Tremayne, *Sidney's private secretary, as a means of demilitarizing the lordships, promoting law and order, and making the civil and military establishment self-sufficient, and was advocated as a panacea by Sidney himself when he entered his third deputyship in 1575. Sidney tried to blackmail the *Pale by demanding a huge cess which he offered to commute to £2,134, a mere £9 per ploughland. The Palesmen refused to pay and sent representatives to court. Sidney, having obtained regional compositions in Connacht and Munster, dispatched an official delegation to London. The Pale's eventual agreement to a one-year composition of £2,000 instead of a permanent tax was a pyrrhic victory for Sidney.

In the 1585–6 parliament *Perrot wanted a total composition of £3,000, the equal rating of ploughlands, and an agreement between landlords and tenants. He gained momentum from his success in Connacht but in the end had to be satisfied with £2,000 negotiated outside parliament, which favoured the Palesmen by spreading the burden to other parts of Leinster. The debate over composition is critical as it involved the state's right to taxation and the subject's right to consent. HM

Composition of Connacht, a tripartite taxation agreement between the crown, lords, and commons of the western province in 1585. It replaced *Malby's composition of 1577, which had been extracted by military threat with the purpose of breaking the power of the magnates. The new composition was negotiated in the lords' favour by Nicholas White and Thomas Dillon, *Old English supporters of Lord Deputy *Perrot, overruling objections from *Bingham, the provincial governor. Lordships were divided by survey into 'quarters' of 120 acres. *Coyne and livery due to the lord from tenants was converted into fixed rents. In turn each quarter paid 10 shillings annually to the president in lieu of *cess, excepting those quarters of the lord declared rent free. The lords were glad to dispense with coyne and livery, but Bingham fumed at the extensive freedoms they were receiving. However, the composition, levied more widely across Connacht than in 1577, yielded £3,645 per annum. This sum, exceeding the *provincial presidency's administrative costs, allowed considerable freedom of action. When the *Nine Years War spread to Connacht in 1595, the collection of composition rent was impeded and the effectiveness of the presidency began to crumble. The composition worked well in Clanrickard and Thomond, where primogeniture was well established, but the attempt to enforce the required abolition of *tanistry as a method of succession caused dangerous revolts, especially amongst the Mayo *Burkes. HM

conacre, land rented for the taking of a single crop, most commonly of potatoes. Conacre was taken by tradesmen, by small farmers, and most commonly by agricultural labourers, who invested all or most of their earnings in potato ground from which to feed their families. The practice thus illustrates the limited role of retail markets in pre-Famine rural Ireland. Conacre rents were a frequent cause of *agrarian violence, as population pressure increased and as farmers, encouraged by price trends to move into livestock, no longer found in such lettings a profitable means of providing for crop rotation.

concealed lands were lands illegally detained from the crown after leases lapsed, rebels were forfeited, and monasteries dissolved. English-run attempts to resume these lands in Ireland were exploited by unscrupulous adventurers and brought acute political problems.

Beginning in the late 1580s Lord Treasurer Burghley in England made grants of Irish concealed lands to encourage their recipients to make discoveries. There were many racketeers but the leading figure was the deputy escheator-general in Ireland, Richard *Boyle, who worked hand in glove with the deputy surveyor-general, Francis Capstock. Having taken advantage of a landholder whose title was not in order, Boyle acquired a cheap lease through a grant of concealed lands.

The campaign for concealments was one cause of the *Nine Years War spreading to Connacht in 1595. Boyle was jailed by Lord Deputy Burgh in 1597 but, aided by Sir Geoffrey Fenton, the secretary of the Irish *privy council, he relaunched the campaign in 1598. After the revolt in Munster, Boyle was again imprisoned and the campaign wound up.

The Commission for *Defective Titles (1606) tried to remedy landholder insecurity but the search for concealed lands continued unofficially. The minor Jacobean *plantation in Wicklow had its origins in the discovery of a 'long slept' royal title. *Old English complaints eventually took shape as one of the *Graces for security of tenure in line with the English Concealment Act of 1624.

A renewed search for crown lands in the 1670s threatened to disrupt the delicately balanced *Restoration land settlement. HM

Confederate Catholics of Ireland, sometimes referred to, after the title of a book by C. P. Meehan (1846), as the 'Confederation of Kilkenny', formed in the aftermath of the *rising of 1641 to administer Catholic-controlled parts of the country pending a final settlement. A meeting of lay and clerical leaders at Kilkenny on 7 June 1642 established a confederation of Irish Catholics bound together by an oath of association asserting their rights as subjects of Charles I. They set up a provisional executive and called an election by sending out writs in customary fashion. The first of nine general assemblies met at Robert Shee's house in Kilkenny on 14 October 1642. Lords and clergy sat together in the same chamber as the commons, who were mostly landowners, lawyers, and merchants. This mix of Old Irish, *Old English, and some New English, debating in English, announced that they were not a parliament. The first assembly wound up by appointing a supreme council to run its affairs and by calling for similar councils at provincial and county level. The motto on the confederate seal of office read *Pro Deo, Rege et Patria, Hibernia Unanimis* (For God, King and Fatherland, Ireland united).

In the supreme council the Old English and lawyers had greater influence and, being based at Kilkenny, the Butler connection was strong. As a result Lord Mountgarrett (*Ormond's grand uncle) and Richard *Bellings were president and secretary respectively of the first five councils. They established four provincial army commands rather than a unified command, minted money, set up a printing press, collected taxes, and raised supplies. Agents were sent to foreign courts for money and arms but the confederation received only some £70,000 in aid. More success was achieved by issuing letters of marque to foreign mariners who protected Irish Catholic trade while attacking English shipping. Administratively the confederation was considered bureaucratic and as the end neared its tax demands became unbearable.

Major divisions emerged over the first *Ormond peace in 1646. The 'Ormondists' on the supreme council, headed by Muskerry (see CLANCARTY) and Bellings, proclaimed the peace. The clerical faction led by *Rinuccini, the recently arrived papal nuncio, along with those affected by the *plantations, wanted the full restoration of Catholicism. A middle group, led by Patrick *Darcy, Bishop *French, and *Antrim, emerged from the majority on the supreme council to repudiate the treaty in favour of confederate unity. After Owen Roe *O'Neill had staged a coup in support of the nuncio in September 1646, this middle grouping got the imprisoned Ormondists released and called a general assembly in January 1647. This rejected the treaty but exonerated its proponents, and altered the confederate oath to give itself the final say in any future such agreement. After the military defeats of 1647, the moderates tried to maintain unity by further strengthening the assembly's power over the executive. Although the *Inchiquin truce broke the confederacy, the last-ditch second Ormond peace subsequently gave the middle group much of what it wanted.

Ohlmeyer, Jane (ed.), *Ireland from Independence to Occupation 1641–60* (1993)

HM

confederate clubs, see IRISH CONFEDERATION.

Confederate War (1641–53), also known as the Irish Civil War, the War of the Confederation, and the Eleven Years War. Developing out of the *rising of 1641, it was part of the 'general crisis' of the mid-17th century, which saw subjects and subject peoples in revolt against absolutist monarchies, with religion often as a complicating or overriding factor. The civil wars in Britain 1642–51 (with which the Confederate War was linked in 'the War of the Three Kingdoms'), and the Thirty Years War 1618–48 (which kept continental powers otherwise occupied), were crucial determinants of the outcome of the Irish struggle.

In December 1641 an alliance between the Ulster Irish and the *Old English of the *Pale saw a general Catholic rising across the country, culminating in the formulation of political demands, and an outline plan for a provisional civil administration, in March 1642. By this time the state and settler interest had regrouped. The sieges of Drogheda and Cork were raised and *Ormond defeated insurgents at Kilrush, Co. Kildare (15 Apr. 1642); a Scottish army landed at *Carrickfergus under Robert Munroe, beating off Sir Phelim *O'Neill and taking Newry. The Pale, east Ulster, and south Munster had been secured for the king, but the outbreak of war between king and parliament in England left royalists in Ireland undersupplied, underpaid, and on the defensive. Meanwhile the insurgents had organized themselves into the *Confederate Catholics of Ireland with an administrative centre at Kilkenny in order to secure law and order in their own areas, to galvanize their war effort, and to negotiate an advantageous resolution to the conflict. Owen Roe *O'Neill and Thomas *Preston, experienced generals, returned from continental exile with veteran soldiers and began training the confederate army.

Confederation of Kilkenny

The English Civil War forced parliament into alliance with the Scots and the king into negotiation with the Confederate Catholics. Ormond opened negotiations in June 1643 and a ceasefire came into operation in September. This allowed him to send the king 5,000 troops but divided the Protestants in Ireland, leaving Munro to fight separately in Ulster and leading to the subsequent defection to parliament of *Inchiquin in Munster and *Coote in Connacht. The confederates gained only limited political recognition from the truce while squandering their military potential. They failed to send Montrose, the royalist commander in Scotland, enough military aid to force Munroe's withdrawal from Ulster and then annoyed their best generals by making the earl of Castlehaven, a political appointee, overall commander. Their scope for action was, however, limited by a shortage of cash to pay troops. With rents and revenue already hit by the 1641 rebellion, the outbreak of the English Civil War and the activities of the parliamentary navy reduced exports to a trickle. The ceasefire enabled a limited trade recovery but not enough to facilitate full-scale war.

The greatest confederate military success coincided with the breakdown of peace negotiations with the king. In 1646 a secret peace negotiated by the earl of Glamorgan was repudiated by the royalists and the first *Ormond peace by the confederates. Buoyed up with money brought from Rome by Rinuccini, O'Neill won a crushing victory over Munroe at *Benburb and Preston took Roscommon, but their successes were not followed up and they signally failed to co-operate in a joint campaign against Dublin. The two generals had their equivalents at sea in the 40 to 50 confederate privateers who, in spite of considerable individual success, never managed the concerted strategy worthy of a navy. On 19 June 1647 Ormond handed Dublin over to the parliamentary command of Michael Jones. Jones in Leinster and Inchiquin in Munster went on the offensive, winning decisive victories over Preston at *Dungan's Hill and over the Munster army at Knocknanuss, Co. Cork (13 Nov. 1647), until their supplies dried up as a result of the recommencement of the English Civil War. O'Neill now detached himself from the confederacy over its truce with the Protestant Inchiquin.

Confederate coffers were empty and the economy at a standstill as famine in 1648 and then plague in 1649 ravaged the country. With Charles I condemned to execution and *Cromwell readying the New Model Army, the confederates and royalists concluded the second Ormond peace in January 1649. Ormond's assault on Dublin was defeated at *Rathmines and *Drogheda and Wexford had already fallen by the time he and O'Neill belatedly patched up their differences. The parliamentarians under Cromwell and later *Ireton and Ludlow made a steady advance across Ireland, facilitated by continuous resupply, naval control of the coasts, and artillery that battered down obstructing fortifications. During 1650 they won victories at Macroom, Co. Cork (10 Apr.), and Scarrifhollis, Co. Donegal (21 June). They gained Limerick in October 1651 and Galway in April 1652, by which time their occupying forces amounted to 30,000 men. Only in its dying embers did the Irish Catholic struggle receive foreign support, and then it was the desultory interest of a minor princeling, the duke of Lorraine.

More generally, the confederate-royalist cause failed due to a narrow economic base, weak leadership, and religious divisions. The divisions were carried into exile and showed up in the differing histories of the confederacy by Bellings and *Lynch on the one hand and O'Ferrall and O'Connor (see RINUCCINI) on the other. The country itself was left devastated—rent and population levels did not regain pre-war levels until the 1670s.

Ohlmeyer, Jane (ed.), *Ireland from Independence to Occupation, 1641–60* (1995)

HM

Confederation of Kilkenny, see CONFEDERATE CATHOLICS OF IRELAND.

conformity, a legal procedure whereby converts from Catholicism to the *Church of Ireland, having read a public recantation of former religious errors and taken Anglican communion, registered their change of religion with the court of *chancery. The original rolls were destroyed in 1922 (see PUBLIC RECORDS), but surviving indexes show a total of 1,853 converts registered in the period 1703–51 and 3,944 during 1752–1800. A legally certified conformity was of evident value to the Catholic upper and middle classes, offering release from the restrictions on property, marriage, and political activity imposed by the *penal laws, as well as the possibility of admission to the legal profession. What proportion of humbler converts recorded their change of religion remains unclear. About a quarter of all recorded converts were women. Detailed studies show an increase in convert numbers at times of tension, such as the *Jacobite scare of 1744–5 and the *Whiteboy disturbances. In some cases, as with the family of Bishop *Butler of Cork, only the heir to the property conformed, and some convert families, like the *Mathews of Tipperary, were perceived as part of a continuing Catholic interest. Legislation in 1728 and 1733 sought to curb the entry into legal practice of recent and nominal converts.

Congested Districts Board, established in 1891 by Arthur *Balfour, and invested with extensive powers to encourage agriculture and industry in parts of the country where, it was believed, acute poverty was inhibiting individual initiative. The congested districts initially covered an area along the west coast from Donegal to Cork but this was later extended inland to take in over one-third of the country. The board comprised ten (later increased to fourteen) members. The *chief secretary and a member of the *Land Commission sat ex officio, with nominated members drawn from the local community and including representatives of the churches, landlords, business, and the professions. Sponsored schemes ranged from the employment of agricultural instructors and the promotion of cottage industries to the purchase of land for resale to tenants. Opinions differ as to the success of the board. It was undoubtedly popular, mainly because of its willingness to spend money. (From 1909 it had an annual sum of £250,000 at its disposal.) The quality of its financial management, however, left much to be desired. Conflict was also to arise between the CDB and the Department of *Agriculture and Technical Instruction, which was attempting to achieve similar ends by somewhat different means. VC

Congregationalists, see INDEPENDENTS.

Congress of Irish Unions, see IRISH CONGRESS OF TRADE UNIONS.

Connachta, otherwise the *Fir Ol nÉcmacht*, were the inhabitants of Connacht. Their name may be derived from the Old Irish *cond*, 'head', i.e. the premier tribe of the region, although Irish tradition derives the element *Conn-* from *Conn Cétchathach. Their capital was at *Cruachain, the modern Rathcroghan in Co. Roscommon. Their rise as a political power is set in the 5th and 6th centuries when they came to dominate *Tara. In the Ulster Cycle (see LITERATURE IN IRISH) the Connachta are portrayed as the hereditary enemies of the Ulstermen, although they are also granted their own set of heroes. JPM

Connaught Rangers mutiny (28 June–2 July 1920), a mass refusal to obey orders involving some 300 members of the regiment stationed in the Punjab. Their protest was inspired by accounts from Ireland of repression by government forces (see ANGLO-IRISH WAR). One private, James Daly, was shot. Others received long prison sentences, although all were in fact released by early 1923.

Conn Cétchathach ('Conn of the Hundred Battles'; also Cétchorach, 'of the hundred treaties'), was a mythical king from whom the *Connachta, including the powerful *Uí Néill, claimed descent. Irish tradition placed him as king of Ireland at *Tara in the 2nd century AD and created a series of tales about his marvellous reign. Among the major events of his career was the division of Ireland in two along the *Eiscir Riata. JPM

Connolly, James (1868–1916), labour leader. Born of Irish immigrant parents in Edinburgh, he imbibed Irish nationalism from a *Fenian uncle and socialism from grim experience of working-class life combined with avid reading of Marx and others. Ironically, he first came to Ireland as a boy soldier in the 1880s. In 1896 he was invited to Dublin to set up the *Irish Socialist Republican Party. He established and edited the *Workers' Republic*, the party organ. A prolific political journalist and pamphleteer, his greatest works are *Labour in Irish History* (1910) and *The Re-conquest of Ireland* (1915). Connolly's advanced socialist-republicanism made little headway and in 1903, disillusioned with his lack of political progress, and with a growing family, he went to America. There, in the burgeoning socialist political scene, Connolly added an international dimension to his thinking.

In 1910 Connolly was invited back to Ireland to run the newly established Socialist Party of Ireland (SPI). Appointed Belfast organizer of the *Irish Transport and General Workers' Union (ITGWU), he successfully organized the dockers and won a pay rise for striking seamen and firemen. Called in by women linen workers during their unsuccessful strike of 1911, he set up the Irish Textile Workers' Union. Aiming to wean the Belfast movement from the labour-unionism of William *Walker's Independent Labour Party, Connolly convened a 'Socialist Unity' conference in Dublin, from which emerged the Independent Labour Party of Ireland (ILP(I)). Only a few Belfast trade unionists, among them Tom *Johnson, became members. Connolly, with Larkin, also played a pivotal role in establishing the more important Irish *Labour Party, based on the *Irish Trade Union Congress (ITUC).

At the height of the *home rule crisis, Connolly achieved notoriety in a debate with Walker on socialism and the national question in the socialist paper *Forward*. He became unpopular with the followers of Joseph *Devlin for opposing the *Nationalist party's acceptance of the temporary exclusion of Ulster from home rule. His return from jail for his part in the 1913 *Dublin lockout was the occasion of a hostile Unionist demonstration at the Great Northern railway station. Connolly underlined his pariah status in Belfast by openly opposing the war in 1914. Both he and his opponents were glad when he was called to Dublin as acting ITGWU general secretary, replacing Larkin, who had gone to America.

Although opposed to an imperialist war, in which the workers on all sides would be the losers, Connolly hoped to turn it with German help into an insurrection against British rule in Ireland. As commandant of the *Irish Citizen Army he reached agreement, in January 1916, with the military council of the *Irish Republican Brotherhood for a joint insurrection. He and his comrades duly took part in the *rising of 1916, in which *Pearse described him as being 'the guiding brain of our resistance'. Connolly sustained leg wounds in the fighting and was propped in a chair to be executed by firing squad.

Although he now passed into the nationalist pantheon, the state that eventually emerged paid him lip-service, while shunning his ideology. Nowadays, for most Irish people, his name is associated with street-names, hospitals, barracks, and train stations. His legacy is disputed even among Ireland's small, faction-ridden left. Labour politicians and trade unionists play down the insurrectionist side. It is only the present-day republican movement that accords his ideas and reputation full credence.

Greaves, C. Desmond, *The Life and Times of James Connolly* (1961)

Morgan, A., *James Connolly: A Political Biography* (1988)

PC

Conolly, William (1662–1729), politician. Extravagant accounts of his rise from humble origins included the claim that he was the son (or grandson) of a Catholic innkeeper in Ballyshannon, Co. Donegal. In fact both he and his father were important enough to be among the Protestants attainted by the *patriot parliament for their adherence to *William III. However, it is clear that shrewd dealings in the chaotic landmarket created by the *Williamite confiscations enabled him vastly to increase his fortune. Up to 1714 he shared the leadership of the Irish *Whig Party with Alan *Brodrick. Thereafter, with their *Tory opponents in eclipse, the two men competed for dominance. Where Brodrick sought to enhance his position by obstruction, and by sporadically espousing what he presented as the Irish interest, Conolly established himself as the reliable servant of successive English ministries, the first clearly identifiable *undertaker. Regarded as the richest commoner in Ireland, he built *Castletown House. His great-nephew and heir **Thomas Connolly** (1738–1803), attached to a major English political dynasty by his marriage to a daughter of the duke of Richmond, was MP for Co. Londonderry 1761–1800, and also sat in the British parliament 1759–80. His politics were self-consciously those of an independent country gentleman, willing to support government but also liable to oppose on *patriot or popular issues. He favoured the admission of Catholics to parliament and supported the Act of *Union.

constitution of Ireland (1937). Largely the work of de *Valera, the constitution was drafted during 1935–7 by a small team of civil servants working under his supervision. He also consulted academic, legal, and religious authorities.

De Valera retained features of the 1922 *constitution of the Irish Free State regarding the *Oireachtas, the government, and the courts, but there were important differences. Article 2 defined the national territory as the 'whole island of Ireland', but in article 3 jurisdiction was limited to the 26 counties. Articles 12–14 provided for an elected *president as head of state with important discretionary powers. To much surprise, the *Senate, abolished in 1936, was reconstituted on vocational lines. The *president of the executive council was replaced by the *taoiseach with strengthened prime ministerial powers.

In a far-reaching provision, article 34 gave the *Supreme Court power to review the constitutionality of new legislation. Articles 40–5, which showed the influence of Catholic social thinking, dealt with fundamental rights concerning family, education, private property, and religion. Articles 46–7 provided for amendment of the constitution by popular referendum.

The most controversial parts of the constitution in 1937 were the role of the president, which opponents claimed had dictatorial aspects; the 'special position' accorded to the Catholic church in article 44 (abolished by referendum in 1972); and the status accorded to women. There were also protests that article 3 recognized *partition. The constitution was submitted to a referendum in July 1937 and passed by 685,105 votes to 526,945. It became law in December 1937. In the referendum that followed the Good Friday Agreement (see PEACE PROCESS) amendments to articles 2, 3, and 29, relating to the status of Northern

Ireland, were approved by 94 per cent of those voting. DMcM

Constitution of Northern Ireland Act (1973), passed by the United Kingdom Parliament following the closing of *Stormont. The act was intended as the basis for a comprehensive settlement in *Northern Ireland, replacing most of the extant clauses of the *Government of Ireland Act 1920. It created a 78-seat Assembly, and sought the support of the Catholic minority through *proportional representation and power-sharing in government. Assembly powers were to be less than those of Stormont, initially excluding policing, justice, and elections. The guarantee enshrined in the *Ireland Act of 1949, that Northern Ireland would not cease to be part of the UK without the consent of the parliament of Northern Ireland, was modified slightly to require 'the consent of the majority of the people of Northern Ireland'. Assembly elections took place in May 1973, and the ill-fated *Sunningdale agreement later sought to implement the power-sharing scheme. ACH

constitution of 1782, see LEGISLATIVE INDEPENDENCE.

constitution of the Irish Free State, drafted by the *Provisional Government and ratified by the *Dáil in December 1922. Initial hopes of producing a document acceptable to republican opponents of the *Anglo-Irish treaty vanished when the British government insisted on the inclusion of clauses relating to the *oath of allegiance, the *governor-general, and appeal to the privy council. Article 2 of the Constitution Act declared void any article or amendment repugnant to the treaty.

Under the constitution, government and authority were derived from the people. The *Oireachtas (legislature) consisted of the king (represented by the governor-general), the Dáil, and the *Senate. Voting was by *proportional representation. Executive authority was vested in the king but exercisable by an executive council, headed by a president, which was nominated by and responsible to the Dáil.

The constitution contained some novel features: the appointment of external ministers from outside the Oireachtas (although this was never implemented); powers of popular initiative and referendum; the qualified dissolution of the Dáil; the vesting in the whole executive council of control over dissolutions of parliament; and the amendment of the constitution by ordinary legislation. This last provision was much criticized because of the implications for citizens' rights at a time of draconian *public safety legislation.

Extensive amendments to the constitution during 1922–36 included the abolition of popular initiative, referendum, and direct elections to the Senate in 1928, and the abolition of the Senate itself in 1936. By the time the constitution was superseded in 1937 (see CONSTITUTION OF IRELAND), 41 of its 83 articles had been amended. DMcM

constructive unionism, or 'killing Home Rule by kindness', titles given to the Irish policy of successive Conservative governments in the period 1895–1905. The policies concerned fall into three broad categories: land, local government, and Catholic university education. Land purchase was a central principle of constructive unionism, and was incorporated into a succession of *Land Acts, culminating in *Wyndham's measure of 1903. Constructive unionists also argued that democratic local government on the English model of 1888 was consistent with Unionist principles, and vigorously supported the *Local Government Act of 1898. The creation of a Catholic *university was debated throughout the period, but the idea foundered on widespread opposition to state-sponsored denominational education. In addition, since constructive unionists sought to demonstrate that Unionist government could address all Irish grievances, it was logical that an imaginative minister such as Wyndham should sponsor the initiatives leading to the *devolution crisis (1904–5): this for many Irish Unionists demonstrated the extent of the paradox which constructive unionism embodied.

Some Unionist ideologues (such as Gerald *Balfour or Horace *Plunkett) linked ameliorative legislation to a broad philosophy of government, arguing that such measures would, especially in the context of a divided Irish parliamentary party, deprive nationalism of impetus, and possibly reconcile Ireland to the Union. However, recent scholarship has tended to pare away the self-congratulatory rhetoric surrounding constructive unionism, seeing it less as a coherent philosophy, and more as a series of distinct legislative responses to political challenges. Thus, Gerald Balfour's Land Act of 1896 has been seen less as a proactive measure, and more as a response to a specific set of demands urged by the radical Unionist politician T. W. *Russell. Equally, the Local Government Act (1898) has been interpreted as a pragmatic response to a parliamentary opportunity, and not as a carefully honed fragment of a broader Unionist programme. The Land Act of 1903 has been interpreted in the light of pressure applied from the *United Irish League and a reactivated Russellite agitation. Constructive unionism may also be viewed as part of a longer tradition of British government in Ireland: the policy was certainly prefigured by *Gladstone's approach to the problems of Irish administration.

Gailey, Andrew, *Ireland and the Death of Kindness: The Experience of Constructive Unionism, 1890–1905* (1987)

AJ

contraception was outlawed in the Irish Free State by the Criminal Law Amendment Act (1935); information about it had already been categorized as 'indecent literature' by the Censorship of Publications Act (1928). Some deputies and senators spoke out against the ban, mainly because they believed that it would drive contraception underground and promote 'immorality'. Some doctors and Protestant clergymen on the Commission on Emigration in 1956 dissented from the commission's disapproval of 'family limitation', on the grounds that large families on low income weakened women's and children's health. From the 1960s doctors were permitted to prescribe the contraceptive pill for menstrual regulation. Many Irish Catholics, however, were mindful of their church's ban on artificial birth control, reinforced by the papal encyclical *Humanae vitae* in 1968. In 1974 the *Supreme Court upheld people's right to import contraceptives for their own use. In 1979 the sale and distribution of contraception information was no longer deemed obscene and indecent, and in the same year the Health (Family Planning) Act legalized the sale and distribution of contraceptives to people for bona fide family planning purposes. Soon afterwards all restrictions on the sale of contraceptives were removed. CC

convention (1660), an assembly summoned following the coup (13 Dec. 1659) that preceded the *Restoration of Charles II. It met between 2 March and 27 May 1660, reassembling briefly in January 1661. The method of election remains unclear, but the 137 members, representing traditional parliamentary constituencies, were all Protestants, including both beneficiaries of the *Cromwellian land settlement and members of longer-established families. Its immediate purpose was to authorize a poll tax to pay the army, but members also considered the imminent political settlement, gradually moving towards an open commitment to the restoration of monarchy and episcopacy. The convention also asserted Ireland's right to tax and legislate for itself through parliament, and commissioned Sir William Domville (1609–89) to prepare a 'disquisition' rejecting English claims of legislative superiority. This part of its proceedings has encouraged interest in the convention as a landmark in the emergence of a distinct Protestant identity, foreshadowing 18th-century *patriotism.

Convention Act (1793). Meetings of elected delegates at the conventions of *Dungannon and at the *Catholic Convention had implicitly challenged parliament's claim to represent the nation. Passed in response to a further assembly planned by the *United Irishmen for Athlone, the Convention Act declared illegal all assemblies for the purpose of soliciting a change in the law that claimed the status of a representative body. The act was used to block attempts in 1811 to give the reconstituted *Catholic Committee a more representative character, and in 1814 to suppress its successor, the Catholic Board.

convocation of the *Church of Ireland, organized on the English model as a bicameral clerical assembly meeting concurrently with *parliament, was first convened in 1613. The upper house comprised the archbishops and bishops, the lower house archdeacons, deans, and 'proctors' representing the other clergy.

While purely advisory, lacking any legislative powers, and dependent on government to convene it, convocation was seen by many clergy as an assertion of the church's independence of parliament and its right to be consulted. Convocation drew up the 104 articles of religion 'agreed upon by the archbishops and bishops and the rest of the clergy of Ireland' in 1615. *Puritan in character, the articles were superseded when, meeting at the same time as parliament in 1634, convocation accepted, under government pressure, the Thirty-Nine Articles of the Church of England.

Convocation met only intermittently from then onwards, in 1636, 1640, and 1661–6. When it convened again, after a gap of over 30 years, from 1704 to 1713, *high-church clergy hoped that it would prove to be an agent of reform, but its debates were frequently acrimonious and inconclusive, and it failed to realize the hopes vested in it. After 1714 *Whig governments, suspicious of its high-church, even *Jacobite sentiments, refused to convene it. While meetings of the convocations of Canterbury and York were restored in the mid-19th century, the Irish convocation never met again, despite calls to have it revived, especially when *disestablishment was under consideration in the 1860s. KM

Conyngham, William (Burton) (1733–96). Born William Burton, the second son of a Co. Clare landowner, he inherited a life interest in the estates in Co. Meath and Donegal of his uncle, the 1st Earl Conyngham. (The title and other lands went to Burton's elder brother, on condition that both legatees changed their name to Conyngham.) He had entered parliament for his uncle's borough of Limavady in 1761 and generally supported government, for which he received appointments to the Barrack Board and elsewhere. In 1785 he began to develop a herring fishery on an island off the Donegal estate, which he renamed Rutland after the 4th duke of Rutland, lord lieutenant (1784–7). He invested in the project £20,000 raised on the Conyngham estate, and £20,000 granted by parliament. The fisheries declined after the first few years, and had collapsed by 1793–4. Also a keen student of antiquities, Conyngham was first treasurer of the *Royal Irish Academy.

Cooke, Henry (1788–1868), *Presbyterian champion of trinitarian orthodoxy and political parson. Cooke emerged as a public figure in 1821, when the appointment of a self-confessed *Arian, William Bruce, to the chair of Hebrew and Greek in the *Belfast Academical Institution, where most of the *Synod of Ulster's ordinands were trained, provoked Cooke, then minister of Killyleagh, Co. Down, to launch a campaign against Arianism in the college and in his church. Initial responses to his campaign were discouraging, but the acknowledgement of Arian opinions by Henry *Montgomery and other ministers during a government inquiry into the affairs of the institution enabled Cooke to attack them in the Synod, eventually achieving their secession and a reaffirmation of theological orthodoxy

This second *subscription controversy had political overtones, and after his victory Cooke became openly identified with conservatism in politics. However, many Presbyterians who had supported him theologically opposed him politically, particularly on the issue of *tenant right. They did not approve his publication of 'the banns of marriage' between presbyterianism and the *Church of Ireland at Hillsborough in 1834, and his deathbed appeal to Protestant electors in 1868 to vote *Tory to save the church from *disestablishment fell largely on deaf ears. Perhaps the only political issue on which he spoke for Presbyterians in general was his opposition to *O'Connell's *repeal movement. Significantly it was *Orangemen and not Presbyterians who erected his statue in the centre of Belfast. In death as in life Cooke has remained a controversial figure in Irish Presbyterianism, honoured by some and vilified by others.

Holmes, R. F. G., *Henry Cooke* (1981)

RFGH

co-operative movement. Unlike British co-operative activity, which centred on urban retailing, the Irish co-operative movement was based on agricultural processing and marketing. The co-operative form of organization involved the pooling of small capitals to create new enterprises which were democratically owned and controlled by the shareholder-farmers. In the eyes of its more visionary leaders, such as the unionist Sir Horace *Plunkett or the nationalist George Russell (AE), the co-operative movement had the potential to reconstruct an agriculture and rural society battered by the economic depression of the later 19th century.

Co-operative societies took three major forms. There were the co-operative creameries producing butter, which were located in the traditional dairying areas of Munster and Ulster. There were agricultural societies which achieved economies through the bulk purchasing of farm inputs. Finally there were the co-operative credit societies which extended credit to the poorer sections of rural society, and which were particularly numerous in the west of Ireland.

From small beginnings in the 1890s co-operative societies spread extensively through Ireland, in the process generating hostility from vested interest groups, in particular shopkeepers, traders, and *home rule politicians. By 1914 there were over 800 co-operative societies on the island. The largest group, and by far the most significant in financial terms, was composed of some 350 dairy or creamery societies. Other types of co-operative went into steep, usually terminal, decline during the *First World War or soon thereafter.

While the future belonged to the dairy co-operatives, the inter-war period proved to be a testing time. Depressed markets faced agricultural producers and exporters. As in the rural economy generally, the name of the game was survival. The period between the *Second World War and Ireland's entry to the European Economic Community (see EUROPEAN UNION) in 1973 was one of consolidation and slow expansion. Some co-operatives diversified into new activities, including the manufacture of cheese and milk powder, and the provision of a range of farm services. This period witnessed also the introduction of the co-operative livestock mart, which was of particular value to livestock farmers.

The decade after entry to the EEC was one of unprecedented prosperity for Irish farmers, though the gains were more muted thereafter. There was a flowering of small industrial and service co-operatives, as well as a renewed interest in co-operative ideas, but the dairy sector retained its predominant position. The process of amalgamation of small dairy co-operatives into larger units gathered pace, culminating in the creation of large agro-industrial enterprises. The largest of these extended their business horizons to European and global markets, becoming in effect multinational corporations owned and controlled from Ireland. Inevitably much of the democratic and participative ethos which inspired the early pioneers declined over time in deference to financial imperatives. Still the journey from crossroads creameries to transnational companies is one of the more remarkable stories of modern Irish enterprise. LK

Coote, Sir Charles (d. 1661), a remarkable survivor and beneficiary of the *Confederate War. With his brother Richard, he established a successful planter army in Leitrim, Sligo, and Roscommon. A defector to parliament over *Ormond's negotiations with the *Confederate Catholics, Coote returned from England as lord president of Connacht to take Sligo town in 1645. Combining his western army with the Laggan army, he defeated the Scots at Lisburn (1649) and the Confederate Catholics at Scarrifhollis, Co. Donegal (1650). He received Galway's submission in 1652 and influenced the settlement of Connacht by having Sligo, Leitrim, and the barony of Tirawly (Co. Mayo) exempted from *transplantation so that western army arrears could be satisfied. This 'Old Protestant' was never trusted by the Cromwellian arrivistes, especially the *Independents. Not surprisingly he was a prime mover at the *convention of 1660 for the *Restoration of Charles II, who rewarded him with lands and the title of earl of Mountrath. HM

copper mines, existing from the *Bronze Age, in Schull and Derrycahon, Co. Cork, and Killarney, Co. Kerry, have been radio-carbon dated to 1500 BC. In modern times, due to rising demand in the late 18th and 19th centuries, there were highly productive copper mines at Allihies, Co. Cork, Bunmahon, Co. Waterford, and Avoca and Ballymurtagh, Co. Wicklow. The price peaked, in the mid-19th century, at £100 a ton, falling to a low of £90 in 1875. By 1899, due to both overseas competition and falling demand, the output for the whole of Ireland had dropped to only 533 tons annually. Production remained low until the start of the *Second World War. Following the Minerals Development Act (1940), the state mining company, Minrai Teoranta, began general exploration. Post-war copper deposits have been found at Avoca, Tynagh, Co. Galway, Gortdrum, Aherlow, Mallow, Ballyvergin, and Silvermines in Munster, and Navan, Co. Meath. PC

Córas Iompair Éireann (CIE), established by the Transport Act of 1944, the result of a merger of the Great Southern railway and the Dublin United Tramway Company. CIE also absorbed many of the smaller bus companies, a process that was eventually to lead to state monopoly. It inherited a rail system dogged by soaring coal prices and wage demands, old stock, unprofitable lines, and a dwindling number of customers due to competition from road transport. The government stipulated that CIE become self-financing and at the same time perform the social service of keeping open non-commercial routes. These contradictory requirements led to repeated overhauls, but in practice political and social considerations have forced successive governments to subsidize CIE to a considerable degree. Under the Transport Act of 1950, CIE absorbed the Grand and Royal *canal companies. In 1953 the government approved a programme of railway modernization, including the change-over to diesel. In 1958 southern lines owned by the Great Northern Railway Company became part of CIE. Under the 1986 Transport Act, CIE became a state-owned holding company, with three highly autonomous subsidiaries, Iarnród Éireann, Bus Éireann, and Bus Átha Cliath. PC

Corish, Brendan (1918–90), *Labour Party leader and government minister. Corish was elected TD for Wexford in 1945, and served in the first *interparty government (1948–51) as parliamentary secretary to the minister for Local Government and Defence. In 1954, when the coalition returned to office, he was promoted to be minister for social welfare. He was elected to the leadership of the Labour Party in 1960, but had to wait until 1973 before returning to office. With the formation of the National Coalition (between *Fine Gael and Labour) in that year, Corish became **tánaiste* and Minister for Health and Social Welfare. On 1 July 1977, following the defeat of the coalition at a general election, and the loss of two Labour seats, Corish resigned from the party leadership. A moderate and sympathetic leader, Corish presided over a left-ward realignment of Labour in the 1960s, and increasing tensions between Dublin radicals and the party's rural base. Despite the electoral setback in 1977, the Corish years were also marked by a strengthening of Labour's popular support. AJ

Cork, the Irish city with probably the longest urban pedigree, and for the last four centuries the most important port south of Dublin. The marshy flood-plain of the river Lee gave the settlement its Gaelic name, *Corcaigh*, but the earliest urban embryo developed on rising ground along the south bank in the 7th and 8th centuries, around St Finbarre's monastery. Two nearby islands formed the lowest fording point across the Lee and they became the site for the second phase of Cork's urban beginnings. Permanent *Viking settlement began on the south island before the mid-9th century, and over the following two centuries a Hiberno-Norse trading community evolved below what was then a prestigious monastery.

The two islands had defensive fortifications and a sea-going fleet when Anglo-Norman grantees of *Henry II captured the town in 1177. Cork was made a royal borough and received a series of charters from 1189 which led to the emergence of Norman-style municipal government in the following century. A simple street system similar to that of the south island emerged on the north, and the city's maritime commerce, based on wool and hides, reached new levels. The wealth of the urban community was evident in new monastic foundations, the switch from timber to stone housing, and the growth of suburbs, Shandon north of the river and the episcopal borough of Fayth to the south. The city was particularly disadvantaged by the general economic and demographic reverses of 14th- and early 15th-century Ireland. The repeated destruction of the suburbs by rival Gaelic and Gaelicized warlords made the walled city even more emphatically an island fortress loyal in its protestations to the distant English crown, if in practice subservient to neighbouring Munster powers.

In the later 16th century the interlinkage of a reassertion of royal authority, the state promotion of Protestantism, and a fresh wave of English colonization across the hinterland turned the urban elite into unlikely champions of the *Counter-Reformation. The city benefited in material terms from the trade boom generated by the *Munster plantation in the following half-century, but the continued dominance of the *Old English burgher families protected its Catholic ambience. All changed midway through the *Confederate War when most of these families were expelled from the town by the royalist commander in 1644. It was, however, only with the *Cromwellian reconquest that a radically new municipal elite was installed from whom were derived a number of the great Protestant merchant dynasties.

The island parishes remained predominantly Protestant and New English for several generations, the suburbs culturally and religiously mixed. During this time Cork forged ahead as centre of Munster's agricultural export trade: the medieval walls were demolished, the sloblands west and east progressively reclaimed, and the suburbs transformed to become the workshop, market, and stockyard zone of a bustling city. Cork's growth curve was steepest from the 1670s (when it contained 10,000–12,000 inhabitants) to the 1770s (when it had probably reached 50,000), and this despite the physical destruction caused by the savage *Williamite siege in September 1690.

Cork's competitive success in processing and supplying beef, butter, pork, hides, and tallow products to commercial and naval markets in southern Europe, the Americas, and later Britain itself made it famous round the Atlantic world and gave it 150 years of urban prosperity and physical expansion, but it was a narrowly based and inequitably distributed economic system. For all the dynamism of the 18th-century port and the complexity of its Atlantic and European commerce, Cork failed to become a shipping or financial centre akin to Glasgow or Bordeaux.

Commercial and industrial growth faltered after the end of the *revolutionary and Napoleonic wars. Cork's salted provisions trade was eclipsed. The reorientation of southern agricultural exports towards England weakened its locational advantages while its wholesale and financial functions were undermined by Anglo-Irish market integration; only its status as centre of Irish butter exports remained. Local industrialization in *brewing and *distilling, *flour milling, *textiles, and *shipbuilding lost momentum in the mid-19th century and failed to offer employment to the pauper flood coming from its overpopulated hinterland, most starkly so during and after the *Great Famine. By then Cork's outport in the harbour, Cove/Queenstown, had become the principal Irish exit point for the mass migration to America, and remained so for a century. The nearly static Victorian city became notorious for appalling standards of housing and public health.

Perhaps more than any other southern Irish city, Cork remained a religious battleground in the 19th century, as a fractured middle class competed for control over municipal government, intellectual life, and philanthropic activity. However, success in securing one of the *Queen's Colleges for Cork in 1845 brought one institution to the city that cut across denominational battle-lines. The college and the city's newspapers reinforced Cork's cultural leadership of Munster society, and the distinctively radical edge of popular politics in the city, demonstrated in every generation between 1830 and 1922, rippled outwards.

The death by hunger strike of the imprisoned lord mayor, Terence *MacSwiney, in October 1920, followed by the burning of central Cork by crown forces in December, were the city's bitter rites of passage to second city in a Free State. Reindustrialization followed in the 1920s and 1930s, the first wave of investment being led by multinationals Ford and Dunlop. The new political order brought with it a housing revolution with the great expansion of local authority building and the explosive growth of the outer suburbs, bound to the centre by a proliferation of bus services. From mid-century Cork harbour emerged as a premier location for new industry, becoming the burgeoning centre of Ireland's chemical industry by the 1970s. Belatedly the exceptional natural qualities of the outer harbour were being exploited, enhanced by the discoveries of massive reserves of natural gas off Kinsale Head. Yet even this commercial resurgence towards the end of the 20th century did not reinvest the city with the strategic international significance it had had 200 years before.

Clarke, Howard (ed.), *Irish Cities* (1995)
Cronin, Maura, *Country, Class or Craft? The Politicisation of the Skilled Artisan in Nineteenth-Century Cork* (1995)
O'Flanagan, Patrick, and Buttimer, C. G. (eds.), *Cork: History and Society* (1993)

DD

Cork Association of Ministers, a grouping of ex-Church of Ireland clergy, founded in 1657 by Edward Worth, closely connected with the local Protestant gentry (particularly the *Boyles) and organized on Presbyterian lines to promote religious uniformity and to facilitate ordination. At the Dublin Convention of Ministers in 1658, which restored *tithes, Henry *Cromwell projected Worth's Munster experiment as a model for Ireland and England. The Cork Association was symptomatic of Old Protestant resurgence in the late 1650s. At the *Restoration Worth was rewarded with the bishopric of Killaloe after leading his ministers back into the established church.

HM

Corkery, Daniel (1878–1964), writer and cultural nationalist. Corkery joined the *Gaelic League as a young schoolteacher, contributed to D. P. *Moran's *Leader* 1901–20, and with Terence *MacSwiney founded the Cork Dramatic Society. He was primarily a cultural nationalist until the Easter rising (see RISING OF 1916). Angered by Republican defeat in the *Civil War and the subsequent reaction against nationalist idealism, he restated his ideals in *The Hidden Ireland* (1924) and *Synge and Anglo-Irish Literature* (1931). His definition of Irishness as rural, nationalist, and Catholic alienated his protégés *O'Faolain and Frank O'Connor. His reputation as the voice of de *Valeran orthodoxy overshadows his role as cultural catalyst.

PM

Cormac mac Airt was a legendary king of Ireland, and the epitome of the royal figure, especially in the 'histories' of his descendants, the *Connachta. His rule in *Tara is placed at *c.* AD 227–66 and the stories concerning him are extremely eclectic, e.g. orphaned before birth, nurtured by wolves, adopted Christianity before his death. He has been treated as emblematic of the Leinster domination of Tara but was later adopted into the tradition of the Connachta. The tales of the legendary Fionn mac Cumhaill were set within Cormac's reign. His reputed burial place was Rossnaree, Co. Meath.

JPM

Cormac's chapel at *Cashel is the most integral example of Romanesque *architecture in Ireland. The chapel is thought to be that built in 1127 by King Cormac *Mac Carthaig of Cashel and consecrated with great ceremony in 1134. The stylistic influence of this innovative building is reflected in the remains of many Romanesque buildings throughout Ireland.

Although the steeply pitched stone roof and small scale of the building are typically Irish, other architectural features demonstrate considerable foreign influence, suggesting the involvement of imported labour in its construction. The chapel consists of a nave and chancel, the junction of the two flanked by twin square towers. Towers such as these were otherwise unknown in Ireland, their closest parallels being found in western England and Germany.

Other elements of the building, in particular the profusion and style of carved ornament, exhibit parallels with coeval buildings in south-west Britain and western France. Wall surfaces are enlivened with string courses, corbel tables, and blank arcading carved with human-mask and scalloped capitals. The three doorways are lavishly carved with chevron ornament and both the north and south doors sport tympana, a rare feature in contemporary Irish buildings. The rib-vaulted choir houses the earliest surviving frescos in Ireland.

RM

Cornwallis, Charles Cornwallis, 1st Marquis (1738–1805). Having confirmed Britain's defeat in the war of the *American Revolution by his surrender at Yorktown, Virginia (19 Oct. 1781),

Cornwallis had more success as governor-general of India (1786–93). In 1797 he refused the command of the Irish army unless guaranteed some progress towards *Catholic emancipation. His appointment in June 1798 as both lord lieutenant and commander-in-chief was thus a recognition of the need both for an effective military response to the *insurrection of 1798 and for a new political initiative. His support for Catholic claims, along with his refusal to countenance indiscriminate violence by loyalists and government forces, alienated conservative Protestants but helped to secure Catholic support for the Act of *Union. He resigned with other members of William Pitt's ministry in February 1801, after George III had vetoed further discussion of Catholic emancipation.

coroner. The primary responsibility of the coroner is, and always has been, to hold inquests into unnatural deaths in order to discover the cause of death and (until very recently) to identify any individuals responsible. In the Middle Ages and later coroners also exercised various other responsibilities: receiving the abjurations of those who had taken sanctuary and who (in return for making a full confession of their offences) were allowed safe passage to the nearest port to go into exile; recording all private criminal accusations (appeals) made in the county court, and outlawries pronounced there. Coroners were also used to execute court orders when local *sheriffs were negligent or thought likely to be biased. The office of coroner was created in England in 1194 and was probably introduced into Ireland early in the 13th century. Coroners were chosen in the county court and elections for the post were still taking place in the second half of the 19th century. Originally, the post was held by members of the local gentry with no professional expertise, but by the early 19th century it was generally held by local solicitors and the requisite medical expertise was normally provided by expert witnesses.

PAB

corporatism, see COMMISSION ON VOCATIONAL ORGANIZATION.

Corrigan, Sir Dominic (1802–80), a leading member of the Irish medical establishment. He studied in Dublin and Edinburgh, qualifying in 1825. As well as conducting a private practice in Dublin, he worked as physician to the Charitable Infirmary, Jervis Street (1831–43), and to the House of Industry hospitals (1840–66). He published many papers, notably an important study of aortic insufficiency (1832) and one on the relationship between famine and fever (1846). As a consequence of the latter work, he was appointed to the Board of Health, set up in 1846 to advise on medical measures to combat fever during the *Famine. He served on the senate of the *Queen's Colleges for thirty years and became vice-chancellor of the Queen's University in 1871. He was the first Catholic to hold the presidency of the Royal College of Physicians in Ireland (1859–64). In 1870 he was elected as a Liberal MP for the city of Dublin, but his energetic support of the *temperance cause and of non-denominational education alienated the drink industry and the Catholic church and he did not stand for re-election in 1874.

ELM

Corrymeela, near Ballycastle, Co. Antrim, established in 1965 as a Christian community promoting reconciliation between Catholic and Protestant.

Cosgrave, William Thomas (1880–1965), first *president of the executive council. Cosgrave was one of the delegates to the first *Sinn Féin convention in 1905, and was elected to Dublin Corporation in 1909. He joined the *Irish Volunteers in 1913, and fought in the South Dublin Union during the *rising of 1916. A sentence of death was commuted to imprisonment. He won the Carlow-Kilkenny seat for Sinn Féin in the 1917 by-election and sat in the first Dáil. He was minister for local government from April 1919 to September 1922. He succeeded Michael *Collins as chairman of the *Provisional Government and minister for finance in July 1922, and Arthur *Griffith as president of the Dáil government in August 1922. His experience in local government was one of the main reasons for his appointment. He was not as flamboyant or as charismatic a leader as his predecessors but was effective and a good chairman who knew how to delegate. In September 1922 he became the first president of the executive council of the Free State. He founded *Cumann na nGaedheal in 1923 and became its first leader. When *Fine Gael was formed in 1933 he stood aside in favour of Eoin *O'Duffy, but succeeded O'Duffy in 1934 and led the opposition to the *Fianna Fáil government until 1944.

Together with his talented right hand man, Kevin *O'Higgins, Cosgrave is generally seen as the stabilizing force in the young Free State. His term in office was dedicated to the establishment of a stable democratic state witnessed by the smooth transfer of power to Fianna Fáil in 1932. His policies have been characterized as extremely careful and conservative, broadly representative of the rural petite bourgeoisie which dominated the new state. His son **Liam Cosgrave** was leader of Fine Gael 1965–77.

Regan, J.M., *The Irish Counter-Revolution, 1921–36* (1999)
Prager, Jeffrey, *Building Democracy in Ireland: Political Order and Cultural Integration in a Newly Independent Nation* (1986)

JA

coshering (Ir. *cóisir*, perhaps from the French *causerie*). In 15th- and 16th-century Ireland this was a custom whereby each of the principal subjects or tenants of a lordship, often including local church dignitaries, had to entertain their lord and his retinue once, twice, or even four times a year, to a feast lasting 24 or 48 hours at a time, accompanied by music, poetry, and story-telling. The last earl of *Desmond is said to have brought 40 to 100 followers with him on such occasions. The custom derived from the earlier *cáe*, a food render owed by clients to their patrons in pre-*Norman Ireland. As in the earlier period, the favourite season for a lord to embark on a feasting tour of his vassals was from New Year's Day to Shrovetide, when winter food stores were running out for lord and vassal alike. 'Cuddy' (Ir. *cuid oidhche*, 'a night's-portion') signified the actual food render involved, sometimes sent direct to the chief's house or commuted to a money payment. The objections of the Anglo-Irish commons to this exaction were particularly vocal, since the leading members of a community suffered most by it. KS

Costello, John A. (1891–1976), *taoiseach 1948–51 and 1954–7. Costello started his career as a barrister in 1914, and became one of the main legal advisers to the Free State government after independence. He was attorney-general from 1926 to 1932, and represented the state at the *League of Nations and imperial conferences between 1926 and 1932. He entered the Dáil in 1933 as a *Fine Gael TD (Dáil deputy) for Co. Dublin, and was the compromise choice as taoiseach in the first *interparty government. Although his term in office is traditionally best remembered for the *Mother and Child controversy and the formal establishment of the *Republic of Ireland, it also recorded some notable achievements, particularly in industrial development, house building, and public health. His second term of office was ended by the IRA *border campaign, which led *Clann na Poblachta to withdraw support. He subsequently retired to the backbenches and again took up his work as a barrister. JA

Cotter, Sir James (*c.* 1630–1705). Of a Catholic landed family in Co. Cork, Cotter fought with the royalists in the English civil wars. In 1664 he organized the assassination at Lausanne, Switzerland, of John Lisle, one of the 'regicides' who had ordered the execution of Charles I. He later served in the West Indies as a soldier and as governor of *Montserrat (1681), and was a leading *Jacobite commander in the south-west during the *Williamite War. His son **Sir James Cotter** (1689–1720) was prominent in a riot by *Tory supporters in Dublin during the general election of 1713, and was reputed to be an active Jacobite. His execution in 1720 for the rape of a Quaker, Elizabeth Squibb, was widely regarded by contemporaries as judicial assassination, although recent evidence suggests that the charge was in fact well founded.

cottier. In its most distinctive sense this meant a labourer paid in land rather than cash. The cottier received from a farmer a cabin, a small plot of land sufficient to raise potatoes for a family, and in some cases limited grazing or turf-cutting rights. His rent, though calculated in money terms, was set against days worked at an agreed wage. In the decades preceding the *Famine, these contracts provided the cheap manpower on which depended the whole system of capital-poor but labour-intensive tillage farming. The term was also used more loosely, to refer to any holder of a small plot of land, or to any occupier of a cabin.

cotton manufacture, initially an ancillary activity to *linen, became firmly established in the last decades of the 18th century. Cotton was fashionable and its rapidly declining price widened its market base. The Irish parliament was also eager to promote it, putting heavy duties on British imports from the early 1780s and making grants to Irish producers. From the 1780s cotton mills with the latest spinning technology were built in *Dublin, *Cork, *Belfast, and a few rural locations; Dublin was the most important centre until after the turn of the century, when it was displaced by Belfast, where there was greater investment in mechanized spinning mills, and a greater supply of skilled weavers who could work on fine cloths. Most of the investment in the Dublin and Cork industry went into large finishing and printing establishments. The coarser cloth types made in the south succumbed more quickly to British competition (notably from Manchester), particularly following the depression of the mid-1820s. The Belfast industry lasted only a little longer, as the linen industry (which did not face the same competition from British manufacturers) was competing for resources. The large, vertically integrated establishment set up in 1825 by the *Malcomsons at Portlaw, Co. Waterford, was unique in surviving these upheavals; it remained a major producer of cotton cloth until its collapse in 1876. AB

council. The king's council in Ireland was constituted following the *Anglo-Norman conquest. A separate institution from the council following the king, it was charged with advising him and, more immediately, his governor of Ireland specifically concerning Irish affairs. Apart from matters expressly reserved to the king, the council was omnicompetent. It exercised all the powers of government in conjunction with the governor, who convened and presided over it; and from 1520 it might also take decisions in the governor's absence as an executive *privy council. Essentially, its work was judicial, legislative, and executive in nature. The council ordered petitions from the king's subjects in Ireland, and it also determined other legal matters referred by the king—work which, eventually in 1563, gave rise to the court of *Castle Chamber. Its legislative functions were from the later 13th century mainly discharged in *parliaments or (to 1494) in great councils which were similar in composition and powers to later medieval parliaments but summoned at shorter notice. Orders in council remained important, however, particularly for war and defence, in connection with which local dignitaries might also be summoned ('afforced councils') to secure more weighty and public backing.

Although the king's greater tenants-in-chief had originally been influential, the council's membership was from the 13th century predominantly ministerial, notably the *chancellor, *treasurer, two chief justices, chief baron, keeper (later, *master) of the rolls, and king's serjeant. These leading officials were by 1300 councillors *ex officio*. In 1479, the king ordered that nothing should be taken as an act of council without their consent. Yet the king could consult whomever he wished; and medieval governors also sometimes appointed councillors and had discretion as to who should be summoned to a particular meeting. Thus leading magnates were regularly sworn of the council. Occasionally too, individuals might be specially paid as councillors. The medieval council was, like the governor, endlessly itinerant, but as Dublin developed as an administrative capital in the 15th century, the council tended more frequently to meet there, particularly in term time, with the chancellor presiding in the governor's absence. The council's clerical work was discharged, already by 1344 apparently, by a specialized clerk of the council. The clerk sometimes doubled as the governor's secretary under the early Tudors. Thus, until 1560, when a new royal seal, the signet, was created for Ireland, the governor's personal seal was commonly used to warrant council orders. The clerk also kept the council's records: a roll of petitions survives from 1392–3, but original registers of proceedings (referred to in 1486) survive only from 1556. As the weight of government increased, separate regional councils (sometimes, in Ireland, called 'presidencies') were established for Connacht (1569) and Munster (1570), following practice in the English provinces, but these councils had more limited powers.

Ellis, S. G., *Reform and Revival: English Government in Ireland, 1470–1534* (1986)

Richardson, H. G., and Sayles, G. O., *The Irish Parliament in the Middle Ages* (1952)

SGE

Council of Europe. Established in 1949 as an intergovernmental forum covering the greater part of non-communist Europe, the council was the most important international organization in which Ireland participated in the decade following the Second World War. Although Ireland joined the council at its inception, however, the opportunities of membership were never properly exploited in this most introverted phase of Irish politics and foreign policy. Sean *MacBride's attempts to use the council to provide an audience for the 'sore thumb' of partition proved wholly counter-productive, merely mystifying—and ultimately alienating—other national delegations rather than winning them to the cause. In the mid-1950s the council was superseded in importance in Europe by the establishment of the European Economic Community (see EUROPEAN UNION), and in Irish foreign policy by admission to the *United Nations. NMacQ

Council of Ireland, established under the *Government of Ireland Act 1920 to promote an all-Ireland parliament. The council was to consist of 20 members each from the parliaments of Northern and Southern Ireland, and would discuss matters of mutual concern, including the administration of services. A president nominated by the *lord lieutenant would have the casting vote.

Although the council was inoperative because of *unionist opposition, it remained in force for both *Northern Ireland and the *Irish Free State under the *Anglo-Irish treaty. In the 1925 Boundary agreement, the Northern Ireland government assumed responsibility for the council's functions regarding Northern Ireland. The governments of north and south were to meet together 'as and when necessary' for purposes of common interest arising out of these powers. This never happened. The council was revived in the 1973 *Sunningdale agreement but never took effect. DMcM

Counter-Reformation. The revival of Catholicism in Ireland, as elsewhere in western Europe, was not just a reaction to Protestantism, but the continuation of a movement already visible before the *Reformation. The impact of the 15th-century *Observant movement on the religious orders had enabled the *Franciscans and to a lesser extent the *Dominicans to present real opposition to Henry VIII's reformation. The continuity provided by these friars, together with the political alienation wrought by the *Tudor conquest and the overwhelmingly colonial nature of the new *Church of Ireland, meant that the failure of the militant Counter-Reformation in Ireland did not matter. As early as 1561 the visiting *Jesuit, David Wolfe, emphasized the need to combat vice not heresy. Likewise the devotional literature produced at the Irish College in Louvain in the early 17th century saw no need to counter Protestant doctrine.

The militant approach, coinciding with European religious wars, had its basis in papal policy towards England. In 1570 Pius V issued the excommunication of Queen Elizabeth, demanding that Catholics forsake their allegiance to a heretic. James Fitzmaurice, sent to Ireland by Pius's successor Gregory XIII, declared a holy war and helped provoke the second *Desmond revolt. Papal reinforcements were massacred at *Smerwick (1580). The high point was Rome's backing for the *Spanish Armada of 1588. By the time of Hugh *O'Neill's revolt, the papacy under Clement VIII (1592–1607) had, unluckily for the Ulsterman, entered a conciliatory phase. Clement hoped to win over Protestant princes by persuasion rather than excommunication and to consolidate the position of Catholics as loyal subjects by disengaging Catholic clergy from any involvement in politics. The militant approach briefly reappeared under *Rinuccini in the 1640s.

The institutional developments of the 1590s were of more importance. Diocesan *seminaries to train priests were a specific Counter-Reformation innovation. In Ireland's case these had to be established abroad, beginning with the Irish college at Salamanca in 1592 (see IRISH COLLEGES). A second major development came in 1598 with the establishment of a permanent Jesuit mission in Ireland, headed by *Palesmen Richard Field and Christopher Holywood, with explicit instructions to avoid politics. The third major development was the appointment from the 1590s of vicars apostolic to take care of dioceses in the absence of resident bishops. However, this policy quickly gave way to the establishment of a full episcopal hierarchy under Peter *Lombard and David *Rothe. By 1630, with seventeen bishops and thirteen vicars apostolic, each of the country's dioceses had a resident ecclesiastical authority.

A resident episcopacy to instil clerical discipline and provide spiritual leadership was a keynote of the Counter-Reformation. Its achievement in Ireland was unique in a Protestant-controlled country. Synods of bishops met regularly, political circumstances permitting. Their diocesan authority was strengthened because the *dissolution of the monasteries and the destruction of Gaelic ecclesiastical tenures simplified parochical structures. By 1623 there were 1,100 Catholic clergy in Ireland, about 30 per cent of whom had been trained in continental colleges. The custom of clerical marriage had been largely suppressed outside Ulster. The Jesuits provided 'workshops' for diocesan clergy and even ran a 'university' for a time in Dublin's *liberties.

Behind the glowing annual Jesuit reports, it is hard to gauge the actual success of the Counter-Reformation. At the popular level this entailed the enforcement of a code of religious observance—mass and the sacraments—within a parish structure. Mass attendance seems to have remained high, despite poor facilities and adverse political conditions. Priests were to teach *catechism on Sundays but this depended on their preaching ability, the availability of catechisms, and the *literacy level of their parishioners. The Counter-Reformation attempted to remove the political, pagan, and promiscuous aspects of communal religion, by reforming christenings and wakes, controlling pilgrimages and gatherings at *holy wells, and preventing veneration of *sheela-na-gigs. The church also set its face firmly against *divorce, hitherto not uncommon in Gaelic Ireland.

The Counter-Reformation had produced a clandestine church in Ireland. There were occasional religious processions and public manifestations of religious zeal, but most religious services happened in a domestic setting or in backstreet mass-houses. Although Catholics reoccupied churches in many parts of the country in the 1640s, no colourful, ornate baroque churches were ever built. Assessments of overall success at a popular level vary, but on balance it seems right to argue that the full 'Christianization' of the lower classes had to await the '*devotional revolution' of the 19th century. Nevertheless the Catholic church in the 1640s was confident enough to move into power as a driving force behind the

*Confederate Catholics and resilient enough to survive *Cromwell, despite the execution, transportation, and flight of many clergy and the *transplantation of supporting gentry to Connacht.

Bossy, John, 'The Counter-Reformation and the People of Catholic Ireland 1596–1641', *Historical Studies*, 8 (1971)
Corish, P. J., *The Catholic Community in the Seventeenth and Eighteenth Centuries* (1981)

HM

counties (shires), territorial divisions created from the late 12th century as part of the *Anglo-Norman colonization. The process of shiring involved the appointment by the crown of a *sheriff, in whom legal, military, and administrative powers were vested. Counties were, and remain, the most important unit of *local government in Ireland. Co. Dublin was created before 1200. Cork, Waterford, and Munster had sheriffs by 1211. By 1240 Munster was divided into Cos. Limerick and Tipperary, and Cos. Louth and Kerry had been constituted. Connacht was created as a county prior to 1247. The later 13th century saw the creation of Roscommon, Kildare, Meath, and Carlow. Crown control fluctuated in the coming years, however, and some areas remained wholly outside the royal prerogative, either as recognized independent *liberties or as autonomous Gaelic lordships. In 1556 King's and Queen's Counties were created by statute. The *Flight of the Earls allowed the shiring of Ulster from 1604, and Wicklow was created in 1606. However, not until the abolition of the *Ormond *palatinate in 1716 were there 32 centrally appointed shrievalties. County identities were reinforced by the mapping of boundaries in 1846. County councils, created in 1898, now exercise considerable powers in the Irish Republic, though they were abolished in Northern Ireland in 1972. In 1993 the county of Fingal was created as an administrative division of the Irish Republic, from territory formerly within Co. Dublin.

NG

Courcy, John de (d. *c.*1219), conqueror of Ulster. Though possibly illegitimate, de Courcy was a member of a family who held lands in Somerset and elsewhere in England. We know little of his early life, but almost all of the many religious houses which he founded in Ulster were affiliated to monasteries in the north of England, especially Cumbria, which suggests that his background lay there, and many of his followers hailed from the same region. He came to Ireland with *Henry II's deputy William *fitz Audelin in 1176, and became part of the Dublin garrison, where he assembled a force of 300 men and, apparently without royal licence, invaded the kingdom of *Ulaid early in 1177. He seized Downpatrick, banished the king of Ulaid, and, in spite of a number of rebuffs, soon brought the province under his sway, helped, no doubt, by his marriage to Affreca, daughter of the king of *Man and the Isles. He instituted an elaborate process of colonization, was a munificent patron of the church, and fostered devotion to the Irish saints, particularly *Patrick. Though contemporaries styled him 'prince of Ulster', and he may have had pretensions to independent rule, he held the post of chief governor of Ireland intermittently between 1185 and 1195. From 1188 onwards he intervened in Connacht and elsewhere in alliance with the de *Lacys of Meath, but by 1201 the latter had become his enemies and, after a number of unsuccessful attempts, they overthrew him in 1204. Hugh de *Lacy was granted Ulster, and the title of earl which John had never held. De Courcy unsuccessfully invaded Ulster from the Isle of Man in 1205, and although he assisted King *John in overthrowing Hugh de Lacy in 1210, he never recovered his Ulster lands and died in obscurity, apparently in 1219, leaving no known legitimate offspring.

Duffy, Seán, 'The First Ulster Plantation: John de Courcy and the Men of Cumbria', in T. B. Barry, R.F. Frame, and M. K. Simms (eds.), *Colony and Frontier in Medieval Ireland* (1995)

SD

court leet, see MANOR.

court martial, see SPECIAL COURTS.

courts of law. For around eight centuries justice has been administered in Ireland through a combination of central and local courts. The earliest central court, known simply as the king's court in Ireland or as the county court of Dublin, was in existence by the 1190s. It was remodelled *c.*1220 to bring it more closely into line with royal courts in England. Initially its sessions (*assise*) were held both at Dublin and elsewhere in the lordship. By *c.*1250 the Dublin sessions were clearly differentiated from those held elsewhere, but it was only in 1274 that there emerged a separate Dublin bench, later called the court of Common Pleas, a permanent and mainly civil court with its own personnel holding regular sessions at Dublin. This was the first of the Four Courts to become permanently established as a law court in Dublin. It remained there for over six centuries, apart from a period between 1364 and 1394 when it moved to Carlow.

The second of the Four Courts, the court of King's Bench, began existence as the *justiciar's court but was renamed the court of King's Bench after *Richard II's visit in 1394–5. Only in the 16th century did this court take up permanent residence in Dublin. King's Bench had both a civil and criminal jurisdiction and played an important role in reviewing cases previously heard in other courts.

A separate Irish *chancery existed from the early years of the 13th century. Initially it was primarily an administrative organization with responsibility for issuing writs in the name of the monarch both for legal and for administrative purposes. Like its English counterpart, by the 14th century its administrative responsibilities had given rise to its exercise of a limited legal jurisdiction but it was only in the second half of the 15th century that it began to act as a court of equity, providing remedies in certain particular circumstances where other courts were unable to act. By 1520 it was holding regular sessions in Dublin and by 1537 it too was accounted one of the Four Courts. It was probably primarily seen as a law court by then, though it continued to exercise administrative responsibilities as well.

The fourth of the Four Courts, the *exchequer, had also existed since the early 13th century. Its primary responsibility was the collection and expenditure of government revenue but already in the 13th century (as in England) this also led to its dealing with some litigation about matters such as disputed liability for debts to the crown. It was probably only in the 16th century that the exchequer came to be seen primarily as a court and only in the late 17th century that it came to exercise a general equity jurisdiction. This competed with that of chancery until its abolition in 1850.

The Four Courts shared accommodation at a variety of venues in Dublin from the early 16th century onwards. From 1609 to 1796 they were located together behind *Christ Church cathedral and in 1796 moved to their new building (see FOUR COURTS) on the former site of *King's Inns. In 1878 the Four Courts were merged into one Supreme Court consisting of a single High Court (with several separate divisions) and a Court of Appeal. The 1920 *Government of Ireland Act created two separate Supreme Courts for Northern and Southern Ireland. In 1924 the latter was abolished and replaced by a new High Court and Supreme Court of the Irish Free State.

From the 1220s onwards royal justice was also brought on an irregular basis to the counties of the lordship by the king's court in Ireland holding local sessions with a wide jurisdiction in civil and criminal pleas and the responsibility of making local inquiries on behalf of the royal administration. After 1274 there was a separate group of itinerant justices who went on eyre to perform this function. However, the last full eyre in Ireland took place in 1322. The eyre was partially replaced by much more regular sessions held locally by justices of assize with a more restricted civil and criminal jurisdiction. The *assizes remained the principal local courts of criminal trial until their abolition in independent Ireland in 1924.

During the Middle Ages and into the early modern period (and in some cases later) there were also a variety of more local courts within the lordship. These ranged from private *liberty courts, whose powers were almost as extensive as those of the royal courts and whose jurisdiction might extend over several modern counties, though more commonly over individual counties or parts of counties, to county courts and city courts and down to local manorial courts. In Ireland the *keepers (or later the *justices) of the peace do not seem to have become the main local group for hearing all but the most serious criminal offences in each county until the early 17th century, when they began holding four yearly sessions (quarter sessions) for this purpose, and it was not until the early 19th century that individual justices of the peace began to try the most minor criminal offences and to hold preliminary hearings into the more serious offences in petty sessions. During the first half of the 19th century the government also began replacing unpaid justices of the peace with salaried *resident magistrates. The minor original civil jurisdiction of the assize courts was transferred in 1796 to an 'assistant barrister' in each county who also provided expert advice to quarter sessions; in 1877 these became sessions of a distinct county court. When the courts were reorganized in 1924 within the new Free State the petty sessions became district courts; the county court and quarter sessions became circuit courts. PAB

Covenanters, see REFORMED PRESBYTERIANS.

Coventry Letter (26 Oct. 1686). Ostensibly a private letter sent to *Tyrconnell by the Catholic attorney-general Sir Richard Nagle, in Coventry on his way to Ireland, this was in fact a public document, intended to counter proposals that *James II should calm Protestant fears by confirming titles to Irish land. Important as a particularly clear statement of Catholic aspirations, it describes the *Restoration land settlement, and argues that only the re-establishment of a substantial landowning class will secure Catholic interests under James's Protestant heirs. Printed in

Historical Manuscripts Commission, *Ormonde MSS*, NS 7 (1912).

Cox, Sir Richard (1650–1733), lawyer and historian. Born into a Co. Cork Protestant family whose wealth had been lost in the *Confederate War, Cox built up a lucrative legal practice, despite not having attended a university, as recorder (a salaried *justice of the peace) of Kinsale. He withdrew to England to escape *Tyrconnell's Catholicizing policies in 1687, but returned with *William III's expedition in 1690. As governor of Co. Cork (1691) he raised a Protestant *militia which effectively crushed Jacobite resistance and wartime disorder. Knighted in 1692, he was a judge in the court of Common Pleas (1690), lord chancellor (1703), and a member of the commissioners who administered the *Williamite confiscations. A firm *Tory, though wholly committed to the Protestant succession, he was removed as lord chancellor in 1707, to placate the *Whigs and facilitate possible concessions to dissenters, and returned to office as chief justice of the Queen's Bench 1711–14. His *Hibernia Anglicana* (1689–90) is a history of Ireland, concerned to show that only the English conquest had rescued Ireland from barbarity. The claim that he imprisoned the poet Hugh MacCurtin (Aodh Buidh MacCruitin) for satirizing his anti-Irish prejudice was made by Charles *Lucas, then engaged in controversy with Cox's grandson **Sir Richard Cox** (1702–66); there is no contemporary evidence to support it.

Cox, Walter ('Watty') (*c*.1760–1837), gunsmith turned radical journalist. A *United Irishman, he published the militant *Union Star* in 1797. His *Irish Magazine* (1807–15) was an important vehicle for popular disaffection in the aftermath of the *insurrection of 1798. Its lurid drawings of flogging, pitch-capping, half-hanging, and other atrocities remain a favourite source for modern illustrated histories. Having failed to suppress the paper by raids and prosecutions, the government paid Cox a pension on condition he left the country.

Coyne, Richard (d. 1856), *printer, bookseller, and publisher in Dublin. He specialized in Catholic literature, and was printer to St Patrick's College, *Maynooth. VK

coyne (coign, coigny) **and livery** was a phrase derived from the Irish word *coinnmheadh* or 'guesting' and the English word 'livery', meaning something handed out, in this case corn and straw for horses (as in the term 'livery stables'). Together the words described a system of billeting used by Irish and Anglo-Irish lords in later medieval Ireland, whereby the lord's *gallowglass and *kern, his 'chief' horses and their grooms, his huntsmen with their hounds, and his other employees were quartered on his tenants or subjects, exacting from their hosts not merely food and lodging but often the money for their wages also. Regional variations meant that sometimes military captains organized their own billeting, using letters of authorization from the lord, sometimes each district owed maintenance for a fixed quota of men, and sometimes liability became commuted to a money payment. Direct billeting suited a subsistence economy, but was open to abuses such as the exaction of 'foyes' or bribes to exempt certain householders, violent or excessive demands, and unwarranted billeting on church lands or independent neighbouring territories. The Anglo-Irish commons constantly opposed the custom, and in 1297 parliament limited magnates' right of quartering their kerns to their own tenants in the 'land of war' or frontier regions of the colony. The 8th earl of Kildare was accused of being the first chief governor to exact 'coyne and livery' from the inhabitants of the *Pale ('the land of peace') since the expeditions of *Richard II, possibly an exaggerated claim. KS

Craig, James (1871–1940), 1st Viscount Craigavon, architect of Ulster *Unionist opposition to the third *home rule bill, and first prime minister of Northern Ireland. The son of a millionaire distiller, he typified the wealthy professional and commercial interests who were enjoying increasing political significance in Edwardian Ulster: he was returned to the United Kingdom House of Commons in 1906, representing East Down until 1918, and Mid-Down until 1921. He was one of the leaders of the Ulster Unionist revival of the mid-Edwardian era, and simultaneously established a reputation within parliament as an unflappable, if prosaic, debater. He was not strong enough to assume the leadership of the Irish Unionist parliamentary party when it became vacant in February 1910; but he was probably responsible for the nomination of Sir Edward *Carson to this position. With Carson he led the Ulster Unionist opposition to home rule: Craig mediated between Carson and the local leadership, and was responsible for the detailed planning of local Ulster Unionist activity. He held junior office in the Lloyd George coalition government between 1917 and 1921, and was able to exercise some control over Irish policy. In particular he was one of the influences behind the *Government of Ireland Act (1920), and was partly responsible for the choice of a six-county territory for Northern Ireland rather than the nine counties favoured by English ministers.

Although reluctant to abandon a promising ministerial career at Westminster, Craig accepted the premiership of Northern Ireland in 1921. He remained in this office until his death in November 1940. He overcame the military and political opposition which the new state faced, especially from the *IRA campaign in 1920–2; he withstood Lloyd George's efforts during the negotiation of the *Anglo-Irish treaty to subordinate Northern Ireland to a Dublin parliament. He sustained powerful Unionist majorities in elections for the devolved parliament held in 1921, 1925, 1929, 1933, and 1938. But these constitutional successes were bought at the price of a tough crimes policy and the neglect of other pressing problems. No sustained effort was made to integrate the disaffected nationalist minority within Northern Ireland; no energetic effort was launched to halt, or compensate for, the decline of the regional industrial economy.

Early assessments of Craig's political achievement tended to divide along party lines, but more recent interpretations emphasize his tactical and administrative skill. He was a talented manager, with an unusually keen eye for political symbolism. He occupied junior ministerial office with distinction. His premiership was, after the troubled early years, marked by an increasing political disengagement: he ruled Northern Ireland in a paternalist and clientilist manner, overriding civil service advice and budgetary constraints in the dispensation of patronage. Spending much time out of Northern Ireland, he kept Unionism in contact with Westminster and with the *Commonwealth. He bridged the transition from a cosmopolitan Edwardian Unionism through to the increasingly parochial Unionism of the Stormont years. Craig helped to create Northern Ireland, but his ambitions were rooted in Westminster, and his convictions were rooted in the empire.

Buckland, Patrick, *James Craig* (1980)
Ervine, St John, *Craigavon: Ulsterman* (1949)
Follis, Bryan, *A State under Siege: The Establishment of Northern Ireland, 1920–25* (1995)

AJ

Craig–Collins pacts, two agreements concluded in response to continuing violence in *Northern Ireland during early 1922. The first, negotiated at a meeting between *Craig and *Collins in London on 21 January, provided for the lifting of the *Belfast boycott, the return to work of Catholics violently expelled from the Belfast shipyards, and negotiations to reach an agreement on boundaries. The second 'pact' was in fact a formal agreement between the British, Northern Ireland, and *Provisional governments, following a meeting on 29–30 March. It repeated the earlier promises of restoration of expelled workers and negotiations on boundaries, called for the cessation of *IRA activity in Northern Ireland, and made detailed provision for policing by a mixed Catholic-Protestant police force. The agreements were a reflection more of British government pressure than of any real spirit of compromise, and had no significant influence on the level of either loyalist or republican violence.

Cranfield Commission (1622), sent to Ireland by Lionel Cranfield, lord treasurer of England, when its government was close to bankruptcy and allegations of corruption widespread. Staffed by English and Irish experts, it revealed slow progress in the *plantations, faulty accounting procedures in the exchequer, neglect of the established church, and a hugely inadequate *judiciary. Although some fiscal retrenchment and judicial change eventuated, serious reform had to await *Wentworth's arrival ten years later. HM

crannog, the archaeological term for an artificial lake island, from the Irish *crannóg*. Early Irish texts, however, almost always use the word *inis*—'island'—for such structures. Upon excavation crannogs have almost always proved to be habitations, constructed for defensive or strategic purposes. They are typically placed close to the shore of the lake, in shallow water, and are approached by a causeway that might be submerged. The waterlogged conditions of a crannog are most conducive to the preservation of ancient artefacts. Some crannogs have been dated to the *Bronze Age, and a few even earlier, but the great majority are of *Early Medieval and *Late Medieval date, apparently lasting until the 17th century when a few carried substantial masonry houses and even castles. Crannogs are shown in use on Bartlett's maps compiled during the *Nine Years War. RW

Crawford, Frederick Hugh (1861–1952), one of the most influential militant *unionists of the *home rule era. As a member of Lord Ranfurly's Ulster Loyalist Union in 1893, Crawford imported small quantities of weapons from England. He created a society, 'Young Ulster', modelled on continental nationalist sporting clubs, and organized drilling and the manufacture of ammunition. A *Boer War veteran, he brought his military experience to the unionist movement. He was a key influence behind the creation in November 1910 of a secret subcommittee of the *Ulster Unionist Council designed to consider the importation of weapons, and in 1914 organized the *Larne gun-running. In 1920–1 he helped to revive the *Ulster Volunteer Force. AJ

Crawford, Robert Lindsay (1868–1945), radical Protestant journalist and politician. Crawford was a product of the popular *evangelical subculture of late Victorian Ireland. He was a co-founder and theoretician of the *Independent Orange Order, as passionately Protestant as T. H. *Sloan, but more nationally minded; he was the author of the *Magheramorne manifesto. In June 1910 he emigrated to Canada. He supported the Irish revolutionary struggle and the *Anglo-Irish treaty, and after 1922 served as the *Irish Free State's trade representative in New York. His determination to marry a passionate Protestantism with revolutionary sympathy was virtually unique. AJ

Crawford, William Sharman (1781–1861), radical politician. A Protestant landowner in Co. Down, William Sharman added his wife's name of Crawford to his own in 1805. From 1830 he campaigned to have the *Ulster custom given legal force throughout Ireland. As MP for Dundalk 1835–7, he criticized *O'Connell for compromising on *tithes to preserve the Whig alliance, and he later advocated *federalism as an alternative to repeal. He participated in the drafting of the People's Charter in London in 1837, and was elected radical MP for Rochdale (1841–52) with *Chartist support. In parliament he regularly proposed land reform bills for Ireland and was a consistent opponent of coercion. He was involved in the establishment of the Tenant-Right Association in Ulster in 1846, and subsequently of the *Tenant League in 1850. After being defeated for Co. Down in the 1852 general election he retired from public life. PHG

cricket is first recorded as being played in Ireland in August 1792. However, both the 'Garrison' and 'All-Ireland' teams which contested the match in Phoenix Park appear to have been composed of visiting Englishmen. Irish cricket clubs, encouraged by officers from local garrisons and schoolboys returning from English schools, were formed from the 1820s in Dublin and Munster. A permanent pitch was established in Dublin from 1838. Ireland's first ever international representative sporting fixture was a cricket match against England in London in 1855. In subsequent years Irish teams toured England and America, and Ireland welcomed numerous teams from England. However, the growing popularity of the sport was curtailed from the 1880s as the *Land War soured relations between playing tenantry and sponsoring landlords, and pitches became harder to find. From 1904 the *Gaelic Athletic Association's ban on 'foreign games' further reduced popular support for cricket. The disruption of the *First World War and the withdrawal of British troops accentuated the decline. The focus of Irish cricket shifted to Ulster, where it remains. There are currently about 130 cricket clubs in Ireland, primarily in the larger urban centres. Though an Irish national team defeated the West Indies at Sion Mills, Co. Tyrone, in 1969, this result was entirely unrepresentative. NG

crime, as opposed to political violence, or to *agrarian and other forms of protest, has attracted little attention from Irish historians. This is partly at least because the destruction of *public records makes systematic discussion of incidence and trends impossible for any period earlier than the past 200 years.

Fragmentary surviving court records suggest that in the second half of the 18th century Irish homicide rates were comparatively high, at a level roughly equivalent to that suggested for England a century earlier. Theft also appears to have been more common in Ireland than in England. On the other hand more serious forms of property crime, burglary and robbery, were no more common, or even less so. This is consistent with the image of a relatively poor society, in which want drove many to petty thievery, but commercial underdevelopment created fewer opportunities for more ambitious criminal ventures. Rising living standards across the century did, however, encourage an expanding *smuggling trade.

Fuller statistics for the 19th century confirm that homicide was more common in Ireland than elsewhere in the United Kingdom. There was, however, both an absolute and a relative decline, from around two-and-a-half times the English level in the first half of the century to around one-and-a-half times by the early 1900s. Assault was also more common in Ireland, as was malicious damage to property, often related to protest or economic conflict. But other forms of property crime, with or without violence, were well below English levels.

Following the violence of the *Anglo-Irish War and the *Irish Civil War, the homicide rate in independent Ireland during the 1920s remained more than twice that in contemporary England. Thereafter, however, it fell to well below the English level. In Northern Ireland the homicide rate from the mid-1920s to the late 1960s was the lowest in any part of the United Kingdom. The *Northern Ireland conflict from 1969 brought a sharp rise in the homicide rate: in the 1980s it stood at 56 per million, almost three times the

English level, though still well below that of the United States (90 per million in 1986).

The general level of recorded crime increased sharply in independent Ireland, particularly in the Dublin area, during the 1970s and 1980s. In particular the appearance of drug-related crime has given rise to much public anxiety. Yet overall Irish crime levels remain significantly below those recorded in Great Britain. In Northern Ireland political conflict has provided the opportunity for racketeering and drug dealing by both loyalist and republican paramilitary groups. Yet, with the exception of homicide, Northern Ireland continues to record the lowest levels of serious crime for any policing region of the United Kingdom.

Garnham, Neal, *The Courts, Crime and the Criminal Law in Ireland 1692–1760* (1996)

Crime Branch Special (1887–1908), the records, collation, and analysis section for political crime at *Royal Irish Constabulary headquarters. Staffed by a handful of RIC officers and clerks, it had no direct investigative function. The limited scope of its activities reflects a chronic difficulty in policing in pre-independence Ireland: because the RIC did not operate in Dublin city, its ability to investigate and appraise political crime was much constricted. The surviving Crime Branch Special Records in the *National Archives provide considerable insight into both subversive organizations and the police's view of them. EO'H

Críth Gablach is a legal tract on status, written in Irish, probably in the first half of the 8th century. It is an ambitious attempt to analyse the sources of status among the ordinary free laity; the church, the professional orders, the unfree and half-free are mentioned only in passing. Free laymen are divided into two principal orders, commoners and nobles; *kings are treated as part of the nobility. Within these two principal orders, however, there are numerous grades, and the author may have exaggerated the complexity of early Irish status. After the discussion of royal status, the text has a virtual appendix on kingship, in which kings are perceived as existing in a contractual relationship with their peoples. TMC-E

Croagh Patrick, a 2,500-foot high mountain in Co. Mayo, associated with St *Patrick, who, according to tradition, fasted there for 40 days. Pilgrims climbed the mountain on the last Sunday of July, close to the old Celtic festival of *Lughnasa, reciting prayers, performing penitential exercises or 'stations', and spending one night in vigil at the summit. The pilgrimage survived the *Reformation and, thanks to its penitential element, which came to include personal confession, won the approval of Tridentine reformers. The pilgrimage was revived in 1903 and its popularity survived the changes in traditional religious practice after *Vatican II. TO'C

Croke, Thomas William (1824–1902), Catholic archbishop of Cashel (1875–1902). Born in Co. Cork and educated in Paris and Rome, he taught theology at Carlow and Paris, and was the first president of St Colman's College, Fermoy, before becoming parish priest of Doneraile in 1867. He acted as theologian to Bishop Keans of Cloyne at the first *Vatican Council, and was bishop of Auckland, New Zealand, 1870–5. Croke was involved in the *temperance movement and supported the *Land War during 1879–80, but, fearing an increase in violence and the withdrawal of proposed new land legislation, opposed the 'no rent' manifesto (1881). His 'No Tax Manifesto' of 1887 made him popular in nationalist circles but provoked the criticism of the government and a rebuke from Rome. He was a firm advocate of *home rule and the *Land League but severely criticized *Parnell's divorce case and worked to have him replaced as leader of the Irish parliamentary party in 1890. An ardent supporter of Gaelic games, he was first patron of the *Gaelic Athletic Association, whose headquarters in Dublin bears his name. TO'C

Croker, Thomas Crofton (1798–1854), antiquarian. Born in Co. Cork, the son of an army officer, Croker left school at 16 for a commercial apprenticeship before becoming a clerk in the admiralty in London (1818–50). His works on Irish folklore, notably *Fairy Legends and Traditions of the South of Ireland* (1825), were widely read. Both contemporary and later critics, however, questioned his fidelity to his sources and his reliability as an editor of such texts as the memoirs of the United Irish leader Joseph *Holt.

Crommellin, Samuel Louis (1652–1727). A prominent member of the colony of *Huguenot refugees at Lisburn, Co. Antrim, Crommellin was commissioned by government to form a royal corporation for the manufacture of *linen. In 1705 he published *An Essay on Linen Manufacture in Ireland*. He was at one time regarded as the founder of the Irish linen industry, but modern accounts see his venture as only part of a broader development taking place at this time in response to the new opportunities created by the removal of duties on Irish linen exports to Britain.

Cromwell, Henry (1628–74). Younger son of Oliver *Cromwell, he governed Ireland between

1655 and 1659 as, successively, president of the council, lord deputy, and lord lieutenant. His objective was stable, civilian government. He culled the *Baptist military clique, despite the continuance of their supporters on the Irish council and, until 1657, of *Fleetwood as lord deputy. Civilian authority was re-established: the Four Courts, commissions of peace, and municipal government were restored, as revenue commissioners and army officers lost their judicial powers. Having tamed the Baptists and kept the *Quakers under control, Cromwell turned for support to more conservative Protestants, such as the Ulster *Presbyterians and Edward Worth's *Cork Association. He continued the policies of *transportation and *transplantation but in a less dogmatic fashion than Fleetwood. The Old Protestants certainly benefited, mainly due to his increasing reliance on them to counter the animosity of well-connected Baptists in Ireland and England. His basic policies were perforce reactionary, because he needed to boost the Irish economy in the absence of adequate funding from the cash-strapped protectorate. The *Restoration settlement allowed him to retain his Irish lands in lieu of army arrears. HM

Cromwell, Oliver (1600–58). Ireland's first and only commoner *lord lieutenant, he campaigned in Ireland between 15 August 1649 and 26 May 1650. Backed by a 20,000 strong army, a huge artillery train, and a large navy, Cromwell projected himself as a providential liberator from Irish barbarism, royalist misrule, and Catholic hypocrisy.

His best remembered actions were the sieges of *Drogheda (11 Sept. 1649) and Wexford (11 Oct. 1649). Giving no quarter to garrisons refusing to surrender was in line with contemporary European practice. However, Cromwell's own explanation of the massacre at Drogheda, which had never been under *Confederate Catholic control, was plainly influenced by religious convictions and propaganda about the 1641 massacres. In Wexford the New Model Army ran amok—killing 2,000 in the market place after an outpost had surrendered whilst a parley was still in progress. Though not responsible, Cromwell once more justified his army's action with reference to massacres of Protestants in the vicinity.

Cromwell's campaign was quickly running out of steam. Sickness and the need to man garrisons reduced his army's size and on 2 December 1649 he was forced to abandon the siege of Waterford. He resumed the next year, as a string of towns surrendered with good terms offered to inhabitants and defenders, only to meet disaster at Clonmel (17 May 1650). When his men poured through the breached walls, they were trapped in a killing ground prepared by Hugh Dubh O'Neill. Estimated losses of 1,000–2,500 were the heaviest the New Model Army had experienced anywhere. Cromwell was conspicuously silent about Clonmel in his dispatches to parliament.

Cromwell's success lay as much with the Old Protestants as with the legendary efficiency of his army. Michael Jones's victory at *Rathmines provided him with Dublin as a bridgehead; subsequently the victories and influence of Charles *Coote and Roger Boyle (see ORRERY) secured Ulster, Connacht, and south Munster. More generally Protestant royalists began deserting in increasing numbers, culminating in significant submissions in April 1650. Nevertheless Cromwell's triumphant return from Ireland, coupled with the revolutionary situation in England, gave him the opportunity for political power that some previous lord lieutenants had merely contemplated and he ruled England as lord protector from 1653 until his death. He continued to exercise influence in Ireland through his sons-in-law *Ireton and *Fleetwood, and later through his younger son Henry *Cromwell.

Although Cromwell's direct connection with Ireland lasted only nine months, his dominance in England has meant that his name is associated with the events of the whole period 1649–58, which saw the ruthless suppression of Catholic and royalist resistance, the execution, *transportation, or imprisonment of substantial numbers of Catholic clergy, and the wholesale confiscation of Catholic lands. Barnard suggests that the black legend of Cromwell the oppressor took its present form only in the 19th century. However, his campaign was evidently controversial at the time, and he himself published an extraordinary defence of his policies in response to the decrees of a Catholic ecclesiastical assembly at *Clonmacnoise in December 1649. Gaelic poets of the 17th century already associated his name with the destruction of the Catholic elite and their replacement by newcomers of lowly social origins. Hence the ironic picture in *Pairlement Chloinne Tomáis* (see LITERATURE IN IRISH) of churls hailing Cromwell as their liberator, and the poet Daithi Ó Bruadair's references to 'Cromwellian dogs'.

Barnard, T. C., 'Irish Images of Cromwell', in R. C. Richardson (ed.), *Images of Cromwell* (1993)

SC/HM

Cromwellian land settlement, the greatest early modern transformation in Irish landownership, creating an estate system which lasted with minor adjustments until the late 19th century. Indeed it is no accident that J. P. Prendergast's pioneer study, *The Cromwellian Settlement of Ireland* (1865), coincided with the emergence of the Irish land question as a contentious political issue.

Although the Act for *Adventurers had raised only £306,718, the Cromwellian conquest of Ireland had cost an estimated £3.5 million. Other state creditors, and arrears of pay due to 35,000 soldiers, had thus to be satisfied out of Irish land. The first object under the 1652 act for the settling of Ireland was to identify 'rebel' landowners for clearance. The most guilty, including 105 named chief rebels, were subject to execution, banishment, and *transportation, while others who had not shown 'constant good affection' to parliament were subject to various levels of forfeiture and *transplantation to Connacht.

In September 1653 the English parliament set aside four counties (Dublin, Kildare, Carlow, and Cork) for the government, and ten counties (Armagh, Down, Antrim, Laois, Offaly, Meath, Westmeath, Limerick, Tipperary, and Waterford) for division between the adventurers and soldiers, with more land to be provided out of other counties if necessary. A tripartite *Civil Survey, by jury inquisition, 'gross' estimation, and mapping supervised by William *Petty, was ordered. In January 1654 1,500 adventurers began dividing their halves of the ten counties by lot. In this way 1,043 adventurers were eventually assigned 1.1 million acres, 5 per cent of total profitable land, the biggest beneficiaries being London merchants who had recently bought out other investors at knock-down prices. The 33,419 debentures issued to disbanding soldiers, theoretically convertible into Irish land at the same 'act-rates' as the adventurers, were worth only 12*s.* 6*d.* in the pound after the adventurers' share-out. More land had to be made available but only 11,804 certificates of possession were taken out, most soldiers having sold their debentures cheaply to their land-hungry officers. Some soldiers, particularly Munster Protestants who had turned coat late in the day, got nothing, as indeed did some adventurers because of the inaccuracies of the 'gross' survey. Petty reckoned that 11 million of Ireland's 20 million acres had been confiscated, but Henry *Cromwell complained that the land and debt problems were still not fully resolved in 1659. The post-Restoration books of *Survey and Distribution show that Charles II confirmed 7,500 soldiers and 500 adventurers in their lands. In the interim land speculation had continued with Old Protestants in particular rounding off their estates.

The Cromwellian land settlement saw no new wave of *immigration. Bottigheimer claims that the adventurers were more interested in a return on their investment than in bringing over English yeomen. By 1657 Catholic tenantry had drifted back into many confiscated territories or had never left, and the 1659 'census' indicates that they still composed three-quarters of the population. However, Catholic landowners had been displaced from Ulster, Munster, and Leinster by victorious army officers and opportunistic Old Protestants.

Bottigheimer, K. S., *English Money and Irish Land: The 'Adventurers' in the Cromwellian Settlement of Ireland* (1971)

HM

crown jewels. On 6 July 1907 the set of jewels known as the Irish crown jewels was discovered to be missing from the safe in which they were kept in *Dublin Castle. Investigation of the theft was reputedly hindered by the discovery of links between a member of the staff of Sir Arthur Vicars, *Ulster king of arms, and a London-based network of socially prominent homosexuals, whose connections may have extended to Edward VII's court. The jewels have never been recovered.

Cruachain (Rathcroghan), the royal capital of the *Connachta, is located 3 miles north-west of Tulsk, Co. Roscommon. It is a large archaeological complex consisting of over 50 monuments centred on Rathcroghan Mound. The monuments comprise enclosures, linear earthworks, and mounds, dating from the prehistoric through the medieval period. The name itself may derive from *cruach*, 'mound', and the site was traditionally known as a royal cemetery, inauguration site of the Connachta kings, and gateway to the Otherworld. Cruachain figures prominently in the Ulster tales as the capital of Queen Medb and King Ailill who warred against the Ulstermen.

JPM

Cruthin (Cruithin, Cruithni), an apparently ethnic descriptor used of a number of *Early Medieval kingdoms, especially in the restricted area of post-4th-century *Ulaid, where the **tuatha* so described (for instance Dál nAraidi of mid-Antrim and Uí Echach Coba of Down) are contrasted with the **Érainn*-descended *tuatha* such as Dál Fiatach and Dál Riata (see ULAID). The Ulster Cruthin were originally located on both sides of the lower River Bann but were pushed east of that river by the *Airgialla after the battle of Móin Daire Lothair in AD 563. They shared the overkingship of Ulaid with the Dál Fiatach until the 10th century and it is probably significant that the inauguration place of the Ulaid overking, at Cráeb Tulcha near Glenavy in Co. Antrim, lay in the hinterland between the two ethno-political groups. The name Cruthin—cognate with Welsh *Prydyn* and probably with Roman (British?) *Britanni*—seems simply to be an early borrowing of *Priteni*, probably a general (non-ethnic?) name for the indigenous peoples of the two islands, first attested in Greek texts of about the 5th century BC. This, rather than any cultural connection, would have been the reason why ancient Irish writers referred to the Picts of Scotland as Cruthin. The early Irish pseudo-historians regarded the Cruthin as amongst the earliest of the Irish peoples, on a par with the *Érainn* and earlier than the *Goídel* (see GAEL). Recently *unionist writers in Northern Ireland, elaborating on this theme, have invented a new form of the ancient 'returning exile' myth by which the Ulster-Scots settlers of the 17th century (see ULSTER PLANTATION) are seen as the lineal descendants of Cruthin who left for Scotland over a thousand years before. Thus the unionists can claim a sort of primacy over the 'newcomer' Gaels. Useful as this new myth might be as a boost to unionist self-esteem it is totally without historical basis. RW

Cuala Press, see DUN EMER PRESS.

Culdee, see CÉILE DÉ.

Cullen, Paul (1803–78), Catholic ecclesiastic. Born in Co. Kildare, Cullen was educated in Rome, becoming professor of Greek and oriental languages in *Propaganda College and from 1832 rector of the Irish College, where he was an influential agent for the Irish hierarchy. As archbishop of Armagh 1849–52 and Dublin 1852–78, he was known for his moderate nationalism, *ultramontanism, and pastoral concern. He summoned the first canonical synod of the Irish church in *Thurles in 1850. Pragmatically acquiescing in growing intimacy between church and state in education and health services, he nevertheless fought his corner when he believed the church could get a better deal, especially in primary education. His opposition to the *Queen's Colleges has been described as bigoted but was based on a narrow ecclesiastical vision rather than religious hatred. Disapproving of clerical involvement in politics, he was opposed to all political movements that did not serve the interests of the church. He used his Roman contacts to influence Irish episcopal appointments but faced opposition from colleagues like *MacHale. In 1866 he became Ireland's first cardinal.

His pastoral, disciplinary, and administrative reforms in Dublin continued those initiated by Daniel *Murray and benefited from the favourable environment created by *Peel's policies. In the same way his strong support for the more standardized, clerically controlled practices associated with the *'devotional revolution' continued a trend already established under *Troy and Murray. Cullen founded the *Irish Ecclesiastical Record* in 1864. Suspicious of *Maynooth's independence, he succeeded in getting episcopal control of the college. He set up Clonliffe College in 1859 to supply priests for Dublin. His episcopate saw the Irish Catholic church assume a form it maintained until the early 1980s.

Bowen, D., *Paul Cadinal Cullen and the Shaping of Modern Irish Catholicism* (1983)

TO'C

Cumann na mBan ('the league of women'), the women's auxiliary corps to the *Irish Volunteers, set up in 1914. Members were mainly white-collar workers, artists, professional women, or women supported by relatives, but also included a significant proportion of working-class women. Although an independent organization, its executive was subordinate to that of the Volunteers, which made Francis *Sheehy Skeffington charge it immediately with 'crawling servility'. Cumann na mBan membership included many feminists who angrily rejected Sheehy Skeffington's evaluation of their organization. But this early acceptance of a subordinate role helps to explain why women, despite the tireless dedication and radicalism which characterized Cumann na mBan, were to be so effectively marginalized in politics after independence.

The radicalism of Cumann na mBan came into evidence when the vast majority of members voted to stay with the Irish Volunteers after the Volunteer split in 1914. The corps played an active, though non-combatant, role in the *rising of 1916, in signals, first aid, and dispatch-running, and it sustained one fatality, Margaretta Keogh, at St Stephen's Green. The surrender was delivered by a Cumann na mBan member, Elizabeth O'Farrell, a midwife from the National Maternity hospital.

From 1916 to 1918 Cumann na mBan were largely in charge of fomenting the cult of the dead leaders through commemorative events. They also raised money for prisoners, canvassed for the 1918 elections, and opposed conscription. During the *Anglo-Irish War they hid arms and other supplies, provided safe houses, helped run *Dáil courts and local authorities, and produced the nationalist newspaper the *Irish Bulletin*. Most members opposed the *Anglo-Irish treaty. The rump who supported it called itself Cumann na Saoirse and included *Ladies' Land League veteran and Free State champion of women's rights Jenny Wyse Power. At least 400 Cumann na mBan members were imprisoned during the *Civil War. It was this organization which initiated the Easter Lily commemorations in 1926. In 1930–2 it was associated with a 'buy Irish' campaign and the foundation of *Saor Eire, and was often attacked with 'red scare' tactics, as was the *Fianna Fáil party it helped to elect. Cumann na mBan continued to be active, mainly on the republican left, but was affected by splits in the *IRA as well as within its own organization.

Ward, Margaret, *Unmanageable Revolutionaries* (1983)

CC

Cumann na nGaedheal ('party of the Irish'), political party formally launched on 8 April 1923. The core of the party consisted of the pro-treaty members of *Sinn Féin returned in the 1922 general election who constituted the government party in the *Irish Free State. A decision to found the party had been taken on 7 December 1922, and organizational work proceeded in early 1923.

The party won its highest ever share of the poll at the first general election it contested, on 27 August 1923 (39.0 per cent, and 63 seats), although its leader, William T. *Cosgrave, was nevertheless able to continue in office as *president of the executive council only because of the absence of anti-treaty deputies from the *Dáil. The party survived in government despite a dip in support in the general election of 9 June 1927 (27.4 per cent of votes and 47 seats) and notwithstanding *Fianna Fáil's entry to the Dáil in August 1927. It re-established its share of the vote (38.7 per cent and 62 seats) in the general election of 15 September 1927; this was sufficient to allow it to continue in office with the support of the *Farmers' Party.

To its great surprise, the party was defeated by Fianna Fáil at the general election of 16 February 1932 (35.3 per cent of the vote, 57 seats), and its support fell back further at the next general election on 24 January 1933 (30.5 per cent, 48 seats). The party subsequently engaged in discussions with the National *Centre Party on a possible merger, and finally agreed this, taking in also a third group, the National Guard (see BLUESHIRTS), to form *Fine Gael in September 1933.

On matters of social and economic policy Cumann na nGaedheal was conservative, and its defence of the constitutional status quo and of the treaty settlement with Great Britain became increasingly committed as the party aged. JC

Cumin, John (d. 1212), archbishop of Dublin 1181–1212. Originally from Somerset, Cumin served *Henry II as administrator, judge, and diplomat. He supported the king in his feud with Archbishop Becket of Canterbury, and was excommunicated for a time by the pope. Following the death of Laurence *O'Toole (Lorcán Ua Tuathail) in 1181, Henry II secured Cumin's election as archbishop of Dublin. He was the first Englishman to be appointed to an Irish see.

In 1186 he held a council for the reform of the church in his archdiocese. He founded the house of nuns at Grace Dieu and acquired the Arroasian house of All Saints from the bishop of Clogher (Louth). He established the collegiate church of St Patrick's, which was consecrated in 1192, and promoted the canonization of Lorcán Ua Tuathail.

In 1197 he excommunicated the justiciar, Hamo de Valognes, and placed his archdiocese under an interdict. He was exiled by King *John from 1202 to 1205. He died in 1212 and was buried in *Christ Church cathedral. BGCS

Cumming, John (d. 1850), *printer, bookseller, and publisher in Dublin. Cumming was in partnership with his brother James for a period as the Hibernia Press, and had extensive contacts with British publishers. VK

curragh, a wicker boat covered with hide or, in modern times, tarred calico. In early centuries such boats were widely used even for long sea voyages. From the *Viking era they were displaced on the high seas by planked wooden ships, surviving only along the west coast, where they were used for fishing and coastal trade, and on some inland waters.

Curragh, the, Co. Kildare, 5,000 acres of unenclosed down land, located just east of Kildare town, containing extensive remains of prehistoric earthworks. 'Curragh', meaning racecourse, indicates a long-standing association with *horse racing, probably as an adjunct to a *fair. Races were organized on a more systematic basis from the 18th century, and the Curragh remains a major horse-racing venue today.

A camp for the training of *militia was established during the *revolutionary and Napoleonic wars, and a permanent military base in 1854. Though technically crown property, the Curragh was *common land, and an act of 1870 recognized the continuing right of neighbouring farmers to graze sheep there.

Curragh incident. Often known as the 'Curragh mutiny', though no direct orders of any kind were disobeyed, this occurred in March 1914 when, led by Brig. Gen. Hubert Gough, 60 British cavalry officers at the *Curragh camp near Kildare resigned their commissions rather than obey orders which they believed were aimed at coercing Ulster *unionists into accepting *home rule. When the government planned to deploy troops throughout Ulster against the possibility of armed unionist action, the commander-in-chief in Ireland, General Sir Arthur Paget, had injudiciously conceded that officers domiciled in Ulster would be permitted to 'disappear' during this operation, but that no concession would be allowed otherwise, even for men like Gough with Irish family connections. The War Office refused to accept the resignations and told the officers that the government did not intend to take offensive action against Ulster. But this assurance was given without cabinet authority, by the secretary for war and the chief of the imperial general staff, both of whom were subsequently obliged to resign. Although the prime minister afterwards repudiated the assurance, in effect the affair meant that the army could not be used to quell Ulster opposition to home rule. KJ

Curran, John Philpot (1750–1817), lawyer and *Whig MP (in parliament 1783–97 and 1800), master of the rolls, and a privy counsellor 1806–14. A consistent supporter of *parliamentary reform and *Catholic emancipation, Curran opposed the Act of *Union. He acted as defence counsel for leading *United Irishmen, including William *Drennan, Napper *Tandy, and Wolfe *Tone, but reacted harshly to his daughter Sarah's liaison with Robert *Emmet. He was also a noted duellist, literary figure, and wit.

Curry, John (*c.*1710–1780), Catholic activist and writer. Curry studied medicine at Paris and Reims and practised successfully in his native Dublin. A founder of the *Catholic Committee, his historical work was mainly concerned to refute charges of past treason and massacre against the Catholics of Ireland. It included pamphlets, in collaboration with Charles *O'Conor, on the *rising of 1641 and other subjects, and *An Historical and Critical Review of the Civil Wars in Ireland* (1775), a reply to *Leland.

Curtis, Edmund (1881–1943), one of the most influential historians of Ireland in the aftermath of independence and author of a durable *History of Ireland* (1936). Born in England of Irish parentage, Curtis was a medievalist who had published a book on Roger of Sicily in 1912. He became a professor at *Trinity College, Dublin, in 1914 and remained there until his death. Curtis identified closely with Ireland. His *History of Medieval Ireland 1110–1513*, first published in 1923, had the unusual merit of tackling both Gaelic and colonial society; despite its insights, a somewhat artless style and a tendency to transport the political concerns of Curtis's own time into the Middle Ages make many of its judgements now seem quaint. An enthusiastic editor of medieval documents, Curtis made much original material—notably the *Ormond deeds, which he calendared in six volumes (1932–43)—accessible, though his editorial practices do not satisfy modern scholars. RFF

Cusack, Sir Thomas (1490–1571), leading Anglo-Irish reformer and author, as the crown's most trusted local adviser, of a series of important reports on Irish affairs. Under *St Leger, Cusack was the speaker of the commons which voted Henry VIII king in 1541 and the architect of *surrender and regrant. A beneficiary from the *dissolution of the monasteries, he became lord chancellor in 1550 and acted as lord justice in 1552–3, but was out of government under Mary because of his Protestantism. Later, in tandem with Kildare, he helped undermine *Sussex's regime. HM

Custom House, Dublin, built to the design of James *Gandon (1781–91), replacing an older building on Essex Quay. Its siting on reclaimed land in the relatively undeveloped north-east of the city met with strong opposition from the established merchant class, who correctly predicted that it would initiate a general eastward shift in the city, away from its medieval nucleus.

The building was designed to be seen from all fronts, but in particular from the east and west sides—the two waterside approaches. All four façades of the building are treated differently, but with equal importance. Continuity in the building is maintained by the presence of a pavilion at each corner. The building is rich in sculptural detailing; of particular note are the fourteen keystone heads by Edward Smyth, which represent the Atlantic Ocean and thirteen Irish rivers—the routes of Irish trade.

The Custom House was extensively burned in an *IRA attack in May 1921, and little of the original interior remains. The exterior was, for the most part, faithfully restored, although details such as the use of darker limestone, rather than the original Portland stone, on the drum of the dome have taken away from the original effect. The building currently houses the principal offices of the Department of the Environment. RM

customs and excise. The Irish customs and excise system derives from that in force in Great Britain, customs being the duties payable on goods either imported or exported, and excise those payable on goods produced within the country, or in respect of the pursuit of particular trades or actions. The foundation of the modern system took place in the 17th century with the establishment by the English crown of a system of tariffs together with rules of procedure governing payment, and the appointment of commissioners to administer their collection. At the close of the 18th century the contribution of Irish taxpayers to the British treasury (around £3.5 million) was raised almost entirely from customs and excise duties. Following the amalgamation of the various customs and excise boards of Great Britain and Ireland in the early part of the 19th century, Irish revenue was collected by English departments. Uniform rates of duty were introduced in 1853.

Responsibility for the management of customs and excise in independent Ireland has rested, since 1923, with the revenue commissioners. With the introduction of betting shops in 1926, a betting duty was imposed, which has since comprised one of the major contributors to excise revenues, along with duties on beer and spirits. Tobacco represents one of the chief contributors as far as customs are concerned. During the period of *protectionism customs duties were levied on a wide variety of imported goods with the aim of nurturing Irish industries. This system was dismantled in the 1960s. Customs and excise duties still provide the Irish exchequer with a major proportion of indirect taxation. The creation of the single market in 1993 rendered the notion of importing and exporting goods within the *European Union technically redundant. Duty-free sales nevertheless continued (and in fact increased) during a transitional period that lasted until 30 June 1999. VC

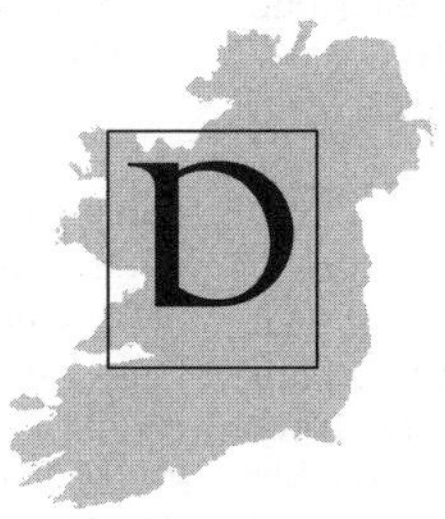

dáil (O.Ir. *dál*, originally a meeting, tryst, or encounter of any kind, sometimes amatory or hostile, was used by extension in the *brehon law tracts for a lawsuit, or legal sentence, and in medieval Irish annals for a political assembly or church synod. The *comhdháil* at Athboy under Rory O'Connor (Ruaidrí Ua Conchobair) in 1167, attended by lay and ecclesiastical leaders of the northern half of Ireland with 13,000 horsemen, which 'reached many good decisions about . . . churches and . . . territories', approximates most closely to an embryonic *parliament rather than a simple church synod, and the *Four Masters' record of this meeting probably inspired the 20th-century use of the term. Later we find the word used in 1433 of a peace conference between hostile territories.

KS

Dáil courts (1919–22), set up by the first and second *Dála to replace the courts of the British administration in Ireland. In 1919 the Dáil established arbitration courts, a Supreme Court, district courts, and parish courts. The impetus for these moves was the escalation of land agitation in the west of Ireland and the threat it posed to the Dáil's authority.

Parish courts dealt with petty criminal offences and civil claims under £10; district courts heard civil appeals from the parish courts and civil claims under £100; the Supreme Court functioned as a final court of appeal from both the district courts and the Land Settlement Commission, which dealt with land cases. More serious criminal cases, theoretically reserved for special sittings of the higher courts, were in practice dealt with summarily by local *IRA units.

The law to be applied by the courts was that existing on 21 January 1919, the first meeting of the Dáil, and citations could be made to the courts, as far as practicable, from early Irish law-codes, Roman law, and the Code Napoléon, but not from any legal textbook published in Britain. Despite the difficulties of *martial law, the courts gradually became established (except in parts of Ulster) and replaced the existing British structures. Their greatest popularity came after the truce of July 1921. After the *Anglo-Irish treaty the situation became confusing, with the crown courts operating side by side with those of the Dáil. In July 1922, following the outbreak of *civil war, the *Provisional Government rescinded the decree establishing the Dáil Supreme Court, which had granted an application of *habeas corpus on behalf of a republican prisoner. The authority of the other Dáil courts was likewise rescinded in October 1922. These steps caused considerable resentment and controversy. The Dáil Éireann Courts (Winding Up) Act 1923 gave statutory recognition to the judgments issued during the courts' period of operation. New courts, incorporating many features from the Dáil courts, were set up under the 1924 Courts of Justice Act.

DMcM

Dáil Éireann, the Irish parliament. Members are *teachtaí dála*, abbreviated as TD. The term Dáil (plural Dála), derived from the name of a council of elders in Gaelic Ireland, has been applied to three separate assemblies.

1919–1922

The first Dáil (Jan. 1919–May 1921) consisted of 73 *Sinn Féin candidates elected in 1918. They abstained from Westminster and set up their own assembly in Dublin. No Unionist or Nationalist members attended and the Dáil was proscribed in 1919.

The first Dáil constitution provided for a unicameral assembly and a ministry (cabinet) headed by a prime minister or president. De *Valera was elected president in April 1919; when he went to America, Arthur *Griffith became acting president. As the *Anglo-Irish War intensified, the work of the ministry became increasingly difficult although some departments, notably finance, local government, and agriculture, were successful. (See DÁIL COURTS.)

In May 1921 Sinn Féin took part in the elections held under the *Government of Ireland

Act and a larger assembly of 125 (including one representative from Northern Ireland) was returned. This became the second Dáil and sat from August 1921 to June 1922.

1922

The *Anglo-Irish treaty created a system of dual government between the Dáil (where Griffith succeeded de Valera as president) and the *Provisional Government. Elections for an assembly to ratify the draft constitution took place on 16 June but the assembly was prorogued until September because of the *Civil War. This assembly (sometimes called the third Dáil) became the parliament of the Provisional Government and was boycotted by republicans. *Cosgrave, now president, abolished dual government. The parliament ratified the constitution and dissolved in December 1922.

1922–

The *constitution of the Irish Free State laid down the main features of parliamentary government in Ireland which were subsequently adapted by the 1937 *constitution of Ireland. Voting was by *proportional representation; constituencies were to be determined by law and revised by the *Oireachtas every twelve years; there was to be not more than one TD per 30,000 population and not less than one per 20,000. The maximum Dáil term was seven years; in 1963 this was reduced to five years. Estimates of government receipts and expenditures had to be submitted annually to the Dáil. The *taoiseach, *tánaiste, and minister for finance had to be members of the Dáil and ministers could attend either house. The Dáil had no power to initiate money votes, bills, or resolutions without a message from the government signed by the taoiseach. However, the consent of the Dáil was needed for a declaration of war. The main differences introduced by the 1937 constitution were the abolition of the *oath of allegiance and university representation, and changes to the dissolution procedure. Before 1937 the Dáil was dissolved by the *governor-general on the advice of the executive council. After 1937 the *president dissolved the Dáil on the advice of the taoiseach.

Although the executive is in theory responsible to the Dáil, it in practice almost completely controls legislation. The use of committees, limited until 1983, has however since then become more important in the legislative process.

Chubb, Basil, *The Government and Politics of Ireland* (3rd edn., 1992)

Farrell, Brian, *The Founding of Dáil Eireann* (1971)

Mansergh, P. N. S., *The Irish Free State: Its Government and Politics* (1934)

DMcM

dairy industry. Down to the late 17th century cattle were valued in Ireland primarily for their milk rather than their beef-producing qualities. From earliest times, milk and dairy products had occupied a prominent place in the diet of the people. No wonder, for the country's temperate climate and regular rainfall effortlessly produced the lush grass necessary to sustain large cattle numbers. However, from around 1700, the growth in population, the increased commercialization of agriculture, and the spread of the potato began to reduce home consumption, although it still remained, and remains to this day, high compared to other countries at comparable income levels. Meanwhile dairy exports in the form of butter—until recently the Irish were never great producers or consumers of cheese—rose as markets opened in Great Britain and her colonies. By the end of the 18th century, butter was Ireland's largest agricultural export. Although production occurred throughout the country, the great butter-producing area was concentrated in Munster, particularly Cork, Waterford, and Kerry.

The relative importance of dairying within the agricultural sector declined from around 1820 as livestock exports increased. The number of dairy cows in Ireland remained roughly stable at 1.5 million for more than a century thereafter. At the same time, the output of beef cattle rose, so that by the last quarter of the 19th century it exceeded that of dairying. Nevertheless, down to the 1870s the market for butter remained buoyant and prices favourable. The end of the decade, though, saw intensified foreign competition for the British market. This feature persisted, despite the relatively rapid adoption in Ireland of the creamery system. The *First World War, by blocking overseas supplies, offered a temporary palliative. But the interwar period, particularly the 1930s, saw an intensification of international competition, mainly from the dominions. Although the Irish domestic market, itself under threat, was secured by *protection, exports could be assured, and then at a reduced level, only by subsidizing them. During the post-war years the burden of subsidies mounted. Ireland had clearly lost its earlier comparative advantage.

This largely remained the situation until Ireland joined the European Economic Community (see EUROPEAN UNION) in 1973. For a period thereafter, the dairy industry, underpinned by the Common Agricultural Policy, which guaranteed high prices while placing few restrictions on output, entered into a period of great prosperity. The Irish contributed their share to the growth of the European butter mountain. The output of dairy products rose rapidly, by 75 per cent in a decade. By the mid-1980s it almost equalled that of cattle, for the first time since the turn of the century. Then, in 1984, the European Commission began to take measures to reduce production. Output fell by 9 per cent over the next four years. The boom years were over. Nevertheless, thanks to the protective shell provided by the EC, the dairy industry was far healthier than it had been two decades earlier, when Ireland had no alternative but to compete on world markets. DJ

Dál Cais, a dynasty which was the dominant force in Munster for much of the 10th, 11th, and 12th centuries, producing a number of claimants to the *high kingship. In the 11th century they adopted the surname Uí Briain after their most famous son, *Brian Bóruma (Boru).

Of humble beginnings, the Dál Cais were originally known as In Déis Tuaiscirt who, having lost their lands south of the Shannon in Co. Limerick, sought to gain a foothold in Clare in the early 8th century. At this period, a number of individual groups within Dál Cais were vying for position but about the beginning of the 10th century the Uí Thoirdelbaig emerged victorious, though it was a member of the Uí Óengusso, Rebachán mac Mothlai, who was first termed 'king of Dál Cais' on his death in 934.

The change of name to 'Seed of Cas' indicates considerable political ambition: by linking themselves to Cormac Cas, supposed son of Ailill Ólum and brother of Eógan Mór, ancestor of the *Eóganacht, this hitherto unknown group was staking a claim to the kingship of *Cashel. That claim, however, could only be realized by military might and political supremacy, and it was under the rule of Cennétig, son of Lorcán (d. 951), and, more particularly, under that of his sons, Mathgamain and Brian Bóruma, that the Dál Cais rose to political dominance, aided by a corresponding decline in Eóganacht fortunes. A succession of able rulers among Brian Bóruma's descendants ensured that the Dál Cais were able to maintain that position more or less down to the early 12th century.

Ever mindful of their humble origins, however, they marked their period in power by the production of a number of literary works which sought to validate their new-found political supremacy. Thus, their genealogies claimed for them an equal alternate right, shared with the Eóganacht, to the kingship of Cashel, while entries reflecting well upon them were inserted retrospectively into the *Annals of Inisfallen*. Eleventh- and 12th-century pseudo-historical compositions such as **Lebor na Cert* and **Cogadh Gaedhel re Gallaibh* were designed to glorify them further. Dál Cais days of glory began to come to an end, however, in the latter years of the reign of Brian Bóruma's great-grandson Muirchertach *Ua Briain (d. 1119). Therafter, the Uí Briain appear merely as one of a number of skilful players on the Munster political scene. MNíM

Dál Fiatach, see ULAID.

Dál nAraide, see ULAID.

Dál Riata, see SCOTLAND; ULAID.

Dallas, Alexander, see SECOND REFORMATION.

dancing. References to dancing in travellers' accounts of rural life in Ireland date from the 16th century, but the development of step dancing as a formal art does not appear to have taken place before the last quarter of the 18th century. Given that the preponderance of instrumental melody which survives in the ethnic repertory is dance music (jigs, reels, hornpipes), it is scarcely surprising to discover that corresponding dance steps rapidly attained a conventional degree of virtuosity. Single, double, and hop (or slip) jigs, reels, and hornpipes were danced as solos, or in group formation. In the mid-19th century, dancing masters adapted continental dances (including the quadrille) to the style of native Irish steps, and 'sets' or 'half-sets' (i.e. the movement of four couples and two couples respectively) thus incorporated European influences which remained in vogue for almost a century.

The formation of the *Gaelic League in 1893 brought fresh impetus to the revival of set dancing, although particular emphasis was given to the solo steps introduced in the late 18th century. The league also cultivated the *céilidh*, a social gathering in which group formations of boys and girls used the traditional steps, accompanied not by solo instruments but by ensembles. This change attested to the urban setting in which many early *céilidh* took place. Although the *céilidh* remained popular after the *Second World War, its gradual decline, especially from the mid-1950s onwards, was unmistakable. Two reasons can be advanced as explanation for this: the supervention of American musical culture in Irish life decisively occluded the appeal of ethnic forms (which nevertheless enjoyed a curious afterlife in *radio and *television programmes); secondly, the revival of Irish music in the 1960s did not address Irish dancing, and the *céilidh* itself was superseded by the new ensemble of instruments initiated by Sean Ó Riada. Nevertheless, Irish dancing continues to enjoy a vigorous existence in amateur festivals throughout the country. In the mid-1990s its projection as a spectacular and brilliantly executed form of professional entertainment (Riverdance, 1994–) offered new vistas of development.

Breathnach, Breandán, *Folk Music and Dances of Ireland* (1989)

HW

Darby, J. N., see PLYMOUTH BRETHRENISM.

Darcy, John (d. 1347), several times *justiciar of Ireland between 1324 and 1336, and for 20 years an important link between the settler elite and the English court. He presided over the *Kyteler witchcraft case in 1324, settled disputes involving the 1st earl of *Desmond in 1329 and 1333, and led Irish forces to serve Edward III in Scotland in 1333 and 1335. During the last decade of his life he rose to become steward and chamberlain of Edward's household. Although he was reappointed to the justiciarship for life in 1341, he ruled by deputy, and surrendered the position in 1344. His son, Roger Darcy, also held important offices in the Dublin administration. In 1329 John Darcy married as his second wife Joan de Burgh, dowager countess of Kildare; their son William founded an Irish branch of the Darcy family, and in 1346 their daughter Elizabeth married the 2nd earl of *Ormond.

RFF

Darcy, Patrick (1598–1668), a Galway Catholic, the most important constitutional lawyer of the 17th century. Educated at the Middle Temple in London, Darcy established a lucrative practice representing a wide range of clients, including the earls of *Clanricard, *Ormond, and Cork (see BOYLE). Blooded politically in *Wentworth's parliament, he became a formidable opponent of the lord deputy as a legal representative and political agent of Galway landowners threatened with confiscation. Imprisonment and debarral ended his campaign.

In the tumultuous 1641 parliament Darcy presented a detailed treatise, known as the 'Argument', defending the legislative independence of the Irish parliament. After the *rising of 1641 he tried to keep the parliament in being; when the Dublin government prorogued it, he suggested the *Confederate Catholic model and subsequently helped draft its constitution. The confederation published his *Argument* in 1643 and a *Declaration* along similar lines in 1644. Serving on the confederate supreme council and in the peace negotiations with *Ormond, Darcy proved a moderate conciliator. He survived Cromwellian rule to resume his legal career but not his lands. William *Molyneux, and later the American colonists, used Darcy's writings to advocate the rights of colonial legislatures vis-à-vis Westminster.

HM

Dargan, William (1799–1867), industrialist. The son of a Carlow farmer, Dargan was educated in England, and trained as a surveyor there. Following experience gained under Thomas Telford in Wales, Dargan returned to Ireland and established himself as a road contractor. In 1831 he became the contractor for the Dublin to Kingstown *railway line, the first in Ireland. Over the next two decades he constructed over 600 miles of railway line, the Ulster canal, and major improvements to Belfast's docks. In 1853 he organized the Irish *Industrial Exhibition, was visited at home by Queen Victoria, but declined a baronetcy. However, the exhibition, and Dargan's later investments in textile manufacture, proved financially disastrous. He finally suspended payment on his debts the year before his death. His widow was subsequently granted an annual civil list pension of £100.

NG

Davey, J. E. (1890–1960). A sometime fellow of King's College, Cambridge, he accepted a professorship in the Presbyterian College, Belfast, in 1916. In 1927 his lectures and publications led to his trial by the General Assembly on a charge of heresy, of which he was overwhelmingly acquitted. His disappointed accusers formed the Irish Evangelical church and Ian Paisley (see FREE PRESBYTERIAN CHURCH OF ULSTER) uses his acquittal as evidence of the apostasy of Irish *Presbyterianism.

RFGH

Davies, Sir John (1569–1626). The third son of a Wiltshire tanner, Davies was already a well-known court poet when he was King James I's choice as Irish solicitor-general (1603–6) and attorney-general (1606–19). In his *Discovery of the True Causes Why Ireland was Never Entirely Subdued* (1612) Davies showed how the common law had finally been extended across Ireland in James's reign. Contemporary writers—Barnaby Riche and Fynes *Moryson—questioned this glowing assessment.

Pawlisch credits his subject with the invention and use of judge-made law to underpin the *Tudor conquest in default of a subservient Irish *parliament. Basically the Irish law officers (most of them New Englishmen) came together and decided key issues (invariably in the interests of the state) as binding legal precedents. Their decisions rode roughshod over vested interests, both Gaelic Irish (cases of *tanistry and *gavelkind) and Old English (cases of *mandates and town charters).

Davies, however, was not wholly responsible for this policy of arbitrary *absolutism, even though he wrote up the cases in his *Reports* (1615). As chief law officer, he was the instrument of the government of *Chichester and not even a member of his privy council. In fact both the *Discovery* and the *Reports* were written to glamorize his own role in order to get a long sought after appointment in the English judiciary, which he eventually achieved.

Sir John's influence was greatest in the *Ulster plantation. Having trumpeted the rights of freeholders, he abandoned them after the *Flight of the Earls and instead advocated full-scale colonization, which the king preferred to Chichester's more conservative proposals. Davies (himself a survey commissioner) received 7,500 acres and the impoverished aristocratic Touchet family, into which he had married, was allotted a further 9,000 acres.

Pawlisch, Hans, *Sir John Davies and the Conquest of Ireland* (1985)

HM

Davis, Thomas (1814–45), *Young Irelander. Son of an English army surgeon and an Irish Protestant mother, Davis was born in Mallow, Co. Cork, and educated at *Trinity College, Dublin. Influenced by Thomas Carlyle and other Romantic writers, he first enunciated his ideas of Irish nationality to the Dublin Historical Society in 1839 and subsequently in the *Citizen* and *Morning Register* newspapers. He joined the *Repeal Association in 1841 and was a founder of the **Nation*. His charisma and powerful articles made him the undisputed leader of the Young Ireland group, and he sought to bring their sense of nationality to a mass public through his popular ballads. Convinced that it was vital to reverse the Anglicization of Irish culture, he argued for the revival of the *Irish language, and attempted to foster a nationality of the spirit uniting the Irish of all religious traditions. Though personally loyal to *O'Connell, he was disappointed by his movement away from repeal in 1844–5 and angered by criticisms of the *Nation* from Catholic O'Connellites. His support for the *Queen's Colleges led to a public clash with O'Connell at the Repeal Association in May 1845, in which Davis, always a poor speaker, was reduced to tears. Despite a subsequent reconciliation, Davis remained a target for Old Ireland polemicists. He died suddenly of an attack of scarlet fever in September 1845.

PHG

Davitt, Michael (1846–1906), nationalist and labour leader. Son of an evicted tenant farmer of Straide, Co. Mayo, Davitt spent his childhood and youth in Haslingden, Lancashire, where he lost his right arm in a factory accident in 1857. He joined the *Fenian movement in 1865 and was sentenced in 1870 to fifteen years' penal servitude for gunrunning. Released on ticket-of-leave, December 1877, Davitt became an architect of the *New Departure, a founder of the *Land League, and leader of the agrarian struggle of 1879–82. He became disillusioned, however, as the emphasis shifted from a general reform of the agrarian system to a defence of the vested interests of the larger tenant farmers. Imprisoned in Portland jail from February 1881 to May 1882, Davitt, under the influence of Henry George, used the time to reformulate his agrarian ideas in the direction of land nationalization, a policy predicated upon an alliance of nationalist and British working-class interests. However, the policy produced an open breach with *Parnell in 1884 and failed to attract popular support. Despite his differences with Parnell, Davitt vigorously supported the Liberal–nationalist alliance. Following the party split 1890, he became anti-Parnellite MP for Meath 1892, and West Mayo 1895–99. He helped found the *United Irish League 1898, but was unattuned to changes in the land question since the 1870s, and bitterly critical of the Wyndham Act, 1903. He published *Leaves from a Prison Diary* (1885), and *The Fall of Feudalism in Ireland* (1904).

JL

Deane & Woodward, *architectural firm, were the principal exponents of the Ruskinian Gothic revival in England and Ireland. The firm was an offshoot of the Cork practice of Sir Thomas Deane, and consisted of the core partnership between Thomas Newenham Deane (1828–99) and Benjamin Woodward (1816–61). Woodward, a native of Tullamore, Co. Offaly, joined the firm in 1845; his involvement in work at Queen's College, Cork (1846–9), and Killarney lunatic asylum (1847–50) reflects his academic interest in the work of the Gothic revivalists. Woodward and T. N. Deane were made partners in 1851. Their first major collaboration, the Venetian Museum building, *Trinity College, Dublin (1852–7), was hailed as the first true embodiment of the ideals of John Ruskin. It incorporates many of the features that were to characterize the firm's work in the following decades: emphasis on structural symmetry, the use of local building materials, polychrome fabric, rich embellishment, and good craftsmanship. The most famous building of the partnership was the Oxford Museum (1855–61); the first public secular Gothic building to be erected in England since the Houses of Parliament (1836–66), it set the trend for many English public buildings in subsequent decades. Other examples of the firm's work include the Crown Life Assurance Company office, Blackfriars,

London (1855–7, no longer extant), the Kildare Street Club, Dublin (1858–61), and extensive alterations to Kilkenny Castle (1858–63). RM

De Blácam, Aodh (1890–1951), journalist and utopian. Born in London of Ulster Protestant parents, he converted to Catholicism and moved in London Irish and separatist circles. In 1915 he went to Ireland and thereafter wrote extensively for Catholic and republican journals, advocating an arcadian neo-Gaelic Catholic socialism. He became a *Fianna Fáil propagandist, associate of de *Valera, and **Irish Press* columnist. De Blácam praised Salazar and Franco as exponents of a Catholic social order free from the evils of capitalism. He defected to *Clann na Poblachta in protest at Fianna Fáil's failure to halt rural decline, and served as speech-writer for Noel *Browne. PM

debtors' prisons. County *prisons housed many small debtors, but in Dublin in the early 18th century there were two prisons specifically for debtors, one on Merchant's Quay, operated by the *Four Courts marshal, and one off Wood Quay, operated by the city marshal. In 1775 a new debtors' prison, the Four Courts marshalsea, was built off Thomas Street, while a new city marshalsea was built beside Newgate prison in Green Street in 1797. Until they could satisfy their creditors, debtors and their families from all over the country were imprisoned in the Four Courts marshalsea, with the rich hiring comfortable chambers, while the poor were crowded into squalid halls. When imprisonment for debt was abolished in 1872, the Four Courts marshalsea was converted into a military barracks. ELM

Decies. The Déisi Muman were a division of the *Déisi who by the 8th century had established a kingdom in what is now Co. Waterford and south Co. Tipperary. King *John granted the territory to Thomas fitz Anthony, from whom it passed to the Fitzgeralds of *Desmond. James, 7th earl (d. 1462), granted Decies to a younger son. Later *FitzGerald lords of Decies sought to preserve their independence from their powerful Desmond cousins by allying themselves with the *Ormond Butlers.

declaration of 1460, a pronouncement in a parliament at Drogheda that 'the land of Ireland is and at all times has been corporate of itself, by the ancient laws and customs used in the same, freed of the burthen of any special law of the realm of England', unless such law was confirmed by parliament in Ireland. There has been some dispute as to whether precedent provided any justification for this assertion, but it was prefatory to an act (subsequently repealed under Edward *Poynings) ruling that no one in Ireland should be compelled to obey a summons from outside Ireland to answer accusations of treason. The immediate beneficiary was Richard, duke of *York, then governing Ireland in defiance of his attainder for treason in parliament in England. The question of whether the declaration was prompted by York himself, or by the strength of aspirations in Ireland for autonomy from English interference, has been the subject of considerable and continuing debate. EAEM

Declaratory Act, 'an act for the better securing of the dependency of the kingdom of Ireland upon the Crown of Great Britain', also known, from the regnal year, as the 6th of George I. Passed by the British parliament in 1720, in response to the **Sherlock* v. *Annesley* controversy, it denied that the Irish House of Lords had any jurisdiction over appeals from the courts, and asserted the right of the British parliament to pass legislation binding on Ireland. Its repeal, confirmed in the *Renunciation Act (1783), was a central part of the 'constitution of 1782' (see LEGISLATIVE INDEPENDENCE).

decorated manuscripts constituted one of the most important branches of the visual arts in Ireland in the Middle Ages. As many more manuscripts have been lost than survive, the development of decoration can be traced only sketchily. In the late 6th-century Gospel book 'Usserianus Primus' (Trinity College Dublin 55), decoration is confined to a framed Chi Rho, surrounded by red dots. The 'Cathach' Psalter (Royal Irish Academy 12.R.33), traditionally attributed to St *Colum Cille (d. 597), but probably written early in the 7th century, employs spiral and trumpet devices, fish and cross symbols, as well as the calligraphic technique of 'diminuendo' (diminishing letter size). In the Book of *Durrow, and later in the Book of *Kells, such devices are integrated with motifs borrowed from metalwork, and with animal and figure drawings derived from Mediterranean prototypes. Fine decoration was practised at other centres, notably *Armagh, where the earliest extant New Testament copied in Ireland, along with a dossier of texts relating to St *Patrick (the Book of *Armagh, Trinity College Dublin 52), was produced around 807 by Ferdomnach and other talented artist-scribes. The late 8th-century Book of Mulling (Trinity College Dublin 60), from St Mullins, Co. Carlow, contains striking portraits of three evangelists. The contemporary Book of Dimma (Trinity College Dublin 59), from Roscrea, Co. Tipperary, contains less naturalistic images. The early 9th-century MacRegol Gospels (Oxford, Bodleian Library, Auct. D.12.19), from Birr, Co. Offaly, employs strong colouristic effects. Manuscripts brought from Ireland to centres such as Bobbio and St Gallen reflect the impact of Irish missionary settlement, while Irish styles exerted enormous influence in Northumbria. Insular styles persisted into the later medieval period, executed with considerable skill in volumes such as the 11th-century *Liber Hymnorum* (Trinity College Dublin 1441) and the late 12th-century Cormac Psalter (British Library Add. 36929). Styles from England, imported following the *Anglo-Norman invasion, are reflected in the Christ Church, Dublin, psalter of 1397 (Oxford, Bodleian Library, Rawl. C.185), and an illustrated early 15th-century missal (London, Lambeth Palace, 213), both probably originating in England. In the late 14th century, the charter roll of the city of Waterford was decorated in a lively manner, perhaps locally, while in the early 15th century a decorated copy of Ranulf Higden's chronicle (Oxford, Bodleian Library, Rawl. B.179) was probably made in Dublin. From the 16th century, the book of the Mayo de Burgo (see BURKE (DE BURGH)) family contains portraits and illustrations drawn with remarkable vigour (Trinity College Dublin 1440).

Alexander, J. J. G., *Insular Manuscripts, 6th to the 9th Century* (1978)
Henry, F., and Marsh-Micheli, G., 'Manuscripts and Illuminations, 1169–1603', in A. Cosgrove (ed.), *A New History of Ireland*, vol. ii (1987)
Meehan, B., *The Book of Kells: An Illustrated Introduction to the Manuscript in Trinity College Dublin* (1994)

BM

defective titles. A Commission for Defective Titles was first issued by James I in 1606 to enable his subjects 'to quietly and privately enjoy their private estates and possessions'. The main object was to prevent prying into land titles caused by the search for *concealed lands. Participating *Old English and Gaelic Irish landholders secured letters patent in return for promising rents and services to the crown. Ironically the same dispensation was exploited by New English adventurers to secure title to formerly concealed lands, to change leases into ownership, and to obtain easier tenures. These sharp practices, which impoverished the crown, continued under a second commission issued in 1615.

The Old English wanted parliamentary confirmation of the *Graces limiting royal claims to land held privately over the previous 60 years, but instead *Wentworth created a Commission of Defective Titles with statutory authority in 1634. Wentworth's object was to boost revenue by forcing landholders, both native and planter, to convert to the higher knight's tenure (see LAND TENURE), which made them not only liable to heavier crown rents but also subject to financial and religious exploitation by the court of *wards.

Furthermore in the case of tenures (1637) the Irish judges questioned the validity of patents issued by the earlier commissions under James. Far from securing land titles, Wentworth was now threatening all land titles prior to 1634. These high-handed land policies were a major grievance against Wentworth in 1641.

In 1684 another Commission of Defective Titles, known as the Commission of Grace, sought to secure the *Restoration land settlement following a renewed concealment campaign. However, when *James II came to the throne, Protestant landholders feared that it would become a weapon to disinherit them. HM

Defence of the Realm Acts (DORA) (1914–18), *First World War emergency legislation empowering the government to make regulations for public safety, breaches of which could be tried by courts martial. Those executed following the *rising of 1916 were sentenced under the acts. During the *Anglo-Irish War DORA regulations were widely used to restrict firearms, to create Special Military Areas within which soldiers could carry out searches, and to substitute courts martial for jury trial. From August 1920 they were superseded by the *Restoration of Order Act.

Defenders, secret society, originally the Catholic opponents of the *Peep of Day Boys in Co. Armagh. From 1790 Defenderism spread into other Ulster counties, and into the northern half of Leinster, including Dublin city. During 1794–5 an explosion of Defender activity in Connacht led to Lord Carhampton's (see LUTTRELL, HENRY) notorious impressment for naval service of over 1,000 suspects. Sporadic contact from the early 1790s with the *United Irishmen (see TANDY, JAMES NAPPER) developed, probably by 1796, into a formal alliance. Defenders as well as United Irishmen participated, though not always harmoniously, in the *insurrection of 1798. The movement continued into the 19th century under the new name of *Ribbonmen.

The Defenders were for long perceived as a largely apolitical adjunct to the United Irishmen, preoccupied with practical economic grievances and religious animosities. Recent work, however, makes clear that Defenderism had a regional and national leadership of a kind never developed by the *Whiteboys or other movements of *agrarian protest. Its members, equally, looked beyond the resolution of immediate economic grievances and sectarian animosities to a general social and political transformation, however crudely imagined. Defenderism can thus be seen as a key stage in the process of *politicization, shaped both by popular awareness of the *French

Revolution and by domestic political events, notably the increasingly assertive activities of the *Catholic Committee and the backlash among conservative Protestants.

Déisi, Old Irish for tenants or vassals, was the name of a number of communities in early Ireland. These included Déisi Temro (of *Tara), otherwise Déisi Breg, who were located in the modern barony of Deece in Meath, the Déisi of Waterford, and the Déisi of Limerick, one branch of which migrated to Clare and subsequently became the *Dál Cais. The Waterford Déisi survived until the *Anglo-Norman conquest. Eoin *MacNeill believed the Déisi were rent paying, a suggestion based in part on the 8th-century compilation *Tairired na nDessi* (Expulsion of the Déisi), which depicts them as subordinate communities, dependent for land on overlords. This text recounts how the Déisi were forced to flee Tara after having blinded King *Cormac mac Airt in one eye. According to the tale, they had various homes in Leinster and Munster before coalescing with other exiled peoples and settling in Tipperary and Waterford. One variant depicts a group of Déisi as migrating to Dyfed in Wales; these are normally seen by scholars as ancestors of a dynasty which ruled Dyfed until the 10th century. Early connections between Dyfed and Co. Waterford are implied by the high concentration of *ogam stones in both areas. CS

Democratic Left, see WORKERS' PARTY.

democratic programme, one of the four major documents approved by *Dáil Éireann at its first meeting on 21 January 1919, setting out its social and economic objectives. It was drafted by William *O'Brien and Thomas *Johnson of the Labour Party, and amended by Sean T. O'Kelly of *Sinn Féin. The introduction of this fairly socialistic document was partly to reward Labour for its decision not to field candidates in the 1918 election, and partly to assist the successful Irish claim to self-determination at the International Socialist Conference in Berne. Although generally ignored by Sinn Féin and its inheritors, the document was to be appealed to by later supporters of a synthesis of *republicanism and *socialism. JA

Democratic Unionist Party, founded September 1971 by Ian Paisley and Desmond Boal as a successor to the Protestant Unionist Party, which had opposed Terence *O'Neill's reformist unionism. The DUP grew rapidly in the 1970s, in the context of a still divided Ulster *unionism and high levels of communal violence: the peak of its electoral support came in the council elections of 1981, when its candidates won 26.6 per cent of votes cast. It opposed the *Sunningdale agreement, and Paisley identified himself closely with the *Ulster Workers' Council strike of May 1974. The DUP were also prominent partners in the Unionist alliance which emerged in opposition to the *Anglo-Irish agreement of 1985. However, their relationship with the Ulster Unionist Party subsequently came under strain, and the two groupings took markedly different approaches to the Downing Street declaration (Dec. 1993), the DUP being more hostile than its rival. This chasm grew wider after 1998, when the DUP emerged as vehement opponents of the Good Friday Agreement (see PEACE PROCESS).

The DUP's command over a section of the unionist electorate remains formidable. Its success has been rooted in the combination of a militant commitment to the Union with often imaginative social policies. The party has a local electoral asset in Paisley, who has consistently polled more highly and across a wider base than other DUP candidates; it also benefits from a relationship with Paisley's *Free Presbyterian church, which has provided a core of party activists. These political tools have allowed the DUP, like earlier populist loyalist movements, to cultivate a constituency neglected by mainstream unionism: the urban working classes, and rural evangelicals. AJ

department stores can be first identified in Dublin during the 1840s although, as the businesses evolved from general drapery or outfitting firms, it is difficult to date their emergence precisely. In 1851, however, W. Neilson Hancock, Whately professor of political economy at Trinity College, Dublin, published a pamphlet on the competition between large and small shops, which suggests that this was a matter of controversy at the time. A wave of pamphlets criticizing the emergence of 'monster stores' appeared in Dublin during the 1860s, coinciding with the expansion and reconstruction of many of these shops. The imposing premises, complete with plate-glass windows, gas lighting, and elaborate façades, were among the most prominent buildings erected in the city during the Victorian era. The fact that most of these stores were owned by foreigners, with Scottish-born David McBirney (a railway director) and Sir John Arnott (proprietor of the *Irish Times*) among the most prominent, was a major cause for criticism. Department stores were also attacked for favouring foreign-made goods, and, somewhat contradicting this, for promoting sweated industries.

Most Dublin department stores appear to have catered for both retail and wholesale markets.

These businesses expanded steadily until the late 1870s when they became victims of the depression in Irish agriculture. In 1884 the Dublin Drapery Warehouse in Sackville Street, owned by Peter Paul McSwiney, a former lord mayor, was wound up. It reopened as Clery's and was later owned by William Martin *Murphy. It was destroyed during the 1916 rising. In Belfast, Anderson & McCauley's business dated from the mid-19th century; the firm renovated and extended its premises *c.*1890. Robinson & Cleaver began business in 1870, moving to a new store, built in Italianate style, in 1888. Both stores played a major role in promoting mail-order sales of Irish linen goods. One leading Dublin department store, Brown Thomas, was briefly owned during the early 20th century by Selfridges of London. During the 1930s branches of British chain stores appeared in Irish cities. However, most department stores remained under local ownership until the late 20th century. MED

depositions, a much cited collection of documents relating to the *rising of 1641, preserved in *Trinity College, Dublin. The collection combines four sets of documents: statements of refugees taken 1641–7 by a commission headed by Henry *Jones, primarily to register claims to compensation for property lost in the rebellion (the controversial depositions relate to robberies from the dead); more depositions taken in Munster in 1642–3 by the English parliament; statements taken for intelligence purposes from both Protestant refugees and captured insurgents; and material collected by the High Court of Justice (1652) to try those responsible for atrocities in the *Confederate War. Jones and his associates had already used the depositions for political purposes when, in 1642, they produced 'The Remonstrance' to solicit relief funds in England and subsequently to promote investment in the *Adventurers' Act. In 1643 they submitted 'The Discourse' to the Irish privy council in an attempt to sabotage the royalist-confederate truce. *Temple published lurid extracts in his popular history of the rebellion (1646). This controversial archive, exploited by scholars in the 18th and 19th centuries to debate allegations of massacre and atrocity, is now being utilized as a source of information on social and economic conditions in the period before the rising. HM

Derrick, John (*fl.* 1578), English engraver whose *Image of Ireland* (1581) contains the most important and widely known representations of 16th-century Ireland. Stolid verse is accompanied by twelve vivid woodcuts. Certain drawings, such as the governor's departure from *Dublin Castle, can be checked for accuracy against contemporary maps, but others are figments of the author's imagination. The main subjects are the depredations of the 'wild Irish' *kern and the glorious exploits of *Sidney. The book, while excluding from its strictures the civil subjects of the *Pale, is heavily laden with anti-Irish, anti-Catholic views. Most notably the friars are shown exhorting and absolving the rebellions of the Gaelic lords. Derrick's woodcuts—their message ignored, sublimated, or misunderstood—have become familiar illustrations in Irish history books. HM

Derry, or Londonderry (Ir. *Doire*, 'place of the oaks'), Northern Ireland, commanding the west bank of the Foyle estuary. The site of a monastery founded by *Colum Cille, which was destroyed by the *Vikings, modern Derry was founded by Sir Henry *Docwra in 1600. The charter granted to London companies in 1613 (see ULSTER PLANTATION) allowed the prefix 'London' to be added: Londonderry remains the official name of the city, and is preferred by unionists. Although the nationalist majority changed the name of the local authority to Derry city council in 1978, the British government refused permission to change the name of the city itself.

Derry's formidable stone walls, completed in 1618, mark it out as the last fortified city to be built in western Europe. During the *Williamite War Protestant resistance to the armies of *James II in the 105-day siege of *Derry, after *Apprentice Boys had closed the city gates, was a decisive moment in European history. Again the city played a key role, as the centre of communications for the North Atlantic campaign, during the *Second World War. With these exceptions Derry's history has been that of an ethnic frontier at the economic margin. The modest success of the port, and the city's role as a source of cheap female labour for the *shirt making industry, caused the population to double, to 40,000, during the second half of the 19th century. But Derry was unable to emulate *Belfast's economic diversification and take-off, nor did it generate large-scale male employment. Although the population doubled again during the 20th century, the economic story was downbeat.

The siege made Derry a symbol of Protestant power in Ulster: for unionists it remains 'the maiden city'. But Catholics were a majority of the population well before 1900, and during the 20th century Protestant power was maintained with difficulty. To immense Catholic disappointment, the *Boundary Commission kept the city within Northern Ireland in 1925, and only gross gerrymandering preserved Unionist control of the city council until 1973. This required a local housing policy restricting Catholics to tenancies in the overcrowded South Ward, and reluctance at *Stormont to promote any growth in the city: in 1965, for instance, the city's Magee College was passed over as the site for a new university in favour of the market town of Coleraine. Driven by such grievances, and by its very rapid population growth in the 1950s and 1960s, Catholic Derry was primed to explode. The renewed *Northern Ireland conflict began there with the televised police violence of 5 October 1968, and continued with the 'battle of the Bogside' (Aug. 1969) and *'Bloody Sunday' (Jan. 1972). Under *direct rule housing in a small city, if not employment, was a problem which the British state had the resources to solve. In the 1970s Catholic Derry expanded northwards and the Protestants moved east: a new sectarian terminology of 'west bank' and 'east bank' emerged to describe the now river-divided city. By the 1990s it seemed that a precarious new equilibrium had been reached, with restabilized ethnic boundaries, improved housing, and increased investment, mainly in consumer services and in a massive expansion of Magee College.

Lacy, Brian, *Siege City: The Story of Derry and Londonderry* (1990)

ACH

Derry, siege of (18 Apr.–31 July 1689), in the *Williamite War. Despite the earlier defiance of the *Apprentice Boys, Derry's open allegiance to *William III began only on 21 March, when the ship *Deliverance* brought arms, supplies, and a new Williamite commission for Robert *Lundy, the garrison commander. On 18 April, after the *Jacobites had overrun the surrounding countryside, *James II appeared in person but was met with gunshots and cries of 'No surrender'. Lundy was now deposed, Major Henry Baker (replaced on his death by John Mitchelburne) and Revd George *Walker taking joint command. The Jacobites, lacking siege equipment, made unsuccessful attempts to force the Butchers' gate on the west wall and to capture the Williamite outpost on Windmill Hill, but relied mainly on starvation to force a surrender. The city's population, normally around 2,000, was swollen by an estimated 30,000 refugees and 7,000 soldiers. Williamite accounts claimed the defenders were reduced to eating rats, mice, and dogs fattened on human corpses, and that 15,000 people, mainly women and children, died of disease and malnutrition. Jacobite attempts to stretch the city's resources further by abandoning Protestant civilians beneath the walls ended when the defenders threatened to hang prisoners in retaliation. On 28 July two ships laden with food broke through the boom with which the Jacobites had blocked the Foyle estuary, effectively ending the siege. The 105-day ordeal of the inhabitants became a central part of *unionist folklore, annually commemorated by the Apprentice Boys.

Desmond, title of the FitzGerald lordship and earldom in Munster, held by the descendants of Thomas fitz Maurice (d. 1213), a younger son of Maurice fitz Gerald, who had landed at Wexford in 1169 as part of the original *Anglo-Norman invasion. Thomas received extensive lands in Limerick from King *John. His son, John fitz Thomas, who was killed at the battle of *Callan in 1261, increased the family's lands and power through a mixture of military action, chiefly against the *MacCarthys, and royal favour. At one time or another he acted as *sheriff of most of the counties of Munster. In 1259, after several visits to court in England, he obtained from the future Edward I a grant of the lordships of Desmond and the *Decies, which had been held by his father-in-law, Thomas fitz Anthony. His death was followed by a long, damaging minority; but his grandson Thomas fitz Maurice (d. 1298), who married Margaret, a daughter of the Gloucestershire baronial family of Berkeley, and served as *justiciar of Ireland in 1295, restored the family's position. It was further extended by Thomas's son (see DESMOND, MAURICE FITZ THOMAS), who in 1329 was granted by the regime of Roger *Mortimer the title of earl, together with *liberty rights over Kerry and the office of sheriff in Cos. Waterford and Cork.

The relations of the earls of Desmond with the crown and, more particularly, its ministers in Ireland were often contentious. There were several reasons for this. The legal basis of the Desmond lordships was not beyond challenge. In making the grant of 1259, Edward had exceeded the powers he had been given by his father, Henry III. The endowments of 1329 were vulnerable to *resumption when Edward III attained his majority and repudiated the acts of the Mortimer government. The intrusion of Desmond power into the de *Clare lordships in Thomond and Cork, which had passed into the hands of *absentees after 1321, was a further source of tension. But above all, the remote, frontier position of the earldom created difficulties. The power of the earls depended on exploiting their lands and liberties in the settled parts of the south-west, but it relied also upon acting as allies and patrons of neighbouring Gaelic leaders. Their lordship was of necessity highly militarized, and based increasingly on exactions such as *coyne and livery. In this respect it differed little from that of their Munster rivals, the Butler earls of *Ormond. But, unlike the Butlers, the earls of Desmond lacked the political advantage of interests closer to Dublin and lands in England.

The authorities wavered in their attitude to the earldom. Usually it was accepted as necessary to the stability of the south-west. Attempts were made to harness the power of the earls, by granting them extensive judicial commissions. They were even, on rare occasions, admitted to the chief governorship, although the last such experiment, in 1463, ended disastrously (see DESMOND, THOMAS FITZGERALD). At other times, the crown and its agents were alarmed by their autocratic behaviour and Gaelic cultural complexion—a view promoted by their rivals and by urban communities in Munster, which regarded their rule as oppressive. In the 16th century, the earls appeared increasingly problematical to the English authorities. Their marriages—since the 1350s almost exclusively to local families such as the MacCarthys, *O'Briens, *Burkes, and Roches—confirmed their roots in south-west Ireland and lack of ties with English society. On the other hand, the openness of Munster to continental influences was reflected in the threatening diplomacy, notably of the 10th earl (see DESMOND, JAMES FITZGERALD). The compromises and ambiguities of earlier periods were difficult to maintain in the age of the more intrusive late Tudor state. The *Desmond rebellions in the reign of Elizabeth I were followed by the obliteration of the lordship in the *Munster plantation. RFF

Desmond, Eleanor, countess of (1545–1638), née Butler. Eleanor married Gerald, 14th earl of *Desmond in 1565. After his imprisonment in the Tower, she ran the estates, contained his rivals, and secured an audience with Queen Elizabeth which facilitated Gerald's move to house arrest. On their return to Ireland, she worked for reconciliation. During the second *Desmond rebellion, she came out of hiding in a number of vain attempts to negotiate the earl's pardon. Widowed without land or money, another audience secured a pension. Fortunately her second husband, O'Connor Sligo, died a loyal subject in 1609 and she lived comfortably thereafter on a large jointure of his lands. HM

Desmond, Gerald, 3rd earl of (*c*.1338–1398). The son of Maurice, the 1st earl, Gerald became earl of Desmond in 1359; at the same time he married Eleanor (d. 1392), daughter of James Butler, earl of *Ormond. His lands covered Kerry (a *palatinate) and substantial quantities in Cos. Limerick, Cork, Tipperary, and Waterford. In February 1367 he was appointed *justiciar, a post he held to June 1369. In July 1370 he was captured in a battle with Brian O'Brien, king of Thomond 1343–75, and freed late in 1371. His son James was sent for fosterage to Conor O'Brien in Thomond in 1388. His reputation in later generations is based on a number of poems in Irish attributed to him; many of them relate to events in his life, including his captivity in 1370–1. GMacN

Desmond, Gerald FitzGerald, 14th earl of (*c*.1533–1583). The son of a usurper, Gerald had little formal education and certainly no training as a courtier, unlike his great rival, Black Tom Butler, 10th earl of *Ormond. Because of disputes with Butler, most notably the pitched battle at *Affane in 1565, he suffered six years' imprisonment in England. In the mid-1570s, having returned with huge debts to a war-torn land, he seemed to have turned the corner by abandoning *coyne and livery and promoting law and order in league with Sir William Drury, the *provincial president. Circumstances, however, catapulted him into the second *Desmond rebellion. After early successes, he took to the woods. Refusing to submit unconditionally, as his lands were already declared forfeit, he was killed near Tralee for head-money by a band of the Moriartys. The Desmond title passed to his son James, but the lands formed the basis of the *Munster plantation. HM

Desmond, James FitzGerald, 10th earl of (d. 1529). James took over the administration of the lordship while his father was still alive in the 1510s and when Desmond power was under heavy pressure from surrounding magnates. He is best known for his contacts with foreign powers. When England went to war with France, he entertained French agents at Askeaton in 1523 and agreed to support the Yorkist pretender, Richard de la Pole, for the English throne. After the Butlers defeated his client Richard Power, and established themselves in Dungarvan, Desmond approached Charles V in 1528. The emperor, then at odds with Henry VIII over his proposed divorce, sent his chaplain to interview the earl. The latter, who was more interested in fighting the Butlers than Henry VIII, made bombastic claims about his military strength. HM

Desmond, Maurice fitz Thomas, 1st earl of (d. 1356), the most turbulent noble of his time. In 1332 Munster juries accused him of conspiracies with Anglo-Irish and Gaelic lords to become king of Ireland. In 1346 he was indicted of treasonable correspondence with Scotland and France, and of offering to rule Ireland as papal deputy. He was imprisoned in 1331–3, and was outlawed again from 1345 to 1349, before being restored by Edward III and becoming *justiciar in 1355. Historians have presented him variously as leader of a colonial 'patriot party', as the archetypal over-mighty magnate, and as an example of *Gaelicization. The more lurid accusations came from those he had oppressed, when Dublin officials were busily justifying their actions against him. They possibly arose from *bardic verse praising him as king-worthy. Edward III seems not to have taken them seriously. While Desmond pushed his power well beyond its legal limits, he was a *frontier magnate who had to strike a difficult balance—maintaining regional dominance through a combination of military force and the cultivation of political links with those outside the peace, while at the same time keeping royal favour. He served the crown during the *Bruce invasion, received his earldom and the *liberty of Kerry in England in 1329, fought in Scotland in 1335, and in 1346–8 lodged with his mother's family, the Berkeleys, in Gloucestershire while negotiating his restoration. The problems he had in reconciling the two aspects of his career arose largely from conflicts over land in *Thomond and Cork, in which royal ministers upheld the interests of *absentees. RFF

Desmond, Thomas FitzGerald, 8th earl of (*c.*1426–1468), the key figure in an unusual attempt to extend the Dublin administration's normal range of operation by associating the most remote of the three Irish earls with the governorship. In 1462, when he became earl, Desmond defeated *Ormond's heir at *Pilltown to end a Lancastrian rising (see WARS OF THE ROSES). Edward IV rewarded him by appointing him deputy in 1463 and he co-operated closely with his kinsman, the earl of *Kildare. Yet his introduction into the English *Pale of *coyne and livery and other Gaelic practices to maintain his troops fuelled opposition from the Meath gentry and eventually proved his undoing. His successor as deputy, Worcester, had both FitzGerald earls attainted of treason, and Desmond was executed at Drogheda. Although the attainder was soon reversed and Desmond's heir became earl, relations with the crown remained strained until 1542. SGE

Desmond rebellions (1569–73, 1579–83), revolts against Tudor centralization which paved the way for the *Munster plantation. The FitzGerald earldom of Desmond was too impoverished and too militarized to make the kind of change demanded by Tudor reformers, and too closely beset by English freebooters to have any real opportunity to adjust. Gerald, the 14th earl, was willing to abandon *coyne and livery and even to assist small-scale colonization. In 1569 James Fitzmaurice FitzGerald, captain general of the earl's forces and previous tenant of St Leger's colony at Kerrycurrihy, led a revolt assisted by dissident Butlers similarly worried by demilitarization and land grabbing. There were short unsuccessful sieges of Cork, Kilmallock, and Kilkenny but the return of Black Tom, earl of *Ormond, brought the submission of most of the Butlers, and *Sidney's appearance had a like effect on the Geraldines. However, Sir Humphrey Gilbert, who was left in charge of Munster, subjected the country to a reign of terror. Sir John *Perrot, who became president of Munster in February 1571, followed a similar policy, executing 800 rebels in the space of two years. Fitzmaurice submitted only in February 1573, after news of the release of the earl of Desmond from the Tower of London.

In 1575 Fitzmaurice went into exile to seek assistance first in France and then in Spain. His efforts were upstaged by those of Thomas Stukeley, a former pirate and English captain, who persuaded Pope Gregory XIII to give him 1,000 men to liberate Ireland. At Lisbon Stukeley opted to join a crusade to Morocco. Fitzmaurice returned to Ireland with the remnant of Stukeley's force on 17 July 1579, proclaiming a holy war, but was killed in a local dispute on the Connacht border. The revolt, however, regained momentum when Sir John FitzGerald brought 2,000 men into the field. *Malby, appointed temporary governor of Munster, defeated Sir John at Monasternenagh, Co. Limerick, but acted in such a provocative fashion that the earl was himself forced into rebellion and proclaimed a traitor. In 1580 *Grey liquidated a papal invasion force at *Smerwick and ordered a scorched earth policy to reduce the insurgents to submission. The famine killed the peasantry but many of the leaders remained at large. Grey was recalled and Ormond, afforded the power to pardon, eventually pacified the country. Resistance ended with the killing of the earl of Desmond on 11 November 1583. HM

Despard, Col. Edward Marcus (1751–1803), born in Queen's County, a naval hero executed 21 February 1803 for an alleged revolutionary conspiracy in London. His activities, long dismissed as a wild personal venture, are now seen as part of the clandestine plotting still kept up, despite defeat in the *insurrection of 1798, by the *United Irishmen and their radical allies in Great Britain, with possible links to Robert *Emmet's venture later the same year.

Devlin, Anne (1780–1851). From a Co. Wicklow farming family, Devlin, a niece of Michael *Dwyer, acted as housekeeper for Robert *Emmet in the period before his insurrection of July 1803, was arrested along with other members of her family, and brutally interrogated. Accounts by R. R.

*Madden, who found her living in poverty in Dublin, and by Brother Luke Cullen (1793–1859), who wrote a first-person life story based on her own account, established her as a nationalist heroine.

Devlin, Joseph (1871–1934), leading Ulster member of the *Nationalist Party. Devlin came from working-class origins in Catholic west Belfast, receiving only primary education from the *Christian Brothers. He worked in pubs until he became, reluctantly, a paid *United Irish League official. Later he donated his parliamentary salary to public causes, and acquired directorships, including the chairmanship of the *Irish News*. A small man with a mane of black hair, his political admirers included many women, but he never married.

His apprenticeship, in divided Ulster during the *Parnell split, provided a double lesson in the importance of organization in politics which he perhaps imbibed too well. His work with emigrant communities made him aware of the power of sentiment and of clientage; he harnessed both to good effect as president of the *Ancient Order of Hibernians. A protégé of John *Dillon, he was after 1903 the main target for William *O'Brien's attacks on the parliamentary party. Entering parliament for North Kilkenny in 1902, he won West Belfast from the Unionists in 1906, losing it through boundary changes in 1922. Alone among the younger Nationalists he established a major parliamentary reputation. *Asquith feared that he would oppose compromise on Ulster, but party loyalty proved stronger than origins. During the attempt to implement home rule after the *rising of 1916, he put his organizational and oratorical skills to their greatest test by persuading six-county activists to vote for temporary *partition. His reputation never fully recovered from this success.

In the 1918 election Devlin brushed aside de *Valera's personal challenge in West Belfast, but was reduced to leadership of six MPs. The Dublin-based *Sinn Féin leadership naturally sought to minimize his influence, which further weakened the northern Catholic position. Not until 1925 did he enter the Northern Ireland parliament. Unsurprisingly, his later years were characterized by disillusion. In 1928 he established the *National League of the North. He failed to enter English politics as an independent in 1922, but spasmodically represented Fermanagh & Tyrone at Westminster after 1929.

Phoenix, E., *Northern Nationalism* (1994)

ACH

devolution crisis (1904–5), a classic example of ministerial responsibility for the actions of civil servants. Encouraged by the appointment of Sir Antony *MacDonnell to *Dublin Castle in 1902, and by their success in inspiring the *Land Act of 1903, Lord Dunraven and other progressive landlords formed the Irish Reform Association. In September 1904 the Association published proposals for the devolution of modest powers to an Irish representative council. MacDonnell was in fact the main author of the scheme. George *Wyndham promptly repudiated the scheme and rebuked MacDonnell. But backbench *Unionist anger continued, MacDonnell was able to maintain that he had acted with Wyndham's tacit approval, and Wyndham resigned. Nationalist reaction to the scheme was mixed, but they later rejected the Liberal government's expanded version, the *Irish council bill. This brief outbreak of southern Unionist conciliation prompted the formation of a distinct Ulster Unionist Council in March 1905.

ACH

Devon Commission (1843–5), familiar title for the Royal Commission on the state of the law and practice relating to occupation of land in Ireland, chaired by William Courtenay, 29th earl of Devon, who had an estate in Co. Limerick. The enquiry was established as part of *Peel's attempt to balance his uncompromising rejection of *repeal with measures of moderate reform. Its most important recommendation was that outgoing tenants be compensated for any improvements they had made. However a bill to this effect, introduced in the House of Lords in June 1845, was effectively killed off. The commission's report was nevertheless of importance in helping to confirm the emerging contemporary belief that Irish rural poverty and low agricultural productivity were primarily the result of an oppressive land system. Its extensive collection of oral and written testimony remains a major resource for historians of pre-Famine rural society.

devotional revolution, term coined in 1972 by the American historian Emmet Larkin to describe what he saw as a sudden and dramatic transformation of popular religious practice in Ireland in the period *c.*1850–75. Other historians argue that the changes concerned were, in fact, part of a long-term modernization of Irish religious life going back to the *Counter-Reformation. They resulted in the replacement of kin-group-centred, lay-controlled, and semi-pagan devotional practices, like *patterns and *wakes, with standardized, usually imported, clerically vetted alternatives, performed in the local church building and integrated into a process of personal sanctification. The decisive instruments of devotional change were Sunday sermons, parish *missions, and confraternities.

The reformed devotions, largely by accident of timing, became part of the new Catholic identity under construction in 19th-century Ireland. Initially, they were best received by better-off, socially and politically active Catholic elites, gradually percolating down the social ladder. By the early 20th century they had made a fairly clean sweep of traditional practices. Because they were so intimately associated with the institutional church, and with a certain phase of Irish nationalism, these devotional practices did not weather very well the process of religious modernization associated with the second *Vatican Council, leaving a gap in contemporary Catholic religious practice. TO'C

Devoy, John (1842–1928), a clerk in Dublin who joined the *Fenians in 1861. For his part in the conspiracy he spent the period 1866–71 in prison. Exiled subsequently, he became the most tireless and effective organizer of Irish-American support for advanced Irish nationalism. He had a key role in the emergence of the *Land League (1879) and in the genesis of the *rising of 1916. His *Recollections of an Irish Rebel* (1929) is a classic (if highly selective) text. RVC

Diamond, battle of (21 Sept. 1795), a sectarian affray taking its name from a crossroads near Loughgall, Co. Armagh. Protestants occupying a strong hilltop position beat off a large force of Defenders drawn from surrounding counties, killing thirty or more. Although the victorious Protestants are frequently described as *Peep of Day Boys, there are also references to a more recently formed, and apparently more politicized, group, the Orange boys, and the immediate sequel was the establishment of the *Orange Order.

Diarmait mac Cerbaill was the ancestor of the two leading dynasties of the southern *Uí Néill. Their tradition recorded in the *annals made him *high king from 544 until his defeat by the northern Uí Néill and his death in 565; he was regarded as the last to celebrate the pagan inauguration known as *Feis Temro. Since the southern Uí Néill dynasties had barely emerged at this date, we should see this as part of their origin-legend. By the time *Adomnán wrote his Life of St *Colum Cille, however, Diarmait had already gained his leading place in their traditions; Adomnán sought to Christianize this, describing him as 'ordained by God's will as king of all Ireland'. He also describes Diarmait's killing on Lough Neagh, which became the subject of a popular tale. He was buried at Connor in enemy territory, but his head was taken back to Clonmacnoise. RS

Diarmait (Dermot) mac Máel na mBó (d. 1072), king of Leinster and contender for the kingship of Ireland. On the death of the king of Leinster, Murchad mac Dúnlaing, at the battle of Mag Mulchet (in the territory of the Loígis) in 1042, the *Uí Dúnlainge dominance of Leinster ended and Diarmait's claim to the kingship was consolidated. From 1048, Diarmait engaged in the affairs of other provinces. He led an army into *Mide (Meath) in 1048 in revenge for raids on Leinster by Conchobar ua Máel Sechlainn (Conor, grandson of Malachy), king of Mide (d. 1073). This action prompted the high king Donnchad mac Briain (Donough, son of Brian) to seek Diarmait's submission. By *c.*1054 Diarmait controlled Dublin, which he entrusted to his son Murchad (Murrough) (d. 1070), who acted as king in his absence. In alliance with Áed Ua Conchobair (Hugh O'Conor), king of Connacht, and with Toirdelbach *Ua Briain (Turlough O'Brien), he challenged Donnchad mac Briain's authority until the high king was ousted and went to Rome in 1064. Diarmait's ally Toirdelbach Ua Briain then assumed the kingship of Munster. With the support of the Munstermen and the Osraige, Diarmait assisted Áed Ua Ruairc (Hugh O'Rourke) (d. 1087) in defeating Áed Ua Conchobair in 1067. Diarmait was killed at the battle of Odba (?Navan, Co. Meath) in 1072 by Conchobar ua Máel Sechlainn, king of Mide. EB

Dickson, William Steel (1744–1824), Presbyterian minister of Ballyhalbert (1771–80) and then Portaferry, Co. Down. He was the personification of 18th-century Presbyterian radicalism: an enthusiastic *Volunteer, an eloquent advocate of political reform and *Catholic emancipation, and apparently a key figure in the military plans of the Co. Down *United Irishmen. Arrested just before the *insurrection of 1798, he spent almost four years in prison without being charged. His remaining years were spent as minister in second Keady congregation, Co. Armagh, but without payment of his **regium donum*. RFGH

diet is fundamental to human existence. What people eat or choose to eat is conditioned by the food-producing capabilities of the country, by trade, income, taste, custom, and culture. In Ireland these influences for many centuries led to a diet dominated by pastoral products. Traditional Gaelic society supported a system of semi-nomadic pastoral farming because Ireland was climatically suited to the rearing of livestock. Meat of all types was eaten in large quantities. Milk in liquid, solid, and semi-solid forms was an important adjuvant, and sour milk, in varying degrees of viscosity, was consumed. Especially popular were curds called 'bonaclabbe'. Butter also formed an essential part of the daily diet. People ate fistfuls of rancid butter rolled in oats, spread butter on oatcakes, and even ate butter on its own. The importance of butter is indicated by the practice of burying stores for future consumption in cool, damp bogs.

Gaelic society was aware of the value of cereals as a useful component of the diet, though until the end of the 16th century the role of tillage crops was no more than as a supplement to meat and dairy produce, particularly in winter. The exception was those areas which overlapped with *Anglo-Norman settlements, where colonists had from the 12th century introduced a different dietary pattern of gruels and puddings based on cereals, peas, and beans, along with bread.

During the course of the 17th century cereals assumed a more central place in diets as arable farming expanded. The process was assisted by the continual influx of people from England and Scotland in the wake of the Munster and Ulster *plantations. This new wave of colonization wrought more fundamental dietary changes than earlier influxes of migrants. English colonial theory required that land be put under the plough. Arable husbandry spread in the east, and the commercial cultivation of oats and other grains developed in many places from early in the 17th century. The spread of *tillage throughout Ireland was gradual. Nevertheless, by the end of the century the land was yielding a variety of grains, fruits, and sweet herbs. *Fisheries had been established along the coasts, netting a variety of bass, mullet, eels, hake, herrings, oysters, cockles, and mussels.

The newcomers to 16th-century Ireland brought with them, not merely their farming methods and their money, but also their prejudices and their tastes. The consumption of blood, in a jellified form or mixed with butter, oats, or salt, was an aspect of Gaelic cuisine that particularly repelled English observers. They were appalled, too, by the willingness of the native population to devour animal entrails and to eat carrion and horse meat, by their partiality for warm milk straight from the cow, adorned with straw and worse, by their habit of eating rancid butter, by their unhopped ale, and by their preference for oatcakes and gruels rather than good wheaten bread.

Changes in taste were powerfully accelerated by the commercial and political developments of which colonization was a part. Several forces were at work. One was a changing perception of food as a commodity. In Gaelic society much food had been distributed as tributes given to overlords or made over to them as rent payments. The lordship system dissolved slowly, although it was still partly intact on the eve of the *rising of 1641. Gradually, however, market mechanisms took over and food became a commercial commodity, its consumption governed by the price and by the incomes and preferences of buyers.

By the 18th century a class distinction in consumption patterns had become pronounced. The diet of the Irish gentry evolved to resemble that of their English counterparts. Their consumption of sugar, tea, coffee, raisins, currants, and confectionery rose sharply, reflecting the growing taste for luxury foods. Although per capita wine consumption declined, that of whiskey and beer increased (see DRINK). The consumption of meat and bread remained important, together with milk, butter, and cheese, but cereals, vegetables, fruit, and other foods were all by now fully integrated into the diet.

Meanwhile, at the beginning of the 18th century, the lower ranks of society still had diets composed principally of dairy products, although with supplements of vegetables and grains. This varied fare was short-lived; contrary trends were at work. As the century progressed labouring-class diets became simpler and distinct from the eating patterns of their social superiors, the process intensifying as the century progressed. By the beginning of the 19th century the poor throughout the country were subsisting principally on *potatoes and milk. Potatoes were consumed in very large quantities; estimates range from 10 to 15 pounds daily for adult men. The potato had become the staple food of at least one-third of the population on the eve of the *Great Famine. During spring and early summer whole milk was sometimes drunk, though skimmed or buttermilk were the more common beverages. Butter was produced for market, leaving the less nutritious buttermilk liquid for home consumption. During the 'hungry months' of summer two foods, oatmeal and herrings, filled the hiatus between the end of the old season's potato crop and the new harvest. There was a regional pattern to oatmeal consumption; more was eaten in northern and eastern counties than elsewhere. Herrings were eaten throughout Ireland, although less extensively in the midlands. Other foods had become occasional, peripheral, and luxurious.

As long as potato harvests were abundant and high yielding, the Irish poor were well fed. Crop yields, however, were variable and throughout the 18th and first half of the 19th centuries the poor occasionally teetered on the brink of *famine. The Great Famine demonstrated just how frail the dietary regime had become. Between 1845 and 1849 the crops failed disastrously in three seasons out of four because of a fungal disease, and the length of the crisis created famine conditions of great severity. In terms of diet, the Famine proved a catalyst, accelerating changes in the food-consumption patterns of the labouring classes as their confidence in the ability of the potato to meet dietary requirements waned.

After the Famine the determinants of dietary change were many. Living standards rose, particularly among the poor. Per capita incomes tripled between the 1840s and 1914. Despite higher household expenditure on rent, advances in wages kept ahead of prices; and from the 1870s to the end of the 19th century food prices were generally falling. Consequently the food-consumption patterns of the poor became more varied and the contrast between their diets and those of their social superiors narrowed, especially in towns.

The rise in purchasing power was reflected in the increasing proportion of food bought in shops and in the growing consumption of imported as opposed to home-grown foods. Shopkeepers often fulfilled a dual, and in some cases triple, role in the food economy of the poor. Not only were they the suppliers of food, but in remote areas they acted as *middlemen, accepting eggs and butter for the export market in exchange for *Indian meal, tea, and sugar. They also provided credit on which the poor depended.

The spread of *railways in the second half of the 19th century greatly facilitated the distribution of groceries and other items to rural areas. As a result sweet strong tea replaced milk as the main beverage, and even the very poorest demanded tea of a high quality. Imports of cheap American wheat stimulated greater consumption of bread, home baked or purchased from bakers' vans that toured the countryside. Roller milling produced several flour grades, though as with tea only a high quality was acceptable (see FLOUR MILLING). Indian meal, a remnant of famine relief, was popular until the end of the 19th century, sometimes mixed with flour for bread making or added to oatmeal for porridge. Fatty American bacon was favoured for its flavour and cheapness. In very poor households bacon fat was rendered down to a sauce for pouring over vegetables. Inferior cuts of meat became weekly treats rather than Christmas and Easter delicacies.

Meanwhile the dominance of the potato declined, though it was still an important item in the daily diet, particularly in the west. A stark demonstration of this pattern was the reappearance of famine conditions accompanied by disease in western counties at the end of the 1870s. Relief committees were set up to dispense Indian meal rations to the starving. A large-scale catastrophe was averted only because potato dependency was confined to that region.

Dietary changes were not always accompanied by improvements in nutritional standards. Paradoxically, at the lower end of the income scale the transition from a monotonous menu to more varied fare resulted in a fall in nutritional quality. The pre-Famine potatoes-and-milk regime had been rich in almost all nutrients, but when it was replaced by cereals, bread, butter, and tea the nourishment was inferior. This new pattern was particularly prevalent in towns, where death rates from diseases of poverty were high. Contemporary commentators noted the deterioration in the nation's health and many ascribed it to poor diet.

By the opening years of the 20th century more dietary improvements were evident. Variety increased further, especially among better-paid urban labourers. Differences between urban and rural diets nevertheless also narrowed as the century progressed, as did the disparity between social classes.

Today most food is bought from retail outlets. Extensive consumer choice has resulted from developments in food-processing technology, trading networks that have become worldwide, and a revolution in the kitchen which has affected both storage facilities and cooking methods. Certain features of the old dietary pattern, however, can be discerned. Potatoes maintain an important role in the diet. And the partiality of the Irish for pastoral products has been retained, prompting the medical profession to speculate on whether the high intake of saturated fat, particularly in the form of butter, contributes to the high incidence of cardiovascular disease.

EMC

Dillon. The family supposedly originated with Sir Henry de Leon's coming to Ireland as Prince *John's secretary in 1185. He was granted lands in Longford, Westmeath, and Kilkenny. This marcher family—Gaelicized clients of the earls of *Kildare at the end of the Middle Ages—managed to establish three noble lines as a result of crown service during the *Tudor conquest.

Sir James Dillon (d. 1642), whose father Lucas was a prominent Elizabethan privy counsellor, benefited from the minor Jacobean *plantations and was created earl of Roscommon (1622). His son Robert, 2nd earl (d. 1642), conformed, served as lord justice three times, and married his heir James, 3rd earl (*c*.1605–1649), to *Wentworth's sister. After the *Restoration, the family regained their estates under the Act of *Settlement. The last earl died in 1850.

Other branches established themselves in Connacht. Theobald Dillon went there *c.*1580 as collector of *Composition, acquired the MacCostello clan lands, and became Viscount Dillon (1622). His daughter Cecily co-founded the Poor Clare *nuns in Ireland (1629). The 12th viscount conformed in 1767, married into an English aristocratic family, and became an absentee. Thomas Dillon, another Elizabethan *presidency official, bought Clonbrock from the O'Connors in Galway. This line, which conformed in the early 1700s, was ennobled in 1790 and died out in 1926.

Other Dillons were *Jacobites, and many saw service in the famous Dillon regiment in the French army. HM

Dillon, James (1902–86), party leader and government minister. The son of John *Dillon, he transmitted some of the *Nationalist Party's values into the politics of the independent Irish state. He was a critic of both the pro-treaty and republican forces in the early years of independence and was a co-founder of the *Centre Party in 1932. The success of this venture meant that Dillon was an important figure in the Dáil; and he was one of the architects of another, and more lasting, force in Irish politics, *Fine Gael (1933). He was a strong opponent of Irish *neutrality during the *Second World War, and resigned from Fine Gael in February 1942, having failed to persuade the party to support the Allies. He was minister of agriculture in the *interparty government of 1948–51, and (while his substantive achievement is open to question) he proved a political success: his Land Rehabilitation Project echoed the concerns of his father, and helped to steal the thunder of *Clann na Talmhan. Dillon held the same ministerial portfolio in the second interparty government (1954–7) and was a lacklustre leader of Fine Gael (1959–65). His politics united the values of the Irish propertied elite with some vestiges of agrarianism. A cautious and conservative patriot, he was often (and unfairly) seen as West British and retrograde. AJ

Dillon, John (1851–1927), MP for Tipperary (1880–3) and for East Mayo (1885–1918), the most influential nationalist politician between *Parnell and de *Valera. Son of John Blake *Dillon, he qualified in medicine but lived comfortably on private means. A lifelong hypochondriac, his melancholia was reinforced by a succession of eight premature family deaths. From 1907 he raised six young children alone.

A militant agrarian in the 1880s, he served four prison terms; anti-landlordism remained a motif throughout his career. He and William *O'Brien often clashed with Parnell over their continued agrarianism, but were reluctant anti-Parnellites in 1890. Dillon became leader of the main anti-Parnellite movement in 1896, giving way to *Redmond in 1900 to facilitate the reunion of parliamentary nationalism. Although not personally close, the two became an effective team: Redmond the dignified orator, living mostly in London and using a hotel when in Dublin; Dillon based in Dublin, at the centre of a great web of grass-roots contacts. He opposed the policy of 'reconciliation' with the landlords which underlay the 1903 *Land Act, almost breaking with Redmond, but the outcome was instead a final split with O'Brien. He remained unplacated by social and administrative reforms, though continuing to expect them from Liberal governments.

Dillon was the *Nationalist Party's most accomplished parliamentarian, a classic radical liberal in his attitudes to imperialism and rearmament. He opposed compulsory Irish in the *National University, and later declined to lend active support to the British war effort. He and Redmond were at the centre of all *home rule negotiations between 1910 and 1916. His bitter speech denouncing the 1916 executions reflected an early awareness of the changing national mood. Solitary, aloof, and fastidious, he lacked the politician's bonhomie, but his vision of Irish nationality was broad and liberal. Earnestly Catholic, he opposed clerical leadership in politics. His analysis of Irish politics was often as accurate as it was pessimistic, and had he led the reunited party after 1900 its defeat by *Sinn Féin in 1918 might have been less complete. That he could not have been that leader is a measure of his limitations.

Lyons, F. S. L., *John Dillon: A Biography* (1968)

ACH

Dillon, John Blake (1814–66), *Young Irelander. Son of a Catholic shopkeeper in Ballaghadereen, Co. Mayo, Dillon was educated at *Maynooth and *Trinity College, Dublin. He was called to the bar and joined the *Repeal Association in 1841. A founder of the **Nation*, he seceded from the Repeal Association with the other Young Irelanders in 1846, but continued to seek reconciliation with Old Ireland, and in 1848 hoped nationalist reunion would effect a bloodless moral force revolution. Following the conviction of John *Mitchel, however, he decided that a rising was the only honourable course. Dillon was a member of the confederate war council, commanded the rebels at Killenaule (see REBELLION OF 1848), and subsequently escaped to New York, where he set up a legal practice with Richard O'Gorman. He returned to Dublin following the amnesty of 1855, entered municipal politics, and collaborated with Paul *Cullen in establishing the *National Association in 1864. Elected MP for Co. Tipperary in 1865, he attacked *Fenianism, and sought an alliance with British radicals for land reform and Irish church *disestablishment. Dillon died suddenly from cholera in September 1866. PHG

direct rule (Northern Ireland 1972–98). On 24 March 1972, after Brian *Faulkner's administration had refused to agree that control of security should be transferred to London, the Conservative government of Edward Heath announced the suspension of the system of devolved government in Northern Ireland. Northern Ireland was now governed directly from Westminster. Cabinet responsibility was transferred from the home secretary to a newly created cabinet post of secretary of state for Northern Ireland. A team of junior government ministers was established to take over the political leadership of Northern Ireland government departments, and a Northern Ireland Office within the British civil service was created to support the new arrangements. The *Stormont parliament, initially prorogued, was abolished, along with the ceremonial office of governor, by the *Northern Ireland Constitution Act in July 1973. Northern Ireland legislation was passed through Westminster, using the somewhat truncated method of order in council rather than the full legislative bill procedure. By the 1990s a fuller method of scrutiny, by a Northern Ireland parliamentary committee, had been established. In 1983 the number of Northern Ireland MPs at Westminster was increased from 12 to 17, raised in 1997 to 18. ACH

discoverer. An Irish act of 1709 created a legal procedure whereby a Protestant who filed a bill in chancery 'discovering' a property transaction prohibited under the *penal laws thereby became entitled to the Catholic party's interest in that transaction. The complex prohibitions on the sale, leasing, and inheritance of land were thus in theory made self-enforcing. But in practice many bills of discovery were collusive, filed by agents of the Catholic party to forestall genuine predators.

disestablishment. The privileged position of the *Church of Ireland had long been resented by both Catholics and Presbyterians. The *Church Temporalities Act and reform of the *tithe system in the 1830s had modified but not removed the anomaly of a state church whose members made up only one-eighth of the population. Following the *Fenian insurrection of 1867 *Gladstone made disestablishment part of his programme for pacifying Ireland. Census returns and a series of parliamentary inquiries confirmed the image of an establishment whose wealth and political prestige contrasted vividly with its minority position and pastoral and administrative inadequacies. Despite strenuous objections by the queen and the Conservative opposition, and in the face of a policy of non-co-operation by the church itself, Gladstone's Irish Church Act became law on 26 July 1869.

The church was largely disendowed. Bishops and clergy were guaranteed their existing incomes for life, but most chose to commute this interest to a capital sum, vested in the Representative Church Body, which thus received a total of £7.6 million. Capital sums were also granted to the *Presbyterian church and *Maynooth College, in place of previous regular endowments. As from 1 January 1871 the Church of Ireland was a voluntary body, governed by the General Synod, with its property and financial affairs in the hands of the Representative Church Body. KM

dissent. Protestant dissent, in Ireland as in England, was a product of the political and social disruption created by the English Civil War and the *Confederate War in Ireland. In Ulster Scots settlers, previously kept within the established church by a policy of mutual accommodation, now set up their own *Presbyterian ecclesiastical organization. In the southern provinces newly arrived soldiers and civilians brought with them the sudden plurality of religious allegiances that had appeared in England. After the *Restoration, dissent came to mean all those, Presbyterians, *Quakers, *Baptists, and *Independents (later Congregationalists), who refused to accept the restored episcopal *Church of Ireland.

In the decades following the Restoration, the government continued to regard the dissenters of the south with suspicion, as potential enemies of monarchy and episcopacy. By the early 18th century, southern dissent, by now heavily concentrated among the respectable middle classes of the towns, had dwindled in numbers and lost this threatening character. Only in Ulster did dissent, in the form of Presbyterianism, retain a wide social base, and it was Ulster Presbyterians that were the main targets of the *sacramental test which continued up to 1780 to exclude dissenters from full participation in public life.

The range of dissenting churches was further increased during the late 17th and 18th centuries by the introduction of immigrant groups, *Huguenots and *Palatines, from continental Europe, and by the appearance of new bodies, the *Moravians and the *Methodists. During the 19th century Methodists completed their separation from the established church and grew to become the third largest Protestant denomination. The growth of *evangelicalism during the 19th century also benefited the other small denominations disproportionately. Yet despite all this Irish dissent continued to be dominated by Presbyterianism. In 1901 there were 443,000 Presbyterians, 62,000 Methodists, and about 60,000 members of all other Protestant denominations together.

Herlihy, K. (ed.), *The Irish Dissenting Tradition* (1996)

dissolution of the monasteries. On the eve of the *Reformation, recruitment to the monasteries was in decline and secularization already in train, with gentry families intruding kinsmen as superiors who dilapidated the properties in their favour. The *Palesmen, led by Patrick Barnewall, rejected an initial bill in 1536 to dissolve eight small Irish monasteries, fearing the loss of interest in estates they were already administering as lawyers or leasing as farmers. The bill passed in 1537, when an equitable distribution of property was agreed. Following the complete suppression of English monasteries in 1538, a commission was appointed in April 1539 which dissolved 42 monasteries and 51 friaries in the Pale and Ormond. The commissioners encountered few problems, despite the war of the *Geraldine League. The last major dissolution was the Knights Hospitallers at Kilmainham, which Prior Rawson surrendered in November 1540 after being granted a life peerage and a pension of 500 marks. *St Leger extended the policy to Desmond and Thomond, but in tune with the conciliatory policy of *surrender and regrant allowed the earls to run the suppression commissions themselves.

The exchequer gained only £1,884 additional revenue from the dissolution. The main beneficiaries were Lord Deputies *Grey and *St Leger, and Treasurer *Brabazon. Palesmen received lands to round off their estates. About 20 *New English landowners arrived in the Pale and in Wexford. The marcher lords extended their holdings as did *Ormond, *Clanricard, Thomond, and *Desmond.

Calculated on the annual income of their monasteries, superiors received pensions ranging from £6 to £50; ordinary monks received between 13*s*. 4*d*. and £3 6*s*. 8*d*. An act of parliament allowed them to work and trade but did not absolve them of their vows of chastity! Socially the dissolution was not a disaster: the monastic provision of poor relief, education, and medical care had all but ceased, and since the end of the 15th century secular charities and municipal bodies had established hospitals, almshouses, and schools. The growing wealth of the Palesmen, which the dissolution accelerated, facilitated further private philanthropy.

Sixty per cent of Irish monasteries and friaries, with a dwindling band of monks but many highly respected friars, remained undisturbed in the Gaelic and Gaelicized parts of Ireland, as potential targets for future land-grabbers.

Bradshaw, Brendan, *The Dissolution of the Religious Orders in Ireland* (1974)

HM

distilling. Whiskey was the most popular drink in Ireland by 1800. In 1700 consumption had been largely confined to those higher up the social scale, but during the 18th century (notably in the last quarter) its appeal became more widespread. Between the 1770s and the 1840s the legal industry became concentrated predominantly in larger distilleries in the major towns. This growth in scale was facilitated by improved technologies, but the main impetus was provided by draconian excise legislation, introduced in 1779–80, which made it impossible for smaller distilleries to operate profitably; the number licensed fell from 1,228 in 1780 to 51 in 1806 and small-scale *illicit distillation flourished. The new legislation suited the larger urban distillers (notably in *Dublin and *Cork, where local demand was sufficient to warrant an increase in scale) who were able to expand their markets as smaller distilleries closed. Power's and Jameson of Dublin are good examples of new concerns which were able to consolidate and expand under the new excise regime. By the 1820s, it was recognized that the 1779–80 legislation had been detrimental to both the legal industry and the amount of excise collected. New legislation introduced in 1823 created more favourable conditions. The arrival of Coffey's patent still in 1830 marked the beginning of a new departure; the northern industry's dramatic expansion over the remainder of the 19th century (centred on *Belfast and *Derry) largely depended on patent still production and blending, which produced a cheaper, lighter whiskey that found a ready sale in the expanding British market. In the south, however, the traditional pot still continued to prevail. The growing export trade enabled the major northern concerns to dominate the Irish industry in the last quarter of the 19th century. However, because of the decline in demand in the British market, much of the Ulster industry had gone out of business by the end of the 1920s. A number of the larger Ulster concerns had merged in 1902, exchanging shares in 1905 with the major player in the British market, Distillers Company Ltd. of Scotland. The Ulster distilleries were taken over and ultimately closed down by DCL. By the end of the 1920s, the Irish industry had experienced significant contraction, and Dublin had once again become the main distilling centre.

Maguire, E., *Irish Whiskey* (1973)
Weir, R., 'In and Out of Ireland: The Distillers Company Ltd. and the Irish Whiskey Trade 1900–1939', *Irish Economic and Social History*, 8 (1980)

AB

divorce was recognized in Gaelic Irish law as a legal procedure for the dissolution of a marriage contract, permitting either party to remarry. The husband or wife could sue for divorce on grounds, specified in detail in legal material from the early Christian period, which include domestic violence, infertility/sterility, or failure of maintenance. By law, the share each partner was entitled to in the settlement depended on his or her status, what wealth was brought into the union, and the amount of work undertaken by either party for the benefit of the marriage. Divorce was not recognized by the church and, as it was viewed as a private and not a public action, couples separated without recourse to the church courts. After divorce the woman returned to the protection of her family, with which contact had been maintained while in the union. In some cases the family might in fact have instigated the divorce to form a more politically advantageous alliance. Although divorce was freely permitted in Irish customary law, the Gaelic Irish in late medieval times often petitioned the ecclesiastical courts in an attempt to nullify an unwanted divorce or to make a separation legal in accordance with *canon law on the grounds of an impediment existing prior to the union.

The frank acceptance of marital breakdown characteristic of Gaelic society was equally unacceptable to the *Reformation and *Counter-Reformation churches. By the late 17th century, if not earlier, Irish customary law had ceased to provide an alternative structure of rules and procedures regulating private behaviour. Yet folklore evidence and statistics on household composition from the 19th century alike suggest that informal separations, where a wife who had proved infertile, or whose dowry had not been paid, was sent back to her family, were fairly common practice. Legal divorce was possible only for the rich, by private act of parliament. Divorce by civil process became possible in England from 1857, but proposals that the act should be extended to Ireland were vigorously opposed by both Catholic and Protestant clergy.

Following *partition the parliament of Northern Ireland continued to receive divorce bills, and legislation for divorce by civil process was introduced in 1939. In the Irish Free State the introduction of private divorce bills in Dáil Éireann during 1922–3 provoked an immediate outcry, and in 1925 the standing orders were revised to rule out further such bills. The 1937 *constitution of Ireland included an unconditional ban on divorce, a prohibition repealed by referendum in 1995.

BNC/SC

Dobbs, Arthur (1689–1765), economic writer and colonial governor. The heir to land round *Carrickfergus, Co. Antrim, Dobbs was MP for Carrickfergus 1727–60. *An Essay on the Trade and Improvement of Ireland* (1729–31) has been taken as identifying him as one of the *commonwealth school, concerned with social improvement and critical of English restrictions on Irish trade. However, he was dismissive of the Irish parliament, and wrote two unpublished pamphlets advocating a legislative *union. The holder of an official post as surveyor-general of Ireland from 1733, he supported government during the *money bill crisis. He was an enthusiastic proponent of British colonial expansion in North America, and persuaded the government to send two expeditions (1741, 1746) in search of a north-west passage to the Pacific. In 1745 he purchased land in North Carolina and energetically sponsored its settlement with immigrants from his own estates and elsewhere. He went to North Carolina himself as governor in 1754, and died there shortly before a planned return to Ireland. **Francis Dobbs** (1750–1811), a great nephew, wrote pamphlets for the *Volunteers. As MP for Charlemont 1799–1800, he opposed the Act of *Union and wrote extensively, in a *millenarian vein, on scriptural prophecy.

Document No. 2, drawn up by de *Valera to reconcile Irish proposals with the provisions of the *Anglo-Irish treaty. But although many of the provisions were identical, notably on finance, religion, and trade, the differences were fundamental. There was no provision for an *oath of allegiance nor for a *governor-general. Ireland would be associated with the *Commonwealth in matters of common concern, including defence, peace and war, and political treaties, and would recognize the king as the head of the association. However, defence facilities would be granted to Britain only for five years. The most striking variations concerned Ulster. The first version of Document No. 2, which de Valera presented to the *Dáil in December 1921, reproduced the Ulster clauses of the treaty. In the second version (occasionally called Document No. 3) presented to the Dáil in January 1922 these were omitted and Ulster was consigned to an addendum which simply promised it privileges and safeguards not less than those offered by the treaty.

Document No. 2 was withdrawn before it could be considered by the Dáil. When de Valera came to power in 1932 it was assumed that he would resurrect Document No. 2. In fact his policy in the field of external relations was much more restricted than that envisaged in 1921. DMcM

Docwra, Henry (d. 1631), leader of the Lough Foyle expedition of 1600–3 during the *Nine Years War. On May 1600 he landed unimpeded with 4,000 men and began the fortification of Derry. He found a formidable ally in Niall Garbh *O'Donnell and gradually widened his control until in June 1602 he was able to effect a rendezvous with *Mountjoy in mid-Tyrone and participate in the spoliation of the country which finally brought O'Neill to submission. Docwra subsequently wrote a 'narration' to indicate that he and his erstwhile allies had been ill-rewarded for their services at Lough Foyle. HM

Dolly's Brae, Co. Down, scene of a bloody sectarian affray on 12 July 1849. *Orange bands marching from Rathfriland to Tollymore Park exchanged shots with *Ribbonmen who confronted them as they passed through the Catholic townland of Magheramayo and then attacked Catholic houses. An estimated 30 persons, all Catholic, were killed. The affair led to the enactment of a new *Party Processions Act (1850).

dolmen, see MEGALITHIC TOMBS.

Dolmen Press (1951–87), *printer and publisher in Dublin, and later Mountrath. It was founded by Liam Miller (1924–87) to provide an outlet for Irish authors. VK

Dominicans (the order of Preachers), established their first Irish house in Dublin in 1224 and by 1305 numbered 25 communities, all but five of which had Anglo-Norman founders. In 1275 the Irish friaries were constituted a vicariate subject to a vicar appointed by the English provincial of the order. Subsequent attempts to gain independence were opposed by English interests and an independent Irish province was not established until 1536.

A further expansion occurred with the foundation of ten new houses, principally in the west of Ireland, between 1385 and 1507. Their isolated locations suggest a desire for reform and their foundation corresponds with the emergence of the *Observant movement. In 1503 an Observant friar from Holland was appointed vicar of the reformed houses in Ireland but the number of these is difficult to determine as reformed and unreformed friars coexisted in many friaries.

In 1536 there were 38 friaries in Ireland, 20 of which were suppressed between 1539 and 1542. Some houses in Gaelic areas were not dissolved until the reign of Elizabeth I (1558–1603).

In the 17th and 18th centuries the friars lived in small communities in the vicinity of their former houses. Novices continued to be received in Ireland and were sent to the colleges at Lisbon (founded 1615), Louvain (1624), and Rome (1677) to pursue studies. The closure of the Irish novitiates in 1751 (see RELIGIOUS ORDERS) initiated a process of decline which lasted until the mid-19th century. CNÓC

Donegall, title of the Chichesters, by the late 18th century the largest landowners in Ireland. The foundations of this fortune lay in the estates disreputably amassed in Antrim and Donegal by the Elizabethan adventurer Sir Arthur *Chichester. However, Chichester never had the capital to match his rapid acquisitions, and tenants were hard to attract to the underdeveloped Ulster of the early 17th century. The family's position weakened after Chichester's death in 1625, and the wars of the 1640s brought further losses. **Edward**, 1st Viscount Chichester (d. 1648), fought with the royalists in the *Confederate War, and his son **Arthur Chichester** (1606–75) was created 1st earl of Donegall by *Ormond in 1647. On Arthur's death, however, the title passed to his nephew **Arthur**, 2nd earl of Donegall (d. 1678), the estate to his daughters. A legal judgment in 1692 reunited title and property under the 3rd earl (1666–1706), who held military commands from *William III and was killed in action in Spain.

Following a fire in 1708 which destroyed the family residence in Belfast Castle and killed three of the 4th earl's sisters, the family moved to England, becoming noted *absentees. **Arthur**, the 4th earl (1695–1757), was feeble-minded. His son **Arthur** (1739–99), created 1st marquis of Donegall in 1791, built an elaborate Palladian mansion at Fisherwick Park, Staffordshire, financed by attempts to increase the yields of his Antrim estates that helped provoke the *Steelboy revolt. **George Augustus**, the 2nd marquis (1769–1844), a hopelessly undisciplined spendthrift, returned to Belfast in 1802 to escape his creditors. However, the family's renewed local influence was decisively undermined by a settlement negotiated in 1822, under which the greater part of the estate was signed away, for immediate cash payments, under perpetually renewable leases. The proceeds were intended to settle the marquis's debts, but instead were secretly appropriated to finance continuing extravagance. The 3rd marquis, **George Hamilton** (1797–1883), was left to dispose of the bulk of the property through the *Encumbered Estates Court.

Donnelly, Dan (d. 1820), boxer. A Dublin carpenter and later publican, he fought celebrated bouts against English challengers in 1814 and 1815, in both cases at the *Curragh, where 'Donnelly's Hollow' is still marked.

Donnybrook fair was held annually, in what is now a Dublin suburb, for six centuries. Established under charter in 1204, the fair reached its peak during the 18th century. Lasting a week, it became a centre for dealing in various goods, as well as providing a focus for popular amusements. However, the fair became synonymous with public disorder, and the phrase 'a donnybrook' passed into the English language as meaning a scene of uproar. By the 19th century the fair's attendant violence was causing concern, and a campaign for its suppression began. This was accomplished in 1855 when a consortium purchased the fair's charter and surrendered it. An attempt to hold a fair in August of that year was successfully opposed by the authorities. NG

Down, battle of (1260). On 14 May at 'Druimdearg' ('Red Ridge') near Downpatrick, the forces of Brian *O'Neill, king of *Cenél nEógain and *soi-disant* 'king of the kings of Ireland', and Áed O'Connor (Ó Conchobair, d. 1274), son and heir to the king of Connacht, were defeated by the English of the county and city of Down, assisted, according to the *annals, by Irish allies. O'Neill and many sub-chiefs from Ulster and Connacht were slain. KS

Downshire, title of the Hill family, major landowners in Co. Down, with smaller properties at Blessington, Co. Wicklow, and Edenderry, King's County. **Moyses Hill** (d. 1630), a landless west country gentleman who came to Ireland with *Essex and later attached himself to Sir Arthur *Chichester, acquired the nucleus of the Ulster estate through grants and by purchase from the O'Neill family. His second son, **Arthur Hill** (d. 1663), bought or leased other lands from the Magennisses, securing his estate in the *Confederate War by supporting first parliament then the *Restoration. The two branches of the Hill estate were united by the marriage of his son **Arthur** (d. 1664) to a cousin. The family's rising status was recognized when **Trevor Hill** (1693–1742) became Viscount Hillsborough in 1717. His son **Wills Hill** (1718–93), a successful courtier and office holder in several English ministries, became marquis of Downshire in 1789.

Arthur, the 2nd marquis (1753–1801), lived almost constantly in England, but opposed the Act of *Union, and was stripped of his local offices. This treatment, and her own Whig inclinations, led the marchioness, **Mary**, Baroness Sandys (1764–1836), to pursue, during her son's minority, a political vendetta against the Stewart (see CASTLEREAGH) family in Co. Down and Carrickfergus. The feud was ended by the 3rd marquis, **Arthur** (1788–1845), more concerned with efficient estate management than the pursuit of electoral advantage, but a strong Tory who hosted a major Protestant demonstration against Whig reforms (see LICHFIELD HOUSE COMPACT) at the family residence at Hillsborough on 30 October 1834. For the rest of the 19th century the Hill and Stewart families dominated Co. Down politics in the Conservative interest. In 1925 Hillsborough Castle became the official residence of the governor of Northern Ireland.

Down Survey. The end of the *Confederate War was followed by confiscations of land affecting nearly half the country. In 1654 Dr William *Petty, physician-in-chief to the Cromwellian army, was made responsible for mapping all the forfeited land previously identified by the *Civil Survey, other than in the western countries already covered by the Strafford inquisitions of 1636. The survey is notable not only for the sheer magnitude of the undertaking but also for the methods of recruitment, training, organization, and remuneration of the surveyors which allowed the work to be completed within five years. It was known as the 'Down Survey' almost from the beginning because it was set down on maps and not just in tabulated form as in some earlier surveys. Drawn by parishes, the maps were more accurate than anything previously attempted, though detail was confined to boundaries, names, acreages, and land quality, which was also recorded in accompanying written descriptions.

In 1685 Petty worked up the results into the first printed atlas of Irish provinces and counties, *Hiberniae delineatio*, though the many blank areas on its maps betray the vast unforfeited lands omitted from the original survey. Its outline appeared in most of the general maps of Ireland published between *c.*1690 and the advent of the *Ordnance Survey. PF

Doyle, Jack (1913–78), showman. Born in Co. Cork, he left the British army to become a professional boxer in Great Britain and America before returning to Ireland with his wife, the Mexican film star Movita Castenada. Their singing act brought a touch of glamour to wartime Dublin. After their divorce in 1945 he returned to London as a wrestler.

Doyle, James Warren (1786–1834), Catholic bishop of Kildare and Leighlin 1817–34. A Co. Wexford-born *Augustinian, he had studied at Coimbra in Portugal and taught at the Augustinian college in New Ross and at Carlow College. A prolific writer, he published his *Vindication of the Irish Catholic* in 1822, *Letters on the State of Ireland* in 1824–5, and *On the Origin, Nature and Destination of Church Property* in 1831. His newspaper correspondence, usually of a controversial nature, was often signed with the initials JKL (James, Kildare and Leighlin). He was instrumental in the setting up of the Catholic Book Society (1827) and supported the *national education system (1831). Doyle was examined by two parliamentary committees on Irish affairs. Although he was the first well-known prelate to join the *Catholic Association, he later opposed *repeal. He was a keen pastoral reformer. TO'C

Drapier's Letters (1724–5), seven pamphlets attacking *Wood's Halfpence, published by *Swift under the pseudonym 'M.B., Drapier'. The first three are concerned primarily with the mechanics of the scheme. However number four, *To the Whole People of Ireland* (22 Oct. 1724), refers back to *Molyneux, rejects the *Declaratory Act as an illegitimate exercise of force, and argues that Ireland and England, though ruled by the same monarch, have an identical right to be governed by laws of their own making. The government issued a proclamation against the author and arrested the printer, John Harding, but was humiliated when two successive grand juries resisted pressure from William Whitshed (1679–1727), chief justice of the King's Bench, to find that the *Seasonable Advice to the Grand Jury* (14 Nov. 1724), in which Swift called for Harding's acquittal, was a seditious libel. Swift nevertheless dropped plans to publish under his own name a more cautiously worded defence of the Drapier's stand in *A Letter to the Lord Chancellor Midleton*. *A Letter to . . . Lord Viscount Molesworth* (31 Dec. 1724) was a mock apology by the Drapier, insisting that he had only followed the principles of the 'real Whig' or *commonwealth school to which Molesworth himself belonged. *An Humble Address to Both Houses of Parliament* called on MPs to hold back finance bills until the coin was withdrawn and outlined other grievances requiring attention. It was abandoned when Wood surrendered his patent, it and the letter to Midleton being published only in 1735.

Drennan, William (1754–1820), *United Irishman and poet. The son of Revd **Thomas Drennan** (1696–1768), who was at one time *Hutcheson's assistant in Dublin, William studied medicine in Glasgow and Edinburgh. *Orellana or an Irish Helot* (1784–5) lamented the loss of reforming momentum following *legislative independence. When radicalism revived following the *French Revolution, Drennan's proposal for a secret 'interior circle' to direct the reinvigorated *Volunteer movement from within was one inspiration for the *United Irish movement. In June 1794 he was tried for sedition, on the basis of an address to the Volunteers published two years earlier, and although acquitted dropped out of active politics. His published poems included a lament for William *Orr and 'When Erin First Rose' (1795), which coined the phrase 'emerald isle'. Later he edited the *Belfast Monthly Magazine* (1808–15), combining literary material and some political comment, and was one of the founders of *Belfast Academical Institution.

dress. A sandstone weight of spindle-whorl form, found in Ballyalton, Co. Down, suggests that, from *neolithic times, *wool was spun and woven in Ireland. The earliest clothing fragments extant are pieces of woollen cloth of about 1000 BC found in Killymoon, Co. Tyrone, in 1995, and wool cloth and a horsehair belt found in Cromagh, Co. Antrim, in 1904 and dated to about 750 BC. These pieces show that in the late *Bronze Age vertical weighted looms, as well as looms for braid, were in use to weave fabrics in plain and sophisticated designs.

According to the *Annals of the *Four Masters* Tighearmas, king of Ireland, was the first person, in 1538 BC, to dye clothes purple, blue, and green, while eight years later Eochaid Eadghadach (Eochaid the cloth designer) ordered that the colours of clothes should denote the wearer's rank in society. The dating is suspect, but the substance carries weight, as in early Ireland the colour and length of the brat (mantle) worn was related to a person's rank in society. Status was also suggested through embroidery and the application of decorative braids, particularly to the colourful brat. The white or *gel* (bright or unbleached) tunic worn throughout the early historic period suggests a *Roman or classical influence, as does the introduction and development of fibulae which indicate the use of fine cloth, possibly linen. The Roman code of hygiene may also have influenced the dictate that certain classes in society had their clothes washed every day. Class rather than gender was thus the main distinguishing feature in dress styles in early Ireland. The less well-off workers wore short tunics and skimpy mantles or tight trews with a small jacket, all dyed in less expensive colours.

As elsewhere throughout Europe, from about the 8th century women in Ireland began to wear layers of tunics and married women started to cover their heads. Men of all ranks changed to favour the styles worn throughout the *Viking world: trews with about knee-length tunics. Irishmen also wore a *cochall* or hooded mantle and a large mantle overall. By the 10th century the regular supply of Andalusian and Byzantine silks, satins, and gold braids added luxury to the homespun and locally dyed woollens and linens.

In the late 12th century the *Anglo-Normans introduced technical improvements such as the horizontal loom and probably the fulling mill, spinning wheel, and carding, much of the machinery known to this day. They also introduced a new dress style. The wealthy followed the modes of London and western Europe: men wore breeches, kirtles (a sleeved full-length garment worn over the smock and under the surcoat), and surcoats (a long, loose outer garment), while women wore a chemise under a kirtle of fine wool. Mantles, tied with a lace on the chest, were worn by both sexes, although of different lengths for each. The clothes worn by both sexes were colourful and the belts were frequently heavy, ornate, and expensive. The clean-shaven, short-hair appearance of the male contrasted with the native Irish who favoured facial hair and a *culan* hairstyle in which the front of the head was shaved and the hair left long at the back. The adoption by the colonists or their descendants of native styles in dress and hair (see GAELICIZATION) was condemned in the Statute of *Kilkenny and other medieval enactments.

The *houpellande*, a colourful, heavy woollen overgarment, worn long by the wealthy and of various short lengths by the less so, evolved about 1375. Superbly tailored and made weatherproof through fulling, it was worn by men, women, and children and was considered such a valuable item that it was included in wills. Fitted to the shoulders it fell in deep tubular folds which were held in place by a belt. Irish women continued to use versions of this *houpellande* into the 17th century. All were worn over a kirtle or chemise. A popular version had a wide V-neck with long front opening ending in a U-shape over the stomach.

The Irish sleeve evolved about this time too. Worn by both sexes it was a band of woollen fabric which stretched from the shoulder along the arm and was secured by buttoning or tying at the cuff. This allowed the display of the voluminous linen sleeves of the kirtle and of the Irish shirt.

Throughout the medieval period Ireland produced and exported 'rugg mantles' or fringed woollen mantles with a thick tufted nap which resembled the wool of sheepskin. Although taxed and disparaged by edicts from 1462 onwards, the rugg mantle was exported regularly to Britain and Europe from the 15th to the mid-17th centuries as it satisfied a market demand for a cheap version of the then fashionable fur-lined woollen cloak. It was criticized regularly in Ireland as unhygienic, being worn by day and night, yet being such a warm outfit it remained in use until at least the late 17th century. It was replaced by another fashion derivative, the home-spun frieze semicircular cloak.

Another distinctive male dress item in late medieval Ireland was the 'Irish jacket'. Of gilded and embroidered leather or of wool, it had a thickly pleated skirt, stand collar, and Irish sleeves. Trews in plain or checked wool were worn as were shoes and hats or caps. The Irish shirt is probably derived from the tunic of the early historic period. In the style of that early time, the long, full skirt was hitched up to the length required by the owner. Irish shirts were said to take 35 yards of linen, which may account for their distinctively full sleeves. By the 16th century they were frequently dyed saffron.

The aim of government from the mid-14th to the 17th century was to make Irish people abandon their own dress styles—styles which retained ancestral comparisons with those worn throughout Europe—and to follow the styles favoured by the middle and upper classes of England. Under Henry VIII there was legislation against the Irish mantle, the use of saffron dye, and the wearing of overly long and full garments. Government also prohibited gowns embroidered or garnished with silk, decorated with couched embroidery, or with applied jewels 'after the Irish fashion'. The use of strong colours at the time and the heavy demand for paste and other jewellery indicates that gaudy medieval fashions survived in Ireland.

Initially it was chieftains and others ambitious for land and wealth who began to adapt English styles, although even then some needed the encouragement of gifts of clothing or promises of preferential treatment to induce them to conform. By the 17th century London fashions were adopted more readily. For men this meant a change to trunk hose (later pantaloons), doublet, long coat, and semicircular cloak. Women's gowns of English styles were of stiff shapes in expensive fabrics but usually in quiet colours. At the same time some obstinately continued to relate to the styles worn by the unpretentious and comfortably off in Europe. An example of this is the red petticoat fashion. Worn with a small brown jacket and a neckerchief crossed on the front, this was a standard style worn by women of all ranks of society throughout Europe—with the exception of Britain—in the 16th and 17th centuries. It survived in use in Ireland to the 20th century.

The coat as an outer garment is generally seen as having evolved in the late 17th century as the long coat for men in the French and English courts. The real origins of the 'Irish coat', however, more probably lay in the medieval gowns that artists such as Brueghel show as having been used generally by the less well off in Europe in the late 16th century. The fabric was measured through wrapping around the wearer's body and then cut to size. The arms were measured in a similar manner and edges joined with cloth buttons rather than a seam. In line with other medieval woollen garments the coat was of unlined frieze, about knee-length, unhemmed, and with unisex stand collars. Irish coats of this distinctive kind were still in use in the late 18th century.

By the late 17th century, the trend throughout Europe was for people not to be restricted in their dress styles by their status in society. The blurring of social distinctions caused consternation in both Gaelic and Anglo-Irish circles, and in 1682 the Irish Council of Trade issued ordinances against women who dressed above their station. By the mid-18th century this barrier had been broken and most people dressed as they could afford—helped by second-hand clothes dealers, locally woven fabrics, and itinerant tailors. The introduction to Ireland in the 17th century of lace-making, machine-knit stockings, silk, and poplin manufacture helped those interested in a luxury image. In the late 18th and early 19th centuries the development of the cotton manufacture allowed even the less wealthy to dress in current fashions.

Some fashions continued to be worn for a long time in rural Ireland. The survival of the tailed coats, knee-length trews, and felt hats of the 18th-century gentleman, for example, was used to caricature Irish men in the mid-19th century. On the other hand long trousers were worn in rural Ireland not long after they were introduced to the fashion world in 1807. Other current fashions were adopted so quickly and fully that they became identified with Ireland. The 'Irish/Kinsale' cloak which evolved from the semi-fitted cloaks fashionable from 1700 to 1730 is a case in point. Similarly the Irish shawl evolved from the Kashmir and Paisley shawls fashionable in the early 19th century. It changed in style in Ireland through the decades until in the 20th century it was the black shawl worn principally by widows.

The greatest breakdown in traditional attitudes to clothing was in the second half of the 19th century, when women in rural as well as urban Ireland began to dress to represent through their clothing the family's position in society. Women thus usurped the role held for centuries by the male head of the family. This happened at a time when fashionable male clothing was conservative, and after the introduction of the sewing machine had enabled women to follow fashions with ease.

Dunlevy, Mairead, *Dress in Ireland* (1989)

MD

Drew, Revd Thomas (1800–70), Church of Ireland clergyman and sectarian rabble-rouser. Appointed to Christ Church, Belfast, in 1833, Drew proved to be a zealous and committed pastor, promoting schools and self-improvement schemes among his mainly working-class congregation. His evangelical fervour brought him into conflict with Bishop *Mant, whose high-church architecture he deplored. A determined anti-Catholic controversialist, he established the Christ Church Protestant Association in 1854, and his polemical preaching was held to be partly responsible for serious sectarian rioting in 1857. He was the father-in-law of William Johnston (see PARTY PROCESSIONS ACT).

drill cultivation, the planting of crops in long, straight, equidistant rows, was believed by contemporaries to be one of the triumphs of 18th-century improved agriculture. Drills allowed more systematic sowing, care, management, and harvesting of crops than had been possible when these were sown broadcast or grown on ridges. The Dublin Society (see ROYAL DUBLIN SOCIETY) strongly advocated the use of drill husbandry. One of its earliest publications was an edition of Jethro Tull's treatise on drill cultivation, and in 1771 the society grant-aided John Wynn Baker's factory near Cellbridge, Co. Kildare, which manufactured drill implements.

In Ireland, the planting of cereals in drills was common only on large farms, but by the 1830s the cultivation of *potatoes in drills had become widespread. In 1852, J. Hanson of Doagh, Co. Antrim, patented a mechanical potato digger which operated by knocking potato tubers sideways out of raised drills. This was arguably Ireland's major contribution to the mechanization of farming during the 19th century. JB

drink. In medieval Ireland the main beverages, aside from milk, seem to have been ale, beer, and mead, with imported wine being drunk among the ruling classes. Whiskey (from the Irish *uisge beatha*, water of life) was probably not introduced until the 14th century and then, mixed with herbs and spices, it was used largely for medicinal purposes. But from the middle of the 16th century the English authorities began to complain at the levels of whiskey being consumed in Ireland. English visitors praised the quality of Irish whiskey, while roundly condemning Irish ale and beer.

Government attempts to control the production, sale, and consumption of alcohol, and especially of whiskey, were partly due to the fact that taxes on drink offered a significant source of revenue in an otherwise undeveloped country; also the authorities wanted to regulate the consumption of grain, channelling it into food production during times of scarcity; but, more importantly, whiskey was seen as giving comfort to Irish rebels, while *public houses offered them important refuges and meeting places.

Patterns of drinking in Ireland differed according to where people came from and what class they belonged to. In the medieval and early modern periods houses selling drink on a regular basis were generally confined to the towns and regular consumption of alcohol was thus an urban phenomenon. Outside the towns, up to the early 19th century, drinking was irregular and often ritualized. It was associated with special occasions; with hospitality and celebration. One 19th-century observer termed this pattern 'circumstantial drinking'. Alcohol was offered to visitors; it was consumed in large amounts at weddings and *wakes; it was freely available during *fairs and markets; and traditional religious festivals, like *patterns, inevitably involved heavy drinking. But outside such special circumstances, alcohol was not a characteristic feature of rural diet. Visitors to Ireland during the 16th and 17th centuries singled out milk as the main beverage consumed in the countryside.

The landed ruling class, first Gaelic lords and later English planters, had readier access to alcohol. There was a substantial trade in wine, as well as wine *smuggling, between Ireland and France and Spain. But, being imported, wine was an expensive commodity compared to home-brewed ale or locally distilled whiskey.

During the 18th century, however, spirits became much more readily available, to the extent that whiskey began to replace wine among the upper classes and ale among the lower. Government attempts to control the *distilling industry, by raising taxes on whiskey and making small stills illegal, helped create a huge illicit industry which flourished up until the *Famine. The development of *illicit distillation undoubtedly did much to promote regular alcohol consumption in rural Ireland. However, both the producers and consumers of poteen were decimated by the Famine and when the Irish constabulary took over policing of illicit distillation in the early 1850s, the illegal industry was finally brought under firm government control.

From the mid-19th century, aided by the spread of the *railway network, commercial breweries and distilleries, which had been operating in the towns for a century or more, began to penetrate the countryside with their products. This was especially true of the brewers. *Guinness's brewery, opened in Dublin in 1759, sold only 21 per cent of its output in rural Ireland in 1855, but by 1880 this figure had jumped to 40 per cent. Indeed, while per capita whiskey consumption in Ireland fell by nearly half between the 1850s and 1900s, the per capita consumption of beer leapt more than sevenfold. Ireland was becoming a nation of beer, ale, and stout drinkers. By 1914 *brewing was the country's largest industry in terms of the value of its output. Major increases in the duty on whiskey during the 1850s had undoubtedly helped to dampen the demand for spirits. The Irish distilling industry in fact only survived by exporting its output: in 1914 two-thirds of Irish-produced whiskey was being sent out of the country.

During the first half of the 20th century drinking in Ireland was generally a male pastime, conducted regularly in public houses in both town and country. But significant changes occurred in Irish drinking patterns during the second half of the century. First, drink consumption in the Republic increased dramatically: it doubled in per capita terms in the years between 1960 and 1980. Partly this was a result of growing prosperity, but it also reflected the fact that women were increasingly challenging the male hegemony of the Irish public house. Before the 1960s few women had entered pubs and, if they did, they were usually confined to discreet snugs. But by the 1980s growing numbers of women were drinking in pubs alongside men and publicans were improving and diversifying their facilities in order to cater for their new customers. The sale of alcohol in off-licences and supermarkets also undoubtedly helped to boost consumption. Drinking was increasingly occurring at home or in clubs and restaurants, rather than in the traditional pubs.

In the 1970s a third of alcohol consumed in Ireland was spirits, about 60 per cent was beer and stout, while wine claimed about 5 per cent. But wine consumption was rising, as the consumption of spirits was falling.

Although the Irish have a reputation as heavy drinkers, alcohol consumption in Ireland is not especially high by international standards. Indeed, the country has the largest population of total abstainers (see TEMPERANCE AND TOTAL ABSTINENCE) in the European Union. But Irish social life does still largely revolve around the pub and there is an unusually tolerant attitude towards drunkenness. This tends often to mean that public drunkenness is more obvious in Ireland than in some other countries, which may help give the Irish their reputation for being excessive drinkers.

Lynch, P., and Vaizey, J., *Guinness's Brewery in the Irish Economy, 1759–1876* (1960)

McGuire, E. B., *Irish Whiskey: A History of Distilling in Ireland* (1973)

Malcolm, E. L., *'Ireland Sober, Ireland Free': Drink and Temperance in Nineteenth-Century Ireland* (1986)

ELM

Drogheda, Co. Louth, the largest urban centre within a day's ride of Dublin. Two walled settlements on the estuary of the Boyne were established in the 1170s by Anglo-Norman grantees on opposite banks of the river, with the principal fortification, Millmount, a converted *Viking fort, located within the smaller town on the south side. The boroughs were united into a single corporation in 1412 by which point they were linked by a bridge. Exceptionally strong fortifications were erected, with walls of over 1.5 miles in length; the surviving barbican known as St Laurence's Gate gives a hint of their scale. At the south-eastern tip of the archdiocese of Armagh, Drogheda was for long the main episcopal residence for the primate at a time when much of his jurisdiction lay outside English control. Drogheda merchants, however, enjoyed a privileged trading position in late medieval Gaelic Ulster. Drogheda became in effect the second centre of the *Pale; *Poynings's Law (1494) was promulgated in one of the many 15th-century parliaments held in the town.

Its role as outport of Ulster extended into more recent centuries, with the maritime links to Chester and later Liverpool underpinning the town's prosperity. During the *Confederate War Drogheda remained in royalist hands; its fall to *Cromwell in September 1649 (see DROGHEDA, SIEGE OF) became the most notorious event of the Cromwellian reconquest.

Drogheda's resurgence as a commercial and manufacturing centre was delayed until the second half of the 18th century when it benefited from the attentions of its then political patron, Speaker John *Foster. Coarse *linen manufacture helped swell the population to over 15,000 by 1821, and the grain trade, *flour milling, and *brewing sustained prosperity until the mid-19th century. Thereafter, despite preserving a diverse industrial base and good port facilities, it lost ground to its northern competitor, Dundalk, and remained in second place to it throughout the 20th century.

Casey, Christine, and Rowan, Alisdair, *The Buildings of Ireland: North Leinster* (1993)

DD

Drogheda, siege of (Sept. 1649), Oliver *Cromwell's first major, and most infamous, action in Ireland. The parliamentarians were anxious to recapture Drogheda, wrested from them the previous July, to prevent a possible juncture between *Ormond and Owen Roe *O'Neill. The royalist–*Confederate Catholic garrison under Sir Arthur Aston defended stoutly until Cromwell's artillery began a bombardment on 9 September. The walls were breached on the third day, the Boyne drawbridge taken, and Aston overwhelmed in a last-ditch stand on the Millmount.

Official figures were 3,500 slain. The quarter given to the Millmount's defenders was ignored. Cromwell tried to vindicate the killing of civilians, of whom possibly 1,000 were slaughtered, on the erroneous grounds of their involvement in the massacres accompanying the *rising of 1641. His other claim, that the action was an expedient to win the war quickly by terrifying other towns into submission, was borne out only in the case of nearby garrisons. HM

druids, the priests of the pre-Christian *Celts. Greek and Roman writers describe the druids of Britain and the Continent as an elite class who presided over sacrifices, foretold the future, and claimed to possess special knowledge concerning the gods, the universe, and the fate of the soul. In Ireland the existence of figures called *druid* (singular *druí*; rendered in Latin as *magus*) is attested in legal writings at least as late as the 8th century: the word is evidently the same, but in sources of the Christian period it is often debatable whether it means more than 'magician, soothsayer'.

In medieval literature druids are often portrayed as followers of pagan kings, whom they usually serve as prophets. Some details resemble the accounts of the classical writers: Cathbad, chief druid of the Ulaid in the Ulster Cycle, is described as having pupils, and a few texts speak of rituals which the druids performed in order to foretell the future. In tales set in the pre-Christian and conversion periods, they figure as defenders of paganism: thus there are several stories of St *Patrick's victories over the druids of *Lóegaire mac Néill. JPC

Druim Cett, the site of a meeting between *Áedán mac Gabráin, king of Dál Riata, and Áed mac Ainmerech, Uí Néill *high king, is traditionally identified with the Mullagh, a small flat-topped hillock less than a mile south of Limavady, Co. Londonderry, which has wide views typical of early medieval assembly places and is located in territory not directly controlled by either king. What the kings agreed is uncertain, but it is clear from *Adomnán's references in his Life of St *Colum Cille that it was an important event, attended also by Colum Cille, a kinsman of Áed and a close associate of Áedán, perhaps also by St Comgall of *Bangor, and by hostages for the subordinates of the two kings. The *Annals of Ulster* retrospectively dated the meeting to 575, at the beginning of Áedán's rule, but Áed was not even king of his own people, Cenél Conaill, until 586, so that a later date, perhaps around 590, would better fit the known historical circumstances. More than four centuries later Ferdomnach, abbot of Kells and *coarb of Colum Cille, seems to have looked back on Druim Cett as an historical antecedent for his installation as coarb in 1007 at a great assembly at Teltown, in imitation of the ancient *Óenach Tailten. This was the occasion when the ancient poem *Amra Coluimb Chille* was provided with a preface that made Druim Cett the meeting at which Colum Cille was said to have saved the poets of Ireland from expulsion. RS

Drummond, Thomas (1797–1840), reforming administrator. Born in Edinburgh, he came to Ireland in 1824 to work on the *Ordnance Survey. As under-secretary (1835–40) he was a key figure in implementing the reforms required by *O'Connell's understanding with the *Whig ministry (see LICHFIELD HOUSE COMPACT), in particular the reorganization of the *police and the steps leading to the dissolution of the *Orange Order.

dual economy thesis, a briefly influential thesis, originating with John Lynch and Patrick Vaizey, *Guinness's Brewery and the Irish Economy 1759–1867* (1960). They divided late 18th- and early 19th-century Ireland into two distinct regions: a 'maritime' cash economy linked to that of Great Britain, which was confined to the eastern coastal fringe, Limerick, and Galway, and a 'subsistence' sector occupying the remainder of the island. Subsequent writing has rejected any such neat geographical division: social groups inhabiting the same region could have very different levels of involvement in the *money economy. The notion of a commercialized sector confined to the east coast also greatly understates the extent to which rural Ireland as a whole in the years before 1845 saw changes in land use, agricultural techniques, and demographic behaviour, all in response to market forces. Indeed one of the most striking features of the pre-*Famine economy was the extent to which poverty was linked, not to economic backwardness, but to exceptionally high levels of commercialization.

Dublin, a huge city-region which at the end of the 20th century contained a third of the population of the Irish Republic and a fifth of the island's population, has a solid claim to be regarded as the most significant Irish urban place for the whole of the last millennium. However, the pre-*Viking beginnings of permanent settlement on the southern edges of what was then the Liffey estuary remain controversial: there may have been two 'proto-towns', a secular settlement, Áth Cliath, on the ridge overlooking the main river to the north and its tributary the Poddle to the south, and Dubhlinn lying south-eastwards on the Poddle's right bank, an enclosed cluster of ecclesiastical foundations. Whether they were in any sense distinctive before the 9th century is unproven. The estuary site lay almost on the border between the kingdoms of Brega and *Laigin and it has been postulated that the long-distance routeways of the early historic period converged on this frontier, indicating its strategic significance. The evidence on routeways remains inconclusive and the claims of *Tara as a central place, culturally and symbolically, however much they may have been exaggerated in later tradition, still seem more plausible.

The Viking/Norse impact on Dublin is clear-cut. For some 60 years after 841 a piratical base was maintained on the river, possibly as far upstream as Kilmainham. The Vikings returned in force in 917 and developed the site of Áth Cliath as a trading town. Archaeological excavation has helped reveal something of the 10th-century urban environment: the core street system of Castle Street/Christ Church Place, intersected by Fishamble and Werburgh Streets, would seem to date from this time; the early town had perimeter earthen fortifications, and property divisions were already evident; the first churches may have appeared before 1000. Both as plunderers and plundered, Dublin's Vikings had become drawn into the mesh of Irish dynastic politics before then; from that time they were subject to an Irish overking.

In the 11th century the urban site expanded westwards, the enclosed area now including a handful of new streets linked to High Street, and the site was more densely settled. Sophisticated craftsmanship and the mushrooming of ecclesiastical foundations were in their different ways indicators of an increasingly affluent town. In the final century of Hiberno-Norse Dublin, its wealth and wider importance were more clearly evident: the proliferation of church foundations *outside* the urban site, several with specific regional associations, was unparalleled in other Hiberno-Norse sites: by 1172 there were some nine churches inside the town and another nine to the immediate south and east across the Poddle; north of the river were two further foundations, linked by a bridge. The elevation of the Dublin bishopric to archiepiscopal status in 1152 (regardless of the immediate political reasons) is another indication of the town's ecclesiastical pre-eminence. But whatever its local autonomy under mainly Norse subkings and its control of a coastal appendage, Dublin was essentially a prized chess-piece in the wider contests for *high kingship, notably in the case of those dynasties whose power base was in

Leinster or Munster. However, eventually even the Connacht men needed Dublin; in 1166 Rory *O'Connor (Ruaidrí Ua Conchobair) organized his public inauguration as high king in the town. Tara was now history.

The exceptional archaeological discoveries which have transformed modern knowledge of pre-Norman Dublin have demonstrated that in commercial terms at least the Normanization of the town was an incremental process, evident in the town's material culture before 1100. At the same period the Normanization of the local church flowed from the close links between the first bishops of Dublin and the archbishops of *Canterbury. Nevertheless the seizure of the city by a Norman-Irish army in September 1170 (see ANGLO-NORMAN INVASION) and the formidable but unsuccessful efforts, first of displaced Norse leaders and then of an Irish army led by O'Connor, to recapture the town the following year mark a sharp disjuncture. The town received its first royal charter several months later and became the seat of the chief of the Norman conquistadors, Hugh de *Lacy.

The confirmation of Dublin as capital of the Norman lordship only came with King *John's decision in 1204 to build *de novo* a royal stronghold on the site of the old Norse fortification beside the Poddle. The construction of the great stone fortress of *Dublin Castle as location for an Irish treasury and seat of royal justice was predicated on John's policy that there should continue to be a separate Irish administration. His ally Archbishop Henry, who oversaw its completion, also secured the elevation of one of the extra-mural churches, *St Patrick's, to cathedral status (*Augustinian canons monopolizing *Christ Church cathedral).

Thirteenth-century Dublin became a city. This was reflected in many ways: the scale and architectural quality of its two cathedrals, the appearance of new suburbs around the great monasteries to the north, south-west, and east of the walled core, and the great expansion of its maritime trade. And although it was only fifth Irish port in terms of exports *c.*1300, it was the busiest in the wine import trade, and had the largest number of urban craftsmen. Over 50 occupations were represented in the trade *guilds which together formed the basis of municipal government as established in the town's royal charters. Its prosperity rested on its embryonic functions as capital and on the activity generated by its very well-endowed monasteries and cathedral chapters.

Municipal government seems to have coped fairly well with the 13th-century boom, but the city's fate in the following century was markedly different: great fires, famines, and the *Bruce invasion were followed a generation later by the *Black Death. The general contraction of the Anglo-Norman colony (see GAELIC RECOVERY) hit Dublin particularly hard, dependent as it was on the political strength of the lordship, not just on a well-defined hinterland. Widely varying estimates exist of Dublin's pre-crisis population (from 10,000 to 25,000), but all are agreed that after several generations of decline the 15th-century town was both much emptier and more akin to the other Irish ports, an urban community dominated by its institutional landowners and its big merchants, yet short of labour and fearful of the world beyond its *Pale: in 1454 municipal efforts were made to exclude those 'of Irish blood' from any city occupation. The most eloquent evidence of late medieval wealth lies not in the city (where even archaeological evidence for the period is scanty) but in the great castellated warehouses built by Dublin merchants at the deep-water harbour of Dalkey—at a time when Dublin Castle was itself in decay.

The *dissolution of the Dublin monasteries in and after the 1540s disadvantaged the poor but enriched many of the city's merchant dynasties. This *Old English elite were valued allies of Tudor government in its slow regeneration of English power in Ireland. Dublin's municipal liberties were extended and its financial privileges strengthened; urban capital entered the rural land market. Yet in the second half of Elizabeth's reign relations between the leading citizenry and New English officialdom in the Castle soured and the Dubliners' religious conservatism began to be a source of friction and suspicion. Even the establishment of a university in 1592 on corporation land (see TRINITY COLLEGE) turned out to be something of a Trojan horse for them. The whittling away of privilege, together with the inconveniences of *recusancy, discommoded many of the old families in the following half-century.

These issues were to an extent obscured by a remarkable burst of urban growth. Internal peace and the consolidation of central authority triggered it; activity in the crown *courts was transformed and *parliament became anchored in Dublin. Prosperity in an enlarged hinterland boosted maritime trade. From a population level of around 10,000 in 1600 the city surpassed its medieval peak well before 1641, and although trade collapsed during the *Confederate War and bubonic plague made a last devastating visit in 1649–51, growth was resumed thereafter at a rate never repeated: by the end of the century its permanent population had reached 50,000–60,000.

In this transformation the Old English were swamped and excluded as effectively as the Norsemen had been over four centuries earlier. Some of course conformed in religion and were absorbed into the multilayered Protestant society which was numerically dominant from the 1640s, thanks to the inflow of migrants, English, French, and Dutch, some of whom were attracted by the open offer of citizenship to Protestant strangers after 1651. Yet despite an almost complete turnover in the families controlling city government there was striking continuity in the form and character of municipal affairs.

Old money and old families were briefly visible in the *Jacobite corporation (1685–90), but until far into the 18th century control of the city was a tussle between different elements of the new Protestant order, mercantile, professional, and landed. From 1672, when the government assumed more direct powers to regulate the affairs of Irish corporations, Dublin aldermen were sucked into parliamentary and national politics. But the existence of the Castle ensured another stratum of citizens—peers, gentry, and office holders—who between them created a counterweight to the civic elite in both the development and governance of the city in the 17th and 18th centuries. This was evident even in some of the earliest development initiatives in *Restoration Dublin, the rival projects of the wealthy merchant Humphrey Jervis on the north bank and that of the functionary Francis Aungier active south-east of the Castle.

By then the timber-framed and densely packed old town was being left aside: a brick-fronted Dublin was far outgrowing its medieval core. New patterns of segregation were visible: to the south, the old monastic lands of Donore and St Thomas, now the privately owned Meath liberties, were assuming a strongly industrial character; to the east the first signs of speculative upper-class residential development; north of the river the market zone. Around the edges of the city large-scale institutional developments placed markers for the future: the college downstream on the south bank, the corporation commons to the south-east which were privatized in 89 lots for development in the 1660s, the great Royal hospital for army veterans to the west erected in the 1680s, the royal Phoenix deerpark to the north-west, lying beyond the huge site marked out for the royal barracks in 1705. To the north-east, private enterprise, led by the *Gardiner family, shaped the future: in the 1720s and for nearly a century after a huge wedge of land, some reclaimed, some elevated, was developed, primarily for high-amenity residence. The controversial relocation of the city *custom house to the north-east riverfront (1791) was the Gardiner group's *coup de grâce*. Similar schemes to the south-east of the old city first imitated and then eventually triumphed over the Gardiner quarter—once the development potential of the crucially located Fitzwilliam estate was exploited in the late 18th and early 19th centuries.

Dublin's second cycle of rapid growth from the 1590s to the 1820s (by which time its population approached 250,000) had rested on a conjunction of factors: its role as leading port and from the 1630s unchallenged national centre of distribution (of goods and printed information); its pivotal position in the provision of financial services during the long commercialization of Irish agriculture; its monopoly of certain professional services—higher education and the higher courts of law; the (intermittent) presence of a viceregal court and a national legislature; and the social imperative that brought the landed classes to Dublin in winter time to live, play, and consume to excess. Their presence, coupled with the city's role as national warehouse, sustained the huge variety of artisanal occupations for men and women, from the most sophisticated stuccadores to the jobbing printers; in employment terms textile trades outnumbered the rest.

The ambiguous aspirations of the 18th-century Irish political establishment (see PATRIOTISM) left a profound mark on the city, both in terms of the set-piece public buildings (*Parliament House, *Four Courts, College, and Castle) and in the refashioning of the central thoroughfares by means of the enlightened despotism of the wide streets commissioners. Thanks to parliament's largesse two trunk canal systems radiating out from the capital were also built. Nearly all the great *palazzi*, from Cork and Chichester Houses in the early 17th century to Ely and Aldborough Houses in the late 18th, were built by active politicians.

Nineteenth-century Dublin has tended to be interpreted by reference primarily to the Act of *Union: this distorts reality. Many changes—the reduced interest of the gentry in winter residence, the declining demand for a commercial and financial centre as Anglo-Irish economic integration intensified, the undercutting of urban artisanal handicrafts by new factory technologies, the flight from an overpopulated countryside—were operating independent of the Union. But nevertheless, given the highly politicized character of the city since the 1740s, which was accentuated in the political cauldron of the 1790s, the symbolism of the loss of parliament rested heavily on the city.

The professions, notably law and medicine, dominated the cultural and political life of a city that more than ever was polarized, vertically by religion, horizontally by class, income, and education. They helped to fund the abundance of new and often spectacular churches, Catholic and Protestant, across the city. Some dominated the corporation, which for 50 years remained the outspoken defender of conservative causes. Others led the political organizations seeking emancipation and reform locally and nationally. The city had actually had a Catholic majority since the mid-18th century but this was translated into political victories only in the parliamentary elections of the 1830s. Municipal reform in 1840 (see URBAN GOVERNMENT) brought fuller power to the Catholic professional and business classes of the city, not however with any very startling results: aside from more effective market management and a high-pressure water supply in 1868, the new corporation only very gradually made an impact on the city.

This was partly because of the progressive flight to the suburbs of a substantial section of Dublin's wealthier households: their relocation beyond the fiscal boundary held back the city's capacity to address public health and housing problems until after 1900. New transport systems (*railways and tramways) allowed middle-class commuting from a swathe of ten independent townships which, in political terms, distanced themselves from the city. Despite this exodus, population density within the city remained high; 49 per cent of city families were in one-roomed accommodation in 1851, 33 per cent in 1911. High-quality housing stock was colonized as tenements and indeed this represented an improvement for the poorest city-dwellers. Dublin's notoriously high mortality rates in the late 19th century were blamed on its slums, but both phenomena in fact reflected the low income and casual employment prevalent in what was a 'warehouse' economy. Despite the international renown of its industrialized distilleries, breweries, and biscuit making, and the strength of its transport sectors, the city could do little for its reserve army of the underemployed, *quondam* dockers, carters, and servants.

Both state and local government intervened more in health and housing by the early 20th century, but the most significant agents of change were charitable—the Iveagh Trust and the Artisans Dwellings Company (which built some 3,300 houses in four decades after 1876 in the inner city). Despite much talk Dublin corporation made only a modest contribution to rebuilding in the 50 years after its first scheme in Benburb Street (1887).

In 1914 the world of petit bourgeois Catholic Dublin was captured in print in Joyce's *Dubliners*, at a time when the city was demonstrably ill at ease with itself. Outshone now by *Belfast in size and self-confidence, it was shaken by the scars of the *Dublin lockout and divided along religious lines as to the consequences of *home rule. Most of the city's banking and business dynasties were Protestant and mainly unionist in sympathy. A return of Irish sovereignty they did not expect.

Dublin's third cycle of growth commenced in the ashes of the *rising of 1916 (an event far more physically destructive for the city than the attempted insurrections in 1798, 1803, or 1848 but one which probably commanded less popular support at the time than any of the others). The rebuilding of the Gardiner-inspired boulevard of O'Connell Street and parts adjacent in the 1920s came when greater Dublin's population stood at about half a million. It had barely doubled in 100 years. The *Irish Free State, with its strong centralist administration, engaged from the beginning in a series of initiatives which indirectly assisted the growth of the city. In the following 60 years the site of the built-up area quadrupled and population doubled, a turnout considerably beyond the projections of the city's planners.

From the 1940s population within the canals fell to early 18th-century levels as a much delayed public housing programme ended or at least banished the slums. New low-density suburbs were created at Crumlin and Cabra, then Ballyfermot and Artane (in the 1950s), Finglas, Ballymun, and Coolock (in the 1960s), and finally the new satellite towns of Tallaght, Clondalkin, and Blanchardstown (in the 1970s). The absence of a single strong metropolitan authority during this period of unprecedented site expansion cost the new suburbs dear in terms of amenities and infrastructure. Only gradually did employment and retail services gravitate westwards in line with the markedly changed distribution of Dublin's population. To the east the port survived as a major terminal, but the communities dependent on employment there were among the many victims of modern technical change.

Such a bursting out of the city was possible thanks to the rise of inter-war bus services, and then to the eightfold growth in private cars between 1930 and the mid-1960s. The early 21st-century city has thus inherited low site densities and a central business district almost completely without high-rise development; even the symbol of the 1980s, the Financial Services Centre, is architecturally restrained. Two-thirds of its citizens had become owner-occupiers by the 1990s as public authorities retreated almost as quickly as they had intervened in housing provision. The enduring importance of private property, private enterprise, and social inequality, timidly mediated by reactive planning, are a somewhat problematical legacy.

Aalen, F. H. A., and Whelan, K. (eds.), *Dublin City and County: From Prehistory to Present* (1992)

Cosgrove, Art (ed.), *Dublin through the Ages* (1988)

Craig, M. J., *Dublin 1660–1860: A Social and Architectural History* (1952)

Daly, Mary, *Dublin: The Deposed Capital 1860–1914* (1984)

DD

Dublin Castle. In 1204 King *John issued a mandate for the construction of a fortress suitable for the administration of the city and, if necessary, for its defence. Until 1922 this castle was the citadel of British authority in Ireland, and official home to the *lord lieutenant or *lord deputy. It was the seat of state councils and was, on occasion, used for meetings of *parliament and the courts of law.

The original castle was built between 1204 and 1268, situated on a hill overlooking the city and flanked on two sides by the rivers Poddle and Liffey. A curtain wall was punctuated with large drum towers, with a rectangular tower in the south-west corner where the castle impinged on the city walls. The whole castle was surrounded by a moat.

Following a fire in 1684 the castle underwent extensive renovations. The medieval fabric was largely replaced with the red brick arcaded buildings of the Upper Castle yard, but retained roughly the layout of the original castle. The Genealogical Office, the Bedford tower (built on the base of one of the original gate towers), the gateways, and the state apartments remain essentially as built in the mid-18th century. Modifications to the last remaining medieval tower (the Record tower), and the construction of a church (the chapel royal, designed by Francis *Johnston), took place during the first two decades of the 19th century.

In spite of its defensive role, the castle never had to withstand a major siege or assault. In 1534 it was unsuccessfully attacked by 'Silken' Thomas FitzGerald (see KILDARE REBELLION), and a plot to seize it as part of the *rising of 1641 was betrayed. It saw some minor skirmishes in the *rising of 1916 and was officially handed over to the Provisional Government of Ireland in January 1922.

RM

Dublin lockout (1913), Ireland's best remembered labour dispute. Commencing in August 1913, a group of employers, headed by William Martin *Murphy, alarmed at the rise of industrial militancy, combined to compel workers to withdraw from the *Irish Transport and General Workers' Union or face dismissal. The ITGWU responded by calling out other workers, and by late September some 20,000 were on strike or locked out. The dispute was prolonged and bitter: *Larkin, *Connolly, and other leaders were arrested for sedition; on 31 August members of the *Dublin Metropolitan Police baton charged strikers in Sackville Street (now O'Connell Street), killing two men; workers drafted in to take the places of strikers were intimidated and attacked. The formation of the *Irish Citizen Army testified to the intensity of the confrontation. The strikers, mainly unskilled labourers, lacked the reserves for a long dispute, and by the end of January 1914 most had returned to work on the best terms they could obtain.

Dublin Metropolitan Police (DMP). A uniformed, armed, and government-controlled *police force had been introduced in Dublin in 1786: the first of its kind in the British Isles. It was opposed by ratepayers, who considered it oppressive and expensive, and in 1795 a locally controlled unarmed force was restored. However, the government, dissatisfied with policing during the *insurrection of 1798, reintroduced the centralized, armed force in 1799 and strengthened it in 1808.

In 1836 the Dublin Metropolitan Police was created, based on the model of the London Metropolitan Police set up by *Peel in 1829. Unlike English borough forces, the DMP was under central not local control, but, unlike the *Royal Irish Constabulary, it was not a paramilitary force. Constables were not armed; they could marry freely; and officers were promoted from the ranks. Recruitment took place largely in rural Ireland.

Mainly concerned with apprehending petty thieves, drunkards, and disorderly persons, the DMP also had a detective division, G Division, which played a significant role in investigating political crime. Reasonably popular, the force however incurred considerable hostility when it brutally suppressed workers' gatherings during the *Dublin lockout.

The DMP was amalgamated with the *Gárda Síochána in 1925.

ELM

Dublin Philosophical Society (1683–1708), founded by William *Molyneux, the 14 founder members rising to 33 by 1685. William *Petty was first president; prominent figures over the years included Narcissus Marsh, William *King and George *Berkeley. Most members were graduates of *Trinity College, Dublin, and they included a higher percentage of clerics than in most other scientific societies; there was at least one Catholic but no Dissenter. The society had external ties, notably with the Royal Society, London, which elected fourteen of the Dublin society to fellowships. Minutes of Dublin meetings were sent to the Royal Society, which published articles from Dublin in the *Philosophical Transactions*.

The society had three periods of activity: 1683–7 (when war interrupted proceedings), 1692–8 (when the society petered out), 1707–8 (a short-lived revival). Most activities were devoted to scientific papers read at meetings, but Petty encouraged programmes of experimentation: as well as studying the mathematical and life sciences, members undertook utilitarian work in agriculture, military technology, textiles, and transportation. Limited as its achievements were, the society was the first attempt to sustain collaborative scientific work in Ireland, and inspired other Irish learned societies of the 18th century. DJS

Dublin University Press (1734–), specialist academic *printer and the oldest printing house in Ireland. It was most successful under the management during 1842–75 of M. H. *Gill, but never engaged extensively in publishing. VK

duelling, like the code of honour from which it derived its impetus and rationale, was introduced into Ireland by the new aristocratic and landed elite that came into being in the late 16th and early 17th centuries. The number of affairs of honour that proceeded to trial by arms increased perceptibly from the mid-17th century, as *Old English royalists embraced the honorific precepts of their continental allies and as the New English elite consolidated its position. Religious and political antipathies lay at the root of many duels in the late 17th century, and it was inevitable that the exodus of thousands of *Jacobite soldiers after the *Williamite War should bring about a temporary falling off, but the number of duels had risen again by the late 1720s.

Duelling peaked in Ireland in the 1770s and 1780s when the confidence of the Protestant elite was at its most assured. This was an era of economic expansion and aggressive political debate. Confrontational politics, rising wealth, and social ambition, along with the unwillingness of the legal authorities to take preventive action, encouraged a growing number of individuals, known and not so well known, to appeal to arms to resolve differences. By the early 19th century *evangelical religion and rising middle-class hostility to the code of honour, along with declining official tolerance, had brought about a decline. The example of *O'Connell, who refused to accept challenges after his dispute with *Peel in 1817, also contributed to the change. Duels continued to occur in the 1830s and 1840s, but the mood was increasingly censorious and the practice had ceased by 1860. JK

Duffy, Charles Gavan (1816–1903), *Young Irelander. Born in Monaghan of a middle-class Catholic family, Duffy became a journalist with the *Dublin Morning Register* in 1836, and editor of the *Belfast Vindicator* in 1839. He was proprietor and editor of the **Nation* from 1842, and produced the Library of Ireland series. He was imprisoned for sedition in 1844, and in 1846 joined Young Ireland's secession from the Repeal Association. Despite his initial caution, the Paris revolution and the threat of coercion led him to support a rising in 1848. He was imprisoned until April 1849, after which he revived the *Nation* and devoted his attention to land reform and the *Tenant League. He was MP for New Ross 1852–5. Disillusioned with Irish politics following the collapse of the Independent Irish Party (see INDEPENDENT OPPOSITION PARTY), Duffy emigrated to Victoria in 1855 and rose to be prime minister in 1871–2 and speaker of the Assembly in 1876–80, receiving a knighthood in 1873. He subsequently retired to Nice to write his extremely influential memoirs and historical accounts of the 1840s and 1850s. PHG

Duffy, James (1809–71), publisher in Dublin and London, specializing in inexpensive publications. He produced the Library of Ireland series for *Young Ireland. The firm continued after his death, ceasing in 1980. VK

Dunbar-Harrison, Letitia. Dunbar-Harrison's nomination in 1930 as Mayo county librarian was attacked by local politicians and Catholic clergy. The ostensible reason for opposing her appointment was that her Irish was inadequate, while there is evidence that opponents were in reality frustrated that the Local Appointments Commission had overridden considerations of patronage and local influence. But references to her position as a Protestant and graduate of *Trinity College, Dublin, gave the episode an additional flavour of sectarianism. The episode, adroitly exploited by *Fianna Fáil, embarrassed the government, which in December 1931 transferred Dunbar-Harrison to the library of the Department of Defence in Dublin.

Dun Cow, Book of (*Lebor na hUidre*), now in the *Royal Irish Academy, Dublin, the oldest surviving manuscript written entirely in Irish. It was associated from the 15th century with the hide of the cow of St Ciarán of *Clonmacnoise. It preserves the earliest surviving versions of Irish tales such as the Voyages of Bran and of Máel Dúin. A large part is devoted to the Ulster Cycle, including a version of the epic *Táin Bó Cuailnge. Linguistic and palæographical evidence suggests that it was compiled in the late 11th century and revised in the 12th. Three scribes worked on the manuscript, one of whom—Máel Muire mac Célechair (d. 1106?) or a later scribe—was responsible for reworking the manuscript. The contents indicate that its scribes probably were connected with Monasterboice, *Durrow, and Clonmacnoise. EB

Dundalgan Press (1859–), Dundalk *printer, bookseller, and publisher. The firm was started by William Tempest, and expanded under his son Henry (1881–1964). It has an extensive list of Irish interest books. VK

Dun Emer Press, established 1902 by Elizabeth ('Lolly') Yeats (1868–1940) as part of Dun Emer Industries, a craft industries partnership she had founded with Evelyn Gleeson and Susan ('Lily') Yeats (1866–1949). The Press produced elegant hand-printed limited editions of texts chosen (and often written) by their brother W. B. *Yeats, its literary editor. The Press also produced hand-coloured greeting cards and broadsheets designed by Jack B. *Yeats. In 1908, having produced eleven titles, the sisters left Dun Emer and took the new name 'Cuala'. The Cuala Press printed 77 titles between 1908 and 1946, including many W. B. Yeats first editions. Cuala prints were produced from 1940 by George Yeats, the poet's widow, and book production resumed 1969–78. Despite persistent tensions between the sisters and between Lolly and W. B. Yeats (who subsidized its financially precarious operations), the Press was a significant product of the *literary revival and a landmark in Irish art printing. PM

Dungannon (Co. Tyrone), **conventions of.** There were three such gatherings, all of *Volunteers from Ulster. The first (15 Feb. 1782), an attempt to revive the flagging *patriot agitation, was attended by delegates from less than half the Ulster Volunteer corps. Its resolutions asserted the exclusive legislative authority of the Irish parliament and called for the amendment of *Poynings's Law, a renewable mutiny act (to secure parliamentary control of the army), and security of tenure for judges. Over the next two months these resolutions were endorsed by numerous other public gatherings. However, it remains unclear how far this renewed agitation, as opposed to the fall of Lord North's government, opened the way to *legislative independence.

A second Dungannon convention on 8 September 1783, followed by similar gatherings in the other three provinces, considered *parliamentary reform, preparing the way for the Volunteer National Convention two months later. A third, on 15–16 February 1793, was initially seen by the *United Irishmen as an important opportunity. In fact its resolutions, balancing calls for a complete overhaul of the electoral system and the enfranchisement of Catholics with a repudiation of *republicanism and a refusal to condemn the war against revolutionary France, revealed the moderation of most advocates of reform.

Dungannon clubs, a nationalist movement launched in 1905 by Bulmer Hobson (1883–1969) and Denis McCullough (1883–1968). Although the initial reference back to the *Volunteers and the constitution of 1782 was quickly superseded, and although both founders were members of the *Irish Republican Brotherhood, the clubs themselves were open not secret, and promoted a more broadly defined advanced nationalism, expressed particularly in a campaign against recruitment for the British *army. In 1907 the clubs merged with another body, Cumann na nGaedheal, to become the Sinn Féin League, forerunner of *Sinn Féin.

Dungan's Hill, battle of (8 Aug. 1647), which saved the *Pale for parliament after *Ormond's departure from Ireland. Michael Jones led an army out of Dublin towards Trim, Co. Meath, which Thomas *Preston was besieging. Preston evaded the relief army and moved towards Dublin but was caught at Dungan's Hill nearby. Jones's cavalry proved vastly superior and the Irish infantry were forced into a bog. Preston's army suffered between 2,000 and 5,000 casualties, shattering the confidence of the Leinster *Confederates. HM

Dún Laoghaire, see KINGSTOWN.

Durrow, in modern Co. Offaly, was founded as a monastery by St *Colum Cille, most likely between 585 and 589. In his time it was administered as part of the family of *Iona and headed by a monk of Iona answerable to the saint. Later Durrow grew into a monastic town with a substantial secular population, so that already in 764 we read in the *annals that 200 men of Durrow were killed in battle against another monastic town, *Clonmacnoise. RS

Durrow, Book of (Trinity College Dublin MS 57), a *decorated manuscript containing a Latin text of the Gospels, along with preliminaries. It is decorated with symbols of the Evangelists, elaborated opening words of certain passages, and 'carpet' pages of ornament based on jewellery designs. Academic debate over its date and origin make it one of the most controversial manuscripts in the field of *insular script and art. Despite its known association with the monastery of Durrow, Co. Offaly, founded by St *Colum Cille, some scholars have argued for an origin in *Iona or in Northumbria. Flann mac Máel Sechnaill (*high king 879–916) encased it in a *cumdach* (shrine). It may date from the late 7th century—making it the earliest surviving fully decorated insular Gospel book—but conflicting views place it in the early 8th century. BM

Dwyer, Michael (1772–1825), leader of a guerrilla band that remained at large in the Wicklow Mountains following the *insurrection of 1798. He surrendered at the end of 1803 and was transported to Australia, where he became high constable of the Liverpool district of New South Wales in 1820.

Dysert O'Dea (O'Dea's hermitage), **battle of** (10 May 1318). Murtagh O'Brien (Muirchertach Ó Briain, *d.* 1343), king of *Thomond, who had fought against the *Bruce brothers and their allies, the O'Briens of Clann Bhriain Ruaidh, later rebelled when forced to share Thomond with a **tánaiste* from rival kindred. His overlord, Richard de Clare, invaded but was defeated and killed by O'Brien and his vassal O'Dea. English lordship in Thomond effectively ended with the death of de Clare's infant son three years later. KS

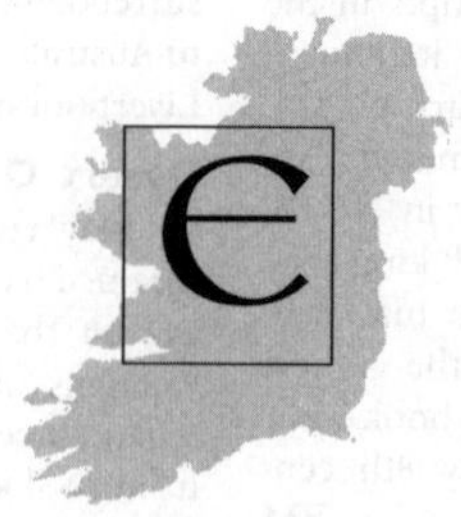

Early Christian period, a popular term for the period now more usually called, by academics at any rate, the *Early Medieval period. The once widely used terms 'Dark Ages' and 'Late Celtic' have now quite properly (see CELTIC IRELAND) fallen into desuetude, and 'Late Iron Age' proved unpopular and short-lived. RW

Early Medieval period (Early Middle Ages), the period following the *Iron Age. Its beginning and end are conventionally defined by 'events' rather than by clear evidence of sudden cultural change and the term, like all 'period' names, must be regarded as a convenience rather than as indicating homogeneity. According to one definition it opens with the beginning of *Christianization and the introduction of *literacy—hence its alternative names of *Early Christian and Early Historic period—and ends with the *Anglo-Norman invasion. It therefore runs from the 5th century to the 12th and includes those sub-periods often called Patrician and *Viking. Most of its historical and social characteristics are dealt with in other entries, but it is particularly noted for its very fine ecclesiastical *metalwork and *decorated manuscripts. The period has been described, with some justification, as Ireland's 'Golden Age', or the 'Age of Saints and Scholars'. Confusion arises from an alternative use of the term 'Early Medieval' only for the period following the Anglo-Norman invasion, which in the definition just outlined belongs rather to the *Late Medieval period. RW

Eason & Son (1886–), nationwide retail and wholesale bookseller and newsagent. The firm was founded by Charles Eason (1823–99) when he took over the Dublin branch of W. H. Smith in 1886. VK

Ecclesiastical Titles Act (1851), forbidding Catholic clerics to assume ecclesiastical titles taken from any place in the United Kingdom. The act was introduced by the *Liberal government of Lord John Russell, in response to the re-creation in 1850 of an English Catholic hierarchy. To Protestants, this was the 'papal aggression', a wholly unacceptable assertion by a foreign power of authority over British territory. Irish Catholics of all shades of opinion, however, regarded the act as a gratuitous insult, and the demand for its repeal provided the main impetus for the creation of the Independent Irish Party (see INDEPENDENT OPPOSITION PARTY).

Economic Development, an official report, published in 1958 under the name of T. K. Whitaker, secretary of the Irish Department of Finance, is commonly credited with providing the blueprint for the transformation of the Irish economy during the 1960s. It signalled a rejection of the policies of *protection, and of government efforts to stimulate the economy by spending money on infrastructural projects, in favour of a return to a more competitive free-trading economic environment. This message was confirmed with the almost simultaneous publication of the government's Programme for Economic Expansion. The impact of both publications was primarily psychological: the modest target for 2 per cent annual growth in GNP was exceeded, and public expenditure was also much higher than planned. However *Economic Development* is generally credited with reversing a mood of pessimism within the state, and with creating a vogue for French-style economic planning. The fact that Sean *Lemass succeeded Eamon de *Valera as *taoiseach less than a year after this report was published reinforced the impression that *Economic Development* signalled the emergence of a more modern and more prosperous state. MED

Economic War, a six-year Anglo-Irish dispute involving economic, constitutional, financial, and defence questions. The dispute began in 1932 when de *Valera abolished the *oath of allegiance and refused to pay the *land annuities. The British government imposed special duties on Irish imports, principally cattle and dairy produce. The Irish government retaliated with emergency duties on British coal, machinery, and iron and steel goods. Both sets of duties inflicted considerable damage on Anglo-Irish trade.

From 1933 to 1935 de Valera passed further controversial amendments to the *constitution. In 1934 the trade war was ameliorated by the first of three coal–cattle pacts. Malcolm MacDonald, appointed British dominions secretary in 1935, established friendly relations with de Valera and pushed the British cabinet towards negotiations. For most of 1936–7, de Valera's new constitution was the focus of attention. Its completion, and the decision that its terms did not after all change Ireland's position within the *Commonwealth, clarified the constitutional issues that had underlain the economic dispute. Neville Chamberlain, prime minister from May 1937, gave added backing to MacDonald's efforts to secure a settlement. Negotiations began in January 1938 and ended three months later with the *Anglo-Irish agreements. DMcM

ecumenism is the name given to the aspiration for the visible union of all Christians throughout the world. Although ecumenical stirrings within the churches can be detected down through the centuries, the modern ecumenical movement dates from the Edinburgh Missionary Conference of 1910. This multidenominational conference generated a number of other international organizations, culminating in the formation of the World Council of Churches in 1948. Similar processes were at work in early 20th-century Ireland, resulting in 1923 in the formation of the United Council of Christian Churches and Religious Communions in Ireland, which in 1966 changed its name to the Irish Council of Churches. The constituent members include the three main Protestant denominations (*Church of Ireland, *Presbyterian, and *Methodist), and a number of smaller churches, including the Lutherans, the *Moravians, and the *Society of Friends. The Roman Catholic church enjoys observer status, and since 1973 there have been regular inter-church meetings between Protestant and Roman Catholic churchmen at Ballymascanlon, Co. Louth, to discuss a wide range of social and theological issues.

Ecumenism, ironically, seems to have prospered amid the social, political, and ecclesiastical divisions of modern Ireland. Organizations unlimited, from the Irish School of Ecumenics and the *Corrymeela community to charismatic renewal movements and local community groups, meet to pray, study, discuss, reflect, and co-operate. There are well over 100 clerical fellowships, ecumenical study groups, and councils of churches issuing discussion documents on almost everything. There is, however, another side to the story. While relations between church leaders remain good, ecclesiastical unification has proved to be a mirage. Moreover, recent polling evidence suggests that while many churchgoers are prepared for social co-operation with members of other churches, fewer are prepared to contemplate joint religious services between Protestants and Catholics, and fewer still have any enthusiasm for church unity. Divisions over education, mixed marriages, and old Reformation doctrines have proved remarkably resistant to ecumenical enthusiasm.

Overall, then, the main denominations in Ireland, Protestant and Roman Catholic, have become far less hostile to one another in the decades since the second *Vatican Council. If a long slow thaw in inter-church relations has begun, however, its progress is as yet uneven. Under pressure from its *evangelical wing, made nervous by Roman Catholicism and trendy liberation theology, the Irish *Presbyterian church in 1980 withdrew from the World Council of Churches, though not from other ecumenical councils. In addition, there remains a formidable *fundamentalist rump in most of the Irish Protestant denominations (proportionately larger in the smaller and more evangelical churches), which regards closer relations with Roman Catholics as a betrayal of Reformation principles. Similarly, conservative ecclesiastics within the Roman Catholic church may no longer regard Protestants as advanced heretics, but they have no wish to see the church relinquish any more of its authority and control. Even the ecumenically well intentioned are now beginning to wonder if a global super-church with impeccable ecclesiastical discipline and almost no popular appeal is a goal worth striving for. Meanwhile, in Ireland, ecumenists continue their efforts to ensure that ecclesiastical diversity is not necessarily the midwife of religious sectarianism. DNH

Edgeworth, Maria (1767–1849), writer and moralist. She was the daughter of **Richard Lovell Edgeworth** (1744–1817), *Enlightenment intellectual, political liberal, and modernizing landlord in Co. Longford. Heavily influenced by her father, she combined a *Whig political project of modernizing Ireland by assimilation to Britain with delight in the Irish peculiarities whose disappearance she advocated. Edgeworth was acutely aware of the responsibilities of her class and the threats of dispossession it had faced; she personally experienced danger from both rebels and ultra-loyalists during the *insurrection of 1798. Once internationally renowned, Edgeworth is now best remembered for her Irish novels, especially *Castle Rackrent* (1800), which pioneered the Big House novel and the use of Hiberno-English dialect. It depicts the vices of an old-style *landlord family as witnessed by an old servant whose unreasoning servility contributes to his master's moral degradation and supplanting by the narrator's own upstart son. PM

Edmundson, William (1627–1712), Quaker. Born in Westmorland, he served in the Cromwellian army in Scotland before setting up as a merchant, in Waterford and then in Co. Antrim. Converted to the *Society of Friends in 1653, he became an itinerant preacher, and from the early 1660s was the recognized leader of Irish Quakerism.

Éire is the Irish-language name of the southern state as prescribed in the 1937 *constitution. Its use in English (like that of the technically inaccurate '*Republic of Ireland') reflects the ambiguity of the official English-language name, 'Ireland'.

Eiscir Riata, the 'running ridge', is a series of eiscirs running east–west across Ireland. Eiscirs were formed at the end of the Ice Age when tunnels in the ice sheets that discharged melt water silted up with sand and gravel leaving exposed ridges. The Eiscir Riata is the most famous as it marks the legendary division of Ireland (see *Leth Cuinn and Leth Moga) along a line running from Clonard, Co. Meath, to Clonmacnoise, Co. Offaly. JPM

elections, see FRANCHISE.

electoral amendment bill (1927). Introduced after the assassination of Kevin *O'Higgins, this required parliamentary candidates to swear that if returned they would take the *oath of allegiance, and provided for the removal of elected members who refused to do so. In response *Fianna Fáil deputies abandoned abstentionism and took their seats. *Cosgrave and other *Cumann na nGaedheal ministers have been praised for thus forcing their main rivals to enter *Dáil Éireann. But they may have hoped to provoke a split in the new party on the issue of the oath.

electricity was first generated on a commercial basis in Ireland in 1880, by the Dublin Electric Light Company. Initially it was used only as a source of lighting; the company supplied *street lighting in the centre of Dublin and won contracts from some leading firms such as Jacobs's biscuit factory. In 1883 the Portrush–Giant's Causeway–Bushmills tram service, on the north Antrim coast, established the first electric railway in Ireland. By the 1890s the majority of electricity generating plants were controlled by local authorities, who were also responsible for distributing current, a situation similar to that in Great Britain. In the Irish Free State the *Electricity Supply Board gradually acquired a monopoly over generation and distribution. In Northern Ireland, however, although the Electricity Board of Northern Ireland (established 1931) acquired ownership of the smaller companies, Derry and Belfast corporations and the Larne Electric Light and Power Company continued to supply the greater part of the province's current. In 1942, in response to wartime emergencies, the Ministry of Commerce assumed control of all generating plants. MED

Electricity Supply Board (ESB), established in 1927 by the government of the *Irish Free State to manage the production and generation of electricity at the *Ardnacrusha hydroelectric station on the river Shannon and the sale and distribution of electricity throughout the state. It was the first Irish *state enterprise: an attempt to combine state ownership and control with a greater degree of autonomy than applied within the civil service. The company's ordinary shares were held by the minister for finance, who nominated the board of directors. The ESB took control of existing electricity generating companies; its monopoly powers have survived until the present day. MED

Emain Macha, capital of Ulster according to medieval Irish tradition, derived its name from the goddess Macha, who also underlies the name of Armagh, 'the heights of Macha'. Its pseudo-historical foundation date ranges from the 7th to the 4th centuries BC and the demise of its ruling dynasty was assigned to the 4th or 5th centuries AD. It provides a setting for many of Ireland's major early heroic tales such as the *Táin.

Anglicized as Navan (<*An Eamhain*), the site is identified with the modern Navan Fort, 3 miles west of Armagh. The main monument consists of a bank and ditched enclosure *c.*1,000 feet across. Settlement is known from the *neolithic to the Middle Ages, but most particularly *c.*400–100 BC when its inhabitants erected a series of round houses and larger enclosures. Within one of the structures was found the skull of a Barbary ape from North Africa, the most exotic prehistoric archaeological find in Ireland, and interpreted as evidence of prestige gift-exchange. About 95 BC the inhabitants erected a ritual structure, formed from concentric rows of 275 timber posts and measuring 130 feet in diameter. This was enigmatically filled with limestone boulders, its timbers set alight, and then covered with a mound of turves, presumably for ritual purposes. Navan was a major ceremonial centre during the prehistoric period, probably the spiritual and political capital of the *Iron Age Uluti, after whom the province of Ulster is named. JPM

Emergency Powers Act (1939). The *constitution of Ireland 1937 exempts from constitutional challenge any act stated to be for public safety in time of war or rebellion. An amendment (2 Sept. 1939) extended this provision to wars in which the state was not a belligerent but in respect of which each house of the *Oireachtas had resolved that a national emergency existed. Resolutions declaring such an emergency were passed on 3 September 1939. The Emergency Powers Act, introduced the same day, provided for *special military courts and the *internment of aliens (extended to Irish citizens by an amendment in 1940), and 'the Emergency' became independent Ireland's term for what the outside world knew as the *Second World War. This resolution of national emergency was rescinded only in 1976 when the government, responding to the *IRA's assassination on 23 July of the British ambassador, Christopher Ewart Biggs, declared a new emergency arising out of the *Northern Ireland conflict.

emigration as a concept in Irish historical writing and social criticism has a set of connotations and contextual limitations different from those which generally apply in European writing. In the world literature, migration, which means out-migration, is joined to in-migration (or *'immigration') to cover the general phenomenon of human movement, usually permanent, from one region or nation to another. The conceptual apparatus is not, for the most part, emotionally loaded and, therefore, dispassionate 'laws' (or, at least, tendencies) for worldwide migration have been articulated by historians and social observers.

'Emigration' from Ireland, however, departs from this world-based conceptual structure in several ways. First, emigration is rarely seen as being part of a general migration process in which in-migration is recognized as being as important as out-migration. Secondly, emigration is usually treated as a singularly Irish phenomenon and not as part of larger processes which, in fact, affected all of western Europe during the same period. Third, emigration in much (though not all) of the literature is treated as something tragic, or as something for which the nation should be ashamed. A synthetic layer of 'exile' is cast over the entire phenomenon, even though it is clear that the majority of those who emigrated from Ireland did so as part of a set of conscious decisions which, in most cases, improved their life-chances.

Historians of emigration in Ireland have yet to resolve two central issues of debate. The first is the extent to which emigrants from Ireland were selected. That is, did the best leave, or the dregs, and what does the answer mean for understanding the Irish society which the emigrants left behind? The second question is whether or not the large-scale migration hurt Ireland economically. On the one hand, economic historians point out that surplus labourers were siphoned off, thus reducing the number of economically dependent individuals. A counter-argument suggests that the individuals who left were those most likely to have been the recipients of social investment (especially primary education) and that their emigration effectively exported to other nations the Irish social capital invested in them.

Although emigration from Ireland began in the pre-Christian era, it became a large-scale phenomenon only in the age of the first English empire, with considerable (but untallied) numbers leaving Ireland during the 17th and 18th centuries, sometimes for the Continent, more often for the British colonies in the western hemisphere.

Mass emigration, however, began only at the close of the *revolutionary and Napoleonic wars. Although sizeable emigration continues to the present day, the era of mass emigration from Ireland was from 1815 to the beginning of the *First World War. A reasonable estimate is that between 1801 and 1921 at least 8 million Irish men, women, and children permanently left the country. Thus, the claim by President Mary Robinson, in December 1990, that there are over all the world 70 million persons who claim as part of their cultural heritage at least partial Irish descent, is not excessive.

As for destinations, a simple formulation is that, prior to the *Great Famine, Canada was the most common destination for Irish emigrants; between the Famine and the First World War, it was the *United States of America; thereafter, it was Great Britain.

Among the most notable characteristics of Irish emigration from 1815 to the present day is that (uniquely among European nations) Irish women were as large a part of the emigrant stream as were Irish men. This had implications both for Ireland (unlike most European countries, a surplus of single females did not develop) and for the new homelands: the numbers of women were sufficiently balanced to make it possible for Irish-born persons to marry within their own ethnic group.

See also IRISH DIASPORA.

Akenson, D. H., *The Irish Diaspora: A Primer* (1993)
Fitzpatrick, David, *Irish Emigration, 1801–1921* (1984)

DHA

Emlyn, Thomas (1663–1743), an English *Presbyterian minister who followed Joseph *Boyse to

Ireland as the countess of Donegall's domestic chaplain and in 1691 joined him as colleague minister of the Wood Street congregation in Dublin. Emlyn's acknowledgement of *Arianism in 1702 brought him deposition from the ministry, a £1,000 fine, and two years' imprisonment. On his release he returned to England, where he defended his Arian opinions until his death. RFGH

Emmet, Robert (1778–1803), *United Irishman. The younger brother of Thomas Addis *Emmet, he was expelled from *Trinity College in a purge of suspected radicals in April 1798, and was one of the new group of leaders to emerge after the defeat of the *insurrection of 1798. He travelled to France in August 1800 to solicit fresh military aid, but returned in October 1802, apparently with no clear plans. By early 1803, however, he was active, in association with such veterans of 1798 as Thomas *Russell, Myles *Byrne, and the Co. Kildare bricklayer Michael Quigley, in recruiting men and stockpiling weapons for a new insurrection.

Emmet's plan was for the seizure of *Dublin Castle and other strategic sites in the capital, to be followed by a largely spontaneous popular rising throughout the country. Despite comments, at his trial and elsewhere, on the danger of exchanging one foreign tyranny for another, he also appears to have counted, initially at least, on French assistance. However, an explosion at his arms depot in Patrick Street on 16 July led Emmet to bring forward the planned insurrection to 23 July. Only a small minority of the expected insurgent force, from Dublin and the surrounding countryside, assembled on that evening, and the attack on Dublin Castle was abandoned following a premature gunshot. About 300 men took control of Thomas Street and James's Street for around two hours, but were dispersed by soldiers after an abortive attack on James's Street barracks. About 50 people were killed, including Lord Kilwarden, the former attorney-general Arthur Wolfe (1739–1803), now lord chief justice, piked to death with his nephew when his coach was surrounded by insurgents.

Emmet, who had fled to the Wicklow Mountains as his plans unravelled, was arrested on 25 August, and executed on 20 September. Twenty-one others, including Russell, were also executed. The defeat marked the end of the United Irishmen as a serious revolutionary conspiracy. Emmet's speech from the dock became a classic of nationalist literature, although there is no definitive text and some much quoted passages are almost certainly later additions. Emmet himself was remembered as a noble but impractical dreamer, his romance with John Philpot *Curran's daughter Sarah contributing to the aura of romantic tragedy. Recent accounts emphasize the place of his conspiracy, like that of *Despard, in a still formidable revolutionary movement. But his talents as a strategist and military planner remain open to question.

Elliott, Marianne, *Partners in Revolution: The United Irishmen and France* (1982)

Emmet, Thomas Addis (1764–1827), *United Irishman. A lawyer and son of a well-connected Dublin physician, he was part of the conservative wing of the United Irish movement, uneasy about lower-class mobilization and consequently reluctant to act without French support. Arrested with other leaders on 12 March 1798, he was imprisoned 1798–1802, then went to France, where he competed unsuccessfully with Arthur *O'Connor for control of the émigré movement. In 1804 he moved to New York, where he had a successful legal career.

enclosure, the division of farmed, cleared, or reclaimed land into individual units surrounded by permanent boundaries. Most enclosure occurred during the 18th and early 19th centuries as part of the gradual modernization of Irish *agriculture, as 'improving' *landlords sought to reorganize the farms on their estates along more commercial and profitable lines. In contrast to England, where most 18th and 19th-century enclosure was sanctioned by act of Parliament, Irish enclosure was piecemeal, and relied extensively on the implementation of leasehold obligations agreed between individual landlords and their tenants. Enclosure Acts were passed for barely 28 parishes, mostly in the former English *Pale, between 1800 and 1840.

Enclosure tended to occur earlier in eastern districts such as the Pale, where it frequently incorporated the results of *engrossing*, or the consolidation of adjacent commonfield strips, undertaken from the 13th century onwards, to create characteristically irregular linear fields. In western districts most enclosure occurred over a shorter period in the first half of the 19th century, as landlords eradicated the *'rundale' system of farming. In both cases the consequence was the replacement of communal settlement and economic activity with a landscape of dispersed farms and fields held in severalty.

See FIELD SYSTEMS. LJP

Encumbered Estates Court, established under the Encumbered Estates Act of 1849 (12 & 13 Vic. c. 77), which superseded the similar act of 1848 (11 & 12 Vic. c. 48). It was designed to facilitate the sale of insolvent landed estates, whose owners had been bankrupted by the *Great Famine, and thereby inject new capital, predicted by the government to be British, into Irish agriculture. The court's three commissioners were empowered, on a creditor's petition, to enforce the sale of any land or lease encumbered with debts worth more than half the net annual rental. Creditors, including the petitioner, were entitled to bid for the land. The eventual purchaser could be awarded indefeasible title by the court. No compensation was offered to existing tenants for their improvements, and many new owners, particularly in the west of Ireland, used the opportunity of purchase to evict tenants. By 1859, over 5 million acres worth some £21 million had been sold by the court and its successor, the Landed Estates Court (established in 1858 under 21 & 22 Vic. c. 72). Contrary to the government's expectations, the vast majority of the 7,489 purchasers were Irishmen. Most of these came from the established landed and professional elites, and were not the commercially minded *arriviste* businessmen that convention suggests. The general tightening up of estate management in the 1850s was engaged in by both old and new owners, and was a consequence of changing economic conditions rather than of the operations of the court.

LJP

enech ('face') is the word used in Irish law from at least the 7th century, both by itself and in various combinations, for 'honour'. An insult and the payment required to compensate for it are *enechruicce* ('face-reddening'); another term for compensation for outraged honour is *enechlann* ('face-cleaning'). In the legal tract **Críth Gablach* there is an elaborate play on this notion of the face: seven things cause a man's *enech* to fall, such as not only committing an offence, but also failing to give a pledge to guarantee compensation, and then being satirized. The threat of satire was claimed to give the poets power through 'the law of the face'. There are likewise three things which wash the dirt of such offences from the face: the 'pumice-stone' of publicly admitting a fault, the 'water' of payment for any damage caused, and the 'towel' of penance according to a *penitential. A freeman's status is expressed by *lóg n-enech* ('the value of the face'). If he is killed, *lóg n-enech* or *díre* is paid to his kinsmen, both patrilineal and matrilineal, in proportion to their status and to their proximity to the dead man. Compensation for the killing, injury, or insult if the victim is one of a freeman's dependants, for example his wife, is fixed as a proportion of the freeman's *lóg n-enech*. A freeman's honour price varies from a very low value up to seven or more slave-women for a *king.

The importance of the concept of honour in early Irish law is illustrated by theft. Compensation for theft is divided into two parts: a payment to the owner of the thing stolen and a payment to the owner of the land or building from which it was stolen. The latter is fixed according to the man's *lóg n-enech*, full *lóg n-enech* if it is his house, and, if the thing was stolen from outside, diminishing fractions according to distance from the house. If, therefore, something is stolen from land owned by the owner of the article taken, the latter is entitled to both payments, for the thing stolen and for the place from which it was stolen. If, however, the article was deposited with someone else, the two payments will go to different people. It is also illustrated by the limits placed by *Críth Gablach* on a freeman's power to perform certain legal acts, such as entering into suretyship for another; he may do so only up to the value of his face.

TMC-E

engineering. In the late 18th century the extension of arable *farming encouraged the growth of foundries and engineering works making plough parts, harrows, and a range of other equipment, as well as ironwork for *flour mills, *breweries, and *distilleries (all of which used grain as their major raw material). The employment of English and Scottish millwrights in Ireland contributed to a high level of technical diffusion from the British engineering industry, so that by the 1830s it had become more convenient and cheaper to hire Irish foundry and engineering works to cast and fit up millwork.

A degree of regional specialization emerged; Wexford's early prominence as an agricultural machine manufacturing centre was a result of its location in one of the major tillage regions. *Dublin, at the hub of the *railway network, dominated railway engineering and ironwork for public works. Most of the major rail companies located their engineering and maintenance works in Dublin; the works of the Great Southern and Western railway at Inchicore (established in 1852) was by far the largest. *Belfast's engineering sector was initially influenced by the demand created by *linen bleaching and finishing. As linen spinning became mechanized a number of firms moved into supplying spinning and preparatory machinery and the number of engineering and foundry works in the city increased from four in 1825 to twelve in 1851. The extent of demand enabled a few Belfast firms to produce steam engines on a regular basis (notably Victor Coates and Rowan). During the second half of the 19th century, as Belfast built up a large trade exporting flax spinning machinery, a number of large firms engaged in machine building emerged, like Combe & Barbour (established in 1845), Mackie's, and Reynolds's. The other industries in and around the city also created a sustained demand for foundry and engineering work, differentiating the engineering sector in the north-east from the remainder of the country.

Cairns, J., 'Inchicore Works', *Railway Magazine*, 43 (1913)

McCutcheon, W., *The Industrial Archaeology of Northern Ireland* (1984)

AB

England. 'Accursed be the day ... when invaders first touched our shores. They came to a nation famous for its love of learning, its piety, its heroism [and] ... doomed Ireland to seven hundred centuries of oppression.' As this quotation from one of Daniel *O'Connell's speeches (1827) suggests, the relationship between 'England' and 'Ireland' is perceived by many as fraught with mutual suspicion and hostility. The preamble to the *constitution of Ireland (1937) speaks of 'the people of Eire, engaged in a heroic and unremitting struggle to regain the rightful independence of our nation'. *Notes for Teachers*, an official publication used up to the 1960s, referred to 'a race that has survived a millennium of grievous struggle and persecution'. The victors of the nationalist revolution of 1916–22, once in power, began to write their own history of the Irish nation. Like similar nationalist interpretations, however, it is open to the criticism that it fails to do justice to the complexities of Irish history and of Anglo-Irish relations.

Until the mid-12th century Ireland's links were more with Scotland and Wales than with England, though there was a short-lived *Viking kingdom of Dublin and York. It was not until well after 1066 that Ireland underwent its own Norman conquest (see ANGLO-NORMAN INVASION), an episode which led to a centuries-long involvement with the English monarchy. Henceforth England's relationship with Ireland was an uneasy mix of colony and *feudal lordship. Professor Rees Davies has shown how the rhetoric of lordship implied patriarchy and mutual obligation, in contrast with a 'two nation' rhetoric of colonialism, which implied the dominance of one nation over the other. English colonialism reached its highest point in the early 14th century. By 1366, however, it was on the defensive, as the Statute of *Kilkenny implied in its attempt to outlaw the spread of Irish practices among the English colonists (see GAELICIZATION; GAELIC REVIVAL). By the later 14th and 15th centuries feudal lordship had become the norm. Such Irish lords as Felim O'Toole and Teig O'Carroll looked to the English crown as their feudal lord for protection against their oppressive neighbours. Until 1541, when the Tudors established themselves as kings of Ireland, the lordship of Ireland was a mosaic of competing feudal lineages and groupings in which short-term survival counted for more than dreams of national independence.

The 16th century brought revolutionary changes, partly the consequence of Elizabethan sea power. With the backing of the 'Creoles' of the Dublin *Pale (to use a parallel from Benedict Anderson's analysis of the Latin American republics), Henry VIII was proclaimed king of Ireland. An Irish-style 'Tudor revolution in government' began which led to the renewal of colonial government. Slowly but inexorably the English common law was introduced throughout Ireland, together with a centralized royal administration in which the *county and the *sheriff replaced the 'country' and the clan chief. Irish customary law (brehon law) lost ground. In themselves these changes would have been revolutionary enough. They were accompanied, however, by radical religious change and in due course by a new wave of colonization. The *'Old English' colonists, still Catholic, had hoped to benefit from administrative and legal revolution. Their hopes were dashed by the success of the Protestant *Reformation in England and by the impact of the papal bull *Regnans in excelsis* (1570) which, by deposing Elizabeth, placed Old English loyalists in an impossible quandary. Ireland became caught up in the struggle of Reformation and *Counter-Reformation, a conflict which lasted until the battle of the *Boyne (1690) and beyond. Reformation was accompanied by the arrival of new English colonists, first in the *Munster plantation, next, after the defeat of *O'Neill and *O'Donnell, in the *Ulster plantation, and finally even in Leinster, as part of the *Cromwellian land settlement. (Scottish colonists also played a key role in the 'informal' plantation of Antrim and Down.)

The new colonists of the 16th and 17th centuries legitimized their presence by a racialist *mentalité*. Such figures as Edmund *Spenser, colonial administrator as well as poet, and Sir John *Davies, attorney-general of Ireland, had no doubt about the superiority of English civilization. Such views were strengthened by the widespread belief, especially among *puritans, that England was an 'elect nation'. But New English colonialism did not go unchallenged. The Catholic Old English lawyer Patrick *Darcy developed an ideology in which he appealed to Magna Carta and the concept of Ireland as an equal though separate kingdom under the British crown. In the 1640s Catholic insurgents, rising against what they saw as a parliament-based puritan despotism, set up the Confederation of Kilkenny (see CONFEDERATE CATHOLICS), which accepted the English monarch as head of state, provided due safeguards could be arrived at for the Catholic elite. Owen Roe *O'Neill, leader of the Gaelic Irish cause in Ulster, also supported this policy. The puritan revolution of the 1650s, however, led to the overthrow of the Catholic Old English, and the *Restoration of 1660 did little to restore their economic and political power. It was this group which supported *James II in his ill-fated attempt to recover his kingdom. '1689' was in many ways the Irish equivalent of the Jacobite rising in Scotland in 1715.

In Ireland, as in Scotland, the hope of the return of the Stuarts persisted well into the 18th century (see JACOBITISM). The Catholic episcopate in particular was closely linked with the Stuart monarchy. So also were the *Irish brigades which fought in British uniform ('England's cruel red') for the French crown throughout the mid-18th century. Such loyalty for the Stuarts indicates that support for 'the rightful independence of our nation' could coexist with acceptance of a three-kingdom framework. To the *'wild geese', a republican separatist future for Ireland would have been inconceivable.

A further twist was given to the complexity of Anglo-Irish relations by the rise of Creole-style nationalism among the Protestant 'New English' colonists. Modern assessments of early 18th-century *patriotism increasingly stress hesitations and hedged bets. Irish Protestants were initially more inclined to appeal to their inherited rights as Englishmen than to Irish history and precedent, and many saw a legislative union on Anglo-Scottish lines as an alternative means of securing proper representation. By the second half of the century, however, Protestant patriotism had become firmly committed to the defence of a specific conception of the Irish constitution, and had even begun to develop a cultural dimension. The *American Revolution provided the opportunity for the achievement of *legislative independence in the 'constitution of 1782', which came to symbolize a widened autonomy if not independence. The Protestant 'Creoles' had decided that they were now a kingdom not a colony. *'Grattan's parliament', however, proved to be a temporary arrangement, unable to survive the challenge of those for whom America and France provided examples of successful *republican government. The ideas of Tom Paine, the East Anglian-born radical, were popularized by the *United Irishmen. Hitherto there had been no republican tradition in Irish history. Traditional Irish ideology was based upon the monarchy of *Tara (see HIGH KINGSHIP). The 'wild geese' had fought to defend the absolutist monarchies of France and Spain. Instead the idea of an Irish republic now propagated by Protestant and Catholic middle-class radicals had its roots in the English puritan revolution of the 1640s, a paradox indeed.

The *insurrection of 1798, 'the Year of the French', ended in defeat for Irish republicanism. Victory went to the forces of the crown. But the colonists themselves suffered defeat when in 1800 the Act of *Union was forced through 'Grattan's parliament' by William Pitt in the teeth of *Orange opposition. Once again the relationship between England and Ireland shifted. Ireland was now fully represented in the Westminster parliament. A United Kingdom of Britain and Ireland had been brought into existence.

In constitutional theory, the Union was an alliance of equal partners. In practice it left in place a colonial-style situation in Ireland, whereby a landlord class looked to the Union as the basis of its political and economic ascendancy. An Anglicized Catholic middle class found itself excluded from power at both national and local levels, a situation which was alleviated only in part by the *Catholic Emancipation Act (1829). Government policy during the years of the *Great Famine of 1845–9 added to the grievances of Catholic Ireland. In retrospect Ireland seems to have been treated more as a colony than as a constituent part of the United Kingdom. (Today the term 'Holocaust' is being used to refer to the Great Famine. This may be unfair. 'Criminal irresponsibility' of the kind often said to have been displayed by some British generals at the Somme may be nearer the truth.)

Throughout the period of the Union, two models of the relationship between England and Ireland persisted. The first of these was that of the unionists, who looked upon their political power as an expression of religious, cultural, and in some cases racial, superiority. As the term '*Celt' came into prominence from mid-century onwards the Irish Celts were seen as a childlike, unpractical race, which would benefit from being ruled by the hard-headed Anglo-Saxons. Such views became part of a wider imperial ideology, adopted by Disraeli and the Conservative Party. A more sinister version of this racialist ideology, resting upon fear of *Fenian terrorism, looked upon the Irish as malevolent subhumans. The second model of Anglo-Irish relations looked to a return to the 'constitution of 1782'. It was this which lay behind O'Connell's *repeal programme, the ideas of Thomas *Davis and *Young Ireland, and the *home rule policies of Isaac *Butt and Charles

Stuart *Parnell. It was also implied in the vision of a 'dual monarchy' espoused by Arthur *Griffith and the first *Sinn Féin. When *Gladstone came to consider home rule as a possibility for Ireland, it was '1782' which he had in mind. However, from the unionist point of view, 'home rule' meant 'Rome rule' since any future Irish parliament, unlike the wholly Protestant 'Grattan's parliament', would have a built-in Catholic majority.

The conflict between these views, dual monarchy and colonialism, was still unresolved in 1914, despite the passing of the Home Rule Act. The constitutional position of Ulster remained uncertain. With the *rising of 1916, however, the future once more changed shape. Colonial-style retribution led to the creation of a new generation of martyrs. The result was to discredit home rule and to arouse a surge of sympathy for the republicans. With the rise of a new Sinn Féin and the *Anglo-Irish War, the cause of separatism became further entrenched. Although the *Anglo-Irish treaty of 1921 stipulated that leaders of the *Irish Free State should take an *oath of allegiance to the crown, the relationship between England and the Irish Free State was now one of constitutional equals. De *Valera's constitution of 1937 reduced the link between 'Eire' and the British *Commonwealth to the minimal gesture of *external association. In 1949 the *Republic of Ireland was formally declared.

De Valera referred to '*Éire' as the national territory, by which he meant the island of Ireland. In fact however Ireland was formally *partitioned in 1920 into a 26-county unit ('the Irish Free State') and a six-county unit (*'Northern Ireland'). Longstanding cultural differences between 'north' and 'south' were now crystallized by a political divide. The division was accentuated by the Free State's *neutrality during the *Second World War, by a drift towards republicanism, and by the strength of the Catholic church. In the north *evangelical Protestantism was dominant, together with a strident unionism which emphasized its loyalty to the crown. Whether this solution was forced upon 'Ireland' by 'England' or vice versa remains a matter for historical debate.

Partition in 1920 seemed an acceptable solution to the Irish problem. In fact, however, it was a difficulty deferred, and, during the radical decade of the 1960s, England and Ireland once more found themselves at loggerheads over the status of the Catholic minority in Northern Ireland. Familiar patterns reappeared: separatism in the shape of the provisional *IRA, constitutional home rule-style politics under the auspices of John Hume and the SDLP (*Social Democratic and Labour Party), and an uncompromising unionism which looked back to the Boyne and the Orangeism of the 1790s. The problems of Ulster proved to be no easier to solve in the 1980s than they were in the 1880s for Gladstone and Parnell.

The impossibility of reducing the Anglo-Irish relationship to a single formula is further illustrated in the complex history of Irish settlement in England. At one end of the spectrum may be placed the figure of Brendan Bracken (1901–58), born in Co. Tipperary, the son of a founder member of the GAA (*Gaelic Athletic Association), who, despite his 'Fenian' family background, became a confidant of *Churchill and member of his war cabinet. At the other stands the lonely figure of the IRA sleeper Ed O'Brien, who in 1996 blew himself up while carrying a bomb on a London bus. The flow and direction of Irish immigration also provides sharp contrasts. After 1945 for example it moved away from *Liverpool, now a depressed area, to London and Birmingham where jobs were more plentiful. A greater middle-class element was also detectable in this post-war immigration, compared to earlier movements.

The 'English-Irishry', like Anglo-Jewry, faced the challenges of assimilation. For many, a religious affiliation became the criterion of Irish ethnic identity, reinforced by attendance at a Catholic school or by living in Irish-dominated 'neighbourhoods' such as were to be found in Kilburn. But Catholicism as such was not a secure mark of Irish identity, and for second and third generations schools and churches became avenues of assimilation into a broader English Catholic identity in which Thomas More loomed larger than Thomas Moore. Those who reacted against what they saw as Anglocentric assimilation were likely to express themselves in 'Irish Studies' programmes provided by some universities or in supporting Ireland in sporting events such as the World Cup. The sports scene is complicated, however, by the fact that all, or almost all, members of Ireland's national football team are regular members of English teams, and that two at least in the 1994 World Cup were recognizably of mixed race. As England becomes multicultural and multiracial, the Anglo-Irish relationship will become even more complex. Clearly an assimilative process is at work, not least in the legal, civil service, medical, and academic professions. This is not to say however that 'the Troubles' in Northern Ireland have not cast a shadow over the life of the Irish community in England.

Over the past 800 years the relationship between Ireland and England has fluctuated. At the beginning of the 21st century a pattern has emerged in which England and the Republic of Ireland are partners within the *European Union. Culturally the two countries remain close. Irish novels, plays, and poetry find a ready audience in England, though the Irish ethnic minority has been slow to make its presence felt in the face of a prevailing anti-Irish sentiment, derived partly from long-standing 'racial' prejudice, and partly from understandable resentment against IRA terrorism. The Irish Republic is an independent nation. In contrast Northern Ireland has until recently been governed as a crown colony.

The need to secure a solution to the problem of Northern Ireland ensures that the future of the two countries will clearly remain closely linked. The 21st century may hold as many surprises as the 20th. For parallels we may well look to Scandinavia and the relationship between Sweden, Norway, and Denmark, or to Spain, where relations between Castile and Catalonia have been as 'fraught' as those between England and Ireland.

Curtis, L. P., *Anglo-Saxons and Celts* (1968)
Davies, R. R., 'Lordship or Colony?', in J. F. Lydon (ed.), *The English in Medieval Ireland* (1984)
Grant, A., and Stringer, K., *Uniting the Kingdom? The Enigma of British History* (1995)
Kearney, H. F., *The British Isles: A History of Four Nations* (1989)
McDonagh, Oliver, *States of Mind* (1992)

HK

English language. Together with Norman-*French, English first came into Ireland with the *Anglo-Norman invasion. Although its use declined with the *Gaelicization of large sections of the settler community, it maintained some currency in the *Pale and in the larger towns, as well as in two rural areas, Fingall (a district north of Dublin; see FINE GALL), and the baronies of *Forth and Bargy in Co. Wexford. This decline was reversed with the distribution of English speakers throughout most of the country during the *plantations (*c.*1550 onwards). Hiberno-English in its present state traces its development from the plantations, when large numbers of English settlers came over to Ireland as managers or tenants in estates and manorial houses.

From then on, the use of English became more widespread, helped by government policies, including the *penal laws, which ensured that the native Irish-speaking population came to regard their own vernacular, together with other elements of their culture, as symbols of failure. Other events confirmed this perception. The Act of *Union of 1800 enhanced the prestige and usefulness of English for those going over to Westminster. Daniel *O'Connell used English as his means of mass communication; the *national schools used English as the medium for instruction, and deliberately discouraged Irish. There was also the *Great Famine, in which so many monoglot speakers of Irish perished, and the ensuing rise in *emigration to countries in which English was the vernacular.

Today there are no monoglot speakers of Irish, even in those areas, known as **Gaeltachtaí*, in which Irish is the common medium of speech. The English language is the principal vernacular and the dialect is known as 'Hiberno-English', which is chiefly characterized by its conservatism (currently employing such archaic or obsolescent English words as 'cog', to cheat in an exam, or 'delph' for crockery), its wide appropriation of words from Irish (e.g. 'ommadhawn' for fool, 'gorsoon' for boy), its retention of older pronunciations (e.g. 'tae' for tea, the aspiration of words beginning with 'wh'), as well as the adoption of Irish sounds for the pronunciation of vowels and consonants (e.g. 'tree' for three). The range of verbal possibilities in Hiberno-English is also increased by its adoption of non-standard patterns, deriving from Irish, in its verbal system (e.g. 'I do be', to signal habituality or 'I was after getting married', which reflects the absence of the verb 'to have' in Irish).

See also LANGUAGE.

Bliss, A. J., *Spoken English in Ireland 1600–1740* (1979)
Dolan, T. P., *A Dictionary of Hiberno-English: The Irish Use of English* (rev. edn. 2004)
—— (ed.), 'The English of the Irish', Special Issue, *Irish University review*, 20 (1990)
—— and Ó Muirithe, Diarmaid, *The Dialect of Forth and Bargy, Co. Wexford* (1996)

TPD

English law, native Irish and, see LAW.

Enlightenment, an 18th-century international philosophical and cultural movement with Paris as its focus. *Philosophes* such as Voltaire and Montesquieu advocated social improvement through the application of scientific and rational principles to social, economic, and political problems, as well as freedom of conscience and religious toleration.

Enlightenment thought was diffused in Ireland through numerous channels. Growing literacy encouraged a demand for books; Voltaire and Montesquieu were widely read. Social gatherings of intellectuals discussed Enlightenment ideas. Travellers from Ireland to the Continent met *philosophes*. (Bishop *Hervey made a favourable impression on Voltaire.) *Presbyterian ministers and sons of Ulster businessmen who attended universities in Scotland, and Irish Catholic priests who studied in Paris, were thereby exposed to the Scottish and French Enlightenments respectively.

The Enlightenment most clearly affected Irish thinking in the areas of economic development and of the *architectural and visual arts. In the former, the *Royal Dublin Society and other bodies advocated economic progress on the basis of Enlightenment principles of agricultural reform and the reduction of trade barriers. In the latter, practitioners embraced the doctrine that artistic creation should enhance 'civilized' living and display moral purpose. The expansion of Dublin and other towns, and the construction of large country houses such as Russborough and Florence Court, provided opportunities for town planners, architects, painters, sculptors, and other artists to put Enlightenment aesthetics into practice.

The question of religious toleration was more problematic—even Voltaire regarded the *penal laws as necessary to check the potentially oppressive Catholic church—and the effects of the Enlightenment in this regard were ambivalent. The 'Protestant ascendancy' generally responded positively to the Enlightenment in its economic and artistic spheres, but supported the civil and religious disabilities under which Catholics and dissenters lived. At the same time, the Enlightenment stimulated calls for toleration, as a matter of principle, from Catholic and dissenting intellectuals who turned for inspiration increasingly to the works of Rousseau and the socio-political ideas surrounding American independence. Much Irish radicalism of the 1780s and 1790s derived from such late Enlightenment thought.

In its totality the influence of the Enlightenment was diverse and complex. Although scholars agree that it manifested itself in Ireland, they are less sure that there developed a specifically 'Irish' Enlightenment with 'national' features. The Enlightenment made little impact upon *Trinity College, Dublin, and it is debatable how much of the literature or *music of Ireland during this period can be regarded as 'enlightened'. Much more research is required before a comprehensive assessment can be attempted.

Porter, R., and Teich, M. (eds.), *The Enlightenment in National Context* (1981)

Yolton, J. W., et al. (eds.), *The Blackwell Companion to the Enlightenment* (1991)

DS

Enterprise of Ulster (1571–5), an attempt to colonize eastern Ulster by allocating the task to private individuals. The main entrepreneurs were Sir Thomas Smith and his son Thomas, who were granted North Down and the Ards, and Walter Devereux, earl of Essex, who received Co. Antrim. Smith, the queen's principal secretary and a leading political thinker, led the most innovative scheme, raising money through a joint-stock company and producing promotional literature. His son's force of 800 had dwindled to a mere 100 by the time he landed in the Ards. Meanwhile Sir Brian MacPhelim O'Neill, the local lord, burned places of shelter and fortification, forcing Smith to winter in Carrickfergus where his troops ran amok. They made little headway during 1573 and Smith junior was killed at Comber. Two subsequent expeditions achieved nothing.

Essex's much larger undertaking was financed by mortgaging his estates in England. By the time Essex arrived at Carrickfergus in August 1573 with 1,100 men, the Ulster Irish had united in opposition to colonization. He was tricked by Sir Brian, who had at first feigned submission, and then found himself in a protracted war against Sorley Boy *MacDonnell. In 1574 the queen sent Essex reinforcements and made him governor of Ulster. He ordered massacres of the Clandeboye O'Neills at Belfast in November 1574 and the MacDonnells on *Rathlin Island in July 1575. Essex's only achievement was the construction of a fort on the river Blackwater to contain the Tyrone O'Neills; he died in Ireland in 1576.

The Enterprise of Ulster was a costly and bloody episode which established no English *plantations. It destabilized Ulster unnecessarily and, because of its semi-autonomous status, got minimal support from the Dublin government.

HM

Eóganacht is the name given to a loose confederation of peoples claiming descent from a common ancestor, Eógan Mór, which provided kings of Munster from the beginnings of recorded history to the time of their overthrow by the *Dál Cais in the mid-10th century. Though the number of affiliated dynasties did not remain constant, at the height of its power the Eóganacht comprised six main groups scattered strategically throughout Munster. In the very west of the province, the Eóganacht Locha Léin were dominant, controlling a large tract of land around Killarney. Their nearest Eóganacht neighbours were the Eóganacht Raithlind who settled along the Lee valley, and further north the Eóganacht Glennamnach had their headquarters at Glanworth near Fermoy. It was over the rich, fertile lands of the Golden Vale that the remaining groups reigned supreme. The Eóganacht Airthir Chliach held sway over an area in East Limerick and Tipperary, while the Eóganacht Áine were centred near Knockainey, Co. Limerick. Finally, the Eóganacht Caisil, as the name suggests, ruled an expansive territory around *Cashel which had been accorded the status of the capital of the kingdom of Munster from the early historic period.

Control of Cashel, however, alternated between the various subgroups, including, until the 8th century, the Eóganacht Áine and the Eóganacht Airthir Chliach. Subsequently, in the person of *Cathal mac Finguine, the Eóganacht Glennamnach gained the kingship only to be usurped at a later date by the Eóganacht Caisil. Kings such as *Fedelmid mac Crimthainn, Cormac mac Cuillenáin, and Cellachán of Cashel ensured that the Eóganacht Caisil remained dominant for much of the 9th and 10th centuries.

Ultimately, however, it was the failure of one particular subgroup to gain absolute control of the kingship of Cashel which led to the downfall of the Eóganacht as a whole. In the absence of a dominant controlling power centre, the *Vikings succeeded in causing maximum disruption and indeed the *Uí Néill sought to interfere in Munster affairs on a number of occasions. Moreover, inherent Eóganacht disunity enabled a new force, Dál Cais, to move to the centre of Munster's political arena on the accession of Mathgamain mac Cennétig to the kingship in 964. It was to be more than a century until an Eóganacht king, Cormac *Mac Carthaig, was to rise to prominence again in Munster.

Ó Corráin, Donncha, *Ireland before the Normans* (1972)

MNíM

éraic, literally 'pay-out', was an early Irish term for the wergild paid to the agnatic kin of a man killed intentionally but not secretly. While *lóg n-enech* ('face-value', see *enech*) was paid to kinsmen, both patrilineal and matrilineal, in amounts varying according to the individual kinsman's status and his proximity to the dead man, the *éraic* was paid to the *derbfhine* (kin group) and was a fixed sum of seven *cumala* ('slave-women') or the equivalent. A client's lord was entitled to a third of the *éraic*. For a woman the definition of those who received *éraic* if she were killed depended on the status of her marital union. TMC-E

Érainn, a name given to one of the ancient peoples of Ireland, was extended to include the entire population of the island. The name is probably reflected in Greek *Iernoi* (later *Iernē*) and ultimately in Latin *Hibernia*, the oldest names recorded for Ireland in classical sources. It also appears as Ériu, a goddess who granted sovereignty to whomever she mated with. As a more specific ethnic name the Érainn are often equated with the Iverni, a tribe which Ptolemy located in Munster. In this more restricted meaning the term was applied to several *septs in Munster and when Érainn was extended to embrace northern tribes such as the *Dál Fiatach of Ulster, these were provided with a fictitious Munster origin. The coincidence of these Munster Érainn with the distribution of *ogam inscriptions indicates that they spoke Irish. The scope of the term varied, however, according to author, date, social status, and political agenda. In the *Táin, for example, the Fir Éireann ('men of Ireland') are contrasted with the *Ulaid ('Ulstermen'), yet annalistic entries from the same period speak of the whole 'island of the Érainn (Ireland)' and the genealogies of the Ulaid indicate that they too were of Érainn stock. In social terms, Érainn was employed to distinguish the common people of Ireland from the aristocracy, especially after the Érainn tribes of Munster were subjugated by the *Eóganacht dynasty of Cashel. By the 7th and 8th centuries the name was replaced by Goídel (*Gael) as the ethnic designation of the inhabitants of Ireland, although Érainn was retained to designate the island itself. JPM

erenach (O.Ir. *airchinnech*, 'head of an ecclesiastical settlement'), an office distinguishing the later medieval *church among the Gaelic Irish from the system obtaining among the English colonists. The erenach, a lay guardian of a parish church, was nominated by the bishop as headman of the family which had hereditary tenure of that church's lands. The emergence of *airchinnech* in the 9th-century *annals and its common occurrence thereafter is usually attributed to secularization of office before and during the age of the *Vikings, in an Irish ecclesiastical system supposedly dominated by *monasticism. Recently, however, this model has been questioned. It is proposed that the *airchinnech* as administrator of ecclesiastical temporalities and dependants is expressly recognized in 8th-century vernacular law and in Hiberno-Latin *canon law of about the same period, where he is often designated *princeps* ('head'). This official might or might not also be a priest or bishop and/or a conventional monastic abbot. If not himself in major orders, however, he was bound to provide for a pastoral ministry, whether resident or visiting, to the community dependent on his church. The office, in the early as in the later Middle Ages, was susceptible to dynastic control. CE

Eriugena, see JOHN SCOTTUS ERIUGENA.

Ervine, St John (1883–1971), writer and political publicist. A Belfast clerk who emigrated to London as a teenager, Ervine became active in the Fabian Society and repertory theatre and was a protégé and biographer of Bernard Shaw. He initially supported *home rule (on social reformist rather than nationalist grounds), denounced *Carson, and criticized Ulster Protestantism for its religious and political narrowness. After serving in the *First World War and witnessing the political upheavals of 1916–23, Ervine reverted to *unionism and combined a metropolitan literary career with praise for Ulster individualism and local values. His idiosyncratic official biography of James *Craig attacks 'Eirean' disregard for individual freedom. PM

escheator, the royal official responsible for lands which came into the king's hands on a temporary basis, by reason of forfeiture, minority of the heirs of a tenant-in-chief (see WARDSHIP), or vacancy in a bishopric. He held *inquisitions and administered the lands, either in person or by appointing custodians, accounting for the revenues at the *exchequer. In the 13th century the income of the escheatry was substantial and the escheator was a senior member of the king's *council. The importance of the office declined in the later Middle Ages, due to the shrinking of the area under the control of the Dublin government, and the duties of the office were often performed by deputy. During the 14th century there were several attempts to abolish the office and to have its functions carried out by the *sheriff in each county. PhC

Essex, Robert Devereux, 2nd earl of (1567–1601), a royal favourite who offered the queen his services after Hugh *O'Neill's victory at the *Yellow Ford. His appointment as lord lieutenant, with an army of over 16,000, aroused popular expectations of success. The key, however, was to be a seaborne expedition to Lough Foyle. When Essex arrived in April, this force was not ready and the English privy council never made available the necessary shipping. Instead he marched southwards winning castles, receiving submissions, and taking hostages. Subordinate commanders, Harrington and Clifford, were defeated. Essex was constantly looking over his shoulder at events at court. Elizabeth rescinded his appointments and criticized the southern expedition as pointless. Ordered northwards against O'Neill, Essex instead contemplated transporting half the army to England to coerce its unsupportive government. Essex foolishly agreed to meet O'Neill alone at the ford of Bellaclinthe on the Louth–Monaghan border, and later patched up a ceasefire. On 24 September he suddenly left his Irish command without permission in a vain attempt to regain royal favour, only to find himself put under house arrest when he reached court. He left Irish affairs teetering on the edge of collapse. Essex never regained royal favour and was executed following an attempted *coup d'état* in 1601. HM

estate villages, the conventional term used by historians and geographers to describe rural settlements founded, refounded, or otherwise modernized by individual *landlord families and wholly or predominantly owned by them. It is estimated that over 600 villages, and 150 towns, were created or improved in this way between *c.*1700 and *c.*1845, and of these approximately one-third were of medieval or *plantation origin. The majority were located in a zone extending from south-east Ulster, through the east midlands, to north-east Munster, and displayed considerable variation in size, design, and formality. Some, such as Castlewellan, Co. Down, or Westport, Co. Mayo, were planned by their owners on broadly Renaissance principles as architectural 'set pieces'. Many more were rebuilt incrementally using building leases and tenant capital, with landlord investment confined to the provision of markets or other utilities. Motivations were complex: improved market facilities enhanced rents and the landlord's control over the local economy; the use of a fashionable architectural repertoire reaffirmed his elite peer-group status; while the demonstration of his ability to transform a geographical locality affirmed his belief in the permanence of his presence in a plural and divided society. LJP

ether drinking was introduced to Ireland in the 1840s, primarily for its supposed medicinal benefits. Ether was also occasionally taken recreationally. By the 1870s its use was more widespread. In some areas ether was now used solely as an intoxicant, often mixed with alcohol. During the 1880s its use became endemic in Cos. Londonderry and Tyrone, encouraged by a decline in the availability of cheap liquor. A select committee examined the problem in 1890–1. From December 1890 ether was scheduled as a poison and became less readily available. In 1923 ether drinking became a criminal offence in Northern Ireland. NG

ethnic music. The preservation and collection of *music in Ireland was originally conceived as an antiquarian enterprise and as an act of cultural redemption. Such motives prompted Edward Bunting to publish his *General Collection of the Ancient Irish Music* in 1797. This volume drew in turn from material which Bunting had annotated at the *Belfast Harp Festival (1792) and from other collectors. The historical significance of this publication was twofold. First, it entered a decisive claim for music as an integral part of Gaelic culture, and second, it proved the frail but unbroken continuity between that culture (in terms of Celtic antiquities) and the circumstances of the present day. Bunting's collection undoubtedly inspired the creation and publication of Thomas Moore's *Irish Melodies* (1808–34), in which some of the airs collected by Bunting were both romanticized and politicized by dint of their association with Moore's verse. Two further collections were issued by Bunting in 1809 and 1840, and throughout the 19th century his practice of collection and publication of the ethnic corpus of melody (vocal and instrumental) was widely emulated.

In the post-Famine period, it was George *Petrie above all others who added significantly to this corpus, having amassed about 1,000 airs hitherto unrecorded. Petrie published a volume of melodies in 1855, and an edition of his entire collection, prepared by Charles Villiers Stanford, appeared between 1902 and 1905. Other notable collectors include Samuel Forde, John Pigot, Peter Goodman, and Patrick Weston Joyce.

This plenitude of ethnic melody was not unproblematic in the history of Irish music. The cult of musical preservation, frequently identified by ideologues of Gaelic culture in terms analogous to the preservation of the Irish language, patently inhibited the growth of original (art) music in Ireland. In addition, the use of the ethnic repertory as an intelligencer of political sentiment entailed a remarkable degree of cultural stasis, by which 'Irish music' and 'folk melody' were judged to be synonymous. This was notably the case in the verbally dominated ambience of the Celtic revival. In the 20th century, the renewed publication of Irish airs, especially by the London-based Irish Folk Song Society, and the systematic archival recordings undertaken by Radio Telefís Éireann, the folklore departments of the universities, and the Irish Traditional Music Archive, have added significantly to an awareness of the corpus of ethnic music. The phenomenal revival of interest in this music as a living tradition since the early 1960s (exemplified by the unprecedented success of music festivals, summer schools, and individual exponents) attests to the cultural significance of the ethnic repertory in contemporary Ireland. The inherent interest of this repertory has at last transcended its symbolic resonances of political and cultural autonomy. The widespread (although not complete) failure of this vast resource to integrate with the techniques and strategies of art music is likewise undeniable.

Breathnach, Breandán, *Folk Music and Dances of Ireland* (1989)

HW

Eucharistic Congress (1932), the 31st in a series of international congresses organized by the Catholic church for the promotion of devotion to the Blessed Sacrament. Held in Dublin 22–6 June 1932 it was sponsored by the archbishop of Dublin, Edward Byrne, and presided over by the cardinal legate, Lorenzo Lauri. The high point of the event was the celebration of mass in Phoenix Park before a crowd of over 1 million persons. The event marked a great fusion of Catholic and national pride and probably made a contribution to healing *Civil War wounds. TO'C

European Community, see EUROPEAN UNION.

European Union (EU) (initially known as the European Economic Community and later as the European Community), a grouping of West European countries formed in 1957 with the objective of economic and political integration. Ireland was admitted in 1973 along with Britain and Denmark. There had long been interest in the prospect of membership as a means of escape from economic stagnation and dependency on the British market. By the late 1950s both *Fianna Fáil and *Fine Gael were committed to seeking membership and willing to accept the diminution of *neutrality that it was expected to involve.

An initial application made jointly with Britain, Denmark, and Norway was rejected in 1962. With the departure of President de Gaulle of France from the political scene in 1969, however, the main obstruction was removed and admission swiftly negotiated. A referendum in 1972 resulted in a vote of five to one in favour of membership.

Membership of the Community brought clear benefits to Ireland. The Common Agricultural Policy boosted Irish farming through production subsidies and higher prices. Industry too gained from the diversification of markets. There was also a major inflow of funds from the European social and regional programmes as well as currency support from the Cohesion Fund. Although Ireland's application for membership was dictated by dependence on the British economy, the effect of membership was sharply to reduce that dependence. Emblematic of this was Ireland's entry to the European Monetary System in 1979 which, with Britain's refusal to participate, ended the 150-year link with *sterling.

Ireland was among the more willing signatories of both the Single European Act of 1988 and the Maastricht treaty of 1992, both of which deepened economic and political integration within the Community. In January 1999 Ireland was in the first group of EU members to move towards European monetary union by adopting the euro.

In the short term this accelerated Ireland's already dramatic growth rates of the time as inward investment increased. Longer-term questions remained, however, about loss of national control over interest rates and the potential impact on investment if and when the United Kingdom also entered the 'eurozone'.

Keatinge, P. (ed.), *Ireland and European Community Membership Evaluated* (1991)

Maher, D. J., *The Tortuous Path: The Course of Ireland's Entry into the EEC 1948–73* (1986)

NMacQ

evangelicalism. Based on the 'evangel' or gospel message, evangelicalism is the generic term for a wide-ranging religious movement that transcended national, denominational, and theological boundaries. It was most often characterized by an emphasis on justification by faith, the Bible as the chief source of religious authority, the centrality of conversion and the New Birth, the importance of religious experience, and the doctrine of assurance of sins forgiven.

Perhaps the most important factor in evangelicalism's international spread in the 18th century is the way in which its formidable religious activism and organizational pragmatism could be adapted to different social and political conditions in a variety of geographical locations. Its roots in Ireland go back to the voluntary religious societies created by committed Protestants in Dublin and elsewhere in the early 18th century. But it was in the 1740s, with the arrival of itinerant evangelists such as John *Cennick, John *Wesley, and George Whitefield, that its conversionist zeal was first manifested. Thereafter, the story is a complicated one, for evangelicalism had the capacity to revive old settlements of European pietists, such as the *Palatines, stimulate missionary zeal among the established Protestant denominations, act as the catalyst in the formation of new religious movements such as *Methodism, and bring forth a vast array of voluntary religious societies for the proclamation of the gospel and the reformation of manners.

Evangelicalism benefited from the political uncertainties of the 1790s and through the so-called *Second Reformation launched a sustained offensive in the 1820s to convert Irish Catholics. But over the course of the 19th century its greatest gains were confined to the north of the country, where conversionism produced a great religious drama in the form of the Ulster *revival of 1859. Evangelical religion undoubtedly played a part in stiffening the anti-Catholic resolve of a significant proportion of Irish Protestants and has contributed much to the distinctive religious and political culture of Northern Ireland from 1920 onwards. Although the religious zenith of evangelicalism is probably past, new forms of enthusiastic popular Protestantism, from pentecostalism to charismatic renewal, continue to enliven the religious landscape of early 21st-century Ireland.

There is a sense in which 'evangelicalism', as opposed to 'evangelicals', is a potentially misleading term, for its adherents are not easily reduced to a particular religious typology. Its boundaries include bellicose, anti-Catholic pulpit politicians as well as pious dispensers of manifold charities: some evangelicals were ardent Calvinists, others were equally ardent Arminians; some were hard and sectarian, others were inclusive and internationalist; and some were rigid denominationalists while others thought denominationalism to be the scourge of 'vital religion'.

Evangelicalism, among contemporaries and historians alike, has evoked strong opinions. Opponents throughout its history have claimed that it elevated enthusiasm far above reason and that it disturbed churches, communities, and families with fanciful notions and socially divisive doctrines. Some historians, equally, have seen it as a pernicious religious movement of counter-enlightenment, while others have drawn attention to its influence in expanding the sphere of religious activity open to the laity, including women and children, and to its admirable, if selective, social conscience. What is not in dispute is its characteristic activism, which reshaped the lives of those who committed themselves to it and led to the expansion of a zealous form of Protestantism throughout the North Atlantic world and beyond in the 18th and 19th centuries. In the words of Francis Newman, himself a committed evangelical with *Plymouth Brethren associations in Dublin in the 1820s, though later a freethinker, religious enthusiasm may be despised, but few dispute its power.

Bowen, D., *History and the Shaping of Irish Protestantism* (1995)

Hempton, D., and Hill, M., *Evangelical Protestantism in Ulster Society 1740–1890* (1992)

DNH

eviction, the physical expulsion by *landlords of tenants from rented property. Normally this was done without their agreement and after serving them with either a civil ejectment process (usually for non-payment of rent or overholding) or a notice to quit (for lease infringements or to terminate an annual tenancy). From 1846 the Irish Constabulary (see ROYAL IRISH CONSTABULARY) made returns of evictions carried out after due legal process and recorded 117,000, affecting approximately 587,000 people, between 1846 and 1887. Other contemporary estimates put the total figure (including voluntary surrenders) at twice this number. The rate of evictions varied regionally and annually and mirrored agrarian crises such as the *Famine and the *Land War. Connacht and Munster consistently experienced the highest incidence. The greatest number, 70,000, occurred between 1846 and 1853, when perhaps a quarter of a million people were permanently evicted, as landlords sought through widespread clearances to rid their estates of pauperized smallholders. The ruthlessness of many of these Famine evictions, and their miserable and often fatal consequences for the tenants, appalled contemporary observers and left an enduring legacy of hatred in the countryside. Arguably, the power to evict was an inevitable concomitant of a land system based on great tenanted estates, but the number and manner of evictions during and after the Famine became a *cause célèbre* in the debate over the land question in the later 19th century. LJP

exchequer, the office headed by the treasurer which dealt with the receipt and payment of royal revenues and the auditing of accounts. First mentioned by name in 1200, in the following centuries it grew in size and complexity and came to consist of two departments. The exchequer of receipt dealt with sums paid in by officials and persons owing money to the crown, and with the disbursement of money on the king's behalf. After the financial scandals of the 1280s (see TREASURER AND TREASURY) it was reconstituted, with two chamberlains and the treasurer's clerk each keeping independent records of receipts and payments to obviate fraud. In the exchequer of account, accounts of *sheriffs and other officials were audited by the barons of the exchequer and enrolled on the *pipe rolls. The barons also heard pleas relating to royal financial interests and cases involving exchequer officials. Despite periodic attempts at reform, the barons were often occupied in the investigation of the misdeeds of other exchequer officials and of sheriffs and other local officers responsible for royal money.

In addition to the barons and chamberlains, the staff of the exchequer included clerks who wrote the pipe and *memoranda rolls and other records; the chancellor of the exchequer who was responsible for the exchequer seal; and the marshal, to whose custody persons might be committed until they had made arrangements for the payment of money owing to the king. PhC

Exeter Hall, London, the headquarters of the militantly anti-Catholic Protestant Association, and later of the Society for Irish Church Missions (see SECOND REFORMATION).

Explanation, Act of (1665), passed by the Irish parliament to resolve the problems created by the Act of *Settlement. Grantees under the *Cromwellian land settlement were required to surrender one-third of their holdings, though *Orrery and other prominent figures were exempted. The land surrendered was used to compensate those displaced by proprietors restored under the Act of Settlement or by direct royal grants, and to pay arrears owed to former royalist officers, the details being worked out by a second court of claims sitting 1666–9.

external association, the idea that Ireland would be associated with, but not a member of, the British *Commonwealth. It was devised by de *Valera as the basis for the Irish proposals during the negotiation of the *Anglo-Irish treaty, formed the basis of his alternative to the treaty proposals, *Document No. 2, and later found expression in his *External Relations Act. The concept of external association was influential in Commonwealth history and was subsequently adopted by newly independent states, notably India, as a way of reconciling their different history and traditions with Commonwealth membership. DMcM

External Relations Act, one of two linked pieces of legislation which de *Valera rushed through the *Dáil during the crisis caused by the abdication in December 1936 of King Edward VIII. The Constitution Amendment Act abolished the remaining legislative, executive, and constitutional functions of the monarch in the internal affairs of the *Irish Free State. However the External Relations Act confirmed his role in external affairs. As long as the Free State was associated with the other *Commonwealth states, the king—recognized by them as 'the symbol of their co-operation' and acting on their behalf for the purposes of diplomatic and consular appointments and the conclusion of international agreements—was authorized to act for the Free State for similar purposes 'as and when advised by the Executive Council'.

The External Relations Act, a variant of de Valera's theory of *external association first set out in *Document No. 2, was unaffected by the 1937 *constitution of Ireland. It was repealed in 1948 when Ireland left the Commonwealth.
DMcM

faction and feuding between rival magnates seems almost synonymous with late medieval politics and administration. English local government was supervised and discharged by officials appointed by the crown, but in practice social cohesion, and thus effective government, rested chiefly on the network of *feudal ties between landlord and tenant, along with the less formal relationships (*'bastard feudalism') that had developed between magnates and their followers whereby the lord upheld the interests of his dependants in return for their service and support. Thus the rule of the provinces was commonly divided between competing magnate affinities. And particularly in a turbulent *frontier society such as Ireland, a magnate's influence and protection was often far more effective than resort to law, since the king's courts were ineffective against violence and disorder from Gaelic Ireland.

Medieval historians have long debated whether bastard feudalism was a generally positive or negative influence on politics and society. The consensus is now that strong kings capable of controlling the magnates could use their bastard feudal connections as an informal alternative system of law enforcement while curbing undesirable features like maintenance (illegal outside interference in lawsuits) and intimidation. In Ireland, however, government was even more dependent on the nobles since the king was almost invariably absent, the Dublin administration's resources were far scantier, and border defence against Gaelic chiefs was a much more pressing priority. Thus faction and feuding were more pervasive and disruptive than in late medieval England.

Major factional conflict included the *Talbot–Ormond feud and the later dispute between *Ormond's Lancastrian son James Butler, 5th earl (1452–61), and York's retainer Thomas FitzGerald, recognized as 7th earl of *Kildare in 1454. The original cause of the latter was possession of ancestral FitzGerald manors in Co. Kildare, but the dispute soon became embroiled in the wider dynastic struggle between Lancaster and York (see WARS OF THE ROSES). Broadly, the Yorkists retained control of the lordship with the support of the two FitzGerald earls of Desmond and Kildare until Henry Tudor's accession. The Butlers supported an unsuccessful Lancastrian invasion in 1462, but thereafter they were effectively leaderless until the 1490s, when another feud began between the 8th earl of Kildare (1478–1513) and James Ormond. Meanwhile factional opposition to Kildare focused on the Meath gentry led by Philip Bermingham and Bishop William Sherwood of Meath; but one reason for Kildare's strong rule after 1496 was the success of Henry VII's settlement in curbing factionalism. The lordship remained peaceful until the accession of a resident Butler earl after 1515 prompted a recurrence of the Geraldine–Butler feud.

The continued existence of Geraldine and Butler networks dents the notion that early 16th-century Ireland was divided into two separate ethnic zones. Factionalism, originating in the pragmatic principle of 'the enemy of my enemy is my friend', was sustained by marriage and *fosterage and underpinned by *coyne and livery in such a way as to unite Gaelic Irish and Anglo-Irish aristocrats into a single political system. The pervasiveness of factionalism is revealed in the allegiance of the MacDonnell *gallowglasses to pro-Geraldine families whereas the *MacSweeneys always served the Butler interest.

The system's continued importance is exemplified by its perpetuation even after the defeat of the *Kildare rebellion. Gaelic Irish lords from both factions united in the *Geraldine League. They hoped to re-establish the status quo ante after Manus *O'Donnell, from a traditionally pro-Butler lordship, gained control of young Gerald, 11th earl of Kildare. Lord Leonard *Grey, the boy's uncle, defeated this coalition but found that he could not rule effectively without the system. He attempted to rehabilitate earlier Geraldine leaders only to fall foul of the Butlers. *St Leger attempted to rule regardless of faction by promoting constitutional relationships with the crown through *surrender and regrant and by bribing the elite with cheap leases of crown lands. To promote stability on the cheap Kildare was allowed to return from exile in 1555 but the following year *Sussex arrived as governor intending to rule with the support of the earl of Ormond and his chief clients, the earls of Thomond and Clanricard. Kildare orchestrated Sussex's failure, encouraging his old allies to frustrate the *Laois-Offaly plantation and promoting the cause of his kinsman Shane *O'Neill at court.

Although Lord Deputy *Sidney defeated Shane, he favoured the Geraldines in general. He tried to clamp down on Ormond and to support the earl of Desmond after the battle of *Affane (1565), while simultaneously forcing both earls to disarm their retainers by abolishing coyne and livery. Ormond's credibility was rocked by the participation of his brothers in the first *Desmond rebellion and by the Clanricard revolts but he regained his reputation by quelling the second Desmond rebellion. The earl of Desmond and his affinity was destroyed in this war while the earl of Kildare was discredited and neutered by the *Baltinglass affair. Essentially Ormond was now a factional leader without opponents and more hindrance than help to incoming governors. The nationwide alliance formed by Hugh *O'Neill gave Ormond a new lease of life in the 1590s, but the system's *raison d'être* had gone, as had the supporting apparatus of coyne and livery.

In the 17th century New English factions sprang up around Richard *Boyle and Lord *Mountnorris but these existed within the fabric of the civil society fashioned by the expanding state and depended more on access to land, office, and pensions than on military might. It might be worth investigating, however, whether the troubles of the Catholic Confederation (see CONFEDERATE CATHOLICS) were in any sense a recrudescence of the earlier Geraldine–Butler rivalry.

Ellis, S. G., *Tudor Ireland: Crown, Community and the Conflict of Cultures, 1470–1603* (1985)
Hicks, Michael, *Bastard Feudalism* (1995)

SGE/HM

faction fighting, between rival groups who met at *fairs, *patterns, and other venues to engage in pitched battles, emerged as a major problem in the early 19th century, until largely, though not wholly, suppressed by the new Irish Constabulary (see ROYAL IRISH CONSTABULARY) in the 1830s. It remains unclear whether this sudden visibility reflects new official attitudes to public order or an actual intensification of conflict. The latter, equally, might be attributed to increasing social tension, or alternatively to the breakdown of conventions (including possibly a degree of upper-class patronage) that had previously kept violence within acceptable limits. The feuds of rival factions, sometimes extending over years, have generally been interpreted as recreational violence, comparable to that of rival groups of football supporters today. But one of the best known such conflicts, between the *Caravats and Shanavests, has been shown to have been based on rural class conflict. In the same way, the frequent and often bloody clashes between Ormond and Liberty Boys recorded in mid-18th-century Dublin, pitting the Catholic butchers of the Ormond market against the Protestant weavers of the Liberties, belong at least partly to the history of *religious conflict.

fairs and markets reflect different patterns of economic activity. A market relies on a settled pattern of trade with an urban infrastructure and a volume of exchange sufficient to maintain its regular, usually weekly, occurrence. A fair by contrast is seasonal, needs little by way of infrastructure, and is often highly specialized. Within the context of the Irish economic structure fairs were more prominent than markets. Early Irish literature records the existence of a number of fairs, such as that at *Tara (held up to 1800) or that at Glendalough, which were often associated with major political events or religious sites. Throughout the Middle Ages there were smaller fairs associated with parochial centres which were held on the patronal feast day. The tradition of holding fairs on the saints' feast days and on one or two of the following days existed by the 16th century, when evidence for such events becomes clearer and merchants from the *Pale travelled to the larger fairs in Gaelic Ireland, and continued into the 19th century.

With the spread of royal authority in the late 16th and early 17th centuries landowners began to take out royal grants of rights to hold markets and fairs, which allowed them to charge tolls. In 1684 503 fairs were recorded as operating, almost half in the more commercialized eastern province of Leinster. By the 1770s over 3,000 fairs were operational but just over a quarter were located in Leinster, reflecting both wider commercialization and the growing importance of regional economies. Many of these fairs grew up by custom and in 1852 37 per cent of all fairs were operating without patents. The first half of the 19th century saw a contraction in the number of fairs, with only 1,297 being recorded in 1852. By 1890 this had contracted yet further to 793.

Fairs were, in the main, seasonal events. Most centres had two or more fairs a year, each of which fulfilled different roles, although over the 19th century smaller centres came to have fewer fairs, most being concentrated in the larger towns. Most important were the livestock fairs, many of which developed in the 18th century with the increased specialization of cattle rearing and dairying, the best known being that at *Ballinasloe. These occurred in May and June for the setting of animals for fattening and in October and November for slaughter. *Hiring fairs were important in the north-west of the country.

Over the 19th century attempts were made to regulate fairs, which were often seen as unruly and sometimes riotous. The most famous of these times of carnival, *Donnybrook fair in Dublin, was suppressed in 1867. A series of enactments, beginning with the 1847 Markets and Fairs Clause Act and followed by the *Local Government Acts of 1872 and 1898, regulated fairs more carefully. By abolishing tolls and regulating weights and measures this legislation removed some of the most common sources of friction.

In contrast to fairs, markets reflect a more established pattern of economic activity. Settler landlords in the early 17th century, anticipating a significant growth in the economy, took out grants for over 500 markets. However, the attraction of cheap land in the surrounding countryside made it difficult to establish market towns, and most markets remained small or disappeared altogether. The development of a more internally specialized regional economy created a greater need for market towns from the late 17th century and inland markets grew at the expense of port towns. This was complemented by the expansion of *road building in the late 18th and early 19th centuries which linked market towns into a trading network. From the early 18th century, meanwhile, improving *landlords began to see the growth of markets as an important part of the improvement of their estates. They invested heavily in the infrastructure required, building market houses and laying out market squares as part of the replanning of their estate towns.

O'Flanagan, P., 'Markets and Fairs in Ireland, 1600–1800: An Index of Regional Growth', *Journal of Historical Geography*, 11 (1983)

RG

famine has afflicted societies since the beginning of history. It may be defined as a persistent failure in food supplies over a prolonged period. It is something experienced by society, whereas starvation is something that affects individuals. During famines more people are likely to die of famine-related diseases than from starvation. The causes are complex. Adverse weather conditions (drought, excessive rain, intense cold) at crucial times, effects of war (scorched earth policies, the provisioning of armies, disruption of trade), pestilence and disease: all these individually or in combination may be to blame.

Famine is generally perceived as the result of a failure of food supplies, typically arising from the Malthusian pressure of population on resources. However some analysts, following the Indian economist Amartya Sen, argue that famine is less commonly caused by an absolute shortage of food than by the lack of 'entitlements'—that is, the existence of large numbers of persons who do not possess the means either of producing food or of acquiring it through purchase or through transfer payments sanctioned by the state or by custom. Famine thus becomes a product of political and social structures, rather than of neutral economic forces.

In Ireland over a period of six centuries from 1300 to 1900 there were up to 30 episodes of severe famine. Between 1290 and 1400 there were around a dozen, mostly clustering in the decades before and including the Great European Famine of 1315–17. Another dozen or so occurred between 1500 and 1750. After 1750 there were several periods of acute regional shortages, culminating in the *Great Famine of 1845–9.

The famines experienced in Ireland over the centuries illustrate their nature both as event and structure. Bad weather in 1294–6 and 1308–10, for example, damaged grain crops, resulting in many deaths. In 1315–17 wet weather produced devastating famine throughout Europe, exacerbated in the Irish case by Edward *Bruce's scorched earth policy. Heavy rains destroyed crops in 1330–1 and the price of wheat and oats rose manyfold. A century later in 1433 a severe famine led to 'the summer of slight acquaintance'. In 1504–5 continual rain and storms ruined crops, and cattle disease decimated livestock. The 17th century was also heralded by bad weather, famine, and disease. The *rising of 1641 ravaged crops and precipitated famine. Two famines in the 18th century, 1728–9 and 1740–1, caused great suffering. The famine of 1740 is noteworthy as the first potato crisis; in terms of mortality rates, it may have been greater than the Great Famine of 1845–9. The latter earns the sobriquet because it was the last and best remembered. But for 'this great calamity', it is doubtful that Ireland would be regarded as more famine-prone than other European countries.

Crawford, E. M. (ed.), *Famine: The Irish Experience 900–1900* (1989)

EMC

Farmers' Party, a political party that appeared before the general election of 16 June 1922. It emerged as the political wing of the Irish Farmers' Union, which had been formed in 1919. With 7.8 per cent of the vote (seven seats) in 1922 and 12.1 per cent (fifteen seats) in 1923, it was a sizeable bloc in the *Dáil and was generally supportive of the *Cumann na nGaedheal government. Its share of the vote dropped in the elections of June and September 1927 (to 8.9 and 6.4 per cent, eleven and six seats, respectively). Following the second 1927 election its leader entered the government and much of its support base moved to Cumann na nGaedheal, though its survivors contested the 1932 general election (2.1 of the vote, three seats) and were eventually absorbed by the National *Centre Party.

The party represented the interests in particular of the larger commercially oriented farmers of the east and south, but was divided on the question of tariff policy (a vital one for farmers), having both *protectionist and free trade wings. It was pro-treaty on the constitutional issue, and its leader, Denis Gorey, defected to Cumann na nGaedheal in 1927 when plans for a merger with that party came to nothing. His successor, Michael Heffernan, became a parliamentary secretary in 1927. JC

farming began in Ireland around 3800 BC. Archaeological evidence suggests that *cattle, *sheep, and *pigs were kept and that cereals have been cultivated since earliest times. Other crops and animals have been introduced at later dates, for example *horses and *flax in the *Bronze Age, *poultry in the *Iron Age, *hay in the medieval period, and *potatoes in the 16th century. New farming methods have also been developed or introduced throughout the millennia. It is probably best to see these as increasing available options for farmers rather than as a simple progression, where a new method immediately rendered earlier techniques obsolete. Some techniques, such as the use of narrow, steep-sided cultivation ridges, which were in use by 2500 BC, are still sometimes found today.

Early literary sources show that by the early medieval period, a stratified, settled agricultural society was well established. Prestige was measured by the number and quality of cattle a farmer owned, but possession of horses and especially the ability to make up a plough team were also important indicators of status. The *Anglo-Normans made a major impact on farming practices. Farm implements, particularly ploughs, changed greatly, and implements such as scythes were introduced. During the late medieval and early modern periods, increasing trade led to the introduction of larger cattle, horses, and other types of livestock, and change of all sorts accelerated in the early 18th century. The foundation of the Dublin Society (see ROYAL DUBLIN SOCIETY) in 1731 can be seen as marking the beginning of this period of great change, which was documented in increasing detail by contemporaries. Most of these were highly critical of farming practices in common use. It was alleged that implements were crude and inefficient, crops low yielding and weed infested, rotations minimal or non-existent, and ground cropped to exhaustion. Animals were claimed to be generally unimpressive in size, breeding uncontrolled, and care and management negligent. Modern historians have argued that these criticisms failed to take into account great variations in practice, related to differences in farm size and regional conditions. Arthur *Young, for example, visited farms in Co. Tipperary during the 1770s which were huge even by international standards, while in other parts of Ireland, and particularly in Connacht and Ulster, farming was done on tiny holdings which could barely provide a subsistence living for their occupiers.

Contemporary commentators also lacked awareness of the limits which size of holding, labour supply, and lack of capital put not only on farmers' ability to make large-scale systemic changes, but also on the potential value of such 'improvements'. Common farming practice required heavy labour inputs, but where these were available the systems followed were often remarkable more for their refinement and adaptability than for their crudity. Spade tillage, or the use of sickles for harvesting grain, for example, allow minute adjustments in response to varying conditions within a field, of a kind which are impossible using mechanized techniques. Evidence for the relative efficiency of 'common' systems can be found in the massive exports of Irish farm produce during the early 19th century, which led to Ireland being described as the granary of Britain.

By the mid-19th century many Irish farmers, responding to changing market conditions, and in particular to competition from North American imports, were turning away from crop production towards livestock farming. This trend accelerated greatly after the *Great Famine, when the sharp decline in the availability of cheap agricultural labour made more capital-intensive livestock farming increasingly attractive. The movement away from *tillage has continued almost uninterrupted until the present day. Paradoxically, the swing away from arable farming coincided with the period of increasing mechanization of farming methods, made possible both by the importation of new machinery, and by the local production of implements in a growing number of foundries (see IRON). Older, labour-intensive methods increasingly gave way to the standardized techniques developed by international experimentation. The complex manual techniques used to prepare marginal land for cultivation began a particularly rapid decline, as the areas concerned, cleared of people by heavy Famine mortality and emigration, were converted by landlords to large-scale sheep farming. During the second half of the 19th century, the number of sheep in Ireland more than doubled.

In richer lowland areas, cattle farming expanded greatly. Throughout Ireland as a whole, the number of cattle increased by over 60 per cent, to 4,673,323 in 1900. The activities of bodies such as the *co-operative movement and the Department of *Agriculture and Technical Instruction led to the organization of *dairy production in creameries, and by the early 20th century Ireland had become a leading exporter in this field.

During the 20th century, Ireland, north and south, developed an international reputation in scientific farming, particularly in the production of new potato varieties. The country has also played a central role in farm technology, especially in the development of tractors. The south of Ireland became an early centre for tractor production when Henry Ford moved production of his company's tractors to a factory outside Cork in 1919. In the north, Harry Ferguson revolutionized tractor design worldwide during the 1930s, with the development of his three-point hydraulic linkage. This allowed farmers to drive the tractor and at the same time manipulate the implement attached behind. By the 1950s, Ferguson tractors were internationally famous. The paradox of Irish farming, noted since the 18th century, still applies, however. Irish farmers now respond rapidly to changes in world conditions, mediated to a large extent by current policies in the *European Union. At the same time, it is still possible to see techniques used, such as ridge making and stone wall building, which were practised 4,500 years ago.

See also AGRICULTURE.

Bell, J., and Watson, M., *Irish Farming* (1986)

Gillmor, D. A., 'The Political Factor in Agricultural History: Trends in Irish Agriculture 1922–85', *Agricultural History Review*, 37/2 (1989)

Kelly, Fergus, *Early Irish Law* (1988)

JB

Farsetmore, battle of (8 May 1567), a catastrophic defeat for Shane *O'Neill. Shane and his army crossed Farsetmore, a ford on the tidal section of the Swilly estuary, to re-establish authority over Tirconnell. He was engaged by Hugh O'Donnell in a pitched battle and forced to retreat. The tide had now risen and many of O'Neill's men drowned trying to escape. Shane's losses are variously reported as 613, 1,300, and 3,000. HM

Faughart, battle of (14 Oct. 1318), fought on a hill north of Dundalk and marking the end of the Bruce invasion. Edward *Bruce, self-proclaimed king of Ireland, was defeated and killed while marching south with an army of Scots and Irish, by some of the Anglo-Irish gentry of Louth and townsmen of Drogheda, under the command of John de Bermingham of Tethmoy. SD

Faulkner, Brian (1921–77), Lord Faulkner of Downpatrick, *Unionist politician. The son of a wealthy shirt manufacturer, he was elected to Stormont in 1949. As minister for home affairs 1959–63 he dealt effectively with the *IRA *border campaign Operation Harvest. He was a highly energetic minister of commerce (1963–9), attracting considerable outside business investment into Northern Ireland. He became deputy prime minister in 1966, but suffered from an ambiguous relationship with the frigid and defensive Terence *O'Neill. Faulkner resigned from office in January 1969, but served as minister of development (1969–71) under O'Neill's successor James Chichester-Clark. As Northern Ireland's last prime minister (Mar. 1971–Mar. 1972), he gained notoriety among nationalists for the introduction of *internment. He was chief executive of the power-sharing administration created under the *Sunningdale agreement. Thereafter Faulkner was marginalized within Unionism, and retired from political life in 1976.

He was a highly gifted politician, who combined an innate pragmatism with (initially) a good command over hardline loyalism. He had some of the same consensual instincts as O'Neill, but possessed much deeper political roots in Ulster Unionism and a much more acute political intelligence. His career suffered because O'Neill misinterpreted his ambition as treachery and successive British governments misinterpreted his breezy pragmatism as weakness. AJ

Faulkner, George (*c*.1703–1775), dominant *printer and bookseller in 18th-century Dublin. He was publisher to Jonathan *Swift and proprietor of the *Dublin Journal*. VK

Fedelmid mac Crimthainn (d. 847) of the *Eóganacht Caisil, ecclesiastic and king of Munster from 820. Seeking to extend his rule, he regularly raided the lands of the *Uí Néill and attacked Brega (Co. Meath, north Co. Dublin, and part of Co. Louth) and Leinster. Recognizing the significance of *Armagh, he sought to influence its politics, and he appointed his own candidate as abbot of *Clonmacnoise. His tactics bore fruit and he can be regarded as the dominant ruler of his day. MNíM

federalism, in an Irish context, meant the creation of a local executive and legislature that would deal solely with domestic affairs, and would remain subordinate to the Westminster parliament. It was proposed in the 1840s, notably by William Sharman *Crawford, as a middle position between *repeal and the maintenance of the Act of *Union in its existing form, but never developed an organized following. Isaac *Butt initially described his proposals for Irish self-government as federalism, but the term was quickly eclipsed by the less precise but, partly for that very reason, more attractive *'home rule'.

feis, a feast often involving the ritual or symbolic mating of a newly installed king with sovereignty as represented by its female aspect. *Feis* is the verbal noun of the verb *foaid* ('spends the night'), related to other Indo-European roots which designate feasting and enjoyment. Two types of *feis* are described in early texts, the *banais* (a compound of *feis* and *ben*, 'a woman') and *tarbfheis* (a compound of *feis* and *tarb*, 'a bull'). The *banais* was the symbolic marriage of the king and sovereignty, while the *tarbfheis* was the ritual, often in the form of a vision, whereby a candidate for kingship was recognized. Symbolic marriages as a form of inauguration of kings continued to be celebrated into the late medieval period. EB

Feis Temro ('The Feast of Tara'), a rite observed by kings of *Tara to celebrate the divine nature of the kingship of Tara and to reiterate its special status in Ireland. Evidence for the celebration of Feis Temro is meagre. The *annals record that it was held on a few occasions in the 5th and 6th centuries. The final and most reliable reference to the celebration of the rite records that it was held in 560 by *Diarmait mac Cerbaill, a king of Tara who reputedly espoused Christian and non-Christian practices. That Feis Temro continued to maintain some legal, if not ritual, significance may be inferred from the 8th-century law tract *Bretha Nemed*, which refers to Feis Temro as one of the three elements which constitute a *rí ruirech* ('king of overkings'). Its ritual aspect may have been demonized by clerics in the 6th and 7th centuries who disliked its non-Christian connotations and who fostered *Óenach Tailten instead. EB

feminism, a term first coined by the utopian socialist Charles Fourier in the 1830s, but not in common use in English until the 1890s, can be defined as advocacy of women's political and social equality. It can trace its beginnings in Ireland to William *Thompson's *Appeal* (1825), which argued for women's emancipation on the grounds of reason. Although Thompson and his collaborator Anna Wheeler were Irish, the *Appeal* was addressed to 'Women of England', and published there; its Irishness was accidental.

As time went on Irish feminism became more rooted in Ireland and came to include all political traditions. The Irish women's campaign against the Contagious Diseases Acts (see PROSTITUTION), while it applied to conditions in Ireland, involved only 49 Protestant middle-class women. The campaign for educational equality, although also confined to middle-class women, was bigger, and towards the end of the century included Catholics as well as Protestants. The first women's suffrage association, the North of Ireland Women's Suffrage Society, was set up in 1873, followed by the Dublin Women's Suffrage Association, later the Irish Women's Suffrage and Local Government Association, in 1876. However, the suffrage movement did not really flourish until the early 20th century, when a range of suffrage organizations appeared, some of which, like the IWSLGA, attracted both nationalists and unionists. The Irish Women's Franchise League, founded in 1908, was the most high-profile of these organizations. Nationalist in its sympathies, it strongly resisted absorption by the British-based Women's Social and Political Union on which it modelled itself. There were some working-class women in the suffrage movement but most of the participants were female white-collar workers or professionals, or the womenfolk of professionals.

It is all the more striking, then, that James *Connolly, champion of the Irish working class, was the most influential feminist in early 20th-century Ireland. Not only did Connolly's *Irish Citizen Army accept women on a strictly equal footing with men; the commitment to sexual equality in the proclamation that accompanied the *rising of 1916 (it addressed itself to Irishmen *and* Irishwomen, and pledged a commitment to universal adult suffrage) was also largely his doing. Besides Connolly, at least four of the proclamation's seven signatories (*Clarke, *MacDonagh, *Pearse, Plunkett) were sympathetic to feminism. It was this, and the involvement of women in 1916, in *Cumann na mBan and in prominent positions in the First and Second *Dáil, rather than unanimous support for women's self-determination among nationalists, which ensured that women in the *Irish Free State gained full equality of citizenship in 1922, six years before British women.

From 1922, feminists opposed women's exemption from jury service, attacks on women's working rights in 1935, and their consignment to a domestic role in Eamon de *Valera's *constitution of 1937. Representatives of the 28,000-member Joint Committee of Women's Societies and Social Workers, the Catholic Federation of Women's Secondary School Unions, and the National Council of Women in Ireland stoutly affirmed their feminism to the *Commission on Vocational Organization in 1940, demanding that 'home-makers' be given an authoritative voice in the proposed vocational assembly. The strong emphasis on 'equality in difference', and the identification of feminism with women's household work, continued into the 1940s. The Irish Housewives' Association (founded in 1942) defined women's issues as everything from consumer issues to children's welfare and women's political representation, and in 1947 incorporated into itself the remnants of the IWSLGA. A small, Dublin-based organization with a high proportion of Protestants, it was regularly attacked by the Catholic sociology journal *Christus Rex* in the late 1940s for its support of school meals and co-operative housekeeping ventures. It supported Dr Noel *Browne's *mother and child bill in 1950–1.

It is misleading to speak of a 'revival' of feminism in the late 1960s. While the high-profile, Dublin-based Irish Women's Liberation Movement (1970–1) attracted the most publicity, the ongoing pressure put on government by the Irish Housewives and the *Irish Countrywomen, among others, to appoint a commission to review women's status probably had more impact. The Commission on the Status of Women in 1970 led to the Council for the Status of Women as a monitoring body in 1973. The feminists of the 1970s and 1980s, while they built upon the earlier feminist concentration on women's household work, prioritized a redefinition of women's legal and social relationship to the family, economic resources, education, employment, and public life. Key reforms followed, while groups like Irishwomen United (1975–7), AIM (1972), the Women's Political Association, Irish Feminist Information, Cherish, Rape Crisis Centres, and many others testified to the renewed popular interest in women's rights.

Owens, R. Cullen, *Smashing Times* (1984)
Smyth, Ailbhe (ed.), *Irish Women's Studies Reader* (1993)
Tweedy, Hilda, *A Link in the Chain* (1992)

CC

fencibles, a military force raised for service within the British Isles only. From 1795 fencibles, mainly Scottish, took the place of regular troops withdrawn for service in the *revolutionary wars, and they were prominent in the fighting arising from the *insurrection of 1798. Earlier, in 1782, the Irish House of Commons had accepted a proposal to raise fencible regiments in Ireland. However the scheme was widely seen as an attempt to undermine the *Volunteer movement, and was withdrawn after strong public protests.

Fenianism, a revolutionary movement originating in the greatly expanding Irish immigrant community of the USA following the collapse of the *repeal and *Young Ireland movements of the 1840s and the discrediting of parliamentary agitation by the collapse of *independent opposition.

Difficulties of integration and prejudice experienced by Irish immigrants kept attention focused on Ireland and her problems while in New York revolutionary groups, which continued to exist after those in Ireland had collapsed, produced men ready to continue the independence struggle. John O'Mahony (1816–77), Michael Doheny (1805–63), and Joseph Deniffe, together with James *Stephens, a veteran of the ineffectual rising of 1848 who had fled to Paris, were chiefly responsible for initiating the Fenian movement.

Stephens, having established a leadership role and with limited financial backing from America, launched a revolutionary society in Dublin on St Patrick's Day 1858, dedicated to secrecy and the establishment of a democratic Irish republic. Initially the organization had no specific title, being known variously as 'The Society', 'The Organization', or 'The Brotherhood'. The name 'Fenian', a reference to the warriors of ancient Ireland, originated with a parallel branch of the organization in America headed by John O'Mahony and, by extension, came to describe the movement in Ireland. Stephens's continental experience was reflected in a clearly defined hierarchical structure with each member's knowledge of the society supposedly limited to the personnel of his own section. In practice neither organization nor secrecy corresponded with intention.

Both Stephens and T. C. Luby (1821–1901), another 1848 veteran, quickly got down to putting the society on a national footing and made significant progress. In the process the movement inevitably attracted police attention, Catholic church opposition, and competition from constitutonal nationalists, especially A. M. *Sullivan and the former Young Irelanders associated with the *Nation* newspaper. Stephens proved adept at wrong-footing Sullivan's attempts to revive constitutionalism; however, his own position was undermined in a split with his American associates when he sought to improve his financial position by starting a newspaper, the *Irish People*. This breach of secrecy resulted in his position within the overall movement being reduced to European representative and organizer of the Irish people. But more seriously, the newspaper offices provided a convenient target for the government, which had successfully infiltrated the movement, and when the end of the *American Civil War released thousands of Irish-American officers for possible Fenian activities in Ireland, it launched a pre-emptive swoop which netted Luby and other prominent members such as John *O'Leary and Jeremiah *O'Donovan Rossa. Stephens was also arrested soon after.

The government strike was effective: 1865 was the optimum year for a rising. The movement had a relatively strong urban base and had recruited successfully in Britain's Irish community and the British army. But by 1866 it was on the defensive and was further weakened by leadership splits in the American body. Stephens, recently sprung from jail, took control of the American organization but lacked the money and arms to put the long heralded rising into effect, and was replaced at the end of the year by military men determined on armed action regardless of the circumstances. A weak attempt in February 1867 was followed by a more significant, but hardly impressive, rising on the night of 4–5 March. All Fenian actions were short-lived, defeated by informers, bad weather, a well-prepared government, and a disciplined army. The rising, however, was not without consequences. Agitation for an amnesty for Fenian prisoners, and outrage at the execution of the *Manchester martyrs, mobilized nationalist opinion on a scale the Fenians themselves had never achieved, and provided the basis for the launching of the *home rule movement. In addition the rising moved *Gladstone to initiate reforms that would culminate in his conversion to home rule.

Traditionally regarded as an uncomplicatedly revolutionary movement, Fenianism has recently been subjected to a revisionist treatment, most notably by Comerford, which dilutes the importance of nationalist commitment and emphasizes the social and recreational role the movement provided for its recruits. This treatment has, in the inevitable reaction to 'anti-nationalist' revisionism, in turn been criticized for distorting reality.

See also IRISH REPUBLICAN BROTHERHOOD.

Comerford, R. V., *The Fenians in Context* (1985)
Moody, T. W. (ed.), *The Fenian movement* (1968)
Newsinger, John, *Fenianism in Mid-Victorian Britain* (1994)

JL

Ferguson, Samuel (1810–86), poet, critic, and antiquarian. Born in Belfast and educated at *Trinity College, Dublin, Ferguson was a regular contributor to the *Dublin University Magazine* (see ORANGE YOUNG IRELAND), in which he published 'A Dialogue between the Head and the Heart of an Irish Protestant' (1833), an attempt to balance sympathy with Irish Catholic claims with his support for *Protestant ascendancy and the Act of *Union. Although a conservative unionist in politics, Ferguson was attracted to cultural nationalism, developed an interest in Gaelic scholarship, and admired Thomas *Davis (for whom he published a *Lament* in 1847). Angered by British policy during the *Great Famine, he became secretary to the cross-party Irish Council in 1847, and was involved the following year in the short-lived Protestant Repeal Association, before withdrawing from political activity. He practised as a QC 1859–67, but remained prominent in Dublin literary circles. His versions of ancient Irish epics, which drew on the antiquarian researches of John *O'Donovan and Eugene *O'Curry, were published as *Lays of the Western Gael* (1865) and *Congal* (1872). Ferguson was appointed deputy keeper of public records in Ireland in 1867, was knighted in 1878, and became president of the *Royal Irish Academy in 1882. PHG

Fethard-on-Sea boycott (1957), an economic boycott of Protestants in Fethard-on-Sea, Co. Wexford, organized after a local Protestant woman married to a Catholic had refused to honour her promise to educate their children as Catholics, fleeing instead to Belfast. Condemned by the *Fianna Fáil government of the day, but supported by a number of Catholic priests and bishops, the boycott is notable as one of the few instances of overt communal sectarianism in independent Ireland.

feudalism. At its broadest this term is used by historians to describe the social, economic, and political structure of north-west Europe in the Middle Ages. More narrowly it serves to define the nature of relations between and within the upper strata of society. It is associated with certain institutions, ceremonies, and attitudes to the ownership and use of property. These include the act of homage and fealty; the holding of fiefs or fees—usually in the form of land—in return for military service; knighthood and chivalry; the use of stone *castles for military and domestic purposes;

reciprocal obligations of protection and service between superiors and inferiors; and hereditary succession to fiefs by eldest sons.

While these features had earlier origins they became more formalized in north-west Europe in the 12th century, an era of economic expansion, population growth, intellectual advance, and more frequent recourse to written documents as legal proof of property transfer. Twelfth-century Ireland shared in many of these developments. Claimants to the *high kingship engaged in military operations which lasted longer, ranged further, involved greater numbers, and depended upon more sophisticated planning than had been the case before. They built castles, employed administrators, issued charters, and granted land in return for homage and military service. The principle of hereditary succession to property by the eldest son of the holder, however, had not been established by the time the English arrived.

In England itself, by the time of the conquest of Ireland, customs concerning the holding and transfer of property, and the rights and obligations which went along with it, were being scrutinized and standardized in law tracts such as *Glanvill* and political documents such as Magna Carta. The assumption that a man who held a fief in return for military service would turn up personally to fight for his lord had been modified long before *Strongbow arrived in Ireland: money payment, known as scutage, was accepted in place of personal military service. The associated idea that a knight's fee or fief should be of a certain size and value had also taken root. These developments were transferred across the Irish Sea in the years after 1170. The size of knights' fees in Ireland, for instance, was not standardized, but they tended to be larger in frontier areas of the lordship than in more densely colonized regions. As regards scutage, this was collected in Ireland from an early stage of the conquest and continued to be taken into the 15th century, even though it provided only a small percentage of the money needed to mount a military campaign.

Some variations of the English pattern were visible in Ireland. From the outset church lands were not expected to provide knights, while types of tenure which did not involve military service, but instead depended upon money payment, were also more common in Ireland. Nevertheless, personal military service remained important. The link between tenure and military service finally ended in England in the early 14th century, but in Ireland *knight service continued to be required into the 15th century, and military tenancies were still being created at an equally late date.

Medieval Ireland was an arena of frequent and small-scale warfare. The flexibility of the system of linked tenure and military service brought in by the English made it possible for the settlers to defend themselves either by personal service or by the payment of money which was used to employ mercenaries, many of whom were Irish. This tenurial system was also the basis of the developing English or common law code, in both England and Ireland. The native Irish had from the outset been almost entirely excluded from the type of tenurial relationship used by the settlers, and this in consequence led to their exclusion from the legal system of the lordship, which had an established set of procedures by the middle of the 13th century.

'Feudalism' in the context of medieval Ireland is perhaps best thought of as a legal approach to property relations between lord and man, introduced by the English, which served to divide the settlers from the Irish and give the former a stronger sense of their separate identity.

O Corráin, D., *Ireland before the Normans* (1972)

Otway-Ruthven, A. J., 'Knight Service in Ireland', *Journal of the Royal Society of Antiquaries of Ireland*, 89 (1959)

Reynolds, S., *Fiefs and Vassals* (1994)

BGCS

fever is an ill-defined term covering a variety of disorders, including, among others, typhus, typhoid, and relapsing fever. By the 18th century, however, fever was identified in particular with typhus, which flourishes in squalid, overcrowded conditions and is spread by lice. Typhus is mentioned in the Irish *annals as early as 1225 and was endemic in Ireland until the late 19th century. During the 17th century, the English referred to it as the *'Irish ague'. Typhus epidemics often accompanied *famines, to such an extent that Irish doctors speculated on a causal link and typhus was popularly known as 'famine fever'. In fact it was overcrowding in institutions and increased vagrancy, such as occurred during the *Great Famine, that helped disseminate typhus. After a major fever epidemic in 1817–18, the government ordered the building of fever *hospitals in every county and borough, but these institutions were overwhelmed during the Famine and numerous temporary fever hospitals had to be erected. The 1851 census estimated that nearly 43,000 people had died of starvation during the Famine, but 193,000 died of various forms of fever. These figures are not reliable, but they are probably correct in identifying fever as a far bigger killer than starvation. By 1900 typhus was still claiming about 100 lives each year in Ireland and not until 1937 was there a year without a typhus death in the country. ELM

Fianna, in Gaelic Ireland a warrior band (see KERN), and more specifically, in Irish mythology, the group that followed the hero Fionn mac Cumhaill (Finn McCool). Fianna Éireann was a nationalist youth organization established in August 1909 by Countess *Markievicz.

Fianna Fáil ('soldiers of Ireland'), a political party formally inaugurated on 16 May 1926. Tensions within the anti-treaty *Sinn Féin party, led by Eamon de *Valera, over the issue of abstention from the *Dáil and the long-term future of the party, came to a head at that party's national convention (*ardfheis*) in March 1926. A proposal from the party leader that, in the event of the removal of the constitutional requirement that Dáil deputies take an *oath of allegiance, it would become 'a question not of principle but of policy' whether Sinn Féin deputies would take their seats, was rejected by the convention, precipitating the withdrawal of de Valera and his supporters.

Though it failed initially to attract the support of a majority of Sinn Féin's Dáil deputies, the general election of June 1927 saw the new party eclipse Sinn Féin (winning 26.1 per cent of votes and 44 seats, to the latter's 3.6 per cent and 5 seats). Under threat of marginalization by the *Electoral Amendment Act, Fianna Fáil took its seats in the Dáil in August 1927. A snap general election in September 1927 reinforced its position (with 35.2 per cent of the vote it won 57 seats). The party's electoral record since then has been impressive. In 1932 (44.5 per cent of votes, 72 seats) it established the position that it was to retain subsequently: easily the largest party in the state, its support normally lying between 40 and 50 per cent. Other unequalled records were broken in 1933, when it became the first party ever to win an overall parliamentary majority (49.6 per cent of votes, 77 seats), and in 1938, when it became the first party to win an overall majority of those voting (51.9 per cent).

The shock of Fianna Fáil's ousting of *Cumann na nGaedheal in 1932 to form its first government was followed by a consolidation of its perception of itself as the 'natural' party of government: it remained in office for a period of sixteen years. Between 1948 and 1957 it alternated with an anti-Fianna Fáil coalition (see INTERPARTY GOVERNMENT), but in 1957 it began a second sixteen-year period in office. The period from 1973 to 1989 once again saw Fianna Fáil alternating in office with a coalition, but in the latter year the party breached its traditional policy of refusing to consider coalition by entering into an alliance with the Progressive Democrats (and in 1992–4 with the Labour Party).

Fianna Fáil's policy position was articulated in 1926 in its constitution, which defined seven basic aims. The first two of these, 'to secure the unity and independence of Ireland as a republic' and 'to restore the Irish language as the spoken language of the people', for long remained central to the party's self-image, however remote the prospects of their attainment. On others, the party reversed its position in practice while retaining the ideal in theory. For example, its third and seventh aims ('to make the resources and wealth of Ireland subservient to the needs and welfare of all the people of Ireland' and 'to carry out the *democratic programme of the First Dáil') imply a level of socio-economic intervention that would be more characteristic of a party of the left than of the right of centre party that Fianna Fáil was to become. By the 1950s the party's position on its three remaining aims (to try to make Ireland economically self-sufficient, to establish as many families as practicable on the land, and to promote the ruralization of industries) had been reversed in practice, though the formal aims themselves remained sacrosanct until the 1990s.

Notwithstanding his own stature and his longevity as party leader (1926–59), Eamon de Valera by no means impeded the evolution of party policy in directions not envisaged in 1926. This was obvious not only in the lack of urgency attached to pursuit of the aims of ending *partition and restoring the Irish language, but in the evolution of industrial policy in a direction sharply at variance with the other party aims. Much of the momentum behind this may be attributed to Sean *Lemass, who as second party leader (1959–66) not only continued policies of economic rapprochement with Great Britain but also sought to improve relations with the government of Northern Ireland, giving de facto recognition to partition. The heritage of the tension between this reorientation of the party and the upsurge of nationalism associated with developing civil unrest in Northern Ireland was managed by the next leader, Jack *Lynch (1966–79), who strove to maintain party unity behind a policy of moderation on Northern Ireland, at the cost of antagonizing more nationalist elements (see ARMS CRISIS). It was this tension that was partly responsible for the succession of the next leader, Charles Haughey (1979–90), though factional divisions and personal factors also had a major impact, as they did in the cases also of later leaders Albert Reynolds (1990–4) and Bertie Ahern (since 1994).

Hannon, Philip, and Gallagher, Jackie (eds.), *Taking the Long View: Seventy Years of Fianna Fáil* (1996)

JC

fiants are warrants to *chancery authorizing the issue of letters *patent, named from the opening of the document, 'Fiant literae patentes' (let letters patent be made). Most were issued by the *lord deputy on his own authority or that of a king's letter. A few were issued by royal commissions or, under Henry VIII, by the king. The fiants were destroyed in 1922 (see PUBLIC RECORDS) but calendars of those for Henry VIII to Elizabeth were published in 7th to 21st *Reports of the Deputy Keeper of the Public Records in Ireland* while those for James I and Charles I were calendared by the *Irish record commissioners.

RG

field systems, the size, shape, and arrangement of *agricultural fields and the way these reflect the social, economic, and environmental circumstances of their creation. Despite recent structural farm improvement programmes, funded since 1973 by *European Union regional aid schemes, Ireland retains its characteristic 'bocage' landscape. In this, numerous, frequently small, fields are separated by banks, ditches, and hedges to produce a highly subdivided agrarian landscape. The variations in the size, shape, and boundaries of the fields in different parts of Ireland provide much of the country's regional distinctiveness, and reflect its varied history of enclosure.

Archaeological research has demonstrated that similarly small and irregular field systems existed during the *neolithic, *Bronze, and *Iron Ages, but no evidence has been adduced to suggest direct continuity from these to the present landscape. Rather, the extant field systems are of relatively recent origin: generally post-*plantation in the east, and immediately pre-*Famine in the west. In eastern districts, farms have traditionally tended to be larger and their fields more extensive (9–10 acres) and more regular than those further west, reflecting the more overtly commercial pressures which historically have affected agriculture in these areas. Over much of east-central Leinster, in counties such as Dublin, Kildare, Louth, and Meath, this regularity reflects the widespread *enclosure carried out in the 18th and early 19th centuries by *landlords and, particularly, their major tenants. This created a landscape of dispersed farms held in severalty, but in so doing largely destroyed the earlier 'champion' or 'commonfield' landscapes which had originated in areas of *Anglo-Norman *manorial settlement and survived in a recognizable form until at least the 17th century.

These commonfields were complex and far from unchanging. Surviving manorial charters from the 13th and 14th centuries suggest that they existed throughout most of Leinster, and west as far as Tipperary, Limerick, and Westmeath, and were characteristically subdivided into scattered strips. A tenant might hold several plots in widely scattered locations throughout the arable area. In return for these and for the grazing rights allocated with them on the meadows and waste, and on the arable itself after harvest, he owed his manorial lord a variety of labour and other services.

It has been suggested that these manorial references amount to evidence for the existence in medieval Ireland of the so-called 'two or three field' commonfield system, in which separate fields were allegedly given over in their entirety to the spring and winter cereal and fallow stages in a three-course rotation. However, this is debatable. What is clear is that the commonfield systems in eastern Ireland experienced widespread engrossing between the 13th and 16th centuries. This consolidated separate strips into larger, compact holdings within the framework of the existing commonfields, suggesting a continuing process of functional adjustment in response to changing socio-economic conditions. Where separate arable strips survived to be enclosed in the 18th century and after, they gave rise to characteristically linear field patterns, as at Rathcoole, Co. Dublin, and Booleyglass, Co. Kilkenny.

In western regions and in marginal areas generally, where the pressures of pre-Famine *population growth and unrestricted subdivision were most acutely felt, other types of field system developed. On the margins of cultivation small, irregular fields developed as hillsides and *boglands were enclosed piecemeal by land-hungry peasants. Where these tenancies were held on a joint basis by extended kin groups, farms might very quickly experience the rapid subdivision and fragmentation of holdings which was the characteristic response of these regions' *'rundale' agriculture to mounting population pressure. The fundamental principles at work here were partible inheritance and the equal allocation of land. Left unchecked, they eventually created a patchwork landscape, not dissimilar to the medieval commonfields of the *Pale, in which individual farmers held numerous widely scattered strips that became increasingly uneconomic in size as subdivision continued. In the worst-affected areas of the west and north, some landlords attempted to alleviate this in the immediate pre-Famine years by unilaterally reorganizing their tenants' farms. At the cost of some population displacement, these landlords replaced the rundale system with smaller numbers of individually larger and regularly laid-out farms, in processes commonly known as 'squaring' and 'striping'. The so-called 'ladder farms' created by the latter remain as a widespread feature of marginal upland areas throughout the west and north, where they run in a characteristic parallel pattern from valley floor to mountain side. Similar rationalization was subsequently undertaken in the later 19th century by the *Congested Districts Board and its successor, the *Land Commission.

Buchanan, R. H., 'Field Systems of Ireland', in A. R. H. Baker and R. A. Butlin (eds.), *Studies of Field Systems in the British Isles* (1973)

LJP

fili (poets). The *fili* of early medieval Ireland evolved from a professional poetic class found in all Celtic societies, the bards, who according to Diodorus Siculus 'singing to the accompaniment of instruments like lyres, praise some and defame others'. Other sources stress the rich rewards paid by Celtic aristocrats for such praise poetry. In early Christian Ireland the advent of literacy caused a cleavage to occur in the poetic order about 700 AD between a literate class of *fili* influenced by the Latin studies of the church, whose surviving compositions are religious or historical rather than simple eulogies of the aristocracy, and on the other hand various grades of oral poets, including the *admall* who composed for minor kings and nobles, the *tuathbard* who served the ordinary landowners, the professional satirist, *dul* or *cáinte*, banned by the church but patronized by warrior bands, and assorted ballad singers and buffoons. The *12th-century reform of the church, which evicted native poetic learning from church schools, coincided with a growing together of learned *fili* and the increasingly well-educated secular bards to form a single, literate, hereditary class of **aes dána* or 'men of the [poetic] art'. This excluded professional satirists and buffoons, who may have gradually become obsolete. These bards of the post-*Norman period styled themselves *filidh* or *fir dhána*. Their schools were run by master-poets or **ollamhain*, whose teaching was not wholly oral, and they have left behind a wealth of *bardic poetry, dating between *c.*1200 and 1660 AD, valuable not only as literature, but as contemporary historical documents. Famous hereditary schools included the O'Dalys (Uí Dhálaigh), O'Higgins (Uí Uiginn), Wards (Meic an Bhaird), and MacNamees (Meic Con Midhe).

Breatnach, L. (ed.), *Uraicecht na Riar* (1987)

Breatnach, P., 'The Chief's Poet', *Proceedings of the Royal Irish Academy*, sect. C, 83 (1983)

KS

Finance, Department of, generally regarded as the most important department within the Irish government service. This primacy was first established under *Dáil Éireann during the years 1919–21, when Michael *Collins served as minister for finance. The department's authority stemmed from the requirement, first introduced in September 1921, that it should be given advance notice of any financial proposal which was to be brought to cabinet; this power was subsequently enshrined in the 1924 *Ministers and Secretaries Act. Finance also had responsibility for recruitment and promotion throughout the Irish civil service. The administrative structures and procedures were almost identical to those exercised by the British treasury, on which they were modelled. Finance's powers were briefly diluted by the existence of a separate Department of Economic Planning and Development between 1977 and 1979, and of a Department of the Public Service from 1973 to 1987.

Until the late 1950s, the Department of Finance appears to have subscribed to the belief that public expenditure was inherently undesirable and should be curbed whenever possible. The publication of the report **Economic Development* in 1958 signalled a more positive attitude towards the role of government in economic development and is generally seen as marking the emergence of a less hostile attitude towards rising public expenditure. MED

Fine Gael ('kindred of the Irish'), a political party founded on 8 September 1933 through a merger of *Cumann na nGaedheal, the National *Centre Party, and the National Guard (see BLUESHIRTS). This realignment was largely a response to the rapid rise of *Fianna Fáil and its victories in the elections of 1932 and 1933. However, the new party performed less well in the next election in 1937 (34.8 per cent of the vote and 48 seats) than the combined support of its predecessors. Since then, the party's share of the vote at general elections has normally been between 25 and 35 per cent. It slumped to 19.8 per cent (31 seats) in 1948, but its participation at that time in the first *'interparty government' has been credited with rescuing the party from electoral eclipse. Indeed, it then began a steady recovery that lasted until the election of November 1982, when it won its largest ever share of the vote (39.2 per cent, 70 seats).

Although the personality of the first party leader, Eoin *O'Duffy, endowed Fine Gael initially with a rather unconventional image, his successors, W. T. *Cosgrave (1935–44) and Richard *Mulcahy (1944–59), reflected the dominance within the party of the pro-treaty, Cumann na nGaedheal tradition. The succession of James *Dillon (1959–65), son of John *Dillon, symbolized the extent to which the party had managed to absorb former supporters of the pre-1918 *Nationalist Party, while his two successors, Liam Cosgrave (1965–77) and Garret FitzGerald (1977–87), were sons of Cumann na nGaedheal ministers. The leadership of Alan Dukes (1987–90) represented a break with the older traditions within the party, but this trend was reversed when John Bruton took over as leader in 1990.

In policy terms, Fine Gael maintained the conservatism of its predecessor, though a centrist wing within the party made its presence felt in the late 1960s and was influential during the leadership of FitzGerald and Dukes. The party described itself in English as the 'United Ireland Party', and was more commonly known by this name in the 1930s. This reflected the party's moderate position on the national question, and it was associated with support for Ireland's position within the British *Commonwealth. In 1948, however, it was a Fine Gael taoiseach, John A. *Costello, who announced the government's decision to leave the Commonwealth. JC

Fine Gall ('territory of the foreigners'), Anglicized as Fingal(l), the name applied to an area of north Co. Dublin settled by *Vikings and Hiberno-Scandinavians between the 10th and 12th centuries. It extended northwards from the Liffey as far as Skerries and westwards to the modern county boundary. It was controlled by the Hiberno-Scandinavian kings of Dublin and included within its bounds the monasteries of Swords and Lusk. Despite the collapse of the kingdom of Dublin, the area retained a tradition of territoriality reflected, for instance, in the creation of the *Plunkett earldom of Fingall in 1628. A *county of Fingal was established as a separate administrative division from 1 January 1994. JB

firearms were first imported into Ireland late in the 15th century, just as their efficiency improved. Artillery (siege and field guns), belonging mostly to the state, was introduced by Gerald FitzGerald (Gearóid Mór), 8th earl of *Kildare. He battered down fortresses, beginning at Balrath Castle in Westmeath in 1488, on annual journeys across the country. Towns bought guns for defence: in 1495 Waterford sank one of Perkin *Warbeck's ships in an exchange of fire. Artillery coming into Gaelic hands was used mainly against local rivals.

Despite a 1494 statute restricting possession of artillery and firearms to the lord deputy and his licensees, it was impossible to stop proliferation. The first recorded use of a handgun was in 1487 when Godfrey O'Donnell killed an O'Rourke. Garret Mór himself died from a gunshot wound gained in battle with the O'Mores. Firearms—handguns, then arquebuses, calivers, and muskets—redressed the state monopoly in artillery by aiding traditional Irish guerrilla tactics. They assisted successful ambushes of *Sussex at Kiltubber, Co. Galway, in 1558 and near Armagh in 1563. By the *Nine Years War 'shot' composed a third of the opposing forces; by the *Confederate War two-thirds of the combatants had guns. HM

fire brigades were formed as a response to the dangers of fire in urban areas. In 1711 the lord mayor of Dublin ordered £6 annually to be paid to one John Oates to organize eighteen men and two 'water engines' to attend at fires in the city. This was the beginning of the first Irish fire brigade. Development was slow. Towards the end of the century Dublin and Cork saw insurance companies provide engines and firemen, but it was only after the local government reforms of 1840 that provincial towns were permitted to provide funds for equipment and full-time firemen. Even so most brigades remained overwhelmingly volunteer organizations, with small professional cadres. In cities with their own police forces, such as Dublin and Belfast, fire brigades became police sub-departments. From the 1890s training improved. In some cities medical training resulted in the founding of the first ambulance services. After *partition brigades remained under county control. However, the wartime failures of the county brigades led to the creation in 1947 of the Northern Ireland Fire Service. In Ireland as a whole, firefighters are primarily part-time volunteers, though major urban centres have full-scale professional brigades. NG

first fruits and twentieth parts, pre-*Reformation papal dues, subsequently paid to the crown, representing the first year's income of a cure, and annual payment of a twentieth part of that income. Following their abolition in England in 1704, the *Church of Ireland petitioned Queen Anne for similar relief. Negotiations, largely conducted by *Swift, led to the establishment of a Board of First Fruits, to fund the building and repair of churches and glebes. Substantial parliamentary grants to the board in the late 18th century, and the good stewardship of William Stuart, archbishop of Armagh 1800–22, and Charles Brodrick, archbishop of Cashel 1801–22, made possible an extensive building programme. In 1833 the board's functions were taken over by the newly formed ecclesiastical commissioners for Ireland (see CHURCH TEMPORALITIES (IRELAND) ACT). KM

First Programme for Economic Expansion, see *ECONOMIC DEVELOPMENT*.

First World War (1914–18). At the beginning of the war the threat of civil conflict in the summer of 1914 was defused when both John *Redmond and Edward *Carson pledged their respective followers to support the British imperial war effort. Redmond's call to nationalists to support gallant (and Catholic) 'little Belgium' was rejected only by a small minority of the *Irish Volunteers. Many thousands of Volunteers joined the two predominantly Catholic and nationalist Irish divisions: the 10th and the 16th. In the north, 30,000 UVF men joined up virtually *en masse* to form the 36th (Ulster) Division. After an initial surge at the start of the war, enlistments fell off sharply, though Irishmen continued to join up until the very end—almost 10,000 men, for example, in the last three months of the conflict. Although Protestants recruited in greater numbers proportionately than Catholics, men—Catholics and Protestants—in industrialized Ulster as a whole were more likely to enlist than those from the rest of Ireland. Urban areas returned more soldiers than rural, and the poorest recruiting area was Mayo. In all some 206,000 men from Ireland served during the war, of whom about 30,000 died. Even taking into account the very many emigrant Irish who joined up in England and elsewhere estimates of up to 500,000 Irish recruits are grossly inflated.

The most enduring legacy of the Irish military involvement in the war came from the Ulster Division's part in the battle of the Somme, which began on 1 July 1916. In the first two days of the battle the division suffered over 5,000 casualties, a 'blood sacrifice' which came to represent for unionists a conclusive demonstration of Ulster's unshakeable loyalty to the Union. The 16th (Irish) Division also fought on the Somme, though not until September 1916, and both divisions remained on the western front in France for the remainder of the war. The 10th Division saw action at Gallipoli, where it sufferd heavy losses at Suvla Bay (August 1915), and later went on to serve in Salonika and Palestine.

At home the First World War provided the opportunity for the republican *rising of 1916, as well as a suitably violent model for political action. Wartime pressures also help to explain the draconian government response to the rising, which contributed to the subsequent emergence of *Sinn Féin. When, in response to a manpower crisis on the western front, London threatened to impose conscription on Ireland in 1918, a broad popular coalition of nationalists and the Catholic church combined to resist it. In doing so Sinn Féin emerged as the leading nationalist political party. The war in general stimulated the Irish economy. There was a heightened demand for agricultural products—food for troops and forage for animals—which brought considerable prosperity to the farming community, and in turn contributed to the relative unwillingness of young men in rural areas to enlist. The *textile industry in the north was kept busy supplying military needs, as were *shipbuilding and *engineering concerns. Activity in some luxury trades and 'non-essential' Irish industries, such as *brewing and *distilling, fell away during the war. The absence of conscription in Ireland meant that a large pool of male labour remained available throughout and that, unlike in Great Britain, comparatively few women were drawn into general employment. Some females, nevertheless, found jobs in Belfast engineering works, and there was increased employment in the textile sector and in more traditional female occupations such as *nursing.

Bartlett, T., and Jeffery, K. (eds.), *A Military History of Ireland* (1996)

KJ

fishing. Ireland occupies a position of rare advantage in relation to the fertile fishing grounds of the North Atlantic. Opportunities existed for several different types of fishery pursuit, including land-based operations involving the capture of crabs and lobsters; land and seafisheries for shellfish and molluscs, the latter important as a source of bait for the line-fishing industry as well as a source of saleable food; seasonal pelagic fishing for migratory species such as mackerel, herring, and, in southern waters, pilchards; and all-year-round boat fishing for demersal species of round and flat fish. However, the development of an Irish fishing industry was shaped by a number of inherent constraints. The sea is an open resource which, apart from coastal waters, must be shared with fishermen of other nationalities. Fish stocks themselves are highly mobile and so subject to localized fluctuations in availability and quality. Most important of all, particularly in the period before refrigeration, has been the highly perishable nature of the product, affecting both the length of time a boat could remain at sea and the marketing of the fish caught.

Evidence from prehistoric kitchen middens testifies to the exploitation of sea and coast by the earliest settlers, while the recognized status accorded to fishermen in early Irish laws and institutions, the *Norse origin of Irish words pertaining to types of fish, boats, and fishing lines, medieval descriptions of the south coast whale fishery, and Gaelic chronicles of western sea cod fisheries indicate the establishment and development over centuries of specialized fishery pursuit. From at least the 14th century Irish boats, merchants, and mariners were highly active in supplying British and European demand for fish and fish products.

Both this trade and the various fishery enterprises which supported it grew apace during the 15th and 16th centuries to make sea fishing one of the key sectors of the early modern Irish economy. In the 17th century, however, commercial sea fishing declined, due both to political upheaval and to unhelpful government policy (for example in relation to Irish duties on the importation of salt). Irish fishermen were nevertheless sufficiently dynamic to be able to exploit the *Newfoundland fisheries once the statutory embargo on their participation was lifted in 1704. The 18th century saw the introduction of a series of government bounties, which particularly benefited the herring industry, with exports of cured herring showing marked increases towards the end of the century. However, herring fishing contracted sharply following the withdrawal of bounties in 1829. Export-based whitefishing in Irish offshore grounds, meanwhile, was very largely carried on by foreign vessels. A parliamentary commission of inquiry in 1836 found an industry in profound decline, its workforce poorly equipped, poorly rewarded, and mostly part-time. A partial exception was the east coast, where the expansion of Dublin supported the establishment of a small whitefishing industry. But overall domestic demand for Irish-caught fish was extremely weak, particularly in inland regions, which were increasingly being supplied from external sources. By 1819 Ireland had become a fish importer.

The mid-19th century saw a 'revolution in the trade in fish', based on the application of steam to land and sea travel, refrigeration to fish carriage, and the trawl to fish capture, and underpinned by population growth and the move towards urbanization. In Ireland, however, severe imbalances between levels of domestic demand and the productivity of local fisheries meant that Irish quayside buyers generally found it more expedient to send their purchases for final sale in Scotland and England, while Irish provincial fish markets, such as Belfast, looked to sources outside Ireland for regular supplies. The exception was Dublin, where the expansion of the whitefishing fleet in the 1830s enabled local fishermen not only to land fish in increasing quantities, but also to hold their own as the major suppliers of the local fish trade. Elsewhere development was limited by weak local demand and the ease with which this could be met within what was now a highly integrated United Kingdom market for fresh fish.

On the east coast a new period of prosperity was heralded by the revival in the 1860s of the Irish Sea herring industry. Unlike earlier herring fisheries, which had been underpinned by the curing sector, this nationally significant enterprise, which attracted vessels from all parts of the British Isles, was directed at supplying domestic fresh markets, particularly in England. Based at first at the two major herring stations of Ardglass, Co. Down, and Howth, Co. Dublin, within a few years participation in this fishery had increased to include most of the fishing harbours on the Irish east coast. The establishment in the 1880s of a similarly cosmopolitan spring mackerel fishery at Kinsale, directed at the export of cured fish to the United States, strengthened the commercial basis of the Irish sea fisheries along the southern Irish coast. At the same time, the efforts of the newly formed *Congested Districts Board were instrumental in the revival at the end of the 19th century of herring curing enterprise in Donegal; by 1906 curers had also re-established bases in Co. Down for the production of fish for export to America and Europe. In the first decades of the 20th century Ireland became a fish exporter, albeit on a modest scale, with a balance of trade which rose from £0.15 million in 1904–7 to £0.45 million in 1915–18.

During the *First World War the withdrawal of British trawl fleets from the North Sea, along with a generous system of government loans and grants directed specifically at the inshore fisheries, brought great improvements in capacity and infrastructure. After 1918, however, the cured herring industry went into steady decline after losing first its Russian and then its German markets. The cured mackerel trade was similarly affected by the loss of American demand during the Depression. The Irish Sea fresh herring trade, however, remained viable. An important new whitefishery based on the Danish seine net and made possible by the previous upgrading of the fleet and the move to engine propulsion emerged on the east coast in the 1920s, and by 1935 had become Northern Ireland's single most valuable fishery.

VP

fitz Audelin, William (*fl.* 1157–98), royal administrator. Sent to Ireland by *Henry II in 1171 in advance of his own expedition, fitz Audelin met Henry on his landing at Waterford. In 1173, when Henry II summoned *Strongbow and Hugh de *Lacy for military service in Normandy, fitz

Audelin returned to Ireland as Henry's procurator in their absence. Following Strongbow's death in 1176 fitz Audelin was appointed custodian of his Leinster lordship. In February 1177 John de *Courcy is said to have left the Anglo-Norman garrison of Dublin without the permission of fitz Audelin who was his superior. *Gerald of Wales presents a very negative view of him as impeding the ambitions of his kinsmen in Ireland, but this is a measure of his success as a royal agent. In 1177 he founded St Thomas's abbey, Dublin, on behalf of Henry II. Recalled to England in 1181, fitz Audelin had no further contact with Ireland. MTF

FitzGerald, see DESMOND; GLIN, KNIGHTS OF; KERRY, KNIGHTS OF; KILDARE.

FitzGerald (Decies). When the *Desmond Geraldine John fitz Thomas (d. 1261) married the daughter of Thomas fitz Anthony, seneschal of Leinster, he was granted lands centred on the honour of Dungarvan, thus establishing the FitzGerald lordship of Decies. It was granted by the 6th earl of Desmond, James (d. 1462), to a younger son, Garret, whose descendants reached the height of their power in the late 16th century, having their seat at Dromana. Although they kept their lands intact through the *Cromwellian settlements, the last lord, John, left only a daughter, who married Edward Villiers, bringing the 400-year-old FitzGerald lordship of Decies to an end. SD

FitzGerald, Lord Edward (1763–98), radical. A younger son of the 1st duke of Leinster, FitzGerald served in the British forces in North America during the *American Revolution. He later became an admirer of the *French Revolution and was dismissed from the army for a toast to the abolition of hereditary titles. He joined the *United Irishmen in 1796 and was one of the militants in the debates on strategy during 1797–8. His arrest on 19 May, during which he was mortally wounded, deprived the *insurrection of 1798 of a key figure. His wife Pamela had been brought up in the household of the radical French nobleman the duc d'Orléans, and was widely believed to be his illegitimate daughter.

FitzGerald, Maurice II (*c.*1194–1257), 2nd baron of Offaly, *justiciar of Ireland 1232–45. Through his father, Gerald FitzMaurice, he possessed Maynooth, and through his mother, Eva de Bermingham, Offaly. He came of age in 1215 and was appointed justiciar in 1232. In 1234 he led the attack on Richard *Marshal on the Curragh and in 1235 he and Richard de *Burgh led the conquest of Connacht. He received land in Galway, Mayo, and Sligo and built a castle and *Dominican friary in the latter place. His attempts to conquer Donegal and Fermanagh failed.

In 1245 he gathered 3,000 men to fight for the king in Wales but arrived too late and lost the justiciarship. In 1248 he fought in Gascony at the bidding of Henry III. Maurice had founded a *Franciscan friary at Youghal in 1224 or 1231 and he died there in the habit of a Franciscan in 1257. BGCS

Fitzgibbon, John (1749–1802), attorney-general 1784–9, lord *chancellor 1789–1802, created earl of Clare 1795. Fitzgibbon was both a determined opponent of *Catholic relief and a savage critic of his fellow Protestants, whose *patriot pretensions he believed endangered the connection with Britain on which their own security depended. Lord Westmorland, lord lieutenant 1790–5, described him as having 'no God but English government'. This commitment, culminating in Fitzgibbon's strong support for the Act of *Union, has been seen as reflecting his doubly marginal position, as the son of a wealthy lawyer who was both a self-made man and a convert from Catholicism, within the Irish elite. Though reputed to be a benevolent and improving landlord, he was also an unrelenting enemy of the *United Irishmen, and a leading advocate of tough security measures in the crisis of the 1790s.

fitz Henry, Meiler (d. 1220), the son of Henry, the illegitimate son of Henry I by Nesta, daughter of Rhys ap Tewdwr, king of south Wales, and thus a first cousin of *Henry II. He was also related to prominent Cambro-Normans, including Robert *fitz Stephen and Maurice fitzGerald, his uncles, and *Raymond le Gros and *Gerald of Wales, who were his cousins. In 1169 Meiler accompanied fitz Stephen to Ireland and received land grants in Leinster from *Strongbow and in Meath from Hugh de *Lacy. In 1199, on *John's accession as king of England, Meiler is found acting as royal *justiciar, an office he exercised until 1208, when disputes with the Anglo-Norman lords of Leinster and Meath led John to remove him. He founded the Augustinian priory of Greatconnell, Co. Kildare, in which he died. MTF

Fitzralph, Richard (*c.*1299–1360). Fitzralph, a noted campaigner against the mendicant orders, died in Avignon. There he had been conducting a legal process against the friars, a task which occupied him for the last decade of his life. Born into an Anglo-Norman family, he was educated, probably by *Franciscans, in his home town of Dundalk, before going to Balliol College, Oxford, about 1315. He became a fellow of the college, gained his doctorate in theology in 1331, and in the following year began a tempestuous two-year period as chancellor, which embraced the 'Stamford Schism', when a group of students decamped from Oxford, out of disgust for the authorities, to set up another *studium* in the town of Stamford. The first of his four visits to Avignon took place in 1334–5. By this time he had made some influential friends, most importantly Bishop Grandisson of Exeter (*c*.1291–1369), to whose nephew he was for a while tutor. Thanks to the influence of Grandisson and that of another patron, Thomas Bradwardine, he became dean of Lichfield in 1335. He spent little time in Lichfield, preferring to work and preach in Avignon (1337–1344). In 1346 he was elected archbishop of Armagh, with which diocese he became so closely identified that he was known as *Armachanus*. Grandisson consecrated him in his cathedral in Exeter in 1347. He went to Avignon on two more extended visits (1349–51, 1357–60) before his death.

All his extant writings, even the sermons originally preached in English, survive in Latin. The inventory of the sermons comprises about 90 items preached from 1335 onwards. The manuscript collections which contain the full set have been described as a 'Sermon Diary', because they contain details of the date and place of delivery, the original language in which a sermon was preached, and the preacher's own title as he moved up the ecclesiastical ladder. Several of the sermons which he preached in his diocese demonstrate his determination to make peace between the two nations, native Irish and Anglo-Norman, but he is chiefly famous for the sermons and treatises he wrote against the friars, especially the Franciscans. His other writings deal with disparate material (e.g. his *Commentary on the Sentences* (*c*.1328–9), or the *Summa de questionibus Armenorum* (*c*.1340–4)).

His anti-mendicancy centred on the way the friars interpreted Christ's poverty. In his dialogue *De pauperie Salvatoris* (1356) he linked the friars' alleged delinquency to the theory of Dominion and Grace: wrongdoing merits dismissal. Many of the anti-mendicant arguments he advanced in this treatise resurfaced in a series of sermons he preached in English in London between December 1356 and March 1357, but the *tour de force* of his career took place on 8 November 1357, in Avignon, when he preached before Pope Innocent VI and the cardinals an address now known as the 'Defensio Curatorum', in which he called into question the justification of the mendicant orders. He lost his case, and because of the power of the friars in the curia the cause for his canonization foundered, except in his native Dundalk, where, in the church of St Nicholas, which contained his tomb, there is a chapel dedicated to St Richard.

Walsh, Katherine, *A Fourteenth-Century Scholar and Primate: Richard Fitzralph in Oxford, Avignon and Armagh* (1981).

TPD

fitz Stephen, Robert, Cambro-Norman adventurer, recruited by Diarmait *Mac Murchada in south Wales in 1167 to help him recover his kingdom of Leinster. He landed at Bannow in May 1169 and captured the city of Wexford. He fought alongside Mac Murchada until the latter's death in 1171. *Henry II placed him in the garrison at Dublin in 1172, but recalled him to England in 1173 to fight on his behalf there. In 1177 Henry II made a speculative grant of the kingdom of Desmond jointly to fitz Stephen and Miles de *Cogan. He died without heirs sometime after 1185. MTF

fitz William, Raymond, see RAYMOND FITZ WILLIAM.

Fitzwilliam, Sir William (1526–99), vice-treasurer (1559–73), lord deputy (1571–5, 1588–94), the most experienced Elizabethan minister in Ireland, and reputedly the most corrupt. When his account was audited in 1571, it was nearly £6,000 short. Fitzwilliam was nevertheless appointed chief governor with orders to cut costs and reduce the army. This gave him little leverage over the *provincial presidencies of Munster and Connacht or over the *Enterprise of Ulster, and as a result he quarrelled with their commanders.

Fitzwilliam was back again to retrench in 1588. He conspired against *Perrot, his predecessor, and presided over massive bribery with relatives and staff acting as receivers. Fitzwilliam's major policy initiative—the *partition of Monaghan (1590/1)—was accomplished in a high-handed fashion. Hugh Roe MacMahon had bribed Fitzwilliam to succeed to the lordship but instead was executed, leading Hugh *O'Neill and other Ulster lords to fear the precedent thus set. Fitzwilliam sparked the *Nine Years War by sending a sheriff into Fermanagh. After he had failed to arrest O'Neill on charges of conspiracy at Dundalk in June 1593, the Ulsterman turned the tables on him with a litany of complaints to commissioners the following March. Fitzwilliam was recalled in the summer of 1594. HM

Fitzwilliam episode, a political crisis centring on the recall on 23 February 1795 of the *lord lieutenant, William Wentworth, 2nd Earl Fitzwilliam. Fitzwilliam's appointment had been part of the terms agreed for the entry into government of the conservative wing of the English *Whig Party. The ostensible reason for his recall was that he had dismissed senior office holders of long standing, ignoring a clear agreement that his appointment was not to inaugurate a general remodelling of the Irish administration. But ministers were also alarmed at his demands for permission to support the *Catholic relief bill that *Grattan had introduced on 12 February. Most modern accounts suggest that Fitzwilliam had shown little appreciation either of the practicalities of coalition government or of the role of a lord lieutenant. But his removal was widely resented by Catholics and Protestant reformers, and his replacement by the more inflexible Earl Camden, lord lieutenant 1795–8, set the scene for a vicious circle of discontent and repression that culminated in the *insurrection of 1798.

flags and the emblems and colours used on them have a complex history. The use of green as the distinctive Irish national colour can be traced back to the 17th century. A standard used by the forces of Owen Roe *O'Neill used a harp on a green background. The royal arms of Ireland, devised for James I, also used a harp, though on a blue background. The harp and crown, along with green and blue but also other colours, featured on many of the flags of the *Volunteers. Green flags and ribbons were widely used by supporters of the *United Irishmen before and during the *insurrection of 1798, while loyalists made equally prominent use of Orange insignia. The idea of combining orange and green colours to symbolize the reconciliation of Catholic and Protestant was first reported in the 1830s. The tricolour, with orange and green separated by white, was first widely adopted by *Young Ireland and in the *rebellion of 1848. It continued to be used in the decades that followed, the occasional replacement of orange by yellow indicating that the symbolism was lost on some users, but was less common as a nationalist emblem than the green harp. It was only after the *rising of 1916 that the tricolour became the distinctive emblem of the newly dominant militant nationalism. It was adopted as the national flag of the *Irish Free State in 1922.

The British government, for its part, sought to deploy green and the harp for United Kingdom purposes, in the flags of Irish regiments and on state occasions within Ireland itself. From 1801 the cross of St Patrick was added to the Union Jack, but this continued to be viewed by all sides, both before and after *partition, as a unionist emblem. The *Flags and Emblems Act testified to the continued potency of rival flags as emblems of dominance and defiance in a divided Northern Ireland.

Flags and Emblems (Display) Act (1954), a law of the Northern Ireland parliament which made it an offence to interfere with the Union Jack in a public place, and gave the *Royal Ulster Constabulary discretionary powers to remove any other flag from public or private property. Introduced to counter Independent Unionist electoral success in 1953, the legislation in practice played into the hands of extremists on both sides, most notably in the fierce Divis Street riots of September 1964 in Belfast, when Revd Ian Paisley forced the police to remove an Irish tricolour from the window of Republican headquarters in Belfast. The issue was apparently trivial but, like the control of marches, it could be exploited to illustrate the absence of parity of esteem between the two communities.

ACH

Flann Mainistrech (d. 1056), lector, or head of the church school at Monasterboice, the most famous of the 10th to 12th century learned poet-historians, whose Irish verses are preserved in the Book of *Leinster and many later manuscript anthologies. He contributed poems on place-name lore to the *Dindsenchus*, and on mythical history to the **Lebor Gabála*, and is credited, not always reliably, with many poems recording genealogies or traditional rights of particular dynasties. His poem on the kings of Ireland, composed in the reign and in the interest of *Máel Sechnaill II, last *high king of the southern *Uí Néill, became influential in promoting the idea of an Uí Néill monopoly of the *Tara kingship.

KS

flax may have been grown in Ireland during the *Bronze Age, and the use of *linen is well attested in the early historic period (see DRESS). Home production of linen continued during the medieval period, but the rapid commercialization of linen production took place in the 18th century, and the major expansion of flax cultivation during the early 19th century. The acreage of flax sown rose from about 70,000 in 1810 to around 175,000 by the early 1850s. Cultivation declined again during the later 19th century, as farmers became reluctant to grow a crop which required so much labour, and which often suffered in the damp Irish climate. By 1900, less than 50,000 acres were grown. The decline was temporarily reversed during both the *First and *Second World Wars, but the crop has now almost completely disappeared.

By 1800, more than 80 per cent of flax was grown in Ulster, most of it produced on tiny holdings rented by weaver-farmers. Seed was mostly imported, from America, the Low Countries, and Russia. Cultivation was very labour intensive. Ground was usually ploughed, harrowed, and rolled before the seed was sown, and harrowed and rolled again after sowing. Flax grown for fibre was generally ready for harvesting about fourteen weeks after sowing. Until the 1940s all flax was pulled by hand, and tied into sheaves or 'beets' using bands made from rushes. Flax-pulling machines became available during the 1940s, but by this time cultivation of the crop had almost died out. JB

Fleetwood, Charles (d. 1692), a son-in-law and principal supporter of Oliver *Cromwell. Coming to Ireland as commander-in-chief of the army and a civil commissioner in 1652, he encouraged his fellow commissioners to recognize Cromwell's protectorate and selected pro-Cromwell Irish MPs for a united British parliament. Fleetwood was made lord deputy in 1654, despite the opposition of those who would have preferred civilian rule. He set up the High Court of Justice to try rebels and implemented the *Cromwellian land settlement. Anxious to satisfy his fellow soldiers when disbanding the army, Fleetwood took a doctrinaire approach to the *transplantation to Connacht, jailing, court-martialling, and seizing the assets of those refusing to transplant. Fleetwood remained lord deputy until 1657, though his tolerance of *Baptists enabled opponents, notably Roger Boyle (see ORRERY), to have him recalled to England in 1655. HM

Flight of the Earls, a popular term for the departure from Rathmullen, Co. Donegal, of Hugh *O'Neill, earl of Tyrone, Rory O'Donnell, earl of Tyrconnell, and Cúchonnacht Maguire, lord of Fermanagh, together with their followers on 4 September 1607. Their decision to leave has never been fully explained. It was probably a combination of government pressure on their seigneurial rights and unwarranted fear that the conspiracy they were hatching with Spain had been uncovered. The escape vessel did not reach Spain. It was driven into a Norman port and the authorities in Paris and Brussels shunted their embarrassing guests off to Rome, where they eked out their days on papal pensions. The government of Ireland declared their flight treasonous and confiscated their lands to make way for the *Ulster plantation. Tadhg Ó Cianáin, who travelled with the earls, left an untitled manuscript account of the journey. *The Departure of O'Neill out of Ireland* (1958), painted by Thomas Ryan, is a good example of the romantic nationalist connotations which the Flight has acquired. HM

Flood, Henry (*c*.1732–91), politician. Born into a landed family, Flood was elected MP for Co. Kilkenny in 1759 and for Callan in 1761. As the son of a prominent office holder, he initially supported government, but by 1763 was a prominent member of the *patriot opposition. His acceptance of the office of vice-treasurer in 1775 was widely seen as a betrayal. Flood himself, a strong admirer of the earl of Chatham, never accepted that patriotism implied permanent opposition to the government of the day. However his ideal of the independent statesman holding office for the public good proved impossible to reconcile with the realities of late 18th-century parliamentary management. Having given only half hearted support to the government's American policy, and supported calls for *free trade and reform, he was dismissed in November 1781. Back in opposition, he was initially overshadowed by *Grattan and others, but the campaign for a *Renunciation Act allowed him to re-establish himself as a popular leader. He effectively directed the *Volunteer National Convention in drawing up its plan for *parliamentary reform, unsuccessfully presenting the result to the House of Commons on 29 November 1783. Thereafter he concentrated on the British parliament, where he had purchased a seat, but remained a marginal figure. He opposed the admission of Catholics to political rights. A will bequeathing his estate to fund the study of Irish at *Trinity College, possibly inspired as much by a family feud as by patriot sentiment, was successfully challenged by a cousin.

Kelly, James, *Henry Flood* (1998)

flour milling. By the early 17th century, *water-powered flour mills had begun to replace domestic production using hand-operated querns. With the expansion of arable *farming in Ireland during the 18th century, and a growing demand for meal and flour, the number of mills increased significantly. Many utilized the new technologies that had been pioneered within the British milling industry; the larger and more sophisticated concerns shelled and sifted the flour prior to grinding. After grinding, the flour was bolted mechanically. Grain and flour were also moved around these mills using mechanical hoists and elevators.

By 1835 there were almost 2,000 corn mills operating in Ireland and it was during this period, when the population was highest and exports to Britain were also significant, that the industry probably reached its peak output. Irish flour had a privileged position in the British market until the repeal in 1846 of the corn laws that had excluded foreign grain from the United Kingdom. Flour milling was largely concentrated in the wheat-growing areas of Munster and Leinster, with a number of very large mills in or near the larger port towns where millers could exploit urban markets and the export trade. Clonmel, situated inland in the heart of a major grain-growing area, was by far the largest milling centre in the country, exporting most of its flour to Britain through *Waterford. The repeal of the corn laws and the transport revolution altered the supply conditions in the UK market and by the late 1870s American wheat began to undermine the Irish trade, damaging the business of inland mills. However, a number of roller mills were established in the decades after 1879, Shackleton's of Carlow being the first, and the industry—increasingly concentrated in large steam-driven mills located in the major ports—was able to make a recovery by milling imported grain.

Cullen, L., 'Corn Milling in Ireland during the Eighteenth Century', *Irish Economic and Social History*, 4 (1977)

Mc Cutcheon, W., 'The Corn Mill in Ulster', *Ulsterfolklife*, 15–16 (1970)

AB

Fontenoy, battle of (30 Apr./11 May 1745), fought near Tournai in modern Belgium during the War of the Austrian Succession (1740–8). British forces under the duke of Cumberland overpowered the French centre, but were repulsed by a dramatic charge spearheaded by the six regiments of the *Irish Brigade under Lieut. Charles O'Brien, 6th Viscount Clare. Later commemorated in a poem by Thomas *Davis, the battle represents the most noted exploit of 'the *wild geese'.

football, see SOCCER.

Forbes, Sir Arthur (1623–96), created earl of Granard 1684. A Scottish-born royalist with lands in Co. Longford, Forbes was an intermediary between the *Restoration government and the *Presbyterians of Ulster, for whom he secured the **regium donum*. His appointment as *lord justice in 1685 was intended to reassure Protestants following the accession of *James II. However, he later supported *William III.

Ford of the biscuits, battle of (7 Aug. 1594), in the *Nine Years War. It is so called in the *Annals of the *Four Masters* because a relief column on its way to the besieged castle of Enniskillen was turned back by Ulster forces under Cormac MacBaron O'Neill and Hugh Maguire and lost its supplies fording the river Arney. Hugh *O'Neill disclaimed responsibility, but information from a camp follower shows that he arrived two days later to collect booty and to ascertain the government losses. HM

foreign armies, Irish in. Military migration from poorer parts of Europe into the armies of great powers was commonplace during the *ancien régime*. Irish recruitment into continental armies, especially of Spain and France, began for political reasons after the second *Desmond War and was sustained thereafter by further defeats and by religious and economic factors.

In 1605 Spain formed a separate Irish regiment under the command of Hugh *O'Neill's sons. Spain created five more Irish regiments in the 1630s and recruited 30,000 ex-soldiers of the *Confederate Catholics in the early 1650s. France first enlisted Irish troops in 1635 but its Irish brigade stemmed from the 16,000 *'wild geese' migrating after the *Williamite War. Initially commanded by *James II, these regiments were later integrated into the French army still wearing their red coats. Replenished by an average of 1,000 recruits per year, mainly from Kilkenny and the Munster counties, they earned fame at *Fontenoy in 1745.

Whereas France and Spain recruited the Irish *en masse*, the Austrian, Swedish, and Russian armies looked for career-minded Irish officers. In the 18th century there were at any one time 500 Irishmen holding foreign commissions. Irish Catholic gentry were able to gain the positions of command and political appointments in continental Catholic countries they were being denied at home.

All ranks experienced heavy casualties in warfare and from camp diseases. By 1649 Spain's first Irish regiment had suffered 17,000 casualties; by 1738 Dillon's regiment in French service had lost 7,000. Spanish and French garrison towns developed identifiable Irish communities which provided a local recruiting base. Strong links existed between the regiments and *Irish colleges.

Dublin's plan of sending *idlemen to continental wars backfired as the likes of Owen Roe *O'Neill, Thomas *Preston, Patrick *Sarsfield, and Justin *MacCarthy returned expert in modern warfare. Émigré Irish regularly plotted invasions of Ireland. Hugh O'Neill in Rome demanded use of Spain's Irish regiment. Four hundred Irish brigade veterans formed the core of the *Jacobite invasion of Great Britain in 1745.

By the late 18th century the Irish regiments in the French and Spanish armies were in practice multinational forces, only their officer corps retaining a distinctive Irish identity. The decline of recruitment from Ireland had many causes: the collapse of Jacobite hopes, the opening up of the British army to Irish Catholic recruits, and greater prosperity, offering alternatives to military service generally. The regiments in French service, associated with the *ancien régime*, were abolished in 1791, following the *French Revolution, although *United Irish exiles later formed an *Irish Legion. The regiments in Spanish service were dissolved in 1818.

See also IRISH BRIGADE.

Henry, Gráinne, *The Irish Military Community in Spanish Flanders, 1586–1621* (1992)

HM

foreign investment has played a major role in the Irish economy. Much of the initial capital for Irish *railway construction was provided by British shareholders, as was the capital for the Belfast *shipbuilding industry. However in the intensely nationalist atmosphere of the newly independent *Irish Free State there was widespread opposition to 'alien penetration' of the Irish economy. When the *Fianna Fáil government took office in 1932, a commitment to protecting Irish-owned manufacturing companies formed an integral part of its industrial policy. The Control of Manufactures Act, passed in 1932 and tightened in 1934, required that the shareholdings and boards of directors of all manufacturing companies operating in the state should be under majority Irish control. Exemption could be granted by ministerial licence, but only to manufacture products that were not produced by an Irish company. In practice the regulations were widely evaded, often with the tacit connivance of both the government and the state-owned *Industrial Credit Company, because the need to secure investment and employment proved paramount.

After the *Second World War attitudes changed. Northern Ireland began to offer financial assistance to foreign investors who established factories in the province; in 1949 the Irish Republic established the Industrial Development Authority to attract overseas investors. Until 1957, however, foreign investors in the Irish Republic remained subject to the Control of Manufactures Act, and licences were only issued for investments located in remote areas. A decisive change of policy came in the years 1956 and 1957 when the Control of Manufactures Act was amended and investors were offered significant tax concessions. Since that time foreign investment has made a significant contribution to economic growth and to exports and employment in both parts of Ireland.

MED

foreign missions. Ireland played little part in Christian missionary activity from the end of its European mission in the 9th century until the post-Reformation period. From the 16th century, the Catholic church was preoccupied with survival, the papacy regarding the kingdom as 'mission' territory. Despite its own domestic problems the *Church of Ireland took foreign mission initiatives. The 'Irish Auxiliary' to the Society for the Propagation of the Gospel was founded in 1714, followed by the Hibernian Church Missionary Society (1817), an Irish offshoot of the *evangelically inspired Church Mission Movement. In 1874 the Leprosy Mission was established while in 1885 the Dublin University Far Eastern Mission was set up. There was also an Irish Presbyterian Mission. Many Irish Protestants were involved in English or international missionary agencies. Today a General Synod Council for the Church Overseas co-ordinates Anglican missionary activity.

Although many Irish Catholic priests worked in *ancien régime* Europe, modern Catholic foreign missions were essentially a post-*Catholic emancipation phenomenon. The orders of female religious came first. Nano *Nagle's Sisters of the Presentation were active in Newfoundland from 1833 and in India from 1841. Catherine *McAuley's Irish Sisters of Mercy had apostolates among Aborigine, Maori, and native American communities, as well as in South Africa, Belize, and Jamaica, beginning in 1839. Frances Teresa Ball's Institute of the Blessed Virgin Mary (Loreto Sisters) had members active in India from 1841 and in South Africa from 1879. Male missionaries came later. While *Maynooth did found a mission to India in 1838, its attention, like that of the remaining continental colleges, was on the domestic church. The growing Irish diaspora's clerical needs were catered for by the local diocesan seminaries at Kilkenny (1782), Carlow (1793), Waterford (1807), Wexford (1819), and All Hallows, Dublin (1842).

The Irish *Christian Brothers, from 1825, and the Patrician Brothers from 1848, served on the diaspora mission. Later in the century, under continental influences, came a drive to produce priests for non-Christian populations, mostly within the British empire. It was the introduction of French missionary congregations like the Holy Ghost Fathers (1859) and the Society of African Missions (1877) which marked the beginning of a larger mission effort. Native foreign mission movements emerged, notably John Blowick and John Galvin's Maynooth Mission to China (1916) and St Patrick's Society for African Missions (1932). Parallel female missionary congregations flourished, like Lady Frances Maloney's Missionary Sisters of St Columban (1922), Agnes Ryan's Missionary Sisters of the Holy Rosary (1924), and Mary Martin's Medical Missionaries of Mary (1937). Lay organizations like the Apostolic Work Society, founded in France in 1838, the *Legion of Mary's Viatores Christi movement, formally established in 1964, and Edwina Gateley's lay Volunteer Missionary Movement, which spread to Ireland in 1972, were also active.

Very recent mission activity has been affected by the growing autonomy of native churches, involvement in justice issues, the growth of government foreign aid programmes, and a decline in the numbers coming forward for missionary work.

Hogan, Edmund, *The Irish Missionary Movement* (1990)

TO'C

foreign policy in independent Ireland took shape under considerable constraints. The former imperial power was both the Free State's closest neighbour and the arbiter of its economic fate, while the 'unfinished business' of the north demanded the most careful diplomatic management. As a consequence, the first two decades of Irish foreign policy were primarily concerned with defining the constitutional relationship with Britain and establishing the nature of Ireland's sovereignty. Despite the Statute of *Westminster in 1931 and an interlude of activism at the *League of Nations, the continuing issue of partition virtually predetermined Ireland's *neutrality during the Second World War.

The diplomatic isolation imposed by neutrality continued virtually undisturbed after 1945. The post-war years were ones in which an introverted, brooding sense of grievance over partition seemed to determine such foreign policy as the state pursued. Access to the *United Nations was, admittedly, denied by a Soviet veto, but withdrawal from the Commonwealth in 1949, and the refusal in the same year to participate in NATO, sharply restricted Ireland's diplomatic opportunities.

There was little to distinguish the foreign policies of the various parties in power during the 1940s and most of the 1950s. However, this lacklustre bipartisanship broke down when *Fine Gael openly opposed the efforts of Frank *Aiken, tacitly supported by de *Valera and then *Lemass, to use the opportunities of UN membership to construct a new international identity for Ireland.

By the late 1960s the prospect of admission to the European Economic Community (see EUROPEAN UNION) had redirected Irish foreign policy towards western Europe. The distinctive party approaches to international relations which had emerged a decade previously gradually lost their definition. Membership of the Community in 1973 merely confirmed this trend. Since then the dominant role of Europe in Ireland's foreign policy has been acknowledged by all parties in government.

Keatinge, P., *A Place among the Nations: Issues of Irish Foreign Policy* (1978)

Keogh, D., *Ireland and Europe, 1919–1948* (1988)

NMacQ

Foras Cosanta Áituil, see LOCAL DEFENCE FORCE.

Forth and Bargy, two baronies in Co. Wexford, noted mainly for the survival into the eighteenth century of an archaic dialect of spoken English, claimed to resemble closely that of the Chaucerian era.

forty-shilling freeholder, a person who met one of the qualifications for the electoral *franchise by owning or holding by a *lease for lives (as opposed to for a term of years) land worth 40 shillings per annum after payment of rent and other charges. The absence of a land tax removed the main potential check on fictitious valuations, and '40-shilling freeholder' was a synonym for the poorest class of voter, until the county franchise was raised to £10 after *Catholic emancipation.

Foster, John (1740–1828), MP for Dunleer 1761–8 and for Co. Louth 1768–1821, created Lord Oriel 1821. As chancellor of the Irish exchequer 1784–5 and *speaker of the Irish Commons 1785–1800, Foster formed, along with *Fitzwilliam and *Beresford, what has been described as an informal Irish cabinet, advising and sometimes dominating successive lords lieutenant. Stripped of office for his uncompromising opposition to the Act of *Union, he had a less successful post-Union career as chancellor of the Irish exchequer 1804–6, 1807–11. A committed opponent of Catholic political rights, he looked to policies of economic improvement (see FOSTER'S CORN LAW) as an antidote to disaffection, while advocating harsh repression in the crisis of the 1790s.

fostering was a popular form of child-rearing in medieval Ireland, whereby a child was sent from the natural home to be reared in another. The age of commencement was a parental decision, for example at 5, 7, 10, though wet-nursing was a common initial phase in the process of fostering. The period of fosterage was completed when the boy reached maturity (at 17) and the girl the age of marriage (at 14). The fosterage fee (*iarraith*) was reflective of the status of the father of the child and consisted of land or moveable wealth, although with 'fosterage of affection' no fee was levied. The education a child received was strictly regulated by customary law and was governed by the social status and needs of the child which ranged from manual skills to aristocratic pastimes. The foster-father (*oide*) and foster-mother (*buime*) were liable if the fosterage was found wanting. The placement of the child could indicate familial links, the maternal kin being particularly popular, or could reflect a political alliance or submission between two families. Bonds created through fosterage were a lifelong commitment, with foster-children being obliged to provide maintenance for their foster-parents in later life. BNC

Foster's corn law (1784), devised by John *Foster to subsidize the export of grain from ports other than Dublin, while restricting imports except at times of scarcity. The act was widely credited with boosting rural prosperity, although tillage farming had in fact already begun to expand in response to rising British demand. The higher subsidy for flour rather than grain did, however, encourage an expansion of provincial *flour milling. Because export subsidies were higher than the bounty paid since 1758 on corn transported by land to Dublin, the city's food supply suffered. In 1797 the inland bounties were abolished while exports through Dublin became eligible for subsidy.

foundling hospitals operated in Cork from *c.*1750 and in Dublin from 1772, developing in both cases out of *houses of industry. The primary motive behind the hospitals, which were financed by local taxes, was to rid the streets of destitute children; providing care was a secondary consideration. Between 60 and 80 per cent of the children admitted died. Conditions in the Dublin foundling hospital were particularly bad and after various attempts at reform its closure was ordered in 1830. The Cork hospital closed in 1854. VC

Four Courts, Dublin, the seat of the state's Supreme Court and High Court. The construction of a records storage building at the west end of the present site began in 1776, under the direction of Thomas Cooley. Cooley died in 1784, and the following year it was decided to enlarge his scheme by transferring the courts of law from St Michael's Hill, beside *Christ Church, to the site. James *Gandon was the architect appointed, in 1786, to complete the scheme.

The Four Courts project presented Gandon with a number of problems. The available site was small, and new construction had to accommodate Cooley's buildings. There were financial difficulties and also, following his involvement with the unpopular new *Custom House, some personalized criticism of Gandon's architectural ability.

Gandon adapted Cooley's original plan for a single quadrangle, by modifying the north and west ranges. Cooley's east range was replaced by a monumental, centrally domed block, and the south side was replaced by a screen wall with a central triumphal arch. The new quadrangle was repeated to the east of the domed block, making it the impressive centrepiece of the building. Inside, the four courts (King's Bench, chancery, exchequer, and Common Pleas) and the rolls court radiated from the central rotunda.

In 1922 the building was severely damaged by shelling and many of the irreplaceable documents from the Public Record Office were destroyed. It was reconstructed by the *Board of Works, who closed off Gandon's open arcades in the quadrangles, and most of the interior was replanned. RM

Four Masters, Annals of the, the popular name for *Annála Ríoghachta Éireann* (Annals of the Kingdom of Ireland), a compilation of earlier *annals produced during 1632–6 by the Franciscan Michael O'Clery (Micheál Ó Cléirigh) and three collaborators. See LITERATURE IN IRISH.

Fox, George (1624–91), founder of the *Society of Friends. Fox visited Ireland in 1669, where he organized Quaker congregations and engaged in public dispute with Catholics.

fox hunting, involving packs of hounds and usually mounted hunters, was introduced to Ireland in the mid-18th century from England. Hunting with hounds was known in Ireland from early times, but hares, stags, and wolves were more usual quarry. Originally packs of hounds for hunting foxes were kept by owners of large estates, the local gentry and *middlemen joining them by invitation. By 1800 subscription packs, funded by the fees of members, were established and fox hunting became more widespread. Encouragement came from resident army officers, and from a rising urban middle class who sought to ape the rural gentry. Hunting remained a sport for the relatively wealthy, however, and in 1877 there were probably no more than 20 fox hunts in Ireland, half being in Munster. Development was hampered by a number of problems, not least a lack of foxes. At least from 1780 there was an internal market in cubs, and in later years foxes were imported from Britain. Coverts were planted and artificial earths created to encourage breeding.

During and after the *Land War hunts, identified as the embodiment of landlordism, were disrupted by agrarian protesters. As late as 1912 hunts were abandoned in Co. Tipperary due to obstruction. The *First World War had no immediate effect, but hunting was suspended 1919–23, as the *Anglo-Irish War again focused hostility on the sport. Thereafter, however, a perceived increase in fox numbers gave the sport a fillip. By 1925 there were at least 25 Irish hunts, again more than half being in Munster. Subscribers were overwhelmingly prosperous farmers. New hunts were formed and some former harrier packs switched to hunting foxes. Foot hunts became more common. By 1980 there were 34 recognized riding fox hunts in Ireland. Huntsmen are still overwhelmingly wealthy as subscriptions and stabling fees are high. However, in many hunts urban professionals now outnumber rural riders.

Lewis, C. A., *Hunting in Ireland* (1975)

NG

franchise. Prior to 1832 the qualifications for voting in parliamentary elections were complex and widely varied, reflecting the gradual and unplanned evolution of law and practice. In the 32 counties, each of which sent two MPs to parliament, an act of 1542 gave the vote to *40-shilling freeholders. The two MPs for *Trinity College, Dublin, were elected by the 22 fellows and 70 scholars. The 117 boroughs that returned the remaining 234 Irish MPs fell into five categories. In 57 corporation boroughs the voters were the members of the corporation, generally 13 in number. In 34 freeman boroughs corporation members were joined by those who had been granted the freedom of the borough. In 12 boroughs 'potwallopers', householders controlling their own front door and cooking facilities, had the right to vote. In 6 manor boroughs the 40-shilling freeholders voted. Finally there were 8 county boroughs, all substantial urban centres, in which the vote was given to members of the corporation, freemen, and 40-shilling freeholders.

One hundred and seven boroughs were *'close', in the sense that a single patron controlled the outcome of the election. In corporation and freeman boroughs this happened because a patron had ensured that the unelected corporation was run by his dependants and that the freedom of the borough, where this carried voting rights, was granted sparingly and only to reliable persons. In manor and potwalloping boroughs, proprietorial control arose from the social and economic influence of a single landlord over all or the majority of voters. The open constituencies were the county boroughs (Dublin, Cork, Galway, Drogheda, Waterford, Kilkenny, Carrickfergus, and Limerick), along with Derry and Swords, Co. Dublin, each of which had an electorate too large for any one patron to dominate. There, as in the counties, there was scope for a genuine contest between rival interests, although the individual voter might be just as much under the control of a social superior as in a close borough.

The Act of *Union, reducing the Irish constituencies to the 32 counties, Trinity College, and the larger boroughs, sharply increased the proportion of open to close constituencies. The granting of *Catholic emancipation in 1829 was balanced by legislation to raise the county franchise to £10, disenfranchising the 40-shilling freeholders whom *O'Connell had so effectively mobilized. This reduced the county electorate from 216,000 to 37,000. The first major *Parliamentary Reform Act, in 1832, retained the £10 franchise in the counties, but admitted some categories of leaseholder. The multiplicity of borough franchises was replaced by a single qualification of occupation of property valued at £10 or more per annum. This brought the county electorate back to around 60,000, and the borough electorate to 30,000. However, the complexities of the registration system, and the use of leasehold as the basic qualification for voting in the counties, produced an arbitrary and unpredictable system. One Irish urban dweller in 26, and one county dweller in 116, had the vote, compared to one in 17 and one in 24 in England. After 1832, moreover, the Irish electorate declined, reflecting both the unwillingness of landlords to grant leases and, later, the ravages of the *Great Famine.

The Irish Franchise Act of 1850 was the single most important reform measure of the 19th century. The borough franchise was reduced to £8. The county franchise was set at £12, but this was now linked to occupation rather than ownership or leasehold. The registration system was thoroughly restructured. The result was to increase the Irish electorate from 45,000 to 164,000, admitted on a reasonably coherent and consistent basis. The Reform Act of 1868, affecting only the boroughs, reduced the franchise to 'over £4', and admitted lodgers occupying premises valued at £10 or more per year. By 1871 16 per cent of the adult male population could vote, compared to 34 per cent in England. The Representation of the People Act (1884) created a uniform franchise of £10 or more for the whole of the United Kingdom. The result was to admit the majority of heads of households among labourers and small farmers, while continuing to exclude lodgers, servants, and adult men living with parents. Meanwhile a Redistribution of Seats Act (1885) abolished all but nine boroughs, replacing them with new constituencies created by dividing the counties and the boroughs of Belfast and Dublin. The electorate rose from 226,000 to 738,000.

The last major extension of the franchise was in 1918, when men over 21 and women over 30 gained the vote. The electorate rose from 700,000 in 1910 to just under 2 million. Women aged between 21 and 29 were enfranchised in the Irish Free State in 1923. In Northern Ireland, as elsewhere in the United Kingdom, they had to wait until 1928.

Hoppen, K. T., *Elections, Politics and Society in Ireland 1832–1885* (1984)
Johnston, E. M., *Great Britain and Ireland 1760–1800: A Study in Political Administration* (1963)

Franciscans (Friars Minor) were established in Ireland *c.*1230. They spread rapidly, chiefly in the towns and boroughs of the Anglo-Irish colony, and by 1325 had founded 32 houses. Racial tension was acute and may have led to the deaths of sixteen friars at the hands of their confrères at the Cork chapter of 1291, though this has been challenged in the most recent study. The province was controlled by Anglo-Irish friars until the emergence of William O'Reilly (Uilliam Ó Raghallaigh) as first Gaelic provincial *c.*1445 and from then on the Gaelic friars were in the ascendant. The *Observant reform, fully established by 1460, had been adopted by 38 (out of 61) communities in 1540. The reformed friars strongly opposed the *Reformation and were closely identified with Gaelic opposition to Tudor expansion. By the early 17th century most of their houses had been suppressed but they continued to work in the localities.

The establishment of colleges in Louvain (1617), Rome (1625), and Prague (1630) allowed the Irish Franciscans to train new members and the intellectual activity of the Louvain friars and of Luke *Wadding in Rome was particularly important for the preservation of Irish culture. Following the closure of their Irish novitiates in 1751 (see RELIGIOUS ORDERS), along with the loss of their continental colleges at the end of the century, the Franciscans went into a decline which lasted until the late 19th and early 20th centuries. CNÓC

Franciscan Third Order Regular. The earliest definite reference to members of the Third Order of St Francis in Ireland occurs in 1425 when they received a copy of the bull *Supra montem* containing their rule from Pope Martin V.

Between 1426 and 1537 48 friaries were founded for male (predominantly) and female tertiaries living in community. These communities, situated almost entirely in the west and north of Ireland, were initially subject to visitation by the Franciscan friars but the appointment of Thomas Oruayn (O'Ruane?) as visitator and provincial in 1456 suggests that by then they enjoyed a large degree of autonomy. Contemporary papal documents indicate that they acted as auxiliaries to the secular clergy in some areas and a 17th-century source records that they were involved in education. Their provincial in 1600 was Donatus Cossaeus and a small number of them still survived in Ulster *c.*1616, but they appear to have died out completely shortly afterwards.

The secular Franciscan tertiaries (lay people living by the rule of the Third Order) also experienced a resurgence in the 15th century. Surviving references to them are few but are sufficiently dispersed geographically to indicate that they were a widespread phenomenon. CNÓC

Freeman's Journal, founded in Dublin in 1763, with Charles *Lucas as a major contributor. From 1786 it was subsidized by *Dublin Castle, but in 1809 it detached itself from Castle control and later supported *Catholic emancipation, *repeal, the *Land League, and *home rule. It took the side of John *Redmond when the Irish parliamentary party split in 1890. In 1921 the newspaper backed the *Anglo-Irish treaty and its presses were destroyed by the anti-treaty *IRA. In 1924 it merged with the *Irish Independent*. M-LL

freemasonry originated in Scotland around 1600, as a blend of medieval and Renaissance mysticism. It expanded rapidly in the 18th century, adapting itself to *Enlightenment rationality and catering for the growing demand, at all social levels, for new forms of sociability. An Irish grand lodge was formed in 1723 or 1724. There are indications of tensions in the early decades between *Jacobite and Hanoverian elements within the movement. Despite explicit condemnations of masonry by successive popes, in 1731, 1758, and 1786, a majority of Irish members in the late 18th century appear to have been Catholic. Daniel *O'Connell became a mason in 1799 but later openly renounced the movement. Masonry spanned all sections of society, from aristocrats like the 1st earl of Rosse, the Irish lodge's first grand master, or the 1st earl of Donoughmore (see HELY-HUTCHINSON, JOHN), also a grand master in his time, to tradesmen and farmers. There were close connections in the 1790s between masons and *United Irishmen, and in the years after the *insurrection of 1798 clashes were recorded between masons and members of the *Orange society. Yet Orangeism also incorporated much masonic symbolism in its rituals and insignia.

Irish masonry revived in the second half of the 19th century. A masonic hall in Molesworth Street, Dublin, was completed in 1869. What was by now its exclusively Protestant character, combined with the secrecy surrounding its proceedings and membership, encouraged some Catholic polemicists, particularly in the decades immediately after independence, to make extravagant claims regarding its supposed clandestine influence.

Free Presbyterian church of Ulster, founded in 1951, ostensibly in protest against *ecumenism and alleged apostasy in Irish *Presbyterianism. Ian Paisley, pastor of the Ravenhill Evangelical Mission church in Belfast, a breakaway from Ravenhill Presbyterian congregation, was invited to conduct an evangelistic mission in the vacant Presbyterian congregation of Lissara in Crossgar. The Down Presbytery refused to countenance Paisley as missioner and, in protest, five Lissara elders published a Free Presbyterian Manifesto and formed a new congregation, 'free' from Irish Presbyterian oversight. The Ravenhill Evangelical Mission church became a second Free Presbyterian congregation and there are now more than 50 congregations with a membership in Northern Ireland of 12,362 (1991 census). The Free Presbyterians also claim to have churches in England, Germany, Spain, Australia, the United States, and the Republic of Ireland. They are unashamedly *fundamentalist in doctrine and practise both believers' and infant baptism. Ian Paisley, whose own denominational background is Baptist, remains permanent moderator. His Ravenhill Evangelical Mission church has been replaced by the commodious Martyrs' memorial church in honour of the Protestant martyrs, illustrating the anti-Catholicism of the Free Presbyterians. Since 1979 the Whitefield College of the Bible, situated near Gilford in Co. Down, has trained Free Presbyterian ministers. The church remains closely linked to the *Democratic Unionist Party. RFGH

free trade agitation (1778–9). Restrictions imposed from England on Irish trade, in particular the *Woollen Act and *Navigation Acts, were a well-established *patriot grievance. Resentment grew from 1776 when an embargo on the export of provisions, imposed in February 1776 to guarantee supplies for the British army and navy, was blamed for what was in fact a general economic depression caused by the *American Revolution. In 1778 the government supported legislation, sponsored by Irish MPs at Westminster, to allow Ireland a free trade with the colonies, but the proposed concessions were attenuated following opposition from British manufacturing interests. During 1779 a systematic non-importation movement promoted a boycott of British goods in Ireland. A major demonstration of armed *Volunteers at the statue of *William III in College Green, Dublin, on 4 November involved menacing demands for 'a free trade or else', while on 15 November a crowd of 3,000–4,000 demonstrated violently outside parliament. MPs responded with a 'short money bill', granting taxes for six months instead of the usual year. On 13 December the prime minister, Lord North, announced that Ireland would be allowed to trade freely with the colonies, and to export glass and wool.

'A free trade' in the late 1770s thus meant, not trade without tariff barriers, but equal participation in the English mercantilist system. For the debate on free trade proper after 1922 see *protectionism.

French, Nicholas (1604–78), Catholic bishop of Ferns and *Confederate Catholic politician. An opponent of the first *Ormond peace, French was dispatched to Rome as crisis mounted. In November 1648 he used the pope's non-committal answer on how peace might be achieved with heretics, and a cardinal's letter about Roman opinion being divided over *Rinuccini's use of excommunication, to swing the Confederate Assembly towards the second Ormond peace. French subsequently persuaded the bishops to acquiesce, citing the compromise between Catholics and Protestants at Westphalia.

By 1650 French regretted his support for *Ormond. He met with other bishops to condemn his conduct and went to Brussels hoping to persuade Charles of Lorraine to assist Irish Catholics. After Ormond revoked his licence to return home, he became the foremost critic of the *Restoration regime, publishing *The Narrative of the Settlement and Sale of Ireland* (1668), *The Bleeding Iphigeneia* (1675), and *The Unkinde Desertor* (1676). HM

French language. Norman-French was introduced to Ireland with the *Anglo-Norman invasion, but came to be replaced by English. However, it continued to be used for formal documentary purposes long after it had died out as the normal language spoken by the settlers. The statute of *Kilkenny (1366), which sought to resist the *Gaelicization of the settler class, was written in Norman-French, even though its purpose was to insist 'that every Englishman use the English language'. TPD

French Revolution. In June 1789 financial crisis forced Louis XVI to summon the French Estates General. The propertied commoners of the third estate, backed by the Paris crowd that stormed the Bastille prison (14 July) and by widespread peasant revolt, forced the king to surrender effective power to a National Assembly. From April 1792 war against Austria and Prussia (joined by Britain, 1 Feb. 1793) undermined this compromise settlement. The king was executed in December, and in June 1793 the ruling Girondin party were deposed by the more radical Jacobins, who organized a successful national war effort but also initiated widespread executions of political opponents ('the Terror'). The Jacobin leader Maximilien Robespierre was deposed and executed in July 1794 ('Thermidor' in the revolutionary calendar). A new constitution in October 1795 vested power in five directors. In 1799 Napoleon Bonaparte overthrew the Directory in the *coup d'état* of 18–19 Brumaire (9–10 Nov.), becoming first consul and from 1804 emperor.

In Ireland, the Revolution inspired radical enthusiasm, official repression, and ultimately civil war (see INSURRECTION OF 1798). From one point of view its influence implanted in Irish popular political culture a strong element of democratic *republicanism. But it must also be recognized that this influence was filtered through existing allegiances and belief systems. The radicalism of the *United Irishmen, for example, had strong roots in long-established *patriot and *commonwealth traditions. Some old light *Presbyterians interpreted the Revolution in *millenarian and triumphalist terms, identifying the overthrow of the popish French monarchy with the defeat of Antichrist. Among the Catholic masses, equally, French radical doctrines seem to have blended with ideas of the overthrow of an unjustly established order derived from the tradition of popular *Jacobitism, with France itself still widely seen as the traditional ally of Catholic Ireland.

French interest in Ireland's potential as a weak spot in British defences began with *Jackson's mission on behalf of the Jacobin-dominated Committee of Public Safety, continued with *Tone's successful appeals to the Directory, but waned after the disappointing local response to *Hoche's expedition. Even the insurrection of 1798 produced only the token response of the *Humbert and *Tandy missions. Although surviving United Irish leaders continued to seek French assistance right up to Napoleon's overthrow (1814, confirmed by defeat at Waterloo, 18 June 1815), they received only sporadic encouragement, and were by now uneasily aware that French intervention might well replace one foreign domination with another.

Elliott, M., *Partners in Revolution: The United Irishmen and France* (1982)

Gough, H., and Dickson, D. (eds.), *Ireland and the French Revolution* (1990)

Freney, James (d. 1788), highwayman. The son of a servant in Co. Kilkenny, he turned to robbery about 1744, after failing to establish himself as a publican. He was arrested in 1749 but pardoned on giving evidence against various confederates. His *Life and Adventures*, a hugely successful autobiography published in 1754, established him as a figure in popular mythology. From 1776 he was employed as a customs official at New Ross.

friendly societies were working class self-help associations, collecting regular subscriptions out of which members could draw financial support at times of illness and from which death benefits and funeral expenses could be paid, while also offering opportunities for sociability and recreation. They received legal recognition in an Irish act of 1797 and a United Kingdom act of 1829. Two hundred and eighty-one Irish friendly societies, 119 of which were in Dublin, registered under the latter act in 1831; however, not all societies necessarily took the opportunity to register. Some Irish friendly societies were branches of English organizations such as the Oddfellows. In the late 1870s, however, the Irish National Foresters, a distinctively Irish body with a strong nationalist tone, seceded from the British-based Ancient Order of Foresters and went on to become the largest Irish friendly society. Membership of societies of all kinds declined after the First World War, as the gradual expansion of state welfare benefits undermined the original self-help function.

Friends of Ireland, a backbench group in the British Labour Party, 1945–51, who supported the Catholic/Nationalist cause in *Northern Ireland. Numbering perhaps 100 MPs at its height, it failed to persuade Attlee's government to intervene. On two occasions, the Northern Ireland bill (1947) and the *Ireland Act (1949), it circumvented the 'speaker's convention' and debated Northern Ireland issues. Friends like Geoffrey Bing saw British intervention and socialist politics as necessary precursors of Irish unity, but Hugh Delargy, chairman of the British wing of the *Anti-Partition League, argued that amelioration could only follow an ending of partition. The Ireland bill flushed out these contradictions as the government guaranteed the position of Northern Ireland in the United Kingdom. The Anti-Partition League broke with Labour and opposed four of its candidates in the 1950 general election, losing Delargy in the process. The Friends faded away. Several, including Bing and Delargy, re-emerged as Bevanites.

ACH

frontier society, in medieval Ireland. Historians have increasingly come to view medieval Ireland, both militarily and culturally, as one of a number of frontier zones which emerged in Europe, and on its fringes, in the late 11th and 12th centuries. These include the Celtic areas of Britain, the Slav lands, the Iberian peninsula, and the crusader states. Although the experience of each was different, all felt the expansionary impact of the dominant Frankish society, whose characteristic features included French language and culture and the reforming church, together with castles and heavily armed cavalry. These features are associated with the English intervention and settlements in Ireland, although the *12th-century reform of the Irish church, developments in *castle building, and changes in the nature of kingship, all testify to the extent to which influences from the Continent had already begun to affect the country before 1170.

The Irish frontier was complex. The physical geography of Ireland ensured that there was no clear, continuous border between the colonized and uncolonized areas. The English encastellated and settled fertile coastal zones and river valleys, predominantly in Leinster, Meath, and east Munster, though there were significant pockets of settlement elsewhere, for instance around Belfast Lough, Galway, and Coleraine. From these cores, they were, particularly during the period up to the mid-13th century, successful in dominating the uplands and boglands where Gaelic society continued to function. It is therefore more accurate to think of Ireland as containing, in the territorial sense, numerous regional and local frontiers. These had distinct histories, which might be shaped partly by the vigour and durability of particular settler magnates, their families, and knightly subtenants. The colonizing powers did not exist in a state of perpetual warfare with their Gaelic neighbours. The segmentary quarrels of native ruling houses permitted a constant criss-cross of alliances, through which lords such as the *Lacys, *Geraldines, and de *Burghs maintained and expanded their influence. In the first generation, marriages between settler lords and native noblewomen were not uncommon. Irish and English troops fought in the same armies, and military equipment and tactics were affected by this experience.

From the late 13th century there was a faltering of colonization in Europe generally, which some have associated with climatic change. Ireland shared this experience. The retreat of the colony, as the initiative passed back into Gaelic hands, although slow and patchy, sharpened contemporary awareness of the frontier. From the 1270s the Irish of Wicklow and Offaly were raiding the settlements in Leinster, creating a serious problem of defence for the Dublin government. But at the same period Richard de *Burgh, the Red Earl of Ulster, was able to expand his power to Derry and beyond, and Thomas de *Clare was establishing a lordship in *Thomond. Even so, the royal records now constantly distinguish between the 'land of peace' (the settled regions where English law prevailed), the 'land of war' (the areas of Gaelic custom, where cattle-raiding was normal), and the 'march', or borderlands, in between.

During the 14th century the 'land of war' and the 'march' expanded greatly at the expense of the 'land of peace'. The most fundamental agent of change was probably the recurrent outbreaks of plague, beginning with the *Black Death of 1348, which seem to have affected the populations of towns and nucleated manorial settlements particularly severely. But disruption caused by the *Bruce invasion of 1315–18, which coincided with a major European famine, was also significant. There was in addition the impact of the subdivision of lordships among co-heiresses and their inheritance by *absentees, which was a particular feature of the first half of the century. The retreat of the frontier is visible in various ways. The Dublin government focused increasingly on the south-east, as *justiciars fought and negotiated with the Irish of Leinster; by 1500 this concentration was to foster the concept of the English *Pale. Easy terms were offered to men willing to take and fortify deserted lands. Legislation urged lords and communities to desist from individual negotiations with the Irish, and to synchronize their military efforts. Towns such as *Waterford, *Cork, and *Limerick portrayed themselves as surrounded by Irish enemies and rebellious English lords. Resident magnates probably weathered the storm better than central government or absentees. Their power had always depended on a combination of exploiting settler communities and establishing networks of clientship among the Irish. During the later Middle Ages the balance between the two activities altered; in the mid-14th century the archives of the earls of *Kildare and *Ormond contain many contracts regularizing their relations with Gaelic lords. In the border zones there was an increasing convergence between lesser noble families of English and Irish origin; both were securing their possessions by building *tower houses.

In the mid-14th century official pronouncements about what historians have come to call *Gaelicization reveal a consciousness that there was a cultural as well as a military threat. Relations with the Irish host society, which had once been taken for granted, were now, fruitlessly, outlawed. This phenomenon is encapsulated in the Statute of *Kilkenny (1366). The image the statute presents, of an embattled 'English Ireland', though oversimplified, reveals the characteristic outlook of a colonial society alarmed by the contraction of its once expanding frontiers.

Bartlett, R., *The Making of Europe: Conquest, Colonization and Cultural Change* (1993)

—— and Mackay, A. (eds.), *Medieval Frontier Societies* (1989)
Lydon, J. F., *The Lordship of Ireland in the Middle Ages* (1972)

RFF

Froude, J. A. (1818–94), historian. Born into an affluent clerical family in Devon, Froude was educated at Westminster College and Oriel College, Oxford. He visited Ireland in 1842 and again in 1845, when he contracted smallpox. He maintained a summer residence in the country after 1865. He also travelled widely abroad on government business, acted as the literary executor and biographer of his mentor Thomas Carlyle, and wrote a number of controversial historical works. His main contribution to Irish historiography was his *The English in Ireland in the Eighteenth Century* (1872). Froude's thesis was that Britain had consistently failed to provide Ireland with firm government or unequivocally to support the Protestant interest there. As a result, 18th-century Irish society was underdeveloped, fractious, and lawless. The effects of the book were unintended. Irish nationalists, while rejecting Froude's ideas of the necessity of an authoritarian, Anglocentric regime, cited his observations on the nature of Ireland's ills to support their own conceptions of British mismanagement. Froude's polemical exaggerations also prompted W. E. H. *Lecky to publish his own work on the period. NG

fuidir, a category of semi-free dependant frequently mentioned in the early Irish *law tracts. He is maintained by a lord in return for his labour. The lord is responsible for any liabilities or fines incurred by the *fuidir* or his family, but he is also entitled to retain any fines for offences against the *fuidir*. Unlike a client of **bó-aire* rank, the *fuidir* cannot make a legal contact without his lord's permission. He is not allowed to part from his lord unless he surrenders two thirds of the produce of his husbandry and leaves no debts behind him.

The texts provide a number of reasons why people were reduced to the status of *fuidir*. A *fuidir* may have been expelled from his kin-group or have been sentenced to death for a serious crime and subsequently been ransomed by a lord. A person whose father and grandfather were of *fuidir* rank is further reduced to the status of **senchléithe*. FK

Fulborn, Stephen de, bishop of Waterford 1273–86, archbishop of Tuam 1286–8, treasurer 1274–85, *justiciar 1281–8. Appointed treasurer of Ireland in 1274 as part of a campaign to reform the administration, he was summoned to the English exchequer in 1285 to answer accusations of corruption arising from an examination of the government of Ireland conducted the previous year. He was found to owe the crown over £13,000, but was pardoned this sum and allowed to continue as justiciar until his death in 1288. He complained about the appointment of sheriffs from England in Irish counties. He established a mint at Waterford in 1281 and in the following year arranged for the murder of Art and Muirchertach *MacMurrough (Mac Murchadha) by the English of Leinster. In 1286 the pope transferred him to the vacant archbishopric of Tuam and made his brother Walter bishop of Waterford. Walter acted as deputy treasurer in the Irish administration. BGCS

fundamentalism, deriving from *The Fundamentals* (1910–15), a twelve-volume, multi-authored, theological protest against trends in modern religion and society published in the USA. The use of the term fundamentalism has changed over time and admits of no easy definition. Described as 'militantly anti-modernist Protestant evangelicalism', fundamentalism is regarded by some as a term of abuse and by others as a proud badge of theological orthodoxy. The word itself came into common currency in the USA in the 1920s. It is in that decade also that it came to have some significance in Irish religious life. The populist evangelist W. P. *Nicholson has been described as a militant fundamentalist who contributed a hard edge to evangelical orthodoxy. Meanwhile the Revd James Hunter orchestrated a campaign against theological professors in the Presbyterian College in Belfast, culminating in the charge of heresy brought against J. E. *Davey and the secession, following his acquittal, of the Irish Evangelical (later the Evangelical Presbyterian) church.

Many of the issues surrounding this split within Presbyterianism were rehearsed in modified forms twenty-five years later with the founding of the *Free Presbyterian church over which Ian Paisley, who thought of himself as the heir of the fundamentalists of the 1920s, quickly established control. To most outsiders Paisley, with his well-maintained connections with strands of American conservative Protestantism, is the embodiment of fundamentalism in Ulster Protestant culture, but in fact fundamentalist attitudes are not confined within the boundaries of the Free and Evangelical Presbyterian churches. This then raises the problem of how exactly fundamentalism should be defined, given that its advocates are not easily separated from hotter forms of *evangelicalism. There is no easy answer to this difficulty, but suffice to say that fundamentalism is usually associated with anti-Catholicism, anti-modernism, anti-liberalism (both theological and ethical), anti-ecumenism, and anti-Darwinism. Such a world-view is not merely the product of rational theological disputation, but has its roots in contests for cultural, political, and religious power. Fundamentalism is therefore as much a cohesive frame of mind as a theological position.

DNH

furniture. Very little is known about Irish furniture made prior to the 18th century since very few pieces have survived. The furniture recorded in early house inventories, which may or may not have been indigenously Irish, has mostly disappeared. The tremendous surge in building of both Dublin town houses and country mansions during the 18th century was matched by increased activity in the furniture trade. Newspapers of the time carried advertisements for cabinetmakers, gilders, japanners, carvers, makers of mirrors, wallpaper, etc., and there is also evidence that furniture was exported from Ireland to America. Unfortunately, little original furniture remains in any of these large houses and it is almost impossible to attribute the majority of the pieces still held in these houses or in public/private collections to specific makers. However trade labels adhering to a piece of furniture can in some cases allow some form of attribution to the manufacturer or retailer of the furniture.

The principal characteristics popularly attributed to 18th-century Irish furniture include grotesque masks elaborately carved on friezes and legs, mainly on mahogany tables; punched and diaper backgrounds behind relief carving; and cabriole legs with square paw feet. However Irish pieces fitting these descriptions exist alongside furniture indistinguishable from English work, either because they are imported pieces, or because Irish craftsmen derived their inspiration from the published trade catalogues of English cabinetmakers such as Thomas Chippendale.

By the last quarter of the 18th century, the fashion for heavily carved mahogany and walnut furniture had given way to the neoclassical style that had begun to pervade English furniture design. Irish characteristics disappeared almost completely as Irish craftsmen sought to follow the prevailing fashions. William Moore was one of the many Dublin cabinetmakers listed in directories of this time who worked in this new style, first at Abbey Street (1785–91) and then at Capel Street (1792–1814). He used fashionable satinwood embellished with marquetry inlays to create furniture that echoed the work of the English architect and furniture designer Robert Adam.

The use of marquetry decoration carried on well into the next century. Dublin cabinetmakers such as Robert Strahan & Co., who had workshops during the mid-19th century, at 24/25 Henry Street and 5 Leinster Street, catered to the Victorian taste for highly decorative furniture with elaborate pieces using marquetry and parquetry. Marquetry was also to feature greatly in one distinctively Irish area of 19th-century furniture making. In the 1850s Killarney became the production centre for a particular style of inlaid furniture that became known as Killarney ware. The local arbutus wood was elaborately inlaid with other woods depicting scenes from around Killarney such as Muckross Abbey. Production declined and ceased during the early part of the 20th century.

Celtic imagery featured prominently in the work of Arthur Jones of Dublin who exhibited his work at the 1851 Great Exhibition in London. Jones, who had taken over the family business in 1840, displayed 20 pieces of excessively ornamental carved 'bog yew' furniture. Towards the end of the century the Victorian yearning for styles of antiquity prompted many cabinetmakers to reproduce furniture from earlier periods. One such cabinetmaker, James Hicks, was extremely skilled at producing furniture in 18th-century styles. He set up business in 1893 at 5 Lower Pembroke Street, Dublin, making fine veneered and inlaid furniture usually to commission. During the 1930s, he also produced some pieces that reflected the Art Deco fashion of the time.

The only Irish furniture designer to have a truly international reputation was Eileen Gray. Born in Co. Wexford in 1879, she originally studied painting at the Slade School before settling in France. A notable feature of her work was her experimental use of oriental lacquer. Her abstract modernist approach to furniture design was highly influential throughout Europe and further afield.

Existing alongside the cabinetmaker's productions was the traditional furniture made to satisfy the needs of rural households. This vernacular furniture was made by the local carpenter who relied on the use of cheap softwoods imported from the Baltic or indigenous gathered wood. Vernacular furniture peculiar to Ireland includes the twisted rope seated súgán chair, the one-piece made dresser, and the settle bed.

Kinmouth, C., *Irish Country Furniture 1700–1950* (1993)
Knight of Glin, *Irish Furniture* (1978)

KMa

Gael (adj. Gaelic), the name of the population of Ireland, particularly those who adhere(d) to the Irish language and native culture. The word appears originally as Goídel and is a loanword from Welsh Gwyddel, 'Irishman', which itself has a pejorative meaning (Welsh *gwydd*, 'wild, savage'). Irish tradition derived the name from Gaedheal Glas, a grandson of Noah who fashioned the Irish (*Gaedhilg*, 'Gaelic') language from the best elements of the 72 languages spoken at the time of the tower of Babel. It appears to have been employed as an ethnic term by the Irish themselves at least by the 8th century, when it first appears in the *annals, and it came to replace *Érainn, which was previously employed to describe the people of Ireland. The *Viking incursions further stimulated the use of 'Gael' as an ethnic designation to contrast the native Irish with the foreign invaders. The term was employed specifically of the Irish as an ethnolinguistic group, while Érainn remained the designation of the island itself. JPM

Gaelic Athletic Association (GAA), founded 1884 by Michael Cusack (1847–1906). Cusack, a teacher and one-time enthusiast for cricket and rugby, had become disillusioned with the social exclusiveness of existing sporting bodies and the association of sport and gambling, and was also convinced that the spread of English games was destroying national morale. The GAA from the start attracted substantial *Fenian support; there are claims that Cusack was in fact only the instrument of an *IRB initiative. By 1886 Fenians dominated the executive and Cusack himself had been ousted from the secretaryship. Open Fenian domination provoked the hostility of the Catholic clergy, especially when the GAA supported *Parnell in 1890–1, and membership slumped badly in the 1890s. From 1901, however, a new generation of IRB-affiliated leaders rebuilt the GAA as an openly nationalist but not explicitly revolutionary movement that could attract clerical endorsement and broad support. Rules excluding from the association anyone who played or even watched 'imported games', and all members of the police and armed forces, quietly dropped during the difficult 1890s, were reinstated during 1902–3.

The GAA was thus part of the *'new nationalism' of the years before 1916. But it was also part of the sudden growth of organized spectator sport seen everywhere in the British Isles from the late 19th century. By the early 1900s attendances of 20,000 at the most important fixtures had become commonplace and entrance charges had replaced affiliation fees from clubs as the main source of revenue. Railway companies provided special trains for important fixtures, and *newspapers gave wide coverage. The purchase in 1913 of a site at Jones's Road, Dublin, subsequently developed as Croke Park, provided Gaelic games with a national stadium. The games themselves also changed their character. Athletics, originally the GAA's main concern, declined in prominence, and from 1922 was to be handed over to the National Athletics and Cycling Association. Among the team games that now took pride of place, *Gaelic football overshadowed the much older but, for spectators, less easily followed *hurling. In both games rules and playing styles were modified to emphasize skill and tactics rather than strength or aggression.

Despite the short-term losses inflicted by large-scale disruption during the *Anglo-Irish War and *Civil War, the GAA retained and consolidated its place as a major part of sporting life in independent Ireland and, for Catholics, in Northern Ireland. The ban on watching or playing 'foreign' games was lifted in 1971. The more controversial Rule 21, excluding members of the police and army in Northern Ireland, was abandoned in 2001.

Mandle, W. F., *The Gaelic Athletic Association and Irish Nationalist Politics 1884–1924* (1987)

Gaelic cultural revival. The literate culture of pre-*Norman Ireland, *Latin and vernacular, sacred and secular, was a creation of the monastic schools. It suffered severely in the *Cistercian reform of the 12th century, which eventually came to oppose the monks' conversing in Irish or writing Irish *annals and laymen's adherence to customary *brehon law. Simultaneously the church-sponsored arts of manuscript illumination (see DECORATED MANUSCRIPTS), sculpture, and *architecture were affected by changing fashions following the *Anglo-Norman invasion. In the 13th century only the art of the praise-poets (*fir dhána*, an amalgam of the earlier orders of *baird* and *filidh*) flourished, suggesting their training and patronage were largely secular—this seems also applicable to the less well-documented musicians. By the opening years of the 14th century, if not earlier, Irish praise-poets and musicians were employed by Anglo-Norman aristocrats as well.

However, the subordination of all Irish chiefs either to the English crown directly, or to an Anglo-Norman earl or baron, undermined the social function of *bardic poetry, which was a celebration of the sovereign powers of a king. A number of poems dating *c.*1340–60 refer to a decline in patronage, either because employers preferred the cheaper services of untrained ballad-singers, or because the church had banned payments to poets. Condemnatory decrees in the legislation of Armagh provincial synods were reinforced for the Anglo-Irish community by the Statute of *Kilkenny in 1366.

Consequently, that Uilliam Ó Ceallaigh (O'Kelly, d. 1381), chief of Uí Mhaine, decided to hold a great Christmas feast for the bardic classes of Ireland in 1351, can be seen as symbolic of the Gaelic political resurgence then taking place (see GAELIC RECOVERY). Other patrons followed suit, notably Margaret, daughter of Ó Cearbhaill (O'Carroll), in 1433. Ó Ceallaigh's *ollamh, Seán Mór Ó Dubhagáin (d. 1372), used the learning of pre-Norman schools in his own historical and genealogical compositions. Scribe in an early part of the Book of Uí Mhaine, Ó Dubhagáin pioneered the movement to copy Old and Middle Irish texts from monastic manuscripts into great anthologies such as the Book of Ballymote, and the Great Book of Lecan, compiled for lay patrons or secular schools of history. Handwriting and illumination in these manuscripts consciously imitate their pre-Norman prototypes. The same revival of 12th-century styles appears in the metalwork of early Christian shrines and relics restored under the patronage of late medieval Irish chiefs, or the carving of the 'Brian Boru harp' in Trinity College, Dublin.

In the 15th century the need to cast an aura of legitimacy over newly independent authority applied to Anglo-Irish earls and barons also, and they too began to patronize the bardic classes and commission great manuscript anthologies including the Book of Fermoy and the Saltair of MacRichard Butler. Only the completion of the *Tudor reconquest rendered bardic schools obsolete.

Cosgrove, A. (ed.), *A New History of Ireland*, vol. ii (1987)
Simms, K., 'Bards and Barons', in R. Bartlett and A. Mackay (eds.), *Medieval Frontier Societies* (1989)

KS

Gaelic football received its first set of codified rules in 1885, following the founding of the *Gaelic Athletic Association in the previous year. References from the 17th century onwards describe a form of football being played in Ireland, in which carrying the ball, as well as kicking it, was common. However, regional variations, including ball shape, were many. By the 1860s rural depopulation had led to a decline in the playing of these games. In urban centres sports such as *cricket and *rugby were now popular. In fact, the resurrection of 'Gaelic football' probably owed much to the popularity of rugby, in which early leading figures, such as Michael Cusack, and clubs, such as Laune Rangers, had previously been involved.

An all-Ireland championship was contested from 1887. By 1915 reduction in team size, the introduction of a lighter ball, the use of hand passing, and new team tactics had made Gaelic football the most popular spectator sport in Ireland: 30,000 watched that year's all-Ireland final. By 1926 the attendance rose to 40,000, with a record 90,000 crowd in 1961. During its early years the sport was dominated by Dublin teams, though from 1903 the focus turned to Munster. The effects of the *First World War and following conflicts were minimal, and the game consolidated its position throughout the country. In 1947 the all-Ireland final was held in New York, while in 1967 an Australian Rules side toured Ireland. Though profitable, these attempts to encourage Gaelic football overseas largely failed. NG

Gaelic Ireland, political and social structures. Early medieval Ireland presents itself as a fragmented entity, in which the basic units were **tuatha* ('peoples') ruled by *kings, kings being abundant. Within the *tuath* rank depended in part on ancestry, in part on personal authority, and in part on property; the same functions were almost always passed on from generation to generation: farmers' sons became farmers, blacksmiths' sons became blacksmiths. All men had in theory an honour price (see *enech*), which governed their capacity to carry out legal acts such as contracts or giving evidence, and to receive compensation for wrongs committed against them.

The highest ranks of society are classed as *nemed* ('privileged'): these are specified as kings and lords, clerics and poets (see *fili*). The abundance of kings in the early medieval period meant inevitably that some kings became subject to other kings, with the consequence that those with subordinate kings had a higher honour price.

Some persons in the population enjoyed a status somewhere between these persons of high status and the ordinary freeman by virtue of the skills useful to society—craftsmen such as a blacksmith or carpenter, or specialists such as a physician or harpist. But the majority of the population is best represented by the ordinary freeman, who had an honour price in his own right by virtue of having sufficient property to maintain himself and his family: the more property, the higher his status. He was normally regarded as being a *client of a lay or ecclesiastical lord, from whom he could accept, for a specified period, a fief of a specified number of cattle and in return render specified services and food rent to his lord. The more clients a lord had, the higher his status; and for the client it was an opportunity to increase his wealth and hence his own standing. Some *law tracts of the period imply that the country's population had been increasing since the mid-6th century, with a consequent increase in dependent freedmen. The rank of a freeman's dependant—his wife, son, or daughter—was a proportion of the freeman's. Below the level of the freeman were various groups of unfree persons, some of whom were tenants at will, others hereditary serfs, and yet others slaves in the strict sense.

This society, while stratified, was not rigidly so: a freeman who misbehaved might be degraded, i.e. have his honour price reduced, without the honour price of his dependants being reduced; and a freeman who acquired sufficient wealth to be able to afford clients (like a lord) went up in the social scale. At this level, however, the greater the number of sons a freeman had, the less their honour price would be when they succeeded to his property, since it would be divided equitably among them.

The early texts go into considerable detail on minute gradations of rank; by the 12th century, however, these have, in common usage, been much simplified, though remaining stratified. The ordinary commoner is classified as a *biatach* (Anglo-Norman *betagh) and corresponds to the client of earlier centuries, paying services and food rent (*biad*) to a lord on a permanent basis; the rare commoner who is independent is known as a *saertach* ('exempt'), and progressively in the 13th and 14th centuries is absorbed into the ranks of the lesser nobility. It is in the ranks of the nobility that are found social shifts betrayed by shifts of terminology. The highest rank of late medieval society is king (*rí*) or chief (*toísech*), but the distinction is fading, and within individual dynasties the title of successive rulers wavers from one to the other. This is perhaps a side effect of the contacts with England before and after the *Anglo-Norman invasion: the upper classes of Irish society copied the official retinue of English kings, as far as their resources permitted. Diarmait *Mac Murchada, in two charters, has a notary and a chancellor; O'Connor of Connacht in a charter of 1224 parades a seneschal, a chancellor, and a royal notary. The household of the early medieval Irish ruler was simple; that of a 13th- or 14th-century Irish ruler complicated, with in some cases ritual offices shared between two or three persons. Where once the status of a noble depended on his property and subjects, it now depended on his rapport with his ruler.

The effect of the invasion on the lower levels of society was variable. In the areas effectively colonized, the ordinary Irishman, previously subject to an Irish lord, was taken by his Anglo-Norman lord to be a serf and treated as such, although in a number of areas the Irish retained practical control at this level as a colony of betaghs and rendered service collectively to their new lords. Outside the colonial areas there are strong indications that a similar depression of social status evolved in the 14th to 16th centuries, with increasing levels of exploitation.

MacNiocaill, G., 'A propos du vocabulaire social irlandais du bas moyen âge', *Études celtiques*, 12 (1970–1)

Ó Cróinín, D., *Early Medieval Ireland 400–1200* (1995)

GMacN

Gaelicization, a term favoured by some modern historians to describe what they see as a key development in the later Middle Ages, the assimilation of the descendants of the *Anglo-Norman settlers by the Irish host society. While the term is not of course contemporary, it does reflect the view of medieval administrators—expressed most notably in the 1366 Statute of *Kilkenny—that the Englishness (and hence the loyalty) of the settler population was being undermined by native influences. Among the socio-political changes often identified—alongside the spread of the Irish language and literary culture—as symptomatic of 'Gaelicization' are the decline of English common law and its replacement over large areas by *brehon or *march law; the presence of extended aristocratic lineages, sometimes practising Gaelic marriage and inheritance customs; the use of Gaelic personal names; the prevalence of cattle-raiding and Irish styles of arms and combat; and the exercise of lordship, including the support of troops, through Gaelic exactions such as *coyne.

The concept of Gaelicization should, however, be employed with caution and discrimination. The official evidence is the product of a period which assumed a closer linkage than before between language, nationality, and political allegiance. Both royal ministers and the settler elites of towns and manorialized lowlands in the south-east might attribute Irishness, with connotations of disloyalty, to lords and lineages who saw themselves as English, and loyal. Ministers were also inclined to lump together all divergences from supposed English norms and view them as the result of specifically Irish influences. Some features—particularly cattle-raiding and march law—need to be understood also as the product of *frontier conditions and a largely pastoral economy; they have parallels in other regions, including the English-speaking Anglo-Scottish borders. Above all, the rhetoric of the sources can obscure the fact that influences passed both ways. Between the 13th and 16th centuries, for instance, Irish law borrowed English terms and procedures; Gaelic lordship and military institutions were influenced by English models; members of some Irish dynasties bore Anglo-Norman personal names. Irish historians have tended to be comfortable with the idea of a settler population progressively absorbed by the Gaelic world, to the point of becoming *'more Irish than the Irish themselves'. The other side of the coin has until recently attracted less attention.

This is not to doubt the impact of Gaelic influences, which affected different areas of the colony in differing degrees, and operated in different ways at various social levels. But the concept of Gaelicization, if used as a glass through which to view the society of later medieval Ireland, is liable to distort. That society was a hybrid one which had emerged through a complex process of interaction and cultural exchange.

Frame, R., 'Power and Society in the Lordship of Ireland, 1272–1377', *Past and Present*, 76 (1977)

Nicholls, K., *Gaelic and Gaelicised Ireland in the Middle Ages* (1972)

Simms, K., *From Kings to Warlords: The Changing Political Structure of Gaelic Ireland in the Later Middle Ages* (1987)

RFF

Gaelic League, Irish-language organization established in 1893 by Eoin *MacNeill and others, with Douglas *Hyde as first president. Unlike earlier movements concerned with antiquarian and folkloric studies, the league sought to revive Irish as a spoken and literary language. It ran language classes and Irish-speaking social gatherings, including from 1897 a national festival, An tOireachtas, modelled on the Welsh Eisteddfod, published a newspaper, *An *Claidheamh Soluis*, and sponsored the publication of contemporary verse and prose. Public awareness of its work was heightened in 1899 when it opposed attempts, headed by John Pentland Mahaffy (1839–1919), provost of *Trinity College, Dublin, to have Irish removed from the intermediate school syllabus. During 1908–9 it campaigned successfully to have Irish declared a compulsory matriculation subject in the *National University of Ireland.

The membership of the league was drawn mainly from the urban lower middle classes of English-speaking Ireland. As such it testifies, like the near contemporary *Gaelic Athletic Association, to the acute need for cultural roots experienced by many at the end of several decades of exceptionally rapid social change. There was an inevitable tendency to idealize the culture and way of life of the surviving *Gaeltacht areas, and the neo-medieval fantasies indulged in by enthusiasts are easy to caricature. Yet if the return to an imagined Gaelic world represented for some an escape from the pressures of *modernization, for others language revival was the means by which Ireland could enter the modern world without losing its identity.

The leadership of the league, notably Hyde, insisted that it should be non-political, and the movement initially attracted significant support from Protestants and *unionists. However, the Mahaffy and matriculation controversies, while boosting membership, gave the language question an inescapable political undertone. Differences in outlook between nationalist and unionist members were evident in debates on whether the league should create links with other parts of the United Kingdom through the Pan-Celtic movement. In 1914 the Church of Ireland clergyman Canon James Hannay (1865–1950) was expelled for what were considered derogatory portrayals of Irish life in works published under his pseudonym George Birmingham. By this time a concerted *IRB takeover of the movement was largely complete, leading to Hyde's resignation as president in 1915. League members took a prominent part in the *rising of 1916 and in the subsequent growth of *Sinn Féin and the *IRA. The league itself was declared an illegal organization in September 1919. Today, generally known by its Irish name Connradh na Gaeilge, it remains active in the promotion of Irish language and literature.

Hutchinson, John, *The Dynamics of Cultural Nationalism: The Gaelic Revival and the Creation of the Irish Nation State* (1987)

Gaelic recovery is a phrase describing the gradual emancipation of many Irish chieftaincies in the later Middle Ages from the control of the English king and the Dublin administration, partly as a result of military action by the chiefs themselves, partly because of internal decline in the Anglo-Irish colony.

Eoin *MacNeill saw this recovery as beginning in the mid-13th century, reflected in military victories like the defeat of the Fitzgeralds by the *O'Donnells at Credran near Sligo in 1257 and the battle of *Callan (1261), in the use of *gallowglasses by O'Connor and O'Donnell leaders, and in the recognition of Brian *O'Neill as king over all the Gaels of Ireland. However this last initiative was to end in O'Neill's defeat at the battle of *Down (1260), and the later 13th century saw further expansion and tightening of colonial control in the west under Richard de *Burgh, earl of Ulster and lord of Connacht, and Thomas (d. 1287) and Richard de *Clare (d. 1318), lords of Thomond.

Ultimately the most significant revolts of the 13th century were those of the Leinster Irish (1271–7, and 1295 onwards). They were closest to Dublin, the administrative centre of the lordship, their territorial expansion was at the expense of the colonized area, and medieval governors never found a lasting solution to the threat they posed. Elsewhere it was the 14th century that was the period of major advance for the chieftains. The invasion of Edward *Bruce hastened the colony's decline and the disruption provided additional opportunities for rebellion. After the battle of *Dysert O'Dea (1318) the O'Brien lordship became effectively autonomous, and the assassination in 1333 of William de *Burgh, earl of Ulster and lord of Connacht, led to the independence of Connacht under his rebel cousins, the de Burgh or Burke lords of Mayo. Meanwhile the *O'Neills of *Cenél nEógain gradually rebuilt a province-wide lordship over the other Ulster chiefs, hindered only by the rivalry of the *O'Donnells, and their own kinsmen, the *O'Neills of Clandeboye.

Outside Leinster, the main gains of the recovery were political rather than territorial. To the Anglo-Irish the chiefs were subjects in the 13th century, enemies and felons in the 14th, and potential allies in the 15th. The effort to rebuild past overkingships meant that much of the fighting took place between the chieftains themselves, and was accompanied by a revival of interest in pre-Norman art and literature (see GAELIC CULTURAL REVIVAL). This interest was shared by the Anglo-Irish marcher lords, whose power also grew with the weakening of royal government (see GAELICIZATION). By the end of the 15th century it was these who came to dominate both Irish chiefs and Anglo-Irish towns beyond the *Pale area.

Cosgrove, A. (ed.), *A New History of Ireland*, vol. ii (1987)
Nicholls, K., *Gaelic and Gaelicised Ireland in the Middle Ages* (1972)
Simms, K., *From Kings to Warlords* (1987)

KS

Gaeltacht is the collective name for areas where Irish is spoken. In 1922 Irish was still the general medium of communication in parts of Cos. Waterford, Cork, Kerry, Galway, Mayo, and Donegal. Scattered pockets of Irish speakers in Cos. Louth, Kilkenny, and Clare were not considered true Gaeltacht. Native governments have given the Gaeltacht preferential treatment, including grants for Irish-speaking children, employment schemes, and since 1979 a development authority. In 1970 a radiostation for the Gaeltacht was established with headquarters in Costelloe, Co. Galway. The decline in the numbers of Irish speakers continued, however, and by the 1980s the actual areas of Irish speech were considerably less than the official Gaeltacht. Indeed many now fear that the true Gaeltacht is on the verge of extinction.

The Irish of the Gaeltacht has been studied in detail by Finck (1899), Quiggin (1906), Sommerfelt (1922), Sjoestedt-Jonval (1931), Wagner (1958-69), and others. The Gaeltacht has produced many writers in Irish, for example, Tomás Ó Criomhthain (1856–1937) from Kerry, Máirtín Ó Cadhain (1907–70) from Galway, and Seosamh Mac Grianna (1901–93) from Donegal.

In the 1930s some Gaeltacht families were resettled in Leinster. The Irish-speaking community in Rath Carn, Co. Meath, is still fairly vigorous.

NJAW

Gallicanism, a theory of state–church relations, favouring the limitation of papal authority by general councils and/or state intervention. It was strong in France where, from the mid-15th century, the emerging state brought the church under its control. This was achieved at the expense both of the Gallican church's relations with Rome and of the independence of its bishops. A milestone in the process was the 1682 Declaration of the Four Articles. In Ireland, a form of Gallicanism emerged in the *Restoration period when *Old English catholics attempted in the *Remonstrances of 1661 and 1666 to reconcile loyalty to the pope with that required by the king. With the re-entry of Catholics into civil life in the late 18th century, the old question of divided loyalties arose once again and some early 19th-century bishops, anxious to speed up the granting of *Catholic emancipation, considered giving London a *veto on episcopal appointments. *Maynooth College, because of its state grant, independent governing structures, and French associations, was held in suspicion by some bishops. In the 1850s Archbishop *Cullen, anxious to increase episcopal control of the college, accused some of its professors of Gallican tendencies. In the longer term, *ultramontanism proved more politically useful to the Irish Catholic community than Gallicanism. TO'C

gallowglass (Ir. *gallóglach*, 'foreign warrior', or 'warrior from the *Innse Gall*, the Hebrides'). In the 11th and 12th centuries Irish sources indicate that some provincial kings already used mercenaries from the Hebrides, chiefly as bodyguards, but from the mid-13th century larger troops, under the name of *gallóglaigh*, or gallowglass, were imported from Argyle and the Western Isles of Scotland by the chiefs of Ulster and north Connacht, where they played a significant role in stiffening Irish resistance to the extension of English settlements. They were armoured foot soldiers, wielding long- and short-handled battleaxes, spears, and two-handed swords, and their value lay in their ability to beat off a cavalry charge, forming a wall of defence across the battlefield from behind which the light Irish horsemen could make short charges before retreating and regrouping. They were led by their own chieftains, MacDonalds, *MacSweenys, MacCabes, MacSheehys, and MacLeods, who received grants of land in various parts of Ireland from the lords who employed them, and became part of the hereditary nobility of Ireland. By the 15th and 16th centuries Irish and Anglo-Irish lords in Munster and Leinster also employed them, often as bodyguards or for policing duties. KS

Galway, the only substantial medieval city in Connacht. It was little more than a fortified ford over the Corrib river when first captured by Richard de *Burgh in 1230; the first mention of a town in the *annals is for the year 1247. Galway thrived over the next century under firm de Burgh protection, a modest walled town of about 35 acres. With the fracturing of that dynasty after 1333 the town sought its independence, receiving a murage charter from the crown in the 1390s and a far stronger municipal charter in 1484. This copper-fastened the autonomy of the town against the encircling magnates, Hiberno-Norman and Gaelic. At the same time the creation of the wardenship of *Galway gave the townsmen control over the large parish church, St Nicholas, and its possessions.

For the next century and a half Galway's mercantile elite, the 'tribes', extended their economic influence across much of the west and beyond. A narrow range of overseas exchanges with Spain and France—hides and fish outwards, wines and fine cloth inwards—created many civic fortunes, and, not unexpectedly, Galwaymen were precociously involved in Caribbean commerce in the early 17th century. These mercantile fortunes were converted into urban castles, rural *tower houses, land purchase, and, in the earlier stages, monastic endowments.

However, where once the English government had emancipated the townsmen, 17th-century religious and political convulsions from across the water impoverished their decendants: Galway citizens went against their garrison and supported the confederate side in 1642 (see CONFEDERATE CATHOLICS OF IRELAND). They capitulated to *Cromwellian forces in 1652 after a nine-month siege; plague and expulsions followed. The urban economy recovered some of its old resilience for a generation, but in the next crisis the city remained *Jacobite until 1691; it surrendered without a siege (see GALWAY, ARTICLES OF) and derived some benefit from inclusion within the terms of the treaty of *Limerick. Thereafter the town became something of a commercial backwater. It lost its former wholesale hinterland to Dublin, and the capital and energies of its erstwhile leading families to foreign and colonial ventures.

Only towards the end of the 18th century did the town begin to expand rapidly, thriving on the demographic explosion in its hinterland (and the agricultural surpluses to which it gave rise) before eventually being nearly overwhelmed by it. Despite the great fishing traditions of the Claddagh, the seafaring suburb to the west of the town, and a programme of docks construction, 19th-century maritime trade never lived up to its promise. But Victorian Galway prospered in a limited way as a commercial, educational, and tourist centre of the west, with a university college (see QUEEN'S COLLEGES) trying to maintain minimum numbers.

Since the 1920s, and dramatically so since the 1960s, Galway has expanded more than any other provincial centre in independent Ireland; this has been a reflection both of state industrial and cultural policies, and of the atrophying of small towns in the region. Its outstanding 20th-century public monument, the Catholic cathedral (1965), remains an ambiguous civic symbol.

Clarke, Howard (ed.), *Irish Cities* (1995)

Moran, Gerard, and Gillespie, Raymond (eds.), *Galway: History and Society* (1996)

DD

Galway, articles of (21 July 1691), agreed at the surrender of the *Jacobite garrison following a brief siege in the *Williamite War. The terms, securing the inhabitants and garrison in their estates and guaranteeing freedom of religious worship and the right of Catholic lawyers to practise their profession, anticipated those of the treaty of *Limerick.

Galway, Henri Massue de Ruvigny, earl of (1648–1720). A French Protestant driven into exile following the revocation of the Edict of Nantes, Galway fought in the army of *William III during the *Williamite War and was granted land at Portarlington, Queen's County (Laois), where he established a *Huguenot colony. He was *lord justice 1697–1700 and was accused, though apparently without justification, of promoting *penal laws in revenge for his own experience of religious persecution.

Galway, wardenship of. In 1484, in response to tensions between English and Irish clergy, the papacy placed the collegiate church of St Nicholas in *Galway under the control of a warden elected by representatives of the town elite. There were regular quarrels over the election of wardens, as well as repeated jurisdictional disputes with the Catholic archbishop of Tuam. In 1831 the church and town were incorporated in a new diocese of Galway, later united with Kilfenora and Kilmacduagh.

gambling in Ireland has uncertain origins, though by the 17th century it was considered a common vice. Regular lotteries were held at least from the 1680s. Following the *revolution of 1688 reforms were attempted. Amongst several parliamentary measures was one of 1708 which made it an offence to play cards or dice for cash. Interestingly it did not apply to the residence of the *lord lieutenant. An act of 1740, citing gambling as a distraction from labour, made *horse racing for small prizes a criminal offence, and lotteries, already deemed nuisances and liable to suppression, completely illegal. Yet lotteries continued to flourish. By the early 19th century the Irish were still portrayed as compulsive gamblers, though religious opposition and economic uncertainty in the following decades did prompt some decline. After *partition both Irish states used gambling as a means of raising revenue. In *Northern Ireland betting was heavily taxed. In the *Irish Free State the existing lottery of the *Irish Hospitals Sweepstake was given government backing from 1930. From 1926 off-course betting on horses and greyhounds was legalized and taxed. Later levies were imposed on on-course betting to support the racing industries. A national lottery, the Lotto, now provides funds for various projects in the Republic. Gambling remains extremely popular throughout Ireland. In the Republic alone IR£223 million was gambled on horse racing alone in 1985. NG

Gandon, James (1742–1823), the most important and influential resident protagonist of the neo-classical style of *architecture in Ireland. A student of Sir William Chambers in London, Gandon established his own practice there in 1765. In 1767, in collaboration with John Woolfe, he began to publish a number of his designs in a two-volume continuation of Campbell's *Vitruvius Britannicus*. In 1769 he was awarded the first gold medal for architecture by the newly founded Royal Academy. His first connection with Ireland dates to around this time when he obtained second place in the competition for the *Royal Exchange building in Dublin. In 1781 he travelled to Dublin to supervise the building of the new *Custom House and remained. In 1786 he replaced Thomas Cooley as architect of the *Four Courts in Dublin. Other work in the city by Gandon includes Carlisle bridge (begun 1791), the east portico of the *Parliament House (1784–9), and initial work on the *King's Inns (begun 1800). Outside Dublin, examples of his work include Coolbanagher church and mausoleum, Co. Laois (*c.*1781–5) and Emo Court, Co. Laois (*c.*1790–1800). Gandon retired in 1808, handing control of his practice to his pupil, H. A. Baker. RM

Garda (pl. Gardai) **Síochána** (Civic Guard), established in February 1922 to police all of independent Ireland outside Dublin city, which until 1925 remained the preserve of the autonomous *Dublin Metropolitan Police. Intended initially as an armed body analogous to the *Royal Irish Constabulary, the force had a disastrous first year: unrest amongst recruits culminated in mutiny in August 1922. The charismatic Eoin *O'Duffy then reconstructed the force as a mainly unarmed one which would police by consent. The force quickly won widespread public acceptance, which it still generally retains in the very different circumstances of the present day. The problem of *political policing was addressed by the establishment of a *Special Branch distinct from the uniformed force.

The Gárda Síochána has always operated under the direct control of the Department of Justice. Promotions above the rank of inspector have to be approved by the government, and allegedly are sometimes subject to party political influence. Furthermore, a number of its commissioners, including Michael Staines in 1922, O'Duffy in 1933, Edmund Garvey in 1977, and Patrick McLaughlin in 1983, were forced out because of their handling of issues with a political dimension.

Since the early 1960s the progressive urbanization and modernization of Irish society has created new policing problems. The Gárdai have had to deal not only with periodic resurgences of political crime, but with the corrosive social effects of urban deprivation. Drug-related crime has become a major feature of inner-city life, while public confidence in the force has slipped even if public respect remains high. The force has grown as crime has risen, from about 2,000 men in 1922 to some 6,000 in 1969, and to about 11,000 men and women in 1994. The 1960s saw the emergence of powerful representative associations, in effect trade unions. These have since succeeded in turning a policeman's lot into a well-paid if not a happy one. EO'H

Gardiner. The banker, property developer, and MP **Luke Gardiner** (d. 1755) was involved in urban building projects from as early as 1712. In the 1740s and 1750s he was responsible, with his son Charles, for the development of a large area of what became central Dublin. O'Connell Street, constructed in the 1740s, was originally called Gardiner's Mall. He further enhanced his fortune by holding the lucrative office of deputy vice-treasurer, which allowed him temporarily to invest official balances on his own account. Charles's son **Luke Gardiner** (1745–98), created Viscount Mountjoy 1795, was MP for Co. Dublin 1773–89. His death at the hands of rebels during the *insurrection of 1798 was seen by many as a fit return for his sponsorship of the first *Catholic Relief Acts in 1778 and 1782. His son Charles became earl of Blessington 1816, and married Marguerite Power (1789–1849), who, as 'Countess of Blessington', established herself after her husband's death as a popular novelist.

Garvagh, 'battle of' (26 July 1813), sectarian affray. Following earlier clashes in March and June, Protestants gathered for the fair at Garvagh, Co. Londonderry, fired on a large party of attacking Catholics, killing one man and wounding others. Nine men were later convicted of manslaughter but discharged.

gavelkind, the English legal term used by government officials to describe the complex and regionally varied forms of collective partible inheritance which characterized communal native Irish *land tenures, before these were formally abolished in 1606. The fundamental principle, of subdivision between all male heirs or kinsmen, was similar to that of gavelkind in medieval England, but was applied to communal *sept land rather than tenements held in severalty. Moreover, the nature and occasion of such subdivision varied widely. In some districts, scrupulous impartiality was observed in the allocation of equal shares among all eligible male heirs; in others, the lord allocated shares at will, frequently retaining the best portion for himself. In some areas, redistribution only occurred on the death of a co-heir; in others it took place annually. As in England, the practice encouraged the rapid fragmentation of landholdings, and has been held to have been a major factor discouraging the erection of permanent buildings. The *penal law of 1704 reimposed gavelkind on Catholic landowners unless the eldest son converted to Protestantism, when he inherited the whole. LJP

gavelkind, case of, a special ruling by the Irish judges in 1606, recorded by Sir John *Davies's *Reports* (1615). This abolished partible inheritance (gavelkind) in Gaelic districts. Hitherto, all lands, except those pertaining to the office of chief or tanist (see *tánaiste*), had been periodically divided between the male members of the clan. The methods varied across the country—divisions could take place annually, after a set number of years, or when the chief died; in some places the shares were equal, in others they were apportioned according to age and status. English rulers found these practices, which created fractionalized holdings and continual shifting of abode, inimical to stable property rights and agricultural improvement.

The Irish system gave full rights to *illegitimate children and disqualified the claims of widows and daughters. Therefore the judges declared that land in Irish parts would henceforth be held and passed according to common law (the eldest legitimate male inheriting). The judgement was converted into an act of state by the Irish *privy council which declared void all gavelkind settlements since the accession of James I.

This ruling allowed an attack on the Gaelic lords of Ulster by the creation of freeholders under common law tenures in Fermanagh and Cavan in 1606. The judicial overthrow of the Gaelic system was consolidated by the 1608 decision in the case of *tanistry. The act of state on gavelkind was claimed by the privy council as a precedent for its capacity to rule on land matters in its dealings with Adam *Loftus in the late 1630s. Ironically, having gone to great lengths to establish primogeniture in Ireland, the Act for Preventing the Further Growth of Popery (1704) (see PENAL LAWS) ordered that the lands of papists who refused to conform should descend 'by nature of gavelkind'. HM

genealogy. Some ancestral names in Irish genealogies suggest the common barbarian practice of deriving the kings' descent from the gods. However, the first surviving texts, 7th-century genealogical poems about Leinster and Munster kings, trace their ancestry to Milesius, allegedly the first Gael to invade Ireland (see MILESIANS), and through Japheth and Noah to Adam, only son of God, the king of heaven. This indicates an early origin for the ecclesiastically inspired myth later elaborated into the **Lebor Gabála*, or 'Book of Invasions'. Native historians defined the whole corpus of Irish genealogies in relation to this doctrine. Subject peoples are traced to the pre-Goidelic inhabitants of Ireland, the Fir Bolg. All dominant dynasties are derived from one of the sons of Milesius—the *Uí Néill, *Connachta, *Airgialla, Osraige, *Déisi, and *Laigin from Éremón, said to be leader of the expedition, and most Munster dynasties from his brother Éber. Smaller kingdoms wishing to emphasize their independence tended to claim descent from some other line. The *Ulaid of eastern Ulster, the O'Farrells of Longford, and *O'Connor of Kerry claimed descent from Ír, another son of Milesius, while the O'Driscolls claimed descent from Ith, Milesius's uncle.

Genealogies validated claims to land and kingship, so the corpus was periodically revised, ignoring later generations of declining dynasties, finding a suitable origin for new arrivals on the political scene, or transferring lines from one ancestor to another to reflect new alliances. Our earliest surviving copy is in the 12th-century manuscript Rawlinson B 502, but later revisions can be found in the 14th-century Books of *Ballymote and *Lecan, and the 17th-century Genealogies of Cúcoigcríche Ó Cléirigh and an Dubhaltach Óg Mac Firbhisigh. Old Catholic families, and some of the incoming planters, continued to commission manuscript genealogies from traditional historians well into the 18th century.

Kelleher, J., 'The Pre-Norman Irish Genealogies', *Irish Historical Studies*, 16 (1968–9)

MacNiocaill, G., *Irish Population before Petty: Problems and Possibilities* (1981)

KS

Geneville (Joinville), Geoffrey de (d. 1314). Geneville, the brother of Jean, Sire de Joinville, the biographer of St Louis, spent a long life in English royal service. He accompanied the future Edward I on crusade in 1270, fought in Wales, and went on diplomatic missions. But much of his career lay in Ireland. One of the Savoyard group at Henry III's court, by 1252 he had married Matilda, granddaughter of Walter de *Lacy, who brought him a half-share of Meath and the Lacy lands in Britain. He was acting *justiciar 1264–6, when he pacified baronial feuds, and justiciar 1273–6, when he had little success against the Leinster Irish. He assiduously defended his *liberty rights in Trim, and defined his tenants' military duties. In 1308, when he was about 80, he resigned his lordship to Roger *Mortimer, the husband of his granddaughter, retiring to the *Dominican priory at Trim, where he was buried. RFF

George IV (1762–1830), king of the United Kingdom of Great Britain and Ireland (1820–30). As prince of Wales he had supported the *Whig opposition and professed support for *Catholic emancipation. By the time he became regent to the incapacitated George III in 1811 he had outgrown this early radicalism, and expectations of a new political era were quickly disappointed. His visit to Ireland (12 Aug.–3 Sept. 1821) nevertheless aroused enthusiasm among all classes, and *O'Connell and other Catholic leaders offered extravagant displays of personal devotion. In the event it took political crisis, and all the efforts of *Wellington and *Peel, to extort the king's consent to the Catholic relief bill of 1829.

Gerald of Wales (Gerald de Barry, Giraldus Cambrensis) (1146–1223), historian of the *Anglo-Norman invasion. Born at Manorbier, Pembrokeshire, Gerald was a younger son of William de Barry by Angharad, granddaughter of Rhys ap Tewdwr, king of south Wales. He was educated as a cleric at St Peter's abbey, Gloucester, and Paris University. He was appointed archdeacon of Brecon *c.*1175, and this was the title which he used of himself. About 1182 he visited Ireland, where many of his Cambro-Norman relatives had acquired lands; he returned in 1185 in the train of *John, son of *Henry II, and remained for a period after John's departure. In 1186 he preached at a provincial synod at Dublin, severely criticizing the Irish clergy. While in Ireland he claimed to have been offered the bishoprics of Wexford and Leighlin, and somewhat later Ossory and the archdiocese of Cashel, all of which he declined. To his two Irish journeys are owed his *Topography of Ireland* (1188), which was dedicated to Henry II, and his *Expugnatio Hibernica*, which appeared shortly thereafter. Both works were written with a strong polemical purpose to justify Anglo-Norman intervention in Ireland; he was highly critical of the Irish, portraying them as barbarians, and barely Christian. He extolled the bravery of his relatives, the *Geraldines, at the expense of other early adventurers, such as *Strongbow, and argued that they were harassed unjustly by royal officials. He outlined strategies for completing the conquest of Ireland, which he hoped to persuade King Henry, and later Richard I (1157–99), to implement in Ireland. His work, inaugurating the colonial historiographical tradition of a negative portayal of the Irish, was to be relied on heavily by subsequent Anglo-Irish and English writers, and stimulated an apologetic response from native authors: Geoffrey *Keating's *Foras Feasa ar Éirinn*, for example, devoted considerable attention to refuting Gerald's portrayal of the Irish. MTF

Geraldine League, an unprecedented Gaelic alliance of the late 1530s led by Manus *O'Donnell and Conn *O'Neill. The league, a reaction to the aggression of Lord Deputy *Grey, wanted the restoration of the house of *Kildare. It rejected royal ecclesiastical supremacy and offered the sovereignty of Ireland to James V of Scotland. The leaguers were decisively beaten at *Bellahoe in August 1539. HM

Geraldines, a term used to describe the FitzGerald family, earls of *Desmond and *Kildare throughout the medieval and early modern period.

Gilbert (d. 1145), appointed first bishop of Limerick about 1106, an important figure in the *12th-century reform. He was also the first native-born papal legate (evidence that Máel Muire Ua Dunáin, d. 1110, had exercised a legateship before Gilbert is unreliable) and in that capacity presided at the Synod of *Ráith Bressail (1111), which outlined a diocesan structure for the Irish church. His treatise *De usu ecclesiastico* (Concerning Ecclesiastical Practice), which focused on episcopal church government, was probably written in association with that synod. He corresponded with Anselm, archbishop of Canterbury, and may be presumed to have been closely associated with Muirchertach *Ua Briain, king of Munster and claimant to the *high kingship. In 1140, on grounds of advanced age, he resigned the office of native papal legate to *Malachy, as well as the see of Limerick. MTF

Gilbert, J. T. (1829–98), historian and archivist. Born in Dublin, Gilbert quickly established himself as a leading historian with his widely acclaimed *History of the City of Dublin* (1861). A series of articles followed criticizing the handling of surviving historical documents, and as a result he was appointed secretary of the new Public Record Office in Dublin in 1867. He was also responsible, as the librarian of the *Royal Irish Academy, an inspector for the Historical Manuscripts Commission, and an employee of Dublin corporation, for the calendaring and publication of a wealth of valuable historical documentation. He was knighted in 1897. NG

Gill, Michael Henry (1794–1879), Dublin *printer, bookseller, and publisher. He managed the *Dublin University Press in the period 1842–75. In 1856 he bought out the publisher, James McGlashan. The firm continues today as Gill & Macmillan. VK

Ginkel, Godard van Reede, Baron van (1630–1703), created earl of Athlone 1692. An experienced Dutch soldier, he commanded the Williamite army from *William III's return to England in September 1690 to the end of the *Williamite War.

Giraldus Cambrensis, see GERALD OF WALES.

Gladstone, William Ewart (1809–98), British prime minister and *Liberal Party leader. The son of a Liverpool merchant, educated at Eton and Oxford, Gladstone first entered parliament as Conservative MP for Oxford 1832. He supported *Peel's increase in the *Maynooth grant but felt that his earlier support of an exclusive Anglican polity required him to resign as president of the Board of Trade. As prime minister 1868–74 he carried through the *disestablishment of the Anglican church 1869, and enacted the symbolically important *Land Act of 1870. His Land Act of 1881 effectively ended the *Land War, while the *Kilmainham treaty signified his acceptance of *Parnell as a nationalist leader with whom a settlement of the Irish question might be made. He attempted, unsuccessfully, to effect this with the *home rule bill of 1886. Gladstone's conversion to home rule split the Liberal Party. His second attempt to enact home rule, in 1893, also failed. In March 1894 he resigned as prime minister.

A complex personality, Gladstone's commitment to Ireland was based on a variety of motives: a profound moral sense; an acceptance, born of the *Fenian rising of 1867, that Ireland was a separate nationality requiring distinctive treatment; and, relatedly, the realization that constitutional reorganization was necessary if the essential integrity of the United Kingdom and its interests were to be safeguarded. Historians' interpretations of Gladstone and Ireland have tended to mirror political divisions, with Conservative views emphasizing self-interest as against Liberal interpretations focused on insight and moral purpose. Later work has combined these views, especially the latter, with due appreciation of personal and contextual limitations. JL

glass was a minor industry until 1780, when restrictions on Irish exports were removed (see FREE TRADE AGITATION), and a duty imposed on glass manufacture in Great Britain was not imposed in Ireland. This led to a period of pronounced growth with glasshouses being established in Dublin, Cork,

Ballycastle, Drumrea, Belfast, Waterford, Newry, and Derry. By 1785 there were nine glasshouses in Ireland; six were for flint glass, two for bottles, and one for window glass. Three-quarters of the workers in these houses came from England, bringing with them new techniques. The industry produced predominately for the home market, displacing British imports. Output increased and the number of glasshouses rose to eleven by 1825, Dublin dominating the industry.

Glass designs in Ireland tended to mirror those produced by English factories according to the fashion of the day. This has led to some confusion over attributing glass pieces to a particular factory. The idea that Irish glass has a certain colour or that it has a different ring when struck is totally inaccurate. Some decanters, finger bowls, and jugs, however, have impressed factory marks on the base giving a firm attribution, although recently decanters bearing spurious Cork marks have come on the market. Genuine marks that occur on Irish glass include 'B. Edwards Belfast', 'Cork Glass Co.', 'Penrose Waterford', 'Francis Collins Dublin', 'Mary Carter & Son', and 'Waterloo Co. Cork'. Some designs, such as the turnover rim bowl, the canoe shaped bowl, and the piggin, do seem to have been made predominately by Irish glasshouses. The heavy cut decoration normally associated with Irish glass was a later phenomenon, when steam-driven cutting machines were introduced into the factories *c*.1820. Earlier Irish glass had much shallower cut designs, giving the pieces a lighter and more delicate appearance.

The imposition of excise duty on Irish glass from 1825 signalled the start of a decrease in production. The number of glasshouses fell from ten in 1832 to six by 1835, and only three (flint glasshouses in Dublin and Belfast, and a bottle works in Dublin) by 1852. The craft-based Irish industry was steadily undermined by cheaper mass produced goods from larger English glasshouses which utilized machinery to a greater degree. Gatchell's of Waterford (the most prestigious works) closed in 1851. The Pugh brothers maintained the production of flint glass in Dublin between 1854 and 1893, but their craft-based concern was unable to survive against British and continental competition. With the closure of the works in 1893, the only type of glass which continued to be manufactured was bottles in Dublin and Belfast.

Table glass manufacture in Ireland was revived in 1951 when the Waterford factory was reopened. The success of the modern heavy cut glass produced by Waterford Crystal has led to other glasshouses being established, including the lead crystal factories at Cavan in 1969, and Tyrone in 1970. As with *ceramics in Ireland, there has been a growth in the rise of individual studio glassmakers in recent years. Simon Pearce was one of the first in 1972 to set up a workshop for blowing studio glass in Co. Kilkenny. He was followed by Keith Leadbetter, who set up Jerpoint glass in 1978.

Boydell, M., *Irish Glass* (1976)
Warren, P., *Irish Glass* (1981)
Westropp, D., *Irish Glass* (1920; 2nd edn., ed. M. Boydell, 1978)

AB/KMa

glebe, a piece of land within a parish that is used to provide income for the priest or minister, either by his farming it himself or leasing it out. Closely associated with the *Anglo-Norman parochial system, glebes were rare in Gaelic areas of the Irish church, where the traditional system of *erenachs and *coarbs provided land to support clerical families. With the *Reformation, the *Church of Ireland tried to establish an Anglicized system of glebes throughout the country, but often found it difficult to prevent the land from being alienated or illegally detained by lay people. Much effort in subsequent centuries was expended in providing glebes and glebe-houses for the support of Church of Ireland clergy. AF

Glendalough, an important early Irish *monastery in Co. Wicklow famed for its picturesque setting in the 'valley of the two lakes'. The settlement was originally eremitical, founded by St Kevin in the 6th century. A large monastery grew up around the cult of the saint, and in 1111 Glendalough was made the seat of a bishopric. Between 1153 and 1162 Glendalough's second saint, Lorcán Ua Tuathail (Laurence *O'Toole), presided over the monastery as abbot. In 1213 the diocese was united with Dublin, with Glendalough being reduced to the status of an archdeaconry. Even after the dissolution of the monasteries the site remained popular with pilgrims until 1862, when the annual *pattern was finally suppressed.

The original hermitage was probably sited on the hillside above the upper lake where a small oratory, Tempall-na-Skellig, now stands. Another church, Reefert, between the two lakes, is associated with the burial of local rulers. The principal monastic remains are located at the far end of the lower lake. These consist of a *round tower, the ruined cathedral, and several stone churches, some of which were drastically restored by the *Board of Works during the 1870s. St Kevin's church retains a steep stone roof with incorporated round belfry. Several of the other churches include fine Romanesque detailing. RM

Glenmalure, battle of (25 Aug. 1580). The newly arrived Lord Deputy *Grey decided on an immediate prosecution of the rebel forces of Viscount *Baltinglass and Feagh MacHugh *O'Byrne, which had withdrawn into Glenmalure in the Wicklow Mountains. Grey sent half his army under George Moore to flush them out. Soldiers fresh from England in bright coats and officers in armour made easy targets, especially for the hundred 'shot' (see FIREARMS) at O'Byrne's disposal. At least 30 Englishmen were killed, including Moore himself. HM

Glin, knights of, a cadet branch of the Fitzgeralds of *Desmond, with lands in north Co. Limerick. The title first appears in the 15th century. Tradition claimed that these knights, along with the knights of *Kerry, and two other minor branches of the FitzGerald family, were descended from liaisons between John fitz Thomas, grandson of the original Maurice fitz Gerald, and the wives of four subordinate Irish chiefs.

Goidelic, see IRISH LANGUAGE.

gold, see METALWORK.

gold mining in Ireland is much less prevalent than the working of alluvial deposits, particularly in Avoca, Co. Wicklow. Indeed, the 12th-century Book of *Leinster describes the Leinster men as 'Lagenians of the Gold'. The Goldmines river area of Avoca was the scene of the 'gold rush' of September 1796, which was abandoned because of the *insurrection of 1798. Subsequently unsuccessful attempts were made to locate a 'mother lode' by mining in the area. Gold has also been found in the Sperrins in Co. Tyrone, though recent prospecting in the area has so far been without success. PC

golf in its modern form was introduced to Ireland by a Scottish teacher of English at the Belfast Academy. In 1881 the first Irish club, the Royal Belfast, was established. By 1891 there were ten clubs and courses in Ireland, nine of which were in Ulster. That year the Golfing Union of Ireland, the first in the British Isles, was founded. A men's amateur championship began in 1893. In 1895 the first professional tournament in Ireland and the first ladies' championship in the world were held at Portrush, Co. Antrim. The sport grew steadily in popularity, encouraged by the availability of land and the patronage of landowners. The social level of players, however, was kept high by the cost of fees and equipment. By 1950 there were 179 courses in the country, and Ireland was promoted as a venue for golfing holidays. Nearly 70 new courses were built over the next 30 years. Golfing tourists now outnumber domestic players, who belong to over 350 recognized clubs. NG

gombeen man, from the Irish *gaimbín*, 'interest', a moneylender. From the late 19th century the term was widely used to describe shopkeepers and other traders, particularly in the rural west, who extended credit to local farmers. The notion of liberating the vulnerable classes of rural society from high interest charges and dependency through indebtedness was one of the aims of the *co-operative movement. Some modern studies have presented the economic power of the gombeen man as the basis of a pervasive structure of ideological domination and political patronage. Others, however, suggest that the scale of economic exploitation was sometimes exaggerated, and have questioned the general applicability of models of debt-based clientelism.

See also BROKERAGE AND CLIENTELISM.

Gonne, Maud (1866–1953), founder of *Inghinidhe na hÉireann and lifelong political activist, was born in Surrey to a British army officer and his wife. The family moved to Ireland in 1867. Maud lost her mother at an early age, and was not sent to school, thus missing two important experiences of socialization into the conventional life of a woman of her time. In 1887 she went to France to be with her Boulangist lover, Lucien Millevoye, with whom she had two children, George (1890–1) and Iseult (1894–1954). Back in Ireland she developed into one of the most prominent and colourful nationalists of the period. In 1903 she married Major John *MacBride, whom she acrimoniously divorced after the birth of their son, Sean *MacBride. At the start of the *First World War she went to France with an ambulance corps, but returned to Ireland after the *rising of 1916. She adopted her ex-husband's name for the first time after his execution, was imprisoned with Kathleen Clarke in 1918, and opposed the *Anglo-Irish treaty. In the 1920s and 1930s she was active in the Women's Prisoners Defence League. She was a lifelong friend of W. B. *Yeats. CC

gospel halls, name given to small meeting places of no particular denominational provenance within a broadly popular *evangelical Protestant tradition. Most commonly it has been used to describe the meeting places of the *Plymouth Brethren, but is used also by those from a pentecostal or independent evangelical background. Mostly confined to the working-class or labouring-class areas of town and country, gospel halls, through *Sunday schools, prayer cells, and gospel meetings, have sustained a vigorous popular Protestant culture in areas not usually accessible to the mainstream denominations. Gospel halls and mission halls (the names are almost interchangeable) grew in popularity in the years after the *revival of 1859 and again in the 1920s, but now show signs of succumbing to the effects of secularization. At the peak of their influence they sustained a peripatetic ministry of lay preachers which sometimes acted as a springboard for other kinds of leadership in working-class neighbourhoods. Revealingly, perhaps, the prefix 'gospel' was never used by the trustees of the great urban citadels of Brethrenism or by those with a predominantly suburban and middle-class membership. Gospel halls, partly because of the size of the buildings and the religious enthusiasm they sustained, have been theatres of popular religious conflict as well as centres of genuine religious devotion. DNH

gossipred means the relationship established by sponsorship at baptism, considered so close in medieval *canon law as to preclude marriage between, for example, the mother of a child and its godfather. Like marriage and *fosterage, gossipred was often used to cement alliances, particularly between Irish chiefs and Anglo-Irish barons. A baron might stand godfather to the child of a chief and vice versa, or both became god-sib, or god-related, by jointly sponsoring the child of a third party. The practice was condemned by the Statute of *Kilkenny in 1366, but persisted, perhaps promoting the spread of English forenames among the Irish. KS

governesses were usually girls and women from middle- and lower middle-class families. Charlotte Brontë has given governessing a bad press, making much of the governess's anomalous social position in the household. This could have had its advantages, however, often giving the working governess a respected, independent position, and by no means confining the ex-governess to 'service'. Like domestic service for working-class women (see SERVANTS), it was often stop-gap work. In Ireland it was common for *nuns to use their social and family networks to find ex-pupils work as governesses in Ireland and abroad. Catholic Irishwomen were in great demand as 'English governesses' in Poland, France, and Spain. Many also went to Russia. Protestant Irishwomen went to Britain and Germany. Two of the most famous accounts of Irish governesses abroad are set in the twilight of governessing, the 1920s and 1930s. In Kate O'Brien's novel *Mary Lavelle* (1932), and Maura Laverty's autobiographical *No More than Human* (1944), breaking free of the governess network is represented as a liberation; Laverty got into journalism and worked for *El debate* before returning to Ireland, marriage, and a lifetime of writing. CC

government and administration. The minimal administration of an early Christian petty *king or *rí tuaithe* is given in the Old Irish *law tracts as a *brethem* (brehon or judge), a *rechtaire* or seneschal of his palace, and a group of freed slaves or pardoned criminals who served as his bodyguard. However, the 11th-century commentaries dealing with kings of larger territories refer to more than one *rechtaire*, to counsellors and foreign mercenaries, mercenaries of native origin, domestic servants, and *maoir*, or bailiffs who collected the kings' tributes and dues.

The establishment of English authority in parts of Ireland following the *Anglo-Norman invasion, and the view (stated explicitly by King *John) that English law should apply in Ireland, produced a system of royal government which mirrored that in England. The king appointed a *justiciar, who headed the administration and exercised royal powers, subject to the king's right to intervene when he saw fit. The justiciar was advised by a *council, which had a ministerial core but expanded to include magnates and leading churchmen as business demanded. From the later 13th century he summoned *parliaments. By 1300 there was a secretariat, headed by the *chancellor, who kept the king's seal for Ireland and normally travelled with the justiciar. An *exchequer, presided over by the treasurer, sat in Dublin to hear the accounts of local officials; it was subject to periodic audits by Westminster. The legal establishment included judges attached to the peripatetic *justiciar's court and to a court of Common Pleas which sat in Dublin (see COURTS OF LAW; JUDICIARY). At local level *sheriffs and county courts existed in the colonized areas from Louth to Cork and Kerry, though in places royal rights were devolved to lords who held *liberty jurisdictions. Alongside the sheriffs there were other local officials such as *coroners and, through time, *keepers of the peace. Central government was staffed by a mixture of appointees from England and Anglo-Irishmen, while local offices tended to be the preserve of settler families; the native Irish had no part in the system.

The formal structure of government changed little in the later Middle Ages. There was some diminution of supervision by Westminster, as the *king's lieutenants, appointed periodically from 1361, were given wide powers over patronage and revenues. More significantly, the contraction of the colony meant that areas beyond the future *Pale had increasingly tenuous links with Dublin, though their position was regularized to some extent by the existence of liberties such as Tipperary and Kerry, the awarding of wide judicial commissions to magnates, and the enlargement of urban privileges.

Anglo-Norman conquest and colonization left a series of districts still under Gaelic rule, though initially subject to the English king or to some baron. These varied in size from a *_tuath_ occupying about a fifth of a modern county (e.g. O'Molloy of Feara Ceall) to an overlordship extending across two or three counties (*O'Neill of Tír Eógain), and their administrative staff varied accordingly. Originally officers directing the king's household and his military campaigns were drawn from his hereditary vassal nobility, who were rewarded with recognized perquisites in relation to tribute, ransoms, etc. Rival candidates for chieftainship recruited different members from the same families to serve as their _aes grádha_ (men of rank, or trust). In smaller lordships the court poet or *_file_, the king's brehon or judge, and the leech or doctor also came from hereditary local families, though the last provincial kings in the early 13th century used clerics as chancellors and notaries, and men of lower social status as _maoir_.

As Irish armies became increasingly mercenary, chiefs employed a professional commander or constable (_constábla_), normally a Scottish captain of *gallowglasses, maintained by grants of land and billeting rights. Supervision of the army's billeting, equipment, and discipline was done by the marshal or _marasgál_, sometimes a hereditary post. Policing duties in the larger lordships were carried out by a small troop of 'household *kerns', the _ceithearn tighe_, again sometimes with hereditary commanders. Over major internal disputes, submission, or war, the chief consulted his *_oireacht_ or vassal nobility, and held an _aonach agus ardoireachtas_ (see *_óenach_) or general assembly of his territory periodically at a customary open air meeting place, where lawsuits were settled and impositions of taxation announced.

Government in early modern Ireland was still essentially royal government and officials were appointed by royal patent. After 1541 authority emanated from the king of Ireland who (unless actually present, as in 1689–90) was represented by the *lord lieutenant or the *lord deputy. During the latter's absence government was controlled by *lords justices. The chief governor was advised by a *privy council appointed by the king and a grand council composed of the nobility, although this did not meet after 1600. The wider representative institution, parliament, was summoned and prorogued by the king although the terms of its business were severely restricted by *Poynings's Law. The infrequency of parliamentary sessions meant that a good deal of Irish business was carried out by proclamation and judicial decision. The enforcement of legislation was carried out by courts, of which two types existed. Prerogative courts, such as *Castle Chamber, were abolished after 1660 leaving the four common law courts of chancery, Common Pleas, exchequer, and King's Bench. Much administrative work was also carried out by these courts. The equity jurisdiction of chancery, for example, was subsidiary to its main function as the secretariat for the Irish administration keeping the *patent and close rolls. Similarly exchequer jurisdiction, from 1625, arose from disputes generated by its main role as revenue gatherer and administrator. In addition to the courts the chief governor's household acted as a civil service. The most important officer was the secretary, later the *chief secretary, who controlled most of the business. A number of other administrative matters were assigned to the church courts, including slander and matrimonial cases as well as the administration of probate. Only once in the early modern period was this structure amended. From 1651–4, following the defeat of royalist and Catholic forces in the *Confederate War, Ireland was governed by parliamentary commissioners and the courts were abolished. From 1653–9 Ireland was represented in the Westminster parliament.

Notwithstanding a gradual but inexorable increase in the scope and personnel of government, the Irish administration in the late 18th century remained on a small scale, with a total workforce (excluding ordnance and crewmen on revenue vessels) of only 2,000. Many official positions were little more than sinecures, any essential duties being performed by deputies. Following *Townshend's defeat of the *undertakers the lord lieutenant, now permanently resident, acquired greater importance. The role of the chief secretary also grew significantly, and the chief secretary's office, subdivided into first two then three sections (civil, military, and yeomanry), became the centre from which the Irish administration was controlled. New public bodies, reflecting the gradual expansion of state functions, included the *Linen Board, the commissioners of inland navigation (1752), and the Wide Streets Commission. Demands by the *Whig opposition for more effective parliamentary scrutiny of public administration and spending led to the creation in 1793 of an Irish Treasury Board. But all such attempts to achieve reform and accountability were overtaken by the Act of *Union.

Although the Union deprived Ireland of the status of a separate kingdom, it did not alter the basic machinery of government. Responsibility for the administration of Ireland remained in the hands of the lord lieutenant, aided by the Irish privy council, the chief secretary, and a body of officials. Day-to-day administration was organized from the chief secretary's office and supervised by the under-secretary. However, the parliamentary union, coinciding as it did with a period of administrative reform in Britain, provided an opportunity for a general overhaul of administrative practice and standards. Sinecures were progressively reduced, and the administration became increasingly professional in character and performance. Qualifying tests were introduced for offices such as that of county surveyor (1833), and from 1871 recruitment to the civil service was by competitive exam.

By the mid-19th century the tendency towards closer integration with Britain had given way to strategies and structures designed to meet Ireland's particular needs. The result was a highly centralized, interventionist system of government quite unlike that in Britain. By utilizing appointed bodies (*'Castle boards'), ministers were able to bypass existing structures of local government. While this helped to broaden the base of local administration, it also lessened democratic accountability. Having been excluded by law from any government post prior to 1793 (see PENAL LAWS), Catholics were recruited in growing numbers from the 1830s, although Protestants continued to predominate, particularly in senior positions.

Public administration in independent Ireland has reflected a combination of British influence and Irish innovation. The *constitutions of 1922 and 1937 in practice followed British example in terms of cabinet government, the role of the legislature, and the position of the head of state. The organization and apolitical ethos of the civil service, similarly, reflected Whitehall values.

The Irish system of government has nevertheless developed its own characteristics. Highly centralized and somewhat authoritarian structures are balanced by a written constitution which can be amended only by referendum, and by the electoral process. Despite *proportional representation, and the prevalence of minority or *interparty governments, however, the cabinet is even more powerful, and the legislature is conspicuously weaker, than in Britain.

The wider public sector has also developed distinctive traits. As the state's role expanded in areas such as *health services, *social welfare, economic planning, and industrial development, many regulatory, promotional, developmental, and other functions were hived off from the civil service to functional state agencies beyond direct ministerial and parliamentary control. Public or *state enterprise has also played an important part in the modernization of the Irish economy. In the early 1990s total public sector employment of all kinds, including health, education, defence and security, stood at about one-fifth of total employment.

McDowell, R. B., *The Irish Administration* (1964)
Nicholls, K., *Gaelic and Gaelicised Ireland in the Middle Ages* (1972)
Richardson, H. G., and Sayles, G. O., *The Administration of Ireland 1172–1377* (1963)
Simms, K., *From Kings to Warlords* (1987)

KS/RFF/RG/VC/EO'H

Government of Ireland Act (1920), an attempt by the *Lloyd George coalition government to create a new structure for Ireland. Its immediate origins lie in the report of the cabinet committee on the Irish question chaired by Walter *Long. Long's committee, and subsequent government policy, tried to reconcile conflicting pressures. *Sinn Féin's success in the 1918 election, followed by the outbreak of the *Anglo-Irish War, made some form of *home rule inevitable. The government also saw the need to help the American president Woodrow Wilson in his campaign for ratification of the Versailles settlement by conciliating Irish-American opinion. But in the 1918 election the Conservatives, who secured 339 seats in the coalition against 136 Liberals, made Lloyd George promise not to implement any policy leading to 'the forcible submission of the six counties of Ulster to a Home Rule Parliament against their will'. Arguing that Britain could not impose unity, Long's committee on 4 November 1919 recommended the creation of two parliaments, one in Belfast for the nine Ulster counties, and the other in Dublin. Such a nine-county *partition, combined with a *Council of Ireland, would encourage moves towards unity. Unsure of Unionist ability to govern Cavan, Monaghan, and Donegal, James *Craig lobbied the cabinet for a six-county partition, and was strongly supported by Arthur *Balfour. On 24 February 1920 the cabinet voted that 'the area of Northern Ireland shall consist of the parliamentary counties of Antrim, Armagh, Down, Fermanagh, Londonderry, and Tyrone and the parliamentary boroughs of Belfast and Londonderry'. The subsequent bill passed its third reading on 23 December 1920.

In the elections which followed for the parliament of Southern Ireland, only the four representatives of Trinity College, Dublin, attended; 124 Sinn Féin members abstained. By contrast, Unionists won 40 of the 52 seats for the Northern Ireland parliament, enabling Craig to form his government. While largely satisfying Lloyd

George's Conservative allies and the unionists of the six counties, the act was bitterly resented by unionists elsewhere in Ireland, and failed to meet the aspirations of Sinn Féin. Nevertheless, it provided the constitutional framework for the creation of Northern Ireland.

Fraser, T. G., *Partition in Ireland, India and Palestine: Theory and Practice* (1984)

TGF

governor-general, representative of the British crown in the *Irish Free State 1922–37. The office was one of the most controversial provisions of the *Anglo-Irish treaty. The British government, aware of Irish sensitivities, allowed the Free State government, unlike the other dominions, to nominate the first incumbent, T. M. *Healy.

Although in theory the governor-general had a position equivalent to the king in Britain, in Ireland his executive powers were more circumscribed. Under the 1922 *constitution, the governor-general summoned, prorogued, and dissolved the *Dáil but at dates fixed by the Dáil itself. He approved money bills on the advice of the executive council. Under article 41 the governor-general could withhold assent to or reserve a bill provided this was in accordance with accepted Canadian practice. Although article 51 declared that executive authority was vested in the governor-general as representative of the crown, the executive council was appointed by the governor-general on the nomination of the president. The most important restriction concerned dissolution. Under article 53, only a president with a Dáil majority could advise dissolution, thus denying the governor-general any discretionary powers.

One important function which the governor-general retained until 1927 was to act as the channel of communication between the dominion government and the British government, but this was discontinued after the 1926 imperial conference (see COMMONWEALTH).

After 1932 James McNeill, who had succeeded Healy in 1928, became the focus of *Fianna Fáil's hostility to the governor-generalship. He resigned in November 1932 and was succeeded by the last incumbent, Donal Buckley (Donal Ua Buachalla), who considerably reduced the visibility of the office. In 1933, de *Valera passed legislation reducing the governor-general's powers, and in 1936 his remaining functions were removed. (See EXTERNAL RELATIONS ACT.) The office was finally abolished by the Executive Powers (Consequential Provisions) Act 1937.

Sexton, Brendan, *Ireland and the Crown 1922–36* (1989)

DMcM

Graces, the, concessions promised to Irish interest groups by Charles I but left largely unratified. The *Old English used the war with Spain in 1625 to request concessions in return for subsidies. Amid complaints from Protestant bishops, provincial conventions selected eight Old English and three Protestant settlers as delegates. A further outbreak of war with France strengthened their negotiating position. In May 1628 51 articles were agreed with the English privy council. Although the Old English were promised legislation to secure property titles, they gained nothing substantial on *recusancy fines or the oath of supremacy. This reassured the Protestant interest who were promised an easing of conditions for Ulster planters. In return the crown received four successive quarterly subsidies of £40,000 sterling.

The crown subsequently used the intricacies of *Poynings's Law and the end of hostilities as excuses not to ratify the Graces. In the 1634 parliament the Old English were misled by *Wentworth when they supported his financial bills in the first session in the hope of getting the Graces in the second. In 1641 Charles I again promised to enact the Graces to obtain support from the Irish parliament but the *rising of 1641 closed the matter. HM

grand juries, introduced as part of the administrative system imposed on Ireland following the *Anglo-Norman invasion, became the primary organ of *local government in the Irish counties. The high *sheriff was responsible for nominating a jury of between 12 and 23 men from amongst the leading property owners in the county, excluding peers. Catholics were excluded until 1793 under the *penal laws, and even after that date there were complaints that they were rarely selected.

One function of the grand jury was to rule on the validity of indictments at the twice-yearly *assizes held in each county. Only after the jury had found a true bill could the case go to trial. In 1634 the grand jury was also empowered to levy a local tax to pay for the upkeep of roads and bridges in the county. Its taxing powers gradually extended to cover matters such as the building and repair of jails and courthouses (1708), and the establishment of county infirmaries (1765). In the early 19th century statutory responsibilities regarding the provision of lunatic asylums and fever hospitals were imposed on grand juries by government. Few checks were made on how money was spent, and as expenditure levels increased so did dissatisfaction with a system which many believed to be both corrupt and inefficient. Reforms in 1818, 1833, and 1836 reduced the opportunities for abuse and allowed *cess payers a limited role in authorizing expenditure.

Grand juries remained the preserve of the *landlord class, and as such never enjoyed popular support in Ireland. They were relieved of their administrative functions under the *Local Government Act of 1898, but retained their role in criminal proceedings. Grand juries were abolished in independent Ireland under the Criminal Justice Act of 1948, but survived at assizes in Northern Ireland until 1969.

Crossman, Virginia, *Local Government in Nineteenth-Century Ireland* (1994)

VC

Grattan, Henry (1746–1820), the most noted of the 18th-century *patriots. The son of a Dublin lawyer and MP, he was called to the Irish bar in 1772 and entered parliament in 1775, sitting first for Lord *Charlemont's borough of the same name and later, from 1790, for Dublin city. In 1778–9, already a leading patriot spokesman, he responded eagerly to the opportunities provided by the *Volunteer movement and the *free trade agitation. The concession of *'legislative independence' in 1782 was a personal triumph, marked by a Commons resolution to vote him £50,000 for the purchase of a landed estate. However, the *renunciation controversy almost immediately afterwards permitted Henry *Flood to undermine Grattan's popularity. Having tried to support government as an independent member, Grattan returned to opposition over the *Commercial Propositions in 1785. The *regency crisis completed his re-emergence as a patriot leader, now active in the new Irish *Whig Party. Though alarmed by the *French Revolution, and hostile to the *United Irishmen, he was increasingly critical of what he saw as government's blindly reactionary response to popular disaffection, particularly after the recall of *Fitzwilliam. He withdrew from parliament in 1797, returning in 1799 to oppose the Act of *Union.

Although he had earlier spoken against permitting Catholics to purchase land, Grattan added to the resolutions prepared for the Convention of *Dungannon a call for the relaxation of the *penal laws. In 1793, after some hesitation, he advocated full *Catholic emancipation. In 1804 he commenced a second parliamentary career, entering the Westminster parliament to support the renewed Catholic agitation. He remained until his death a leading parliamentary advocate of emancipation, as well as a prominent Whig spokesman on other issues. However, his support for the *veto as a means of reassuring Protestant opinion put him increasingly at odds with *O'Connell and other Catholic leaders.

Nineteenth-century constitutional nationalists looked back to the Irish parliament of 1782–1800 (despite Grattan's own almost permanent position on its opposition benches) as *'Grattan's parliament'. The government of independent Ireland, less sympathetic to this particular brand of Irishness, refused in 1943 to preserve his house intact. Modern assessments see Grattan as representative of the Protestant patriotism undermined by the religious and political polarization of the 1790s. They also note the lack of administrative ability that made him a natural opposition politician, the extent to which some of his famous speeches were rewritten for posterity, and the opportunism occasionally evident in his advocacy of popular causes.

Kelly, James, *Henry Grattan* (1993)

Grattan's parliament, a later name for the Irish parliament in the period between the achievement of *legislative independence and the Act of *Union, perceived by later nationalists as a golden age of prosperity through self-government. Modern assessments more frequently emphasize the illusory nature of legislative independence, parliament's rejection of the electoral reforms that might have made it a genuinely representative body, and the continued exclusion of the Catholic majority from political rights (see PENAL LAWS). The economic prosperity of the 1780s and 1790s, once seen as a direct result of legislative independence, is also now viewed as largely independent of political arrangements.

Gray, Sir John (1816–75), MP for Kilkenny city 1865–75, a proprietor of the *Freeman's Journal* from 1841, and a highly influential politician. A Mayo-born Protestant with a medical degree from Glasgow, he campaigned for *repeal in the 1840s, and subsequently for *tenant right and *disestablishment, contributing significantly to the achievement of the latter. As a member of Dublin city council from 1852 he advanced various projects of municipal improvement, for one of which—the Vartry water supply scheme—he was knighted in 1863. RVC

Great Famine (1845–9), caused by the failure, in three seasons out of four, of the *potato crop. The harvest of 1845 was one-third deficient. In 1846 three-quarters of the crop were lost. Yields were average in 1847, but little had been sown as seed potatoes were scarce. In 1848, yields were only two-thirds of normal. An alternative measure of the crop loss is demonstrated by the fall in potato acreage. Before the Famine it was 2 million acres, falling to around a quarter of a million acres in 1847.

A fungal disease, *Phytophthora infestans*, commonly called potato blight, damaged the crops. Its origins are unclear, though bird droppings imported as fertilizer from South America have been suggested as a likely source. The first region of Europe to be affected by blight was Belgium in June 1845. Transmission to Ireland was swift, the first signs appearing in September 1845.

To cope with the loss of a large part of the staple diet of one-third of the population, relief measures were implemented by private organizations and by government. The *Society of Friends was at the forefront, providing food, clothing, cooking equipment, seeds, and money. Their kitchens dispensed soup in towns, cities, and rural districts. Religious houses, churches, and some local gentry were also involved in philanthropic work.

Government's response to the crisis was circumscribed by a range of influences. The prevailing ideology of *laissez-faire* held that any tampering with market forces would bankrupt *landlords and dislocate trade. There was the belief that the collapse of the potato economy provided an opportunity for agricultural reorganization, through the consolidation of smallholdings and the removal of surplus population. (For many, indeed, the Famine, in line with the prevalent *evangelical theology of the day, was seen as the workings of divine providence, acting to correct the ills within Irish society.) The government was also concerned to make Irish landlords meet the cost of a crisis widely blamed on their greed and negligence, and to ensure that local taxpayers did not evade their share of the burden of financing relief. As the crisis continued, repetition blunted the response of the British public to reports of Irish misery. Severe economic recession in Great Britain itself during 1847 further limited sympathy for Ireland's problems, as did the apparent ingratitude for help given displayed in the return of 36 *repeal MPs in the general election of 1847 and the *Young Ireland *rebellion of 1848.

In the first year of famine, 1845–6, Sir Robert *Peel's Tory government purchased *Indian meal from America for sale from government depots, and inaugurated a programme of public works managed by *grand juries and the *Board of Works. The *Whig government of Lord John Russell, which took office in June 1846, greatly extended the public works schemes, while refusing to interfere either in the internal market in food or in the export of agricultural produce. In February 1847 ideology was at last set aside and kitchens opened throughout the country to supply cooked food directly to the starving without cost or imposition of a 'work test'. This operation at its peak supplied 3 million meals daily. From September 1847, however, the government wound up the soup kitchens, insisting that further relief should come from the greatly expanded but still wholly inadequate *workhouses run under the *poor law.

The severity of the Great Famine is indicated by the widespread incidence of disease. The potato-eating population had become accustomed to a diet rich in vitamin C and quickly succumbed to scurvy. Symptoms of marasmus and kwashiorkor, although not identified as such, were described in the medical journals. The lack of vitamin A in the famine-constrained diet was manifest in xerophthalmia—a disease causing blindness—among workhouse children.

Typhus and relapsing fever were the most common diseases afflicting the weakened population. Both were transmitted by the body louse and famine conditions provided an ideal environment for spreading the infection as starving masses congregated in urban centres searching for food. Typhus affected the small blood vessels, especially the brain and skin vessels, which explains frequently described symptoms of delirium and stupor and the distinctive spotted rash. Relapsing fever, as the name implies, was characterized by numerous relapses. It usually invaded its victims through the skin. Popular names included 'gastric fever' and 'yellow fever', as some patients became jaundiced. Typhus and relapsing fever were no respecters of persons, afflicting rich and poor, old and young, though mortality among the rich was particularly high.

In the absence of official figures we will never know precisely how many died. Neither was there systematic enumeration of emigrants. Estimates of excess mortality range from half a million to just over 1 million; recent research supports the latter figure. The highest levels of mortality occurred in Connacht, and the lowest in Leinster. More died of disease than starvation; the old and the very young were particularly vulnerable.

The pace of *evictions increased during the Famine. The ruthlessness of many landlords stemmed from two problems: drastic reduction in rent receipts and rising taxation. Experience varied from district to district. Reliable figures are unavailable before 1849, but in that year the constabulary recorded the eviction of over 90,000 people, increasing to over 100,000 in 1850.

The legacies of the Famine were several. The *population declined by one-fifth between 1845 and 1851, and never regained its pre-Famine level. The *cottier class was decimated, altering the social structure of Irish society. Many thousands escaped hunger by emigrating to Britain, North America, and Australia, accelerating an outward flow already established.

The immediate cause of the Great Famine was blight, but there were underlying forces that had resulted in 3 million people subsisting on the potato. One view would be that the disasters of 1845–9 represented the culmination of a long-term crisis resulting from rapid population growth against a background of economic decline. More recently some economic historians, pointing to the levelling off in population growth, to the progress of new, agriculturally based manufacturing industries such as *brewing, *distilling, and *flour milling, and to improvements in transport, communications, and *banking, have argued that the pre-Famine economy had not in fact 'ground to a halt'. In this perspective the failure of the potato should be seen as a massive exogenous blow dealt to an economy that had begun to adjust to changing market conditions. These contrasting perceptions are central to the debate on how far the Famine changed the course of Ireland's development in the 19th century. They also have at least an indirect bearing on the equally disputed question of whether the government of the United Kingdom, notwithstanding prevailing ideology, could have been expected to have done more to alleviate distress in a part of the world's richest nation.

Daly, Mary, *The Famine in Ireland* (1996)

Kineally, Christine, *This Great Calamity: The Great Famine 1845–52* (1994)

EMC

Greatrakes, Valentine (1628–83), faith healer, 'the Irish stroker'. The heir to a small property in Affane, Co. Waterford, Greatrakes served under *Orrery in the Cromwellian army. His apparent power of healing by touch, first reported in 1662, provoked much debate in scientific circles, particularly during and after a visit to England in 1666.

green has been identified as the Irish national colour since at least the 17th century (see FLAGS). Suggestions that prior to the 19th century blue was the generally accepted Irish colour appear to derive from the colour chosen to represent Ireland in Stuart flags and coats of arms, rather than tradition within Ireland itself.

Green, Alice Stopford (1847–1929), historian. Daughter of a Church of Ireland clergyman, she married the English popular historian John Richard Green and became a leading figure in London intellectual circles. A close friend of *Casement, she assisted in raising the money that financed the *Howth gun-running. Her passionate Irish nationalism found expression in three influential works, *The Making of Ireland and its Undoing* (1908), *Irish Nationality* (1911), and *A History of the Irish State to 1014* (1925), all of which sought to establish the highly developed state of Ireland's political institutions before the *Anglo-Norman invasion.

Gregg, John Allen FitzGerald (1873–1961). As archbishop of Dublin 1920–39, Gregg held high office in the *Church of Ireland at a time of critical importance. While encouraging his community to accept with good grace the reality of independence, he left the *Irish Free State authorities in no doubt as to Church of Ireland discomfort over many issues, including compulsory Irish. De *Valera, to whom he bore a striking physical resemblance, respected him, and consulted him in the formulation of article 44 of the 1937 *constitution.

As archbishop of Armagh 1939–59, Gregg presided over the General Synod with notable authority, having a profound and meticulous understanding of the letter and spirit of the church's written constitution. He showed himself highly competent in the financial affairs of the church, as he was in matters theological. He was a robust exponent of the Church of Ireland's doctrinal position: courteous in debate with Rome, and strongly opposed to any ecumenical involvement with Protestant churches that would, in his opinion, compromise the catholic elements in Anglicanism. KM

Gregg, Revd Tresham (*c*.1800–81), Church of Ireland clergyman and religious controversialist. In 1841 he launched the Dublin Protestant Operative Association, to co-ordinate working-class Protestant opposition to *O'Connellite and liberal politics.

Gregory, Lady Augusta (1852–1932), author. Born Augusta Persse, from a Galway landowning family, she married Sir William Gregory (see GREGORY CLAUSE) in 1880. After his death she administered his estate at Coole Park, Co. Galway, for their son and developed nationalist sympathies. Coole became a centre of the Irish *literary revival through her friendship with W. B. *Yeats, who idealized the aristocratic traditions of the Gregorys and encouraged her interest in folklore. In 1899 Gregory co-founded the Irish Literary Theatre, remaining a leading *Abbey board member and playwright until the late 1920s. She wrote 27 plays employing a synthetic dialect known as 'Kiltartanese'. Her light comedies were popular; she also wrote plays on historical and mythological themes. Gregory produced Kiltartanized book versions of Gaelic sagas and folklore. Her history of the Abbey theatre and posthumous autobiography and journals are significant sources for the history of the literary revival. Her grandmotherly, slightly condescending image disguises her stature and individuality. Coole was demolished after her death. PM

Gregory, William (1762–1840). The son of a Co. Galway landowner, Gregory was under-secretary at *Dublin Castle 1812–30, an efficient administrator and strong opponent of Catholic emancipation. He was removed in 1830 at the insistence of *Wellesley. His grandson gave his name to the infamous *'Gregory clause'.

Gregory clause, an amendment to the Poor Law Act of 1847, named after its proposer, Sir William Gregory (1817–92), MP for Dublin city and later husband of Lady Augusta *Gregory. Also called 'the quarter-acre clause', it prohibited the relief from poor rates of anyone occupying more than a quarter-acre of land and also (until the rules were changed in May 1848) of their dependants. The restriction facilitated those landlords who wished to take advantage of the *Great Famine to clear their estates of surplus tenants, but added significantly to misery and loss of life, as smallholders stubbornly refused to give up their foothold on the land.

Grey, Lord Leonard (d. 1541), lord deputy, 1536–40. Grey supervised the Reformation parliament (May 1536–Dec. 1537), but is better known as the military-minded governor who provoked the Gaelic Irish into forming the *Geraldine League. He traversed the country each year with his artillery, battering down castles as the *Kildares had formerly done. Rather than extracting peace treaties from the Gaelic lords like earlier deputies, Grey now demanded formal submission to English overlordship with heavy tribute and homage. The reformers in Dublin complained that Grey was more interested in initiating a conquest than reorganizing the lordship. In 1540 Conn *O'Neill himself wrote to the king about Grey's aggressive style of government. The Butlers (see ORMOND (BUTLER)) denounced him as 'the earl of Kildare newly-born again'. Grey, as brother-in-law to Gearóid Óg, 9th earl of *Kildare, had tried to gain influence by taking over and utilizing the old Geraldine network. However, it was the threat posed by the Geraldine League which damaged him. Despite the victory at *Bellahoe, Henry VIII felt constrained to dispatch money and reinforcements in November 1539. Grey was removed from office in April 1540 and executed for treason in June 1541. HM

greyhound racing as a sport has its origins in the hunt. Irish hounds were reputedly known in ancient Rome and in Elizabethan England. Formal coursing events were held in Ireland from the 17th century. The success of Irish dogs in English hare coursing in the 19th century reinforced their reputation. However, the sport in its modern form came to Ireland in 1927, when electric hares were run in Belfast and Dublin. This development transformed greyhound racing from a popular rural pastime to a major urban attraction. By 1960 Ireland had 22 registered venues, four of which were in Northern Ireland. In 1980 1.2 million spectators attended meetings in the Irish Republic and £23 million was placed in wagers. The Irish Greyhound Racing Board was established in 1952, supported by a betting levy. It oversees racing and breeding, and began the formal industrialization of the sport. Between 1960 and 1980, 7,000 greyhounds were exported annually from the Republic, with breeding on a lesser scale also taking place in Northern Ireland. NG

Grianán of Ailech is a large multi-period, fortified site in north-east Donegal. Early excavations and extensive restorations have tended to obscure rather than illuminate the antiquity of the site. The three outer earthen ramparts are perhaps a late *Bronze Age hillfort but the Middle Ages saw the construction of a massive stone fort *c.*75 feet in diameter. The site on Greenan Mountain has been popularly identified as Ailech, the seat of the northern *Uí Néill dynasty, which was destroyed in the 12th century, but nearby Elagh, Co. Londonderry, which preserves the name 'Ailech', also has a claim. JPM

Grierson, George (*c.*1680–1753), *printer and bookseller in Dublin. Grierson was the first of a family dynasty to hold the king's printer patent from 1732. He married Constantia Crawley (?1705–33), celebrated under her married name for her editions of the classics. VK

Griffith, Arthur (1871–1922), journalist and politician. Born in Dublin, Griffith was a printer by trade, but turned writer and journalist. Strongly influenced by *Parnell, Thomas *Davis, and John *Mitchel, he was a founder member of the Celtic Literary Society in 1893 and was active in the *Gaelic League and the *Irish Republican Brotherhood, which he left in 1910. He edited several radical newspapers, including the *United Irishman* and *Sinn Féin*. Although his ideas attracted little support in this period, they had a long-term influence on the public mind. In 1904 he wrote *The Resurrection of Hungary: A Parallel for Ireland*, in which he set out his ideas on Irish independence under a dual monarchy. His protectionist economic programme was heavily influenced by the German economist Friedrich List. These two elements became central to the political programme of *Sinn Féin, set up on 28 November 1905.

In defence of *home rule Griffith joined the *Irish Volunteers on its foundation and took part in the *Howth gun-running. However, he rejected the use of force to establish a republic and did not take part in the *rising of 1916. The authorities, like much of the population, nevertheless thought the rebellion was inspired by Sinn Féin and arrested Griffith. After his release he became vice-president of the revived Sinn Féin party which now became a republican organization.

He was again arrested in 1918, and while imprisoned was elected MP for East Cavan. He became acting president of the *Dáil when de *Valera toured the USA from June 1919 to the end of 1920. He was rearrested in November 1920 and released shortly before the truce which ended the *Anglo-Irish War. He was appointed head of the plenipotentiaries assigned to negotiate the *Anglo-Irish treaty, and regarded the resulting agreement as the best that could be achieved for Ireland. He was elected president of the Dáil on 10 January 1922 after de Valera resigned. He became increasingly weakened under the strains and died of a cerebral haemorrhage on 12 August 1922.

Although generally seen as one of the founding fathers of the democratic Republic of Ireland, Griffith was a nationalist before he was a democrat, and believed that the rights of nations came before those of the individual. The feasibility of his proposals for dual monarchy and economic self-sufficiency has been questioned, and it has recently been shown that he had little appreciation for the position of unionists, assuming that there was no real conflict of interest within Ireland.

Maume, Patrick, 'The Ancient Constitution: Arthur Griffith and his Intellectual Legacy to Sinn Féin', *Irish Political Studies*, 10 (1995)

Younger, Calton, *Arthur Griffith* (1981)

JA

Griffith, Sir Richard (1784–1878), engineer and public servant. Born in Naas, Co. Kildare, he began his career with the commission set up in 1809 to study the possible exploitation of Irish bogs and later worked on the upgrading of roads in the south-west for the *Board of Works. His greatest monuments are the *Geological Map of Ireland* (1839) and the *Primary Valuation.

Guild of St George, see BROTHERHOOD OF ST GEORGE.

guilds were associations of merchants and craftsmen in cities and towns, for the mutual benefit of members and for the purpose of regulating their trade or craft. Their members had an exclusive right to practise a craft or engage in trade within the boundaries of the city or town.

Prince *John's charter to Dublin in 1192 granted the city the right to have guilds, and it is probably to this that the earliest Dublin guild dates. This, known as the guild merchant, included not only merchants, but also craftsmen of various kinds. Membership was not restricted to inhabitants of the city; many of those who became members were foreign traders. Separate craft guilds developed in the 15th century, each under the patronage of a different saint and with its own chapel. The guild, which was composed of master craftsmen, charged membership fees and maintained a common chest to pay for legal costs and feasts and other celebrations, and to support members in time of need. The wealthier guilds had their own guild halls.

The guilds took an active part in the social life of the city, performing in mystery plays and pageants. They regulated apprenticeship, the quantity and quality of production, wages, and prices. Catholics were precluded from joining by insistence on the oath of *supremacy, but a class of associate members, called quarter brothers, was instituted, which enabled both Catholics and Quakers to participate in guild membership (see QUARTERAGE DISPUTE). From the beginning of the 18th century onwards the economic power of the guilds began to decline with the movement towards decontrol and deregulation. Another factor was the growth of journeymen's clubs, combinations of skilled workers for their own mutual benefit, which came into conflict with the guilds and the municipal authorities. These were to be the ancestors of the modern *trade union movement.

By the middle of the 18th century guilds were more important for their political role in municipal and parliamentary politics than for their economic influence. Guild members were eligible for the municipal franchise, and the guilds were represented on the governing body of the city or town (see URBAN GOVERNMENT). The political importance of guilds led to the admission of non-tradesmen for political purposes. Guild involvement in municipal government was ended by the Municipal Corporations (Ireland) Act (1840), and many guilds were abolished shortly afterwards because of their failure to co-operate with the *Catholic Relief Acts.

PC

Guinness, *brewing dynasty and one of Ireland's greatest commercial success stories of the 19th century. **Arthur Guinness** (1725–1803), son of a land agent from Co. Kildare, commenced brewing in Leixlip in 1756, and three years later took over a disused brewery at St James's Gate, Dublin. His son **Arthur Guinness** (1768–1858), inherited the brewery, along with his father's extensive *flour milling interests. He became a director of the Bank of Ireland in 1808 and governor from 1820. Like his father a committed member of the Church of Ireland, and active in a range of philanthropic ventures, Arthur II supported *Catholic emancipation and *parliamentary reform, but declined to back *O'Connell's *repeal agitation. His son **Benjamin Lee Guinness** (1798–1868), created a baronet in 1867, was lord mayor of Dublin 1851 and Conservative MP for the city from 1865. He financed and directed the restoration of *St Patrick's cathedral. On his death the business passed to his sons **Arthur** (now Sir Arthur) (1840–1915) and **Edward Cecil** (1847–1927). Sir Arthur withdrew in 1876. Created Baron Ardilaun in 1880, he devoted himself to public causes, including the restoration of Marsh's library and the Coombe hospital and the construction of artisans' dwellings. He was Conservative MP for Dublin 1868–9, 1874–80. Edward Cecil, manager of the company to 1889 and subsequently chairman of its board, also continued the family tradition of philanthropy, contributing almost £1 million to slum clearance and housing projects, as well as donations to medical and other causes. He was created Baron Iveagh in 1891.

Guinness's Dublin brewery initially produced ale and beer, to which by the 1790s it had added the darker drink porter. From the 1820s its better porters had begun to be described as 'stout', 'double stout', and later 'triple stout'. Initially it produced mainly for the Dublin market, but English outlets expanded rapidly from the 1820s and by 1840 accounted for more than half of total sales. The period of most dramatic growth was from the 1850s. By increasing the scale of its operations, while retaining a high quality, and so reducing costs below those of its rivals, Guinness succeeded in extending sales in both the British and Irish markets. When it was incorporated as a public company in 1886, applications for shares totalled over £100,000,000, and by the 1930s it was among the seven largest companies in the world.

Lynch, Patrick, and Vaizey, John, *Guinness's Brewery in the Irish Economy 1759–1876* (1960)

AB/SC

Gwynn, Stephen (1864–1950). An Oxford educated Protestant and grandson of William Smith *O'Brien, Gwynn was *Nationalist MP for Galway 1906–18 and saw active service in the *First World War. He published biographies, literary criticism, and historical works.

habeas corpus, a writ requiring the production in court of a detained person. An English act of 1679 confirmed the procedure's status as a defence against imprisonment without trial. The absence of comparable Irish legislation was first raised as a grievance in 1692 (see SOLE RIGHT), and became a central patriot demand until remedied by Sir Samuel Bradstreet's Liberty of the Subject Act (1782).

In response to the challenges of the *Defender and *United Irish movements, *Young Ireland, and the *Fenians, the right of habeas corpus was suspended by act of parliament for most of the period 1796–1806, during 1848–9, and again in 1866–9. The Protection of Life and Property Act or Westmeath Act (1871), permitting the detention without trial of suspected *Ribbonmen in Westmeath and adjoining counties, was seen as a novel use of the power of suspension outside periods of political emergency (although there was in fact one precedent, in response to agrarian disturbances, during six months of 1822). The Protection of Persons and Property Act of March 1881 temporarily reintroduced detention without trial; but the necessity of maintaining those so detained in relatively comfortable conditions led government to rely thereafter on the summary jurisdiction of the 1887 Crimes Act (see COERCION ACTS). *Internment was however to reappear in the *Anglo-Irish War, and in the security policies of both Northern Ireland and independent Ireland.

Hackett, Thomas (d. 1697). A native of England but a graduate of *Trinity College, Dublin, Hackett became Church of Ireland bishop of Down and Connor in 1672 but resided almost continually in England. In 1694 an episcopal commission appointed by the government deprived him of his see and suspended several of his clergy for a range of abuses.

hagiography, the writing of Lives of the saints, was a genre of literary activity of the first importance in the Latin church in the early Middle Ages. The cult of saints flourished in Ireland and, in particular, there was a strong focus on native saints. The writing of their Lives forms a distinctively Irish strand in the tradition of Latin hagiography, and from the 9th century the use of the Irish language gives Irish saints' Lives a special interest.

From the second half of the 7th century there survives a group of four Lives whose authors are known. Of these *Adomnán's Life of St *Colum Cille, written in or soon after 697, is the richest in accessible historical information. Weaving together stories collected in the saint's community, in terms that look back to the well-known Lives of St Antony, St Martin of Tours, and St Benedict, Adomnán depicts Colum Cille as an idealized abbot in a style that would be recognized by a European audience. The Life of St *Brigid by Cogitosus is earlier, simple in style, but lacks the biographical information: it is no more than a series of miracle stories, often pointing to a biblical precedent, framed by opening and closing passages that claim the highest status for St Brigid's church at Kildare. Two Lives of St *Patrick, both extant in the Book of *Armagh, belong to the same period. Muirchú's life, full of fantastic stories that owe much to Irish secular tales and to folklore, was composed before 700. That by Tírechán is very much simpler, little more than a narrative of Patrick's supposed missionary journey around Ireland founding churches, a literary device that allows the writer to claim a historical link with churches Armagh sought to control. The only clue to the date of Tírechán's work is a reference to plagues, which make dates around 670 or the mid-680s equally plausible. These four Lives have little in common, so that one cannot say that at this date there is a recognizable Irish style of saint's Life.

The anonymous first Life of St Brigid shows a close verbal relationship to the Life by Cogitosus, allowing one to infer that it was one of the texts used as a source. A third Life of Brigid, known in part from an Old Irish version of the 9th century, provides a glimpse of a further early account. Both of these Lives, minimalist in style, bear a generic similarity to the greater bulk of Lives of Irish saints known in Latin from three late medieval compilations and in Irish from a number of collections made between the 15th and 17th centuries. Analysis of the Latin collections has shown that the collectors used for some of the Lives a manuscript written probably no later than the 9th century. One of the collections has preserved without alteration the Lives of ten further saints written between the late 7th and the 9th centuries, among them St Ailbe of Emly, St Munnu of Taghmon, and St Colmán Alo of Lynally. For a few Irish saints we have Lives composed in Latin in the 12th century, among them the Life of St *Malachy by no less a writer than St Bernard of Clairvaux. However, the best known of the later collections, compiled by an antiquary at Ferns in the 13th century, was a sympathetic rewriting of some thirty Lives from various dates.

The vernacular tradition of hagiography, first evident in the 9th century, produced a number of homiletic Lives in Irish, among them the long Tripartite Life of St Patrick, a synthesis of the earlier Latin Lives. Most of the Irish Lives survive only in late copies, and many of them were evidently rehandled in the later Middle Ages. The apogee of the vernacular tradition of saints' Lives is perhaps the long and very full Life of St Colum Cille by Manus *O'Donnell, compiled from Latin and Middle Irish sources in 1532. Manuscript copies of some Lives in Irish continued to circulate into the age of modern printing: the 12th- or 13th-century Life of St Finbarr, for example, was still being copied commercially at Cork in the 1890s. RS

Hamilton, William Rowan (1805–65), mathematician. The son of a Dublin solicitor, he entered *Trinity College, Dublin, in 1823 as a mathematical prodigy: when an undergraduate he gave lectures (including the famous 'Theory of Systems of Rays', 1827) to the *Royal Irish Academy. In 1827 he was appointed astronomer royal of Ireland and professor of astronomy at Trinity College, Dublin; he later received honours from scientific societies throughout the world. His finest achievements were in the algebra of quaternions, on which he published his *Lectures* (1853) and his *Elements* (1866); he also worked in optics and dynamics. Influenced by Kant, Coleridge, and Boscovich, he adopted an anti-materialist philosophy. DJS

handball was certainly played in Ireland in the 18th century. By the mid-19th century Irish immigrants had taken the sport abroad, though it had become uncommon in Ireland. Irish handball became extremely popular in America, primarily as a focus for gambling. The first modern court was built in Brooklyn, New York, in 1880. The semi-professional status of top-level players and the prominence of policemen in the sport made the *Gaelic Athletic Association reluctant to become involved in its administration within Ireland. Thus it was not until 1924 that a governing body was formed. Later sponsorship by the GAA, Free State army patronage, government provision of courts, and the establishment of all-Ireland and international competitions boosted the popularity of the sport. By 1980 there were 210 clubs in Ireland and around 2,800 players. NG

Hanna, Hugh (1821–92), pugnacious *Presbyterian minister and *Orangeman whose open-air preaching allegedly contributed to sectarian riots in Belfast. Ordained for missionary outreach in north Belfast in 1851, he formed a congregation in Berry Street. When this outgrew its building, St Enoch's church, accommodating 2,000 worshippers, was built for him. An ardent *evangelical, he figured prominently in the *revival of 1859. A statue in his honour in Belfast was destroyed by explosives in 1970. RFGH

Harland, Sir Edward James (1831–95), *Belfast *shipbuilder. Between 1846 and 1851 he served an engineering apprenticeship with Robert Stephenson & Company of Newcastle upon Tyne. In 1854 he was appointed manager of Robert Hickson's shipyard on Queen's Island, Belfast.

In 1858 Harland purchased Hickson's yard. Three years later he went into partnership with Gustav Wilhelm *Wolff. After William James *Pirrie joined the partnership in 1874, Harland gradually withdrew from day-to-day involvement in the firm in order to pursue wider interests. He was chief harbour commissioner for Belfast 1875–87, and then became an alderman for the city in 1884, mayor in 1885 and 1886, and finally *Unionist MP for North Belfast from 1887 until his death in 1895. The baronetcy was conferred in 1885. FG/WJ

Harland & Wolff, the *Belfast *shipbuilding firm, was formed in 1861 by Edward James *Harland and Gustav Wilhelm *Wolff.

From 1905 to 1913 inclusive Harland & Wolff's launchings placed it in the top five UK firms on seven occasions. As with other UK shipbuilding firms, growth was facilitated by linkages, both formal and informal, between shipbuilders and shipping lines. These linkages enabled a considerable degree of product specialization and a high level of output to be maintained. The former resulted in Harland & Wolff being one of a small number of yards equipped to construct the largest vessels, and the latter helped the firm to sustain unit cost advantages over competitors. Under the chairmanship of William *Pirrie, these linkages culminated in Harland & Wolff's participation in 1902 in J. P. Morgan's International Mercantile Marine, which sought (and failed) to corner a dominant share of the lucrative market for North Atlantic shipping services. By 1914 Harland & Wolff had also forged links with the Sheffield steel firm of John Brown, and extended its shipbuilding and repair operations to the Clyde, Liverpool, and Southampton.

In the inter-war years all UK shipbuilding firms confronted the problems of excess world capacity and growing foreign competition. Following Pirrie's death in 1924 the firm experienced severe financial difficulties under its new chairman, Lord Kylsant of the Royal Mail shipping group. In 1930 the company was placed under the control of trustees for its creditors. Despite these difficulties the firm maintained its share of UK launchings, though the latter declined as a proportion of world tonnage launched. In these years Harland & Wolff entered the market for oil tankers and diversified by entering into partnership in 1936 with *Short Brothers to produce aircraft.

In the *Second World War, as in the First, the firm benefited from admiralty orders for warships. Its financial position improved and by 1945 the creditors' trustees had been stood down. From the late 1940s to the mid-1970s world output rose almost continuously, driven by a boom in the construction of oil-tankers and bulk carriers. While output on the Lagan increased relative to that of the UK it fell as a proportion of world output. Tonnage launched by Harland & Wolff reached a historical high in the 1970s with the new capital-intensive production of oil tankers and bulk carriers.

Unfortunately the firm had re-equipped and modernized its yards too late to take full advantage of the boom. Losses were sustained from 1964 onwards and the firm was in receipt of government financial support from 1966. In 1975 the Northern Ireland government became the sole shareholder in the company and continued to give financial support. In 1989 Harland & Wolff was privatized through a management and employee buyout. Since then the company has survived by diversifying its product mix and catering for specialist markets, such as offshore production vessels for the oil industry.

Geary, F., and Johnson, W., 'Shipbuilding in Belfast, 1861–1986', *Irish Economic and Social History*, 16 (1989)

Moss, M., and Hume, J. R., *Shipbuilders to the World: 125 Years of Harland and Wolff, Belfast 1961–1986* (1986)

FG/WJ

harvest in Ireland during at least the last three centuries has gone on throughout the summer, depending on the crop grown and the seasonal weather. *Potatoes, *hay, and *flax could be harvested during July, while cereal crops were commonly reaped or mown during August and September.

Harvest techniques varied with the crop grown and the period considered. Flax was almost all pulled by hand, while after the 1850s potatoes could be dug mechanically. Before 1850, hay was commonly mown using scythes, while most grain was reaped using toothed sickles or smooth bladed reaping hooks. However, after *horse-drawn American reaping/mowing machines were exhibited in Belfast in 1852, and Dublin in 1853, their use spread quickly, the availability of these labour-saving machines coinciding with a continuing fall in the number of *agricultural labourers. By 1895, it was estimated that there were 15,000 such machines in use in Ireland.

Before 1800, grain was entirely threshed by hand, but during the early 19th century threshing machines, which removed grain seeds from the straw mechanically, became common. These could be operated manually, or powered using horses, water, or steam. By the 1840s, several Irish foundries (see IRON) were manufacturing threshing machines, and by 1875 it was estimated that there were 10,000 horse-operated machines in Ireland.

During the twentieth century, an increasing number of grain-harvesting tasks came to be carried out in a single operation, first with the introduction of reaper-binder machines, and later, since the *Second World War, with the extensive use of combine harvesters. JB

Harvey, Beauchamp Bagenal (1762–98). A Co. Wexford landowner and early member of the *United Irish society, he commanded the rebel forces in the county during the *insurrection of 1798. He was executed despite his claims—not necessarily to be believed—that he had been forced to assume the leadership.

Haslam, Thomas (1825–1917) and **Anna** (1829–1922), two of the most active *feminists in 19th- and early 20th-century Ireland. Both were *Quakers, from Laois and Cork respectively; they married in 1854 and settled in Dublin. They were involved in many feminist campaigns, but their most enduring achievement was the Dublin Women's Suffrage Association (later the Irish Women's Suffrage and Local Government Association), which they founded in 1876, and which lasted in one form or another until 1947. Anna Haslam was also a co-founder of the Women's Liberal Unionist

Association, but worked side by side with nationalist and Catholic suffragists in the early 20th century. The IWSLGA was a non-militant association but it kept close links with the more militant suffrage organizations during the high point of suffrage agitation 1910–12. CC

Haughton, Samuel (1821–97), polymath. In 1859, while already professor of geology at *Trinity College, Dublin, he enrolled as a medical student, becoming registrar of the college's medical school immediately on qualifying. He published papers on mathematics, geology, and medicine, was secretary of the Royal Zoological Society of Ireland, and in 1866 published a formula for calculating the drop needed to cause instantaneous death at hangings.

Hawarden kite, the indiscreet statement of *Gladstone's son Herbert that his father was about to declare his support for Irish *home rule. Gladstone, then privately entreating the Tories to take up the home rule issue, immediately repudiated the statement when it appeared in the London press on 17 December 1885, but failed to dispel the impression that he had inspired it. The kite served to clarify the division in British politics on the home rule question. JL

hay making was probably introduced to Ireland by the *Normans, but as late as 1838 it was claimed that some small farmers in Connemara did not know that it was possible to use dried grass as fodder. In the 19th century, agricultural improvers often criticized the length of time Irish farmers left the hay crop to ripen before cutting, and the length of time it stood drying in the field, arguing that this led to a loss in nutritional value. Farmers, however, pointed out that the damp climate and the lushness of the crop meant that *harvesting had to be extended.

The swing towards livestock farming which occurred in Ireland during the second half of the 19th century (see FARMING) led to a great expansion of the acreage set aside for hay, and by 1900 it was the largest crop produced. During the twentieth century, the production of grass seed became an important part of farming. JB

Hay, Edward (*c.*1761–1826), Catholic activist and radical. Born into a propertied Catholic family in Co. Wexford, Hay studied in France and Germany and was active in the campaign that secured the *Catholic Relief Act of 1793. His brother **John Hay**, a former officer in the French army, was a rebel commander in the *insurrection of 1798. Edward Hay was also tried for treason but acquitted; modern accounts conclude that he was in fact involved in the insurrection. He was later active in Catholic politics and served as secretary to the revived *Catholic Committee (later Catholic Board) until dismissed following a dispute in 1819. His *History of the Insurrection in the County of Wexford* (1803) is now treated with caution, as one of several subsequent accounts that seek to play down the element of active disaffection in 1798, and to exculpate both the *United Irish leaders and the Catholic clergy, by emphasizing official repression as the main cause of the outbreak.

heads of bills, a procedure designed to permit draft legislative proposals to be introduced and debated in either house of the Irish *parliament, despite the restrictions of *Poynings's Law. Heads of bills differed from regular acts in the inclusion of the supplicatory opening 'we pray it may be enacted', rather than the instructional 'be it enacted', and in that they could originate in either house, although most in fact took their origin in the Commons. If passed by the house in which they originated, heads were transmitted to the Irish *privy council, where they could be approved, amended, postponed, or respited. 'Heads' that passed this hurdle became bills, and were sent with the Irish great seal attached to the English privy council, which had the same options. Those that were approved were returned to Ireland, engrossed, as acts with the great seal of England attached, and a commission empowering the *lord lieutenant to give them royal approval—thus making them law—if they passed both houses of the Irish parliament unaltered.

Hayden has traced this form of proceeding back to 1615, but the tone and content of the exchanges between parliament and council, and parliament and the lord lieutenant, during 1634–5, 1640–1, and 1661–6 indicate that it was initially hotly disputed. The differences had largely been ironed out by the 1690s, when it became established practice for most legislation to originate as heads of bills. This practice remained current until 1782 when *Yelverton's Act (see LEGISLATIVE INDEPENDENCE) made it redundant. JK

health services. At the beginning of the 20th century Ireland apparently had well-developed health services, especially for the poor. In the cities there were prestigious Catholic and Protestant voluntary *hospitals, while each county had its own infirmary. The *workhouses offered free infirmary care to the poor, who could also consult salaried dispensary doctors without charge.

But, although this system looked impressive on paper, it had serious weaknesses. Standards in county infirmaries varied, while many workhouse infirmaries were primitive. Even the famous voluntary hospitals, catering for paying patients, were often old-fashioned and short of money. Dispensary doctors were poorly paid and frequently worked from rundown premises. Public health was neglected by local authorities and a number of infectious diseases were still endemic.

The creation of *Northern Ireland and of the *Irish Free State in 1920–2 at first saw only limited improvements in health services. In the south workhouses were closed or converted into county homes and county, district, and fever hospitals. But no extra money was initially forthcoming to improve hospital services. Dilapidation and overcrowding therefore continued. In 1926 the procedures for appointing dispensary doctors were reformed, but the dispensary system continued to operate until 1972 when it was finally replaced by a choice-of-doctor and fee-for-service scheme. County medical officers of health were appointed from 1927 to improve public health. They took the initiative in upgrading the school medical service, but little was done regarding maternal and infant health and the *tuberculosis death rate actually increased in the late 1930s.

From 1930 the *Irish Hospitals Sweepstakes provided money to maintain voluntary hospitals, as well as allowing the government to replace or extend county and district hospitals. Small hospitals thus proliferated. It was not until the 1970s that a concerted campaign began to rationalize the Irish hospital system by closing and amalgamating smaller and older hospitals.

Although the poor had access to free medical services, others did not. National insurance had been introduced in 1911, but in Ireland, unlike Britain, this did not include free general practitioner treatment and free medicines. In 1930 Northern Ireland extended such medical benefit to all insured workers, but in the south this step was thwarted by the opposition of doctors, the Catholic clergy, and many politicians. It was not until 1953 that insured workers in the Republic became eligible for medical benefit. In 1957 a system of voluntary health insurance was introduced to cover the remainder of the population and within twenty years over half a million people were insured. Major Health Acts passed in 1947 and 1953, in the face of determined opposition from both the medical profession and the Catholic hierarchy, who opposed state regulation, contributed substantially to the creation of an up-to-date health service in the Republic.

Northern Ireland passed two important Health Acts in 1946 which finally swept away the old poor law system and laid the basis of a modern health service. British legislation establishing a national health service was applied simultaneously in the province in 1948, although substantial British subsidies were essential to its operation.

Gormley, M., *Ireland's Community Health Services* (1988)

Hensey, B., *The Health Services of Ireland* (4th edn., 1988)

ELM

Healy, Cahir (1877–1970), nationalist politician. A member of *Sinn Féin, Healy was interned 1922–4. He was Nationalist MP in the parliament of Northern Ireland for Fermanagh-Tyrone 1925–9 and Fermanagh South 1929–65, and in the United Kingdom parliament 1922–4, 1931–5, and 1950–5. His internment during the *Second World War outraged nationalists.

Healy, Timothy Michael (1855–1931), politician. Healy combined membership of the 'Bantry band', a tight political clan, with a record as the most independent of all *Nationalist MPs. Scarcely ever out of parliament between 1880 and 1918, he represented six constituencies and four different allegiances. A leading Dublin barrister and KC, his high income, sharp tongue, and courtroom prowess equipped him for a maverick role. He attacked *Parnell savagely in 1890–1, and later sought to destroy the anti-Parnellite faction from within through his People's Rights Association, whose call for a return to local constituency power was grounded in clerically based conservative nationalism. Isolated after the 1900 reunion, he was sustained by Cardinal *Logue and the press magnate W. M. *Murphy. From 1910 he took sanctuary in William *O'Brien's All for Ireland League. His long record of opposition to the parliamentary party, albeit from a conservative perspective, endeared him to *Sinn Féin, which he cultivated (but did not join) after 1916. This new link, and his older ones with the British legal-political establishment, made him a mutually acceptable choice as first *governor-general of the *Irish Free State, 1922–8.

ACH

Hearts of Steel (Steelboys), a movement of *agrarian protest. Originating in conflict over the general reletting of the *Donegall estate in Co. Antrim in 1770, it spread during 1771–2 to Cos. Down, Londonderry, and Armagh, as a general protest against rent levels and *evictions, as well as against local taxation (*cess) and food prices. On 23 December 1770 500 or more Steelboys invaded Belfast and forcibly rescued a prisoner. As a movement of social protest that insisted on its exclusively Protestant character, the Steelboys have been seen as a precursor of both the *United Irishmen and the *Orange Order.

hedge schools (pay schools) were so designated because, especially in the early 18th century, when the prohibition against Catholic schools and teachers was stringently enforced (see PENAL LAWS), the masters taught their pupils clandestinely in makeshift classrooms, sometimes consisting of little more than the shelter of a hedge or barn. The name continued in use even when a hut or the home of a pupil was a more usual location. Though by no means restricted to Catholic pupils, especially in the Presbyterian north, hedge schools were particularly identified with the Catholic population. Official figures suggest that in the 1820s between 300,000 and 400,000 children attended, the number of schools rising to 9,000 by 1824.

The masters, usually self-taught or former hedge scholars themselves (contemporaries give contrasting accounts of teachers of academic distinction, and of others who were subversive, intemperate, and brutal), were often itinerant, setting up school in a cottage or lodging with a family in return for teaching the children. Other parents paid a modest fee in coin or in kind. Attendance was erratic.

The curriculum was generally in English and comprised the customary three Rs, though there were masters who had some competence in classics and modern languages. Such books as were used were often simply what lay to hand, e.g. religious literature or novels. Children were taught individually, though William Carleton, himself a hedge school pupil and teacher, claimed that a system close to the monitorial was quite common by the early 19th century. KM

heiresses, see WIDOWS AND HEIRESSES.

Hely-Hutchinson, John (1724–94). A Co. Cork-born lawyer he entered parliament in 1759 and was prime serjeant 1761–74. During the *free trade agitation he produced an influential memorandum detailing the damage done to the Irish economy by English commercial legislation. His appointment in 1774 as provost of *Trinity College, Dublin, made in order to liberate the office of prime serjeant for other purposes, was widely viewed as the extension of political patronage into an inappropriate area. His son **Richard**, 1st earl of Donoughmore (1756–1825), was one of the liberal Protestant sympathizers through whom Irish Catholics put their case before parliament in the period prior to the *veto controversy.

Henry II (1133–89), king of England (1154–89). Within a year of his accession, Henry II discussed a possible conquest of Ireland leading to the issue of **Laudabaliter*. However he did not act on this grant until *Strongbow's acquisition of Leinster, and the failure of Ruaidrí Ua Conchobair (see O'CONNOR, RORY) to assert control over his activities, raised fears that Strongbow might use this new Irish lordship as a base from which to retake forcibly the earldom of Pembroke, of which Henry had deprived him. Henry mounted a large-scale expedition to Ireland, where he remained from October 1171 to April 1172. It was successful in so far as Strongbow acknowledged Henry as his overlord for Leinster, a significant number of Irish kings voluntarily submitted to Henry, and the Irish bishops also endorsed his intervention. Henry left Ireland hurriedly because his younger son, Henry, had revolted against him in league with King Louis of France. But prior to his departure he reserved Dublin, Waterford, and Wexford as royal demesne and made a grant of the kingdom of *Mide (Meath) to Hugh de *Lacy.

By the treaty of *Windsor (1175) Ruaidrí Ua Conchobair acknowledged Henry's overlordship of Leinster, Meath, Dublin, Waterford, and Wexford. The task of ruling not only England but extensive continental dominions, and of overcoming opposition from within his own family, precluded Henry from allocating adequate resources to his Irish lordship; he was forced to rely on colonists such as Hugh de Lacy to uphold his interests in Ireland. In 1177 Henry designated his youngest son, *John, lord of Ireland, with the intention of eventually having him crowned king and so providing resident personal lordship. In 1185 he sent John to Ireland with a main aim of asserting control over Hugh de Lacy, whose independent activities were causing concern. Henry's last act in relation to Ireland was to promise Isabella, daughter of Strongbow and of *Aífe, and heiress of Leinster, to the powerful landed magnate William *Marshal. While such men had the resources to implement colonization, they were also difficult to retain under royal control; the tensions between colonists and royal officials which surfaced during Henry's reign were to remain an enduring feature of the medieval colony. MTF

Henry of London, archbishop of Dublin 1213–28, *justiciar of Ireland 1213–15, 1221–4. A member of the London patrician family of Blund, he was archdeacon of Stafford by 1194. He served King *John as administrator, royal justice, and diplomat, travelling to Navarre, Ireland, and Germany before 1208. He supported the king during the interdict and in 1209 was elected bishop of Exeter, but this was declared invalid. He was elected archbishop of Dublin in 1213. Before 1215 he had rebuilt *Dublin Castle and went on to rebuild the cathedrals of *Christ Church and *St Patrick's in Dublin, as well as founding the hospital of St James in the city. He witnessed Magna Carta in 1215 before attending the fourth Lateran Council in Rome. He was papal legate in Ireland from 1217 to 1220. He advocated the creation of a completely English hierarchy for the Irish church, and granted his nephews land and ecclesiastical office in Ireland. BGCS

Henry, Paul (1876–1958), the most influential Irish landscapist of the 20th century. Born in Belfast, he was educated at Belfast Government School of Art, the Académie Julian, and Whistler's Académie Carmen, Paris. In 1900 he began working as an illustrator on various journals in London, while also exhibiting charcoal drawings of landscapes at the Goupil Gallery and other venues. He was a founder member of the Allied Artists' Association (1908). In 1910, at the recommendation of a friend, he went to Achill Island, an experience that shaped the rest of his career. He remained there for a decade. The island, its people, and their way of life, which he recorded with a Post-Impressionist rigour, at first dominated his subject matter, but from about 1917 he travelled more widely in Connemara, painting the landscape itself in scenes usually empty of people yet redolent of humanity, a characteristic which lends a universality to his work. In 1919 he moved to Dublin and the following year founded the Society of Dublin Painters as a forum where young and experimental artists could show their work. He achieved popular acclaim during the 1920s and 1930s, but thereafter his work became repetitive.

Kennedy, S. B., *Paul Henry* (2000)

SBK

heraldry is a system of identification based on armorial insignia. When armoured knights participated in battles, sieges, and tournaments, easy methods of recognition were necessary. Hence, beginning in the 12th century, distinctive markings were placed on shields, pennants, surcoats, helmets, and crests. These insignia were subsequently transferred onto seals; 'supporters' were added at the sides and mottoes, originally derived from family battle cries, below. Since heraldry indicated not only one's family but also one's position within it, pedigrees were crucial. By the end of the Middle Ages, when the right to bear arms was still the mark of a gentleman, a coat of arms was a desideratum. Institutions, originally corporate families, also adopted coats of arms as marks of status. The system was regulated by heralds (in Ireland the *Ulster king of arms) who had originally been liveried messengers and official pronouncers.

As an integral part of the *feudal system, Anglo-Norman Ireland rapidly adopted armorial insignia, many of which are extant as carvings on medieval tombs and gravestones. Use of heraldry amongst the Gaelic Irish is more debatable. From the 13th century some Gaelic Irish had seals with heraldic insignia, most famously the silver seal of Donal *O'Neill (d. 1325). This development may reflect attempts to establish lineal successions. In 1542 two heraldic standard-bearers were captured in Ulster and later, when Gaelic and Gaelicized lords conformed to the procedure of *surrender and regrant, many affixed armorial seals.

The Ulster king of arms (established 1552) mostly confirmed existing insignia and created new coats of arms for the rising *New English planter families and for the many knights made by English lord deputies. Ironically native Irish demand for heraldry increased just as official interest began to wane. From the 1690s foreign armies required coats of arms and attested pedigrees from Irishmen seeking promotion. Between 1690 and 1725, James Terry, the exiled Athlone pursuivant, serviced the *Jacobites, and Roger O'Feral drew up *Linea antiqua* (1708), with coats of arms of most native families.

More recently, the historian Edward MacLysaght created coats of arms for the 'chiefs of the name' whom he authenticated as chief herald. In 1961 the Republic presented the visiting American president, John F. Kennedy, with a coat of arms. Since the 1980s insignia have been much sought after by status-conscious families, institutions, and companies. HM

Hervey, Frederick Augustus (1730–1803), Church of Ireland bishop, peer, radical politician, and eccentric. Appointed bishop of Cloyne when his brother, the 2nd earl of Bristol, was briefly *lord lieutenant (1766–7), he was translated to Derry in 1768. In 1779 he succeeded his brother as earl. He appeared with great ceremonial at the *Volunteer National Convention of 1783, and took a leading part in the proceedings, much to the alarm of *Charlemont, who consciously used his position as commander-in-chief to negate Hervey's influence. He was an open supporter of *Catholic emancipation, and cultivated good relations with *Methodists and *Presbyterians in his diocese. A lover of fine art, he spent much of his time in Italy.

Hibernian Bible Society, see LONDON HIBERNIAN SOCIETY.

Hidden Ireland, The (1924), a study of 18th-century Gaelic Munster by the Gaelic revivalist Daniel *Corkery. The title sums up Corkery's image of an oppressed and impoverished but culturally rich Gaelic world, coexisting with yet wholly distinct from the Ireland of the Protestant ruling class.

More recent work has questioned Corkery's depiction of unrelieved poverty and his reliance on highly conservative literary sources as a reflection of social and political realities. Studies of *hurling and other sports have also revealed a degree of interaction between elite and popular culture that runs counter to Corkery's model. But the idea that 18th-century Ireland was characterized by unique cultural divisions between rulers and ruled remains an influential one.

Higgins, Francis (1746–1802), proprietor of the *Freeman's Journal*, which he transformed from a radical to a government paper. His origins are obscure, and traditional accounts are coloured by the lurid account of trickery and deceit published in 1789 by a rival editor, John Magee of the *Dublin Evening Post*, against whom Higgins subsequently won a legal action. The label 'the sham squire', bestowed by the judge in an earlier prosecution for fraud, was frequently used. A magistrate until he resigned (or was dismissed) shortly after irregularities in the papers on the Magee case came to light, Higgins throughout the 1790s kept the government supplied with a flow of secret intelligence, not always reliable, on the activities of Dublin radicals.

high-church movement, a movement common (though with different emphases) to the Church of England and *Church of Ireland of the late 17th and early 18th centuries, which sought to restore the traditional prerogatives of the established church. As such it appealed to clergy alarmed at the erosion of the church's power to regulate morals and behaviour, the rise of deism and infidelity, and the growing influence of dissent. High-church writers also restated the traditional Anglican concept of a divinely appointed monarchy working in close partnership with the church, making them natural allies of the *Tory Party, and leading to accusations of *Jacobitism from opponents.

As in England, Irish high churchmen looked to *convocation to reassert the church's traditional prerogatives and disciplinary powers. They fiercely defended the *sacramental test as an essential defence against the numerical and organizational strength of *Presbyterianism, supported the withdrawal of the **regium donum* in 1714, and successfully resisted the introduction of a *Toleration Act until 1719.

The movement's concept of the church, emphasizing its divine origins, its sacramental system, and its due place in the life of the state, was an exalted, 'high' one, but its expression was primarily political. In this it contrasts with the 19th century, when 'high church' came to denote in common parlance an emphasis on *ritualism in worship. KM

High Commission, court of (Ecclesiastical Commission), a group of secular officials and Protestant clergy granted special powers to enforce the *Reformation in Ireland. After an inconclusive trial in 1539, four commissions (23 May 1561, 6 Dec. 1562, 6 Oct. 1564, 27 Nov. 1593) were issued, on the authority of the Act of *Supremacy, during the reign of Elizabeth I. Although it was seen by its advocates as a means of cutting through the obstruction, corruption, and conservatism that prevented the Reformation from gaining widespread support, infighting, local hostility, and the inadequacies of the central and local systems of government prevented the court from ever being an effective means of spreading Protestantism. The fifth commission, issued on 11 February 1635, proved, however, much more formidable. Under the firm central control of Lord Deputy *Wentworth, the commissioners concentrated, not on attacking *recusancy, but on establishing uniformity within the *Church of Ireland and restoring the church to its rights, privileges, and property. The success of the court in driving out *Presbyterian clergy and in forcing landowners, both Catholic and Protestant, to disgorge church property that they had illegally detained aroused great hostility, and when Wentworth fell in 1641 the court was abolished. AF

high crosses, free-standing stone crosses, often of monumental proportion, associated principally with Irish *monastic sites. On the basis of style and occasional inscriptions the majority of crosses are dated to the 9th or 10th centuries, a time when high-quality stone carving was rare in the rest of Europe. A revival of cross carving was experienced during the 12th century.

The crosses generally consist of a tall shaft and ringed cross head mounted on a solid stepped base. Some crosses are also surmounted by a capstone. The ring is the most distinctive feature of the crosses. Its origins are obscure; it may have symbolic connotations, or reflect the form of wooden prototypes.

Many of the crosses are elaborately carved. The surfaces of those dating from the 9th or 10th centuries are often divided into panels, some depicting biblical scenes, others with abstract ornament comparable to contemporary *metalwork and *illuminated manuscripts. Decoration on the later 12th-century crosses is less contained and extends over the entire surface of the cross.

The function of the crosses is uncertain. They may have served as boundary markers, as didactic aids during outdoor masses, or as monastic status symbols. RM

high kingship is the term used to describe the most powerful Irish kings of the pre-*Norman period. The historical reality behind the phrase is disputed, largely because the primary texts use a variety of words and phrases and are not internally consistent. Three of the most common are *ardrí* (high king), *rí Érenn / rex Hiberniae* (king of Ireland), and *rí Temro* (king of *Tara). Although these overlap semantically to some degree, it is helpful to consider high kingship under each heading.

Ardrí Érenn (high king of Ireland) was used by the 17th-century historian Geoffrey *Keating to refer to heads of the *Uí Néill confederation. In earlier sources, *ardrí* could be used indiscriminately for any ruler above the rank of *rí túaithe* (king of a **tuath*), whether they were Uí Néill or not. In annalistic death notices for Uí Néill leaders it is both rare and relatively late. In the original hand of the *Annals of Ulster*, for example, it is used only for Domnall ua Néill (d. 980), *Máel Sechnaill mac Domnaill (d. 1022), Domnall Mac Lochlainn (d. 1121), and Muirchertach *Mac Lochlainn (d. 1166). An earlier form, *airdrí*, occurs in the 7th-century legal tract *Cáin Fuithirbe*, where it refers to *Lóegaire mac Néill, but this form, too, is used elsewhere simply to describe overkings. Keating's usage is, therefore, far more specific than that in pre-Norman sources and represents a modification of an earlier, more generalized meaning.

Rí Érenn / rex Hiberniae (king of Ireland) is a title used sparingly in the original hand of the *Annals of Ulster*: only six times prior to the 11th century. The concept of an island-wide overkingship, however, is well attested by the 7th century; it is associated with Lóegaire mac Néill by Patrician hagiographers, with *Diarmait mac Cerbaill by *Adomnán, with Conchobar mac Nessae, king of the *Ulaid, in the early *law tract *Míadslechta*, and with Cathal mac Áedo of Munster in 8th-century regnal synchronisms. Though the majority of early sources link kingship of Ireland to an Uí Néill overlordship, it is apparent that other dynasties aspired to this honour from the beginning of the historical period. Despite this, the surviving lists of 'kings of Ireland', all apparently 12th century in date, limit this title entirely to the Uí Néill prior to the 11th century, a distortion that has influenced modern historical interpretations. The *Míadslechta* reference may cast doubt on Binchy's contention that a kingship of Ireland was unknown in early law tracts. His wider conclusion, that the title was aspirational rather than effective until the mid-9th century, remains plausible, and has been endorsed by F. J. Byrne. Byrne further suggests that the concept was fostered by clerics from *Armagh and *Iona but that its realization was due to the political prowess of the Uí Néill in establishing hegemony over most of the island.

The most problematical title is *rex Temoriae / rí Temro* (king of Tara). The current orthodoxy, developed by Binchy and Byrne, argues that it originally designated an archaic religious monarchy, located at the pre-Christian site of Tara and ruled by a priest-king. It held national prestige although the exact nature of its authority is unknown. Kings of the *Laigin claimed that they had occupied Tara prior to the emergence of the Uí Néill while the law tract *Bechbretha* claimed that Congal Cáech, overking of the Ulaid, had ruled there as late as the 7th century. The current orthodoxy sees Congal as exceptional and argues that from the days of *Niall Noígiallach (early 5th century) a new genre of dynastic federation was formed, at the apex of which stood an Uí Néill king of Tara. This was originally a pagan monarchy whose inauguration rite, *Feis Temro, was identified by Binchy as a primitive fertility rite culminating in the apotheosis of the sacred king; its disappearance in the mid-6th century has been seen as marking the *Christianization of the Tara monarchy. Colmán Etchingham, however, has pointed to an 8th-century legal reference which implies rather that Feis Temro was a mark of supreme kingship, open to all contenders in the Christian era, even those of Munster. The political cohesion enjoyed by this far-flung congeries of kindred Uí Néill dynasties was such that its kings eventually became effective rulers of Ireland, as exemplified by *Máel Sechnaill mac Máele Ruanaid's achievement in exacting hostages from Munster in the mid-9th century. Meanwhile, medieval literati, attempting to fill the gap separating Irish tradition from accepted world history, had developed the notion of a pseudo-historical kingship, the list of which gradually became packed with Uí Néill ancestors. One of the most active exponents of this doctrine was Cúán ua Lothcháin, the *file* (poet) patronized by the Uí Néill ruler Máel Sechnaill mac Domnaill.

For analytical convenience, this entry has considered three distinct designations of high kingship. It is important to reiterate that this does not reflect pre-Norman usage. The pseudo-historical kings of the pre-Christian era are sometimes termed 'kings of Tara', sometimes called 'kings of Ireland', and sometimes have no title. (They are rarely, if ever, termed *ardrí*.) The *annals differ in the titles ascribed to specific individuals and anomalies in the use of Old and

Middle Irish forms imply that some at least of the designations concerned have been added retrospectively. The literary sources, many of which have been seen as representing a continuum from the archaic Indo-European era, are now interpreted by some scholars as reflecting more closely the specific circumstances of the period in which they were composed. Difficulties in the dating of Irish linguistic forms hamper the chronological evaluation of texts, and consequently of the historical period to which they refer. Despite this, there still exists a vast potential for further investigation of Irish high kingship: the evidence of *genealogies and law tracts has barely been touched upon, and even the annals still await detailed study.

Bhreathnach, E., *Tara: A Select Bibliography* (1995)

Byrne, F. J., *Irish Kings and High-Kings* (1973)

Etchingham, C., 'Early Medieval Irish History', in K. McCone and K. Simms (eds.), *Progress in Medieval Irish Studies* (1996)

CS

Hill, see DOWNSHIRE.

hillfort, a large, roughly circular enclosure surrounded by one or more earthen banks and external ditches, or stone walls. Where there are two or more banks they are usually concentric and widely spaced. The innermost, or only, enclosure must be not less than 495 feet (150 metres) internal diameter to qualify as a hillfort. Furthermore a hillfort is always (by definition) positioned in a high, defensive, often strategic location, the bank(s) usually encircling a substantial portion of a prominent hill. Several dozen hillforts are known, the majority lying in the northern part of Munster. A remarkable cluster exists near Baltinglass, Co. Wicklow. Irish hillforts were once, wrongly, regarded as evidence of *Iron Age settlement, but excavation now indicates that most are of Late *Bronze Age date, especially from the 12th to the 10th centuries BC. It has been suggested that they might represent a defensive response to social stresses brought about by a seriously deteriorating climate at that time. Ritual deposits of weapons and gold ornaments, and evidence of a ritual obsession with lakes, rivers, and bogs, appear to support this hypothesis. It also seems probable that hillforts acted as centres of local power. There is much confusion amongst the uninitiated between hillforts, *ringforts, and *monastic enclosures. However, there is little overlap in the typological descriptions and careful consideration of form, context, and definition will almost always satisfactorily identify the class of an enclosure. The shared characteristic of all these types is their defensive nature (for instance the external ditch, where a ditch exists), and in this respect hillforts should not be confused (though they often are) with the large, ritual, internally ditched enclosures of *Neolithic or Iron Age date (see EMAIN MACHA). RW

hiring fairs were a source of farm labour. The hiring of farm servants was widespread in Ireland by the early 18th century (see AGRICULTURAL LABOURERS). However hiring fairs, at which farmers and those seeking employment negotiated type and hours of work, lodging, and wages, seem to have been most common during the late 19th century, when they were held in about 80 towns, mostly in Ulster. Fairs were usually held twice a year, on or near 12 May and 12 November, the contracts made running for six months, to the next hiring day. Those looking for work, mainly the sons of small farmers, would gather at a central point in the town where they were approached by prospective employers.

The largest fairs were held in west Ulster, in towns such as *Derry, Strabane, Omagh, and Letterkenny. These fairs attracted hundreds of young people from west Donegal, for whom hiring represented a stage in a career which might end in permanent *emigration, or a return to the family farm. In east Ulster, fairs were generally smaller, and servants and farmers often knew one another in social contexts other than work. Hiring of farm servants almost disappeared during the early decades of the 20th century. The *First World War, the introduction of minimum wages, and unemployment benefits meant that day labouring contracts became more attractive to both farmers and workers. By the 1930s, surviving fairs had become holiday occasions rather than a source of labour. The last hiring fair was probably one held in Milford, Co. Donegal, in 1947. JB

historical fiction. In the 19th century Sir Walter Scott provided a model for writers in many countries who looked to historical fiction as a means of creating both a distinctive national identity and a usable past, and there were frequent calls for 'an Irish Scott'. Yet Irish attempts in this direction, even in the hands of talented writers like John Banim (*The Boyne Water* (1826)) and J. S. Lefanu (*The Cock and Anchor* (1845) and *Turlough O'Brien* (1847)), were notably unsuccessful. One reason for their failure was that the Irish intellectual and literary milieu was not as well developed as that of Scotland. Despite outlets such as the *Dublin University Magazine*, Irish writers of any literary pretensions were usually published in Great Britain and wrote with an English audience in mind: 19th-century Irish novels are often presented through the eyes of an English visitor who serves as stand-in for the reader. This need not by itself have been fatal (Scott often uses this sort of 'mediocre hero' as reader-surrogate when describing unfamiliar societies), but it imposed constraints not only on the amount of knowledge that could be assumed but on the attitudes that could be expressed.

Secondly, and possibly more important, it proved much harder to construct an 'acceptable past' in 19th-century Ireland, where religious and political divisions ran deeper than in Scotland. This was exacerbated by the use of historical fiction in verse and prose as a medium of mass political instruction (exemplified by Thomas *Davis's proposal for the systematic composition of 'a ballad history of Ireland'), which naturally encouraged unwillingness to enter imaginatively into other points of view or confront the fact that the idealized past had contained factors which produced the detestable present. Apart from those writers who confined themselves to straightforward politico-religious propaganda (e.g. Charlotte Elizabeth, *Derry* (6th edn. 1836); P. G. Smyth, *The Wild Rose of Lough Gill* (1883)), some were frightened away from historical fiction by its political implications (like Sydney Owenson, Lady Morgan (*c.*1776–1859), who began but then abandoned a novel about Red Hugh *O'Donnell), while others found the form disintegrating in their efforts to depict extreme violence and cultural disruption (Emily Lawless, *Maelcho* (1894)). Many, by facile use of the Scottian motif of the reconciliation through marriage of opposing traditions, or by the reduction of the past to a picturesque backdrop for romance, evaded the implications of the conflicts which they described and severed the linkage of private and public spheres associated with the best historical novels.

Twentieth-century Ireland continued to produce historical fiction of varying degrees of merit, but the form no longer has the same degree of expectation attached to it. In Ireland, as elsewhere, the historical novel as a genre has lost much of the critical respectability it enjoyed in the 19th century, when Scott was placed on the same level as Shakespeare. The image of Irish history as a single great narrative leading to a predestined conclusion has been intensively deconstructed. There has been widespread debate about how far Irish culture and society should still be seen as suffering from the effects of its *colonial past rather than from problems characteristic of modern developed society as a whole. Many writers have anatomized the inevitable subjectivity of historical self-images. There has been a general tendency to move away from the great story and its protagonist (and from the respectable, Whiggish Scottian viewpoint) to focus on history as experienced from below through its impact on everyday lives. Joyce's Stephen Dedalus called history 'a nightmare from which I am trying to awaken'; *Birchwood* (1973) by John Banville has been described as presenting Irish history as an enormous black joke.

The Scottian tradition has, however, survived and even been revivified by greater willingness to face up to pain, loss, and defeat. Significant historical fictions have continued to be produced, whether in support of accepted self-images (W. F. Marshall, *Planted by a River* (1948); Francis MacManus, *The Greatest of These* (1943)) or more critical (Sam Hanna Bell, *A Man Flourishing* (1973); Thomas Kilroy, *The Big Chapel* (1971)). William Buckley's *Croppies Lie Down* (1902), now almost entirely forgotten, is seen by some critics as significant in the move towards naturalism. There has also been a shift in the historical themes which attract fictional treatment. For example, the dismantling of the post-1690 political settlement during the 19th century means that the *Williamite War is now of little interest to writers outside Northern Ireland, while the *Great Famine and the *Land War, which for 19th-century writers were contemporary, have become the subjects of 20th-century historical fiction (Liam O'Flaherty, *Famine* (1937), *Land* (1946); Tom Murphy, *Famine* (1968)) because of their formative influence on contemporary society. Irish writers will continue to draw on the past to illuminate present discontents.

Cahalane, J. N., *Great Hatred, Little Room: The Irish Historical Novel* (1983)

PM

history and historians. The writing of analytical history, as opposed to the compilation of chronicles or annals, had its origins in the *Renaissance and the scientific revolution, advanced significantly during the *Enlightenment, and came to maturity with the new awareness of the need for critical appraisal and objective assessment of sources that developed in the 19th century. Its extension to Ireland was impeded by religious and political divisions. That *Spenser, *Campion, *Davies, and later *Cox wrote supposed histories that were in fact justifications of English conquest and colonization is hardly surprising; a similar propagandist function was evident in historical writing everywhere and these authors met a response in kind in the writings of the *Four Masters and of Geoffrey *Keating, who used legendary accounts of the assimilation of successive waves of invaders to promote the unity of *Old English and Gaelic Irish (see LITERATURE IN IRISH). What is more striking is the failure over a century later of Thomas

*Leland's attempt to produce an Irish counterpart to David Hume's successful history of Great Britain, a generally acceptable analytical account of a shared national past.

Political divisions continued to be evident in the historical writing of the early 19th century, most notably in the attempts of Protestant writers to appropriate for themselves the early Christian past by creating an image of a 'Celtic church' independent of Roman control (see BEDE). By this time, however, serious antiquarian and historical work was also being done, by scholars like *O'Donovan, *O'Curry, and *Petrie, supported by the *Royal Irish Academy and other learned bodies. In the second half of the century *Froude and *Lecky offered scholarly yet accessible works of general narrative. Although both were unionist in their politics, their extensively documented accounts of past poverty and conflict were repeatedly drawn on by nationalist propagandists. Their near contemporary Richard *Bagwell, and in the next generation Eoin *MacNeill, Edmund *Curtis, and G. H. *Orpen, carried out solid work on original sources that laid the foundations for much of what was to come. Meanwhile more politicized versions of the Irish past were offered by Alice Stopford *Green, Daniel *Corkery, and others.

The establishment in 1938 of **Irish Historical Studies* is generally seen as inaugurating a revolution in Irish historical scholarship. Unfortunately the declared commitment to new standards of professional rigour was not always matched by the production of significant scholarly work. Indeed it could be argued that the transformation of Irish historical writing owed more to the succession of sober monographs produced over several decades by J. C. Beckett of Queen's University, Belfast, and by R. B. McDowell and J. G. Simms at Trinity College, Dublin, than it did to the programmatic statements and agendas for future work produced by more flamboyant, and more highly placed, figures. The collaborative volume *The Great Famine*, edited by R. Dudley Edwards and T. D. Williams, provides an instructive case study: commissioned by the Irish government in 1943, it appeared thirteen years later, as a series of disconnected essays, to which the nominal editors had not contributed a word. By 1968 it was possible to contemplate a multivolume history, to be published by the mid-1970s, that would sum up a generation's work. But the first volume of the *New History of Ireland* appeared only in 1976, and at the time of writing the project is still uncompleted.

In contrast to the rather narrow focus on administrative and constitutional history that characterized the *Irish Historical Studies* generation, the 1970s saw a marked broadening in the concerns of historians of Ireland. A specialized journal, *Irish Economic and Social History*, began publication in 1974; *Saothar*, the journal of the Irish Labour History Society, appeared two years later. Political historians shifted their attention from high politics to popular movements, historians of religion from the intricacies of church–state relations to the beliefs and practices of the ordinary church member. In all areas there was a new openness to concepts and methods borrowed from related disciplines, notably anthropology and sociology, and a new willingness to place Irish developments in a comparative perspective. The price paid for this sudden expansion was a growing tendency to fragmentation. In particular the quantitative techniques employed by demographic and economic historians have made their work increasingly inaccessible to non-specialists. More recently the rise of literary theory has threatened to cut off what was previously one of the most rewarding areas of interdisciplinary co-operation. (See LITERATURE AND THE HISTORIAN.)

More recent discussion of the writing of Irish history has been dominated by the controversy over 'revisionism'. This had its origins in objections, first voiced in the mid-1980s, to a specific body of recent writing that was seen as openly hostile to the traditional nationalist understanding of the Irish past. Since then the debate has expanded to include a broader critique of the way in which Irish history in general has been written since the late 1930s. Essentially the argument is that the concern of academic historians to distance themselves from a nationalism identified with propagandist myth making and violence has led them to produce a bland, 'value-free' history that has failed to do justice to crucial aspects of Irish experience. The apparent eagerness of most writers to minimize the responsibility of the British government for massive loss of life during the *Great Famine is one often cited example. This process of self-censorship is seen as intensifying from the 1970s, in response to the resurgence of physical force nationalism in Northern Ireland. An alternative argument, more political in character, is that 'revisionist' history, denigrating the nationalist tradition, is a conservative attempt to undermine the forces of political change in Ireland north and south.

None of these charges need be accepted without question. The more critical approach to traditional understandings of the Irish past evident from the 1970s arguably owed less to developments in Northern Ireland than to the new perspectives opened up by more extensive research, and by a greater willingness to view what were supposedly peculiarly Irish problems in a comparative context. Nor is it self-evident that to write critically of the key assumptions of nationalism is necessarily to engage in counter-revolutionary polemic: in independent Ireland, it could be argued, nationalism has been for most of the past 80 years the official ideology, and historians who have drawn attention to its evasions, blind spots, and untested assumptions have only discharged the proper function of any society's critics and thinkers. At its best the campaign against 'revisionism' has encouraged a healthy revival of debate on important issues of interpretation. At its worst it has provided a bogus mantle of radicalism for what is in fact the refurbishment of traditional myths and preconceptions.

Brady, Ciaran (ed.), *Interpreting Irish History: The Debate on Historical Revisionism* (1994)

history painting. The visual representation of Irish history was conditioned by ideological outlook and visual convention. Netherlandish artists provided the initial models for descriptive scenes, as in Jan Wyck's *Battle of the Boyne* (1693), promulgating the imagery of Protestant supremacy. James *Barry's London history subjects relate to the history of England, but he touched on the beginnings of the Irish medieval era in *St Patrick Baptizing the King of Cashel* (1763). The political activity of the late 18th century is recorded in Francis *Wheatley's *The Dublin Volunteers in College Green* (1779) and other paintings. The *insurrection of 1798 lacked a strong pictorial record, with the exception of Thomas Robinson's *Battle of Ballinahinch*. It was in the field of popular prints that key events like the arrest of Lord Edward *FitzGerald were recorded. The official ideology of the Act of Union was celebrated formally in Vincent Waldre's three ceiling paintings in St Patrick's Hall, *Dublin Castle (early 19th century), which include certain antiquarian details and depict St *Patrick, *Henry II, and George III.

The breakthrough to a greater interest in Irish history and its representation came with the rise of a Romantic and antiquarian movement, typified by *Young Ireland. Thomas *Davis appealed to Irish artists to turn to patriotic and historical themes. Daniel *Maclise was the principal artist to turn to Irish folklore and history in his early book illustrations of the 1830s and in his great painting *The Marriage of Strongbow and Aoife* (1854), which was based on antiquarian research. A related history painter in this mode was James Ward, who painted twelve panels in Dublin City Hall on the history of the city, completed by 1919. Other minor 19th-century artists took themes from contemporary history, such as Henry McManus in *Reading the Nation* and Edwin Hayes in *The Emigrant Ship*. By contrast the *unionist point of view was represented by images of British ceremony and life in Ireland by Joseph Peacock, Michelangelo Hayes, James Mahony, and Richard Moynan. Few paintings on Irish historical subjects appeared at the exhibitions of the *Royal Hibernian Academy, although the 1888 Irish Exhibition at South Kensington did show several.

The conventions of late 19th-century realism are evident in the Irish subject paintings by Lady Butler (Elizabeth Thompson) and Aloysius O'Kelly. However, by far the most common representations of Irish history in its many forms were images in popular prints and magazines like *The Illustrated London News* (from which most of the *Famine images come). There was highly politicized imagery in the lithographic illustrations of the *Weekly Freeman*, *United Ireland*, and *The Irish Pilot* of the late 19th century. Mass circulation *printing, a result of the industrial revolution, rather than painting, became the main medium for representing Irish history.

The *rising of 1916 and the *Anglo-Irish War were mainly represented by film and *photography, although some painters made records, such as Kathleen Fox's *The Arrest of the College of Surgeons Garrison*. Sean Keating's *Men of the West* (1917) and other images of fighting men provided the clearest representations of the struggle. The building of the Free State's Shannon Scheme at *Ardnacrusha was recorded by a series of paintings by Keating, while John *Lavery too created records of state events. On the unionist side, Robert Ponsonby Staples depicted the shipyards and Stanford Merrifield recorded Ulster resistance to *home rule in the *Carson reliefs outside *Stormont. The nationalist canon of the representation of Irish history culminated in the Douglas Hyde collection of historical pictures (and prints) housed in the official residence of the president, Aras an Uachtaráin (1944). At the 1966 commemoration of the Rising, Modernist artists, like Charles Harper, showed a new more subjective mode of representing the past. However Tom Ryan adhered to traditional realism. In the later 20th century, Michael Farrell and Robert Ballagh explored Irish historical themes in a questioning and ironic manner. By contrast the violent political and adversarial atmosphere of the *Northern Ireland conflict has continued to produce nationalist and unionist murals, as well as more intellectually reflective imagery by artists like Willy Doherty.

Crookeshank, Anne, and The Knight of Glin, *The Painters of Ireland 1660–1920* (1978)
Turpin, John, 'Irish history painting', *The GPA Irish Arts Review Yearbook* (1989–90)

JT

hobelar, meaning a mounted infantryman armed with a spear, was a term derived from the light horse (ME 'hobin', 'hobby') which he rode. Originally typical of warfare in Ireland, they were adopted into English armies under Edward I, though replaced by mounted archers in the mid-14th century. In Anglo-Irish armies Robin Frame calculates that hobelars outnumbered the heavier men-at-arms by an average of 4.5 : 1. They were well adapted to driving off or protecting cattle on rough terrain, and utilized the small, native breed of horse rather than the expensive imported strains of 'chief horses' required by the knights. KS

Hoche expedition. In December 1796 the Directory (see FRENCH REVOLUTION), responding to *Tone's appeals, dispatched 14,450 troops on 43 vessels, commanded by General Lazare Hoche (1768–97), to Ireland. Following a disastrous storm 36 ships arrived at Bantry Bay, Co. Cork (21 Dec. 1796), but did not attempt a landing. The episode dramatically boosted *United Irish numbers and morale. But the French, disillusioned at the apathetic popular response, never again committed so large a force to Ireland.

hockey in Ireland may have its roots in the older game of *hurling, and was to absorb the variant of it known as 'hurley'. Whatever its origins, the modern game emerged prior to 1893, when the Irish Hockey Union (IHU) was founded. The first men's international followed in 1895 against Wales. A cup competition, which is still current, was begun in 1894. The Irish Hurley Union, founded in 1879, and the Ulster Hockey Union (1896) had been subsumed into the IHU by 1898, when interprovincial games began. British army teams were prominent from an early date. The *First World War led to the demise of many clubs, and the later withdrawal of troops accelerated hockey's decline. However the provision of new facilities in Dublin from 1934 led to a resurgence. The *Second World War isolated Irish hockey, but provided only a short-term impediment. Despite financial crises in the sport local league and cup competitions continued to flourish, especially in Dublin and Ulster. Women's hockey has developed in parallel to the men's game. The Irish Ladies' Hockey Union was formed in 1894, following a representative game against England. Hockey is currently the most popular women's sport in Ireland. NG

Hogan, Patrick (1891–1936). As minister for agriculture 1922–32 Hogan was on the conservative wing of *Cumann na nGaedheal, opposing *protectionism, and advocating minimal taxation, in order to keep down the price of Irish agricultural exports. However, he also introduced close regulation to maintain the standard of Irish produce, and in 1923 put through the last of the *Land Acts that since the 1870s had changed the ownership of rural Ireland. A fatal car crash prematurely ended his political career.

Holt, Joseph (1756–1826), the son of a Protestant farmer, a leading figure in the *insurrection of 1798 in Wexford. Transported to Australia, he returned to Ireland in 1814 to pursue an unsuccessful career as a publican. His *Memoirs*, published in 1838, present him as having been driven into rebellion, but there are suggestions that both Holt himself and his editor, Thomas Crofton *Croker, deliberately played down his prior involvement in radical conspiracy.

holy wells, in Ireland as elsewhere, were a common feature of popular tradition. Visitors could seek supernatural protection, relief from illness, or other benefits by drinking the water, by performing one or more circuits round the site, possibly reciting prayers or charms, and often leaving behind them a piece of cloth or other token. On the feast day of the saint to whom it was dedicated, a well might be the focus of more elaborate festivities at a *pattern. The origin of most wells is obscure. Some may represent survivals from the pre-Christian era, later made acceptable by the attachment of a saint's name and a veneer of orthodox ritual; others may be associated with the sites of early Christian churches. But there are also examples of wells acquiring a reputation as holy only in the 18th or 19th centuries, as circumstances led the loose general body of belief and custom to attach itself to a new site.

Home Government Association, launched by Isaac *Butt on 1 September 1870 to campaign for a *federalist system of Irish self-government. It was superseded from November 1873 by the *Home Rule League.

home rule, the objective of constitutional nationalists from 1870 to 1918. The term was believed to have been coined by Revd Joseph A. Galbraith, a member of the *Home Government Association, and was carefully chosen to maximize the appeal of a movement which, in the wake of Anglican *disestablishment, was attracting significant support from the Protestant middle and upper classes. Its political usefulness has been described in terms of a 'transfiguring vagueness' which enabled the most extreme nationalists, as well as the most moderate, to invest the term with their own meanings.

The most authoritative statement of what home rule meant was made by Isaac *Butt, who envisaged an arrangement whereby Ireland, Scotland, and England would have a common sovereign, executive, and 'national council' at Westminster for the purposes of statehood in the international arena, while each country would have its own parliament for domestic affairs. In Ireland's case the specific form of parliament would be decided by an Irish assembly elected on the basis of household suffrage. Throughout his leadership Butt refused to commit his ideas to the precise form of a parliamentary bill, believing it best to campaign for the principle of home rule rather than have to defend every detail of its implementation.

Butt's approach to the home rule question was followed by his successor *Parnell, and the vagueness of 'home rule' took on an enhanced importance as the character of the movement changed in the 1870s, with the decline in landlord involvement and the growing prominence of *Fenians, Catholic clergy, and, from 1879, agrarian radicals. Indeed vagueness on the specific meaning of home rule was especially suited to Parnell, whose politics in general were based on ambiguity. Home rule took a concrete form only when *Gladstone became converted to the policy and used Butt's ideas, together with colonial precedents, especially those of Canada, as the groundwork for the home rule bill of 1886. This plan envisaged a local assembly consisting of two chambers, charged with responsibility for Ireland's internal affairs, while Westminster retained control of such areas as imperial and foreign affairs, armed forces, currency, security, and major taxation.

However, there were problems inherent in the very concept of home rule, and these became part of the case against Gladstone's plan. Most difficult was the question of taxation and representation. Since Ireland would continue to pay an imperial contribution, it was accepted that Irish MPs would continue to sit at Westminster; but this would give them a voice not only in imperial policies but in the making of governments at Westminster and in the domestic affairs of the British mainland. This was a problem that was never resolved.

Gladstone's plan of 1886 failed to get the unanimous support of the Liberal Party. A section led by Joseph Chamberlain (see CENTRAL BOARD) allied with the Conservatives to defeat it in the Commons. Nevertheless, despite its weaknesses, it became the template for the second home rule bill, rejected by the Lords in 1893, and for the third, introduced by a Liberal government dependent on Irish nationalist support in 1912. Politically, as distinct from constitutionally, the most significant weakness of the home rule schemes was the failure to cater for the specific interests of Protestant north-east Ulster; and it was from that quarter that the most strenuous opposition to home rule came in the pre-war period. The enactment of the third home rule bill in 1914, despite Ulster Unionist opposition, was purely formal, its implementation being suspended until the end of the *First World War, by which time the Irish parliamentary party and home rule had been superseded by *Sinn Féin and the demand for a republic. By a supreme historical irony the only part of Ireland to be given home rule (see PARTITION) was Unionist Ulster, which had done so much to oppose it.

Kendle, John, *Ireland and the Federal Solution: The Debate over the United Kingdom Constitution* (1989)
Loughlin, James, *Gladstone, Home Rule and the Ulster Question 1882–93* (1986)

JL

Hope, James ('Jemmy') (1764–*c.*1846). A Presbyterian weaver from Co. Antrim, he was sent to Dublin in 1796 to extend the *United Irish movement there. He fought in Co. Antrim during the *insurrection of 1798, then took refuge in Dublin until he could return to Belfast in 1806. He wrote his *Memoirs* in 1843, at the request of R. R. *Madden, and was apparently still alive when they were published in 1846.

horse racing in Ireland takes two main forms: steeplechasing and flat racing. Steeplechasing began in Co. Cork in 1752. This racing over fences became popular amongst the county elites, encouraged by huntsmen and cavalrymen. The sport spread rapidly to England. The English rules were adopted in Ireland in 1864, but an independent Irish National Hunt Steeplechase Committee (INHSC) was established in 1869. Permanent courses were built at Punchestown, Co. Kildare, and Fairyhouse, Co. Meath. Popular interest in steeplechasing exploded after the *First World War, following the successes of Irish horses in English racing. Irish interest in English steeplechasing remains high.

Flat racing is mentioned in 14th-century manuscripts, though its roots are probably much older. During the 18th century it was both encouraged as an important aspect of horse breeding and suppressed as promoting idleness and disorder. By 1790 the Turf Club of Ireland had been founded to improve the sport by introducing universal rules. Throughout the 19th century meetings, especially those at the *Curragh, drew enormous crowds. Irish racing imitated English formats. An Irish Derby was run from 1886, and an Irish Oaks from 1895. While racing standards were extremely high, prize moneys remained lower than in England.

All Irish racing enjoyed a boom during the First World War due to an influx of English stock and personnel. However from 1918 civil disorders began to disrupt meetings. Eventual partition did not affect the organization of racing and, despite the association of the ruling bodies with the military and the Protestant ascendancy, racing remained popular in independent Ireland. Always of some economic importance, racing and breeding in the Irish Free State were overseen from 1945 by the Racing Board, a government organization funded by a betting levy. Though said in 1986 to be in 'a perilous financial state', the racing industry remains a major employer in the Republic, and a considerable earner of foreign income through training and the export of stock.

D'Arcy, F. A., *Horses, Lords and Racing Men: The Turf Club 1790–1990* (1991)

NG

horses were probably introduced into Ireland during the early *Bronze Age. Harness trappings from archaeological sites and early medieval literature both suggest a connection between horsemanship and high social status. During the later medieval period small riding 'hobby' horses were highly valued, and small dual-purpose horses (*gearrain*), for working and riding, became common. Descendants of the latter survived into the 20th century in hilly areas such as west Kerry and the Glens of Antrim.

*Horse racing has been a major sport in Ireland since the 18th century, and the Irish thoroughbred industry is now world famous. Large working horses such as Clydesdales were introduced to lowland farms in Ireland during the early 19th century. Between 1846 and 1871 there were 206 Irish Clydesdale sires registered in the breed's stud book, and the breed remained popular until the 1950s. On smaller farms, however, lighter dual-purpose horses remained most common. In the late 19th century it became accepted that these constituted a distinctively Irish type of working horse. During the 1880s, the *Royal Dublin Society began an organized breeding programme to upgrade these horses, and by 1905 an 'Irish Draught' horse was generally recognized. A stud book for the breed was established in 1917.

In 1901, there were 564,916 horses in Ireland, and numbers remained at this level until after the *First World War, when tractors, lorries, and motor cars slowly began to compete. It was not until *c.*1960, however, that the number of tractors exceeded the number of working horses in Ireland. The modern horse-breeding and -training industries are based on horse racing and other leisure pursuits. Irish Draught horses survive as basic stock for cross-breeding with thoroughbreds to produce the world-famous Irish Hunter. Half-bred cobs and riding ponies, notably the Connemara, are bred for riding and trekking. JB

hospitals and dispensaries. With the development of towns in Ireland from about the 9th century temporary houses began to be set aside for the victims of epidemics; most permanent hospitals appear to have been lazarettos, for the care of lepers. Many houses of *religious orders also contained general hospitals or infirmaries. The largest was probably the hospital of the priory of St John the Baptist without Newgate in Dublin, an *Augustinian foundation established in the mid-1180s. By the early 14th century this hospital had 155 beds, but at its suppression in 1539 only 50 remained.

With the *dissolution of the monasteries, the sick were left with only small leper, plague, and poor houses. It was not until the more settled conditions of the early 18th century that the Protestant elite in the towns began to build substantial institutions for the care of the sick poor. Hospitals then proliferated. In *Dublin eight appeared in 40 years, including Jervis Street, Dr Steevens's, Mercer's, the Incurables', the Lying-in (later *Rotunda), the Meath, the Lock (later Westmoreland), and St Patrick's for the mentally ill (see INSANITY AND THE INSANE). In *Cork the South and North Charitable Infirmaries opened during the same period. But *Belfast lacked a general hospital until 1817, when Frederick Street (replaced in 1903 by the Royal Victoria) opened, and *Limerick until the opening of Barrington's in 1831. Most of the above were so-called voluntary hospitals, largely financed by donations, fund-raising, and investments, and run by the Protestant upper and middle classes.

Early in the 19th century new Catholic female religious orders (see NUNS), supported by a reviving church and a growing Catholic middle class, also began to open voluntary hospitals. The Sisters of Charity established St Vincent's in Dublin in 1834, while the Sisters of Mercy opened the Mercy in Cork in 1857, the Mater Misericordiae in Dublin in 1861, and the Mater Infirmorium in Belfast in 1883. As well as nursing in Catholic hospitals, female religious began to nurse in *workhouse infirmaries from the 1860s and soon dominated the Irish *nursing profession.

Fear of the spread of infectious diseases among the poor also prompted the state to play a major role in the establishment of Irish hospitals from the late 18th century onwards. In 1765 an act was passed to facilitate the opening of county infirmaries, while other acts in 1807 and 1818 made provision for fever hospitals. In 1805 *grand juries were empowered to fund dispensaries. Most of the 130 workhouses built in the decade after 1838 contained an infirmary for the house's pauper inmates.

The medical disaster of the *Great Famine persuaded the state to develop the dispensary system further. The 1851 Medical Charities Act divided Ireland into over 700 districts, each with at least one salaried medical officer and in many instances also a midwife (see CHILDBIRTH), under the control of the *poor law guardians. The workhouse infirmary system was also significantly expanded in 1862 when the sick poor, not solely the destitute, became eligible for admission.

This system of voluntary religious hospitals and government infirmaries and dispensaries operated into the 1940s with minimal change in both the *Irish Free State and *Northern Ireland, although the Free State did replace poor law guardians with local authority boards of health in the 1920s. In 1946, however, Northern Ireland hospitals were placed under the jurisdiction of a new Hospitals Authority, although the Mater in Belfast, the only Catholic voluntary hospital in the province, remained outside this system until 1972. In the Republic free hospital care was extended to the majority of the population from 1953.

In 1968 a report criticized the Republic's network of 169 hospitals, many of which were small, ill-equipped, and inadequately staffed. As a result a major consolidation of hospitals began, which saw the closure of many of the country's smaller and older hospitals and their gradual replacement by larger regional and general hospitals.

See MEDICINE; HEALTH SERVICES.

Barrington, R., *Health, Medicine and Politics in Ireland, 1900–70* (1987)

Fleetwood, J. F., *The History of Medicine in Ireland* (2nd edn., 1983)

ELM

hostages were human pledges handed over by an inferior to a superior, more rarely exchanged by two parties of equal standing, to guarantee fulfilment of a contract. An early Irish king's base *clients jointly delivered a human pledge to guarantee payment of his food rents, and the word for base clientship, *giallnae*, from *giall*, a hostage, suggested to D. A. Binchy that this practice once applied to the clients of every lord. But in historic times hostages normally guaranteed political contracts, for instance the oaths of allegiance taken at a king's inauguration by his own leading nobles, and the promises of tribute and military service given when a defeated territory submitted to an overlord. Hostages were closely related to the submitting parties, as sons and daughters, or foster-children, or else were close relatives of their principal supporters. They could be honourably treated while the submitting party remained loyal, but chained, blinded, or executed in case of rebellion. Anglo-Norman kings and barons were familiar with the practice of hostage-taking, and continued to use this as a way of controlling Irish chieftains in the later Middle Ages. Angry protests rose from the colonists when government officials sometimes released hostages for ransom instead of retaining them to guarantee peace. KS

Houghers (1711–12), a movement of protest against the extension of stock rearing at the expense of small-scale tillage farming, commencing in *Iar Connacht and spreading to other western counties. Large numbers of sheep and cattle were killed or houghed (disabled by cutting their hamstrings). The houghers anticipated many of the methods—notably the use of disguise, and the issuing of formally worded letters and proclamations in the name of a mythical leader (Ever Joyce)—employed by the *Whiteboys and other groups. But there is evidence of a degree of connivance and encouragement from local gentry that set them apart from later movements of *agrarian protest.

houses of industry. The first house of industry was erected in *Dublin in 1704 as a refuge for the destitute and a place of detention for beggars. Increasingly taken up with the care of deserted children, it was converted into a *foundling hospital in 1772. The same year the Irish *parliament made provision for the establishment of a house of industry in every county and city, supported by local *taxation and voluntary subscriptions, to provide accommodation and work both for the 'helpless' poor and for beggars and vagrants. At the beginning of the 19th century only a handful of such institutions were operating, and a number of these, such as the *Belfast house of industry, were supported solely by voluntary subscriptions. The promptitude with which the act was implemented in Dublin, where a new house of industry opened in 1772, reflected contemporary anxieties concerning the problem of poverty in the city, and more particularly the large number of beggars. Sixty-five per cent of those entering the Dublin house of industry 1773–5 did so under duress. From 1777 parliamentary grants were made towards its upkeep. A number of houses of industry were transferred to the *Poor Law Commission in 1838; others, now redundant, closed. VC

housing. Shelter and sustenance are the fundamental human needs in Ireland's climate. So, as the ubiquitous feature of the built environment, housing reflects cultural continuities as well as historical changes wrought by developing social perspectives and by external influences.

Studies of housing are customarily built on a rigid distinction between vernacular design, rooted in customary practice, and formal *architecture. In reality 'vernacular' and 'formal' represent opposite ends of a spectrum of design possibilities, with a considerable area of overlap between them. In Ireland, for example, most housing in country and town was until recently locally inspired within vernacular norms which had little to do with its external appearance. From the mid-18th century, however, there was a growing tendency towards symmetry in handling the relationships of mass and void in the façade. Together with detailing of doors and windows, this betrays influence from formal architecture. Change in the vernacular interior developed much more slowly. If external influences slowly changed vernacular design, equally, traditional practices—for example, the use of internal walling rather than timber roof trusses to support the roof ridge—persisted in formally designed construction.

Since *c.*1600 interior space relationships have provided a basis for distinguishing between two widespread rural house types. In both cases houses were one room deep from front to back and one storey high; they rarely had a gable entrance, were built with mass walls of earth or stone but rarely of brick, and had their hearths placed on their long axis. In circumstances of modest prosperity accommodation was increased by adding a room at one or both gables. A second storey was unusual anywhere until the late 18th century, and in the Atlantic coastal counties and in the north became common only after about 1860. These characteristics also dominated the dwellings of most urban working people, producing the characteristic 'ribbon' housing of mainly one-storey, thatched buildings along the sides of roads leading into the towns.

The basic types are defined by the relationship between the principal entrance and the position of the main (often the only) hearth used for preparing food. Houses of *direct-entry* type have the entrance, or opposite entrances, in front and back walls, at the end of the kitchen away from the hearth. The door was usually placed about centrally in the front wall, so the hearth was at one gable end whether the house was undivided internally or had separate spaces for living and sleeping. A third room added behind the hearth altered the external appearance because the hearth position, evident externally from the smoke-hole or chimney, was no longer at a gable. However, in some places like the Loop Head district in Co. Clare and the kingdom of Mourne in south Co. Down, some two-room houses were entered at one end and had a central hearth position.

Internally unpartitioned direct-entry houses in western and northern Ireland often accommodated both people and cattle, using the same entrance(s). Some of these survived in use into the 20th century, although most late examples did have internal division and independent entrances for people and cattle. Population pressure in the early 19th century was accommodated by exploiting increasingly difficult terrain, with houses often built on sloping sites. In some such cases internally partitioned byre dwellings were adapted to have the byre at the low end underneath a loft or bedroom, and the kitchen at the upper end. In these cases, known in Cos. Tyrone and Donegal, separate access for cattle was essential. Recognition of the existence of these byre dwellings is vital to interpreting the housing data in the 1841 *census. High incidences of Class IV one-room dwellings in north-west Ireland were accounted for by internally unpartitioned byre dwellings, while elsewhere the statistics exclusively represent the tiny cabins and hovels of the landless poor.

In north Connacht and much of Ulster some direct-entry houses had a bed at one side of the kitchen hearth. This was built into the gable and hearth walls, which were slightly recessed to accommodate it. Alternatively, when accommodated in an externally expressed outshot which created a distinct niche in the kitchen corner, the bed intruded less into the living space. Such kitchen beds may once have been more widespread, even in eastern Ireland, in hill and mountain districts; three examples were discovered in the Armagh/Louth borderland. Bed outshots were also known elsewhere in Europe's Atlantic coastlands.

Direct-entry houses had antecedents earlier than 1600. Few earlier rural house sites have been identified, but one in Co. Antrim with a direct-entry house form produced a radio-carbon date in the 13th century. Excavated medieval urban houses in *Dublin and elsewhere show a different form, with doors in gables, aisled interiors, and some constructional techniques unknown in later vernacular housing. Nevertheless there were also some continuities between the two, in the use of wattled non-load-bearing walling, and cruck trusses (A-shaped frames springing from ground level to support the roof ridge), both features identified in *Viking period houses in Dublin.

The second Irish vernacular house type juxtaposes the (often only) entrance and the principal hearth, and a screen ('jamb wall') separates them parallel to the building's long axis, forming a lobby inside the entrance. This entrance/hearth complex is usually in the centre of the house, only very occasionally at one end. These *lobby-entry* houses could not accommodate cattle due to the restricted space within the lobby. Essentially they were a lowland house type, unknown in the mountains of Wicklow and Munster, but otherwise common throughout Ireland, except in the west from Kerry to Donegal, and in north and east Ulster.

Introduction of lobby-entry houses from England to Ulster is documented in the 17th century. Further south the innovation may have arrived slightly earlier. The type developed in south-east England, where it was perceived in the 16th century to be the modern small rural house, and settlers took it also to Tidewater America. These houses diffused from English settlement cores, spreading north and west in Ireland until the early 19th century. The type was commonest in single-storey form with either a hipped or gabled roof. Some *landlords favoured formally designed versions of them as gate lodges, or as estate dwellings for tenants.

Antecedents of the lobby-entry house in England were usually of two storeys with stairs at the rear of the central chimney stack. Occasional two-storey 17th-century examples have been discovered in areas of English settlement, including one excavated at Dungiven, Co. Londonderry. Thatched lobby-entry farmhouses in Co. Wexford, one-and-a-half or two storeys high with hipped roofs, may have resulted from early introduction of the type there.

Materials for vernacular building until after 1750 were what was locally available: earth, turf, and peat, stone, occasionally slate, timber, thatch materials, and fired-clay products where knowledge of their manufacture and use had been introduced in the 16th century or later. Timber-framed walls were an innovation mostly in towns, without any apparent connection with earlier Irish timber-framing traditions, for example in ecclesiastical buildings. In contrast, there was continuity from early and medieval times in the

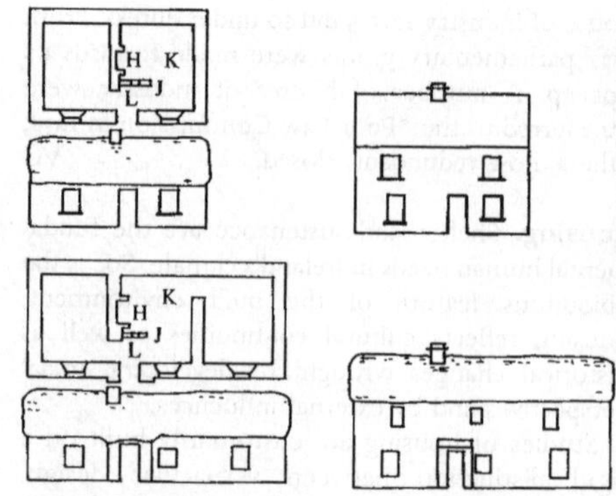

Schematic plans and elevations of lobby-entry houses. Left: 2- and 3-room thatched houses. K: kitchen; H: hearth; J: jamb wall; L: lobby. Right: *above*, slated-roof, *below*, thatched enlargements with upper bedrooms.

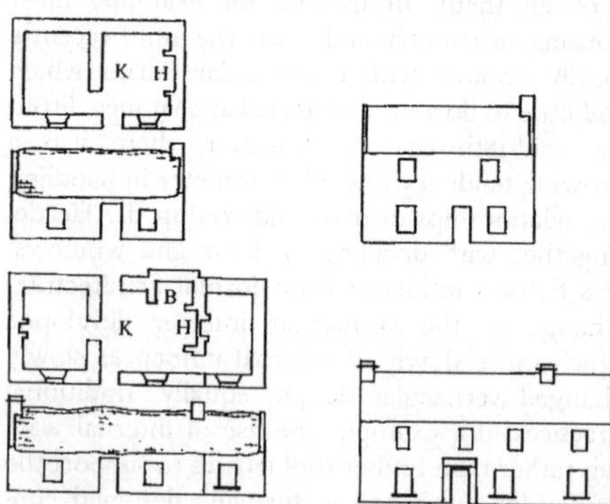

Schematic plans and elevations of direct-entry houses. Left: *above*, 2-room thatched house; *below*, 3-room thatched house with bed outshot and opposite entrances. K: kitchen; H: hearth; B: bed outshot. Right: slated-roofed enlargements with upper bedrooms.

use of clay-plastered wattlework for internal partitions. After 1600 vernacular housing was dominated by mass walls of compacted earth, or of stone where it was readily available from rock outcrops or glacial deposits. Native 'green' timber provided roof framing until the early 18th century; the latest dendrochronologically dated use of native oak in roofing is about 1720. Fossil wood from *bogland was widely used thereafter, also poor scrub timber for light scantling. After about 1760 imported softwoods became available for building, first from Baltic lands and later from America. Driftwood was used in building in coastal areas, but probably commonly so only in western districts by the 19th century.

Gabled and hipped roof forms coexisted. The latter was more extensive down to the early 19th century but it had become rare in most of Ulster by 1850. Thatch was much the commonest roof covering and, except in some parts of Leinster, it was applied over a layer of turf. Thatched roofs provided excellent insulation from both heat and cold. Wheat, rye, and flax straws were recognized as longer-lasting materials, but poor people resorted to using a wide variety of inferior materials. Two thatching techniques predominated, each being Ireland's variant of widespread European traditions. Along the western and northern coasts, thatch was tied down with a close network of ropes. Elsewhere straw was pinned in place with bent lengths of pliable wood thrust into the lower layers of the roof.

Beaten earth floors were commonplace until late in the 19th century, when fired-clay tiles, either locally made or imported, came into use where they could be afforded. Chimneys were introduced in the 16th century in *castles and *tower houses and descended socially to vernacular housing where they became common only in the late 19th century. Statistical sources of the 1840s, including detailed estate surveys by Maurice Collis of the lands owned by *Trinity College and other estates which included the prosperous *Londonderry estate in north Co. Down, show that unimproved housing typified many parts of Ireland. Most rural houses were still of one storey with a clay floor, and many lacked glazed windows and chimneys. Until chimneys were introduced, smoky interiors in housing rendered lofts unusable and the addition of upper storeys impossible. Consequently sleeping upstairs was unknown to most rural dwellers until late in the 19th century.

Functional specialization of interior space developed quickly after about 1860 at vernacular level, by subdivision within the traditional small house of two or three rooms, as well as by addition of new spaces. Bedrooms multiplied, facilitating segregation of unmarried males and females. Parlours became socially desirable. Internal entrance lobbies were elaborated or external porches added, indicators of the increasingly clear division between family and community in a more commercialized and socially stratified rural society.

The consequences of the *famine of the 1840s revolutionized Irish housing standards. By 1851 most of the inadequate one-room houses of the very poor had disappeared, their occupants having either died or emigrated. By 1900 one-room dwellings had virtually disappeared, and three-room or larger houses predominated everywhere. Some landlords were concerned about the living standards of their tenantry earlier in the 19th century, but effective legislation to enforce improvements came only in the 1890s, implemented in the construction of the 'labourers' cottages' by rural district councils (see LOCAL GOVERNMENT). Standards were improved in western districts with aid from the *Congested Districts Board and later, and more widely, there was assistance through the Irish *Land Commission. Yet within these improved houses, interiors remained traditional in design.

Some enlightened owners also experimented with improved housing standards for industrial workers, including development of model villages like Bessbrook in Co. Armagh and Portlaw (see MALCOLMSONS OF PORTLAW) in Co. Waterford. Minimum standards for industrial housing were set in *Belfast as early as the 1840s and were enhanced three decades later, but in Dublin, *Cork, and *Limerick improvements commenced only in the 1880s. Until after 1920, however, the emphasis in public housing remained on rural problems.

Vernacular approaches to housing ended mainly between the world wars, and after 1950 vernacular design had ceased. By the 1920s *suburban housing estates were developing, proliferating after 1960 when modes of housing new to Ireland were introduced. Tower blocks and other mass housing schemes were built in the cities, bringing social problems in part attributable to an overemphasis on housing provision at the expense of creating the physical infrastructure of new urban communities. Rural housing changed quite fundamentally too. Bungalow and suburban villa dwellings introduced new design idioms constructed of industrially produced and often imported materials. Building technology freed the siting of dwellings from environmental constraints and the appearance of housing in the landscape broke radically with the past.

Aalen, F. H. A., 'Public Housing in Ireland, 1880–1921', *Planning Perspectives*, 2 (1987)

Gailey, A., *Rural Houses of the North of Ireland* (1984)

RAG

Howth gun-running. In May 1914 Darrell Figgis and Erskine *Childers travelled to Germany to purchase 1,500 rifles and ammunition for the *Irish Volunteers. Part of the consignment was landed without incident on the Wicklow coast in early August. The remainder, in a publicity stunt devised to rival the earlier landing of weapons at Larne by the *Ulster Volunteer Force, was brought ashore at Howth, just north of Dublin, on 26 July and distributed to waiting Volunteers. Soldiers sent to intervene succeeded in seizing only a handful of weapons (which were subsequently returned, on the grounds that their seizure had been illegal). On their march back to barracks some soldiers, baited by a hostile crowd, opened fire, killing three and wounding 38.

Huguenots, French Protestants granted religious toleration under the Edict of Nantes (1598), but in the late 17th century subject to increasing persecution, culminating in 1685 in the revocation of the edict and the flight of many Huguenots from France. A small Huguenot community already existed in Dublin by 1665, when a chapel in *St Patrick's cathedral was set aside for their use. A more substantial immigration, involving an estimated 10,000 persons, took place in the 1690s. Twenty-one Huguenot communities were established, of which the most notable, consisting mainly of veterans of the Huguenot regiments in the Williamite army (see WILLIAMITE WAR), was on the earl of *Galway's estate at Portarlington, Queen's County (Laois). At its peak, in 1703, the colony had 489 residents. By 1720 this had fallen to only 205. However, the French character of Portarlington was still evident to visitors up to the end of the 18th century, and the town continued even longer to be noted as the site of several genteel boarding schools. Near Lisburn Louis *Crommelin and other Huguenots contributed to the emerging Ulster linen trade, while in Dublin the *La Touche family achieved prominence both in banking and in political life. Some Huguenot congregations adopted the liturgy of the *Church of Ireland. Others insisted on maintaining their own forms, at the price of incurring some hostility from the established church, and being denied the financial assistance which the state gave to conformist congregations.

Humbert, Gen. Jean Joseph Amable (1767–1823). A relatively junior officer, he sailed precipitately at the head of what should have been one of three French expeditions sent in belated support of the *insurrection of 1798, landing at Killala Bay, Co. Mayo, on 22 August with 1,019 men. The French were taken aback by the indiscipline and lack of political awareness of local people, but nevertheless raised 3,000 or so local volunteers and established a provisional government under John Moore, son of a local Catholic merchant and landowner. Ignoring instructions to remain on the defensive until reinforced, Humbert routed government troops at Castlebar ('the races of Castlebar') on 27 August, but was encircled at Ballinamuck, Co. Longford, on 8 September. Government forces accepted the French surrender, but massacred some 2,000 accompanying Irish supporters.

Hundred Years War. The Anglo-French wars (1337–1453) affected Ireland mostly indirectly. They ensured that its problems had a relatively low priority for English kings, interventions such as those of *Lionel of Clarence in 1361 or *Richard II in the 1390s tending to coincide with truces. Irish trade was affected by *piracy, and by royal manipulation of *wool exports for diplomatic purposes. Anglo-Irish lords occasionally served abroad, as at the sieges of Calais (1347) and Rouen (1418). But the lordship's resources, now much shrunken, were not exploited as they had been for earlier wars in Wales and Scotland. RFF

hunger strike, as a protest tactic by prisoners, has been fancifully traced back to early Irish traditions of shaming an enemy by fasting in protest at his actions ('fasting upon' him). A more likely derivation is from the example of the suffragettes (see FEMINISM). On 25 September 1917 Thomas Ashe died after force feeding following a hunger strike in protest at conditions in Mountjoy jail, Dublin. A second strike in 1920 was suspended following the deaths of Terence *MacSwiney and two others. Another, in October–November 1923, by republican prisoners still held following the end of the *Civil War, collapsed in disarray, with two dead. De *Valera's refusal to grant political status to *IRA men imprisoned during the *Second World War led to the death of two hunger strikers in April 1940 and a third in May 1946. In Northern Ireland the withdrawal of 'special category' status from IRA prisoners convicted after March 1976 provoked an immediate 'dirty protest', followed by a hunger strike during May–October 1981. The election to parliament of the strike's leader, Bobby Sands, initiated *Sinn Féin's entry into electoral politics, while nationalist outrage at the death of Sands and nine others helped ensure some dramatic early successes at the polls.

hurling has a long history in Ireland. *Brehon law is thought to have recognized the sport, and 12th-century manuscripts mention comparable ball and stick games. The Statute of *Kilkenny legislated against English colonists playing the game. Nevertheless the sport persisted, and is mentioned in a law of 1527 and in the Sunday Observance Act of 1695. During the 18th century hurling remained popular. In 1755 the *lord lieutenant attended an intercounty match. By the early 19th century, however, social and sectarian tension and changing gentry lifestyles had eroded upper-class patronage, while popular participation declined as part of the general contraction of traditional amusements (see SPORT), especially following the *Famine. The game was still played only in isolated pockets when, in 1870, the first laws of hurling were drawn up by the Dublin University Hurley Club. The Irish Hurley Union was founded by six Dublin clubs in 1879, and contact was made with *hockey clubs in

England. The establishment of the *Gaelic Athletic Association offered an alternative for would-be hurlers. The Hurley Union, seen as elitist and pro-Union, dissolved prior to 1892. Under the auspices of the GAA, all-Ireland championships were instituted in 1887. By 1913 the rules of the game had been rewritten, reducing teams to fifteen a side, and restructuring the scoring system. The sport spread rapidly from Dublin, becoming most popular in Munster. In Northern Ireland, where hurling has continued to be perceived as a nationalist and Catholic sport, clubs came to enjoy significant success only after 1960. NG

Hussey, Thomas (1746–1803), first president of *Maynooth College and Catholic bishop of Waterford 1796–1803. Born in Co. Meath, educated in Seville and Salamanca, he was ordained priest in 1769. While chaplain to the Spanish embassy in London he built up a network of contacts which included Edmund *Burke, and was a member of the Royal Society of London. With Burke's son Richard, he worked as an agent for the *Catholic Committee, winning the trust of the London government. He also negotiated the setting up of Maynooth College. Canny and capable in diplomatic affairs, he found it difficult to adjust on his return to Ireland. He was rarely in Maynooth and clashed with the government over his defence of the right of Catholic troops to absent themselves from Anglican services. A pastoral letter in 1797, with its criticism of the established church and its reference to 'the remnants of old oppression', also strained relations. Politically conservative, Hussey advocated *Catholic emancipation but was hostile to the *French Revolution. TO'C

Hutcheson, Francis (1694–1746), *Presbyterian moral philosopher. The son and grandson of Irish Presbyterian ministers, he studied for the ministry in Glasgow but chose to run a dissenting academy in Dublin for ten years, during which he published his *Inquiry into Beauty and Virtue* (1725) and *Essays on the Passions with Illustrations on the Moral Sense* (1728). Appointed to the chair of moral philosophy in Glasgow in 1730, his teaching earned him the title of Father of the Scottish *Enlightenment. His views of God and man were more optimistic than those of the Westminster Confession (see SUBSCRIPTION CONTROVERSIES) and he maintained contacts with the Irish non-subscribers. Moral philosophy included political and economic questions as well as ethical theory, and Hutcheson's teachings that the end of government was 'the greatest good of the greatest number', and that victims of unjust regimes had the right to rebel, contributed to the ideology of revolution in Ireland and colonial America. RFGH

Hyde, Douglas (1860–1949), academic and cultural revivalist. The son of a *Church of Ireland clergyman, Hyde was brought up first in Co. Sligo and then, from 1867, at Frenchpark, Co. Roscommon, both areas rich in antiquities and where some spoken Irish survived. He entered *Trinity College in 1880, switching from an initial course of divinity to law. 'The Necessity for De-anglicizing the Irish People' (1892), his inaugural lecture as president of the National Literary Society, called for action to arrest the decay of Irish, denounced the imitation of English manners, but also recommended Anglo-Irish literature as superior to imported mass-circulation works. Though not the founder of the *Gaelic League, Hyde became its first president in 1893. He was professor of Irish at University College, Dublin, 1909–32, a member of the *Irish Free State Senate from 1925, and first *president of Ireland 1938–45.

Hyde published extensively, drawing both on oral tradition and on manuscript sources. His most important collections included *Love Songs of Connacht* (1893) and *The Religious Songs of Connacht* (1906). He collaborated with *Yeats and Lady Gregory on a number of theatrical productions, commencing with *Casadh an tSúgáin* ('The Twisting of the Rope') (1901), the first Irish-language play performed in a theatre, and published a highly successful *Literary History of Ireland* (1899).

Hyde's public insistence that the Gaelic League should avoid politics, leading eventually to his resignation as president in 1915, has encouraged the image of an unworldly and apolitical idealist. Such a portrayal hardly does justice to the organizational and strategic capacity displayed in Hyde's promotion of the league, or to the skills as a public performer revealed in his highly successful fund-raising visit to America during 1905. Hyde's own political sympathies were nationalist, and he was to comment subsequently that he had sought to resist the politicization of the league only because he did not foresee the triumph of *Sinn Féin.

Dunleavy, J. E. and G. W., *Douglas Hyde: A Maker of Modern Ireland* (1991)

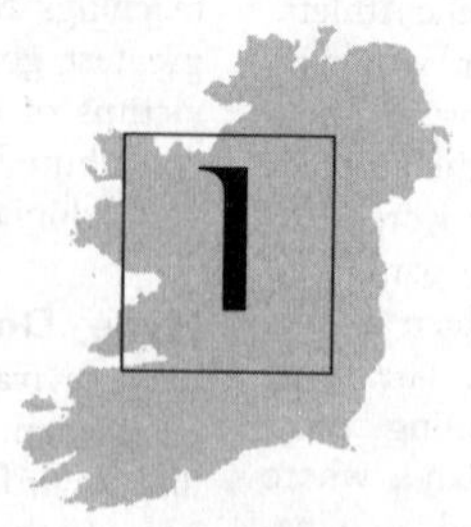

Iar Connacht, a district in west Co. Galway, consisting of the baronies of Moycullen and Ballynahinch and the half-barony of Ross. Noted up to the middle of the 18th century as a wild and lawless region in which aspects of the Gaelic social order survived unchanged, it was the original centre of the *Hougher disturbances, and was described in a 'Chorographical Description' prepared for William *Molyneux by Roderick *O'Flaherty but not published until 1846.

idlemen were soldiers, previously maintained by *coyne and livery, left redundant after their lords were either defeated and expropriated or had agreed to their disbandment through *composition. An estimated 24,000 professional swordsmen existed in the mid-16th century. Government policy was either to send them to *foreign armies or to execute them. Between 1609 and 1614 *Chichester shipped 6,000 to Sweden and executed many others. Remilitarization during the *Confederate War caused the Catholic ecclesiastical congregation at Clonmacnoise (1649) to excommunicate 'idle boys' plaguing the roads as highwaymen. The Cromwellians subsequently cleared the defeated confederate soldiery by *transportation and foreign enlistment. HM

illegitimacy. The concept of illegitimacy had little meaning in Gaelic Ireland. In the early Christian period all children were legitimate as long as the child was conceived within a recognized union. A wide spectrum of unions were permitted in customary law and as a result the offspring of primary wives, secondary wives, and concubines were all accorded equal rights, though the social status of the mother might affect the eligibility to succeed to a chieftainship. In addition, in late medieval Ireland a custom referred to as 'naming' a child developed. This was an official recognition of the offspring of a casual relationship after the mother of the child had made an official declaration which was then accepted or rejected by the alleged father. Once a child was acknowledged by its father, it was entitled to participate in succession issues and also eligible to receive a share in the family inheritance, in accordance with the Gaelic-Irish custom of gavelkind (equal division between sons). In the later medieval period the Gaelic Irish often resorted to the church courts to obtain marital dispensations in order to secure the inheritance rights of a child or children who might otherwise have been labelled illegitimate in canon law.

Accounts of Gaelic Irish society in the 16th and 17th centuries, though inevitably coloured by the prejudice of New English observers, seem to indicate that attitudes to sexual activity and pregnancy outside the bounds of formal marriage remained relatively relaxed. The first available Catholic *parish registers, on the other hand, dating from the mid-18th century, suggest that by this time illegitimacy was relatively uncommon, accounting for 3 per cent or less of Irish births. The same figures indicate that less than 10 per cent of Irish Catholic brides were pregnant at the time of marriage, as compared to 40 per cent or so in contemporary rural England. Evidence collected in the 1830s by the *Poor Inquiry makes clear that women who did become pregnant outside marriage were generally ostracized by family and neighbours. The apparent change in attitude can presumably be attributed to the transition from a pastoral agrarian economy to a more settled rural society, as well as to the reshaping of popular Catholicism brought about by the *Counter-Reformation.

The proportion of illegitimate births recorded in the first years of *civil registration, at just over 3 per cent, was half or less of that recorded in most other European societies. The exceptions were the predominantly Protestant areas of Ulster, and the south-east, where illegitimacy rates of 5–6 per cent were closer to those recorded in contemporary England. Illegitimacy rates in Northern Ireland stood at between 4 and 5 per cent up to the Second World War, dipped below 3 per cent in the period 1950–65, then began to rise again to 6 per cent by 1980. Rates in independent Ireland, consistently below 4 per cent and in the late 1950s lower than 2 per cent, showed a similar rise in the 1960s and 1970s, reaching 5 per cent by 1980. By the 1990s the proliferation of long-term partnerships outside marriage had arguably made the concept of illegitimacy meaningless. In 1993, for example, 18 per cent of all births in the Irish Republic were to women who were not married. BNC/SC

illicit distillation, using barley or other grain to produce a colourless spirit (poteen), expanded rapidly following the Revenue Act of 1779, which banned small stills and imposed a minimum duty on others. Poteen not only provided a cheap spirit, superior in quality to the often unpalatable 'parliament whiskey'; income from its sale was a crucial element in the survival strategy of many smallholders and occupiers of marginal land. Attempts at suppression were thus fiercely resisted. Further increases in duty during the *revolutionary and Napoleonic wars exacerbated the conflict. Indeed one of the first deployments of the new *Peace Preservation Force, in Inishowen, Co. Donegal, in 1817, was against distillers rather than agrarian protestors. Problems of enforcement continued up to the 1860s. Thereafter illicit distillation, though practised to the present day, became less common. The decline was due both to better law enforcement, particularly after 1857, when the *Royal Irish Constabulary took over the functions of the not always effective Revenue Police, and to the improved quality of legally produced whiskey.

Illicit distillation, and a taste for its products, is often thought of as characteristic of Irish culture in general. In fact early 19th-century inquiries suggested that it was very largely confined to the northern half of the country, and a similar regional concentration was revealed in the pattern of convictions and seizures up to at least the 1950s. The divide presumably reflects both the prominence of beer rather than spirits in the drinking habits of the southern population, and the easier availability of grain away from the main dairying and cattle-fattening regions.

illuminated manuscripts, see DECORATED MANUSCRIPTS.

Imbolg (1 Feb.), the first day of spring and one of the four traditional 'quarter days', important in the calendar customs of Goidelic-speaking areas up to the present century. The name's derivation is uncertain; medieval etymologists fancifully explained it as *oí-melc* ('ewe-milk'): 'that is, it is then that sheep's milk comes.' Since the later Middle Ages the day has been known as Lá Fhéile Bríde, 'St Brigid's Day': the saint's great popularity is doubtless responsible for the disappearance of the older term. JPC

immigration constitutes a central theme in the history of Ireland. Early movements of population, up to and including the arrival of the *Celts, are obscure, but the assumption is of successive waves of newcomers, reinforcing existing populations and modifying existing cultures. The scale and impact of *Viking settlement from the 9th century is better documented. The *Anglo-Norman invasion is now recognized as initiating more than a military and political conquest. Coming at the peak of a great wave of European economic and demographic expansion, it also brought a significant movement of English and Welsh settlers into parts of Ireland (see ANGLO-NORMAN COLONIZATION AND SETTLEMENT). The 16th and 17th centuries saw a much larger inward flow. Formal schemes for colonization and *plantation, in Munster, Ulster, and elsewhere, were reinforced and eventually overshadowed by large-scale spontaneous migration, as a thinly populated and underdeveloped hinterland, particularly in Ulster, was opened up for settlement and exploitation. Given the resistance to the *Reformation of both native Irish and *Old English, statistics of religion provide a rough guide to the scale of the influx, suggesting that by the early 18th century somewhere over a quarter of the population were descendants of English and Scottish migrants who had arrived within the previous 200 years.

Other inward movements were more modest. Settlement by *Huguenots and *Palatines in the late 17th and early 18th centuries brought a touch of continental European cultural influence, but failed in its main aim of significantly reinforcing Protestant numbers. Immigration from eastern Europe in the late 19th and early 20th centuries significantly increased Ireland's *Jewish community, and also produced some ugly manifestations of anti-Semitism. The other distinctive immigrant group from this period were Italians. Overwhelmingly drawn from the Lazio region, and in particular from the town of Casalattico, these arrived from the 1880s, establishing themselves principally in the catering trade. More recent, and rather different in character, has been the appearance of German and Dutch natives seeking in Ireland a less industrialized and cleaner environment. Ireland also received some eddies from the mid-20th-century immigration from India to Great Britain. By the 1980s there were some 1,000 Indians in Northern Ireland and 600 in the Irish Republic, working mainly in the retail drapery trade and, more recently, in catering.

impropriations, ecclesiastical benefices that were annexed either to a corporation (typically a *monastery or abbey) or to a layman as private property. Income from the benefice went to the holder of the impropriation, or impropriator, as did the responsibility for paying a curate to serve the cure. Impropriations became an important source of wealth, and were bought and sold as pieces of property, particularly in the years after the *Reformation, when many of the monastic impropriations fell into royal and thence into lay hands.

AF

Inchiquin, Murrough O'Brien, 1st earl of (1614–74), controversial soldier and politician. He converted to Protestantism as a royal ward between 1628 and 1635. In the *Confederate War he succeeded his father-in-law, Sir William St Leger, as governor of Munster, holding Cos. Cork and Waterford and winning battles at Liscarroll and Bandonbridge in 1642. As the English Civil War developed, the need for supply drew Inchiquin towards the parliamentary side (1644). Although the parliamentarians never trusted him, and encouraged his rival Roger Boyle (see ORRERY), the soldiery remained loyal, enabling a decisive victory over the confederate army at Knocknanuss, Co. Cork (13 Nov. 1647). Inchiquin subsequently rejoined the royalist side and forced a truce with the *Confederate Catholics, who split over rapprochement with an enemy who had evicted Catholics from Co. Cork (1644) and massacred the defenders of Adare and Cashel (1647).

When the royalist cause failed, Inchiquin went into exile in 1650. Catholic émigré hostility thwarted his desire to take unified command of the Irish regiments in France. He became governor of Catalonia (1654) and converted to Catholicism (1657).

Inchiquin returned to his restored Munster estates in 1663. He signed the loyal Catholic *Remonstrance (1666) but mended relations with Orrery in a double marriage alliance through his elder Protestant children.

HM

Incorporated Law Society, the professional body representing Irish solicitors. Its origins go back to the Law Society of Ireland established in 1830. This was a Dublin pressure group for promoting the interests of attorneys and solicitors but it soon gained control of rooms at the *Four Courts and in 1852 secured a charter of incorporation. In 1888 it took its present name and changed its constitution to ensure representation on its council of members from outside Dublin. In 1898 legislation gave it control of the education of solicitors and important disciplinary functions over the profession.

PAB

Independent Irish Party, see INDEPENDENT OPPOSITION PARTY.

Independent Opposition Party (Independent Irish Party), the realization of an idea occasionally mooted during the *O'Connell era but difficult to achieve because of the affinity of Irish Catholic MPs (including the Liberator himself) for the fellowship and patronage of the *Whig–*Liberal family. The *ecclesiastical titles bill so alienated some Catholic members that they systematically opposed not only the bill but unrelated government measures also. Most prominent among them were John *Sadleir, William *Keogh, G. H. Moore, and Thomas Reynolds; they were dubbed 'the *Irish Brigade'.

The Irish *Tenant League (founded 1850) intended to field candidates at the next elections, so that its leaders had little choice but to come to an arrangement with the Brigadiers, which they did in August 1851. The alliance won widespread support in the general election of 1852; subsequently, at one or other of two conferences in Dublin, 42 MPs formalized their election promises by pledging to remain 'independent of and in opposition to' any government that would not make specific concessions. The group voted as a bloc in the defeat of the *Tory government in December 1852. In the same month rudimentary party structures were agreed upon but these were never implemented.

When a new government emerged in January 1853 it offered no concessions but, being led by Lord Aberdeen (who had opposed the Ecclesiastical Titles Act), it was more favourably disposed towards Catholic interests than any conceivable alternative. It was supported by a number of the 'pledged' MPs, and two of them, Sadleir and Keogh, actually accepted appointments. A bitter split ensued, with those faithful to the pledge adopting the designation of 'Independent Opposition', while the others reverted to the Whig–Liberal allegiance.

The Independent Oppositionists were drawn preponderantly from the tenant right group, but their more prominent members included G. H. Moore. Any semblance of countrywide organization the party possessed was provided by the Irish Tenant League. With the advent of a minority Tory government in 1858 the party enjoyed some leverage but only about a dozen members remained and they split almost equally in the crucial reform bill vote on 31 March 1859.

Down to 1865 Independent Opposition had a significant following at the polls. Its last and best recruit was John Blake *Dillon, elected for Tipperary in 1865, who reunited the scattered remnant in the Commons and led it in 1866 into an alliance with the reforming Liberals. RVC

Independent Orange Order, founded in June 1903 as a breakaway movement from the mainstream *Orange Order. Its immediate origins lay with the populist revolt of T. H. *Sloan and the Belfast Protestant Association: in July 1902 Sloan angrily confronted the grand master of the Belfast Orangemen, Col. Edward *Saunderson, accusing him of failing to represent Irish Protestant interests in the House of Commons. These accusations were elaborated in Sloan's successful campaign in the South Belfast by-election of August 1902, and emerged as a full critique of a trimming and inefficient Irish Unionist leadership. Sloan and his allies were suspended from the Orange Order, and on 11 June 1903 they defiantly established the Independents.

The Independent Order gave expression to popular loyalist resentment at the unrepresentative nature of early Edwardian Unionism, symbolized by the collusion between Ulster Unionism and the 'romanizing' policies pursued by the Conservative government. The Independents also secured support from Protestant elements within organized Belfast labour. The adherence of Robert Lindsay *Crawford brought to the order a liberal Protestant ideologue, who was able to bind it to the northern tradition of farmer protest. However, while the Independent Order had the potential to develop in a liberal, or even secular labourist, direction, it remained fundamentally a Protestant protest movement.

Although the order grew rapidly in the mid-Edwardian period, its geographical base was confined to Protestant working-class Belfast and the liberal Protestant stronghold of North Antrim. The order enjoyed some electoral influence: Sloan was MP for South Belfast until January 1910, and Independent votes helped to return R. G. Glendinning for North Antrim in 1906. But increasing division within the leadership deprived the order of both talent and the capacity to grow in any other than a conventionally Protestant direction. This, combined with the revitalization of mainstream Unionism and the re-emergence of the home rule threat, served to undermine the order's appeal. It reached a peak of membership, with 38 affiliated lodges, in 1907; only 12 of these remained by the beginning of the third home rule crisis, in 1912. The order had fallen into abeyance by the early 1920s. It was later revived, and remains in existence as a small organization associated with the Revd Ian Paisley, who left mainstream Orangeism in 1962. If the contemporary Independent Order reflects little of the thought of Lindsay Crawford, then it retains the authentic popular loyalist and evangelical Protestant hallmark supplied by Sloan.

Patterson, Henry, 'Independent Orangeism and Class Conflict in Edwardian Belfast: A Reinterpretation', *Proceedings of the Royal Irish Academy*, 80c/4 (May 1980)

AJ

Independents were members of an elitist religious sect which emerged during the English Civil War. Influenced by New England congregationalism, these Protestants believed in liberty of conscience and the independence of each congregation. They were numerically inferior to *Presbyterians on the parliamentarian side, but converts in the upper echelons of the New Model Army gave them a heightened political profile. They believed in the political dominance of England in the three kingdoms, included a high percentage of *adventurers, and produced much of the propaganda urging a reconquest of Ireland. First evident in Ireland during Lisle's short lord lieutenancy in 1646–7, the Independents returned in force with Cromwell. His expedition was justified by the poet John Milton, a leading Independent, in *Observations upon the Articles of Peace* (1649), a triple broadside against Irish Catholics, Ormond's royalists, and Scots Presbyterian settlers.

During the Interregnum there was no established religion in Ireland. In Dublin Samuel *Winter established Independency at St Nicholas within the walls and John Rogers at *Christ Church; in all about 30 Independent churches operated, especially in garrison towns. The Independents lost ground in the army to the *Baptists during *Fleetwood's government and more generally to the Presbyterian-style Cork Association under Henry *Cromwell. They nevertheless survived after the *Restoration as a minor dissenting sect, protected from official harassment by their insignificant numbers and sustained by a degree of co-operation with the southern Presbyterians. In 1695 there were reported to be six Independent congregations. Like other minor sects the Independents, now more commonly called Congregationalists, enjoyed a revival in the 19th century, their numbers rising from 162 in 1861 to more than 10,000 by 1901. SC/HM

India provided a career for Irishmen of all classes and religious denominations. Key figures in the extension of British rule included Laurence Sulivan (1713–86), born in Co. Cork, dominant from the 1750s in the affairs of the East India Company, and the Co. Antrim landowner George Macartney (1737–1806), later Earl Macartney of Lisanoure, who as governor of Madras 1780–5 reformed the financial administration of the territory. During the Indian Mutiny (1857) Sir Henry Lawrence (1806–57), educated at Foyle College, Derry, won fame for his defence of Lucknow. His brother John (1811–79), later viceroy of India 1863–9 and 1st Lord Lawrence, presided over the reimposition of order in the Punjab, in which the Dublin-born Brig. Gen. John Nicholson (1821–57) played a prominent and ruthless part. Later Sir Michael O'Dwyer (1864–1940), son of a Catholic landed family from Co. Tipperary, was lieutenant governor of the Punjab 1913–20, where he directed the vigorous suppression of protest, including the shooting dead of at least 379 Indians at Amritsar (13 Apr. 1919). The Ulster-born Sir Claude Auchinleck (1884–1981) was the last commander-in-chief of the Indian army (1943–7), overseeing the transition to independence and partition. Irishmen also made up a significant proportion of the army rank and file on which British power ultimately depended.

The introduction from 1855 of recruitment by competitive examination opened the way for enthusiastic Irish participation in the Indian civil service. Between 1855 and 1863 24 per cent of recruits were Irish, compared to less than 5 per cent before 1850. Recruitment was reduced after 1864 by new procedures deliberately designed to favour entry from English public schools rather than Irish universities or English 'crammers'. Between 1880 and 1914 between 5 and 10 per cent of recruits were Irish. Despite this narrowing of overall opportunity, Irish recruitment became over time less aristocratic and more middle class, while the proportion of Catholics rose from 8 per cent in 1855–84 to 30 per cent in 1885–1914.

Indian grievances attracted some attention from the *Nationalist party, particularly F. H. O'Donnell (1848–1916), MP for Dungarvan and brother of an Indian civil servant, who in 1883 proposed that Dadabhai Naoroji of the Indian National Congress be found an Irish parliamentary seat. Later there were inconclusive contacts between Congress and *Sinn Féin. On the other side *Carson and other Unionists gave unreserved support to O'Dwyer's administration of the Punjab, on the grounds that failure to support firm action in India would weaken the struggle against militant nationalism in Ireland.

Cook, S. B., 'The Irish Raj: Social Origins and Careers of Irishmen in the Indian Civil Service', *Journal of Social History*, 20/3 (1987)

Indian meal (maize meal) was first imported from America into Ireland in 1799 as a relief food for the poor when *potatoes were scarce. During the *Great Famine large quantities were distributed to the hungry. Initially difficulties in grinding produced poorly refined meal which caused digestive discomfort to consumers: hence the popular name 'Peel's brimstone'. Once properly ground, Indian meal became popular, outstaying the Famine to form part of labouring diets until the early decades of the 20th century. EMC

indulgence, declarations of, decrees suspending by royal authority all *penal laws against Catholics and dissenters, issued on 15 March 1672 and 4 April 1687. The first, ostensibly a bid for national unity on the eve of war with the Dutch republic, may have reflected Charles II's desire to improve the position of Catholics (see RESTORATION). The second confirmed *James II's abandonment of his former *Tory supporters for an attempted Catholic–dissenter alliance.

Industrial Credit Company (ICC), a state-owned merchant bank established in 1933, as part of the drive for industrial self-sufficiency, to provide capital for Irish industry by way of public flotation, direct investment, or contract loans. However its initial capital allocation of £500,000, increased to £1 million in 1936, proved insufficient to provide long-term capital, and from an early stage the ICC concentrated on underwriting share issues by protected companies. It was largely responsible for the major expansion of share activity on the Dublin *Stock Exchange during the 1930s. MED

industrial exhibitions, inspired by the success of the Great Exhibition of 1851 in London, were organized by individuals and groups anxious to promote the revival of Irish industry, by providing showcases for its products and encouraging technological innovation. A first exhibition in Cork in 1852 attracted 140,000 visitors and was seen as a reasonable success. A much larger exhibition in Dublin in 1853, sponsored by William *Dargan and staged in a temporary building erected in the grounds of the *Royal Dublin Society, was less successful: the Irish market was too small to tempt adequate numbers of foreign manufacturers, and the deficiency was made up by a greatly expanded arts and antiquities section, along with overseas exotica, which between them overshadowed the displays of Irish raw materials, machinery, and manufactured goods. Despite the patronage of Queen Victoria and Prince Albert, who during a week-long stay in Ireland visited the hall four times and also paid a visit to Dargan's home, overall attendances were low and Dargan underwrote a substantial loss. Further exhibitions, on a smaller scale, were held in Dublin in 1865, 1872, 1895, and 1907, and in Cork in 1883, and there were also exhibitions of Irish industry in London (1888) and Glasgow (1901).

industry. See MANUFACTURING INDUSTRY.

Inghinidhe na hÉireann ('daughters of Ireland'), *nationalist women's organization founded by Maud *Gonne in 1900. It grew out of the Patriotic Children's Treat Committee, created to provide a nationalist response to the Phoenix Park treat organized for children during Queen Victoria's visit in the same year. The Inghinidhe were proactively nationalist—as well as running Irish classes, and putting on plays and tableaux vivants, they promoted Irish-manufactured goods and opposed recruitment to the British army. Their newspaper, *Bean na hÉireann*, appeared 1908–11; among other things it supported the introduction of school meals in 1908, going against the Catholic church and majority opinion in the *Nationalist party. It also supported women's suffrage, though it prioritized national independence. Many of the women prominent in the non-parliamentary nationalist movement from 1912—Constance *Markievicz, Helena Molony, Louise Gavan Duffy—started off in the Inghinidhe, as did actresses Sara Allgood and Máire O'Neill, cartoonist Grace Gifford, journalist Sydney Gifford, and many others. IE took part in the meeting of all Irish women's organizations to consider the failure of the conciliation bill on women's suffrage in 1912. *Cumann na mBan, if it did not actually replace IE, became the major magnet for nationalist women after 1914. CC

inquisitions are sworn statements by local juries as to the value and ownership of moveables or property, returned to *chancery or *exchequer by the *escheator, who made the inquiry. They were taken for a wide range of reasons including attainder, proof of royal title, or after death to establish royal rights. Inquisitions were also used to compile land surveys. Most inquisitions were destroyed in 1922 (see PUBLIC RECORDS), but both the chancery and exchequer series were calendared by the *Irish record commissioners. Two volumes of the chancery series, for Ulster and Leinster, were published in 1829 and a volume of the exchequer series appeared in 1991. RG

insanity and the insane. Until the 19th century, most Irish people regarded as insane were looked after by their families or wandered the countryside as beggars. Some found their way into the houses of correction, opened from 1634, into the county infirmaries, opened from 1765, and into the *houses of industry, opened from 1772. The accumulation of the mad in institutions not specifically intended for their care fuelled a demand in the late 18th century for specialist hospitals.

In 1757 St Patrick's hospital, Dublin, the first such hospital in Ireland, was opened with money left by Jonathan *Swift. But fears that lunacy was increasing led the government after 1800 to embark on a major asylum-building programme, unprecedented in the United Kingdom. The Richmond asylum was opened in Dublin in 1814 and 22 district asylums were built throughout the country between 1824 and 1869.

By 1870 Irish asylums had 7,500 beds and by 1914 over 21,000. This increase in patients was partly due to a dramatic decline in the number of discharges in the latter half of the 19th century. By 1911 nearly as many people were dying in the Irish asylums each year as were being discharged.

Despite a critical report in 1925, little was done in independent Ireland until the Mental Treatment Act of 1945, which made admission a medical, not a legal, procedure and introduced the concept of voluntary admission. Within a short time the vast majority of admissions were voluntary. The Northern Irish laws had been overhauled in 1932 along similar lines. Another act in the Republic in 1981 further reformed the system. At the same time the numbers of psychiatric in-patients fell dramatically, from a peak of 21,000 in the late 1950s to around 12,000 by the early 1980s.

The Irish government is in the process of closing all the older mental hospitals and plans to cater for the mentally ill in the future through a network of psychiatric units in general hospitals, out-patient clinics, day centres, and hostels.

Finnane, M., *Insanity and the Insane in Pre-famine Ireland* (1981)

Malcolm, E. L., *Swift's Hospital: A History of St Patrick's Hospital, Dublin, 1746–1989* (1989)

Robins, J., *Fools and Mad: A History of the Insane in Ireland* (1986)

ELM

insular script. The origins and development of insular art and script have attracted fervent academic debate—and assertion—for more than 150 years. The term 'insular' was originally applied in 1901 by the German palaeographer Ludwig Traube to styles of script which began in Ireland and spread to Britain and Europe between the 6th and 9th centuries; the term has subsequently been extended to characteristics of the style in art and artefact. 'Insular', as Traube intended, has the advantage that it can be used as a neutral designation, avoiding commitment to particular national attributions in the case of the most controversial objects such as the Book of *Kells.

Probably developed from late Roman 'literary cursive', insular scripts present such varied characteristics that palaeographers have differed on appropriate terminology and classifications. E. A. Lowe divided them into 'majuscule', a higher grade, and 'minuscule', a less formal grade. Refinements to this broad division by T. J. Brown are not entirely satisfactory. Majuscule, seen at its most accomplished in the Book of Kells, is a rounded script, with the uprights of *b*, *l*, and *t* forming curves, and with pronounced wedge-shaped serifs on many letters. The *a* characteristically takes an *oc*-shape. The earliest Irish majuscule to have survived is in the 'Cathach' Psalter (Royal Irish Academy 12.R.33) and in an early 7th-century copy of Orosius's chronicle (Milan, Biblioteca Ambrosiana D.23 sup), while the script of the 6th-century waxed writing tablets from Springmount Bog, Co. Antrim (National Museum of Ireland SA 1914: 2) and the contemporary 'Usserianus Primus' (Trinity College Dublin 55) can be characterized as half-uncial. Minuscule, found first in the Bangor Antiphonary of 680 × 691 (Milan, Biblioteca Ambrosiana C.5.inf.) is a more compressed, angular script, with longer descenders and ascenders. In the form it took as the dominant script of the early 9th-century Book of Armagh, minuscule persisted in Ireland into the modern period.

Brown, T. J., 'The Irish Element in the Insular System of Scripts to circa A.D. 850', in *A Palaeographer's View: Selected Writings of Julian Brown*, ed. J. Bately, M. Brown, and J. Roberts (1993)

O'Sullivan, W., 'Insular Calligraphy: Current State and Problems', *Peritia*, 4 (1985)

—— 'Manuscripts and Palaeography', forthcoming in *A New History of Ireland*, i

BM

insurance in Ireland was traditionally provided by London or Scottish houses. During the 18th century, when Irish merchants traded on their own account, both insurance and credit were generally effected through London. By the mid-19th century English and Scottish firms dominated the Irish market for life and fire insurance. In the 1920s over 80 per cent of insurance business conducted in the *Irish Free State was controlled by British firms, and most Irish firms were insolvent. From 1926 Irish governments sought to strengthen the indigenous insurance industry and to prevent the overwhelming majority of insurance premiums being invested outside Ireland. Draft legislation adopted in 1934 provided for the amalgamation of weak companies and the creation, with state assistance, of one or more Irish firms; only companies with at least 60 per cent of their shareholdings under Irish control would be permitted to engage in non-life insurance. Many British insurance companies sold their Irish operations and the Irish Life Insurance Company was established, with the government as majority shareholder. During the *Second World War the government formed a specialist marine insurance company to provide cover for the fleet of *Irish Shipping Ltd. However, the failure to establish an Irish reinsurance company meant that insurance companies continued to invest substantial sums in London. MED

Insurrection Act. First introduced 1796, the act imposed the death penalty (replaced in 1807 by transportation for life) on persons administering illegal oaths. It also allowed government to proclaim specific districts as disturbed, thereby imposing a curfew, suspending trial by jury (see SPECIAL COURTS), and giving magistrates sweeping powers of search and detention. The act was in force during 1796–1802, and was reintroduced, with modifications, in 1807–10, 1814–18, and 1822–5. From 1833 a new type of *Coercion Act took over as the standard response to Irish disorders.

insurrection of 1798, the culmination of the revolutionary activities of the *United Irishmen. There were four main outbreaks.

1. Risings in Co. Dublin, Kildare, and Meath on the night of 23–4 May. Apparently triggered by the interception of mail coaches leaving Dublin, and possibly envisaged as leading to a descent on the capital, the insurrection was undermined by lack of co-ordination and the failure to capture strategic local centres. Government forces killed 350 at *Tara (26 May) and 200 at the *Curragh (29 May), where troops attacked surrendering rebels. The rising spread to Carlow on 25 May; an attack on Carlow town was bloodily defeated next day.

2. Risings in eastern Ulster, following a rank and file revolt against provincial United Irish leaders who had failed to respond to events in Leinster. In Co. Antrim 4,000 men under Henry Joy *McCracken captured Randalstown and Ballymena, but were defeated at Antrim town (7 June) and dispersed when Gen. George Nugent offered an amnesty to all except ringleaders. In Co. Down Henry Munro (1758–98), a Lisburn linen draper, raised 7,000 men but was defeated at Ballynahinch (13 June).

3. In Co. Wexford, insurgents massacred militia and yeomanry at Oulart on 27 May, going on to capture Enniscorthy and on 30 May Wexford town, which remained for the next three weeks the headquarters of an improvised revolutionary government. However, the failure of attacks on New Ross (5 June) and Arklow (9 June) left the insurgents confined to this south-eastern corner to await the counter-attack, culminating in the battle of *Vinegar Hill (21 June) and the recapture of Wexford town (22 June).

The Wexford insurrection, in a region where religious conflict was exacerbated by a comparatively large Protestant population, involved acts of nakedly sectarian violence, most notably the burning to death of 200 Protestant prisoners in a barn at Scullabogue and the mass execution of 93 more in Wexford town. Partly as a result, the county's insurgents have been portrayed as a largely unpoliticized peasantry, driven to rebellion by the indiscriminate violence of local loyalists and turning for leadership to sympathetic Protestant gentlemen like Bagenal *Harvey and priests like John *Murphy. More recent accounts point to evidence of some prior United Irish organization, and argue that the insurrection was more disciplined, and clearer in its political goals, than has been generally recognized.

4. The Connacht rising, sparked off by *Humbert's arrival.

The insurrection included several lesser episodes: the activities, continuing into 1803, of Michael *Dwyer and Joseph *Holt in Co. Wicklow; a small outbreak, inspired by Humbert's landing, in Cos. Longford and Westmeath on 2–6 September; and *Tandy's brief appearance in Co. Donegal.

Following the insurrection, some 1,500 persons were executed, transported, or flogged, and there were also unofficial reprisals by loyalists, particularly in the south-east. Overall the rebellion, involving an estimated 30,000 deaths, represents the most violent episode in Irish history since the 17th century. Polemical accounts by writers such as *Musgrave and Watty *Cox perpetuated a legacy of bitterness on both sides. Disillusionment and renewed insecurity following the apparent degeneration of the movement into a priest-led anti-Protestant crusade were central to the collapse both of Protestant *patriotism and of the Protestant popular radicalism represented by the United Irishmen.

International, short name for the first International Workingmen's Association, founded in London by Karl Marx in 1864, and its successors, the second International (1889–1940) and third International or Comintern (1919–43). The first International declared its support for the *Fenian movement, and called for the release of prisoners. J. P. MacDonnell (1847–1906), a journalist and *IRB member, was elected to the council of the IWMA in 1871 and became secretary for Ireland, but an attempt to establish branches in Irish cities (1871–2) achieved limited and ephemeral success. The third International had a succession of Irish affiliates, commencing with the first *Communist Party of Ireland (1921–4), none of which achieved significant popular support.

internment. In the 18th and 19th centuries detention without trial had been provided for by the suspension in times of emergency of *habeas corpus. Following the *rising of 1916, 1,841 persons were interned according to regulations made under the *Defence of the Realm Acts. The same regulations were used to intern about 100 *Sinn Féin and *Irish Volunteer activists between May 1918 and March 1919. A fresh wave of arrests, initiated by the army in January 1920, led to the internment of over 250 'rebel leaders'. Following *'Bloody Sunday' (21 Nov. 1920), the army (now acting under *Restoration of Order in Ireland Act regulations) made more widespread use of internment, detaining a total of 4,454 persons between January and July 1921.

During and after the *Civil War the Free State government, acting first under *martial law powers then under the *Public Safety Acts of 1923 and 1924, made extensive use of internment, the numbers detained peaking at 11,480 on 1 July 1923. Internment was next used, under the *Offences against the State and Emergency Powers Acts, to detain over 500 republican activists (as opposed to over 600 imprisoned for offences under the former act) during the *Second World War. More were interned during the IRA *border campaign of 1957–62.

In Northern Ireland internment under the *Special Powers Act was used to detain 728 men, almost all nationalists, between May 1922 and December 1924. Around 320 were detained during the Second World War, and an average of 150 during 1957–9. Internment was reintroduced, in response to the renewed *Northern Ireland conflict, in 1971. The initial wave of arrests, on 9 August, was based on inaccurate identifications of key activists and was accompanied by methods of 'interrogation in depth' later categorized in a government inquiry as 'brutality', and by the European Court of Human Rights as 'inhuman and degrading treatment'. The operation provoked widespread nationalist alienation while wholly failing to curb republican violence. 2,060 republicans and 109 loyalists were detained in the period up to December 1975, when internment was suspended, the enabling legislation lapsing in 1980.

interparty government (coalition), government in which two or more parties share posts and agree on a common set of policy priorities. Though not so called, the *Cosgrave government formed in October 1927 was the first such example in Ireland, in that the *Farmers' Party was formally brought into government and given a junior post (its leader became a parliamentary secretary).

In February 1948 a coalition of *Fine Gael, *Labour, *National Labour, *Clann na Poblachta, and *Clann na Talmhan that also incorporated some independents took office as the 'interparty government', but broke up in early 1951. In June 1954 a 'second interparty government' comprising Fine Gael, Labour, and Clann na Talmhan took office, and survived until 1957.

The next three coalitions were alliances between Fine Gael and Labour: the 'National Coalition' led by Liam Cosgrave (Mar. 1973–July 1977) and the coalitions of 1981–2 and 1982–7 led by Garret FitzGerald. In a significant development in July 1989, Charles Haughey led *Fianna Fáil into its first-ever coalition, with the Progressive Democrats; the coalition survived the succession of Albert Reynolds to the Fianna Fáil leadership in February 1992, but deteriorating relations between the parties led to its collapse later that year. Following the election of December 1992, a Fianna Fáil–Labour coalition was formed in January 1993, but interparty suspicions culminated in the fall of the government following a dispute regarding the extradition to Northern Ireland of a Catholic priest accused of sexual offences. It was replaced in January 1995 by a three-party coalition of Fine Gael, Labour, and Democratic Left, headed by the Fine Gael leader John Bruton. This was a significant landmark, the first occasion on which the European model of coalition formation without a general election was followed. JC

Invincibles, an extremist society of *Fenian background devoted to political assassination. The Dublin section, organized in November 1881 by James Carey, David Curley, James Mullett, and Edward McCaffrey, carried out the *Phoenix Park murders, atrocities which provoked a very intensive police investigation. By July 1882 Carey was identified as a prime suspect and within seven months the Dublin group was smashed. Carey's evidence, with that of others, helped to hang five of his comrades and imprison eight others. Freed for betraying his accomplices, Carey was later shot dead by Patrick Donnell, whom he had met on board ship to Cape Town. JL

Iona, a small island off the western tip of the Isle of Mull in western Scotland, was the location of St *Colum Cille's principal monastic foundation. Established in 563 it remained the centre of the Columban family of churches until the early 9th century. Iona played an important part in the Christianization of the Pictish kingdom in eastern Scotland. In the early 7th century it provided a retreat for exiled Northumbrian royalty and thereby became the instrument for introducing Irish clergy into England under Abbot Ségéne (623–52). After the synod at *Whitby in 664 the Iona clergy withdrew from Northumbria, though under Abbot Adomnán (679–704) there may have been hopes of a return, and in 717 they were expelled from Pictland. During the 8th century, therefore, Iona was more involved with affairs in Ireland than with Britain, though its annals continue to take a close interest in Scottish matters. In this period it flourished as a centre for manuscript art, stone sculpture, and metalwork. Exposure to Scandinavian raids from 795 (see VIKINGS) may have played a part in reducing the importance of Iona within the Columban community, but the migration of the *coarb of Colum Cille to Kells in 812 has more to do with increasing links with the southern *Uí Néill. After the martyrdom of Bláthmac in Iona in 825, the island monastery declined into obscurity. RS

IRA, see IRISH REPUBLICAN ARMY.

IRB, see IRISH REPUBLICAN BROTHERHOOD.

Ireland, names for. The commonest name for 'Ireland' is Old Irish *Ériú*, Modern *Éire*, which may mean 'fertile country' (<Indo-European [*]*Piweriya-*, compare Greek *Pieria*). The dative *Éirinn* (Anglicized 'Erin') is the origin of 'Ierne' of classical geographers and, by contamination with *hibernus*, 'wintry', of Latin *Hibernia*. The stem *Ériu* is also the origin of the first element in English 'Ireland'.

Other early names for Ireland include *Banba*, *Elg(a)*, and *Fótla*. The first is possibly a reflex of earlier [*]*Bannomagos* ('the plain small heights, Meath') used for the whole country. The others, of uncertain origin, are probably divine names. All four were taken by colonists to Scotland, where they are attested in toponyms, e.g. Strathearn <*Srath Éireann*, Banff <*Banbha*, Eilgin <*Elg*, and Atholl <*Athfhótla* or 'New Fótla'). Ireland was sometimes known in Latin sources as Scotia. This name, based on Scot(t)i, a name for the Goidels (cf. O. Ir. *scuchaid*, 'moves'), was later applied exclusively to Scotland. Roderic O'Flaherty (1629–1718) used an obscure Greek toponym as a name for Ireland in the title of his work *The Ogygia Vindicated*.

In bardic poetry Ireland is frequently referred to by kennings, e.g. *Clár Coinn* ('plain of Conn'), *Gort Gaedheal* ('field of the Gaels'). Particularly important in this connection was the name of the stone at *Tara, the *Fál* or *Lia Fáil*, which was believed to scream beneath the true king. Ireland was often known as *Fál* or *Inis Fáil* ('island of Fál'). Geoffrey *Keating calls the *Lia Fáil* the *saxum* *fatale* ('stone of destiny'), an unwarranted translation, which persists in the mistaken notion that *Fianna Fáil, literally 'war-bands of Ireland', means 'soldiers of destiny'.

In later poetry Ireland is often personified as a young woman who awaits her rightful husband. This is the origin of such names as *Caitlín Ní Uallacháin* and *Mo Róisín Dubh*. The latter, a title of a patriotic song, was rendered into English by James Clarence Mangan as 'My Dark Rosaleen'.

See also ÉRAINN. NJAW

Ireland Act (1949), the British government's response to Ireland's departure from the *Commonwealth. Special citizenship status and trade preferences were maintained but the act also declared 'that in no event will Northern Ireland or any part thereof cease to be part . . . of the United Kingdom without the consent of the Parliament of Northern Ireland'. This guarantee, unwelcome in Dublin, was attributed to British resentment at the lack of consultation over the sudden decision to leave the Commonwealth. DMcM

Ireton, Henry (1611–51), *lord deputy and commander of the New Model Army after his father-in-law Oliver *Cromwell left Ireland in May 1650. Ireton continued the conquest, taking control, in quick succession, of Carlow, Waterford, and Duncannon fort (which commanded the sea approach to Waterford). His greatest success was capturing Limerick. After an abortive two-month siege in 1650, Ireton took outlying forts the following year and commenced a naval blockade and military encirclement to starve the city into submission. He played on Limerick's peace and war factions until a bombardment targeted on a weak section of the walls eventually brought submission in October. A military tribunal ignored Ireton's wishes by refusing to execute Hugh Dubh O'Neill and the other defiant leaders. Ireton had also gained a reputation for cheap and speedy justice in his other role as *provincial president of Munster. He died in Limerick, of the plague raging within the city, within a month of having captured it. HM

Irish Agricultural Organization Society (IAOS), set up in Dublin in 1894 to propagate the idea of *co-operative organization among Irish farmers and to co-ordinate the activities of existing co-operative societies. The prime mover was an Irish unionist, Sir Horace *Plunkett. In his view Irish agriculture faced a dire threat in the form of competition in its traditional British export markets from foreign producers. Co-operative action on the part of farmers was the means to meet this competition and to better living conditions on the land. Since 1894, and without interruption (other than a name change to the Irish Co-operative Organization Society in more recent times), the IAOS has served as the central organization for rural co-operatives, making representations to government and other public bodies on their behalf. It has also worked to promote reform within the co-operative sector. From the 1950s in particular it sought to accelerate the process of consolidating small, inefficient societies into larger, more viable organizations. These efforts were attended by mixed success, though it is fair to add that throughout most of its history the central organization has been poorly supported financially by co-operative societies affiliated to the IAOS. This has meant dependence on state subsidies for its day-to-day operations, an anomalous position for a voluntary society devoted to the principle of self-help. LK

Irish ague, a disease reported as affecting both natives and foreigners in the 16th and 17th centuries. Gerard *Boate, in 1652, described it as 'commonly accompanied with a great pain in the head and in all the bones, great weakness, drought, loss of all manner of appetite and want of sleep and for the most part idleness or raving and restlessness or tossings but no very great or constant heat' and as 'hard to be cured'. One suggestion is that it was typhus, but malaria is also a possibility, since the country had more *bogs than today. HM

Irish Amateur Athletic Association (IAAA), founded in 1885 to regulate and organize athletics in Ireland. Some Irish clubs had already affiliated to the English Association, and the *Gaelic Athletic Association had been formed the previous year. Athletics was already the most popular spectator sport in Ireland. Regular local meetings were well established and Irish championships had been held in 1873. From 1885–6 the GAA and IAAA barred their affiliated athletes from participating in each other's meetings. After a period of constrained hostility, from which the IAAA emerged in the ascendant, the two bodies embarked from 1895 on a decade of co-operation, in which joint record committees were established, and bans enforced. This ended in 1906, following the GAA's establishment the previous year of its own Athletics Council. The GAA was by now clearly identified as a militant nationalist organization, while the IAAA was portrayed as unpatriotic. In 1913 the GAA's Athletics Council was reorganized, and all-Ireland championships were established under its auspices. *Partition and independence led to a split in Irish athletics. In the south the IAAA was replaced by the National Athletics and Cycling Association, in *Northern Ireland by an Amateur Athletics Association of Ireland, succeeded from 1931 by the

Northern Ireland Amateur Athletics Association. It was not until 1967 that the Irish Athletics Board was founded to organize international athletics in the Republic. NG

Irish-American nationalism, a product of the Irish emigrant experience from the 1840s, shaped by national identity, nostalgia, Anglophobia, and social rejection in a new homeland. Between 1845 and 1891 3 million Irish arrived in the country. By the 20th century Irish-American propagandists spoke of their community in general as numbering 20 million. The concentration of this large and growing population in the great urban centres of Pennsylvania, New York, New Jersey, and New England facilitated the maximization from the late 19th century of Irish-American influence. The Irish-American press became powerful and Irish-Americans came to dominate the Democratic Party. They not only supported a large number of Irish dependants but produced a variety of extreme and moderate organizations dedicated to the achievement of Irish independence. In the pursuit of this objective Irish-Americans were to contribute significantly to American Anglophobia and profoundly to influence Anglo-American relations.

The *famine experience encouraged a tendency to explain mass emigration to America largely in terms of English oppression. This alone would have ensured that Irish-American nationalism was a significant political force. But its growth was powerfully reinforced by the reception Irish immigrants received from a hostile Protestant host community. Nativism enhanced the Irish-American sense of being Irish and fed the idea that the fulfilment of their self-respect as a community was dependent on the achievement of Irish independence. The conditions of existence in a hostile environment also encouraged the development of a large number of Irish-American fraternal, religious, sporting, political, and benevolent societies. The interests of these bodies were addressed by three main groups: the Catholic clergy, Irish-American politicians, and Irish nationalists. The latter two groups, not always with identical interests, shaped the political development of the Irish-American community. The former, concerned as much with the integration of their community into American society as with the Irish question, found that the American nativist strain of Anglophobia offered a means of mitigating, to some extent, the effects of anti-immigrant sentiment, while at the same time serving the cause of Irish liberation.

Irish-American nationalism displayed its vibrancy in the plethora of organizations it threw up as each stage of the Irish struggle developed, from *O'Connellism, through *Fenianism, *home rule nationalism, the Gaelic revival, and *Sinn Féin to the Irish war of independence and after. Both kinds of Irish struggle, the militant and the constitutional, received influential support, especially financial backing, from the Irish-American community. But until the development of a mass struggle for an Irish republic after 1916, which brought a united Irish-American response in support, constitutional movements such as Parnell's in the 1880s tended to appeal to a wider section of the Irish-American community than did physical force groups dedicated to bombing outrages.

To its direct influence on Irish and British politics can be added the way in which the Irish-American lobby in the USA was able to damage English interests through its impact on American government policies, and especially in defining the parameters beyond which American foreign policy could not go. For example, it effectively inhibited Anglo-American co-operation on arbitration treaties in the period 1897–1911, and more generally during the *First World War; while British acceptance of Irish-American political influence was an important factor in eventually persuading them that the Irish question would have to be settled. With the *Anglo-Irish treaty of 1921, Irish-American influence as a political force substantially diminished. The history of the *Northern Ireland conflict since 1969, however, has demonstrated how deep-seated, resilient, and politically exploitable the sentiments that have shaped Irish-American thinking since the 1840s can be.

Brown, Thomas N., *Irish-American Nationalism 1870–1890* (1966)

Carroll, Francis M., *American Opinion and the Irish Question 1910–1923: A Study in Opinion and Policy* (1978)

Ward, Alan J., *Ireland and Anglo-American Relations 1899–1921* (1969)

JL

Irish brigade. The original 'Irish Brigade' comprised regiments in the service of France after 1691 (see FOREIGN ARMIES, IRISH IN). A variety of later ventures sought to capitalize on this romanticized tradition. Irish brigades fought for the pope in the era of *Italian unification, on both sides during the *American Civil War, and for the *Boers. During the *First World War, Roger *Casement attempted to form an Irish brigade from prisoners of war in Germany. Eoin *O'Duffy led an Irish brigade which fought for Franco in the *Spanish Civil War. During the *Second World War *Churchill, much to the chagrin of the Northern Ireland government, formed an Irish brigade which fought with distinction in North Africa and Italy. Away from the battlefield, the title was also appropriated, in the early 1850s, by Irish opponents of the *ecclesiastical titles bill. HM

Irish Citizen Army (ICA), set up by the *Irish Transport and General Workers' Union (ITGWU) to protect demonstrating workers and pickets from the often violent attentions of the *Dublin Metropolitan Police during the 1913 *Dublin lockout. This was a few weeks before the foundation meeting of the *Irish Volunteers. Drilling began at the union's retreat at Croydon Park, conducted by Capt. Jack *White. In 1914 James *Connolly, now union acting general secretary, became ICA commandant. The ICA was the first ever socialist militia and the bulk of its *c.*350 members were union members. It was also dedicated to Irish self-determination. The ITGWU HQ, *Liberty Hall, became the centre of ICA activity and its arsenal. Michael Mallin was appointed chief of staff. The ICA made joint preparations, with the military council of the *Irish Republican Brotherhood, for the *rising of 1916. Although much smaller than the Volunteers, it played a crucial role in Easter week. Connolly was commandant-general of the insurgents' Dublin Division. Sean Connolly of the ICA was the first insurgent casualty. Mallin and James Connolly were executed after the rising. ICA lieutenant Countess *Markievicz was sentenced to death, later commuted to life imprisonment. Other ICA insurgents, along with many ITGWU members, were interned in Britain. PC

Irish Civil War (1922–3), fought between two factions of the *republican movement over the acceptance of the *Anglo-Irish treaty. Although widely supported by the population, the treaty split *Sinn Féin and the *IRA. The pro-treaty side dominated the political arena and established the *Provisional Government, while the majority of the IRA went anti-treaty and became known as the Irregulars. The latter included the most experienced and numerically strongest units from the south-west and Dublin. The factionalism and local independence which had developed in the *Anglo-Irish War allowed individual units to go against the decision of the politicians and their own central leadership regarding the treaty. The long stand-off which followed its signing gave invaluable time to the *Provisional Government under Michael *Collins to set up an army with the aid of the British government, undermining the initial numerical superiority of the Irregulars.

Hostilities finally broke out on 28 June 1922 when government troops attacked the headquarters of the Irregulars in the *Four Courts building. The factionalism of the Irregulars seriously affected their success on the battlefield. Due to a lack of co-ordination their opponents were able to take out their strongholds one by one. Fighting in Dublin was over in less than two weeks, and by August the pro-treaty side had taken control of all the urban areas. The Irregulars then reverted to the guerrilla tactics employed during the Anglo-Irish War, but despite some initial successes they were virtually defeated by December. The stringent measures taken by the government, including large-scale *internment and the introduction in September of the death penalty for those found in possession of arms, played a major part in this process. However, an end to the hostilities became possible only after the death of Liam *Lynch, the irreconcilable chief of staff of the Irregulars. His successor Frank *Aiken called a unilateral ceasefire on 30 April 1923, and on 24 May 1923 the IRA ordered its men to dump their arms and wait for another day.

Although the fighting now stopped there was no negotiated peace and consequently the Civil War was never officially ended. Recent research has revealed that the Civil War was not as bloody as previously thought. After a summer of heavy fighting, the number of casualties dropped sharply, leaving a total of 927 people dead by June 1923, including 77 executed by the government. Nevertheless, the depth of the divisions left a lasting legacy on the Irish political scene.

In historiography the Civil War has long been treated as the consequence of the actions of individuals, or alternatively as an inevitable result of the independence struggle which had brought a disparate group of people together. Both the inevitability of the Civil War and the crucial role of individuals in its making are now slowly being contested, but the legacy of the conflict is still so divisive that historical research remains far behind that into the Anglo-Irish War.

Kissane, Bill, *The Politics of the Irish Civil War* (2005)
Garvin, Tom, *1922: The Birth of Irish Democracy* (1996)
Hopkinson, Michael, *Green against Green: The Irish Civil War* (1988)

JA

Irish colleges, the continental *seminaries, founded in the wake of the Council of *Trent, which trained the Catholic clerical elite in the 17th and 18th centuries.

The first Irish college was founded with Philip II's encouragement at Salamanca in 1592 by the Jesuit Thomas White. A similar college was founded in Lisbon the following year. In 1611 there were twelve Irish colleges in Spain, France, and the Low Countries; by 1690 there were 30 colleges throughout the Continent.

Many colleges were run by religious orders. The *Dominicans, Capuchins, *Augustinians, and *Carmelites all had colleges, but the *Franciscans and *Jesuits played the leading role. The Franciscan college of St Anthony's, Louvain, which cut a font for printing in Irish in 1611 and became famous for its devotional publications, was the most politicized. Jesuit colleges were accused of picking the brightest students and, even where they were not in control, their famous *ratio studiorum* influenced the courses of logic, philosophy, and theology on offer.

Ireland's regional and ethnic problems were prominently exhibited amongst staff and students. Salamanca was accused of favouring Munster students and denying places to Ulster and Connacht. Despite the advent of St Anthony's, Louvain, Leinster kept a strong grip on the Low Country establishments. There was trouble between students at Douai, Antwerp, Bordeaux, and St Isidore's in Rome. These regional biases were accentuated by endowments specifying sponsorship of students from particular parishes or dioceses.

Long-term finance was problematic. Colleges in Spanish realms had grants from the crown or local universities and occasionally received contributions from municipalities, local alms, and Irish regiments. However, the financial difficulties of the Spanish monarchy in the 17th century hit the colleges hard, especially in the Low Countries. The establishment of the *Irish brigade in France's army, and the presence of a rich expatriate merchant community, ensured that the French colleges were reasonably well endowed after 1691.

Under Tridentine rules priests needed dismissorial letters from diocesan colleges signed by the ordaining local bishop to get a parish. This was impossible with priests educated abroad. By 1600 40 priests were returning home each year. In 1623 college superiors were given permission to ordain clergy, which led to complaints from Irish bishops. After the *Restoration many priests were ordained in Ireland on condition of going to the Continent for further education. Their resort led to the foundation of a second Paris college (1677) and another at Nantes (1689).

Circumstances conspired against the Irish colleges in the late 18th century. In 1764 and 1767 the Jesuits were expelled from France and Spain and in 1773 the pope himself suppressed the order. French colleges survived the first religious dissolutions of the *French Revolution only to find themselves suppressed in 1793. *Maynooth was founded as a counter-revolutionary alternative in 1795.

Today Paris's Irish College is available to visiting academics and students; St Anthony's, Louvain, is a conference centre for Irish businessmen and policy-makers in the *European Union; only the Roman college still operates as a seminary.

Walsh, T. J., *The Irish Continental College Movement* (1973)

HM

Irish Confederation, established 13 January 1847 by the *Young Irelanders who had seceded from the *Repeal Association. Smith *O'Brien hoped to work for the reform of the association and eventual reunion, but in practice the split within the nationalist movement was formalized. The confederate clubs emerged from summer 1847 to defend confederation meetings from O'Connellite attacks; they spread in Irish cities and larger towns and amongst the Irish immigrant communities in Britain, and became the focus of militancy within the movement, but made little impact in the countryside. In early 1848 the confederation split as John *Mitchel and his associates resigned in protest at the social conservatism of O'Brien and *Duffy. The French revolution of February 1848 encouraged the Young Irelanders to agree on the desirability of a rising, but divisions over strategy continued. In July the confederation reunited with the O'Connellites in the abortive Irish League, while at the same time forming a secret war council to plan a rebellion. The clubs were suppressed by government proclamation on 26 July, just before the abortive *rebellion of 1848. PHG

Irish Congress of Trade Unions. An Irish Trade Union Congress was established in 1894. Following the decision in 1912 to create a political party it became the Irish Trade Union Congress and Labour Party, changed in 1918 to the Irish Labour Party and Trade Union Congress, and then reverted in 1930, following the separation of party and congress, to Irish Trade Union Congress.

Even after 1922 British-based unions (colloquially referred to as 'amalgamated unions') continued to account for a large proportion of Irish union membership. In 1944 these affiliated 108,000 members to congress, compared to 80,000 for Irish-based unions. William *O'Brien of the *Irish Transport and General Workers' Union had already made clear his opposition to the influence of the British-based unions, taking particular exception to the challenge to the ITGWU of the Amalgamated Transport and General Workers' Union, established in 1921. In 1945 he led the secession of ten unions which joined with other, non-affiliated unions to form the Congress of Irish Unions. In 1959 the rival movements united as the Irish Congress of Trade Unions.

Irish Convention (25 July 1917–5 Apr. 1918), one of several attempts by *Lloyd George to improvise an Irish settlement as the *Nationalist Party lost ground to *Sinn Féin in the aftermath of the *rising of 1916. Over 100 delegates, representing different parties, met under the chairmanship of Sir Horace *Plunkett. The main outcome was the assent of both nationalists and southern *unionists to a scheme for immediate domestic self-government, although the two groups were unable to agree on whether this should include fiscal autonomy. But the opposition of Sinn Féin, which boycotted the convention, and of the Ulster unionists, who demanded the exclusion of six or nine counties from any proposed Irish legislature, condemned the proceedings to irrelevance.

Irish council bill (1907), an unsuccessful attempt at administrative *home rule. The Conservative government had disclaimed Sir Antony *MacDonnell's ideas during the *devolution crisis of 1904–5, but in 1906 the incoming Liberals seized on them as a possible way of placating their Nationalist allies without becoming ensnared in a home rule crisis. MacDonnell and *Chief Secretary James *Bryce hoped that a modest version of the scheme might pass the House of Lords. Under Bryce's successor Augustine *Birrell, in 1907, there was more consultation with the Nationalist leaders, and the proposed assembly became more powerful and representative. But on publication the bill was attacked as inadequate by rank and file Nationalists, and by priests who were concerned at the loss of clerical control over education. The Nationalist leaders, who had privately been inclined to accept the measure in principle and press for amendments, thus denounced it at a national convention on 21 May. It was withdrawn without a second reading, and the idea of governmental reform in Ireland short of home rule was abandoned. ACH

Irish Countrywomen's Association, set up as the United Irishwomen by Anita Lett in Bree, Co. Wexford, in 1911. Early patrons included Horace *Plunkett and Ellice Pilkington. The association saw as its mission the reform of Irish society through the improved home lives of its rural people. It became the Irish Countrywomen's Association in 1935, affiliated to the International Countrywomen. Its interests ranged from the promotion of health and hygiene to the preservation of local traditions, and from poultry-keeping to public speaking. It called, as early as 1940, for rural houses to be connected to electrical and water supplies as a convenience for women, and was a prime mover in the subsequent drive for both. A 'countrywoman' was defined as a woman of any age or class who lived in the country or in a town of less than 3,000 people. The ICA, in its evidence to the *Commission on Vocational Organization in 1940, argued that countrywomen needed to be represented on the proposed vocational committee as both producers and consumers. Total membership in 1940 was 2,442 but it soared in the 1950s and 1960s and has remained buoyant since. CC

Irish diaspora. Diaspora is a concept that during the 1990s became fashionable in world history and in the specific Irish context as well. Indications of each of these phenomena are: that in 1995 the International Congress of Historical Sciences denominated 'Peoples in Diaspora' as one of the three central themes of historical research for the 1990s; and, in her inaugural speech as president of Ireland in December 1990, Mary Robinson articulated a concern with the Irish diaspora, one which remained a major theme of her presidency.

'Diaspora' comes from the Greek word for 'dispersal'. Its primary reference until the later 20th century was to the diaspora of the ancient Israelites and their descendants, the Jewish people. The term came to be used during the 1970s by historians of peoples whose historical origin was Africa. It also became common currency among Armenian historians. Thence it spread to almost every group that has had a history of widespread out-migration. Political scientists tend to limit the term to groups who are minorities (frequently refugee minorities) in larger polities and who identify more with their former homelands than with their new homes. Historians, however, have not limited the concept in that way.

Whether the concept will replace the older one of *'emigration' in the context of Irish history is uncertain. 'Diaspora' has the advantage of removing the Irish homeland as the metropole through which all Irish dispersal must be apprehended. Unlike emigration, 'diaspora' permits a multigenerational study of the dispersal of Irish culture around the world. On the other hand, if it becomes simply another word for 'out-migration', then nothing is gained.

Akenson, D. H., *The Irish Diaspora: A Primer* (1993)

DHA

Irish Folklore Commission, a state-funded body established in 1935. It collected material on popular custom, tradition, and belief, using full- and part-time collectors throughout the country. A representative sample of its work may be found in the journal *Bealoideas* (1927–). The commission was disbanded in 1971, but its work is carried on by the Department of Irish Folklore at University College, Dublin, where its archives are housed.

Irish Free State, the first name of the Irish state 1922–37. It was suggested by Arthur *Griffith to Lord Birkenhead during the negotiation of the *Anglo-Irish treaty.

The treaty gave Ireland the same constitutional status as Canada, Australia, New Zealand, and South Africa. The Free State's relationship with the imperial parliament was governed by Canadian law and usage, but this relationship rested on very different historical and geographical factors and created tensions in Irish policy. The Free State government was determined to assert its autonomy. In 1924 it issued its own *passports, registered the treaty as an international agreement with the *League of Nations, and appointed an Irish minister to the USA, the first dominion representative to be accredited to a foreign state. It also worked, in collaboration with other dominions, to enhance its status within the *Commonwealth, contributing significantly to the enhancement of dominion status achieved in the Balfour declaration (1926) and the Statute of *Westminster.

In the 1937 *constitution the title 'Irish Free State' was superseded by 'Éire (Ireland)', though it continues to be used, often with derisive connotations, by both unionists and republicans to refer to the southern Irish state. DMcM

'Irish Fright' (Dec. 1688), a mass panic in England caused by reports of imminent pillage and massacre by Irish Catholic soldiers brought over to support *James II's crumbling regime, and now left leaderless following his flight. The panic, beginning in London on 13 December and spreading over six days or more to at least nineteen counties, led to attacks on real or suspected Catholics and the hasty assembly of armed parties.

Irish Historical Studies (1938–), the leading Irish historical periodical, published jointly by the Ulster Society for Irish Historical Studies and the Irish Historical Society. Its founders were T. W. Moody (1907–84), from 1939 professor of modern history at *Trinity College, Dublin, and Robert Dudley Edwards (1909–88), from 1944 professor of modern Irish history at University College, Dublin. Both were concerned to promote rigorous, source-based historical writing of the kind practised at the University of London's Institute of Historical Research, where they had worked as research students. Though recognized as a landmark in the professionalization of Irish history, the journal was to be criticized for its rather narrow concentration, continuing up to the 1970s, on political and constitutional history. More recently some critics have argued that the tone of dispassionate neutrality it established amounted to a form of self-censorship, in which themes of oppression and exploitation were evaded or unjustifiably minimized.

Irish Hospitals Sweepstake, a lottery on major horse races held three times a year, between 1930 and 1986, the proceeds of which went to selected Irish *hospitals. It was initiated by a group of small Dublin voluntary hospitals and legalized by the government in 1930, with the provision that a portion of the proceeds also went to local authority hospitals. The 201 sweeps held raised nearly IR£134 million and permitted a major hospital-building programme between the 1930s and the 1950s. The sweep also allowed many small hospitals, which might not otherwise have been financially viable, to survive into the 1980s. ELM

Irish Industrial Development Association, (IIDA), an informal federation of local industrial development associations. The first was established in *Cork in 1903; others subsequently emerged in major towns and cities such as *Belfast, *Dublin, *Galway, and *Derry. In 1906 the IIDA registered an Irish national trade mark, consisting of a Celtic motif inside a circle that contained the words *Déanta in Éirinn* (made in Ireland); by 1920 there were over 700 licensed users. The association sought to make Irish manufacturers aware of the value of advertising and of the importance of producing high-quality goods. It also tried to encourage shopkeepers, wholesalers, and commercial travellers to stock Irish-made goods; it collected data on Irish trade and lobbied for direct shipping links between Ireland and foreign countries. Although the organization was part of the Irish-Ireland movement (see MORAN, DAVID PATRICK), it drew support from some Ulster manufacturers, notably the Belfast cigarette-manufacturing firm of Gallaher's. MED

Irish language. Irish and its offshoots, Scottish Gaelic and Manx, constitute the Gaelic or Goidelic branch of the Celtic languages. Welsh, Cornish, and Breton form the Brythonic or Brittonic group. The extinct languages of the *Celts of mainland Europe are known collectively as Continental Celtic. It was once assumed that Brythonic and the Celtic of Gaul formed a unity separate from Goidelic. More recent research suggests that Goidelic and Brythonic have much in common and that the two branches shared a common prehistory as Insular Celtic.

Apart from geographical names in classical authors our earliest evidence for Irish is to be found in *ogam inscriptions. These are written in a script consisting of horizontal and diagonal lines and exhibit an archaic form of the language. When the Latin alphabet was introduced by Christian missionaries the history of Irish proper begins. The language is usually divided into the following periods: Old Irish AD *c*.650–*c*.900, Middle Irish *c*.900–*c*.1200, Early Modern Irish *c*.1200–*c*.1600, Modern Irish *c*.1600–.

In the pre-Old Irish period inherited unstressed syllables were shortened and in many cases lost altogether. As a result consonantal quality became an essential part of the language. In Irish consonants are either pronounced with lip rounding and velar articulation or with spread lips and palatal articulation (cf. the hard/soft difference in Russian). This opposition survives in full vigour into the modern period. Since Irish uses the roman alphabet or variations of it, the broad–slender distinction can be indicated in writing only by using vowels. It is for this reason that contemporary Irish orthography presents unusual collocations of vowels, for example in *tuíodóireacht* 'thatching', *deartháireacha* 'brothers'.

Another consequence of the loss of unstressed syllables was the emergence of the system of initial mutation. The tendency was probably already present in Insular Celtic, since a similar series of phenomena is attested in Brythonic. In Irish initial mutation means that the first consonant of a word can change according to grammatical function. Initial mutation also continues into the modern language where the initial consonant of *bó* ('cow'), for example, is lenited to bh (pronounced as v or w) after the definite article (*an bhó*, 'the cow'), and is nasalized to mb (pronounced m) in *leis an mbó* ('with the cow').

From the Old Irish period until the 13th century the language underwent a prolonged period of regularization and simplification. Among the more important changes one could cite the loss of the neuter gender and analogical reshaping of the verbal and pronominal systems. In early Irish 'he seized me' is rendered by *rom-gab* where *ro* is a preverbal particle, *gab* is the verb, and *m* is an infixed object pronoun. By the 13th century this has become *do ghabh sé mé*, where *do* is the particle, *ghabh* the verb, *sé* the subject pronoun, and *mé* the object pronoun.

Although they had existed in the language since earliest times, dialects do not come into view to any degree until the 17th century. This is because the literary standard language was common to the entire Gaelic-speaking area. With the collapse of the *bardic schools, however, writers began to use spoken rather than literary forms. Using such forms, *place names, and Irish words surviving in Hiberno-English, it is possible to deduce something about the dialects spoken throughout Ireland.

It seems that there were essentially three main dialects. The Ulster dialect was spoken north and east of a line drawn from Leitrim to the Boyne valley. The centre of this dialect was probably Inishowen and Co. Londonderry. The southern dialect was spoken in Munster, southern Clare, Kilkenny, and part of Co. Laois. The epicentre of this dialect was the territory of the *Eóganachta. A third dialect, 'Galeonic Irish', was spoken in Connacht, in Westmeath and south Longford, across to Dublin and south to Wexford.

The position of the accent and concomitant weakening of syllables were the chief distinguishing features of the three dialects. In Old Irish word-stress was generally upon the initial syllable. The word *scadán*, 'herring', for example, is or was pronounced as *SCADan* in the north, as *scuDAN* in Munster, but as *SCUdán* (with a weakened but stressed first syllable and a long unstressed syllable) in the Galeonic area. Although the surviving dialects in Ulster, Connacht, and Munster conform to this pattern of stress, in other ways all three forms of speech are somewhat atypical of the Irish spoken elsewhere in Ireland.

Irish and indeed the Gaelic languages in general are very unlike other European languages in syntax and idiom. Irish lacks any single word for 'yes' or 'no', the question being repeated instead. Thus the answer to 'Did you see him?' is either *Chonaic* ('[I] saw') or *Ní fhaca* ('[I] did not see'). Irish does not emphasize by use of intonation but by bringing the item to be emphasized to the head of its clause after the copula (one of the two verbs 'to be'): 'I don't live in Dublin any more' is rendered *Ní i mBaile Átha Cliath atá cónaí orm a thuilleadh* (lit. 'It is not in Dublin that dwelling is on-me any more'). Similarly 'Do you want a stamp?' is *An stampa atá uait?*, literally 'Is it a stamp that is from-you?' Many Irish idioms survive in Hiberno-English, ' 'Tis true for you', 'Not a bother on me', etc.

Although Irish was not much cultivated during the 19th century, its status as an official language since 1922 has helped to modernize it. All writers now employ the *Caighdeán Oifigiúil* or Official Standard, a regularized spelling and grammar developed by the translation staff of the *Oireachtas. The terminological committees of the Department of Education have over the years provided speakers of Irish with technical vocabulary in a wide range of subjects. The Gaeltacht radio service, Raidió na Gaeltachta, has disseminated much modern terminology as well as familiarizing native speakers with dialects other than their own.

See also LANGUAGE.

Greene, D., *The Irish language/An Ghaeilge* (1966)
Ó Cuív, B., *Irish Dialects and Irish-Speaking Districts* (1951)
Ó Murchú, M., *The Irish Language* (1985)

NJAW

Irish Legion, established in August 1803, under the command of Bernard MacSheehy, as a force recruited among *United Irish exiles to prepare for a possible invasion of Ireland by Napoleonic France (see REVOLUTIONARY AND NAPOLEONIC WARS). Over time, though still commanded mainly by Irishmen, it became a multinational force, increasingly integrated into the French army. It was disbanded in 1815, following the restoration of the French monarchy.

Irish (National) Volunteers, a militia founded 25 November 1913 at the Rotunda in Dublin, often seen as a direct response to an article by Eoin *MacNeill in the *Gaelic League paper **Claidheamh Soluis*. In this article nationalists were called upon to arm themselves in defence of *home rule as the *Ulster Volunteer Force had done to prevent home rule the year before. Although branches were set up throughout the country, the initial response was strongest in the north. A heavy *IRB involvement in the foundation of the force made John *Redmond, leader of the *Nationalist Party, hesitant to support it. However, after he was allowed to nominate half the seats on the organizing provisional committee in June 1914, he gave his assent. Subsequently Volunteer membership rose to about 160,000.

With the start of the *First World War the movement split when Redmond called upon all Irishmen to support the British war effort. Redmond's supporters broke away with the bulk of the Volunteers and formed the *National Volunteers. The radical nationalists in the Irish Volunteers were left with only a skeleton organization of about 2,000–3,000 members. They slowly reorganized until they comprised about 15,000 men by 1916. Against the will of Eoin MacNeill, the chief of staff, an IRB-led section of the organization had begun to plan an uprising, which became the *rising of 1916. JA

Irish News Agency. Established in 1949 by Sean *MacBride with a government grant of £82,000, the agency's purpose was to channel Irish news worldwide, particularly on the issue of *partition. Although de *Valera had supported the possibilities of such an agency, an Irish News Agency run by MacBride was anathema to him and to *Fianna Fáil. The first managing director, Conor Cruise O'Brien, brought together a group of astute journalists. However, the technical limitations of the agency, and its public image as a government propaganda vehicle, made foreign news editors unwilling to buy its material. It closed in 1957.

M-LL

Irish parliamentary party, see NATIONALIST PARTY.

Irish Press, a Dublin daily newspaper founded in 1931 by Eamon de *Valera, with American funds, to provide a platform for *Fianna Fáil. Its editorial policy was always closely controlled by the de Valera family. It was addressed to lower middle-class workers and made a special appeal to women. Its Irish-language section gave it national appeal and it provided the first full coverage of Gaelic games. In the 1980s the paper was increasingly badly managed. An award for damages and compensation that could not be met, and a dispute with its journalists, led to the paper's closure in 1995.

M-LL

Irish Record Commission, established in 1810, modelled on the British Record Commission, to examine the surviving official records in Dublin government offices and archival repositories and to improve their housing, calendaring, and indexing. The repositories in question were the Birmingham tower, rolls office, chief remembrancer's office, auditor-general's office, and parliamentary record office. The work of the commission was hampered by lack of consultation between repositories, the inexperience of some transcribers, and the decision to prepare calendars for publication before documents were fully sorted. The commission dealt with patent rolls, *acta regia*, *chancery and *exchequer, *inquisitions and decrees, plea rolls, *fiants, *memoranda rolls of exchequer, statutes, parliamentary records, and regal visitation books. After the commission's patent was revoked in 1830, the unpublished calendars and transcripts which had been produced lay largely unused in Dublin Castle until 1922 when the loss of many of the original documents (see PUBLIC RECORDS) gave them a value which had not been anticipated. Most IRC files are now in the National Archives, Dublin, with the remainder in the National University of Ireland, Maynooth. BC

Irish Republican Army (IRA). The *rising of 1916 left the *Irish Volunteers in disarray. However, the organization was quickly re-established on a wave of popular support, due to the events surrounding the rising and a fear of conscription. The new leadership did not envisage starting another uprising for the time being. At their first post-rising convention in October 1917 it was determined that the Volunteers were primarily to be used to exert political pressure on the British government to recognize the Irish Republic. For this aim the Volunteers were to arm, train, and organize. However, the public drilling exercises which started at the end of 1917, particularly in the south-west, brought them into conflict with the authorities. The increasingly harsh measures taken by the government during 1918 drove the organization underground. The concurrent success of the politicians in *Sinn Féin made the militarists in the Volunteers feel left out, and, without the sanction of their leadership, they began to take increasingly violent action which slowly led to the start of the *Anglo-Irish War.

After the foundation of *Dáil Éireann in January 1919 the organization became increasingly known as the Irish Republican Army, but also retained the name Irish Volunteers. This highlighted the ambivalent relationship between individual Volunteer units and their military and political leadership. Although now officially the army of the Republic, Volunteers never fully accepted the central power of their GHQ, established only in March 1918, or the political control of the Dáil government, despite swearing an oath of allegiance to it.

The Volunteers/IRA were unevenly distributed over the country. They attracted the largest membership in the west, closely followed by Munster. Membership was limited in the more prosperous east, and extremely low in Ulster, where the Volunteers were a largely marginal organization concentrated in a few small areas. Membership was young, aged mainly between 20 and 30, and overwhelmingly Catholic. Volunteers were broadly representative of Irish Catholic male society, coming from most sectors of the working and middle classes, although rarely from the upper middle or upper classes, and few were unemployed or indigent. Officers tended to be older, more urban based, and of a higher status—better educated, more skilled, and financially better off. In Dublin the majority of officers and men had working-class backgrounds. There are clear changes in the composition of membership after the fighting started. The average age of Volunteers decreased, and in the most active areas the rank and file became more working class and urban, while officers became more middle class. The difference in backgrounds which had existed between areas in the early period largely disappeared in 1920–1.

Losing the *Civil War, which followed the signing of the *Anglo-Irish treaty of 1921, showed the IRA that for the moment it could not achieve its objective through a military confrontation. However, neither did it accept the legitimacy of the *Irish Free State or of Northern Ireland, nor did it hand in its arms. All it could do now was to try to maintain the organization and mobilize support through Sinn Féin, but the 1916–22 period left it with a difficult legacy. Abstention had become the benchmark of true republicanism, the organization had acquired an inherent suspicion of involvement in politics, and memories of James *Connolly and the *democratic programme gave rise to a strong socialistic tendency within its ranks. These elements combined made it nearly impossible to obtain the wide public support necessary to make a military campaign a success.

In 1925 the link with Sinn Féin was broken when a large section of the party under de *Valera decided that abstention from parliament would lead them nowhere. The subsequent political success of *Fianna Fáil, and the IRA's inability to launch a military campaign, soon made it clear that the IRA needed its own political party. This led to the launch of several unsuccessful political initiatives, including Comhairle na Poblachta in 1929 and *Saor Éire in 1931. The left wing of the movement subsequently broke away in 1934 and formed *Republican Congress. A more traditional republican party, Cumann Poblachta na hÉireann, was then launched by Sean *MacBride in 1936, again without success.

The takeover of government by Fianna Fáil in 1932 led to a large increase in enthusiasm for the IRA. However, after slowly undermining their strength by satisfying many of their supporters' demands, de Valera banned the organization, now no longer needed as possible allies against the *Blueshirts, in 1936.

In a final attempt to regain its relevance the hard-line remnants of the IRA under Sean *Russell embarked on a *bombing campaign in Great Britain in January 1939. Their hope of forcing Britain to renegotiate the treaty soon proved futile. Some damage was done to economic targets but the campaign soon ended with relatively few casualties (7 deaths and 137 injured). Attention then turned to Northern Ireland but by December 1944 the movement there was virtually wiped out by a combined effort of the British, Irish, and Northern Irish governments.

After the Second World War the IRA was re-established by some of its former members. The organization renewed its links with Sinn Féin, but again dedicated itself to reuniting Ireland by physical force. The subsequent *border campaign, launched in 1956, failed due to a lack of public support. Hoping to attract a mass following the movement slowly moved to the left during the 1960s, becoming involved in economic and social agitation. These attempts to rouse the masses inevitably led those involved to a desire to become more fully engaged in politics through existing institutions. This in turn meant conflict with the more traditional abstentionists in the organization.

A formal split came about under pressure of the violence which erupted in the north in 1969. At the Army Convention of 1969 the militarists broke away over the issue of abstention and formed the provisional IRA, which became the dominant grouping, while the remainder became known as the officials. The official IRA suspended military operations in May 1972, although it remained in existence for some years, carrying out bank robberies and similar operations for fund-raising purposes. A breakaway group unwilling to accept the ceasefire became the Irish National Liberation Army (INLA).

Although the provisional IRA sustained the campaign of violence for much longer than in the past, the tensions between abstentionism, political action, and physical force that have characterized the republican movement since the Civil War continued to dog it. The initial belief that a full-scale military campaign with a maximum of civil disorder could bring about an early British withdrawal gave way from the mid-1970s to the concept of the 'long haul', which would gradually sap the British will to remain; this change coincided with the adoption of a tighter cellular structure. From the early 1980s the continued use of violence was combined an attempt to establish Sinn Féin as a force in national, local, and community-based politics. This fusion of military and political action in the two-pronged approach of the 'armalite and the ballot box' was challenged by supporters of traditional abstentionism, who broke away to form Republican Sinn Féin in 1986. By 1994 successful involvement in social and political action had brought about a serious reappraisal of the role of physical force, leading to the formal suspension of the military campaign. This cleared the way for Sinn Féin to enter into a compromise political settlement, the 1998 'Good Friday Agreement' (see PEACE PROCESS). However, the reluctance of unionists to accept Sinn Féin as a genuine political party and the continued uncertainty surrounding the implementation of the agreement have given a boost to supporters of continued violence and abstentionist politics. The emergence of the Continuity Army Council, connected to Republican Sinn Féin, and the formation of the Real IRA in 1995, show the potential for further conflict. The political success of Sinn Féin has so far constrained them, but in the long run the dominance of political tactics among republicans will depend on the success of the new power-sharing institutions.

Bell, J. Bowyer, *The Secret Army: The IRA* (1996)
English, Richard, *Armed Struggle: The History of the IRA* (2003)
Hart, Peter, *The I.R.A. at War 1916–1923* (2003)
Smith, M. L. R., *Fighting for Ireland? The Military Strategy of the Irish Republican Movement* (1995)

JA

Irish Republican Brotherhood, a revolutionary organization that grew out of the *Fenian movement of the 1850s. Fenianism originally developed in the absence of a viable constitutional movement, but for much of the period from 1867 to 1916 the IRB had to coexist with a dominant *home rule movement and accordingly led a rather submerged existence seeking opportunities to exploit.

Following the failed rising of 1867 the Fenian movement was confused. Lack of opportunity for an effective rising was compounded by internal divisions, especially over the leadership of James *Stephens, whose failure to appear in Ireland in 1867 caused continuing controversy and complicated attempts at organizational reconstruction. Division also existed over whether it was best to hit at England in Ireland or Canada, a dispute only resolved after the succession of failed interventions in Canada in 1866, 1867, and 1871. Reorganization began slowly from 1871, with the release from prison of effective leaders such as *O'Donovan Rossa and *Devoy. Devoy especially was to be at the centre of every leading movement for Irish independence until 1921. By 1873 the IRB had acquired a formal constitution which provided for an elaborate, secret society organized on a democratic basis and governed by a partially elected supreme council. Nevertheless, with the prospects for revolutionary activity poor, many Fenians were attracted to practical action in agrarian agitation, a reality formalized in the *'New Departure' during the *Land War of 1879–82. For the IRB this was a compromise which allowed individual members to become involved in agrarian struggle while the organization formally remained aloof and committed to the revolutionary path: a path pursued chiefly in the 1880s through bombing outrages in England.

Such was the strength of the *Parnellite movement at this time, however, that the revolutionary tradition was effectively overshadowed. Many IRB men either were expelled or left the organization while in America splits emerged at leadership level between Devoy, who was reluctant to abandon his arrangement with Parnell until it had clearly proved fruitless, and Rossa, who remained resolutely committed to physical force. Even with the constitutional movement weakened and divided in the 1890s, following the Parnell divorce scandal, the IRB failed to capitalize on the situation. Only at the turn of the century, with a new generation and new organizations such as *Sinn Féin, did the revolutionary tradition revive. It found inspiration in 1907 with the arrival in Ireland of Tom *Clarke, a committed revolutionary who had spent fifteen years in English jails, and further impetus in 1910 with the launching of *Irish Freedom*, a militantly separatist newspaper.

The opportunity republicans had been waiting for came in 1914 with the formation of the *Irish Volunteers. John *Redmond's commitment of this body to the British war effort produced a split, and it was from the ranks of the dissident group which rejected Redmond's lead that the forces which carried out the Easter *rising of 1916 would largely come. The rising was organized mainly by the supreme council of the IRB which, led by Patrick *Pearse and joined by James *Connolly and his tiny *Irish Citizen Army, decided that England's engagement in a foreign war gave them the best opportunity they could hope for. As the struggle for independence widened, however, so the scope for conspiratorial action diminished, and the influence of the IRB during the *Anglo-Irish War was due chiefly to the fact that Michael *Collins was its president. The organization came to an end with the failed Irish *army mutiny of 1924.

Since 1800 Ireland's struggle for independence has tended to oscillate between constitutional, mass movements and usually small, conspiratorial, revolutionary groups. It was the specific contribution of the IRB to persevere doggedly in the most unfavourable circumstances in the ultimately well-founded belief that, given the right conditions, it could communicate its radical conception of Irish independence beyond its own narrow confines to a mass movement dedicated to its realization.

O'Broin, Leon, *The Story of the Irish Revolutionary Brotherhood 1858–1924* (1976). JL

Irish Shipping was set up in 1941 as a semi-state enterprise (see STATE ENTERPRISE) by Sean *Lemass, minister for supplies, in response to the wartime ban on British merchant ships carrying goods to Ireland. This was a necessary crisis measure as British ships had carried 95 per cent of Irish imports. Nine ships, mostly old, were bought and six chartered. After the war, this nucleus was expanded into a national merchant fleet. Due to government pressure, Irish Shipping Ltd. in the 1970s became fatally embroiled in loss-making bulk carrier and ferry ventures. It was placed into liquidation in November 1984. PC

Irish Socialist Republican Party. The ISRP, maliciously described as having more syllables than members, was established in 1896 by James *Connolly out of the Dublin Socialist Society, which had employed him as its organizer. Inspired by the Marxist Social Democratic Federation in England, it published a newspaper, the *Workers' Republic*, and sent delegates to the second *International, but collapsed after Connolly's departure for America in 1903.

Irish Society. This was responsible with its shareholders, the London companies, for the development of Co. Londonderry as part of the *Ulster plantation. James I and his ministers cajoled the City of London and its wealthy guild-companies into making a patriotic investment to fortify and plant this strategic region. The Irish Society took charge of the towns, customs, and fisheries, and devolved the rest of the county to the companies in twelve proportions.

Rapid progress was made at Coleraine and, after a false start, the walls of Derry were constructed between 1614 and 1618. Apart from bringing over a few London orphans as apprentices, the City relied on creating the necessary infrastructure. The companies kept up their profit margins by retaining many Irish inhabitants.

By 1630 there were about 1,930 British settlers in the whole county. The 1622 *Cranfield Commission accused the Londoners of slowness in clearing, fortifying, and colonizing. Sir Thomas Phillips of Limavady, originally a promoter of London's involvement, assembled evidence against the City. This formed the basis of the crown's prosecution in the Star Chamber in 1635. Although the City's accounts showed that it had spent £140,000 where only £20,000 was originally demanded, it was found guilty and subjected to fine and confiscation.

*Cromwell returned the plantation to the Irish Society in 1658. Thereafter the investors obtained a steady return. The liquidity crisis caused by the South Sea Bubble (1720) forced the companies either to sell their proportions, in the case of the Goldsmiths and Vintners, or to let them at heavy entry fines. The Irish Society itself continued to invest in the towns, building bridges over the Bann and the Foyle. The years before the *Great Famine saw considerable philanthropic investment by the companies, most notably the rebuilding of Moneymore, Draperstown, Kilrea, and Eglinton. Six companies sold up during the 1870s and 1880s, in response to land agitation; the purchase provisions of the *Land Acts brought the dissolution of the remaining proportions. The Irish Society sold its last major asset, the Foyle Fisheries, in 1952.

Moody, T. W., *The Londonderry Plantation* (1939)

HM

Irish Sugar Company (Comhlucht Siúicre Éireann Teoranta), established in 1933 as a state-owned company with the object of manufacturing sugar from Irish-grown sugar beet. During the 1920s a Belgian company opened a sugar beet factory in Carlow, which received substantial government subsidies. When it failed, the *Fianna Fáil government replaced it with a state-owned company, which would implement the government's objectives of increasing tillage acreage and of making Ireland self-sufficient in sugar. The company was required to disperse sugar beet production throughout four factories, one in the west of Ireland, in keeping with the policy of decentralizing industry, though economic criteria would have dictated otherwise. MED

Irish Times, founded in Dublin by Major Laurence E. Knox in 1859 as Ireland's first daily penny newspaper. Knox perceived the poor quality of the Dublin conservative papers at a time when the principles and possessions of the *Protestant ascendancy were under threat. The paper quickly outstripped its conservative rivals but it was soon overtaken in circulation by the nationalist **Freeman's Journal*. On Knox's death in 1873, it was sold to the industrialist Sir John Arnott who also owned the **Northern Whig*. It is now Ireland's most widely read liberal daily paper and prints an Irish-language column. M-LL

Irish Trade Union Congress, see IRISH CONGRESS OF TRADE UNIONS.

Irish Transport and General Workers' Union (ITGWU), established in December 1908 following a final breach between James *Larkin and his employers, the British-based National Union of Dock Labourers. The new union, combining an ability to cater for the rapidly developing mood of industrial militancy with a distinctly nationalist flavour, grew rapidly. By mid-1913 membership had risen to 10,000. Having survived defeat in the *Dublin lockout of 1913, the ITGWU entered a second phase of dramatic growth from 1918, as it became the main organization for those who aspired to see social as well as political revolution emerge out of the developing *Anglo-Irish War. By 1920 membership had risen to 120,000. Much of this growth took place among a previously almost wholly unorganized group, the *agricultural labourers. During this period *syndicalism played a significant role in ITGWU strategy, and the union was involved in most of the *soviets and local general strikes that took place. After 1922, however, labour militancy receded, and the ITGWU leadership, under William *O'Brien, was drawn into a bitter conflict with Larkin's Workers' Union of Ireland. Aspirations to make the ITGWU the 'One Big Union' called for in syndicalist strategy faded. By 1923 membership had fallen to 87,000, and by 1929 to 15,453. Despite this the ITGWU remained the largest union in Ireland. Rapid post-war growth brought membership back to an estimated 120,000 by 1950, and during the 1970s and 1980s it absorbed a number of smaller unions.

Irish Volunteers, see IRISH (NATIONAL) VOLUNTEERS.

Irish Women Workers' Union. Set up in 1911 as a sister organization to the *Irish Transport and General Workers' Union, with Delia Larkin as its first general secretary, this women-only union lasted until 1984 when it was amalgamated with the Federated Workers' Union of Ireland. Under Louie *Bennett's secretaryship (1917–55) the union, while it organized steadily, emphasized the commonality of worker–employer relations. However, the IWWU laundry workers' strike of 1945 won the important right to a fortnight's paid holiday. Although it opposed the Conditions of Employment Act (1935) and de *Valera's *constitution of 1937 for their encroachments on women's working rights, the IWWU, in common with many women's unions worldwide at this period, did not think in terms of the individual woman's right to work, but conceived of jobs as a public resource. This was evident in the controversy in 1932 over whether married women with employed husbands should be admitted to the union. From the 1950s, with new leadership and changing economic conditions, the union became more democratic, organized in a range of new trades, and supported married women's right to work and equal pay. CC

Irish Workers' League. Established by James *Larkin in 1924, it replaced the *Communist Party set up three years earlier as the *International's Irish affiliate but was largely inactive. A later Irish Workers' League (1948) was a revival of the Communist Party.

iron. Because of the abundant supply of charcoal from the clearance of Irish *woodlands, and encouragement from Irish landlords, iron smelting grew rapidly during the 17th century. By the end of the century, however, the industry began to contract with the disappearance of the last extensive woodlands.

In 1788 an ironworks was set up at Arigna in Roscommon, using coke from the Connacht coalfield. Operations here were never very successful and the works closed in 1838. Most of the iron used in Ireland was imported from Britain and Sweden. Irish ironworks tended to be located close to the major ports, as the cost of transporting imported coal and iron inland was prohibitive. They were also usually located close to rivers which provided motive power. The agricultural sector provided much of the demand for castings and implements; the forges of local blacksmiths all over the country provided a range of tools and implements for farmers, as well as shoeing horses and repairing iron equipment. From the mid-18th century specialized spade mills emerged, predominantly in Ulster but also close to Dublin and Cork. These were larger and more technically sophisticated than the traditional forge, utilizing *water power extensively to drive bellows, shearing machinery, grindstones, and trip hammers. Increased demand due to the growth in arable *farming encouraged the emergence of a number of small foundries close to the major ports from the last decades of the 18th century, producing heavier castings like plough parts and harrows. Urban development in the larger ports also provided a demand for ironwork for construction purposes, such as gates, railings, plumbing, copper work and ironwork for ships; more specialist ironworkers like bell founders, and those producing for the transport sector like *coach makers, also tended to locate in the larger urban centres. *Dublin was the main iron working centre by the end of the 18th century, and during the 19th century it remained the main centre for supplying castings for public works and the *railways. By 1824 there were thirteen iron foundries in the city. Overall, however, the greater *Belfast region gradually displaced Dublin as the principal ironworking centre during the 19th century.

Coe, W., *The Engineering Industry in the North of Ireland* (1969)

AB

Iron Age (or Early Iron Age), the techno-cultural term for the period that follows the *Bronze Age and precedes the *Early Medieval period. Its beginning, defined by the earliest significant use of iron, is unclear. It was no later than the 3rd century BC, when *La Tène material began to arrive, but might have been several centuries earlier, when iron was in use amongst British and continental cultures which were in contact with Ireland. The end of the period is defined, rather arbitrarily, as the beginning of *Christianization, which event is given a notional 5th-century date. While the Irish Iron Age is well represented by metal artefacts (ornaments, harness-pieces, and weapons), almost all of which indicate high-status owners, its settlements and mundane artefacts remain undiscovered. It is certain, however, that its ritual elements—great internally ditched enclosures (such as *Emain Macha) and ring-barrows—are indigenous in origin. The types of settlement, *hillfort, and pottery characteristic of Iron Age cultures on the Continent are entirely absent from Iron Age Ireland. For these and other reasons the notion of a major population intrusion into Ireland from the *Celtic world, or from anywhere else, at the inception of, or during, the Iron Age is unsupportable.

The Irish Iron Age is now believed to have consisted of a number of separate cultural elements. The rich Irish La Tène assemblage, probably indicating cattle-rearing warrior groups, consists of objects and art styles originally derived from Britain and the Continent. But while such objects are without doubt the best known and most visible part of the cultural assemblage of the Irish Iron Age they have a limited distribution. A geographically distinct, apparently artefact-impoverished, cereal-growing population can be demonstrated over much of the country by the wide distribution of rotary querns of a distinctive type. Strong *Roman influences can also be seen in certain areas. Curiously, in the southern third of the country (most of Munster and southern Leinster), it has proved virtually impossible to identify or describe an Iron Age at all. The La Tène and Roman assemblages are best explained as the result of the intrusion of limited numbers of warrior adventurers and there can be no doubt that the bulk of the population remained genetically unchanged from the Bronze Age, and continued thus into the Early Medieval period.

RW

issue rolls record payments made out of royal revenue by the *treasurer and chamberlains of the *exchequer, each of whom kept his own record of the transactions. The entries were originally chronological, but from 1291 onwards were arranged by category, such as fees to officials, wages of war, works on royal castles, and gifts and rewards. They were originally compiled on a yearly basis, but from 1339 onwards a roll usually covers the period for which the treasurer accounted at the English exchequer. The issue rolls of the English exchequer contain payments for military expeditions to Ireland and for royal messengers sent there. PhC

Italian unification. In 1859 Piedmontese and French forces, and Italian nationalist volunteers, defeated the Austrians in northern Italy and the Spanish Bourbons in the south. Rome and the surrounding territories, governed by the pope, were threatened with forcible incorporation into the united kingdom of Italy thus created. In Ireland a campaign of mass meetings orchestrated by the Catholic hierarchy raised £80,000 for the defence of the papal states. A total of around 1,000 volunteers travelled to Italy, where they were enrolled in the Battalion of St Patrick and fought in unsuccessful actions against the Piedmontese at Spoleto and Castelfidardo in September 1860.

itinerants, see TINKERS.

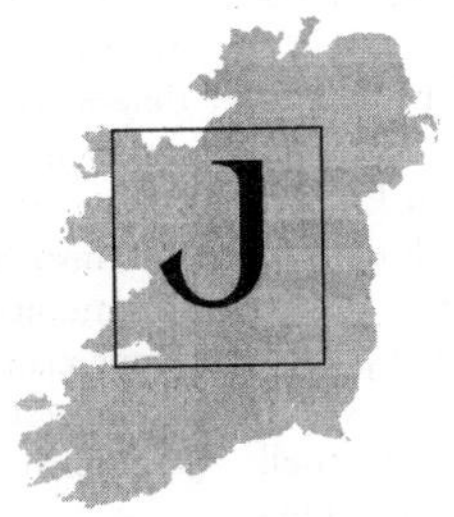

Jackson, Revd William (1737–95), Dublin-born Church of Ireland clergyman turned radical journalist. In April 1795 Jackson returned from France to Ireland to sound out responses to a possible invasion, unaware that his travelling companion, John Cockayne, was a government spy. His conversations with leading Irish radicals provided evidence sufficient to send *Tone into exile and to help justify the suppression of the Dublin *United Irishmen. Arrested and tried for treason, Jackson committed suicide by poison while in the dock.

Jacobitism, support for the Stuart dynasty, following the *revolution of 1688. *James II and his son James Francis Edward (1688–1766), otherwise James III or 'the Old Pretender', maintained a court in exile while their supporters, relying on the backing of France or other sympathetic powers, plotted the recovery of the British and Irish thrones. There was a minor Jacobite rising in Scotland, the main centre of British Jacobitism, in 1708, a larger insurrection there and in northern England in 1715, and projected invasions, in each case aborted, in March 1719 and in early 1744. In July 1745 James III's son Charles Edward (1720–88), 'the Young Pretender', landed in Scotland and raised an army which marched south as far as Derby before retreating to Scotland, where it was crushed at Culloden (16 Apr. 1746).

A number of Irish Protestants were involved in Jacobite conspiracy in England. These included the 2nd duke of *Ormond, James Barry, 4th Earl Barrymore (1667–1747), arrested in 1715 and again in 1745, and the 4th and 5th earls of Orrery (see BOYLE). In Ireland itself *Tory and *high-church partisans, in particular students at *Trinity College and some clergy of the *Church of Ireland, indulged in an occasional rhetorical Jacobitism. Most Irish Protestants, however, saw the revolution settlement and Protestant succession as their only defence against renewed Catholic domination. Irish Catholics, by contrast, remained strongly committed to the Stuarts. Up to 1766 appointments to Catholic bishoprics in Ireland were made on the nomination of the Stuart court in exile, while recruitment in Ireland for the *Irish Brigade provided potential military support for the Jacobite cause. Four of the 'seven men of Moidart' who landed with Prince Charles in 1745 were Irish; one of them, John William O'Sullivan (1700–*c.*1760), born in Co. Kerry, served as quartermaster and adjutant general of the prince's army, which was also reinforced by some 400 men raised from Irish regiments in France. Such connections, along with the perceived threat of invasion or insurrection, helped to legitimize the *penal laws. In reality, however, Ireland, strategically peripheral and with its Catholic population disarmed and leaderless, played little part in Jacobite planning.

Following defeat in 1745–6, Jacobitism quickly lost credibility both in Britain and abroad. In Ireland too leading Catholics became from the 1750s notably more willing to offer declarations of unqualified allegiance to the Hanoverian dynasty. At popular level, however, Jacobitism survived in poems and songs lamenting the exile of the rightful monarch and looking forward to his eventual restoration with the aid of France and other Catholic powers. There has been much speculation about how far this literary tradition contributed to popular disaffection, and receptiveness to French-inspired radicalism, in the 1790s.

Lenman, Bruce, *The Jacobite Risings in Britain 1689–1746* (1980)

Ó Buachalla, Breandán, 'Irish Jacobite Poetry', *Irish Review*, 12 (1992)

James II (1633–1701), a convert to Catholicism since 1669, succeeded his brother Charles II as king of England, Ireland, and Scotland in February 1685. Contrary to later claims, he did not aspire to either absolutism or forcible religious change, believing that the use of his prerogative to suspend anti-Catholic legislation would be enough to promote a Catholic revival in England. However, suspicion of his intentions led to his overthrow in the *revolution of 1688.

In Ireland James, initially restrained by fear of alienating English and Irish Protestant opinion, and by his own unwillingness to weaken English control, came increasingly under the influence of *Tyrconnell, who advocated making the kingdom a secure Catholic stronghold. Policy thus passed through four broad phases. In May 1685 the Protestant militia was disarmed and Tyrconnell began to purge the army of supposed dissidents and install Catholic soldiers and officers. From March 1686 Catholics were appointed to the privy council, commission of the peace, urban corporations, and judiciary, magistrates were ordered to leave Catholic ecclesiastics unmolested, salaries began to be paid to Catholic bishops, and the replacement of Protestant by Catholic soldiers intensified. From February 1687 Tyrconnell, now lord deputy, created an overwhelmingly Catholic army, judiciary, and civil administration. In August 1687 he secured James's consent to a parliament that would revise the Acts of *Settlement and *Explanation.

Having fled to France in panic following *William III's landing, James was sent to Ireland by Louis XIV. Landing at Kinsale on 12 March 1689 he made a triumphal progress to Dublin, but disappointed supporters by his resistance to the demands of the *patriot parliament. His hasty flight from Ireland after defeat at the *Boyne—apparently a second mysterious failure of nerve in a man noted for his courage as a soldier in the 1650s and a naval commander in the 1660s—confirmed his low standing in both Protestant and Catholic eyes.

Miller, John, *James II: A Study in Kingship* (1978)

Jansenism, a 17th-century current of Catholic theological thought, originating in the Low Countries and associated with Cornelius Jansen (1585–1638), characterized by a pessimistic religious anthropology. Many Irish scholars, such as Florence Conry (1560–1629), contributed to the early theological phase of Jansenism. However, because of its divisiveness, Jansenism was viewed with great suspicion by Rome, and 17th-century Irish synods toed the Roman line. Indeed, while its moral rigorism made it attractive to elements of the *Counter-Reformation church, Jansenism's theological and political radicalism alienated both local hierarchies and Catholic monarchs. This was especially the case in France and most Irish clerical students there associated with milieux hostile to the movement. Indeed their anti-Jansenist opinions were singled out for criticism by the pro-Jansenist journal *Nouvelles ecclésiastiques*, Irish clerics, in general, being more attracted to Jesuit-style humanism. The success of the anti-Jansenist bull *Unigenitus* (1713) marginalized the movement but it survived as a popular millenarian-cum-miracle cult. Neither as a theology nor as a political attitude did Jansenism recommend itself to the Irish Catholic community, either at home or abroad. The frequent claim that Irish Catholicism was Jansenist-influenced springs from the tendency to confuse Jansenism with mere moral rigorism. TO'C

Jellett, Mainie (1897–1944), painter of genre scenes, religious subjects, and abstract compositions. She was educated at the Metropolitan School of Art, Dublin, the Westminster School, London, under Sickert, and in France with André Lhote and Albert Gleizes. While Sickert, Lhote, and Gleizes provided the 'three revolutions' of her career, as she once commented, it was Gleizes—with whom she worked on and off for many years—with his deeply spiritual approach to picture making, who had the lasting influence on her work. Back in Dublin she became a member of the Dublin Painters' Society and there, in 1923, first exhibited cubist and abstract canvases which had resulted from her studies with Gleizes. She was at once recognized as the most avant-garde painter in Ireland, although she was only later accorded full recognition for her achievements. Her pioneering work often brought her into conflict with the moribund Dublin art establishment and so, with Louis le Brocquy, in 1943 she founded the Irish Exhibition of Living Art as a venue where the progressive painters could show their work. She was, in Bruce Arnold's words, 'the greatest woman painter [Ireland] has ever produced'.

Arnold, Bruce, *Mainie Jellett and the Modern Movement in Ireland* (1991)

SBK

Jesuits, popular name for priests of the Society of Jesus, founded in 1534 by the Spaniard Ignatius of Loyola (1491–1556). Along with the usual vows of chastity, poverty, and obedience, Jesuits took a special vow of obedience to the pope. Society priests were strictly selected and trained according to the programme Ignatius laid out in his *Spiritual Exercises*. The Jesuits played a large part in the 16th-century reform movement of the Catholic church. Their speciality was education and their rigorous but flexible methods, systematized in the *Ratio et institutio studiorum* (1599), became models for Catholic education. Active as missionaries in India and Japan, they experimented with the inculturation of Catholicism in China. In Paraguay they set up closed missionary villages, the Reductions. Bowing to Bourbon and other pressures, Clement

XIV reluctantly suppressed them in 1774, but they were re-established by Pius VII in 1814 and have been to the fore of every major church initiative since. Active in Ireland from 1542, the first native Irish Jesuits were effective agents of the papacy and Tridentine reforms, identifying inadequate popular understanding of the faith and Protestantism as major threats. Predictably hounded by the government, small numbers remained active during the penal period. They founded Clongowes Wood College in 1812. Intellectually influential, especially through journals like *Studies* (1912), they took over University College, the successor to Newman's *Catholic University, in 1883. A period of complacency in the wake of independence was followed by a renewal in the 1960s marked by involvement in domestic and international justice issues. TO'C

Jews have a long, but by no means continuous, history in Ireland. Scattered references to their presence have been discovered between the 11th and 13th centuries. In 1290 Jews were expelled from the dominions of the English crown, though there are stray references thereafter to individuals, including some refugees from Spain and Portugal in the 16th century. Jews began to resettle in England from 1656 and had reappeared in Ireland by the 1660s. Dublin had a rabbi by 1700, and a Jewish cemetery opened in 1718. By the mid-18th century Cork also had an organized community. Jews were by now sufficiently numerous, or at least noticeable, for their status to become a political issue. Proposals to permit their naturalization were debated in the Irish parliament on four occasions between 1743 and 1747, but rejected each time. A British act of 1753, which would have permitted naturalization in both Great Britain and Ireland, was repealed after eight months due to hostile agitation. The Irish Naturalization Act of 1784 explicitly excluded Jews, a provision repealed only in 1816.

The Jewish presence in Ireland remained a volatile one, highly responsive to economic and other circumstances. From the 1690s Dublin had attracted a group of wealthy merchants originally based in London; most of these, however, returned to England during the depressed years of the late 1720s. At the end of the 18th century the Dublin community largely collapsed, due partly to conversion and intermarriage with Christians, but also to emigration at a time of political unrest and economic uncertainty. In 1818 there were said to be only two Jewish families in the city. From the 1820s a new Jewish population appeared, of German and Polish origin but coming to Ireland via England. A high proportion were goldsmiths, silversmiths, and watchmakers, or dealers in tobacco, cigars, and snuff. In 1874 Lewis Harris (1812–76), merchant and jeweller, stood successfully for election to Dublin corporation. Overall numbers remained small: the *census recorded 393 Jews in 1861 and only 285 in 1871. From the 1880s, however, there arrived a much larger group of immigrants from eastern Europe, mainly refugees from persecution in Tsarist Russia. By 1901 Jewish numbers had risen to 3,769. This influx of mainly poor eastern Europeans encouraged a degree of anti-Semitism, notably in Limerick, where inflammatory preaching by a Redemptorist priest, John Creagh, inspired a two-year boycott of the city's Jewish shopkeepers and traders.

Jinks, John (d. 1934). Returned as *National League member for Leitrim-Sligo in June 1927, Jinks achieved momentary fame when his absence allowed *Cumann na nGaedheal to survive a vote of no confidence (16 Aug.) in a *Dáil evenly divided following *Fianna Fáil's decision to take its seats. His absence, engineered by R. M. Smyllie, editor of the *Irish Times*, and the independent Dáil deputy Major Bryan Cooper, has been attributed both to successful persuasion and to generously administered drink. Jinks stood again, as an independent, in September 1927, but was not elected.

Jocelyn, Percy (1764–1843), third son of the earl of Roden, Church of Ireland bishop of Leighlin and Ferns 1809–20 and Clogher 1820–2. In 1822 Jocelyn was the subject of an ecclesiastical scandal when he was discovered in compromising circumstances with a soldier in a London public house, leading to his removal from his see.

John (1167–1216), king of England (1199–1216). John was the youngest son of *Henry II; in 1177 Henry designated him lord of Ireland, with the intention of raising him to royal status. A crown for Ireland was subsequently sought from the papacy and delivered to England by papal legates around Christmas 1185. However, Henry, about to depart for Normandy, deemed the time inopportune and it was not used. In March 1185 Henry had supplied John with a personal household of experienced administrators and dispatched him to assume the lordship of Ireland in person. John alienated those Irish kings who had been prepared to enter into a personal association with him and signally failed to assert control over the principal Anglo-Norman landholder, Hugh de *Lacy. Plans to send John back to Ireland were abandoned following de Lacy's assassination.

During the reign of Richard I (1189–99), John's private household was responsible for those areas of Ireland under Anglo-Norman control, apart from a brief period in 1194 during John's rebellion against his brother, when Richard assumed direct responsibility for Ireland. In 1199, on John's accession as king of England, Anglo-Norman Ireland was attached to the royal government, resulting in the elaboration of English administrative structures, including the establishment of an *exchequer at Dublin. In 1210 John mounted a second expedition to Ireland. The outcome was markedly different from that of his earlier visit. Walter de *Lacy and Hugh de Lacy were deprived of their lordships of Meath and Ulster, while William de *Braose lost Limerick, and William *Marshal was obliged to accept a diminution of his liberties as lord of Leinster. Much of this enhancement of royal control was to be compromised by the baronial revolt in England from 1212 which allowed the Anglo-Norman barons in Ireland to negotiate a series of restorations and privileges. The favourable position they thus attained is exemplifed by the appointment of William Marshal as regent for John's successor, the young King Henry III. MTF

John Scottus Eriugena (d. 877) was one of a group of Irish scholars who worked in the area of Reims in the 9th century. He first comes to notice when asked by Hincmar of Reims to refute Gottschalk, who argued for 'a double predestination' (851). From then until his death he can be linked to Reims itself, Soissons, Laon, and Charles the Bald's palace at Compiègne. Eriugena is a typical teacher of the period: concerned with teaching the arts, exegesis, and the standard theological questions. However, aside from handling these areas with originality, he stands apart from contemporaries in his range of sources, especially Greek sources. Thus he produced in his *Periphyseon* a Christian presentation of reality that is unlike any other medieval Latin work. Yet despite, or because of, his brilliance, he made little impact on the tradition. When read, he was little understood, and hence was open to suspicions of heresy. The recovery of his thought began only in this century.

Van Riel, G., et al., *Johannes Scottus Eriugena: The Bible and Hermeneutics* (1996)

TO'L

Johnson, Thomas (1872–1963), Labour leader. Born in Liverpool, a commercial traveller in Belfast from 1900, he became president of the Irish Trade Union Congress (see IRISH CONGRESS OF TRADE UNIONS) in 1916 and took an active part in the campaign against conscription in 1918. As Dáil deputy for Co. Dublin 1922–7 he was the first leader of the parliamentary *Labour Party. He subsequently sat in the *Senate of the Irish Free State 1928–36.

Johnston, Francis (1760–1829), one of the leading *architects of the early 19th century in Ireland. Trained by English architect Thomas Cooley, Johnston succeeded his tutor in the patronage of Primate *Robinson in his native Armagh. Johnston travelled little, and the bulk of his work was influenced by local example, particularly the designs of James Wyatt and James *Gandon. His stylistic versatility is reflected in the range of his classical work, from the austere, Greek revival, Townley Hall, Co. Louth (1790s), to the General Post Office in Dublin (1815–18), and St George's church, Dublin (1802–*c*.1817), inspired by the English architect James Gibbs. He was a pioneer of the picturesque 'castle style' of country house; amongst his earlier works in the style were the influential Charleville Forest, Co. Offaly (1801–12), and Killeen Castle, Co. Meath (1802–3). His Chapel Royal at *Dublin Castle (1807–14) is perhaps the best example of his Gothic revival work. In 1805 he was appointed architect of the *Board of Works and Civil Buildings and as such was responsible for the design of a number of institutions including Richmond penitentiary (1811) and Armagh and Belfast lunatic asylums (1820, 1826). He was an avid art collector, and a founder member of the *Royal Hibernian Academy, of which he was president between 1824 and 1829. RM

joint-stock companies assumed an important role in Irish business life during the first half of the 19th century. In 1800 the only company stocks trading on the Dublin *Stock Exchange were the Bank of Ireland and the Grand and Royal canals. By 1844, in addition to several joint-stock banks, 47 other companies were in existence; gas, water, other utilities, and *rail, shipping, and mining stocks predominated. The 1844 Companies Act, which applied throughout the United Kingdom, defined a joint-stock company and established a register of companies with an office in Dublin. Legislation passed in 1855 and 1856 extended limited liability to incorporated companies. Between 1856 and 1906 a total of 2,850 companies were registered in Ireland, with a nominal share capital of almost £110 million. In 1906 there were 1,387 companies on the Dublin register. By 1931, despite the loss of companies based in Northern Ireland, this figure stood at 1,803, and it increased to 2,832 by 1939. Company formation was particularly strong during the 1890s, which was prompted by a mania for cycle shares, and after 1932, when businesses responded to *Fianna Fáil's drive for self-sufficiency. MED

Jones, Henry (1605–82), clergyman and political survivor. The son of Lewis Jones, Church of Ireland bishop of Killaloe 1633–46, he was appointed bishop of Clogher by *Ormond in 1645, served the *Cromwellian regime as scoutmaster-general, but in 1661, following the *Restoration, was promoted to the bishopric of Meath. A vehement anti-Catholic, he was a firm believer in the reality of the *Popish Plot and played an important part in the proceedings that led to the execution of Oliver *Plunkett.

Jones, Richard (*c.*1638–1712), earl of Ranelagh. A nephew of *Orrery, he headed the opposition in the Irish parliament of 1661–6, but later joined the administration as chancellor of the exchequer (1668). In 1671 he undertook to manage the revenues and financial obligations of the crown in Ireland. Although there were complaints concerning both Ranelagh's methods of raising revenue and his failure to make payments, he was able to remit significant amounts of money directly to Charles II, who in return protected him from inquiries and repercussions. After the *revolution of 1688 Ranelagh was paymaster general of *William III's army from 1691 until 1702, when irregularities in his accounts led to his resignation and expulsion from the English parliament.

Joy, Francis (*c.* 1697–1790), *printer, bookseller, *newspaper proprietor in *Belfast. Joy founded the **Belfast News-Letter* in 1737, and was succeeded in 1748 by his two sons, **Henry** (d. 1789) and **Robert** (d. 1785). VK

Joyce, James (1882–1941), novelist. Joyce's father was a middle-class Parnellite activist whose gentlemanly pretensions contrasted with the squalor he inflicted on his family. Joyce was expected to restore the family fortunes. In Jesuit schools and University College he mixed with aspiring Catholic professionals who shaped the ethos of the new Irish state. Though fascinated by scholasticism and the Catholic liturgy, Joyce rejected faith as conformism, asserting artistic individuality at all costs. In 1904 he left Ireland for the Continent, returning seldom and briefly. Short stories of restricted lives, *Dubliners* (1914), and the semi-autobiographical *Portrait of the Artist as a Young Man* (1916), established Joyce as a major modernist writer. *Ulysses* (1922), a meticulous reimagination of Dublin on 16 June 1904, is one of the great literary explorations of the textures of urban life. Its sexual and cloacal frankness provoked attempts at censorship. It is disputed whether the dream-novel *Finnegans Wake* (1939) is a further breakthrough or a retreat into solipsism.

Joycean academic commentary and tourism have become growth industries; the re-enactment of Leopold Bloom's wanderings on 16 June ('Bloomsday') is a major social occasion. Joyce is often hailed in his own terms as secular patron saint of modern Ireland, his plurality contrasted with the strained dreams of the literary revival. PM

judiciary. The Irish judiciary of the present day is, institutionally, the direct descendant, not of the *brehons of pre-Norman Ireland, but of the justices appointed to give judgments in the royal courts of the Anglo-Norman lordship of Ireland from 1221 onwards. The first Irish justices had no prior connection with Ireland. However, a pattern was soon established of appointing a mixture of Englishmen and of men of Irish birth and upbringing. In most periods the latter were the larger group, though the early years of the 17th century (when the exclusion of Catholics and the difficulty of finding alternative local candidates meant that almost all judicial posts were held by English appointees) provides one marked exception to this general pattern. The practice of appointing Englishmen with no prior Irish connections to the Irish bench ceased only around 1750, and there was a small-scale resumption of the practice during the first half-century after the Act of *Union, when the *chancellorship of Ireland was normally held by Englishmen. The exclusion of Catholics from the higher judiciary lasted (with a brief intermission during the reign of *James II) until the *Catholic Emancipation Act of 1829.

Initially, royal justices in Ireland (like their counterparts in England) were not drawn from the ranks of professional lawyers and were not apparently required to have any special prior legal expertise. In Ireland, as in England, the first professional lawyers had been appointed to the bench before the end of the 13th century but the full 'professionalization' of higher judicial posts which was accomplished in England by the middle of the 14th century was not completed in Ireland till the 16th. Even then, it still remained possible, as late as the second half of the 17th century, to appoint men without legal training to the lord chancellorship of Ireland: the last non-professional lord chancellor of Ireland (Michael Boyle, archbishop of Armagh) did not leave office till 1689.

Prior to the 15th century Irish justices were normally appointed during pleasure and could in theory be removed from office at any time. A number of justices in the 15th century tried to strengthen their hold on their posts by obtaining appointments or confirmations in office giving them tenure during good behaviour or for life. A statute of 1494/5 explicitly prohibited future life appointments and the practice of making appointments to act during good behaviour died out until it was reintroduced by an Irish statute of 1782, thus giving Irish judges the same security of tenure which their English counterparts had possessed since 1701. The same act also protected Irish judges against removal on the death of the monarch, when formally they required re-appointment, a protection which their English counterparts had enjoyed since 1760.

Ball, F. Elrington, *The Judges in Ireland, 1221–1921* (1926)

PAB

justice of the peace. The term first appears in Irish law in 1410, as a new name for the *keeper of the peace. Although the military dimension of the original office continued strongly into the 16th century, justices also held the power by 1415 to convene courts of quarter session for the trial of minor civil and criminal cases, and were required to be active in enforcing the law. Serious offenders were to be bound over or remanded in custody to appear in the superior courts. The post was unpaid, and jurisdiction was limited by *county boundaries. Appointments, generally made on the nomination of local magnates, were by the *lord chancellor, who issued a commission in the name of the monarch. In some *boroughs, charters made provision for certain townsmen to act as justices. By 1638 it was thought viable to publish a handbook for Irish justices, who now operated more regularly and took on a greater role in the kingdom's administration.

During the 18th century justices acquired new duties, including a limited summary jurisdiction, and a role in tax collection. Their numbers rose from 2,000 in 1760 to 3,000 by 1798. Around 10 per cent of justices were clergymen, the rest mainly members of the resident gentry. Catholics could not hold the commission of the peace, and suspected *Jacobites were also excluded, although the relatively small number of resident gentry available meant that exclusion on party political grounds was less common than in contemporary England. Fairly frequent accusations of corruption in the early part of the century were attributed by critics to the recruitment of men of inadequate social standing. It is also clear that only a minority of those in the commission of the peace at any one time (one estimate is as low as one in five) actively exercised their powers.

With the intensification of sectarian and political conflict in the last decades of the century, the rural gentry came to seem increasingly inadequate as agents of law enforcement. Before and during the *insurrection of 1798 some justices absconded, while others were criticized for indiscriminate brutality. Reforms of the commission of the peace in 1822–3, and again in the period of the *Lichfield House compact, sought to weed out the inactive and conspicuously partisan. The belated appearance of petty sessions (see COURTS OF LAW) also reduced the scope for individual abuses of power. But the long-term solution was to bypass the local magistracy in favour of officials, *resident magistrates, and the *Royal Irish Constabulary, under central government control.

During the *Anglo-Irish War republican intimidation and the appeal of the *Dáil courts undercut the remaining authority of the justices. *Partition led to the abolition of the office in the *Irish Free State, though the concept was continued through the offices of district justices and peace commissioners. In *Northern Irelandjustices of the peace continued to play a role, though from 1935 they lost their judicial powers, which were entirely delegated to the resident magistrates.

Mc Dowell, R. B., *The Irish Administration 1801–1914* (1964)

NG

justiciar, more properly 'chief justiciar', the normal title of the governor of Ireland from the late 12th to the mid-14th centuries. It mirrored usage in England, where from the reign of Henry II until 1234 the justiciar was a bishop or magnate who headed the administration and ruled during royal absences. The justiciar of Ireland was administrator, military commander, and judge. The office was held sometimes by settler lords and sometimes by ecclesiastics, but from the mid-13th century more commonly by English knights connected with the king's military household. By the later 13th century the justiciar received an annual salary of £500 from the Irish *exchequer, from which he retained his own small military household, and presided over a court roughly equivalent to the English King's Bench. Except in emergencies, when a governor might be chosen by the Irish council, he was appointed by the king, who remained free to intervene in all matters, and usually forbade the justiciar to dismiss other high officials or to exercise rights of patronage above a certain value. In the late Middle Ages, the title of *king's lieutenant was increasingly adopted for high-born governors, and that of justiciar came to denote a stop-gap appointment.

RFF

justiciar's court, a law court which accompanied the chief governor as he travelled round the medieval lordship of Ireland and of which he was the chief justice. There is no clear evidence for the existence of a permanent justiciar's court holding regular sessions before 1282. Between 1282 and 1324 the justiciar was assisted in the work of his court by a single full-time justice and thereafter by two. The work of the court was recorded on the *justiciary rolls. After *Richard II's visit to Ireland the court became known as the court of King's Bench.

PAB

justiciary rolls. These record a variety of administrative and legal business conducted by or in the name of the chief governor of the medieval lordship as he travelled round Ireland. The earliest such roll to survive until modern times came from 1295. Only two original justiciary rolls (for 1312–13 and 1318) survived the destruction of the Irish *public records in 1922: both are as yet unpublished. Much of the contents of a number of other justiciary rolls of the period between 1295 and 1318 is known from calendars prepared (and in part published) prior to their destruction.

PAB

Kane, Sir Robert (1809–90), scientist. A graduate of *Trinity College, Dublin, Kane was the first president of *Queen's College, Cork, and president of the *Royal Irish Academy (1877). His *The Industrial Resources of Ireland* (1844) offered a highly optimistic assessment of the prospects for Irish development, widely cited by later proponents of economic nationalism. He established a Museum of Irish Industry (1847), and was one of the three-man scientific commission established in October 1845 to find a cure for potato blight (see GREAT FAMINE).

Keating, Geoffrey (Seathrun Céitinn) (*c.*1570–*c.*1644), priest and historian. Born in Co. Tipperary, he received his doctorate at Reims, taught at the Irish College at Bordeaux, and by 1613 was serving as a priest in Co. Tipperary. His major work *Foras Feasa ar Éirinn* (literally 'Compendium of Wisdom about Ireland') synthesized the biblical account of the Flood and the repeopling of the world, the narrative of the **Lebor Gabála*, and the work of *Gerald of Wales, to recount the history of Ireland from earliest times. Although Keating's reliance on legend and acceptance of the fabulous left him open to criticism from both Catholic and Protestant contemporaries, his work circulated widely in manuscript, offering Gaelic Irish and *Old English a shared origin legend, and encouraging them to see themselves as joint heirs to a glorious historical past. An English translation by Dermot O'Connor appeared in 1723. Keating also wrote poetry, and two religious tracts: *Eochairsgiath an Aifrinn*, a polemical defence of the mass against the arguments of Luther and Calvin, and *Trí Biorghaoithe an Bháis* (Three Shafts of Death), a homily on mortality and the afterlife.

See also LITERATURE IN IRISH.

keening, from Irish *caoineadh*, also referred to as the 'Irish cry', the custom of delivering a lament, accompanied by wailing and cries of grief, over the body of a dead person. The keen could be performed by friends and relatives of the deceased, or by specialist performers hired for the occasion. Although observers as late as the early 19th century commented admiringly on the fluency with which those involved extemporized in verse on the qualities of the departed and the tragedy of their death, it is difficult to see how this could have been done without heavy reliance on standard formulae. The most famous keen in Irish literature, for the ex-soldier Art *O'Leary, ostensibly delivered over his body by his wife, is now seen as the work of one or more specialist hands, possibly completed in its present form only decades after the event.

keeper of the peace (*custos pacis*), the officer appointed in Irish counties from the early 14th century to assist the sheriff to maintain order and provide defence. There were several in each county, chosen from the leading gentry families; an earl or other magnate might head the commission. Their duties included regular musters and inspection of horses and weapons, and they had authority to negotiate and make truces with the Irish. From *c.*1400 they were sometimes known as *justices of the peace, and performed some of the judicial duties of English JPs, but their main function remained military. RFF

Kells, Book of (Trinity College Dublin MS 58), a copy of the Gospels in a Latin text based on the Vulgate but intermixed with readings from the Old Latin translation. The Gospels are preceded by prefaces, summaries, and Eusebian canon tables. The book is lavishly decorated with full-page depictions of the Evangelists and their symbols; portraits of Christ and the Virgin and Child; and illustrations of the temptation and arrest of Christ. Its text is enlivened with interlinear drawings and decorated initials composed of human and animal figures, most of which carry symbolic resonances. As one of the key manuscripts in the debate over *insular script and art, the Book of Kells has attracted a great deal of scholarly disagreement over its date and origin. The current majority opinion attributes it to the scriptorium of *Iona (Argyllshire), though it remains unclear whether its production took place there or (wholly or partially) at Kells, Co. Meath, where the monastic community moved after it was attacked by *Viking raiders in 806. BM

Kells, Synod of (1152), culmination of the pre-Norman church reform movement. Sitting first at Kells and later at Mellifont, the synod legislated for payment of *tithes and other reforms of the kind initiated at the Synod of *Cashel. It reassigned Irish dioceses to four provinces, Dublin and Tuam being added to Armagh and Cashel, the archbishoprics established at the Synod of *Ráith Bressail. Cardinal John Paparo, papal legate, arrived with pallia (insignia) for the four archbishops. CE

Kenmare, title of the Browne family. **Sir Valentine Browne** (d. 1589) came to Ireland as surveyor-general in 1559, and his son and grandson acquired lands in Cos. Kerry, Cork, and Limerick. Although its origins were thus those of *New English colonists, the family subsequently reverted to Catholicism. **Sir Valentine Browne** (d. 1691) supported James II, who in 1689 made him Viscount Kenmare. Sir Valentine's son, the 2nd viscount, also an active Jacobite, forfeited his life interest in the estate, but on his death in exile in 1720 the lands passed to his heir. The Kenmare title, one of several granted when James had been deposed in England but was still de facto king of Ireland, was granted limited official recognition by 18th-century Irish governments. **Sir Thomas Browne** (1726–95), 4th viscount, took an active part in Catholic politics, leading the conservative secession from the *Catholic Committee in 1791. In 1798 the government bestowed a new title of Viscount Kenmare, ignoring the Jacobite creation, quickly following this with promotion to an earldom in 1801. In 1883 the Kenmares, with 119,000 acres, had the 19th largest aristocratic estate in the United Kingdom, measured in terms of acreage, and the 24th largest in terms of rental income.

Kenyon, Fr. John (1812–69), curate, and later parish priest, of Templederry, Co. Tipperary, who was strongly associated with *Young Ireland from 1845 and was elected to the council of the *Irish Confederation in 1847. As a militant nationalist close to John *Mitchel, Kenyon denounced the *O'Connells and urged an early rebellion in 1848. Suspended by his bishop in April 1848, Kenyon continued to agitate, but in July declared that the confederate rising was hopeless, and refused to assist the rebels. PHG

Keogh, John (1740–1817), Catholic activist. A merchant whose self-made fortune allowed him to purchase land, Keogh was the dominant figure in the *Catholic Committee of the 1790s. A *United Irishman, he was briefly detained in 1796 and temporarily dropped out of public life. He returned to Catholic politics from 1805, but retired about 1810 having been overruled on questions of tactics.

Keogh, William Nicholas (1817–78), politician and judge. A Catholic barrister and MP for Athlone 1847–56, Keogh sparkled in the opposition of the *Irish Brigade to the *ecclesiastical titles bill. Pledged to *independent opposition in 1852, he nevertheless accepted office (Dec. 1852) in Aberdeen's government as solicitor-general for Ireland. For this he was denounced as a pledge-breaker and a place-seeker. He became judge of the court of Common Pleas in 1856. His conduct of a number of cases, including *Fenian trials, evoked criticism. RVC

kern (Ir. *ceithearn*, 'a warband'). Although the Irish word is a collective, with an individual member of the troop being described as a *ceithearnach*, the Anglo-Irish used the word both for a band of light-armed native Irish mercenary soldiers and for the individual members of such a band. In pre-Norman times, *ceithearn* might describe a band of *fianna*, young men who left their homes to join a warrior cult, but from the last years of the 12th century onwards kerns are small freelance bands of mercenaries, typically numbering around 20, organized under their own captains, who wander the countryside looking for military employment, and meanwhile intimidate peasants into offering them hospitality. Fighting without armour or helmets, often equipped only with a sword and a bunch of wooden throwing-darts, kerns were not suited to pitched battles, but were chiefly employed in harrying civilian populations, burning houses, and plundering cattle. In the mid-14th century accounts of the *justiciar Ralph *Ufford these troops were paid a mere penny a day, where foot archers earned twopence. They were, however, indispensable in Irish conditions and formed the bulk of the rank and file in any Irish army. KS

Kerry, knights of, title of a cadet branch of the Fitzgeralds of *Desmond, hereditary collectors of the Desmonds' rents in the county. As with the knights of *Glin, the origins of the title, which first appears in the 15th century, are obscure.

Kettle, Thomas (1880–1916), poet and essayist, *Nationalist MP for East Tyrone 1906–10 and from 1909 professor of national economics at University College, Dublin. When the *First World War began Kettle was in Belgium purchasing weapons for the *Irish Volunteers. Outraged at the German invasion, he transferred his support to the war effort. Initially employed in recruiting, he applied to go to France after the *rising of 1916, and was killed in action.

Kickham, Charles J. (1828–82). A member of a prosperous shopkeeping family in Mullinahone, Co. Tipperary, he was involved from 1848 onwards in nationalist politics and journalism at local level. He joined the *Fenians in 1861 and moved to Dublin in 1863 to become a leader writer for the organization's weekly, the *Irish People*. Having been arrested in November 1865 he emerged from jail in March 1869 as the leading Fenian at liberty in Ireland. He supported the new Fenian organization that had been emerging since 1867 and was president of the supreme council of the *Irish Republican Brotherhood from about 1873 until his death. He opposed (with limited success) the involvement of Fenians in the *home rule movement and in the *Land War. A successful ballad-writer, he was the author of a number of books, one of which, *Knocknagow, or the Homes of Tipperary* (1873), struck a deep chord with several subsequent generations of Irish people. RVC

Kildare, see BRIGID.

Kildare, title of the FitzGerald earldom (later a marquisate) of Leinster, the most long-lived, though by no means consistently the most powerful, of the three great dynasties stretching back to the *Anglo-Norman conquest (see DESMOND, ORMOND). The earldom was created in 1316, but it was the 7th earl (see KILDARE, THOMAS FITZGERALD) who laid the foundations for the family's power, recovering lost lands and serving repeatedly as chief governor. The family fortunes reached a peak under the 8th earl (see KILDARE, GERALD FITZGERALD) but were destroyed when his grandson launched the disastrous *Kildare rebellion. Gerald FitzGerald (1525–85), younger son of the 9th earl, was restored as 11th earl in 1554, but was suspected of treasonable conspiracy with his cousin Shane *O'Neill, and later of complicity in *Baltinglass's rebellion.

The Kildare family returned to political prominence in the 18th century. Robert FitzGerald (1675–1744), 19th earl, served as a *lord justice in the tense period after the death of Queen Anne in 1714 and built a new residence at Carton to replace the castle at Maynooth. James FitzGerald (1722–73), 20th earl of Kildare, enjoyed a popular reputation as a *patriot politician. He supported Henry Boyle during the *money bill dispute, but subsequently came to terms with the administration, serving as lord justice 1756–7 and master-general of the ordnance 1758–66. He became marquis of Kildare in 1761 and duke of Leinster in 1766. His Dublin town house, Leinster House, is now the headquarters of *Dáil Éireann.

Kildare, Gerald FitzGerald (Gearóid Óg), 9th earl of (1487–1534). Garret óg, operating in the straitened conditions of the early Henrician period, never attained the greatness of his father Gearóid Mór. His three lord deputyships (1513–20, 1524–8, and 1532–4) were interspersed with periods of detention in England. He extended his family's landholdings and added to his father's list of Gaelic tributaries, but faced increasing opposition from the *Pale over *coyne and livery and a long-running feud with Piers Butler, earl of *Ormond.

Early Tudor government in Ireland was impossible without FitzGerald's co-operation—he frustrated *Surrey's experiment in direct rule, rendered Ormond's deputyship a failure, and had Lord Delvin kidnapped by O'Connor Faly, his son-in-law. In 1530 Kildare returned home with the new deputy, Sir William Skeffington, but eventually undermined him so that there was no alternative to his own reappointment. Wary of the ascendancy of Thomas Cromwell at court, Kildare began removing ordnance from Dublin Castle in August 1533. Early in 1534 he reluctantly answered a summons to England and appointed his son Thomas as his deputy. Gearóid Óg died in the Tower of London in September, the *Kildare rebellion already under way. HM

Kildare, Gerald FitzGerald (Gearóid Mór), 8th earl of (1456–1513), the dominant figure in English Ireland from 1478 until his death. Kildare was governor of Ireland for over 30 years (1478, 1479–92, 1496–1513), serving under five kings and crowning a sixth, 'Edward VI' (Lambert *Simnel) in 1487. The key to an understanding of the earl's turbulent and colourful career was his tripartite relationship with successive English kings and both Englishry and Irishry in Ireland: his ultimate success reflected his ability to reconcile the divergent interests of these three parties.

English kings valued Kildare's ability to deploy his extensive *manræd* (his connection and tenantry available for military service) for the good rule and defence of the English *Pale and saw in the earl a potentially cheap and effective instrument of provincial government—provided his reliability could be assured. Edward IV's reforms of the Dublin administration in 1479 had this in mind, but Henry Tudor's later efforts to wean Kildare away from his Yorkist sympathies (see WARS OF THE ROSES) were much more protracted. By 1496, however, Sir Edward *Poynings had eliminated Ireland's potential as a Yorkist bridgehead. Kildare was married to the king's cousin, Elizabeth St John, and reappointed governor, leaving his son at court as pledge for his good conduct.

Such evident marks of royal favour also raised the earl's standing among the English of Ireland, damping down *factional rivalries and promoting stronger government which tipped the military balance in the lordship's favour. Yet Kildare's success also rested on forging cross-border alliances with Gaelic chiefs, often cemented by marriages, to stabilize the lordship's defence. Indeed, from a Gaelic perspective, Kildare's dealings with border chieftaincies differed little from relations between a Gaelic overlord and his *uirríghthe* (sub-chieftains). The earl's court included a Gaelic entourage, but concurrently he was extracting *black rents from chiefs and ejecting clansmen from disputed marchlands.

Earl Gerald's extended connection was most visibly and effectively deployed in the battle of *Knockdoe (1504), for which Henry made Kildare in reward Knight of the Garter. He eventually died of a gunshot wound and his son Lord Gerald succeeded him as earl and governor.

Ellis, S. G., *Tudor Frontiers and Noble Power: The Making of the British State* (1995)

SGE

Kildare, Thomas FitzGerald, 7th earl of (d. 1478). Kildare laid the foundations for the later *Kildare ascendancy. He was recognized as 7th earl probably in 1454 and, through his association with the Yorkists (see WARS OF THE ROSES), gradually recovered all the ancestral FitzGerald estates, both those acquired by the Butlers (see ORMOND (BUTLER)) and also marchlands in the Kildare–Carlow region reoccupied by Gaelic clans during the earldom's abeyance from 1432. Altogether, he served as governor of Ireland for over eleven years (1454–9, 1460–2, 1464, 1470–5, 1478), and as lord *chancellor for three more (1464–7). With his wife Joan, the earl of *Desmond's daughter, he founded the *Franciscan friary at Adare, Co. Limerick. Attainted of treason by Worcester's parliament in 1468, he was soon restored to favour and was instrumental in the establishment in 1474 of the English *Pale's standing defence force, the *Brotherhood of St George. He was buried in All Hallows' monastery, Dublin, and was succeeded by his son *Gerald, the 8th earl. SGE

Kildare Place Society. Encouraged by the success of Sunday and day schools on the English model in several Dublin parishes of the *Church of Ireland, a group of philanthropic businessmen and lawyers, *Quakers prominent among them, sought to widen the scope of their work by founding (1811) the Society for the Promoting the Education of the Poor in Ireland. Consistent with government policy to assist with the provision of popular, non-sectarian, education in Ireland, the society quickly attracted state funding. Applying the methods of Joseph Lancaster, the English educationist, it pioneered the monitorial system and soon had an ambitious programme of *teacher-training, publishing, and inspection, based on its headquarters in Kildare Place, Dublin.

Initially supported by some prominent Catholics, including Daniel *O'Connell, the society came under increasing criticism from the Roman Catholic church, which found unacceptable its key principle that the Bible should be read by all children together 'without note or comment'. This, together with evidence both of direct proselytism in some schools and of financial assistance by the society to the schools of openly proselytizing societies (see SECOND REFORMATION), brought Catholic opposition and government disenchantment to a head. From 1831 state support was diverted from such voluntary bodies to the *national schools. KM

Kildare Poems, the name given to a group of sixteen poems written in English, preserved in British Library Ms Harley 913, which consists of a miscellaneous selection of mainly religious and/or satirical material, in verse and prose, written in Latin, French, and English. One of the English pieces is a poem whose author names himself 'Friar Michael of Kildare'. Nothing is known of this man, or of his or others' authorship of these poems. Another, however, is a poem on 'Pers of Birmingham', who was buried in the Franciscan friary in Kildare. From these ascriptions comes the title 'The Kildare Poems'. The manuscript is dated to about 1330. From dialectal evidence, the fact that it once contained a poem beginning 'Yung men of Waterford', and that it was once owned by George Wyse, a 16th-century mayor of Waterford, it is likely that the manuscript was compiled in the city of Waterford, probably by Franciscans, whose order features in references and entries in the manuscript. This suggested provenance is supported by the evidence of a Franciscan concern for the poor and dislike of monks, especially in 'The Land of Cokaygne'. This is a satire on the libidinous delinquency of a house of monks, probably the *Cistercian abbey at Inislounaght, a community not far from Waterford. The monks have no concern for chastity, poverty, and obedience. Everything conspires to help them enjoy an unascetic life: their walls are made of choice food, geese fly in, already cooked, and the local nunnery supplies willing sexual partners. TPD

Kildare rebellion (1534–5). There are two views of the causes of this outbreak. Brendan Bradshaw argues that it was a reaction to deliberate Tudor policies of centralization, directed against overmighty subjects and encouraged by local humanist reformers. S. G. Ellis offers a more contingent explanation, amounting to Kildare miscalculation in an unstable situation. *Surrey's experiment and the chopping and changing of governors had dented the confidence of the 9th earl of *Kildare, Gearóid Óg. Thomas Cromwell's appointments in Ireland during Kildare's final deputyship caused further resentment. The announcement of his replacement by Skeffington in 1533 was not a deliberate challenge, because he was the only Englishman willing to serve in Ireland. Furthermore Cromwell had no radical administrative overhaul in mind, because Skeffington's *Ordinances for the Government of Ireland* were a mish-mash of previously issued instructions.

It was a message from Gearóid Óg rather than false rumours of his execution that resulted in the stage-managed resignation and denunciation of royal policies before the Irish privy council of his son Lord Offaly, 'Silken Thomas', on 11 June 1534. This demonstration of *Geraldine frustration was intended to force negotiations, but with the crown pushing through the *Reformation in England such defiance had to be taken seriously and so Kildare was sent to the Tower. On 27 July Offaly's men murdered Archbishop John *Alen and began a siege of *Dublin Castle. Silken Thomas proclaimed a Catholic crusade, made contacts with English and Welsh Catholics, and requested support from the pope and Emperor Charles V. Skeffington finally arrived with an army of 2,300 in October. The 'pardon of *Maynooth' on 25 March 1535 saw effective resistance collapse. With no imperial aid forthcoming, Thomas surrendered on 25 August to Lord Leonard *Grey on promise of his life. He was sent to London where in February 1537 he was executed with five of his uncles. Although the rebellion cost £23,000 to suppress, remarkable leniency was shown, with only 75 executions. With Kildare lands confiscated and the large Geraldine affinity leaderless, the crown perforce embarked on radical administrative reform which entailed the more expensive alternative of ruling directly with an English governor and garrison.

Bradshaw, Brendan, *The Irish Constitutional Revolution of the Sixteenth Century* (1979); Ellis, S. G., *Tudor Ireland* (1985)

HM

Kilkenny has the distinction of being the only true inland city in the country. Urban beginnings were pre-Norman: Kilkenny was the ecclesiastical and political centre of the kingdom and diocese of Ossory. However, it was in the 13th century—as focal point of Anglo-Norman power in south Leinster—that the city first achieved prominence, reflected in a remarkable cluster of monastic foundations and the reconstruction of its cathedral. Four contiguous boroughs nestled together, but only the urban core of 'Hightown', adjacent to the great castle of the *Marshals, was walled. The town's prosperity was linked to the *wool trade of its hinterland, a measure of that prosperity being the recurrent meeting of the medieval Irish *parliament within its walls.

Kilkenny had a second cycle of expansion in the late 15th, 16th, and early 17th centuries, becoming in effect capital of the *Ormond lordship and benefiting from sustained Butler patronage. The unique survival of civic architecture and funereal monuments from that period is a pointer to the wealth of its merchants and their patrons. The choice of Kilkenny as location for the assembly of the *Confederate Catholics (1642–8) was tribute both to the strength of its Catholic burghers and to its civic prestige.

After the wars, trade passed to Protestant hands, but 18th-century Kilkenny retained its Catholic and *Old English ambience. Population grew from around 2,000 in the 1660s to about 18,500 in 1821, a transformation linked to the growth of woollen blanket manufacture in the town, together with *brewing, *flour milling, and marble stone-cutting. In addition Kilkenny became a regional service and consumption centre and continued a long tradition of outstanding schools. Until the coming of the *railways it was also the busiest resting point on the Dublin–Cork road.

Industrial decline and transport change after 1830 froze, then sharply reduced, Kilkenny's size; but during this time much of the castle was spectacularly rebuilt and the city continued its distinctive cultural history: the Kilkenny Archaeological Society was founded in 1849 and became a highly influential national organization. In the mid-20th century Kilkenny re-emerged to become a provincial leader in the arts, craft design, and urban conservation.

Clarke, Howard (ed.), *Irish Cities* (1995); Nolan, William, and Whelan, Kevin (eds.), *Kilkenny: History and Society* (1990)

DD

Kilkenny, Confederation of, see CONFEDERATE CATHOLICS OF IRELAND.

Kilkenny, Statute of (1366), the most ambitious legislation produced by the medieval Irish *parliament. Its 36 clauses cover a variety of topics but they are remembered mainly for their preamble with its deprecation of the increasing *'Gaelicization' of the English colony and for those clauses aimed at halting and reversing that trend. These required all living within the colony to use the English language and English personal names and to ride their horses in the English manner. They also required the use of English methods of dispute settlement, by litigation in the courts of the lordship rather than by self-help through distraint or violent retaliation in accordance with *march or native Irish law. Further 'contamination' of the colony by the native Irish from outside the area of the lordship was to be avoided by prohibiting their presentment to ecclesiastical benefices within the lordship and their admission to religious houses, and by the prohibition of the creation of social relationships between colonists and native Irish through marriage, standing as godparents, *fostering, and concubinage. Even minstrels and other entertainers who came from outside the lordship were no longer to be allowed to travel freely within it.

The legislators did not expect the colony to enjoy peaceful relations with its Irish neighbours. Other clauses, therefore, were concerned with making proper preparations for future wars. Non-martial games were prohibited, as was the export of horses or armour to the native Irish. There were to be regular monthly reviews of all men of military age and their weapons. Other clauses were aimed at avoiding unnecessary wars caused by breaches of truces and treaties and by the conclusion of treaties whose clauses did too little to avoid future conflict. Wars were only to be commenced after proper deliberation and by the colony as a whole (not by individual counties), and peace was also to be made only after proper consultation. Since the colony was also threatened with disorder by internal forces, other measures prohibited colonists retaining *kerns, *hobelars, and *idlemen in their service within the colony or supporting other kinds of malefactor, and allowed the disregarding of jurisdictional boundaries when felons were being pursued. Still other clauses made a variety of reforms in local and central administration and attempted to create a system for regulating the price of imported goods and the payment of labourers.

Much of the legislation was not novel. As many as 20 of the 36 chapters of the statute were re-enactments (some in identical words) of ordinances enacted by a great council at Kilkenny in 1351 during the period Thomas *Rokeby was chief governor of the lordship. Others re-enacted clauses from a 1357 English ordinance for Ireland. An older generation of scholars saw this legislation as marking a major turning point in the history of the medieval lordship, when its rulers finally turned their backs on the native Irish and excluded them from the colony. More recent writers have emphasized its essentially defensive nature, as a reaction to the growing threat posed to the colony by the cultural and military encroachments of the resurgent Irish. Its wider European context is the series of measures adopted in many states in the aftermath of the first attacks of the *Black Death and intended to preserve the existing social and economic order. Within a few years licences were being granted by the government for breaches of some of its regulations but the statute was re-enacted on several occasions during the 15th century and unlicensed breaches continued to be investigated and punished until the legislation was repealed in the parliament of 1613–15. PAB

Kilmainham treaty (1882), an understanding between *Parnell and the *Gladstone government which marked the end of the *Land War. The arrest of Parnell and leading nationalists in October 1881, for attacking the *Land Act of that year, had initiated a great increase in Irish agrarian crime. The government now sought to secure the restoration of order by agreeing, effectively, that Parnell and his followers would be released in return for his acceptance of the act and his influence in quelling unrest. In addition, the Land Act was extended to leaseholders and better terms offered to tenants whose rent was in arrears. JL

kincogish (Ir. *cin comocuis*, 'the offence of a kinsman') is a term referring to the liability of a kinsman to pay compensation if an offender has evaded payment or has been unable to pay. Similarly, it was possible to distrain a kinsman if pressure could not be brought on a defendant directly. Because this principle by which kinsmen were contingently liable for each other's offences was strange to *Anglo-Norman settlers, it was known by the Anglicized Irish term 'kincogish'. TMC-E

king. *Rí* is the Irish word for king. Traditionally, Irish kingship has been seen as retaining archaic features deriving from Indo-European custom. These include inauguration ceremonies which involve killing horses or bulls and drinking and/or bathing in the resulting soup, chariot-riding, especially on hilltops associated with the *síd* (otherworld), phallic stones, and marriages between king and sovereignty goddesses, symbolized by gifts of ale. The texts describing these practices vary in specifics, date, and geographical location; the belief that they reflect prehistoric ceremonies derives ultimately from 19th-century scholars of myth (notably J. G. Frazer in *The Golden Bough*) and is currently a matter of debate. References to taboos on royal activities and the need to be physically unblemished are common in secondary literature but less so in early sources. More substantial evidence exists for a widespread Irish belief that a kingdom's fertility and success was directly related to royal righteousness (*fír flathemon* or the justice of a ruler).

Mid-20th-century scholarship argued that Irish annals depicted powerful warriors who had superseded what have been called the 'priestly vegetables' of sacral kingship. This change is often termed the transition from tribal to dynastic kingship, exemplified by the 8th-century disappearance of *moccu*-names and by *Uí Néill territorial expansion. The timing of change has been left unclear, but there is general agreement that it had occurred by the 11th century, when Irish kings are seen as exercising a rule similar to that of their counterparts elsewhere in Europe. In contrast to the generally static view of royalty for the early period, kingship in Ireland is seen as developing rapidly in the centuries immediately prior to the *Anglo-Norman invasion.

More recent doubts about this model have been fuelled by the work of Liam Breatnach, Kim McCone, and Donnchadh Ó Corráin, which has undermined Daniel Binchy's contention that Irish *law tracts delineated a society pre-dating that in which the tracts themselves were written. The description of kings in 7th- and 8th-century legal texts is now being harmonized with the evidence of other medieval sources to produce a picture of rulers who were entitled to tribute from all free families, had the right to hospitality for themselves and their retinues, were forbidden to undertake servile work, helped to promulgate law and often enforced it, occasionally acted as judges, and were served by a mandarin class of clerics and *fili* (poets), who attempted to provide a Christian ideology concerning royal office. Accession depended as much on control of resources and proximity to the political centre as it did on lineage. Royal power is thus seen as developing along lines similar to elsewhere in Europe.

The perceived hierarchy of kingship has also been modified. Eoin MacNeill and Daniel Binchy argued for a three-tier model: *rí tuaithe* (king of a **tuath*), *ruiri* or *rí tuath* (overking or king of more than one *tuath*), and *rí ruirech* (king of overkings). The *rí cóicid* (king of a province) was seen as paralleling the *rí ruirech*, although this is not specified in the sources. The status of each is mirrored in his *lóg n-enech* (honour-price—see ENECH), the fine payable to him for offences committed against himself or those under his protection. In contrast, recent scholars have underlined the inconsistency of terminology used to describe both kings and territories as well as the categorization of both lords and kings simply as members of the *grád flatha* (grade of nobility). They tend to make a functional distinction between king and overking, with the proviso that some overkings were more powerful than others. Liam Breatnach has also adduced evidence disproving Binchy's contention that a kingship of all Ireland was unknown to early lawyers.

Regardless of the exact status of either overlord or subordinate king, all scholars are apparently agreed that submission to a superior was indicated by entry into his house or acceptance of *rath* (gift made by overking to applicant). The king became a *céile* (*client) of his overking, engaging to pay tribute (usually cattle), provide hospitality for the overking and forces for his army, and attend his **óenach* (assembly). Exactions varied, depending on the status of the subordinate and his dynastic links to the overking.

Binchy, D. A., *Celtic and Anglo-Saxon Kingship* (1970)
Charles-Edwards, T., 'Early Medieval Kingships in the British Isles', in S. Bassett (ed.), *The Origins of Anglo-Saxon Kingdoms* (1989)
Kelly, F., *A Guide to Early Irish Law* (1988)

CS

King, William (1650–1729), theologian and bishop. Though born into a Presbyterian background in Co. Antrim, he was ordained in the Church of Ireland and became dean of *St Patrick's cathedral in 1674. During the *Williamite War he remained in Dublin, and was imprisoned by the Jacobites. He became bishop of Derry in 1690 and archbishop of Dublin in 1703. *The State of the Protestants of Ireland under the Late King James's Government* (1691) is often read as an anti-Catholic polemic. But its real purpose was to justify the extreme step of having withdrawn allegiance from a legitimate monarch, on the grounds that the position Irish Protestants had been placed in had left them no other choice. King in fact voted against most of the *penal laws introduced after 1691, and strongly condemned the incomplete ratification of the treaty of *Limerick. On the other hand he strongly opposed concessions of any kind to Presbyterians. *A Discourse Concerning the Inventions of Men in the Worship of God* (1694) attacked Presbyterian claims to be a separate denomination. Two other important tracts were *De origine male* (On the Origin of Evil) (1702) and *A Sermon on Predestination* (1709). Within the Church of Ireland he was a consistent, if somewhat fussy and self-righteous, promoter of internal reform and conscientious churchmanship.

King's unwavering commitment to the Protestant succession assured him of the favour of the incoming *Whig government after 1714, and he was four times lord justice during 1714–22. However, his hostility to any move to improve the position of dissenters put him at odds with English ministers. In addition he was increasingly seen as an over-zealous defender of Irish national interests. Already during 1697–9 a legal dispute with the *Irish Society had involved him in constitutional controversy, when he had refused to accept the right of the English House of Lords to overturn an Irish verdict in his favour. He strongly opposed the *Declaratory Act, and displayed open hostility to English recipients of Irish ecclesiastical patronage. That he was passed over in favour of *Boulter for the archbishopric of Armagh was due to politics as well as age.

kingdom of Ireland, officially established by the Irish parliament in June 1541 under 'the act for kingly title'. 'Kingdom' had appeared in some official documentation of the early 13th century but the usual designation was the 'land' of Ireland. This was a hereditary dependency, like the duchy of Gascony, over which the English king exercised 'lordship' as an inalienable parcel of the crown of England. The terms 'kingdom' and 'realm' obviously denoted a higher status—for instance in 1487 the independently minded Irish parliament crowned the pretender Lambert *Simnel king of Ireland as well as king of England.

English sovereignty over Ireland rested not only on conquest and submission but also on papal donation in 1156 under the bull *Laudabiliter*. By 1541 Henry VIII had broken with Rome (see REFORMATION) and the *Geraldine League had threatened to transfer sovereignty to the Catholic king of Scotland. Henry VIII's new title, celebrated by bonfires in Dublin, coincided with the policy of *surrender and regrant under which the Irish were to be transformed from enemies into subjects. However, the reformers had themselves to persuade Henry VIII, who worried about the expense of ruling the whole island and keeping an estate there worthy of the new designation.

Some of the ideological shine was taken off the 1541 development when Queen Mary obtained a papal bull approving the new title. Furthermore the change in status made little difference in practice because the English privy council, chancery, and parliament still claimed superiority over their Irish counterparts. In the 17th century Patrick *Darcy and his *Catholic Confederate colleagues wanted the kingdom made a reality. In fact the concept of Ireland as a kingdom provided a new focus of loyalty for Irish Catholics, particularly those of Gaelic background, after the Stuart succession. They claimed that one of their own race—a descendant of the mythical Míl Espáine (see MILESIANS)—was on the English throne and that Ireland was a more ancient kingdom than his British realms. This was celebrated in poetry; in the *Annals of the Kingdom of Ireland* by the *Four Masters, and in other histories by *Rothe, *Keating, and *O'Flaherty.

Ireland arguably operated as a kingdom between 1782 and 1801 with the modification of *Poynings's Law and the revocation of the *Declaratory Act, although the actual method by which it was governed scarcely changed (see LEGISLATIVE INDEPENDENCE). HM

King's Inns. In 1539 judges and leading legal practitioners joined together to lease the buildings of the recently dissolved Dominican friary in Dublin as term-time accommodation. The lawyers lost possession of the renamed 'King's Inn' in the later 16th century but regained it, this time on a permanent basis, in the early 17th century. An organized society of the King's Inns was in existence by 1607. Membership did not become compulsory for barristers practising in the Four Courts until 1629 and for other barristers until 1635; by 1629 membership was also (in theory at least) compulsory for attorneys practising in the Four Courts. During the 18th century King's Inns acquired control over entry into both branches of the legal profession, and also disciplinary powers over both branches. However, it subsequently lost the power to control admissions to the 'lower branch' of the profession, and disciplinary power over it, to the *Incorporated Law Society.

By the mid-18th century the original King's Inn(s) had ceased to be habitable and in 1776 the new *Four Courts were built on their site. The society began work on its present building at Henrietta Street in 1800. PAB

king's lieutenant, the title given to the more socially exalted governors of Ireland in the later Middle Ages. It was also borne by nobles sent to rule English Gascony, and by those whom French kings appointed to govern regions of their kingdom. The first king's lieutenant in Ireland was Piers Gaveston, earl of Cornwall, the favourite of Edward II, who was sent as a form of exile in 1308. The second was Roger *Mortimer, who arrived in 1317 to resist the *Bruce invasion. William de *Burgh, earl of Ulster, held the position in 1331–2. A *justiciar continued to serve under these early lieutenants. The title became more common from 1361, when *Lionel, the second surviving son of Edward III, was sent to Ireland with some 800 troops whose wages were paid from England. The habit of financing Irish wars from English resources, and of appointing members of the royal family or higher nobility to the lieutenancy, continued in the 15th century. These lieutenants made contracts with the king to serve for a fixed term and to receive wages for a specified number of troops; they were given wider powers, especially of patronage, than justiciars. RFF

Kingstown, the new name given in 1821, in commemoration of the visit of *George IV, to Dunleary, south of Dublin, from which the king embarked to return to England. In 1922 it was renamed Dún Laoghaire. In the 18th century a minor harbour village, Dunleary/Kingstown grew very rapidly from the 1820s to the 1870s, by which point it had a population of some 18,000; the smaller and shorter-lived autonomous townships of Blackrock and Dalkey were immediately contiguous.

The town's rise rested on a number of factors—the construction of the huge artificial harbour for the mail and packet services to Holyhead in the 1820s; its fashionable status as location for upper-class yacht racing; and its attractions as a salubrious maritime retreat from an often sickly city. The most important factor was, however, the building of a rail link from the city in 1834 and the entrepreneurial skills of the *railway company concerned; not by coincidence did Kingstown become an independent township in the same year. Underpinning all of this was a history of competent management of the estate on which most of the town lay, jointly owned by the Longford and de Vesci families.

Local government remained in the hands of Protestant businessmen and property developers, *unionist in their politics, until 1914 when *Nationalist Party supporters won control of the town. The 20th-century town retained its independence until local government reform in 1993, by which time it had become an indistinguishable part of the south-east wing of the Dublin conurbation. DD

Kinsale, battle of (24 Dec. 1601), the decisive battle of the *Nine Years War. In September 1601 a Spanish expeditionary force disembarked at Kinsale but was quickly besieged by *Mountjoy. The arrival of Hugh *O'Neill and Red Hugh *O'Donnell left the crown forces trapped and dying of disease between the Irish and Spanish armies. However, the Irish were routed while mounting a disastrous dawn attack and on 2 January 1602 the Spaniards agreed to withdraw. HM

knight service, a duty the medieval lay elite owed for tenure of their lands. Royal grants in Ireland were specific: in 1172 Hugh de *Lacy received Meath for the service of 50 knights. In the late 13th century the entire service of Ireland was assessed as *c.*427 knights. Lords granted land on similar terms to their followers; indeed lordships tended to contain more knights than services owed to the king. Service normally involved 40 days on campaign, but occasionally took the form of castle-guard. The crown increasingly commuted it to a tax, known as 'royal service' or 'scutage'. RFF

Knights of Colombanus, an association of Catholic lay men founded in 1915 by Canon James O'Neill in Belfast 'to secure adequate recognition for Catholic doctrines and practices in all phases of life'. Influenced by Catholic social action, its main activity was fund-raising for charitable purposes. It spread to Dublin in 1917 and the Colomban Knights joined it in 1922. Recognized by the Catholic church in 1934, it helped fund the chair of Catholic sociology at *Maynooth College from 1937. Traditionally conservative in outlook, attached to corporate ritual, and narrowly based socially, the association has worked in recent years to diversify both membership and activities and to shed its aura of secrecy. TO'C

Knights Templars, created to protect pilgrims to Palestine and combining a military function with life according to a religious rule, were present in Ireland before 1180, when they were granted the vill of Clontarf by *Henry II. This became the chief house or preceptory of the order in Ireland and five other preceptories were established by 1200. The Templars' lifestyle was modelled on that of the *Cistercians and the preceptories were religious houses in which novices were received and instructed and to which older members could retire. Nine other smaller houses (cameras) were established in the late 12th and 13th centuries. All the foundations were in areas controlled by the Anglo-Normans and their role in Ireland was to protect the colony from the attacks of the native population, though some Templars from Ireland fought in the Holy Land. The native Irish were initially excluded from membership but this ban was later lifted.

In 1307–8, as part of the wider campaign against them, the Templars in Ireland were imprisoned and in 1310 fifteen of them were brought to trial in Dublin. In 1311 three preceptories were assigned to accommodate members of the order; the rest of their property, in accordance with the decisions of Clement V and the Council of Vienne, passed to the Knights Hospitallers after 1312. CNÓC

Knock, a parish in Co. Mayo where a vision of the Blessed Virgin was reported by fifteen local people on 21 August 1879. Two ecclesiastical commissions examined the affair, one in 1879, the second in 1936, their conclusions permitting Knock's establishment as a centre of Marian pilgrimage. The Knock Shrine Committee was set up in 1935, and a folk museum in 1973, while a basilica was completed shortly afterwards. Knock's early success was part of the worldwide growth in devotion to the Virgin Mary and, in Ireland, was an arm of the so-called *devotional revolution. The devotion associated with Knock was personal with a strong emotional appeal. Since the second *Vatican Council more attention has been paid to its theological content and Knock's mission has extended itself into a broader pastoral programme. Like *Croagh Patrick and *Lough Derg, it has retained its popularity despite the changes in devotional practice associated with Vatican II. TO'C

Knockdoe, battle of (19 Aug. 1504), the defeat of Ulick Burke of Clanricard by Gearóid Mór FitzGerald, 8th earl of *Kildare, on a punitive expedition into Connacht after Burke's seizure of Galway city. Ten thousand men took part in this largest ever battle between Irishmen; most of the fighting was undertaken by *gallowglasses; about 2,000 fatalities resulted. The battle saw the first recorded use in Ireland of a handgun (see FIREARMS), which a Dublin soldier used as a bludgeon. HM

Knox, Alexander (1757–1831), *Church of Ireland layman and theologian. Largely self-taught, Knox was much influenced in his early life by John Wesley, with whom his family was intimate. However, his theological studies led him to a position very much in tune with that of the Oxford movement; while claims that he was a key figure in this attempt to reassert the Catholic element within Anglicanism have been challenged, none deny that his views on the nature of the church influenced many. After an early interest in politics, which brought him the position of private secretary to *Castlereagh, then Irish *chief secretary, he abandoned a promising public career for a life of study and reflection. Much of this was spent in his rooms in Dawson Street, Dublin (where he was much sought after as a conversationalist), and with the *Latouche family in Delgany, Co. Wicklow. As a young man, he wrote on politics, but is best remembered for his published *Remains* (1834–7) and correspondence with John Jebb (bishop of Limerick, 1823–33). KM

Kyteler, Alice (*fl.* 1324), the subject of the most famous of Irish *witchcraft trials. Alice was a Kilkenny matron of Flemish descent, who had married four husbands. She was alleged by Richard Ledrede, the English Franciscan bishop of Ossory (who had been educated in France and who shared to the point of obsession Pope John XXII's preoccupation with heresy and sorcery) to have lain with a demon incubus named 'Robin FitzArt', and to have cast spells to advance the career of William Outlaw, her son by her first marriage. Outlaw was a merchant and moneylender related to Roger Outlaw, the prior of the Hospitallers and *chancellor of Ireland, and was connected with leading Kilkenny figures. Alice was accused of sorcery by the families of her later husbands, who were hostile to Outlaw. Her case became caught up in disputes between the bishop and elements of the local elite, led by Arnold le Poer, the *seneschal of Kilkenny, who is said to have denounced Ledrede as a 'vagabond from England'. Ledrede later excommunicated both le Poer and Roger Outlaw on improbable charges of heresy. Alice escaped to England but her associate, Petronilla de Midia, was executed. RFF

Labour Court, created by the Industrial Relations Act (1946), one of a number of measures by which *Lemass sought to improve relations with the trade union movement in the immediate post-war period. Its main functions have been to appoint conciliation officers (later industrial relations officers) who can mediate in industrial conflicts, and to investigate disputes and recommend terms of settlement. Although the court has the power to summon witnesses under penalty and take evidence under oath, these have never been used, and its recommendations remain non-binding.

Labour Party. 'Labour' candidates had contested local elections since 1899, and the Irish Trade Union Congress (see IRISH CONGRESS OF TRADE UNIONS) had voted in 1912 to form a Labour Party. Two years later the congress changed its name to 'Irish Trades Union Congress and Labour Party', but no party organization was established and the movement stood aside at the general elections of 1918 and 1921. The party enjoyed a dramatic success at the general election of 1922, when it won 21.3 per cent of the vote and all but one of its eighteen candidates were elected (see PACT ELECTION). The party was never able to match this performance subsequently, and has normally won in the region of 10 per cent of the vote at general elections (though dropping as low as 5.7 per cent in 1933 and reaching a record 19.3 per cent in 1992). The formal organizational unity of the party and the *trade union movement lasted until 1930, when the party and congress separated.

The weakness of the Labour Party has been remarkable from a comparative perspective. One explanation, that 20th-century Irish society long remained agrarian and lacked a sizeable industrial working class, is unconvincing; powerful socialist movements developed elsewhere (for example, in Scandinavia) in similar conditions, based substantially on a rural proletariat. The prevalence of conservative, Catholic values can offer little more than a partial explanation; this has not been incompatible with a powerful strand of political radicalism in Ireland, and has coexisted with socialism in other predominantly Catholic societies. The fundamental explanation appears to lie in the dominance of the national question, on which the party had difficulty in taking an unambiguous and distinctive stance; this issue was a central one at elections for many years after 1918. Strangely, industrial workers have consistently been more attracted to *Fianna Fáil than to the Labour Party.

In addition to being much weaker than its west European counterparts, the Irish Labour Party has been rather less radical. Party policy has normally been reformist, though it has occasionally made more explicit use of *socialist rhetoric, as in the mid-1930s and from the late 1960s. It has included a range of opinions on the national question, and in the domain of *foreign policy has been attached to the policy of military *neutrality.

The party's early leaders, Thomas *Johnson (1918–27), T. J. O'Connell (1927–32), and William Norton (1932–60), were well known for their trade union involvement, and in many ways saw the party as the political arm of the organized labour movement. Their successors, Brendan *Corish (1960–77), Frank Cluskey (1977–81), and Michael O'Leary (1981–2), though coming from similar backgrounds, tended to have a more ambitious vision of the party's electoral potential, and to be less cautious on policy matters. Dick Spring, who took over as leader in 1982, brought with him the image of a professional politician rather than a trade unionist, but he was only a little more successful than his predecessors in shaking off the image of his party as a sectional one with a strong regional base in Munster and Leinster. It is, however, of some significance that in recent elections the party has managed to increase its representation significantly in cities (including Dublin) outside its traditional area of core support.

Gallagher, Michael, *The Irish Labour Party in Transition 1957–82* (1982)

JC

Lacy. The Herefordshire branch of the Lacy family, which originated from Lassy in Normandy, was prominent in Ireland during the first two generations of the *Anglo-Norman settlement. Hugh de *Lacy I (d. 1186), who had lands in England, Wales, and Normandy, accompanied *Henry II to Ireland, and in 1172 was granted Meath. His lands were inherited by his eldest son, *Walter (d. 1241), while his second son, *Hugh II (d. 1242), was made earl of Ulster by King *John in 1205. Walter and Hugh II fell foul of John and suffered forfeiture in 1210. Meath was restored to Walter in 1215, but Hugh did not recover Ulster until 1227, after a failed rising in 1223–4. Their half-brother, William 'Gorm' de Lacy, born of Hugh I's second marriage to a daughter of Rory *O'Connor (Ruaidrí Ua Conchobair), supported Hugh II's rebellion. But William, who had married a daughter of Llywelyn the Great, the prince of north Wales, went on to serve Henry III in Brittany in 1230, before being killed in warfare against the Irish of *Bréifne in 1233. Neither Walter nor Hugh II left direct male heirs. Ulster reverted to the crown, while Meath passed to Walter's two granddaughters, who married Geoffrey de *Geneville (d. 1314) and John de *Verdon (d. 1274). A cadet branch of the family, descended from Robert de Lacy of Rathwire (possibly another son of Hugh I), survived in Meath. The Lacys of Rathwire were outlawed for supporting the *Bruce invasion (1315–18), probably out of hostility to Roger *Mortimer, who had become lord of Trim through marriage to the Geneville heiress. RFF

Lacy, Hugh de (d. 1186). De Lacy accompanied *Henry II on his expedition to Ireland in 1171 and was granted the kingdom of *Mide (Meath), along with custody of the city of Dublin, which Henry retained as royal demesne. In 1172 Tigernán Ua Ruairc, king of Bréifne, who had been expanding into the pre-Norman kingdom of Mide, was killed while parleying with de Lacy on the Hill of Ward, Co. Meath. Hugh then set about encastellating Mide, choosing *Trim as his principal castle, and planting Meath with tenants drawn from his English and Welsh estates. About 1180 he married a daughter of Rory *O'Connor (Ruaidrí Ua Conchobair), thereby incurring the suspicions of Henry II that he aspired to the kingship of all Ireland. He was recalled to England to answer charges in 1181, but was sent back with a royal clerk, Robert of Shrewsbury, to oversee him. In 1185 King Henry sent his son *John to assert control over Hugh, but his expedition failed in this aim. When news reached the English court that de Lacy had been murdered by an Irish member of his household, who had struck him with an axe while he was inspecting the building of a castle at Durrow, Henry is reported to have been overjoyed. Hugh's burial in Bective abbey was disputed by St Thomas's abbey, Dublin, which in 1195 secured his head; in 1205 his body was also recovered and laid to rest alongside his first wife, Rose of Monmouth. He was succeeded by his son Walter, who had to invoke the aid of King Richard in 1194 against his brother John, who sought to deny Walter the lordship of Meath. MTF

Lacy, Hugh de (d. 1242), 1st earl of Ulster. Hugh was in Ireland from 1195 and involved himself in the politics of Connacht. King *John used him to destroy his former ally John de *Courcy and in 1205 made him earl of Ulster. John became suspicious of Hugh and his brother Walter and in 1210 chased them from Ireland into Scotland. They travelled to France where Hugh participated in the Albigensian crusade until 1219. In 1220 he joined Llywelyn ap Iorwerth of Gwynedd in attacking William *Marshal II in Wales. He invaded Ireland late in 1223 and plundered his enemies in Meath. The following summer the *justiciar, William Marshal II, captured *Trim Castle from adherents of Hugh and forced him to abandon the siege of *Carrickfergus. After destroying the castle of Coleraine and harrying lands around Dundalk, Hugh surrendered to Marshal in October 1224. In April 1227 Ulster was restored to him as earl. In 1228 he was summoned by the king to fight in France and in 1234 he participated in the murder of Richard Marshal on the Curragh. In 1235 he was involved in the conquest of Connacht by Richard de *Burgh. His reward was the revival of the grant made to him almost 40 years earlier by Richard's father, William. He received lands in Sligo, but apart from founding the manor of Meelick did not involve himself in Connacht, preferring to grant most of his interests to other English lords.

In 1230 Hugh's ally and client Aodh Méith O'Neill (Áed Méith Ó Néill), king of Cenél nEógain, died and was eventually succeeded by an opponent of Hugh's, Brian *O'Neill (Ó Néill). Hugh died before February 1243. He had no surviving sons and his lands reverted to the crown. He married first Lesceline, daughter of Bertram de Verdon, and second Emeline, daughter of Walter de Ridelisford. BGCS

Lacy, Walter de (d. 1241), lord of Meath, a durable baron in Ireland and the Welsh marches who had a stormy relationship with King *John. Walter succeeded to the Irish lands of his father Hugh de *Lacy I (d. 1186) only in 1194, after backing Richard I during John's unsuccessful rebellion. He was a target of John's Irish expedition in 1210, when he forfeited Meath, but served him in France and was soon restored. Between 1216 and 1223 he

supported the young Henry III, and became sheriff of Hereford. Thereafter he constantly crossed the Irish Sea and was a source of stability for the crown, remaining loyal in 1223–4 when his brother Hugh de *Lacy II rebelled. Walter gave the new town of *Drogheda a charter in 1194, advanced the building of *Trim and other castles, and consolidated the settlement in Meath. On his death his lordships were divided between his two granddaughters.
RFF

Ladies' Land League (LLL), set up in 1881 at Michael *Davitt's invitation to run the *Land War in the event of its leaders being jailed. Headed by *Parnell's sister *Anna, the LLL resisted evictions, held public meetings, distributed *United Ireland*, provided temporary accommodation for evicted tenants, and tried to implement *Land League policy. It was wound up in 1882 at Anna Parnell's insistence, as she believed it had responsibility without power. The LLL was the first time Irish women became formally involved in nationalist politics. As well as relatives of key nationalists (Anna Parnell, John *O'Leary's sister Ellen), it included other women who were starting out on a long life of political activism—Jennie O'Toole (later Wyse Power), Hanna Reynolds, Hannah Lynch—almost all of them from middle-class backgrounds. Davitt claimed later that the LLL were 'honester and more sincere than the men'.
CC

Laigin, a people and confederation of dynasties claiming common ancestry from Labraid Loingsech and his grandfather Lóegaire Lorc. The derivation of the name Laigin is not certain, despite its traditional association with the word *láigen* ('a spear'). This etymology is more likely to explain the supposed alternative name for the Laigin, *Gáileóin*. A third group associated with the Laigin, the Domnainn, recalls the British Celtic tribe, the Dumnonii. The Lleyn peninsula in north Wales is cognate with the name Laigin. Among the dynasties regarding themselves as Laigin and descended from Labraid Loingsech were the Uí Garrchon, the Uí Máil, the Uí Failge, the Uí Bairrche, the *Uí Dúnlainge, and the *Uí Chennselaig, all of whom held the kingship of Leinster intermittently from the early historic period onwards. The last four of these dynasties claimed closer genealogical kinship, less likely than the 'prehistoric' genealogical connections to be wholly spurious, through their common eponymous ancestor Cathaír Már. The territory occupied by the Laigin, *cóiced Laigen* ('the province of the Leinstermen') in the south-east of Ireland, extended as far as the Shannon and the Boyne until the 6th century, when it contracted under pressure from the midland and northern *Uí Néill dynasties and from Munster. A division between the northern and the southern parts of the province (Laigen Desgabair and Laigen Tuathgabair) was reflected in the title *rí diabul-Laigen* ('king of double Laigin').
EB

Lake, Gerard (1744–1808), British general. As commander of the army in Ulster during 1797 Lake oversaw the campaign of repression that partially broke the *United Irish organization there. Having succeeded *Abercromby as commander-in-chief in March 1798, he initiated a policy of terror to force the surrender of arms in the counties round Dublin. Following the outbreak of rebellion, he ordered subordinate commanders to take no prisoners. He later served in India and became Viscount Lake of Delhi in 1807.

Lalor, James Fintan (1807–49), nationalist writer. Son of a Catholic *middleman farmer in Queen's County (Laois), Lalor injured his spine in infancy and suffered from recurrent ill health. Influenced by the agrarian radical William Conner, Lalor rejected his father's *repeal politics. However, the formation of the *Irish Confederation and the worsening of the *Great Famine stimulated him to contribute a series of letters to the *Nation* in 1847 calling for a rent strike by small farmers followed by a popular social and political revolution. His attempt to organize a Tenants' Association at Holycross, Co. Tipperary, in 1847 failed, but his idea of agrarian-led revolt was taken up by *Mitchel. Following Mitchel's conviction, Lalor wrote a series of militant articles for the *Irish Felon*, was involved with the confederate clubs, and was imprisoned for five months in 1848. He was involved in unsuccessful attempts to revive the clubs in 1849. Lalor was later appropriated by James *Connolly and Patrick *Pearse as the forerunner of socialist republicanism, although his objective of peasant proprietorship fell short of real agrarian socialism.
PHG

Lancaster, Thomas of (*c*.1388–1421), duke of Clarence, second son of Henry IV and lieutenant of Ireland. When Lancaster was appointed in 1401, aged 13, Sir Stephen Scrope, already experienced in Irish campaigning, served alongside him as his deputy. Scrope, and deputies who served in his absence, had some success in tackling the widespread disorder. Lancaster, resident in England from 1403, returned to Ireland in 1408, when he conducted a campaign in Leinster. In March 1409 he left Ireland for good, although remaining lieutenant until 1413. Thomas Butler, prior of Kilmainham, then served as his deputy, and was the subject of many complaints. Lancaster's lieutenancies, handicapped initially by his youth, were dominated by financial difficulties. Irish exchequer receipts were inadequate for the payment of military forces, and desertion from his retinue forced him in 1402 to sell personal goods. Despite efforts to secure him assignment of revenues in England, he was by 1407 owed more than £20,000. The level of default limited any possibility of a military recovery. DBJ

Land Acts passed over a period of more than half a century transformed landholding from a system of territorial landlordism to one of owner occupancy.

The Landlord and Tenant (Ireland) Act 1870 (Gladstone's first land act) gave the force of law to customary *tenant right where it existed and created similar rights elsewhere in the country, provided for compensation for disturbance of tenants evicted other than for non-payment of rent, and made provision for compensation for improvements in the case of a departing tenant. Its so-called 'Bright clauses' allowed tenants to purchase their holdings.

The Land Law (Ireland) Act 1881 (Gladstone's second land act) granted the *three Fs and instituted the *Land Commission, with authority to adjudicate on fair rents and to make loans of up to 75 per cent of the purchase price to tenants purchasing their holdings.

The Purchase of Land (Ireland) Act 1885 (the Ashbourne Act) increased the loan limit to 100 per cent.

The Purchase of Land (Ireland) Act 1891 (the *Balfour Act) introduced land bonds as an alternative form of payment of landlords selling land to tenants, thereby extending the scope of sales without an equivalent increase in the burden on the exchequer. It also set up the *Congested Districts Board with wide powers to divide and amalgamate holdings with a view to relieving congestion in impoverished areas.

The Irish Land Act 1903 (*Wyndham's Act), unique in that its contents were the product of agreement between representatives of landlords and tenants, laid down financial parameters within which an agreement between a landlord and tenant would be automatically approved by the Land Commission. The act appealed to the farmers because it guaranteed annual repayments lower than existing rents, and to the landlords because it gave a 12 per cent government bonus on the sale price of an entire estate, ensured payment in cash, and allowed them to retain demesne farms now mortgaged to the Land Commission on favourable terms.

The Irish Land Act 1909 (the *Birrell Act) was designed to limit the cost to the exchequer of the success of the Wyndham Act. The terms were disimproved and payment by land bonds was reintroduced. The pace of transactions subsequently slackened.

In the Irish Free State, the Land Act of 1923 (the *Hogan Act) converted rents into payments to the Land Commission, pending compulsory transfer of ownership of remaining tenanted land, abolished the Congested Districts Board, and gave the Land Commission reponsibility for redistribution. The Northern Ireland Land Act (1925) provided for compulsory completion of tenant purchase of land in that jurisdiction. RVC

land agent, the *landlord's local representative, responsible for the day-to-day running and, frequently, the strategic management of his estate. Agents became increasingly important in the early 19th century as the numbers of *middlemen decreased. Their duties varied according to the estate's size and complexity, but normally included collecting rents, setting leases, valuing property, and generally enforcing their employers' property rights. During *elections, an agent might act for his employer's candidate. On very large and widely scattered estates, several land agents could be employed under the direction of a central administrator.

Significant figures of authority in their own right, agents on larger estates frequently acquired additional local status as justices of the peace or *poor law guardians. Eighteenth-century Irish land agents tended to be of higher social standing than their English counterparts; many were of minor gentry stock. During the 19th century, an increasing degree of professionalism became apparent, as first lawyers, and latterly full-time agents, were employed. Land agents have become notorious in the popular historical imagination for their alleged dishonesty and ruthlessness. While such agents did exist, the low reputation of the body as a whole owes more to their unenviable position as representatives of an increasingly discredited landed elite, with whom they were closely identified. LJP

land annuities were repayments to the British government for loans advanced to Irish tenant farmers to purchase their land under the *Land Acts of 1891–1909. The *Government of Ireland Act 1920 provided that the governments of both Northern and Southern Ireland would retain the revenue from land annuities, but for the south this was superseded by the *Anglo-Irish treaty and subsequent instruments. Under the 1923 Anglo-Irish financial agreement, confirmed in the Ultimate Financial Settlement of 1926, the Irish government agreed to collect the annuities from tenants and pay them to the British government.

In 1925 Peadar *O'Donnell, editor of the *IRA newspaper *An Phoblacht*, began a campaign to abolish the annuities which was subsequently taken over by *Fianna Fáil. When de *Valera took office in 1932, he refused to pay the annuities, the main reason being that the 1923 and 1926 agreements had not been approved by the *Dáil. He refused to accept *Commonwealth arbitration. The British government retaliated with special duties on Irish imports, initiating the *Economic War. DMcM

Land Commission, set up by the *Land Act of 1881 as a body charged with fixing rents that would be binding on landlord and tenant. It was also empowered to purchase estates with a view to transferring ownership to tenants, to whom it could advance a proportion of the purchase price by way of a loan. In accordance with the quasi-judicial function of the body one or more of the commissioners had the status of a judge of the High Court. The Church Temporalities Commission charged with disposing of the property of the established church following *disestablishment had completed the bulk of its work by 1881: the Land Commission now assumed its remaining functions and inherited its clerical personnel and headquarters.

With agrarian issues being so central to Irish public life the various functions of the Land Commission had a large political significance. It can be seen as a stabilizer in volatile circumstances, mediating change with an imperturbability unachievable by politicians increasingly susceptible to public pressures. Thus, in determining the thousands of cases referred to it in 1881 and 1882, the commission tacitly took 'fair rent' to mean 'politically acceptable rent' and was the main agent in the deflation of the *Land War.

Facilitating the transfer of land ownership from landlords to farmers under the terms of the Land Acts was to be the commission's largest area of activity. This transfer was one of the key socio-political transformations of modern Irish history. The 1903 act assigned newly appointed members designated as 'estates commissioners' to specialize in this work. By 1921 the title deeds of most of the land of Ireland had been processed by the commission, the period of most intensive activity having begun with the 1903 act. This work resumed in the 1920s.

The distribution of land, as distinct from its ownership, was the third main area of commission activity and one likewise loaded with political implications. The commission was given powers of redistribution under the 1903 act but it was the acquisition of the functions of the *Congested Districts Board under the 1923 act that placed this work at the centre of the commission's activities. The same act gave wide powers for the compulsory acquisition of untenanted land anywhere in the state deemed necessary for relief of congestion. Redistribution took off in earnest in the 1930s as land prices plummeted and de *Valera's supporters looked to the fulfilment of his populist promises. The most eye-catching of a number of measures taken was the transplantation of many thousands of migrants from western counties to small farms carved out of confiscated ranches in Cos. Kildare and Meath. This was an important piece of social engineering; it also amounted to piecemeal concession to a radical policy until (in the 1970s) the policy lost credibility. In 1984 the scope of the commission's activities was drastically cut back. The Land Commission (Dissolution) Act of 1992 tied up most of the loose ends. RVC

Land League (Irish National Land League), the key organization in the main phase of the *Land War, founded in Dublin in October 1879. Its chief architect was Michael *Davitt, who intended it to promote and co-ordinate a countywide campaign against *landlordism. The decision of Charles Stewart *Parnell to accept the presidency of the organization greatly widened its potential scope and facilitated the absorption of the existing Central Tenants' Defence Association. The league had a widely representative committee of 54, but this had no mechanism for controlling the executive, which was dominated by men of advanced nationalist views. Starting from its original stronghold in Co. Mayo the league extended its network of branches throughout the country (except for the predominantly Protestant areas of Ulster), aided where necessary by the work of travelling organizers remunerated from the league's plentiful American funds. The weekly *United Ireland* was launched in August 1881 as the organ of the league.

While peasant proprietorship was a stated objective of the Land League, some of its supporters had more revolutionary aims. The majority of tenants entertained the less ambitious hope of rent reductions and the concession of this under the *Land Act of August 1881 undermined the unity of the league. That in turn emboldened the government to lodge Parnell and most of the executive in Kilmainham jail. When the prisoners issued a 'no rent' manifesto the authorities responded by outlawing the league, on 20 October 1881. Following his release in May 1882 Parnell effectively dismantled what remained of the Land League and also the *Ladies' Land League. RVC

landlords, the owners or leaseholders of property who rented some or all of this out to others. We may thus distinguish between landlords who were land*owners*, and who held a permanent fee simple interest in their land; those who held land on perpetuity leases or for terms of several hundred years, and whose property interests were, in effect, nearly as permanent (see LAND TENURE); and *middlemen. The term is, however, widely used as a synonym for the first group, and it is this usage which is adopted here.

Landlords have acquired a negative resonance in the popular historical imagination, reflecting the long-standing emphasis, in *nationalist writing, on their colonial origins and allegedly predatory attitudes. By 1703, the vast majority of Ireland's landowning landlords were of English or Scots origin, and had acquired their property during the *plantations and subsequent land confiscations of the 16th and 17th centuries, at the expense of the existing Gaelic Irish and *Old English landowners. These land transfers constituted a cultural as well as an economic revolution in landownership. Previously, land had provided the basis for complex social and familial ties which linked titular landowners and their dependants in ways frequently reinforced by their shared confessional and cultural identity. In contrast, the landlord class created by *c.*1700 was, for the most part, linked to its tenants by economic rather than social ties, and, in most parts of Ireland, separated from them by language (English), religion (Anglican or Episcopalian), ethnicity, and culture. Many but by no means all landlords were titled. By 1703, only 14 per cent of land remained in Catholic ownership, a figure reduced still further during the 18th century by the *penal laws.

Despite these distinguishing characteristics, Ireland's landlords were neither homogeneous in wealth and attitude nor unchanging in number. As elsewhere in *ancien régime* Europe, they constituted a numerically insignificant elite who nevertheless derived enormous economic, social, and political authority from their virtual monopoly of landownership. Their numbers rose from an estimated 5,000 families in the 1780s, when they owned over 95 per cent of all productive land and could be accurately described as a *Protestant or Anglo-Irish ascendancy, to around 9,000–10,000 by the mid-19th century. Their aggregate rent roll reflected the overall performance of the agricultural economy. Head rents rose from *c.* £5 million in the 1780s to *c.* £9 million in 1800, and more slowly to £12 million in the early 1840s. By 1870 they were around £10 million. Behind these figures lay extreme variations in the size and value of individual landlords' estates. The government returns of 1876 list 5,000 proprietors as owning between 100 and 1,000 acres; 3,400 as owning between 1,000 and 10,000; and 300 as owning over 10,000 acres.

Although individual proprietors such as Lord Farnham in Co. Cavan or John *Foster in Co. Louth were active advocates of farm improvement, in general little landlord wealth was reinvested in agriculture; Ó Gráda suggests an average of 3 per cent by the mid-19th century. More seems to have been spent on maintaining a social 'presence' during the Dublin or London 'seasons', or on status-enhancing projects such as the construction (or reconstruction) of country houses and their associated parklands, or on improving control of agrarian marketing by laying out *estate towns and villages.

Irish landlords were also divided politically: between *Whigs and *Tories in the 18th century, and various shades of Conservative, Liberal, *home rule and *Unionist opinion in the 19th. They were at their most powerful during *Grattan's parliament (1782–1801), when Anglican landlords saw themselves as the embodiment of (Protestant) Irish *patriotism. By surrendering their political independence at the Act of *Union, they consigned themselves thereafter to a progressively more marginalized role in the imperial British parliament. Here, the increasing challenge to the landlords' interests culminated in the passage of successive *Land Acts between 1870 and 1909, which ultimately divested them of their land and the residual authority derived from it.

Ó Gráda, Cormac, 'The Investment Behaviour of Irish Landlords 1830–75: Some Preliminary Findings', *Agricultural History Review*, 23 (1975)

Vaughan, W., *Landlords and Tenants in Mid-Victorian Ireland* (1994)

LJP

land reclamation, as distinct from land clearance, brought under cultivation previously unfarmed land by remedying major deficiencies in the soil's natural structure, drainage, or fertility. Land clearance achieved the same objective on a wider scale but did not involve this element of rehabilitation. Land reclamation was therefore a comparatively expensive business, whether in terms of capital or labour investment, and consequently tended to take place only after all easily cleared land had already been brought into use. Accordingly, it invariably occurred on the margins of existing cultivation and in response to a pressing demand for increased agricultural land. Its occurrence was thus as much a function of socio-economic pressure as of environmental opportunity.

In Ireland, land reclamation was particularly widespread between *c.*1750 and 1845, when it was designed to extend the area of cultivation in response to *population growth and, prior to 1815, the growing profitability of agriculture. While most reclamation was undertaken by tenants and their *landlords, other institutions such as town corporations and the government were occasionally involved. In 1809–14 the government surveyed Ireland's *bogs with a view to reclaiming them in order to alleviate pressure on land. Although nothing came of this scheme, marginal uplands and bogs, particularly in the west of the country, witnessed widespread incremental reclamation by tenants in response to locally extreme pre-*Famine population growth. Arguably, the availability of this reservoir of minimally fertile land encouraged such growth, as may have those landlords who were prepared to facilitate reclamation by letting land at low rents. Thus rising population pressure pushed an impoverished peasant class onto progressively more marginal hillsides and boglands. Here they applied a variety of labour-intensive appropriate technologies, including the spade cultivation of 'lazy beds' and the use of natural fertilizers and soil conditioners such as seaweed and crushed seashells, to raise *potato crops on land of inherently limited fertility. With the release of population pressure by the Famine, these newly reclaimed lands were quickly abandoned, and the margins of cultivation receded to environmentally less hostile lowland areas.

Elsewhere, individual 'improving' landlords undertook the reclamation of lowland heaths and other marginal areas by underdraining and liming the soil, while by the mid-19th century coastal and estuarine salt marshes, such as those on the Foyle, Blackwater (Co. Waterford), and Fergus (Co. Clare) rivers, were being reclaimed on a large scale using more modern civil engineering technologies. LJP

land tenure in early medieval Ireland was generally determined by kinship. It is, however, necessary to disentangle the notion of land tenure, since there is a serious danger, especially for pre-Norman Ireland, of anachronism. It is here taken to comprise first-order rights to use, and to control the use of, land; it may also include second-order rights to alienate and to prevent alienation of the first-order rights. Which of these rights are recognized will vary from one society to another.

Inheritance was a right enjoyed by an individual as against his kindred. This came in two stages: first, when sons divided the land of their father; secondly, when they had a right to ask for a redistribution within their generation of the kindred. An inheritor had the exclusive right to the products of the land, unless a contract had been made with a lord whereby an annual food render was due. It was not expected that a kinsman would always cultivate his land by himself; ploughing was normally done in collaboration with other kinsmen and even non-kinsmen might be involved in arrangements for joint herding of livestock. On the other hand, a kinsman had an obligation to his kindred to cultivate the land in such a way as not to reduce its value or harm his fellow kinsmen. In other words, inheritance involved obligations as well as rights.

No kinsman had the right to alienate his inheritance without the consent of the kindred. Acquired land could be alienated more freely, but even here the kindred had a right to a proportion of a man's acquisitions, more if they were made by using his inheritance, less if they were not. Broadly, therefore, the individual held the rights to use land, the kindred to alienate it, while legal rules governed the transference of land within the kindred.

There were various forms of temporary tenure of land. One was enjoyed by the *banchomarbae*, 'the female heir'. She was someone who had inherited land in default of brothers. (Women could, of course, own acquired land outright and regularly inherited moveable property.) The *banchomarbae* had possession of the inheritance for her lifetime. So far she was no different from any kinsman. What distinguished her case and made her possession seem more temporary than the norm was that she could not transmit her land to her sons, since they belonged to her husband's kindred and not to hers. The danger of the land passing out of her kindred was met by requiring her to give guarantors that it would return. Her possession thus assumed a contractual character, although it was, within its limits, as good an inheritance as any other.

Still more contractual was the tenure enjoyed by the client (see CLIENTSHIP) by virtue of a grant from his lord. Normally this grant consisted of livestock, but sometimes, perhaps especially for younger men who had not yet inherited, it might consist of land. This was then held under the terms of the contract of clientship. The **fuidir* or half-free may have held land from a lord at will, but evidence is scarce. Land could also be held for rent, in other words, under the terms of a contract which, unlike clientship, did not involve any personal subjection of the rent-payer to the owner of the land.

*Anglo-Norman invasion and settlement brought a new system of tenure. This was rooted in lordship rather than ownership. Social status was determined by tenure, together with the rights and obligations attached to it. The medieval *manor was not an estate in the modern sense: it was a society defined by its relationship to a common lord.

The Anglo-Norman state was a manor writ large. The king reserved certain counties (e.g. Dublin, Waterford, and Louth before 1200), manors, and towns in demesne. The rest he granted to his immediate vassals, the great tenants-in-chief, like *Strongbow (Leinster) and de *Lacy (Meath), to hold by military service of 100 and 50 knights respectively. They were bound to the king by the same nexus of *feudal rights and obligations as the humblest military vassal of the humblest lord in the realm: 40 days' military service, wardship, relief, licence to marry, suit of court, and the payment of scutage and tallage when required. In return the vassal held his fief by the immutable laws of feudal inheritance and received his lord's protection.

Further down the tenurial scale were the honorial barons, particularly in Meath and Leinster, who held entire *cantreds from their tenant-in-chief overlord. These were divided into smaller manorial units held by knights or free tenants.

Apart from fief-holding military tenants, whose tenures were governed by feudal law, there were six classes of tenants commonly encountered on Anglo-Norman manors: free tenants, *burgesses, farmers, gavillers, cottiers, and *betaghs. All, except betaghs, enjoyed free status, though some were burdened with labour services in addition to rents.

Free tenants ranked next to the military tenants. In 14th-century manorial extents the largest free tenements are listed indiscriminately with the fiefs, suggesting that earlier social distinctions were blurring, perhaps because free tenants were obliged to bear arms in proportion to their wealth. Their duties were normally confined to payment of rent and suit at the manor court every fortnight. By virtue of their tenures the burgesses could sell their burgage land or marry without licence of the lord, but they were commonly obliged to transport salt, wine, or iron at the lord's behest. The privilege of pleading in the hundred court (town court) instead of the manor court protected them from interference by manorial officials. Farmers, who were probably recruited from other classes of tenant, held their lands on lease, often with suit of court and labour services on the lord's demesne. Lowest on the social scale were the gavillers and cottiers, who lived on smallholdings, paying rents and performing labour services on the demesnes. The humble cottiers lived in cottages in the lanes of the towns, unlike the burgesses who lived on the high street. Betaghs, unfree tenants of Irish origin living in communities called betaghries, paid rent for their common lands, and by 1300 normally paid rent in lieu of services. Generally, they seem to have been better off than cottiers and gavillers of English origin.

Early modern land tenure, as in England, continued to be dominated by the assumption that all land was owned absolutely by the king and that others held from him either directly or indirectly by letters patent or royal lease. In theory Gaelic Ireland had no such hierarchy of tenures, land being held absolutely by freeholders who rendered services to overlords. By the middle of the 16th century the increasing influence of English common law and the adoption of English ideas by the greater native Irish lords had undermined this older system.

Under common law two types of tenure, freehold or leasehold, were available to any landholder, including the crown, wishing to create tenancies on land. Freehold was of two types, a fee simple which subsisted for ever, and a fee tail which was restricted to the immediate descendants of the original grantee. Royal grants were usually fee simple and held under one of two main sets of conditions, *knight service and common soccage. Knight service was the more burdensome and the more common in 16th and 17th-century Ireland. It involved liability for homage, *wardship, and reliefs, such as the payment made to a lord by a tenant of full age on succeeding to land by descent. Soccage tenures were less burdensome. They were used in grants made under *plantation schemes to encourage settler landlords to move to Ireland, but in the 1630s *Wentworth attempted to convert soccage grants to knight service using the Commission on *Defective Titles. The distinction between knight service and common soccage was abolished by the Tenures Abolition Act (Ireland) 1662.

The second type of tenure was leasehold, the characteristic of which was that it subsisted for a fixed period, usually years or named lives, over which a rent was paid and certain conditions, negotiated between landlord and tenant and set down in the lease, were observed. The final main category of tenancy was a tenancy at will which, although it might continue indefinitely, might also be terminated by either party at any time. All three tenures, freehold, leasehold, and tenant at will, were in use in early modern Ireland and were seen as an appropriate reflection of social distinctions. In both the Munster and Ulster plantations, for example, the government prescribed a predetermined mixture of tenures as a means of creating a balanced social hierarchy.

Economic conditions in 17th-century Ireland produced a new form of tenure unknown in other areas, combining elements of both leasehold and freehold. This, first appearing in Ulster during the late 17th century, became known as a three life lease renewable for ever. The freehold element derived from the fact that, since lives could be continuously inserted on payment of a fine the lease was, in effect, a perpetuity. But it also contained the normal stipulations of a lease relating, for instance, to distraint and re-entry for non-payment of rent. In this way the interests of landlords were protected while allowing long leases which encouraged substantial tenants to settle on an estate.

Irish land tenures in the 18th and early 19th centuries were diverse, reflecting long-term changes in the balance of supply and demand for land, the attitude of individual landlords, and the effect of government legislation. During the 18th century, the usual tenure for *middlemen and the larger tenant farmers was leasehold, but this varied widely in its terms and conditions. The most favourable leases were those for lives renewable for ever, or for named terms of several hundred years, either of which made the tenants concerned landowners in all but name. Most leases were much shorter, and were either for a named term of usually 21 or 31 years, or for two or three lives with or without a concurrent or consecutive reversionary term of years. The reversionary term safeguarded the tenant's interest. If his named lives died prematurely, he retained the farm for the balance of the stated period. Leases became shorter towards the end of the 18th century as landlords sought to retain a larger proportion of the increasing value of their property for their own use.

In the 18th century, vacant leaseholds were frequently 'canted', or offered to tender by the highest bidder. Both new and existing tenants were often expected to pay an additional sum or 'fine' on entry or renewal. Leases usually also stipulated levels of tenant investment and other obligations. Up to 1850 the parliamentary *franchise in the counties was restricted to tenants (until the *Catholic Relief Act of 1793 Protestant tenants) holding leases for lives.

During the early 19th century, the pattern of tenure changed rapidly. Many landlords replaced leaseholds with annual tenancies, while the *Great Famine bankrupted most remaining middlemen. Annual tenancies allowed rents to be raised each year and placed the tenant on six months' notice to quit, enhancing both the landlord's economic control over his estate and its profitability. In towns and villages, monthly and weekly tenancies became increasingly widespread. By *c.*1870, approximately 80 per cent of Ireland's 500,000 tenants held annual tenancies, while the relatively few newly created leaseholds were for no more than 21 or 31 years. A loophole in the 1870 *Land Act, permitting tenants of land worth more than £50 to forgo their claim for compensation for improvements, temporarily encouraged the granting of more leaseholds, as landlords pressurized tenants into accepting leases with appropriate excluding clauses. With the passage of later Land Acts, however, the existing system of tenurial landholding was abolished and replaced by owner occupation.

See also LANDLORDS.

Empey, C. A., 'Medieval Knocktopher: A Study in Manorial Settlement', *Old Kilkenny Review*, 2 (1982–3)

Gillespie, Raymond, *Settlement and Survival on an Ulster Estate* (1988)

Otway-Ruthven, A. J., *A History of Medieval Ireland* (2nd edn., 1980)

Vaughan, W. E., *Landlords and Tenants in Mid-Victorian Ireland* (1994)

Wylie, J. C. W., *Irish Land Law* (1975)

TMC-E/CAE/RG/LJP

Land War, a campaign of *agrarian protest, commencing in 1879, in which tenant demands for rent abatements in consideration of a serious downturn in agricultural incomes were transformed into a campaign against *landlordism *per se* orchestrated by the *Land League. Starting in Co. Mayo, where the distress was greatest, the militancy had spread to most of the southern provinces and parts of Ulster by autumn 1880. When landlords did not concede the reductions demanded by their tenants, rents were refused and the attempts to recover them were thwarted by a variety of expedients. Much activity centred on the matter of evictions: delaying them by legal means, physically impeding them, and preventing the replacement of evicted tenants. Thus the power of landlords to control their tenants and to secure a proportion of the income of the soil was nullified. This was backed by rhetoric which challenged the legitimacy of landlordism in Ireland and identified it with the British connection. The revolutionary political implications of the rhetoric reflected the ulterior objectives entertained by the majority of the Land League executive, if not by its president, Charles Stewart *Parnell.

Economic motivation was linked with a sense of resentment against privilege to give the Land War a distinctly democratic flavour. Indeed it was the occasion of a very impressive nationalist mobilization providing the basis for Parnell's subsequent political triumphs. Mass meetings, marching bands, and speech-making were the hallmarks of the Land War as much as the social ostracization to which Captain *Boycott and numerous others were subjected. In addition to non-violent activities there were violent actions, not officially approved by the Land League. Crime figures rose dramatically and the challenge to the civil authority was serious.

Gladstone's incoming government of 1880 acknowledged the need for concessions and established a parliamentary commission of inquiry under the earl of Bessborough (see PONSONBY). The consequent delay placed a premium on tenant militancy. The government felt obliged to put coercive legislation in place before introducing the 1881 *Land Act. This, particularly when complemented by the Arrears Act of 1882, conceded enough to the tenants to take the steam out of the anti-landlord campaign. Yet what ended in 1882 was only the first phase of the Land War. Politicized agrarian strife on a serious scale was to occur intermittently down to 1923, as in the *Plan of Campaign, the agitation of the *United Irish League, and the land seizures and rent strikes of the period 1917–23.

Clark, S., *Social Origins of the Irish Land War* (1979)
Donnelly, J. S., *The Land and the People of Nineteenth-Century Cork* (1975)

RVC

language. Nothing is known of the pre-*Celtic language(s) of Ireland. By the first centuries of the Christian era the inhabitants of Ireland were speaking an early form of Irish. Colonists took the language to Scotland and constant maritime contact ensured that Irish and Scottish remained mutually intelligible until the 13th century. Christian missionaries in the 5th century brought a knowledge of *Latin, which became the language of the liturgy. The *Viking settlers of the 9th and 10th centuries brought *Norse with them, though they seem to have learned Gaelic—albeit overlaid with Norse features—within a few generations. Nordic Gaelic was swamped everywhere in Ireland and Scotland though it survived in the Isle of *Man.

The *Cistercian reforms of the Irish church and the *Anglo-Norman invasion had a profound effect on Irish; native learning was no longer cultivated in the monastic centres. The secularization of Irish learning gave rise to the great bardic families and their standard and archaizing literary dialect, known by modern scholars as Early Modern or Classical Irish. This artificial literary diction common to Ireland and Scotland was taught in the native schools until the collapse of the Gaelic order after the battle of *Kinsale (Dec. 1601). In western Scotland the literary medium survived until the early 18th century.

*English was introduced by the Anglo-Normans. Although some of the higher nobility may have spoken *French, the bulk of the colonists must have been monoglot English speakers. There is evidence for French as a literary language but no clear indication that it was ever widely spoken. Indeed the total absence of French place names in Ireland suggests that French was never a vernacular in the country.

The weakening of the English colony and the Gaelic recovery of the 14th and 15th centuries eliminated English from much of Ireland. English was known in the larger towns at this period and in the *Pale and south Wexford. Everywhere else Irish was spoken. As late as 1515 many of the nobility, Gaelic and Old English alike, knew no English. Nor did the *Reformation alter the picture immediately; it is apparent from those involved in translating Anglican devotional works in the late 16th and early 17th centuries that many of the native literati had accepted the reformed faith while remaining Irish speakers.

English was reintroduced gradually following the *Tudor conquest. Yet Irish remained the language of the majority of Irishmen and women until *c.*1745. Thereafter the language began its inexorable decline, as many monoglots learned English from the local *hedge schoolmasters. Immediately before the *Great Famine, however, Irish was still spoken by about half the population of 8 million. In the first decade or so after the founding of St Patrick's College, *Maynooth, in 1795, a quarter of the students knew no English on arrival. Many more were bilingual. English was the everyday language of the college, however, and Latin was the medium of instruction. Daniel *O'Connell himself was a native speaker of Irish but was dismissive of the language.

Irish was widely spoken in much of Ulster. Many of the planters were themselves Gaelic speakers from Scotland and a significant proportion of Ulster Protestants were of native Irish stock. As late as 1835 the *Synod of Ulster made Irish a necessary subject for the training of all Presbyterian ministers. In 1841 the Presbyterian General Assembly published a handbook for teachers of Irish, which was described as 'our sweet and memorable mother tongue'.

The shift from the indigenous language (Irish) to the language of the conquerors (English) weakened the attachment of the Irish to their own country. Indeed it can be argued that the loss of the Irish language is the decisive event in Irish history, since it altered radically the self-understanding of the Irish and destroyed the continuity between their present and their past. This view was implicit in *Hyde's project for the de-Anglicization of Ireland, though Hyde was unable to distinguish *modernization from the speaking of English. Although the revival has not been wholly successful, all surveys show that a majority of Irish people value the language as a mark of identity. There is some evidence that the weakening of traditional Catholicism is leading to a reassessment of Irish as a central element in the national identity.

de Fréine, S., *The Great Silence* (1965)
Ó Snodaigh, P., *The Hidden Ulster* (1973)
Tovey, H., Hannan, D., and Abramson, H., *Why Irish? Irish Identity and Irish Language* (1989)

NJAW

Lansdowne, Henry Petty-Fitzmaurice, 5th Marquis (1845–1927), politician. Though based mainly in England, he enlarged and developed the family house and demesne at Derreen, Co. Kerry. Initially a follower of *Gladstone, from whom he accepted the post of governor-general of Canada (1883–8), he moved from the Liberals to the Conservative Party over *home rule. He was viceroy of India 1888–94, secretary of state for war 1895–1900, foreign secretary 1900–5, and then leader of the Conservative opposition in the Lords. In the period following the introduction of the third home rule bill, he was initially, along with Midleton (see BRODRICK (MIDLETON)), a key spokesman for the southern *unionist interest within the Conservative Party. However, a letter to the *Daily Telegraph* (29 Nov. 1917) deprecating the notion of all-out war against Germany destroyed his political career.

Laois-Offaly plantation, the first and most troublesome of the Tudor colonial projects. It had its basis in the garrison policy to impose order in the lands of the *O'Connors and O'Mores. Allotments were made to leaseholders in the vicinity of the forts in 1549 and then to copyholders in 1556, but revolts by the original occupiers meant few colonists remained when *Sussex put the plantation on a more permanent footing in 1563. He made 44 grants to New English soldiers, much to the annoyance of the *Old English who received only 15. Lands given to 29 Gaelic recipients continued to diminish through confiscation and indebtedness. The colony was ill begun, composed of soldiers who made reluctant farmers, and initiated without a proper survey, the co-operation of the powerful earl of *Kildare, or permanent freehold grants. In 1575 Lord Deputy *Sidney complained that the revenue of King's and Queen's counties, as the former Gaelic lordships were now known, was less than a twentieth of what they cost the government to maintain. In 1608 *Chichester, reflecting on the eighteen revolts in the last 60 years, attempted to transplant the native inhabitants, beginning with the O'Mores to Kerry, but they soon returned home. HM

Larkin, James (1876–1947), labour leader. He was born into the Irish working-class community in Liverpool. Working in the docks, he became a convinced trade unionist and socialist. In 1907 James Sexton, leader of the National Union of Dock Labourers, sent him to Belfast as union organizer. The dockers were unorganized, dispirited, and divided by sectarianism. Larkin, through his fiery eloquence, energy, and organizational ability, soon established a strong union branch. However, to break the union, the employers locked out members, provoking the dockers' and carters' strike, lasting from May to late November 1907. Most of the city's industries were closed. 'Blacklegs' were attacked and had to have police protection. Three hundred Royal Irish Constabulary, led by Constable Barrett, mutinied in support of the strikers. Troops shot dead two young people during a riot on the Falls Road. Although supported by the *Independent Orange Order, Larkin was subjected to a campaign of sectarianism, designed to divide the workers. Because Sexton justifiably feared that continuing strike pay would bankrupt the union, he settled over Larkin's head, on capitulation terms.

Feeling betrayed and wishing to break free of the English union leadership, Larkin founded the *Irish Transport and General Workers' Union (ITGWU), in 1909. His combination of socialism, *republicanism, and trade unionism became known as 'Larkinism'. Larkin helped persuade the *Irish Trade Union Congress to set up a congress-based Irish *Labour Party. In 1914, worn out and depressed by his failure in the *Dublin lockout, Larkin headed for the United States, leaving *Connolly in charge. In America he spoke at anti-British meetings on behalf of Irish and German-American organizations, and was a delegate to the founding convention of the American Communist Party. In a climate of 'red scare' hysteria, he was sentenced to three years in prison for 'criminal anarchy'.

On his release in 1923, Larkin returned to a very different Ireland, with Connolly dead and the *Irish Free State enmeshed in the *Civil War. ITGWU membership, 5,000 when Larkin left for America, now approached 100,000, largely due to the efforts of Connolly's successor, William *O'Brien. O'Brien had no intention of stepping down for Larkin. Following a bitter dispute, Larkin was suspended as general secretary by the union executive. In 1923, he founded the *Irish Workers' League which, flying in the face of public opinion, supported the USSR. In 1924, Larkin became founding general secretary of the Workers' Union of Ireland. He attacked the labour leadership for careerism and betraying the original ideals of the movement. They in turn viewed him as a left-wing loose cannon.

Larkin later joined the Labour Party and he and his son James Jnr. were elected to the *Dáil in 1943. However, O'Brien and his supporters, claiming Communist infiltration, took the ITGWU out of both the Labour Party and the Congress. Larkin's opponents accused him, with some justification, of splitting the movement because he could not accept less than complete power. On the other hand, he was largely responsible for making labour a formidable industrial and political force.

Larkin, E., *James Larkin, 1876–1947: Irish Labour Leader* (1965)

PC

Larne gun-running (24–5 Apr. 1914), organized by F. H. *Crawford for the *Ulster Unionist Council. Although weapons had been imported since late 1910, pressure for a more significant operation came only in the context of the constitutional impasse of late 1913 (see HOME RULE). Twenty-five thousand rifles and 3 million rounds of ammunition were bought in Germany, shipped in the vessels *Fanny* and *Clydevalley*, and landed at Larne, Donaghadee, and Bangor. The weapons were of three different types (although Austrian Mannlichers predominated); this, combined with the comparative scarcity of ammunition, meant that the *Ulster Volunteer Force remained inadequately armed. The gun-running was therefore more important as a political coup for the Unionist leaders than as a military feat. AJ

Late Medieval period, or Late(r) Middle Ages, is an ambiguous chronological label. One common usage defines the *Early Medieval period as extending from the 5th to the 12th century. Late Medieval Ireland then begins with the *Anglo-Norman invasion, and takes in the period of *Anglo-Norman colonization and settlement, as well as the subsequent period of *Gaelic recovery. Others, however, reserve the term 'Late Medieval' for a period beginning around the mid-14th century, as the demographic and military contraction of the English colony becomes apparent. The end of the 'Late Medieval period is also problematic. Political historians generally place the transition from Late Medieval to Early Modern Ireland in the early 16th century, with the *Kildare rebellion, the creation of the *kingdom of Ireland, and the transition to rule by English chief governors. Yet in terms of demography, economic and social structures, and material culture, the significant discontinuity comes considerably later, around the start of the 17th century. From these perspectives the later medieval period is better seen as extending from the Anglo-Norman invasion to the *Nine Years War or the *Flight of the Earls. RW

La Tène in Ireland. The most distinctive artefacts and art styles of the Irish *Iron Age have their ultimate origin either in the La Tène cultures of transalpine Celtic Europe, or in the British Iron Age cultures that drew material and influences from that milieu. The earliest such influences seem to have arrived in the north-east, perhaps via northern Britain, in the 3rd century BC, although few actual imports have been found. The failure of other archaeological traits (such as settlement and pottery types) from those origin areas to appear in Ireland suggests that only small bands of settlers (warriors and metalworkers) arrived. This undermines the orthodox belief that the La Tène material, and the Celtic language, were the result of an overwhelming 'Celticization' of Ireland (see CELTIC IRELAND). It is, however, likely that these people would have spoken Celtic dialects. The Irish La Tène assemblage is rich, but rather unevenly distributed, occurring in concentrations in the north-east, the east midlands, and the west midlands. A high proportion of the La Tène objects are harness pieces and weapons (and their fittings) confirming that this cultural group included a horse- and chariot-using warrior elite. RW

Latin. Although Ireland had not been wholly isolated from the *Roman world, Latin came to Ireland with the 5th-century *Christianization. The earliest surviving Latin works written in Ireland are St *Patrick's *Confession* and *Letter to Coroticus*. Recent research suggests that Patrick's apology, in the former, for his rusty Latin should not be taken at face value, the apparently awkward style concealing a close attention to the number of syllables in each phrase.

Writings in Latin by native Irishmen first appear in the 7th century. The Irish, unlike inhabitants of the former Roman empire, had to learn their Latin from scratch. Hence their writings reveal a particular interest in grammar, while their written Latin, though recognizably medieval in its grammar and syntax, is generally correct, with very little borrowing from Irish, other than in place and personal names. The same fascination with language, and particularly with Greek and Hebrew, led Irishmen in the early medieval period to employ what is sometimes called 'Hisperic Latin', distinguished by its exotic vocabulary, mainly

Latinized forms of Greek words. Two products of this fascination with language are the *Hisperica famina* (*Western Sayings*), and the enigmatic writings of Virgilius Maro (*fl. c.*650), whose work is thought to parody the pedantry of contemporary grammarians. Saints' lives were mostly, though not always, written in Latin, beginning with Cogitosus's Life of *Brigid (written *c.*680). *Columbanus was the first Irish Latinist to write outside Ireland. Although he was probably not the author of the poems traditionally attributed to him, with their echoes of classical Latin verse, his five surviving letters reveal a good knowledge of patristic authors and a fine command of Latin. The Irish played a role in the revival of Latin learning that marked the reign of Charlemagne and his successors. Most influential was the philosopher and translator of Pseudo-Dionysius, *John Scottus Eriugena. Sedulius of Liège produced around 80 lively poems, displaying a knowledge of several classical authors, and other scattered poems by Irishmen survive in Carolingian manuscripts. Dicuil's *De mensura orbis terrae* (On the Measurement of the Earth) (*c.*825) describes voyages by Irish monks in the north Atlantic, while Virgil (Fergal), bishop of Salzburg (d. 784), has been credited with the influential *Cosmography* attributed to Aethicus Ister.

Latin writings by Irishmen tail off by the 11th century. After the partial colonization of the *Anglo-Normans, Latin writings, mostly the work of the settlers, offer isolated examples of particular genres. The intellectual life of the universities is reflected in the writings of Richard *Fitzralph, in Maurice O'Fihelly's commentaries on Duns Scotus, and in the brief philosophical treatises of Peter of Ireland, who taught Thomas Aquinas at Naples. However, it is now suspected that William of Drogheda, author of *Summa aurea* (Golden Compilation), a casebook of ecclesiastical law, may not have been Irish. Richard de Ledrede, bishop of Ossory (1317–*c.*1361) left a collection of lively hymns as well as an account of his feud with the *Kyteler family, while Simon Fitzsimon (Simeon Simionis) gives an account of his journey from Clonmel to the Holy Land. There are also some half-dozen chronicles in Latin, notably those of John *Clyn and the so-called *Annals of Multyfarnham*.

Latin remained the language of learning and intellectual debate into the early modern period, being employed for example in the historical writings of Philip *O'Sullivan Beare, John *Lynch, and Richard *Stanihurst. The controversies surrounding the *Confederation of Kilkenny provoked a lively pamphlet war in Latin, while the *Commentarius Rinuccianus*, compiled by Richard O'Ferrall and Robert O'Connell, is an invaluable, if biased, source for the history of the confederation. Luke *Wadding's *Annales ordinis minorum* (History of the Franciscan Order) (1625–54) and *Scriptores ordinis minorum* (Writers of the Franciscan Order) (1650) are still consulted by scholars. John Colgan's *Acta sanctorum Hiberniae* (Acts of the Saints of Ireland) (1645) and *Trias thaumaturga* (1647), Lives of Patrick, Brigid, and Columba, helped initiate modern hagiographical studies. Other important Latin works were the historical and bibliographical writings of Sir James *Ware, and Roderick *O'Flaherty's *Ogygia*, with its bizarre mixture of Irish and classical mythology.

During the 17th century Latin gradually gave way to English as the language of scholarship. Archbishop *Ussher's vast output of scholarly works contained rather more Latin than English writings. In 1692, on the other hand, William *Molyneux made a last-minute decision to write his *Dioptrica nova* (New Optics) in English. Latin continued to dominate the curricula of schools, universities, and seminaries well into the 19th century, and was abandoned as the liturgical language of the Roman Catholic church only after the second *Vatican Council. References by Edmund *Campion, Richard *Stanihurst, and several 16th- and 17th-century visitors to Ireland to the use of an ungrammatical spoken Latin among the rural Irish must be viewed with scepticism, but should not be totally discounted.

Bieler, L., 'Hibernian Latin', *Studies*, 43 (1954)
Lapidge, M., and Sharpe, R., *A Bibliography of Celtic-Latin Literature 400–1200* (1985)
Millett, B., 'Irish Literature in Latin 1550–1700', in T. W. Moody et al. (eds.), *New History of Ireland*, iii (1991)

ABS

Latin America. Early Irish involvement in South and Central America was a by-product of the employment of Catholic Irishmen in the service of the Catholic powers of Europe. Don Ambrosio O'Higgins (*c.*1720–1801), marquis de Osorno, born Ambrose Higgins, probably in Co. Sligo, went first to Spain and then to South America, where he became a successful military commander and colonial administrator. He was governor of Chile 1787–95 and viceroy of Peru 1795–1801. His natural son Bernardo O'Higgins (1778–1842), educated in England, led the successful Chilean struggle for independence against Spain and headed the first national government 1817–23. Meanwhile the *United Irish veteran John Devereux (1778–1860) had raised an Anglo-Irish legion of 5,500 men, about half of whom were Irish, to support the revolt of the Spanish American colonies. The legion, strongly endorsed by Daniel *O'Connell, whose teenage son Morgan was an officer on Devereux's staff, saw action in Simon Bolivar's war of liberation in Venezuela. During the Mexican–American war of 1846–8 a St Patrick's Battalion composed of some 200 Irish deserters from the United States army fought on the Mexican side.

One Latin American country, Argentina, provided a minor destination for Irish *emigration during the 19th century, receiving a total of around 7,000 settlers up to 1870, and another 3,600 by 1895. The prominence among these settlers of migrants from Cos. Westmeath, Longford, and Wexford suggests a classic pattern of chain migration, in which existing settlers encouraged and assisted the arrival of relatives and former neighbours. Up to *c.*1870, Irish settlers were in many cases able to build up substantial cattle ranches in a rapidly expanding economy; thereafter this type of spectacular upward mobility became more difficult to achieve.

La Touche, a prominent banking family of *Huguenot origin. **David Digues** (1671–1745), who took the name of the family estate of La Touche, was a veteran of the *Williamite War who had settled in Dublin as a cloth dealer and merchant. His banking business developed out of his responsibility for handling pensions and remittances payable to his fellow Huguenot refugees. His eldest son **David La Touche** (d. 1785) bought out his father's partners to make the bank a family-owned and highly profitable enterprise, and also acquired extensive landed property. Another son, **James La Touche** (d. 1763), a cloth merchant, joined with Charles *Lucas in a campaign to reform Dublin muncipal politics. David II's son, another **David La Touche** (d. 1817), was first governor of the Bank of Ireland. In 1761 he purchased a seat in the Irish parliament, where he was a prominent opponent of *Catholic relief. He later acquired control of his own parliamentary borough, and was joined in parliament by his two brothers and by two nephews. In the two decades after the Act of *Union five members of the family sat for Irish seats at *Westminster. The La Touche bank lost its financial dynamism from the 1840s, and was absorbed by the Munster Bank in 1870.

Laudabiliter, a papal letter issued in 1155 by the English Pope Adrian IV (1154–9) to *Henry II, authorizing a conquest of Ireland in the interests of reforming the Irish church. It takes its name from the first word of the document, the authenticity of which has been the subject of much historiographical controversy lasting into the 20th century. Whether or not the text, as now surviving, is wholly authentic, there is independent evidence that proposals for a conquest of Ireland were discussed at an English royal council at Winchester in 1155, following which John of Salisbury, secretary of Theobald, archbishop of Canterbury, sought papal authorization for Henry's intervention in Ireland, and that a papal document giving consent was issued. The proposal almost certainly originated with the archbishop, reacting to the recent diminution of *Canterbury's control over the Irish church. *Laudabiliter* was subsequently to be used to argue against English intervention on the grounds that the English kings had not advanced religious reform; most notably it was cited in the *Remonstrance of the Irish princes, addressed to Pope John XXII by Domnall *Ó Néill *c.*1317. MTF

Lavelle, Fr. Patrick (1825–86), parish priest of Partry, Co. Mayo. A strong opponent of the *Second Reformation, Lavelle attacked the harsh treatment of tenants on the estate of the evangelical bishop of Tuam, Thomas Plunkett, in *The War in Partry* (1860). In the early 1860s he became notorious as a *Fenian fellow-traveller, preaching at the funeral of Terence Bellew *MacManus, becoming vice-president of the Fenian front organization the Brotherhood of St Patrick, and delivering a public lecture (11 Feb. 1862) on 'The Catholic Doctrine of the Right of Revolution'. However, he was protected from *Cullen's hostility by his archbishop, *MacHale. Conflict with his parishioners led to his transfer to Cong, Co. Mayo, in 1869. In the Galway by-election of 1872, the outcome of which was overturned in a controversial judgment by William *Keogh, Lavelle was one of the priests accused of spiritual intimidation.

Lavery, Sir John (1856–1941), portrait and landscape painter. Born in Belfast, he was educated in Glasgow, London, and at the Académie Julian, Paris. In 1883 he paid the first of many visits to Grez-sur-Loing, south of Paris, where he was influenced by *plein air* painting, then much in vogue. A year later he was back in Glasgow and was associated with the group of avant-garde painters subsequently celebrated as 'The Glasgow Boys'. This marked the beginning of his meteoric rise to fame, a success that dazzled even Lavery himself. In 1888 he was commissioned to paint the royal visit to the International Exhibition in Glasgow. The commission comprised more than 200 portraits, including that of the queen, thus establishing him as a society portrait painter. In 1896 he settled in London, remaining there till near the end of his life. During the *First World War Lavery was appointed an official war artist with the Royal Navy and afterwards was knighted for his work. He was elected an academician of the Royal Academy in

1921. His portrait of his second wife Hazel (1880–1935) as Kathleen Ni Houlihan, personification of Ireland, was used on Irish banknotes up to the 1970s. Hazel, Lady Lavery, also entered popular legend for a supposed liaison with Michael *Collins during the negotiation of the *Anglo-Irish treaty. Following her death Lavery spent much time with his stepdaughter in Ireland.

McConkey, Kenneth, *Sir John Lavery* (1993)

SBK

law.

Early Ireland

Our knowledge of pre-Norman law in Ireland derives largely from the Old Irish *law tracts, which date from between the 7th and 9th centuries AD. Less detailed information on legal topics is provided by sources such as *annals, saints' lives (*hagiography), gnomic material, and sagas. Practically no case law has survived from this period, so it is sometimes difficult to be sure how early Irish legal theory worked out in practice. Linguistic evidence shows that many basic features of early Irish law go back to Common *Celtic times (*c.*1000 BC). For example, Old Irish *macc*, 'surety', is cognate with medieval Welsh *mach* of the same meaning. This indicates that a system of suretyship was in operation in Common Celtic law.

The coming of *Christianity in the 5th century had a profound impact on early Irish society, and the law tracts of two or three centuries later are thoroughly Christianized. Some of the material in these tracts comes directly from *canon law, and clergy are accorded positions of legal privilege. None the less, the law tracts do not invariably reflect the teachings of the church: concubinage is tolerated and *divorce is permitted in a wide variety of circumstances.

In early Irish society, split as it was into numerous petty kingdoms, with no overall authority, the administration of law was essentially a private matter: offences were dealt with, not by a higher authority, but between persons, in a process in which sociolegal status played an important part. There was no distinction between criminal and civil offences: where such had occurred it was up to the injured party, or his kin if homicide was involved, to bring a legal action against the offender for compensation. Compensation was proportional to the standing of the victim of the offence, i.e. to his 'honour price' (**enech*); where homicide was involved a further payment, the **éraic* ('body fine'), was payable also. The normal procedure was to hire an advocate skilled in the law; but before the case could proceed both parties had to produce a pledge or surety that the decision of the judge would be accepted. Where offender and offended were subjects of the same king or lord, matters were relatively simple; where they were from different jurisdictions matters were more complicated, and depended on agreements between the jurisdictions.

In all cases pledges played an important part, both for payment and enforcement, in both criminal and civil matters. Almost any crime could be atoned for by payment: restitution first, followed by a penalty fine. Where the offender was unable to pay, his kin-group, usually descendants in the male line of the same great-grandfather, was liable, starting with his next of kin and extending, if these were unable to pay, to degrees further out. If payment was not made voluntarily, the plaintiff could distrain it from a kinsman of the guilty party, and the person so distrained was entitled to compensation from the guilty party. If the latter failed to pay this, he could be formally disowned by his kin, and lose his legal rights in society—in effect, anyone could kill him without being brought to justice. If there was no kin to pay for him, he could be put to death by the relatives of the victim, or enslaved either by them or (if surviving) by the victim of the original offence.

Sureties also played a key role in all legal matters. One very common one was the *ráth* or 'paying surety' normally used in contracts: the *ráth* guaranteed with his own property that his principal would fulfil his side of the contract within the term specified. If he did not, the surety had to pay, and his principal was liable to heavy penalties. A second type of surety was the *naidm* or 'enforcing surety', who had no financial liability if the principal defaulted, but was entitled to compel the principal by distraint or imprisonment or violence.

Minor cases were normally heard by a single judge, but major ones by several; in each petty kingdom there was usually an official judge, but his functions were not limited to official matters, since he could hear cases which did not involve the king, and there were usually other judges making a living from their knowledge of law, probably by arbitrating for a fee. In such hearings oaths played a crucial part, not merely in support of evidence, but because the oath of a person of high rank overrode that of anyone of lower rank. In extreme cases, where there were no witnesses and oaths on either side cancelled one another out, matters could be settled by casting lots, or by ordeals.

In actions at law, personal status was crucial; and status depended on property and authority:

on property, because status was to some extent proportional to the amount a man possessed; on authority, because a man who had committed his surplus property to *clients who rendered him services and food rents outranked the man who had no clients. Moreover the authority attributed to a king, a cleric, or a judge increased their rank and gave them special legal privileges and immunities. Women, with the rarest of exceptions, had no status in their own right, but derived it from their husbands, if they had fully formal marriages; concubines had only half the status.

Matters of succession were complicated by the fact that most land was owned by the kin-group as a whole, rather than by individuals; other land could largely be disposed of as the acquirer wished, but the passage of kin-land from one generation to the next was governed by rigid rules. Where there was more than one male heir, the land had to be equitably divided: the youngest son divided up the land, but the eldest had the first choice, and so on down to the youngest. Where there were no male heirs, daughters were entitled to hold the land for life, but thereafter it normally reverted to the kin-group. The rules for succession to land were obviously not applicable to succession to the kingship: theoretically all the king's sons had an equal right to succeed, but commonly the strongest or least scrupulous did so.

Medieval Ireland

During the first half-century after the *Anglo-Norman invasion there is comparatively little evidence about the law or legal custom that was being followed in those parts of Ireland controlled by the new settlers. It is, however, clear from such fragmentary evidence as does survive that in this earliest period some of the characteristic remedies of English law, and some of its characteristic modes of proof, were already being used for disputes between the settlers, and that the settlers had also brought with them some of the characteristic rules of English medieval land law and criminal law. In 1210, during King *John's visit to Ireland, the king drew up a charter laying down as a general principle that English law was to be followed within the lordship of Ireland and describing in detail some of its more important rules. During the following century a number of other positive measures were taken to ensure that the Irish common law was (and remained) in keeping with that of England. On his return to England John sent a formulary (a Register of Writs) to Ireland, based on the standard writs then available from the English chancery, for the initiation of litigation in the king's own courts and in the county courts, with instructions allowing the *justiciar to issue writs of the various kinds given in Ireland. Further orders were given in 1234 and 1236 for making available in Ireland particular forms of writ available in England, and in 1246 the general principle was stated that all writs 'of common right' should be available in Ireland as they were in England.

During the same period there is also evidence of the communication of specific legal rules and procedures from England to Ireland with instructions that they be applied in the courts of the lordship. These mandates are probably evidence, not so much of ignorance of the rules and procedures in Ireland, as of the determination of the English government to ensure that the Irish courts did not develop their own variant local rules. There is also evidence from 1236 owards of English legislation being sent to Ireland with orders that it be applied in the lordship. This ensured that the Irish common law was not left behind as the English common law was remodelled by legislation. In the 14th century this process became much less common and the last occasion on which English legislation was simply sent to Ireland with instructions for its application was in 1411. However, much the same effect was achieved, albeit with Irish agreement, through the adoption or re-enactment of English legislation by the Irish *parliament. The last comprehensive measure of this kind (the 'statutory' *Poynings's Law) was enacted in 1494–5. This adopted all general, public legislation enacted up to this time in England for future use in Ireland. Uniformity between the English and Irish common laws was also promoted by the practice (attested from the mid-13th century onwards) of removing cases by writs of error from the courts of the lordship to the court of King's Bench in England, where judgments were upheld or overthrown on the basis of the current English legal rules, and by the practice (attested from the later 13th century onwards) of Irish lawyers going to England to receive their legal education (see LEGAL PROFESSION).

The courts of the lordship did not, however, slavishly follow English law in all respects. Even in the 13th century (the period when we find the greatest emphasis on uniformity) there is some evidence for the existence of distinctive Irish institutions and for legal rules different from those of England being enforced within the lordship. From the later 13th century onwards there was also an Irish parliament possessing (down to 1494–5) unfettered freedom to enact its own separate legislation. Other differences between the law followed in the two jurisdictions resulted from separate legislation being made specifically for Ireland in England itself.

Throughout this period English law coexisted with the system of Gaelic law. The initial assumption seems to have been that even the Irish living within the areas of English settlement would continue to use Irish law, at least in their disputes with each other. In general the native Irish were debarred from using English law even for litigation with the English settlers. From the early 13th century an exception was made for members of five major Irish royal families, ecclesiastical dignitaries, and those granted the right to use English law. Between 1277 and 1280 there were abortive negotiations for a more general grant of English law and in 1331 such a general grant was made to all except the unfree peasantry. With the decline of the lordship after 1300 (see GAELIC RECOVERY) came a decline in the size of the area within which English law was effective, and the intermingling of the descendants of the settlers and of the earlier inhabitants through intermarriage and other social contacts led to some of the former adopting Gaelic law (see GAELICIZATION) even for the transmission of family property and in dealings with other settler families: the alarm this caused the rulers of the lordship is reflected in the Statute of *Kilkenny. There had also been some borrowings from Gaelic Irish law into the law of the lordship as early as the 13th century. These included the concept of family responsibility for the wrongdoing of family members (*kincogish). Even during Elizabeth's reign there was some accommodation of native Irish custom (especially regarding the descent of land) in the practice of the court of *chancery. It was only in the first decade of the 17th century that this policy was reversed in two significant decisions, the case of *gavelkind (1606) and the case of *tanistry (1607).

Early Modern Ireland

The area within which the 'English law' of the lordship was effective had never, even at the height of the medieval lordship, covered anything like the whole of the island, and declined steadily from the early 14th century onwards. By the early 15th century English law was the law only of a relatively small area around Dublin, the 'English *Pale', though English legal custom was also a significant part of the mixture of legal rules applicable within the great lordships of *Ormond, *Desmond, and *Kildare, and made a lesser contribution to the legal customs of other lordships. By 1691, however, the courts of the king of Ireland were exercising jurisdiction over all parts of Ireland and the church courts (although still enforcing what was largely the previous system of canon law) had been brought under the ultimate control of the state.

The destruction of local autonomy and extension of the common law throughout Ireland took little more than half a century, between *c.*1540 and *c.*1610. The policy of *'surrender and regrant' adopted in the 1540s encouraged major Irish lords to receive a regrant of their lands under the rules of English law and to acknowledge the authority of the king's courts. A more drastic tactic for spreading English rule and with it English law, first adopted in the 1550s, was *plantation. A third mechanism for ensuring that English law was brought to parts of Ireland which had hitherto been largely outside its territory was the establishment early in the reign of Queen Elizabeth (1558–1603) of *provincial presidencies in Munster and Connacht, with their own courts and their own military forces, to establish law and order on the English model. The Court of *Castle Chamber, established in 1563 on the model of the English court of Star Chamber, may also have played a role. Symbolic of the success of these measures was the fact that by 1617 the justices of *assize were holding regular sessions twice yearly in all 32 counties. The court of Castle Chamber none the less went on sitting until the 1640s and the presidency courts themselves survived until 1672, exercising a wide jurisdiction within their respective provinces. The destruction of the links between the Irish church courts and the papacy was theoretically accomplished by legislation of the 1530s, but was not fully effective until the early 17th century.

The courts of the lord (later the king) of Ireland throughout the early modern period applied a system of law that was ultimately derived from the English common law but none the less differed in some respects from the law of the contemporary English common law courts. This was partly because of the existence of a separate Irish parliament making its own distinct legislation, a corpus of law better known to both lawyers and the courts once it began (from 1572 onwards) to be available in print; partly because the Dublin parliament was often slow to enact major legislation paralleling that enacted in England. It was not, for example, until 1634 that the Irish parliament enacted legislation equivalent to the English Statutes of Uses and Wills of 1536 and 1540. Although the English court of King's Bench continued to exercise an appeal jurisdiction for cases from Ireland, this was virtually the only formal mechanism to ensure that Irish courts followed English common law precedents and rules; informally, however, substantial uniformity in most matters was probably ensured both through the much readier availability (in print) of English reported decisions and by the practice of requiring barristers to receive their legal education at the inns of court in England, even after the foundation of the *King's Inns in Dublin.

Modern Ireland

From the late 17th century the Irish parliament held much more frequent sessions, producing a substantial volume of legislation. The English (from 1707 the British) parliament also insisted on its power, reaffirmed in the *Declaratory Act, to make legislation binding on Ireland. In practice the exercise of this power was comparatively infrequent, albeit generally controversial. It was not renounced until the Declaratory and Renunciation Acts of 1782–3 (see LEGISLATIVE INDEPENDENCE). After 1800, under the Act of *Union, it was the United Kingdom parliament at *Westminster (to which Ireland now sent representatives) which gained sole power to legislate for Ireland. Although some legislation was enacted which was binding on the whole United Kingdom, much legislation continued to be passed specifically for Ireland, particularly in the politically sensitive areas of land law and landlord and tenant law. Thus, despite the disappearance of the Irish parliament, there continued to be a distinctive Irish statute law. The Irish House of *Lords had asserted its claim to stand at the head of a largely separate Irish court system by acting as court of appeal for Irish cases from the 1660s onwards. This claim was challenged by the English House of Lords in a 1698 case and the Irish House of Lords was deprived of its powers under the Declaratory Act. Their restoration in 1782 lasted only until the Act of Union came into force in 1801, when the United Kingdom House of Lords became the final court of appeal for Irish as for English and Scottish cases. It is unclear how far this led to a greater uniformity between the jurisdictions, but there is some reason to suppose that the greater availability of specifically Irish law reports in print (see LAW REPORTING) may actually have helped to reinforce the distinctiveness of the Irish legal system.

The *Anglo-Irish treaty of 1921 and the adoption of the *constitution of the Irish Free State led to the creation of the *Oireachtas, an independent legislature with 'sole and exclusive' power to make legislation for the 26 counties included in the new state. The constitution specifically made provision for the continuation of all existing laws in force in Ireland, except in so far as these were inconsistent with the terms of the constitution. This preserved almost all the pre-1922 legislation of the United Kingdom parliament, and of the earlier Irish parliament, then in force in Ireland, but did not preserve the legislation of the first *Dáil. It was also held to provide constitutional authority for the continuation of the existing Irish common law, as stated in pre-1922 judicial precedents from both islands. The *constitution of Ireland (1937) made similar provision for the continuation of existing legislation and common law in Ireland. Both constitutions included a series of specific guarantees of personal rights. Since the 1960s the Irish courts (partly under the influence of American constitutional practice) have also recognized and protected a series of additional rights not specified in the constitution, such as a right to marital privacy and a right to withdraw one's labour. The 1922 constitution contained a provision allowing a right of appeal from the Irish courts to the judicial committee of the British privy council, but in practice this was a little used and mainly ineffective, if controversial, power and it was abolished by constitutional amendment in 1933. Under the terms of Ireland's admission to the *European Union in 1973, the law of the Community takes precedence over Irish domestic law and appeal now lies on questions of European law to the court of the Community.

The *Government of Ireland Act devolved legislative power in the six counties of Northern Ireland to a separate parliament of Northern Ireland which first met in May 1921. That parliament was given power to make laws for the 'peace, order and good government' of Northern Ireland but made subject to a number of specific safeguards against potential abuse of its powers. It was also subject to the continuing overall sovereignty of the United Kingdom parliament at Westminster, to which Northern Ireland continued to send MPs. The United Kingdom parliament also retained the sole ability to legislate on matters relating to peace and war, foreign relations, coinage, and weights and measures. The 1920 act created a separate Supreme Court for Northern Ireland (both a High Court and a Court of Appeal) from which appeal lay initially to an all-Ireland High Court of Appeal (soon abolished), and beyond that to the United Kingdom House of Lords. The judicial committee of the privy council was given power to adjudicate any disputes about the validity of Northern Ireland legislation. In 1972 the United Kingdom parliament used its legislative sovereignty to suspend the operation of the Northern Ireland parliament and substitute legislation for Northern Ireland by order in council. The *Constitution of Northern Ireland Act (1973) devolved legislative powers back to a new Northern Ireland Assembly, but the experiment lasted only until July 1974. Thereafter order in council became the normal mode of legislation for Northern Ireland.

Binchy, D. A. (ed.), *Studies in Early Irish Law* (1936)
Donaldson, A. G., *Some Comparative Aspects of Irish Law* (1957)
Kelly, F., *A Guide to Early Irish Law* (1988)
Ó Corráin, D., Breatnach, L., and Breen, A., 'The Laws of the Irish', *Peritia*, 3 (1984)

FK/GMacN/PAB

Lawless, Valentine, see CLONCURRY, VALENTINE LAWLESS, 2ND BARON.

Lawrence, Richard (d. *c.*1684). Lawrence arrived as a colonel in Oliver *Cromwell's army. Appointed governor of Waterford, he had the task of settling 1,200 soldiers on forfeited lands in south Leinster. He staunchly defended army interests in print against those, such as Vincent Gookin and William *Petty, who opposed the wholesale *transplantation of the Irish to Connacht. Receiving little land himself, Lawrence gravitated, like many other discontented officers, from *Independency to *Baptism. After the *Restoration, he abandoned politics for trade, advocating the cultivation of hemp and flax and publishing in 1682 *The Interest of Ireland in its Trade and Wealth*. HM

law reporting. The first published reports of cases heard in Irish law courts and of decisions made by the judges are those contained in Sir John *Davies's *Reports*, published in 1615. Davies was attorney-general and a participant in most of the cases (of the period 1604–11) which he reported. Over one-and-a-half centuries were to elapse before the publication of the next significant collection of Irish reports (covering the years 1786–8) by G. W. Vernon and J. B. Scriven in 1790. During the intervening period some collections of reports circulated in manuscript, but only individual reports (such as the *Case of Tenures* published in 1637), or small groups of reports (such as the ten Irish equity cases reported by Gilbert and published in 1734), found their way into print. After 1790 law reporting was erratic and variable in quality, as there was no real attempt to supervise the quality of published reports. The era of the 'official' law report began with the establishment of the Irish Law Reporting Council in 1867 and its publication of an official series of annual *Law Reports*. PAB

law tracts. Most of our knowledge of early Irish *law comes from the Old Irish law tracts, mainly composed in the 7th and 8th centuries AD. Some of these tracts have survived in a complete form in later manuscripts (generally of the 14th to 16th centuries), but many are only partially preserved.

The most extensive collection of law tracts is that of the *Senchas Már* school. This collection is divided into three parts. The first contains tracts on distraint, *hostageship, *fosterage, lordship, *marriage, and the relationship between *church and laity. The middle third starts with the *Heptads*, a collection of miscellaneous legal information arranged in groups of seven. There are also tracts on kinship, the semi-free classes, bee-keeping, watermills, theft, and other topics. Most of the last third is lost, but two tracts on illegal injury have survived. There are also fragments of tracts on the law relating to hunting, dogs, and cats.

It has been suggested by D. A. Binchy that some other tracts surviving in legal manuscripts belong to a different school, which had particular associations with the poetical profession. Of special importance in this group are *Bretha Nemed toísech* and *Bretha Nemed déidenach*. These lengthy tracts provide much information on the rights and obligations of poets (**fili*), as well as many other legal matters. There are also law tracts which do not fit into either the postulated *Senchas Már* or *Nemed* school. Of particular importance among these is **Críth Gablach*.

Different styles are used by the authors of the early Irish law tracts. Most of the *Senchas Már* tracts are in prose, but there are also passages in unrhymed alliterative verse. This style of verse is regular in texts attributed to the *Nemed* school. Little is known about the authors of the law tracts, but it is likely that they worked in monastic scriptoria: some may have been clerics.

From about the 9th century, the practice arose in the law schools of adding glosses and commentary to the Old Irish tracts. These are mainly explanations or expansions of the original text, and sometimes provide evidence of legal change. In his *Corpus iuris Hibernici*, Binchy has provided a diplomatic edition (without translation) of practically all the existing law tracts and associated material.

Many law tracts were edited in *Ancient Laws of Ireland*, i–v (1865–1901), but there are numerous errors of transcription and translation, particularly in the first two volumes. Thurneysen, Binchy, and other scholars have published improved editions of some tracts in the journals *Zeitschrift für celtische Philologie*, *Ériu*, and *Celtica*.Two law tracts have been edited in the Early Irish Law Series, and further editions are in preparation.

Binchy, D. A., *Corpus iuris hibernici*, i–vi (1978)
Breathnach, L., *Uraicecht na ríar: The Poetic Grades in Early Irish Law* (1987)
Charles-Edwards, T., and Kelly, F., *Bechbretha: An Old Irish Law-Tract on Beekeeping* (1983)

FK

League of Nations, established by the treaty of Versailles in 1919 as a vehicle for the regulation of international relations through collective security. The Irish Free State entered the league in September 1923. Its first years of membership were dominated by uncertainty as to how far dominion status permitted an independent national position at the league. The Statute of *Westminster cleared the way for a phase of Irish activism. In 1932 the presidency of the League Council passed by rotation to Ireland. This coincided both with a transfer of power from *Cumann na nGaedheal to *Fianna Fáil, and also with a change in the nature of the international system the League was established to regulate. The relative calm of the post-First World War decade was giving way to the ideological and territorial instabilities that preceded the Second World War. From the beginning Eamon de *Valera, who acted as his own minister for external affairs, laid claim to the moral high ground as spokesman for the 'small powers' in the league. In a series of speeches to the Council and Assembly between 1932 and 1936 he presented Ireland as champion of collective security and enemy of unrestrained power politics. This assertion of international rectitude clashed on occasion with the domestic political mood in Ireland. De Valera's enthusiasm for sanctions against Mussolini's Italy after the invasion of Abyssinia in 1935, for example, was ill-regarded by a considerable section of political and public opinion reluctant to oppose a fellow Catholic country and its incontestably anti-communist leader.

The growing irrelevance of the league in an international system moving inexorably towards breakdown led Ireland to abandon its declared commitment to collective security and to prepare for wartime neutrality. It was, however, an Irishman, Seán Lester, who presided over the final, moribund years of the league. Successively Irish permanent representative and league high commissioner in Danzig, Lester became its last secretary-general from 1939 to 1946.

Barcroft, S., 'Irish Foreign Policy at the League of Nations', *Irish Studies in International Affairs*, 1 (1979)
Keatinge, P., 'Ireland and the League of Nations', *Studies*, 59 (1970)

NMacQ

leases, see LAND TENURE.

Lebor Gabála, literally 'Book of Taking' or 'Book of Settlement', but usually rendered as 'Book of Invasions': a legendary history of Ireland and the Gaels, of fundamental and enduring importance to the shaping of Irish historical thought. The original *Lebor Gabála*, itself largely an amalgam of earlier materials, was probably composed in the second half of the 11th century. The text begins with the creation of the world and the origins of the Gaels; then describes Ireland's successive settlements by Cesair, granddaughter of Noah, Partholón, Nemed, the Fir Bolg ('Men of Bags'), the Tuatha Dé Danann (the pagan gods, here euhemerized as magicians), and the Gaels or Milesians; and concludes with an account of the subsequent kings of Ireland. JPC

Lebor na Cert (the Book of Rights) is concerned with the rights of Irish kings and purports to record a list of tributes and stipends due from and owed to a number of provincial kings. The text can be divided into seven main sections, each consisting of a series of poems accompanied by a prose introduction and focusing on a particular kingship. Since the section on *Cashel is both the first and the most detailed, the redactor appears to have been a Munsterman writing for an *Uí Briain patron some time in the late 11th century. It has been suggested that the text was in fact put together specifically for the Synod of *Cashel by a scribe in the employ of Muirchertach *Ua Briain. MNíM

Lecan, Book of. Like many other Irish manuscript miscellanies, the Book of Lecan (or 'Great Book of Lecan') was a product of the *Gaelic cultural revival, written between 1390 and 1418 by Giolla osa Mór Mac Firbhisigh, head of a west Sligo school of *seanchaidhe* or traditional historians, and scribe of the texts of many Old Irish sagas in the Yellow Book of Lecan. The contents of the Great Book, however, which Giolla osa transcribed for his own use with the help of a number of assistants or pupils, include a poem of his own composition on the landowning families of O'Dowda's country, a comprehensive corpus of updated *genealogies of the Irish nobility, and the texts of many pre-Norman historical tracts. KS

Lecky, W. E. H. (1838–1903), historian. The heir to a small landed property in Queen's County and Carlow, Lecky attended *Trinity College, Dublin, 1856–60, and travelled in Europe before settling in London and Dublin. *The Leaders of Public Opinion in Ireland* (1861) lamented the decline of Irish public life after the Act of *Union. Lecky's first major works, *History of the Rise and Influence of the Spirit of Rationalism in Europe* (1865) and *History of European Morals from Augustus to Charlemagne* (1869), were attempts at sociological history, concerned to discover the laws of human development, but he later turned to analytical political narrative. His *History of England in the Eighteenth Century* (1878–90) included his influential treatment, later separately published, of 18th-century Ireland. Lecky's detailed refutation of *Froude's negative portrayal of Irish character, his catalogue of Irish grievances, and his glorification of *Grattan's parliament won the praise of nationalists. But Lecky himself, horrified at the rise of the *Land League, abandoned his liberal patriotism to become a leading polemicist against *home rule. He sat as *Unionist MP for Trinity College 1895–1902. His last major work, *Democracy and Liberty* (1896), located the golden age of the British constitution in the years between the reform bills of 1832 and 1867.

legal profession. Although there had been professional lawyers expert in native Irish law for several centuries before the *Anglo-Norman invasion of the 12th century, and such experts continued to exist down to the early 17th century, the modern Irish legal profession is descended from the legal profession of the lordship of Ireland, whose expertise was in the Anglo-Irish common law. From the earliest days of that profession it has been divided, like its English counterpart, into two separate groups: specialists in legal argument and those doing other types of legal work.

By 1300 a group of professional *serjeants*, who were specialists in legal argument, can be identified at work in the Dublin bench and in the *justiciar's court and the eyre, and other professional serjeants were at work in city, county, and *liberty courts. The professional serjeants of the royal courts appear to have been a 'closed' group, able to exclude non-members from offering their professional services to litigants in those courts. Entry into a similar group of serjeants associated with the Westminster bench came during the 14th century to be controlled by the crown, and its members gained a monopoly of higher judicial appointments. Neither development was paralleled in Ireland. There was still a small group of Irish serjeants at the end of the 15th century but it had evidently disappeared before 1580, when there was a proposal to create an Irish 'order' of serjeants at law on the English model.

A different (and larger) group of specialist pleaders becomes visible in Ireland from the first half of the 16th century, men known as *counsellors (at law)* or *barristers*. The Irish Statutes of Jeofails of 1542 and 1569 imposed one basic requirement for membership of the group (though initially only for those wishing to practise as such in the Four Courts in Dublin): attendance at one of the inns of court in London. The inns were where legal education was given and an elite within the Irish legal profession had attended them from the 14th century onwards. By 1628 the minimum period of attendance at the inns was fixed at five years. The requirement continued long after the inns had themselves abandoned any attempt to provide legal education and was only removed by statute in 1885. From 1629 Irish barristers were also required to become members of *King's Inns. Catholics were excluded from practising as barristers after 1613 by the enforcement of a requirement that all practising barristers take the oath of *supremacy. This was suspended after 1626 as one of the *Graces. After 1691 all practising barristers were required to take an oath of *abjuration and a declaration against transubstantiation. This again effectively excluded Catholics, who were only readmitted to the practising bar in 1792. The first king's counsel in Ireland were created in the early 17th century. Initially they provided specific legal services to the crown. The title seems soon to have become purely honorific and a recognition of seniority and superior standing at the bar. After 1924 the title was changed within the *Irish Free State to that of senior counsel.

By 1300 there seems also to have been a small group of professional *attorneys* practising in the Dublin bench. There may also have been such attorneys in other courts of the medieval lordship. Attorneys acted for their clients at the preliminary stages in litigation and attended to much of the associated paperwork; they probably also engaged and briefed serjeants on behalf of those clients. The subsequent history of the group is obscure though there were probably professional attorneys in Ireland throughout the later Middle Ages. It seems likely that they acquired their expertise mainly through clerical service to justices, court officials, serjeants, and existing practitioners. By the later 17th century attorneys had to be specially admitted to practice in each of the Four Courts and an act of 1715 also restricted practice as an attorney on the assize circuits to those previously admitted as attorneys of one of the Four Courts. The earliest surviving set of court rules (from 1671 for the Dublin bench) required five years of service to a judge or official of the courts, or to a member of either branch of the profession, in England or Ireland, before admission.

By the end of the 17th century legislation also acknowledged the existence of a separate, but related, group of *solicitors*. Their main function was the management of litigation, acting as an intermediary between litigants and attorneys and barristers, especially in the court of chancery, where a small group of clerks had an official monopoly of acting as litigants' attorneys. An act of 1733 required all those acting as solicitors who had not been admitted as attorneys or appointed as court officials to obtain a licence. The same legislation imposed similar qualifications for licensing as a solicitor or admission as an attorney: a formal apprenticeship of five years to an attorney or solicitor or chancery clerk. A further act of 1773 required a prior inquiry into an apprentice's morals and qualifications before admission as an attorney in any of the three common law courts in Dublin. The closeness of the connection between attorneys and solicitors was underlined by a chancery rule of 1791 requiring prior admission as an attorney to one of the Dublin courts and residence in Dublin as qualifications for admission as a solicitor of the court of chancery. After the unification of the Irish courts in 1878 the formally separate attorneys and solicitors of the various courts became a single group of solicitors. After 1898 both the education of solicitors and their discipline came under the control of their own professional body, the *Incorporated Law Society.

Hogan, D., and Osborough, W. N. (eds.), *Brehons, Serjeants and Attorneys* (1990)

Kenny, C., *King's Inns and the Kingdom of Ireland* (1992)

PAB

Legion of Mary, an association of lay Catholics, founded in 1921 by Frank Duff (1889–1980). Its members' practical Christian action is rooted in a theologically based spirituality, inspired by the writings of St Louis Marie Grignion de Montford (1673–1716). Organizationally influenced by the Society of *St Vincent de Paul, it consists of a network of local conferences, called *praesidia*, under regional *concilia*. Members attend weekly meetings and engage in practical mission work. Because it was lay run and theologically sophisticated, it excited, for a time, the suspicion of Dublin archbishops Edward Byrne and John Charles *McQuaid. The movement has been extraordinarily successful abroad. TO'C

legislative independence, a term used to describe the changes in the constitutional relationship between Great Britain and Ireland introduced in 1782.

Following the granting of *'free trade' in 1779, some *patriot politicians took up the issue of Ireland's subordination to Great Britain. The earl of Carlisle, lord lieutenant 1780–2, and William Eden, chief secretary 1780–2, though ordered to resist all agitation on constitutional issues, chose not to oppose *heads of a bill for what became *Yelverton's Act, as well as other heads clarifying *habeas corpus and giving judges security of tenure. Popular agitation following the *Volunteer Convention of *Dungannon (15 Feb. 1782) increased the pressure for change. In March Lord North, prime minister since 1770, was replaced by a *Whig ministry under the marquis of Rockingham, leading figures in which had already expressed sympathy with Irish grievances. On 16 April the Commons unanimously accepted *Grattan's amendment to the address to the throne asserting Ireland's constitutional rights. The British *Declaratory Act was repealed on 21 June, Yelverton's Act (27 July) modified *Poynings's Law, and other measures secured the independence of judges, declared the Irish House of Lords a court of final appeal, and made the legal basis of army discipline dependent on regular parliamentary renewal by limiting the duration of the Mutiny Act.

Contemporaries, and later constitutional nationalists, liked to speak of the 'constitution of 1782'. In fact the patriot leaders ignored the new ministry's appeals for time to negotiate a comprehensive redefinition of constitutional relationships. The loose ends left by the resulting settlement were revealed in subsequent uncertainties as to the role of the Irish parliament in foreign affairs, in the failure to agree the *Commercial Propositions, and in the *regency crisis. The term 'legislative independence' is also misleading. Under Yelverton's Act Irish bills could still be vetoed by the English privy council, though this power, already employed sparingly before 1782, was used only four times during 1782–1800. More important, the Irish executive continued to be headed by British politicians, the lord lieutenant and chief secretary, accountable to the British cabinet rather than to the Irish parliament.

Leinster, Book of (*Lebar na Núachongbála*), now in *Trinity College, Dublin, and the Franciscan Library, Killiney, Co. Dublin, an important collection in Irish of *genealogies, poetry, pseudo-history, and sagas. An inscription in the text notes that Áed Ua Crimthainn, abbot of Tír dá Glas (Terryglass, Co. Tipperary) wrote and collected it from many books, probably in collaboration with Bishop Find of Kildare (d. 1160). It was assembled after 1151 during the reign of Diarmait *Mac Murchada and completed in the late 12th century. Scholars disagree on the number of scribes involved, either regarding Áed as the sole scribe or identifying four main hands. When Terryglass was destroyed in 1164, the manuscript may have been brought to Cluain Eidnech (Clonenagh, Co. Laois) and thence to Núachongbháil (Oughavall, Co. Laois). EB

Leinster House, Dublin, was designed by Richard *Castle in 1745 for the earl of Kildare (see FITZGERALD). Built on the then unfashionable, and largly undeveloped, south side of the city, the Palladian mansion has the appearance of a country rather than a town house. In 1815 the house was sold to the *Royal Dublin Society. The patronage of the society led to the establishment of a number of cultural institutions around Leinster House, including the *National Library, the National Museum, the School of Art, and the National Gallery. In 1922 the government of the new *Irish Free State obtained a portion of the building for parliamentary use, and two years later acquired the entire building. The house is currently the seat of *Dáil Éireann. RM

Leland, Thomas (1722–85), *Church of Ireland clergyman and historian. Born and educated in Dublin, Leland became a fellow of *Trinity College in 1746. Following a dispute, he was appointed to the parish of Bray, Co. Wicklow, in 1768, though he maintained his links with the university. He subsequently held various livings in Wicklow, Dublin, and Tyrone. His *History of Ireland from the Invasion of Henry II* (1773) was more balanced than earlier Protestant histories. However, its treatment of the 1641 rebellion dismayed liberal Catholics, such as Charles *O'Conor, who had assisted Leland's research, and John *Curry, who published a rival account in 1775. NG

Lemass, Sean (1899–1971), The son of a prosperous Dublin retailer, Lemass was a teenage combatant in the *rising of 1916. Interned for *IRA activities 1920–1, he fought on the anti-treaty side in the *Civil War. His brother Noel was murdered in October 1923, allegedly by Free State *political police. Lemass became abstentionist *Sinn Féin TD (Dáil deputy) for South Dublin 1924, and went on to play a key organizational role in the successful establishment of *Fianna Fáil.

As minister for industry and commerce 1932–9 Lemass energetically promoted domestic manufacturing through protective tariffs and the exclusion of foreign capital. From 1939 he was minister for supplies (while also resuming control of industry and commerce from 1941), coping efficiently with the acute shortages created by the *Second World War. By 1944–5 Lemass was already impatient with the limitations imposed by *protectionism and state support for small-scale agriculture, but was restrained by the conservatism of cabinet colleagues. In 1959 he succeeded de *Valera as party leader and *taoiseach, and gave full support to the new strategy of industrial development, largely financed by inward investment, outlined in the *First Programme for Economic Expansion.

The rapid modernization of the 1960s, replacing the stagnation of the de Valera era, encouraged perceptions of Lemass's premiership (1959–66) as a new era. Modern accounts emphasize the pragmatism, and at times opportunism, that allowed him to work for so long with a party largely out of sympathy with his goal of economic, and in particular industrial, development, and to respond to the new ideas taking shape in a variety of quarters at the time he became taoiseach. In the same spirit he promoted friendlier relations with *Northern Ireland, notably in his exchange of visits with Terence *O'Neill (1965), while continuing to insist that economic progress in independent Ireland would eventually permit the peaceful ending of *partition.

Leth Cuinn and Leth Moga are names for the two halves of Ireland, the dividing line running from Dublin to Galway Bay. As terms they were designed to represent the political hegemony of the *Uí Néill in Leth Cuinn (Conn's half) in the north of the island, and that of the *Eóganacht (Leth Moga—Mug Nuadat's half) in the south, a division which was supposed to have taken place in remote prehistory when the sons of Míl conquered Ireland. This model reflects the aspirations of Eóganacht kings of Munster rather than political realities, since Munster kings only rarely controlled the peoples of Leinster. CS

Leth Moga, see LETH CUINN AND LETH MOGA.

Liberals, successors to the *Whigs as one of the two main British *political parties, until relegated to third place, from the early 1920s, by the rise of Labour. Despite the survival of Liberal loyalties among a diminishing minority of mainly affluent Presbyterians, the Irish Liberal Party relied mainly on Catholic votes, even though all its candidates in Ulster, and a disproportionately large minority elsewhere, were Protestants. Following the collapse of the *Independent Irish Party, the Liberal share of Irish seats rose from 48 in 1857 to a record 66, on the basis of *Gladstone's promise of 'justice for Ireland', in 1868. Thereafter, however, Liberalism was eclipsed by the rise of the *home rule party. The one exception was Ulster, where its commitment to agrarian reform gave Liberalism unprecedented electoral success, among Catholics and Protestants alike, until the home rule crisis of 1886 split the electorate between Nationalist and Unionist.

See also ULSTER LIBERAL PARTY.

liberties, a term applied to Anglo-Norman lordships in Ireland that exercised jurisdiction normally reserved to the crown. Since the invasion was a seigniorial rather than a royal enterprise, *Henry II permitted *Strongbow (Leinster), de *Lacy (Meath), and de *Courcy (Ulster) to exercise full jurisdiction within their lordships.

Initially no limitation was imposed, but in 1197 *John, while still lord of Ireland, seized the temporalities of the see of Leighlin, thereby affirming his lordship over the temporalities of the church even when they lay within the liberties. This claim was affirmed in John's charter restoring the liberty of Ulster in 1205, followed three years later by the additional reservation to the crown courts of four 'royal' pleas: rape, arson, treasure trove, and forestall. The exclusions were significant. First, by reserving church lands to his immediate jurisdiction, the king excluded the great lords from having a say in the appointment of bishops. Second, by retaining the pleas he underlined the inferiority of private jurisdictions. Third, a writ of right could remove actions begun in a liberty court to a royal court, with the result that the legal system in the former, unlike the marcher lordships in Wales, had to conform to the norms of common law. In effect, the liberty courts became extensions of the royal system of justice. John's measures ensured that the Irish liberties, which, unchecked, would have followed the Welsh pattern, developed more on the lines of the English immunities.

Royal officials were normally excluded from the liberties, where the lord's peace prevailed, not the king's. Courts were summoned, and writs ran, in his name. At times in the 13th century it would have been possible to travel from Hook Head in Wexford to Dunluce on the coast of Antrim passing through only one narrow strip of royal territory in Louth. Some Henrician liberties were subsequently converted into royal counties (Kildare, Carlow, and Kilkenny), while new ones, like Tipperary and Kerry, were created as political favours in the 14th century. Yet even those that endured were subject to periodic forfeiture, as happened in Tipperary in 1331, 1415, 1462, and 1494. They were, moreover, routinely reintegrated into the county system during the minority of the lord.

Basically, the liberties were privately governed counties that formed part of the system of royal administration. The chief official of the liberty, the *seneschal, had to report to the exchequer at the same terms as the royal *sheriff, and had to swear to serve the king faithfully. Like the sheriff, he was subject to fines and liable for debts due to the crown.

Internally, the liberties were organized like counties. The seneschal, as chief officer, presided over the liberty court, while the sheriff presided over the county court and the sessions of the tourn. He was assisted by serjeants and *coroners in each *cantred. In lieu of royal officials, chancellors and treasurers were regularly appointed. In the 15th century a justice of the liberty of Tipperary, who presumably discharged some of the legal functions of the seneschal, appears for the first time.

See also PALATINE JURISDICTION.

Otway-Ruthven, J., 'Anglo-Irish Shire Government in the Thirteenth Century', *Irish Historical Studies*, 5 (1946)

—— *A History of Medieval Ireland* (2nd edn., 1980)

CAE

Liberty Hall, on Eden Quay, Dublin, headquarters of the *Irish Transport and General Workers' Union. The original building, formerly a hotel and offices, was acquired in 1912. Though seriously damaged in the *rising of 1916, it remained in use until 1956. It was demolished in 1958 and replaced by the present 17-storey glass and steel building, opened in 1965.

Liberty League, a short-lived political movement launched in April 1917 by George Noble Plunkett (1851–1948—Count Plunkett by a hereditary papal title). Plunkett's son Joseph Mary had been executed following the *rising of 1916, and he himself had been returned in North Roscommon (5 Feb. 1917), in the first of a series of by-election defeats for the *Nationalist Party. His attempt to supersede *Sinn Féin with his own movement caused temporary confusion, but was abandoned within months.

libraries, public. Restrictions on access to the college and diocesan libraries that developed in the 17th century may have motivated Narcissus Marsh, Church of Ireland archbishop of Dublin 1694–1703, to found a library there in 1701. Open to all 'graduates and gentlemen', its claim to be the first public library seems justified, though the limited range of its holdings may have ensured a small membership. The town library founded by Archbishop *Robinson in Armagh in 1770 served a broader membership, as did the libraries organized by voluntary subscriber democracies in Belfast (1788—see LINEN HALL LIBRARY), Dublin (1791), and Cork (1819), as well as in smaller towns and villages. Elsewhere the demand for reading material was partly filled by commercial libraries and by parish and church libraries. In the 1830s and 1840s the libraries of *temperance societies, *repeal clubs, and *mechanics' institutes revealed a growing reading public but there was also anxiety regarding its reading matter. In 1849 a parliamentary committee advocated rate-funded free public libraries. This led to the Public Libraries and Museums Act (1850), whose provisions—periodically extended—applied to Ireland from 1853. The first library thus funded opened in Dundalk in 1858, followed by two others in Dublin in 1884, and another in Belfast in 1888. Local authorities were slow to allocate funds but grants by Andrew Carnegie and by the Carnegie United Kingdom Trust between 1897 and the early 1950s facilitated substantial capital projects. By 1945 all the counties of both independent Ireland and Northern Ireland had established a library service, while those urban or borough councils without a service had passed their power to an adjacent county council. In 1973 responsibility for the Northern Ireland service passed to five regional education and library boards. Levels of funding and provision continue to vary, as does membership, though uneven record-keeping has obscured the long-term trend. By the 1970s between one-tenth and one-fifth of all adults were members of a public library, but in the Republic a pattern of growth was halted in the early 1980s by budget constraints which led to substantial charges, stock reductions, and restricted opening hours. JnL

Lichfield House compact, taking its name from the London residence of Lord Lichfield, where *Whig, radical, and *repeal MPs met several times during February and March 1835 and worked out tactics to bring about the fall of *Peel's *Tory ministry. Although both *O'Connell and the Whigs denied that any formal agreement had been reached, there was a tacit understanding that he would support a minority Whig government in exchange for measures of practical reform. The results, from O'Connell's point of view, were mixed. Municipal reform (1840) permitted O'Connell himself to become the first Catholic lord mayor of Dublin since the reign of *James II, while the reform of *tithe (1838) made payments a little less burdensome. But neither these measures nor the new *poor law (1838) met his aspirations, partly because all bills had to pass through the Tory-dominated House of Lords. The real gains were in the day-to-day administration of Ireland under the earl of Mulgrave, lord lieutenant 1835–9, his chief secretary Viscount Morpeth (1835–41), and the under-secretary Thomas *Drummond. Some 30–40 per cent of Irish appointments under the new executive went to Catholics, and many others to liberal Protestants. Law enforcement became more impartial and the *Orange Order dissolved itself to avoid suppression. O'Connell's ingenious rationalization of the arrangement as a test of whether Ireland could be well governed under the *Union, with a promise to drop repeal permanently if the experiment was successful, need not be taken at face value. But the episode clearly illustrates the pragmatism that was later to bring him into conflict with the doctrinaire nationalism of *Young Ireland.

lighthouses in Ireland date back to the 5th century, when the monks of St Dubhan established a fire beacon at Hook Head, Co. Wexford. Indeed nearby is the oldest still-operational lighthouse in Ireland and Great Britain, which has stood on the same site from the 12th century. Lighthouses were in private hands until 1717, when the land they stood on was vested in the crown. Central control of lighthouses came with the establishment of the commissioners of Irish lights in 1867. This all-Ireland body maintains 80 lighthouses, all but one now automatic, around the entire coastline. PC

'Lilliburlero', satirical verses representing two Irish Catholics gloating over *Tyrconnell's appointment as lord deputy (Jan. 1687). It begins 'Ho Brother Teague dost hear de decree' and ends 'Now, now de Hereticks all go down . . . By Chreist and St Patrick the Nation's our own'. The refrain 'Lilli Burlero Bullen-a-la' was said to represent passwords used in the *rising of 1641, but has also been taken to refer to the lily, symbol of the *Orange party. *Swift, in 1712, named the *Whig leader Thomas Wharton as the author, quoting him as claiming to have whistled a king out of three kingdoms. The tune, attributed to Henry Purcell but if so adapted by him from a popular air, replaced an earlier one as the song gained popularity, and was subsequently used for 'The Protestant Boys' and other Orange ballads.

Limerick, treaty of (3 Oct. 1691), ending the *Williamite War. In exchange for the surrender of their last stronghold in Limerick, Jacobite soldiers were offered free passage to France, where they could continue the war in what became the *Irish Brigade. Those remaining in Ireland were secured in their estates and guaranteed the right to practise their trades or professions and, if gentlemen or nobles, to carry arms. Catholics in general were guaranteed such religious freedoms 'as are consistent with the laws of Ireland', or as they had enjoyed under Charles II (see RESTORATION). There was also a ban on lawsuits for plunder or trespass committed during the war.

To *William III and *Ginkel these concessions were a fair price for freeing resources tied up in what had always been a diversion from the main struggle against France. Irish Protestants, however, were outraged both by the denial of redress for wartime losses and by the failure to secure the final destruction of Catholic political power. Their resentment encouraged the *sole right agitation of 1692, as well as a bitter campaign against Sir Charles Porter, lord chancellor 1690–6, one of those who had signed the treaty. The act by which the Irish parliament eventually ratified the treaty, in 1697, omitted the reference to freedom of religion, as well as an undertaking that Catholics would be obliged to take no oath other than a pledge of simple allegiance. Also omitted was an important clause, left out of the fair copy of the articles but acknowledged by letters patent four months later, that extended the full protection of the treaty to civilians in Jacobite-held territories. Despite these concessions to Protestant feeling the provisions of the treaty relating to Jacobite estates (including those covered by the 'missing clause') were scrupulously observed, sharply limiting the scope of the *Williamite confiscations. Legislation forbidding Catholics to possess arms or to practise law also exempted those covered by the treaty. Catholics nevertheless argued that the *penal laws enacted from 1695 breached the treaty's guarantee of religious freedom, but their case was weakened by the vagueness of the relevant clause. This in turn reflected the extent to which the main preoccupation of Sarsfield and the other Jacobite leaders had been with the removal of the army intact to France. It was only in retrospect that the other articles, seen at the time as the terms of a temporary truce, came to be interpreted as a statement of the terms on which Catholics might have been willing to live permanently under a Protestant government.

Simms, J. G., *The Treaty of Limerick* (1961)

Limerick city began as a *Viking settlement on the south-west part of King's Island, close to the lowest fording point across the Shannon. For two centuries before the Anglo-Norman invasion Limerick had been under the sway of the *O'Briens, becoming in effect their capital in the 12th century and not passing permanently out of their control until Domnal Mór's death in 1194. The walled island settlement was then drawn into firmer English control with its first charter (1197), its royal castle (1210), and the relocation of many of its former inhabitants south across the Abbey river to 'Irishtown'. The latter suburb was eventually enclosed within a second set of walls. St Mary's in 'Englishtown' is the only medieval cathedral surviving largely intact in a provincial Irish port; its pre-Norman elements were mostly eradicated in the 13th-century reconstruction, but the quality and range of its 15th-century additions is evidence of the city's late medieval revival.

The political agility of its old patrons, the O'Briens, protected Limerick from some of the harsher swings of fortune in the course of the 17th century—until 1690. The choice then of the city as rallying point for *Jacobite and French forces and the twelve-month siege (see WILLIAMITE WAR) was a tribute both to the apparent impregnability of the site and to the strength and cohesiveness of the old order in the city. Sections of the walled city suffered badly in the conflict, but the siege was remembered for the manner of its ending: the departure of the *'wild geese' and the controversy over the half-honoured peace terms (see LIMERICK, TREATY OF) which still reverberated a century later.

In the post-siege reconstruction, brick replaced the stone and timber of the walled city. The walls themselves remained until 1760, by which time Limerick had developed as a centre of Atlantic trade, gentry consumption, and *woollen manufacturing. The city at that stage burst its claustrophobic bounds and over the following 70 years a grid-iron network of residential and commercial streets was constructed to the south-west of the Irishtown and outside the jurisdiction of the corporation. Appropriately this became known as Newtown Pery, after the ground landlord of the new zone and the very successful general patron of the city, Edmond Sexton Pery (1719–1806). The city's social and commercial centre was transplanted; even the new town hall in 1843 was located in the Newtown. But in this period of expansion the physical limitations of the Shannon as a trade artery (despite a canal link to Killaloe) denied Limerick the opportunity of becoming the great outport many believed was its destiny.

Always a preponderantly Catholic city, Limerick in the 19th century witnessed a pronounced growth in the visibility and range of its Catholic institutions which helped to mould its distinctive religious culture. The industrial traditions in textiles and milling adapted to changed times (e.g. the development of army clothing and lace manufacture) but the pervasive poverty of the old city remained. Even in the second half of the 20th century, with the old slums swept away and Limerick (as part of the mid-west region) one of the most successful centres of modern industrial development, it remained a city of extremes.

Clarke, Howard (ed.), *Irish Cities* (1995)

Hill, Judith, *The Building of Limerick* (1991)

DD

linen was Ireland's most important *manufacturing industry during the 18th and 19th centuries. It was heavily concentrated in Ulster, where it became the lead sector in the industrialization of the eastern half of the province during the 19th century.

There had been a tradition of flax cultivation and linen manufacture, largely for domestic consumption, prior to the *Ulster plantation. The plantation brought a number of experienced artisans and merchants into the Irish industry from Britain and to a lesser extent from continental Europe. Their new skills and knowledge of trade networks enabled linen to become the dominant export from the Ulster region by the end of the 17th century. Duty-free access to the British market from 1696, and to that of Britain's colonies from 1705, gave Irish linens the edge over German and Dutch rivals. In addition to these official measures and the establishment of the *Linen Board (1711), the industry received support from many *landlords who initiated local schemes such as the provision of market facilities.

Participation in extra-regional markets made linen more resilient and dynamic than other Irish industries. Exports increased from about 2 million yards in 1713 to over 47 million yards in 1796. By the latter year linen, flax, and hemp products accounted for over 56 per cent of the value of all Irish exports.

Linen was well suited to Ireland as, during the 18th century, it was (with the exception of bleaching and finishing) labour intensive rather than capital intensive. The cultivation of flax, the spinning of yarn, and the weaving of linen cloth were all well suited to the economy of rural smallholders, being activities that could occupy the slack periods of the *farming year. From the 1740s yarn spinning began to spread westwards into Connacht and also into north Leinster, increasing the supply of yarn to the major weaving districts in Ulster. Facilities for bleaching and finishing, and the core markets in the industry, tended to be located in east Ulster, in an area (known as the linen triangle) linking *Belfast, Dungannon, and *Armagh. Despite Ulster's predominant position in the industry, most of the exports were channelled through *Dublin factors until the end of the 18th century, when Ulster factors began to deal directly with London.

By the end of the 18th century, bleaching had become the most centralized and mechanized process within the industry. The bleachers who controlled the final stages of production and the early stages of marketing were a powerful group within the industry, capable of financing the larger capital outlays required to introduce mechanized finishing processes. Spinning and weaving, by contrast, remained predominantly a cottage industry. Although Belfast had become the main centre of mechanized cotton spinning in Ireland by the 1820s, the mechanization of flax spinning took place more slowly; dry spinning techniques produced a yarn which was too coarse for most cloth types. Wet spinning, pioneered in England, produced a finer yarn more suitable for the finer cloth types made in Ulster, and in the second half of the 1820s a number of bleachers and cotton manufacturers in the region began to invest in the new technology. Mulholland's (ex-Belfast cotton spinners) were the first commercially successful wet spinners to undertake the new process on a large scale from 1829. By the mid-1830s, linen had displaced *cotton as the main employer of factory labour in the Belfast area. The proprietors of spinning mills gradually began to displace bleachers as the principal employers of labour within the industry, though many bleachers also began to invest in spinning. The factory industry was even more concentrated in east Ulster. The adoption of powerloom weaving from the 1850s completed the process of mechanization.

By this time Belfast had become the largest linen manufacturing centre in the world; the expansion of mechanized production was most rapid during the 1860s when a shortage of cotton wool resulting from the *American Civil War undermined the rival cotton industry. Peak 19th-century spindlage had already been reached in 1870. Between 1860 and 1914 all but one of the five firms who dominated the industry (the York Street Spinning Company, the Brookfield Linen Company, Ewart & Son, the Linen Thread Company, and the Ulster Spinning Company) carried out all aspects of the manufacture from spinning to retailing cloth. Smaller firms tended to specialize. By the end of the 19th century the making-up trade had also become significant so less cloth was exported directly, and more was made up into handkerchiefs, sheets, table cloths, *shirts, and so on. Over the course of the 19th century, linen had become a luxury item; it was particularly suited to warm climates. By the end of the century the USA rather than Britain had become the main destination for Irish exports. The industry did reasonably well until after the end of the *First World War, but international demand for linen contracted dramatically over the following decades. Fashions changed and people used fewer linen sheets, table cloths, and underwear. This decline was permanent and the linen industry never recovered.

Cohen, M., *The Warp of Ulster's Past: Interdisciplinary Perspectives on the Irish Linen Industry 1700–1920* (1997)

Crawford, W., 'The Evolution of the Linen Trade in Ulster', *Irish Economic and Social History*, 15 (1988)

AB

Linen Board, set up in 1711 to regulate and finance the expanding *linen industry. The board was composed of 72 trustees, 18 from each of the four provinces. They were drawn from the episcopacy of the *Church of Ireland, the nobility, and gentry. Trustees generally knew little about the industry, leaving the day-to-day work of the board to permanent officials. Nevertheless, in the early days of the board, the trustees' influence in parliament and with the government was very useful in winning preference for the linen trade. The board gave grants and prizes for outstanding work by spinners, weavers, and bleachers and also encouraged the spread of new methods and inventions. Money was granted to establish new bleach greens. In time, as the industry grew and became more complex, some saw the regulations of the board and the activity of its officials more as a hindrance than as a help. While the board's work undoubtedly helped to establish linen in its initial base in Ulster, the aim of disseminating its manufacture throughout Ireland was never achieved. The Linen Board lasted until 1828, by which time spinning was entering into its mechanized phase. PC

Linen Hall Library, Belfast, created by the Belfast Reading Society (1788), which in 1792 became the Belfast Society for Promoting Knowledge. From 1802 the library was granted the use of space in the city's white linen hall, from which it took its familiar name. It moved to its present premises, a former linen warehouse in Donegall Square, in 1892.

linen halls were markets at which drapers sold linen. The *Linen Board built the first white linen hall, to handle bleached linen goods, in Dublin in 1721. Ninety per cent of its business was with English buyers. Much of the industry was concentrated in the north and, after a falling-out with the Linen Board in 1782, Ulster drapers erected white linen halls in Armagh, Newry, and Belfast. These were not a success, as many drapers were already dealing directly with buyers in England. The white linen hall in Belfast was demolished in 1896 to make way for the new city hall. PC

Lionel of Clarence (1338–68), *king's lieutenant 1361–6, the third son of Edward III, held large estates in Ireland through his marriage to the heiress of the earldom of *Ulster. His appointment, after the conclusion of peace with France in 1360 had enabled Edward III to turn his attention to Ireland, marks the beginning of a half-century of English military intervention in Ireland, financed primarily out of English revenues.

The army which Lionel brought to Ireland was supplemented with local forces and the tactics used were a combination of garrisons and attacks on specific objectives. Although Lionel's wife had estates in Ulster and Connacht, as well as in Kilkenny, the main areas of military activity were Leinster, the midlands, and the south-west. After a promising start, the initial impetus faded. The size of the army declined and the military gains were reversed after Lionel's return to England in 1366.

The programme of reform concentrated on the financial administration, with the aim of maximizing the amount of money at the disposal of the lieutenant. However, the resulting increase in revenues depended on the maintenance of stable conditions and did not survive the departure of Lionel's army. The Statute of *Kilkenny, enacted in 1366, was an attempt to promote greater social and political stability by preventing further causes of dispute and increasing central control over local warfare. PhC

literacy. The initiation of *printing promoted the adoption of a standard written form, notwithstanding the extent to which different dialects continued to be spoken, and it also increased the contexts within which reading and writing might be used. The progress of literacy in English outside the urban commercial and professional classes is charted with difficulty, but the incidence of written names and marks as signatures on leases, depositions, and petitions partly indicates its diffusion. In the early 17th century the majority of male members of the gentry, particularly those of Scottish or English origin, had writing skills. At mid-century perhaps a third of the larger leaseholders could write their names, though striking variations, influenced by sex and race, were evident. At the end of the century up to a quarter of artisans and of smaller leaseholders may have been able to write. In the towns literacy was more widespread than in the countryside, though the ability to write a name was rare amongst the poorer inhabitants, and almost entirely absent in those who were female.

Literacy levels may have risen slowly in the first half of the 18th century. They undoubtedly grew more rapidly during the second half, and at the end of the century practically all larger leaseholders and most artisans and shopkeepers had reading and writing skills. Formalized *school instruction had become more common and brought literacy into households unable to afford a private teacher, but dissemination further down the social scale proved difficult without a significant increase in school supply. This was met, in part, by the teacher proprietors of *hedge schools. Their unregulated methods often elicited a hostile response, particularly from those who believed that popular education would aggravate social and political discontent. Yet the appeal of literacy could not be denied nor its dissemination prevented. Evangelical philanthropists and landlords extended patronage to teacher proprietors and to teaching congregations, though at a level hardly sufficient to keep pace with increasing demand in an expanding population. In the first two decades of the 19th century a swelling coalition of political and religious interests led to substantial levels of state support for such initiatives, and from 1831 the centrally regulated and locally managed *national schools became the main conduit through which an increasing proportion of the population acquired elementary skills.

Literacy in 19th-century Ireland may be measured by *census data (from 1841), and, following compulsory *civil registration of marriages from 1864, by the proportion of bridegrooms and brides who signed their name. Although the usefulness of both sets of data has been questioned, they indicate, at the very least, the availability and diffusion of minimal skill levels. Moreover the results in each case show a high degree of internal consistency, while the long-term trend, sex differences, and patterns of regional variation revealed in both sets of data are broadly similar. In 1841 47 per cent of persons over 5 were returned by heads of household as able to read; by 1911 the proportion was 88 per cent. (Throughout the early modern period the ability to read was more widespread than the ability to write, particularly amongst women, and the 19th-century census data revealed the persistence of that differential.) Sixty-one per cent of grooms and 49 per cent of brides in 1864 were able to sign by writing their name; the disparity between men and women had gone by 1891, when 82 per cent of all spouses wrote their names. Thereafter marking of the register is rare and in 1931, when the data series ends, 98 per cent wrote their name. Census and marriage register data also help to confirm the view that the school was the principal means through which literacy was disseminated, though not the argument that it was its sole cause. In general, higher levels of school enrolment and higher literacy levels were strongly associated with the degree to which a region experienced urbanization, with higher incomes, and with the prevalence of English.

The adoption of a compulsory elementary school attendance policy in Northern Ireland in 1923 and in the Irish Free State in 1926 led to the widespread belief that basic literacy would very soon become universal. That assumption has been successfully challenged by educationists who have shown that, notwithstanding a compulsory state curriculum in reading and writing, literacy skill in adulthood is formed and modified by occupational and social need, and that in some groups, including linguistic minorities, travellers, and the urban poor, it is frequently present at a low level or absent altogether. The debate on the precise meaning of literacy continues, intensified by the development of new information technologies and the evolving forms of the spoken language in its different social contexts. JnL

literary revival, one of several terms used to refer to a movement of poets, prose writers, and playwrights (see ABBEY THEATRE) *c.*1890–*c.*1914, who looked for inspiration to Irish mythology, folklore, and popular culture. The domination of the movement by writers from middle- and upper-class Protestant backgrounds (*Yeats, John Millington Synge (1871–1909), and Augusta, Lady *Gregory, and its concern to use Gaelic material as the basis of a revitalized Irish literature in English, has encouraged the alternative label 'Anglo-Irish revival'. The popular nickname 'the Celtic twilight' was derived from a book of this title published by Yeats in 1893.

The revival reflected the same acute concern with questions of cultural defence seen in other near contemporary movements, the *Gaelic Athletic Association, the *Gaelic League, and D. P. *Moran's 'Irish Ireland' campaign. But there was no consensus on how identity was to be defined or preserved. Irish-language supporters dismissed the idea of a national literature in English. Moran and others rejected what they saw as the claim to cultural leadership by an Anglo-Irish elite. Depictions of 'traditional' Irish life that failed to present a suitably idealized image in harmony with middle-class Catholic values came under attack: in particular Synge's plays *In the Shadow of the Glen* (1903) and *The Playboy of the Western World* (1907) provoked outrage and protest. The question of how far art should be related to politics divided leading protagonists both from other groups and from one another. These often bitter controversies contributed to what in retrospect can be seen as the highly charged atmosphere of the years before 1914 (see NEW NATIONALISM), and continued to influence cultural policy and attitudes in both parts of Ireland after 1922.

literature and the historian. History is both an art and a science, dealing with ideas and assumptions as much as the more tangible records of administration. Ireland has provoked many writers of stature: for many people, indeed, Irish history is better known through literature than through the formal works of historians. For this reason, and because Irish writing has long been deeply implicated in politics, it is impossible for historians to do full justice to Ireland's past without coming to terms with its literature.

At one time Irish universities contained joint chairs of history and literature. This reflected not only a relative lack of academic specialization, but also a definition of literature which extended beyond purely imaginative works to cover other types of public discourse such as parliamentary speeches and historical texts. The divide between the two relates both to the development of history as a professional discipline modelled on the sciences (a doctrine articulated in its extreme form by the Irish classicist J. B. Bury (1861–1927)), and the increasing identification of literature with the private and subjective. In recent years both disciplines have again extended their ranges to take in much of the material excluded by the previous tightening of boundaries: this cross-fertilization has produced some valuable new approaches but has also created a certain amount of interdisciplinary tension between historians and literary critics.

The use of literature as a resource for historical analysis presents a range of problems. There is a natural tendency to focus more on the great individual writer than on the wider conditions governing the production of literature. In addition, certain viewpoints are by their nature under-represented in literature. Like any other source, writing produced at a certain time and place for a particular purpose requires critical and sometimes sceptical interrogation. But there is also the particular problem, illustrated for example in current debates on the significance to be attributed to the political sentiments expressed in medieval *bardic poetry or in the 18th-century *aisling* (see LITERATURE IN IRISH), of distinguishing between intended representations of reality and the observance of literary convention.

Literary merit and historical value are not conterminous; the obscure or mediocre writer, when placed in the right context, can be a valuable source. Yet the bulk of 19th-century Anglo-Irish literature, to take one example, remains in the obscurity to which it was dispatched by the pre-1914 *literary revival; much of the information on lesser-known writers accumulated by literary historians and by feminists looking for evidence of women's achievements has yet to be assimilated by mainstream historical scholarship.

Current debates on the relationship between literature and history are overshadowed by an earlier attempt, partly successful and partly catastrophic, to subsume the latter into the former. Owing to the colonial/romantic identification of England with rationality and Ireland with art and dreaming, there is a strain of Irish thought which regards 'history as science' as a colonial imposition and sees literature as a superior substitute. This is related to the fact that the 19th-century pioneers of Irish professional history, because of differential access to higher education, the state-centred outlook of early professional historians everywhere, and the nature of surviving archives, were predominantly of Protestant/ *unionist background, concentrated on the history of the Anglo-Irish colonial elite and the British administration in Ireland, and equated their political position with reason, progress, and modern civilization. On the other hand, much 19th-century nationalist history was the product of a self-conscious counter-culture, propagated through mass produced literature, often heavily polemical, and regarding the ideals of progress and rationality as masks for a parasitic elite. For many writers in this tradition, their uncertain social position and the absence of a coherent literary ancestry mirrored the plight of a nation cut off from a heroic past where art, religion, and society had complemented one another; the presentation of that past could inspire its re-creation. From a different perspective some unionists, alarmed by the inroads of metropolitan values and by their own social and political marginalization, also looked to literature as a solution. From both viewpoints, history in the modern sense was a gigantic imposture, while literature had privileged access to Irishness: indeed Ireland itself became a gigantic unfinished artwork, to which its inhabitants/characters are subordinated like the builders of a Gothic cathedral. Thus Standish *O'Grady said that those trying to write history from archives were like a man observing a stained-glass window from outside, while the artist saw the same window from within; Daniel *Corkery wrote that those acquainted with 18th-century Munster Gaelic poetry could not possibly see state papers as anything more than a tedious irrelevance.

At the same time, literature seen as a protest against British utilitarianism was often wielded in a surprisingly utilitarian manner. For example, the *Young Ireland concept of 'a ballad history of Ireland', conceived as romantic protest, was carried out through the systematic dissemination of didactic mass literature using methods borrowed from English radicals. Sixty years later Gaelic revivalists were to protest that by disseminating nationalist literature in English their predecessors had actually promoted Anglicization and undermined the Gaelic identity which they were trying to preserve; yet Irish Ireland images of Ireland were themselves heavily influenced by preconceptions inherited from those same predecessors.

These suspicions were inherited by post-independence professional historians who tried to separate Irish history from the controversies of the past by studying its materials dispassionately.

For traditional nationalists this amounted to treason; in the 1940s the Republican balladeer Brian O'Higgins (1882–1963), who inherited the pedagogic methods of the Young Irelanders, called for the removal of 'unpatriotic' academics from their positions and demanded that the expression of unorthodox views on Irish history should be made a criminal offence. More recently (and reasonably) it has been pointed out that the ideal of a definitive and purely dispassionate history is unattainable: sources bear different interpretations; selection is unavoidable and must take place in accordance with some order of priorities, explicit or unstated. Thus the historian must always be to some extent an artist employing techniques of persuasion: yet at the same time few would argue that no interpretation is truer than any other.

To some extent this dispute between 'history' and 'literature' lies behind recent debates over 'revisionism', in which some of the most impassioned 'anti-revisionists' have been literary critics rather than professional historians (though practitioners of both disciplines are found on each side). 'Anti-revisionists' accuse 'revisionists' of positivistic reverence for state documents, producing an unacknowledged identification with the wielders of power against the voiceless and restless oppressed, and dismissing popular versions of history out of hand as irrational. 'Revisionists' complain that 'anti-revisionists' wish to ignore the complexities of Irish history, supersede professional standards, impose their own arbitrary will on the people whose experiences they profess to recover, and raise their own preconceived ideas above criticism, much as nationalist protestors of the early 20th century objected when writers failed to conform to their preconceptions about national literature. While recent developments in literary theory can make important contributions to decoding the assumptions implicit in certain texts (for example, the colonial rhetoric of self-justification, the maintenance of gender roles) they are sometimes applied simplistically (e.g. the equation of appeals to a romanticized past by previous generations of nationalists opposing colonial claims to represent 'modernity' with present-day postmodernism and the privileging of this over other past expressions of nationalism less appealing to postmodernist sensibilities). It is to be hoped that a new generation of cultural historians will ultimately produce a synthesis of the contending positions.

Dunne, Tom (ed.), *The Writer as Witness* (1987)
Kiberd, Declan, *Inventing Ireland* (1995)
McCormack, W. J., *Ascendancy and Betrayal* (1994)

PM

literature in Irish. Ireland has the oldest vernacular literature in western Europe. Apart from inscriptions the earliest surviving writings in Irish are interlinear glosses in Latin religious texts. The earliest manuscript entirely in Irish is *Lebor na hUidre*, 'the Book of the *Dun Cow', written in *Clonmacnoise *c.*1100.

Of major importance are the early prose sagas, classified by modern scholars into four separate cycles.

1. The Mythological Cycle tells of the Tuatha Dé Danann, originally the deities of the pagan Irish but reinterpreted after the coming of Christianity as earlier inhabitants of the country. They included Lug, Nuadu, the sea-god Manannán, and the Dagda (literally the 'good god'). The foremost mythological tale is Cath Maige Tuired (The Battle of Moytura), in which the Tuatha Dé are first oppressed by and finally defeat the race of giants known as the Fomori, a struggle reminiscent of the similar conflict between the Olympians and Titans of classical mythology.

2. The Ulster Cycle recounts the exploits of the heroes around Conchobar mac Nessae, king of the *Ulaid. The foremost tale is *Táin Bó Cuailnge (The Cattle-Raid of Cooley), in which the young hero Cú Chulainn defends Ulster alone against the invading army of Queen Medb. The Ulster Cycle is heroic in the strict sense. War is the chief activity of its heroes and loyalty and prowess are their main virtues. There are numerous other Ulster tales, of which the tragic story of Deirdre and Naoisi is perhaps the best known.

3. The stories concerning early rulers of Ireland are collectively known as the Cycle of the Kings. They cannot always be entirely distinguished from the mythological tales, containing as they do much mythological and legendary material. The tale of the birth and early life of *Cormac mac Airt is a good example. Perhaps the finest king tale is *Togail Bruidne Da Derga* (The Destruction of Da Derga's Hostel), which tells how Conaire, king of Tara, is induced to break his *gesa* or 'taboos' one by one, with disastrous consequences.

4. The Ossianic Cycle deals with Fionn mac Cumhaill, his son Oisín, his grandson Oscar, and the other heroes of his *fian* or 'war-band'. Unlike the Ulster heroes who occupy a central place in society and fight from chariots, the Ossianic heroes live in the forest as outlaws and travel exclusively on foot. The Ossianic Cycle, itself of ultimately mythological origin, is poorly attested in the earlier literature. The turning point is the late 12th-century text *Acallam na Senórach* (The Colloquy of the Ancients), in which St *Patrick meets Oisín and Caoilte, two surviving heroes of the *fian*, and accompanies them around Ireland.

The *Acallam* is thus a work of *dinnsenchas* or toponymic lore. As each story is told, Patrick enjoins that it be written down lest it be lost. The *Acallam* is almost certainly a Gaelic counterblast to the contemporary *Cistercian reforms. The anonymous author, by making St Patrick the preserver of the pagan past, is protesting at the Cistercian expulsion of native learning from the monasteries.

**Lebor Gabála*, 'the Book of Invasions', though not a saga, deals *inter alia* with the Tuatha Dé Danann. The work, which underwent constant revision, relates the synthetic history of Ireland, a largely spurious account of the various peoples to have inhabited Ireland before the coming of the Gaels themselves. The various sources of this 'history' include the Bible, Isidore of Seville, and much native tradition. The synthetic history was not seriously questioned until the 19th century.

The classical ethnographers noticed that the Celts sang eulogies and satires to the accompaniment of the lyre. The *bardic poets of medieval Ireland are direct inheritors of this ancient tradition, for the poet (Ir. **file*, 'seer') is a transmutation of the pagan *druid. The oldest poetry consists of stressed alliterative lines, often without stanzaic form. The bulk of early poetry, however, is syllabic and is composed for the most part in four-line stanzas. Such a metrical form is based on Christian Latin metres. Whether the rhyme of Irish syllabic poetry derives from Latin models is less certain.

We have a certain amount of nature poetry associated with early *monasticism as well as several didactic poems on Christian themes, *Félire Oengusso* (The Martyrology of Oengus) (*c*. 800), for example, and the biblical *Saltair na Rann* (Metrical Psalter) (late 10th century).

By the early 13th century praise poetry had reached its fullest development, involving a high degree of metrical adornment. None the less the pagan origins of this poetry are reflected in the way the poets composed reclining in the dark. The main function of bardic encomium was to legitimize the rule of the chieftain addressed. Since poets were well rewarded for their poems, they were prepared even to support the lordship of the Anglo-Norman nobility.

A large corpus of Ossianic lays in syllabic metres survives together with much personal poetry. Noteworthy are the so-called *dánta grádha*, love poems that exhibit the influence of the European Renaissance.

The first book printed in Irish, John Carswell's *Foirm na nUrrnuidheadh*, was a translation of the Presbyterian Book of Common Order and appeared in Edinburgh in 1567. The Catechism of Seán Ó Cearnaigh, published in Dublin in 1571, was the first book printed in Irish in Ireland. Ó Cearnaigh plagiarized Carswell but unlike the Scottish book, which was in roman type, the Irish catechism was printed in a specially cut Gaelic font, which was also used for the New Testament in 1602 and *Leabhar na nUrnaightheadh gComhchoidchionn* (the Book of Common Prayer) in 1608. William Daniel saw both through the press, though several hands are to be seen in the two works. The 1608 Irish Prayer Book is an excellent translation, regrettably never reprinted.

The Catholics, prevented from publishing in Ireland, produced devotional works on the Continent. The Franciscans of St Anthony's College in Louvain were the pioneers, publishing *Teagasg Críosdaidhe* or Catechism by Giolla Brighde Ó hEodhasa, but based on Canisius and Bellarmine, in Antwerp in 1611. St Anthony's College acquired its own press and the first books printed there were *Desiderius* by Florence Conry (1616), an adaptation of a Spanish devotional tract, and Mac Aingil's *Sgáthán Shacramuinte na hAithridhe* (1618), an original composition on the Tridentine understanding of penance. Mac Aingil is a consummate stylist and his work enjoyed great popularity. Theobald Stapleton's Latin and Irish *Catechismus seu doctrina Christiana* printed in Brussels in 1639 is unusual since it uses roman characters for the Irish and a simplified spelling.

The secular priest Geoffrey *Keating produced two devotional works, *Eochairsgiath an Aifrinn*, an explication and defence of the Counter-Reformation doctrine of the eucharist, and *Trí Biorghaoithe an Bháis* (Three Shafts of Death). This latter sought to deflect the Irish Catholics from sin, for Keating believed that the English conquest was divine punishment. Keating's most important work was *Foras Feasa ar Éirinn* (*FFÉ*), a narrative history of Ireland from the beginning till the coming of the Normans, whose object was to defend the Irish against the calumnies of the foreign historians and to explain how Irish and *Old English had fused to become the Catholic Irish nation. Keating's historical writing is therefore as religious as his religious tracts are political. Since Keating accepted without question the synthetic history of the *Lebor Gabála*, *FFÉ* compares unfavourably with that of his English-speaking contemporaries. Although Keating did not publish his works but circulated them in manuscript, they were widely read.

Another important historical work was *Annála Ríoghachta Éireann*, an annalistic history of Ireland from the biblical flood to the 16th century. The chief compiler of the work was Michael O'Clery, a Franciscan friar (b. *c*.1590), who was sent to Ireland to gather material for a history of the country. Since he was not a priest, O'Clery was unlikely to be proscribed. Indeed it appears from his colophons that he worked among other places in the library of Archbishop James *Ussher. O'Clery had three collaborators: Farfassa O'Mulconry, Peregrine O'Duigenan, and Peregrine O'Clery. After years of collecting material O'Clery and his colleagues settled in Drowes, Co. Donegal, in 1632 and there produced their annals, more commonly known as the *Annals of the Four Masters*.

Duald Mac Firbis (1600–71) was a member of a well-established family of historians. He compiled a genealogical compendium *The Great Book of Genealogies* and also assisted Sir James *Ware in his historical researches. Irish lexicography began in earnest in the 17th century. The most important work perhaps was the Latin–Irish dictionary of Richard Plunkett, completed in Trim in 1662. Although Plunkett's work was never printed, the Celtic scholar Edward Lhuyd published material from it in his *Archaeologia Britannica* (1707), whence some entries found their way into later dictionaries, misprints and all.

A completely new departure in prose writing was *Pairlement Chloinne Tomáis* (*PCT*), a savage satire upon the labouring classes of Gaelic society. As well as describing the demonic origins of 'Clan Thomas' and incidents from their history, the author gives an account of two sittings of an assembly in north Kerry in 1632 and 1645. It has been thought that *PCT* was written after the second of these dates, but internal evidence indicates that both are projections and that the work was composed *c.*1615. *PCT* parodies Irish story-telling and owes much to medieval English and continental writing. A sequel to *PCT* was written by a different author in Leinster *c.*1662 and appended to the original work. *PCT* clearly struck a chord with the Irish-reading public for it survives in many manuscripts and gave rise to a whole new class of Irish writing.

The prose writers of the earlier part of the 17th century were often trained poets and composed in the traditional syllabic metres. Mac Aingil's poem to the infant Jesus, for example, is deservedly famous. As the 17th century progressed the looser stressed metres gained in importance. Geoffrey Keating composed chiefly in such metres, though syllabic poems of his also survive. Patrick Hackett (*c.*1600–1654), a Dominican priest from Tipperary, excelled at invective. The Munsterman David O'Bruadar (1625–98) was a master of poetic language in a variety of metres. *PCT* is sometimes erroneously ascribed to him.

The political upheavals of the 17th century gave rise to the *caoineadh*, a long poetic lament consisting of four-stressed lines and the same end-rhyme throughout. Among the best-known examples are *Tuireamh na hÉireann* by Seán Ó Conaill (*fl.* 1650) and the anonymous *Síogaí Rómhánach*, composed 1650–3. Poetry flourished in south-east Ulster in the 17th and 18th centuries, the first *Oriel poet being Séamas Dall Mac Cuarta (1647–1733). The most important poet of the late 17th century was the Munsterman Egan O'Rahilly (*c.*1675–1729). O'Rahilly is an evocative and accomplished poet who produced the first fully developed *aisling*, a poem in which a maiden, the personification of Ireland, appears to the poet, laments her present condition, and looks for the return of the Stuarts (see JACOBITISM) and a new age.

By 1800 the Irish language was apparently in terminal decline. The only works printed in the language were *catechisms, sermons, and translations of scripture. In the first half of the 19th century manuscripts continued to be transcribed and folk poets still composed in some places. The most famous of these was the Mayoman Antaine Ó Reachtabhra or Raftery (1784–1835), many of whose songs are still remembered.

From the end of the 18th century a number of scholars published editions of texts and anthologies of poetry, but it was not until *c.*1875 that the revival of Irish as a spoken medium was seriously contemplated. The foundation of the *Gaelic League in 1893 was crucial, not least because the league encouraged the creation of new literature. Many of its early members were scholars of the language, e.g. Douglas *Hyde and Patrick Dinneen (1860–1934), whose second dictionary (1927) was for long the standard work, or creative writers in it, such as Patrick *Pearse and Peter O'Leary (1839–1920). The latter, more commonly known as an tAthair Peadar, was the first to abandon the archaizing classical language in favour of the simple diction of everyday speech. His literary folk tale *Séadna* (1910) quickly became a classic.

The native government, established in 1922, took responsibility for the cultivation of the language and an ambitious plan of translating prose works was undertaken. Unfortunately many of the originals selected were of second rank and the Irish versions remained unread.

One of the most important figures of the early 20th century was Pádraig Ó Conaire (1882–1928). Though from Galway and the child of Irish-speaking parents, Ó Conaire eschewed the folk tale as a model for his short stories and consciously wrote in a modern idiom. The *Gaeltacht produced a number of autobiographies in the 1920s and 1930s.

After the *Second World War a new generation of writers, both native speakers and others, came into being, assisted in part by the foundation of the Irish-language magazine *Comhar*. Máirtín Ó Cadhain (1907–70), Liam Ó Flaitheartaigh (1897–1984), and Seosamh Mac Grianna (1901–93) are particularly significant in prose, and Máirtín Ó Direáin (1910–88) and Máire Mhac an tSaoi (1922–) in poetry. Seán Ó Ríordáin (1917–77) was discouraged from writing by the reception of his first collection *Eireaball Spideoige* (1952), but he is considered by some the greatest poet in Irish for three centuries.

The present state of Irish literature is anomalous since the reading public for Irish is very small, but the output in both verse and prose is relatively large. The contemporary literature is varied in content and much of it compares favourably with writing in English in Ireland. Noteworthy are the prose writers Diarmuid Ó Súilleabháin (1932–85) and Eoghan Ó Tuairisc (1918–82), for example, and the poets Nuala Ní Dhomhnaill (1952–), Biddy Jenkinson (1949–), and Liam Ó Muirthile (1950–). Literary criticism has flourished in the periodical *Irisleabhar Mhá Nuad* and elsewhere. NJAW

Liverpool, like Bristol, owed its rise to its involvement in trade with Ireland (though its link with the slave trade in the 18th century was another key element). Individual migrants from Ireland came regularly to Liverpool but it was during the *Great Famine that migration occurred on a massive scale. Many of these refugees continued on to Canada and the United States but others remained, earning a living as dock workers, as seamen, or as casual labourers in the Scotland Road area. A strongly Irish ethnic identity survived and in the 19th and early 20th centuries the Irish community in the Scotland parliamentary division regularly returned the *Nationalist Party MP T. P. *O'Connor to Westminster. A good deal of sectarian hostility between 'Orange' and 'Green' also existed, particularly in the Netherfield Road area of Everton. During the *Second World War, however, in the wake of heavy bombing by the Luftwaffe during 'May Week' 1941, the level of sectarian feeling declined. In the second half of the 20th century the links between Liverpool and Ireland became more attenuated. Immigrants from Ireland now preferred to seek work in London or the Midlands rather than the depressed area which Liverpool had become. 'Liverpool Irish' was increasingly transformed into a 'Liverpudlian' identity made familiar by the Beatles, by television series, and by the success of Liverpool Football Club. The memory of Bill Shankly overwhelmed that of St Patrick. HK

Lloyd George, David (1863–1945), *Liberal politician and British prime minister 1916–22. Apparently prompted by his Welsh nonconformist sympathies, Lloyd George argued in cabinet from February 1912 for special treatment for Ulster under *home rule. In May 1916 he was directed by *Asquith to negotiate with *Redmond and *Carson for immediate home rule with the exclusion of six Ulster counties. Succeeding Asquith in December 1916, he split the Liberals but led Britain to victory in the *First World War. As leader of the coalition government from November 1918, he was immediately confronted by the Irish problem but his ability to manœuvre was limited by his dependence on *Bonar Law's Conservatives. His *Government of Ireland Act secured a settlement with the Unionists and in 1921 his contacts with de *Valera led to the negotiation of the *Anglo-Irish treaty. Conservative discontent with the Irish settlement contributed to his overthrow in October 1922 and despite his reputation as a war leader he never again held office. TGF

Local Defence Force (LDF), established under *army command in 1940 as a part-time security force to assist the national defence effort by carrying out static guard and security duties in each locality, freeing first-line and reserve troops to concentrate on training to resist an invasion. The LDF contributed to the sense of national mobilization which characterized Irish reactions to the first years of the *Second World War. It was succeeded by An Fórsa Cosanta Áituil (FCA), established in 1946, which also functions as the army's first-line reserve. EO'H

local government. Although considerably changed, the *county and the *borough remain the focus of local administration seven centuries after they were introduced by the Anglo-Normans.

The county (French *comté*) was first introduced into the areas of Ireland that were reserved to the crown by *Henry II and *John, lord of Ireland. Dublin was organized as a county by the 1190s, if not earlier. In 1206 a boundary commission was established to determine the border between the kingdoms of Cork and Limerick, no doubt with a view to dividing Munster into the two counties that appear in the records shortly afterwards: Cork with Waterford, and Limerick with Tipperary. Outside the royal demesne, the *liberties or *palatinates of Leinster and Ulster were subsequently subdivided into counties under private jurisdiction, so that by the end of the 13th century only the Gaelic north-west remained unshired. A uniquely Irish aspect of the county system was the introduction of the counties of the cross in the 14th century. Governed by royal *sheriffs, they consisted of scattered church lands ('crosslands') inside the liberties. Thus, for example, there were two counties of Tipperary: the county of the liberty of Tipperary under a sheriff appointed by, and answerable to, the earl of *Ormond; and a county of the cross of Tipperary, under a sheriff appointed by the crown.

The county was divided into *cantreds or *baronies, which corresponded to the hundreds in English counties. In each cantred the sheriff presided twice a year over a court called the tourn, where he inquired into the alienation of royal jurisdiction by feudal or ecclesiastical courts, breaches of the peace, burglaries, homicides, and abuses of power or neglect of duty by royal officials such as serjeants, who served writs, or *coroners, who kept a record of the pleas of the crown.

The county court, summoned once a month, was attended by those who owed suit in virtue of their tenure. While its judicial importance was greatly reduced by the introduction of the *assizes in the 13th century, it retained important public functions: proclamations, elections, outlawries, and (probably) consent to local subsidies in time of war.

The second pillar of local government was the Anglo-Norman borough. Every borough had its own hundred court and corporate protections against outside interference secured by charter. Between 1171 and 1229 Dublin achieved a large measure of self-government through successive royal charters, including the right to elect a mayor.

Early modern local government continued to be organized through the counties, those of medieval origin being supplemented by a larger number created between 1542 and 1606. A few medieval towns, such as *Dublin, *Galway, and *Carrickfergus, were regarded as counties. Within the county the principal royal official was the sheriff, appointed annually from the landowners of the county by the *privy council with the advice of the justices of assize. The sheriff was the link between central government and the localities, receiving and executing writs from Dublin and collecting certain royal taxes for which he accounted at the *exchequer at the end of his term. He was assisted by a number of subsheriffs. The sheriff was also responsible for the operation of law within the county, including jail delivery at the assize, and for executing writs from the assize. In time of war the powers of the sheriff were considerably augmented by grants of *martial law which might be exercised by provosts marshal. During the 17th century another county institution, the *grand jury, emerged. Originally drawn from the freeholders to approve indictments at the assizes, it became responsible for bridge building and raised local *taxes (the 'county charge', later *'cess') for this purpose.

Two areas were exempt from these structures. The palatinate of Tipperary, finally abolished in 1716, had its own officials and procedures, as had the major ecclesiastical liberties of Dublin, such as St Sepulchre's (abolished 1856). The second exemption was the *provincial presidencies of Connacht and Munster (abolished in 1672) which had their own system of administration. At a local level three institutions were important. Where there was a *Church of Ireland presence the *parish, through the meeting of the *parish-vestry, exercised some local government functions through its officials, including the churchwardens and parish constable. The vestry was responsible for local taxation, *poor relief, and the maintenance of roads, and in some larger urban parishes watches were established. Secondly, the great estate through its manorial structures such as the court leet and court baron provided ways of obtaining legal redress for grievances and in some small Ulster towns formed a layer of urban government. Thirdly, *urban government through corporations, of which over 80 were erected in the reign of James I, provided a wide range of services including franchisal courts.

During the 18th century the grand jury became more significant as more duties were assigned to it, including responsibility for roads and provision for the sick and the poor. Concern about standards of public health in the early 19th century led to legislation requiring grand juries to provide certain facilities, such as fever hospitals, under the supervision of central government.

After 1838 *poor law boards took over responsibility for the provision of health and welfare services and grand juries resumed their original role of maintaining the local infrastructure. In contrast to grand juries, which were composed of members of the predominantly Protestant landed gentry, poor law boards combined elected guardians with magistrates sitting ex officio. The boards were to provide a training ground for Catholic/nationalist politicians, and, from 1896, were to give women their first experience of local government office. Under the *Local Government Act of 1898 the administrative responsibilities of grand juries were transferred to popularly elected county councils, while poor law boards were absorbed into rural district councils.

Local government in independent Ireland has seen the gradual narrowing of its traditional roles and the loss of functions, in matters such as public health, vocational education, *social welfare, road development, physical planning, and most recently environmental protection, either to central government or to national or regional administrative boards. Its structure has remained largely unchanged: county borough corporations for city government, and county councils for county government. Beneath county councils the only effective administrative units are urban district councils and a handful of borough corporations: rural district councils were abolished in 1925, while no new electoral 'towns' (legally defined as between 1,500 and 8,000 in population, and therefore too small to administer increasingly complex local services themselves) were established between 1900 and 1978. Since then a court decision has forced the government to provide for elected town commissioners in a number of towns.

Since the 1920s, reforms including the *city and county management system have wrought a shift in power from politicians to officials. The funding base of local authorities has also undergone change. The bulk of revenue now comes through block grants from central government rather than from local property taxation and other discretionary sources: domestic rates were removed in 1978, and those on agricultural land in 1982.

Local government occupies a peculiar place in the Irish political system. Elected on a universal adult franchise since 1934, it remains the main stepping stone to a seat in the *Dáil, yet local politicians have little direct power. Local elections should be held every five years. They have frequently been postponed by central government, yet very few people bother to protest. With central government as the dominant funder, the democratic link between local representation and local taxation has all but gone, and is not much mourned: there has been intense communal resistance to efforts to supplement revenue through charges for specific local services. Furthermore, while local politicians of all parties have routinely condemned what they term administrative and political overcentralization, those who have later achieved national office seldom do much to reverse that trend.

Crossman, Virginia, *Local Government in Nineteenth-Century Ireland* (1994)

Feingold, W. L., *The Revolt of the Tenantry: The Transformation of Local Government in Ireland 1872–86* (1984)

Otway-Ruthven, A. J., *A History of Medieval Ireland* (2nd edn., 1980)

CAE/RG/VC/EO'H

Local Government Act (1898), one of a number of reforming measures introduced by Gerald *Balfour when chief secretary (see CONSTRUCTIVE UNIONISM). The act swept away the existing system of county government whereby *grand juries looked after the local infrastructure while *poor law boards administered welfare services and acted as rural sanitary authorities. Modelled on the English Reform Act of 1888, the act introduced a two-tier system of democratically elected county and district councils. Rural district councillors served also as poor law guardians. In urban areas municipal corporations and town councils were retained, together with separate poor law boards. The *Local Government Board was given the task of supervising the activities of councils, and its approval was required for many of their acts, including appointments and dismissals. All councillors and poor law guardians were elected on a parliamentary *franchise, with the addition of women and peers. Following vigorous lobbying by women's organizations women obtained the right to stand for election as district councillors, though not, until 1911, as county councillors. (Some 30 women were returned as district councillors in 1899.) One of the most important effects of the act was to substitute *nationalist-dominated councils for *unionist-dominated grand juries, and significantly to reduce unionist representation on boards of guardians. VC

Local Government Board, created in 1872 to replace the Irish *Poor Law Commission. The board, which was made up of the *chief secretary, the under-secretary, a vice-president, and two commissioners, took over responsibility for the operation of the poor law, and of public health legislation generally. It was further empowered to alter local government boundaries and to approve applications from town councils to levy additional rates and amend or repeal local acts. Based in Dublin, the board relied on a staff of regional inspectors and auditors to supervise and report on the activities of poor law boards and other local authorities. The board retained its supervisory role under the *Local Government Act of 1898, which required many of the acts of the newly established county and district councils to be submitted to the board for approval. It was thus in a position to act as a check on the activities of the predominantly *nationalist councillors. To this end the vice-president and permanent head of the board, Henry Robinson, endeavoured to ensure that a majority of his staff were *unionist and Protestant. In 1908 the board became the pensions authority for Ireland under the old-age pensions act of that year.

VC

Lóegaire mac Néill (d. 462 according to the *Annals of Ulster*). Lóegaire is portrayed in 7th-century and later sources as the son of *Niall Noígiallach and as king of Ireland during St *Patrick's mission. The texts differ as to whether Lóegaire himself converted to Christianity. He is also depicted in early legal sources as the king who presided over the creation of a synthesized law-code, amalgamating Christian and native Irish material. CS

Loftus, Adam (*c.*1533–1606), the dominant leader of the *Church of Ireland under Elizabeth I. Born in Yorkshire, educated at Cambridge, he first came to Ireland in May 1560 as chaplain to the lord deputy, the earl of *Sussex. A committed Protestant and capable administrator, his ascent to high office was rapid: dean of *St Patrick's cathedral (1561), archbishop of Armagh (1563), moving finally to the archbishopric of Dublin (1567), which he combined, from 1581 to his death, with the influential secular post of Lord *Chancellor. A strong believer in the use of civil and ecclesiastical power to enforce religious conformity, his efforts to spread the Reformation were hampered by a shortage of Protestant clergy, the weakness of the Dublin government, and the poverty of the established church. He was closely involved in the establishment of *Trinity College, Dublin, in 1592. AF

Loftus, Adam (*c.*1568–1643), lord chancellor of Ireland and first Viscount Ely, a typical *New English careerist in the Irish church–state apparatus. Brought over in the 1590s by his uncle and namesake Adam Loftus, archbishop of Dublin 1567–1606, he was quickly granted an archdeaconry, church lands, a knighthood, and headship of the Irish marshal court. In the 1610s he received a plantation grant in Wexford and became lord chancellor, a position he allegedly bought from Buckingham, the royal favourite. He fell out with Viscount Falkland, lord deputy 1622–9, but was subsequently appointed *lord justice with Richard *Boyle, the leader of a rival planter faction. *Wentworth had Loftus suspended and imprisoned, on dubious grounds, in 1637, but the English House of Lords quashed this judgment following Wentworth's own impeachment. HM

Logue, Michael (1840–1924), Catholic bishop of Raphoe 1879–87, archbishop of Armagh 1887–1924, made a cardinal in 1893. Born in Co. Donegal, Logue had been ordained in Maynooth in 1866 and had taught in the Irish College, Paris. A pragmatic prelate, he was anxious that neither domestic politics nor Roman directives should compromise the interests of the Irish church. The opinion that he sacrificed the interests of Northern Catholics for enhanced episcopal influence in the *Irish Free State probably overestimates his freedom of political manœuvre. TO'C

Lombard, Peter (1554–1625), the major Irish figure in the *Counter-Reformation. An *Old English native of Waterford, he studied at Louvain, graduating first in the school of arts (1575) and staying on to become professor of philosophy and theology. On university business in Rome in 1598–9, he doubled as Hugh *O'Neill's agent and wrote *De regno Hiberniae sanctorum insula commentarius* (published posthumously 1633) to encourage papal support. Talent-spotted by Pope Clement, he was made archbishop of Armagh instead of O'Neill's Ulster candidate. Lombard became one of the chief theologians in the curia, involved in the congregation on grace (1602–7), the condemnation of Copernicus's heliocentric theory (1616), and the approval of nativist conversion techniques in India (1623). Lombard's influential position-papers argued for a recognition of James I to ease pressure on Irish and British Catholics. At first he favoured the appointment of vicars-general rather than bishops in Ireland, to avoid affronting the civil authorities. Not surprisingly, the exiled Hugh O'Neill disagreed with him over invasion plans and ecclesiastical appointments.

Lombard left the day-to-day running of the Irish Catholic church to his one-time secretary David *Rothe, whom he instructed to hold synods of the clergy to remind them of their parochial duties, to reconcile seculars and regulars, and to stamp out popular superstitions. In 1621 he made preparations to return home, hoping to take up the vacant see of Waterford and Lismore rather than rough it in Armagh, but never went. HM

Londonderry, see DERRY.

Londonderry (Stewart), landed family and political magnates in Co. Down from the 18th century. The family initially received land in Co. Donegal during the *plantation of Ulster. **Robert Stewart** (1739–1821) purchased the Co. Down estate in 1744, his failure to acquire with it political control of the borough of Newtownards creating a celebrated legal dispute (see NEWTOWN ACT). He was MP for Co. Down 1771–83. In their long rivalry with the Hillsborough/*Downshire family for dominance of country politics, the Stewarts initially enjoyed the support of the independent and dissenting interest. By the 1790s, however, Robert

Stewart had abandoned Presbyterianism and became a government supporter, advancing in the peerage from Baron Londonderry in 1789 to marquis of Londonderry in 1816. His son Viscount *Castlereagh was returned for Co. Down as a *Whig champion in 1790, but went on to become a key figure in successive *Tory ministries.

Castlereagh's brother **Charles William** (1778–1854), the 3rd marquis, served with distinction in the *revolutionary and Napoleonic wars, and was ambassador to Austria (1814–23). He married Lady Frances Vane Tempest, heiress to land, and to what became highly profitable collieries, in Co. Durham. Thereafter the family were to divide their time between residences at Wynard Hall (Durham), Holdernesse House, later Londonderry House, in Park Lane, London, and Mount Stewart, in Co. Down, begun by the 1st marquis in 1804. The 6th marquis, **Charles Vane-Tempest-Stewart** (1852–1915), was *lord lieutenant of Ireland 1886–9. His wife Theresa (1856–1919) was president from 1912 of the Ulster Women's Unionist Council.

Charles, 7th marquis (1878–1949), was chairman of the standing committee of the Ulster Unionist Council during the home rule crisis 1912–14. He was a junior minister for aviation 1919–21, resigning to enter the Senate of the new Northern Ireland parliament and become minister for education. In 1923 he introduced an education bill intended to provide for non-denominational primary schooling. Concerted opposition from Protestant churches and the *Orange Order forced the government to include compulsory Bible instruction, ensuring that Catholics would reject the state schools, which in consequence became de facto denominational. Londonderry returned to British politics as secretary of state for air (1931–5). His wife Edith (1879–1959) was a leading society hostess and an advocate of women's suffrage. During the *First World War she founded the Women's Legion. In the 1930s both marquis and marchioness showed a degree of sympathy towards Nazi Germany.

London Hibernian Society, Protestant missionary society established 1806, a prominent agent of the *Second Reformation. By 1823 it had 61,387 day pupils in its schools. The **Hibernian Bible Society**, which by 1874 had distributed 3.9 million English and Irish bibles, was established in the same year but was claimed to be a wholly separate body.

Long, Walter (1854–1924), another of the highly placed members of the British Conservative Party, along with *Lansdowne and the earl of Midleton (see BRODRICK (MIDLETON)), who were actively associated with the Irish *unionist cause in the period before and during the First World War. The son of a Wiltshire landowner, whose mother was from a Co. Wicklow gentry family, Long was in parliament from 1880 and in the cabinet from 1895. Having served as chief secretary for Ireland in the last months before the Conservatives lost office in 1906, he succeeded *Saunderson as leader of the Unionist parliamentary grouping 1906–10, during which period he sat as MP for South Co. Dublin. He was back in the cabinet from 1915, and joined with Lansdowne in overthrowing *Lloyd George's attempts to negotiate an immediate settlement based on *home rule for 26 counties in May–July 1916. In 1919 he chaired the cabinet's Irish Situation Committee, whose report of 4 Nov. laid the foundation for the *Government of Ireland Act.

longphort, a defended enclosure designed originally to protect ships. The word was first used in 841 to describe the *Viking encampments at Dublin and Linn Duachaill (Annagassan, Co. Louth). It was also used to describe the new Scandinavian settlements established at Waterford in 914 and at Limerick in 922. The sites are characterized by a sheltered harbour which was easily defended and had immediate access to the sea. Subsequently the term was applied to any fortress or stronghold. Among modern scholars the earliest period of Viking occupation at Dublin (841–902) is usually referred to as the longphort phase. JBr

lord chancellor, see CHANCELLOR.

lord deputy came into use as the term for the chief governor of Ireland during the reign of Henry VII. In some cases holders were nominally deputies to a lieutenant, often a royal prince; in other cases they held office directly under the monarch. The office retained immense patronage, which expanded as the whole country was taken under control, and considerable prestige as the monarch's representative.

At first lords deputy were local magnates, usually the earls of *Kildare. After *Poynings's intervention these were bound to consult their *privy council and restricted in their interference with lands, pardons, parliaments, and coinage. However, the Kildares still enjoyed great power and patronage in exchange for using their own resources in the service of the crown. The 9th earl of *Kildare was the last chief governor with authority to appoint his own deputy.

For a century or so after the *Kildare rebellion only Englishmen were trusted. The post attracted ambitious politicians who sought not only personal enrichment in Ireland but also a political stepping stone to greatness in England. However, these chief governors depended on the confidence of the monarch and continual subvention from England, which was lost by the earl of *Sussex (lord deputy 1556–8) and Sir Henry *Sidney because of opposition from the *Old English, and by *Perrot and Viscount Falkland (lord deputy 1622–9) because of infighting with their privy councils. Ireland was a poisoned chalice which destroyed the careers of *Gray, *St Leger, Perrot, and *Wentworth.

Although most early modern chief governors were lords deputy, the more prestigious title of *lord lieutenant was kept alive: Sussex, having served as lord deputy 1556–8, was promoted to lord lieutenant in 1560; *Mountjoy was likewise promoted in 1603, and Wentworth in 1640; *Essex was appointed lord lieutenant from the start. All the chief governors in the quarter-century following the *Restoration, from *Ormond to the earl of Clarendon (1685–7), held office as lords lieutenant. *James II's decision to revive the title of lord deputy for *Tyrconnell in 1687 was seen as a deliberate attempt to hold back from giving him too much power. The last lord deputy was Sir Henry Capel (1695–6); all subsequent chief governors were lords lieutenant. HM/SC

lord lieutenant, the most common name for the chief governor of Ireland in the period after the *Restoration, replacing *justiciar, *king's lieutenant, and *lord deputy. Lords lieutenant in the 18th century were invariably English politicians who came to Ireland as a stage in a ministerial career or occasionally, as with Baron Carteret 1724–30, as a form of exile from the domestic political scene for a rival too powerful to be dispensed with completely. In the 19th century, Irish peers also served as lords lieutenant: the 4th earl of Bessborough (see PONSONBY) 1846–7, the marquis, later duke, of *Abercorn 1866–8, 1874–6, and the 6th marquis of *Londonderry 1886–9.

With a salary of £12,000, rising to £20,000 in 1783, lords lieutenant enjoyed similar powers and patronage to the former lords deputy. Until 1767 the lord lieutenant came to Ireland only for the meetings of parliament held every second year. Consequently the task of establishing a government party in the Commons, and ensuring that revenue bills sanctioning adequate levels of taxation were enacted, devolved largely on the *lords justices and *undertakers. Following Lord *Townshend's viceroyalty 1767–72 lords lieutenant were permanently resident and, aided by the *chief secretary, took over direct responsibility for parliamentary management. Despite *legislative independence in 1782, they remained accountable to the cabinet in London rather than to the Irish parliament.

The Act of *Union, removing the need to manage a separate Irish parliament, significantly reduced the importance of the lord lieutenancy. Its possible abolition, as no longer appropriate to a part of what was now a united kingdom, was debated in parliament in 1823, 1830, and 1844. Yet a combination of inertia and the manifest need to make some special provision for the direction of Irish affairs ensured that the office survived up to 1922. As the political significance of the lord lieutenancy declined, the viceregal court, its elaborate ceremonial enhanced by the Order of St Patrick from 1783 and the construction of the Vice-Regal Lodge in Phoenix Park, became, if anything, more important. The requirement to reside permanently had considerably increased the expenses of the office, and the duke of Richmond (1807–13), who had incurred debts of £50,000, had the salary raised to £30,000.
HM/SC

Lords, House of. The Lords came into being as a separate house of the Irish *parliament in the late 14th century when prelates and lay lords were hived off from the *privy council. Since the Irish parliament represented only those parts of the country under English control, and since the Irish peerage was small and ill-defined, the Lords did not make a major impact in either the 14th or 15th centuries. Despite this, the House gradually acquired a distinct identity, as the elaboration of voting by proxy attests.

For most of the 17th century the increasingly Protestant character of the House did not prevent the development of an aristocratic identity which transcended ethnic differences. After the *revolution of 1688, however, the Lords, which met biannually or annually between 1692 and 1800, became emphatically Protestant in outlook as well as composition. Its membership comprised 22 spiritual peers, all bishops of the *Church of Ireland, and an increasing number of temporal peers. Since many of those ennobled in the 18th century were Englishmen or *absentees, the bishops, as more faithful attenders, exercised an influence disproportionate to their numbers and ensured that the House caused the government few problems. By the 1750s the era of the political prelate, exemplified by Archbishop *King and Primate *Boulter, had come to a close, and control of the Lords passed into lay hands. Because so many peers were former MPs who had supported government policies in the Commons, however, *Dublin Castle continued to have few problems securing a working majority, despite the efforts of the small *patriot rump led by *Charlemont.

The House of Lords was not without power. All legislation had to be ratified there, and it could initiate *heads of bills. The restoration after 1782 of the appellate jurisdiction taken away by the *Declaratory Act contributed to the increase in the standing of the Lords in the final two decades of the 18th century, though it would be an exaggeration to claim that this signalled the commencement of a new vital era. The House of Lords journals and standing orders amply attest to the efforts of members to maintain the dignity of the upper house. But, in practice, the real power and influence of Irish peers rested in their ability to influence the returns to the House of Commons and in their membership of the privy council.

James, F. G., *Lords of the Ascendancy: The Irish House of Lords and its Members 1600–1800* (1995)

JK

lordship of Ireland, the title of the medieval English dominion of Ireland. Pope Adrian IV gave *Henry II permission to subject the Irish to his authority in 1155 (see *laudabiliter*), though Henry did not do so until 1171–2. The title 'lord of Ireland', was first used by *John, Henry's youngest son, to whom he granted Ireland in 1177. Plans to invest John as a king were not carried out, although Henry obtained a crown from Rome; even so, Ireland was occasionally called a kingdom, as in 1213 when John surrendered England and Ireland to Innocent III, receiving them back as papal fiefs. After John became king of England in 1199, 'lord of Ireland' was a permanent part of the royal style. In 1254, when Henry III gave Ireland, Gascony, and other lands to his heir, the future Edward I, he declared that they were inalienably annexed to the crown. This remained the constitutional position: a medieval ruler became lord of Ireland by becoming king of England.

Lordship of Ireland implied authority over the whole island. Originally this involved the direct allegiance of colonial magnates and of the surviving Gaelic kings. By Edward I's time, however, further grants meant that all Ireland was *theoretically* in the hands of English lords, whose homage sufficed to express the king's authority: in the 1317 *Remonstrance the Irish complained to the pope about the English barons that stood between them and the crown. The *Gaelic recovery of the late Middle Ages made the theory increasingly anomalous; and the renewed submissions taken from Gaelic leaders by *Richard II during his 1394–5 expedition were a significant confirmation of royal lordship. The submissions were to be cited in 1541 when, after his break with Rome, Henry VIII proclaimed Ireland a kingdom.

Frame, R., 'England and Ireland 1171–1399', in M. Jones and M. Vale (eds.), *England and her Neighbours 1066–1453* (1989)

Lydon, J. F., 'Ireland and the English Crown 1171–1534', *Irish Historical Studies*, 29 (1995)

RFF

lords justices were temporary governors of Ireland in the absence or death of a *lord lieutenant or *lord deputy. In the 16th century there were generally two lords justices, normally appointed by their fellow *privy counsellors, and most commonly consisting of the lord *chancellor and lord chief justice. As stop-gaps they made no major policy changes but often had to cope with military emergencies such as the *rising of 1641.

Between 1690 and 1700 the government of Ireland was placed entirely in the hands of successive teams of two or three lords justices, although in 1692–3 and 1695–6 Viscount Sidney and Sir Henry Capel, initially lords justices, became respectively lord lieutenant and lord deputy. From 1700 lords justices were once again deputies for absent lords lieutenant, but since these were now invariably English politicians who up to 1767 resided in Ireland only during the parliamentary session, the scope of the office was substantial. Lords justices enjoyed a salary of £1,500 a year each, controlled a staff, dealt with law and order, and advised on offices, honours, and pensions. Up to the mid-1720s they were generally chosen from among leading local figures; William *Conolly, Lord Midleton (Alan *Brodrick), and Archbishop *King all served repeatedly. Following the *Wood's Halfpence crisis, when the lords justices had joined in frustrating the government's plans, authority was more cautiously bestowed. It became normal practice to appoint three lords justices: the lord chancellor and the archbishop of Armagh, both of whom were for most of the remainder of the century Englishmen, and the *speaker of the House of Commons, who was generally the leading *undertaker. HM/SC

Lough Derg ('St Patrick's Purgatory'), Co. Donegal, a place of severe penitential *pilgrimage where, reputedly, *Patrick fasted to expel demons. Although there probably was an earlier cult, the legend originates with Henry of Saltrey's *Tractatus de Purgatorio Sancti Patricii* (1184). He told of the pilgrimage of a knight, Owein, to where Patrick fasted, and of a deep cave which was the gateway to hell. Soon this was a standard piece of information about Ireland, mentioned, for example, by *Gerald of Wales. Prior to the 16th century, we have many accounts not only of Irish, but of European pilgrims; it is prominent on medieval maps; and copies of the *Tractatus* were widespread in Latin and translation. Pope Alexander VI forbade the pilgrimage (1497), but to little effect. Lough Derg was destroyed by the *Cromwellians as a place of superstition, but was well established again by the mid-18th century and grew in popularity during the 19th, in what has been seen as a local manifestation of the *devotional revolution. By this time the cave had been sealed, and the focus of the modern pilgrimage shifted to the church building. The pilgrimage, differing from the western model in its exclusive focus on penitence, continues today between June and August. TO'L

Lucas, Charles (1713–71), Co. Clare-born apothecary. Lucas was elected to the common council of the corporation of Dublin in 1741 and began a campaign, in alliance with James Digges Latouche of the *Huguenot banking family (see LA TOUCHE), against the oligarchic control of city politics by the lord mayor and aldermen. As a candidate in the Dublin by-election of October 1749 he published election addresses and a newspaper, the *Censor*, reviving *Molyneux's arguments concerning the independence of the Irish parliament. A series of resolutions in the Irish House of Commons declared Lucas an enemy of his country, forcing him to flee to the Isle of Man, and subsequently to continental Europe, where he qualified as a doctor in 1752. He returned in 1760 to contest and win a Dublin seat, and became a leading figure in the emerging *patriot opposition. He also assisted in the establishment of the initially liberal **Freeman's Journal*. Although recent work suggests that his anti-Catholicism has been exaggerated, his active support for the corporations in the *quarterage dispute is a reminder that his definition of liberty was of the sectional variety characteristic of 18th-century patriotism.

Lucas, Frederick (1812–55), an English convert to Catholicism and founder of the Catholic periodical the *Tablet* (1840), whose offices he transferred from London to Dublin in 1850. He was one of the leaders of the *Tenant League, and energetically promoted the concept of *independent opposition, becoming MP for Co. Meath in 1852. In 1854 he appealed to Rome against what he saw as the obstructionism of Cardinal *Cullen, achieving a theoretical confirmation of priests' right to take part in political agitation but embroiling the independent opposition movement in a damaging controversy.

Lucy, Anthony (d. 1343), *justiciar of Ireland 1331–2, after Edward III escaped from Roger *Mortimer's tutelage. His rule was intended to prepare for a royal expedition to Ireland. He imposed a *resumption of grants made to Anglo-Irish lords by Mortimer, arrested the 1st earl of *Desmond, and executed William de *Bermingham. Lucy was a Cumbrian baron and border soldier; the renewed *Anglo-Scottish war led to his withdrawal from Ireland and the abandonment of Edward's expedition. RFF

Lughnasa (1 Aug.), the first day of autumn and one of the four traditional 'quarter days', important in the calendar customs of Goidelic-speaking areas up to the 20th century. The name means 'festival of Lug' and the day must originally have been sacred to this god, versions of whose name are found throughout the Celtic world. In modern times Lughnasa has been a time for the holding of fairs; legends associated with the day deal largely with St *Patrick's victory over a representative of paganism. JPC

lunatic asylums, see INSANITY AND THE INSANE.

Lundy, Robert (d. before July 1717), Scottish commander of the Protestant troops installed in Derry in the name of *James II following the closing of the gates by the *Apprentice Boys. On 21 March Lundy accepted a new commission from *William III, but when the Jacobites overran the surrounding countryside following the battles of Clady and Lifford (15 Apr. 1689), he advocated surrender, sending away two regiments of reinforcements just arrived by sea. Deposed by advocates of continued resistance, he fled the city. Modern accounts suggest that he was at worst faint-hearted, and possibly only realistic, in his assessment of Derry's prospects, and he was in fact later to be employed on English pay in the Portuguese service. But 'Lundy' survives in *unionist rhetoric as a synonym for 'traitor', his effigy being burned annually by the Apprentice Boys of the city.

Luttrell, Henry (*c*.1655–1717), initially a leading supporter, with his brother Simon, of *Sarsfield and the *Jacobite militants in the *Williamite War, but arrested after *Aughrim for corresponding secretly with the enemy. Following the treaty of *Limerick, he brought his regiment into the Williamite army, receiving in exchange his brother's Co. Dublin estate. Retrospective claims that he had treacherously failed to prevent the Williamite breakthrough at Aughrim confirmed him as the *Lundy of Jacobite Ireland, though his eventual assassination in a Dublin street may have been for private motives. The violation of his grave in 1798 was attributed to the activities of his grandson, **Henry Lawes Luttrell**, Lord Carhampton (1743–1821), who impressed suspected

Connacht *Defenders for naval service in 1795 and directed further repression as commander-in-chief 1796–7.

Lynch, Jack (John) (1917–99), taoiseach 1966–73, 1977–9. Jack Lynch was born into a Cork family which had initially supported William *O'Brien before transferring its allegiance to *Fianna Fáil. There was no deep-seated *IRA tradition within the family, but Lynch's brilliant career as a hurler and footballer provided an alternative form of popular legitimacy. This success, allied with his blossoming career as a barrister, propelled him into the Dáil in 1948, when he was immediately appointed as secretary to the Fianna Fáil parliamentary party. He served as parliamentary secretary to the taoiseach during the Fianna Fáil government of 1951–4; and when his party returned to power in 1957 he was minister for the Gaeltacht (March–June 1957) and then minister for education. When, in 1959, Sean *Lemass succeeded as taoiseach, he selected Lynch to inherit his own department, Industry and Commerce. Lemass again indicated his personal favour when he promoted Lynch to the Finance portfolio in 1965. It was at Lemass's insistence that (in November 1966) Lynch ran for the Fianna Fáil leadership, beating George Colley by 52 votes to 19.

Lynch's record as taoiseach and as party leader was ambiguous. He had a considerable measure of success at the polls: he led his party to victory in June 1969, and increased its popular vote at the election of February 1973 (even though a coalition of *Fine Gael and *Labour took sufficient seats to form a government). His economic track record was more problematic: he inherited problems (a slowing growth rate, rising unemployment, spiralling inflation) which had been brewing in the Lemass years. His handling of the fallout from the developing *Northern Ireland conflict betrayed a certain steeliness of character. The timing and extent of Lynch's knowledge of the *arms crisis remains unclear, but he eventually acted to dismiss the ministers who were implicated (C. J. Haughey and Neil Blaney). In doing so, he helped to preserve the Irish state from embroilment in Northern Ireland.

Lynch was returned to power in 1977. However, victory was secured only on the strength of an election manifesto which promised increased state expenditure and simultaneous tax reductions. The result, particularly when combined with the oil crisis of 1979, was spiralling debt and unemployment. Lynch's political strength began to ebb, and when Fianna Fáil lost two by-elections in the taoiseach's home territory of Cork his enemies turned the screw. In 1977 Lynch had brought Haughey back into government; and it was Haughey who in December 1979, after two years of intrigue, succeeded as taoiseach.

Lynch is generally regarded as a man of considerable personal integrity and popularity. He was a reluctant leader, who brought to his office no fiery political vision. The zenith of his statesmanship—the arms crisis—simultaneously underlined his strengths and weaknesses: he had no roots in the republican traditions of Fianna Fáil, and this meant that, while he was sometimes out of touch, he could distance himself from hard-line colleagues. Despite some re-evaluation at the time of his death, it seems likely that Lynch will continue to be overshadowed by his more gifted and fortunate patron, Lemass, and by his more ruthless and unscrupulous successor, Haughey.

Collins, Stephen, *The Power Game: Fianna Fáil Since Lemass* (2000)

AJ

Lynch, John (*c.*1599–*c.*1677), a Catholic historian and controversialist. Archdeacon of Tuam, Lynch became warden of the College of St Nicholas in Galway under the *Confederate Catholics. There he patronized the work of his former schoolmate, Duald MacFirbis. After the surrender of Galway in 1652, he lived in exile in France. His most famous works were in Latin: *Cambrensis Eversus* (1662), in which he followed up Geoffrey Keating's attack (see LITERATURE IN IRISH) on *Gerald of Wales with a full-scale refutation, and *Alithinologia* (1664–7), a defence of the pro-*Ormond confederates against the apologists of *Rinuccini. HM

Lynch, Liam (1890–1923), commander of the Cork No. 2 Brigade and the 1st Southern Division in the *Anglo-Irish War. As leader of the strongest division of the *IRA, Lynch was one of the most important opponents of the *Anglo-Irish treaty. He became chief of staff of the Irregulars, but was anxious to avoid a conflict. Once the *Irish Civil War had started, however, he refused to accept the possibility of defeat. As a result an end to the hostilities could be achieved only after he had been killed in action in April 1923. JA

Maamtrasna murders (8 Aug. 1882), the murder in Connemara of five members—husband, wife, and three children—of the Joyce family. The killings were apparently motivated by *Ribbon Society politics and bitter personal feuds over grazing rights. Three of the alleged perpetrators were hanged and five sentenced to penal servitude for life. These convictions became controversial following well-founded allegations of perjury by prosecution witnesses. The case subsequently formed part of the nationalist critique of Liberal rule in Ireland. JL

Macardle, Dorothy (1889–1958), historian, republican, novelist, and journalist, born into the Dundalk brewing family. An important republican publicist during the *Anglo-Irish War and *Civil War, she sat on the first executive of *Fianna Fáil, although this did not stop her protesting about the conditions of employment bill (1935) which limited women's working rights. She was also interested in refugees, and in 1951 was president of the Irish Association for Civil Liberties. Her best-known work is *The Irish Republic* (1937). CC

McAuley, Catherine (1778–1841), founder of the Sisters of Mercy, one of the two largest and most widely distributed orders of *nuns in Ireland. Born in Dublin into a mixed Catholic/Protestant background, she inherited a considerable fortune. Initially concerned with the accommodation and protection of working girls in houses of mercy, run by a group of ladies living in community and praying together, her sisterhood was persuaded by local priests and the bishop to adopt a formal religious identity in 1828, and eventually took on a wider range of activities. CC

MacBride, John (1865–1916). A long-standing republican activist, MacBride fought with the pro-Boer Irish Brigade in the *Boer War, where he reached the rank of major. He married Maud *Gonne in Paris in 1903. Though not involved in the planning of the *rising of 1916, he joined the fighting and was subsequently executed. JA

MacBride, Sean (1904–88), son of Maud *Gonne and John *MacBride. He had a long and chequered career as a radical republican, a barrister, a politician, and a human rights and peace campaigner. He joined the *Irish Republican Army during the *Anglo-Irish War. Although remaining a prominent figure in the organization after the *Irish Civil War, he leaned towards the use of political means and was involved in several political projects in the inter-war period. He became IRA chief of staff in 1936 but left the movement after the enactment of the *constitution of 1937, which he felt satisfied republican demands. He then took up life as a barrister and soon won a national reputation for defending republicans. He founded *Clann na Poblachta in 1946 and was minister for external affairs in the first *interparty government 1948–51. He caused the fall of the second interparty government in 1957 over its handling of the IRA campaign in the north (see BORDER CAMPAIGN). He subsequently failed to be re-elected and left politics in 1961, after which he became deeply involved in human rights and peace organizations. He was secretary-general of the International Commission of Jurists (1963–70), and chairman of Amnesty International (1961–74). He was awarded the Nobel peace prize in 1974 and the Lenin peace prize in 1977. He formulated the MacBride principles, aimed at eliminating discrimination by employers against Catholics in Northern Ireland.

Although eulogized in later life as an international jurist and statesman, he was an ineffectual leader and often a controversial figure, both for republican hard men, who mistrusted his intellectual and political inclinations, and for more constitutional-minded sections of society, because of his radicalism. JA

McCabe, Edward (1816–85), Catholic archbishop of Dublin from 1879, having earlier (1877–9) served as *Cullen's auxiliary, made a cardinal in 1882. He published a circular on the question of *university education for Catholics in 1879. An urbanite, he had little sympathy for agrarian problems, opposing both the *Land League and the 'no rent' manifesto. He never imposed himself on his episcopal colleagues as successfully as Cullen had done. TO'C

Mac Carthaig, Cormac (d. 1138). King of Munster from 1124, Cormac succeeded in restoring *Eóganacht fortunes by curbing the power of the Uí Briain (see DÁL CAIS), and by challenging the supremacy of the Connacht king, Toirdelbach *Ua Conchobair (Turlough O'Connor). Though he suffered setbacks in his struggle against the latter, most notably in 1127 when Ua Conchobair removed the kingship from him and banished him to Lismore, his authority over the Uí Briain remained secure. Indeed, it was Toirdelbach and Conchobar Ua Briain who restored Cormac to power by agreeing to accept him as consensus king of Munster. However, this alliance came to an end in 1134 and the Uí Briain, with the aid of the Leinster king Diarmait *Mac Murchada (Dermot Mac Murrough), turned upon Cormac. He was murdered at their behest in 1138. Monuments to his notable career include *Cormac's chapel, and the political propaganda tract *Caithréim Chellacháin Chaisil*, written during his reign. MNíM

MacCarthy. The MacCarthy kings of Desmond, were the greatest of the Gaelic lords in Munster throughout the medieval and Early Modern period. They descended from the kings of *Eóganacht Caisil in the 11th century.

The Desmond kingdom remained undiminished until the early 13th century, despite frequent succession disputes among the extended lineage. For example, the first MacCarthy king of Desmond, Tadhg (ruled 1118–23), was deposed by his brother Cormac, who remained in power until his death in 1138. He was succeeded by his brother Donnchadh, who was eventually deposed in 1143 by his nephew Diarmuid, son of Cormac. Diarmuid's long rule between 1143 and 1185 was temporarily disrupted when he was deposed by his son Cormac Liathanach (1175–6). Another son, Donal Mor, succeeded in 1185 as king of Desmond, until his death in 1206. The resultant succession dispute undermined the cohesion of the MacCarthy lordship, and facilitated the Anglo-Norman advance into the south-west.

It is from this common ancestor, Donal Mór MacCarthy (d. 1206) that the several branches of the MacCarthy are descended. These are, the MacCarthy Mór kings of Desmond, and later earls of Clancare (*fl.* 1262–*c.*1598); the MacCarthy Muskerry, lords of Muskerry, and later earls of *Clancarty (*fl.* 1359–1734); the MacCarthy Reagh, lords of Carbery (*fl.* 1366–*c.*1600); and the lesser MacCarthy septs of Duhallow and Coshe Mang that emerged in the late 14th century. MacCarthy Mór claimed nominal lordship over these other MacCarthy lineages.

In 1232 Donal Got MacCarthy conquered the O'Mahony territory in south-west Cork. His son Fineen (ruled 1252–61) consolidated these territorial gains, and also pushed back Anglo-Norman settlement, recovering much of the frontier regions. By 1280 the senior MacCarthy lineage (MacCarthy Mór) conceded Carbery, the lands south of the Lee, to Fineen's successor. The grant provided the landed basis of the MacCarthy Reagh lineage. The marriage of the MacCarthy Reagh and Eleanor, daughter of the 9th earl of *Kildare, in 1513, brought the lineage into the Geraldine affinity. The lordship remained a political force in the region into the late 16th century.

From the mid-13th century the MacCarthy Mór variously aligned with the colonists and the administration. Donal Roe (ruled 1262–1302) probably allied with the Anglo-Normans against the MacCarthy Reagh, to retain his position as head of the lineage of the (Gaelic) Desmond kingdom. His grandson, Cormac (ruled 1325–59), campaigned with the *justiciar, Sir Thomas *Rokeby, against his MacCarthy (Duhallow) kinsmen and their allies the earls of *Desmond. In 1352/53 Cormac received a crown grant of Macroom, the basis of the lordship of Muskerry, and other lands which later provided the basis of the MacCarthy Cosh Mang, founded by the descendants of his younger sons, Dermot and Owen. MacCarthy Mór secured title to their lands under common law in 1365, by a grant of confirmation from the lord lieutenant.

The comparative stability of the MacCarthy Mór lineage in the Late Medieval period is evident in the uninterrupted father–son succession, from Cormac's accession in 1325 until the death of his great-great-great-grandson Donal, son of Tadgh Liath, in 1508. Descent passed to the line of Donal's brother after a brief succession dispute between 1508 and 1516. In 1565 the crown created the MacCarthy Mór as earls of Clancarty, but the lineage foundered, as a dispute arose from the divergence of the brehon and common law concerning right of succession.

The MacCarthy Muskerry expanded east from Macroom throughout the 15th and 16th centuries, and consistently aligned with the administration. They survived the *Nine Years War, and were created earls of Clancarty in 1658. FF

MacCarthy, Justin (*c.*1643–1694), created Viscount Mountcashel 1689, third son of the 1st earl of *Clancarty, *Jacobite soldier. After serving in British and Irish regiments employed by France, he played a major part in *Tyrconnell's Catholicization of the Irish army, and in early 1689 suppressed Protestant revolts in Munster. Captured following his defeat at Newtownbutler, he escaped and in April 1690 sailed to France as commander of the 5,000–6,000 Irish soldiers exchanged for French troops supplied to James II in Ireland. He later commanded this force, the nucleus of the *Irish Brigade, in Italy, Spain, and the Rhineland.

McCarthy, Michael (*fl.* 1890–1910), religio-political controversialist. The son of a Co. Cork farmer active in the *Land League, he was a barrister and parliamentary lobbyist for the drink trade in the 1880s. He became a *unionist by 1891 and subsequently converted to Protestantism; from 1898 he achieved notoriety through a series of extensively researched controversial books denouncing Catholicism as the source of Ireland's misfortune. McCarthy was associated with Ulster Unionist critics of *'constructive unionism'. He went to England in 1904 after an unsuccessful parliamentary candidacy, but continued to write for fringe unionist and ultra-Protestant groups until 1923. PM

McCracken, Henry Joy (1767–98), radical. He was a member of a leading Belfast commercial family; his maternal grandfather was Francis *Joy. He joined the society of *United Irishmen in 1795, and was imprisoned 1796–7. He returned to Ulster from Dublin in June 1798 to take charge of the rising in Co. Antrim, and was subsequently hanged. His sister **Mary Anne McCracken** (1770–1866) was also a keen supporter of radical causes. She and her sister Margaret managed their own textile business from the late 1780s until 1815. Mary Anne was subsequently active in a range of philanthropic causes in Belfast.

MacCurtain, Thomas (1884–1920). As commander of the *Volunteers in Cork city MacCurtain, aided by Terence *MacSwiney, engaged in a week-long stand-off with the military authorities during the 1916 *rising, ending with a negotiated surrender of weapons. On 30 January 1920 MacCurtain, by now commandant of the Cork No. 1 Brigade of the *IRA, was elected *Sinn Féin lord mayor of Cork. He was murdered, almost certainly by police, on 19 March.

MacDermott, Seán (Seán MacDiarmada) (1884–1916), a leader of the *rising of 1916 and a signatory of the proclamation with which it began. MacDermott was born in Leitrim, and worked as a barman in Belfast, where he joined the *Ancient Order of Hibernians. He moved from Catholic constitutionalism towards republicanism, joining the *Dungannon clubs and later (at the instigation of Bulmer Hobson and Denis McCullough) the *Irish Republican Brotherhood. MacDermott was an enthusiastic recruit to Fenianism and—as secretary and a member of the executive—he wielded enormous influence within its ranks. He was a co-founder and (for a time) the editor of *Irish Freedom*, which was Fenian in its sympathies. In 1915 he was recruited to the Military Council of the IRB, and was intimately involved with the planning of what became the Easter Rising. He tried hard to persuade pragmatists like Eoin *MacNeill to facilitate his plans: he helped to forge the 'Castle Document' which purported to be a British scheme for the suppression of the Irish Volunteers. In the end, however, it was a minority of hard-liners who rose against the British on Easter Monday, 24 April 1916. MacDermott fought in the GPO building until *Pearse's surrender on 29 April. He faced a British firing squad on 12 May, and was the last of the rebel leaders to be executed. MacDermott had a passion for conspiracy and intrigue, which was facilitated by a gift for friendship and personal charisma: he was a tireless and experienced organizer. He had a critical impact upon the design of the Rising; and—through his protégé, Michael *Collins—he exercised an influence on the Irish revolution from beyond the grave. AJ

MacDonagh, Thomas (1878–1916), one of the signatories of the 1916 proclamation. MacDonagh had a lifelong involvement in the Irish-language movement. He aided Patrick *Pearse in founding *St Enda's School, lectured in Irish in University College, Dublin, was editor of the *Irish Review*, and was a founder member of the Irish Theatre. He joined the *Irish Volunteers on its formation and became its director of training in 1914. He was sworn into the *Irish Republican Brotherhood in 1915 and became a member of the military council which organized the *rising of 1916. Like Pearse he believed in the need for a blood sacrifice to awaken the Irish nation. He was executed after the rising. JA

MacDonlevy (Mac Duinn Shléibhe), the surname of the 12th-century rulers of *Ulaid, was restricted to the descendants of the king Donn Sléibe Ó hEochada (d. 1091) of the Dál Fiatach dynasty, whose line eventually monopolized power, excluding other Ó hEochada and Ó Mathgamna claimants. They repeatedly resisted domination of their province by the *MacLochlainn high kings, and the blinding of Eochaid, son of Cú-Ulad Mac Duinn Sléibe, by Muirchertach Mac Lochlainn precipitated the latter's deposition. Eochaid was suceeded by his brothers Magnus (d. 1171), Donn Sléibe (d. 1172), who submitted to *Henry II, and Ruaidrí (d. 1201), who struggled against John de *Courcy's invasion of Ulster before submitting as vassal to the Anglo-Norman conqueror. The last recorded MacDonlevy 'king of the Irish of Ulster' attested a letter of support for William FitzWarin, seneschal of Ulster, in 1273, after which the family apparently died out, or according to doubtful tradition crossed to Tír Conaill to found the medical family of Ó Duinn Shléibhe. KS

MacDonnell, the Irish offshoot of the Scottish Highland family of MacDonald, lords of the Isles of Islay and Kintyre, later earls of Antrim. In 1399 John Mór MacDonnell married Margery Bisset, heiress to the Glens of Antrim. In the 16th century the family, now under growing pressure from a hostile Scottish monarchy, began to expand in Co. Antrim, overrunning the neighbouring lands of the MacQuillans ('the Route') to form a formidable territorial base. Randal MacDonnell (d. 1636), younger son of Sorley Boy *MacDonnell, maintained a carefully ambiguous relationship with his father-in-law Hugh *O'Neill during the *Nine Years War. After the battle of *Kinsale he submitted to the crown, and then aided in the suppression of a rebellion by his Scottish MacDonald cousins. He was rewarded with a grant of over 300,000 acres in the Route and the Glens of Antrim, and in 1620 became 1st earl of Antrim.

Randal MacDonnell, 2nd earl and 1st marquis (see ANTRIM), survived the political upheavals of the 1640s and 1650s, and the hostility of *Ormond, to regain his estates at the *Restoration. The 3rd earl, Alexander MacDonnell (1615–96), supported *James II in the *Williamite War: it was against his troops that the *Apprentice Boys of Derry closed the city gates. His estates were protected under the treaty of *Limerick. The 4th earl, Randal MacDonnell (1680–1721), was suspected of *Jacobite conspiracy in the political crisis of 1714–15, but nothing was proved. His son Alexander (1713–75), 5th earl, was brought up as a Protestant by his uncle, the 3rd Viscount *Massereene.

MacDonnell, Sir Antony Patrick (1844–1925), Baron MacDonnell of Swinford, a Catholic gentleman from Co. Mayo who became an Indian proconsul. Knighted in 1893, he retired in 1902 but was appointed by the Conservative George *Wyndham as under-secretary for Ireland with a special dispensation to initiate policy—although a civil servant, a Liberal, and a home ruler 'in principle' whose brother was a Nationalist MP. He sought a general Irish settlement, based on reconciliation and administrative reform. The 1903 *Land Act was partly his achievement, and certainly his main success. The *devolution crisis ended Conservative interest in his ideas, but in 1907 the Liberal government introduced his *Irish council bill. Neither this, nor his plan for a university settlement based on a second college in Dublin University with a Catholic ethos, was implemented. Augustine *Birrell and the Nationalist leaders both found his autocratic style irksome and his faith in 'moderate landlords' unrealistic. He went to the House of Lords in 1908. ACH

MacDonnell, Finola, alias Iníon Dubh ('dark daughter'), daughter of a powerful Highland Scottish family who married Hugh O'Donnell of Tirconnell (1569), bringing a dowry of *redshanks. She held onto power after the premature ageing of her husband and the kidnapping of their son, Red Hugh *O'Donnell. Her exploits include the murder of Hugh O'Gallagher (1588) and the defeat of Donnell O'Donnell (1590). Her military support facilitated Red Hugh's election as O'Donnell (1592). After the *Flight of the Earls, she implicated Niall Garbh *O'Donnell, the enemy of her sons, in Sir Cahir *O'Doherty's rebellion. She received 600 acres in the plantation of *Ulster. HM

MacDonnell, Randal, see ANTRIM, RANDAL MACDONNELL, 2ND EARL AND 1ST MARQUIS OF.

MacDonnell, Sorley Boy (Somhairle Buidhe) (*c.*1505–1590). He completed the conquest of the part of Co. Antrim known as the Route from the MacQuillans and secured English recognition of his family's rights in Ireland. After the assassination of Shane *O'Neill, he repeatedly requested agreements with the crown but the lands claimed by the MacDonnells were included in the *Enterprise of Ulster. In 1575 he retaliated for the *Rathlin massacre by descending on Carrickfergus, a frequent object of MacDonnell plunder. In the 1580s Lord Deputy *Perrot again tried to eject Sorley and the MacDonnells but neither expeditions nor garrisons could keep the Scots out. Finally, in return for a solemn submission in Dublin in 1586, Perrot made him a denizen of the crown, constable of Dunluce Castle, and owner of half the Route. In the winter of 1588 Sorley gave *Spanish Armada survivors passage to Scotland and helped himself to guns and possibly treasure from the *Girona*. HM

McEntee, Sean (1889–1984), born in Belfast. Sentenced to death for his part in the *rising of 1916, but reprieved, McEntee was one of the few who opposed the *Anglo-Irish treaty because of *partition as opposed to on grounds of sovereignty. As minister for finance (1932–9, 1951–4), industry and commerce (1939–47), and health and social welfare (1957–65), he was a formidable spokesman for the conservative wing of *Fianna Fáil, and as such *Lemass's most consistent long-term rival within the cabinet.

McEoin, Sean (1894–1973), leader of North Longford Flying Column in the *Anglo-Irish War, known as 'the Blacksmith of Ballinalee'. Under

McEoin's leadership Longford became one of the more active counties in Ireland. He supported the *Anglo-Irish treaty and joined the Free State army of which he became chief of staff. He resigned in 1929 to enter the *Dáil. He was a minister in both *interparty governments, and an unsuccessful candidate for the presidency in 1945 and 1959. JA

McGee, Thomas D'Arcy (1825–68), *Young Irelander. Born in Carlingford, Co. Louth, McGee emigrated to Boston in 1842 but returned in 1845 to write for the **Freeman's Journal*. He joined the **Nation* in 1846 and was secretary of the *Irish Confederation from June 1847. As a member of the confederate war council he sought to raise support in Scotland in July 1848, but fled to America when the rising failed. Moving to Montreal in 1857, McGee became prominent in the movement for Canadian confederation. He was assassinated in 1868 after condemning *Fenianism. PHG

MacGeoghegan, James (1702–64), priest and historian. Born in Co. Westmeath, he studied at Reims, where he was ordained, and remained in France as one of the large body of expatriate Irish clergy working there. A three-volume *History of Ireland* (1758–62), published in Paris, combines *Jacobitism with Irish patriotism, asserting the royal title of the Stuarts while condemning English misgovernment of Ireland, insisting on Ireland's status as a kingdom, and praising its past cultural achievements. Available in English translation from 1831–2, the *History* was popular among 19th-century Irish nationalists. John *Mitchel called his *History of Ireland* (1868) a continuation of MacGeoghegan's work.

McGilligan, Patrick (1889–1979). Born in Coleraine, Co. Londonderry, the son of a *Nationalist MP, McGilligan contested North Derry for *Sinn Féin in 1918. As minister for industry and commerce 1924–32, he promoted the creation of the *Electricity Supply Board. He also acted as minister for external affairs 1927–32, and was a key figure in the expansion of dominion status through the *Commonwealth. Returning to office as minister for finance in the *interparty government of 1948–51, he adopted a modestly expansionist fiscal strategy that contrasted with the conservatism of his earlier ministerial career.

McGrath, Joseph (1887–1966), politician and businessman. One of the less conservative members of the *Cumann na nGaedheal government, McGrath was minister for labour 1922 and industry and commerce 1922–4. During the *army mutiny he mediated between the discontented officers and the government, while himself resigning in protest at what he saw as the government's neglect of legitimate grievances. He and eight other Dáil deputies resigned from Cumann na nGaedheal to form a short-lived 'national group', all nine of whom resigned their seats in October 1924. The *Irish Hospitals Sweepstake, which he launched in 1930, made him a rich man. He was subsequently a noted owner and breeder of race horses.

MacHale, John (1791–1881), Catholic bishop of Killala 1825–34, archbishop of Tuam 1834–81. While professor of dogmatic theology at *Maynooth (1820–5), he began a series of public letters critical of the established church and the government's neglect of the poor. In Killala and Tuam he faced problems of poverty, clerical shortages, and a partially successful *evangelical Protestant mission (see SECOND REFORMATION). One of *O'Connell's staunchest supporters in the *repeal campaign, he supported *tithe abolition and *tenant right in the 1830s. Although most of the bishops accepted the *national schools system as the best deal available, MacHale came out against it on the grounds that it facilitated proselytism. His opposition was a serious misjudgement, and by 1852 he was forced to accept the system. He also opposed the *Charitable Bequests Act and the *Queen's Colleges, was critical of Newman's appointment to the *Catholic University in 1851, and argued against papal infallibility at the first *Vatican Council (1870). He was hostile to the *Land League, fearing the unrest generated by 'godless nobodies'. Although he approved of *Cullen's appointment relations between them cooled as Cullen's influence grew. MacHale's style of direct political involvement, ecclesiastical management through family networks, and charismatic, headstrong leadership belonged to an age which had died before he did. TO'C

Maclise, Daniel (1806–70), Ireland's most important practitioner of *history painting in the 19th century. Born in Cork, he began his education by drawing plaster casts of the Vatican marbles. His enthusiasm for Irish antiquities and folk-life, developed under the influence of Richard Sainthill and Thomas Crofton *Croker, can be seen in his book illustrations, paintings, and antiquarian drawings. He sketched Sir Walter Scott on a visit to Cork in 1825, which led to his success as a portraitist. He studied at the Royal Academy Schools, London, from 1828 to 1831, when he was awarded the gold medal for history painting. He became a friend of the young Benjamin Disraeli and subscribed to his Young England Toryism. He was much affected by the Victorian theatre, as seen in his paintings of Shakespearian subjects. During the 1830s he supplied caricature portraits to *Fraser's Magazine* and became friendly with Charles Dickens, whose books he illustrated. His finest illustrations were for Thomas Moore's *Irish Melodies* (1845). During the 1840s and 1850s he was deeply involved with the commissions for the new Houses of Parliament, Westminster Palace, providing murals for the House of Lords and the Royal Gallery, where his work shows the influence of French and German monumental painting. He produced a number of related paintings on the history of Britain and Ireland, notably *King Alfred in the Camp of the Danes* (1852), *The Marriage of Strongbow and Aoife* (1854), and his series of drawings (1857) on the Norman conquest of England, published as engravings in 1866. He also made designs for the applied arts. He had a strong sense of Irish identity, but for him, as for Moore, this was within a larger United Kingdom context. JT

Mac Lochlainn. Despite the existence of two alternative pedigrees, the Mac Lochlainn kings of Ailech or *Cenél nEógain in the late 11th century probably sprang from Lochlainn mac Máelsechnaill (d. 1023), king of Inis Eógain, to replace their *Tullaghoge-based *O'Neill kinsmen as overkings of the north of Ireland and claimants to the *high kingship. While Domnall Mac Lochlainn (1083–1121) repeatedly challenged the supremacy of Muirchertach *Ua Briain, his own title to high kingship, if justified at all, comes after that king's death in 1119. Domnall's grandson Muirchertach *Mac Lochlainn, however, won acknowledgement as high king from 1150 until he was killed by an insurrection among his northern vassals in 1166. The new high king, Rory *O'Connor (Ruaidrí Ua Conchobair), divided Cenél nEógain between one of Muirchertach's sons and an O'Neill, leading to prolonged interdynastic strife, only settled by a massacre of Mac Lochlainn leaders by Brian *O'Neill at the battle of Caimeirghe in 1241, after which the family lapsed into obscurity. KS

Mac Lochlainn, Muirchertach (d. 1166), king of *Cenél nEógain, eventually penultimate *high king of Ireland, came to power in 1136 and by 1149 was in a position to challenge Toirdelbach *Ua Conchobair for the kingship of Ireland, a position he held after the latter's death in 1156. His leading ally was Diarmait *Mac Murchada of Leinster, and his main rival for the kingship was Rory *O'Connor (Ruaidrí Ua Conchobair), whose submission Muirchertach secured in 1161, when the annals declared him 'king of Ireland without opposition'. When he blinded the king of Ulaid in 1166, Tír Eógain was invaded by the forces of *Bréifne and *Airgialla, and Muirchertach was killed in battle. His death weakened the Mac Lochlainn family and paved the way for the restoration of the *Ó Néills. Since his ally Mac Murchada was immediately banished overseas, it also indirectly brought about the *Anglo-Norman invasion of Ireland. SD

Mac Máel su (Mac Maol Iosa), Nicholas, archbishop of Armagh 1272–1303. A native of the diocese of Ardagh, he was consecrated as archbishop by Pope Gregory X in 1272 and probably attended the Council of Lyons in 1274. He defended his rights as archbishop against both the English and the Irish lords of his diocese and quarrelled with Edward I, provoking an adviser to the king in 1285 to urge that 'it would be expedient . . . that no Irishman should ever be an archbishop or bishop, because they always preach against the king and always provide their churches with Irishmen'. In 1291 he persuaded all the bishops of Ireland, both English and Irish, to agree to resist pressure from the lay power. In fact Nicholas was a committed supporter of the English order in Ireland, acquiring English *law for his relatives, settler husbands for his nieces, and grants of land from the English for his church. BGCS

MacMahon (Mac Mathghamhna) is the surname of two unrelated families of medieval chieftains, the MacMahon vassals of the *O'Brien princes of Thomond or north Munster, and the MacMahon kings of *Oriel (Oirghialla), approximately Co. Monaghan. In the 12th century the Monaghan and Louth areas were ruled by the Ua Cerbaill (O'Carroll) family, whose power was extinguished by the Norman colonization of Louth. Then in the early 13th century the annals identify a new military power in the Monaghan area, as wielded by Niall MacMahon 'with his bandits'. An early genealogy traces Niall to a collateral kinsman of the Ó Cerbaill kings, though the MacMahons were later to claim direct descent. Vassals of the *Pipards and de *Verdons in the 13th century, and of the earls of *Ulster in the early 14th, the MacMahons won a brief independence before becoming subordinate allies of *O'Neill from the late 14th to the 16th centuries. KS

MacMahon, Heber (1600–50), Catholic bishop of Clogher, a representative of the militant *Counter-Reformation. A product of the *Irish colleges in Flanders, he recruited mercenaries for continental service under Owen Roe *O'Neill. MacMahon was a delegate to the Synod of Kells (March 1642), which declared the *rising of 1641 'a just and pious undertaking', and subsequently member of the *confederate supreme council. Supporters of the *Ormond peace tried to appoint him a foreign ambassador but he refused to go and later broke with them over the *Inchiquin truce. The compromise choice to succeed O'Neill as general of

Ulster, he was executed following defeat at Scarrifhollis (see CONFEDERATE WAR). HM

MacManus, Terence Bellew (1823–60), *Young Irelander. Born in Co. Fermanagh, MacManus became a successful shipping agent in Liverpool, and was active in the *Repeal Association. In 1848 he returned to Ireland, fought at Ballingarry (see REBELLION OF 1848), and was *transported to Tasmania. Escaping with *Meagher in 1852, MacManus died in poverty in San Francisco. His funeral in Dublin in 1861 was the occasion of a major *Fenian demonstration. PHG

Mac Murchada, Diarmait (Dermot Mac Murrough) (d. 1171), king of Leinster. He succeeded to the kingship of Leinster no later than 1132 and ruled until 1166 when he was deposed and went into exile. Rivalry between him and Tigernán Ua Ruairc, king of *Bréifne, originating from Diarmait's abduction of Tigernán's wife Derbforgaill in 1152, traditionally has been offered as a main cause of his deposition, but more realistically it was occasioned by his failed bid for the *high kingship in 1166 which was won by Rory *O'Connor (Ruaidrí Ua Conchobair), king of Connacht. Diarmait sought military aid from *Henry II to recover Leinster and was granted permission to recruit soldiers within Henry's dominions. He concentrated on raising forces in south Wales, the most significant ally whom he secured being Richard fitz Gilbert alias *'Strongbow', to whom he offered his daughter *Aífe in marriage. Although his sobriquet 'Diarmait na nGall' (Dermot of the Foreigners) has often been interpreted as referring to his association with the Anglo-Normans, it more likely derived from the overlordship which he had asserted over the Hiberno-Norse kingdom of Dublin. Despite Diarmait's negative posthumous reputation as the instigator of English rule in Ireland, he enjoyed a considerable contemporary reputation as a patron of the church reform movement: he endowed the *Cistercian abbey of Baltinglass (receiving a letter of commendation from St Bernard of Clairvaux), as well as a series of *Augustinian houses in Leinster. MTF

MacMurrough (Mac Murchadha). On the death of Diarmait *Mac Murchada, his nephew Murtough was recognized by *Strongbow as king of Uí Chennselaig. From the late 13th century MacMurroughs claimed to be kings of Leinster. Their most successful leader, Art *MacMurrough, succeeded in creating a strong territory in Wexford and Carlow from which he and his descendants were able to menace the *Pale, and extract regular *black rents, until they were brought under control in the late 16th century.

MacMurrough, Art (Art Caomhánach Mac Murchadha) (d. 1416/17), king of Leinster, the chief military target of *Richard II during his expeditions to Ireland. Art came to power in the 1370s, when the English settlements were weakened by Irish raids and outbreaks of plague. The *Gaelic recovery, which was symbolized by the revival of the title 'king of Leinster', had not been halted by the execution of several of Art's recent predecessors by the Dublin government. Within his own society Art was very much a king, overlord of other Gaelic leaders and the recipient of praise-poetry. His power also depended on interaction with the colonial world. He raised *black rent from Castledermot and New Ross, and sought an annual fee from Dublin, together with recognition as 'captain of his nation'. His marriage to the Anglo-Irish heiress Elizabeth Calf brought a claim to her inheritance in Kildare. In 1395, after defeating him, Richard conceded his fee and his wife's barony, in return for a promise to vacate the lands he had conquered and earn compensation through military service against other Irish. This came to nothing, and Art resisted Richard successfully in 1399, retaining to the end his power among the Leinster Irish and his ambivalent relationship with the crown. RFF

McNally, Leonard (1752–1820), barrister and author of comic operas. A member of the *United Irish society, he defended *Tandy and other radicals in court, but was revealed after his death to have been a government informer. He appears to have been motivated partly by panic at having been dangerously compromised by the Revd William *Jackson, and partly by genuine alarm at the direction the United Irish movement was taking.

MacNeill, Eoin (1867–1945), historian and political activist. A Co. Antrim-born Catholic, he was a founder of the *Gaelic League, first editor of *An *Claidheamh Soluis*, and from 1909 professor of early and medieval Irish history at University College, Dublin. His article 'The North Began', pointing to the example of the *Ulster Volunteer Force, provided the inspiration for the *Irish Volunteers. As commander-in-chief of the Volunteers, he opposed participation in the *First World War, but insisted that armed resistance was justifiable only if the government attempted to suppress the movement or impose conscription. When he learned, at a late stage, of the planned *rising of 1916, he was initially persuaded to acquiesce, partly by an apparently forged official plan for the suppression of the Volunteers ('the Castle Document'), and partly by the argument that matters had gone too far to retreat. His last-minute order countermanding all plans for 'special action', issued after he had learned of the loss of the *Aud* and the capture of *Casement, was too late to prevent the Dublin rising, but destroyed any hope of a nationwide insurrection.

Imprisoned after the rising, MacNeill was a minister in the first *Dáil, and then minister for education 1922–5. His service as the Free State's representative on the *Boundary Commission ended his career: MacNeill may have recognized that he was to take the blame for the inevitable failure to achieve a united Ireland.

MacNeill's historical works, *Phases of Irish History* (1919) and *Celtic Ireland* (1921), pioneered the serious study of early Irish society. He was also the main force behind the establishment of the Irish Manuscripts Commission.

McQuaid, John Charles (1895–1973), Catholic archbishop of Dublin from 1940. Born in Co. Cavan and a member of the Holy Ghost order, he was earlier dean and then president of Blackrock College, and had been consulted by de *Valera during the drafting of the 1937 *constitution. His first concern as archbishop was to improve Catholic social services, founding the Catholic Social Welfare Bureau in 1942 and expending great energy in building up the physical fabric of his diocese. After the war he frequently acted as mediator in industrial disputes. Committed to denominational education, he founded the Dublin Institute of Catholic Sociology in 1950 and was a firm advocate of Catholic social action. He opposed Noel *Browne on the *Mother and Child Scheme in 1950. Deeply conservative, he found difficulty in adjusting to the reforms of the second *Vatican Council, but his obedience to Rome helped him to weather the change. TO'C

MacRory, Joseph (1861–1945), Catholic bishop of Down and Connor 1915–28, archbishop of Armagh from 1928, made a cardinal in 1929. Earlier he had been president of Dungannon Academy, then professor of moral theology and scripture at Oldon Seminary, Birmingham. From 1889 he was professor of scripture at *Maynooth, where he wrote a commentary on St John's Gospel (1897) and was co-founder of the *Irish Theological Quarterly* (1906), becoming college vice-president in 1912. He supported *Collins's strategy of refusing to recognize the new Northern Ireland state (although he served on the Catholic–police liaison committee set up under the *Craig–Collins pact) and was reluctant to condemn *IRA activities. As archbishop he proved much more hardline than his predecessor *O'Donnell, continuing to regard dealings with the new government as collaboration with the enemy. TO'C

MacSweeny (Mac Suibhne). The most famous of the *gallowglass families, the MacSweenys of Castle Ween in Argyle were fosterers to Domhnall Óg O'Donnell (king of Tír Conaill 1258–81), who subsequently married a daughter of MacSweeny and was succeeded by a son of this marriage, Aodh O'Donnell (d. 1333). According to their traditional history, *Leabhar Chlainne Suibhne* (early 16th century), MacSweeny gallowglasses at first hired themselves out as free-lances to various Irish kings, and a tradition in the 16th-century *Leabhar Eoghanach* that Donal *O'Neill (d. 1325) was the first to billet them on his subjects may explain their official genealogy, which links the family to the *O'Neill family tree. They were rewarded with land grants by both sides during a war of succession among the *O'Donnells, and by the end of the 14th century the MacSweeny chief ruled Fanad as O'Donnell's vassal, subject to a levy of two gallowglasses for every quarter of land in his territory. An extension of this arrangement in the 15th century installed another leader of the kin in the Trí Tuatha (MacSweeny na Doe), and by 16th century a third chief, MacSweeny Banagh, ruled Tír Boghaine. Other members of the family received lesser estates in return for military service in Connacht and Munster. KS

MacSwiney, Mary (1872–1942). Born in England, MacSwiney lived most of her life in Cork. Educated by the Ursuline nuns, she later taught for them, but lost her job as a result of her nationalist activity in 1916. Initially a suffragist, by 1914 she had decided to prioritize nationalism and joined *Cumann na mBan. She came to prominence as a publicist for her brother *Terence, and was elected to the second *Dáil, where she is best remembered for her long speech against the *Anglo-Irish treaty. A lifelong political activist, she also ran a girls' school in Cork. CC

MacSwiney, Terence (1879–1920). MacSwiney, who had succeeded Thomas *MacCurtain as *Sinn Féin lord mayor of Cork, died at Brixton prison, London, on 25 October on the 74th day of a hunger strike following his imprisonment for possessing a *Royal Irish Constabulary cipher.

Madden, R. R. (1798–1886), historian and administrator. Born in Dublin, the son of a successful Catholic silk merchant, Madden studied medicine in Paris, Naples, and London. From 1833 he began a varied career as a colonial administrator and foreign correspondent. While in Portugal he published *The United Irishmen, their Lives and Times* (1843–6). This sympathetic account of the *insur-

rection of 1798, for which he is best remembered, installed the *United Irishmen as icons of Irish nationalist rhetoric. In 1850 he returned to Ireland to become secretary to the Loan Fund Board, a post he continued to hold for the next 30 years.
NG

Madden, Samuel (1686–1765), Church of Ireland clergyman, a nephew of William *Molyneux and friend of *Berkeley and *Swift. He was co-founder of the Dublin Society (see ROYAL DUBLIN SOCIETY), and was nicknamed 'Premium Madden' for the prizes he established to encourage excellence in artistic and technical work. *Reflections and Resolutions Proper for the Gentlemen of Ireland* (1738) set out his ideas on agricultural and economic improvement

Máel Sechnaill I (d. 862), king of *Mide, belonged to the Clann Cholmáin branch of the southern *Uí Néill and succeeded to the kingship in 846. Having enforced his authority in territories close to home, he turned his attention further afield and succeeded in taking the *hostages of Munster in 858. Áed Finnliath of the northern Uí Néill challenged his supremacy. Nevertheless, on his death in 862 he had considerable claim to the title 'king of Ireland' (see HIGH KINGSHIP) which the *annalists accorded him.
MNíM

Máel Sechnaill (Malachy) II (d. 1022), high king, of the Clann Cholmáin branch of the southern *Uí Néill, came to power in 980. For much of his reign, he was involved in an ongoing struggle against the Munster king *Brian Bóruma (Boru), who sought to extend his authority northwards. The two kings came to an agreement at a meeting in Clonfert in 997, whereby each recognized the other's supremacy in his own half of the country. The truce was short-lived, however, and as a result of Brian's incessant attacks, Máel Sechnaill was forced to submit in 1002. Despite subsequently acting as Brian's ally, Máel Sechnaill's support for the Munster king was conditional and he withdrew his forces from Brian's camp on the eve of the battle of *Clontarf. That battle left Brian dead and Máel Sechnaill the most powerful king in Ireland in his wake, so that he is justifiably termed *ardrí Érenn* (*high king of Ireland) on his death.
MNíM

Magee, William Connor (1821–91). An Irish-born clergyman whose grandfather William Magee had been archbishop of Dublin 1822–31, he served in both Ireland and England, and was much in demand as a conference speaker. He quickly made a reputation for himself as a man of strong principle: while serving in Enniskillen he upbraided the *Orange Order for being less than true to its principles, and supported the *national schools rather than the rival *Church Education Society. From being dean of Cork, he was appointed bishop of Peterborough by Disraeli in 1868 on the eve of the Liberal electoral victory that brought Irish *disestablishment to the fore. While the Irish bishops refused to treat with *Gladstone, Magee argued the Church of Ireland's case with government, both privately and in the House of Lords. His opinion was that disestablishment would result in a 'lay tyranny', and, like Archbishop Trench of Dublin, he was fearful that the inevitable revision of the Prayer Book would undermine the Church of Ireland's Anglicanism. He also predicted that disestablishment would follow in England in a matter of years. Magee died within weeks of his preferment to York in 1891.
KM

Magheramorne manifesto (July 1905), written by Robert Lindsay *Crawford for the *Independent Orange Order. The manifesto indicted all forms of clericalism, appealing to Catholics and Protestants to unite on the basis of shared nationality. It condemned the newly created *Ulster Unionist Council, dismissed unionism as a 'discredited creed', and endorsed compulsory land purchase. The manifesto embodied a reaction against the social exclusivity and intellectual narrowness of early Edwardian unionism: it was a protest document, rather than a successful appeal to nationality. Although endorsed by the Independent Orange Order, it later proved an embarrassment.
AJ

magic is the manipulation of the supernatural for immediate practical purposes. This in theory distinguishes it from religion, which offers a general explanation of the universe, and whose rituals are symbolic rather than instrumental in purpose; in practice the line is not always so easy to draw. Magical beliefs were widespread in both Catholic and Protestant popular culture. They included belief in the fairies, who could be angered by an incautious act or word, whose dwellings (generally former *ringforts) and thorn bushes must be left strictly untouched, and who sometimes kidnapped children or adults leaving a sickly simulacrum (a changeling) in their place. The major festivals marking turning points in the agricultural year (see CALENDAR CUSTOM) were occasions when good luck or other favours could be obtained by appropriate performances. There were also charms and rituals by which sick persons or animals could be healed, or misfortune brought on an enemy (see WITCHCRAFT), and a multitude of minor prescriptions for or against lucky and unlucky acts. Practitioners of such magic, such as Biddy Early (1798–1873) in Co. Clare, could achieve considerable fame.

As with other poor and technologically unsophisticated societies, the prominence of magical beliefs in Irish popular culture is most convincingly accounted for in terms of the need for an explanation of, and a sense of control over, what would otherwise have been an incomprehensible pattern of good and bad fortune. The relationship of such traditions to orthodox religion was complex. In some cases, as with many *holy wells, Christianity was 'folklorized' by magical accretions; in others, as with the many local festivals (including *Croagh Patrick) that are clearly continuations of the ancient feast of *Lughnasa, it is non-Christian practices that were given a veneer of religious respectability. Observers in the middle decades of the 19th century reported a sharp decline in magical beliefs and practices, as well as in *wakes and *patterns, reflecting both the growing hostility of the Catholic church and the cultural changes associated with Anglicization and commercialization. Yet many such traditions remained alive, if in modified form, well into the 20th century.

'Magna Carta Hiberniae', a version of Magna Carta as reissued after the death of King *John in November 1216, which purports to be a contemporary adaptation of the charter to Irish circumstances. It substitutes 'Ireland' for 'England', 'Dublin' for 'London', and 'the Liffey' for 'the Thames' and 'the Medway' throughout, but otherwise differs in no significant respect from its English counterpart. Although it was copied into the semi-official 'Red Book of the Irish Exchequer', and was printed by Berry in 1907 among the genuine legislation of the Irish lordship, scholars now believe that the 'adaptation' was made as late as the early 14th century and without any official authorization. PAB

Magrath, Miler (*c.*1523–1622), a long-serving prelate noted for his flexible religious principles. As a *Franciscan friar he was appointed by the papacy to the sees of Down and Connor in 1565. In 1570, however, he conformed to the established church and was appointed bishop of Clogher by Queen Elizabeth. The following year he was made archbishop of Cashel, which he held with the diocese of Emly till his death. During the periods 1582–9 and 1592–1608 he also administered the sees of Waterford and Lismore. Magrath became an influential political figure during the latter part of Elizabeth's reign, and was an important mediator between the Gaelic world and the Dublin government. By the early 17th century, however, he was viewed with suspicion by the leading English-born bishops of the *Church of Ireland and was accused of pluralism, rampant nepotism, and widespread alienation of see property. Though he acquired two further dioceses, Achonry in 1607 and Killala in 1613, he had by this stage little influence in either church or state. AF

Maguire (Mág Uidhir). The chiefs of this family ruled Feara Manach (Fermanagh) from the reign of Donn Óg Mág Uidhir (d. 1302) to 1607. Like their Ó hEignigh predecessors in the kingship, they claimed descent from Colla fo Chrí via Cenél Lugáin. Before 1333 the Maguires' lordship of Lough Erne was subject to the de *Burgh earl of *Ulster, but they regained independence when the earldom passed in that year to an underage absentee. By the later 14th century, however, they had been brought into an enduring relationship of subordinate alliance with the *O'Neills of Tír Eógain. As with the O'Neills, the Maguire chieftainship at first tended to pass from father to son, with younger sons acquiring lands of their own by replacing the unrelated vassal chiefs who had been ruling the 'seven *tuatha*' of Lough Erne. By the end of the 15th century the descendants of Pilib 'the Tánaiste' Maguire (d. 1470) had acquired lordship over most of Fermanagh west of Enniskillen and were powerful enough to displace the senior line descended from Pilib's elder brother Tomás Óg (d. 1480). This reflected the growing influence of the O'Donnell lordship over west Fermanagh at a time when the O'Neills were divided and weak. The dominance of Clann Philib was confirmed under Cúchonnacht 'the *Coarb' Maguire (d. 1537), who bolstered his power by amassing control of church lands. His grandson Aodh (d. 1600) was a leader in the *Nine Years War, succeeded by his brother Cúchonnacht Óg, who joined the *Flight of the Earls in 1607. In the *Ulster plantation some branches of the family were allotted lands, notably Brian Maguire of Tempo, brother to Cúchonnacht Óg, and a rival kinsman, Conchobhar Ruadh (Conor Roe) Maguire. Their descendants remained as patrons of Gaelic literature and history well into the 18th century.

Livingstone, P., *The Fermanagh Story* (1969)
Simms, K., 'The Medieval Kingdom of Lough Erne', *Clogher Record*, 9 (1977)

KS

Mahon, James, see O'GORMAN MAHON.

Malachy, St (Máel Máedóc Ua Morgair) (d. 1148), archbishop of Armagh. The most prominent advocate of the *12th-century reform of the Irish church, Malachy was born into an ecclesiastical family in 1094–5 and trained as a monk at Armagh, where he came under the influence of the ascetic Imar Ua hÁedacáin, abbot of SS Peter and Paul,

Armagh. He was ordained priest at the age of 25, notwithstanding that the canonical age for ordination was 30 years. He spent a period of time at Lismore, under the ecclesiastical discipline of the monk bishop Máel su Ua hAinmire (Malchus). He inaugurated his public career as a church reformer by reviving conventual life at the secularized monastery of *Bangor, although he faced strong local opposition. In 1124 he was consecrated bishop for the see of Connor, but was forced into exile to the monastery of Lismore in 1127, where he met another refugee, Cormac *Mac Carthaig, king of Desmond, whom he persuaded to return to the kingship, and with whom he subsequently collaborated in promoting church reform. Cellach, archbishop of Armagh, had designated Malachy as his successor, but when he died in 1129, Malachy encountered great difficulty in ousting the hereditary secularized ecclesiastical dynasty of *Clann Sínaich, which had asserted an almost 200-year monopoly of clerical offices at Armagh. He was unable to take possession of either the insignia or temporalities of the church of Armagh until 1134. Having asserted the case for reform and canonical consecration at Armagh, he resigned the see in 1137 in the interests of conciliation to Gilla Meic Liac (Gelasius), abbot of the important Columban monastery of Derry, and assumed the bishopric of Down.

In 1139 he undertook a mission to Pope Innocent II to request formal papal recognition (signified by the granting of palls) for the archbishoprics of Armagh and Cashel, visiting on the way the *Cistercian abbey of Clairvaux, where he formed a friendship with his future biographer, St Bernard. Pope Innocent II did not accede to his request, but instructed Malachy, whom he commissioned as a papal legate, to return to Ireland and summon a general church council so that a more formal and demonstrably unanimous request for papal endorsement could be made. On his homeward journey Malachy again visited Clairvaux and left four of his associates to be trained as monks in the Cistercian observance. The first Irish Cistercian monastery was founded under his auspices at *Mellifont in 1142. Malachy also visited the monastery of Arrouaise in Flanders, whence he introduced the *Augustinian rule according to the Arroasian observance into Ireland, the first Arroasian community in Ireland being founded at St Mary's abbey, Louth, in 1142. Both Mellifont and Louth abbey were situated in the kingdom of *Airgialla, the protection and patronage of whose king, Donnchad Ua Cerbaill, enabled Malachy to introduce these continental monastic observances. Malachy's brother, Gilla Críst, acted as bishop of Airgialla, alias Clogher, 1135–8. In 1148, availing of the fact that Pope Innocent II had summoned a church council at Reims, Malachy undertook a second journey to the Continent, having first convened a synod on the island of Inis Pádraig (Co. Dublin) for the purpose of making a formal request for palls. Reaching Clairvaux in October he fell ill and died there, aged 54, in the arms of St Bernard on 2 November 1148. The monks of Clairvaux initiated proceedings for his canonization which Pope Clement III confirmed in 1190, his feast day being set as 3 November, so as to avoid All Souls' Day (2 Nov.). Bernard of Clairvaux's biography of Malachy, as well as letters written to him during his lifetime, and commemorative sermons preached on his feast day, are the most important sources for his life. MTF

Malby, Sir Nicholas (*c.*1530–1584), soldier and administrator. Originally serjeant-major general in *Sidney's army and a minor player in the *Enterprise of Ulster, Malby was appointed military governor of Connacht in 1576 and promoted to *provincial president in 1578. His actions included the suppression of *Clanricard's sons, campaigns against *O'Rourke, the settlement of the Mayo Bourkes' succession dispute, and the establishment of a *composition in Connacht to finance its administration. Malby's military rigour and judicial equity won the respect of the Gaelic Irish and the praise of their *annalists. Not only did Malby turn a blind eye to Catholic religious practices and monastic survivals, he also used Gaelic methods including the *fostering out of his children to establish personal ties with the lords. His ambitions extended to Ulster and Munster. The queen was critical of his aggressive actions in the latter, which contributed to the second *Desmond rebellion. Malby's 17,000-acre grant in Roscommon was the nucleus of a small New English colony. HM

Malcolmsons of Portlaw, the most notable, if still mysterious, exception to the general tale of 19th-century deindustrialization outside the north-east. David Malcolmson, a Quaker (see SOCIETY OF FRIENDS), originally from Lurgan, Co. Armagh, set up in business as a *flour miller in Co. Tipperary before establishing a *cotton spinning mill at Portlaw, Co. Waterford, in 1826. This survived the crisis that almost immediately afterwards gripped the rest of the Irish cotton industry, and reached its peak of productivity in the 1850s, when the firm employed 1,600 workers. The family also owned mills in Manchester and Belfast and the Neptune ironworks in Waterford, and had interests in steam shipping and other concerns. In 1876 the whole complex of business interests suffered a general collapse which, like the family's earlier success, has not yet been fully explained. The mill continued as the Portlaw Spinning Company, but at a much reduced level, and closed down in 1904.

Man, Isle of. This island, which may take its name from the Irish mythical figure Manannán mac Lir, has played a prominent role in Irish history and legend through the centuries. The Manx language is a dialect of Gaelic, which probably indicates Irish settlement, and we know, for instance, that the late 6th-century king of *Ulaid, Báetán son of Cairell, controlled the island for a time. Man was probably christianized from Ireland, which may account for the cults of Irish saints reflected in the names of some of its medieval church sites. During the *Viking period there were close relations between Man and Dublin, with a series of rulers governing both jointly, and occasional allusions thereafter to the archbishop of Dublin's jurisdiction over the diocese of Sodor. While political contacts diminished following the English annexation of Man in the 14th century, there were continued ecclesiastical and, increasingly, trading links. By the 16th century Man begins to feature as a haven for privateers preying on Irish shipping, while in the 18th century in particular it was an important centre for the activities of *smugglers. More recent links have been dominated by Man's role as a tourist destination and a centre for the financial services sector. SD

Manchester martyrs. On 18 September 1867 Thomas Kelly and Timothy Deasy, two leading *Fenians, were being transported from the courthouse in Manchester to the county jail when the police van containing them was attacked. The prisoners escaped, but an unarmed police sergeant was shot dead. Twenty-nine arrests followed, and in November five men were convicted of murder. One was subsequently pardoned and another's sentence was commuted, but three men, William O'Meara Allen, Michael Larkin, and William O'Brien, were hanged. The deaths of these 'Manchester martyrs' prompted a partial reconciliation between the *Catholic church and Fenianism, and a groundswell of popular sympathy for the Fenian movement in Ireland. NG

mandates, letters sent in October 1605 to sixteen leading Dublin *recusants by Lord Deputy *Chichester requiring them to attend Protestant services. When they refused, they were hauled before the Court of *Castle Chamber, fined, and imprisoned until such times as they conformed. The mandates campaign, subsequently extended to Kilkenny, Cork, Galway, and Drogheda, was suspended only when *Old English conspiracies with Hugh *O'Neill were uncovered after the *Flight of the Earls. HM

Mannix, Daniel (1864–1963), Catholic ecclesiastic. Born in Co. Cork, he taught at *Maynooth and became president there in 1903, before being appointed coadjutor archbishop of Melbourne in 1912 and archbishop in 1917. During the *First World War he opposed conscription and was a loud advocate of Irish independence and a vociferous critic of *Black and Tan atrocities. The British navy prevented his landing in Ireland in 1920. Active in Catholic Action, he oversaw a massive church-building programme in Melbourne. He issued a famous criticism of the 1945 bombing of Hiroshima. TO'C

manor, an institution, introduced into Ireland by the Anglo-Normans at the end of the 12th century, that provided the framework within which a radically reorganized society came into existence. The social structure of manorial society was determined by *land tenure and the rights and duties attached to it.

The medieval manor was primarily an instrument of lordship. Once a territory was conquered, structures had to be put in place urgently to defend and exploit it. For example, the Butler lordship, founded by *Theobald Walter between 1185 and 1206, comprised some 750,000 acres in Leinster and Munster. This enormous area was divided into seven 'capital' manors—Nenagh, Caherconlish, Dunkerrin, Thurles, Gowran, Tullow, and Arklow—each with its castle and lands reserved as the lord's demesne. The territory of each capital manor was in turn divided into smaller manors (fiefs)—perhaps 3,000 to 5,000 acres on average—held by tenants (knights) owing military service. At this primary level the manor was a tenurial structure to provide the means to defend and retain a recent conquest.

The manor was also the institutional means of exploiting the agriculture and trade of the lordship. The rising population of Europe in the 12th and 13th centuries stimulated the development of demesne farming, enabling Ireland to export large quantities of grain and *wool in the 13th century. Anglo-Norman lords likewise sought to profit from trade in their lordships by founding towns, creating a network of towns and villages that survive to this day, such as those already mentioned in association with the Butler lordship.

Fundamentally, lordship had to do with the population rather than the territory of the manor. Every class was subject to the lord, and that relationship was expressed by the terms of tenure: knights held their lands by military service, free tenants by rent, *burgesses by burgage tenure, and *serfs by tenures that owed labour services. The place for resolving disputes involving tenure, minor breaches of the peace, or custom was the manor court (or court leet), where custom was declared on disputed points by the suitors (another tenurial obligation). Since the record of the court was the memory of the suitors, seldom written, our knowledge of this institution governing the lives of most of the population is extremely limited. A unique archive of social custom and daily life in medieval Ireland perished with the society that sustained it.

Empey, C. A., 'Medieval Knocktopher: A Study in Manorial Settlement', *Old Kilkenny Review*, 2 (1982–3)

CAE

Mant, Richard (1776–1848), English-born *Church of Ireland bishop of Killaloe (1820–3) and Down and Connor (1823–48). He came to Ireland with a considerable reputation as preacher and lecturer. His first visitation address, containing trenchant references to Roman 'error', caused much offence to Catholics, though—according to his son's account—his discomfiture in Killaloe, and consequent translation to Down and Connor, owed more to *agrarian than sectarian unrest. A 'Caroline' churchman, in the old *high-church tradition, his writings stressed the prerogatives of the historic episcopate, dignity in worship, eucharistic practice, and the daily offices, much of which did not commend him in evangelical circles. The Church Architecture Society, over which he presided, was influential at a time of considerable church building in his diocese, and was suspected of tractarian leanings by its critics. He published many hymns, several of which remain in use, but is best remembered for his two-volume *History of the Church of Ireland* (1840), most valued today for its extensive reprinting of original material. KM

manufacturing industry. Given the lack of substantial mineral-based natural resources, and a smaller and poorer domestic market, Ireland's industrial history was quite different from that of neighbouring Britain. Only in the north-east, in *Belfast and its hinterland, was Ireland to experience large-scale factory-based industrialization. Elsewhere the limited industrial development that took place depended mainly on organically based industries, predominantly those engaged in processing raw materials from the agricultural sector.

In the pre-*Anglo-Norman period there is only limited archaeological evidence for industries such as high-quality *metalworking, jewellery, and souterrain-ware pottery production in rural settlements such as *ringforts. With the setting up of major *Viking trading towns from the 10th century, mainly along the east coast, industrial production increased in size and intensity. In Hiberno-Norse *Dublin there is much evidence for industrial quarters: wood-turners and coopers in Winetavern Street, leather working in High Street, and bone, antler, and metalworking in the adjoining area of High Street and Christchurch Place. Other Hiberno-Norse towns such as *Waterford have produced comparable material.

With the coming of the Anglo-Normans the indigenous pottery industry expanded considerably, with kilns located at Downpatrick, Co. Down, and *Carrickfergus, Co. Antrim, as well as probable examples at Adare Castle, Co. Limerick, *Trim Castle, Co. Meath, and near major urban centres such as Dublin. Ceramic floor tiles mainly produced for religious houses were also being produced in Ireland at places such as *Drogheda and in the *Kilkenny city area. Cloth production was also important, especially that based on the *wool supplied from the great *Cistercian houses of south-east Ireland. Other industries important to the medieval economy included leather-making: excavations in Dublin and Cork have produced many items of worked leather such as footwear, scabbards, and other personal adornments, mainly of 13th- and 14th-century date. Towns would also have been the centres of large *iron and bronze metalworking industries, based largely on imported ores, but with centres such as Carrickfergus relying on local iron ore for their raw material. Coopering and woodworking were other industries which were located in both rural and urban settlements, testifying to the importance of wooden structures and artefacts in medieval Ireland.

Manufacturing industry in early modern Ireland remained limited in variety and scale. At the beginning of the 16th century commercial output included some manufactured items such as coarse *linen cloth and iron goods for local consumption. Most exports were of unprocessed material such as linen yarn. The principal reason for this was a skill shortage combined with the lack of a marketing structure. During the 16th century central government encouraged Irish manufactures by limiting the export of linen yarn and introducing Flemish tanners to Ireland. These measures had limited success. The expansion of colonization in the early 17th century saw some growth in manufacturing with the expansion of ironworking, some *glass production, and local promotion of cloth manufacture, but this was limited since land yielded a greater return than manufactures. Most economic activity consisted in exploiting unprocessed natural resources.

In the later 17th century there was a growth in manufacturing activity. The passage of the

*Cattle Acts encouraged the production of butter and processed beef and the woollen cloth trade expanded dramatically. *Landlords, in order to ensure that a growing population would have enough cash to pay their rent, actively promoted manufacturing projects. This took the form of encouraging linen production through competitions and providing a guaranteed market for linen cloth, exports of which grew from 14,750 yards in 1665 to 131,568 yards in 1686. The *Woollen Act of 1699 hit an expanding woollen cloth trade badly and the economic recession of the early 18th century affected other manufacturing activity. *Brewing was disadvantaged by high local taxation. To combat this the *Royal Dublin Society tried to promote local manufacturing activity by encouraging consumption of locally produced manufactured goods and promoting technical innovation.

During the second half of the 18th century a growing population and a steady rise in agricultural prosperity based on the demands of the expanding Atlantic trade provided the basis for a healthier and more broadly based manufacturing sector. Glass making, *flour milling, brewing, and the luxury trades all expanded significantly. Wool production for the domestic market remained important in the towns of Munster and Leinster, while *cotton grew rapidly in the last decades of the century. Most important of all was the growth of linen, which by the end of the century had expanded far beyond its original heartland in Ulster and accounted for more than half of all Irish exports.

Linen remained largely a cottage-based industry until well into the 19th century, although bleaching and finishing had become more centralized during the 18th century. Cotton spinning in contrast had already become quite mechanized by the end of the 18th century, and its concentration around Belfast initiated the first phase of industrialization in the city. However, most of the cotton industry in Belfast (and in the rest of the country) succumbed ultimately to competition from the Lancashire industry. Machine spinning of linen yarn became firmly established only during the 1830s, taking over many of the factories previously used for cotton spinning. The mechanization of linen production led to a major decline over the following decades in the number of flax spinners working by hand in rural Ireland. Powerloom weaving in linen from the 1850s led to further concentration within factories in east Ulster and undermined the role of the domestic handloom weaver. The making-up trade also developed in east Ulster, creating greater added value in the industry and intensifying the process of industrialization close to the strongholds of power spinning and weaving, while in west Ulster the *shirt making industry emerged, centred largely around *Derry.

In the second half of the 19th century the transport revolution facilitated an increase in trade with Britain in processed foodstuffs. Although population fell significantly, the average standard of living rose, increasing the demand for processed foodstuffs like bacon, *bread, and butter, as well as for *tobacco and beer. Most industrial development in the south of Ireland (outside *Dublin) was geared towards producing for the home market. In Ulster, by contrast, a large proportion of industrial production was for export, particularly in the east, where the exportation of linen cloth and *ships provided the backbone of the region's industrial development; Belfast also exported a range of other goods, such as whiskey, tobacco, textile machinery, and rope. British competition across the industrial sector as a whole became much more intense after the main parts of the *rail network had been built between the 1840s and the 1870s. Prior to this transport costs were too high to enable British producers of heavier and less valuable goods to penetrate the Irish market.

Although employment in the Irish industrial sector declined during the second half of the 19th century, industrial output increased. Productivity in Irish industry improved as it became more capitalized and more technically sophisticated. Many craft industries declined in the face of competition from low-priced British mass produced goods. However, this decline was more than offset by the larger industries in which Ireland began to specialize (like linen, ships, beer, spirits, tobacco, bacon, and other foodstuffs), which were generally concentrated in technically sophisticated factories producing commodities which could compete in terms of price and quality with British goods. A number of non-traded industries emerged to serve the needs of the domestic market; construction, railway engineering, printing, and flour milling are good examples of significant industries oriented almost entirely to the home market. These industries were well represented in the south where Dublin was the main industrial centre. Belfast, Ireland's only major industrial city, dominated the export trade, accounting for about two-thirds of Ireland's industrial exports by 1907.

*Northern Ireland's staple industries experienced contraction in the inter-war period; demand for shipbuilding declined in the 1920s due to world overcapacity and competition from Scandinavia and Japan. The industry revived only with the outbreak of the *Second World War. With changing fashions, linen went out of favour after the First World War, resulting in the beginning of a permanent decline in Northern Ireland's staple industry. After a brief upturn in the 1960s, Northern Ireland's industrial base contracted significantly, and its traditional role as the major industrial centre on the island has been eclipsed by industrial expansion in the south.

In independent Ireland attempts to boost the low degree of industrial development through *protectionist measures intensified under *Fianna Fáil after 1932. While there were some short-term employment gains from this policy, its long-term impact on industrial development was limited. A greater degree of industrial expansion took place following the abandonment of protectionism in the 1960s (see *ECONOMIC DEVELOPMENT*). Much of this growth was achieved by encouraging export-oriented multinationals to locate in Ireland, and such firms continue to account for a large share of industrial employment, exports, and output.

Cullen, L., *An Economic History of Ireland since 1660* (1972)
Gillespie, Raymond, *The Transformation of the Irish Economy, 1550–1700* (1991)
Kennedy, L., *The Modern Industrialisation of Ireland 1940–1988* (1989)
Ó Gráda, C., *Ireland: A New Economic History 1780–1939* (1994)

TB/RG/AB

maps. Irish cartography begins no earlier than the 16th century, with the advent of separate maps of Ireland. Before that, the mapping of Europe's outermost Atlantic fringe belongs to the history of other nations and other cultures, with Great Britain and Ireland taking an inconspicuous place successively in Claudius Ptolemy's *Geography* of the 2nd century AD, in the diagrammatic *mappaemundi* characteristic of early medieval Christendom, and in the sea charts produced by Italian and Iberian navigators in the 14th century and after. The latter provided the information on Ireland which appeared on the first printed maps of Great Britain and Ireland, such as Martin Waldseemüller's map of 1513.

Only after *c.*1540 did Ireland acquire a definite cartographic identity in the many English military and political maps that were the surveyors' and engineers' contribution to the forward policy pursued by Tudor governments. In this connection the maps of Robert Lythe (1567–71), the two John Brownes (uncle and nephew, 1583–90), Francis Jobson (1587–98), and Richard Bartlett (1601–2) are particularly notable. Many of these maps remained buried in government offices. However some, such as those by Lythe of central and southern Ireland, were used without acknowledgement in the compilations of foreign cartographers like Gerard Mercator (1564, 1595), Abraham Ortelius (1573), and Jodocus Hondius (1591), and later in the maps of the Englishman John Speed (1611), whose version of Ireland found general acceptance for much of the 17th century.

By Speed's time military campaigns had become a less important cartographic influence than the confiscation of landed property. The emphasis now was on the measurement and plotting of numerous small territorial divisions at large scales. After the *Flight of the Earls in 1607 land in six Ulster counties was confiscated (see ULSTER PLANTATION) and a hasty survey was made by Josias Bodley to show the divisions in which the land was to be apportioned among its new owners; in Co. Londonderry land granted to the London companies was mapped in more detail by Thomas Raven in 1622. The *Down Survey, organized by Sir William *Petty in the 1650s, is preeminent among these 17th-century surveys of confiscated land. Petty's bequest to the future included not only accurate printed maps of the outline and counties of Ireland, but also a flourishing class of land surveyors who specialized in the manuscript mapping of estates and farms on behalf of their new proprietors. Estate mapping remained an Irish preoccupation even after the visit to Dublin in 1754–60 of the celebrated Anglo-French cartographer John Rocque, who through his pupils (especially Bernard Scalé) exercised more influence in Ireland on estate surveying than on the kind of printed map that Rocque himself had specialized in. Thereafter estate maps began to reflect more closely the growing elaboration of towns, country houses, demesnes, and other artefacts in the Irish landscape, rather than the bare boundaries of the Down Survey.

The long ascendancy of Petty's county maps was gradually undermined. The *Physico-Historical Society encouraged the production of maps of Down, Kerry, Waterford, and Cork in the 1740s, and Rocque published maps of Cos. Dublin and Armagh. However, it was not until printed maps of counties received limited funding from *grand juries under an act of 1774 that 25 counties were mapped at scales of between 1 and 2 inches to the Irish mile. These maps varied greatly in content and accuracy, and the high point of the genre was achieved in Bald's 25-sheet map of Mayo, completed in 1830. However, no Irish cartographer ever equalled the magnificent town plan of Dublin which Rocque published in 1756. Lesser Irish towns were more usually mapped, if at all, as part of estate surveys, though printed maps do exist for Armagh, Belfast, Cork, Derry,

Drogheda, Enniskillen, Galway, Limerick, Newry, Tralee, and Waterford.

Another generation of innovators, several of them Scotsmen or with Scottish connections, appeared in Ireland after the *Union, and were especially active in the mapping of roads, canals, and harbours, exploiting new cartographic techniques and achieving new standards of accuracy. Prominent in this group were William Bald, Richard *Griffith, William Duncan, and William Edgeworth. Most of them spent some time practising as independent civil engineers under central or local government control, particularly in surveys for the Irish Bogs Commission of 1809–14 and in several county maps that were by-products of the bogs survey. Some engineers tried to apply improved standards of precision to the traditional subject-matter of Irish estate surveying, but their efforts were overtaken in 1824 when central government took an active role in Irish cartography through the establishment of the *Ordnance Survey.

Private large-scale cartography in Ireland was stifled by Ordnance Survey competition and land surveyors largely became copyists thereafter; on the other hand, commercial publishers, mostly outside Ireland, found it profitable to reduce and restyle the survey's small-scale work.

Andrews, J. H., *Plantation Acres: An Historical Study of the Irish Land Surveyor and his Maps* (1985)
—— *Shapes of Ireland* (1997)
Ferguson, Paul J., *Irish Map History: A Select Bibliography, 1850–1983, on the History of Cartography in Ireland* (1983)

JHA/PF

marble in Ireland comes in many varieties and colours. Black marble is carboniferous limestone, coloured by a small percentage of graphitic carbon. This comes from Menlo (Co. Galway) and Archer's Grove (Co. Kilkenny) quarries. The former yields pure black stone, while the latter provides a striking contrast of white fossil brachiopods against a black background. Oxidized limestone, brownish in variegated flecks and patches, due to the introduction of iron and magnesium, was used as ornamental marble. Co. Cork's red varieties were in great demand for decorative work, the most richly coloured coming from Little Island. With its flowing lines and veins, it was often used for columns and panelling, as in St Finbarr's cathedral, Cork. The most famous is the unique green variety of Connemara. Mineralogically unsuitable for outdoor use, it is much sought after for indoor ornamental work. Sent all over the world, in ornaments and jewellery, countless pieces have been purchased by tourists as keepsakes or gifts. There are many variations in texture and colour such as 'Irish Green', yellow-green stones from Ballynahinch, and the tinted and striped masses from Lissoughter. Irish marbles were used extensively in the decorative work of public buildings, notably the *National Library and Museum. PC

march law, a set of compromises arrived at in the border areas hovering between Anglo-Irish colonization and native Irish rule, particularly from the later 13th century, when the Anglo-Irish administration had been weakened by Edward I's drainage of resources from Ireland to support his Scottish campaigns. Since the two kinds of area were intermingled to a great degree (e.g. on the edge of the Wicklow Mountains, which had been largely left to the native Irish), march law is found scattered widely. In substance it consists of the acceptance by the Anglo-Irish of aspects of Irish law when there was no practical alternative. The colonial administration was often powerless to recover cattle driven off by Gaelic Irish cattle raids or Anglo-Irish felons. The alternative was to grant a licence to those persons thus robbed to enter negotiations with the thieves. In the same way, Irish felons from the marches or border areas, whose crimes would under English law be punished by hanging, were increasingly permitted to settle, when caught, by paying a fine or ransom. There is evidence for Irish law seeping into family law both in the law of succession, for example in the case of the Rochfort family in 1299, and in the case of individuals involved in crime and imprisoned by their families. GMacN

Marcus Ward & Company (*c.*1840–1899), Belfast *printing, stationery, and bookbinding firm. Its contract to print Vere Foster's copybooks for use in *schools contributed much to its early success. Later it specialized in chromo-lithography. VK

Maria Duce, a conservative Catholic movement founded in 1942 by Fr. Denis Fahey of the Holy Ghost Fathers (1883–1954), professor at the Spiritan Seminary, Dublin. It published a journal called *Fiat*. Initially inspired by Catholic social teaching, which it interpreted in a fundamentalist fashion, it was rabidly anti-communist and spearheaded a campaign to amend article 44 of the 1937 *constitution to recognize the unique truth of the Catholic church's teaching. Although Archbishop *McQuaid of Dublin had been Fahey's pupil and was sympathetic to the aims of the movement, he was unenthusiastic about its methods and nomenclature. When Fahey died he withdrew support. The movement survived until the 1960s as An Fhírinne (the Truth). TO'C

Marisco, Geoffrey de (d. 1245), *justiciar of Ireland 1215–21, 1226–8, 1230–2. A member of a Somerset family and nephew of Archbishop *Cumin, he held Adare in Limerick and Killorglin in Kerry. In 1210 he accompanied King *John against Hugh de *Lacy. He was appointed justiciar in the summer of 1215 but was accused of financial irregularities and resigned in October 1221. In 1224 he fought against Hugh de Lacy and in June 1226 was reappointed justiciar and built castles at Rindown and Ballyleague (Roscommon) on the Shannon. He supported Richard *Marshal in 1234 and was jailed for a time. In 1235 he was excommunicated by the bishop of Limerick for keeping church land. In 1238 he was suspected of involvement in an assassination attempt on Henry III. He fled to Scotland but was forced to leave by Alexander II in 1244 and died in France in 1245. BGCS

Markievicz, Constance Gore-Booth, Countess (1868–1927), a leader of the *rising of 1916 and one of the most romanticized political figures of the early 20th century. The daughter of a landed Sligo family who had separated amicably from her Polish husband Casimir Markievicz, she became involved initially in *Inghinidhe na hÉireann. Later she worked closely with James *Connolly, ran a soup kitchen in *Liberty Hall during the *Dublin lockout of 1913, set up the Fianna as a male youth organization for the *Irish Volunteers in 1909, and took part in the 1916 rising as commandant in the *Irish Citizen Army. Released from prison in 1917, she was honorary president of the *Irish Women Workers' Union. She was the first woman ever elected to the House of Commons in 1918, but as a member of *Sinn Féin did not take her seat, serving instead as minister of labour in the first *Dáil. Like most women active in politics she opposed the *Anglo-Irish treaty, and later joined *Fianna Fáil. She died in a public ward of a Dublin hospital, and the working-class people of Dublin lined the streets for her funeral. CC

marriage. The institution of marriage followed several traditions in medieval Ireland which reflected the composite nature of the population: a native tradition evident from early Christian times which was strong enough to resist radical change in the face of the *12th-century church reform, and an Anglo-Irish tradition reflecting the influence of English common law and *canon law introduced by the coming of *Anglo-Norman conquest and settlement. In Gaelic-Irish law (*brehon law) ten unions were recognized in early Christian times, all of which were formal contracts, varying in the status of the persons concerned and in the contribution both parties brought to the coupling. The strongest marital ties were with the first wife (*cétmuinter*), but because of the recognition of secondary wives, who were in many cases concubines, polygyny was a feature of pre-Norman Ireland. Polygynous tendencies decreased, probably under church pressure, but this did not create the monogamous lifelong marital pattern advocated by the church.

In Gaelic-Irish society consecutive marriages became a prominent feature, facilitated by the ready availability of *divorce. Women were subordinate to the leading male member of their family (a father, an uncle, a brother), which greatly diminished any personal choice in deciding a match. This was particularly the case among the nobility where marriage almost invariably accompanied a political settlement (alliance, the pacification of an enemy, submission). A woman in Gaelic-Irish society however, could achieve more influence through the acquisition of wealth. In a divorce settlement the woman withdrew what she brought into the marriage and received a share of the profits generated while within the union. Economic factors were also taken into consideration when forming a match. In both traditions the bride brought to her husband goods in the form of land or moveable wealth. In Gaelic-Irish custom the bride received a gift in return. Marriage was also contracted in exchange for goods, property, or services.

Depending on her social status the bride in Irish customary law had certain rights in relation to contract making and responsibilities within the domestic realm. As a result of ties to her family which remained throughout the course of the union she retained a certain degree of independence. In Anglo-Irish tradition the family of the bride relinquished all responsibility for the bride to the husband, with the property of the bride being transferred to her husband's estate. When the sole child left to inherit was a daughter, Gaelic-Irish custom encouraged the heiress to marry within her kin group in order to prevent the alienation of family land, as was advised in the Old Testament. This custom stood in direct opposition to the church's teachings on unions within specific degrees of consanguinity and affinity. Likewise intermarrying within the forbidden degrees among the Anglo-Irish was common, in particular amongst the nobility, where a limited number of families utilized intermarrying to consolidate power and wealth.

In accordance with canon law and common law the consent of both parties to a union was the sole mandatory requirement which constituted a legally binding marriage—preferably declared in the presence of witnesses and followed by a church ceremony. This eliminated the many difficulties which arose with the prevalence of *clandestine marriages. Cross-cultural marriages occurred, which were prohibited in legislation on the grounds of protecting the Anglo-Irish colony from degenerating through contact of this manner with the Gaelic-Irish (see KILKENNY, STATUTE OF). As a result of the growing influence the church brought to bear on social issues, the spread of common law which required legitimate children to inherit, and the increasing contact between the two traditions, the gap between Gaelic and Anglo-Irish marital practices in late medieval Ireland was slowly diminishing.

Marriage in early modern Ireland, although theoretically subject to the restrictions imposed by *canon law, and from the 1530s to renewed secular legislation, was still regarded by many as a private contract between individuals, and clandestine marriages remained common. The Council of *Trent's *Tametsi* decree (1563), invalidating marriages not celebrated by the couple's bishop or parish priest, or a clergyman authorized by them, was not implemented in early modern Ireland because it complicated marriages between Catholics and Protestants, which were normally celebrated without the involvement of Catholic clergy.

The canon law on consanguinity, which excluded close relatives as potential marriage partners, had significant social implications in what were still small-scale societies in which marriage was often a means of strengthening existing ties of kinship. Evidence from 15th-century papal letters shows steady demand for dispensations from both Gaelic and Anglo-Irish applicants. Many requests were from cohabiting couples with children, indicating that dispensations were sought to regularize pre-existing marriages. Second and third marriages were common in a society where life expectancy at birth was 28 for males and 34 for females. Second or subsequent marriages while a partner was still alive were not unusual. While the church imposed impediments on marriage if one party had a living spouse, evidence of aristocratic marriages among the Gaelic community in 16th-century Ireland suggests an ongoing tension between canon law and social and political realities. Marriage practices which did not find sanction in canon law continued to be socially and politically acceptable in Gaelic Ireland down to the end of the 16th century. Women classified as concubines under canon law were accorded the same status as wives within Gaelic society, and their children were not deprived of rights of inheritance. On the other hand, the abandonment of wives without recourse to divorce or annulment left women vulnerable, and such cases were sometimes appealed to the ecclesiastical courts.

The extension of English common law throughout Ireland in the early modern period gradually influenced concepts of marriage and legitimacy. In particular, there was a growing concern among those who owned property, and who wished to ensure valid title to land under the common law system of inheritance, that marriages could be shown to have been legally contracted.

Choice of marriage partner was influenced by a range of social and political considerations. Among the elite, marriage contracts were most likely to be negotiated with political allies. The 1537 legislation, which included a restatement of the medieval prohibition on intermarriage between individuals of Anglo-Irish and Gaelic origin, in an attempt to protect the *Pale, had scant impact. The level of intermarriage between Gaelic Irish and *Old English families varied from one region to another, and was determined more by the availability of partners of appropriate social status than by concerns over ethnicity. By the 17th century the level of intermarriage was such that traditional ethnic distinctions had become irrelevant. In a period of religious and cultural change, there is plentiful evidence, too, of a divergence of religious practices between the partners to a marriage.

Marriage across social groups was rare, and little evidence survives about the marriages of the poorer classes. In regions where land was held on annual tenures reallocated in May, this was also the matchmaking season when marriages of young couples of all social levels might be arranged. Marriage was an economic as well as a social contract. The amount of money, land, or other property to be brought to the marriage was agreed in advance.

Older historical accounts, commencing with Connell's classic study of 1950, suggested that the 18th and 19th centuries saw dramatic shifts in attitudes and behaviour. From the mid-18th century, it was argued, age at marriage fell dramatically as the growth of labour-intensive tillage farming, subdivision of holdings, and dependence on the potato liberated young couples from economic and family restraints. After the disaster of the *Great Famine, on the other hand, an obsessive concern with security, and with the preservation and extension of the family holding, led to a new pattern of late and often arranged marriages. Modern research has played down these suggested discontinuities. Such evidence as is available indicates that in the mid-17th century the average age at first marriage was already relatively low (22–3 for women, 27–8 for men). The average age in the late 18th and early 19th centuries was probably not very different: contemporary accounts of widespread teenage marriages reflect growing concern at the sharp rise in *population and the increase in poverty that had accompanied it, rather than reliable observation. It is also clear that long before the Famine arranged marriages, negotiated between the families of the prospective partners on the basis of the assets each would bring with them, were common among graziers and farmers.

By the 1830s there are signs that marriages were becoming fewer and later, as falling agricultural prices and pressure of numbers reduced economic opportunity: in this as in other respects the Famine accelerated rather than initiated change. The increasing prominence of the arranged marriage or 'match' in post-Famine Ireland, similarly, may be evidence less of a change in behaviour than of the growing dominance in a smaller population of the farming class, among whom matchmaking was already well established. That said, the pattern of marriage that now took shape was on the margins of European experience. By the First World War the average age of marriage had risen to 33 for men and 28 for women, while more than a quarter of both men and women over 45 were still, and probably permanently, unmarried.

It is impossible to generalize about the nature of the marital relationships that resulted from this demographic pattern. From the late 18th century the new idea of the 'companionate' marriage, of mutual inclination and constant negotiation, challenged the older idea of the authoritarian husband and the submissive wife. Folklore, song, and story give us to understand that pleasurable wooing followed by lifelong support and co-operation was the popular ideal; mercenary 'matches' were deplored. In practice, the everyday companionship of some husbands and wives, and the tyranny of one spouse (male or female) over another, both existed at all social levels.

For all but the very wealthy, the marital state involved hard work: making a living, and maintaining life from day to day, to say nothing of reproduction and childcare. Even with separate spheres of work for husband and wife, burdens could be eased if the couple 'agreed'. The despised 'matches' often worked out if the two people got on well together. Emotional power reinforced economic power and vice versa; the younger wife ruled by a much older husband often went on to enjoy a vigorous and powerful widowhood administering her property and the lives of her offspring. In the 1940s and 1950s government commissions, churches, and other organizations concerned at population decline identified these powerful widows as serious obstacles to marriage among farmers and property owners.

By this time, however, patterns of marriage were already beginning to change. The idea that the marital home should be inhabited solely by the couple and their children, without permanently resident parents or adult siblings, had begun to permeate all social classes. The popularity of female *emigration, the rise in opportunities for (single) women's white-collar work, and external cultural influences combined to undermine the practice of matchmaking. Education, skills, and the woman's own savings took the place of the dowry that would previously have been demanded. From the late 1950s the average age of marriage began to fall. There was less generational discontinuity in the marriage practices of the propertyless and wage earners. But for them too the introduction in both jurisdictions of supports like family allowances, better housing, and health and educational benefits played their part in encouraging earlier marriage.

Connell, K. H., *The Population of Ireland 1750–1845* (1950)
Cosgrove, Art (ed.), *Marriage in Ireland* (1985)
Jackson, Donald, *Intermarriage in Ireland, 1550–1650* (1970)
O'Dowd, M., and Wichert, S. (eds.), *Chattel, Servant or Citizen: Women's Status in Church, State and Society* (1995)
Simms, Katharine, 'The Legal Position of Irish Women in the Later Middle Ages', *Irish Jurist*, 10 (1975)

BNC/BC/SC/CC

Marshal family, earls of Pembroke and lords of Leinster, during the first half of the 13th century the most powerful noble house in Britain and Ireland, and a crucial link between the two islands. William *Marshal I (d. 1219) rose through royal favour, which in 1189 enabled him to marry Isabel de Clare, *Strongbow's daughter and heiress. From 1207 he and then his eldest son *William II (d. 1231) spent considerable periods in Ireland, partly because of the loss of their Norman estates and the undermining of their position in Wales after 1212 by Llywelyn the Great. They made grants in Leinster to members of their circle, including John Marshal, William I's bastard nephew, whose descendants held the office of marshal of Ireland; promoted the towns of *Kilkenny and New Ross; endowed the abbeys of Tintern and Graiguenamanagh (Duiske); acquired royal charters clarifying their *liberty rights in Leinster; and organized the administration of Leinster around their castles of Carlow, Wexford, Kilkenny, Kildare, and Dunamase. William II had no children, and was succeeded in turn by his four childless brothers: *Richard (d. 1234), Gilbert (d. 1241), Walter (d. 1245), and Anselm (d. 1245). In 1247 the Marshal lordships underwent the first of several partitions between the heirs of William I's five daughters. This increased the number of English noble houses with Irish interests, bringing Kilkenny to the *Clare earls of Gloucester, Carlow to the Bigod earls of Norfolk, Wexford to the *Valences, and Kildare to the *Vescys. But the successive partitions ultimately weakened the lordship of Leinster. RFF

Marshal, Richard (d. 1234), earl of Pembroke and lord of Leinster. Marshal was fatally wounded on the *Curragh, where he and his men had been confronted by Maurice *FitzGerald, the *justiciar of Ireland, and other lords, probably on Henry III's orders. Marshal, who inherited his lands in 1231, had quarrelled with Henry and withdrawn to Ireland after a conflict in the west country and Wales during 1233. His death provoked opposition to both king and justiciar. RFF

Marshal, William I (*c.*1147–1219), lord of Strigoil, earl of Pembroke, and lord of Leinster. Born in either Wiltshire or Berkshire, he was sent to Normandy to be fostered in 1160 and was knighted there in 1167. In 1168 he entered the household of Queen Eleanor and in 1170 moved to that of Henry, son of *Henry II. He knighted the young Henry in 1173, supported him against his father, and was with him when he died in 1183. William then travelled to the Holy Land and joined the household of Henry II when he returned. He supported the king against his son Richard, but when Richard became king in 1189 he also employed Marshal. In the same year William married Isabel, the heiress of *Strongbow, thereby eventually acquiring Chepstow, Pembroke, and Leinster. When he fell foul of King *John for doing homage to King Philip of France for his Norman lands in 1205 he went to Ireland, but became embroiled with the king's justiciar, Meiler *fitz Henry. William supported John against his barons and was made regent of England in 1217. He died in 1219. At the time he was under sentence of excommunication by the bishop of Ferns. BGCS

Marshal, William II (1190–1231), *justiciar of Ireland 1224–6. His father William *Marshal I gave him as a hostage to King *John after doing homage to King Philip of France for his Norman lands in 1205. He opposed John and his father during the civil war, and was excommunicated. He supported the invasion of England by Louis, son of Philip, and captured Worcester before changing sides. In 1220 and 1222 his Welsh lands were ravaged by Llywelyn ap Iorwerth of Gwynedd. In 1224, as justiciar, he subdued Hugh de *Lacy's rebellion in Ireland. He was removed in 1226 for opposing the treatment of Aodh O'Connor (Áed Ó Conchobair) in the run-up to the conquest of Connacht. He founded the *Dominican priory of the Holy Trinity in Kilkenny in about 1225 and began construction of the castles of Carlow and Ferns. He died in April 1231. His second wife Eleanor was Henry III's sister. BGCS

Marshall Plan (1948–52), officially the European Recovery Programme. Named after United States secretary of state George Marshall, it was intended to guard against communist gains by assisting the reconstruction of European economies. Ireland, which could claim neither war damage nor an imminent communist threat, received mainly loans rather than grants, which made a significant but limited contribution to capital investment and economic development.

Martello towers, round stone structures with emplacements for cannon, constructed round the British and Irish coasts between 1804 and 1812 to protect against possible French invasion (see REVOLUTIONARY AND NAPOLEONIC WARS).

martial law, the supersession of ordinary legal process by military law, including courts martial, in times of war or rebellion. Originally based on the government's inherent right to repel attack, its evolution into an instrument of policy, adopted in conditions short of full-scale military conflict, raised difficult constitutional issues.

Some 19th-century *Coercion Acts provided for trial by military courts. The provisions of the *Defence of the Realm Acts (DORA) and the *Restoration of Order in Ireland Act were also sometimes described as forms of martial law. However, martial law proper was introduced in Ireland on only three occasions during modern times: in March 1798, continuing until 1806, immediately after the *rising of 1916, and from 11 December 1920, when it was proclaimed in Cos. Cork, Tipperary, Limerick, and Kerry, with Clare, Kilkenny, Waterford and Wexford being added from 4 January 1921. Its employment in 1916 is generally seen as contributing substantially to the growth of disaffection; the courts martial that ordered the execution of the rebel leaders were, however, held under DORA. Its restriction to eight counties in 1920–1, and the failure to give the army control of the police or immunity from scrutiny by the courts, greatly weakened its effectiveness, while at the same time betraying continued official confusion as to its nature. By contrast the proceedings of military courts during the *Civil War, founded on a resolution of *Dáil Éireann, and upheld by the civil courts on the grounds that a state of war existed, came much closer to the classical theory of martial law.

See also SPECIAL COURTS.

Massereene. The viscountcy of Massereene, granted to Sir John *Clotworthy, passed under a special clause in the original grant to his son-in-law John Skeffington (d. 1695). Several subsequent heirs to the title were given the name Clotworthy. **Clotworthy Skeffington**, 5th viscount (d. 1757) was created earl of Massereene in 1756.

The 2nd earl, **Clotworthy Skeffington** (1743–1805), suffered from a mental instability reputedly caused by a fall from a horse. When imprudent financial speculations led to his imprisonment for debt in Paris in 1770, his mother, in an attempt to force him to place his affairs in reliable hands, refused to advance money for his release. He eventually escaped in 1789, with the aid of a Frenchwoman whom he subsequently married. He later formed a relationship with a servant in London, who had to be expensively bought off after his death.

On the death of the 4th earl (1816) the title passed to his daughter Harriet (d. 1831), who married Thomas Foster (*c.*1772–1843), a son of John *Foster, who subsequently took the name Skeffington. On the death of his mother in 1824 he became Viscount Ferrard, and the family were thereafter known as Viscounts Massereene and Ferrard.

mass rocks. The idea of hunted priests illegally celebrating mass at remote open air sites is firmly lodged in popular folklore. Open air mass sites did exist, particularly in Ulster, up to the mid-19th century, but this reflected lack of resources rather than persecution. The 18th-century *penal laws did not prohibit ordinary parochial worship. 'Mass rock' traditions, if they have any historical basis, probably relate instead to the short-lived religious repression of the *Cromwellian era.

master of the rolls. The office developed out of the earlier office of keeper of the rolls of chancery, whose holder bore responsibility for safe custody of chancery records and was the most senior of the clerks of chancery. The new title was first used in the late 15th century and was in regular use by the second quarter of the 16th century. By then the master of the rolls was also playing a significant part in the functioning of chancery as an equity court, as one of its two judges, and was a trained common lawyer. During the last quarter of the 17th century and for much of the 18th century the office became a valuable sinecure whose duties were discharged by deputy. This practice ceased after 1801. During the 19th century the holders of the office included a number of distinguished lawyers. The master of the rolls became responsible for all Irish *public records in 1867 and his office survived the major reorganization of the Irish judiciary in 1877. The last master of the rolls retired in 1924 when a new system of courts was created under the Courts of Justice Act. PAB

Mather, Samuel (1626–71), *Congregationalist minister. Born in Lancashire, educated in America, and having preached in England and Scotland, Mather was employed in Dublin from 1653 as a government preacher. He was appointed a senior fellow of *Trinity College in 1654, and ordained in 1656. Suspended following the *Restoration, he established a meeting house in Dublin. His preaching, interrupted by a short spell of imprisonment in 1664–5, continued until his death. He is best remembered for his pamphlets, mainly published posthumously, written in defence of Protestant dissent. His more renowned brother Increase (1639–1723), later president of Harvard College (1684–1701), also briefly resided in Dublin in 1658, during which time he was admitted MA at Trinity College. NG

Mathew, prominent Catholic landed family in Co. Tipperary. **George Mathew** of Glamorgan (d. 1636) married Elizabeth, widow of Viscount Thurles. The protection of the duke of *Ormond, whose brother had been Lady Thurles's first husband, ensured that the family emerged from the *Restoration with its lands intact. Lady Thurles's second son **George Mathew** (d. 1689/90) subsequently managed Ormond's estates. In the first half of the 18th century the estate was divided between three branches of the family. The head of one of these, **George Mathew** (d. 1738), conformed to the Church of Ireland and was MP for Co. Tipperary in 1713, when he sat as a *Tory and supporter of the second duke of Ormond, and again in 1727–36. The other two branches remained Catholic. In 1760 the whole estate came into the hand of **Thomas Mathew** (d. 1777), who was returned as MP for Co. Tipperary in 1761. Although he had converted to the Church of Ireland in 1755, his election was perceived as a victory for a crypto-Catholic interest. The resulting increase in sectarian tension provides the background for the judicial murder of Nicholas *Sheehy and others during the *Whiteboy outbreak that followed shortly after. Thomas Mathew's son **Francis Mathew** (1744–1806) followed him as MP for Tipperary. In 1783 he became Baron Landaff of Thomastown, and in 1797 earl of Landaff.

Mathias, Revd B. W. (1772–1841), a leading figure in the *evangelical movement in the *Church of Ireland. Though for a time prevented by episcopal inhibition from preaching elsewhere in the diocese, he drew great congregations to the Bethesda chapel in Dublin. At Bethesda he and others founded the interdenominational *Hibernian Bible Society (1806), on whose behalf he travelled widely throughout the country, and he was a founder member of the Hibernian Church Missionary Society (1814) for evangelism overseas. KM

Maynooth, pardon of. During the *Kildare rebellion, the constable of the besieged castle of Maynooth, Christopher Paris, agreed to its betrayal for money. When the castle was overrun on 23 March 1535, the lord deputy, Sir William Skeffington, executed Paris and 25 other prisoners, as an example to other rebels. By reneging on the deal with Paris, Skeffington made 'the pardon of Maynooth' an ironic term for every subsequent breach of trust. HM

Maynooth, St Patrick's College, the principal seminary for the training of Irish Catholic priests, created by act of parliament (1795) at a time when the *French Revolution had caused the closure of many continental colleges, and the government was seeking to woo moderate Catholic support. Its lay college functioned until 1817, its theological school was declared a pontifical university in 1896, and its arts and science schools have constituted a recognized college of the *National University of Ireland since 1910.

Maynooth's early structure and discipline followed French models and the first generation of academic staff included refugees from the Revolution. By 1826 it had over 400 students and by 1853 half the priests serving in Ireland had been trained there. Many contemporary commentators claimed that the creation of Maynooth had led to the appearance of a new breed of priest, of humbler social origins and stronger political prejudices than those trained in the continental seminaries, but recent research suggests that any such contrast should not be overstated.

The bishops resented Maynooth's legal and financial independence, which seemed far too *Gallican to prelates like Paul *Cullen. He and his supporters worked tirelessly, and successfully, to increase episcopal control, taking advantage of the severing of Maynooth's links with the state at *disestablishment. By the end of the 19th century the college had assumed the architectural, organizational, and governmental form it would retain until the 1960s, when its recognized college and pontifical university were opened up to lay students. This strained old structures. While the recognized college coped as well as any university with increased student numbers and meagre resources, the pontifical university struggled to identify a properly contemporary theology while the seminary, with a reduced student body, sought to modernize its training and formation programmes. TO'C

Maynooth Grant, political controversy arising from the act of parliament (June 1845) increasing the state grant to *Maynooth College from £8,928 to £26,360, with additional funds for building. The proposal, like the *Charitable Bequests Act and the *Queen's Colleges, was part of *Peel's strategy of detaching moderate Catholics from the *repeal movement. But the measure provoked strong anti-Catholic protest, and contributed to the Conservative split that was to bring down Peel's government in June 1846.

Meagher, Thomas Francis (1823–67), *Young Irelander. The son of a merchant in Waterford, his attack on Daniel *O'Connell's peace resolutions in 1846 earned him the title 'Meagher of the Sword'. A member of the war council of the *Irish Confederation, he was *transported to Tasmania, but escaped in 1852. He became a journalist in New York, and commanded the pro-Union Irish Brigade during the *American Civil War. He was appointed temporary governor of Montana territory in 1866, but was drowned in the Missouri the following year. PHG

meat processing. With the growing transatlantic trade during the 18th century, the larger Irish ports (notably *Cork) built up a profitable provisions trade in barrelled beef and pork. This declined from the 1780s, but the slack was taken up by the growing needs of the British army and navy, which accounted for much of the new investment in meat processing from the 1770s, particularly during the French wars 1793–1815. Exports of beef and pork declined after the war. Exports of bacon and ham to Britain became significant from the 1820s, when bacon curing began to be organized on a factory basis. Materson's set up a factory in *Limerick, followed by Shaw's in 1831. In 1832 Lunham's established a factory in Cork. A number of other curers emerged at this time all over the country. During the second half of the 19th century bacon and ham exports more than trebled and the factory trade became more centralized in Limerick, Cork, *Waterford, and *Belfast. Methods of curing changed radically from the 1860s, when brine was pump injected into the meat, which improved taste. The industry became more highly capitalized and some of the larger firms began utilizing the best techniques available. The major Munster curers dominated the London trade. While Irish bacon was more highly rated in regard to taste, Danish competition became significant in the last decades of the 19th century; but with 20 bacon curing factories the Irish industry was still larger than the Danish at the turn of the century. AB

mechanics' institutes, mainly founded by middle-class radicals and philanthropists, and catering for the cult of self-improvement among skilled workers, provided libraries, reading rooms, and courses of lectures in the arts and sciences. A Belfast mechanics' institute was founded in 1825, only two years after the first such ventures in London and Glasgow, but by 1837 it had ceased to function. Other Irish institutes, in Carrick-on-Suir, Clonmel, Coleraine, Downpatrick, and Dundalk, likewise failed to achieve long-term success. After *c.*1850 mechanics' institutes everywhere gradually lost ground to libraries and more specialized institutions of adult education.

medical schools. A large number of different institutions have offered medical education in Ireland since 1600. Medicine was, in theory, taught at *Trinity College, Dublin, from at least the early 17th century, but not until 1711 was a purpose-built medical school opened and then students appear to have been few. Only with the appointment of Dr James Macartney (1770–1843) as a professor in 1813 did the Trinity College medical school become a major teaching establishment.

Dissatisfied with teaching at Trinity, Sir Patrick Dun (1642–1713), a noted Dublin physician, left money in his will to endow a professorship in the College of Physicians. This became three professorships in 1747, but not until the opening of Dun's hospital in 1816 was the college able to conduct adequate clinical teaching. In 1785 the newly established College of Surgeons appointed professors and instituted training in anatomy and surgery.

For most of the 19th century a variety of private medical schools also flourished in Dublin, operated by noted doctors. Such schools, particularly prior to the 1830s, offered a great deal of work to the large Dublin community of resurrection men or grave robbers.

Cork and Belfast also had private schools, but these were superseded in 1849 with the opening of medical schools in the new *Queen's Colleges. The *Catholic University had its own medical school. This was the Cecilia Street School, which flourished between 1855 and 1931, when it was absorbed by University College, Dublin.

ELM

medicine has been practised in Ireland for thousands of years, but the modern Irish medical system is essentially a product of the post-1700 period.

It is not easy to describe Irish medicine during the pre-Christian era reliably, as the main sources available are myths and sagas. The *Celtic pantheon of gods included a doctor or leech (*liagh*) called Dian Cecht, who cured by means of therapeutic herbs and magic. The Irish sagas refer to leeches on numerous occasions. In the most famous of the Ulster Cycle of sagas, the *Táin Bó Cuailnge, the hostile armies of Ulster and Connacht were both accompanied by leeches. Conchobar mac Nessae, king of Ulster, had his own personal leech, Fingin Faithliaig, who was in charge of the Ulster medical corps. But a leech's job had its peculiar dangers: one warrior in the Táin, informed by a succession of leeches that his wounds were mortal, killed each in turn before Fingin was able to pacify him.

Even for the medieval period (AD 500 to 1500) literary sources, such as *annals and *law tracts, are still major sources of information on Irish medicine. The Irish annals mention a variety of disorders, including plague, leprosy, *smallpox, *tuberculosis, ague (malaria), dysentery, pneumonia, gout, colic, palsy, erysipelas, paralysis, epilepsy, cancer, and flux (diarrhoea). Some of these diseases, like bubonic plague and smallpox, struck Ireland as major epidemics, creating widespread panic and disorder. Such outbreaks were seen as visitations of God, rather than as medical disasters, and from the 8th century the church sought to counter them by circulating holy relics through affected areas.

Doctors did, however, play a significant role in the treatment of wounds and injuries and of endemic diseases. Irish chieftains employed doctors as honoured members of their households. Often such doctors came from medical families, as medicine was largely a hereditary occupation. Leech books compiled over generations by medical families, such as the O'Hickeys, the O'Lees, and the O'Shiels, and mainly surviving from the late medieval period, are vital sources for the early history of Irish medicine. These show that Irish doctors were well aware of developments in European medicine, while they continued to practise their own treatments.

As important as leech books in understanding medicine in medieval Gaelic Ireland are legal tracts, setting out patients' rights and dictating the fees doctors could charge. Patients could be treated at home, in a doctor's house, or, in the case of a wound, in the house of the person who had inflicted the injury. The doctor's house had to be well ventilated and have access to a plentiful supply of fresh water. Medical fees varied according to the rank of the patient, but if the patient did not recover then the doctor could be fined.

In terms of treatments, early Irish doctors made extensive use of herbs, baths, cupping, bleeding, and sweating. Leech books often contain long lists of herbs, with descriptions of their medicinal properties and of the correct modes of preparing and administering them. Doctors carried cupping horns and probes intended to clear and clean wounds. Herbal baths and sweating houses were also employed extensively in cases of fever or skin diseases.

In the 16th and 17th centuries, with the decline of Gaelic power, Irish medicine underwent major changes. Increasing numbers of would-be doctors began to seek training in formal medical schools. Catholic students were largely to be found in medical schools attached to universities, such as Paris, Montpellier, Reims, Louvain, Padua, and Bologna, while Irish Protestants favoured Oxford, Cambridge, Leiden, and, from the early 18th century, Edinburgh. Not until the 19th century did Irish students patronize Irish *medical schools in any large numbers.

Irish doctors, whether trained in England or on the Continent, soon felt the need of a body to represent their interests and regulate the practice of medicine. In 1654 Dr John Stearne (1624–69) established a fraternity of physicians, which received royal charters in 1667 and 1692, transforming it into the present Royal College of Physicians in Ireland. The 1692 charter stipulated that no one could practise physic in Ireland who was not a licentiate or fellow of the college, and it gave the college power to supervise surgeons, apothecaries, and midwives (see CHILDBIRTH).

The surgeons and apothecaries had already been organized before the setting up of the College of Physicians. In 1577 the *Guild of Dublin Barber-Surgeons received a royal charter and in 1687 a further charter added apothecaries and wigmakers to the guild. But, by the 18th century, many surgeons were unhappy with their lowly status and with attempts by the physicians to control them. They therefore began to organize themselves into separate companies. This trend culminated with the granting of a royal charter to the Irish College of Surgeons in 1784.

The creation of the two colleges, which both sought to ensure that practitioners were adequately trained, helped raise the quality and status of Irish medicine. At the same time the establishment of voluntary and state *hospitals in Irish cities and towns during the 18th century gave doctors greatly increased opportunities to practise their profession.

By the early 19th century there was a recognized Irish school of medicine centred on Dublin, competing for prestige with the medical establishments of London and Edinburgh. The Irish school was particularly strong in fields like midwifery and anatomy. The *Rotunda hospital pioneered with regard to the former, while the College of Surgeons set high standards in the teaching of the latter. Large numbers of Irishmen served in the British army and navy: the advent of the Napoleonic wars brought a great demand for military and naval surgeons, which stimulated the teaching of anatomy and surgery in Dublin.

A number of Dublin surgeons made significant contributions to medicine during the early and mid-19th century. James Macartney (1770–1843) pioneered the teaching of pathology and revitalized the medical school at *Trinity College, Dublin; Abraham Colles (1773–1843) identified a common fracture of the wrist (Colles's fracture); Arthur Jacob (1790–1874), a pioneer of ophthalmology, described the neutral layer of the retina (Jacob's membrane); William Wallace (1791–1837) was the first to establish the contagious nature of secondary syphilis; Robert Adams (1793–1875) recognized the significance of disorders in cardiac rhythms; Francis Rynd (1801–61) gave the first hypodermic injection in 1844; and Sir William *Wilde was a pioneer in ear surgery.

Dublin-based physicians also made major contributions to medicine. John Cheyne (1777–1836) made important studies of the fever epidemic of 1817–19; Robert Graves (1796–1853) identified exophthalmic goitre (Graves's disease) and published an influential collection of clinical lectures in 1843; William Stokes (1804–78) wrote the first book in English on the stethoscope and described Cheyne–Stokes respiration (intermittent breathing which usually indicates the approach of death) and Stokes–Adams syndrome (a slowed pulse with fainting attacks); Sir Dominic *Corrigan (1802–80) first recognized the signs of incompetence in the aortic valves.

Yet, despite the considerable achievements of Irish medicine and the existence of a network of hospitals, infirmaries, and dispensaries throughout the country, far more people died of disease during the *Famine of the late 1840s than succumbed to hunger. Typhus, relapsing fever, dysentery, and smallpox reached epidemic proportions and were followed by a *cholera epidemic in 1848–9. A series of Fever Acts were passed and a Central Board of Health set up in 1847 charged with establishing fever hospitals throughout the country. But these efforts were to little avail. It has been estimated that there were 2,600 doctors in Ireland in the late 1840s, some 380 of whom died in the three years 1845–7, two-thirds of them succumbing to fever and dysentery.

A Medical Act of 1858 established a council which was responsible for compiling and policing a register of practitioners. Despite protests, women were excluded from the register and it was not until 1876 that an act was passed to remove restrictions on medical education based on sex. In 1877 the College of Physicians licensed its first woman practitioner, although women were not eligible for fellowships in the college until 1924. The College of Surgeons opened its medical school to women in 1885 and elected its first female fellow in 1893. The *Royal University agreed in principle to admit women students in 1882, but women did not begin studying medicine in Belfast until 1889, in Cork until 1892, and at Cecilia Street medical school in Dublin until 1896. Trinity College, Dublin, took even longer, not admitting women medical students until 1904.

The Famine had highlighted the inadequacies of public health in Ireland, but these inadequacies remained obvious well into the 20th century. In 1878 a major Public Health Act was passed. The act's comprehensive provisions relating to sanitation, water, food, housing, offensive trades, markets, and infectious diseases were, however, largely permissive. Many town councils and rural boards of guardians, who were charged with enforcing the act, were more concerned with keeping down the rates; and dispensary doctors, who were empowered under the act to control infectious diseases, were already underpaid and often overworked.

Poor living conditions, particularly in towns and cities, were at the root of Ireland's dismal public health record. In Dublin during the 1880s 17 per cent of infants died before reaching the age of 1 year, while in Belfast the figure was 15 per cent. (In the 1980s in Belfast only 1 per cent of infants died.) During the 1880s, similarly, 30 per cent of deaths in Belfast were due to infectious diseases, half being due to tuberculosis. The comparable figure in the 1980s was 0.5 percent.

In 1925 the Irish Free State appointed county medical officers, charged solely with promoting public health measures, and many of the provisions of the 1878 act were at last made compulsory. Even so tuberculosis, and maternal and infant mortality, remained alarmingly high throughout the 1930s and 1940s. The controversial Health Acts of 1947 and 1953, which were opposed by the medical profession and the Catholic church, who feared a state-controlled health service, finally introduced more effective disease prevention measures. In Northern Ireland a Public Health Act of 1946 transferred powers from boards of guardians to county and borough health authorities, which opened the way for more rigorous enforcement of public health regulations.

Barrington, R., *Health, Medicine and Politics in Ireland, 1900–70* (1987)

Fleetwood, J. F., *The History of Medicine in Ireland* (2nd edn., 1983)

Jones, G., and Malcolm, E. (eds.), *Medicine, Disease and the State in Ireland, 1650–1940* (1999)

ELM

megalithic tombs. The most visible remains of Ireland's *Neolithic communities are the megalithic tombs (from the Greek: *megas*, great; *lithos*, stone). These tombs are popularly referred to by a range of names including 'dolmen', 'giant's grave', and 'cromlech', but it is more correct to refer to them as 'megaliths' or 'megalithic tombs'. The tombs are associated with a communal burial rite, both cremation and inhumation being practised. Most tombs would have been covered by a mound of earth (barrow) or stone (cairn). There are four distinct tomb forms, each architecturally defined: court tomb, portal tomb, passage tomb, and wedge tomb.

The court tomb is defined by the semi-circular court-like area at the entrance to a gallery divided into several burial chambers. There are around 400 tombs, located mainly in the northern half of the country. In the dual court tomb at Audleystown, Co. Down, the remains of over 30 individuals were discovered together with pottery and flint tools.

Portal tombs are architecturally the simplest of the tomb types. They are defined by two tall portal stones at the entrance and a lower back stone that hold a massive roof stone, creating a single burial chamber. Nearly 200 portal tombs are known and these are also mainly distributed in the northern half of Ireland. The best known is that at Poulnabrone on the Burren in Co. Clare, where recent excavations revealed the remains of 20 individuals, including a newborn baby. An arrowhead was found embedded in the hip bone of an adult male.

Passage tombs are defined by a passage, lined by large stones (orthostats), leading to one or more burial chambers within a circular mound, often edged with more large stones. They are sometimes grouped into 'cemeteries' and their distribution is mainly in the north and east of Ireland. They have many parallels in western Britain, in Scotland (particularly the Orkneys), and in Brittany, Spain, and southern Scandinavia.

The most famous example is Newgrange, Co. Meath, where for a short period during the midwinter solstice, the rising sun shines through the roof box and down the passage to illuminate the burial chamber. A feature of passage tombs is the carvings or art (including arcs, spirals, circles, and lozenges) on some of the stones. The meaning and significance of this artwork is unclear.

Wedge tombs, of which there are around 500, represent the largest group of megaliths, and are mainly concentrated in the south and west of Ireland. They are wedge-shaped, being taller and wider at the entrance and becoming shorter and narrower towards the back of the tomb. One of the best known is Labbacallee, Co. Cork. The occurrence of these tombs in areas of copper ore outcrops has prompted some archaeologists to suggest they are associated with early metalworkers.

Neolithic burials are not only found in megalithic tombs, but have also been discovered on settlement sites, in caves, and in cists (stone-lined graves) known as Linkardstown tombs. The latter appear to be the focus for the interment of small numbers of individuals and single inhumed adult males.

Megalithic tombs, particularly the more elaborate forms such as Newgrange, illustrate not only great engineering skills, but also considerable organizational capabilities. The development of sophisticated tombs and burial types may reflect increasing social stratification and complexity in Neolithic society. SMcC

Mellifont, the first *Cistercian abbey in Ireland, and ultimately head of an affiliation of over 20 Irish Cistercian foundations. Founded in 1142 at the instigation of St *Malachy of Armagh, this essentially European foundation was part of the wider *12th-century reform of the Irish church which led to the eventual demise of traditional Irish *monasticism. In its first years the community was composed of a mixture of French and Irish monks trained at the mother house of Clairvaux. In its layout and planning the abbey demonstrated considerable French influence. The octagonal lavabo (*c.*1210), the chapter house (*c.*1220), and the late medieval gate house remain partly intact; the form of the other buildings can be seen from foundations revealed during excavation. RM

Mellifont, conspiracy of, contemporary term for the crisis among the Irish *Cistercians between 1216 and 1228. Following the foundation of Mellifont in 1142 the Cistercians expanded rapidly and numbered fourteen houses by 1170. The new *monasticism was radically different from earlier Irish forms and the order's general statutes indicate that key aspects of observance were soon ignored by the Irish monks. Non-attendance of Irish abbots at the annual chapter at Cîteaux also led to increasing isolation from the order. The foundation of ten Anglo-Norman houses between 1180 and 1222 created a rival filiation to Mellifont and introduced an element of racial tension.

Following complaints in 1216 the general chapter ordered a visitation of the Irish houses. The scale of the breakdown became apparent when the visitors were refused entry to Mellifont and were greeted by rioters at Jerpoint. The abbots of both monasteries were deposed but further efforts at reform in 1220–1 and 1226 were rebuffed. The abbots of Mellifont and five of her daughter houses were deposed in 1227 for opposing visitation. In 1228 Abbot Stephen of Lexington conducted a visitation and managed to restore some degree of order despite opposition; at Monasternenagh (Co. Limerick) the monastery was fortified against him and one of his assistants was wounded in an ambush organized by the prior of Inislounaght (Co. Tipperary). The Mellifont filiation was broken up and the houses placed under English, Welsh, and French mother houses. Where possible no Irish abbots were to be appointed for three years and Stephen personally supervised the election of Jocelyn of Bec as abbot of Mellifont. Most importantly, he ruled that no one was to be admitted to profession unless they could make confession in either French or Latin. Though his visitation solved some problems, tension remained high; in 1230 the Anglo-Norman abbot of Fermoy (Co. Cork) was reputedly murdered by his community. The Mellifont filiation was restored in 1274.

O'Dwyer, B. W., 'The Crisis in the Cistercian Monasteries in Ireland in the Early Thirteenth Century', *Analecta Cisterciensis*, 31/2 (1975)

Stalley, R., *The Cistercian Monasteries of Ireland* (1987)

CNÓC

Mellifont, treaty of (30–1 Mar. 1603), ending the *Nine Years War. *Moryson's account has Hugh *O'Neill making an unconditional surrender to *Mountjoy, unaware of the death of Queen Elizabeth. However, it has been shown that, while the queen's death was indeed kept secret, O'Neill's submission was the result of hard bargaining at *Tullaghoge and later Mellifont. O'Neill avoided confiscation, gaining a pardon and a new patent for his lands. He abandoned the O'Neill title but crucially retained control of *O'Cahan, his principal **uirrí*. His position was consolidated at a subsequent meeting with the English privy council. HM

Mellows, Liam (1892–1922), republican and socialist. Mellows was involved with the organization of *Fianna Éireann and the *Irish Volunteers. He fought in the *rising of 1916 and afterwards fled to the USA, where he aided de *Valera. He returned to Ireland in 1921 to become *IRA director of purchases. Leading the anti-treatyites in their occupation of the Four Courts, he was arrested after its fall (see IRISH CIVIL WAR). Influenced by James *Connolly's thinking, he called upon republicans to develop a more radical social programme to attract support. He was executed as a reprisal for the shooting of two Dáil deputies by Irregulars in December 1922. JA

memoranda rolls record details of *exchequer business, particularly those which might be needed for future reference. The entries relate to exchequer control over *sheriffs and other persons who were involved in the collection and expenditure of royal revenue locally, and include copies of letters sent and received by the exchequer, appointments of officials, details of cases heard in the exchequer affecting the king or exchequer officials, acknowledgments of debts, and items concerning different stages in the auditing of accounts. The memoranda rolls of the English exchequer contain detailed information relating to the audit of the Irish treasurers' accounts there. PhC

mendicity institutes. Concern about the extent of poverty in the early 19th century, particularly in urban areas, prompted the inhabitants of a number of towns (including Birr, Coleraine, *Derry, *Drogheda, *Dublin, Newry, Sligo, and *Waterford) to establish voluntary associations to relieve destitution and prevent the nuisance of street begging. Such associations, also known as mendicity institutes, were funded by subscriptions and donations, and managed by committees of subscribers. Relief was given in the form of money, food, and in some cases accommodation. Applicants were normally required to be resident in the town, but no restriction was made as to religion, age, or trade. A number of associations established asylums to house the destitute. Inmates were generally required to work and children sent out to school. Total numbers relieved were relatively small. The Drogheda asylum, for example, housed around 130 people, with provision also being made for 20 out-poor, while in Derry 82 people were supported in the asylum and a further 137 provided with daily rations of food. Women and children, together with the elderly, made up the majority of those relieved. All mendicity institutes suffered from lack of funds and many ceased to function following the passage of the *Poor Law Act in 1838. VC

Mercier Press (1944–), Cork publisher, founded by John M. Feehan. Initially it specialized in Catholic literature, but in the mid-1960s moved into paperback editions of Irish interest. VK

Mesolithic Ireland. The Mesolithic (Middle Stone Age) is the period defined by postglacial prefarming hunter-gatherers. Regional variants of their culture are found all over Europe and in Ireland they represent the earliest period of human settlement of the island. There is no conclusive evidence to indicate that an earlier Palaeolithic (Old Stone Age) colonization of Ireland occurred, although the possibility exists that this evidence may one day be discovered, particularly in Munster, where large areas of land remained ice free during the last Ice Age. It is therefore assumed that Mesolithic hunter-gatherers were the first people in Ireland.

As the ice melted and the climate became warmer plants and animals colonized Ireland, creating an environment and landscape very different to that which exists today. The rising sea levels drowned the landbridges that once existed to Britain, and finally, by 10,000 years ago, Ireland was isolated as an island. Isolation has resulted in a limited range of Irish flora and fauna and this affected the subsistence activities of the Mesolithic hunter-gatherers and the development of the Irish Mesolithic.

At first, meadows of grasses, meadowsweet, and docks covered the land, followed by shrubs such as juniper, willow, birch, and hazel. Later, pine, oak, ash, and elm trees spread to form a tall, dense forest canopy with hazel undergrowth and it was into this densely forested landscape that the first colonists arrived. The forest provided many food resources including fruits, nuts, berries, wild boar, and brown bear, together with smaller mammals and game birds. The rivers and the sea provided plentiful supplies of fish, birds, sea mammals, and shellfish. Contrary to belief, red deer may not have existed in Ireland during this time as recent research indicates that the earliest red deer remains date to the *Neolithic period.

The earliest colonists arrived after isolation from Britain, by boat. The capabilities of a wooden dugout canoe would have been very limited on the open seas and it is assumed that skin-covered boats were used for such journeys, with dugouts being used only for travel closer to the shore, in the estuaries, and on the rivers and loughs. It is not entirely clear from where the first colonists came, but most were probably from different parts of western Britain and possibly from mainland Europe.

At Mount Sandel, on the eastern bank of the River Bann and near its upper tidal limits, archaeologists have excavated the remains of Ireland's earliest human settlement, radiocarbon dated to between 7000 and 6600 BC. Several circular huts, possibly four, each measuring approximately 20 feet in diameter with a central hearth, were found. These huts were not occupied continuously or contemporaneously, but instead the evidence suggests repetitive use of the site over a period of time. It is believed that not more than fifteen people could have occupied each hut. To the west of these huts an area of flintworking was found. 'Microliths' (from Latin 'small stone') were the dominant type of flint tool and included a range of different forms including scalene triangles, rods, and needle points. Microliths are known as composite tools as several were used together, for example in wooden handles for cutting or sawing, or in wooden shafts to create an arrow with multiple barbs. Other artefacts included flake and core axes, pointed implements, awls, and ochre-stained blades. Food remains were also recovered including the bones of wild pig and dog (the latter was probably used for the hunting of other animals). Extensive quantities of fish bones were also recovered with salmon, trout, and eels predominating. Amongst the bird bones were thrush, pigeon, red-throated diver, and the earliest known example of capercaillie. Traces of plant foods recovered include hazelnut shells, water-lily seeds, and a seed of apple/pear. These food remains suggest that the site was occupied for a substantial part of the year with salmon indicating possible early summer occupation and the young and foetal pig bones suggesting late winter or early spring activity, while the hazelnuts had to be collected during the autumn period. These early hunter-gatherers, therefore, appear to have led a settled lifestyle rather than a highly mobile one, but were still reliant on seasonal food resources.

After 6000 BC the character of the Irish Mesolithic changed dramatically. This is most notable in the stone technology where the method of manufacture changed and a range of new tools were produced. Microliths were no longer in use and appear to have been replaced by a leaf-shaped flake with trimming at the butt-end, commonly referred to as the 'Bann flake' because of the vast numbers that have been found in the Bann Valley. Why this change in stone technology occurred is unknown. It clearly reflects a change in hunting techniques with the possible demise of the bow, since it is unlikely that the relatively heavy 'Bann flake' would serve as an efficient arrowhead. It has been suggested that changing environmental conditions, possibly even the limited range of native mammals suitable for exploitation, may have prompted a change in subsistence activities and hunting strategies.

Late Mesolithic hunter-gatherers repeatedly visited the sheltered bay of Ferriter's Cove, on the Dingle Peninsula, in Co. Kerry, during the late summer/autumn and left behind traces of hearths, shell dumps (indicating shellfish exploitation), stakeholes, and pits. They made tools, including 'Bann flakes', picks, polished axes, borers, and notched pieces from a variety of raw materials such as flint, volcanic tuffs, rhyolites, and siltstones. This range of raw materials indicates that the later hunter-gatherers were not solely reliant on flint, but could exploit whatever raw materials were available. Uniquely, the remains of an adult, of unknown sex, but aged between 20 and 30 years, were recovered. Isotope analysis of the remains suggests that this individual survived on a diet of predominantly marine protein. This site has also raised important questions about the Mesolithic–Neolithic transition as it has produced the earliest dates for domesticated cattle in Ireland.

Woodman, P. C., 'Problems in the colonisation of Ireland', *Ulster Journal of Archaeology*, 49 (1986)

SMcC

metalwork. The period between *c.* AD 450 and *c.* AD 1200 marked the pinnacle of Irish fine metalworking. Metalwork objects were made under both ecclesiastical and secular patronage. Archaeological evidence suggests that metal workshops were attached to *monasteries (*Clonmacnoise) and royal sites (Clogher, Co. Tyrone), but also existed independently (Moynagh Lough, Co. Louth). The lack of inscriptions, particularly on earlier work, has led to difficulties in attaching specific dates to many pieces. Dating is often achieved by stylistic comparisons with other media such as *decorated manuscripts and stone carving.

Objects were seldom made entirely from precious metals. A common base for smaller pieces was cast or sheet bronze gilded or plated with a more precious metal. Bigger objects, such as reliquaries, often consisted of a wooden core with applied metal plaques.

Metalwork objects made up to *c.*650 are recognized by style and object type. Curvilinear patterns reminiscent of the *Celtic La Tène period are common, often set in red *champlevé* enamel or raised above a cut-away background. Objects typical of this period are 'latchet' cloak fasteners, penannular (broken-ring) brooches, small pins with hand-shaped terminals, and escutcheons (small decorative mounts). Colours of enamel other than red, and polychrome millefiori glass, appear to have been a post-*c*.650 innovation.

From the 7th century, increased contact with Anglo-Saxon Britain and continental Europe introduced new techniques and motifs to Irish metalwork. Gold filigree (fine soldered wire) and granules, knitted wire, stamped foils, and engraving were applied to enliven surfaces. Coloured glass studs with metal inlay, amber, and enamelling added a dramatic polychromatic effect. Zoomorphic motifs and Christian symbols were mixed with purely abstract design. The 'Tara' brooch (*c*.700) and Derrynaflan paten (8th century) incorporate most of the techniques typical of the period.

During the 9th and 10th centuries polychromatic insets were replaced by amber studs (the Derrynaflan chalice) and later by metal bosses. The arrival of the *Vikings led to an increase in the availability of silver, reflected in a number of cast silver penannular and kite-shaped brooches.

The 11th and 12th centuries saw the repair and creation of a number of important reliquaries. Several showed the influence of Viking motifs, probably introduced via Danish England, and a revival of the polychromatic effects of the 7th and 8th centuries. Some of the reliquaries made during this period, such as the cross of Cong, carry informative inscriptions.

With the *Anglo-Norman invasion came a change in the style of Irish fine metalwork. Silver and gold alloys replaced bronze as the principal material, and sparing use was made of semi-precious stones such as rock crystal. The small body of material, mainly liturgical, from the later period that has survived the melting pot shows the influence of English fashion as well as a gradual awareness of broader European trends. Examples include the de Burgo/O'Malley chalice (1494), in the National Museum, and the mitre and crozier of Bishop Cornelius O'Dea of Limerick (1418), in the Hunt Museum, Limerick. The latter, although made by an Irishman, Thomas O'Carryd, demonstrates a full and competent adoption of current European style.

From the end of the 12th century English goldsmiths were recorded in Dublin and by the 15th century smiths both native and foreign were working from other towns. In 1637 came the complete organization of a company of goldsmiths in Dublin, with the issue of a royal charter and a new assay mark.

Church plate, some domestic silverware, and civic regalia remain from the 17th century. However it was during the 18th century that Irish domestic silver craftsmanship reached its peak, following English styles quite closely, but at the same time developing localized characteristics. Refinements due to *Huguenot influence can also be seen in the work of the time. Silver dish rings, helmet-shaped cream jugs, and three-legged sugar bowls are considered to be peculiarly Irish. Centres of production thrived not only in Dublin but also in Cork and Limerick, and to a lesser extent in Galway, Kinsale, Youghal, and Waterford.

Following the Act of *Union there was a decline in native silver production due to competition from mass produced English imports.

Ryan, Michael, *Metal Craftsmanship in Early Ireland* (1993)

Youngs, Susan (ed.), *The Work of Angels: Masterpieces of Celtic Metalwork 6th–9th Centuries AD* (1989)

RM

Methodism. Originally a term of abuse applied to the so-called 'Holy Club' in Oxford in the 1730s, Methodism came to be used as a generic term for the system of religious belief and practice promoted by John and Charles *Wesley. It began as a religious movement within the established church and was usually characterized by *evangelical Arminian theology, itinerant and lay preaching, a cell structure of societies and classes, a connexional form of church government, and a disciplined commitment to holy living and social duty. Methodist influence in Ireland pre-dated Wesley's first visit in 1747, but its disciplined growth began in the 1750s. Although Methodism benefited from generational pulses of religious revivalism in 1784–6, 1799–1802, and 1819–21, growth was generally steady and unspectacular until it reached a peak of 44,314 members in 1844. Even allowing for the fact that Methodist membership is conventionally multiplied by three for a more realistic estimate of adherents, Methodism in Ireland never achieved success comparable with its growth in England, Wales, and the United States. Denuded by annual emigration, and largely confined to old Anglican settlements in south and west Ulster, Methodism never made much impression on the Presbyterian heartlands of Antrim and Down or, despite the extensive employment of Irish-speaking evangelists, on the Roman Catholic population of the south and west. It nevertheless acted as a catalyst for a much wider evangelical movement in 18th- and 19th-century Ireland and introduced into Irish society a new form of voluntaristic, associational, and non-credal religion. Irish Methodist migrants and missionaries also helped carry Methodism to the American colonies and many other parts of the world during its first century of international expansion.

Within Ireland, Methodism suffered a serious division in 1816 over the issue of separation from the *Church of Ireland. Primitive Methodists (not to be confused with English Primitive Methodism) chose to remain within the established church, but the two branches of Methodism were reunited in 1878. Since then Methodism has remained an influential (especially in the spheres of education and social action), but relatively minor, Protestant denomination with a membership concentrated in the north of the country. In the 20th century Methodism's distinctive emphasis on itinerant preaching and class meetings has been diluted, as has its conversionist zeal. Such developments have helped promote greater ecumenical co-operation with other churches without adding much to its popular appeal.

Hempton, D., *The Religion of the People: Methodism and Popular Religion c.1750–1900* (1996)

Jeffery, F., *Irish Methodism: An Historical Account of its Traditions, Theology and Influence* (1964)

DNH

middlemen, tenants who held large properties directly from *landlords on long leases (see LAND TENURE), and who in their turn sublet these to their own undertenants for shorter periods and at advanced rents. The difference between these aggregate rents and the fixed head rent paid to the landlord provided the middleman's income. Middlemen holding under the long leases and low rents offered by landlords in the depressed late 17th and early 18th centuries were able to benefit spectacularly from the rapid rise in land values after *c.*1750 by raising their own tenants' rents in line with changing market conditions, but were increasingly criticized for rack-renting. In fact, throughout the 18th century in dairying regions such as Kerry and Cork, many middlemen had played an important role in financing their undertenants' cattle buying. With the rise in agricultural values in the later eighteenth century, and the growth of a capitalized 'strong farmer' class, the importance of middlemen declined, as landlords increasingly let directly to occupying tenants, and their role as facilitators of agrarian investment was subsumed by *land agents. The *Great Famine completed the process by bankrupting those middlemen responsible for paying the poor rate on behalf of their own numerous impoverished smallholders. LJP

Mide, originally the territory of Clann Cholmáin, and subsequently part of the southern Uí Néill lordship. Later 'Mide' was used for the whole southern Uí Néill territory, the original kingdom being known as Iarthar Mide (west Meath, from which derives the name of the modern county). Later still Mide became the de *Lacy lordship of Meath.

Midgley, Harry (1892–1957), politician and trade unionist. Apprenticed in a Belfast shipyard in 1906, Midgley soon became involved with the emergent Independent Labour Party. After service in the *First World War he became a full-time union official. Having stood unsuccessfully in West Belfast as an anti-partitionist Labour candidate, he was instrumental in 1924 in forming the disparate labour groups in Northern Ireland into the *Northern Ireland Labour Party (NILP). Representing the Dock ward, Midgley was elected to Belfast city council in 1925, and in 1929 to the more powerful city corporation. Becoming chairman of the NILP in 1932, he gained a *Stormont seat in 1933. In 1937, disillusioned by the social conservatism of the *Irish Free State, and the growing influence of the Catholic church there, he stated that the NILP's future lay within the United Kingdom. The following year, largely deprived of Catholic electoral support, he lost his seat. He re-entered Stormont in 1941, as member for an East Belfast constituency. In 1942 Midgley split from the NILP over the issue of *partition and, forming the pro-Union *Commonwealth Labour Party, held cabinet office in the wartime Unionist administration (1943–5), before taking the Unionist whip in 1947. His career highlights the innate sectarianism of Northern Ireland politics, and the dominance of the constitutional issue. NG

Milesians, the Gaels. The term is derived from *Milesius*, a late Latinization of the name of Míl Espáine, whose sons according to **Lebor Gabála* led the Goidelic conquest of Ireland. The number of Míl Espáine's sons varies in different sources: the most important were Éber Donn, who died during the invasion; Amairgen, the judge and poet whose wisdom enabled the new settlers to take possession; Éremón, ancestor of the Uí Néill, and of the rulers of Leinster, Connacht, and Airgialla; and Éber Finn, ancestor of the *Eóganacht overkings of Munster. JPC

military intelligence, in the shape of the *army's intelligence directorate, has intermittently played an important role in Irish national affairs, while also serving the army's own operational needs. During the *Civil War the army assumed responsibility not only for intelligence regarding its armed opponents but also for monitoring the political activities of republican, revolutionary, and pro-British groups, and for counter-espionage. These functions were ceded to the Gárda *Special Branch in 1926, but army intelligence resumed counter-espionage work in 1938 to deal with German activities in Ireland directed against Britain. During the *Second World War army intelligence controlled telephone tapping, postal interception and censorship, and other forms of overt and covert state intrusion into citizens' affairs. In 1945 it lost most of its investigative functions, although it retained responsibility for counter-espionage. Army intelligence has since played only a limited role in internal security questions, while continuing to perform its conventional military intelligence functions, although an officer was involved in the *'arms crisis' which convulsed Irish politics in 1970. EO'H

military revolution, a thesis first proposed for Europe as a whole by Michael Roberts, and subsequently elaborated upon by Geoffrey Parker, suggesting that developments in warfare transformed early modern government and society. The effect on a peripheral region like Ireland was slow and patchy. Artillery was one reason for *Kildare dominance of early 16th-century Ireland. However, opponents of the state did not respond with expensive thick fortifications, but instead chose to pull down their *castles when the army approached. Similarly, with the Irish unable to mount long sieges, the state had no need to replace thin medieval town walls (see WALLED TOWNS). Hugh *O'Neill transformed traditional Irish tactics with trained units of shot and pike, but his victories remained large-scale ambushes rather than textbook pitched battles. Modern stone fortifications were built for external and internal security at Duncannon, near Waterford (1578–9), and later at Derry (1610s). The *Confederate War saw larger armies in action and naval power a factor. Limerick, Galway, Wexford, Dublin, and Belfast improved their defences. Thomas *Preston used modern siege methods at Duncannon, but the best example was *Ireton's circumvallation of Limerick. English control of Ireland had always required a peacetime standing *army—a feature of the military revolution not visible in England—and this saw the construction of the Royal hospital for army veterans at Kilmainham in Dublin (1684), before the similar establishment of Chelsea in London. The *Williamite War (1689–91) witnessed the completion of the military revolution in Ireland, with traditional Irish tactics becoming synonymous with *toryism. Ireland also played a key role in England's military revolution. The modernization that helped to secure the victory of the parliamentary army was partly financed by the subsequent *Cromwellian land settlement.

See also FIREARMS. HM

militia. The first Irish militia, a part-time military force composed exclusively of Protestants, was raised at the outbreak of war with France in 1666. Mainly sponsored by *Orrery, it was treated with suspicion by *Ormond, who feared subversion by religious and political radicals. This Protestant militia was disarmed following rebellions against *James II in England and Scotland (1685). Its weapons were subsequently distributed to a Catholic militia raised by *Tyrconnell.

A new Protestant militia was raised during the *Williamite War and given a statutory basis by an act of 1716 requiring all Protestant males aged between 16 and 60 to muster for four days each year. It was mobilized to repel possible invasion in 1739–40 and 1745, and formally arrayed in 1719 and 1756. In the second half of the century the state of the now moribund militia became an issue of political controversy, with government reluctance to accede to *patriot demands for the revival of what was seen as a citizen army providing the background to the rise of the *Volunteers.

A new Irish militia, a full-time force liable for service within the British Isles, was established in 1793. An initial system of recruiting by compulsory ballot provoked widespread and often violent resistance. The rapid substitution of voluntary recruitment permitted the raising by 1795 of over 12,000 soldiers, growing by 1800 to 25,000. Although most militia offices were Protestants, the rank and file were predominantly Catholic. During summer 1797 evidence of widespread penetration by *Defenders and *United Irishmen led to a series of courts martial and executions. In the event militia units deployed during the *insurrection of 1798 performed creditably against insurgents. Yet suspicion as to their reliability continued. After 1800 the militia was increasingly regarded as a feeder for the regular army, leaving peacekeeping and defence duties to regulars and the *yeomanry. From 1908 militia battalions, in Ireland as elsewhere, were absorbed into the regular army's special reserve.

millenarianism, a version of the Christian belief that history will end with the establishment of a 1,000-year reign of the kingdom of God on earth, to be established by means of a cataclysmic struggle between the forces of good and evil. Such beliefs, implying the imminent transformation of the world by direct supernatural intervention, were widespread among the common people of medieval and early modern Europe, particularly at times of social or political crisis. Their most notable appearance in Ireland was in the late 18th and early 19th centuries. While some Ulster Presbyterians found in the radicalism of the *United Irish movement a political outlook that matched their New Light religious views (see OLD LIGHT AND NEW

LIGHT), others were theological conservatives, for whom the *French Revolution was to be interpreted in millenarian terms, as the defeat of Antichrist in the form of the absolutist and popish Bourbon monarchy. The circulation among both Catholics and Protestants of political *prophecies added further to the sense of impending crisis in the years before the *insurrection of 1798. During 1822–4 the prophecies of *Pastorini, in which the Book of Revelation was interpreted as foretelling the violent destruction in 1825 of the forces of Protestantism, gave the Rockite movement in Munster and Leinster a tone of revolutionary excitement, and a sectarian edge, not seen in other *agrarian movements.

Ministers and Secretaries Act (1924), a cornerstone of the Irish administrative system. Its genesis lay in the conviction of the first generation of Irish officials that the machinery of government inherited from Britain was uncontrollable and inefficient. Their solution was to reduce the number of departments, from over 40 to just 11, and to enshrine in law the doctrine that each minister was a 'corporation sole', responsible for all the acts of his officials (other than in certain areas of tax and social welfare administration). The Devlin Report of 1969 was highly critical of this, claiming that it engendered overcentralization in government and meant that ministers and their top officials became mired in detail at the expense of Olympian consideration of long-term policy. Critics have so far been unable to formulate an alternative principle for national administration which would secure greater flexibility without diluting either political control or public accountability. EO'H

missions, in a domestic context, were courses of sermons and services to supplement ordinary parochial catechesis, given by specially trained teams of priests. Originating in the *Counter-Reformation, they became popular in Ireland from the 19th century. Organized at intervals of several years, they were designed to encourage confession, deepen devotion, and catechize. Confraternities were often set up to continue the mission's work in the longer term. Missions contributed greatly to the standardization of religious practice in 19th-century Ireland sometimes called the *devotional revolution, and, in mid-century, were often part of local offensives against the *Second Reformation. Since the 1960s missions have declined in both frequency and intensity. TO'C

Mitchel, John (1815–75), *Young Irelander. The son of a Unitarian minister, Mitchel was educated in Newry and at *Trinity College, Dublin. He practised as a solicitor at Banbridge, was attracted by the writings of the Young Irelanders, and joined the *Repeal Association in 1843. In 1845 he succeeded Thomas *Davis as political leader writer for the **Nation*. Deeply influenced by Thomas Carlyle and James Fintan *Lalor, and traumatized by his experience of the *Great Famine, Mitchel became an outspoken advocate of a peasant-led revolution to establish an independent Irish republic. Increasingly at odds with more socially conservative Young Irelanders, he resigned from the *Nation* in December 1847 and later, when his call for a rent and rates strike was rejected, from the *Irish Confederation. He began publishing the *United Irishman* specifically as an organ of revolution in February 1848. In May he was convicted of treason-felony by a packed jury and *transported. Escaping from Tasmania to America in 1853, Mitchel was involved in Irish-American politics and was a leading supporter of slavery and the southern cause during the *American Civil War. In 1865–6 he was the financial agent of the *Fenian Brotherhood in Paris, but he disapproved of that movement's leadership and subsequently criticized it. In 1875 he returned to Ireland and, although disqualified as an undischarged felon, was elected MP for Co. Tipperary shortly before his death. His *Jail Journal* (1854) and other writings had an immense impact on subsequent nationalist thinking. PHG

model schools, founded by the commissioners for *national schools as the basis of their *teacher-training programme. Male and female model schools in Dublin, the central training institutions, were opened in 1834. By mid-century there were 25 district model schools, each making residential provision for the candidate teachers during their six-month training period. The schools were vested in the commissioners and under their direct control, which the Catholic authorities regarded as unsatisfactory, as they did the provision for religious education in the schools. In 1863 the clergy were ordered to withdraw Catholic pupils and in 1866 Catholics were forbidden to attend. A number of the model schools, chiefly attended by Protestant pupils and no longer having a training function, remained in operation until recent years. KM

modernism is an aesthetic movement related to the process of *modernization. It is a complex and troubled response to the reality of rapid change. The emergence of modernism is often located at the end of the 19th century and encompasses art, literature, and *architecture in particular. Modernism is internationalist in intent and challenges not only the past and tradition but the validity of the local and national. In Ireland, particularly after independence, modernism was seen as a corrosive influence on the attempt to create a national culture and was kept at bay by *censorship and rhetoric. The establishment of the Film Censorship Board (1923), the passing of the Censorship of Publications Act (1929), and the anti-jazz campaign of the 1920s were all examples of attempts to keep modern culture at bay. The main Irish contribution to modernist culture was in the field of literature. However, both James *Joyce, whose work *Ulysses* is a key text, and Samuel Beckett, who wrote in French, spent their adult life on the Continent. The effect of modernism on the visual arts was derivative and diluted, and it was not until the building of Michael Scott's Busarus in Dublin (1952) that the country received its first clearly modernist building. A general agreement with *Yeats's exhortation to 'stem the filthy tide' characterized the cultural reality of both parts of Ireland until the latter decades of the 20th century. JS

modernization. The discourse on modernization has been dominated by normative considerations. Modernization is seen as a process leading towards greater equality in the social, political, and cultural arenas, which distinguishes modern from traditional societies. This definition has its roots in the 19th century and is inseparable from the idea of progress. As a theory, it is itself part of the process it purports to describe, in that it legitimizes a particular path of change and delegitimizes others. In reality the path to modernity is neither unilinear nor unitary, and is characterized by blockages and 'pathological' developments such as nationalism.

In the traditional model of modernization class and class struggle play a central role, along with differentiation and rationalization, in the definition of the path to be followed. The central problem (most explicitly addressed in the debate on German development) is whether there is a normal road to modernity. The Irish case is structured by two factors: the blockage of class conflict by the national struggle and the ability of the *Catholic church, in the wake of the *Great Famine, partly to restore the pre-modern hegemony of religious institutions and ideology. The attitude of the Catholic church and the nationalist intelligentsia towards modernization was ambivalent, as was that of the northern *unionists. The latter embraced capitalist economic modernization, but insisted on denying civil liberties to Catholics, while the former embraced civil liberties while attempting to negate the class question. During the latter half of the 19th century the Catholic church consistently opposed and undermined the 'moral economy' of the Irish peasantry, and accepted *O'Connell's slogan, 'our religion from Rome, our politics from Ireland', fostering the rise of a Catholic and nationalist middle class dedicated to economic growth. This policy of fostering modernization in the socio-economic arena was balanced by a near hysterical opposition to the development of the cultural forms of modernity. While the rationalization of education, health, and welfare services, the promotion of economic growth, and the establishment of a modern class structure were promoted and supported by the Catholic church, the cultural forms of modernization, *modernism, were bitterly opposed. The displacement of pre-modern practices by a secular and cosmopolitan culture was countered by an increasing emphasis on religious and devotional practice.

With the establishment of the *Irish Free State, the modernizing impulse which had come from London—particularly in areas of social legislation and the general trend towards secularism—was halted, largely through the influence of the Catholic church. In Northern Ireland, the establishment of a local administration and parliament gave free rein to those intent on curtailing civil liberties for the minority. The blocked process of modernization remains a central dynamic of politics on both sides of the border. In the north the agenda is still dominated by the language of justice and equality. In the south social questions such as *contraception, *divorce, and *abortion have been to the fore. On both sides of the border the question of modernization is still fatally entangled with questions of ethnicity and religion. Indeed, it could be argued that the rhetoric of modernization, or anti-modernization, is often a verbal smoke screen for a continued obsession with the problems of ethnicity and nationality.

Fennell, Desmond, *Heresy: The Battle of Ideas in Modern Ireland* (1993)

Lee, J. J., *The Modernisation of Irish Society* (1973)

JS

Modus tenendi parliamentum, a document relating to the procedure for holding parliaments in Ireland, found in the possession of Christopher *Preston on his arrest in 1418 and of importance for what it may reveal of Anglo-Irish constitutional aspirations at that period. The document was traditionally seen as an adaptation for Ireland of an English original. A recent suggestion that it is the various English texts of a similar nature that are derivative of an Irish original has not found general acceptance. In 1692 Anthony Dopping, Church of Ireland bishop of Meath, published a text of the *Modus*, taken from a different manuscript, bequeathed to him by Sir William Domville, who had reported on the powers of the Irish parliament for the *convention of 1660. The timing of this publication can be related to the new concern with Irish constitutional rights reflected in the *sole right controversy of the same year.

Molesworth, Robert (1656–1725), Viscount Molesworth, Whig writer and politician. The son of an *adventurer who had received 2,500 acres in Co. Meath, he was MP for Dublin 1695–9 and for Swords (where he had an estate at Brackenstown) 1703–14. He also sat for various English constituencies, initially as a country Whig but forced by financial necessity into compromise with government. *An Account of Denmark as it Was in the Year 1692* (1694), written after a controversial diplomatic mission and describing the subversion of representative institutions by absolute monarchy and clerical power, established him as a leading *commonwealthman. The preface to the second edition (1721) of his translation of François Hotman's *Franco-Gallia* (1573) was reprinted in 1775 as *The Principles of a Real Whig*.

In the 1720s Molesworth was patron to a group of writers and intellectuals, mainly New Light Presbyterians (see OLD LIGHT AND NEW LIGHT), such as James Arbuckle (d. 1742), editor of the *Dublin Weekly Journal* (1725–7), John Smith (d. 1771), Irish publisher of leading works in the Commonwealth tradition, and Francis *Hutcheson. Some historians refer to a 'Molesworth circle', though the precise character of any such network remains unclear.

Molyneux, William (1656–98), scientist and political writer. Molyneux belonged to an English family that had come from Calais to Ireland in the 1570s. Educated at *Trinity College, Dublin, and the Middle Temple, he was joint surveyor-general and chief engineer, supervising civil and military construction projects during 1684–8. He resumed both posts after 1691, as well as becoming commissioner of army accounts and MP for Trinity College, Dublin, 1692–8. A founder of the *Dublin Philosophical Society and correspondent of John Locke, he published important works on optics and mathematics, but is best known for his *The *Case of Ireland . . . Stated* (1698). His brother **Thomas Molyneux** (1661–1733) was a noted doctor, antiquarian, and scientist. **Samuel Molyneux** (1689–1728), son of William, undertook diplomatic work for the Hanoverian court before 1714, was MP for Trinity College 1727–8, and also sat in the British parliament 1715–22 and 1726–8.

Monaghan, partition of (1590–1). In September 1590 Hugh Roe MacMahon was executed for breaking his *surrender and regrant agreement amid allegations of bribery, broken promises, and tyrannical government by *Fitzwilliam. The lordship was divided between seven chief lords and 287 freeholders, each holding from the crown by letters patent. Church lands were granted to government officials and cronies, most notably Marshal Henry *Bagenal, and a garrison was established at Monaghan town. Hugh *O'Neill was left aggrieved at the loss of income and influence over this neighbouring territory.

Alarm at this settlement was a major cause of the *Nine Years War. Gaelic lords, who continued traditional practices, rather than keep to surrender and regrant, faced execution for treason and the conversion of their lordships into a society of property holders great and small after the English model. The partition of Monaghan survived the subsequent war and was re-established in 1606.

HM

monasteries, Irish, in continental Europe. From the late 6th century Irishmen are associated with continental monasticism in many ways, and this presence is a celebrated theme in Irish history. Irish monks perceived themselves as living on an island in the ocean surrounding the inhabited world. Christianity had come from the centre, through the provinces, and finally out to them in the far west (cf. Luke 24: 47 as echoed in *Patrick and Muirchú). Thus there was an impulse to travel in towards that centre in which the great events they read about had taken place, and where books and learning were perceived to exist in a way they did not in Ireland. This was expressed religiously as the desire to pilgrimage for Christ, and act as teachers and missionaries. Travels by monks/teachers about Europe were not unusual, but those of the Irish were seen as distinctive as they were recognized as belonging to a nation that was part neither of the old Roman empire nor of the invading peoples. This strange status, of being not old and yet not new, seems to have given them certain advantages in relating to other cultures where Christianity was being absorbed from outside.

The regions with Irish links can be broken into three groups: (1) other Celtic-language areas such as Brittany; (2) north-east France, Switzerland, and northern Italy; and (3) some places further east in German lands, e.g. Salzburg. The second group of contacts is the most significant by far. These places are linked by the river routes, which, following maps from the period, we can view as arteries linking the centre of Europe with the ocean and its islands. And it was through these monasteries that the main contributions of the Irish to Latin Christianity were made.

Their level of involvement also varies. *Columbanus, the most famous, is atypical, in having travelled, preached to rulers, founded houses, and evolved a monastic pattern of his own. In contrast, others contributed indirectly to monastic life. Gall, for instance, was a hermit, and it was only after his death that his hermitage was chosen by others as the site for a monastery which they named after him (St Gallen). The second level of involvement, and quantitatively the most important, was the presence of groups of Irish monks in houses not specifically linked with Ireland. We find them as groups of teachers whose presence is usually known only through lists of names that have accidentally survived, or through their literary works. Thus we know the names of many teachers in the north-east of France from the period, we know that books written by them were in use in monasteries in the area, and we have evidence of their work in book production in places like Peronne (*Perrona Scottorum*). In a similar way we know of the presence of Irish monks elsewhere through texts copied in an Irish manner, the presence of glosses in Old Irish in books, or, more indirectly, theological topics handled in ways that were particularly popular among the Irish.

Lastly, there are places where there are traces of the Irish, but no evidence that there was an Irish group in the area. An individual name in a list, one glossed manuscript, or one reference to an Irishman has often been enough to 'establish' that the monastery was 'Irish', but continental monasteries often welcomed both Irish brothers and their ideas. It has often been assumed that Irish *monasticism was more extreme than that found among 'Benedictines'. However, the classic Benedictine monastery appeared only with Benedict of Aniane (d. 821). Before then there were various styles of monasticism, although Benedict of Nursia's *Rule* was steadily growing in prestige. The Irish monastic pattern was thus only one strand of monasticism. Several Irish monks might give a house a distinctive character; yet a single Irishman might still fit easily into a Frankish monastery. We should note that, while there were Irish missionaries throughout the period, it is only in a small number of cases, particularly in the eastern Carolingian empire, that this was their principal reason for being there.

Much writing on this topic has been flawed by romanticism. A balanced view will need a comprehensive list of Irish links with continental monasteries, along with a prosopography (even if it is just a name and a place) of Irish monks there. TO'L

monastic enclosures. During the *Early Medieval period the majority of monasteries (see MONASTICISM) were surrounded by defences consisting, like the contemporary *ringforts, of earthen banks and ditches or of massive stone walls. The enclosures are usually roughly circular and they may cover many acres, reflecting the importance of the monastery. The most important monasteries consisted of up to three concentric and widely spaced banks (or walls), and in these cases the central enclosure contained the church, graveyard, and *round tower, whereas the outer enclosures have produced evidence of domestic and industrial use. RW

monasticism has long been seen as dominating the Irish *church before the *12th-century reform. Since this view is now controversial, the received wisdom is presented first, followed by the recent revision.

The 5th-century missionary church was assumed to have been organized in territorial dioceses. However, the absence of towns and Roman administrative infrastructure supposedly rendered Ireland infertile ground for such a system. On the other hand it is maintained that monasticism, which gained popularity in the western church in the 6th century, was suited, by virtue of its ascetic spirituality, exclusivity, and organizational autonomy, to the Irish temperament and to a politically archaic and kin-dominated Irish society. Accordingly, by the 7th century, if not before, abbots controlled the Irish church, bishops were marginalized, and the diocese was superseded by the dispersed filiation or *paruchia* of monasteries. The peculiarly monastic nature of their church reputedly led Irish missionaries into conflict abroad. Around AD 600 *Columbanus fell foul of the Frankish bishops for resisting episcopal jurisdiction. It has also been inferred that rival episcopal and abbatial models of ecclesiastical government were at issue in the 7th-century *paschal controversy. Despite the triumph of the Easter computation approved by Rome, the prevalence of abbatial government and monastic *paruchiae* in the Irish church was unaffected. In the 8th century and during the *Viking age, Irish monasticism is portrayed as succumbing to secularization. Abbots were so in name alone and increasingly not even in name, as titles such as *airchinnech* (*erenach) and *comarbae* (*coarb) and their Latin synonyms became common in the *annals after the 8th century to designate heads of churches who were not usually in major orders and were simply lords of ecclesiastical assets and of *manaig* (literally 'monks'). These latter were really little more than lay *clients or vassals, who were married (though monogamous), held property and transmitted it to their heirs, and supplied food renders and labour services to their churches. The church settlements of this period have been characterized as monastic towns or proto-towns, though the existence of pre-Viking *urbanization in Ireland is disputed. The abuses attendant on secularization, including pluralism and hereditary office-holding, led to pressure for change in the 11th century. The 12th-century reform movement is represented as ending the peculiarity of the Irish church, establishing dioceses and a conventional episcopal hierarchy, combating secularization, and distinguishing between regular and secular clergy.

Recent scholarship questions much of this sequence of change, reaction, degeneration, and reform. The existence of a conventional diocesan system in the 5th century and its replacement during the 6th and earlier 7th centuries by an all-embracing monasticism and a system of dispersed filiations are seen as inferences drawn from much later sources, for there is virtually no demonstrably contemporary evidence for the 5th or 6th centuries. That a conflict between two systems of government, abbatial and episcopal, was any part of 7th-century controversies is also held to be no more than inference. Modern research would suggest that when the church emerges into the full light of day, as it does for the first time only in the 7th century, it presents rather an aspect of diversity within a single system, in which clerical and monastic functions and the administration of temporalities could be combined in various permutations. The bishop's importance would seem to have been greatly underestimated in the traditional account. He alone, apparently, epitomized the highest ecclesiastical status in Hiberno-Latin and vernacular *law. He supervised a clerical pastoral mission, the significance of which has but recently been realized. Moreover, there are indications that bishops exercised jurisdiction within territorially defined spheres (the basic connotation of *paruchia*) and that there was a nascent episcopal hierarchy. The leading clerics (bishops and priests) dwelt in church settlements, the assets and dependants of which were administered by an erenach or coarb, which function would appear to be other than a later secularization of true abbacy, since it is expressly recognized as early as the 7th century. Either or both clerical orders and administrative headship might be combined with the function of abbot of the strictly regular element (in all likelihood a minority of the community in larger ecclesiastical settlements), but all three roles were in principle separate.

If the model of diversity within a single system postulated by recent scholarship were accepted, this would necessitate revising the characterization of the pre-Norman Irish church as peculiarly monastic and regarding it instead as a local variant of the early medieval western church.

Etchingham, Colmán, †*Church Organisation in Ireland AD 650 to 1000* (1999)

Hughes, Kathleen, *The Church in Early Irish Society* (1966)

Sharpe, Richard, 'Some Problems Concerning the Organization of the Church in Early Medieval Ireland', *Peritia*, 3 (1984)

CE

monastic schools. Since so much early Irish material is monastery related, there is a tendency to see monastic learning as covering all we know of learning in the period. We should note that there was a definite academic agenda at work in western monasteries, from the outset, as places where men dedicated themselves to the praise of God and the pursuit of wisdom. As a place of wisdom, the monastery had to assist its monks to grow in the 'fear and knowledge of God' by understanding his 'mighty acts'. In this study, scripture had a central role. But this was accessed through language, so grammar was seen as the portico to wisdom—and to the extent that *Latin was, as in Ireland, a foreign language, its importance increased. In turn, the monks were expected to master the classical quadrivium as a tool of theological discovery in making the scriptures clearer to them.

This agenda presupposed that the monastery was a place were students came to learn, so teaching was a central activity. This accounts for the enormous amount of teaching materials which survives from these monasteries. It is against this background that we should view Irish monastic learning. Its apparently disparate products—*biblical exegesis, grammar, and computistics are the topics often listed as characteristically Irish—actually form an intellectual unity. Moreover, the forms that are found in Irish materials can be seen as linked to their intellectual agenda. Thus they provided many works on grammar intended for those for whom Latin was a second language. Likewise, their exegesis was usually reworkings of patristic materials in the forms of epitomes and collections (e.g. the Irish epitome of Augustine on Genesis, or Laidcenn's *Ecloga* of Gregory on Job). Similarly, they produced works in Latin and Irish where complex patristic discussions were turned into simple question-and-answer dialogues (e.g. the Old Irish treatise on the Psalms). Manuals and textbooks on specific topics—and several of the most interesting examples from the period before 800 come from Ireland (e.g. the pseudo-Isidorian *De ordine creaturarum*, one of the earliest works of formal systematic theology, *Adomnán's *De locis sanctis*, or the anonymous *De mirabilibus sacrae scripturae*)—reveal the desire for texts for the average student, as well as the belief that they were the followers of earlier 'illustrious writers'. It was this adherence to the monastic ideal as set out by Cassian and Cassiodorus, rather than isolated feats of intellectual genius, that gained Irish monks their medieval reputation for learning, and enabled them to take an important part in the intellectual build-up to the Carolingian renaissance. While the position of the monastery within the society changed, especially after the arrival of the *Vikings, this aspect of Irish monasticism continued, and this early pattern probably survived longer in Ireland (well into the 12th century) than elsewhere.

Hughes, K., *Early Christian Ireland: Introduction to the Sources* (1972)

O'Loughlin, T., *Celtic Theology: Humanity, World and God in Early Irish Writings* (2000)

TO'L

money, in the form of coins and banknotes, appeared in Irish society only gradually. Even when money sums are mentioned in historical records, it is not always wise to assume that the payments referred to were made in coin or its analogues.

The first coins found in Ireland are Roman. Single examples are probably modern losses, and others may represent non-monetary usage in the past. However, Roman hoards, concentrated on the north-east coast, seem to represent more than casual contact in the 2nd century AD, though the function of these silver denarii in a society where the primary indicator of value seems to have been gold is hard to guess.

By the 8th century Ireland existed in a world where coin use, based on the silver penny or denier, was common. The earliest deniers found in Ireland date from the reign of Offa, king of Mercia 757–96, and mark the beginning of a series of finds of Anglo-Saxon and, to a lesser extent, Carolingian pieces. From the late 9th century coin hoards appear with increasing frequency. Many were the result of incursions by *Vikings, among whom coins were still at this stage a source of bullion, rather than a token of exchange.

The start of Irish coinage proper can be dated to *c.*997, when pennies closely imitating an English issue were struck under Sitric, king of Dublin 989–1036. Hiberno-Norse issues had initial international acceptance, but later became primarily an internal currency. Some later issues may have had ecclesiastical links.

Following the *Anglo-Norman invasion the new rulers appear to have imposed their monetary as well as their political practices with remarkable speed. Coins were first struck in Dublin *c.*1185, with larger issues of mainly halfpennies with a few farthings from Dublin, Waterford, Kilkenny, and Limerick, as well as a separate issue from John de *Courcy at Carrickfergus and Downpatrick. From *c.*1207 new coins, mostly pennies, appear to have been used for collecting and transferring money rather than for local consumption. A fresh coinage, intended as a complete renewal of the circulating medium, was struck in Dublin *c.*1252–4, for a total of £43,000. By the second half of the 14th century, in response to political changes (see GAELIC RECOVERY) money had begun to devalue in weight and condition, and poor-quality foreign coin was tolerated. Enactments by the Irish parliament in 1460 probably at best legitimized the existing situation, and standards of production of Irish coin continued to deteriorate.

In the 16th century both Henry VIII and Elizabeth issued debased coin to raise revenue. Ireland was flooded with poor-quality coin, including issues demonetized in England; good coin, internationally negotiable and commanding a premium within Ireland, remained in the hands of a privileged few. Under James I this policy was reversed. Irish silver shillings and sixpences were minted, English sterling was given a one-third premium, and base coin was valued at slightly below bullion content.

From the middle of the 17th century foreign, mainly Spanish, silver, given legal tender at officially stated values from 1641, began to play a growing part in the Irish economy, reducing Irish and English coin to a small part of the circulating medium. *Petty and others identified the lack of specie as a major obstacle to economic development. The problem intensified from the 1690s, as rising silver prices inhibited the issue of small coin in Britain. Proposals for a copper issue in the 1720s were overwhelmed by political controversy (see WOOD'S HALFPENCE), but the issue of halfpennies from 1736 eased the situation. Despite the shortage of coin, most banknotes remained of high denominations. Outside Dublin, particularly in the north, trade depended instead on a sophisticated system of discounting bills and reliance on mutual obligation.

Since 1701 the official value of the Irish pound had been fixed by proclamation at £108 6*s.* 7*d.* to £100 (English) (13*d.* Irish to an English shilling), although in practice the rate given for money moving between the two kingdoms varied with economic conditions. In 1797 the *revolutionary war led to the suspension of gold payments in both kingdoms. Gold continued to circulate in

Ulster, but elsewhere banks flooded the market with low-value notes. By 1803–4 the amount of paper money in circulation had trebled, and the premium on Irish bills in London had risen to 20 per cent. Exchange rates stabilized from 1805, though with a further temporary depreciation following the end of the war. From 6 January 1826 the two currencies were amalgamated, although the Irish pound lingered on in accounts for many years.

Notions of a *dual economy in pre-*Famine Ireland, with geographically separate commercialized and subsistence sectors, have been largely abandoned. But the progress of monetarization, as opposed to commercialization, remained uneven, as was evident in the continued prevalence up to the 1840s of *cottier tenancies. In the second half of the 19th century rising bank deposits, growing numbers of shops and commercial travellers, and a widening range of consumer goods all testified to the extension of the money economy into even the most remote areas. By this time the Irish and British monetary systems were largely integrated, although minor regional differences, such as the prevalence (shared with Scotland but not England) of the £1 note, remained.

*Partition had little immediate effect. The first coins of independent Ireland were dated 1928, designed to a definite brief, in a very modern style. Although made in the Royal Mint, the shillings, florins (two-shilling pieces), and half-crowns were 750 pure silver, better than the 500 that the *First World War had forced on the United Kingdom. British coins continued to circulate, and those of the new state became fully acceptable in Northern Ireland by the late 1930s. The last silver issue was in 1943, replaced by cupro-nickel when coinage resumed in 1951. Decimalization followed the British pattern, but following the break with *sterling the opportunity was taken to use coins of different size and shape.

See also BANKING.

Seaby, P., and Purvey, F., *Coins and Tokens of Ireland* (1970)

RJH

money bill dispute (1753–6). In 1753 the Commons rejected a bill applying surplus revenue to the payment of the national debt, because the English privy council had inserted words suggesting that such appropriations required the king's consent. The ostensible issue was thus the parliamentary control of financial legislation asserted in the *sole right controversy of 1692 and consistently defended since. However, the rejection of the bill was organized as a show of strength by Henry *Boyle, to deflect the growing challenge to his dominance of the *Ponsonby family and Archbishop *Stone. Boyle was supported by the prime serjeant, Anthony Malone (1700–76), and the master of the rolls, Thomas Carter, both of whom combined office with a reputation for moderate *patriotism, and by the earl of *Kildare, the more erratic leader of a small parliamentary faction. When the *lord lieutenant, the duke of Dorset, dismissed Boyle and others, they appealed to public opinion as defenders of Irish interests against English encroachments. In 1755 Dorset's successor, the 4th duke of Devonshire, negotiated a settlement: Boyle and others were compensated or restored to office, the Ponsonbys gained the speakership of the Commons and a share of power, while Stone was excluded. This successful defiance of a lord lieutenant by the *undertakers who nominally served him, along with the mobilization of popular *patriotism for political purposes, has been seen as the beginning of a breakdown in relations between British government and the Irish Protestant elite that was to lead to the constitutional crisis of 1779–82 (see LEGISLATIVE INDEPENDENCE) and ultimately to the Act of *Union.

Montgomery, Henry (1788–1865), *Presbyterian liberal, *Arian, and non-subscriber. He combined the pastorate of Dunmurry, Co. Antrim, with the headmastership of the English school in the *Belfast Academical Institution, and was Henry *Cooke's main antagonist in the second *subscription controversy. A champion of *Catholic emancipation, Montgomery influenced *Peel in the legislation to secure members of the *Remonstrant Synod and other anti-trinitarians in the possession of their congregational properties—the Dissenters' Chapels Act of 1844. A conservative radical, he was disturbed in later life by the full-blown unitarianism of some of the younger non-subscribing Presbyterians.

RFGH

Montserrat is a small (39 square miles) island in the Lesser Antilles. Its interest to scholars of Ireland is that for a time it was the only colony in the first English empire to have been peopled mostly by individuals from Ireland and their descendants and to have been governed chiefly by persons of Irish origin. Thus, it serves as a laboratory study of how an Irish empire might have operated.

The island, which had no Amerindian inhabitants at the time of its colonization, was settled between 1632 and 1634: the exact date is uncertain. The earliest settlers, most of whom were Irish, came from three sources: direct migrants from Munster, refugees from various European ventures in the Caribbean, and, probably, Irish Catholic settlers who had been rejected by the

Virginia colony. Slightly later the numbers were augmented by Irish Catholics who had first settled on St Christopher, by considerable numbers of migrants from Munster, and by English and Scots, mostly indentured labourers. Later, a limited number of refugees from the *Cromwellian settlement may have found their way to the island. The importation of black slaves from Africa became significant in the 1660s.

The historical value of Montserrat is that its 17th- and 18th-century history reveals that the Irish and their descendants acted in no significant way differently, as imperialists, from the English and the Scots. They became brutal slave-owners and enemies of the Amerindians on neighbouring islands, whose extermination they encouraged.

Today, the tourist industry of Montserrat promotes the idea that Montserrat is a uniquely Irish location in the Caribbean and, among other things, encourages the myth of the Irish as 'nice' slave-holders. DHA

Moore, Henry (1751–1844), Wesleyan *Methodist preacher who collaborated with Thomas Coke on the first official *Life of Wesley* (1792) and later, when Wesley's private papers became available, published a two-volume *Life* of his own in 1824. Born in Drumcondra, near Dublin, the son of a farmer, Moore was converted in 1777 and entered the Methodist itinerancy in the same year. Though stationed first in Irish circuits, he spent the most important part of his career as a Methodist preacher in England. He became John Wesley's travelling companion and literary executor, and served twice, in 1804 and 1823, as president of the Methodist Conference. Unintentionally, he found himself at the centre of the most bitter conflict in Methodism after Wesley's death when he administered the sacrament at a chapel in Bristol in 1792, thereby provoking five years of debate within Methodism about its relationship with the Church of England, culminating in de facto separation in 1797. DNH

moral agent, an official appointed by various *evangelical *landlords, particularly in south Ulster, to oversee the moral and spiritual welfare of their tenantry. Notable examples included the Farnham and *Saunderson estates in Co. Cavan, and the Roden estate in Co. Down. A phenomenon of the *Second Reformation of the 1820s and after, moral agents attempted to enforce conformity to the biblically inspired codes of behaviour required by the landowner, and encouraged Catholic tenants to convert to Protestantism. Criticized by both the Catholic church and moderate Protestants, these attempts met with little long-term success, and had ended by the 1860s. LJP

Moran, David Patrick (1869–1936), Waterford-born journalist and editor, inventor of the phrase 'Irish Ireland'. He worked in London 1888–99, and joined the *Gaelic League in 1896. Moran first attracted attention through a series of articles in the *New Ireland Review* 1898–1900 (republished 1905 as *The Philosophy of Irish Ireland*), arguing that political nationalism was an invention of the *Protestant ascendancy which had led to Anglicization, snobbery, and economic decay. Instead Moran advocated cultural nationalism based on Catholic and Gaelic values. ('The Gael must be the element that absorbs.')

In 1900 he founded the Dublin weekly paper the *Leader*, which became an instant success through forceful writing and aggressive pursuit of Irish industrial advertisers. Contributors included dissident Munster Gaelic Leaguers and intellectuals associated with University College, Dublin. Moran excelled in vendettas and damaging nicknames, denouncing Protestants/unionists ('sourfaces'), the drink trade ('Bung'), W. B. *Yeats, and Arthur *Griffith. Linked to Catholic Action groups, he highlighted anti-Catholic discrimination by Protestant employers and denounced 'evil literature'. After several years' success the *Leader* went into a long slow decline but adapted sufficiently to outlive Moran: it survived until 1971.

Some commentators regard Moran as purely destructive; others see him as a 'reactionary modernizer'. He embodied some of the darker aspects of the Irish Ireland movement. PM

Moravians. Part episcopally organized ancient church, part revivalistic sect, and part interconfessional renewal movement, the Moravians played a pivotal role in the international 'Great Awakening' of the 18th century. Their roots in Ireland go back to the Moravian evangelist John *Cennick, who was instrumental in the formation of over 200 religious societies, mostly in Co. Antrim, in the 1740s and 1750s. Thereafter, Moravianism declined in importance despite, or possibly because of, the establishment of a Moravian model village called Gracehill at Ballykennedy. Moravians acquired a formidable reputation as educationalists and pietists, but they were never able to fulfil the evangelistic promise of their first decade in Ireland. DNH

'More Irish than the Irish themselves' (*Hiberniores Hibernis ipsis*), a phrase describing the *Gaelicization of the *Anglo-Norman settlers, apparently coined in its Latin form in 1803 by Francis *Plowden. Although not current in the Middle Ages, it echoes the rhetoric of legislation such as the 1366 Statute of *Kilkenny about the erosion of the English identity, and also the hostility of later commentators such as Edmund *Spenser and Sir John *Davies. Ironically, in the 19th century the cliché passed into the armoury of nationalist writers, including Thomas *Davis, who cited it approvingly as evidence of the convergence of the two traditions. RFF

Moriarty, David (1814–77), Catholic bishop of Kerry from 1856 (coadjutor 1854–6), having earlier served as vice-rector of the Irish College in Paris and rector of All Hallows, Dublin, where he was a firm advocate of the Sulpician system of seminary education. A unionist, he opposed *home rule and proclaimed that hell was not hot enough nor eternity long enough for the 'godless' *Fenian leadership. TO'C

Mormons, members of the church of Jesus Christ of Latter Day Saints, which has its origin in an American populist revolt against official religion in the 'burned over district' of upstate New York in the early 1830s. The first Mormon missionaries arrived in Britain in 1837 and in Ireland three years later. In terms of membership statistics the Mormons made a modest impression in the period 1840–55, then underwent a century of relative stagnation before experiencing a period of remarkable growth after 1950, when missionaries from the USA arrived in considerable numbers. The first purpose-built Mormon chapel in Ireland opened in Belfast in 1963, and in 1985, in a quaint ceremony at Loughbrickland, Co. Tyrone, where the first Irish convert had been baptized in 1840, Ireland was solemnly dedicated for the preaching of the Mormon gospel. DNH

Mortimer, a family immensely important in later medieval Ireland. By a series of marriages they had become by 1368 theoretical lords of almost half the country. They formed the chief link between the English and Anglo-Irish aristocracies, and often governed Ireland for the king. A Norman family who acquired Wigmore and other lands in the Welsh marches during the generations after 1066, their Irish connection began in 1247, when as one of the heirs of the *Marshals they gained lands in Laois. Their active involvement dates from 1308, when Roger *Mortimer, later 1st earl of March, became lord of Trim. After Roger's fall in 1330, the family suffered an eclipse until 1354. In 1368 his great-grandson Edmund *Mortimer, 3rd earl of March, married Philippa, daughter and heiress of Edward III's son *Lionel of Clarence and Elizabeth de Burgh (see BURKE (DE BURGH)), heiress of Ulster and Connacht. Edmund was lieutenant in 1379–81, and his brother Thomas Mortimer deputy in 1382–3. *Roger, the 4th earl, held the lieutenancy 1395–7 and 1397–8, his brother Edmund serving in his place during 1397. The line ended with *Edmund, the 5th earl, lieutenant in 1424–5. Edmund's sister carried the Mortimer inheritance, together with a claim to the throne through Lionel, to her son Richard, duke of *York, the father of Edward IV. With Edward's accession in 1461, Ulster, together with the Mortimers' other Irish estates and claims, reverted to the crown. RFF

Mortimer, Edmund (1351–81), 3rd earl of March and 6th earl of Ulster, pre-eminent in the 1370s because of his inheritance of the lordship of Meath and his claim to Ulster and Connacht through his wife, the heiress to *Lionel of Clarence and Elizabeth de Burgh. Mortimer combined the elements sought in many appointments of chief governor during a period of weak defence and financial crisis, having both private resources to supplement his stipend and a strong personal interest in pursuing an effective military campaign. First suggested as a suitable appointee in 1373, he arrived in Ireland as lieutenant in 1379 with a large military force. He achieved some success in Ulster, Connacht, and Meath, but unrest in Leinster and Munster drew him south in 1381. His sudden death at Cork in December 1381 prompted an extreme military crisis, leaving the lordship without effective leadership. Without his personal presence, the gains made in Ulster were soon lost. DBJ

Mortimer, Edmund (1391–1425), 5th earl of March and 8th earl of Ulster. Following the death of the 4th earl in 1398, another long minority further weakened the Mortimer interest in Ireland, limiting the chances of effective control of the inheritance in Ulster and Connacht as well as Meath. At the same time, Edmund Mortimer's position in England was of unusual political interest. Recognized by the childless *Richard II as heir presumptive, he was a potential focus for anti-Lancastrian feelings under Henry IV. His first military service was in France, but his Irish interests made it inevitable that he would be required to support the defence of the lordship and in 1423 he was appointed lieutenant for nine years. He arrived in Ireland in late 1424, and had achieved the submissions of *O'Byrne, *O'Neill, and *O'Donnell when in January 1425 he died at Trim of the plague. His estates passed to his nephew Richard, duke of *York. DBJ

Mortimer, Roger (d. 1330), 1st earl of March, lover of Queen Isabella, the wife of Edward II, and ruler of England during Edward III's minority (1327–30). He was closely associated with Ireland. Through marriage to the heiress of de *Geneville, he became lord of Trim in 1308, and visited Ireland before serving as governor in 1317–18 and 1319–20, during and after the *Bruce invasion. Although he was not in office when the Scots were defeated at *Faughart (Oct. 1318), he restored government control in the south. After a period of exile in France, he and Isabella returned in 1326 and deposed Edward II. They found difficulty in controlling Ireland; the creation of the earldoms of *Ormond (1328) and *Desmond (1329) was an attempt to win friends there. Before his overthrow by Edward III in 1330, Mortimer further expanded his Irish interests, and his links with Ireland made Edward initially suspicious of the Anglo-Irish lords. RFF

Mortimer, Roger (1374–98), 4th earl of March and 7th earl of Ulster. The earl's inheritance in Meath, Ulster, and Connacht gave him an inescapable role in Irish history. In 1382, aged 7, he served briefly as nominal lieutenant on the death of his father Edmund Mortimer, the 3rd earl. He spent his minority on his English and Welsh estates, and his interests in Ireland suffered accordingly. Appointed lieutenant in 1392, Mortimer came to Ireland in 1394 with *Richard II's expedition. Assisted by the king's presence, he achieved the submission of the Gaelic Irish of Ulster, but Richard delayed judgement on outstanding issues between Mortimer and *O'Neill. As lieutenant in Ireland after the expedition, Mortimer attacked O'Neill, apparently defying royal wishes. His momentum was soon lost as he faced reduced military resources, and the distraction of concern about Richard's policies in England. Richard replaced Mortimer in office and was already considering a second royal expedition when the earl was killed in 1398 in Leinster. DBJ

Moryson, Fynes (1566–1630), English travel writer, best known for his description of the Irish at the end of Elizabeth's reign. After an extended grand tour, he joined Lord Deputy *Mountjoy's entourage in Ireland as official historian, later becoming his private secretary. His travel memoirs, *An Itinerary* (1617), included a detailed account of Mountjoy's victory in the *Nine Years War from official papers and Moryson's own eye-witness memoranda. In this he inflated his patron's reputation and criticized preceding and succeeding regimes. With the exception of Irish whiskey, Moryson had nothing good to say about the country or its inhabitants. HM

Mother and Child controversy. In 1950–1 Noel *Browne, minister for health in the *interparty government, drew up proposals for free medical care for mothers and children under 16. Although Browne apparently believed that he had secured the acquiescence of the Catholic bishops, they denounced the scheme as contrary to the Catholic principle of subsidiary function, i.e. that the state should not intervene in cases where a lower organization, in this case the family, could provide what was needed. John A. *Costello, as *taoiseach, and Sean *MacBride, as Browne's party leader, joined in forcing Browne's resignation. Their action, accompanied by extravagant declarations of their obedience to church teaching, enshrined the episode as a demonstration of the political power of the Catholic church in independent Ireland. But it is also suggested that the bishops were themselves manipulated by the powerful Irish Medical Association, whose members were reluctant to lose fee-paying patients to a state service. In 1953 Browne's *Fianna Fáil successor, James *Ryan, successfully introduced a broadly similar scheme, but excluding the 15 per cent of families in the highest income bracket.

motor car history in Ireland mirrors that of most developed countries in the social, economic, and environmental changes it effected. Motor transport effectively replaced other forms of transport, notably the *railways, not least in the haulage sector. The car was the preserve of the well-off until the 1930s. Although traffic greatly increased, it remained behind that of most developed countries. This reflected Ireland's comparative economic backwardness in the first half of the 20th century. The smallish *population and comparatively short distances kept Ireland's roads still relatively uncrowded. There were 5,058 registered motor cars, buses, and lorries in 1911. By 1983 there were approximately 900,000 registered vehicles in the Republic. In the north, the figure had reached 558,000 by 1991.

Pollution from petrol fumes and the despoliation of the environment by multi-lane highways and roadside hoardings is also markedly less than elsewhere. This draws favourable comments from foreign visitors. Motor transport has made great inroads into the parochialism and sense of isolation of rural Ireland. Car ferries allow ordinary families to take touring holidays abroad. Other consequences have been the growth of new *suburbs and dormitory towns around Dublin, Belfast, and other cities, and more recently the proliferation of out-of-town shopping centres. PC

motor car manufacture and assembly. As early as 1897 a large-scale factory manufacturing cars, amongst other items, was proposed for Dublin by Joel C. Pennington, an American entrepreneur. The actual development of the industry in Ireland, however, was comparatively slow, though by 1904 numerous coachbuilders were manufacturing bodies for imported chassis. In that year the Chambers brothers of Co. Down produced their first vehicle, entirely manufactured in Ireland. Eventually trading as Chambers Motors Ltd., and having established a large factory in Belfast, they continued the production of 'all Irish', high-quality cars until 1929, when the company entered receivership. In 1917 Henry Ford had established a tractor factory at Cork. Between 1922 and 1928, and again from 1932, the manufacture of components and car assembly replaced tractor production. Small-scale production continues. These two ventures represent the most successful among a litany of projects that were otherwise uniformly disastrous. Since 1945 at least ten Irish companies have assembled cars from kits provided by foreign manufacturers, but none were ultimately profitable. In 1959 a plan to assemble cars for the American market in Co. Monaghan foundered after a mere eight machines were built. In 1982 the heavily subsidized De Lorean Car Company, based in Belfast, entered receivership after fewer than 10,000 cars were built in under two years' production. Even under *protectionism the small internal market and lack of raw materials fatally inhibited growth. In its absence the competition of large-scale manufacturers in Great Britain and elsewhere has been impossible to withstand. Car component manufacture remains important at a local level, however. NG

motor sport in Ireland has a comparatively long but chequered history. The first road race for cars in the United Kingdom was held in Leinster in 1903. There followed a period of inactivity. Between the wars regular road racing was encouraged both by Irish motor trade organizations and by governments, to boost car sales and tourism. The Irish Grand Prix was held in Phoenix Park 1929–31. After the war road racing resumed, but was ended following fatal accidents at the *Curragh in 1954 and Dundrod (Co. Antrim) in 1955. In Northern Ireland racing moved to former wartime airfields. From 1968 racing in the Republic centred on the purpose-built Mondello Park course, near Naas, Co. Kildare.

Hill-climbing is as old as road racing. A sport for aficionados, its major event is the Craigantlet climb, begun in 1925.

Organized rallying, first begun in 1928, now provides the country's only international standard motoring event, the Circuit of Ireland Rally.

Motorcycle racing began with locally organized 'runs'. The Motor Cycle Union of Ireland, founded in Dublin in 1902, became active in racing after the *First World War. Development was similar to that of car racing, though road circuits remain in use. NG

motte and bailey. These were the major type of earthwork *castle introduced into Ireland by the *Anglo-Normans at the end of the 12th century, just over a century after their use in the Norman conquest of England. The 'pudding-shaped' mound was called the motte and was usually constructed from the earth thrown up by the construction of a fosse (ditch) around it. Its flat top often contained a wooden tower or bretasche in the centre, with a wooden palisade encircling its edge. The bailey was usually attached to it by a wooden bridge, and was a lower, more extensive enclosure, often rectangular in shape, also surrounded by a fosse and an internal bank surmounted by a wooden palisade. Built both because of the speed with which they could be constructed and because of the ready availability of earth and wood, most of the 350 known examples are located along the eastern side of Ireland. Irish ones are generally smaller than European examples, with most mottes being less than 15 feet high and with very few surviving baileys. Many functioned as the centres of *manors, but by the start of the 13th century they were increasingly being replaced by stone castles. TB

Mountjoy, Charles Blount, Lord (1563–1606). Mountjoy claimed the victory in the *Nine Years War which his friend *Essex had signally failed to achieve. Arriving as lord deputy in 1600, he refused parleys and truces and adopted different tactics from his predecessors. He concentrated on reducing Leinster and south Ulster, leaving *Docwra in the north-west and George *Carew in Munster with virtually independent commands. In mid-1601 the Irish currency was debased to keep down the escalating costs of the war, though Mountjoy and most Irish officials objected. Inflation leapt 80 per cent in six months, damaging the economy and Mountjoy's attempt to root out army corruption. Critically he defeated the Irish at *Kinsale and forced the withdrawal of their Spanish allies. The cost of 25 garrisons in Ulster was crippling, but only in February 1603 did Queen Elizabeth I take up the fugitive Hugh *O'Neill's offer to submit. Mountjoy agreed the treaty of *Mellifont but the *revolt of the towns postponed his trip to court to claim the laurels as conqueror of Ireland from the new king, James I. James created him earl of Devonshire and appointed him lord lieutenant of Ireland. Mountjoy's governorship was chronicled by his secretary Fynes *Moryson. HM

Mountnorris, Francis Annesley, Lord (1585–1660), best known for his struggle with *Wentworth. Arriving in Ireland in 1606, he accumulated lands and offices, becoming secretary of state in 1618. He opposed Lord Deputy Falkland (1622–9), gaining control of the treasury and eventually engineering Falkland's recall. By adopting moderate views on the *Graces, he courted popularity.

Wentworth initially used Mountnorris, one of the symbols of *New English corruption, to make overtures to the Catholics and attack Richard *Boyle, a rival planter. When charges were brought against him in 1635, Mountnorris and his relatives launched a tirade of abuse against the lord deputy. Wentworth court-martialled Mountnorris (a military officer in his capacity as treasurer-at-wars) and condemned him to death for insulting his commanding officer. The English privy council then stripped him of his offices.

The English Long Parliament made Mountnorris's case a prime instance of Wentworth's arbitrary government. He succeeded a distant kinsman as Viscount Valentia (1643), and regained his secretaryship of state from Henry *Cromwell (1655). HM

Moylan, Sean (1887–1957). An *IRA leader in Co. Cork during the *Anglo-Irish War, and one of the more articulate and less militaristic opponents of the *Anglo-Irish treaty, Moylan was *Fianna Fáil Dáil deputy for Cork North 1932–57. As minister for lands he joined with *Lemass in an unsuccessful attempt in 1944 to challenge the policy of unconditional support for uneconomic small-scale farming.

Mulcahy, Richard (1886–1971). A Waterford-born Post Office employee, Mulcahy fought with Thomas Ashe in north Co. Dublin in the *rising of 1916. As chief of staff of the *Irish Volunteers from March 1918, he sought to impose central control on the developing *IRA campaign during the *Anglo-Irish War. Following the *Anglo-Irish treaty he became minister for defence, and also succeeded *Collins as commander-in-chief. Despite having tried desperately to avoid military confrontation, he was inevitably associated with the crushing of the anti-treaty forces in the *Civil War. Forced out of the *Cumann na nGaedheal government following the *army mutiny, he returned in 1927 as minister for Local Government. During 1944–59 he was leader of *Fine Gael, but hostility to his civil war past ruled him out as head of the *interparty governments, in which he was instead minister for education.

Mullaghmast, massacre of (Nov.–Dec. 1577), the slaughter of Moris O'More and at least 40 others after they had been summoned to the fort of Mullaghmast, Co. Kildare, by the soldier-colonists Francis Cosby and Robert Hartpole to do military service. This bloody episode in the troubled relations between the *Laois-Offaly planters and the displaced O'Mores and O'Connors occurred at a time when Lord Deputy *Sidney was trying to quell the revolt of Rory Óg O'More. HM

Munster plantation. Following a small private colony established at Kerrycurrihy near Cork in the late 1560s, opportunity arose for a major *plantation after the second *Desmond War, with the confiscation of rebel lands in a wide arc from Cork to Limerick. In a project directed from London, undertakers would receive seigniories up to 12,000 acres, remove the Irish, and bring in a set number of English settlers. Thirty-five undertakers (soldiers and officials serving in Ireland and courtiers, merchants, and country gentlemen recruited from England) were granted 298,653 acres.

Inaccurate and incomplete land surveys led to a torrent of complaints after the inclusion of Desmond freeholders and those who had been promised pardons. There was large-scale litigation which dragged on after special commissions in Munster in 1588 and 1592. By 1611 the locals had regained 70,000 acres.

Some undertakers were content to take rents from existing Irish tenantry; others invested, brought in settlers, *enclosed lands, and introduced new breeds of livestock. The plantation had a population of 3,030 by 1592 and the crown was receiving *c.* £1,900 in rent by 1594. When the *Nine Years War broke out sporadic killings of settlers began; in October 1598 the scattered seigniories were overrun and reoccupied by former owners led by James FitzThomas FitzGerald. With the settler militia only a fifth of its paper strength of 1,575, the colonists fled to the safety of the towns and to England.

After 1601 the colony was re-established and eventually prospered. Eleven seigniories changed hands between 1598 and 1611. Richard *Boyle bought out Sir Walter *Raleigh and went on to own six seigniories and portions of four others. Towns developed, notably Boyle's at Bandonbridge, and outside the formal plantation considerable settlement occurred along the coast. Youghal and Kinsale encouraged English settlers and Baltimore, with its flourishing pirate trade, was incorporated in 1612. In the early days the colonists asset-stripped their lands of exhaustible supplies of timber and iron ore, but in the longer term success lay in the export of wool and cattle. By 1632 Youghal's custom returns from exports were second only to Dublin's. The plantation's population has been estimated at 14,000 in 1611 and 22,000 in 1641. A wealthy, influential, and Anglicizing Protestant minority had thus been established in Munster, but there was some intermarriage, with four of the original undertaker families, including Edmund *Spenser's descendants, having become Catholic.

McCarthy-Morrogh, Michael, *The Munster Plantation* (1986)

HM

Murphy, Fr. John (*c*.1753–1798), curate of Boolavogue, Co. Wexford, one of the leaders of the *insurrection of 1798 in the south-east, but not a *United Irishman. In the lead up to the outbreak Murphy had encouraged his parishioners to surrender weapons, and appears to have advocated resistance only when the violence of local loyalists and government forces seemed to leave no other option. His prominence in popular memory is attributed to attempts by 19th-century clerical writers to capture 1798 from contemporary republicans by presenting it as a defensive Catholic uprising. After the defeat of the insurgents, he was captured at Tullow, Co. Carlow, and hanged.

Murphy, William Martin (1844–1919), capitalist and politician. Born in Co. Cork, the son of a building contractor, Murphy acquired a large fortune from railway contracts and investments in Britain, South America, and Ireland. He established the Dublin United Tramways Company, before purchasing two nationalist newspapers, the *Irish Catholic* and *Irish Independent*, in 1904. He was *home rule MP for the St Patrick's division of Dublin 1885–92. Murphy was the main influence behind the Irish International Exhibition of 1907, but refused a knighthood in that year. As founder of the Dublin Employers' Federation (1912), he led the counter-attack against the growing labour militancy represented by the *Irish Transport and General Workers' Union, culminating in the defeat of the unions in the *Dublin lockout of 1913. On the outbreak of the *First World War Murphy actively supported recruitment to the British army, even advocating the sacking of able-bodied men who refused to enlist. Invited to the *Irish Convention, he opposed *partition, advocating dominion status. Murphy was typical of the affluent, conservative nationalists who dominated the *Nationalist party.

NG

Murray, Daniel (1768–1852). As curate of Arklow, Co. Wicklow, he narrowly escaped death at the hands of government forces in the *insurrection of 1798. He became Catholic archbishop of Dublin in 1823, having served from 1809 as coadjutor to the increasingly infirm *Troy. He continued his predecessor's work of institutional reform and expansion, but his willingness to seek accommodation with the government, and particularly his acceptance of the *national schools and *Queen's Colleges, earned him the hostility of more militant colleagues, notably *MacHale.

Musgrave, Sir Richard (*c*.1757–1818), writer and parliamentarian. The proprietor of a Co. Waterford estate, Musgrave entered the Irish *parliament in 1778 as a member for Lismore. He proved a loyal friend to the administration, and in 1782 received a baronetcy. In Waterford in the 1780s he took an active part in suppressing the *Whiteboys, going so far as to flog one convicted offender personally, while acting as high *sheriff of the county. By the 1790s Musgrave was predicting both a domestic rebellion and French invasion, and published two pamphlets to this effect. In the immediate aftermath of the *insurrection of 1798, Musgrave anonymously published a pamphlet praising the executive and countering allegations that they had deliberately precipitated the rebellion. In 1800, though attached to the administration, he spoke against the Act of *Union. The following year he published his *Memoirs of the Different Rebellions in Ireland*, the book for which he is best remembered. His depiction of the rebellion as a priest-led conspiracy, continuing the pattern of consistent Catholic treachery earlier seen in the *rising of 1641 and the reign of *James II, strongly influenced conservative Protestant thinking. Numerous replies followed, notably that of Francis *Plowden.

NG

music. The condition of music in modern Irish history can briefly be characterized as a more or less polarized development of colonial and ethnic ideologies of culture.

Sources which preserve Irish music prior to the mid-17th century are remarkably few, although the literature of early and medieval Ireland repays close scrutiny with regard to the presence of music as a vital seam in the fabric of pre-Christian and early Christian culture. The oral transmission of the music itself (sacred as well as secular) poses considerable problems for the historian: the few manuscript sources which appear to record elements of the (sacred) Celtic rite, for example, date from the 15th century, and must thus be regarded with circumspection, in terms of recovering what in probability was a rich tradition of monophony. Sporadic but instructive comments by outsiders, from *Gerald of Wales in the 12th century to *Spenser in the 16th, clearly attest to the prominence of music in Gaelic tribal culture. Gerald's remarks are disinterested, in so far as he was concerned with the technical prowess and civilizing influence of musicians, but Spenser's famous antagonism towards bardic culture apostrophizes that reading of Irish music as an instrument of political resistance which was to endure in the minds of English and Irish commentators alike.

The radical changes wrought in Irish society by the defeat of the Gaelic aristocracy at *Kinsale in 1601 were reflected not least in the fragmentation and decline of music. Although Gaelic literature in the 17th century retained its learning and technical complexity (notwithstanding the permanent sense of dispossession and expectation which it evinced), the status and condition of music markedly deteriorated. Set against the newly imported icons of English musical culture, the art of the native executant, 'illiterate and blind', seemed peripheral and (at best) an object of curious delight.

The comparative stability enjoyed by the Protestant interest in Ireland after the *Williamite War produced a corresponding measure of musical continuity from within the *Pale throughout the 18th century. Although the *Protestant ascendancy did not espouse a taste for serious *opera in Italian, it patronized other forms of high musical culture, and a number of gifted musicians (among them, Matthew Dubourg, Johann Sgismond Cousser, and Francesco Geminiani) settled for long periods in Dublin. The distinctive feature of ascendancy taste, apart from the popularity of ballad opera, was the promotion of major choral works (oratorios, odes, and anthems) for charitable purposes, including the support of hospitals and the relief of prisoners in the city jails. The choirs of *St Patrick's and *Christ Church cathedrals provided the backbone of many of these performances, with distinguished soloists invited from London. The climax of these activities was the extended visit which George Frideric Handel paid to Dublin in 1741–2, which culminated in the premiere of *Messiah* on 13 April 1742 in Neal's music hall, Fishamble Street. Nevertheless, a continuing disdain for art music as a harbinger of popery ensured that it occupied a marginal place in Irish intellectual life. Attempts towards the end of the century to narrow the gulf between Gaelic and ascendancy musical cultures vividly illustrated the differences between them. While Joseph Cooper Walker, in his *Historical Memoirs of the Irish Bards* (1786), sought to identify Turlough Carolan (1670–1738) as the proper focus of Irish musical endeavour, Charles Burney, in 1787, contemptuously dismissed the role of the Irish bard as 'little better than that of piper to the *Whiteboys, and other savage and lawless ruffians'.

A small number of collections of ethnic music had been published throughout the 18th century (beginning in 1724) but it was not until the appearance of Edward Bunting's *General Collection of the Ancient Irish Music* (3 vols., 1797, 1809, 1840) that the anglophone tradition took any real cognizance of the native repertory. Thomas Moore's (1799–1852) *Irish Melodies*, which appeared in ten volumes between 1808 and 1834, drew liberally from Bunting's publication, and in the process provided further evidence of disparity between two traditions of Irish music. Whereas Bunting (and the collectors who succeeded him) laboured to preserve the ethnic repertory essentially as an antiquarian, Moore politicized this repertory from within the fold of the colonial establishment. Although Bunting deeply resented this interpretation of Irish music, its appeal gathered momentum through the 19th century. When Moore's projection of Irish melody was cross-fertilized with the ballad tradition (via the efforts of *Young Ireland and the musical publications of Thomas *Davis in particular), the polarized condition of ethnic music as the intelligencer of nationalism *vis-à-vis* the colonial status of art music was complete. Although several composers in the period 1760–1830 introduced the popular tradition of arranging Irish melodies, 'the ostentation of science and mere trick execution' appeared to be substituted for 'the wonderful charm of melody' (J. Gamble in 1819).

With the passing of the Act of *Union in 1801, the cultivation of music within the art tradition notably waned. Choral societies developed in Dublin from 1810 onwards and gained considerable strength in the Victorian period, while the lack of professional music-making found some compensation in the surge of amateur activity fostered by the Robinson family and Robert Prescott Stewart, among others. The Theatre Royal in Dublin, which opened in 1821, was perhaps the most important of a number of similar venues in Dublin, Cork, and Belfast, where the international operatic successes of the day (including operas by Irish-born composers such as Wallace and Balfe) were regularly given within a few years of their British or European premieres. The improved condition of Roman Catholics after *Catholic emancipation (1829) was reflected in the surge of music associated with the *devotional revolution. In particular Paul *Cullen's steady drive towards the Romanization of the Catholic liturgy inspired a musical reanimation of astounding proportions. The strong connections which the Irish Society of St Cecilia (1878–) formed with European associations also devoted to the scholarly and pragmatic dissemination of plainchant and High Renaissance church music attests to a vital chapter in Irish music which the colonial–ethnic division tends to occlude. In essence, 'Cecilianism' speaks to the aspirations of a strong Catholic middle class in Ireland which sought and found in Church music an aesthetic *raison d'être*. One of its chief proponents was Edward Martyn, better known as co-founder of the Irish Literary Theatre and sometime president of *Sinn Féin.

The inauguration in 1897 of an Irish music festival, the Feis Ceoil, is illustrative of the division which continued to attend music in Ireland at the close of the century. Although the Feis did espouse ethnic music to a degree, it quickly became apparent that two kinds of music—however nationalistic the motivation of the Feis—required two kinds of festival. Efforts to merge the resources of European art music and the indigenous repertory languished, despite the prominence of music as a symbolic intelligence during the heyday of the Celtic revival. Music functioned in Irish poetry and drama as a commonplace metaphor of the literary imagination, but the development of Irish music itself was nugatory. The incidental music written by John F. Larchet for plays given at the abbey (including Synge's *Deirdre of the Sorrows* (1910)) and the Irish opera *Eithne* (1910) by Robert O'Dwyer reflect efforts at synthesis which only partly succeeded. The early compositions of Arnold Bax were directly inspired by Yeats and the *literary revival, but escaped the burden of the ethnic tradition.

After 1922, the cultural oppressiveness of the ethnic repertory worsened, in so far as composers were caught between the crisis of (musical) modernism abroad and that of nationalism at home. While critics recognized that a cosmetic arrangement of Irish melodies was a poor substitute for a wholly developed yet manifestly Irish art music, the raw politicization of Irish traditional music as national resource continued to inhibit composers. And as late as 1950, Brian Boydell could write (with justification) that 'music in Ireland . . . is in a shocking state'. Boydell's concern was with the dearth of infrastructures which marked musical life throughout the country, a lack repaired in significant measure by Radio Telefís Éireann (the expansion of its orchestras) and by the improvement in educational facilities and opportunities for performance which followed upon the economic growth of the 1960s.

The 1960s also witnessed the troubled career of Sean Ó Riada (1930–71), perhaps the only composer to have been comfortably received by the verbally dominated cultural matrix of modern Ireland. Ó Riada's own crisis of artistic growth, in which he abandoned art music for a new and enduring recreation of the ethnic repertory, was undoubtedly born of that colonial–ethnic fissure which has been the signature of music in Ireland for three centuries. Although younger Irish composers (notably Gerald Barry, Raymond Deane, and John Buckley) have escaped the anxiety of his influence (both as to Ó Riada's own preoccupations and the expectations which his music created), none has overcome the paradox of a musical tradition which appears to remainder the enterprise of original composition.

See also MUSICAL INSTITUTIONS AND VENUES; OPERA; BALLADS; POPULAR MUSIC; ETHNIC MUSIC; BELFAST HARP FESTIVAL; DANCING.

Daly, Kieran, *Catholic Church Music in Ireland, 1878–1903* (1995)
Fleischmann, Aloys (ed.), *Music in Ireland* (1952)
Gillen, Gerard, and White, Harry (eds.), *Irish Musical Studies* (1990–)

HW

musical institutions and venues (1700–1990). The development of music in Ireland in the period immediately after the *Restoration was notably indebted to English precedents. Before the building of Crow Street music hall in 1731, the chief venues for concert music in Dublin were the cathedrals (*St Patrick's, *Christ Church) and the larger churches in the city, including St Andrew's Round church. Mr Neal's Great Room in Fishamble Street was built by the Charitable Musical Society in 1741; it was converted into a theatre in 1777. As the city's first purpose-built concert hall, it was much used for the promotion of charity benefits and other regular performances of instrumental and choral music. The first performance of Handel's *Messiah* was given there on 13 April 1742. The gardens in Great Britain Street laid out by Dr Bartholomew Mosse, master of the Lying-in hospital in 1749, were modelled on London's Vauxhall Gardens and became the venue for a series of summer concerts which were given annually until 1791. The opening of the Rotunda Room in 1767 provided another important venue for concert performances.

A number of charitable societies were closely associated with the promotion of music in Dublin in the 18th century. The performance of ballad opera in the theatres in Smock Alley and Aungier Street (actually in Longford Street) was followed by the broader cultivation of opera in the 19th century, particularly at the Theatre Royal in Hawkins Street (1821–80).

The sharp decline of ascendancy patronage after the Act of *Union notably affected the promotion of art music, which thereafter survived largely through the foundation of amateur societies for the performance of large-scale choral works. These societies include the Sons of Handel (1810) and the Philharmonic Society (1826–78). The latter also promoted occasional professional appearances by visiting artists, as did the Antient Concerts Society (1834–63). In 1875 Joseph Robinson founded the Dublin Musical Society which gave its performances in the Exhibition Hall at Earlsfort Terrace (rebuilt and opened in 1981 as the National Concert Hall). It was succeeded by the Dublin Orchestral Society in 1899. The *Royal Dublin Society inaugurated a series of concerts in 1886 which continues to the present day.

Important educational musical institutions include the Royal Irish Academy of Music (1856) and the Dublin College of Music (1890). The inauguration of festivals (*feiseanna*) of music in Dublin, Cork, Belfast, Derry, Sligo, and other centres from 1897 onwards was a crucial step in the dissemination of art music. The Oireachtas, a literary festival inaugurated at the same time as the Feis Ceoil, likewise fomented revival of the ethnic tradition. Since 1900 the Belfast Music Festival, the Queen's University Music Festival, the Dublin Festival of Twentieth-Century Music, and the Cork International Choral Festival have been preeminent in the cultivation of Irish art music and the presentation of the international repertory of contemporary music in this country. The establishment of professional orchestras in Dublin (Radio Éireann Symphony Orchestra (1926), reorganized as the National Symphony Orchestra in 1989), Belfast (BBC orchestra (1926); the Ulster Orchestra (1966)) and Limerick (the Irish Chamber Orchestra (1995)—originally established in Dublin as the New Irish Chamber Orchestra (1970)) has significantly increased the presence of art music throughout the country. The role played therein by Radio Telefís Éireann through its sponsorship of choirs, ensembles, and individual composers has been seminal. The development of RTE FM3 (a radio channel shared with Radio na Gaeltachta) marks a new degree of commitment since the mid-1980s to the dissemination of art music.

Boydell, Brian, *A Dublin Musical Calendar, 1700–1760* (1988)

Hogan, Ita, *Anglo-Irish Music, 1780–1830* (1966)

HW

music halls in Ireland, as in England, developed from taverns and inns rather than from the conventional *theatre. Henry Connell's Dublin tavern was offering food and drink, accompanied by a number of short entertainments, in 1855. In such early halls drinking was undoubtedly more important, for both patrons and proprietors, than entertainment. In 1871 Ireland's first purpose-built music hall, the Alhambra, was opened in Belfast. Its owner was Daniel Lowrey, an Irish-born Yorkshireman, already established as a music hall proprietor and performer in Liverpool. In 1878 Lowrey acquired Connell's former Dublin premises, which he rebuilt. Cork did not acquire a large-scale music hall until 1897. Halls differed from theatres in that they permitted drinking and eating in the auditorium. They also required no drama licences, as programmes consisted only of a series of short acts. Programmes were versatile enough to include *circuses, *boxing matches, and topical sketches. Irish halls employed local performers, but were also part of a circuit followed by famous British acts such as Marie Lloyd and Harry Lauder (although the latter was booed off stage at his first Belfast performance). All classes attended shows at the halls, though they were condemned by churchmen and *temperance campaigners. By 1910 music halls were the premier entertainment venue for Ireland's growing urban population, though most Irish halls were now owned by British conglomerates. Their decline, almost complete by 1923, was precipitated in part by the disruption of the *First World War and following conflicts, but also by several other factors. Though the halls themselves were now more luxurious, many established 'turns' had either died or retired, and new acts did not replace them. Theatres began to stage musical reviews that rivalled the halls. Most importantly, *cinema, previously a frequent component of music hall presentations, began to draw its own audience.

Watters, E., and Murtagh, M., *Infinite Variety: Dan Lowrey's Music Hall 1879–97* (1975)

NG

mystery plays, see THEATRE.

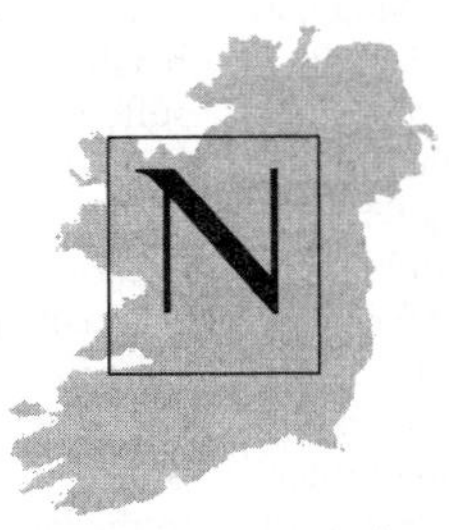

Nagle, Nano (1718–84), founder of the Presentation *nuns. Nagle was the daughter of a Catholic landowning family in Ballygriffin, Co. Cork. She operated six poor-schools in Cork city from the 1750s, and in 1771 invited the French Ursulines to take over one of these. Unsatisfied with their performance, she set up her own congregation, the Sisters of the Charitable Instruction of the Sacred Heart of Jesus, in 1776; the first of the modern, socially active congregations in Ireland, it was intended as a sisterhood without enclosure, and with a multidimensional function of work among the poor. The formal papal recognition of the congregation as the Presentation nuns in 1802, some years after Nagle's death, imposed strict enclosure upon the sisterhood, limiting them to the work of teaching. The congregation nevertheless holds 1776 rather than 1802 as its foundation date. CC

Nangle, Edward, see SECOND REFORMATION.

Napoleonic wars, see REVOLUTIONARY AND NAPOLEONIC WARS.

Nary, Cornelius (1658–1738), Catholic priest and controversialist. The son of a Co. Kildare farmer, he was educated at the Irish College, Paris, and became parish priest of St Michan's, Dublin, around 1699. His best-known work, *The Case of the Roman Catholics of Ireland*, arguing that proposed new *penal laws were unnecessary and a breach of the treaty of *Limerick, though commonly said to have been published anonymously in 1723, first appears in a collection printed in 1742. Nary engaged in public debate with several Protestant clergymen, including Edward Synge, archbishop of Tuam. His translation of the New Testament (1718) was condemned in Rome as unsound.

Nation, a weekly newspaper founded in October 1842 to promote the campaign for *repeal and to disseminate the ideas of cultural nationalism. Owned and edited by Charles Gavan *Duffy in collaboration with Thomas *Davis and John Blake *Dillon, the *Nation* was the mouthpiece of *Young Ireland. With an initial print-run of 12,000 copies, the paper was widely distributed through repeal reading rooms, and claimed a readership of 250,000. The *Nation* was suppressed in 1848 and revived by Duffy in 1849. It continued until 1897, but never regained the impact of its early years. PHG

national anthems, like *flags, have a contentious history. 'God Save the King', accepted from the early 19th century as the British national anthem, became in Ireland, and in *Northern Ireland has remained, an important expression of *unionist allegiance. Up to 1914, its most popular nationalist rival was T. D. Sullivan's 'God Save Ireland' (1867), commemorating the *Manchester martyrs, which became the unofficial anthem of the *Irish parliamentary party. From 1912, however, the *Irish Volunteers chose as their marching song 'The Soldier's Song' (first published 1912), by Peadar Kearney (1883–1942) and Patrick Heeney (d. 1911). In 1926 this was adopted, despite apparent reservations concerning its suitability, as the national anthem of the *Irish Free State. De *Valera's appropriation for a political party of the opening words of the 1923 Irish version ('Sinne Fianna Fail'—'we are the soldiers of destiny') was apparently unintentional, but attempts to replace 'Fianna' with 'laochra' (heroes) never gained general acceptance. The resurgence of political violence in Northern Ireland from 1969 has sharpened reservations concerning the anthem's romantic militarism.

National Archives, see PUBLIC RECORDS.

National Association, formally instituted in Dublin in December 1864 to facilitate co-operation between Irish Catholics and English radicals, specifically with a view to promoting *disestablishment. The initiative had come from William J. O'Neill Daunt (1807–94), a former aide of *O'Connell, who had established contact with John Bright and the English Liberation Society and then drawn in Archbishop Patrick Leahy of Cashel, John Blake *Dillon, and a group of Dublin Liberals. The approval of Paul *Cullen, archbishop of Dublin, as indicated by his attendance at the inaugural meeting, was hard won. *Independent Opposition interests, including John *MacHale, archbishop of Tuam, used the National Association as a forum in which to settle old scores with Cullen and others. The consequence was an extended and debilitating row over the rules of the association. The association's purpose triumphed with the election in 1868 of *Gladstone, pledged to Irish disestablishment. However, the association contributed little directly to this. Dillon was elected to parliament in 1865 and made some use of the National Association's meetings in bringing the remnant of the Independent Opposition Party together in support of the emerging Liberal Party. Gladstone's appeal for Irish Catholics in 1868 transcended all existing organizational arrangements. RVC

National Council, formed in 1903 by Arthur *Griffith, Maud *Gonne, and others to organize opposition to the forthcoming visit to Ireland of Edward VII, and continued as an advanced nationalist forum. In 1908 it merged with the Sinn Féin League (see DUNGANNON CLUBS) to form *Sinn Féin.

National Group, see MCGRATH, JOSEPH.

National Guard, see BLUESHIRTS.

National Health Service, see HEALTH SERVICES.

national identities in early and medieval Ireland. While the inhabitants of early and medieval Ireland had no concept of themselves as *'Celts', they had a strong sense of belonging to one nation, the Goídil (or in Latin Scotti), a sense intensified by a common language, Goídelg. The Goídil were not the inhabitants of Ireland but speakers of the *Irish language, which, since the early centuries AD, included a considerable portion of the population of what is now *Scotland; the homeland of the Goídil was, however, the island of Ireland, the Goídil of Scotland being regarded as exiles. By the 7th century, the Irish had devised a prehistory of their nation (culminating in the composition of the **Lebor Gabála Érenn*, 'The book of the taking of Ireland'), in which the various tribes and dynasties were all linked by a common line of descent from the mythical Míl, or *Milesius, of Spain, and thence back to Noah and Adam. In spite of this sense of unity, early medieval Ireland was notoriously divided politically, though the leading dynasty in the country, the *Uí Néill, were able to exploit the sense of common ancestry to assert the existence of a *high kingship, rightfully theirs, with its symbolic capital at *Tara.

Irish awareness of racial distinctiveness was heightened when, in the 9th century, the island suffered sustained *Viking assault, which at times looked likely to overwhelm the country, and which saw the establishment of a number of enclaves and towns. Although the Vikings were gradually integrated into Irish society, becoming Christian, marrying into Irish dynasties, and commissioning Gaelic verse, the Vikings continued to be regarded as *Gaill*, 'foreigners', until, in the late 12th century, Ireland was again invaded and colonized, this time by people of *Anglo-Norman origin. The communities of Viking extraction were absorbed by the new settlers (some of them gaining recognition as Englishmen in the eyes of the law, a law denied for the most part to the native Irish); and, to the Irish, the English colonists now became the *Gaill*. Society in later medieval Ireland was, therefore, again dominated by two peoples regarding themselves as distinct nations, whose relationship was dogged by racial antagonism.

In time many of the new colonists too were assimilated into Irish life (and, indeed, were dubbed 'the middle nation' by the Irish author of the *Remonstrance sent to the pope in 1317). Yet despite what has been seen as a process of *Gaelicization, they never, in the medieval period, came to see themselves as Irish, preferring to call themselves 'the English of the land of Ireland'. The English government in Ireland repeatedly legislated to prevent further acculturation, most famously in the Statute of *Kilkenny (1366), though this proved largely ineffective. Even during the late Middle Ages, in what was at one time seen as the era of *'aristocratic home rule', a sense of Englishness remained uppermost. It was only from the mid-16th century onwards, when both faced the prospect of dispossession by a new wave of English Protestant *plantation, that what soon after came to be called the *Old English began to discover a common identity with the native population.

Frame, R., ' "Les Engleys nées en Irlande": The English Political Identity in Medieval Ireland', *Transactions of the Royal Historical Society*, 6th ser. 3 (1993)

Lydon, James, 'The Middle Nation', in id. (ed.), *The English in Medieval Ireland* (1984)

Ó Corráin, Donnchadh, 'Nationality and Kingship in Pre-Norman Ireland', in T. W. Moody (ed.), *Nationality and the Pursuit of National Independence* (1978)

SD

nationalism has provided the central theme of much Irish historical writing. Yet the point at which its Irish history begins continues to be debated. The issue can in part be resolved by distinguishing between national consciousness, an awareness of belonging to one nationality rather than another, and national*ism*, a political philosophy and programme for action built round the proposition that national consciousness finds its only proper expression in the achievement of a nation state. In Ireland the sense of a single people, united by a common language and legal code (see BREHON LAW), and with well-developed origin myths (see MILESIANS), is evident from an early period, although the relationship between such ideas and the sporadic attempts from the 9th century to establish political unity under a *high kingship continues to be debated. It is also necessary to distinguish between nationalism and the sort of movements for the defence of local, sectional, or corporate liberties that were characteristic of the multiple kingdoms and overlapping jurisdictions of late medieval and early modern Europe. Examples of the latter would include episodes like the resistance to the Acts of *Resumption and the parliamentary *declaration of 1460; these testified to the emergence among the English of Ireland of a distinct identity, but one that did not extend beyond their own ethnic and cultural group.

A further element in what can be considered the prehistory of Irish nationalism was provided by the notion of **patria* or fatherland, developed from the early 16th century by *commonwealth reformers within the *Pale. The same concept, linked to a militant *Counter-Reformation Catholicism, was deployed in the revolts of James Fitzmaurice FitzGerald and Hugh *O'Neill. In the 1640s the alliance forced on *Old English and Gaelic Irish by the hostility of the Protestant state provided the background to a new assertion of Irish national rights by Patrick *Darcy and others. Yet the bond between the *Confederate Catholics was based above all on religion, while their political self-definition was built around their loyalty to the crown. In the same way *Jacobitism, the main political allegiance of Irish Catholics for two generations after the Glorious *Revolution, was undoubtedly a vehicle for the indirect expression of a sense of religious and (for some) ethnic separateness. But it was also a British ideology, founded on the assumption of a continued link between Ireland and Great Britain. The Protestant *patriots of the 18th century developed a more explicit defence of Irish constitutional rights. Yet their sense of Irishness remained intriguingly ambivalent, looking forward in some of its rhetoric and symbolism to the concerns of modern nationalism, yet looking back, in its social and religious exclusiveness, to earlier defences of sectional liberties.

As a mass movement Irish nationalism can be traced to the 1790s, when the strong sense of lost ancestral rights inherited from Gaelic tradition by the *Defenders fused with the broader vocabulary of popular and national rights derived from the *American Revolution and *French Revolution by the *United Irishmen. The durability of the popular consciousness thus created is confirmed in the persistence of the *Ribbon tradition. Revolutionary nationalism was revived half-heartedly by *Young Ireland in 1848, and more purposefully by the *Fenians. *O'Connell's *repeal movement made popular nationalism a powerful electoral force. Yet later attempts to revive a separate Irish parliamentary identity, *independent opposition and the *National Association, were less successful, and there remained at least the possibility, in the prosperous and relatively tranquil 1850s and 1860s, that the ethnic distinctiveness, social conflicts, and denominational rivalries of Ireland, like those of Wales and Scotland, might be integrated into the broad-based alliances constituted by the main British *political parties, Liberal and Conservative. It was not until the 1880s, and *Parnell's achievement in transforming the *home rule party into a disciplined parliamentary grouping with a well-organized popular base, that Irish politics became polarized round the dichotomy of nationalist and *unionist.

Irish nationalism differed from most continental European nationalisms in not having a strong basis in language or culture. From the United Irishmen to the Fenians, organized nationalist politics were consistently stronger in the commercialized and Anglicized south and east than in the Gaelic west, and offered no consistent challenge to the progressive Anglicization of Irish society. The greatest interpreters of Gaelic tradition and Irish history, such as *Ferguson, *O'Grady, and *Lecky, were unionist in their politics. It was not until the very end of the 19th century that political nationalism came to be associated with cultural revivalism. However, the importance then achieved by movements like the *Gaelic Athletic Association and the *Gaelic League ensured that a commitment to cultural revival became a central element in nationalist ideology.

Nineteenth-century Irish nationalists emphasized the perceived contrast between the prosperity enjoyed under *Grattan's parliament and the economic decline that followed the Act of *Union, presenting self-government as the key to economic regeneration. Yet nationalism, in Ireland as elsewhere, was a cross-class alliance, avoiding identification with specific economic interests. Parnell was briefly able to link the cause of home rule, in both practical and rhetorical terms, with that of the tenant farmer (see LAND WAR). Once the *Land Acts had transferred ownership from a small, isolated Protestant elite to a large class of medium and small farmers, however, proposals for further social and economic change threatened to divide rather than unite the nationalist population. The democratic programme of the first *Dáil offered vague promises of a more equal society. But land seizures and workers' soviets during the *Anglo-Irish war and after were repudiated, and in some cases forcibly suppressed, by nationalist leaders anxious both to assert the primacy of the national issue and to avoid antagonizing vested interests within Irish society. Later attempts to give militant nationalism a social base, in *Saor Eire and *Republican Congress, were short-lived and unsuccessful.

If nationalism muffled class differences, it exacerbated religious ones. The defence of Irish constitutional rights in the 18th century, up to and including resistance to the Act of Union, had come almost entirely from the Protestant middle and upper classes. Already by the 1830s, however, the great majority of Protestants had come to see the Union as their only defence against a *politicized and increasingly threatening Catholic majority. Instead support for the repeal movement came overwhelmingly from Catholics, reacting to economic decline and failure to make good promises of rapid progress towards religious equality. Across the 19th century, concessions to Catholic education, and a more even-handed approach to official appointments, progressively widened the circle of Catholic opportunity. But progress was gradual and constantly lagged behind rising Catholic expectations. A minority tradition of Protestant nationalism survived in Young Ireland, and later in the home rule movement. But constitutional nationalist movements, from repeal to the Irish parliamentary party, were to enjoy a close working partnership with the Catholic church, and Catholicism was to remain a central, if rarely acknowledged, element in the imagined community of the Irish nation.

Boyce, D. G., *Nationalism in Ireland* (2nd edn., 1991)

Garvin, T., *Nationalist Revolutionaries in Ireland 1858–1928* (1987)

nationalist literary societies. Irish *nationalism, like other revolutionary movements, drew heavily on those who no longer fitted into the social categories of the old regime and felt themselves excluded by the existing system from the respect and security to which their talents entitled them. Hence it is not surprising that from the late 19th century to the present day literary societies should have played an important part in the efforts of nationalist movements to articulate and disseminate their ideologies and implement these through political organization.

These societies, especially those most explicitly separatist, were often inspired by desire to create a nationalist subculture of self-reliance which would preserve its members from corrupting social and intellectual influences. They were primarily drawn from adolescents and young men with some older mentors; individual women were active in nationalist movements of this type—though not necessarily in the club milieu—from the *Young Ireland period, and from the 1880s separate women's groups appeared, often associated with patriotic children's groups such as the Children's Land League and *Fianna Éireann.

Such societies were not peculiar to Ireland. Late 18th-century French local literary and debating societies were important in the intellectual and forensic development of the future leaders of the *French Revolution. Nor were they confined to nationalist groups: the Catholic church, for example, tried to establish social clubs and reading rooms under its control, and sometimes directly attacked rival bodies. (Such rivalries were not always purely political; the social function of nationalist clubs often produced tension, especially in rural areas, over clerical claims to supervise dances and other activities.) In towns, these societies served as social and intellectual centres for young clerks and artisans. Papers were read and debated; sometimes manuscript journals were compiled and circulated. Nationalist *anniversaries were commemorated, and as transport methods improved excursions were made to historic sites.

A recurring charge made by separatists against constitutional nationalists was that while separatists, as part of their commitment to self-reliance, taught themselves to think out the basic principles of Irish nationality by study of classic texts, constitutionalists had to resort to windy oratory and authoritarian personal leadership to hide their unprincipled incoherence. In fact, the two shared common terms of reference. (Much of the literature studied by separatists was written by constitutionalists such as T. D. Sullivan; William *O'Brien praised the popular nationalist publishing firms of Denvir, *Duffy, and Cameron & Ferguson for providing the material for an alternative 'national' system of education opposed to that provided by the British state.) Branches of constitutionalist organizations often presented themselves as literary societies, and there was a certain amount of overlap.

In the 1790s local literary societies were often front organizations for the *United Irishmen (especially in Ulster) and came under government attack. In the 1840s *repeal reading rooms and literary societies were adjuncts to the attempts of the Young Irelanders to produce a mass nationalist literature and educate the population in nationalist ideas. Among the artisans of the towns (the mainstay of separatist politics throughout the 19th century) these societies became the confederate clubs which made up the Young Ireland political organization, and some survived the suppression of the movement to operate as centres of nationalist activity thereafter. (The Young Ireland Society of early 20th-century Tralee claimed to have existed continuously since the 1840s.) When the body of the Young Irelander T. B. *MacManus was brought back to Ireland for burial as a *Fenian political gesture and the corpse was refused admission to Dublin churches, it was waked in the hall of the *mechanics' institute (later the premises of the *Abbey theatre), the base of a society of this type.

In the 1880s Young Ireland societies of this type served as centres of *Parnellite / separatist activity; most took the Parnellite side in the 1890s. Notable among these was the Dublin-based Leinster Literary Society (later the Celtic Literary Society), whose members included William Rooney (1873–1901) and Arthur *Griffith. The political turmoil of the 1890s led to an increasing emphasis on the literary aspect of nationalism, and some writers (notably W. B. *Yeats) saw in the societies the basis of an Irish literary movement which under their direction might supersede the introspective high culture and jaded commercial art of Britain. The rise of the *Gaelic League should be seen in this context.

The centenary celebrations of 1898 led to a revival of explicitly separatist societies. Many '98 clubs were founded, and the *Sinn Féin movement began as a network of groups such as the Celtic Literary Society, held together at first by the Belfast-based monthly paper the *Shan Van Vocht* and later by Griffith and Rooney's weekly the *United Irishman*. The separatist subculture at this time also developed a network of women's societies, *Inghinidhe na hÉireann.

It was from this milieu that many early members of the Irish National Theatre Society were drawn, and this helps to explain the tensions which developed between artists and nationalists over the Abbey. For those like Arthur Griffith (initially supportive of Yeats, later a bitter critic) who saw the literary movement as inseparable from the demands of nationalism, the professionalization of the Abbey represented the transformation of a democratic movement into the dictatorship of a few aesthetes, and the calling in of the police to suppress organized nationalist disruption of Synge's *The Playboy of the Western World* (1907) marked the use of imperial power against outraged defenders of the values which the literary movement had initially claimed to represent.

These societies should not be romanticized. In many cases they were simply social or political clubs, and their intellectual activities were often narrow or ill-informed. (Their limitations are satirized in Synge's unpublished skit *National Drama: A Farce* and *Corkery's play *The Embers*). Nonetheless, their social role should not be seen as incompatible with political significance, and their role in Irish politics under the Union deserves more detailed research than it has hitherto received.

Davis, R. P., *The Young Ireland Movement* (1987)
—— *Arthur Griffith and Non-Violent Sinn Féin* (1974)
Nic Siubhlaigh, Maire, *The Splendid Years* (1955)

PM

Nationalist Party (1882–1922), the generic term for the Irish parliamentary party and its successive constituency organizations. From Isaac *Butt's loose group in the 1870s it grew into a strongly centralized party under *Parnell and his successors. The party was tightly structured: Parnell's aristocratic authority being reinforced by control of the funds made available to needy MPs, and by strict enforcement of 'the pledge' by all candidates to 'sit, act, and vote' as directed. In Ireland the party was sustained first by the *National League, a constituency organization which replaced the *Land League in 1882, and which was itself overshadowed during the 1890s by the anti-Parnellite Irish National Federation; both were replaced in 1900 by the *United Irish League (UIL), supported later by the *Ancient Order of Hibernians. The Irish vote in Great Britain was organized by the Irish National League of Great Britain until 1900 and thereafter by the United Irish League of Great Britain (UILGB) under the leadership of T. P. *O'Connor. Except during the 1890s, party funds raised from the Irish abroad exceeded the totals raised at home.

In parliament after 1882, weight of numbers replaced disruptive tactics. After the electoral changes of 1884–5, up to 86 of Ireland's 103 parliamentary seats (plus one in Liverpool) went regularly to Nationalists. In the 1880s most MPs were young agrarian militants, but the average age rose from 40 in the 1880s to 55 in 1918. Outside the divided north, over 60 seats often went uncontested. The party usually included about ten Protestant MPs, but its record in securing northern Protestant votes was minimal: Ulster's segregated society dictated that elections would be sectarian headcounts where the crucial contests were not those fought by politicians on the hustings but those between rival party solicitors at the annual revision courts which maintained the electoral register. In the north as in the south the route to maximum support lay through the social institutions of Catholic Ireland: a majority of the hierarchy supported the party, while at the local level priests played key roles, and made up about a third of the attendance at conventions.

The party had two weapons: the 'Irish vote' in British constituencies; and the 'balance of power' at Westminster, which after the Conservatives espoused *unionism in 1885–6 meant a Liberal alliance. Nationalist leaders probably exaggerated their influence over the Irish vote in Britain, but despite the rival appeal of Conservatives on Catholic schools and liquor licensing, and of Labour to trade unionists, the UILGB maintained its official commitment to the Liberals. Legislative *home rule, the party's overarching aim, was scarcely on the parliamentary agenda between 1886 and 1910: although the balance of power might be achieved, the House of Lords' veto continued. During its long wait the party developed a role as parliamentary advocate of Catholic interests, its most notable success being the creation of the *National University in 1908. More central to its authority in these years was a continued dependence on agrarianism and the UIL: but although still serviceable, 'the land for the people' was becoming an increasingly rickety slogan as the social structure of rural Ireland diversified.

Explanations for the party's decline fall into two categories. One emphasizes the impact of the *First World War, while the other places more stress on earlier failings and on underlying social changes already beginning to be apparent before 1914. There is little serious evidence that the futility of the 1890s Parnellite split did the party long-term damage: the later breakaway by William *O'Brien and T. M. *Healy in 1910, though restricted to the south-west, created as many dissident nationalist MPs, yet coincided with the party's greatest years.

More important than these divisions among the older generation of Nationalist politicians were generational and social changes. First, electoral reform and the passage of years meant that fewer than one-third of the 1918 electorate which rejected the party so resoundingly had been electors in 1910. Secondly, although about half of the Irish party in the 1880s came from humbler occupational backgrounds than their British counterparts, a further third were university educated and many were men of high local standing. The party did not take up cultural nationalism after 1900 as convincingly as it had embraced agrarianism a generation earlier, but this was less because it failed to identify the issues than because its involvement was not welcomed: those who took up the new movements most enthusiastically came mainly from more modest backgrounds—typically farmers' sons with an education and a job in the public service, for whom the small-town notable so characteristic of the Nationalist Party seemed to represent less an ideal of patriotism than an uninspiring *gombeenism.

But from 1910 to 1914 the party played the balance of power card very effectively, restoring home rule to centre stage. Its dramatic collapse from over 70 seats in 1910 to 6 seats in 1918 stemmed not from its adherence to parliamentary methods but from its failure to develop an effective Ulster policy—a failing shared by *Sinn Féin. Having adhered to an ostrich-like policy on Ulster Unionism until 1914, the party compounded its difficulties at home by a misguided attempt to make active support for the war the foundation for a new sense of unity in Ireland. Instead the opposite happened: economic hardship recruited the urban poor for the British army but elsewhere, especially in rural areas, the call for sacrifice merely sharpened the sense of national difference. As in continental Europe, the war weakened a liberal ethnic movement and nurtured more strident articulations of national sentiment. It is unlikely that, without its influence, the new would have overcome the old either so completely or so rapidly.

Bew, Paul, *Conflict and Conciliation in Ireland, 1890–1910* (1987)

Lyons, F. S. L., *The Irish Parliamentary Party, 1890–1910* (1951)

O'Brien, C. C., *Parnell and his Party* (1957)

ACH

Nationalist Party (of Northern Ireland), successor to the all-Ireland *Nationalist Party (1882–1922) and its grass-roots organizations, the *United Irish League and the *Ancient Order of Hibernians. At the first elections to the Northern Ireland parliament in 1921 it secured rather less support than *Sinn Féin, but following its merger with the pro-treaty wing of the latter in the *National League of the North, it consolidated its position as the main political voice of northern Catholics. Its first leader, Joseph *Devlin, retained considerable political stature in Belfast and London, but he had little influence with Dublin after 1922, nor with west Ulster Catholics who believed that a different political strategy might have put them on the other side of the new Irish border. In Devlin's last years, and especially under his successors T. J. Campbell and later James McSparran, both barristers, the party became increasingly rural and socially conservative. It was closely associated with the Catholic church, and focused its rhetoric heavily on well-worn demographic and historical arguments against *partition; it lost all foothold in Belfast. Condemned to perpetual opposition at *Stormont, its members frequently lapsed into abstention.

For much of their existence the Nationalists were scarcely a political party at all: there was little party discipline, and vital matters such as abstention decisions were taken not at the top but at constituency level. There was no regular party organization in the constituencies, which mostly operated through electoral registration committees chaired by Catholic clergymen, with 'representative conventions' to nominate candidates and take key decisions. During the British Labour government of 1945–51, the *Anti-Partition League briefly gave Nationalists rather more organization and dynamism, some of the inspiration for which came from a *Derry accountant, Eddie McAteer, who later became Party leader. Under McAteer the party moved towards professionalism and normalization: a socio-economic programme was published; in 1965 it accepted the role of official opposition at Stormont for the first time; and in 1966, annual party conferences were instigated. But the party failed to associate itself effectively with the *civil rights movement, and was easily supplanted by the *Social Democratic and Labour Party after 1970. It was opposed to violence throughout its history, but the fact that McAteer's elder brother Hugh had at one time been chief of staff of the *IRA was for many years a delight to Unionists.

Phoenix, E., *Northern Nationalism, 1890–1940* (1994)

ACH

National Labour Party, a political party founded by a group of deputies who were expelled from the *Labour Party on 2 February 1944 following their earlier resignations from the parliamentary party. These deputies, members of the *Irish Transport and General Workers' Union, had objected to the presence of radical socialist James *Larkin in the party since 1941; personal rivalries and power struggles within the trade union movement apparently reinforced ideological disagreements. (See IRISH CONGRESS OF TRADE UNIONS.)

The party maintained its small *Dáil presence after the general elections of 1944 (2.7 per cent of the vote, four seats) and 1948 (2.6 per cent, five seats), and following the latter it entered the *interparty government, where its leader, James Everett, was given a post. This was followed quickly by reconciliation with the Labour Party, which National Labour rejoined in June 1950.

JC

National League, a nationalist organization formed in October 1882 as a replacement for the suppressed *Land League. Few of the former controlling members of the Land League were on the executive of the new body, while local branches tended to have a wider social mix than their Land League predecessors. Local branches existed ostensibly to represent local nationalist opinion, especially in the selection of parliamentary candidates, but in reality leadership opinion usually prevailed. In fact the league, as a movement shaped in accordance with Parnell's desire to abandon agrarian struggle and pursue a purely constitutional campaign for *home rule, was very much under his control. Only very occasionally, and most seriously in Galway in February 1886, when Parnell sought to impose Capt. *O'Shea on unwilling local activists, did serious conflict between leadership and constituencies arise. Nevertheless, the growth of the National League was, until the approach of the 1885 general election, slow. Following the *franchise reforms of 1884–5, however, the number of local branches expanded threefold to reach 1,200 by 1886. The National League remained the organization through which the authority of the Parnellite movement was exercised until the movement split in 1890. JL

National League, a political party founded on 12 September 1926. Its founding leader, William Redmond, was a son of John *Redmond, leader of the *Nationalist Party, to whose former supporters the new party sought to appeal. It performed creditably in the general election of June 1927 (7.3 per cent of votes, eight seats), and a parliamentary stalemate opened the prospect of its participation in a minority coalition government. It failed to capitalize on its position, and in the election of September 1927 its support dropped back (1.6 per cent of votes, two seats). The party dissolved in 1931. It was a conservative party, supporting the *Anglo-Irish treaty. JC

National League (of the North) (1928–34), an attempt by Joseph *Devlin and Cahir *Healy to create a united and structured nationalist movement in Northern Ireland and to establish a basis for collaboration with *Fianna Fáil. Devlin was a barrier to unity with bishops and republicans, and though his participation brought some structure, it died with him. Despite the shared name, the movement had no connection with the party founded in the Irish Free State by William Redmond in 1926. ACH

National Library of Ireland. The 1877 Science and Art Museum Act established the former *Royal Dublin Society Library as a national reference library for Ireland. In 1891 the library's holdings were transferred from *Leinster House to purpose-built premises in Kildare Street, Dublin. An Irish legal deposit library since 1927, the National Library aims to collect all material published in Ireland, including newspapers, material published abroad which relates to Ireland, and works by Irish authors. The collection includes manuscripts, both historical and literary, photographs, maps, and microfilms of manuscripts of Irish interest from repositories outside Ireland. BC

national schools were the government's response to the demand for an acceptable system of state-funded elementary education, especially on the part of the Catholic community which rejected the existing provision by largely Protestant and sometimes proselytizing voluntary societies. The national schools were also intended to supersede the sporadic and largely unsupervised provision previously made by *hedge schools and parish schools. The government established a Board of Commissioners for National Education (1831) which comprised three members of the *Church of Ireland (including the duke of Leinster (see KILDARE) as chairman), two Catholics, and two Presbyterians. Both archbishops of Dublin were among the commissioners.

The principles on which the system was based were set out by Lord Stanley, the lord lieutenant, in a letter to Leinster. They provided for state support for local initiative, and while it was open to persons of standing such as landlords and clergy to apply for recognition of their schools, there was a particular welcome for applications from denominationally mixed groups, in line with the commissioners' policy that children should receive 'literary' education together and 'religious' education separately.

The local sponsors were expected to provide the site and to contribute to maintenance costs and the salaries of teachers (whom they appointed and dismissed). The commissioners contributed most of the costs of building and of salaries, operated an inspectorial scheme, and published textbooks. Their practice in both inspection and publishing owed much to the *Kildare Place Society model, as did their emphasis on teacher-training and *model schools.

The principle of 'mixed' education, on which the system rested, fell short of the expectations of the churches. Presbyterians objected to the right of clergymen of different denominations to have access to the schools. The established church resented the infringement of its prerogatives in popular education, and set up its own system, under the *Church Education Society. The Catholic authorities, though supportive at first, became increasingly critical, especially under *Cullen's leadership, of some textbooks and of other features of the scheme. Gradually, the churches won concessions that moulded the national schools to meet their demands. The report of the Powis Commission (1870) accepted the denominational nature of most schools.

Powis made wide-ranging recommendations, which introduced 'payment-by-results' for teachers. However, this practice was abandoned, as being harmful in effect, on the advice of the Belmore Commission (1898), which also advocated a broader curriculum that took more cognizance of children's aptitudes and introduced manual and practical subjects.

The number of pupils grew from 107,000 in 1833 to over half a million by the end of the century. Though falling short of some of the ambitions of its founders, and open to criticism for an undue emphasis on the didactic and for neglect of the children's Irish environment, the national schools, a form of state intervention in popular education that was unique for its time in these islands, played a major part in promoting literacy in Ireland. KM

National University of Ireland, successor to the *Royal University, and the British government's final attempt to solve the *university question. Ignoring schemes proposed by the Robertson (1903) and Fry (1907) commissions, the Irish Universities Act (1908) dissolved the Royal University and established the Queen's University of Belfast and the National University of Ireland, the latter a federal body comprising University College, Cork, University College, Galway, and a reconstituted University College, Dublin. (*Maynooth became a 'recognized' college in 1913.) Religious tests and the use of funds for theological chairs were prohibited, but the act stipulated that the composition of the senate and the governing bodies of the constituent colleges should be acceptable to the members of the predominant denomination in each institution. KM

National Volunteers, formed when the *Irish Volunteers split in September 1914 on the question

whether Irishmen should fight for the British in the *First World War. The greater majority of the original 160,000 Irish National Volunteers joined the National Volunteers. However, the organization soon became defunct through enlistment and demoralization. Although the National Volunteers were not allowed to form their own regiment as the *Ulster Volunteer Force had been, around 35,000 to 40,000 of them joined the British army. At the same time their function as defenders of *home rule became irrelevant when the Home Rule Act was shelved for the duration of the war.
JA

naval service. The naval service of independent Ireland, a subordinate arm of the *army, was established in 1946. It succeeded the ill-starred marine service, hastily improvised in 1939 and dismissed by the army chief of staff as 'unreliable' in 1945. It suffered monumental neglect—for some months in 1970 it had no operational craft—until its fleet of three elderly corvettes was gradually replaced by modern patrol vessels, some Irish built, in the 1970s and 1980s. The expanded service is now engaged mainly on fisheries protection duties in Ireland's extensive sector of *European Union waters, and it also assists the civil authorities in operations against arms runners and drug smugglers. EO'H

Navan Fort, see EMAIN MACHA.

Navigation Acts, English legislation protecting trade with overseas colonies, introduced under *Cromwell and re-enacted following the *Restoration. Although the first act (1661) gave equal status to Irish and English vessels, the second, in 1663, restricted exports to the colonies to goods shipped from English ports. Ireland was, however, allowed to export horses, victuals, servants, and (from 1705) linen. An act of 1671 forbade the direct import into Ireland of sugar, tobacco, and other named colonial products. This expired in 1681, but the ban on imports was renewed in 1685 and in 1696 was extended to all colonial produce. Imports of unenumerated goods were again permitted from 1731.

Recent assessments suggest that the impact of the acts on Irish economic development was limited: the exceptions made permitted a flourishing export trade in linen and provisions, while Ireland in any case lacked the resources to develop a large trade in colonial consumer goods. Contemporaries, however, saw the acts as a major grievance. Following the *free trade agitation of 1778–9 a British act of 1780 permitted Ireland to trade with the colonies on equal terms with Great Britain. An act of 1793 permitted Ireland to re-export colonial products to Great Britain itself. A new British Navigation Act of 1786, taking account of the independence of the United States, was quietly replicated in an Irish act of the following year, side-stepping the constitutional sensitivities that had wrecked the *Commercial Propositions.

Neolithic Ireland. The Neolithic period (New Stone Age) is often viewed as a mainly economic phenomenon, and is sometimes referred to as the 'Neolithic Revolution'. It began in Ireland around 4500 BC, slowly displacing the *Mesolithic, and ended with the transition to the *Bronze Age at around 2500 BC. It is the combined traits of changes in food production, settlement forms, burial practices, and material culture that essentially define the Neolithic. It is now recognized that the Neolithic was not homogeneous throughout Europe, or even Ireland, and that regional variation occurred.

The mechanisms for the spread and establishment of farming are a point of some contention. Non-native domesticated cereals (primitive forms of wheat and barley) and animals (cattle, pig, and sheep/goat) were imported into Ireland. This may have been done by new groups of people who arrived in boats from Britain, and maybe mainland Europe. Alternatively some of the indigenous Mesolithic hunter-gatherers may have imported the concept and tools for an agricultural lifestyle. Most probably what occurred was a combination of both processes. In any case hunting and gathering remained important and provided supplementary foods.

Many new skills and crafts developed during this time. Polished stone axes increased in importance during the Neolithic period. They were required to clear the native forests for land to grow crops and to create pastures, and to build houses, fences, and trackways. There was intensive exploitation of specific stone sources, such as porcellanite at Tievebulliagh Mountain near Cushendall and at Brockley on Rathlin Island, Co. Antrim, for the large-scale production of polished axes. Wood and stone points were placed in simple ards (ploughs) to break up the ground for planting; flint tools were used for harvesting crops, and stone saddle querns for grinding the grain. Flint remained an important stone for the production of tools and weapons, and fine flint leaf and lozenge-shaped arrowheads were used for both hunting and warfare. Some objects such as flint javelin heads, mace heads, and large finely executed polished axes (similar to those in the Malone Hoard from Belfast), were probably symbols of power, wealth, and prestige, rather than utilitarian objects. Pottery makes its first appearance in Ireland during the Neolithic and production is believed to have occurred on a small, localized scale. The pots were handmade, coil-built, and fired in bonfires or firing pits. The earliest pots were mainly undecorated round-bottomed bowls, although decoration became more common in the later part of the period. Towards the end of the Neolithic a great diversity in pottery styles existed and flat-based pottery was introduced.

The development of farming greatly impacted on both society and the landscape. Field divisions, probably once extensive, have been found in a number of places preserved under peat such as the expansive Céide field systems in north-west Mayo. The forests provided wood for the construction of trackways that provided access across wetland areas to higher and drier land. Timber was also used in the construction of houses and circular (or oval) and plank-built rectangular forms are known. An average sized house could have accommodated a family group of between five and ten individuals and the variation in house sizes may be linked not only to the numbers of occupants, but also to function and social status. At some sites, such as Ballygalley, Co. Antrim, more than one house is known and they may have been occupied contemporaneously. In general, however, the pattern appears to have been one of dispersed settlement linked to a sedentary existence.

Short-term, specialized habitations are also known and some appear to be linked to specific activities such as exploiting marine resources, flint, and other stone sources. Enclosed settlements also existed, such as that at Lough Gur, Co. Limerick, where low banks retained by stone walls may have had some type of social significance. A small number of hilltop enclosures, including Donegore Hill and Lyles Hill, both in Co. Antrim, probably had a defensive role.

The most enduring monuments of the Neolithic are the *megalithic tombs. Great earthen monuments known as henges were also constructed and at the Giant's Ring, Co. Down, an impressive henge, enclosing an earlier megalithic monument and a nearby timber-post complex, suggest the area was used by large numbers of people, probably for ritual purposes. These monuments indicate status, a knowledge of engineering, and the ability to organize resources, including labour. Ritual practices can also be discerned at sites such as Goodland, Co. Antrim, where a small ditch and over 170 pits, filled with flints, pottery, charcoal, and stone cobbles were excavated. It has been suggested that this material was deliberately deposited in the pits for ritualistic purposes, possibly linked to fertility ceremonies.

Ireland was not isolated during the Neolithic and evidence suggests that communication networks existed between Ireland and Britain and mainland Europe. Irish-made objects such as porcellanite axes have been found as far away as the Shetland Islands, south-west England, and the Isle of Man. Equally, stone axes from Britain, a flint axe from Scandinavia, pitchstone from Scotland, and jadeite axes from the Alpine area of northern Europe have been found in Ireland.

Cooney, G., and Grogan, E., *Irish Prehistory: A Social Perspective* (1994)

SMcC

Ne temere, a papal decree of 1908 governing marriages where one of the partners was not a Catholic. Its main provision was that the non-Catholic partner must agree that children be brought up as Catholics. This and other stipulations largely restated existing Catholic teaching, and had been anticipated in the regulations on mixed marriage laid down at the Synod of *Thurles. The decree was nevertheless frequently cited by *unionist and *Orange polemicists as evidence of Catholic intolerance and spiritual tyranny.

neutrality has been an element, implicit or explicit, in Irish foreign policy since the foundation of the state. Between the First and Second World Wars intimations of neutrality as national policy were evident in the Irish positions at the League of Nations where, in the 1930s, Eamon de *Valera was an insistent advocate of collective security as an alternative to great power-led alliance systems.

The Second World War saw the transformation of this diplomatic tendency into a legal status. Although neutrality was the favoured stance of the greater number of small powers at the beginning of the war, Ireland could gloss this self-preservatory pragmatism with moral principle in view both of its pre-war diplomacy at the league and of the continuing issue of *partition. However, while the formal requirements of neutrality were strictly adhered to throughout the conflict, Ireland's position was rather less than equidistant between the belligerents and, in effect, favoured the allies. This form of neutrality, a degree short of 'benevolent' but some distance from the rigour of, for example, the Swiss or Portuguese approaches, seemed to commend itself to public opinion, especially after the entry of the United States to the war.

Nevertheless, the simple fact of its non-belligerence left Ireland in some disfavour with the western allies in the atmosphere of the immediate post-war years. Diplomatic isolation at this time was not eased by the continuation of neutrality into the Cold War era. The rejection of NATO membership in 1949 by the first *interparty government on 'constitutional' grounds failed in its evident purpose of eliciting American support for the anti-partitionist cause. Consequently, for the first half of the 1950s, Ireland was forced to maintain an uncomfortable foreign policy stance in which fiercely pro-western ideological affinities were complemented, on grounds bewildering to many abroad, by a refusal to participate in the western alliance.

From the later 1950s, however, neutrality found a more comprehensible diplomatic expression. The combination of United Nations membership in 1955 and the return of *Fianna Fáil to power in 1957 gave rise to a reassertion of the international activism of the 1930s. Ireland emerged as a considerable 'middle power' player in UN diplomacy. Positions were taken which were frequently at odds with 'western' interests on issues such as the representation of China at the UN and nuclear disengagement in Europe.

The question of neutrality featured prominently in the national debates over entry to Europe in the 1960s (see EUROPEAN UNION). In the event, however, the status of sole neutral in the Community posed no great difficulties. Similarly, Ireland was able to navigate its way through the final, tense phase of global bipolarity in the 1980s with its declaratory commitment to neutrality intact. At the end of 1999 the Irish government signed up to NATO's 'Partnership for Peace' programme, which was originally designed to provide the former communist states of eastern Europe with a half-way house to full membership. Official assurances that this would not affect Ireland's traditional neutrality were questionable—but they remained largely unquestioned in a diplomatic environment in which the stance had ceased to have much meaning.

Fisk, R., *In Time of War: Ireland, Ulster and the Price of Neutrality* (1983)

Keatinge, P., *A Singular Stance: Irish Neutrality in the 1980s* (1984)

Salmon, T., *Unneutral Ireland: An Ambivalent and Unique Security Policy* (1989)

NMacQ

New Departure, a compact arrived at between *Parnell, *Davitt, and the *Fenian leader John *Devoy in June 1879 which provided the basis for the effective prosecution of the *Land War. It was predicated on the acceptance that a fundamental link existed between the land and national questions; but there were unarticulated differences about the nature of that link. The Fenian case was that no Westminster government would solve the land question on the tenants' terms and that realization of this would produce mass support for their *republican objective. Parnell, while giving the impression that he concurred in this view, believed that under sufficient pressure Westminster would make an adequate settlement, one that would further his own, more realistic, objective of *home rule. The New Departure maximized Parnell's ability to engage all shades of nationalist opinion in the agrarian struggle of 1879–82. JL

New English, see OLD ENGLISH AND NEW ENGLISH.

Newfoundland. Fishermen from the south-east of Ireland began to travel regularly to the rich fishing grounds off Newfoundland from the second half of the 17th century. In the first decades of the 19th century the long-standing connections established by seasonal and temporary migration provided the basis for a wave of permanent emigration. An estimated 30,000–35,000 people, drawn overwhelmingly from Waterford and its hinterland, settled in Newfoundland 1800–30, giving its popular culture and spoken English a distinctive flavour.

Newgrange, see MEGALITHIC TOMBS.

New Light, see OLD LIGHT AND NEW LIGHT.

Newman, John Henry (1801–90), a former fellow of Oriel College, Oxford, and the most celebrated English convert to Catholicism of his day, chosen by Archbishop *Cullen as first rector of the *Catholic University. His most celebrated work, *The Idea of a University, Defined and Illustrated* (1852), was based on lectures delivered at the Rotunda, Dublin, in preparation for the opening of the university. Newman was installed as rector on 4 June 1854, but resigned in 1858. His withdrawal in part reflected the gulf between his vision of 'a Catholic Oxford in Ireland', which would attract English as well as Irish students, and the more narrowly domestic and vocational institution which Cullen and other bishops were prepared to support. However Newman had always stressed that he intended to serve for a limited period only, and continued throughout to spend more than half his time in England, where he remained superior of the Birmingham Oratory.

new nationalism, a term coined to describe the rise, in the quarter-century before 1914, of a more radical nationalist sentiment. The long-term background to this development was the disillusionment with parliamentary nationalism created by the fall of *Parnell, the factional conflict that followed, and the apparent decline of the reunited

*Nationalist Party into a conservative counter-establishment. An immediate stimulus was provided by three events: the centenary of the *insurrection of 1798, the *Boer War, and the visit of Queen Victoria, with accompanying counter-demonstrations, in 1900. The chief manifestations of changing attitudes were the growth of new forms of cultural nationalism (the *Gaelic Athletic Association and *Gaelic League), the appearance of the first *Sinn Féin, and the takeover of the *Irish Republican Brotherhood by a new generation of activists. What remains unclear is whether these developments, involving small if highly committed groups, were in themselves sufficient to undermine the constitutionalism of the Nationalist Party, or whether it was only the novel circumstances of the *First World War that allowed radical nationalism in its different forms to move from the fringes of Irish politics to the very centre.

new rules, regulations governing the composition of urban corporations introduced in 1672. The original aim was to impose order following Charles II's brief experiment with religious toleration (see RESTORATION). Members of corporations were to take the oath of supremacy, unless the *lord lieutenant issued a dispensation. In practice this power to admit Catholics was not used, except during the reign of *James II. The rules also required that the *privy council approve the appointment of mayors. During 1711–14 efforts to impose a Tory mayor on the predominantly Whig corporation of Dublin gave rise to a prolonged dispute.

newspapers. The earliest newspaper to be published in Ireland was probably *An Account of the Chief Occurrences of Ireland* printed in Dublin in February 1660. This was succeeded by a number of ephemeral journals until the early 1690s, when the *Dublin Intelligence* was the first of a number of papers to be supported by *Dublin Castle and to publish both English and Irish news.

In the first half of the 18th century 165 newspapers were launched in Dublin. Richard Pue started *Pue's Occurrences* in 1703; *Faulkner's Dublin Journal* was begun by George *Faulkner (*c.*1703–75) in 1725, and the **Freeman's Journal* was established in 1763. Early Dublin newspapers recognized the commercial importance of advertisements; their contents are an important source for the social and commercial history of the period. Many papers were an extension of their proprietor's interests: *Pue's Occurrences* specialized in sale notices for country estates, the *Dublin Courant* (founded 1724) in booksellers' advertisements.

In 1774, later than in England, taxes were imposed on newsprint, advertisements, and paper. After the Act of *Union, the Irish press was more heavily taxed than that in England and proprietors had to lodge securities for good behaviour. These duties lasted until 1865—again rather later than in England. Continuing a practice of the Irish parliament, secret service moneys were voted to buy support for the Castle, and contracts to publish proclamations and official advertisements became valuable subsidies. The *Freeman's Journal* was a prime example of a 'patriotic' paper purchased by these means. In the face of such opposition, the founding of their own newspaper, the **Northern Star*, was an important part of the *United Irishmen's drive to build up popular support.

Daniel *O'Connell made 'a cheap and enlightened Press' one of the aims of the *Catholic Association, which spent part of the *Catholic rent on advertisements in both the English and Irish press. Later *repeal reading rooms were established in provincial towns to spread the movement's propaganda but were suppressed after the *rebellion of 1848. The establishment of **Nation* was likewise crucial to the rise of *Young Ireland, first as an adjunct, later as a rival, to the repeal movement. The *Tenant League was, however, the first political association in Ireland to understand how to use the press to its fullest extent. Newspaper owners like Charles Gavan *Duffy and John *Gray of the *Freeman's Journal* organized the conference which founded the league in 1850. John Francis Maguire (1815–72) of the *Cork Examiner* (1841–) and James M'Knight (1801–76) of the *Banner of Ulster* (1842–70) were acute analysts and strong supporters of the league's programme.

*Fenianism came late to the use of newspaper propaganda. After initial hesitation, James *Stephens founded the *Irish People* in Dublin in 1863 as the official Fenian paper, but it was suppressed in 1865 and succeeded by the *Irishman* (1858–81), owned by Richard Pigott (see 'PARNELLISM AND CRIME'). During the *Land War Pigott used his paper to attack the leadership of *Parnell. To silence him, the *Nationalist party in 1881 purchased the *Irishman*, along with another Pigott paper, the *Flag of Ireland*, which under the new title *United Ireland* (1881–98) became Parnell's main support. Following the split precipitated by the *O'Shea divorce, *United Ireland* was captured for the Parnellites by the forcible occupation of its offices. In 1891 Parnell founded the *Irish Daily Independent*, but this was challenged by William Martin *Murphy, who financed the anti-Parnellite *National Press* (1891–2), which amalgamated with the *Freeman's Journal*. Murphy founded the *Daily Nation* (1897) which, when it merged in 1900 with the *Irish Daily Independent*, became a cheap mass circulation daily imitating the 'new journalism' of the Northcliffe Press in Britain. After some difficulties, it became the *Irish Independent* (1905–), which later supported *Cumann na nGaedheal. It is now the largest-selling morning newspaper in Ireland. The **Irish Times*, the bulwark of *Protestant ascendancy, was founded in 1859.

In 1853 *Gladstone abolished the tax on advertisements; he went on to abolish taxation on newspapers in 1855 (although Irish newspapers sent by post had to be printed on stamped paper until 1865) and on paper in 1861. The consequent drop in prices, together with increasing *literacy and a rise in consumer spending, led to an explosion in the number of titles. In 1850 there were 68 newspapers published outside Dublin; by 1879 there were 127. The provincial press was influential in the spread of nationalism and its editors were important figures in their communities. Early provincial proprietors had been stationers and patent medicine vendors, but in the 19th century local and national politicians often ran the press. The transition from elite to mass politics meant a sharp rise in the number of nationalist provincial papers. In 1861 there were no nationalist papers outside Dublin; by 1891 there were 34. Many provincial newspaper editors went on to figure in national politics, including John Francis Maguire of the *Cork Examiner* and Edward Harrington and Timothy Harrington (1851–1910) of the *Kerry Sentinel* (1878–1918).

With the exception of the liberal *Belfast *Northern Whig*, 19th-century Ulster newspapers reflected the sectarian divide. The *Belfast Telegraph* (1870–) group of papers were founded to further the interests of the *Orange Order; the short-lived *Banner of Ulster* was the organ of the *Presbyterian church. This division of allegiance continues today, with the unionist **Belfast News-Letter* and the nationalist *Irish News* (1891–). From the mid-19th century, newspapers began to print columns in Irish and *An *Claidheamh Soluis* was founded by the *Gaelic League as its official newspaper. However, there has never been a successful mass circulation Irish-language paper.

In the Republic today there are two national morning dailies, a regional daily, and four Sunday papers. Dublin and Cork have evening papers and there are about 50 local papers, mainly published weekly. Belfast has four morning papers and one evening paper. Sales of English newspapers, the backbone of the Irish wholesale business in the mid-19th century, had declined by the 1880s, expanded in the early 20th century, but declined again under *protectionism. Since 1965, with the use of air transport, English titles have had an increasing share of the Irish market.

Aspinall, A., *Politics and the Press c.1780–1850* (1946)
Inglis, Brian, *The Freedom of the Press in Ireland 1784–1841* (1954)
Munter, R. J., *The History of the Irish Newspaper 1685–1760* (1967)

M-LL

New Tipperary, a development in the *Plan of Campaign initiated by William *O'Brien. In response to the action of the largest landlord of Tipperary town, A. H. Smith-Barry, who pursued wholesale evictions against tenants withholding rents, nationalists resorted to the extreme measure of building a substitute 'town' nearby. Opened with great fanfare on 12 April 1890, New Tipperary was a disastrously expensive venture, greatly depleting Plan funds and undermining the whole strategy.

JL

Newtown Act (1748), confirming that non-residents could be members of *borough corporations. Passed after the Colvill estate in Co. Down and the right to nominate new members to the corporation of Newtownards had been sold to different purchasers, the act confirmed that such a separation between lordship of the soil and political control of a parliamentary borough (see FRANCHISE) was legal.

New Zealand. The Irish presence in New Zealand began with the earliest white settlement. Levels of migration of 2,000 persons or more annually characterized most of the period 1870 to 1914. Thereafter, Irish migration dropped sharply. In 1881 the Irish as a multigenerational ethnic group comprised about 18.9 per cent of the pakeha (that is, non-Maori) population. That was their high point and the proportion slid slowly downward thereafter, but as late as 1951 it was 16.7 per cent. Roughly three out of four persons of Irish ethnicity were Catholic. In the period of heaviest Irish migration to New Zealand (1870–1914) Munster and Ulster were the largest sources of migrants. Roughly equal numbers came from each. Taken together, these two provinces supplied over 80 per cent of Irish migrants.

The level of ethnic consciousness of the Irish in New Zealand has never been very high. The most important Irish influence has been the century-long pressure of Irish-descended Catholics to have the government fully fund a religiously segregated school system. This battle, begun in the 1870s, was finally won in 1975. DHA

Niall Glúndub ('Niall Black-knee') (*fl.* 896–919), king of the *Cenél nEógain, king of Tara 916–19, one of twelve pre-*Norman kings entitled *rí Érenn* (king of Ireland—see HIGH KINGSHIP) in the original hand of the *Annals of Ulster*. After building up power in Ulster and northern Connacht, he attained the kingship of Tara after the death of Flann Sinna (of the *Clann Cholmáin), whose queen, Gormlaith, Niall married. He died fighting the Dublin Norse in 919. CS

Niall Noígiallach ('Niall of the Nine Hostages'), eponymous ancestor of the *Uí Néill, reputed to have flourished in the early 5th century. The earliest traditions about his career are 9th century in date, when he was remembered as a raider of Britain. The texts ascribe the nine hostages to varying locations in Ireland, Britain, and the Continent. In genealogical and saga materials, he is identified as brother to the ancestor of the *Connachta kings. CS

Nicholson, W. P. (1875–1959), a remarkably effective evangelist, particularly in Ulster, in the early 1920s. After experience in Scotland, Australia, and America, where he was ordained, Nicholson returned to Ulster, where large working-class audiences responded to his homely, if sometimes vulgar, preaching. The results of his missions recalled the *revival of 1859. Some claim that he saved *Northern Ireland from sectarian civil war; others charge him with dividing congregations and churches. RFGH

Nine Years War (Apr. 1593–Mar. 1603), also known as Tyrone's rebellion, after the state's main antagonist in the conflict, Hugh *O'Neill, 2nd earl of Tyrone. It arose from *Fitzwilliam's partition of *Monaghan, which broke up the MacMahon lordship and threatened other Ulster lordships with a similar fate. The state's other main antagonist, Red Hugh *O'Donnell, was O'Neill's son-in-law. Their alliance transcended traditional rivalry in Ulster and came to include many other Gaelic lords in an oath-bound confederacy which initially took the form of a secret conspiracy.

The first action of the war was an exercise in manipulation and deceit by O'Neill. After the ejection of a sheriff from Fermanagh, O'Neill fought on the side of the government while simultaneously directing his brother Cormac, and other relatives whom he allegedly could not control, against the state. This was a delaying tactic, because the northern lords were hoping for aid from Spain, where they had sent agents as early as 1592. O'Neill disclosed his true role in February 1595 when he ordered the destruction of the garrison on the river Blackwater. The state finally proclaimed him a traitor in June 1595.

Irish tactics during the war were primarily defensive. The **buannacht* system used to accommodate *redshanks was reoriented to put local troops into the field. These were well trained and leavened with English and Spanish veterans. Up to a third of the confederates fought with *firearms, supplied by Scottish and *Old English merchants, which enhanced their traditional guerrilla-style tactics. A major lack was artillery, which made the taking of forts and towns, other than by ruse or betrayal, impossible. The English army, surprised by the discipline of their opponents, suffered from a divided command, between Lord Deputy Russell and Lord General Norris in 1596–7, and between Black Tom Butler of *Ormond and Henry *Bagenal in 1598. Their offensive tactics usually amounted to no more than a single expedition to establish or relieve outlying garrisons. The resulting Irish victories were in fact large ambushes—the *Ford of the biscuits (1594), *Clontibret (1595), the *Yellow Ford (1598). These successes, together with the fall of Sligo and Cavan, allowed the war to spread to Connacht and Leinster in 1595 and to Munster in 1598.

For the Irish, politics was an extension of war. O'Neill used ceasefires and long-drawn-out negotiations as a delaying tactic in which the hard-pressed and factionalized state acquiesced. A compromise, which would have left O'Neill supreme in Ulster, was negotiated in 1596 but aborted by the timely arrival of Spanish agents. Further negotiations, prolonged in the case of Ormond in 1598, and short and secret in the case of *Essex in 1599, worked to O'Neill's advantage. After the débâcle of Essex's lieutenancy, O'Neill and his confederates controlled the greater part of Ireland. Unable to take the towns by force, O'Neill now tried to win over the Old English Catholics. In November 1599 he issued a proclamation requesting the Old English to join his fight for faith and fatherland. A final negotiating position with the crown, which would have provided for an autonomous Catholic Ireland run jointly by its great lords and the Old English, was drawn up. Cecil, the English secretary of state, marked these 22 demands with the word 'Utopia'.

O'Neill's adoption of **patria* frightened the crown more than it encouraged the Old English. *Mountjoy was rapidly dispatched to Dublin and *Docwra established at Lough Foyle behind confederate lines. The strategy was now the establishment of small garrisons, closely placed and mutually supporting, to wear down the economy that supported the irregular warfare of the Irish. The long-heralded Spanish expedition finally landed at *Kinsale, only to withdraw ignominiously after O'Neill and O'Donnell abandoned their defensive tactics and risked all in a pitched battle. The garrisons in Ulster brought famine in their wake. One by one O'Neill's allies sued for peace and he went into hiding. In September 1602 Mountjoy destroyed the symbol of his authority at *Tullaghoge. However, the garrison policy was proving very expensive and could be sustained only by the debasement of the Irish currency. The state was therefore glad when O'Neill submitted at *Mellifont in March 1603. The war had cost the English exchequer nearly £2 million—eight times as much as any previous Irish war and as much as Elizabeth's continental wars. But it had given England complete control of Ireland for the first time since the *Anglo-Norman invasion.

Morgan, Hiram, *Tyrone's Rebellion* (1993)

HM

non-jurors, clergy of the established church who refused to accept the legitimacy of the *revolution of 1688 by taking oaths of allegiance to the new monarchs. Non-jurors were far fewer in the *Church of Ireland than in the Church of England. The best known were William Sheridan (1636–1711), bishop of Kilmore and Ardagh, and Charles Leslie (1650–1722), chancellor of the cathedral of Connor, who subsequently debated the legitimacy of the revolution with William *King. The Irish-born Henry Dodwell (1641–1711) likewise forfeited the Camden chair of history at Oxford rather than take the oath of allegiance. 'Non-juror' is also sometimes used for those refusing to take the later oath of *abjuration.

Norbury, Ist earl of, see TOLER, JOHN.

Normans, the term applied to the men from Normandy and surrounding parts of northern France who conquered England under Duke William in 1066, and by extension to those from England and Wales who invaded Ireland a century later. G. H. *Orpen, writing in the early 20th century, included the whole period 1169–1333 in his four seminal volumes entitled *Ireland under the Normans*. A. J. Otway-Ruthven wrote in 1965 of 'Norman' settlement in Ireland. 'Normans' are even to be found in the pages of authors concerned with the 14th and 15th centuries; indeed R. Dudley Edwards placed the collapse of something he christened 'Hiberno-Norman civilization' in the 16th century. Yet the identity of the settlers in Ireland is far more complicated than this extension suggests: some had Welsh, Flemish, or Breton forebears, and many had English; few came to Ireland directly from the Continent, let alone from Normandy; and the epithet favoured by contemporary writers on both sides of the Irish Sea was, quite simply, 'English'. Nevertheless, the usage is firmly established among Irish historians and archaeologists, though some prefer hybrids, unknown to contemporaries, such as 'Anglo-Norman' or 'Anglo-French'.

These historiographical conventions partly reflect the sheer conservatism of Irish scholarship: many Victorian historians of England, echoing Sir Walter Scott's *Ivanhoe* (1819), imagined a far more enduring distinction between Anglo-Saxons and Normans than is envisaged by their modern successors, who have shown that the descendants of the conquerors of 1066 adopted the English past and manufactured their own version of Englishness during the 12th century. It may also reflect other influences: on the one hand, the snobbery that led late medieval Gaelic poets to stress the French ancestry of the settler nobility; on the other, the reluctance of Irish medievalists to use the term 'English', because it had been hijacked by those who sought to reduce Irish history after 1170 to an undifferentiated tale of English oppression. Orpen in particular—as the descendant of long-established Irish Protestant gentry, and as a linguist whose first major venture as a medievalist was to edit and translate from the original Anglo-Norman French the verse chronicle known as the *Song of Dermot and the Earl*—would not have found it natural or agreeable to see the lordship of Ireland as merely 'English'. Ironically, the *Song* itself calls the 12th-century invaders *les engleis* ('the English').

In so far as the term 'Norman' helped historians to set medieval Ireland in the European context of its own time, and to achieve distance from crude English imperialist or Irish nationalist interpretations of the past, it may have served a useful purpose. As a description of contemporary realities, however, it is profoundly misleading. For historians studying language and elite culture, 'Anglo-Norman' or 'Anglo-French' is a defensible alternative; for those concerned with politics, government, and national consciousness, 'English' is probably the least inaccurate way of describing those involved in the invasions of 1167–71 and the colonization that followed. It is unlikely, nevertheless, that such a well-rooted usage will be readily expelled from the Irish historian's vocabulary.

Thomas, H. M., *The English and the Normans: Ethnic Hostility, Assimilation and Identity 1066–c.1220* (2003)

Frame, R., '"Les Engleys nées en Irlande": The English Political Identity in Medieval Ireland', *Transactions of the Royal Historical Society*, 6th ser. 3 (1993)

Gillingham, J., 'The English Conquest of Ireland', in B. Bradshaw, A. Hadfield, and W. Maley (eds.), *Representing Ireland: Literature and the Origins of Conflict* (1993)

RFF

Norse, the language of the *Viking invaders and settlers, substantially influenced the Irish language, after an initial period when the differences between the two languages made mutual communication impossible. The invaders were mainly Norwegian in origin (known as the *Fingaill*, i.e. the 'fair' foreigners, as distinct from the smaller number of Danish settlers, known as the *Dubhgaill*, i.e. the 'dark' foreigners). By the middle of the 9th century, a population group known as the *Gall-Gáidil* ('Norse-Irish') was identified. Settlement, intermarriage, and the sharing of each other's way of life encouraged linguistic assimilation, and the vocabulary of Irish was enriched through the adoption of many Norse words, particularly those associated with the preoccupations of the invaders, such as seafaring, fishing, and commerce. Examples of loanwords in these categories include Ir. (Irish) *acaire*, 'anchor' (ON (Old Norse) *akkeri*), Ir. *dorú*, 'fishing line' (ON *dorg*), Ir. *stiúir*, 'rudder' (ON *styri*), Ir. *mál*, 'excise, tax' (ON *mál*), Ir. *mangaire*, 'hawker, huckster' (ON *mangan*), Ir. *margadh*, 'market' (ON *markar*), Ir. *beoir*, 'beer' (ON *bjórr*), Ir. *fuinneog*, 'window' (ON *vindauga*), Ir. *iarla*, 'earl' (ON *iarl*), Ir. *laincis*, 'fetter, hobble' (ON *lang-festr*), Ir. *lochta*, 'loft' (ON *lopt*), Ir. *pónaire*, 'bean' (ON *baunir*). A number of Norse names, such as ON Magnus (Ir. Maghnus), also entered the Irish lexicon, and place names, such as Wicklow (ON *Vikingaló*), Howth (from ON *Hoved*, 'head'), supply further evidence of the Norse influence. TPD

Northern Ireland, a province created by the *Government of Ireland Act of 1920, made up of the six Ulster counties of Antrim, Armagh, Down, Fermanagh, Londonderry, and Tyrone, and retained within the United Kingdom after the rest of Ireland achieved dominion status by the *Anglo-Irish treaty of 1921. Following the successful resistance of Ulster unionists to *home rule in 1911–14, it was only the separation of the predominantly Protestant segment of Ulster in 1920 that made it politically possible for a Conservative-dominated British coalition government to reach agreement with *Sinn Féin on constitutional arrangements for the south. Although the Ulster Unionists sacrificed the remaining three counties of Ulster with their significant Protestant minorities, the new six-county province included a reluctant Catholic minority amounting to more than one-third of its population (which by the 1990s was to rise to more than two-fifths). After some abortive attempts at minority protection through the *Craig–Collins pacts, the British government gave the Unionists unequivocal support: in effect those who had objected so strongly to home rule under Dublin in 1914 were given an extended opportunity to run the north's divided society. The Unionists had wanted initially to be governed directly from London, but in 1921 accepted a devolved parliament in Belfast and came quickly to like it.

While Unionist governments delivered stability in Northern Ireland British governments of all parties let them get on with it: when this stability disappeared after 1968 the dissolution of the Northern Ireland parliament quickly followed. After 1972 Northern Ireland retained a devolved administration, but politically it was governed by *direct rule from London, until a new form of self-government was attempted in 1998. Although the constitutional arrangements of 1921–72 failed to achieve lasting or deep-rooted communal harmony, they do represent the most sustained attempt at devolved regional government ever attempted in the United Kingdom.

The Northern Ireland parliament, created under the 1920 act, was opened by King George V in Belfast city hall on 22 June 1921, following elections to a 'House of Commons' on Empire Day, 24 May. It later moved to Assembly's College before occupying the imposing purpose-built premises at *Stormont (which became the standard way of referring to the Northern Ireland parliament or government), on the edge of the city, in November 1932. Partly deriving from the legislation, partly as a result of decisions taken by the first prime minister, Sir James *Craig, Stormont followed the Westminster model very closely. The main differences were that the body was in practice part-time, meeting for only a couple of months each year, and that government ministers were entitled to speak in both the House of Commons and the upper house or 'Senate'. This consisted of the lord mayors of Belfast and Derry, who sat ex officio, and of 24 other members elected by the House of Commons. Not surprisingly, it failed to establish a reputation as an effective revising chamber. There was also a governor, representing the crown.

Returned to the first House of Commons in 1921 were 40 *Unionists, 6 *Nationalists, and 6 Sinn Féiners, a government majority of 28. Although the number of Unionists was sometimes reduced by challenges from the *Northern Ireland Labour Party and other minor parties, only in 1925 did the party's overall majority fall below 20. Soon after the government replaced *proportional representation based on nine multi-member constituencies with first-past-the-post elections in 48 single seaters; PR was retained in the four-seat Queen's University constituency, which survived until 1968. No nationalist members took their seats prior to 1925, and organized nationalist abstention occurred frequently between 1932 and 1945. The system of majoritarian democracy, though based closely on the Westminster model, operated in the circumstances of Northern Ireland's divided society to produce a one-party state, in which the interests of the state and the interests of the Unionist Party became dangerously intertwined. In local government, until 1973, almost 100 separate authorities operated, including an upper tier of six county councils. The local government franchise was restricted to ratepayers, and permitted multiple votes for business voters. After 1946 this was out of line with practice in Britain, where almost all adults were enfranchised compared with less than 80 per cent in Belfast (1966). Universal suffrage in local government elections was a major issue for the *civil rights movement, and was attained in 1972; in the following year local government was restructured into a single tier of 26 district councils, now with far more limited powers than was the case in Britain.

The devolved powers of the Northern Ireland parliament included all major aspects of domestic policy except major taxation. By 'the convention' operated at Westminster, members of the United Kingdom parliament were effectively precluded from debating the internal affairs of Northern Ireland except on very isolated occasions. Defence matters, however, were reserved to the Westminster parliament (including the decision not to include Northern Ireland in the provision for compulsory military service during the *Second World War). Once the British army was called out in aid of the civil power, from August 1969 onwards, it was only a matter of time before Westminster demanded control over the province's internal security policy. The refusal of Brian *Faulkner's government to agree to this led to the prorogation of Stormont in March 1972, and its dissolution the following year.

The disentanglement of Northern Ireland's finances after 1921 proved more problematic than the establishment of devolved legislative powers. Revenue was allocated from the British treasury by a joint exchequer board. While the 'imperial contribution' soon effectively disappeared, the British government proved distinctly reluctant to make the large injection of funds necessary to raise Northern Ireland's level of welfare provision to the British level. It was agreed by the Colwyn Committee in 1925 that in future per capita welfare spending for the province would be increased 'step by step' with improvements in Britain, but Northern Ireland's relatively low base point meant that the great burden of inter-war unemployment weighed very heavily on the province, while the quality and volume of urban and rural housing stock, school buildings, roads, and public health fell further behind. In effect Colwyn's arbitration of 1925 and the Unemployment Insurance Agreement of 1926, while both making financial concessions to Northern Ireland, implicitly accepted that devolution justified lower levels of provision in the province, on grounds both of historic factors and of higher per capita take-up of welfare services than in Britain.

Full equalization of public spending provision did not come until 1946, when 'step by step' gave way to the principle of 'parity' of social services, so that welfare state provisions applied equally in Britain and in Northern Ireland. The impact of this was noticeable both in improved health statistics and in education, where free grammar schooling was available for the first time to those able or fortunate enough to pass the 11-plus examination. In economic policy also, the post-war era offered opportunities for devolved government to demonstrate its worth.

The staple industries of *linen and *shipbuilding, the major urban employers in the province, which had struggled during the inter-war period, went into steep decline—linen from 1953 (due to competition from other materials and cheaper labour markets) and shipbuilding by the end of the same decade (due to over-conservative management in the face of technological and market changes). Agriculture too, the province's largest employer, shed labour massively in the face of mechanization. These changes constituted a rigorous test for devolved regional government—could its closeness to the problems facilitate more effective responses than could have been offered by a more remote central government? Though the evidence is mixed, the overall answer must be 'no'. Shipbuilding fared no better than in Britain. The man-made fibre industry did constitute a major innovation, benefiting many centres in the east of the province, and in *Derry City, from the 1950s to the 1970s, an achievement for which regional planning can claim some credit. But in this, the golden era of state planning, the lack of political consensus between nationalist and unionist in the province was an increasingly serious problem. While the economic case for concentrating new developments in the predominantly Protestant east of the province, as argued in the Matthew Plan for Greater Belfast (1962) and the Wilson Report (1964), may have been strong, Stormont's chances of gaining the confidence of the nationalist community were slimmer than those of central government would have been. Equally, the Unionist government and local authorities, most notably in Derry City, were reluctant to risk damaging their electoral position by economic or social policies that might increase the numerical or economic strength of the Catholic community. While it is not easy to control for the effects (negative and perhaps also positive) of the post-1969 troubles on the regional economy, it seems clear that the suspension of political devolution after 1972 brought more effective public investment and no worse a performance in terms of economic management.

Buckland, Patrick, *The Factory of Grievances: Devolved Government in Northern Ireland 1921–39* (1979)

ACH

Northern Ireland conflict (1969–). Northern Ireland was born in violent conflict, but with the exception of savage riots in 1935 (see RELIGIOUS CONFLICT) the conflagrations which had recurred regularly, especially in *Belfast, during the later 19th century were avoided between 1923 and 1968. The *IRA's *border campaign of 1956–62 failed either to provoke the Protestants or to interest the Catholics very much. But almost half a century of *Stormont government, while it had been successful in managing the ethnic divide, had done little to mitigate it. After 1930 the funding of Catholic schools has been put on a basis acceptable to the Catholic church, but no effort was made to dissuade Catholics from the early acquired belief that posts in the Northern Ireland civil service were not for them, to address the housing shortage in areas where houses meant voters, to alleviate unemployment in Catholic areas, or to persuade the majority of Catholics that the *Royal Ulster Constabulary and the *Ulster Special Constabulary exercised their responsibilities even-handedly. Inspired by a wish to modernize, and under pressure from the British government, Terence *O'Neill sought to bring in reforms after 1963. Expectations were raised but not met, while a powerful Protestant backlash was aroused, led by Revd Ian Paisley, whose militant Protestant Unionist Party (renamed the *Democratic Unionist Party in 1971) became, paradoxically, the main beneficiary of the reintroduction of *proportional representation in 1973.

During the late 1960s the *civil rights movement took up many of the main Catholic grievances, but the successive governments of O'Neill, James Chichester-Clark, and Brian *Faulkner proved unable to deliver reforms, contain growing Catholic street action, or keep Protestant militants in check. British troops were called out 'in aid of the civil power' in August 1969, an intended short-term measure which is still in place more than 30 years later. Mass rioting between Catholics and the police and at Catholic–Protestant interfaces in Belfast, Derry, and other centres was brought under more effective control after three summers of rioting and other major incidents such as *Bloody Sunday, in January 1972. But during 1970 the conflict took an even more serious turn as the provisional *IRA began a campaign of terrorist warfare against both the security forces and major commercial centres. The death toll rose from 25 in 1970 to 173 in 1971 (all but 30 of which occurred after the introduction of *internment on 9 August) and 467 in 1972, before levelling off at an average of about 100 deaths per year from 1977 until 1993. From 1972 onwards Protestant counter-violence from within the *Ulster Defence Association and the *Ulster Volunteer Force also became a major feature of the conflict.

Where British government strategy is concerned, early hopes that *direct rule would be a short-term expedient were dashed following the failure of the *Sunningdale agreement and the Constitutional Convention of 1975–6. After this governments gave up serious hope of achieving an internal settlement between the constitutional parties within Northern Ireland. From 1980 a new strategy began to develop, based on direct links between London and Dublin, within the context of the *European Union. This at last bore fruit in the *Anglo-Irish agreement of 1985. In the meantime another quixotic attempt at an internal settlement, the Northern Ireland Assembly of 1982–6, had failed. Sustained paramilitary violence from both sides continued for almost another decade, and the 1985 Agreement was bitterly opposed by all shades of Unionism. It contained within it, however, the basis for what later became known as 'the *peace process'.

Arthur, Paul, and Jeffery, Keith, *Northern Ireland since 1968* (1988)
Bardon, Jonathan, *A History of Ulster* (1992)

ACH

Northern Ireland Labour Party (NILP), founded in 1924. It was based on the Belfast Labour Party, originally founded in 1893 as part of the Independent Labour Party. Before the *First World War, labour politics in Belfast made advances comparable to those achieved in British cities, but thereafter the *partition question hindered further progress. NILP policy was to argue the primacy of social and economic issues over the national question: prior to 1949 it sought to achieve this by having no position on the national question, and allowing its candidates considerable leeway according to personal preference and electoral circumstance; after that date it pursued the same end by endorsing the province's existing constitutional position. The two approaches delivered similar results: flashes of hope followed by disappointment. Many of Labour's ablest political leaders ultimately sought salvation elsewhere, including William McMullen (James *Connolly's Belfast Protestant convert who ended up a Dublin trade union official and member of the Irish *Senate), William *Walker, and Harry *Midgley.

The party's activities were mainly confined to Belfast. It had some early success in city council and Northern Ireland parliamentary politics, brought to an end by intra-left disputes and by the abolition of *proportional representation (PR) in 1929; it repeated this success briefly in 1945 and for a more extended period in 1958–65. Although never formally linked with the British Labour Party nor with the Northern Ireland *trade union movement, its main support lay among unionized working-class electors. Its political fortunes were quickly and utterly destroyed by the disturbances which began in 1968–9, and it had ceased to be of any political importance long before its demise in the early 1980s. Far from reviving it, the reintroduction of PR in 1973 undermined its position further by creating a party political culture in which class differences could be expressed within a sectarian framework. ACH

Northern Star, a *newspaper launched in Belfast in January 1792 by the *United Irishmen, edited by Samuel Neilson. Its vivid and accessible accounts of domestic and foreign politics were popular and influential; its peak circulation of 4,000 copies was larger than that of any other contemporary newspaper. Publication ended when its offices were wrecked in a raid by the Monaghan militia in 1797.

Northern Whig, founded in Belfast in 1824 by Francis Dalzell Finlay. During the 19th century it became one of the foremost liberal Ulster papers. It was the first platform for Sharman *Crawford's views on *tenant right. From 1866 to 1891, under the editorship of Thomas Macknight, who had been influenced by the Christian Socialist F. D. Maurice, the paper held a unique position in Ulster, advocating civil and religious equality, and endeavouring to stand above sectarian argument, supporting causes and candidates on their merits. In 1874 it was bought by the industrialist Sir John Arnott. It ceased publication in 1963. M-LL

Norton, William (1900–63), Labour leader. Born in Dublin, he was full-time secretary of the Post Office Workers' Union 1924–48, TD for Co. Dublin 1926–7 and for Kildare 1932–63, and leader of the *Labour Party 1932–63. He was **tánaiste* and minister for social welfare in the first *interparty government (1948–51), and *tánaiste* and minister for industry and commerce in the second (1954–7).

Nugent, a family that had arrived in Ireland with Hugh de *Lacy in the 1170s and established themselves in Delvin, Co. Westmeath, and came to prominence in the 15th century. Richard, 10th Baron Delvin, was lord deputy in the 1440s; his grandson, also Richard, held the same post in 1527–8. The Nugents were aligned with the *Talbot, later Butler, *faction against the Geraldines (see DESMOND), often in proxy struggles with the *O'Connors and *Dillons. Grants of monastic, rebel, and plantation lands in the Elizabethan and Jacobean eras allowed for the establishment of cadet branches in Cavan, Longford, and Mayo.

Christopher, the 14th baron, wrote a famous Irish primer for Queen Elizabeth, but got into trouble as a leader of *Pale protests over *cess and died (1602) imprisoned, wrongly suspected of treason with Hugh *O'Neill. He had earlier been arrested during the *Baltinglass revolt which saw the involvement of his brother William and the execution of his uncle Nicholas, chief justice of the Common Pleas, on charges instigated by Robert and Lucas Dillon. Christopher's son Richard won the favour of James I, who created him earl of Westmeath (1621). He stayed loyal to the crown in 1641 but his grandson and successor became a pro-*Ormond *Confederate, ending up as commander of Leinster in 1650. The 5th earl, Richard (1671–1754), having fought at the *Boyne and *Limerick, was one of the many Nugents who became *wild geese. He fought for France for the next half-century; his son Thomas, the 6th earl (1714–92), became a Protestant. HM

nuns. Though consecrated virgins were present in the Irish church from the time of St *Patrick little can be said about their way of life. Secular *law tracts indicate that nuns enjoyed a privileged status in society of which some details can be gleaned from the *hagiographies. Reluctance to alienate land into the hands of women may have led to a system of small communities, gathered around a foundress, which disbanded when the land reverted to her kin group on her death, so that few survived into the later medieval period.

Those which survived generally became houses of Arroasian Augustinian canonesses whose chief house at Clonard, Co. Meath, was founded *c.*1144. This is listed as having thirteen daughter houses in 1195 but went into decline in the 14th century and by 1383 the abbacy had been transferred to Odra, Co. Meath. In 1223–4 the convent at Kilcreevanty, Co. Galway, emerged as head of the canonesses in Connacht and a number of the Clonard houses were transferred to its jurisdiction. Other important houses were the *O'Brien foundation at Killone, Co. Clare, and those of St Mary de Hogges (founded *c.*1146) and Grace Dieu (*c.*1190) in Dublin. It is difficult to ascertain when monastic life ceased in many of these houses; some of those in the *Pale continued to the *Reformation with the superiors and small communities receiving pensions at the *dissolution of the monasteries; others, particularly in Gaelic areas, had ceased to be conventual at an earlier period.

There were Cistercian nunneries at Derry and Ballymore (Co. Westmeath) and the presence of nuns at the male houses of *Mellifont, Jerpoint, and Inislounaght was criticized by Stephen of Lexington (see MELLIFONT, CONSPIRACY OF) in 1228. Of the mendicants only the Franciscans seem to have had any impact on female religious life in the late medieval period. In 1316 six houses of the order of St Clare were listed in Ireland; a list of 1384–5 gives three which have been tentatively identified as Youghal (Co. Cork), Fooran (Co. Westmeath), and Carrick-on-Suir (Co. Tipperary). There are 15th-century references to male and female members of the *Franciscan Third Order and it is possible that the communities at Court (founded 1454) and Killeenbrenan (founded *c.*1426) were mixed. The community of Franciscan nuns in Galway in 1511 were also probably Third Order.

The Reformation brought the suppression of all religious orders, male and female. As the Irish *Counter-Reformation gained pace there are occasional references to revived or newly established congregations of women living together under a religious rule, but overall numbers remained small: a nationwide inquiry in 1731 reported only nine 'nunneries'. From the early 19th century, on the other hand, the number of nuns expanded enormously, as the religious life became the career choice of growing numbers of women. In 1851 there were 1,160 nuns in Ireland; by 1911, despite a decline in the overall Catholic population, this had risen to 8,887. By 1961, nuns made up 4.6 per cent of the female workforce, and one-third of all women in 'professional and technical' occupations.

This expansion was largely due to the new wave of active female congregations that developed in Ireland from the late 18th century. Nano *Nagle's Presentation congregation (1776) was, in its original form, modelled on the French Daughters of Charity (1633). The development of the Brigidines (1809), the Irish Sisters of Charity (1815), the Loreto nuns (1821), and the Sisters of Mercy (1828) owed more to the zeal and buoyancy of Irish Catholicism in the early 19th century than to continental influences. Meanwhile older established congregations like the Poor Clares, Carmelites, and Dominicans sometimes took on activities like schoolteaching and orphanage care. Confident and able upper middle-class women like Mary *Aikenhead, Catherine *McAuley, and Frances Ball (founder of the Loreto nuns) were in regular contact with dynamic bishops like Daniel *Murray, and all were part of a lively social scene where Catholic philanthropy had a strong nationalist dimension. These foundresses and their companions dealt with bishops and priests on a level of equality. Later, as numbers expanded and the church gained in self-confidence and central authority, relationships became less personal and more authoritarian.

The Presentation and Mercy nuns made up over half of all the convents in Ireland in 1850, but other congregations also grew. Foreign congregations like the Ursulines and the Sisters of St Louis (to name but two) established many convents. Houses of religious depended upon a concentration of local, wealthy Catholics for support for their ongoing projects, so there was a much higher concentration of convents in cities, in large towns, and in the east and south of the country.

A substantial minority of nuns ran exclusive fee-paying boarding-schools, but most Catholics would have encountered nuns as they worked with the poor and working class in educational, refugial, or custodial institutions, or in outreach work. Nuns were also important agents of the expanding state, as they taught in *national schools, ran industrial schools and *reformatories, and nursed in *poor law hospitals.

Most women entering convents brought substantial dowries with them. Working-class women could enter most congregations as lay sisters, the religious who performed mainly manual and service work. They had inferior ecclesiastical status, did menial household and garden work, and often dressed in a distinctive way. This distinction between ranks of religious, which also operated in most male religious orders, was not abolished until the second *Vatican Council.

Clear, C., *Nuns in 19th-Century Ireland* (1987)

CNÓC/CC

Nunziatura di Fiandra, the papal embassy at Brussels between 1596 and 1795, which dealt with Ireland, England, Scotland, Denmark, and Norway, as well as the affairs of the Low Countries. Headed by a nuncio or an internuncio, it supplied intelligence, often in the form of newsletters (*avvisi*), gathered from merchants and travellers, in addition to information on its own political and ecclesiastical transactions, to the secretariat of state and congregation of *Propaganda Fide in Rome. Material of Irish interest in its archive was extensively calendared in the journal *Collectanea Hibernica* between 1958 and 1970. HM

nursing. Before the 19th century most nursing of the sick took place at home, sometimes with the help of a traditional female healer or 'wise woman'. Only with the development of *hospitals during the 18th century did professional nurses begin to appear. Initially, however, these were untrained, often illiterate women, and sometimes also men, who were regarded as little more than domestic *servants. In 18th-century Irish hospitals nurses spent much of their time cleaning wards, washing linen, and delivering meals. As for treating the sick, they simply carried out the doctors' orders. When *workhouse infirmaries began to appear after 1838, nurses were at first pauper inmates who received increased rations for looking after patients.

The *Rotunda hospital had pioneered the training of midwives in 1774 (see CHILDBIRTH), but the first training scheme for lay nurses was not established until 1858 in the Adelaide hospital in Dublin. Shortly before the Sisters of Charity opened St Vincent's hospital in the same city in 1834, three nuns were dispatched to a Paris hospital for instruction. But Vincent's did not begin formal training of lay nurses until 1892 nor of nursing nuns until 1897. Yet nuns had started to take over nursing in the workhouses from 1861 and by 1903 were employed in half of them. The slowness with which nurse training was introduced in Ireland reflected the widely held belief that nursing was a moral and spiritual vocation, not an occupation requiring extensive technical education.

As well as working in hospitals, other nurses, including nuns, worked in private homes, while others still were employed in district schemes, like the Queen Victoria Jubilee Institute for Nursing the Poor in their Own Homes, established in 1889.

In an attempt to improve and standardize nurse training a General Nursing Council was set up in 1919 to produce a uniform syllabus of instruction and to keep a register of trained nurses. A similar Central Midwifery Board had been established in 1918. A Joint Nursing and Midwives Council was created for Northern Ireland in 1922, while the council and the board in the south were finally replaced in 1950 by An Bord Altranais (the Nursing Board), with responsibility for training and registering both nurses and midwives.

Scanlin, P., *The Irish Nurse. A Study of Nursing in Ireland: History and Education, 1718–1981* (1991)

ELM

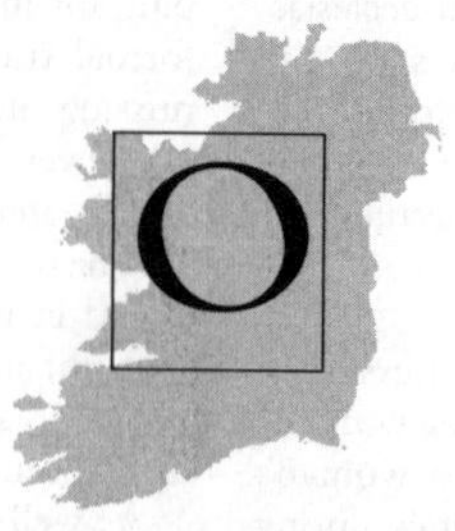

Oakboys (Hearts of Oak), a movement of popular protest in Cos. Armagh, Tyrone, and Monaghan in 1763. The main grievances were county *cess, which was rising as the growth of the *linen industry created a need for better roads and bridges, and the lesser *tithes demanded by the clergy of the *Church of Ireland. Presbyterians, Anglicans, and Catholics all took part in the protest.

oath of allegiance. Following the *Remonstrance controversy of the 1660s there were various attempts over the century that followed to agree a formula whereby Catholics could attest their loyalty to the monarch. Such a formula, it was argued by Protestant supporters, would make it possible to progress from the indiscriminate, and slackly enforced, *penal laws to measures that would discriminate effectively between loyal and disloyal Catholics. Although the idea had some appeal to the Catholic gentry, the clergy were held back both by scruples over the claims of the exiled Stuarts (see JACOBITISM) and by the fear that explicitly to repudiate doctrines such as the power of the pope to depose heretical princes might give credence to Protestant charges that these were in fact Catholic doctrine. In 1774 an act of the Irish parliament permitted Catholics to swear allegiance to the king and to make a declaration disavowing the pope's deposing power and the doctrine that faith need not be kept with heretics. The Catholic archbishop of Cashel and several bishops, mainly in Munster, took the oath along with their clergy, while the archbishop of Dublin condemned it as unacceptable. The *Catholic Committee likewise split into jurors and non-jurors. The controversy was effectively ended when the first *Catholic Relief Act (1778) restricted its provisions to those who had taken the oath, leading opponents quietly to drop their objections.

oath of allegiance, prescribed in article 4 of the *Anglo-Irish treaty for members of the *Irish Free State parliament. In form it differed from that of the other dominions: 'faith and allegiance' were sworn primarily to the constitution; fidelity to the king was sworn by virtue of common citizenship with Britain and membership of the *Commonwealth. Despite these modifications, the oath was the treaty provision most resented by opponents. Attempts were made to exclude it from the draft *constitution but after pressure from British ministers it was incorporated into article 17. Following the *Electoral Amendment Act (1927), de *Valera was forced reluctantly to take the oath and enter the *Dáil. When he came to power in 1932 he immediately introduced a bill to abolish the oath, which contributed to the start of the *Economic War. Rejected by the *Senate, the bill became law in 1933. DMcM

O'Brien (Ua/Ó Briain), successors of the *Dál Cais as kings of Thomond in modern Co. Clare. Donogh (Donnchad Cairprech), king 1210–42, accepted a charter from King *John for this reduced portion of the former O'Brien territory. Fresh royal grants of land in the region to Thomas de *Clare in 1276 initiated a further cycle of English expansion, leading to several decades of conflict, until the battle of *Dysert O'Dea ended the de Clare challenge. Thereafter the O'Briens continued to make periodic war on the English of Munster. Teig O'Brien (Tadhg Ó Briain), king 1459–66, extended his lordship into adjacent parts of Cos. Limerick and Tipperary. In 1543, under the policy of *surrender and regrant, Murrough O'Brien became 1st earl of Thomond and Baron Inchiquin. The Inchiquin title descended in a junior line, raised to an earldom in 1654 (see INCHIQUIN, MURROUGH O'BRIEN, 1ST EARL OF). In 1663, following the *Restoration, Daniel O'Brien, third son of the 3rd earl of Thomond, was created Viscount Clare. His great-grandson Charles O'Brien, 5th viscount (d. 1706), followed *James II to France after the *Williamite War, and gave his name to a regiment in the French service. By contrast his cousins, the earls of Thomond and Inchiquin, were firm supporters of the Protestant succession, allowing the O'Briens to survive as one of the few families of Gaelic origin to become part of the 18th-century landed elite. The earldom of Thomond became extinct in 1774; in 1800 the 5th earl of Inchiquin was made marquis of Thomond.

O'Brien, Murrough, see INCHIQUIN, MURROUGH O'BRIEN, 1ST EARL OF.

O'Brien, William (1852–1928), nationalist and journalist. O'Brien represented various Cork seats in parliament, 1883–95 and 1900–18. A Catholic educated at a Church of Ireland seminary and at the 'godless' *Queen's College, Cork, he always retained a somewhat anticlerical reputation. During the 1880s, he and fellow agrarian militant John *Dillon became *Parnell's leading lieutenants. Reluctantly, but crucially, they joined the opposition to him in 1891. O'Brien's marriage to a rich Frenchwoman, together with the ramshackle state of nationalism in the 1890s, caused his temporary retirement. But his most important contribution to politics was the creation of the *United Irish League in 1898. After 1903 he broke with *Redmond and Dillon over his programme of continued conciliation with southern unionists. He later founded the All-for-Ireland League, which won eight parliamentary seats in Co. Cork in 1910 despite very little clerical support, notwithstanding a bizarre alliance with the ultra-clericalist Tim *Healy. Like Healy he was sympathetic to *Sinn Féin after 1916.

A volatile personality, O'Brien was a compulsive founder of newspapers and a prolific writer of memoirs. He was dismissed in his later years as 'screaming William' by the *Nationalist Party and its historians. In recent years his policy of conciliation has attracted more interest, although his lack of adherence to any consistent line lends support to the view that the splits in post-Parnellite nationalism were mainly about personalities. ACH

O'Brien, William (1881–1968), labour leader. Born in Co. Cork, a policeman's son, O'Brien became a tailor in Dublin. Although his early trade union experience was in his own craft union, he strongly supported the organization of unskilled and casual workers, assisting *Larkin in the creation of the *Irish Transport and General Workers' Union and sponsoring *Connolly's return to Ireland in 1910. He was also a leading figure in the launching of the *Labour Party, and secretary of the workers' committee in the *Dublin lockout of 1913. Though not a participant in the *rising of 1916, he had agreed to serve on the provisional government to be set up in the event of success, and was interned. On his release he assisted in reconstructing the ITGWU, becoming acting general secretary in 1918.

Following Larkin's return to Ireland in 1921 a power struggle quickly developed, based partly on the contrast between Larkin's revolutionary socialism and O'Brien's reformism, but also involving an increasingly bitter personal hostility. O'Brien's determination to deny his rival a role in the Irish labour movement led him in 1944 to disaffiliate the ITGWU from the Labour party, after it had selected Larkin as a prospective candidate, leading to the creation of the rival *National Labour Party. Fear that the growing influence in the Irish Trade Union Congress of British-based unions would undermine opposition to Larkin's readmission there likewise played a part in O'Brien's decision to lead a secession from congress in 1945 (see IRISH CONGRESS OF TRADE UNIONS).

O'Brien, William Smith (1803–64), nationalist politician. Born into a Protestant gentry family, O'Brien inherited estates at Cahermoyle, Co. Limerick, and was educated at Harrow and Cambridge. He was elected MP for Ennis in 1828 as a Tory, but supported *Catholic emancipation and gravitated towards independent liberalism. In parliament he advocated assisted emigration, education reform, and an Irish poor law, but became convinced that justice for Ireland could not be attained under the *Union. He joined the *Repeal Association in October 1843 and acted as leader during *O'Connell's imprisonment in 1844. O'Brien saw himself as a 'Middle-Aged Irelander', mediating between O'Connell and the *Young Ireland group, but felt obliged to secede with the latter in 1846. O'Brien hoped to win the patriotic gentry to repeal, and opposed social radicalism. Having reluctantly put himself at the head of the *rebellion of 1848, he was convicted of high treason and *transported to Tasmania. He was pardoned in 1854 and returned to Ireland in 1856, playing no further role in politics except to denounce *Fenianism. PHG

Observant movement. The Observant reform emerged among the mendicant friars in Gaelic areas between 1390 and 1433. It stressed strict observance of the rules and constitutions of the various orders and was part of a wider reaction to the laxity of discipline known as Conventualism. Among the *Franciscans dispute centred on the observance of the vow of poverty which eventually led to the triple division of the order in 1517 and 1528. The reformers were accommodated by establishing a hierarchy of reformed superiors nominally subordinate to the unreformed Conventual authorities of the various orders. This system had a political attraction for the Gaelic friars who, by adopting the reform, could legitimately withdraw from the jurisdiction of the Anglo-Irish Conventual superiors who had governed them since the 13th century. This may explain why the Observance was initially more successful in Gaelic than in Anglo-Irish areas but should not be overstated: many of the older friaries in the *Pale adopted the reform in the 16th century and it is clear that the Observants were highly regarded by all sections of contemporary Irish society.

The *Augustinian Observants established their first foundation at Banada (Co. Sligo) in 1423 and the reform numbered eight houses in 1517. The *Dominican Observance may have been established in Drogheda by 1390 but Portumna (1414) and Longford (1420) were founded for the reformers. Later developments are obscure but a distinct Observant congregation had emerged by 1503 which was confirmed in 1518 and 1529.

A reform group is discernible among the Franciscans by 1417 and reformed houses were established at Quin (1433) and Muckross (*c.*1448), but the movement proper began in 1460 with the institution of Nehemias O'Donoghue as first Observant vicar provincial. Between 1460 and 1540 ten houses were founded for the Observants and 28 of the existing Conventual houses accepted the reform. Closely associated with these were the Franciscan Regular Tertiaries who founded 49 houses between 1426 and 1540.

There is slight evidence for a Carmelite reform group in the mid-15th century.

With notable exceptions like the Augustinian Richard Nangle, first Anglican bishop of Clonfert, the Observants proved hostile to the *Reformation and provided an important link between the medieval church and *Counter-Reformation Catholicism.

Martin, F. X., 'Irish Friars and the Observant Movement', in *Proceedings of the Irish Catholic Historical Committee* (1960)

CNÓC

O'Byrne, Feagh MacHugh (*c.*1544–1597), the main leader of the O'Byrnes of Wicklow after 1580, and a major obstacle to the extension of crown government. In the *Baltinglass revolt, O'Byrne defeated a government column at *Glenmalure and burned the southern suburbs of Dublin. He made pragmatic token submissions to *Perrot in 1584 and to *Fitzwilliam in 1588. In 1594 O'Byrne was held responsible after a murder was committed by his son-in-law, Walter Reagh FitzGerald. Sir William Russell, the new lord deputy, mounted a surprise winter attack on his mountain fastness, capturing his house at Ballincor and his wife Rose O'Toole, and hanging Walter Reagh. Hugh *O'Neill now claimed O'Byrne as an ally as the Irish of Leinster grew restive. O'Byrne was eventually killed on 8 May 1597. His head was displayed on the battlements of *Dublin Castle and later sent to England, but this did little to redeem Russell's failed governorship.

HM

O'Cahan (Ó Catháin). The first O'Cahan on record was Ragnall (d. 1138), ruler of Fir na Craîbe, Ciannachta, and Fir Lí (the baronies of Coleraine and Keenaght, Co. Londonderry). The family were sub-chieftains of *Cenél nEógain, then closely associated with the *Mac Lochlainn dynasty, but in the early 13th century sided with the *O'Neills, supporting Brian *O'Neill at the battle of *Down and subsequently joining Aodh Buidhe O'Neill (see O'NEILL OF CLANDEBOYE) as fellow vassals of the earl of *Ulster. Their lands were partially colonized by the de *Burghs until the rising of the Ulster colonists in 1333 freed them from English ties and they reverted to being the most influential of O'Neill's vassals. Their leader Maghnus joined in negotiations with *Richard II (1395) and 16th-century observers describe them as empowered to inaugurate each new O'Neill chieftain. The family played a role in the rise of the line of Turlough Luineach *O'Neill (d. 1595), and they were also closely allied to the *MacDonnells of the Glens. O'Cahan's lordship formed the basis of the county of Coleraine (or Londonderry) at the Ulster plantation.

KS

O'Connell, Daniel (1775–1847), political leader. Born in Co. Kerry, the nephew (and eventually heir) of a local Catholic landowner, O'Connell studied briefly at Douai but fled to escape the developing extremism of the *French Revolution. He read for the bar in London during 1794–6. Allegations of *United Irish sympathies led him to withdraw from Dublin to Kerry in November 1797, but he expressed what appears to have been genuine horror, both at the time and later, at the *insurrection of 1798.

O'Connell's first political appearance was in January 1800, when he was one of the minority of Catholics openly hostile to the proposed Act of *Union. From 1805 he was prominent in a succession of movements for *Catholic emancipation. His strong opposition to the *veto, along with his rising fame as a barrister, established him as a popular Catholic champion. However, it was not until 1824 that the introduction of the *Catholic rent transformed the *Catholic Association into a nationwide mass-based movement. O'Connell's mastery of events during the period that followed should not be exaggerated: for example, it was only after *Wyse and others had already mobilized the Catholic voters of Waterford and elsewhere that O'Connell, who a year before had been prepared to see the *40-shilling freeholders disenfranchised (see 'WINGS'), belatedly recognized the potential of such tactics. But his oratorical and organizational skills, capacity for brinkmanship, and mastery of political theatre were nevertheless crucial to the eventual success of the campaign.

Following the general election of 1832 O'Connell became the leader of a small party of 39 Irish MPs pledged to secure *repeal of the Act of Union. However, he continued to hold out the possibility of co-operating with the *Whigs to promote measures of practical reform. From 1835 such co-operation was formalized in the *Lichfield House compact. When the Tories came to power in 1841, O'Connell reverted to the campaign for repeal, which reached its climax during 1843. After the collapse of the agitation he was convicted of conspiracy and imprisoned from May 1844 until his release in September following a successful appeal. The experience produced a physical decline, and a new cautiousness that helps to explain the rupture soon after with the *Young Ireland movement. But he continued up to his death to explore the possibility of new initiatives and alliances, negotiating among others with both Whigs and *federalists.

O'Connell remained throughout the 19th century a hero for moderate nationalists. The laying of the foundation stone of the statue that stands in what is now O'Connell Street, Dublin, was attended by a reputed half a million people, the largest political meeting recorded in 19th-century Ireland. Today his development of a wholly new style of mass agitation is recognized as a major contribution to the process of *politicization. Despite his genuine desire to gain Protestant support for repeal he is also seen as having contributed, through his political alliance with the Catholic clergy and also, at times, through his rhetoric, to a growing polarization of politics along religious lines. Attempts to present O'Connell as an exemplar of non-violence are misleading: his rejection of physical force was based on a belief that it was likely to lead, in the Irish case, to disaster for those involved, and did not prevent him endorsing both the Belgian revolt of 1830 and the wars of liberation in South America. On the other hand criticisms of O'Connell for abandoning the pursuit of self-government for the short-term gains of a Whig alliance are anachronistic. O'Connell himself must be recognized as a figure in British as well as in Irish radicalism, active in promoting parliamentary reform, Jewish emancipation, the abolition of slavery, and a range of other progressive causes. And his career must be located in the context of what can in retrospect be seen as a transitional phase in Irish political development, in which Catholics had not yet finally decided whether their interests were best served by the politics of nationalism or by participation in movements for reform within the United Kingdom.

MacDonagh, Oliver, *O'Connell: The Life of Daniel O'Connell 1775–1847* (1991)

O'Connor (Ó Conchobhair). The Connacht royal family (to be distinguished from the unrelated Offaly dynasty of *O'Connor Faly) descended from Conchobar (d. 973) of the Uí Briúin Aí, one of the lines claiming descent from Brión, legendary elder brother of *Niall Noígiallach. When not controlling the whole province they ruled Síl Muiredaig (approximately Co. Roscommon). However, during the 11th century they finally ended rival claims to provincial kingship from the *O'Rourkes (Uí Ruairc) of *Uí Briúin Bréifne (Leitrim/Cavan area) and O'Flahertys (Uí Fhlaithbertaig) of Uí Briúin Seola (Tuam–Galway region). At the same time successive O'Connor kings, Áed in Gaí Bernaig (Áed 'of the Gapped Spear', d. 1067) and Ruaidrí na Soide Buide (Ruaidrí 'of the Yellow Bitch', deposed 1092, d. 1118), attempted vainly to shake off the overlordship of the O'Brien high kings, a conflict partially resolved by the inauguration in 1106 of Toirdelbach Mór *Ua Conchobair (d. 1156) as king over Síl Muiredaig in the first instance, sponsored by his maternal uncle, the high king Muirchertach *Ua Briain.

Toirdelbach Mór soon rose to be provincial king, and from c. 1120 displaced the O'Briens in the role of '*high king with opposition'. Although he had to give way *c.*1150 to the northern high king Muirchertach *Mac Lochlainn, on the latter's death in 1166 Toirdelbach's son Rory *O'Connor (Ruaidrí Ua Conchobair, deposed 1186, d. 1198) seized control of all Ireland, banishing the recalcitrant king of Leinster, Diarmait *Mac Murchada, and thus unknowingly precipitating the *Anglo-Norman invasion, when Diarmait brought in foreign auxiliaries in 1167 and 1169. By the treaty of *Windsor (1175) between Rory and King *Henry II, O'Connor retained the province of Connacht and a fleeting overlordship of the uncolonized west and north of Ireland, but in succession struggles after his retirement, Rory's sons were ousted by the much younger, perhaps posthumous, son of Toirdelbach Mór, Cathal Crobderg *O'Connor. Cathal held all Connacht by a royal charter, and in 1223 requested a renewal in favour of his eldest son Áed (d. 1228), but

Richard de *Burgh also held charters and by 1235 had conquered Connacht, the five cantreds nearest to Athlone (approximately Síl Muiredaig) being reserved to the English crown and farmed out to Cathal's younger son Fedlimid (d. 1265). Since Fedlimid's son Áed (d. 1274), who fought at the battle of *Down (1260), left no heir, the later *O'Connor Don and *O'Connor Roe lines descended from Áed (d. 1228).

Orpen, G. H., *Ireland under the Normans* (4 vols., 1911–20)

KS

O'Connor, Arthur (1763–1852), *United Irishman. He was youngest son of Roger Conner, a Co. Cork gentleman of English descent. ('O'Connor' was a later affectation adopted by Arthur and his brother Roger.) As MP (1791–5) for the borough of Philipstown, controlled by his uncle Richard Longfield, later (1795) Baron Longueville, O'Connor initially supported government, but turned to radicalism from 1792. In 1796 he travelled to France to discuss invasion plans, and was subsequently one of the advocates of early revolutionary action, clashing with the more cautious Thomas *Emmet. He was arrested with *Coigley at Margate in February 1798, but acquitted of treason (at the cost, some felt, of incriminating Coigley). Detained on new charges in Ireland, he was deported with other United Irish prisoners in 1802, and spent the rest of his life in France.

O'Connor, Cathal (d. 1224), king of Connacht, nicknamed Crobderg ('the red-handed'). He was a brother of Rory *O'Connor, the last *high king of Ireland, whom he challenged for the kingship of Connacht from 1189, emerging victorious from the succession struggle following the latter's death in 1198. Cathal generally maintained friendly relations with the Dublin government, serving in King *John's army during his 1210 expedition, and sought to hold his kingdom as a heritable estate, which he could hand on to his son Áed at his death. To the extent that he did this, and was able to forestall the intrusion of the de *Burghs into Connacht (albeit by ceding much of the province to the crown), Cathal's reign must be deemed a success. He died on 27 May 1224, aged 72. SD

O'Connor, Feargus (1794–1855), *Chartist leader, a nephew of Arthur *O'Connor. He was *repeal MP for Co. Cork 1832–5, until expelled for failing to meet the property qualification for members. Aided by his newspaper, the *Northern Star* (established 1837), he emerged as leader of the Chartist movement, relying on the support of handloom weavers and other depressed groups in the north of England to eclipse the London-based artisans who had initiated the Charter. His influence waned after 1848, and from 1850 he was mentally ill.

O'Connor, Rory (Ruaidrí Ua Conchobair) (d. 1198), last *high king of Ireland. He became king of Connacht in 1156, then sought to gain dominance over his northern rival, Muirchertach *Mac Lochlainn, his reign as king of Ireland being dated from 1166, the year of the latter's death. One of his first acts as high king was to secure the banishment of the Leinster king, Diarmait *Mac Murchada, which led to the *Anglo-Norman invasion. When Mac Murchada returned with mercenary aid in 1167 Rory was initially conciliatory, though he reacted strongly to the arrival of the main body of Anglo-Norman forces in 1169, and made two unsuccessful attempts to dislodge them from Dublin. He did not submit to *Henry II during his expedition to Ireland in 1171–2, but reached an accommodation under the 'treaty' of *Windsor in 1175, which secured Rory's rule over the unconquered parts of the country. The treaty, however, was soon broken and O'Connor's position was gradually eroded. He suffered mounting opposition from within his own family and abdicated in favour of his son Conchobar in 1183. Though he later sought to regain power, he never recovered his former status. He died at Cong and was buried in *Clonmacnoise. SD

O'Connor, T. P. (1848–1929), nationalist politician. He left Ireland in 1870 for a career as a London journalist and was from 1883 leader of the *Nationalist Party in Great Britain. He became MP for Galway in 1880, transferring in 1885 to Liverpool (Scotland), which he represented as an Irish Nationalist for the rest of his life, retaining the great affection of his constituents with a minimum of effort. Unlike his colleagues he was personally close to *Lloyd George and other Liberal and Labour figures. His paid appointment in December 1916 as president of the Board of Film Censors did not prevent him spending the following year fundraising for the Nationalist Party in the USA.

ACH

O'Connor Don (Ó Conchobhair Donn) ('the Brown-haired') and *O'Connor Roe (Ruadh, 'the Red-haired') were both representatives in later medieval and early modern Connacht of the royal line of Cathal Crobderg *O'Connor, provincial king of Connacht (d. 1224). In 1384 the two houses ended a long succession struggle by making a permanent division of their shrunken patrimony. By this date overall control of the province was disputed between MacWilliam *Burkes of Mayo and the Clanricard Burkes of Galway, with

O'Connor Roe in support of the Mayo Burkes, and eventually of *O'Donnell, while O'Connor Don was more closely associated with Clanricard. The O'Connor Don family retained considerable property and influence into the mid-17th century, when together with their neighbours, the *O'Rourkes, and a newcomer to Roscommon, William O'Molloy, they patronized a group of *bardic poets whose work is seen in *Royal Irish Academy MS 540 (c). This interest in Gaelic culture continued in the 18th century with Charles *O'Conor of Belanagare, who commissioned and purchased many manuscripts, including the large 17th-century collection of bardic verse now known as the 'Book of O'Conor Don'. KS

O'Connor Faly (Ó Conchobhair Failghe). By the mid-11th century the O'Connor Faly lordship was established in the central midlands region. *Anglo-Norman settlement and colonization in the 13th century confined the lordship to the area that corresponds to present north Co. Offaly. By the late 14th century a strong dynastic line emerged under Murrough O'Connor Faly (d. 1421), consolidated by his son Calvagh (ruled 1425–58). The second half of the 15th century saw the temporary decline of O'Connor's regional influence, and internecine succession disputes, due in part to the lack of strong internal lordship between 1458 and 1520. A related factor was the rise of the *Kildare ascendancy after the 1470s. The Kildare earls reduced O'Connor Faly to a client jurisdiction, and between 1511 and 1520 appointed their own candidates as lords of Offaly. The emergence of Brian O'Connor in 1520 marked the return of strong lordship. Brian renegotiated his client status with Kildare, based on the Offaly lordships' militarily strategic position on the borders of the *Pale. The alliance was crucial to Geraldine unrest and rebellion between 1528 and 1535 (see KILDARE REBELLION). The O'Connor Faly remained loyal to the Geraldine affinity even after the attainder of the Kildare earls. The government's scheme for the *plantation of Offaly and Laois enacted in 1557 removed O'Connor Faly's land base, and eroded their power in the region. FF

O'Connor Roe (Ó Conchobhair Ruadh). The lines of *O'Connor Don and O'Connor Roe grew out of a succession struggle between the descendants of the Connacht kings. When Áed na nGall ('of the Foreigners' (see GALLOWGLASS) (d. 1274)) left no direct heir, the line of Cathal Crobderg *O'Connor was represented in kingship by a cousin Áed (1296–1309), son of Eógan, against the claims of remote kinsmen, the Clan Murtagh O'Connors of Bréifne, and the descendants of Brian Luignech from north Sligo, who continued to challenge his two sons, Fedlimid (king 1310–16) and Toirdelbach (king 1317–18, 1324–42, 1342–5). Dynastic rivalry between the descendants of the brothers was exacerbated by their *Burke overlords until in 1384 their shrunken territory was divided between Toirdhealbhach Ruadh ('the Red-haired', d. 1426, grandson of Fedlimid and ancestor of O'Connor Roe), and Toirdhealbhach Donn ('the brown-haired', d. 1406, grandson of Toirdhealbhach (d. 1345) and ancestor of O'Connor Don). O'Connor Roe, whose lands were somewhat more northerly, tended to ally with MacWilliam Burke of Mayo, while O'Connor Don allied with the Burkes of Clanricard. KS

O'Connor Sligo (Ó Conchobhair Sligigh). The title O'Connor Sligo was a 16th-century innovation, but this line of chieftains had a long history in north Connacht, being descendants of Brian Luignech ('of Leyney' (Co. Sligo), d. 1181), a younger son of the *high king Toirdelbach *Ua Conchobair (d. 1156), whose descendants are recorded in the barony of Carbury, Co. Sligo, from the early 14th century. Domhnall son of Tadhg (d. 1307), who allegedly ruled from the Erne to the Curliew hills, was styled **tánaiste* of Connacht, and his son Cathal (d. 1324) briefly became the nominal king of Connacht, but from 1395 to 1536 the descendants of Cathal's brother Muircheartach ruled Carbury with the title Mac Domhnaill mac Muircheartaigh, until Tadhg Óg (d. 1545) changed his title to Ó Conchobhair 'to ennoble his line'. From the mid-14th century the family held Sligo Castle (originally built by the Fitzgeralds), though in 1470, 1516–33, and again through a celebrated agreement between Tadhg O'Connor and Manus *O'Donnell in 1539, O'Donnell as overlord was to garrison it. KS

O'Conor, Charles (1710–91), antiquarian and Catholic activist. He inherited an estate at Belanagare, Co. Roscommon, but had later to buy off a Protestant brother who attempted to gain possession. A founder, with John *Curry, of the *Catholic Committee, he published pamphlets arguing against the *penal laws as economically damaging and, given Catholic loyalty to the state, unjustified. His historical writings, notably *Dissertations on the Ancient History of Ireland* (1753), challenged the prevailing hostile stereotype by presenting pre-Norman Gaelic Ireland as an advanced civilization and a fit object of study in the age of the *Enlightenment.

Octennial Act (1768), requiring a dissolution of *parliament, previously mandatory only on the death of a monarch, at least every eight years. Agitation for a seven-year limit, as in Britain, had grown during the 1760s. However, the act eventually passed, part of *Townshend's attempt to build up Irish support, chose eight years as more appropriate for a parliament that met only in alternate years.

O'Curry, Eugene (1794–1862), historian and scholar of Irish. Born in Co. Clare, the son of a farmer versed in the Irish language and music, O'Curry claimed an exotic and noble Celtic ancestry. A slight disability reportedly made him unsuited to farm work, but allowed him the time to study Irish, and did not prevent him becoming employed at a lunatic asylum. The years 1834–7 saw him working for the historical and topographical section of the *Ordnance Survey. Here he gained further valuable experience of dealing with ancient Irish manuscripts and made some useful academic contacts. He also met John *O'Donovan. In the following years he was employed by various institutions, including the British Museum, the Bodleian Library, the *Royal Irish Academy, and *Trinity College, Dublin, in examining, copying, and translating Irish manuscripts. From 1851 his publications began to generate a new interest in Irish literature. On the founding of the *Catholic University in 1854, O'Curry was appointed professor of Irish history and archaeology. His lectures, as well as works on the *brehon laws, were subsequently published. NG

O'Devany, Conor (1533–1612), *Franciscan and Catholic bishop of Down and Connor (1583–1612), hailed as a martyr when executed in Dublin. O'Devany, who had been imprisoned 1588–90, was re-arrested in 1611. *Chichester accused him of abetting the treasons of Hugh *O'Neill. Although little substantive evidence was adduced against him, the jury—eleven of them British—found him guilty. A more convincing case was made against Patrick O'Loughlin, O'Neill's chaplain, who was also convicted and executed. Upper-class Dubliners publicly displayed their Catholicism as O'Devany processed to the gallows and ended up in an undignified scramble for relics. Far from cowing the *recusants, the government found itself confronting a triumphant *Counter-Reformation. HM

O'Doherty (Ó Dochartaigh). Until the early 14th century the O'Dohertys were chieftains of Ard Midair (Ardmire, barony of Raphoe, Co. Donegal). They were sub-chiefs of the *Cenél Conaill, though at the end of the 12th century, during an interregnum between the fall of the Ó Máeldoraid (Dorrian) dynasty, and the rise of the *O'Donnells, two of their leaders, Echmarcach (d. 1197) and Domnall Carrach (d. 1203), were briefly recognized as kings of all Tír Conaill.

When the *Anglo-Norman colonization of Derry and Inishowen was halted by the murder of Earl William de *Burgh in 1333 and the absenteeism of his heirs, the O'Dohertys of Ardmire expanded into the peninsula. Domhnall O'Doherty (d. 1342) was styled high chief of Ardmire and lord of almost all Inishowen and the cantred of Tír Éanna ('the Laggan'). It is noticeable that both he and the late 16th-century O'Doherty are praised for their large cavalry troop, which was at the service of their O'Donnell overlords.

After the *Flight of the Earls (1607), the hitherto pro-English Sir Cahir *O'Doherty, knighted and appointed 'the Queen's O'Doherty' in 1602, found himself accused of treason. In 1608 he raised an unsuccessful rebellion leading to his own death and precipitating the *Ulster plantation. KS

O'Doherty, Sir Cahir (1587–1608). The last Gaelic lord of Inishowen, he owed his position to Sir Henry *Docwra's arrival in 1600. His fortunes changed when Docwra sold his governorship of Derry to Sir George Paulet in 1606.

O'Doherty was foreman of the jury which found Hugh *O'Neill guilty of treason after the *Flight of the Earls (1607). However, officials feared further conspiracies. Paulet tried to arrest O'Doherty, who had landed near Derry to cut wood, for treason. When Cahir complained to Dublin, Lord Deputy *Chichester decided to make an example of him and imprisoned him in *Dublin Castle. Bailed for £1,000, O'Doherty was provoked beyond endurance when Paulet struck him during a visit to Derry in April 1608.

O'Doherty's response was to take Culmore Fort, burn Derry, and kill Paulet. He gathered about 800 followers but Niall Garbh *O'Donnell, who may have encouraged him, stood aside. O'Doherty was eventually shot dead at Kilmacrenan in July 1608. His revolt enabled hardliners to argue successfully for a more wide-ranging *Ulster plantation than originally envisaged. Inishowen was granted to Chichester. HM

O'Donnell (Ó Domhnaill) became lords of Tír Conaill on the decline of the lordships of O'Maoldoraidh and O'Canannáin in the late 12th and early 13th centuries. In the medieval and early modern period, successive O'Donnell lords extended the traditional boundaries of Tír Conaill, which remained under their rule, independent of the crown, until 1603. The success of the O'Donnell lordship was underpinned by a strong dynasty, despite occasional succession disputes. The heavy military organization of Tír Conaill was also a key factor. O'Donnell's vassal lords and chiefs paid their overlord a *buannacht* to maintain his army of mercenaries. By the mid-14th century, the Scots *gallowglass family of MacSweeny had settled in Tír Conaill. They became key supporters of O'Donnell lordship, and contributed armed soldiers to their O'Donnell overlord, in addition to the required *buannacht*.

This level of militarization probably enabled O'Donnell to resist repeated invasions and even limited settlement in the 1250s by Maurice FitzGerald, 2nd baron of Offaly and lord of Sligo, who had received a speculative grant of Tír Conaill from the de *Lacy earls of Ulster. Indeed, in the course of the wars with FitzGerald, Gofraidh O'Donnell (ruled 1247–58) actually extended the southern boundary of Tír Conaill as far as the Drowes estuary, land previously part of Fermanagh.

The Anglo-Norman threat to Gaelic power in Ulster diminished with the contraction of the colony in the early 14th century. Between 1333 and 1380, a serious succession dispute affected the internal security of Tír Conaill. In 1342 Niall O'Donnell murdered his brother Conor. Opposing factions within the O'Donnell sept subsequently bribed the MacSweenys to back their rival claims to lordship. This effectively undermined the cohesion of Tír Conaill, so that in 1359 the O'Connors of Sligo defeated O'Donnell's army, and briefly ruled the territory until 1362. The succession dispute among the O'Donnells was not resolved until 1380 when Turlough an fhíona, son of Niall, killed his cousin Shane, son of Conor, in battle.

Under Turlough's strong rule, O'Donnell influence was now extended into Connacht, and from the 15th century the northern part of the province paid a permanent tribute to the O'Donnell lords. The decline of the *Maguire lords and of Lower MacWilliam (see BURKE) in the early 16th century facilitated O'Donnell's sustained influence in the region. O'Donnell success also created rivalry with the other Ulster power, *O'Neill, and in the 15th century a dispute arose between the two lordships over the tribute from the Inishowen peninsula, though also concerning control of the district of Ceneal Moen. The resolution of this latter issue established the regional boundaries between the two lordships, later reflected in the county boundaries of Donegal and Tyrone. In 1522 O'Neill unsuccessfully tried to break O'Donnell's regional power, through a confederation of Ulster and Connacht lords.

The comparative stability of the O'Donnell lordship in the early modern period is evident in the almost uninterrupted father–son succession, from the accession of Hugh Roe in 1461. He was succeeded in 1505 by his son Hugh Dubh, who was in turn succeeded by his son Manus *O'Donnell in 1537. In 1555, however, Manus was deposed by his son Calvagh *O'Donnell, who assumed the lordship in opposition to his brothers and their O'Neill allies. The resultant succession dispute continued until 1566, and weakened O'Donnell lordship. However the cessation of the tribute from north Connacht, as the crown extended its control there, proved a more serious threat to O'Donnell dominion.

The O'Donnells aligned with O'Neill during the *Nine Years War, and the *Ulster plantation permanently removed their land base in the province. FF

O'Donnell, Calvach (d. 1566), a weak lord of Tirconnell whose control depended on external support. He ousted his father Manus O'Donnell in 1555, with the assistance of an expeditionary force and a large siege-gun from the earl of Argyll. In 1561 Shane *O'Neill captured Calvach and his wife Catherine Maclean. Shane made Catherine his mistress and moved Calvach, manacled, around Tyrone to prevent his rescue. Released in 1564, he travelled to Dublin and London seeking redress. *Sidney restored him to his patrimony in 1566. Calvach died in a riding accident before receiving the crown charter creating him earl of Tyrconnell. HM

O'Donnell, Hugh (Aodh Ruadh Ó Domhnaill) (1572–1602), called 'Red Hugh', lord of Tirconnell from 1592. Son of Hugh O'Donnell and Finola *MacDonnell, he saw his first military action at the age of 12. In 1587 *Perrot, fearing the implications of Red Hugh's betrothal to a daughter of Hugh *O'Neill, had him captured by sending a ship to Rathmullen, on board which he was lured to drink. He languished for four years in *Dublin Castle until he escaped, at the second attempt, with the connivance of O'Neill. Upon his return in 1592 his mother arranged the deposition of her senile husband in his favour.

During the *Nine Years War the betrayal of Sligo Castle into O'Donnell's hands allowed him to exercise overlordship in north Connacht and to mount further raids into Clanricard and Thomond. Only in 1600, with the establishment of *Docwra's garrison at Derry, did his authority begin to wane. When Spanish forces landed at Kinsale in 1601, O'Donnell marched his army to Munster, evading George *Carew, who blocked his passage at Cashel, by a brilliant flanking manœuvre across the Slievefelim Mountains. After the Irish defeat at *Kinsale, Hugh went to

Spain to seek further help but died at Simancas. Allegations that he was poisoned are probably unfounded.

Red Hugh was immortalized soon afterwards in Lughaidh Ó Cléirigh's *Beatha Aodha Ruaidh Uí Dhomhnaill* (Life of Red Hugh O'Donnell). This biography, which portrays Red Hugh at the centre of events, has distorted historical interpretation. O'Donnell was certainly more impulsive than O'Neill, but he generally played second fiddle to the older man. HM

O'Donnell, Hugh Ball Dearg (d. 1704), soldier in the Spanish army. O'Donnell returned to Ireland in 1690 to participate in the *Williamite War. Popular excitement at his arrival, arising out of a *prophecy that an *O'Donnell with a red mark ('Ball dearg' means red spot) would save Ireland, allowed him to raise a private army in Ulster. He later defected to the Williamites, accepting a pension for his services, and returned to the Spanish army in 1697.

O'Donnell, Manus (d. 1563), lord of Tirconnell, a Gaelic chief with pretensions to statesmanship and scholarship. In 1538 O'Donnell married Eleanor MacCarthy, protectress of Gerald FitzGerald, the *Kildare heir, made overtures to Scotland, and formed the *Geraldine League with Conn *O'Neill. After defeat at *Bellahoe, he packed Gerald off to France and opened negotiations with Dublin. However, his hopes of becoming earl of Sligo to substantiate his claims to overlordship in north Connacht were not realized. Manus not only composed poetry but also commissioned and probably edited *Betha Colaim Chille*, a Life of *Colum Cille, the patron saint of the O'Donnells, in 1532. This project, because of its commitment to sources and interest in religious reform, has been claimed as an example of *Renaissance humanist influence. Manus was deposed by his son Calvach O'Donnell in 1555. HM

O'Donnell, Niall Garbh (1569–1626). A grandson of Calvach *O'Donnell, he sided with the crown in the *Nine Years War, backing *Docwra's landing at Derry against Red Hugh *O'Donnell after being promised a grant of Tirconnell. However, the post-war settlement favoured Hugh's brother Rory. Their mother Finola *MacDonnell implicated Niall in Cahir *O'Doherty's revolt (1608). After an Irish jury refused to convict him, he was detained for the rest of his life in the Tower of London.

O'Donnell, Patrick (1856–1927), bishop of Raphoe 1888–1922, coadjutor archbishop of Armagh 1922–4 and archbishop from 1924, made a cardinal 1925. A keen agrarian reformer, O'Donnell supported *Redmond and was a friend of *Dillon. He was prominent in the *Irish Convention, strongly opposed conscription, but was equally opposed to radical republicanism. His espousal of constitutional methods immobilized him during the *Anglo-Irish War. A political realist, he accepted *partition as inevitable but continued to hope for unity through peaceful means, an aspiration which his nationalist opponents found naive. He was more open to accommodation with unionists than most of his episcopal colleagues and, in a period of deep hostility between northern Catholics and Protestants, managed to develop a *modus vivendi* with the new northern state on matters such as Catholic teacher-training. TO'C

O'Donnell, Peadar (1893–1986), socialist-republican, activist, and writer. O'Donnell started off as a trade union organizer but became involved in the *IRA during the *Anglo-Irish War. A lifelong and prominent career in various republican and socialist organizations, including *Saor Éire and *Republican Congress, followed. His concern for the oppressed and his belief that only socialism could bring a fully independent republic to Ireland is reflected in his writings as editor of radical journals like *An Phoblacht* and *The Bell*, and in his novels and short stories, often depicting the harsh conditions of rural life in his native Co. Donegal. JA

O'Donoghue, Daniel (1833–89), alias 'The O'Donoghue of the Glens'. O'Donoghue was head of a family with lands in Cork and Kerry. A great-nephew of Daniel *O'Connell, he studied at Stonyhurst. As *Independent Opposition MP for Co. Tipperary 1857–65 he seemed set to lead a new radical, open, nationalist movement, but his plans were thwarted by the *Fenians. His transfer to the borough of Tralee, which he represented 1865–85, marked a permanent switch of allegiance to the Catholic–*Gladstonian alliance. RVC

O'Donovan, John (1806–61), historian and scholar of Irish. Born in Kilkenny, the son of a Catholic tenant farmer, O'Donovan was educated in Dublin. A family claim to noble Irish lineage, and the influence of an uncle, allegedly gave him an interest in ancient Irish history and tradition. From 1827 he was employed in the Irish Record Office, and from 1830 in the *Ordnance Survey, for whom he compiled a list of over 140,000 place names. From 1832 he published numerous articles, notably a series on Irish surnames. In 1841 he co-founded the Irish Archaeological Society. A series of translations of Irish poetry and *annals followed, along with a series of maps delineating ancient boundaries and settlements. In 1845 he produced an Irish grammar. He was called to the Irish bar in 1847, but does not seem to have practised. From 1852, while acting as professor of Celtic studies at the *Queen's College, Belfast, he was employed on a project to publish the ancient *brehon laws. The *Annals of the Four Masters* (1848–51) remain his most important work. Along with *O'Curry (whose wife's sister he married) and *Petrie, O'Donovan made an immeasurable contribution to the preservation of Ireland's past, and laid some of the foundations for the rise of a cultural nationalism in the later 19th century. NG

O'Donovan Rossa, Jeremiah (1831–1915). A grocer in Skibbereen, Co. Cork, he founded in 1856 a literary and political group, the Phoenix Society, which was absorbed into the *Fenian movement. Imprisoned 1865–71, he went to America, where he organized a 'skirmishing fund' to finance terrorist operations, and later directed the first nationalist *bombing campaign in mainland Britain during 1881–5. His funeral at Glasnevin cemetery, Dublin, following his death in New York, provided the occasion for a notable graveside oration by Patrick *Pearse.

O'Duffy, Eoin (1892–1944), soldier and politician. O'Duffy joined the *Irish Volunteers in Monaghan in 1917. He became director of organization on the *IRA GHQ staff in 1921 and was deputy chief of staff at the time of the truce. He was also a member of the supreme council of the *Irish Republican Brotherhood and sat for Co. Monaghan in the second *Dáil (1921–2). He became the first commissioner of the *Gárda Síochána, and was appointed head of the army during the *army mutiny. Responsible for much of the repression of republicans during the *Cosgrave administration, he became one of the people republicans most detested. Dismissed from office after de *Valera's second election victory in 1933, he became leader of the Army Comrades Association (see BLUESHIRTS), which protected *Cumann na nGaedheal politicians against the reinvigorated IRA. The organization was banned in 1933 and O'Duffy subsequently became president of *Fine Gael. However, his increasingly corporatist and radical anti-government stance forced his resignation and he left Fine Gael to form the National Corporate Party. In 1936 he organized the *Irish Brigade to fight on Franco's side in the *Spanish Civil War. JA

óenach, a periodic assembly of the population of a **tuath*, or group of *tuatha*, for *horse racing and athletic contests. *Óenaig* apparently originated as funeral games, a number of the traditional sites being associated with mythical burials. In Old Irish *law tracts the presiding king uses this assembly for publicly binding announcements of war, treaties, or emergency legislation, and enforces clearance and maintenance of the site as a public duty. The 11th-century poem on the *Óenach Carmain* adds that tributes were discussed there, and that there were musicians, story-tellers, and markets for foodstuffs, livestock, and the wares of foreign merchants. However, after the 9th century the provincial gatherings at Teltown (*Óenach Tailten) and Carmun were abandoned, though occasionally revived for political propaganda purposes. Instead assemblies of the surrounding population at major church sites on liturgical feast days acquired commercial and political associations, becoming known in their turn as *óenaig*. These are probably the forerunners of the early modern *aontaí* or Irish country *fairs, although more overtly political gatherings of subjects summoned by later medieval lords to the green outside their castle on rent-days (May Day and All Hallows) could be termed *aonach* as well as **oireachtas*, and were also festive occasions attended by minstrels and beggars. KS

Óenach Tailten was an annual assembly for racing and athletic contests held at Teltown, Co. Meath, for a week around 1 August, once feast day of the god Lug. It was presided over by the king of *Tara, and the 9th-century tract *Baile an Scáil* links its celebration to a Tara kingship relevant to the whole island (see also HIGH KINGSHIP). However, D. A. Binchy has pointed out that recorded participants between the 8th and 11th centuries were drawn only from lands subject to the northern and southern *Uí Néill, the dynasties which monopolized the 'Tara' title throughout that period. The annals occasionally note riots between population groups who attended, and in 811 the monks of Tallaght successfully organized a boycott of the proceedings to avenge an Uí Néill violation of their sanctuary. Violent rivalry between northern and southern Uí Néill dynasts for the Tara title in the late 9th century may lie behind repeated failures to celebrate the *óenach* at that time and certainly contributed to its long-term abandonment after what was described as the 'black' *óenach* of 927. Sporadic revivals in 1007, 1120, and 1168 were propaganda exercises by claimants to the Tara kingship, resulting in more overtly political assemblies. See also TAILTEANN GAMES. KS

O'Faolain, Sean (1900–91), novelist, short story writer, and commentator. O'Faolain rebelled successively against the deferential loyalism of his *Royal Irish Constabulary father and the elegiac Gaelic revivalism of his early mentor Daniel *Corkery. He fought in the *Anglo-Irish War (which he saw in retrospect as a struggle of youth for liberation from petty social hierarchies) and on the anti-treaty side in the *Civil War. As an author, he conducted a long-running conflict with the new state over literary *censorship and other intellectual restrictions. From the late 1930s he advanced an interpretation of Irish history emphasizing a decisive discontinuity between the Gaelic-aristocratic past, destroyed for ever in the 16th century (*The Great O'Neill* (1942)), and the modern liberal culture whose first great spokesman was Daniel *O'Connell (*King of the Beggars* (1938)). This controversial view to some extent echoes earlier disputes between separatists such as Arthur *Griffith and purely cultural nationalists such as Corkery's mentor D. P. *Moran.

In the 1940s O'Faolain provided an outlet for dissent and social criticism as editor of the **Bell*. In later life he moved away from polemics to become a cosmopolitan writer dealing with the *haute bourgeoisie*, accepted by the new establishment of a changed Ireland. He published an autobiography, *Vive Moi!*, in 1964. PM

Offences against the State Act (1939), security legislation, replacing the *Public Safety Acts of the *Cumann na nGaedheal government, introduced in response to the *IRA *bombing campaign in Great Britain. The act gave a new definition of unlawful associations and provided for the establishment of a *special court to try both specific types of cases and any others referred to it by the government. Clauses permitting *internment without trial were declared unconstitutional, but were successfully reintroduced in an amending act (1940). The act was used extensively against the IRA during the *Second World War, during the *border campaign, and, from 1972, in response to the *Northern Ireland conflict.

O'Flaherty, Roderick (1629–1718), a historian trained under John *Lynch and Duald MacFirbis, impoverished by the *Cromwellian land confiscations. O'Flaherty contributed a much-quoted description of his native *Iar Connacht to a survey of Ireland co-ordinated in 1684 by William *Molyneux. O'Flaherty's most famous work was *Ogygia, seu rerum Hibernicarum chronologia* (1685). Dedicated to *James II, it attempted to apply the recent developments in chronology to the mythological period of Irish history, to argue that the kingdom of Ireland was older than those of Scotland and England, and to elaborate on existing accounts of the Irish descent of the Stuart kings. HM

O'Flanagan, Fr. Michael (1876–1942), nationalist priest. Initially a supporter of Count Plunkett (see LIBERTY LEAGUE), he became vice-chairman of the second *Sinn Féin but was relegated to the sidelines after the establishment of the *Dáil, at whose first meeting he read prayers. He was one of those known to be unhappy with the drift towards violence during 1919 (see ANGLO-IRISH WAR). His attempt in December 1920 to initiate peace talks with the British government was repudiated by the Sinn Féin leadership.

ogam (ogham) is an early Irish system of writing, preserved on stone but, according to literary sources, also employed on wood. It represents the oldest form of script in Ireland and consists of an alphabet of originally 20, later 25, letters, which might be incised along the edge of a stone pillar. The signs are slashes, differentiated by their number, their length, and by which side (or both) they appeared on. There are over 300 ogam stones known in Ireland, primarily concentrated in Munster, and in areas colonized by the Irish such as Wales. The inscriptions, memorial markers with the name and descent of an individual of the 'X son of Y' type, are generally dated from about the 4th century to the 7th century, the period of transition from paganism to Christianity in Ireland. The language employed is Primitive Irish, an elevated and very archaic form the use of which was probably confined to the older pagan priestly class for rituals and more formal oral renditions. The language of the ogam inscriptions was subsequently replaced by Old Irish, the more common vernacular, probably with the introduction of Christianity which had its own elevated language, Latin. JPM

O'Gorman Mahon, the, title affected by **James Mahon** (1800–91), a Catholic gentleman from Co. Clare who took a leading part in *O'Connell's campaign there in 1828. A noted duellist who saw military service in Europe, Latin America, and the United States, Mahon was MP for Ennis 1847–52, and *home rule MP for Co. Clare 1879–85 and Carlow 1887–91.

O'Grady, Standish James (1846–1928), journalist and popularizer of Gaelic myth. The son of a clergyman of aristocratic descent, O'Grady grew up in west Cork. After becoming aware of Gaelic sagas in his early twenties, he published several romanticized 'histories' of 'the heroic period', which he later reworked as boys' stories. O'Grady also wrote about the Elizabethan conquest and commented on contemporary politics, particularly as editor of the *Kilkenny Moderator* (1898–1900), and proprietor of the *All Ireland Review* (1900–7). A 'Fenian Unionist' admired by nationalists, O'Grady attacked British overtaxation of Ireland and denounced *landlords as degenerate for failing to lead Irish plebeians against bourgeois commercialism. At different times he called himself Tory democrat, imperialist, and socialist, but consistently despised commercial values and praised agrarian warrior societies. His political views influenced *Yeats; his histories inspired *literary revival writers such as George Russell (AE), though O'Grady distanced himself from the mainstream of the revival. He was a maverick more notable for influence than personal achievement. PM

O'Halloran, Sylvester (1728–1807), noted antiquary and pioneer in the study of eye diseases. Born in Limerick, O'Halloran studied surgery in London, Leiden, and Paris, returning to Limerick in 1749. He wrote important medical texts dealing with glaucoma and cataracts (1750), amputation (1765), and head injuries (1793), and helped establish the Limerick county infirmary, where he practised for many years. He was a prolific letter and pamphlet writer and his criticisms of the state of Irish surgery in 1765 are considered to have been influential in the foundation of the Irish College of Surgeons in 1784. But he was also deeply interested in Irish history and archaeology. He was an early and active member of the *Royal Irish Academy, and published major studies of Irish antiquities (1770) and Irish history (1774). ELM

O'Hanlon, Redmond (1640–81), the leading Ulster *Tory of the *Restoration period, subsequently a figure in popular legend. A former tax collector turned outlaw, O'Hanlon was active in Armagh and surrounding counties from at least 1674, until shot by a confederate and foster brother. Contemporary and later references to 'Count Hanlon' may have originated with inaccurate French reports of his exploits, or may reflect a persona adopted by O'Hanlon himself.

O'Hara, lords of modern Co. Sligo, one of the few Gaelic families to be absorbed into the 18th-century Protestant landed elite. Cormac O'Hara (d. 1616) obtained a regrant of his lands from the crown shortly before his death. His two sons, Tadg and Kean (d. 1675), were brought up as Protestants. Kean's son Kean (d. 1717) maintained what some saw as an ambiguous position during the *Williamite War. The younger Kean's son Charles O'Hara (*c.*1705–1776) was a noted patron of horse racing, a friend of the English *Whig leader Lord Rockingham, and a regular correspondent of Edmund *Burke. His son Charles O'Hara (1746–1822) was MP for Dungarvan 1776–83 and then for Co. Sligo, first in the Irish and then in the United Kingdom parliament, 1783–1822.

O'Hegarty, P. S. (1879–1955), historian and civil servant. Born in Co. Cork, O'Hegarty worked in the Post Office in London, where he was a major contributor to the *IRB-controlled paper *Irish Freedom*. He resigned in 1918, following the imposition on crown servants of an oath of allegiance, and returned to Ireland. He was later secretary of the Department of Posts and Telegraphs (1922–44). His historical works, strongly nationalist in tone, include *The Victory of Sinn Féin* (1924) and *A History of Ireland under the Union* (1952).

O'Higgins, Kevin (1892–1927), strong man of the first *Cumann na nGaedheal governments. O'Higgins was elected to the first *Dáil for Co. Laois in 1918 and became assistant to the minister for local government, W. T. *Cosgrave. After the establishment of the Free State he became one of the leading forces in the new administration, combining the position of vice-president of the executive council first with the Ministry for Home Affairs and later with the Ministry for Justice and External Affairs. He was a ruthless and dedicated politician, a committed democrat who attempted to foster a civic culture in Ireland. As a free trade proponent he rejected the interventionist ethos of the *democratic programme, which he described as poetry and communist doctrine. His boast that the government consisted of the most conservative revolutionaries who had ever been successful has often been used to characterize the Cumann na nGaedheal administrations.

His uncompromising attitude towards the *IRA gained him both respect and hatred, but little popularity. He was killed by republicans in 1927, without IRA sanction. Ironically his death forced *Fianna Fáil to enter the Dáil (see ELECTORAL AMENDMENT BILL), thereby ensuring the ultimate stability of the Free State. Although probably not personally opposed to the monarchy, he played a prominent part in extending the powers of the dominions in the *Commonwealth Conference of 1926, laying the foundations for later progress towards the establishment of an Irish republic. JA

oireacht (O.Ir. *airecht*), perhaps originally an assembly of every freeman (*aire*), signified a law court in Old Irish *law tracts. In 11th- and 12th-century annals it figures as a territorial council under the regional king, involved in treaties and depositions. In the 13th century *oireacht* (Anglo-Irish 'eraght') is applied to the body of vassal nobles in receipt of a chief's *tuarastal*, or wages of submission, while the more abstract derivative *oireachtas* described the council meeting itself, a term that was to be revived in the 20th century both for the festive gatherings of the *Gaelic League and for the Irish legislature. From the 14th century onwards *aireachta* ('urraghts') described the leading nobles of any district ruled by an Irish chief, while in the 15th and 16th centuries *oireacht* was also used of the chief's territory. KS

Oireachtas. Under the *constitution of the Irish Free State the Oireachtas (legislature) consisted of the king, the *Dáil, and the *Senate. It had 'sole and exclusive power' to make laws, although provision was made for subordinate legislatures and vocational councils. In the 1937 *constitution of Ireland the only major change was that the king was replaced by the *president. DMcM

O'Keeffe case, a Catholic ecclesiastical controversy 1869–79, with constitutional implications. It began when Robert O'Keeffe (1814–81), parish priest of Callan, Co. Kilkenny, was suspended for having sued two fellow priests in the course of a dispute over competing schools within the parish. Refusing to accept the suspension, O'Keeffe went on to take civil actions against two successive bishops of Ossory and against Cardinal *Cullen, while continuing to officiate in Callan with the support of a section of the congregation. He won militant Protestant support by presenting himself as the victim of a renewed papal aggression (see ECCLESIASTICAL TITLES ACT), publishing *Ultramontanism v. Civil and Religious Liberty* (1874), and the government was much criticized when his suspension led to his removal from the positions of manager of the local *national school and chaplain to the *workhouse.

Old English and New English, terms expressing the new divisions created by the arrival during the *Tudor conquest of a new cohort of soldiers, settlers, and officials. Tension mounted steadily from the 1550s but was not fully articulated until the 17th century. In 1500 the descendants of the Anglo-Norman conquerors referred to themselves as 'Englishmen born in Ireland'. Scholars tend to call them 'Anglo-Irish', the analogy being with the 18th-century elite who allegedly possessed a similar sort of *colonial nationalism founded on the local parliament. This term is used up to 1603, especially for magnates inhabiting the borders with the Irish. Scholars use the term 'Old English' for *Palesmen and townsmen after the mid-16th century, though they are actually called 'Anglo-Hiberni' (*Stanihurst) and 'English-Irish' (*Moryson) in the literature of the period. Only in the 1620s does the term 'Old English' make its appearance to cover all descendants of the Norman conquerers as opposed to the recent Elizabethan and Jacobean settlers, the 'New English'. Similar terms—*sean Ghaill* and *nua Ghaill*—came into use in Irish.

New arrivals had also aroused resentment during the Middle Ages but they quickly integrated by marriage into the local Englishry. Many of the newcomers attracted to Ireland, particularly by the distribution of lands following the *dissolution of the monasteries, during Henry VIII's reign likewise assimilated, being essentially state Catholics. Over time, however, successive English lords deputy used their powers of patronage to fill posts in the military–state–church apparatus with compatriots who were increasingly Protestant and less likely to intermarry with the local elite. The Old English, proud of their associations with the original conquest, not only felt a loss of control to arrivistes but also an erosion of their rights in the *cess and *composition disputes. Their discontent was visible in the *Baltinglass revolt, which had a *Counter-Reformation political dimension.

The New English, who could only succeed by displacing the Old English, now began their systematic denigration, depicting them as disloyal servants of Rome, gun-runners to the Irish, and corrupters of the common law. These critics, notably Edmund *Spenser, sought to tar the Old English with an Irish brush, alleging that they had degenerated from their original Englishness through marriage and *fosterage to the point where they now spoke Irish and had become even more incorrigible than the Irish themselves.

The Old English were on the horns of a dilemma. The state was demanding conformity to Protestantism from a population traditionally loyal to the English crown who had committed themselves to the spiritual leadership of the pope. For a moment, with the *Graces, the Old English seemed to have secured their rights as Englishmen. In fact common religion and mutual threat was accelerating an alliance between themselves and the Gaelic Irish. This coming together, long feared by the Protestants and prefigured in *Rothe's *Analecta* (1616–19) and *Keating's *History* (see LITERATURE IN IRISH), was eventually realized at Knockcrofty during the *rising of 1641 and in the subsequent Catholic Confederation (see CONFEDERATE CATHOLICS) for God, king, and country.

Ironically, the New English, who had completed their assumption of power under *Chichester (1605–15) and his successor Sir Oliver St John (lord deputy 1616–22), were themselves threatened by further incoming groups of high Anglicans under *Wentworth in the 1630s and most significantly by soldiers and *adventurers of the English parliament in the 1650s. However, the Old and New Protestant groupings apparent at the *Restoration rapidly coalesced as they united to resist the claims of the dispossessed Catholics.

Canny, N. P., *The Formation of the Old English Elite in Ireland* (1975)

HM

Old Light and New Light, names given to conflicting parties in 18th-century Irish *Presbyterianism. The Old Lights were conservative Calvinists adhering to the Westminster formularies which they believed ministers and ordinands should subscribe. New Lights were liberals, unhappy with the Westminster formularies and the practice of *subscription. The terms emerged in the 1720s when the Revd John Malcolme of Dunmurry accused the Revd John Abernethy and the avant-garde Belfast Society of offering 'new light' to the world. The New Light party dominated the *Synod of Ulster in the 18th century; subscription fell into disuse and the conservative *Seceders grew rapidly. In the early 19th century the New Lights became tainted with *Arianism and were driven out of the synod to form the *Remonstrant Synod, while the Synod of Ulster joined the Seceders in 1840 to form the General Assembly of the Presbyterian Church in Ireland.

RFGH

O'Leary, Art (1747–73), a former officer in the Austrian army who returned to Co. Cork in 1767 and was killed six years later by followers of a local magistrate, Abraham Morris. His death, generally attributed to his refusal to sell a horse to Morris for £5, has been seen as exemplifying the oppressed condition of Catholics under the *penal laws. In fact Morris had invoked this legal technicality (intended to prevent Catholics from keeping horses fit for military use) only as part of a much longer feud with both personal and sectarian dimensions. O'Leary, moreover, was never outlawed, despite Morris's attempt to have him indicted, and Morris, though subsequently acquitted, had to stand trial for murder. A celebrated lament in Irish, 'Caoineadh Airt Uí Laoghaire', is conventionally attributed to O'Leary's wife Eibhlin Dubh Ní Chonaill, an aunt of Daniel *O'Connell. But although she is the ostensible speaker in the poem, the sophisticated literary conventions deployed in the surviving text, which dates only from the 1820s, make it unlikely that she was actually its author.

O'Leary, Revd Arthur (1729–1802), Capuchin friar and controversialist. Educated in France, O'Leary returned to Cork in 1771, where he published pamphlets defending the *oath of allegiance, repudiating the threatened French invasion of 1779, and denouncing the *Whiteboys. *An Essay on Toleration* (1780) made the case for liberty of conscience. Although he supported the *Volunteer movement, his loyalist writings earned him a secret government pension, to which was added a further £100 per year from 1784, in exchange for information on the affairs of the *Catholic Committee. In 1789 he was transferred to London as chaplain to the Spanish embassy.

O'Leary, John (1830–1907). Born into a Catholic middle-class family in Co. Tipperary, O'Leary was associated with the *Young Ireland movement, and briefly imprisoned in 1848. Although he refused to take the *Fenian oath, he travelled to America on Fenian business and was joint editor of the *Irish People*, joining with *Kickham in a sustained polemic against clerical interference in politics. He was imprisoned 1865–74 then lived in exile in Paris until permitted to return to Ireland in 1885, where he became an important influence on *Yeats and other leaders of the *literary revival.

ollamh (perhaps from O.Ir. *oll*, 'great') signified master of an art, especially poetry, but originally including even a master of martial arts. To hold the 'chair of ollamhship' (*cathaoir ollamhnachta*) signified a royal appointment as court poet, judge, physician, or historian. In practice the tax-free lands endowing such a post often became hereditary within a local learned family, whose kin-head in each generation was chosen on the basis of his learning, and confirmed (or not) by the local king. Consequently all fully qualified junior members of such a family were called *adhbhar ollamhan*, 'eligible to be ollamh'.

KS

O'Malley, Donogh (1921–68), politician. An engineer, O'Malley became *Fianna Fáil TD (Dáil deputy) for Limerick East in 1954, minister for health in 1965, and minister for education 1966. A flamboyant figure, his main achievement before his premature death was the abolition from September 1967 of fees in post-primary education.

O'Malley, Ernest ('Ernie') (1898–1957), writer and republican. O'Malley joined the *Irish Volunteers during the *rising of 1916, became one of its first organizers in 1918, and was appointed commander of the 2nd Southern Division in April 1921. He took the anti-treaty side in the *Irish Civil War, and became assistant chief of staff of the Irregulars in October 1922. Apart from his republicanism, he is known for the literary quality of his autobiographies, which provide a revealing but highly personal account of Volunteer life during the *Anglo-Irish War and Civil War.

JA

O'Malley, Grace (*c.*1530–*c.*1603), alias Granuaile, legendary pirate-queen of Connacht, celebrated in popular tradition as a nationalist heroine and now a feminist icon. She married first Donal O'Flaherty, and later Richard 'Iron Dick' Bourke, but was a power-broker in her own right due to the unique naval power of the O'Malleys. Despite clashes with the crown, which imprisoned her in 1577–9, she urged her husbands and sons to seek accommodations with the encroaching state. While in London in 1593 with other Connacht notables complaining about *Bingham's government, she petitioned the queen for a grant of lands, because under Gaelic law she was not entitled, as a widow, to any part of her husband's estate. HM

O'More, Rory (*fl.* 1620–52), a principal plotter and leader of the *rising of 1641. As an army officer with lands in Kildare and Armagh, descended from the former lords of Laois and married into the leading *Pale family of Sir Patrick *Barnewall, Rory was a crucial link between the Gaelic Irish and *Old English parties. He initiated the conspiracy behind the rising of 1641 when he approached Lord Maguire. Forewarned of the discovery of their plot to seize Dublin Castle, he managed to escape the city. O'More led the insurgent army to victory at Julianstown, Co. Meath (29 Nov. 1641), and won over the Pale gentry at a conference at Knockcrofty near Drogheda, by assuring them that the struggle was to defend the king and to save Catholicism. In the *Confederate War he commanded a force in Laois and Offaly and favoured negotiations with the royalists. At the end of the war he took refuge on Bofin Island, off Co. Galway, and was last heard of escaping from there disguised as a fisherman. HM

O'Neill. Descended from *Niall Glúndub (d. 919), high king from the *Cenél nEógain branch of the northern *Uí Néill, the O'Neills suffered a prolonged eclipse *c.*1033–1170 at the hands of their *Mac Lochlainn kinsmen. Their restoration to power began in 1167 when Rory *O'Connor divided Tír Eógain in two, between the MacLochlainn claimant and Áed 'an Macaomh Tóinleasc' O'Neill (d. 1177). The latter's son, Áed Méith O'Neill (d. 1230), achieved province-wide kingship, leading the forces of Tír Conaill and *Airgialla as well as Tír Eógain against the attempts of Bishop Grey, the justiciar, to conquer mid-Ulster 1211–12. Áed Méith's nephew Brian *O'Neill eliminated the MacLochlainn threat at the battle of Caimeirghe (1241), before taking submissions from the heirs of O'Connor and O'Brien at Caoluisce near Belleek (1258) in an unsuccessful attempt to revive the *high kingship which ended in his defeat and death at the battle of *Down in 1260.

Brian was succeeded by Áed Buidhe O'Neill (d. 1283), grandson of Áed Méith, who co-operated with the Anglo-Normans of Ulster rather than resisting them. His death was followed by a prolonged feud between his immediate kin, the Clann Aodha Buidhe or Clandeboye O'Neills, and Brian's son Domhnall (d. 1325), who was to ally with Robert and Edward *Bruce against the earl of Ulster and the English king Edward II. Even after the defeat at Faughart (1318), Domhnall retained his position in western Tír Eógain, though his son Aodh Reamhar (or Aodh Mór, d. 1364) had to contend with the rivalry of Henry O'Neill of the Clann Aodha Buidhe (d. 1347) during the earlier part of his reign.

However, the close relations between the Clandeboye O'Neills and the Ulster colonists led to Henry O'Neill's involvement in rebellion following the assassination of the de *Burgh earl in 1333, so in 1344 the justiciar, Ralph *Ufford, deposed him and recognized Aodh Reamhar as king. The title on Aodh's extant seal reads 'king of the Irish of Ulster'. Formerly a *MacDonlevy title, this implies overlordship of the Irish east of the Bann, which would now include the Clandeboye O'Neills themselves, but there is better evidence for Aodh's dominance of *O'Donnell, *Maguire, *MacMahon, and O'Hanlon.

Aodh's son and successor Niall Mór O'Neill (d. 1397) mounted an aggressive campaign against the Ulster earldom, continued by his son Niall Óg (d. 1403) when he partnered his father in kingship *c.*1390. This led to strife with Earl Roger *Mortimer when the O'Neill father and son submitted to *Richard II in 1395. It was probably to distinguish the father from his son of the same name that the expression Ó Néill Mór (the Great O'Neill, or O'Neill Senior) was first used, but the Anglo-Irish continued to employ the expression 'The Great O'Neill' in the reign of Niall Óg's nephew and successor Domhnall Bog O'Neill (d. 1432), apparently to contrast him with *O'Neill of Clandeboye (Brian Ballach, d. 1425).

The succession of Domhnall Bog, made possible by the premature death of Niall Óg's eldest son Brian (d. 1404), led to a crippling civil war between Domhnall and Eoghan (d. 1456), a younger son of Niall Óg, during which much land in western Tír Eógain was annexed by O'Donnell. Eoghan, however, began to take back control even before Domhnall Bog's murder by some O'Cahans. He recovered territory from O'Donnell, added O'Reilly to his list of vassal chieftains, and imposed a regular tribute of *black rent on Dundalk. His son Henry (d. 1489) ruled over an area equivalent to all nine counties of Ulster, including the remnants of the Ulster colony, and in 1463 received a present of livery to attach him to the service of King Edward IV, who was also absentee earl of Ulster.

In 1480 Conn Mór (d. 1493), son and heir of Henry O'Neill, married Elinor, sister to the 8th earl of *Kildare, and received a grant of full rights under English law. Consequently, after Conn's assassination by his own brother Henry Óg, the earl became closely involved in the subsequent war of succession. Ultimately Elinor's son Conn Bacach *O'Neill succeeded to the chieftaincy in 1519. A staunch ally of the 9th earl of Kildare, he participated in the *Geraldine League before surrendering his lands and rights and receiving them back from Henry VIII (1542) with the title earl of Tyrone and remainder to his illegitimate son Matthew, Baron Dungannon. A rebellion by Conn's legitimate son Shane *O'Neill resulted, followed by a succession struggle for the chieftaincy between Turlough Luineach *O'Neill (d. 1595), great-grandson of Conn Mór, and Matthew's son Hugh *O'Neill, from 1593 recognized as 'the Great O'Neill', one of the chief leaders in the *Nine Years War (1594–1603). After the treaty of *Mellifont (1603) Hugh O'Neill's jurisdiction as a chieftain ended and his departure to seek help on the Continent in the *Flight of the Earls (1607) proved fruitless. Although Hugh's nephew Owen Roe *O'Neill, and the more distantly related Phelim Roe *O'Neill of Kinnaird (d. 1653), were prominent in the *Confederate War, neither was formally inaugurated as chief.

Mathews, T., *The O'Neills of Ulster* (1907)
Simms, K., ' "The King's Friend": O'Neill, the Crown and the Earldom of Ulster', in J. Lydon (ed.), *England and Ireland in the Later Middle Ages* (1981)

KS

O'Neill (Ó Néill), Brian (*d.* 1260). Perhaps briefly installed as king of *Cenél nEógain by Hugh de *Lacy in 1238, Brian really reigned from 1241, when with Melaghlin O'Donnell (Maol Seachlainn Ó Domhnaill, d. 1247) he massacred his dynastic rivals, the *MacLochlainns of Inishowen, at Caimeirghe, north of Omagh. Subsequently marriage alliance with the MacLochlainns led to war with O'Donnell, and in 1248 Brian supported an Ó Canannáin claimant to Tír Conaill. He sheltered King Fedlimid O'Connor (Ó Conchobair, d. 1265) from the English in 1249, withheld after 1253 the tribute he owed as a vassal of the earldom of *Ulster, and launched repeated raids against Co. Down. In 1258 Brian met Aodh, son of Fedlimid O'Connor, and Tadhg, son of King Conor O'Brien of Thomond, at Caoluisce near Belleek. Aodh recognized O'Neill as king of the Irish of Ireland, gaining support for his own claims over *Bréifne in exchange. However, in 1260 O'Neill and O'Connor lost the battle of *Down, where Brian was slain. KS

O'Neill, Conn (*c.*1484–1559), 1st earl of Tyrone. Conn owed his succession as O'Neill in 1519 to his cousin, Gearóid Óg FitzGerald, 8th earl of *Kildare. Having supported the *Kildare rebellion and the *Geraldine League, he was forced to participate in *St Leger's *surrender and regrant scheme. He was created earl of Tyrone after being refused the royal earldom of *Ulster. Poets and annalists noted the degradation of sovereignty involved in abandoning the O'Neill title, but Conn had gained advantage over his internal rivals and a feudal connection with the crown to replace the familial one with the Kildares. The real mistake was the designation of an adopted son, Matthew Kelly, as heir, in flagrant disregard for the claims of the eldest legitimate son, Shane *O'Neill. This brought civil war in Tyrone and left Conn a refugee in the *Pale, apparently regretting his rapprochement with England. HM

O'Neill, Donal (Domhnall Ó Néill) (d. 1325). A son of Brian *O'Neill (d. 1260), Donal thrice seized the kingship of *Cenél nEógain (1283–6, 1291, 1296) from the brother and subsequently the son of his father's rival Aodh Buidhe O'Neill (d. 1283), after which Earl Richard de *Burgh as overlord ceased to oppose his rule. The English, however, treated with his sub-chieftains independently, and the earl began to annex and colonize lands west of the Bann. Contacted by the *Bruce brothers, Donal welcomed Edward's invasion of Ulster in 1315, and transferred to him the O'Neill claim to the *high kingship of Ireland, justifying his actions by a *'Remonstrance' to Pope John XXII. After Bruce's defeat at *Faughart (1318), de Burgh and the Clann Aodha Buidhe O'Neill temporarily deposed Donal, but he had recovered at least western Tír Eógain by his death. KS

O'Neill, Hugh (*c.*1550–1616), 2nd earl of Tyrone and last inaugurated O'Neill. Hugh was raised in the *Pale after the assassination of his father Matthew in 1558. The crown re-established him in Ulster ten years later as a bulwark against the pretensions of Turlough *O'Neill. When it tried to curb his growing power after 1587, Hugh resorted to bribing officials and opened up contacts with Spain. *Fitzwilliam's partition of *Monaghan proved the decisive break. O'Neill tried to entangle the main beneficiary of government reform, Sir Henry *Bagenal, in a marriage alliance by eloping with his sister Mabel. In 1592 Red Hugh *O'Donnell, his son-in-law, assisted him in the encirclement of Turlough and the achievement of supremacy in Ulster.

At the start of the *Nine Years War O'Neill managed an outward show of loyalty while using proxies to oppose militarily the implementation of further reform. Victory at the *Yellow Ford in 1598 enabled the extension of his authority through the midlands and into Munster. A major stumbling block was the *Old English, to whom O'Neill appealed unsuccessfully on the grounds of common nationality and religion. O'Neill and O'Donnell were defeated at *Kinsale and he himself surrendered at *Mellifont in 1603. The subsequent *Flight of the Earls was a gamble by O'Neill which went badly wrong. He died in Rome in 1616.

That Hugh O'Neill enjoys such an enigmatic reputation is largely the result of 19th-century misinterpretation. Uncritical use of Ó Cléirigh's life of O'Donnell, and the mistaken idea that O'Neill was brought up in England, fashioned a vacillating figure caught between two cultures. In fact O'Neill was an adept politician and gifted soldier who made the most of limited resources in a period of rapid change.

Morgan, Hiram, *Tyrone's Rebellion* (1993)

HM

O'Neill, Owen Roe (*c.*1582–1649), the Catholic confederacy's (see CONFEDERATE CATHOLICS) most successful general, and its most dogmatic politician. A nephew of Hugh *O'Neill, Owen joined the Irish regiment in Spanish Flanders in 1604, received his own regiment in 1633, and distinguished himself in the defence of Arras (1640). Following the *rising of 1641, he left Spanish service to return home, aiming to reverse the *Ulster plantation and achieve full religious liberty for Catholics.

With their insurrection in danger of collapse, an Ulster Irish assembly selected him general to replace Sir Phelim *O'Neill. Defeated at Clones (13 June 1643), Owen retired to Connacht where he forged an effective Ulster army. Although never co-operating successfully with his fellow generals, *Preston and Castlehaven, he won a stunning victory at *Benburb on 5 June 1646 and then marched south, enabling Papal Nuncio *Rinuccini to depose the supreme council members who favoured the *Ormond peace. The decision to support Rinuccini over the confederation's contentious truce with *Inchiquin (May 1648) left his army isolated for over a year and forced him to truck with the parliamentarians Jones and Monck, even saving the beleaguered *Coote at Derry. After Cromwell's arrival, he belatedly accepted an alliance with *Ormond, but died the following month. HM

O'Neill, Sir Phelim (*c.*1605–1653), leader of the *rising of 1641. As MP for Dungannon, Phelim sat on a number of parliamentary committees, but in late summer 1641, disenchanted with constitutional methods of resisting further repression of Catholics, he joined the plotting of Rory *O'More and Conor Maguire. On the night of 22 October he surprised Charlemont fort by the ruse of inviting himself to dinner with Lord Caulfield. O'Neill made clever use of a forged royal commission, ancient *prophecies, and kinship networks to legitimize his struggle and galvanize supporters. He proved unable to prevent the murder of settlers, including Lord Caulfield.

The rebellion soon faltered. Phelim was repulsed at Lisburn in November, had to break off the siege of Drogheda in April 1642, and retained only Charlemont by June. In August 1642 Owen Roe *O'Neill arrived from the Continent and took over command. Phelim in turn sought a marriage alliance with Thomas *Preston, Owen's rival and a fellow supporter of the *Ormond peace.

Phelim surrendered Charlemont in August 1650 and fled to an island hide-out in Tyrone which was eventually betrayed in February 1653. At his trial, much to the chagrin of the Cromwellian judges, he admitted the forgery of the royal commission, thereby forfeiting any chance of escaping execution. HM

O'Neill, Shane (*c.*1530–1567), an innovative Ulster leader for a dozen years until his early death. In 1558 he killed his rival Matthew, whom the state had recognized as Conn *O'Neill's successor when Tyrone was *surrendered and regranted. The following year he claimed the O'Neillship as the electee of the clan freeholders, but still wanted the earldom as Conn's eldest legitimate son. *Sussex mounted three costly offensives (1560, 1561, and 1563), which Shane either side-stepped or harried. These developments fed Shane's expansionist tendencies, not only against the urraghts (see OIREACHT), but also against Calvach *O'Donnell, whom he imprisoned and cuckolded. In 1562 Shane submitted to Elizabeth in London and in 1563, at the peace of Drumcree, the state acceded to his demands for the O'Neillship and an investigation into Matthew's parentage. Then, in a self-interested show of loyalty, Shane attacked the *MacDonnells, winning a resounding victory at Glenshesk.

*Sidney's arrival put paid to the 1563 agreement. With Shane making appeals to Scotland and France, the government sapped his strength by establishing a garrison at Derry. He was eventually defeated at *Farsetmore and in desperation made overtures to the MacDonnells, who murdered him on 2 June 1567. English and Irish accounts see this as a revenge killing, but there is strong evidence to suggest that the MacDonnells assassinated O'Neill after getting a better offer from Sidney.

Shane's spectre continued to haunt the country. His posthumous attainder by the 1569 parliament, far from facilitating the *Enterprise of Ulster, merely hindered relations with future lords of Tyrone by banning the O'Neill title. He was survived by as many as twelve landless MacShanes, whom the state feared more than the rest of the O'Neills because of their bellicosity and *redshanks connections.

Brady, Ciaran, *Shane O'Neill* (1996)

HM

O'Neill, Terence (1914–90), Lord O'Neill of the Maine, prime minister of Northern Ireland 1963–9. A member of an Anglo-Irish landed family with a protracted (if undistinguished) parliamentary record, O'Neill represented the seigniorial tradition of *Unionist politics. He was returned to Stormont in November 1946, and was minister of finance 1956–63. As prime minister, he was anxious to revitalize the ailing Northern Irish economy, and embraced technological improvement and economic planning with a will. He was equally anxious to improve community relations within Northern Ireland: he was the first prime minister to visit a Catholic school (in Ballymoney, Co. Antrim, Apr. 1964), and he hosted the visit of Sean *Lemass to Stormont on 14 January 1965. But the rhetoric of consensus was not accompanied by any substantial reform initiative, so that Catholic expectations were raised but not satisfied. It was not until 1968 that the violence arising from the *civil rights movement and loyalist counter-demonstrations converted O'Neill to desperate legislative action. In December he announced a five-point programme of reform designed to defuse communal tensions. However, he faced mounting criticism within his own, previously sympathetic, party. O'Neill sought to rout his critics through a general election, held in February 1969: but this merely consolidated Unionist division. He resigned from office on 28 April 1969.

O'Neill had political vision, but lacked the personal charm and strategic skill necessary to enact his ideals. He was closer in temperament to 18th-century Irish *Whiggery than to his Butskellite admirers in Britain. Called a technocrat, O'Neill can best be understood within the tradition of improving landlordism: he was paternalist, occasionally authoritarian, but ultimately detached from those whom he sought to benefit. AJ

O'Neill, Turlough Luineach (*c.*1531–1595), one of the most effective 16th-century lords of Tyrone, despite being caricatured as a hen-pecked drunkard. Based at Strabane rather than Dungannon, he had more power in western Ulster than other chiefs of his name. Having made his first bid for power in 1562, he succeeded as O'Neill in 1567 because of Shane *O'Neill's premature death. The key to his subsequent success was his 1569 marriage to Agnes *Campbell, which brought him a constant supply of mercenaries. The *Enterprise of Ulster gave him the opportunity to assert provincial hegemony, and the 1575 peace with Essex gave him control of the principal O'Neill urraghts (see OIREACHT). During the second *Desmond rebellion Turlough was at the height of his power, making demands and threatening the *Pale. Afterwards the state had to prop him up because of the growing power of Hugh *O'Neill and the threat from Shane's sons.

HM

O'Neill of Clandeboye (Clann Aodha Buidhe). This subdivision of the *O'Neill family descended from the king Aodh Buidhe ('Hugh, the yellow-haired') O'Neill (d. 1283), notable for his close co-operation with the earldom of *Ulster, in contrast to his cousin Brian *O'Neill (d. 1260). His brother Niall Cúlánach (d. 1291), his son Brian O'Neill II (d. 1296), and his grandson Henry (d. 1347) were likewise maintained by the Ulster colonists against Donal *O'Neill, son of Brian I, a supporter of Edward *Bruce. Henry's implication in the Anglo-Norman rising of 1333, although it gained him much land in south Antrim, led to his deposition, and none of his descendants ruled Tír Eógain. Instead from the 15th century they had an independent chieftainship in south Antrim and north Down. Aodh Buidhe II (d. 1444) and Conn, son of Aodh Buidhe (d. 1482), seriously menaced the residual Ulster colony, and in 1574 Sir Brian mcPhelim Bacagh O'Neill was hanged for opposing a local plantation. But the family survived and in the late 17th century still sponsored Gaelic literature including the *Leabhar Cloinne Aodha Buidhe* or 'Book of Clandeboye'. KS

open borough, see 'CLOSE' AND 'OPEN' BOROUGHS.

opera. Although the cultivation of opera in Ireland was slow to develop, the performance of John Gay's *The Beggar's Opera* in March 1728 established a lively tradition of ballad opera through the 18th century. Works by Thomas Arne, William Shield, Thomas Coffey, and John Lampe were among the most popular operatic 'mainpieces' or 'afterpieces' sung between the acts of spoken plays. From 1760 visiting companies from Britain and the Continent presented serious operas in Italian and English at Smock Alley and Crow Street theatres and (from 1820) at the Theatre Royal in Hawkins Street. Many of these works (including operas by Mozart) were adapted and altered to meet local requirements.

After the demise of the Crow Street theatre in 1819, the Theatre Royal became the focus for presentations of grand opera in Italian (Bellini, Donizetti) as well as of English grand opera. The latter included *The Bohemian Girl* (1843) by Michael Balfe (1808–70), *The Lily of Killarney* (1862) by Benedict, and *Maritana* (1845) by William Vincent Wallace (1812–65). Although Balfe and Wallace were Irish, their careers were made abroad.

The decline of operatic performance in the late 19th century coincided with the enormous appeal of individual singers who visited Dublin, Cork, Belfast, and other centres from the Continent. In the early 20th century, touring companies (the Carl Rosa, Moody-Manners, O'Mara, etc.), revived the popularity of the genre itself. The presentation of regular seasons of opera was achieved only in 1941 by the founding of the Dublin Grand Opera Society, based at the Gaiety theatre, Dublin. The Wexford Opera Festival, established in 1951 by T. J. Walsh, explores little-known works and enjoys an international reputation. Touring companies and smaller companies such as the Irish National Opera (1965), Opera Theatre Company (1986), and Opera Northern Ireland have significantly advanced both opportunities for young Irish singers and the dissemination of the standard repertory. At the time of writing (1995) Dublin still lacks an opera house.

Given the sporadic condition of opera performance in Ireland, few Irish composers have succeeded with this genre. Charles Stanford's (1852–1924) *Shamus O'Brien* (1895) perpetuates a stage Irishry more memorably explored by Hollywood and the English music hall. Robert O'Dwyer's *Eithne* (1910) is an early example of an opera which sets a text in Irish. Since the Second World War, however, a number of composers have written substantial operas, including Gerard Victory (*Chatterton* (1971)), A. J. Potter (*The Wedding* (1981)), and Gerald Barry (*The Intelligence Park* (1981–90)).

Walsh, T. J., *Opera in Dublin 1705–1797* (1973)
—— *Opera in Dublin 1798–1820* (1993)

HW

Operation Harvest, see BORDER CAMPAIGN.

Opus Dei, a Catholic lay organization founded in Spain in 1928 by José Mariá Escrivá de Balaguer to 'spread to all sectors of society an awareness of the universal call to holiness and apostolate in and through everyday work'. Introduced into Ireland by Joseph Madurga in 1947, it received papal approval in 1950 and was made a personal prelature in 1982. Members give time to prayer, go on a yearly retreat, and engage in apostolic work, the latter usually on their own initiative. In Ireland, the organization is particularly active in education and youth work. Theologically conservative, it is noted for its obedience to the Holy See. TO'C

O'Rahilly, Alfred (1884–1969), academic, polymath, and public intellectual. A former *Jesuit novice from a middle-class Catholic family, O'Rahilly became professor of mathematical physics at University College, Cork, in 1917. He supported *Sinn Féin, was imprisoned by the British, and became a pro-Treaty TD (1923–4). O'Rahilly later denounced *Cumann na nGaedheal for downgrading economic nationalism and supported *Fianna Fáil. He influenced the *constitution of 1937, quarrelled with de *Valera, and supported *Clann na Poblachta. For several years O'Rahilly, a 'lay theologian' and slightly patronizing advocate of Catholic social reform, edited and virtually wrote a Catholic weekly, the *Standard*. He polemicized against Einstein, defended the Turin Shroud, and urged Ireland to abandon *sterling for a non-convertible fiat currency. A capable, sometimes visionary administrator, as registrar (1919–43) and president (1943–54) he shaped the ethos of UCC for decades. He became a Catholic priest in 1955. His brilliance was marred by aggressive self-certainty. PM

O'Rahilly, Egan (Ó Rathaille, Aodhagán), see LITERATURE IN IRISH.

O'Rahilly, Michael Joseph (1875–1916), nationalist and journalist. The son of a well-off Co. Kerry family, he called himself 'the O'Rahilly'. An associate of Arthur *Griffith, he had a long involvement with *Sinn Féin and the *Gaelic League. He became editor of the league's journal *An *Claidheamh Soluis* in 1913. As one of the founder members of the *Irish Volunteers he was appointed its director of arms. He was unaware of the preparations for the *rising of 1916 and aided Eoin *MacNeill in his attempt to call it off, but when this failed he joined in and was killed in the fighting. JA

Orange Order, a Protestant political society dedicated to sustaining the 'glorious and immortal memory' of King *William III and of his victory at the *Boyne. It was instituted in September 1795, following the victory of the Orange Boys, an offshoot of the *Peep of Day Boys, over the *Defenders at the battle of the *Diamond: the Protestant victors retired to the village of Loughgall, where, in the inn of James Sloan, they formally established the Orange Order.

Although the immediate origins of the order lay in the heightened sectarian animosity of the

1790s, it benefited from a longer 18th-century tradition of Protestant reverence for the memory of William III; it also drew on the ritualistic and organizational precedents established by the *Freemasons, and indeed by the Defenders. The bitter combination of sectarian and economic resentments which fuelled the order is evidenced by the *Armagh outrages that followed its creation. The order spread rapidly through south and west Ulster in the late 1790s, penetrating both the *yeomanry and regular army: in addition it spread socially, recruiting landed gentlemen.

The order was at first both brutally loyalist and intensely anti-unionist: it was associated with the bloody suppression of the *insurrection of 1798, and—because of the prospect of *Catholic emancipation—with opposition to the Act of *Union. Politically suspect, and a threat to public order, Orangeism was a highly ambiguous asset to the British government, and successive chief secretaries (such as Robert *Peel) sought to counter its influence. In 1825 the order was suppressed under the terms of the Unlawful Societies Act. It survived in the form of the *Brunswick clubs, and was revived on the lapsing of the act. However, in 1835 a parliamentary select committee, set up by a Whig government dependent on *O'Connell's support (see LICHFIELD HOUSE COMPACT), delivered a highly critical report: it was demonstrated that the order had successfully infiltrated both the yeomanry and the army. The English lodges disbanded in February 1836; and later, in April, the Grand Lodge of Ireland also voluntarily dissolved.

Orangeism survived, albeit at a local level, and—certainly in the mid-19th century—without broad support from the Protestant gentry or middle classes. The movement benefited from success in several minor but bloody sectarian clashes, notably at *Dolly's Brae (1849). The order was also sustained in the mid-19th century through a pervasive popular culture which brought its symbolism and rhetoric into many Irish loyalist homes. In 1867 Orangeism found a champion in William Johnston, who led the movement in a defiance of the *Party Processions Act.

Johnston prefigured a wider landed interest in the Orange Order. Faced with the challenge of the *Land League, the landlords of southern Ulster joined the order in the early 1880s: of these new landlord recruits, the most significant was Edward *Saunderson, who used the order to promote a broadly based unionist movement in 1885–6. This genteel patronage combined with the *home rule crisis of 1886 to encourage the massive growth of Orangeism in late Victorian Ulster. The Orange Order provided an organizational resource for Ulster Unionism during the second and third home rule crises and in 1920–2, during the first years of the Northern Irish state.

The order remains an essential adjunct to Ulster Unionism. However, its political role resists glib definition. The order has been formally represented within the structure of the *Ulster Unionist Party since 1905. All leaders of the Ulster Unionist Party have been members of the order, as were all but three Unionist cabinet ministers between 1921 and 1969, and 87 out of 95 Stormont backbenchers and junior ministers in the same period. Yet, equally, there are Unionist traditions which have been deeply antagonistic to the order; and for some Unionist representatives (Terence *O'Neill and his followers) membership of the order has seemed merely a political device.

There has also been a recurrent, though still unsuccessful, effort to dissociate the Ulster Unionist Party from the order: this has gained momentum since 1995 in the context of the controversial Orange protest at Drumcree, Portadown, over marching rights on the nearby Garvaghy Road. If contemporary Ulster Unionism remains bound to its late Victorian, and evangelical Protestant, roots, the formal link with the Orange Order may remain. If the party is able to choose a more secular and reasoned constitution, then the order need no longer function as the touchstone of Unionist integrity.

Dudley Edwards, Ruth, *The Faithful Tribe: An Intimate Portrait of the Loyal Institutions* (1999)

Haddock-Flynn, Kevin, *Orangeism: The Emergence of a Tradition* (1999)

Senior, Hereward, *Orangeism in Ireland and Britain, 1795–1836* (1966)

AJ

'Orange Young Ireland', a joking label applied to a group of authors, including *Butt and *Ferguson, associated with the *Dublin University Magazine* (established 1833) who combined an interest in Irish culture and antiquities, and frequent frustration with the mismanagement of Irish affairs from London, with a strong commitment to the established church and the defence of the Act of *Union.

Ordnance Survey. Established under the Board of Ordnance in 1791, the Ordnance Survey was given the task of mapping Britain to new levels of accuracy in anticipation of a feared invasion from France. However, it was civil rather than military needs that brought the survey to Ireland in 1824. Inequities in the local taxation system pointed to the need for an official map of the names, boundaries, and acreage of the 60,000 or so *townlands as a prelude to the revaluation of rateable property. The average size of a townland, less than 300 acres, necessitated the adoption of the unprecedented scale of 6 inches to 1 mile for what was officially called 'The Townland Survey of Ireland'.

The larger scale entailed refined methods for the detailed survey, and for a brief period Dublin was at the cutting edge of cartographic innovation. At the height of the project 2,000 staff were employed, including men of the calibre of Thomas *Drummond, John *O'Donovan, Eugene *O'Curry, and George *Petrie, supervised by officers of the Royal Engineers and Royal Artillery under director Col. Thomas Colby in London and Thomas Larcom in local charge at Phoenix Park. The survey was carried out county by county between 1825 and 1841, starting in Derry and completed with the maps of Kerry published in 1846. Townland boundaries were determined in advance by a separate department under Richard *Griffith, who also conducted the subsequent valuation. Additional information was collected on antiquities, place names, geology, and industry, only some of which ever appeared on the final maps. Completed on the eve of the *Great Famine, the 1,900 or so maps show the Irish landscape as it approached its population climax, detailing every road and house, field and settlement, in a finely engraved topographical portrait that is austerely beautiful.

On completion the focus of the survey shifted back to Britain, but sufficient staff remained in Ireland to insert field boundaries omitted from the maps of the first eight counties. Their value to government, local government, and landowners ensured that the maps continued to be revised and their range expanded to include detailed town plans as well as small-scale maps aimed at the growing tourist and recreation market. After 1921 the southern Irish survey became wholly independent and the Ordnance Survey of Northern Ireland was established in Belfast.

Andrews, J. H., *A Paper Landscape: The Ordnance Survey in Nineteenth-Century Ireland* (1975)

—— *History in the Ordnance Map: An Introduction for Irish Readers* (2nd edn., 1993)

PF

O'Reilly, Edmund (1598–1669), Catholic ecclesiastic. O'Reilly studied at Douai and Antwerp and became vicar-general of Dublin in 1636. During the *Confederate War, he became one of *Rinuccini's strongest supporters, his opposition to advocates of accommodation with the king leading him into complex intrigues, as agent for Owen Roe *O'Neill, with the parliamentarian forces. These contacts may explain why he was banished rather than executed after being tried and convicted in 1653 for allegedly encouraging the massacre of Protestant prisoners in Wicklow. Appointed archbishop of Armagh in 1657, he reorganized the church in Ulster during 1659–61, but was forced to leave Ireland due to the particular hostility, encouraged by his old opponent Peter *Walsh, with which he was regarded by the *Restoration government. *Ormond allowed O'Reilly to attend the convention of Catholic clergy in Dublin in 1666, but had him arrested and deported when the meeting failed to approve the *Remonstrance.

Oriel (Oirghialla) emerged from the contraction of the northern territory of *Airgialla between the 5th and 12th centuries. By this latter date Oriel, ruled by the *MacMahon lords, comprised the subkingdom of Fernmag (modern Co. Monaghan) and the territory of modern Co. Louth. During the *Anglo-Norman invasion Louth was conquered and later shired as the county of Uriel within the *Pale. Attempts to settle Fernmag itself were unsuccessful, although the MacMahons nominally leased the lesser lordship of Farney from the crown. In the later medieval period the MacMahons reasserted many of their former claims of lordship. From the late 14th century they exacted protection money (see BLACK RENT) from the English of Louth, and by the late 15th century had reconquered northern Louth. Succession disputes split the cohesion of the MacMahon lordship and after 1513 the lesser lordships of Dartry and Farney were ruled by minor branches. In 1592, crown government settled Oriel as Co. Monaghan. FF

Ormond (Butler), a premier Anglo-Norman family deriving its name from the office of an ancestor, *Theobald Walter, butler in the household of Prince *John, whom he accompanied to Ireland in 1185. The title 'earl of Ormond', though not bestowed till 1329, referred to the *cantred of Ormond, where the castle of Nenagh, the principal seat of the family before 1391, was situated. The prominent historical role of the Butlers was due in part to their capacity to produce an unbroken succession of male heirs down to 1515, and subsequently to 1715, long after other leading families had run out in daughters or come to political grief. In this way they preserved intact the lordship granted to them in 1185 and augmented by Theobald's successors, including the *palatinate of Tipperary. This power base secured for their members a significant role in the history of Ireland and England.

The Walter family owed its rise to court connections. Theobald's maternal uncle was Ranulph de Glanville, *Henry II's great justiciar, while his brother Hubert, archbishop of Canterbury, governed England during the long absences of King Richard I. Ranulph and Theobald received from John a grant of some 750,000 acres in north Munster, no doubt with the king's approval. The Butler lordship in Munster and Leinster, where Theobald also held important fiefs, was organized rapidly into seven seigniorial centres in Nenagh, Thurles, Dunkerrin, Caherconlish, Gowran, Tullow, and Arklow. Theobald shared his distinguished relatives' flair for administration.

Although the Butlers were from the beginning important tenants-in-chief, they remained in the political background in the 13th century. This situation changed dramatically in the next century when Scottish and French affairs, combined with declining revenues in the Irish administration, forced the crown to leave the government and defence of Ireland increasingly in the hands of the resident magnates. The absentee lords of Leinster, Meath, and Ulster, the great players in the previous century, left the political stage vacant by default, leaving the Butlers and Fitzgeralds (see DESMOND; KILDARE) to fill the vacuum. The *Bruce invasion thrust Edmund Butler onto centre stage. His son James, the 1st earl of Ormond, was granted the liberty of Tipperary together with the earldom in 1328, perhaps to secure his acquiescence in the *Mortimer regency. In spite of territorial losses to the renascent Irish *septs in the mid-century, the earls took advantage of the weakness of absentee lords to acquire their lands, so that by 1391, when the 3rd earl bought Kilkenny Castle, they dominated the Barrow–Nore–Suir basin.

The summit of their influence in the medieval period was attained by James, 3rd earl of Ormond (1385–1405), and his son James, the White Earl (1411–52). By means of marriages and frontier alliances with Irish and Gaelicized Anglo-Norman septs their influence extended well beyond their lordship, anticipating the kind of suzerainty exercised by the earls of Kildare at the beginning of the 16th century. It was for this reason, as much as for his fluency in Irish, that *Richard II selected the 3rd earl as his chief adviser and go-between during his first Irish expedition (1394–5).

This period of dominance ended with the execution of James, 5th earl of Ormond and Wiltshire, following the defeat of the Lancastrians at Towton in 1461 (see WARS OF THE ROSES). His absentee successors John and Thomas failed miserably to control the feuds of the cadet branches of the family that reduced the Butler lordship to chaos, and did little to check the power of Desmond and Kildare. When Thomas died in 1515, the title to the earldom was contested fiercely by Piers Butler and Thomas Boleyn, earl of Wiltshire and father of Henry VIII's second wife Anne. Piers's title was paper thin, but the king needed him as much as he needed the king. In the event he won recognition as earl of Ormond, and in the process recreated Butler domination of the Irish political stage, thanks to the political skills of his son James, the 9th earl, and grandson Thomas ('the Black Earl'), who died in 1614. This remarkable renaissance coincided with the destruction of their medieval rivals, Desmond and Kildare, leaving the Butlers in unchallenged possession of the field.

It is sometimes suggested that the Butlers, unlike the Fitzgeralds, owed their survival to their association with English interests. But the politics of the royal court could bring destruction as quickly as fortune: only the most experienced players survived. The Butler lordship repeatedly faced extinction: the attainder of 1462, the Boleyn challenge in the reign of Henry VIII, the Preston challenge in the reign of James I, and the *Cromwellian period. The reality is that they survived because at such critical moments the interests of the family lay in the capable hands of Piers Butler (1515–39), Walter Butler (1614–33), and the great James, 1st duke of Ormond (1633–88). Ormond's grandson the 2nd duke (1665–1745) seemed initially set to follow in his grandfather's footsteps, acting as a leader of the *Tory interest in Great Britain and as its centre in Ireland. In 1715, however, faced with the threat of impeachment by the Whig government, he fled to France and embraced what proved to be the lost cause of *Jacobitism. His brother Charles Butler, earl of Arran (1671–1758), was permitted to purchase the forfeited estate, which passed on his death to the Butlers of Kilcash. In 1791 John Butler (1740–95) secured recognition as 17th earl of Ormond, on the grounds that since the 2nd duke had never been attainted by the Irish parliament his Irish titles had not been forfeited. (The marquisate and dukedom had nevertheless become extinct on the death of Charles Butler in 1758). The marquisate was revived in 1816 and again, following another failure of male heirs, in 1825. CAE

Ormond, James Butler, 4th earl of (*c.*1390–1452), called 'the White Earl', son of the 3rd earl (d. 1405), eight times chief governor (*king's lieutenant 1420–2, 1425–6, 1442–4, *justiciar 1426–7, and deputy in 1407–8, 1424, 1441–2, and 1450–2), and protagonist in the *Talbot–Ormond feud. He showed energy and skill both in dealing with Gaelic chiefs and in governing with little or no financial help from England. As earl, his rule of the Butler lordship is noted for his seigniorial ordinances for its government and defence. After the death in 1430 of his first wife Joan Beauchamp, he acquired the greater part of the lands of Gerald, 5th earl of *Kildare, through his second marriage to the latter's only legitimate child, Elizabeth FitzGerald, in 1432. However he made a number of enemies. Besides John and Richard *Talbot, these included Giles Thorndon, treasurer of Ireland, and Thomas FitzGerald, prior of Kilmainham, who curtailed Ormond's third lieutenancy in 1444 by making charges in England, respectively, of misappropriation of Irish exchequer funds and of treason and necromancy. None were proved, but before the earl was acquitted in 1447 abortive arrangements were twice made to settle the FitzGerald–Ormond case by judicial duel in London.

Both a patron of Gaelic culture and a frequent visitor to England, Ormond also served three times (1412–13, 1418–19, 1430) with English armies in France. Although he did not scruple to circumvent unwelcome royal orders, he twice (1421 and *c.*1436–8) pressed, unsuccessfully, for a major English military effort to perfect the conquest of Ireland under the crown. EAEM

Ormond, James Butler, 12th earl and 1st duke of (1610–88), three times lord lieutenant of Ireland. Ormond was raised a Protestant under the auspices of Abbot, archbishop of Canterbury. His first achievement was marriage to Elizabeth Preston, which reunited his Ormond title with her Ormond lands. Political attachment to *Wentworth brought court connections and command of the army in Ireland at the age of 30. Despite defending his patron in the Irish House of Lords, Ormond survived Wentworth's fall and the baleful influence of lords justices who leaned towards the English parliament. As commander of royalist forces during the *Confederate War he has been accused of dilatory generalship, but his forces were never well supplied or financed. His appointment as lord lieutenant in January 1644 made him the first Irish chief governor in over a century, and his family connection gave him leverage in negotiations with the *Confederate Catholics. However, he staunchly upheld the Protestant interest in the first *Ormond peace in 1646, and even delivered Dublin to parliament the following year. Charles I's defeat in the English Civil War forced him into concessions to Catholics in the second Ormond peace. Following defeat at *Rathmines, he lost stomach for the war against Cromwell and left Ireland in December 1650.

In exile throughout the 1650s, Ormond became a principal confidant and envoy for Charles II; meanwhile Cromwell permitted his wife to manage truncated Ormond lands in Kilkenny. Massively in debt, he was rewarded at the *Restoration with the dukedom of Ormond and the lord stewardship of England. As lord lieutenant 1662–9, he oversaw the Restoration land settlement, in the acts of *Settlement and *Explanation. Ormond himself complained that the multiplicity of commitments that had to be honoured would have required 'a new Ireland' to satisfy them all. However, Catholic disappointment—Ormond had himself benefited at the expense of Catholic relatives—led Bishop *French to write *The Unkinde Deserter of Loyall Men and True Friends* (1676). Meanwhile the resentment of Cromwellian adventurers at the prospect of being forced to give up part of their gains was expressed in *Blood's plot; later, in 1670, Blood was to attempt the assassination of Ormond himself in London. Out of office Ormond opposed any relaxation of penal legislation against Catholics or a land revision in their favour. During his third period as lord lieutenant (1677–85), however, he prevented the extension to Ireland of the anti-Catholic hysteria associated with the *Popish Plot. Where earlier writing portrayed him as the quintessential royalist, recent work stresses the extent to which his loyalty coincided with self-interest. Today his legacy is most obvious in Dublin, where he laid out St Stephen's Green, built the Royal hospital at Kilmainham, and founded the Irish College of Surgeons. HM

Ormond, 'Black' Tom Butler, 10th earl of (1532–1614), the most adept magnate survivor of the *Tudor conquest. The upbringing of this handsome distant cousin of royalty as a Protestant at court was the key to his success, establishing him as one of Elizabeth I's favourites. This gave him the influence to resist any governor who threatened his interests, at a time when many *New Englishmen targeted him as a great obstacle to reform. The queen made him her commander in Munster at the close of the second *Desmond War and her lieutenant-general of Ireland in 1597 during the *Nine Years War. He executed these commissions with a mixture of conciliation (protections and pardons) and ruthlessness (frequent use of martial law) even towards his close relations.

Restrained by the queen from curbing Ormond after *Affane, *Sidney took advantage of the involvement of the earl's brothers in the first Desmond revolt. Ormond put down their outbreak with ferocity, pulled strings to get Sidney recalled, and had his brothers pardoned in 1574. When Sidney returned with a vengeance in 1575, imposing Francis Lovell, a draconian New English sheriff, on Kilkenny, the earl was involved in his sacking in 1578. During the Nine Years War

Ormond used royal military power to keep his own territories free of conflict. When he was captured by Owney O'More in 1600, the local gentry raised £3,000 for his release and seventeen of the most prominent stood hostage. After Elizabeth's death, central government pressure on Ormond's territories increased. He died a Catholic in 1614. HM

Ormond deeds, a collection of manuscripts, formerly preserved in Kilkenny Castle, the family seat of the Butlers, earls and later dukes of *Ormond, now in the National Library of Ireland. The manuscripts include the most important Anglo-Norman family archive in Ireland, which were edited in six volumes by Edmund *Curtis for the Irish Manuscripts Commission (1932–43). Other medieval deeds from this collection were edited by N. B. White in *The Red Book of Ormond* (1932) and *Irish Monastic and Episcopal Deeds, A.D. 1200–1600* (1936). In addition, there still exists in the National Library an extensive collection of 16th- and 17th-century deeds, unpublished, sometimes uncatalogued, and largely unresearched. CAE

Ormond peace, two agreements (1646, 1649), intended to reconcile Irish Protestant royalists and *Confederate Catholics so that their combined forces could be deployed for the king.

After Charles I repudiated the secret treaty negotiated with the confederates by the earl of Glamorgan, *Ormond managed to achieve a treaty in March 1646 with no concessions on Catholic worship or clerical benefices, promising instead the *Graces and a parliament untrammelled by *Poynings's Law. However, changing English circumstances and Irish Catholic opposition led by *Rinuccini quickly rendered this first Ormond peace a dead letter.

In 1649, after parliament's victory in the English Civil War, Ormond conceded recognition of Catholic worship and church organization pending a free parliament. He became supreme commander and commissioners of trust took over from the Catholic confederacy. Owen Roe *O'Neill's army was subsequently included, on the assurance that the proposed parliament would reconsider the *Ulster plantation. These compromises came too late to stop the *Cromwellian juggernaut. HM

O'Rourke (Ó Ruairc). The O'Rourke lords of Bréfny (otherwise Bréifne), descended from the Uí Briúin Bréifne, scions of the royal Connacht dynasty, were established in east Connacht by the late 7th/early 8th centuries. Four of the provincial kings of Connacht between the 10th and 12th centuries were O'Rourke lords. In the mid-12th century, Tiernan O'Rourke (ruled *c.*1124–72) reoriented the focus of his lordship eastward into the kingdom of Meath. At the time of the *Anglo-Norman invasion, the O'Rourke lords controlled the eastern frontier of the Meath kingdom, present Co. Meath.

In 1172 Hugh de *Lacy received the Meath kingdom by a royal grant. De Lacy claimed he was entitled, by this grant, to all lands in the jurisdiction of Meath at the time of the conquest, including O'Rourke's kingdom of Brefny. By 1220 the de Lacy lords, assisted by O'Rourke's O'Reilly vassals, extended their influence into Brefny. In a bid to curb the colonists' expansion, the English crown now granted Brefny to Aodh O'Conor, who allied with O'Reilly to bring the region back into the sphere of influence of a much reduced Connacht kingdom. The O'Rourkes were caught in a pincer movement between O'Conor in Connacht, and O'Reilly on their eastern frontier, and by 1233 the O'Reillys were *de facto* rulers of Brefny. However the O'Reillys' expanded regional influence threatened their former Connacht allies. O'Conor realigned with the northern *O'Neill, and in 1256 reinstated O'Rourke as ruler of a reduced kingdom. Henceforward Brefny was divided into the western lordship of Brefny O'Rourke and the eastern lordship of Brefny O'Reilly.

O'Rourke consolidated control of west Brefny, underpinned by the Clan Murtough, a branch of the O'Conors, but repudiated the alliance in the second half of the 14th century. After 1458, the O'Rourkes were gradually absorbed into the affinity of the *O'Donnell of Tír Conaill. FF

Orpen, Goddard Henry (1852–1932), historian of Anglo-Norman Ireland. Born into a legal family in Dublin, he took a classics degree in Trinity College, Dublin, then trained as a barrister in London but never practised. His chief work, the four-volume *Ireland under the Normans* (1911–20), remains the best narrative account of the period 1169–1333, though, in the contemporary context of the *home rule controversy, it provoked hostile criticism from Eoin *MacNeill, who accused Orpen of exaggerating both the 'tribal anarchy' of pre-Norman Ireland and the positive benefits of Anglo-Norman intervention. Reflecting his emphasis on source-based history, Orpen produced an edition of an important Old French poem, dealing with the period 1169–75, to which he gave the title *The Song of Dermot and the Earl*. He focused on the contribution of the Anglo-Norman settler community rather than on royal government and administration, and it is regrettable that he made no use of the governmental records in the *Public Record Office of Ireland prior to their destruction in 1922. He made a major contribution to medieval

Irish archaeology by identifying Anglo-Norman *mottes as of that period, and not of either prehistoric or *Viking origin as had previously been held. MTF

Orpen, Sir William (1878–1931), portraitist and painter of subject pictures. One of the most celebrated Irish artists of his generation, he had an enormous—some say overwhelming—influence on Irish painting up to the mid-20th century. He was educated at the Metropolitan School of Art, Dublin, and the Slade School of Art, London, where he won the coveted Life Painting and Composition prizes. Although he lived in London from 1902, Orpen visited Dublin regularly till 1914, teaching at the Metropolitan School. His artistic prowess brought him many honours and he was an academician of both the Royal Academy and the Royal Hibernian Academy. A war artist during the *First World War, his experiences had a profound effect on him and he recorded some of the most stirring images of that conflict. Afterwards, however, he never quite recovered the confidence of his earlier days. He was knighted in 1918 and the following year was resident artist at the Paris Peace Conference. Also an author, in 1924 he published his war memories as *An Onlooker in France* and this was followed by *Stories of Old Ireland and Myself* (1924). In Kenneth McConkey's words, Orpen was 'the essential Edwardian painter'.

Arnold, Bruce, *Orpen: Mirror to an Age* (1981)

SBK

Orr, William (1766–97), a prosperous Co. Antrim farmer hanged at Carrickfergus on 14 October 1797 for having allegedly administered the *United Irish oath to two soldiers. He was defended at his trial by *Curran and sentenced to death by Baron *Yelverton. The evidence against him was less flimsy than sympathizers claimed, but his death outraged radical opinion and was commemorated in a poem by *Drennan.

Orrery, Roger Boyle, 1st earl of (1621–79), formerly Baron Broghill, fifth son of Richard *Boyle, 1st earl of Cork, and leader of the Old Protestants in Munster. Loans to Charles I by his father brought Boyle onto personal terms with the royal family. He was deputy in *Inchiquin's Munster command during the *Confederate War, becoming his pro-parliamentary rival after the appearance in Cork of the parliamentarian Lord Lisle, lord lieutenant of Ireland (1646–7).

During the king's trial and execution, Boyle retired to Somerset. Oliver *Cromwell gave him the choice of service in Ireland or the Tower. Boyle brought key Munster towns and most of Inchiquin's soldiers over to parliament just as Cromwell's campaign was flagging. In April 1650 he destroyed Lord Muskerry's (see CLANCARTY) royalist-confederate force at Macroom and executed the Catholic bishop, Boethius MacEgan.

Boyle served as governor of Scotland (1655–6) and was the chief sponsor of the Humble Petition and Advice (1657), an appeal to Cromwell to assume the crown. In Ireland he propped up Henry *Cromwell's rule and was granted Muskerry's lands at Blarney. As the protectorate fell apart in 1659–60 he became a supporter of the *Restoration.

As a lord justice he helped lay down the Act of *Settlement. Subsequently, as lord president of Munster and major-general of the army, he disputed defence allocations with *Ormond but got his way over a long-cherished *militia scheme. Amid fears of land redistribution and disgruntlement about being ignored as Ormond's successor, Boyle embarked on a vigorous anti-Catholic persecution in Munster in 1671, which helped to provoke his dismissal as provincial president.

Boyle wrote a *Treatise on the Art of War* (1677) and several allegorical plays on the theme of regicide for the London stage. HM

O'Shea, Capt. William (1840–1905), politician, and **Katherine** (1845–1921), mistress and later wife of *Parnell. Born in Dublin, son of a Catholic solicitor, O'Shea married Katherine, youngest daughter of Revd Sir John Page Wood, in 1867. As *home rule MP for Clare 1880–5, he connived at his wife's affair with Parnell while exploiting his connection with the nationalist leader for political advantage. As a political intermediary O'Shea made the initial contacts which resulted in the *Kilmainham treaty, but was an untrustworthy contact between Parnell and Joseph Chamberlain on the *Central Board scheme, 1884–5. Refusing to vote for home rule in 1886, he resigned his seat. Hoping to benefit from a legacy due on the death of Katherine's Aunt Ben, O'Shea did not expose his wife's adultery until the will (1889) disappointed his expectations. He then instituted the divorce petition that destroyed Parnell's career. JL

O'Sullivan Beare, Philip, Catholic historian, poet, and polemicist, born in Co. Cork in the 1590s and last heard of in Portugal in the 1630s. O'Sullivan Beare's major work, *Historiae Catholiciae Iberniae compendium* (1621), is an important reflection of Irish *Counter-Reformation mentality, with miracles, *prophecy, and providence to the fore. This patriotic history gives pride of place to the role of his own family—his uncle Donal O'Sullivan's heroic defence of Dunboy and epic wintertime march to Leitrim after the defeat at *Kinsale. He launched scathing attacks on *Gerald of Wales, Richard *Stanihurst, and James *Ussher, wrote hagiographies of St *Patrick and St Mochua, and included an early account of Irish flora and fauna in his *Zoilomastix*, written in 1625. HM

O'Toole, Laurence (Lorcán Ua Tuathail) (d. 1180), archbishop of Dublin. Son of Muirchertach Ua Tuathail, king of Uí Muiredaig, he was abbot of *Glendalough before becoming archbishop of Dublin in 1162. In 1167 he attended the convention of Athboy which endorsed the high kingship of Rory *O'Connor, but he also supposedly approved the intervention of *Henry II in Ireland at the Council of Cashel in 1172. In 1175 he witnessed the treaty negotiated at *Windsor between Rory and Henry II. In 1179 he attended the third Lateran Council in Rome and returned to Ireland commissioned as native papal legate, holding a reform synod for the province of Connacht at Clonfert later in the same year. He was instrumental in securing the translation of Rory O'Connor's nephew Tommaltach (Latinized as Thomas) from the see of Elphin to the see of Armagh in 1180. In the same year he undertook an embassy to Henry II on behalf of Rory O'Connor, accompanied by one of Rory's sons. While on this mission, he died at Eu in Normandy on 14 November. He was canonized at the petition of the canons of Eu by Pope Honorius III in 1226. His early 13th-century Latin biography depicts him as an ascetic supporter of church reform. MTF

Ouseley, Gideon (1762–1839), the most important *Methodist itinerant preacher in the generation after John *Wesley's death in 1791. The son of a freethinking, anticlerical father of minor gentry status and a pious mother, Ouseley was born in Co. Galway and experienced an emotional religious conversion under the preaching of Methodist soldiers in 1791. His ambition was to preach to every human settlement in Ireland in the language of its people, in pursuit of which he travelled several thousand miles a year and preached twelve to fifteen times a week. Ouseley's suspicion of ecclesiastical institutions and their clergy scarcely endeared him either to the ministerial elite within Irish Methodism or to other denominations. His chief quarrel, however, was with the clergy of the Roman Catholic church with whom he carried out a vigorous pamphlet war until his death in 1839. Ouseley's anti-Catholicism pre-dated his *evangelical conversion, was part of a more general anticlericalism, and was rooted in a professed concern for the condition of the Irish rural poor. His most significant contribution to Irish society, however, was as an indefatigable missionary evangelist who found himself at the centre of remarkable religious revivals in south and west Ulster in the aftermath of the *insurrection of 1798. DNH

outdoor relief, term used for *poor relief given outside the *workhouse. No provision was made for outdoor relief under the terms of the *Poor Law Act of 1838, since it was feared that granting assistance without requiring recipients to submit to the rigours of the workhouse regime would swell the number of claimants and destroy the incentive to work. During the early years of the *Famine a number of boards of guardians did provide additional relief, in the form of money and food, to assist the large numbers of people who could not be accommodated in workhouses. An amending act in 1847 permitted the granting of outdoor relief to certain specified groups, such as the sick and disabled, and widows with two or more legitimate children. The *Poor Law Commission was also empowered to authorize the granting of outdoor relief to the able-bodied during periods of 'unusual distress', to be provided wherever possible in the form of cooked food. Applications for relief were made to local relieving officers. Under a partial liberalization of outdoor relief provision in the later decades of the 19th century it became possible for the able-bodied to receive financial assistance in cases of urgent necessity. In 1923 outdoor relief was replaced in the independent Irish state by home assistance, and relieving officers by assistance officers, though the procedure for obtaining relief remained fundamentally unaltered. VC

Outdoor Relief Protests, a campaign waged in Belfast, 4–14 October 1932, by unemployed workers and their supporters for an improvement in welfare benefits. The movement, which had widespread Catholic and Protestant support, was organized by the *Revolutionary Workers' Group, northern wing of the Irish *communist movement. Most of its leaders, including Tommy Geehan and Betty *Sinclair, had previously split from the *Northern Ireland Labour Party. Local property taxes and relief rates were considerably lower in Belfast than in the main British industrial cities, and unemployment in the city was above 25 per cent. After massive demonstrations, leading to serious rioting and two deaths when the police intervened, the local authorities made major concessions to head off further trouble. Relief was raised from a minimum of 8 shillings per week (max. 24 shillings) to a minimum of 20 shillings (max. 32 shillings). Geehan correctly claimed the outcome as a 'glorious victory', and indeed it represents one of communism's few successes in Irish (or British) history. But it did not lead to electoral advances for the Communists, nor to a general lowering of the sectarian divide in

Belfast, let alone imply any incipient harmonization of the views of Catholic and Protestant workers on the national question. ACH

overseas trade. There is very limited historical evidence on this subject before the 12th century, although it is known that hides, hunting dogs, slaves, and possibly *wool were important exports. In the pre-*Norman period it is the *Viking towns such as *Dublin and *Waterford that provide much of the archaeological evidence of the extent of overseas trade. From the workshops of these towns Ireland exported ring pins and other *metalwork objects, as well as bone and antler combs and jewellery all over Viking Europe. The import trade was dominated by wine, iron, salt, and amber, along with other raw materials for Ireland's urban industries.

Following the *Anglo-Norman invasion the towns of the east and south coasts, from Waterford to Kinsale, dominated Ireland's international trade, with wool being the single most important export until it declined in the later Middle Ages. The next most important export commodity was arguably hides, which undoubtedly became more important than wool or cloth in the later Middle Ages. The main market was Europe, with Pisa alone taking many thousands of these hides to supply her growing tanning industry in the 15th century. Flanders took many annually, as did France and England, the latter importing them through the port of Bristol, the main gateway to Ireland. In the 13th and early 14th centuries Ireland was also exporting her surplus cereal crop to England and to the royal armies fighting in Scotland. Again the main centre of this trade was in the south-east, especially from the *manors of the earls of Norfolk in Co. Wexford. But by the second half of the 14th century this trade was in decline because of the general economic downturn, until by 1437 Bristol was shipping grain back into Ireland. However, by then both salt and freshwater *fish had become a major Irish export. As early as the 13th century an Irish fishing fleet was operating along the eastern and northern coasts and in the Manx herring fishery. Waterford was the main centre of this trade in Ireland and exported mostly to Bristol and Chester in Britain, from where the fish were sold on to inland towns. Because of the socio-economic difficulties in the 14th century (see BLACK DEATH; GAELIC RECOVERY) Ireland's export trade, much of which had been based on the cereal trade, became almost entirely dependent on hides and fish, with the continued export of wool and woolfell (sheep skin with the wool still attached) at a reduced level.

Throughout the period the greatest import was arguably wine, especially from La Rochelle and Bordeaux. Ports like Waterford made large profits re-exporting wine to the English army fighting in Scotland. In the 14th century the port of *Galway prospered as a result of its trading links with the Iberian peninsula, especially in Spanish wine. Salt also was imported in large amounts, again through Bristol and from the European mainland, in order to preserve meat and fish. Iron also had to be imported from Brittany, the Iberian peninsula, and England. The remainder of the import trade was made up of manufactured goods and luxury commodities like spices and fine cloths.

The structure of Irish overseas trade in the early 16th century changed little from the late medieval pattern. Over the course of the century the volume of trade seems to have grown, although the evidence is sketchy. A report on Irish trade in 1611 identifies corn, frieze, tallow, hides, and pipe-staves as the main exports, much of which went to Spain. Wine, iron, and salt were the main imports. Most 16th-century Irish overseas trade was conducted in English ships through ports in the south and east of the country to the English ports of Bristol or Chester. French and Spanish ports were also used when international diplomacy allowed. Merchants from Spain and France also traded with individual Irish chiefs in the north and west of Ireland.

The expansion of royal authority in the early 17th century eroded the trading rights of local Irish lords and this, combined with the expansion of the population through colonization, meant that overseas trade grew dramatically as natural resources were more intensively exploited. There were some new elements in this trade. The most important innovation was live cattle, which had not been exported at all in 1600. By 1640 15,000 live cattle were exported annually, representing over half the value of Irish trade, together with exports of between 1.5 and 2 million sheep. The volume of wool landed at Chester grew from about 100–200 stone a year in the 1580s to 6,666 stone in 1639. More limited in its expansion was the trade in fish and timber. Overall, exports consisted mainly of raw materials which were little processed.

The outbreak of the *rising of 1641 was accompanied by a commercial crisis which brought overseas trade almost to a halt, from which Ireland recovered only slowly during the 1650s. Changes in the structure of the Irish economy during the 1650s, reinforced by the *Cattle Acts, encouraged a move from dependence on live cattle and sheep exports towards more processed goods such as barrelled beef, butter, and cheese. These comprised over 50 per cent of Irish trade down to the 1720s. There was also a significant increase in wool and woollen cloth exports, until this was curtailed by the *Woollen Act.

Overall Irish exports, in value terms, rose by some 50 per cent in the late 17th century. In the early 17th century England had been the main market for livestock exports, and hence the main market for Irish trade generally. The new trade in processed goods was directed more to North America. In 1664 about 74 per cent of all Irish exports were destined for England but by 1683 this had fallen to 30 per cent, rising by 1700 to 42 per cent. Towns such as Cork became important centres of the provisions trade. New Irish imports arose as a result of this trade, the most important of which was *tobacco, leading ultimately to the balance of trade favouring the colonies.

While the crisis of the 1690s disrupted trade its effect was limited in comparison with the economic slump of the first 30 years of the 18th century. Depressed export prices and bad harvests slowed export growth, but these decades also saw the emergence of *linen cloth and yarn as an important element in Irish trade. By the middle of the 1720s linen accounted for about a third of all Irish trade by value. As Ireland recovered from that slump the twin supports of the trading economy emerged as cattle production and domestic linen manufacture. Older elements in the traded economy such as fish, timber, and iron became much less significant with the rise of cheaper sources elsewhere.

The pattern of late 18th-century Irish overseas trade was still dominated by the demand for foodstuffs and linen cloth. Despite political developments which guaranteed *free trade for Ireland in the 1770s, Britain had by now re-established itself as Ireland's most important trading partner, as the growth of American agriculture reduced transatlantic demand. This is reflected in the growth of Irish grain exports, the value of which doubled in the later part of the 18th century as a result of demand for food from a growing British urban population. Despite this the largest single element in Irish overseas trade by the 1790s was linen cloth. This buoyant demand prompted a considerable improvement in the Irish balance of trade. In the 1730s and 1740s Irish trade had been roughly in balance, with a slight surplus of exports over imports. By the 1790s the export surplus represented about a quarter of the total annual import bill.

Following the Act of Union Ireland ceased to be a separate unit for trading purposes. Figures collected in the first decades of the 19th century indicate that exports of agricultural produce, both livestock and tillage crops, grew very rapidly in the period up to the *Great Famine. Exports of grain became insignificant after 1850, but the export of cattle and other livestock to the British market grew rapidly to become the main support of the Irish rural economy. By 1914 cattle exports were four times what they had been in the 1840s. Meanwhile growing imports of manufactured goods from Great Britain and elsewhere brought about the partial deindustrialization of Ireland outside the north-east. However, those industries that survived and prospered, notably linen, shipbuilding, distilling, and brewing, were strongly export based. In 1907 half of all manufactured output (including food and drinks) was exported.

Political independence did not radically alter the pattern of Irish overseas trade. Despite the emphasis laid in nationalist ideology on *protectionism as a strategy for national industrial development, and on the primacy of the small (implicitly tillage-based) family farm, *Cumann na nGaedheal accepted the overriding importance of livestock exports as Ireland's main earner of foreign currency. *Fianna Fáil, after 1932, embarked on a radical programme of protection, the fostering of native industries, and the promotion of tillage. The result was a sharp contraction of Irish trade with the outside world: exports and imports together fell from 75 per cent of Gross National Product in 1926 to 54 per cent by 1938. But the attempt to change the composition or direction of trade was less successful. Live cattle, 43 per cent of exports in 1926, accounted for 50 per cent by 1938, and Great Britain remained by far the country's most significant trading partner.

During the 1940s and 1950s independent Ireland continued to rely on relatively high tariffs to protect what were generally small domestic industries, while securing an outlet for its agricultural produce by trade agreements (1938, 1948, 1960) with Great Britain. The price paid for this strategy, according to some analyses, was that Ireland failed to benefit from the dramatic expansion of the world economy following the Second World War. The abandonment of protection in the 1960s (see *ECONOMIC DEVELOPMENT*), combined with a new strategy of promoting industrial growth and foreign investment, permitted a sharp rise in exports of manufactured goods. Entry into the EEC (see EUROPEAN UNION) completed Ireland's abandonment of economic self-sufficiency, while offering subsidies and guaranteed prices for agricultural exports. Although Great Britain remained Ireland's largest single trading partner, its dominance was significantly reduced, its share of Irish exports falling from three-quarters in 1960 to 47 per cent by 1977.

Barry, Terry, *The Archaeology of Medieval Ireland* (1994)

Oxford

Cullen, L. M., *Anglo-Irish Trade, 1660–1800* (1968)
Gillespie, Raymond, *The Transformation of the Irish Economy* (1991)
O'Neill, Timothy, *Merchants and Mariners in Medieval Ireland* (1987)

TB/RG/SC

Oxford, Council of (May 1177). Following the death in 1176 of Richard fitz Gilbert, alias *Strongbow, lord of Leinster, administration of his lands became the responsibility of the English crown during the minority of his heirs. At the Council of Oxford Leinster was divided into three areas centred on Dublin, Waterford, and Wexford, to which royal administrators were assigned. *Henry II also designated his son *John 'lord of Ireland' and made speculative grants of the kingdom of Cork (Desmond) to Robert *fitz Stephen and Miles de *Cogan, and of Limerick (*Thomond) to Philip de Braose. MTF

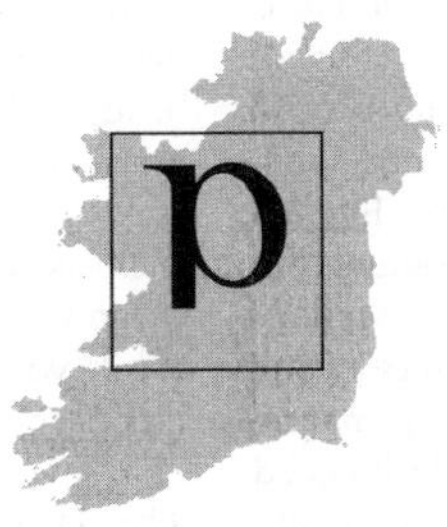

pact election (16 June 1922). The election was for a parliament to ratify the draft *constitution of the new *Irish Free State. The pact was an agreement between *Collins and de *Valera (20 May), under which the two wings into which *Sinn Féin had been split by the *Anglo-Irish treaty were each to nominate candidates in proportion to their existing strength in *Dáil Éireann. A coalition government would then somehow resolve the constitutional question. The agreement, reflecting Collins's desperate desire to avoid *civil war, alarmed the British government and dismayed his cabinet colleagues. The election result, with 239,193 votes cast for pro-treaty pact candidates and 133,864 for anti-treaty pact candidates, made clear that public opinion was on the side of the pragmatists. The most striking feature of the outcome, however, was the large number of votes (247,276) cast for candidates—*Labour, *Farmers' Party, independents—who did not belong to either wing of Sinn Féin.

painting

1660–1900

The fine arts first blossomed in Ireland following the *Restoration. Prior to that, the development of art had been hindered by political upheavals and outbreaks of war. However, under the first viceroy of the Restoration, James Butler, duke of *Ormond, the situation improved. A noted patron of the arts, he decorated his seat at Kilkenny Castle with paintings and furniture and thereby set an example to others. His viceroyalty also ushered in a period of prosperity to Dublin: between 1660 and 1685 the population doubled, new buildings were erected, and the city became a focus for artists and craftsmen. In this improved artistic climate, a number of portrait painters were enabled to pursue careers, notably Garret Morphey (*fl.* 1680–1716), the first Irish-born artist of note, and visiting painters like Gaspar Smitz (d. *c.*1707) from Holland and the Scot John Michael Wright (1617–94).

The first half of the 18th century brought a rise in the standard of portraiture and the development of landscape painting. The former genre was dominated by James Latham (1696–1747), an Irishman who had studied abroad and whose style displayed a realism and sophistication new to Irish portrait painting. With landscape, a genre which did not emerge until the 1720s, the first important figure was Willem van der Hagen (*fl.* 1700–40), whose output included imaginary views and classical landscapes. His contribution was significant as the depiction of scenery in Ireland had hitherto been purely topographical and the preserve of map makers, engravers, and travellers. Appropriately, with this increased flourishing of the fine arts came the establishment of the first art educational institution in the country, namely Robert West's drawing school (see ART SCHOOLS).

The second half of the 18th century saw sufficient patronage in the country to maintain several portrait and landscape painters and a number pursued successful careers in Dublin. Amongst portraitists, Robert Hunter (*fl.*1752–1803) occupied the leading position from the 1750s to the 1780s, until supplanted by Hugh Douglas Hamilton (1739–1808), probably best known for his portraits of Lord Edward FitzGerald. Visiting portrait painters also made an important contribution to the art world, possibly none more so than the Londoner Francis *Wheatley, whose pictures of Volunteer gatherings and of the Irish House of Commons during *Grattan's parliament have assumed almost iconic significance as images of the fight for *legislative independence from England. Other visiting portraitists included Robert Home (1752–1834) of Hull and the American Gilbert Stuart (1755–1828). Their sitters were mainly connected with *Trinity College and the Irish House of Commons.

During these years, landscape reached its peak with the work of Thomas Roberts (1748–78), William Ashford (1746–1824), and George Barret (1728/32–1784). Roberts, probably the most brilliant of the three, died at the age of 30. He is best remembered for his picturesque views of parks of the Irish nobility. Ashford, who moved from England to Dublin, likewise painted well-ordered estates, always with a distinctly English air. The foremost landscapist in the country, he seldom executed the wild and romantic scenery favoured by most Irish landscape painters of the time. Of those who specialized in romantic landscape, Barret was the best known. Influenced by Edmund *Burke's theories of the Sublime and Beautiful, he found the mountains and glens in Co. Wicklow ideal to illustrate the Sublime in nature, that is, its wild and overpowering forces. He is now recognized as one of the forerunners of the genre. With this flourishing of art, it was perhaps inevitable that an exhibiting society—the first in the country—was established in 1765, namely the Society of Artists in Ireland. Its exhibitions were to continue until 1780.

During the early years of the 19th century, a number of other art societies were set up, only to fold after a short time. Finally, in 1823, the *Royal Hibernian Academy, the country's premier art society, was founded, modelled on the lines of the Royal Academy in London. It remains in operation and is an important focus of the Irish art world. In the matter of portraiture, of the many practitioners in Dublin during the first half of the 19th century, the leading exponent was Martin Cregan (1788–1870), first secretary of the above-mentioned Academy. Extremely prolific, he showed 334 pictures in its various exhibitions between 1826 and 1859, an indication of its value and importance to the artistic community. Other portraitists of the period included Martin Archer Shee (1769–1850) and the miniaturist, Adam Buck (1759–1833). The second half of the century was dominated by Sir Thomas Alfred Jones (*c.*1823–1893), who maintained studios in Dublin and Belfast for a time, one of the few Dublin-based painters to do so. As a result, there are numerous portraits by him in the north, chiefly of merchants and professionals.

Landscape painting also continued in popularity, the best-known figure being probably James Arthur O'Connor (1792–1841) who, despite settling elsewhere, continued to paint scenes of his native land from memory. His work passed through a variety of styles, from the topographical to the picturesque and finally, in the 1830s, to a brooding Romanticism. Amongst his contemporaries were Joseph Peacock (1783–1837), who specialized in crowd scenes amidst landscape backgrounds, and William Sadler II (1782–1839), who also painted historical subjects. These and others of their contemporaries worked in the academic tradition, characterized by tight brushwork and attention to detail. The post-1870s brought far-reaching changes to the genre as a number of Irish artists, influenced by studies abroad, brought back to Ireland avant-garde traits such as loose, impressionistic brushwork and a greater emphasis on the effects of light. Their break with tradition was to herald exciting new trends in the next century. EEB

The Twentieth Century

The 20th century was a period of unprecedented change in Irish painting as traditional ideas were gradually overtaken, first by influences from 19th-century French painting and, secondly, by the onslaught of international *modernism, both continental and American. Consequently Irish artists were divided in their aspirations, some fighting a rearguard action, others adamant in their espousal of modernism.

From the 1850s Irish artists had worked in France and had absorbed the influences of *plein air* (open air) painting and of Impressionism and Post-Impressionism. Nathaniel Hone (1831–1917), John *Lavery, Walter Osborne (1859–1903), and Roderic O'Conor (1860–1940), the most important Irish artists of their generation, had all been in France and the ideas they brought back home from there—a love of the outdoors, of light, colour, shape, and the existential act of painting—contrasted with the narrow academic work of their fellow-countrymen. By the early 1900s, with Hugh Lane busy establishing a gallery of modern art in Dublin and the *literary revival in full swing, Ireland was a volatile place, culturally and politically.

From this background emerged the two strands of thought that shaped the future course of Irish art, namely, modernism and a longing for a distinct Irish school of art. In 1920 Paul *Henry, Jack B. *Yeats, and a few others founded the Society of Dublin Painters, representing all that was progressive in Irish art. There, for example, Mainie *Jellett first exhibited cubist and abstract paintings and Cecil Salkeld (1904–69), Harry Kernoff (1900–74), and others exhibited experimental compositions that would have been rejected, say, by the Royal Hibernian Academy. Yet concurrent with these developments Henry, J. H. Craig (1877–1944), Frank McKelvey (1895–1974), and Charles Lamb (1893–1964) evolved a landscape genre—mainly to do with the West—of great force which had a lasting effect and which, in company with works by Dermod O'Brien (1865–1945), Sean Keating (1889–1977), and Maurice MacGonigal (1900–79), was to be the nearest materialization to a native school.

In 1943 the establishment of the Irish Exhibition of Living Art brought Louis le Brocquy (b. 1916), Norah McGuinness (1903–80), Colin Middleton (1910–83), Gerard Dillon (1916–71), and younger painters to the fore. Principally through genre works and landscapes they dominated the scene till the arrival in the early 1960s of American-inspired abstraction and Op and Pop Art influences from Britain. The new art forms, successively with their gestural emphases, mechanical procedures, and, finally, high realism—Micheal Farrell (1940–2000), Roy Johnston (b. 1936), Felim Egan (b. 1952), and Robert Ballagh (b. 1943) come to mind—predominated till the 1980s when, with the persistence of the *Northern Ireland conflict and the rise of a new generation, there was a widespread return to representational painting. This development brought, too, a renewed interest in landscape as subject matter, although in truth Irish painting, even at its most abstract, retains vestiges of the landscape. But in these years, at the hands of artists such as David Crone (b. 1937), Joseph McWilliams (b. 1938), Rita Duffy (b. 1959), and John Kindness (b. 1951), the troubles spawned works of force and importance which, paradoxically, link the socio-political concerns of the present with those of earlier years.

Crookshank, Anne, and The Knight of Glin, *The Painters of Ireland* (1978)

Kennedy, S. B., *Irish Art and Modernism 1880–1950* (1991)

SBK

Pairlement Chloinne Tomáis, see LITERATURE IN IRISH.

palatine jurisdiction, a 17th-century term applied to major medieval seigniorial jurisdictions that included all or most of the pleas and prerogatives elsewhere reserved to the crown (see LIBERTIES). Although palatinates were ultimately subject to royal authority, in practice royal officials were excluded from them. However, four royal pleas and some prerogatives were reserved to the crown. The palatine lord issued writs in his own name, and appointed justices to determine pleas in his court. The last major palatinate, in Tipperary, was abolished in 1716, following the flight and attainder of the 2nd duke of *Ormond. CAE

Palatines, Protestant refugees from the Rhineland palatinate in Germany who arrived in England in 1709. Eight hundred and twenty-one families, containing more than 3,000 persons, were sent on to Ireland. By 1720 only 162 families remained. Of these 103 were settled on the Southwell estate in Co. Limerick, and 35 on the estate of Abel Ramm in Co. Wexford, with smaller groups in Co. Cork and in Dublin. The relative failure of the project was attributed by some to fraud on the part of the commissioners entrusted with the settlement's finances. A more important reason, apart from the inherent difficulties of promoting settlement in an underdeveloped and unwelcoming environment, was possibly that the settlement of foreign Protestants was a *Whig enthusiasm; *Tories were less susceptible to appeals for international Protestant solidarity, and suspicious of potentially dissenting incomers. The Limerick Palatines, despite some defections to Catholicism, remained culturally and religiously distinctive, with high rates of endogamy. They responded enthusiastically to early *Methodist preaching, and *Wesley visited them several times. In the 1820s they became the targets of sectarian hostility from local *agrarian societies. This exacerbated an already high propensity to emigrate, and by the end of the 19th century they had largely ceased to exist as a separate group.

Pale, more correctly 'English Pale', a term applied to the region around Dublin, asserting its character as a fortified area of English rule. Recent research points to a statute of *Poynings's parliament in 1495 for 'diches to be made aboute the Inglishe pale' as the term's earliest application to Ireland. (An earlier purported reference in a document of 1446 has been exposed as a Tudor interpolation.) As the English crown moved after 1400 towards a defensive, containing strategy against Gaelic Ireland, the area which was firmly under the Dublin government's control—'the land of peace' or 'maghery', as opposed to the marches or 'the land of war'—was increasingly equated with 'the four obedient shires' around Dublin. In this lowland region, comprising the medieval counties of Dublin, Meath, Louth, and Kildare which later constituted the English Pale, conditions more closely accorded with contemporary lowland English norms in respect of language, culture, law, social structures, and government than with any other part of the English dominions. For administrative and military reasons the region was increasingly divided into marches and maghery (a transliteration of the Gaelic *machaire*, meaning 'a plain'). Yet a march was essentially an open border region defended by castles and peles, whereas a pale denoted a defensive ring of fortifications; and despite earlier proposals for enclosing the four shires, the first systematic attempt to apply this defensive concept to Ireland was apparently the 1495 statute. It was probably inspired by the defensive arrangements at Calais where the first reference to a 'Pale' occurs in 1494. Sir Edward Poynings was then deputy lieutenant at Calais, immediately before his appointment as governor of Ireland: probably he or his officials first applied the term to the Dublin region in token of its apparently similar character as an English stronghold. It remained a politically distinct region until the dismantling of the medieval frontier with the *Tudor conquest of Ireland. SGE

Palladius was, according to the contemporary chronicler Prosper, sent to the Irish by Pope Celestine as their first bishop in AD 431. As a deacon Palladius was responsible for inducing Celestine in 429 to appoint Germanus, bishop of Auxerre, as his representative in combating the *Pelagian heresy in Britain. In the late 7th century, Muirchú, writing to glorify Armagh and *Patrick, claimed that Palladius rapidly gave up his mission and soon died. This is rendered improbable by two pieces of evidence. About 434 Prosper wrote in his *Contra Collatorem* that Celestine 'having ordained a bishop for the Irish, while he labours to keep the Roman island [Britain] catholic, has also made the barbarian island [Ireland] Christian'. Palladius's achievements were probably still a matter for celebration in Rome in the 440s, when Leo cited the missionary achievements of the see of Peter beyond the Roman empire in a sermon delivered on the feast of SS Peter and Paul. The likelihood is, therefore, that Palladius came from an anti-Pelagian group in Gaul, supported by Prosper and by Pope Celestine and centred around Germanus of Auxerre; that he made significant progress in a mission to the Irish, perhaps centred in Leinster, the area of Ireland most open to Roman influence; and that his achievements were stolen by Patrician hagiographers. Whether he belonged to the Palladii mentioned by Sidonius Apollinaris is uncertain. TMC-E

papacy. The popes, as bishops of Rome, enjoyed a primacy in the western church. Its purpose was to ensure unity of faith. In 431 Pope Celestine (422–32) sent *Palladius as bishop to the Christian Irish. *Patrick does not appear to have been dispatched by the papacy. Over time the isolated Irish church developed distinctive practices, retaining, for instance, an older method of calculating the date of Easter. In the ensuing *paschal controversy, Nativists (*Hibernenses*) clung to the old ways while Romanizers (*Romani*), encouraged by Pope Honorius I (625–38), who received an Irish embassy in 630–1, opted for the Roman practice. The Irish conformed to Rome after the Synod of *Whitby (664). How deep this conformity was is difficult to say, but according to recent research an early 8th-century *brehon law text unambiguously endorsed Roman primacy.

There is little evidence of Roman-Irish contact until the 11th century when the papacy embarked on a reform drive to strengthen its jurisdictional claims. In Ireland this culminated in the Synod of *Kells (1152), presided over by Cardinal Paparo, which confirmed a European-style diocesan system. In 1155 Hadrian IV's letter **Laudabiliter*, probably issued at the behest of *Canterbury, placed Ireland under the lordship of *Henry II, ostensibly in the hope of furthering reform. The incompleteness of the *Anglo-Norman conquest produced differences of organization and culture within the Irish church, and complicated papal relations with Ireland. The papacy continued to uphold the English title to the island; John XXII, for instance, rejected the argument of the 1317 *Remonstrance that the failure of the English to honour the terms of *Laudabiliter* justified the Irish in transferring their allegiance to Edward *Bruce. But the same pope urged Edward II and Edward III to treat Irish grievances seriously.

The loss of papal revenue during the popes' exile in Avignon (1305–78) and the loss of authority during the Great Schism affected Ireland. Hungry for revenues, papal bureaucrats granted dispensations for the ordination of sons of priests, and native Irish clergy in particular, among whom the hereditary system persisted, became accomplished 'Rome-runners'. By the early 16th century reform was in the air. In 1536 the Irish parliament declared Henry VIII supreme head of the church. The papal response was indecisive. Ecclesiastical penalties, such as Pius V's *Regnans in excelsis* (1570), and support for *Counter-Reformation crusaders like James FitzMaurice FitzGerald, were accompanied by internal reform initiatives. The Council of *Trent (1545–63) elaborated reform programmes which slowly affected Ireland. The reformed papacy targeted episcopal appointments, establishing a special congregation for that purpose by 1572. It nominated bishops to Irish sees even where temporalities were alienated and the new bishops' faculties often extended beyond inherited ecclesiastical boundaries. In the absence of an established Catholic church, Irish affairs were channelled through the Nunciature in Brussels (see NUNZIATURA DI FIANDRA) to *Propaganda in Rome. By the 1590s an Irish Counter-Reformation religious community had been established, committed to the papacy.

The papacy was anxious lest Irish Catholics' efforts to find a political accommodation with the Protestant state might dilute its authority. These fears were realized during the complex political struggles of the 1640s, when *Old English *Gallicans were ready to compromise on papal authority, but the Old Irish, encouraged by the papal nuncio *Rinuccini, pushed for an established Catholic church. Old English Gallicanism surfaced again in the *Remonstrances of 1661 and

1666, but the *Revolution of 1688 hardened attitudes. For the Irish Protestant state, continued loyalty to pope and Stuarts (see JACOBITISM) made Catholics ineligible for basic civil rights. Throughout the era of the *penal laws, the papacy remained active in Irish church affairs through episcopal appointments and the regulation of disputes between regular and secular clergy. Clement XIII's refusal to recognize the Stuart succession in 1766, ending the Stuart right to episcopal nomination, opened new possibilities for Irish relations with Rome.

As Catholics regained civil status the question of papal loyalty was again politically topical. In 1772 parliament approved an oath of loyalty for Catholics but its anti-papal phraseology divided bishops and laity. Reform came anyway but the *French Revolution and the *insurrection of 1798 changed everything. The papacy swung in behind established authorities and during the *veto controversy was more anxious than the Irish bishops to appease London. It was the genius of 19th-century Irish Catholicism to blend domestic political liberalism with staunch *ultramontanism. The papacy never intervened directly in Irish affairs but was the focus of ecclesiastical politicking as episcopal factions lobbied Rome on questions of church–state co-operation, notably in education. The Syllabus of Errors (1864) condemned the separation of church and state. Yet even Cardinal *Cullen realized that separation with voluntary co-operation was in fact the relationship that best served the interests of the Irish church. While most Irish bishops accepted the definition of papal infallibility (1870), they saw its limits when applied to political matters. When Leo XIII declared the *Plan of Campaign unlawful in 1888, Archbishop William *Walsh of Dublin made his objections known to Rome.

After independence, elements of social Catholicism found their way into legislation but their effect was minimal. The *Eucharistic Congress (1932) probably marks the high point of Irish ultramontanism. A new phase of *modernization in Irish society coincided with *Vatican II. Apparent doctrinal confusion and pastoral indecisiveness followed, giving way to a period of consolidation under John Paul II, who visited Ireland in 1979. He paid special attention to episcopal appointments and doctrinal renewal.

Keogh, Dermot, *Ireland and the Vatican: The Politics and Diplomacy of Church–State Relations, 1922–1962* (1995)

TO'C

paper manufacturing grew rapidly during the 18th century. *Dublin dominated the industry with mills concentrated on the outskirts of the city on the rivers Liffey, Camac, and Dodder. The other important centres were *Cork and east Ulster; in the country at large there were about 50 paper mills by the 1780s. Although a few mills around Dublin produced fine paper, most of the output of the Irish industry was not of a high quality; little was exported and most of the fine paper consumed came from England. During the third quarter of the 19th century production became more concentrated in larger mills; machinery was increasingly introduced and smaller mills using traditional techniques began to close, although total output was growing. With mechanization the industry became even more concentrated around the main centres of demand. However, despite a few success stories (like the Ballyclare Mills in Co. Antrim), the industry as a whole experienced rapid decline from the 1860s and by 1907 there were only seven mills left in the entire country (five in Dublin and two in Co. Antrim). The capital costs of entering the industry and maintaining competitiveness had become very high, which made it difficult to compete with English, German, and American paper imports. AB

parish, a territorial subdivision with both ecclesiastical and civil significance. An ecclesiastical parish structure came relatively late to Ireland, following the creation of a diocesan structure as part of the *12th-century reform. The first parishes were probably conterminous with the lands of Gaelic family groups. English settlement began before the pattern was complete, and in colonized areas parishes became coincident with the new *feudal tenureships. A divergence in the Catholic and *Church of Ireland parish structures may have begun from the 16th century. The established church took over the medieval pattern, while the Catholic church created its own network, only partially based on the pre-Reformation predecessor. Both systems were then modified in response to social and demographic change. Civil parishes were originally coincident with the medieval parishes, which in turn became those of the established church, but they did not change along with their religious counterparts. Civil parish divisions served as bases for surveys, and in later years for *censuses, but for little else. They frequently transgressed *county and *barony borders, and by the 19th century were essentially irrelevant to settlement patterns. There are 2,445 civil parishes in Ireland. NG

parish registers, recording births, marriages, and deaths, are a major source for both family and demographic historians. *Church of Ireland registers for the period up to *disestablishment are public records. They survive for between 600 and 700 parishes, most of them beginning in the early 19th century or later, but with about a quarter covering some part of the period before 1800. Although the keeping of registers was required by the Council of *Trent, the slow progress of the *Counter-Reformation, and the effects of recurrent political disruption, have meant that only a handful of Catholic parish registers, generally from urban areas, exist for any part of the 18th century. In many parishes, particularly in western districts, registers were not kept until the 1840s or later. *Presbyterian church registers date mainly from the early 19th century. The most complete set of demographic records for any religious denomination are those of the *Society of Friends, extending back to the beginnings of the society in the 1650s.

parish vestry, meetings of parishioners to provide for the collection and expenditure of parochial rates. The *Church of Ireland's status as an established church should in theory have made its parishes units of local government as well as ecclesiastical organization. In practice, with church members accounting for one in eight or less of the population, this was often not possible. In parts of Ulster, in some of the larger towns and cities, and in a few other areas, the parish vestry nevertheless became involved in a range of civil functions: the relief of poverty and the control of vagrants, the appointment of constables and provision for a night-time watch, sanitary services, and the upkeep of roads. In some cases a distinction was maintained between the select vestry, consisting of ratepayers who were members of the Church of Ireland, which dealt with matters relating to the upkeep of the church and its staff, and the general vestry, which all ratepayers could attend, and which dealt with secular functions.

parliamentary papers, the printed reports of select committees and royal commissions and other accounts and papers laid before parliament. From the Act of *Union to 1922 they include a huge variety of material on every aspect of Irish society. Particularly notable sources are the *Poor Inquiry, the *census taken every ten years from 1821, the *Devon Commission (1845) which inquired into Irish land, and numerous inquiries into agrarian crime and political disturbance.

parliamentary reform, in the sense of the refashioning of the electoral system, first became a major issue in the second half of the 18th century. Previously critics of the political system had concentrated on means of eliminating corruption among MPs and office holders. A different emphasis first appeared in the campaign during the 1760s for more regular elections, culminating in the *Octennial Act. Parliamentary reform on a larger scale first became an issue following the successful campaigns for *free trade and *legislative independence. Detailed proposals were drawn up by the *Volunteer Convention at *Dungannon in September 1783 and by the National Convention in November, and by the *Whigs in 1793–4. Though differing in detail they shared the same objective of strengthening the electoral power of the small property owner. The *franchise was to be made more uniform, while retaining a property qualification; proposals to increase the boundaries of small boroughs, and, in the case of the Whig plan, to give an extra parliamentary seat to each county and to the cities of Dublin and Cork, would have increased the proportion of open to *closed constituencies. The Dungannon Convention also advocated the secret *ballot. It was only the *United Irishmen who moved beyond such limited schemes to real (if still gender-bound) democracy: their plan, finalized in early 1794, called for universal manhood suffrage, equal electoral districts, and the secret ballot.

The Act of *Union, though opposed by most *patriots and radicals, was in fact a major measure of reform, at a stroke reducing the representatives for closed constituencies from more than two-thirds to less than one-third of Irish members. *O'Connell's wholehearted participation in the reform agitation of the years before 1832 reflects both his own position as a figure within British as well as Irish radicalism and his perception, borne out by events, that British reforms would not necessarily be replicated in Ireland. Subsequent extensions to the Irish franchise, in 1867, 1885, and 1918, were more closely in parallel with changes in the English and Welsh and the Scottish electorate, and the cause of reform attracted correspondingly less interest from Irish politicians.

Parliament House, later Bank of Ireland, Dublin. Built between 1729 and 1739 to the designs of Edward Lovett *Pearce, it was one of the most influential public buildings of the century. The Palladian south façade, with Ionic portico and projecting gallery pavilions, is the most important survival of Pearce's work. Inside, his House of Lords remains in a slightly altered state. Pearce's House of Commons was an octagonal room, surmounted by a low dome; it was destroyed by fire in 1792 and was replaced by a circular chamber designed by Vincent Waldré.

Between 1784 and *c.*1789 the building was extended eastwards by James *Gandon, who erected the Corinthian portico as a new entrance for the House of Lords, and joined it to Pearce's façade by a niched screen wall. The building was also extended to the west by Richard Parke, who continued Pearce's use of the Ionic order in his portico and linking screen wall.

Following the Act of *Union, the government sold the buildings to the *Bank of Ireland. Francis *Johnston, the architect selected to make the necessary alterations, blocked up the central doorway and windows of Pearce's south façade and added the statues of Commerce, Hibernia, and Fidelity to the portico. The House of Commons was replaced with the bank boardroom, the governor's office, and the accountant-general's office. Johnston also replaced Gandon's screen wall and altered Parke's west façade. RM

parliaments are first mentioned in Ireland in the 13th century, following closely on their appearance in England. The word *parliamentum* meant 'parley' or 'discussion', and seems to have been a new-fangled term for the long-established colloquies between kings and their leading lay and ecclesiastical subjects. It acquired additional significance during the disputes between Henry III and his barons (1258–65). Edward I (1272–1307) used English parliaments for royal purposes—hearing and answering petitions, promulgating legislation, and seeking consent to the taxes he needed for his wars. On occasion the forwarding of his business required the presence of representative knights from the shires and burgesses from the towns, alongside the magnates and higher clergy who received individual summonses. Similar development took place in Ireland, where the first clearly documented parliament met in 1264. In 1278 ordinances were promulgated in parliament with the assent of the magnates. In 1297 the *justiciar summoned knights from the counties as well as lords or their stewards to the Dublin parliament, probably because a reorganization of shire government and the formulation of peacekeeping regulations was being planned. In 1300 the king's request for taxation towards the *Anglo-Scottish War saw the first known summons of both knights and burgesses. Parliaments did not, however, yet *require* the presence of elected representatives. Annalists continued to present them as primarily aristocratic occasions, when the justiciar might compose differences between the great lords and obtain their agreement to discipline their followers. It should be noted, too, that similar business to that transacted in parliament continued to be handled in 'great councils', which could be called at short notice (parliament involved 40 days' warning), and so tended to have a more regional attendance.

In England the 14th century saw the role of parliament change. The king's need for resources, especially after the beginning of the *Hundred Years War, made taxation a frequent occurrence. Edward III (1327–77) used parliament to publicize and gain support for his activities, and an unspoken link appeared between the granting of taxes and the redress of grievances. Particularly from the 1370s, when the war went badly, some English parliaments saw magnates and knights combine to criticize royal ministers and policy. Broadly parallel developments are visible in Ireland, where the Gaelic threat to the colony led to more frequent taxation from the 1350s onwards. During the 1370s *William of Windsor's heavy fiscal demands provoked opposition in parliament; when the king tried to bring representatives of the Irish counties and towns to England in the hope of unlocking their purses, their electors reacted by denying them authority to make grants. By this time country and borough representatives were a normal part of Irish parliaments, as were representatives of the lower clergy. (In England, by contrast, the clergy met separately in convocation.) The special problems of government in Ireland set a distinctive agenda for parliaments and great councils, which became, as the Statute of *Kilkenny shows, an arena where royal ministers and the colonial elites dealt wth issues such as security, *absenteeism, and *Gaelicization. The Anglo-Irish also used them as occasions to formulate appeals to the king and accredit messengers to the English court: in 1385 meetings at Dublin and Kilkenny sought to convince *Richard II that without his personal intervention the colony would be lost.

The 15th century saw the appearance of an enhanced sense of parliament's status. This was sufficiently developed by 1460 to be exploited by Richard, duke of *York, when the Drogheda parliament issued its *declaration asserting Ireland's jurisdictional identity under the crown, and denying the validity in Ireland of English statutes unless these were accepted 'by the lords spiritual and temporal and the commons of [Ireland] ... in great council or parliament there held'. Such major political and constitutional issues, however, arose infrequently. The normal role of parliament was as a high court where legislation particular to Ireland was enacted, and where petitions from the lords, gentry, and communities of the lordship were dealt with. As the colony shrank geographically, it became rare for parliaments to be held outside the future *Pale; but they still attracted attendance and petitions from south Leinster and Munster, and compensated in some degree for the declining effectiveness of other royal courts. The support in Ireland for Yorkist pretenders (see WARS OF THE ROSES) to Henry VII's throne helped prompt the enactment of *Poynings's Law, which gave the English government unprecedented control over the business of the Irish parliament, and may be regarded as bringing the medieval phase of Irish parliamentary history to a close.

In the period of reconquest and renewed colonization that followed during the 16th and early 17th centuries, the crown wanted a compliant parliament voting taxes for its increased expenditure and legislating for its policies on religion, land, and social regulation. Changes in representation generally favoured the state. The representation of the lower clergy by proctors was abolished after these had opposed royal ecclesiastical supremacy in 1536. The gradual extension of shire government saw new Commons constituencies, providing not only space for Gaelic Irish MPs but also room for government officials. The most dramatic change took place in *Chichester's parliament (1613–5) when new boroughs, most little more than villages or projected plantation towns, were created. This gave 38 new MPs from Ulster, 18 from Munster, 16 from Leinster, and 12 from Connacht, and a government majority of 32. This majority was reduced to six after successful *Old English objections to the late issue of borough charters, but became fully operational in *Wentworth's 1634–5 parliament. For his 1640 parliament Wentworth eliminated 16 more Old English seats by disenfranchising boroughs. In the *Restoration parliament of 1661–6, following the devastating Cromwellian attack on Catholic property rights, only one Catholic member was returned, and his election was subsequently overturned.

These changes in representation sprang from growing Old English resistance to government policies. In *Grey's Reformation parliament of 1536–7, the state confidently suspended Poynings's Law. The local elite had little ideological objection to establishing Henry VIII as head of the church and, when its worries about monastic land distribution and new taxes were dispelled, the response was positive. *St Leger's parliament (1541–3), which established Ireland as a *kingdom and saw the attendance of many Gaelic and Gaelicized lords in response to the new policy of *surrender and regrant, was euphoric. *Sussex's two parliaments bringing back Catholicism under Mary (1557–8) and establishing Anglicanism under Elizabeth (1560) saw little opposition. But *Sidney's parliament (1569–71) hit problems when the Commons objected to non-resident New Englishmen being elected and refused the suspension of Poynings's Law in an atmosphere vitiated by the first *Desmond revolt and the ongoing *cess controversy. Sidney's subsequent plan to replace cess by *composition encountered so much opposition that a second parliament intended for 1577–8 had to be abandoned. In *Perrot's parliament (1585–6) Old English fears about recusancy laws and composition ruined most of the lord deputy's plans.

Parliament was not called for another quarter-century. In Chichester's parliament, penal legislation was widely expected in the light of his *mandates policy. In fact the anti-Catholic proposals were mild but the parliament took place under an armed guard in Dublin Castle. The Old English minority sabotaged proceedings by attempting to elect their own *speaker; when he was ejected, they withdrew from the house. Parliament reconvened only after concessions from James VI. In 1628 the Old English seemed on the point of getting a parliament to approve the *Graces. The writs of summons had been dispatched but failure to follow the procedure laid down by Poynings's Law meant the parliament was called off and that run by Wentworth six years later was to be quite a different event. Wentworth's second parliament, however, went completely awry. After he left Ireland the government party disintegrated and Old and New English united against his arbitrary methods. They accrued authority as the executive power evaporated, culminating in Patrick *Darcy's famous 'Argument' that the Irish parliament had power to make law and control the courts notwithstanding the claims of either royal prerogative or English parliament.

Many of these aspirations were evident in the subsequent development of the *Confederate Catholic assembly, which was technically not a parliament since it was not called by the king and itself made no legislation. However, the claims of the English parliament, which had applied 36 acts to Ireland between 1532 and 1640, were amply demonstrated by the unprecedentedly wide-ranging *Adventurers Act of 1642. The logical consequence of the growing assertiveness of the English body was parliamentary union in 1654, in which Ireland and Scotland each received 30 elected representatives at Westminster. The *convention of 1660, which restored the king, shows that the Protestant interest in Ireland favoured its own parliament. Ironically the parliament of 1661–6, in which representatives of pre-1641 Irish Protestants were joined by 16 adventurers and 50 Cromwellian soldiers, was no more compliant than formerly. It passed the Act of

*Settlement (1662) but protested as the Court of Claims proceeded to find large numbers of Catholics innocent and passed the Act of *Explanation (1665) only with extreme reluctance. MPs were, however, willing to grant *customs duties and the hearth tax in perpetuity rather than for a term of years. This, along with buoyant receipts for most of the next two decades, ensured that it was not necessary to summon another parliament until *Tyrconnell's *patriot parliament of 1689.

The 1690s began a new phase in the history of the Irish parliament. The rhetoric of representative government that had accompanied the *revolution of 1688 had created new expectations among the Irish propertied classes. Meanwhile the need for additional grants of *taxation, as the cost of prolonged war against France pushed government spending far beyond the traditional revenues of the crown, gave parliament, in both Great Britain and Ireland, new bargaining power. Both influences were evident in the *sole right controversy of 1692, and in the compromise that followed in 1695. Parliament met at roughly two-year intervals up to 1714, and regularly every second year thereafter until 1785, when annual sessions commenced.

The Irish parliament throughout the 18th century represented the Protestant propertied classes. Landowners and their relatives made up a substantial majority among MPs; there was also a sizeable contingent of lawyers and smaller numbers of bankers and merchants. In parliament members operated either as independent individuals or as part of informal groups or connections, based on family, friendship, or mutual interest. The only exceptions were the period *c.*1704–14, when parliamentary politics were dominated by the conflict of *Whig and Tory, and the 1790s, when the formation of a new Whig Party once again introduced an element of conflict between *political parties.

Up to 1782 the powers of the Irish parliament were still nominally restricted by Poynings's Law and, from 1720, the *Declaratory Act. In practice, the Irish executive, and the British ministry to which it answered, found it preferable to proceed by co-operation and mutual accommodation. Up to the late 1760s the Irish parliament was managed through *undertakers. *Townshend's much publicized conflict with these powerful intermediaries did not remove the need to construct parliamentary majorities by negotiation, consultation, and the careful distribution of patronage. Instead those functions were now taken over directly by the *lord lieutenant and *chief secretary. Nor did *legislative independence in 1782 substantially change the relationship between executive and legislature.

This type of 'management' was made possible by the restricted electoral system on which the Irish House of Commons was elected. No fewer than 234 out of 300 members sat for *'close' boroughs, where the return of members was wholly under the control of a single patron; the rest were elected on a narrow, property-based *franchise. The unrepresentative character of the Commons, the prominence of patronage in parliamentary management, and the eventual willingness of parliament to vote itself out of existence by accepting the Act of *Union have all contributed to the low historical reputation of parliamentarians. More recent writing, however, acknowledges the extent to which the pursuit of profit and influence was nevertheless regulated by notions of honour and duty, while episodes like the resistance to *Wood's Halfpence, and the agitations for *free trade and legislative independence, remind us that parliament was not wholly detached from what its members accepted as legitimate public opinion.

Ellis, S. G., *Reform and Revival: English Government in Ireland 1470–1534* (1986)

McCracken, J. L., *The Irish Parliament in the Eighteenth Century* (1971)

Richardson, H. G., and Sayles, G. O., *The Irish Parliament in the Middle Ages* (1964)

RFF/HM/SC

Parnell, Anna (1852–1911), nationalist and founder of the *Ladies' Land League. Anna's political beliefs, like those of her brother *Charles and her sister *Fanny, came partly from their Irish-American mother, who also introduced the young Parnells to American anti-slavery and women's rights activism. The Parnell women were active in Irish-American political circles in the 1860s and 1870s. Michael *Davitt asked Anna to come back to Ireland to head a Ladies' Land League early in 1881. Anna proved a fearless leader, travelling the country to hold public meetings, resist evictions, and organize accommodation for the evicted. *The Tale of a Great Sham*, written in 1907 but published only in 1986, reflected her later disillusionment with what she saw as the *Land League's attempts to placate the larger tenants while making empty promises of land redistribution to the smaller ones. She was drowned while swimming in Devon in 1911. CC

Parnell, Charles Stewart (1846–91), nationalist leader. Born into a Protestant landlord family in Avondale, Co. Wicklow, and educated at Magdalene College, Cambridge, he was *home rule MP for Meath 1875–80, and for Cork city 1880–91. He established his reputation as an advanced nationalist through 'obstruction' tactics in parliament in association with J. G. *Biggar and progressed to the leadership of the nationalist movement via the *New Departure, presidency of the *Land League (1879), and chairmanship of the *Irish parliamentary party (1880). The passing of the 1881 *Land Act, the suppression of the Land League, and the *Kilmainham treaty allowed Parnell to pursue a purely constitutional campaign for home rule, a change of direction marked by the inauguration of the *National League in 1882. The general election of 1885, which returned 86 Nationalist MPs, was an impressive demonstration of Parnell's power, and an important factor in *Gladstone's conversion to home rule, which inaugurated the Liberal–nationalist alliance.

The year 1886 marked the height of Parnell's power. Thereafter, a combination of poor health, his affair with Mrs *O'Shea, and a refusal to support the *Plan of Campaign removed him from the centre of nationalist affairs. The charges made in the *'Parnellism and crime' letters in *The Times* 1887, and his subsequent vindication by the special commission 1890, served to unite all shades of nationalist opinion around him. However his career was destroyed soon afterwards in the party split that followed his citation as co-respondent in the O'Shea divorce petition of December 1889. Parnell married Katherine O'Shea in June 1891 and died in Brighton the following October after an exhausting by-election campaign.

The key to Parnell's career lies in his exceptional personal and political qualities: qualities all the more striking given a highly nervous disposition and superstitious nature. His leadership of the Land War established a firm basis for his political power: leadership grounded in a myth of himself which could appeal to both extremists and moderates and which was exploited to maximum effect through an uncanny ability to assess the most that could be obtained in any political context. His political achievements can be charted in terms of his role in obtaining the enactment of land reforms, especially the 1881 Land Act; and the creation of a disciplined and independent Irish parliamentary party which brought the home rule issue to the centre of British politics and established an alliance with Gladstonian Liberalism to obtain it.

Parnell's failures, however, are also significant. The abandonment of agrarian struggle, especially during the Plan of Campaign, together with the absences from Ireland necessitated by his affair with Mrs O'Shea, inevitably diminished his authority. Accordingly, Parnell was already politically weakened before the scandal surrounding the O'Shea divorce developed. Also, despite a highly sensitive political antenna, Parnell failed to appreciate adequately the obstacle to the achievement of his home rule ambitions presented by the Ulster problem. Historically, however, his reputation did not suffer the same fate as that of his successor as party leader, John *Redmond, when constitutional nationalism became discredited after 1916. Just as the 'penumbra of revolution' which surrounded Parnell during his political career served to retain militant support, so too, after his death, it was possible for Arthur *Griffith, Patrick *Pearse, and Eamon de *Valera to focus on the militant strand in his political persona to claim him, effectively, for the *republican tradition. Assessments of Parnell have traditionally focused on a brilliant career brought to a tragic end. More recent work has looked beyond the personalities of the split to the conflict of liberal and conservative forces that it symbolized.

Bew, Paul, *C. S. Parnell* (1980)
Callanan, Frank, *The Parnell Split 1890–91* (1992)
Lyons, F. S. L., *Charles Stewart Parnell* (1977)

JL

Parnell, Fanny (1849–82), sister of *Charles and *Anna, and founder of the New York Ladies' Land League (1880). Her poem 'Hold the Harvest' was described by *Davitt as 'the Marseillaise of the Irish peasantry'. Like Anna and their mother Delia, she spent most of her life in America. Although Anna is most remembered for political activism, Fanny was more involved initially, having close links with Irish-American *Fenians. She understood Irish life less well than Anna, and was frustrated at the lack of response to her letter to the *Nation* newspaper (1 Jan. 1881) calling for a women's land organization. She died of a heart attack. CC

'Parnellism and crime', a series of articles published in *The Times* in 1887 while an Irish coercion bill was before parliament and appearing to demonstrate, in letters supposedly written by *Parnell, his connection with terrorism. The most damaging link was in a letter of 15 May 1882, in which he apparently expressed regret at having to condemn the *Phoenix Park murders. Parnell denounced the letters in the House of Commons and demanded a select committee to investigate their authenticity. The Conservative government, however, preferred to establish a special commission to investigate the charges they contained, thus putting the whole nationalist movement on trial. This move largely backfired. The desired link between nationalism and terrorism was inadequately established; the forger of *The Times* letters, Richard

Pigott, was exposed under cross-examination and the credibility of *The Times* severely damaged. JL

Parnell special commission, see 'PARNELLISM AND CRIME'.

Parsons, William (1800–67), 3rd earl of Rosse, astronomer and politician. Born in York, he was brought up at the ancestral home in Birr, Co. Offaly. After Trinity College, Dublin, and Oxford (where he excelled in mathematics) he entered Parliament as member for King's County (Offaly) (1821–34); from 1831 he was lord lieutenant of King's County, and in 1841 entered the House of Lords. His intellectual passion was astronomy, particularly the design of large telescopes in which regard he expanded on the work of William Herschel. In 1842 he constructed at Birr the famous 72-inch telescope ('Leviathan') with which he made many important observations, principally of nebulae. DJS

partition, noun deriving from the Latin *partitio*, a division. It began to be used in a political sense in the 18th century, notably in 1751 when Voltaire referred to the 1700 accord of London as 'ce traité de partage', and then in connection with the partitions of Poland of 1772, 1793, and 1795. By the 19th century it was well understood in a political sense, as in the partition of Africa. In Ireland it did not surface as a significant issue in the first two *home rule controversies, although some form of county option was discussed in the *Liberal Party in 1887. It can be argued that the emergence of a specifically Ulster unionist organization (see ULSTER UNIONIST COUNCIL) following the *devolution crisis foreshadowed division, the more so as southern unionism declined as a political force.

The first overt proposal to exclude part of Ulster from the jurisdiction of a Dublin parliament came during the committee stage of the home rule bill in June 1912, when Thomas Agar-Robartes, Liberal MP for St Austell, proposed that its terms should not apply to Antrim, Armagh, Down, or Londonderry. When *Carson moved an amendment in December 1912 for nine-county exclusion it was clear that some form of partition would be seriously discussed. By the time of the Buckingham Palace conference of 21–4 July 1914 the issues had come to focus on whether exclusion would be temporary or permanent and on the number of counties involved. It was during *Lloyd George's negotiations with *Redmond and Carson in May 1916 that the prospect of a six-county partition came clearly into view. Even so, in 1919 the cabinet committee on the Irish question recommended a nine-county division as a means of minimizing the partition of Ireland on religious lines. The terms of the *government of Ireland bill proposed a six-county Northern Ireland, the course northern unionists had come to accept. Debates in the House of Commons revealed that both unionists and nationalists saw this as leading to a permanent partition of the island.

The opening of the Northern Ireland parliament by King George V on 22 June 1921 seemed confirmation of the reality of partition, though Irish unity remained a priority for *Sinn Féin in the negotiation of the *Anglo-Irish treaty. Failure to break off negotiations on the issue of unity was the basis of much criticism of *Griffith and *Collins. Their belief that the *Boundary Commission would end partition by truncating Northern Ireland proved baseless. With the collapse of the commission in 1925 partition became an established, if controversial, fact.

Fraser, T. G., *Partition in Ireland, India and Palestine: Theory and Practice* (1984)

TGF

Party Processions Act (1850), the most controversial of a series of measures designed to outlaw provocative sectarian meetings and parades, passed in the aftermath of the bloody confrontation at *Dolly's Brae (1849): it was complemented by the Party Emblems Act (1860), passed after a sectarian riot at Derrymacash, Co. Armagh. Although the legislation was at first grudgingly accepted by the *Orange leadership, the rise of the *Irish Republican Brotherhood, and increasingly frequent *Fenian processions, brought a shift of attitude. In the 1860s William Johnston of Ballykilbeg (1829–1902), a minor landlord and radical Orange leader, led a campaign of defiance. Johnston's imprisonment for leading an illegal Orange procession between Newtownards and Bangor, Co. Down, on 12 July 1867 reinvigorated demands for the act's removal, and the measure was repealed in 1872. In contemporary Northern Ireland, the question of the right to march remains a deeply divisive one, the underlying issues of territorial supremacy and civil rights remaining much the same as in the mid-19th century. AJ

paschal controversy, an argument over the calculation of the date of Easter that constitutes a prominent theme in the ecclesiastical affairs of the 7th century. Easter was defined as the Sunday following the full moon of Pesach, the Jewish Passover, but because the Jewish calendar was based on lunar months, its date in relation to the western solar calendar is variable. Different methods of calculation for correlating the two calendars were tried in the 5th and 6th centuries.

The Celtic churches of western Britain and Ireland adhered to an 84-year cycle when Rome adopted what Irish computists judged to be a less accurate system; they continued to use this after Rome and the rest of the western church (and some eastern churches) had changed to a better nineteen-year cycle. In the year 600 *Columbanus in Italy had clashed with the local church over the date on which Easter was to be celebrated, and wrote to Pope Gregory the Great forcefully defending the Celtic position. Gregory's successors formed the mistaken impression that the Celtic churches celebrated Easter heretically on the day of the paschal moon rather than the Sunday following, and for thirty years there were strenuous efforts to persuade the Irish church to adopt the Roman practice. Attempts by Roman missionaries in England to move the Irish and the Welsh churches were resisted. By the late 620s, however, the matter was discussed by Irish synods. Envoys were sent to Rome and returned in 633 persuaded by the merits of unity and orthodoxy. As *Bede indicates, most of the churches of Munster and Leinster conformed about this time. In the 660s Irish and Roman practice clashed again in Northumbria, where the Roman method was adopted following a synod at *Whitby in 664. The churches of midland and northern Ireland did not adopt the Roman practice until persuaded to do so by *Adomnán, who had been won over during a visit to Northumbria in the 680s. His own community in *Iona was the last of the Irish churches to follow the older Celtic method, adopting the Roman practice only in 716. The Welsh church remained conservative until the late 8th century. RS

passage grave, see MEGALITHIC TOMBS.

passports. The first Irish passports were issued in 1924, despite British objections that they ignored common British citizenship. They identified the bearer as a citizen of the *Irish Free State and British *Commonwealth of Nations. Passports were initially issued by the *governor-general in the name of the monarch. After 1930 they were issued by the minister for external affairs in the name of the monarch, from 1939 solely in the name of the minister. There is no Irish passport law. The granting of passports derived from crown prerogative and this function was assigned to the Department of External Affairs under the *Ministers and Secretaries Act 1924. DMcM

'Pastorini, Signor', pseudonym of Charles Walmesley (1722–97), an English Catholic bishop whose *General History of the Christian Church* (1771), an elaborate interpretation of the Apocalypse of St John, formed the basis for a dramatic outbreak of *millenarian excitement in the 1820s.

patent and close rolls contained the letters patent and letters close issued by *chancery. The former include land grants, corporate charters, peace treaties, king's letters, and deeds. The latter consist mainly of authorizations for making *exchequer payments, although earlier rolls contain a variety of other orders and instructions. The original rolls were destroyed in 1922. Calendars for the reigns of Henry II to Henry VII, and for James I, were printed by the *Irish record commissioners; calendars for the reigns of Henry VIII to Elizabeth and part of Charles I were published by James Morrin in 1861–3. Additional material is available in manuscript calendars and in John Lodge's records of the rolls, both in the National Archives (see PUBLIC RECORDS). RG

patria, the Roman concept of the fatherland, entered Irish political discourse under the impact of the *Renaissance. First used by a Protestant radical, Edward Walshe, in 1545, it increasingly bolstered the claims of Catholic reactionaries, notably James Fitzmaurice. In 1579 he combined the concepts of fighting for Ireland and Catholicism in the second *Desmond revolt. The same combination was used by Hugh *O'Neill in a vain attempt to rally *Old English support during the *Nine Years War, and was further elaborated by subsequent accounts of the period by *Lombard, *O'Sullivan Beare, and O'Clery (the *Annals of the *Four Masters*, see LITERATURE IN IRISH). *Patria* emerged again as a slogan of the *Confederate Catholics in the 1640s. HM

Patrick (Patricius) was a native of late Roman Britain and is Ireland's patron saint. The dates of his birth and death are disputed; that he flourished in the 5th century is agreed. Two Latin texts written by Patrick are the oldest documents in Irish history and the sole contemporary witness to his life. Neither is autobiographical. The *Confession*, the longer of the two, is a defence of his mission in answer to detractors. That mission, by his own testimony, was to bring to the faith the pagan Irish living 'at the ends of the earth' (*in ultimis terrae*), 'as far as where there is no one beyond' (*usque ubi nemo ultra est*). In putting the case Patrick identifies himself as the son of a deacon and the grandson of a priest. He elaborates only to mention his capture at the age of 16 during a raid on his father's estate, his enslavement for six years in Ireland, his escape from the country, and his eventual decision to return. Patrick tells of a dream in which people living beside *Silva Vocluti*, near the 'western sea' (*mare* *occidentale*—literally the 'sea of the setting [of the sun]', i.e. the Atlantic), besought him to 'come and walk once more' among them. He answered the call, returned to Ireland, and seems never to have left. His ambit, apparently, was Ireland's northern half. Irish Christian communities already existed (see PALLADIUS), but Patrick's mission was to the unconverted.

In the *Confession* Patrick sets out his creed and claims his episcopate to be divinely inspired. Those he addresses are probably British clergy, seemingly suspicious of his evangelical role and/or of the scope of his jurisdiction. The second Patrician text is a letter of excommunication to the soldiers of one Coroticus, a British chief (presumably resident in Britain, but conceivably in Ireland) who had murdered some of his converts and enslaved others. Patrick uses the weight of his authority to denounce.

Patrick declares himself to be 'untaught' (*indoctus*) and lacking in fluency, and scholarship has traditionally acquiesced. But this orthodoxy is challenged by Howlett, who argues that Patrick has so constructed the *Confession* (using, among other devices, chiasmus and division by extreme and mean ratio) as simultaneously to damn his detractors with faint praise, display the scope of his Latinity, and ensure the accurate transmission of his text. An analogous case is made in respect of the *Letter*, a composition of exactly 1,300 words. Wide implications also attend the biblical, patristic, and magisterial apparatus published by Conneely.

Among the saints' cults of medieval Ireland that of Patrick is paramount. The oldest relevant document, perhaps of the early 7th century, is 'Audite omnes amantes', a hymn in Patrick's praise. A letter of the 630s refers to him as 'our father' (*papa noster*). Three texts in the Book of *Armagh are more explicitly devoted to his cult: the *Book of the Angel*, *c*.680, is the oldest witness to a claim on the part of *Armagh to be the see of Patrick and Ireland's primatial church; a life by Muirchú and a 'memoir' by Tírechán (both of whom used written sources) belong to the later 7th century and form the oldest extant horizon of the Patrician legend. The 9th-century *Bethu Pátraic* or Tripartite Life (the first in the vernacular) built upon its predecessors and represents the apogee of Patrician hagiography. Armagh had by now monopolized the cult of Patrick in liaison with the *Uí Néill kings of the north; in 1111 the primacy of Armagh was papally endorsed. (See PRIMATIAL CONTROVERSY.)

The abbots of Armagh, the *comarbai Pátraic*, exhibited the insignia of the saint: Patrick's bell, crozier, and 'canon'. The latter is the Book of *Armagh, written in 807 and enshrined in 937 (although the shrine has since been lost). The archaeology of the bell is uncertain and a date earlier than the 10th century could hardly be defended. The crozier is first mentioned in 789 and was destroyed in 1538.

The cult of Patrick entered a new phase under *Anglo-Norman patronage in the 12th century. At Downpatrick in 1185 John de *Courcy engineered the discovery and translation of what were held to be Patrick's remains (which Armagh never claimed to possess), together with those of *Colum Cille and *Brigid. The existence of 'St Patrick's Purgatory' at *Lough Derg, Co. Donegal, is attested for the first time in the same century and rapidly became a destination for continental as well as Irish pilgrims. The vernacular tradition so completely absorbed the Patrician legend as to ensure its survival beyond the *Reformation. Growing nationalist sensibilities thereafter found a focus in Patrick as figurehead of an Irish identity. The 20th century has seen the entrenchment of a popular and largely unhistorical view of Patrick as well as scholarly appraisals of great refinement. In parallel with consensus (or indifference) in today's Republic, the relative importance of Patrick to its two communities continues to exercise minds in the divided north.

Bieler, L., *Libri epistolarum Sancti Patricii episcopi* (1952)

Conneely, D., *St Patrick's Letters: A Study of their Theological Dimension* (1993)

Howlett, D. R., *Liber epistolarum Sancti Patricii episcopi: The Book of Letters of Saint Patrick the Bishop* (1994)

CB

patriot and patriotism. Patriotism, in an Irish context, generally refers to the new awareness of Irishness, and commitment to the defence of Irish interests, that emerged among Protestants during the 18th century. Some sense of Irish identity had existed among settlers or their descendants since the Middle Ages (see NATIONAL IDENTITIES IN EARLY AND MEDIEVAL IRELAND). Ireland's constitutional status as a separate kingdom had been defended by both *Old English and New English opponents of *Wentworth 1640–1, and was reaffirmed by the *convention of 1660. The *revolution of 1688, however, enhanced the status of the Irish *parliament and encouraged novel constitutional aspirations, while Protestant self-confidence grew with the final defeat of Catholic political power in the *Williamite War. The revolution also made Ireland's long-standing political subordination to England less tolerable because it was no longer mediated through the personal rule of a shared monarch. In particular, Irish Protestants resented the restrictions on Irish trade imposed by the *Cattle Acts, the *Woollen Act, and other measures, the subordinate status of the Irish parliament under *Poynings's Law and the *Declaratory Act, and the large numbers of Englishmen being appointed to desirable positions in the Irish civil, military, and ecclesiastical establishments.

In response to these grievances patriots argued that Ireland, though a possession of the British crown, was a separate kingdom, to be governed solely according to its own laws and institutions. Such ideas were first systematically outlined by *Molyneux, with later contributions by *Swift, *Lucas, and others. Popular patriot sentiment was evident in the *Wood's Halfpence affair (1722–5) and in the *money bill dispute (1753–6). By the 1770s a patriot grouping had emerged in the Irish parliament, its members including *Flood and *Grattan in the Commons and *Charlemont in the Lords. Between 1779 and 1782 the *American Revolution, the *Volunteer movement, and the *free trade agitation provided the opportunity to mobilize public opinion, achieving commercial freedom and apparently extensive constitutional concessions (see LEGISLATIVE INDEPENDENCE).

The patriot identity that thus emerged was complex and in some ways contradictory. Early patriot argument relied heavily on the claim that Irish Protestants, the descendants of Tudor and Stuart settlers, retained the inherited constitutional rights of Englishmen. Even as patriotism became more assertively Irish, moreover, the 'nation' to which it appealed remained a distinctively Protestant one. Some individual patriots, like Grattan, favoured *Catholic relief, but others, like Flood, were strongly opposed. It is this sectional nature of patriot identity that is highlighted in the frequent use of the term *'colonial nationalism'. Leerssen, in an alternative formulation, emphasizes the specific 18th-century meaning of patriotism, as an attachment to a particular political community—not necessarily a nation—and its institutions. Yet patriot argument, as early as Molyneux's **Case of Ireland*, also based its constitutional claims on historical rights supposedly inherited from the Gaelic Ireland of the Middle Ages. By the end of the 18th century, moreover, a growing enthusiasm for Gaelic literature and antiquities, seen for example in the establishment of the *Royal Irish Academy with the Volunteer earl of Charlemont as its first president, had given patriotism a cultural and historical dimension that brought it closer to modern *nationalism.

Although Protestant opposition to the Act of *Union testified to the continued strength of patriot sentiment, the passage of the act reflected the extent to which the robust assertiveness of the 'Protestant nation' had been undermined by the crisis culminating in the *insurrection of 1798. The survival into the 19th century of a version of the patriot tradition can nevertheless be seen in the *Young Ireland movement of the 1840s and in the initial support of some Protestants for the *home rule movement of the 1870s, with the career of Charles Stewart *Parnell as a last, if atypical, flourish.

Leerssen, J. T., 'Anglo-Irish Patriotism and its European Context', *Eighteenth-Century Ireland*, 3 (1988)
Vance, Norman, 'Celts, Carthaginians and Constitutions: Anglo-Irish Literary Relations 1780–1820', *Irish Historical Studies*, 22 (1981)

'patriot parliament' (7 May–18 July 1689), summoned by *James II after his arrival in Ireland. Thanks to *Tyrconnell's preliminary work in remodelling borough charters, all but 6 of the 230 MPs returned were Catholic, over two-thirds of them *Old English. Five Protestant lay lords and four Protestant bishops also sat. James assented reluctantly to bills outlawing Protestant supporters of William III, restoring landed estates to the families that had held them in 1641, and denying the right of the English parliament to legislate for Ireland. He also approved acts proclaiming liberty of conscience and requiring Catholics, and probably Presbyterians, to pay *tithes only to their own clergy. However he refused to agree to the repeal of *Poynings's Law or to any further transfer of property or privilege from the Church of Ireland to the Catholic church. Williamites denied the legitimacy of the parliament, and an act of 1695 annulled its proceedings, but the assertion of legislative independence attracted 19th-century nationalist writers, the term 'patriot parliament' being coined by Gavan *Duffy in his 1893 edition of articles published by Thomas *Davis in 1843.

pattern, a local festival celebrated at a holy well or other significant venue on the feast day of the saint (hence 'pattern', from Ir. *patrún*, meaning patron) to whom the site was dedicated. By the 18th century patterns were a major venue for popular sociability, while the larger gatherings, like that at *Glendalough, were also important commercial occasions. Participants typically combined prayers and ritual observances at the well or other site with dancing and other forms of celebration. The resulting combination of religious observance and festive gathering has been seen both as the product of a partial secularization of Christian parochial festivals and as evidence of pagan origins concealed beneath a superficial Christian veneer. By the early 19th century patterns had come under attack from the Catholic clergy, previously tolerant or actively supportive but now more concerned both to purge popular religion of unorthodox elements and to impose a tighter moral discipline. More effective policing, *Famine disruption, and the social changes associated with the development of a more literate and affluent rural society further contributed to their decline. By the 1870s most patterns had fallen into disuse, although a few survived, in reformed guise, as officially approved parochial festivals.

pawnbroking was first regulated in Ireland by an act of 1786, which required pawnbrokers to take out an annual licence at a cost of £100, issued subject to the applicant providing proof of good character. Subsequent legislation required pawnbrokers to execute a bond of £1,000 and to provide three independent sureties, approved by the police, of £300 each. Regulations also limited the maximum value of any article pledged and the rate of interest charged. Evidence collected by the *Poor Inquiry shows that by the 1830s pawnshops were conducting business in most Irish towns. Personal clothing and bedclothes were the items most commonly pledged, and the shops were regarded as offering credit to the poor on better terms than other sources at the time. MED

Peace Preservation Force, established by *Peel in 1814 to counter widespread rural unrest. These first 'peelers' were appointed by the government and, under the command of a stipendiary magistrate (forerunner of the later *resident magistrate or RM), they could be dispatched to any district proclaimed as disturbed. The local ratepayers had to pay for the force whether they had requested its presence or not. This made the peelers extremely unpopular with landlords. They were deployed in sixteen counties up to 1822, but did not have a major impact on agrarian crime. When a national constabulary was created in 1822 (see POLICE), many peelers joined the new force. But the Peace Preservation Force was revived in 1831 during the *Tithe War and dispatched to the ten most disturbed counties. In 1836 it was amalgamated with the reorganized Irish Constabulary. ELM

peace process (1993–), the agreed label, partly designed to mask very differing interpretations of what is involved, for the political arrangements that brought an apparent end to the *Northern Ireland conflict. On 24 April 1993 negotiations between *Social Democratic and Labour Party leader John Hume and Gerry Adams of *Sinn Féin, intended to draw the republican movement into the political process, culminated in a joint statement of nationalist principle. On 15 December the Downing Street Declaration, issued by the British and Irish prime ministers John Major and Albert Reynolds, outlined a way forward based on three proposed strands. Once the *IRA had responded by declaring a ceasefire in August 1994 (quickly followed by *Ulster Defence Association and *Ulster Volunteer Force ceasefires), the way was clear for further progress, and in February 1995 the two sovereign governments published a detailed scheme, *Frameworks for the Future*. As in 1973 the proposal was for power-sharing between major political parties representing the two traditions within Northern Ireland (Strand One), accompanied by an 'Irish dimension' of cross-border collaboration, sufficient to give full recognition to the sense of Irish identity felt by most Northern Catholics while retaining the United Kingdom membership valued by Ulster Protestants (Strand Two). Strand One was of more substance than Strand Two, and there was some truth in the wry nationalist characterization of the scheme as '*Sunningdale for slow learners'. Where the new proposals differed from those of the 1970s was in the addition of Strand Three, which built on the 1985 *Anglo-Irish agreement to put the Dublin–London axis firmly in charge of the process. A further difference was in the intention of ending violence by involving Sinn Féin in the political process, rather than by using that process to isolate them.

Various developments made this possible. Twenty years of European collaboration had created a new context for Anglo-Irish relations; militant nationalist rhetoric had less resonance than previously in the Irish Republic; the republican movement was in the hands of veterans from 1969 who wished to escape from the stalemate of 'the long war'. The new American president, Bill Clinton, helped to bring Sinn Féin into the political process. There was also the new global context created by the end of the Cold War and the apparently successful peace initiatives in South Africa and in Israel.

The *Ulster Unionist Party, led after 1995 by David Trimble was, as ever, divided in its response to reformist pressures, not least because it feared a challenge from the uncompromising *Democratic Unionist Party. The Unionists pressed for 'decommissioning' of IRA weapons before they would begin talks with Sinn Féin. Meanwhile the Conservative government had become dependent on Unionist MPs at Westminster to keep them in office. A tacit agreement emerged among constitutional politicians that further progress could not be made prior to a UK general election. The

Republicans were less patient, and on 9 February 1996 the IRA ceasefire ended with a devastating bomb at Canary Wharf in London. Further incidents followed, although violence still remained considerably below its pre-ceasefire level, and did not return in any significant way to Northern Ireland itself.

The election of a Labour government with a strong parliamentary majority changed the context once again, so that when a new IRA ceasefire began on 20 July 1997 the Ulster Unionists reluctantly took the risk of going into all-party talks with Sinn Féin prior to any 'decommissioning' of weapons. The 'Good Friday (or Belfast) Agreement' of 10 April 1998 accepted the three-strand approach. It confirmed that Northern Ireland would remain within the United Kingdom unless and until a majority of its voters determined otherwise; the Irish government agreed to revise the territorial claim in clause 2 of the *constitution of 1937 to reflect this new understanding. Important powers would be devolved to the Northern Ireland Assembly and a power-sharing executive of ministers, led by a 'first minister'. The fact that the Labour government was at the same time implementing devolution schemes in Scotland and Wales provided a context of 'normality' in which this part of the scheme could be set. Strand Two of the Agreement provided for the establishment of a North-South ministerial council in Ireland, which nationalists could read as a first step towards ending *partition, and unionists could characterize as merely practical co-operation with a neighbouring state. Strand Three provided for a British–Irish Council, or 'Council of the Isles', drawing in the two sovereign governments and the three devolved ones.

Although there was fierce debate over Strands Two and Three, the most important practical outcome was the evolution of measures which might transform Northern Ireland itself into a polity which would be *de facto* acceptable to Catholics as well as Protestants. By summer 2001, the Unionist Party had survived the spectre of 'Republicans in government', the devastating bomb in Omagh planted by a Republican splinter group on 15 August 1998, the release of virtually all IRA (and UDA and UVF) prisoners, repeated challenges to Trimble's leadership from within the Unionist Party, and the continued refusal of the IRA to 'decommission' its weapons. The future character of the police service in Northern Ireland was a substantive issue which remained unresolved (see ROYAL ULSTER CONSTABULARY), and support for anti-Agreement Unionists within the party showed no sign of abating. The rerouting of *Orange Order parades away from nationalist areas and the lack of progress on IRA decommissioning were also recurring threats to stability. In October 2002 the discovery of an alleged IRA spy ring within Stormont led to the collapse of the power-sharing executive. Over the next five years the DUP and Sinn Féin steadily gained electoral ground. New elections in March 2007 confirmed that they had decisively overtaken the UUP and SDLP but seemed to open the way to a new executive in which they would predominate. How far this outcome will bring an end to the earlier pattern of walkouts, suspension of devolution, and paramilitary brinkmanship remains to be seen.

Darby, J., and MacGinty, R. (eds.), *The Management of Peace Processes* (2000)

ACH

Pearce, Edward Lovett (*c*.1699–1733), Ireland's earliest and most important Palladian *architect. Born in England of Irish descent, Pearce joined the army when he was 16 or 17 and travelled extensively through Europe, probably arriving in Dublin in 1726. He was a relative of one of the foremost English architects of the day, Sir John Vanbrugh, and it is probable that at some point Pearce came under his tutelage. Pearce's first known work in Ireland was his collaboration with Italian architect Alessandro Galilei in the design of *Castletown House, Co. Kildare. In 1727 he became a member of parliament for Ratoath, Co. Meath. The following year, despite his young age and relative lack of experience, he was commissioned, in preference to the surveyor-general, Thomas Burgh, to design the new *Parliament House for Dublin. By 1730, having built up a substantial private practice, he succeeded Burgh as surveyor-general. Amongst the domestic buildings attributed to Pearce are Drumcondra House, Co. Dublin (1727), Cashel Palace, Co. Tipperary (begun 1729), and Bellamont Forest, Co. Cavan (*c*.1730). He died suddenly in 1733, his practice passing to his assistant Richard *Castle. Despite the brevity of Pearce's career he was instrumental in the introduction of Palladian architecture to Ireland.

RM

Pearse, Patrick (1879–1916), educationalist, writer, and revolutionary. Although best known as leader of the *rising of 1916, Pearse's nationalism was initially more cultural than political. He became involved with the *Gaelic League as a teenager and edited their journal, *An *Claidheamh Soluis*, from 1903 to 1909. He also lectured in Irish at University College, Dublin. Influenced by continental practices in bilingual education he founded *St Enda's in 1908, a bilingual secondary school which fostered all things Irish.

Initially willing to accept *home rule as a step towards independence, he became convinced that Britain would never voluntarily grant Ireland autonomy when faced with unionist opposition and began to favour the use of force. He was involved in setting up the *Irish Volunteers and became their director of operations. He joined the *Irish Republican Brotherhood and was co-opted onto the supreme council and the secret military council. His graveside oration at *O'Donovan Rossa's funeral in 1915, ending with the much quoted line, 'Ireland unfree shall never be at peace', was influential in the build-up to the rising. He became commander-in-chief of the Volunteers during the rising and president of the Provisional Government. As such he signed the unconditional surrender, and was subsequently court-martialled and executed.

Pearse wrote extensively in Irish and English. In his writing he described bloodshed as a cleansing and sanctifying thing, and stated that a blood sacrifice was needed to awaken the Irish nation. In his eyes slavery was more horrible than bloodshed. This thinking, which can be seen as a response to the realization that a successful rising was unlikely, is largely responsible for the controversial reputation he has enjoyed in recent decades. JA

Peel, Robert (1788–1850), British politician. He spent the first three years of his parliamentary career as MP for the Irish rotten borough of Cashel, transferring to an English constituency when he became *chief secretary for Ireland. As chief secretary (1812–18) he initiated the early 19th-century transformation of law enforcement with the *Peace Preservation Force (1814), co-ordinated relief measures during the harvest failure and typhus epidemic of 1816–17, and emerged as the most formidable parliamentary opponent of *Catholic emancipation. A narrowly averted duel with Daniel *O'Connell in August 1815 laid the foundations of a lifelong mutual hostility. As home secretary (1822–7, 1828–30) Peel remained closely interested in Irish affairs, although the County Constabulary (see POLICE) created in 1822 was not his work but that of his successor as chief secretary, Henry Goulburn. By 1825 Peel accepted that emancipation could not be postponed indefinitely, and was ready to withdraw from office while it passed. His decision, in January 1829, to remain in government and give the measure his active support was crucial in securing the consent of *George IV.

As prime minister (1841–6) Peel combined firm action against the *repeal movement with a series of measures (a threefold increase in the *Maynooth Grant, the *Charitable Bequests Act, and the *Queen's Colleges) intended to detach moderate Catholic support from the agitation. His handling of the first year of the *Great Famine (1845–6) is often favourably compared to the more doctrinaire approach of his *Whig successors, although the crisis Peel had to cope with was significantly less formidable. Hunger in Ireland provided the occasion for Peel to abandon his earlier defence of the corn laws, which protected domestic agriculture against imported grain. Tory resentment at this apostasy, and at the Maynooth Grant, led to the defeat of Peel's government, on an Irish coercion bill, in June 1846.

In British history Peel is seen as the creator of modern conservatism, bringing his party to terms with a changing social and political order. His Irish policies anticipate in some respects the *'constructive unionism' of a century later. Yet the balance between principle and pragmatism remains difficult to set. As chief secretary Peel bitterly criticized the venality of Irish parliamentarians and the crass triumphalism of the Protestant party, while remaining an efficient manipulator and, where necessary, defender of the system he affected to despise. In the 1840s his declarations on the necessity of conciliating moderate Catholics alternated with private comments suggesting that he was in practice content to create controversy and division in Catholic ranks.

Kerr, D. A., *Peel, Priests and Politics* (1982)

Peep of Day Boys, first noted by Arthur *Young (*c.*1779) in the context of *agrarian protest, but best known as the Protestant party in the sectarian conflict that developed in Co. Armagh from *c.*1784. This resurgence of religious hostilities has been attributed to the entry of Catholics into *linen weaving at a time when the livelihood of Armagh's farmer-weavers was threatened by land hunger and competition from the mechanized *cotton industry. But the determination of plebeian Protestants to reassert their traditional supremacy can also be seen as a response to the repeal of some *penal laws and failure to enforce others. Thus raids on Catholic houses, the main Peep of Day tactic of the period 1784–7, were accompanied both by the sabotage of linen weaving equipment and by the seizure of firearms, possession of which was until 1793 theoretically confined to Protestants. From 1788 Catholic resistance to such attacks, through the *Defenders, produced mounting confrontation. Although the *Orange Order repudiated the lawlessness of the Peep of Day Boys, it in practice superseded them after 1795.

Pelagianism is *the* Latin heresy. Pelagius is usually said to have come from Roman Britain, but a contemporary, Jerome, held that he was of the Irish people (*Scotticae gentis*) from the vicinity of the

Britons; so the question of where he came from must remain open. Augustine perceived him as denying Original Sin and holding that man saved himself. Pelagius's exact teaching is unclear, but Augustine's reaction has reverberated down to this day. Hence every reference to Pelagius has been seized upon as evidence of the extent of his influence. In Ireland the name occurs in two contexts: first, in that Pelagius's commentary on Paul's epistles was used by name in Irish writings; and second, a letter from Pope-elect John IV in 640 referring to a revival of Pelagianism in Ireland. However, neither constitutes evidence for a survival of support for Pelagius. The survival of his commentary in insular circles is probably accidental; and it was used because it was a good commentary rather than controversially. In John IV's letter, the issue is the date of Easter (see PASCHAL CONTROVERSY) and Pelagianism is used as a rebuke—no doubt remembering that Pelagius came from these islands. TO'L

penal laws or (the more common contemporary term) popery laws. For most of the 17th century the continuing political influence of Irish Catholics, and the desire of successive monarchs to retain a free hand, had been sufficient to block attempts to pass anti-Catholic legislation similar to that in operation in England. Periodic repression of Catholic worship, and the increasing exclusion of Catholics from political and administrative office, had been implemented on an ad hoc basis (or, in the case of the Cromwellian regime, by the de facto application in Ireland of English law). The enactment from the 1690s of a series of discriminatory measures directed against Catholic clergy and laity reflected the hardening of Irish Protestant attitudes following their experiences under James II, the enhanced importance of the Irish parliament as a forum for their demands, and the new primacy, following the *revolution of 1688, of statute over prerogative.

The first Irish penal laws were two statutes in 1695, both part of the bargain that ended the *sole right controversy, and both reflecting Protestant fears that lenient treatment of the defeated Jacobites had left Protestants dangerously open to renewed attack. One forbade Catholics not covered by the treaty of *Limerick to keep weapons. The second, concerned mainly to sever links between Irish Catholics and their continental allies, forbade Catholics to go overseas for purposes of education, but also banned Catholics from teaching or running schools within Ireland. The Bishops' Banishment Act (1697) required all regular clergy, and all bishops, vicars-general, and others exercising ecclesiastical jurisdiction, to leave the kingdom by 1 May 1698. Other clergy were permitted to remain, but an act of 1704 required them to register with the authorities, limited their number to one per parish, and forbade the entry of further priests into the kingdom. The Act to Prevent the Further Growth of Popery (1704), the most important single penal statute, prohibited Catholics from buying land, inheriting land from Protestants, or taking leases for a period of longer than 31 years. (Protestant heiresses marrying Catholics had already been disinherited under an act of 1699.) The act also required that the estates of a deceased Catholic landowner should be divided equally among the male heirs. An act of 1709 strengthened these provisions, particularly by the introduction of the *discoverer. Other legislation prohibited Catholics from practising law, from holding office in central or local government, from membership of *grand juries and municipal corporations, and from service in the army or navy. Catholics were excluded from parliament (under an English act) from 1691, but did not completely lose the right to vote until 1728.

The penal laws were traditionally seen as victimizing the entire Catholic population. More recent work emphasizes the selective nature of their operation. The Catholic aristocracy and gentry, who in 1703 still owned 14 per cent of the profitable land of Ireland, were both the main targets of the legislation and its main victims. Over the next few decades most of these surviving Catholic landowners, deprived of the opportunity to extend their estates by marriage or purchase, excluded from local and national politics, and threatened with the progressive fragmentation of their properties, conformed to the Church of Ireland. By contrast the laws did not seriously affect the wealth of the Catholic mercantile and manufacturing classes. Catholic tenants suffered some disadvantage, but the laws did not prevent the emergence during the 18th century of a Catholic leasehold interest among large farmers and *middlemen, or the growth of a Catholic tenant farmer class. Strictly enforced, the banishment of Catholic bishops, combined with the ban on ordained priests entering the kingdom, should have caused the Irish clergy to die out in a generation. In practice, despite the efforts of individuals like John Richardson, there was no sustained attempt either to enforce the laws or to promote the conversion of the Catholic masses to Protestantism. By the 1720s priests and bishops operated freely, if discreetly, in most areas.

Agitation for the repeal of the penal laws commenced with the foundation of the *Catholic Committee in 1760. *Catholic Relief Acts were passed in 1778, 1782, and 1792–3, with the remaining formal disabilities being repealed ('Catholic emancipation') in 1829.

Power, T. P., and Whelan, Kevin (eds.), *Endurance and Emergence: Catholics in Ireland in the Eighteenth Century* (1990)

penitentials, lists of sins and the fixed penances needed for their forgiveness, possibly appearing first in Wales, but developing their characteristic form in Ireland in the 6th to 8th centuries. They spread to the Anglo-Saxons and the Franks, and eventually throughout Latin Christendom. At a time when the Latin church was struggling to find a workable theology of the remission of sins, these lists offered a new approach based on two sources. From Irish *law came the notion that an offence carried with it a price, varying with the status of the parties, to be paid by the offender to the one injured. From monastic spirituality came the idea of penitence as an ongoing therapy. The penitentials looked on a sin as a crime with a debt attached to it, and in paying this debt the offender is healed. So penances (e.g. fasting for a fixed time) were graded by the deed, and the status of offender. Sins, as crimes against God, became private matters which could be put behind one through a process repeated many times in a lifetime. Behind these provisions lay a new understanding of sin as *culpa* (to be overcome by inner conviction of sorrow—the Irish developed the notion of 'the penance of tears' that anticipates the notion of 'contrition') and *poena* (the debt to justice and the requisite penitential therapy). The penitentials were a crucial step in the development of sacramental penance, and, since longer penances could be commuted to less demanding ones, the later practice of indulgences developed. They were the most significant Irish contribution to the western church.

O'Loughlin, T., *Celtic Theology: Humanity, World and God in Early Irish Writings* (2000)

TO'L

Penn, William (1644–1718), Quaker and founder of the colony of Pennsylvania. His father, Admiral Sir William Penn (1621–70), originally granted part of the *Clancarty estate in Co. Cork by the *Cromwellian regime, supported the *Restoration and was compensated by an alternative grant in the same county. William Penn joined the *Society of Friends while living on his father's Irish estate, and later found places for Irish Friends in the development of Pennsylvania.

People's Democracy (PD), a grouping formed at *Queen's University, Belfast, in response to the *Royal Ulster Constabulary's suppression of a demonstration in Derry on 5 October 1968. In its early days a ginger group on the flank of the *civil rights movement, it added to the American influences on that body something of the flavour of the international student movement. Its 'long march' of January 1969, from Belfast to Derry, involved only a few dozen marchers but provoked an ambush by Protestant counter-demonstrators at Burntollet Bridge in Co. Londonderry which sharply escalated the developing *Northern Ireland conflict. PD won 4 per cent of the vote in the Northern Ireland general election of 1969. Initially aiming for a radical break with 'sectarian politics', it soon diverted into a socialist republicanism which restricted its appeal to radicals in the Catholic community. It resurfaced spasmodically as an independent republican ginger group in local elections and in pamphleteering until the early 1980s.

ACH

Perrot, Sir John (*c.*1527–1592). Perrot began his Irish career with a ruthless suppression of the first *Desmond rebellion as *provincial president of Munster (1571–3). He returned as lord deputy (1584–8), with orders to hold a parliament to confiscate the Desmond lands and to agree a *composition with the *Palesmen. His team's failure to get *Poynings's Law suspended meant most intended legislation had to be abandoned.

Perrot wanted to introduce English law and land tenure into Ulster. Shiring, composition, and *surrender and regrant were accomplished in theory but not in practice. Even his partition of Cavan was maintained only by keeping the *tánaiste* imprisoned in Dublin Castle. When war broke out with Spain in 1585, Perrot was forced to compromise with Sorley *MacDonnell, whom he had earlier tried to evict.

Perrot's activism brought many enemies. He disagreed with Archbishop *Loftus over plans for Dublin university, with Black Tom Butler (10th earl of *Ormond) over the extension of the composition to Kilkenny, with *Bingham over jurisdiction in Connacht, and with Nicholas *Bagenal over Ulster policies.

In 1592 Perrot was convicted of treason on evidence trumped up by his successor *Fitzwilliam, but Queen Elizabeth refused to execute him and he was rehabilitated in the 1620s. HM

Petrie, George (1789–1866), antiquary. Born in Dublin, the son of a successful portrait painter, Petrie also trained as an artist. He developed an interest in antiquities from an early age, and from 1808 began to make notes and sketches of ancient earthworks and ecclesiastical buildings. Success as a landscape artist led, from 1820, to commissions to illustrate various printed guides and tours of Ireland. By 1830 he had produced a number of noted paintings of Irish subjects, and in that year was appointed to the council of the *Royal Irish Academy (RIA). In the following years he developed the academy's library and museum, as well as publishing a number of antiquarian articles. From 1835 to 1846 Petrie worked for the *Ordnance Survey and here met Eugene *O'Curry and John *O'Donovan. In 1837 he published an *Essay on the Antiquities of Tara*, and in 1843 an *Essay on the Origin and Uses of the Round Towers of Ireland*. Both were awarded gold medals by the RIA. The latter work became *The Ecclesiastical Architecture of Ireland* (1845). He received an honorary doctorate from the University of Dublin in 1847, and a civil list pension in 1849. A posthumously published volume of Irish inscriptions completed his works.

NG

Petty, William (1623–87), political economist, born at Romsey, Hampshire, the son of a clothier. A devotee of Francis Bacon's writings on 'useful knowledge', he learned navigation at sea, attended the Jesuit College in Caen, studied medicine in the Netherlands, and in 1645 was tutored by Hobbes in Paris (where he met leading French scientists gathered around Mersenne). In England (1646) he established links with the German refugee Samuel Hartlib, who advocated the application of science to social and economic needs. Petty completed his medical studies at Oxford (1649–50), where he was a member of the scientific group around John Wilkins, the warden of Wadham College. In addition to Petty the group included figures such as Seth Ward, Thomas Willis, and Robert Hooke, and was a forerunner of the Royal Society. Petty was appointed professor of anatomy at Oxford, but left for Ireland in 1652 as physician-general to Cromwell's armies.

In Ireland Petty completed the *Down Survey (1654–9) and thereafter abandoned medicine in favour of cartography, surveying, demography, and economics. He viewed Ireland as a testing ground for Baconian principles of improvement. His practical and theoretical works were rewarded by Cromwell with grants of land, chiefly in Kerry; Charles II continued to favour him and awarded a knighthood (1662). In 1659 Petty returned to London and, like *Boyle whom he knew in Ireland, was one of the first members of the Royal Society (founded 1660). Thereafter he divided his time between London and Ireland, where he resided 1666–73, 1676–85.

Petty produced remarkable socio-economic studies based on statistical and scientific methods. Among his best-known works concerning Ireland are the *Treatise of Taxes and Contributions* (1662), which discusses the economies of England and Ireland, and makes suggestions as to their improvement; and *The Political Anatomy of Ireland* (written 1672, pub. 1691), which describes the land, people, politics, and natural resources. His *Hiberniae delineatio* (1685), which had its origins in the Down Survey, was the first general atlas of Ireland. Between 1682 and 1687 he wrote ten essays on the populations of various cities, including Dublin (1682). Petty also embarked on practical projects in Ireland. He invested in ironworks in Kerry, developed fishing grounds off the coast, and continued trials with double-hulled ships in Dublin bay. Petty was first president of the *Dublin Philosophical Society, whose utilitarian character owed much to his influence. He is significant both for his analysis of aspects of Irish life, and more generally for his pioneering work in political economy.

Strauss, E., *Sir William Petty: Portrait of a Genius* (1954)

DJS

Phaire, Robert (*c.*1619–1682), the only Irish born among the 'regicides' responsible for the execution of Charles I. A lieutenant-colonel in Munster in 1648, Phaire refused to switch sides with *Inchiquin and was allowed to join the parliamentary army in a negotiated exchange. Charles I's execution warrant was addressed to him and two others. Returning as a regimental commander, he captured Youghal, fought at Macroom, and held the governorship of Cork (1651–4). He retired in 1655, dissatisfied with the Cromwellian regime. After dabbling in Quakerism (see SOCIETY OF FRIENDS), Phaire became a follower of Ludovic Muggleton, having met the self-appointed prophet while a prisoner in the Tower of London after the *Restoration. He subsequently escaped punishment for involvement in *Blood's plot. HM

philanthropy, see CHARITY.

Phoenix Park murders (6 May 1882), the assassination with surgical knives of the newly appointed Irish *chief secretary, Lord Frederick Cavendish, and the under-secretary, T. H. Burke, carried out by the *Invincibles. Horrifying British opinion, the murders forced *Gladstone to maintain coercion in Ireland at a time when, following the *Kilmainham treaty, it was about to be dropped, and impelled a depressed *Parnell momentarily to consider resigning from parliament.

JL

photography was pioneered in Ireland by a Belfast engraver, Francis Beatty, who announced in the **Northern Whig* on 6 August 1840 that he had made a 'photogenic drawing', or 'calotype', of Belfast's Long Bridge. This process, published in England in late 1839 and later patented as the 'Talbotype', used a paper negative to produce a positive image on paper. A few months earlier Louis Daguerre in Paris had unveiled the daguerrotype process, which fixed a positive image onto a polished metal plate. The first commercial studio in Ireland opened in Dublin in October 1841; a year later, Beatty's daguerrotypes became the first professionally shot photographs produced in Belfast.

Although the patents which protected these techniques did not apply in Ireland (allowing Irish itinerant photographers to practise illicitly in England), a number of Dublin daguerrotype studios were set up under licence by Richard Beard, a London coal merchant who had bought the concession for England and Wales and engaged Beatty as his European operative. The most long-lived of these was Professor Leon Gluckman's 'Daguerrotype Portrait Institution' in Lower Sackville Street, Dublin, thought to have been responsible for the series of portraits, of doubtful veracity, of imprisoned *Young Irelanders.

The invention in 1851 of the faster, simpler, and unpatented wet collodion or wet plate process by Frederick Scott Archer effectively made both the daguerrotype and Talbotype obsolete, and opened up photography to increasing numbers of professional and amateur photographers. By the end of the decade 60 new studios had opened in Dublin, 24 of which were in Grafton Street alone. Belfast lagged behind but still managed to more than double its complement during the same period from 6 to 12. This commercial expansion was largely due to the growing popularity of portrait photography, especially after the availability from 1861 of the carte-de-visite: small photographs the size and shape of visiting cards, mounted on stiff card and varnished, used both for personal portrait sittings and as collectible sets of images of local and national personalities. Commercial landscape photography also had its beginnings in these decades, with firms offering prints of scenery, mansions, and ruins, often as fashionable stereoscopic views, small twin images taken with a double-lensed camera and viewed through a stereoscope to give an impression of depth. One of the key producers and importers of these images was John Fortune Lawrence; his trade was taken over by his brother William, who established what was to become Dublin's most successful photographic firm in his mother's Sackville Street toyshop in 1865.

The wet collodion process brought recreational photography to the gentry and aristocracy, with the novelty of the pursuit allowing women such as Mary, countess of Rosse, of Birr Castle, the first woman member of the Dublin Photographic Society (established 1854), and Lady Augusta Crofton of Clonbrock House to make important aesthetic and technical contributions. The invention of a successful dry plate process by Richard Leach Maddox in 1878 did away with the need to transport darkroom and chemicals to the scene of action and paved the way for the true popularization of the medium. In America George Eastman began working on the production of film negatives, introducing in 1885 a roll holder which could be fitted on standard plate cameras and in 1888 (under the slogan 'you press the button we do the rest') the first 'Kodak' box camera. Capable of taking 100 circular pictures which were returned to the makers for processing, this sold in its thousands in Ireland for £5 each. In 1892 John Joly, professor of biology at Trinity College and a member of the Photographic Society of Ireland, produced the world's first practical colour photograph.

The new transportability of dry plate equipment paved the way for the photographing of Ireland by image makers such as Robert French, chief photographer to William Lawrence, who travelled all over the country photographing its towns and villages for publication as postcards and printed views, and was responsible for most of the 40,000 views now preserved as the Lawrence collection in the *National Library of Ireland. In Ulster near contemporaries were R. J. Welch (1859–1936) and his equally well-known assistant W. A. Green (1870–1958), followed somewhat later by A. R. Hogg (1869–1939).

The bulk of material in the major historic Irish photographic collections dates from *c.*1880 onwards. Whilst genre images dominate, the introduction of hand-held cameras during the 1890s encouraged documentary photography and the production of visual narratives of political events such as the labour disputes of 1907 and 1913, the *home rule crisis, the *Anglo-Irish War, and the *Irish Civil War. Populated images of commerce and industry become more common in the 20th century, with many large Irish firms, such as *Harland & Wolff, commissioning official photographers. At the same time, photography became more widely used in advertising and promotion and, of particular importance, in journalism. VP

Physico-Historical Society, founded in 1744 and active until the mid-1750s. Like the *Dublin Philosophical Society and *(Royal) Dublin Society, it advocated 'improvement'; its aim was to survey every Irish county, thereby encouraging economic growth. Its 20 founder members included nobles, fellows of *Trinity College, members of the Dublin Society, clerics, and 'gentlemen'; membership soon rose to 226. The society never completed its countrywide survey, but did publish accounts of individual counties. The chief author was Charles Smith (*c.*1715–1762), who prepared volumes on Down (1744), Waterford (1746), Cork (1750), and Kerry (1756); John Rutty published two volumes on Dublin (1772), by which time the society no longer met. DJS

pigs have been kept as livestock in Ireland since the *neolithic period. Archaeological evidence and early medieval texts both suggest that they were a relatively cheap source of meat, as they could be fed largely on household refuse and natural food supplies such as autumn leaf mast. After the 16th century, however, the *potato rapidly became their basic fodder. The close relationship between the two was evident during the *Famine, when the failure of the potato also led to a dramatic fall in pig numbers, from 1,412,813 in 1841 to 565,629 in 1848. Numbers recovered rapidly after the Famine, rising to 1,084,857 by 1851.

Pigs flourish in the same temperature conditions as humans, and the lack of purpose-built outbuildings on many small farms led to the practice of keeping pigs in the farm kitchen, especially when sows were farrowing. Carcasses were also commonly cured on the farm, for home use. The best-known type of pig in 19th-century Ireland was the Irish Greyhound Pig, which was described as long-legged, bony, and coarse-haired, but selective breeding with imported pigs such as the Berkshire led to the development of one of the most successful of all Irish livestock breeds, the Large White Ulster. The herd book for the breed was established in 1908, and during the early decades of the 20th century Ulster pigs were a major source of pork and bacon for industrial centres in England. Because Large Whites were bred for fat their bodies bruised easily, so that many farmers, especially in the north of Ireland, preferred to have pigs slaughtered on the farm to prevent the damage which might arise in moving live animals to market. Fat pigs were wet cured, the hams being steeped in brine. However, the growing consumer preference for lean meat led to the adoption of the dry Wiltshire method of curing and the eventual disappearance of the Large White Ulster breed, which became extinct during the 1960s.

Pig production remains an important element in Irish farming. In the early 1990s, more than 2,000,000 pigs were kept on farms, north and south.

Watson, M., 'Standardisation of Pig Production: The Case of the Large White Ulster', *Ulster Folklife*, 34 (1988)

JB

pilgrimage, a phenomenon found in many religions, in Ireland should be viewed primarily in Christian terms. The early monks (e.g. *Colum Cille, *Columbanus, or Gall) saw themselves on 'pilgrimage for Christ' as penitents or missionaries. By *c.*750 such wandering, unfitted to newer church structures, was being criticized on the Continent as out of harmony with Benedictinism. It was also attacked in Ireland by the **Céili Dé* as a distraction from genuine fervour. While journeying as a specific religious activity ceased, the memory lived on in liturgy (*Litany of the Pilgrim Saints*) and religious imagination (the voyage stories or *Immrama*).

The other notion of pilgrimage (trip, short stay at the holy place, and return) can be seen in references to journeys to Rome and Jerusalem, as well as to more local sites (trips to *holy wells, and the devotions/traditions attached, being the simplest form of pilgrimage). Of these, the two most famous invoke the *Patrick legend: *Croagh Patrick and *Lough Derg. Pilgrimages of more recent origin (e.g. *Knock) are connected with the cult of the Virgin Mary. TO'L

Pilltown, battle of (1461), a bloody clash near Carrick-on-Suir, Co. Tipperary, echoing the Yorkist–Lancastrian strife in England (see WARS OF THE ROSES), at which the forces of Sir John Butler of *Ormond were defeated by the 8th earl of *Desmond. Edmund MacRichard Butler of Polestown, who had lost 400 men at Pilltown, ransomed himself by giving Desmond the manuscript books of Pottlerath and Carrick from his library in part payment. HM

Pim, Jonathan (1806–85), proprietor, with his brother William Harvey Pim, of the Dublin firm of Pim Brothers, drapers and textile manufacturers. During the *Great Famine he was joint secretary, with Joseph Bewley, of the central relief committee of the *Society of Friends. He was Liberal MP for Dublin 1865–74, the first Irish Quaker to sit in parliament.

Pipard, family of. **Gilbert Pipard** served as sheriff of Gloucester and Hereford and guardian of Chester before travelling to Ireland with *John, son of *Henry II, in 1185 and receiving grants of Ardee in Louth and most of Monaghan. He went on crusade with Richard I and died at Brindisi in 1191. His wife Alice was a descendant of Duncan, king of Scots. By 1188 Gilbert had transferred his Irish lands to his brother **Peter**, who also received from John a grant of Fermanagh. Peter was *justiciar in 1194 when he was captured by John's opponent, Walter de *Lacy. He was in conflict with the bishop of Louth (Clogher) about the building of a castle at Donaghmoyne (Monaghan). Peter's lands came to his brother **Roger**, who married Alice, a sister of Walter and Hugh de *Lacy. He was succeeded in 1225 by his son **William** who died in 1227, leaving a daughter, Alice, who was placed in the wardship of Ralph fitz Nicholas. She married Ralph's son and their child, **Ralph Pipard**, inherited the Irish lands in the 1260s. In 1301 he exchanged these for property in England. Junior branches of the family remained important in Louth and Meath for the rest of the Middle Ages and beyond. BGCS

pipe rolls, *exchequer records recording the audited accounts of officials answerable for the collection and expenditure of royal revenue. The accounts show the amount which should have been collected, payments into the treasury, and local expenditure authorized by royal writ. Those accounting at the Irish exchequer included the *escheator, *sheriffs, collectors of customs, city and town officials, receivers of royal manors, and custodians of lands in the king's hands; the rolls also contain accounts relating to expenditure on military expeditions and royal castles. The English pipe rolls record the accounts of Irish treasurers audited at Westminster. PhC

pirates were common on the Irish coast from the time of St *Patrick. Irish seaborne raids against the late Roman empire, *Viking attacks, and Scots naval actions during the *Bruce wars were also often akin to piracy. Pirates usually captured the vessel, sold its merchandise, and ransomed the crew and passengers.

In the 15th century Spanish and Breton pirates regularly congregated at Lambay Island off Co. Dublin to menace the shipping of the *Pale. Periodically fleets were assembled to sweep the seas and levies put on customs to pay for protection. In the late 15th century Kinsale became a freebooting centre with the breakdown of central authority. Amongst the Irish the O'Driscolls, O'Flahertys, and O'Malleys were known for their piratical actions with Grace *O'Malley keeping twenty galleys.

During Elizabeth's war with Spain, Raleigh, Drake, Grenville, and other English privateers (officially licensed pirates) sold their prizes in southern Irish ports. When the war ended in 1604, many west country privateers decamped to Baltimore which Thomas Crooke leased from the O'Driscolls. There a large New English (see OLD ENGLISH AND NEW ENGLISH) settlement suddenly sprang up to service the 1,000-odd pirates attracted to the vicinity. Ireland had no specific legislation against piracy until the 1613–15 parliament, local *admiralty officials were corrupt, and the occasional English naval vessel proved a puny threat to the large, well-organized pirate fleets. The Dutch navy, sanctioned by King James, finally broke the pirate stranglehold in 1616. Ironically, in June 1631, 107 inhabitants of Baltimore were carried off into slavery by Algerian pirates led by a Dutch renegade, Jan Jansen.

In the 1640s a *Confederate Catholic navy was created using privateers from Dunkirk. The establishment of the royal navy in the second half of the 17th century eventually reduced piracy, although enemy privateers remained a regular hazard in wartime throughout the first half of the 18th century. HM

Pirrie, William James (1847–1924), Viscount Pirrie, *Belfast *shipbuilder and shipowner. In 1862 he was apprenticed to the shipbuilding firm of *Harland & Wolff. Twelve years later he was made a partner in the company, becoming chairman on Harland's death in 1895. Pirrie was concerned with improved vessel design, which included ways to facilitate port entry and to enhance passenger comfort; the latter process culminated in the building of luxury liners such as the *Olympic* and the **Titanic*. He excelled at salesmanship and developed links with international shipping lines, including the ill-fated International Mercantile Marine in 1902 and Lord Kylsant's Royal Mail group after 1918. Under his leadership Harland & Wolff became one of the largest shipbuilders in the world.

In March 1918 Pirrie was made comptroller-general of merchant shipbuilding, and he was rewarded for his work in increasing wartime ship production with a viscountcy in 1921. Pirrie's involvement in politics led to his becoming lord mayor of Belfast in 1896 and 1897. Although a *Unionist supporter at the time of the second *home rule bill, he had by 1905 become a Liberal home ruler, and in the following year was raised to the peerage with a barony. After 1918, however, Pirrie was once again a Unionist and became a senator at *Stormont. WJ/FG

place names. The vast majority of Irish place names are Gaelic in origin. The names of rivers are mostly feminine since they contain the names of the tutelary deities, e.g. *Bóinn* (Boyne)<[*]*bowinda*, 'cow-white goddess', *Banna* (Bann)<[*]*bandewa*, 'goddess'. Among the other important elements that refer to natural features one should mention: *loch*, 'lake' (e.g. *Loch nEachach*, 'Lough Neagh'), *sliabh*, 'mountain' (e.g. *Sliabh Bladhma*, 'Slieve

Bloom'), *Inis*, 'island, low-lying country' (e.g. *Inis Toirc*, 'Inishturk'; *Inis*, 'Ennis'), *doire*, 'oak wood' (*Doire Buí*, 'Derryboy'), *áth*, 'ford' (e.g. *Áth I*, 'Athy'), and *maigh*, 'plain' (e.g. *Maigh Cuilinn*, 'Moycullen'). The commonest elements in settlement names are *dún*, 'fort' (e.g. *Dún na nGall*, 'Donegal'), *cill*, 'church' (e.g. *Cill Dara*, 'Kildare'), and *baile*, 'dwelling, town' (e.g. *Baile Móta*, 'Ballymote'). 'Bally' is not infrequently also the Anglicization of *béal átha*, 'the mouth of, dry land near a ford' (e.g. *Béal Átha na Sluaighe*, 'Ballinasloe').

*Viking settlers introduced *Norse names to the south and east coasts, e.g. Howth<Old Norse *hofuð*, 'head', Waterford<'weather fjord'. The second syllable in 'Leinster', 'Munster', and 'Ulster' is probably the Norse genitival -s- followed by Irish *tír*, 'land'. The absence of -ster from the name Connaught/Connacht is indicative of the dearth of Viking settlement in the western province. The name Dublin<*duibhlinn* ('black pool') is Gaelic but was used by the Norsemen for the town they built between the pool on the Poddle river and the Liffey. *Baile Átha Cliath* ('the ford of the town of the wattles') was the older Gaelic settlement to the west of *Duibhlinn* at a point where the Liffey could be forded over wooden hurdles on the river bed.

The *Anglo-Normans introduced English toponyms, many of which contained the element *-town(e)* (e.g. Cheeverstown, Mitchelstown). Some of these names were Gaelicized during the Gaelic recovery of the 14th and 15th centuries (e.g. *Baile an Fheirtéaraigh*, 'Ballyferriter'). Although the Norse must have been largely Gaelicized by the 12th century, the invaders from Britain were familiar with the Norse names of the south and east coasts and continued to use them, rather than the Irish names which would have been in current use in Ireland.

The Anglo-Normans introduced the system of *counties and divided counties into *baronies. Since the baronies often corresponded to the area of the earlier Irish **tuath* or people, the baronies not infrequently continue ancient population names e.g. Corcomroe<*Corca Mrua*, Decies< **Déisi*, etc.

Plantation in the 16th and 17th centuries introduced a new wave of English names, for example Maryborough (Co. Laois), Philipstown (Co. Offaly), and Virginia (Co. Cavan), named for Mary Tudor, Philip II of Spain, and Elizabeth I of England respectively. The planters of Ulster often replaced Gaelic names with unrelated English ones, e.g. Cookstown for *an Chorr Chríochach*, Draperstown for *Baile na Scríne*. London was added to the English name Derry (<Irish *Doire*) in honour of the London companies that colonized the city. The form *Londan-Doire* is attested in Irish poetry.

The Anglicization of Irish place names had begun with the Anglo-Norman invasion. Names were either respelt, e.g. *Sligeach*>Sligo, or translated, e.g. *Baile Coimín*>Blessington (as though from *comaoin*, 'gratitude'). Some English forms are hybrids, e.g. *Cloch na Rón* ('stone of the seals')>Roundstone. The English versions of Irish place names were standardized by the *Ordnance Survey of 1824–46. Later place names are of assorted origin. Portobello and Rialto in Dublin are Italian borrowings. Ranelagh is in imitation of the Ranelagh Gardens in London, sited on land originally owned by Lord Ranelagh (see JONES, RICHARD), who took his title from Ranelagh in County Wicklow. Bangor in Mayo is borrowed either from Bangor in Co. Down or from Bangor in north Wales.

On Irish independence an attempt was made to divest all toponyms in the state of their imperial connotations. In many cases the results were unobjectionable. *Kingstown and Queen's County, for example, became *Dún Laoghaire* (pronounced Dunleary) and Co. Laois/Leix respectively. Some other changes were less happy. Charleville, Co. Cork, was given the unhistorical name *Ráth Loirc*, and King's County was renamed Offaly. Since Offaly is the name of two baronies in Co. Kildare the new name was unjustified.

NJAW

Plan of Campaign, a Nationalist response to the problems of agricultural depression, tenant distress, and evictions that continued despite the *Land Act of 1881. Initiated by William *O'Brien and other leading Parnellites, though not *Parnell, the plan was published in *United Ireland* in October 1886 and proposed that where a landlord refused rent reductions tenants would offer rents they considered to be fair. On these being refused the sums involved would go into an 'estate fund' for the support of tenants who could then expect to be evicted, with further financial support coming, as needed, from the *National League. Operating chiefly in the south and west of Ireland during 1886–90, the plan met with well-organized landlord and government opposition. It heavily depleted Nationalist funds and was less than wholly successful. Disputes on 84 of 116 estates involved were resolved by agreement, some after conflict; 15 were settled on the landlord's terms, while 18 were still unresolved in 1891.

JL

plantation, one of the Tudor options for 'reforming' Ireland, becoming the predominant policy under James I. Policy-makers saw advantages in colonization: for Ireland colonies would be models of civility and religion for the 'barbarous' natives, stimuli to economic growth, bulwarks against foreign invasion, and centres of command and control; for England (and later Scotland) they would provide advancement for landless younger sons and outlets for surplus population.

The earliest Tudor plantation projects were small conservative schemes, many proposed by *Old English reformers such as Thomas Finglas, Edward Walshe, and Rowland White, and not considered out of step with other policies such as *surrender and regrant. Later, larger designs attracted the ambitions of lords deputy and English secretaries of state eager for enrichment and aggrandizement, of James I, concerned with state-building and princely reputation, of *Wentworth for fiscal purposes, and of *Cromwell to meet the cost of large-scale military operations.

Large crown plantation schemes such as *Munster and *Ulster, which tended to have strategic and infrastructural goals, were never quite so successful as the private, informal settlements of the 17th century. The latter, officially encouraged and often reassured by the proximity of government plantations, were less tied by regulations and more flexible in responding to market opportunities. The private planters involved in the *'Enterprise of Ulster' were unable to conquer Antrim and Down, but in the peaceful conditions of the early 17th century Hamilton, Montgomery, and others were able to take over most of the lands of the Clandeboye *O'Neills, who had weak titles and who ran into debt in the new capitalist environment. Similar pressures on Gaelic landholding elsewhere provided other such opportunities.

By 1641 22,000 English had settled in Munster and 15,000 English and Scots in Ulster, but there was *immigration into all parts of the country with even native landlords like *Clanricard, Thomond, and *Antrim bringing in settlers. The economy was boosted: markets proliferated; Youghal and Carrickfergus expanded; Bandon, Derry, Coleraine, and Belfast were established. Early planters exploited the local forests and *fisheries. The object had been to encourage arable farming as a sign of civility, but the real money was in cattle exports, for which new breeds were introduced.

Government, having encouraged settlement to reform the country, now had the problem of defending colonists who often disregarded basic precautions of fortification, armament, and training. Natives who had been dispossessed, exiled, made redundant, or had collaborated but eventually lost out, were a threat. The *Laois and Offaly planters met frequent resistance; the Munster plantation was overthrown in 1598; and there was a conspiracy against the Ulster one in 1615. A twenty-year peace followed until all were attacked in the *rising of 1641.

The significance of the plantations lies in the establishment of a large body of Protestants in Ireland, most notably the establishment of Lowland Scots in Ulster, something that the state was regretting as early as the 1630s. Prosperity was promoted by new skills and capital, but arguably the Old English, given their head, would have created a market economy in any case, without the traumas engendered by colonization. Historiographically, the Irish plantations have been seen by D. B. Quinn, and more recently by Nicholas Canny, as prototypes for English activities in America.

Canny, Nicholas, *Kingdom or Colony* (1988)
Quinn, D. B., 'Ireland and Sixteenth-Century European Expansion', *Historical Studies*, 1 (1958)

HM

plantations, minor Jacobean. These originated in the 1610 discovery by *New English adventurers of crown title to lands in north Wexford. In 1618, following government intervention and local objections, regrants were made to native freeholders with over 100 acres, with the smaller freeholders becoming leaseholders. One-quarter of the land went to undertakers, mostly servitors in the Dublin government. Discovery and regrant were similiarly used in Leitrim, Longford, and parts of King's and Queen's Counties (Laois and Offaly) in 1619–20. These plantations, with few settlers and mostly *absentee owners, merely imposed a new set of landlords on the native population. HM

plasterwork, the practice of covering interior walls and ceilings with designs in relief, made from a mixture of gypsum or pulverized marble and slaked lime. Fragmentary remains at Carrick-on-Suir Castle (*c.*1565), Bunratty Castle, Co. Clare (*c.*1620), and the chapel of the Royal hospital at Kilmainham near Dublin (1680) indicate that the craft was practised at least from the 16th century in Ireland. However it reached its peak during the 18th century, when new styles introduced by foreign stuccadores were adopted by native craftsmen.

During the early years of the century the compartmented, coved ceiling was the vogue, for example at no. 9 Henrietta Street, Dublin, and the House of Lords (1729), both by a plasterer working for Edward Lovett *Pearce. Around 1735 the Swiss Lafranchini brothers arrived in Ireland, bringing with them an international late baroque style. Much of their work is characterized by large-scale figure sculpture, fruit, and foliage, a complete departure from the native style. Their association with Richard *Castle led to their decoration of some of the greatest houses of 18th-century Ireland: of particular note is the salon at Carton House, Co. Kildare. During the 1750s a native plasterworker, Robert West (d. 1790), came to the fore. He was famed in particular for his modelling of birds in high relief, such as at no. 20 Lower Dominick Street, Dublin (*c*.1758).

The influence of the great English neoclassical architects such as Wyatt and Adam led a new trend in plasterwork during the period 1760–75. Dublin artists were slow to lose the flamboyant rococo style, but the grander new houses were decorated with the more internationally fashionable geometrical patterns and plaques associated with ancient Greece and Rome. Powerscourt House and Ely House both had examples of this style executed by Irishman Michael Stapleton (d. 1801).

With the Act of *Union, the Dublin building boom ceased, and thus much of the heavier, early 19th-century work is to be found in public buildings and country houses. An example of this can be seen at the chapel royal, *Dublin Castle, where George Stapleton (son of Michael) worked for the architect Francis *Johnston. RM

Plowden, Francis (1749–1829), cleric and writer. Born in Shropshire, Plowden was educated by *Jesuits in France and became the master of their college at Bruges until the suppression of the order in 1773. A legal career followed, and he subsequently published a series of legal and political texts, notably his *Historical Review of the State of Ireland* (1803). Sponsored by the government, this supported the Act of *Union, and also sought to refute *Musgrave's allegations that the *insurrection of 1798 had been a Catholic conspiracy. Further writings followed. In 1813, under threat of bankruptcy from libel damages, Plowden fled to France, working until his death at the Scots' College there. NG

Plunket, William Conyngham (1764–1854), 1st Baron Plunket, distinguished *Whig/Liberal lawyer, attorney-general 1805–7, 1822–7, and lord chancellor 1830–41. Born in Enniskillen, Co. Fermanagh, the son of a Presbyterian minister, he was MP for Charlemont (having insisted that Lord *Charlemont tolerate his support for *Catholic emancipation) during 1798–1800, and vigorously opposed the Act of *Union. He was prosecuting counsel in the trial of Robert *Emmet. Having sat for two months for an English constituency in 1807, he was MP for *Trinity College, Dublin, from 1812. In 1821 he introduced a *Catholic relief bill which passed the Commons but was rejected in the Lords.

Plunkett family, originally Anglo-Norman invaders who settled at Beaulieu, Co. Louth, and later established branches at Killeen and Dunsany, Co. Meath. The senior branch, ennobled in 1541, were in the front line against the Gaelic Irish. Patrick, 3rd Baron Louth, was slain by MacMahon in 1578. This line, having suffered temporary confiscation under *Cromwell and exclusion from the House of Lords in 1698, conformed to the *Church of Ireland in the 18th century.

The cadet lines descended from Sir Christopher Plunkett, deputy governor of Ireland in 1432–4. The Plunketts of Dunsany (ennobled 1439) counted themselves the most English of the *Palesmen. Patrick, 7th baron (d. 1602), was one of the few Palesmen not involved in the *cess agitation and was a staunch opponent of Hugh *O'Neill. The 9th baron, also Patrick, was imprisoned by the lords justices in 1642 despite his protestations of loyalty. Randall, the 11th baron (d. 1735), took advantage of the articles of *Limerick; his only son and heir conformed.

The Plunketts of Killeen (ennobled 1449) increased in status when Luke, the 9th baron (d. 1637), was created earl of Fingall in 1628. Christopher, his successor, became a *Confederate cavalry commander but was captured at *Rathmines and died soon after confined in Dublin Castle. Christopher's son was restored in 1662 and his grandson avoided *Williamite confiscation being a minor. Robert, the 6th earl, died in Flanders in 1739 after a career in Berwick's regiment in the French service. Arthur, the 8th earl (1759–1836), was leader of the conservative faction in Catholic politics in the early 19th century, and a supporter of the *veto. A yeomanry commander in the suppression of the *insurrection of 1798, he gained a UK peerage as Baron Fingall in 1831. HM

Plunkett, Horace (1854–1932), the pioneer of agricultural co-operation in Ireland. Born into the Anglo-Irish nobility, Plunkett managed the family estate at Dunsany, where he established a co-operative shop in 1878. From 1879 to 1889 he ranched in Wyoming: this work, in addition to his inheritance, provided financial independence and a detailed knowledge of farming. Returning to Ireland in 1889, Plunkett launched a successful *co-operative movement, recruited *Unionist and *Parnellite politicians to the *Recess Committee (1895), and became first vice-president of the Department of *Agriculture and Technical Instruction (1899).

Plunkett was also active in constitutional politics. In 1892 he was elected as Liberal Unionist MP for South Dublin. However, despite his successful appeal to Irish farmers, he had little political dexterity: he was defeated in the general election of 1900 owing to the intervention of a rival Unionist candidate. His most influential publication, *Ireland in the New Century* (1904), created widespread offence because of its baleful reflections concerning the influence of the Catholic church. He remained a nominal Unionist until *c.*1911. He was chairman of the *Irish Convention (July 1917–Apr. 1918), and the founder, in 1919, of the Irish Dominion League. He was a great agrarian reformer, but an indifferent party politician: he was an Edwardian centrist who, in common with others of this type, was a victim of the increasing polarization of Irish politics.

AJ

Plunkett, Oliver (1625–81), Catholic archbishop. The son of a minor Catholic landowner in Co. Meath, he was educated and ordained in Rome, where he taught at the College of *Propaganda Fide until appointed archbishop of Armagh in 1669. In Ireland he became the most noted of a new generation of bishops concerned to restore ecclesiastical discipline after the disruption of the *Confederate War. His *Old English background led to opposition from some native Irish clergy, particularly in the *Franciscan order, against which he gave judgment in a controversy with the *Dominicans in 1671. He also clashed with Peter Talbot, archbishop of Dublin 1669–80, over their respective jurisdictions (see PRIMATIAL CONTROVERSY), stating his case in *Ius primatiale* (1672). He was on good terms with Baron Berkeley, lord lieutenant 1670–2, with whose approval he arranged for a number of Ulster *Tories to leave Ireland for military service in France or Flanders. He had to go into hiding when policy changed in 1673. (See RESTORATION.) Following the unveiling of the *Popish Plot Plunkett was arrested on 6 December 1679, and subsequently accused of planning a French invasion. The witnesses included several priests whom Plunkett had suspended or otherwise antagonized, among them John Moyer, former vicar of the Armagh Franciscans. A first trial in Dundalk (July 1680) collapsed when the accusers withdrew, but Plunkett was transferred to London, tried there, and convicted. Although the Popish Plot was now losing momentum, and the witnesses against Plunkett wholly discredited, Charles II refused to jeopardize his recovering political fortunes by a pardon. Executed on 1 July 1681, Plunkett was beatified 1920, and canonized 1975.

Plymouth Brethrenism, a religious movement with origins in Dublin in the 1820s but named after the town of its most substantial early congregation. It has its roots in a well-educated (mostly Oxford and *Trinity College, Dublin) generation of religious enthusiasts born *c.*1800 who were influenced by *evangelicalism, European warfare, and the spread of *foreign missions. Impatient of rigid denominationalism, whether the establishmentarian claims of Anglicanism or the narrow membership criteria of the dissenters, and intrigued by the implications of a close study of biblical *prophecy, the most important tenets of early Brethrenism were the unity in Christ of all true believers and the absence of any form of ordination. Brethren meetings were thus built around the simple sharing of bread and wine and lay ministry of the word, unencumbered by ordained clergy or ecclesiastical structures. Disagreements over points of doctrine and interpretations of prophecy soon shattered the early emphasis on unity and gave rise to one of the most fissiparous of Protestant traditions. In Ireland the early growth of Brethrenism in Dublin, inspired by A. N. Groves, J. N. Darby, and Edward Cronin, was given a much needed boost by the Ulster *revival of 1859. Thereafter its greatest strength lay in the north of Ireland.

Throughout its history Brethrenism has attracted a social elite of Anglo-Irish landowners, eminent lawyers, and academics, as well as a more humble membership. Although it has retained some of its early commitment to international missions and the priesthood of all believers, Brethrenism in Ireland has settled into a minor and relatively exclusive Protestant sect with a pessimistic eschatology and otherworldly social attitudes.

DNH

Pococke, Richard (1704–65), *Church of Ireland bishop of Ossory (1756–65), antiquarian, and traveller, who published accounts of his visits to the Middle East, Scotland, and England. His *Tour in Ireland in 1752* (pub. 1891) recorded religious practices, agricultural improvements, and industrial development. He endowed a *charter school, 'the Lintown Factory', in *Kilkenny, to bring up Catholic boys in the tenets of the established church and train them in the *linen trade.

KM

Poer, a minor baronial family from Somerset, and originally perhaps from Picardy. The le Poer (Power) connection with Ireland dates from the early phase of the *Anglo-Norman invasion, Robert le Poer appearing in Ireland in 1171–2. The family held the title 'baron of Dunoil', taking its name from their chief manor at Dunhill, Co. Waterford, from which they dominated the central areas of that county. Other branches, such as the Poers of Grannagh, of Ballydurne, and of Kilmeadan, held land in north-east Waterford. They also acquired lands further afield, as testified by Powerscourt,

Co. Wicklow, held in the 13th century. The Poers rank as one of the top half-dozen or so Anglo-Irish baronial families, although by the 14th century they were increasingly fractured into collateral lineages functioning in a manner not dissimilar to that of native Irish *septs. In this period, which represented the peak of their power, they dominated the office of sheriff of Co. Waterford (and are found feuding with the inhabitants of Waterford city). Despite the post-*Reformation upheavals, the *Civil Survey shows that several families of Powers were still among the most significant landholders in Co. Waterford in the mid-17th century. SD

police. The concept of a police force was unknown in medieval Ireland, the law in both Irish- and English-controlled parts of the country being in the main enforced collectively. The Statute of Winchester (1285) introduced *justices of the peace (magistrates), constables, and night watchmen, but also obliged householders to keep arms and to participate in the hue and cry. The act, extended to Ireland in 1308, defined the basis of law enforcement for the next 500 years.

By the 18th century, this system of locally controlled self-policing was in decline, having become both corrupt and ineffective. A growth in *agrarian protest from the 1760s and in political agitation from the 1770s spurred central government to attempt major reform. In 1773 and 1787 efforts were made to bolster the *Baronial Constabulary, while in 1786 the first modern police force in the British Isles was established in Dublin (see DUBLIN METROPOLITAN POLICE). But, in the face of opposition from magistrates and *grand juries, who controlled law enforcement locally, these innovations had only a limited impact.

In 1814 Robert *Peel successfully introduced a *Peace Preservation Force, to be dispatched to counties proclaimed as disturbed, while in 1822 a permanent, national constabulary was finally established. These two forces were amalgamated and brought fully under central control in 1836 as the Irish, later *Royal Irish, Constabulary (RIC). Until it was disbanded in 1922, this armed, paramilitary force policed most of the country. The Dublin Metropolitan Police, an unarmed, civilian force, also established in 1836, policed the capital.

After the Famine, and increasingly from the 1890s, the RIC began to lose its military effectiveness, due to more settled and peaceful times. Thus, despite being reinforced by *Auxiliaries and *Black and Tans during the *Anglo-Irish War, the force was no match for the guerrilla tactics of the *IRA.

After *partition new police forces were established. In the north the *Royal Ulster Constabulary, supported by an *Ulster Special Constabulary, was formed along similar lines to the RIC and, indeed, with large numbers of former RIC men in its ranks. In the south an unarmed, civilian force, the *Garda Síochána, was created in 1922 and took over the policing of Dublin in 1925. These two forces policed the two parts of Ireland for the remainder of the century, until the RUC was reconstituted at the beginning of the 21st century.

Allen, G., *The Garda Siochana* (1999)

Breathnach, S., *The Irish Police from the Earliest Times to the Present Day* (1974)

McNiffe, L., *A History of the Garda Siochana* (repr., 1999)

Palmer, S. H., *Police and Protest in England and Ireland, 1780–1850* (1988)

ELM

political parties first appeared in Ireland with the conflict between *Whig and *Tory, which spread into Ireland from around 1704 and reached a peak of bitterness in the threatened succession crisis of 1714 (see REVOLUTION OF 1688). After 1714, with the Tories permanently excluded from office, party allegiances, even more completely than in contemporary England, lost their relevance. Instead factions or connections based on ties of kinship, region, or personal attachment, of the kind led by Alan *Brodrick, William *Conolly, the *Ponsonbys and the *Boyles, competed with one another for the spoils of office.

Between the 1760s and the 1830s British politics gradually moved towards a new party division between moderately reformist Whigs and Tory defenders of the status quo. In Ireland, despite the creation of an Irish Whig Party in 1789, the shift to party-based politics was considerably slower. Even after the Act of *Union most Irish MPs at *Westminster were distinguished by their mercenary readiness to support whatever government held office, committing themselves to a clear party affiliation only when the crisis surrounding *parliamentary reform in 1830–2 made such identification inescapable.

From the 1830s until the success of the *home rule party in 1874, most Irish MPs defined themselves as supporters of one of the two main British parties, Conservative or Liberal. There were attempts, by *O'Connell in the 1830s and 1840s, and by supporters of *independent opposition in the 1850s, to create a distinctively Irish political grouping. However, the distinction between *repealers, independent oppositionists, and Liberals was often conveniently vague. A similar enlistment of former Liberals under a temporarily popular banner was evident in the early stages of the home rule party.

The turning point in the history of Irish political parties came in the 1880s. The widening of the electoral *franchise made necessary the development of new forms of constituency organization to secure and retain the support of a much larger electorate. Legislation for the elimination of corrupt practices at elections (1883), by limiting expenditure by individual candidates, provided a further impetus for the development of party structures. Meanwhile the home rule crisis of 1885–6 polarized politics along religious lines. The *Nationalist and *Unionist parties that emerged from this combination of influences were at the same time tightly disciplined parliamentary parties and effective popular movements whose appeal was based on their claim to represent entire communities rather than pragmatic coalitions of sectional interests. *Sinn Féin, which displaced the *Irish parliamentary party after 1918, presented itself in similar terms.

Politics in Northern Ireland after 1920 continued the pattern established in the 1880s. Electoral contests were dominated by the opposition between a dominant Unionist Party, representing most shades of Protestant opinion, and what is generally referred to as a Nationalist Party, though in fact this had few of the organizational features of a modern political party (see NATIONALIST PARTY (OF NORTHERN IRELAND)). Challenges to these green and orange establishments by independent unionist and republican candidates met with little success, particularly after the abolition in 1929 of *proportional representation. Nor did the *Northern Ireland Labour Party enjoy more than marginal success in its attempts to substitute the politics of class for those of ethnicity and religion.

The party system of independent Ireland, by contrast, broke sharply with its predecessor. Its core stemmed from Sinn Féin, which controlled all except four of the seats in the House of Commons of Southern Ireland elected (under the *Government of Ireland Act) in 1921. Following the *Anglo-Irish treaty, the pro- and anti-treaty factions of Sinn Féin consolidated into parties that have since constituted the poles of electoral competition in Ireland. The pro-treaty wing, initially the party of government, organized itself as *Cumann na nGaedheal in 1923 and, following its loss of office in 1932, it amalgamated with two smaller groups a year later to form *Fine Gael. Its anti-treaty opponents retained the name Sinn Féin, the most vibrant faction of which broke away in 1926 to form *Fianna Fáil and proceeded in the 1930s to establish an unchallengeable position as the dominant party.

While the initial basis of the cleavage between these two parties was the treaty and they continued to be divided by the national question, they were also to some extent differentiated by other ideological and social factors. Cumann na nGaedheal tended to be conservative on social and economic matters, and this heritage was taken over by Fine Gael. Fianna Fáil was a radical, populist party in its early days, though it later adopted a more pragmatic or even conservative position. These differences were reflected in the parties' support bases, with Fianna Fáil showing a much greater capacity to appeal to small farmers and industrial workers than its rival, especially in its earlier years. The form taken by the two party organizations was compatible with these differences, with Fianna Fáil always maintaining a much higher level of organization in terms of numbers of members and of branches. These two parties have collectively dominated Irish party political life since 1922, their combined share of the vote normally ranging between 60 and 80 per cent.

Next in electoral importance has been the *Labour Party, which since 1922 has normally ranked third in the party system. Its linkage to the *trade union movement and working-class support base predisposed it favourably towards Fianna Fáil until the late 1940s, but from 1948 until the 1980s it more often found itself aligned with Fine Gael. In contrast to its European sister parties, the Labour Party has been extremely weak; like them, it has also had a left-wing rival in the shape of a tiny *communist movement that has appeared under various names since the 1920s but which has attracted virtually no electoral support since then. The only serious challenge was the *National Labour Party, a faction that broke with the Labour Party in 1944 as part of a dispute within the trade union movement but which rejoined the party in 1950.

Rather surprisingly, the two parties that had dominated political life since the 1880s, the Nationalists and the Unionists, made little impact in the south after 1922. This was particularly surprising in the case of the Nationalist Party, which had almost completely controlled southern Irish parliamentary representation from 1885 to 1918. The party organization, the *United Irish League, collapsed completely in the south, and after 1922 this tradition was represented only by a handful of independent deputies. An effort to revive it in 1926 (as the *National League, led by William Redmond, son of the nationalist leader John *Redmond) prospered briefly in the June 1927 election but faded shortly afterwards. The unionist tradition was also represented after 1922 by independent deputies, especially in the border counties.

Other sectional interests have been represented only occasionally in the party system. In the 1920s the most significant were the *Farmers' Party (which attracted the support especially of larger, commercial farmers) and the less significant Business Men's Party, both of which also appealed to ex-Unionist and ex-Nationalist support. Farming interests resurfaced briefly in the early 1930s in the form of the National *Centre Party. The agrarian tradition reasserted itself again in the 1940s, in the shape of *Clann na Talmhan, whose support was particularly pronounced among the small farmers of the western counties.

One of the most significant challenges to the three-party dominance of Irish politics came from the anti-treaty tradition. This was represented continuously by the Sinn Féin party, which survived the split in 1926 that led to the creation of Fianna Fáil, and later splits in 1970, 1974, 1986, and 1992. The consequences were the appearance respectively of 'Provisional' Sinn Féin, the Irish Republican Socialist Party, Republican Sinn Féin, and *Democratic Left; the parent party is now known as the Workers' Party. Other minor parties generated at least in part by the national question have been *Clann na Poblachta in the 1940s and the 1950s, Aontacht Éireann in the 1970s, and the *Progressive Democrats after 1985.

Gallagher, Michael, *Political Parties in the Republic of Ireland* (1985)
Hoppen, K. T., *Elections, Politics and Society in Ireland 1832–85* (1984)
Mair, Peter, *The Changing Irish Party System* (1987)
Sinnott, Richard, *Irish Voters Decide* (1995)

SC/JC

political policing has been fraught with controversy since the foundation of the Irish state. The *Civil War saw the spawning of a number of armed plain clothes security organizations, neither police nor military, to tackle anti-state activities. They earned the collective sobriquet of 'Oriel House' (after one of their headquarters buildings), as well as a justified reputation for brutality towards—and the occasional murder of—suspects, and were quickly disbanded once the war was over. *Military intelligence became the government's main source of information on subversion for a few years, until both intelligence and investigative work were placed in the hands of the *Special Branch of the *Gárda Síochána. When the *Blueshirts threatened state security in the mid-1930s, the *Fianna Fáil government swore in hundreds of former anti-treaty IRA men, soon dubbed the 'Broy Harriers' after the new Gárda Commissioner Col. Eamonn Broy, as armed plain clothes policemen. These political appointments caused tensions within the Gárda Síochána which took years to die down. The Special Branch has remained the government's main peacetime weapon against political subversion, although military intelligence dominated security affairs during the *Second World War. The Special Branch has always taken a broad view of what might constitute subversion, and this has led to controversy where trade unionists, civil libertarians, people involved in protests against foreign governments, aliens, and others have come under surveillance apparently because of the views which they espoused rather than because there were good grounds for thinking that they had broken Irish law or were planning to overthrow the state. On the other hand, Irish political history indicates that a proportion of the republicans, communists, and fascists of previous generations amply merited the police attention which they received. There is always a difficult balance to be struck between the rights of the state and the rights of the individual, particularly where no actual crime has been committed but where national interests could arguably be harmed. EO'H

politicization. The growth of popular political consciousness is a complex process. It requires an awareness of political structures and issues, a perception of these as relevant to one's daily life, and (what will generally follow) a demand for participation in public affairs. These developments are often closely linked to the spread of *literacy, the decline of traditional attitudes of deference towards social superiors, and other aspects of *modernization.

Levels of political awareness in early modern Ireland are difficult to assess. The 17th century saw mass mobilizations of Catholics and Protestants during the *Confederate War and the *Williamite War. But the basis of their participation, presumably involving some combination of ethnic and religious allegiance, obedience to traditional leaders, and possibly coercion, is scantily documented and as yet unexplored. The first clear-cut instances of purposeful popular involvement in organized political activity belong to 18th-century urban Protestantism, to a limited extent in popular backing for the campaign against *Wood's Halfpence, and more positively in support for *Lucas's assault on Dublin's unrepresentative corporation.

The pace of politicization quickened in the late 18th century, as economic development raised growing numbers above the daily struggle for subsistence, created an expanding middle class whose awareness of its own economic importance was not matched by political influence, and contributed to the rise in literacy and the breakdown of traditional attitudes of localism, fatalism, and deference. The mobilization of small property owners and independent petty producers in the *Volunteer movement initially depended on the backing of landlords, MPs, and other persons of consequence. In its last phase the movement had lost this elite patronage, and with it much of its political effectiveness, but mobilization had expanded to draw in a wider social circle, and to include Catholics as well as Protestants. The creation of a broadly based and assertive public opinion was confirmed by the presence throughout the 1780s and 1790s of an urban crowd ready to take to the streets in support of popular causes.

The *United Irish movement was a landmark in the development of popular politics. The creation of a network of local clubs, later replaced by conspiratorial cells, and the use of the **Northern Star* and other publications to disseminate ideas and propaganda, revealed the new potential for mobilization. The willingness of middle-class radical leaders to use ballads and even *millenarian *prophecies, and to broaden their political programme to include some promise of social as well as political change, testified to the compromises that had nevertheless to be made if that potential was to be realized. The *Catholic Committee, meanwhile, embarked on a similar, if smaller-scale, exercise in the mobilization of popular support, notably in the elections to the *Catholic Convention. These proceedings probably contributed indirectly to the third major manifestation of a new style of popular politics, the *Defender movement, whose revolutionary ideology, however crude, represented a significant advance on the pragmatic, defensive protest of the *Whiteboys and similar *agrarian societies.

Politicization was neither uniform nor unidirectional. Support for the advanced doctrines of the United Irishmen was far stronger in eastern counties, and in particular in the hinterlands of Dublin and Belfast, than in other regions. The two decades after the Act of *Union saw radicalism in abeyance and *landlord influence once more dominant at elections. The survival of a tradition of popular radicalism, but also its definite limitations, are evident in the activities of the *Ribbon societies. From the 1820s *O'Connell's agitations for *Catholic emancipation and *repeal represented a new and more controlled mobilization of the masses. But O'Connellism too was stronger in the towns than in the countryside, in the commercialized and Anglicized east than in the impoverished and Gaelic west. Nor was the level of popular political involvement sustained after O'Connell's death. The quarter-century after the *Famine, a period of general prosperity, saw a revival of the politics of localism, personality, and deference, as repeal and reform slipped into the background, and a reinvigorated landlord class once again assumed largely unchallenged control of county politics.

The rise of the *home rule movement from 1874, and its transformation during the 1880s, can thus be seen as the last stage in a long and uneven process. The launching of the *Land War in Co. Mayo dramatically announced the political awakening of the previously supine west. The general elections of 1885 and 1886 revealed a mass electorate organized through new *political party machines in support of two clearly defined ideological blocs. Parliamentary representation, first among nationalists, a little later among unionists, was no longer dominated by landlords and wealthy professional men, but had passed into the hands of a more broadly based middle-class and even lower middle-class elite, attentive, as their predecessors had never quite had to be, to the demands of voters and constituency activists.

Hoppen, K. T., *Elections, Politics and Society in Ireland 1832–1885* (1984)
Smyth, J., *The Men of No Property: Irish Radicals and Popular Politics in the Late Eighteenth Century* (1992)

Ponsonby, one of the major political connections of the 18th century. The Irish family was founded by Col. **Sir John Ponsonby** (1608–78), from Cumberland, who served under *Cromwell and received land at Kildalton, renamed Bessborough, Co. Kilkenny. Its political eminence began with Sir John's grandson **Brabazon Ponsonby** (1679–1758), who attached himself to the duke of Devonshire, lord lieutenant 1737–45, under whom he became earl of Bessborough and 1st commissioner of the revenue. The alliance was sealed when two of Devonshire's daughters married Brabazon's sons **William** (1704–93), later 2nd earl of Bessborough and a reputed lover of George III's daughter Princess Amelia, and **John Ponsonby** (1713–87), who succeeded his father on the Revenue Board in 1744. In 1753 the Ponsonbys joined with Archbishop *Stone to challenge the dominance of Henry *Boyle. In the compromise which ended the resulting *money bill dispute, John Ponsonby became *speaker and a leading *undertaker, until displaced by *Townshend.

The family returned to political favour under the duke of Portland, lord lieutenant 1782, under whom John Ponsonby's sons **William Brabazon Ponsonby** (1744–1806) and **George Ponsonby** (1755–1817) became respectively postmaster-general and 1st counsel to the revenue commissioners. Both were dismissed for their stand on the *regency issue, and became prominent in the Irish *Whig Party. As such they supported *Catholic emancipation and *parliamentary reform, although their commitment to both may well have been largely opportunistic. From 1808 to 1817 George led the Whig Party in the Commons of the United Kingdom parliament, and in 1806 was lord chancellor of Ireland during a brief period of Whig participation in government.

John William Ponsonby (1781–1847), 4th earl of Bessborough, was a liberal and an improving landlord. Well regarded by *O'Connell, he was a popular choice as lord lieutenant, but his administration (1846–7) was overshadowed by the *Famine. His sister **Caroline Ponsonby** (1785–1828) married William Lamb, chief secretary 1827–8 and afterwards, as Lord Melbourne, a Whig prime minister; she achieved notoriety by her adulterous affair with Byron. **Frederick Ponsonby** (1816–95), the 5th earl, maintained his family's Whig/Liberal allegiance and gave his name to a commission of inquiry at the height of the *Land War.

Poor Inquiry, a commission of inquiry into Irish poverty, chaired by Archbishop *Whately, established in 1833. It used questionnaires and public hearings before itinerant 'assistant commissioners' to collect a huge mass of information, printed in the *parliamentary papers, on a wide range of subjects, from employment to diet, and from illegitimacy to pawnbroking. However, its final report, published in 1836 and recommending a huge programme of government expenditure, was ignored in favour of a *poor law based closely on the English model.

poor law. The Irish poor law (1838) was modelled on the new English poor law of 1834. Its introduction followed the rejection by *Whig ministers of the report of Archbishop *Whately's commission, which had recommended a package of reforms, including large-scale public works and state-sponsored emigration, designed to address the problems of overpopulation and underdevelopment. Whilst the English act had curtailed provision for the poor, the Irish act represented a considerable advance on the existing situation. It created a nationwide system of poor relief financed by poor rates paid, in large part, by Irish landowners. There was not, as in England, a legal right to relief. Instead relief, provided within the *workhouse, was granted at the discretion of local poor law guardians, with preference being given to the aged, the sick and disabled, and children. The guardians operated under the direction and control of the *Poor Law Commission, though the commission could not interfere in individual cases. The country was divided into 130 unions, with a workhouse in each, and 2,049 electoral divisions (later increased to 163 unions and 3,438 divisions). Boards of guardians were composed of elected guardians chosen by those paying poor rates, and local magistrates sitting ex officio. An amendment to the act in 1847 recognized the right of some vulnerable people to relief, and made provision for the granting of *outdoor relief under certain circumstances. In the post-Famine period the scope of the system was substantially extended. From 1851 the poor rate supported not only the workhouse system but also a network of dispensary stations (see HOSPITALS AND DISPENSARIES) staffed by qualified medical officers. Poor law boards also became responsible for administering and enforcing the growing body of sanitary and other public health-related legislation, and their role in *local government now rivalled that of *grand juries. Poor law expenditure rose from around £0.5 million in 1859 to over £1 million in 1876, and reached £1.5 million in 1895.

Notwithstanding the increasing influence of Catholic and nationalist representatives in its administration, especially after the *Local Government Act of 1898, the poor law remained an unpopular form of welfare. The first *Dáil declared its intention of abolishing 'the present odious, degrading and foreign poor-law system' and replacing it with a 'sympathetic native scheme'. Boards of guardians were formally abolished in 1925 and replaced by county boards of health and public assistance, empowered to grant outdoor relief to all needy persons. However, the anxiety of the new local authorities to limit expenditure prevented the needy from deriving any significant benefit from the changeover. The poor law remained in operation in Northern Ireland until 1946.

Barrington, R., *Health, Medicine and Politics in Ireland 1900–1970* (1987)

Burke, H., *The People and the Poor Law in Nineteenth-Century Ireland* (1987)

VC

Poor Law Commission. When the new English poor law was first introduced to Ireland in 1838, its administration was placed under the control of the English Poor Law Commission, operating through commissioners based in Ireland. In 1847 a separate Poor Law Commission for Ireland was created comprising the *chief secretary, the under-secretary, and the chief commissioner, and serviced by a staff of assistant commissioners, inspectors, and clerks. The commission supervised the election and proceedings of poor law boards, and was empowered to dissolve boards whose members were incompetent or inactive. Thirty-nine boards were suspended during the *Famine and paid officials appointed. In the decades after the Famine, the commission was made responsible for overseeing a wide range of health and welfare services, from the management of dispensaries to the appointment of sanitary inspectors. Conflict between the commission and local poor law boards, evident from the earliest days of the poor law, increased as the century continued and more particularly as representation of Catholics among poor law guardians increased. The commission was abolished in 1872, and its functions transferred to the newly constituted *Local Government Board for Ireland, a clear acknowledgement of the vital role the poor law system now played in local administration. VC

poor relief. There was no organized system of poor relief in Ireland until the 19th century. The Elizabethan English poor law, which established parochial responsibility for the care of the aged and destitute and for the suppression of begging, never extended to Ireland. *Parish vestries could raise money for local relief measures, such as the care of deserted children, and in the early 18th century a number of vestries experimented with a badging system designed to distinguish the local 'deserving' poor from 'foreign' beggars and vagabonds. Most parishes, however, were reluctant to incur any additional expenditure, some even going so far as to arrange for abandoned children to be removed to the *foundling hospitals in Dublin and Cork. Another group for which special provision was made was the sick poor, who were catered for in voluntary *hospitals supported by private charity, and from 1765 in county infirmaries maintained by local taxation. In *Belfast accommodation for the sick and destitute was available from 1774 in a poor house opened by the Belfast Charitable Society. *Houses of industry were established by act of parliament in Dublin (1703) and Cork (1735), but a more general act passed in 1772 was only patchily implemented. At the beginning of the 19th century *mendicity institutes were established in a number of towns. There was now growing pressure on government to relieve poverty on grounds both of natural justice and of economic utility, though there was disagreement over the best methods of achieving this. The promotion of public works as a way of reducing poverty without encouraging dependency led to the creation of the *Board of Works in 1831. From 1838 a statutory system of poor relief was provided by the *poor law, replaced in the 20th century by new forms of *social welfare.

Black, D. C., *Economic Thought and the Irish Question, 1817–70* (1960)

O'Connor, J., *The Workhouses of Ireland: The Fate of Ireland's Poor* (1995)

VC

Popish Plot (1678–81), a supposed English Catholic conspiracy to assassinate Charles II (see RESTORATION), invented by Titus Oates, a disgraced Anglican clergyman briefly turned Catholic seminarian, and vigorously exploited by the *Whig Party. In contrast to England, where eighteen priests and several laymen were executed, reactions in Ireland were relatively restrained, partly at least because there was no meeting of parliament there. *Ormond's government issued a proclamation (16 Oct. 1678) banishing bishops and members of religious orders, and closing Catholic churches in cities and towns. A number of bishops and regulars were imprisoned, including Peter Talbot, archbishop of Dublin, who died in custody. But charges against Lord Tyrone and other Catholic laymen were rejected by grand juries, and there were no executions. The most famous Irish victim of the plot, Oliver *Plunkett, drawn in only because he was brought to Shaftesbury's attention at a time when the English plot needed new momentum, was tried and executed in London.

popular music. The development of commercial *music in Ireland since the 1960s represents two distinct phenomena which have sometimes merged. One is the rapid assimilation of post-war American musical culture which itself divides into two phases (the showband as an Irish purveyor of country and western music; the rock group and solo rock performer); the other is the vigorous revival of traditional Irish music, which can be regarded as an outgrowth of the preoccupation with folk music in Europe and North America throughout the 1960s and early 1970s. A third phenomenon is the taste for and skilful cultivation of 'easy listening', which reflects a domestically produced mode of bourgeois musical entertainment. This third category is aptly symbolized by Ireland's repeated victories in the Eurovision Song Contest from 1970 onwards. Easy listening apart, the success enjoyed by traditional and ballad groups including the Dubliners, the Chieftains, the Clancy Brothers (with Tommy Makem), and the Wolfe Tones in the 1960s and 1970s is expressive of a wide spectrum of political opinion and inherent musicianship. The Chieftains, for example, were the natural (in many cases literal) successors to Sean Ó Riada's Ceoltóirí Chualann, and the style which they explored depended on a degree of virtuosity and finesse perhaps unrivalled by the plethora of ensembles spawned by the folk revival. During the same period, the development of Irish rock music likewise resulted in a wide range of ability, from brutal noise to the witty if overexposed talents of Phil Lynott and Horselips. As with the Chieftains, Rory Gallagher's guitar playing transcended the Irish context, to the extent that he became one of a small number of Irish musicians to attain enduring international significance.

In the 1980s and early 1990s, the respective profiles of rock and traditional styles softened in Ireland (notwithstanding the sovereignty of U2 as exponents of unadulterated hard rock), with the result that certain artists and groups, notably Clannad, Planxty, and Mary Black, blended elements of American and Irish style into different syntheses, depending on the expressive emphasis in question.

No such subtlety attaches to the strident revival of political *balladry which followed in the wake of the Northern Ireland conflict, although it is fair to point out that ballads such as 'Stand beside me' (the Wolfe Tones), which borrows the Verdi chorus 'Va pensiero' (*Il Trovatore*), enjoyed widespread approval in certain nationalist areas.

HW

population. Estimates of numbers of inhabitants for any period prior to the development of the modern state are inevitably speculative. Tentative suggestions put the population at the end of the *neolithic period at 100,000 to 200,000, and by the coming of Christianity at about 250,000. Estimates for *c.*1300, largely based on extrapolation from English figures, range from 675,000 to 1.4 million. There is general agreement that from the early 14th century plague (see BLACK DEATH), *famine, and warfare caused a sharp loss of numbers. Somewhat more confident estimates for the early modern period suggest that numbers rose from about a million in 1500 to 1.4 million in 1600 and to 2.1 million by 1641. By 1672 population had fallen back to around 1.7 million. It had risen again to between 2.0 and 2.3 million by 1712, but remained close to this level until a new phase of growth commenced in the 1750s.

While the size of the population at any one point in time is uncertain, the broad chronology of change is well defined. During the 16th century population rose at a rate well within the normal pre-industrial experience. The influx caused by the plantation of *Munster was largely offset by the emigration to England or continental Europe promoted by the effects of the *Nine Years War and by harvest crises and plague in 1601–5. In the early 17th century the rate of growth increased as a result of formal plantation schemes and more informal colonization. By the 1630s there are indications of *emigration to America from Munster, suggesting that growth there had peaked. Much of this early 17th-century expansion was undone by the emigration which followed war in 1641 and the plague of the early 1650s. In the late 17th century population rose again. In Ulster this was mainly by migration from Scotland, especially in the 1690s, but in Munster the rate of increase, though still significant, was much slower. Since migration to Ireland was over a relatively short distance, compared with transatlantic movement, whole families migrated, ensuring that the sex ratio within the Irish population was not excessively skewed towards males. This, combined with a low land–labour ratio, permitted earlier marriage than in England and a longer child-bearing period for women. From the evidence of *Quaker families average completed family size in Ireland was 5.4 compared to 4 in England. The stability of the population in the early 18th century seems due to a number of factors. The rise of emigration to America from Ulster provided an escape valve for a surplus population but depressed economic conditions generally may also have lowered the marriage rate. Two major subsistence crises in the 1720s and 1740–1 also had the effect of keeping population low, the latter crisis probably being more severe in its demographic impact than the *Great Famine of the 1840s.

Change in the size of the population was paralleled by shifts in its distribution. In the 16th century Ulster was the least densely populated area, followed by Munster and Connacht, with the greatest density of population in the Leinster *Pale. The 1660 poll money returns suggest that Ulster was now well settled and north Leinster was also densely populated. Connacht, by contrast, was falling behind in relative terms. By the end of the 17th century a new pattern, with the population gradient running east–west rather than north–south as it had done in the 16th century, was well established. This shift was accompanied by a greater concentration of population in towns, with the expansion of older centres such as *Dublin and the establishment of new ones such as *Belfast and *Derry.

From the middle of the 18th century population began to expand at an unprecedented rate. By 1791 numbers had risen to around 4.4 million, and by 1821 to 6.8 million. Growth was clearly related to economic prosperity: the expansion of agriculture in response to the opening of new overseas markets, first in the British and French colonies across the Atlantic, later in the rising industrial cities of Great Britain, and the growth of *linen and other manufactured goods. The precise mechanisms, however, remain unclear. An older tradition of explanation suggested a sharp fall in the age of marriage, made possible by subdivision of agricultural holdings and increased reliance on a *potato diet. More recent work suggests that early modern Ireland was a 'high pressure' demographic system, in which already low marriage ages were balanced by high mortality. What disturbed this equilibrium was a marked decline in mortality, especially infant mortality, reflecting increased resources, better mechanisms of poor relief, and medical improvement.

After 1815, as agricultural prices fell following the end of the *revolutionary and Napoleonic wars, and rural manufacturing contracted, the pressure of rising numbers became increasingly difficult to sustain. With increased emigration and a likely rise in marriage ages population growth began to level off. Numbers rose from 6.8 million in 1821 to 7.8 million in 1831, but to only 8.2 million by 1841. Even if the potato crop had not failed catastrophically from 1845, population might well have declined from mid-century. As it was, death and emigration during the Great Famine reduced population to 6.5 million by 1851.

The pattern of a falling and then stagnant population established from the 1840s continued for well over a century. In a more prosperous but restrictive society marriage was strictly tied to resources, with men waiting to obtain possession of the family farm, and women for the provision of a suitable dowry, before marrying, often by means of an arranged 'match'. A substantial minority never married at all. Heavy emigration carried away those for whom no provision could be made under this system, as well as those displaced by the move from labour-intensive tillage to pasture, and those for whom the new awareness of emigration as an option opened up the possibility of a better life abroad. Population fell to 4.4 million by 1911.

To the consternation of many, for whom the annual haemorrhage of Irish youth by emigration had been one of the great indictments of British rule, political independence did little to stem the outward flow, or to alter other demographic patterns. The population of the Irish Free State declined from just short of 3 million in 1926 to 2.8 million in 1961. (Northern Ireland had a gradual but steady increase, from 1.25 million in 1926 to 1.4 million in 1956.) Official concern at the pattern of decline was reflected in the establishment of the Commission on Emigration and Other Population Problems, which reported in 1954. It was not until the 1960s, following the sudden prosperity associated with new economic policies (see *ECONOMIC DEVELOPMENT*), that emigration fell off, allowing population in independent Ireland to rise to 3.5 million by 1986. Even today Ireland's population density remains strikingly below the European average.

Cullen, L. M., 'Population Trends in Seventeenth Century Ireland', *Economic and Social Review*, 6 (1974–5)

Dickson, D., Ó Gráda, C., and Daultry, S., 'Hearth Tax, Household Size and Irish Population Change', *Proceedings of the Royal Irish Academy*, 82 (1982)

Kennedy, R. E., *The Irish: Emigration, Marriage and Fertility* (1973)

RG/SC

Porter, Revd James (1753–98), Presbyterian minister of Greyabbey, Co. Antrim, and *United Irish propagandist. A series of letters in the **Northern Star* satirizing local landlords was reprinted as *Billy Bluff and Squire Firebrand* (1796). Although Porter insisted that he had taken no part in the *insurrection of 1798 he was arrested and subsequently hanged. His family attributed his death to the hostility of Lord *Londonderry, who had been the model for Squire Firebrand's patron, Lord Mountmumble.

Portlaw, see MALCOLMSONS OF PORTLAW.

ports and harbours really began in Ireland in the 9th century, with the establishment of *Viking settlements in Dublin, Wicklow, Wexford, Waterford, Cork, and Limerick. The Vikings built quays, whereas the Irish had simply beached their *curragh-type vessels. By the *Norman era, there were some 80 active ports including *Carrickfergus, Carlingford, Ardglass, Dundalk, *Drogheda, Arklow, Youghal, Kinsale, *Galway, and Sligo. Many had merchant *guilds with their own, often locally built, fleets. In the Middle Ages, there was a flourishing *overseas trade, and continental maps indicated major Irish ports.

In the 16th century Drogheda and *Dublin traded with *Liverpool and Chester respectively. Galway's links with Europe are symbolized in the Spanish Arch. Youghal served the *Munster plantation, while *Derry was the chief port for the English campaign in Ulster in 1600. Monopoly control of ports like *Waterford, Galway, *Cork and *Limerick, by almost exclusively Catholic and *Old English merchant oligarchies, was ended by *Cromwell. Irish sea trade was menaced by Dutch, North African, and even Irish *pirates, such as Grace *O'Malley. Indeed in 1631 Baltimore was sacked by Barbary pirates.

In the 19th century many east coast ports handled the cross-channel ferries that proliferated after the introduction of steam. Following the *Great Famine, Derry, Moville (after 1860), and Queenstown (Cobh) became important *emigration ports for North America. Harbour commissioners in the larger ports looked after maintenance and expansion, for instance cutting channels to allow the larger steamships to berth at their docks. Belfast rose from third largest port in Ireland in 1800 to third in the UK in 1900. In the late 19th and early 20th centuries, the strategic importance of Ireland was underlined by the building of navy yards and bases at Cobh, Berehaven, and Lough Swilly (see TREATY PORTS). In the 1960s Irish ports adapted to deal with the drive-on market of car ferries and container services. Due to the holiday boom, Rosslare and Cork became important car-ferry ports, linking Ireland to the Continent. PC

postal communications are a relatively modern phenomenon. Prior to the 17th century important people might succeed in using royal messengers, by special permission or payment, with the alternative of handing letters to ship captains or travellers on an ad hoc basis. From 1635, partly in order to spread costs, the Royal Mail was made available to the public. Charges were standardized, a single sheet to Ireland costing 9*d*. From 1638 Evan Vaughan took charge of the posts in Ireland and established routes out of Dublin. By 1653 the main areas had a twice-weekly service. The General Post Office of England, Scotland, and Ireland was established with a monopoly in 1657. Rates were reduced to 2*d*. for up to 40 miles from Dublin. There was a system of foot and horse posts, with dedicated boats on the Dublin–Holyhead route. As usual offices were farmed, with £3,600 a year paid for the inland office alone in 1682.

In 1711 the five main letter offices of home and colonies, including Dublin, were put under a single postmaster-general, and local postmasterships ceased to be farmed. The frequency of posts, and the area served, increased progressively, with a daily service from 1760. Dublin had a local penny post in some form from 1765. In 1784 a separate Irish postal system was set up. Charges, usually paid by the recipient, were based rather erratically on mileage.

The growth of postal services provided an important stimulus for wider infrastructural developments, encouraging improvements in roads, harbours, and ships. *Bianconi's transport empire depended heavily on contracts for the carriage of mail, as did early *railway development. The Post Office also invested early in the fastest ships, which from 1821 meant steam. Following the amalgamation of the British and Irish post offices in 1831, services expanded further. A uniform penny post was introduced in 1840. The number of letters delivered annually rose from 9.25 million in 1839 to 65 million by 1870. The spread of rural post offices brought sections of the population into direct contact with government in ways never before possible, ranging from the payment of pensions to the gathering of intelligence. Post Office savings banks, introduced in 1861, played a part in the growth of the *money economy.

After the *Anglo-Irish treaty of 1921 British stamps were rapidly overprinted with the name of the *Irish Free State, but were replaced from December 1922 with new designs, although much of the personnel and equipment of the Irish Post Office remained intact.

Reynolds, M., *A History of the Irish Post Office* (1983)

RJH

potatoes (*Solanum tuberosum*) originated in the South American Andes. Wild potatoes were brought into cultivation some 2,000 years before the Spanish conquest. They reached Europe in the late 16th century and were cultivated in English gardens a few years later. Their arrival in Ireland is obscure. A Spanish origin is hinted at by the early Irish name for the potato: *an spáinneach*. There is no certain evidence about the date or means of arrival, although tradition gives Sir Walter *Raleigh the credit. The earliest documentary reference to potato cultivation in Ireland is in a lease dated 1606 granting Scottish immigrants land in Co. Down.

Initially potatoes were grown as a garden crop. In the 1640s and 1650s they were common in Munster and Leinster gardens. The most plausible explanation for transition from gardens to fields is that potatoes were an excellent clearing crop on newly tilled land and valuable as a rotational crop to restore the fertility of land used for cereals. As the demand for Irish cereals increased, potatoes entered cultivation regimes. The process accelerated from the mid-18th century under the stimulus of rising cereal prices. Potatoes in Ireland served similar functions to those of turnips in England, but they were better suited to Ireland's cool climate and wet soils. To cultivate, ridges, called 'lazy beds', were dug in which the sprouting tubers were placed. Several varieties were grown. 'Black', 'cup', and 'apple' varieties were highly prized, but the poor cultivated the high-yielding though watery 'lumper'. By the early 19th century over 2 million acres were under potatoes, yielding from 6 to 8 tons per acre.

The chronology of potato diffusion within Irish *diet has generated debate. Until cultivated as field crops on a large scale, potatoes were never more than a dietary supplement. However by the early 19th century they were the staple food, assuring the poor of a highly nutritious diet. The most common method of cooking was boiling. Consumption was between 10 and 15 pounds daily, sometimes eaten at two meals, at other times three, depending on the season. Potatoes, accompanied by milk or herrings, were rich in the nutrients required for human existence.

Between 1845 and 1849 the potato crop was ruined three times by *Phytophthora infestans*, commonly called potato blight. Since over 3 million people were totally dependent upon potatoes for food, famine (see GREAT FAMINE) was inevitable. The dominant role of the potato in the Irish diet was not restored. EMC

poultry were probably introduced to Ireland from Roman Britain. From earliest times they have been kept for both meat and eggs. Intensive, large-scale poultry keeping, however, developed only during the late 19th century. By 1900 there were about 18.5 million poultry in Ireland, more than three times the number recorded in 1850.

During the 1890s, there was much official debate on the necessity of reorganizing the Irish egg trade. Poultry-keeping had become a major source of income for farm women, who used the profits to obtain items such as tea, sugar, or clothing. By 1900, even tiny western farms might keep flocks of around 100 chickens. It was estimated that 20 hens equalled a cow in value, and on many of these smallholdings only one cow was kept. Irish eggs, however, had a very poor reputation with retailers. Poultry breeds were not systematically improved, and there were allegations that both farm women and the shopkeepers or egg merchants with whom they dealt held on to eggs until prices rose, with the result that they were often inedible by the time they reached urban markets. In 1897, merchants in Liverpool and Glasgow threatened to boycott Irish eggs if the situation did not improve.

Public bodies, including the *Congested Districts Board and the Department of *Agriculture and Technical Instruction, attempted to improve poultry breeding by distributing cockerels, pullets, and eggs to small farmers. This succeeded to the extent that breeds such as the Leghorn, Dorking, Brahma, and Frizzle became common. Poultry keeping classes and egg-laying competitions were organized, and these also had a significant effect. After 1897, the *Irish Agricultural Organization Society began to encourage the formation of local societies to collect, grade, and pack eggs. By 1900, 21 specialist egg societies were established. This development had a major effect, despite complaints from farm women that it would lead to the transfer of income to the control of men. During the 1920s, legislation in both the Irish Free State and Northern Ireland required eggs to be tested and graded before packing, and intensive poultry farming became one of the most profitable aspects of Irish farming.

Bolger, P., *The Irish Co-operative Movement* (1977)

JB

Powell, Humphrey (*fl.* 1548–67), first *printer in Ireland. *The Boke of *Common Praier* (1551) was his first book. VK

Power, John O'Connor (1848–1919), nationalist politician. Born in Ballinasloe, Co. Galway, into great poverty, he emigrated to Rochdale, joined the *Fenians, and was involved in the raid on Chester Castle 1867. An impressive orator and early advocate of Fenian involvement in agrarian agitation, he joined the *Home Rule League 1873, became MP for Mayo 1874, and was expelled from the *IRB in 1877. An early exponent of parliamentary obstruction, his political career was destroyed in an open breach with *Parnell over *Land League neglect of the small farmers' interests. JL

Poynings's Law (1494), introduced by Sir Edward Poynings, lord deputy 1494–5. It required the lord deputy and council to seek the king's permission to summon an Irish parliament and his approval of proposed draft bills. The king and English privy council sent back a licence to hold parliament at a specified time with the approved bills. The object was to restrict the autonomy of lords deputy—the earl of Kildare having used the 1487 parliament to ratify his coronation of the pretender Lambert *Simnel—rather than to curb the law-making potential of parliament itself. An Irish government councillor normally travelled with the proposed legislation to secure its transmission from England. There bills were often altered and occasionally new ones inserted. The Irish parliament in turn amended and even rejected transmitted bills.

English lords deputy after 1534 regarded Poynings's Law as an impediment to their management of parliament because local opponents used it as a delaying tactic. It was suspended in 1536 to put through the complicated *Reformation legislation. In the 1541–3 parliament, amended bills had to be re-transmitted to England and passed in a later session. The next parliament (1557) modified the statute to take account of this development. Lords deputy *Sidney (1569) and *Perrot (1585) encountered problems when parliament refused to suspend Poynings's Law, fearing anti-Catholic legislation. James I's apprehensions prevented *Chichester demanding a suspension in the 1613–15 parliament, which saw the amending process in full swing and the first use of the *heads of bills procedure.

*Wentworth turned Poynings's law into a weapon against the legislature. Rather than risk losing control by asking for suspension, he used it as an executive instrument to guide legislative activity and parliamentary debate. In 1634–5 he refused the nobility prior sight of proposed enactments and later turned down their proposals on the *Graces on the grounds that only the executive could initiate legislation. Wentworth prevented parliament acting unilaterally as a court of law and converted the single bill it rejected into an act of state. He used the same interpretation to railroad his programme through the 1640–1 parliament, but after his departure opposition developed. Parliament began demanding the statute's clarification so that it could draw up its own bills without government interference. Poynings's Law proved a stumbling block in the *Ormond peace negotiations during the ensuing *Confederate War.

When parliament next met, in 1661–6, renewed attempts by members of both Commons and Lords to play a more active role in the legislative process once again created controversy. In 1662, for example, the Irish privy council, in response to some ill-chosen observations by the Commons, vigorously asserted its sole right to transmit bills. Despite this, the role of parliament in preparing and considering legislation through the heads of bill procedure now became more clearly defined. MPs (for it was the Commons rather than the Lords that were to the fore on this issue) were careful not to trespass unduly on the sensitivities of either the council or the lord lieutenant. Ministers in London and their deputies in Ireland were content that Poynings's Law should operate in this manner, since it facilitated the operations of parliament while upholding both the crown's authority to determine when and if an Irish parliament should be convened and the privy council's right to veto any measures forwarded to it.

The mood of MPs was less accommodating in the early 1690s. Their claim to possess the *'sole right' to initiate financial legislation was not conceded, but their assertiveness ensured that thereafter the bulk of Irish legislation originated in the form of heads of bills in the House of Commons. In practice, only a small proportion of such bills were respited or postponed, generally on the grounds of incompatibility with existing British legislation, egregious drafting error, or the lobbying of vested interests. By contrast, the proportion of Irish bills that were amended was high. In most cases, the amendments were minor clarifications of syntax or meaning, but a significant proportion had important provisions added, deleted, or recast to bring them into line with English law or to meet the objections of interested parties. Poynings's Law thus continued to ensure that the Irish legislature did not threaten the inherently subordinate position of the kingdom of Ireland. Its operation was nevertheless accepted by most Irish MPs, despite the objections of the *patriot minority, throughout the early and mid-18th century. It was not until 1782 that *Yelverton's Act terminated the need for a heads of bills procedure by empowering the Irish legislature to propose legislation. The Irish privy council was deprived of its power to amend or to respite bills, and while the English privy council retained the right to refuse the royal assent, it exercised this judiciously until the Act of *Union abolished the need for Poynings's Law.

Clarke, Aidan, 'The History of Poynings's Law 1615–41', *Irish Historical Studies*, 18 (1972)

Edwards, R. D., and Moody, T. W., 'The History of Poynings's Law, Part I: 1494–1615', *Irish Historical Studies*, 2 (1941)

JK/HM

pre-Christian religions. The absence of literary evidence from the pre-Christian period means that any discussion of its religious beliefs must remain conjectural; and such conjecture becomes more hazardous the further removed we are in time from the period under consideration. The earliest indications of a concern with the supernatural are more or less elaborate burial customs: thus the *neolithic passage graves in the Boyne valley testify to the great skill and effort which their builders were prepared to invest in the housing of the dead. The most remarkable of these tombs, that at Newgrange (*c.*3000 BC), is aligned with the winter solstice, suggesting that a connection was believed to exist between the fate of those interred there and the movements of the sun.

*Iron Age artefacts, especially those in the Celtic La Tène style, may provide some indication of the inherited beliefs of the first Irish converts to Christianity. Precious objects recovered from bodies of water were probably often ritual depositions, as seems to have been the case with the *Celts of Britain and the Continent; this in turn may reflect belief in divinities dwelling in the depths. Carved stones, although difficult to interpret, are also likely in many cases to have had a ritual significance. Some, such as the Turoe Stone near Galway, are decorated with abstract designs;

there are also a few figures, such as the images of one-armed men associated with Tandragee, Co. Armagh. One of the most important ceremonial sites of this period is Navan Fort, Co. Armagh (earlier *Emain Macha): *c*.90 BC a large structure was erected here, then deliberately burned and carefully buried.

Greek and Roman testimony concerning the Celts of Britain and the Continent, together with inscriptions and images from these areas, provides evidence which helps to supplement the gaps in the Irish data: the *druids of Ireland, for example, probably had much in common with their counterparts to the east. The same sources can serve to corroborate the pre-Christian background of medieval accounts of the Tuatha Dé ('Tribes of the Gods') or *áes síde* ('people of the hollow hills'; fairies): thus Irish Ogma has a counterpart in the Gaulish god of eloquence Ogmios, Nuadu in the Romano-British deity Nodons, and Lug in the Lugus attested throughout the Celtic world.

By far the largest body of evidence is to be found in the medieval literature. Here there is a wealth of tales and traditions concerning the Tuatha Dé, variously interpreted as demons or (as in **Lebor Gabála*) as human beings; the invocation of their names in magical texts indicates that even monastic scribes had some belief in their supernatural efficacy. In addition, such extensive bodies of narrative as the Ulster and Fenian cycles are set in the pre-Christian period and purport to describe the society of that time, furnishing details of divination rituals, spells, and the sacral dimension of kingship.

In assessing this material, however, due account must be taken of the fact that its authors were Christians, and that their own connection with earlier traditions was ambivalent and often tenuous. Much has been lost, whether through oblivion or deliberate suppression; and in many cases the record has been embellished and confused by the invention of clerical authors. The last decade has witnessed a vigorous critique of perceived 'nativist' tendencies to see medieval Irish culture as having been primarily a continuation of its pre-Christian antecedents: sometimes this revisionist case has been overstated, but the cautionary note sounded has been a valuable one.

Mac Cana, P., *Celtic Mythology* (2nd edn., 1983)
McCone, K., *Pagan Past and Christian Present in Early Irish Literature* (1990)

JPC

Premonstratensian canons were established in Ireland from Dryburgh in Scotland by 1182. Initially patronized by Anglo-Normans, they received much support in the west of Ireland from Gaelic patrons; the houses at Lough Key (*c*.1215), Kilross (*c*.1233), and Lough Oughter (1250), in Co. Roscommon, were founded by Clarus Mac Mailin, archdeacon of Elphin (d. 1251). Approximately six abbeys and five smaller priories or cells were founded between 1182 and 1260 but conventual life in many houses had collapsed by the 15th century.

A foundation was made at Kilnacrott, Co. Cavan, in 1924. CNÓC

Prendergast, Maurice de, Cambro-Norman adventurer from the Flemish settlement of Rhos in Pembrokeshire, who landed at Bannow about May 1169 to fight for Diarmait *Mac Murchada, but subsequently defected to Diarmait's enemy, Domnall Mac Gilla Pátraic, king of Osraige; he went on to fight for Richard fitz Gilbert, alias *Strongbow, who succeeded to Leinster after Mac Murchada's death in 1171, and as a reward for military service was endowed with lands in Co. Wexford. MTF

Presbyterianism. Irish Presbyterianism is largely the result of a movement of population from Scotland to Ireland in the 17th century. Some Presbyterian ministers followed these Scots settlers and took livings in the episcopal *Church of Ireland, many subsequently being ejected during *Wentworth's campaign for greater ecclesiastical uniformity. In 1642 a presbytery was constituted in Ulster by the chaplains of a Scottish army which had arrived to crush the *rising of 1641. During the *Cromwellian regime congregations multiplied and new presbyteries were formed. Nonconforming ministers were ejected from parishes after the *Restoration, but the minority colonial administration in Ireland could not afford to alienate such a substantial proportion of the Protestant population and Presbyterianism was allowed a precarious existence, its ministers supported by the **regium donum*.

*William III rewarded Presbyterian support against *James II with an increased *regium donum*. From the 1690s, despite the rearguard action of the *high-church movement, Presbyterian congregations, now organized in the *Synod of Ulster, enjoyed practical freedom of religion, confirmed in the Toleration Act of 1719. Yet their members remained highly conscious both of continuing disabilities and of economic hardship, most of them being tenant farmers chafing under rent increases and payment of *tithes. Presbyterians consistently made up the majority of emigrants from Ulster to colonial America. Others became involved in movements for reform, culminating in the *United Irish movement, in which Presbyterians played a prominent part.

Meanwhile the synod was divided by tensions between New Lights and *Old Lights, often centring on the issue of *subscription to the Westminster Confession of Faith which the synod, following the Church of Scotland, had adopted as its statement of doctrine. The triumph of non-subscription in the synod enabled conservative Scottish Presbyterian dissenters, *Seceders and *Covenanters, to establish a strong presence in Ulster.

In the 19th century awareness that some non-subscribers were in fact *Arians initiated a new phase of the conflict, ending when seventeen ministers opposed to subscription seceded with their congregations to form the *Remonstrant Synod. This led to the restoration of obligatory subscription and union with the Seceders to form the General Assembly of the Presbyterian church in Ireland (1840). The united church displayed great creative energy in foreign missionary outreach and in establishing new institutions in Ireland, including two theological colleges. A revival of *evangelical religion in 1859 breathed new life into dry Presbyterian bones but also sharpened traditional anti-Catholicism.

The victory of theological conservatism did not mean the eclipse of political liberalism. In the 1820s, as in the 1790s, theological and political loyalties did not always coincide. Conservatives in theology might be liberals in politics and vice versa. Many Presbyterians continued to support the *Liberal Party until Gladstone's conversion to home rule in 1886. *Partition left them the largest Protestant denomination in Northern Ireland with some 390,000 members in 1926; numbers in independent Ireland, where Presbyterians had never put down strong roots, fell from 32,000 in 1926 to only 16,000 by 1971. While some Presbyterians have been prominent in recent movements for reconciliation in Ireland, Irish Presbyterianism has become increasingly exclusivist, as evidenced by withdrawal from the World Council of Churches in 1980, and refusal to join the recently formed British and Irish Council of Churches.

Brooke, Peter, *Ulster Presbyterianism* (1987)
Holmes, Finlay, *Our Irish Presbyterian Heritage* (1992)

RFGH

president of Ireland. Under articles 12–14 of the 1937 *constitution, the president is the head of state, elected by popular vote for a seven-year term. The president is also commander-in-chief of the armed forces, though this command is 'regulated by law'. De *Valera stated in 1937 that the president's function was 'to guard the people's rights and mainly to guard the constitution'. Most of his or her powers and functions are exercised on the advice of the government and on the advice of the council of state, whose function is 'to aid and counsel the President' on matters defined by the constitution. There are other restrictions on the incumbent: he or she cannot leave the state without the government's permission; an address to the *Oireachtas must be approved by the government; and the president can be impeached, although this process requires a two-thirds majority of the Oireachtas.

The most important discretionary powers exercised on the president's own initiative are (1) to refuse 'in his absolute discretion' a dissolution to a *taoiseach who has no *Dáil majority; (2) to convene a meeting of the Oireachtas after consulting the council of state; and (3) to refer a bill to the *Supreme Court for a decision on its constitutionality. DMcM

president of the executive council, title of the prime minister of the *Irish Free State 1922–37. Under the 1922 *constitution he was nominated by the *Dáil. He could nominate the vice-president but the other members of the executive council had to be approved by the Dáil. If the president lost a majority in the Dáil, the executive council had to resign and, an important restriction, dissolution was on the council's advice, not his. DMcM

Preston, of Gormanston, Co. Meath, a Catholic noble family founded by Roger of Preston who arrived from Lancashire in 1326 to pursue a legal career in Ireland. His son Robert, who purchased Gormanston in 1363, became lord *chancellor. Another Robert was created the first Viscount Gormanston after being appointed deputy lieutenant in 1478. Although a Geraldine backer of the Yorkist pretender Lambert *Simnel, he was again deputy lieutenant in 1493–4. His son William led the *Pale forces at *Knockdoe and was lord justice in the absence of the 8th earl of *Kildare in 1515.

When Kildare hegemony ended and as the *Old English position deteriorated, the Prestons frequently found themselves in opposition to the government. Christopher, 4th viscount and father of Thomas *Preston (d. 1600), opposed *cess; Jenico, 5th viscount (d. 1630), led an Old English delegation to London after the farcical first session of the 1613–15 parliament, and Nicholas, 6th viscount (d. 1643), was an opponent of *Wentworth and a *Confederate Catholic commander. His son Jenico, 7th viscount (d. 1691), was a *Jacobite, but his nephew Anthony, 9th viscount (d. 1716), managed to regain the family estates under the treaty of *Limerick. Jenico, 12th viscount (1775–1820), was an active member of the *Catholic Committee.

In the 19th century the Gormanstons became part of the United Kingdom establishment. Edward, 13th viscount, was sheriff of Meath and Dublin and gained a UK peerage in 1868. His son Jenico, 14th viscount (1837–1907), was a colonial governor in various minor territories terminating with Tasmania (1893–1900). HM

Preston, Christopher (d. 1422). The alleged 'conspiracy' of Sir Christopher Preston in 1418 took place against the background of the *Talbot–Ormond feud. It was said that Preston, with the earl of Kildare and Sir John Bellew, had 'sought to commune with the prior of Kilmainham', Thomas Butler. Whether they did indeed plan to replace the lieutenant, or whether they intended merely to bring complaints about Talbot to England, they were arrested and their lands forfeited. The case was resolved, apparently in their favour, after a hearing in England. The incident is remembered mainly for the discovery that Preston had in his possession when arrested copies of the coronation oath and of the *Modus tenendi parliamentum, suggesting a constitutional dimension to the affair. DBJ

Preston, Thomas (1585–1655), *Confederate Catholic general of Leinster. An expert at siege warfare, he took Birr (1643), Ballinakill (1643), Duncannon (1645), Roscommon (1646), and Carlow (1648), and made honourable defences of Waterford (1650) and Galway (1652), but lost disastrously in the field at New Ross (1642) and *Dungan's Hill (1648). Quarrels with Castlehaven and Owen Roe *O'Neill aborted important campaigns. Excommunicated by *Rinuccini, he found the royalists, who made him Viscount Tara, more amenable allies.

See CONFEDERATE WAR. HM

Primary Valuation, also known as Griffith's Valuation, after its director, Richard *Griffith. Initiated to provide a basis for the calculation of rates levied under the *poor law, it was carried out county by county between 1848 and 1860. The results (though subject to appeal—hence the term 'primary') were set out in printed volumes, showing the occupants of land and houses, the persons from whom these were leased, and their area and value. Spokesmen for tenant farmers frequently appealed to the valuation as evidence that rents were excessive, although the reality was that Griffith's valuations were based on the unusually low agrarian prices recorded during 1849–52.

primatial controversy. Armagh's primatial claims were articulated in the 7th century and rested on recognition of *Patrick as apostle of Ireland and acknowledgement of papal primacy. Churches such as Kildare resisted but by the 9th century Armagh's theoretical pre-eminence was accepted and exercised through tribute collection.

A challenge to Armagh's primacy emerged after 1074 when archbishops of *Canterbury consecrated Dublin's bishop-elect. The canonical oath used implied that Ireland lay under Canterbury's primacy. In 1096 a new twist came when Dublin's Bishop Samuel made primatial claims against Armagh. When his successor Gréne was in Canterbury for consecration, Cellach, the reformist archbishop of Armagh, occupied Dublin. The *papacy's erection of four archdioceses (1152) did not settle the question. After the *Anglo-Norman invasion, Dublin's primatial claim was influenced by the ecclesiastical politics of the Anglo-Norman colony, though a desire for provincial autonomy seems to have cut across any simple ethnic division. In 1182, at John *Cumin's behest, the papacy abolished Armagh's right to all-Ireland tribute and restricted its jurisdictional claims over Dublin. These measures were reiterated in 1216 and 1221, but in 1244 Pope Innocent IV ordered an investigation of the question. At this stage the papacy was sympathetic to Armagh. In the 14th century Edward III intervened first for Armagh (1349) and later for Dublin (1352). In 1365 he appears to have advised the Irish to settle their dispute by adopting the English formula, giving Armagh primacy of All-Ireland and Dublin the primacy of Ireland.

The controversy died down in the 15th century but in 1533 Armagh again claimed primacy. In 1551 Edward VI transferred primacy outright to Dublin but Mary reversed this in 1553. Dublin's Archbishop Bulkeley (1619–50) clashed with Christopher Hampton and James *Ussher on the question but King Charles I, on the basis of Ussher's scholarly investigations, ceded primacy definitively to Armagh.

Despite persecutions, Catholic archbishops continued the dispute. In 1670 Armagh's Oliver *Plunkett and Dublin's Peter Talbot quarrelled over who should be first to sign the proposed declaration of loyalty to Charles II. Plunkett published *Ius primatiale* (1672) and, although *Propaganda imposed a silence on the question, Talbot, exiled in Lille, published *Primatas Dubliniensis* (1674). Penal rigours did not prevent Hugh McMahon of Armagh (1714–37) publishing *Ius primatiale Armacanum* in 1728. In the late 18th century Archbishop *Troy of Dublin took precedence in government negotiations, and Dublin maintained a practical primacy, especially under Paul *Cullen, the first Irish cardinal. But from 1893, Rome, by conferring the red hat on Armagh archbishops only, ceded the titular primacy to Armagh. TO'C

printing and publishing. Printing was a late arrival in Ireland, introduced by government for administrative and propaganda purposes. The first book, printed in Dublin in 1551 by Humphrey *Powell, was *The Boke of *Common Praier.* For almost a century there was never more than a single press in operation, and the output was small.

From 1604 government control was exercised through the king's printer's patent, which granted to the holder a monopoly over all printing and bookselling. In theory this monopoly held, except for a short period in the 1640s, until 1732; in fact the stranglehold it created was effectively ended by the legal challenge offered in 1680–1 by Joseph *Ray, permitting a rapid expansion thereafter in the book trades.

In the provinces during the troubled 1640s the propaganda needs of the warring factions of king, parliament, and *Confederate Catholics led to presses being established in Waterford (1643), Kilkenny (1646), and Cork (1648). We have firm evidence of a press in only one other town in the 17th century—Belfast (1694).

In 1670 the few booksellers working in Dublin joined together with two other trades, the cutlers and the painter-stainers, to found the Guild of St Luke. Although it continued in existence until 1841 the guild never really became a regulatory force.

The British Copyright Act of 1709 did not extend to Ireland, and so cheap reprints of London publications became the staple of the Dublin book trade. The 18th century proved to be the most successful period in its history. The printer-bookseller predominated, George *Faulkner being the prime example. Specialist printers, like Samuel Powell, were the exception.

Up to the early 1780s most of the books printed were sold on the domestic market. When export restrictions were fully lifted in 1783 there was a huge increase in overseas trade, especially to America. *Wilson's Dublin Directories* record an expansion in book trade businesses from 70 in 1781 to 118 in 1793. But the 1790s saw a disastrous decline, the crucial factor being the expense and lack of paper. A wave of key figures emigrated to America. The decline was compounded by the fact that many in the book trade were members of the *United Irishmen, and were imprisoned or exiled after the *insurrection of 1798.

Beyond the capital only the cities could support specialist printer-booksellers, Eugene *Swiney and James Haly in Cork, and the *Blows and the *Joys in Belfast being examples. The establishment of provincial *newspapers was the impetus to the spread of the printing press beyond the main cities. By 1800 presses had been established in 34 provincial towns.

The output of these provincial presses was of local interest, and they seldom undertook reprints of London works. Thus they were not affected by the extension of the Copyright Act to Ireland in 1801, and the period up to 1840 was one of further expansion. The loss of the reprint trade, however, had a devastating effect on the Dublin printers. The publication of books plummeted 80 per cent, it is said, in the first half of the century and booksellers relied heavily on the sale of imported books. John *Cumming was the largest importer in this period and a publisher of note. The printers who survived best were those that had government contracts, or were official printers to learned bodies or societies.

The publication of William Carleton's very popular *Traits and Stories of the Irish Peasantry* by Curry & Company of Dublin in 1830 was a watershed in the revival of native publishing. It proved that an Irish writer could be successful without having to appear under a London imprint. The lesson was learned by James *Duffy, who in the following decade published many of the authors of the *Young Ireland movement in his series The Library of Ireland. Also in the 1840s the long-established Belfast firm of *Simms & M'Intyre took on the British market with their revolutionary Parlour Library series of cheap fiction.

Parallel with these developments, from 1831 onwards the commissioners of national education (see NATIONAL SCHOOLS) started to issue their schoolbooks, Alexander *Thom being the principal printer. Their phenomenal success led to a large export trade to Britain and the colonies.

The recovery of the book trade was interrupted by the devastations of the *Great Famine of 1845–9, and some of the largest firms in Dublin went bankrupt, Milliken, Folds, Coyne, and Curry among them.

Provincial presses suffered a decline in the second half of the century. The improved *postal service and the spread of the *railway network meant that the bigger towns could supply the printing needs of wider areas. However, improved communications also allowed the larger Irish firms to print and publish for the British market and the colonies. Starting in 1846 James McGlashan published jointly with many of the large British houses, and Michael Henry *Gill, at the *Dublin University Press, printed for many of them. The Dublin branch of W. H. Smith, booksellers and newsagents (taken over in 1886 by

*Easons), established a nationwide wholesale network. Printing works, such as *Marcus Ward and Guys of Cork, both founded in the 1840s, and later Bairds in Belfast (1862), were established and expanded over the years.

The second half of the century was one of stability and steady growth, but it ended, and the new century began, with the trade in the slough of a general economic depression. The Irish literary revival did encourage the foundation of Maunsel and the *Dun Emer/Cuala Press, but these were peripheral to the main trends. The circumstances of the *First World War led to rampant inflation in printers' wages (265 per cent between 1913 and 1920) and huge rises in printing costs.

The depression continued after independence in 1922. The *Censorship of Publications Act (1926) tempered any adventurousness that publishers may have had. The dominant Dublin houses were the Talbot Press, Duffy, and Gills, whose output was a mixture of schoolbooks, light literature, and Catholic piety. The *Dundalgan Press in Dundalk was one of the few provincial houses undertaking any significant publication. Irish-language publishing (e.g. An Gúm, the government's imprint, founded in 1926, and Sáirséal agus Dill, started in 1945), buoyed up by state encouragement, could afford to be more innovative.

The poor standard of Irish typography was a recurrent complaint throughout the 1920s, 1930s, and 1940s. A beacon of good taste at this time was Colm Ó Lochlainn's *Three Candles Press, founded in 1926.

During the *Economic War large tariffs on imports led to a printing boom. But with the settlement of 1938 the industry was thrown back into recession. Unemployment among Dublin printers was six times higher than in previous years. Stasis continued during and after the *Second World War, the foundation of the *Mercier Press being an exception.

Many Irish authors still had to go to London to be published. Liam Miller founded the *Dolmen Press (1951–87) to provide an outlet for them. At the same time his high standards of typography lifted the design standards in the industry as a whole.

Publishing languished in the 1950s and 1960s. The recurrent need for textbooks meant that the educational houses weathered the storm better than the general trade houses. In contrast, by 1960 the printing trade was booming, riding the crest of industrial revival. However, the revolution then happening in printing technology was soon to disrupt matters. The full impact in Ireland took place during the oil crises of the mid-1970s, and led to recession and much industrial unrest.

In 1974 one of the largest firms, the Irish University Press, went bankrupt. Ironically its failure helped fuel the revival in Irish publishing then under way. Several of its redundant staff went on to establish their own publishing ventures, Irish Academic Press, Wolfhound, and the periodical *Books Ireland* among them. At the same time the Blackstaff Press was founded in Belfast, to be followed a few years later by Appletree. The revival can be attributed to improvements in economic conditions and educational levels, and to changes in printing technology. During the 1980s the number of publishers increased by a third.

In 1970 Clé, the Irish Book Publishers' Association, was founded to promote the output of the industry. Centralized distribution was an innovation of the 1980s, and Gill & Macmillan Distribution now handles the output of the largest trade publishers. In 1990 the demand from the publishing industry was such that the first specialist book printer, ColourBooks, could be launched and has proved a success thus far.

Farmar, Tony, *A Brief History of Clé [the Irish Publishers' Association] 1970–1987* (1995)
Pollard, M., *Dublin's Trade in Books 1550–1800* (1989)
Wheeler, W. G., 'The Spread of Provincial Printing in Ireland up to 1850', *Irish Booklore*, 4/1 (1978)

VK

printmaking, using wooden or metal plates, provided not only a means of producing multiple copies of a given work, but an alternative way of creating a visual image. Mezzotint engraving, where the surface of a plate was roughened to create tones and half-tones, flourished in Ireland during the 18th century. The first artist to practise mezzotint in Dublin, the obscure Thomas Beard (active *c.*1728), went there from London. Thomas Frye (1710–62), trained in his native Dublin, went to London early, and established himself as a portrait painter. Later turning to mezzotint, he published two impressive series of life-size decorative heads in 1760–1. Captain William Baillie (1723–1810), born in Carlow, produced a small group of mezzotints, but is chiefly known as an etcher. In 1776 he reworked the original plate of Rembrandt's *Hundred Guilder Print*.

The prolific John Brooks (active 1730–56) and his assistant Andrew Miller (d. 1763), both trained by Faber in London, started mezzotinting in Dublin in 1741, where their star pupil was James McArdell (1728/9–1765). McArdell left for London with Brooks in 1746, and quickly established himself, engraving over 200 plates, including 38 mezzotints after Reynolds, before his early death.

Edward Fisher (1722–c.1785) went to London early and may have worked in McArdell's studio. Other Brooks pupils combined artistic achievement with debauchery. Richard Houston (1721/2–1775), who followed his master to London after 1746 and became McArdell's main rival, engraving a good series of plates after Reynolds, spent time in the Fleet Prison. Charles Spooner, who went to London in 1752, died through habitual drunken brawling in 1767. Richard Purcell, active 1746–66 and lured to London in 1755, produced many plates but ended his short life in debt and living under a false name.

Back in Ireland Michael Ford (d. 1765) took over Brooks's shop in Cork Hill. His plates are all rare. Some of Robert West's pupils in the Dublin Society's Schools became outstanding mezzotinters. West taught through the medium of pastel, which has particular affinity with mezzotint scraping. One of his pupils, John Dixon (d. 1811), engraved John Rocque's *Map of County Dublin* in 1760. Dixon moved to London about 1765, and engraved many mezzotints after Reynolds and Gainsborough. He moved in the circles of *Burke, Johnson, and Garrick. Another of West's pupils, James Watson (d. 1790), went immediately to London, where he probably learnt mezzotinting from McArdell. A perfectionist, he engraved 56 plates after Reynolds. His daughter Caroline made stipple engravings after Reynolds and others, and in 1785 was appointed Engraver to Queen Caroline. James *Barry, remembered more as a painter, was also one of the most original printmakers of his time. The etchings relating to his murals for the Royal Society of Arts in London, finished in 1783, rank as independent works of art.

Apart from the topographical aquatints by such artists as Jonathan Fisher (d. 1809) and Denis Sullivan, published in book form, the 19th century in Ireland has little to show in printmaking. The situation alters in the early 20th century, with the revival of wood engraving. Robert Gibbings (b. Cork 1889; d. London 1958) founded the Society of Wood Engravers and the Golden Cockerel Press, publishing many beautiful books. The Lady Mabel Annesley (b. in Castlewellan, Co. Down 1881; d. 1959) became a member of the Society of Wood Engravers in 1924. In 1932 and 1939 she presented the Belfast Museum with her fine collection of contemporary wood engravings before emigrating to New Zealand. John F. Hunter (1893–1951) and E. M. O'Rorke Dickey (1894–1977), while important art educators, were masters of woodcut and wood engraving.

Many 20th-century painters or sculptors also made prints, including the southerners Harry Kernoff, Louis le Brocquy, Cecil King, Micheal Farrell, Patrick Hickey, Anne Yeats, John Behan, and Robert Ballagh, some of whom have collaborated with poets on folios. Comparable northerners include Colin Middleton, Roy Johnston, Felim Egan, Victor Sloan, and John Kindness. Specialist printmakers grew in number. Tim Mara (1948–97), professor of printmaking at the Royal College of Art from 1990, became one of the most skilled technical exponents of screenprinting in Britain. An important Irish-American printmaker, Mary Farl Powers, died young in Dublin in 1992.

Chaloner Smith, J., *British Mezzotinto Portraits*, 4 vols. (1878–83)
Mara, T., *Thames and Hudson Technical Manual of Screen Printing* (1979)
Wax, C., *The Mezzotint* (1990)

MA

prison. Before the mid-18th century most Irish offenders were not punished by imprisonment. *Capital and corporal punishments, fines, and *transportation were widely employed. Prisons were used largely to hold people awaiting trial. Houses of correction, controlled by *grand juries, began to appear in Ireland from 1635, but initially these were intended to confine beggars. Only during the 18th century did they evolve into prisons. By the end of the century Ireland had 41 county and borough prisons and 112 bridewells for petty offenders and *debtors. Criticisms of Irish prisons by the English reformer John Howard in the late 1770s led to major changes and in 1786 an inspector-general, Sir Jeremiah Fitzpatrick, was appointed to supervise the whole Irish prison system.

At the end of the 18th century emphasis began to be placed more on the regulation of the mind of the prisoner rather than on the punishment of his or her body. This led to the establishment of penitentiaries: institutions in which every aspect of the inmate's behaviour and thought could be closely monitored and strictly controlled. As the number of capital offences was reduced drastically in the 1820s, a programme of prison building began in Ireland, influenced by the penitentiary concept. The Crumlin Road jail (1846) in Belfast and Mountjoy jail (1850) in Dublin were built along these lines.

The Irish prison population increased substantially around 1850, due to the curtailing of transportation and to the *Famine. In 1854 a new convict prisons board was established, under the chairmanship of Sir Walter Crofton, who pioneered the so-called 'progressive stage' or Irish system of incarceration, which was widely copied in Europe and America. Convicts progressed through four stages during their sentences: first, solitary confinement; then hard labour; thirdly, training in an intermediate prison; and finally release on licence, under strict police supervision. Women convicts went through a somewhat similar regime, being sent prior to release to refuges run by religious organizations.

In 1877 the Irish Prisons Board was established to regulate the whole system and the number of prisons was reduced from 137 in 1877 to 23 by 1914 In the latter year they included a *borstal and an inebriates' reformatory.

In 1921 the Ministry of Home Affairs took charge of the prison system in *Northern Ireland and developed the Crumlin Road jail as a major prison to replace Mountjoy and Portlaoise, which remained the main prisons in the south. In 1928 the Prisons Board was abolished in the *Irish Free State and its responsibilities transferred to the Department of Justice.

McDowell, R. B., *The Irish Administration, 1801–1914* (1964)

ELM

privy council, the main executive and administrative organ of state in Ireland between 1534 and 1800. It assisted the chief governors (see LORD DEPUTY; LORD LIEUTENANT; LORDS JUSTICES) and carried on routine administration under instruction from the monarch's privy council in London. It often had over 20 members, including leading bishops and peers, but only half, usually the principal office holders, were active participants. 'Grand councils', enlarged by the nobility, also met in the 16th century to approve military 'hostings' and *cesses and for ceremonial occasions such as the swearing-in of the chief governor.

In 1560 the privy council acquired a seal, the signet of Ireland, which had to be affixed to all major documents along with the lord deputy's signature. This seal, in the hands of a newly created secretary of state, downgraded the importance of the governor's seal and secretary. The secretary became a key figure, especially with Sir Geoffrey Fenton's tenure, 1579–1608. He controlled correspondence with London and with the rest of Ireland and was the principal intelligence gatherer and spy-master. Furthermore the privy council acquired a regular meeting place when in 1567 Lord Deputy *Sidney built a 'stately drawing-room' in *Dublin Castle.

In the conquest and colonization period the Irish privy council supervised the extension of the common law, the maintenance of order, and attempts to increase revenue and manage *parliament. However, the principal initiators and developers of the policy remained the chief governors, while the privy council's own authority was restricted by the creation of *provincial presidencies. The number of Irish-born privy counsellors steadily declined; although most survived the ramifications of the *Baltinglass revolt, the remnant was purged in the early 1590s. Ironically New English-dominated councils proved a major obstacle to active governors such as *Perrot and Falkland until *Wentworth broke their power.

The privy council continued to decide disputes over land and property rights and where public order was threatened, despite the attempt to separate its judicial functions from routine business by the establishment of the court of *Castle Chamber in 1571. It also issued proclamations, many effectively new laws; some of these were its own acts of state, others were simply dispatched from London. At the close of the 16th century it was known as 'the state', perhaps symptomatic of bureaucratization and centralization.

During the 18th century the duties in the preparation and transmission of bills assigned to the Irish privy council by *Poynings's Law gave it a central role in running parliament. There were frequent complaints at the alteration or suppression of *heads of bills, and bills prepared for parliament by the council sometimes encountered resistance. *Legislative independence after 1782 abolished this part of the Irish privy council's duties, while the increasing importance of the *chief secretary diminished its executive importance.

HM

Progressive Democrats, political party founded in 1985 by Desmond O'Malley and other dissident members of (mostly) *Fianna Fáil. The party urged neoliberal economic strategies, and a moderate line on the partition question: it proposed that the territorial claim on Northern Ireland in the *constitution of 1937 be excised. The PDs achieved massive success at an early stage, carrying fourteen seats in the election of 1987: this total quickly fell to six seats in 1989, when they entered into a coalition government led by Charles Haughey and dominated by Fianna Fáil. In January 1992 the PD ministers helped to force Haughey into resignation; and later that year they removed their support from his successor, Albert Reynolds, finally withdrawing from the coalition government. At the election of November 1992 the party returned ten TDs: but though it was able to maintain this strength until 1997, its place as a junior coalition partner (first to Fianna Fáil and later to *Fine Gael) was taken by *Labour. Although only four PDs were returned at the general election of 1997, they held a tactically crucial position; and three of these deputies served as ministers in the coalition government led by Bertie Ahern and Fianna Fáil. The main achievements of the party have been to moderate some profligate impulses within Fianna Fáil, and to soften the asperity of its stand on Northern Ireland. AJ

Propaganda Fide, congregation of, the central government department of the Catholic church, charged with the direction of missionary activity in Protestant and non-Christian countries. A product of the *Counter-Reformation, it met as a congregation from 1622, centralizing missionary activity in an era of unprecedented European expansion overseas. Because post-Reformation Ireland did not have a properly established hierarchy it fell under Propaganda's jurisdiction until the curial reforms of 1908. Propaganda's influence was important as it handled Irish affairs which, in normal circumstances, would have been dealt with by the local church hierarchy and other Roman congregations. TO'C

prophecies, oral or written texts foretelling future events, were a prominent part of popular culture in many early modern societies, giving apparent shape and purpose to human events and in some cases, like *millenarianism, lending the credibility of supernatural authority to fantasies of radical social change. A papal nuncio in 1640 noted the tendency of the Irish to trust in political prophecies, and their continued power was evident in the career of Baldearg *O'Donnell. Prior to the *insurrection of 1798 prophecies of a coming cataclysm, attributed in one case to St *Colum Cille and in the other to the 13th-century Scottish poet Thomas the Rhymer and the 17th-century Covenanter Alexander Peden, circulated among both Catholics and Presbyterians, with the encouragement of the *United Irishmen. The most influential political prophecies in 19th-century Ireland were those extracted from *Pastorini's *General History*. However texts attributed to St Colum Cille were reported as in circulation among *Ribbonmen in the 1820s, and continued to be printed up to at least 1866, when they were denounced in a pamphlet by R. R. *Madden.

proportional representation (PR), an electoral system designed to ensure that the composition of collective bodies reflects accurately the composition of those electing them, especially in terms of their party political make-up. In its original and simplest form, as it emerged in continental Europe in the 19th century, PR was based on voting for discrete lists of candidates proposed by political parties; seats were allocated to parties by means of a simple mathematical formula in proportion to their share of votes.

An alternative system devised by Thomas Hare in Britain achieved, in adapted form, widespread influence in territories of British influence, beginning with Tasmania (1896) and extending to Ireland for local elections (1919–20) and general elections (1921). This is based on the single transferable vote in multi-member constituencies; voters rank candidates in order of preference, and seats are allocated to candidates winning an electoral quota on the basis of complex rules for the counting of votes and transfer of lower preferences. The aggregate effect of this system is proportional, in that the political composition of elected bodies tends to reflect closely that of the electors.

This system of PR set down deep roots in independent Ireland. It was incorporated in the *constitutions of 1922 and 1937, and survived government-sponsored attempts in 1959 and 1968 to replace it by the British plurality system, which tends to favour larger parties. In *Northern Ireland it was abolished for local elections in 1922 and for elections to the House of Commons in 1929; but it was restored at both of these levels in 1973. JC

Prosperous, Co. Kildare, site of a *cotton spinning factory established *c.*1780 by Richard Brooke. The Irish parliament, anxious to promote industrial development and also attracted by the prospect of relocating part of the capital's disorderly artisan population to a safe distance, made substantial loans and grants, but the venture collapsed in 1786.

prostitution was an accepted feature, particularly of urban life, for centuries. In the second half of the 19th century, however, there was growing concern, reflecting fears of physical and moral contamination, with 'the great social evil'. There was an increase in the numbers of 'penitent asylums' or 'Magdalen asylums' run by Catholic and Protestant organizations to 'reform' women of the streets. Meanwhile concern over the effects of venereal disease on military manpower led to the Contagious Diseases Acts (1864, 1866, and 1869) which applied to specific garrison centres, including, in Ireland, the *Curragh, Cobh, and Cork city. Under these acts any woman suspected of being a prostitute could be arrested and forcibly examined. If infected she would be detained until cured, then issued with a certificate and obliged to return for periodic check-ups. The acts were opposed, in both Great Britain and Ireland, as infringing individual liberty, legitimizing the sexual double standard, and conniving at prostitution. They were repealed in 1887. By this time the Criminal Law Amendment Act (1885) had already brought in more stringent penalties for brothel-keepers and raised the age of consent. Protestant and Catholic vigilance associations regularly claimed success in closing down brothels in the later decades of the 19th century, though they seem often to have merely moved them on. The Legion of Mary seems to have made a genuine impact in Dublin in the 1920s, by providing temporary accommodation and crèche facilities for the women, and helping them to find work, but at this stage, due to greater supervision of youth, and cultural changes generally, comparatively fewer women were working as prostitutes.

For some women prostitution was a temporary, clandestine strategy in difficult times; others, such as the Curragh 'Wrens', living under furze bushes on the perimeter of the Curragh camp, or in the 'Bush' in Cobh, were readily identifiable and miserably poor. Prostitution flourished wherever there was both a concentration of high female unemployment and a throughput of men working in poor conditions far from their homes, if they had any—ports, garrison towns, big cities, short-term engineering works. Prostitutes in Dublin in the 1910s and 1920s are remembered by those who grew up in the nearby tenements as good-looking and well dressed, but virtual prisoners in the brothels, and very generous with the poor children of the locality. Only a minority of prostitutes were ever in 'kip-houses', however; most were street-walkers either working on their own initiative or controlled by men.

Kearns, K., *Dublin Tenement Life: An Oral History* (1994)

Luddy, Maria, *Women and Philanthropy in 19c Ireland* (1995)

CC

protectionism, or the belief that Irish economic interests were best served by policies which protected native producers against foreign competition, first surfaced in the late 17th century, when Irish interests held British mercantilist policies, such as the *Navigation Acts or *Cattle Acts, responsible for economic distress. Since then arguments in favour of protection have surfaced on many occasions, most notably in times of economic recession, and the protectionist case has been argued by many Irish writers, including *Swift, *Berkeley, *Mitchel, and *Griffith.

Irish nationalists have tended to blame the collapse of many Irish industries during the 19th century, and the high level of emigration after the *Great Famine, on the existence of a free-trading area between Britain and Ireland. The belief that protection would stimulate a revival in the Irish economy gained strength from the opinion that the Irish economy prospered during the final decades of the 18th century, as a result of the protectionist measures made possible by *legislative independence. At the beginning of the 20th century, Sinn Féin leader Arthur Griffith provided a blueprint for economic revival which was based on giving protection to 'infant industries'. Although this gained widespread support at the time, during the years 1922–32 the government of the *Irish Free State was loath to embark on widespread protection because of the potential damage to agriculture, the country's largest exporter, and because protection would alienate many established business interests, such as the *brewing industry.

In 1932 the incoming *Fianna Fáil government embarked on a policy of widespread protection for both agriculture and industry. This was consistent with the party's intense nationalism and with its desire to break the remaining ties with Britain, the main source of Irish imports and the destination of over 90 per cent of exports. It was also in keeping with the policy of cultural protectionism, as expressed by the *censorship of films and publications, and indeed with the growth of protectionist measures throughout the world, as a result of the post-1929 Depression. Although the futility of a small country pursuing such a policy became evident during the *Second World War, when the country suffered from shortages of imported fuel, food, raw materials, and manufactured goods, it was continued in the post-war era.

By this stage, however, world economic trends favoured freer trade. Ireland duly joined GATT (the General Agreement on Tariffs and Trade) but otherwise did nothing to end its protectionist ways. The publication of the White Paper **Economic Development* in 1958 marked the first official commitment towards freer trade; however moves in that direction were delayed due to Ireland's failure to join the EEC (see EUROPEAN UNION) in the early 1960s. The first real steps towards dismantling Irish protective tariffs came only with the 1965 *Anglo-Irish trade agreement, in which the United Kingdom and Ireland undertook to establish a joint free-trade area by the mid-1970s. Irish entry to the EEC in 1973 set in train the process of dismantling protective barriers against member countries; this was completed by 1980 despite a significant loss of employment in protected industries during the 1970s.

See also CUSTOMS AND EXCISE; FREE TRADE AGITATION.

MED

Protestant ascendancy, commonly used to describe the Protestant landed elite that dominated Irish society under the *penal laws. The term is also used in relation to the 19th and early 20th centuries, though here the emphasis shifts from political realities to subjective identification, 'the ascendancy' being seen as an exclusive caste whose sense of being the natural leaders of Irish society was increasingly challenged by the rise of Catholic political power.

The term had been traced back to the debate on the *Catholic relief bill of 1782, when Sir Boyle Roche MP (1743–1807) advocated liberating Catholics 'so far as is consistent with the Protestant ascendancy'. It was taken up by defenders of the *Church of Ireland during the *Rightboy attack on the *tithe system in 1786–8, and became firmly established as a slogan during the bitter campaign against the Relief Acts of 1792–3. In all cases what was referred to was a state of affairs: the ascendancy of Protestants over Catholics. It was only later that the term came to refer to an imagined social group, *the* Protestant ascendancy, and that a slogan expressing Protestant anxieties at a time of revolutionary change was retrospectively applied to the 18th century as a whole. The characterization of this 'ascendancy' as a landed elite also obscures the strong middle-class element in Protestant political activism, and Irish Protestant society generally, in the late 18th century and after, while the term 'Protestant', which in the 18th century meant Anglican, leaves the status of Presbyterians and other Protestant dissenters unclear.

provincial presidencies were regional administrations intended to establish English law and order in the outlying parts of Ireland. First proposed by *Cusack as councils run by local lords, they were established in modified form by *Sidney in Connacht and Munster in the late 1560s and early 1570s. Each president had a small military force, two judges, and the advice of a provincial council of local lords and bishops. Permitted discretionary use of *martial law, his main tasks were to extend the common law, search out *concealed lands, dispense justice cheaply, and remove *idlemen. Finance came from regional *compositions, extracted initially by force, later through negotiation with local lords.

Early officials were Englishmen and *Palesmen, who exploited their positions to acquire land in the provinces. In the early 17th century the situation was somewhat reversed, with the local magnates *Clanricard and *Thomond being appointed president. When compositions became payable to the Dublin exchequer, and *assize circuits were extended into Munster and Connacht, the presidencies lost autonomy. However, their equity, summary criminal, and arbitration facilities remained inexpensive and popular, and their military role came to the fore again during the *Confederate War.

Abolished by *Cromwell, the presidencies were revived in 1660 as rewards for Roger Boyle, Baron Broghill (see ORRERY), and Sir Charles *Coote, who were the main Irish agents of the *Restoration. The Munster presidency was particularly vigorous under Orrery, but the whole system was abolished in 1672 to prevent his anti-popery campaign damaging Anglo-French relations. HM

Provisional Government (1922). Under article 17 of the *Anglo-Irish treaty, Southern Ireland MPs elected under the *Government of Ireland Act met in January 1922 to ratify the treaty and appoint a Provisional Government, to which were transferred administrative powers and machinery. Michael *Collins was chairman, succeeded after his death by W. T. *Cosgrave. Until September 1922 the Provisional Government existed side by side with the *Dáil in a system of dual government. The Provisional Government had two tasks: to draft a new *constitution, and to arrange elections for a constituent assembly. These were achieved by June 1922 but owing to the Civil War it was not until 5 December 1922 that the constitution was passed and the Provisional Government ceased to function. DMcM

public houses. Houses selling alcohol for consumption on the premises first appeared in Irish towns during the medieval period. Merchants sold wine in their cellars, while women made and sold ale in their homes. The town authorities regulated the price and quality of the drink sold, but it was not until the 16th century that central government began to license retailers. Ireland's first major Licensing Act, which empowered magistrates to license alehouse keepers, was passed in 1635 and an act of 1665 extended these provisions to retailers of wines and spirits as well.

But unlicensed selling undoubtedly continued on a large scale and increased during the course of the 18th century. It is probably no coincidence that the Irish word 'shebeen' entered the English language in the late 18th century. Effective government control of public houses was not really possible until the 1830s when a national *police force was created. Licensing Acts passed between the 1830s and 1870s gave the Irish constabulary wide-ranging powers to suppress shebeens, regulate the hours of licensed premises, and control drinking at outdoor gatherings.

By the early years of the 20th century the publican was a powerful and respected figure in Ireland, while his house was the focus of community life. Publicans, as independent small businessmen, dominated *local government in many areas and were vital sources of credit for farmers. Public houses not only sold drink, but groceries as well, and they were major meeting and socializing centres, especially for men, in both town and country.

See also DRINK. ELM

Public Record Office of Ireland and Public Record Office of Northern Ireland, see PUBLIC RECORDS.

public records are archival materials produced by the various branches of government. Archives of the central government of England and Wales, subsequently of the United Kingdom, including material relevant to Ireland, are managed by the Public Record Office, London, established in 1838 to preserve legal records, its responsibility being extended in 1852–4 to include records of government departments.

In Ireland, most government departments and officials retained their own records, although the Birmingham tower in *Dublin Castle was a central repository for the records of the Rolls Office, and a State Paper Office was created in 1702 to preserve copies of the records of departing chief governors. A fire in the Custom Office in 1711 and another in the Birmingham tower in 1758 destroyed some early records, and drew attention to the need for proper provision for the preservation of public records. The Public Records (Ireland) Act 1867 provided for the establishment of a new Public Record Office in Dublin. The Public Record Office building in the *Four Courts was completed by 1869 and records were transferred there from Dublin Castle, the *Custom House, and the *courts. Records more than 20 years old from central and *local government also began to be centralized. The bulk of the archives deposited in the Four Courts were destroyed when the building was bombarded at the start of the *Civil War. The most extensive records to survive were those of the *chief secretary's office for the period after 1790, which had been retained in the State Paper Office.

The National Archives Act (1986) established the National Archives by merging the Irish Public Record Office and the State Paper Office. It provided for official records to be transferred to the National Archives after 30 years, and made available for public consultation. The National Archives also holds some parochial records and documents acquired from private sources

The Public Records Act (NI) 1923 established the Public Record Office of Northern Ireland. In addition to holding government and court records, it also acts as a centralized repository for non-departmental records such as school records, church records, and family and estate papers acquired from private sources.

Wood, H., 'The Public Records of Ireland before and after 1922', *Transactions of the Royal Historical Society*, 4th ser. 13 (1930)

BC

Public Safety Acts, in the *Irish Free State. The first two measures of this name (1923, 1924) were temporary acts permitting *internment during and after the *Civil War. The Public Safety (Emergency Powers) Act (1926) was a permanent measure conferring powers of internment, but only following the proclamation by government of a state of emergency. The Public Safety Act (1927—repealed 26 Dec. 1928), introduced following the assassination of Kevin *O'Higgins, provided for *special courts, the imprisonment of members of proscribed organizations, and detention of suspects for up to three months. The Constitution (Amendment No. 17) Act (1931), also commonly referred to as a Public Safety Act, permitted the establishment of a military tribunal and the proscription of dangerous organizations. De *Valera strongly opposed the bill in opposition, suspended it on coming to power, but revived it for use against both the *Blueshirts and the *IRA.

puritanism. In popular usage 'puritan' is a term of mild abuse for an overly strict religious killjoy. Historians use it more neutrally to describe a group of 'godly' or 'precise' laity and clergy in England in the 16th and early 17th centuries who were unhappy at the lack of progress towards establishing a firmly Protestant Church of England, saw the Elizabethan religious settlement as incomplete, and wanted to reform the Church of England along more 'biblical' lines. Many of the 'godly' had certain attitudes in common: a belief in a Calvinist doctrine of double-predestination and in the primacy of grace and word in salvation, a concern to identify the presence of God's grace in oneself, sabbatarianism, a commitment to Presbyterian disciplinary structures, the rejection of 'popish remnants' and 'superstitious practices' in worship, and the apocalyptic belief that the pope was Antichrist. Many were persecuted in England during Elizabeth's reign, particularly those seeking to establish *Presbyterianism within the Church of England.

The rigour of ecclesiastical discipline in England and Scotland led some puritans to seek refuge in Ireland, where their commitment to preaching and their fierce anti-Catholicism were welcomed by an established church desperate for zealous clergy. The firm Calvinism of the first comprehensive confession of the *Church of

Ireland, the Irish Articles of 1615, made it still easier for the Irish church to accommodate puritanism. However, under Charles I, Archbishop William Laud and Lord Deputy Thomas *Wentworth took firm measures to stamp out puritanism within the Irish church, imposing on it in 1634 the English Thirty-Nine Articles and stricter disciplinary canons. This was followed by the dismissal of puritan ministers with Presbyterian sympathies.

Puritan influence reached its peak in Ireland following the execution of Charles in 1649, when, after the suppression of the Church of Ireland, the various Protestant religious sects and groups were free to seek converts and influence. Following the *Restoration puritans generally looked to create separate non-conforming churches: Presbyterian, *Baptist, *Quaker, and *Congregational. 'Puritanism' thus becomes 'nonconformity'. Nevertheless, the distinctly low-church tenor of the established church during subsequent centuries can still be linked to its early tolerance of puritan ideas.

Ford, Alan, 'The Church of Ireland 1558–1641: A Puritan Church?', in Alan Ford, James McGuire, and Kenneth Milne (eds.), *As by Law Established: The Church of Ireland since the Reformation* (1995)

AF

Quakers, see SOCIETY OF FRIENDS.

quarrying in Ireland has mainly produced slate, granite, and limestone. Irish slate stood at a huge commercial disadvantage to the mass outpouring from north Wales, especially of the omnipresent 'Bangor Blue'. Nevertheless Clasnasmuth quarry, near Carrick-on-Suir, was famed for the decorative effect of its rich green slate. Similar slate was quarried at Kilmoganny, Co. Kilkenny. Killaloe, near Limerick, provided a rich supply of roofing slates. 'Carlow Flags', from the extremely durable, fine-grained bedded sandstones of the Upper Carboniferous age, were quarried in south-west Clare and Co. Kilkenny. Carboniferous slate was also raised near Clonakilty, Co. Cork. A particularly firm, tough slate, quarried at Valentia Island, was used for large flags and slabs.

Sandstone was used in main buildings in the cities, some of the very best being quarried in Cos. Donegal and Fermanagh. Mount Charles stone, from Co. Donegal, could be used in delicate moulded work. However, soft Triassic sandstone was not suitable in the corrosive atmosphere of big cities. Nevertheless the sandstone quarry at Scrabo, Co. Down, was an important working, which provided stone for *Belfast in the late 1880s, notably in the Robinson Cleaver building.

The problem of atmospheric corrosion in cities was solved by the use of granite and other hard igneous rocks. Granite, from the Leinster chain, was used in the basement-course of many dwellings in *Dublin, which were completed in brick. It also provided façades and ornamentation in the construction of more prestigious buildings. In the 19th century granite from the Newry-Bessbrook area competed successfully, in the London building market, with the better-known Aberdeen and Peterhead granite. The quarry, on the estate of Viscount Charlemont, supplied granite blocks, not only to the nearby model linen village of Bessbrook, but also the town hall in Manchester and the great steps of St George's Hall, Liverpool.

Limestone is widely available in Ireland. Its main ingredient is calcite. Deposits of high purity are not so common. Lime is a by-product after kilning. Most limestone is used for aggregate, roadstone, and cement manufacture. This has increased massively this century. Ground limestone is used in agriculture. Almost all quarries are in the carboniferous limestone areas, although chalk is exploited in Ulster. Limestone was traditionally used for building. The grey carboniferous type, best exemplified by the uniform, fine-grained variety of Roscommon, was used for large structures and decoration. The shaly black limestone, known as 'calp', was only suitable for common walls, as it did not weather out equally along its planes of stratification. More recently, the building industry has used hydrated lime. Smaller amounts of limestone have been used in a wide variety of industries, from glass and chemicals to foodstuffs.

Bauxite, which is an important ore of aluminium, is usually mined. It was discovered in Co. Antrim and as the only source in the British Isles was mined extensively at Clinty, near Ballymena, from the outbreak of the *Second World War.

Nowadays most quarrying is for road building.
PC

quarterage dispute. Although Catholics were not eligible to become freemen of boroughs, they were permitted to become 'quarter brothers' of *guilds, and practise the relevant trade or profession, on payment of a fee. By the 1760s Catholic merchants and manufacturers had begun to refuse these fees, and the courts refused to uphold the demand for their payment. Seven quarterage bills, all unsuccessful, were introduced in the House of Commons between 1768 and 1778. The campaign against these impositions has been seen as an important stage in the rise of a more assertive Catholic middle class.

Queen's Colleges, created by *Peel's government in 1845 as one of a series of reforms intended to undermine the demand for *repeal. Established following private consultation with church leaders in Ireland (including those Catholic prelates with whom lines of communication existed), they were intended to meet clerical and lay Catholic demands for the provision of acceptable *university education, while respecting the objections of Protestant opinion in England to the establishment of denominational colleges in Ireland, as well as Protestant sensitivity where the interests of *Trinity College, Dublin, were concerned.

Under the Colleges (Ireland) Act (1845), three colleges were to be incorporated, all non-residential (though privately funded halls of residence were provided for), free from religious tests, and without theological faculties. Theology might, however, be taught by private endowment and subject to the visitational powers of the crown. Professors were to be appointed by the crown. The degree-granting Queen's University of Ireland was incorporated in 1850, by which time the Queen's Colleges at Belfast, Cork, and Galway had opened.

From the outset, the colleges attracted the opprobrium of the more militant Catholic bishops and clergy. Papal rescripts in 1847 and 1848 condemned them as a system 'to train the youthful mind in indifferentism to every creed' and admonished the hierarchy to have nothing to do with them. In 1850 Rome forbade clergy to hold office in the colleges and required the bishops to discourage Catholics from attending. *O'Connell (to the consternation of the *Young Irelanders) denounced the 'godless colleges'. In 1879 the Queen's University was replaced, as part of a fresh attempt to solve the problem, by the *Royal University. KM

quo warranto writs, challenging the warrant for an exercise of jurisdiction, were used under *James II to compel boroughs in England and Ireland to accept new charters that allowed government to nominate corporation members, so ensuring the return of compliant MPs.

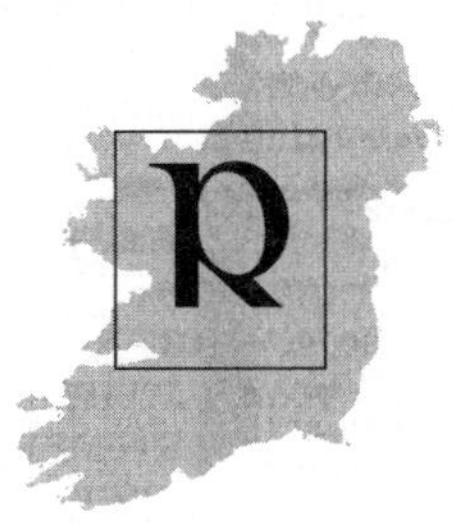

Radcliffe, Thomas, see SUSSEX, THOMAS RADCLIFFE, EARL OF.

radio. Broadcasting in independent Ireland began with the Dublin Broadcasting Station, generally referred to by its call sign 2RN, which began transmitting on 1 January 1926. A second station in Cork, broadcasting some local programmes along with relays of 2RN, opened in 1927 but closed again in 1930. From 6 February 1933 2RN was superseded by Radio Athlone, whose high-powered broadcasts reached a wider geographical area. From 1937 the station was generally known as Radio Éireann, although this did not become a legal entity until the Broadcasting Act of 1960 created the Radio Éireann authority.

Widespread evasion makes the number of radio licences an inadequate guide to audience size. However, drives against unlicensed sets pushed licence numbers up from 100,000 in 1937 to 139,000 in 1938, and from 187,000 in 1947 to 261,000 in 1948. In 1961, the last year before the advent of *television, 502,000 licences were issued. In 1979 the authority belatedly responded to consumer demand by launching a pop music station, 2FM. An Irish language station, Radio na Gaeltachta, began broadcasting in 1972.

In Northern Ireland, transmissions by the British Broadcasting Corporation began in 1924, and the opening of a new transmitter at Lisnagarvey near Lisburn, Co. Antrim, in 1936 permitted reception beyond the 50-mile radius round Belfast. By 1939 124,000 licences had been issued, suggesting that perhaps half of all Northern Ireland families had a radio, compared to around one in four in the Irish Free State.

As a body under state control, 2RN and its successors played an important part in the dissemination of an official culture, notably through Irish language broadcasts, and through programmes devoted to traditional music and Gaelic games. In Northern Ireland, by contrast, efforts to promote a distinctive local culture were inhibited by intense political and public hostility to anything suggestive of an 'Irish' identity.

railway transport began in Ireland with the opening of the Dublin and *Kingstown (Dun Laoghaire) railway on 17 December 1834. This first line provided a link between the capital and the ferry to Holyhead, which in turn was connected to London by road. Its contractor, William *Dargan, became the 'Father of the Irish Railways'. He was involved in the financing and building of most lines up to his death in 1867. Although the Dublin and Kingstown line was a success, investors were slow to put their money into railways, because there was not the same need for cheap, efficient transport as in industrial Britain. In the industrial north-east, however, manufacturers set up the Ulster Railway Company, which launched the second Irish line, Belfast–Lisburn–Portadown, in 1842, and the pace of railway building greatly increased thereafter. During the 1840s, Ireland experienced something of the railway mania then sweeping Britain. From a figure of just over 31 miles in 1842, lines already open or under construction totalled 700 miles in 1850. Investment from 1831 to 1852 amounted to £12.5 million. Government loans were made available under both *Peel and his *Whig successor Lord John Russell.

Although never carrying the huge volume of traffic of British railways, Irish companies flourished because of the comparatively low cost of land and labour. The lines out of Dublin and Belfast were lengthened. Drogheda was reached in 1844. Armagh came on line with the Ulster railway in 1848. By 1850 Belfast was connected to Holywood, Comber, Newtownards, Carrickfergus, and Ballymena. A line from Derry, down the Foyle valley, opened up west Ulster. The Great Southern and Western Dublin–Cork rail link opened in 1849. Cork was also linked to Bandon. The Dublin–Galway line opened in 1851. The Dublin–Belfast link was completed with the building of the Boyne viaduct, at Drogheda, in

1855. There were also many local narrow gauge railways.

By the 1850s most of Ireland's railway network was thus in place. The ramifications for the economy and society were unprecedented. Bridges, viaducts, and track excavations impacted dramatically on the landscape. Travel was greatly speeded up. For instance the Belfast to Dublin train, in 1857, took 5 hours 20 minutes, half the time of the stage coach. Even the poor could travel on the admittedly spartan third class. Savings of time and money were even greater for goods haulage. Commodities became ever more plentiful and cheaper, particularly in rural Ireland. Railways allowed Irish *agriculture easier access to the huge English market. However, the much stronger English manufacturing sector could now flood the Irish market, in the process sending many Irish concerns to the wall. Railway employment accounted for a considerable proportion of the national wage packet. Social changes included standardization of *time, the spread of national daily *newspapers, and the growth of *seaside resorts. A whole new class, the commuter, could now live in purpose-built city *suburbs. Grand railway stations and hotels underlined the importance and the wealth of the railways. This 'golden age' lasted to the end of the *First World War.

By 1919, there was a total of 3,442 miles of rail. But a process of decline was already under way, due to competition from *motor transport, which in a predominantly rural and thinly populated society was more convenient for passengers and goods. Also damaging was the commitment of both governments, after *partition, to the promotion of road over rail. The decline continued despite rationalization in 1925, when 26 companies merged to become the Great Southern Railway Company. After the *Second World War, nationalized integrated road and rail networks (*Córas Iompar Éireann and the Ulster Transport Authority) were set up. Despite a shift to diesel, the railways continued to lose out to the roads. The axe fell in both jurisdictions, though more ruthlessly in the north. By 1977, the total rail mileage had declined to 1,550. Recent collaboration between Iarnród Éireann and Northern Ireland Rail, underpinned by European money, has led to an upgrading of rail services between Belfast and Dublin. Also, with the environmental cost of the move to road from rail at last being recognized, the future for rail now seems more secure.

Nolan, Kevin B. (ed.), *Travel and Transport in Ireland* (2nd edn., 1993)

PC

Ráith Bressail, Synod of (1111). This saw the first formal establishment by a single authority of a comprehensive network of dioceses. Assembled under Muirchertach *Ua Briain, king of Munster, and attended by numerous ecclesiastics, the synod divided Ireland into two provinces, headed by archbishops of Armagh and Cashel. This, as well as the twelve dioceses into which each province was divided, reflected both the model of English diocesan structures and contemporary Irish political realities. CE

Ralahine. In Co. Clare in 1831 the landlord John Scott Vandeleur set up the Ralahine Agricultural and Manufacturing Co-operative Association with 52 tenants and their dependants. Though partly concerned to mitigate local agrarian unrest, Vandaleur was also influenced by having met, in Dublin, Robert Owen, the leader of British cooperatism, socialist factory owner, and founder of several utopian communities. The estate was handed over to a commune, which was governed by a committee of nine, elected half-yearly. The estate and property was to belong to Vandeleur 'until the Society accumulates sufficient funds to pay for them; they then become the joint property of the Society'. The experiment ran successfully for two years, but since these coincided with better than average harvests opinion on its long-term viability remains divided. In 1834 Vandeleur bankrupted himself gambling. His creditors refused to recognize the rights of the commune and the estate was sold off to pay his debts. PC

Raleigh, Sir Walter (*c.*1584–1618). Having served at *Smerwick as a captain of foot, this courtier was favoured with the largest grant (42,000 acres) in the *Munster plantation. Usually working through agents, Raleigh settled his full quota of English tenants and exported much of the local woodland as staves and planks. After disputes with Lord Deputy *Fitzwilliam, he eventually sold his seigniory to Richard *Boyle. Raleigh's other ventures to North and South America have led to his being often quoted as an example of the connection between *plantations on the two sides of the Atlantic. HM

ranch war (1906–9), a campaign of *agrarian protest directed against large-scale stock rearing, at its strongest in Cos. Meath, Westmeath, Galway, Roscommon, and Clare. The main tactic used was 'cattle driving', in which herds were illegally scattered or taken away, combined with *boycotting and a certain amount of intimidation and damage to property. The agitation was vigorously supported by Lawrence Ginnell, Nationalist MP for Westmeath North and a leading figure in the

*United Irish League, and by a handful of other political representatives. In general, however, the *Nationalist party and even the UIL, while condemning graziers as a major cause of rural poverty and depopulation, were unwilling to support effective action against a powerful rural interest whose members were in many cases pillars of the local nationalist establishment. In this sense the ranch war illustrated both the failure of the *Land Acts to fulfil the aspirations of the landless and land poor, especially in the west, and the limits of the agrarian radicalism professed by nationalist leaders.

rapparee, see TORY.

rath, a term sometimes used for an earthen *ringfort. Derived from the Irish word for an earth bank (*ráth*) it is frequently found as the first element in place-names. RW

Rathlin is an L-shaped island in the Sea of Moyle, 3 miles from Ireland and 13 from Scotland. Inhabited since the Stone Age, fortified by 1,000 BC, it featured in Irish mythology and appeared on Ptolemy's map. Rathlin may have suffered the first *Viking raid on Ireland in 795; Robert the *Bruce took refuge there in 1306. Acquired by the *MacDonnells in 1399, it became their refuge when attacked on the mainland. In the Tudor–Stuart period the inhabitants were massacred by *Sidney (1557), Essex (1575—see ENTERPRISE OF ULSTER), and the Campbells (1642). In 1617 George Crawford, laird of Lisnorris, claimed Rathlin under a Scottish grant of 1500, but Randal MacDonnell proved that the territory was Irish—historically part of the Glens and of the diocese of Connor, and snakeless. The Gages bought the island in 1746 and, although despotic landlords at times, were benevolent during the *Great Famine. *Piracy, *smuggling, and the kelp industry had boosted the economy from time to time, but emigration now took its toll, with the population declining from 1,010 in 1841 to 103 in 1981. In 1898 Marconi tested his radio invention between Rathlin and the mainland as a commercial application for Lloyd's of London. HM

Rathlin massacre (26 July 1575), the result of an amphibious operation against the island stronghold of the *MacDonnells, carried out during the *Enterprise of Ulster by John Norris and Francis Drake, on the orders of the earl of Essex. After the surrender of Bruce's castle, the English soldiery massacred its 200 occupants and proceeded to kill 400 others hiding in caves and cliffs. Queen Elizabeth congratulated Essex and his captains on their success. HM

Rathmines, battle of (2 Aug. 1649), a victory over the earl of *Ormond's forces by the parliamentary garrison of Dublin under Col. Michael Jones, ending royalist hopes of taking the city (see CONFEDERATE WAR). Edmund *O'Reilly, later Catholic archbishop of Armagh, was subsequently alleged to have aided Jones by having Ormond's men led astray by their guide.

Ray, Joseph (d. 1709), *printer and bookseller in Dublin. In 1680–1 he challenged the monopoly in Ireland of the king's printer (see PRINTING AND PUBLISHING). Although a hearing before the *lord lieutenant ended in a verdict against Ray, the monopoly was in practice broken. VK

Raymond fitz William, called 'le Gros', Cambro-Norman adventurer, and associate of *Strongbow, who sent him to Ireland around May 1170 in advance of his own expedition. On landing, Raymond erected a fortification at Dún Domnaill, alias *Baginbun, and successfully defended himself against an attack by the men of Waterford. He acted as Strongbow's emissary to *Henry II before the English king intervened in person in Ireland. He left with Henry in 1172, returned in 1173, left again dissatisfied at his lack of rewards, but returned to assume command of Strongbow's troops on being promised Strongbow's sister Basilia in marriage and lands in Leinster. His military exploits are recorded in exaggerated detail by his kinsman *Gerald of Wales, who also described his overweight, which accounted for his nickname. He died without heirs sometime after 1189. MTF

reading societies were established in Ulster and elsewhere in the late 18th and early 19th centuries. One of the earliest such bodies recorded was in Doagh, Co. Antrim, in 1770. Members' subscriptions permitted the purchase of a varied library; there were also meetings for discussion and sociability. The most durable legacy of the movement is the *Linen Hall Library, Belfast, which grew out of the Belfast Reading Society.

rebellion of 1848. *Young Ireland first gave serious thought to a rising in the wake of the Paris revolution in February 1848, but failed to win the support of the French revolutionary government, or to co-operate effectively with the *Chartists. It was only after the conviction of John *Mitchel for treason-felony in May that a conspiracy was formed for a rising after the harvest. A war council of the confederate clubs was elected consisting of *Dillon, *Meagher, Richard O'Gorman, D'Arcy *McGee, and Thomas Devin Reilly. The government, fully informed by its spy network, responded quickly by swamping Dublin with troops and announcing the suspension of *habeas corpus (21 July). Abandoning Dublin for the southern countryside, Dillon and Meagher persuaded a reluctant

Smith *O'Brien to put himself at the head of the rising. The confederates sought to raise forces in Cos. Kilkenny and Tipperary, but lacked a coherent plan of action; crowds of poorly armed peasants assembled to hear the leaders, but dispersed rapidly in the face of clerical opposition and the failure to distribute food or confiscate private property. After a bloodless encounter with troops at Killenaule, Co. Tipperary, on 28 July, many of the confederate leaders dispersed to their own regions, in the hope of staging diversionary risings. O'Brien decided to make a stand at Ballingarry, Co. Tipperary, and on 29 July with about 100 followers confronted a party of police who had taken refuge in the widow McCormick's farmhouse. The police refused O'Brien's call for them to surrender, and two of the insurgents were killed. The rebels dispersed as military reinforcements arrived, and the rising collapsed without further bloodshed. Several of the leaders escaped to America, but O'Brien and others were arrested and tried at Clonmel. The rebels were convicted of treason, but the government commuted the death sentences to *transportation in 1849. PHG

receipt rolls record payments of money made into the *exchequer and received there by the *treasurer and chamberlains, each of whom kept his own record of the transactions. Sums were entered in chronological order with details of the city or county, the reason for the payment, and the name of the person making it. The rolls were essentially a record of the issue of tallies, wooden sticks with notches denoting the amount paid, which were given as receipts to the person making the payment and later produced by him when his account was being audited at the exchequer. PhC

Recess Committee, a body organized by Horace *Plunkett in the parliamentary recess of 1895–6 to discuss the future economic development of Ireland. Bringing together *Nationalist and *Unionist MPs, it pioneered the limited consensual politics of Edwardian Ireland. Its report, submitted in August 1896, urged the creation of an Irish department of agriculture and industries (later partly realized in the Department of *Agriculture and Technical Instruction), and the extension of technical education. AJ

recusancy, the refusal to attend the services of the established *Church of Ireland, was punishable by 12*d*. fines under 1560 legislation. 'Recusant' became an official synonym for Catholic.

At the start of Elizabeth's reign most clergy adapted the Anglican rites to suit themselves and their congregations. They ignored the 'church papistry' developing among the urban patriciate, who were having Catholic baptisms and masses at home and beginning in the 1570s to send their children to *Irish colleges in Catholic Europe.

The *Baltinglass crisis and the coincidental return of continental students as ordained priests proved the turning point. There was a widespread desertion from Protestant services by existing priests and parishioners in the *Pale in the mid-1580s. Similar developments took place in the Munster towns in the early 1590s.

The Dublin authorities were powerless to prevent the growing nonconformity. The tougher English legislation of 1581, though planned for the 1585–6 and 1613–15 parliaments, never reached the Irish statute book but did influence the treatment and fines meted out by prerogative courts. The court of Ecclesiastical *High Commission (established 1564) was never effective because recusants bribed its officials.

After the *Nine Years War *Chichester embarked on the *mandates campaign, now known to have been more wide-ranging and of a longer duration than historians had hitherto surmised. Not only were hefty fines imposed and exacted, but the policy was having the desired effect of forcing the population to attend Protestant services. Chichester's second drive against recusancy in 1611–12, which this time extended to the countryside, culminated in the executions of Conor *O'Devany and Patrick O'Loughlin.

Dublin aldermen, pressurized by the oath of *supremacy, began to elect the Protestants among them as mayor. After 1615 the government deposed and fined recusant town officials in Munster and Leinster and imposed a governor upon Waterford as an example. Recusancy fines were extended to women, but were difficult to collect outside Dublin. Royal plans for a Spanish marriage followed by the *Graces eased the pressure on Catholics until the lord justiceship of Richard *Boyle and Adam *Loftus in 1629.

Lennon, Colm, *The Lords of Dublin in the Age of the Reformation* (1989)

McCavitt, John, *Recusant History* (1991)

HM

Redmond, John E. (1856–1918), Catholic gentleman of a political family, barrister, and leader of the *Nationalist Party 1900–18, MP for New Ross 1880–5, North Wexford 1885–91, and Waterford City 1891–1918. Like his father, he was educated by Jesuits and at *Trinity College, Dublin; his mother was a Protestant, his first wife (d. 1889) an Irish-Australian, and his second (m. 1900) an Englishwoman. A gifted orator and lifelong parliamentarian, he made his maiden speech and was ejected from the House of Commons within 24 hours of taking his seat. In 1888 he was briefly imprisoned for incitement.

Despite his relative closeness to *Parnell, Redmond was not one of the more prominent lieutenants of the Parnell era. Reserved and prone to indolence, his aloofness as leader of the Parnellite rump helped distance him from the squabbles of the 1890s. *Dillon was clear that only Redmond could lead the reunited party. Although inclined to welcome the *Land Act of 1903, Redmond decided to stay with Dillon and the critics of the act, rather than resist their influence alongside William *O'Brien. This set the pattern for the rest of his career: O'Brien was marginalized, and the Redmond–Dillon axis, though not based on personal closeness, was rock solid until 1914, characterized by long, urgent letters from Dillon and stiff, formal replies from Redmond.

From 1909 until 1913 Redmond, as the well-funded 'dollar dictator', played a strong hand well in negotiating the parliamentary path to the third *home rule bill. But once Ulster *Unionist resistance became the key issue, his strategy was less robust, offering the government 'good behaviour' in contrast to the near-rebellion of the Ulstermen. His war policy followed from this: unlike Dillon, he believed that common sacrifice for the British war effort would create a new basis for Irish unity. The outcome was personally and politically disastrous. He encouraged recruiting, but his son was slighted in his first bid for a commission; his brother was killed at the front in 1917; and his policy of imperial loyalty brought not home rule but the *rising of 1916, reluctant acceptance of the principle of six-county *partition, the collapse of his movement, and his own early death.

Bew, Paul, *John Redmond* (1996)
Gwynn, D., *The Life of John Redmond* (1932)

ACH

redshanks were light infantrymen usually hired for the summer months from the Highlands and Islands of Scotland during the 16th century. These mercenaries, known as redshanks because they went bare-legged in kilts, were available because of poverty in the overpopulated Isles and because of the break-up of its lordship. Mostly MacLeans, MacDonalds, Campbells, MacQuarries, and MacLeods, they fought mainly in Ulster and Connacht. Maintained by the **buannacht* system on three-month contracts, the redshanks became increasingly important auxiliaries for Gaelic lords as the century progressed. To ensure a regular supply, O'Neill and O'Donnell maintained good offices with the influential earls of Argyll and began marrying Scottish wives, the first such match being Conn *O'Neill's to Mary MacDonald in the late 1530s. In the 1590s the English state persuaded Argyll to deter mercenary recruitment, distributed subsidies in the islands to keep the men at home, and deployed shipping in the North Channel to intercept them.

HM

Reformation. The European Reformation of the 16th century was an immensely complex phenomenon. Beginning in 1517 as Martin Luther's theological challenge to the orthodoxy of the later medieval Catholic church, based upon the primacy of justification by faith and the Bible, it developed into a widespread reform movement. It was soon sucked into the vortex of diplomacy and politics, as kings and princes sought to impose religious uniformity upon their subjects and exploit the Reformation for their own ends. Finally, it became inextricably linked to the changing social and economic circumstances of the transition from medieval to early modern Europe.

Each country was unique in the way these forces combined. In England, secular issues predominated: it was Henry VIII's desire for a divorce which led him to break with the papacy. In Ireland, similarly, the Reformation was initially a product of dynastic politics, imposed on those areas of the country subject to the English king. But, though the English Reformation provided an influential model, the Irish context was substantially different, and the end result totally contrary. In England, state, church, and people became Protestant: in Ireland, church and state adopted the Reformation, but the people remained resolutely Catholic. The failure of the popular dimension of the Reformation created a basic and often bitter divide. Into this framework of religious division, the further variables of political, social, ideological, and economic divisions have to be woven, giving rise to the subtle complexities of Irish early modern and modern history.

Traditionally there was a tendency, not unnatural given the depth of the religious divide in later centuries, to read later confessional attitudes back into the reign of Henry VIII and to write off the prospects of the Reformation almost before it had begun. Catholic historians attributed the country's loyalty to the pope to its 'fundamentally Catholic disposition', and repeatedly pointed to the intense popular distaste for and resentment at the imposition of religious changes. Protestant writers, on the other hand, attributed the failure of the Reformation to the 'backwardness and superstition' of the Irish people, and even their 'slipshod ... moral conduct'. More recent scholarship has revised this stark picture, re-evaluating casual assumptions about the inevitability of the success of Catholicism and the failure of the Reformation, suggesting that confessional divisions arose more slowly in a series of distinct stages.

The early Reformation under Henry VIII (1536–1547)

This was primarily concerned with the issue of jurisdiction. The Act of *Supremacy passed by the Irish parliament in 1536 declared Henry VIII to be the supreme head of the *Church of Ireland. Modern scholars have concluded that the Dublin government was relatively successful in gaining support for royal supremacy, even from bishops outside the *Pale, though allegiances in this period were far from clear-cut. The most obvious practical use of the supremacy was the *dissolution of the monasteries, an event which modern studies have concluded was not the sweeping social, cultural, and religious calamity once assumed.

The Protestant Reformation under Edward VI (1547–1553) and Elizabeth I (1558–1603)

The reign of Edward VI marked the first efforts to establish a doctrinal Reformation, as Protestant liturgy and bishops were introduced to Ireland. The hostile reaction of previously conformist clergy and laity pointed to the continuing strength of religious conservatism and survivalist Catholicism even within the established church. After the untroubled restoration of Catholicism under Mary (1553–8), the Elizabethan religious settlement of 1560, comprising the Act of Supremacy and the Act of *Uniformity, again sought to impose Protestantism. The English monarch was declared the supreme governor of the Church of Ireland. All citizens were to attend their parish church on Sunday where they were to worship according to the Book of *Common Prayer or face a fine of 12*d*. The civil and ecclesiastical courts were to ensure that the population obeyed.

In England the enforcement of the Reformation at central and local level slowly created a Protestant nation during the reign of Elizabeth. In Ireland this never happened, for three reasons. First, the weakness of government: the authority of the Dublin administration was limited to only a part of the island and even there it was repeatedly challenged by risings and revolts. As a result it was never possible for the state consistently to enforce religious uniformity. Second, the weakness of the established church: short of committed Protestant clergy, with many of its benefices impoverished by lay encroachment and its churches ruinous, it proved incapable of providing adequate pastoral care. When the church did manage to procure Protestant preachers, they often came from England, which strengthened the image of the Reformation in Ireland as a foreign imposition rather than an indigenous movement. Finally Protestant weakness provided a breathing space in which Catholicism could regroup and ensure that it retained the loyalty of the Irish population. Increasingly during the reign of Elizabeth conservative-minded native Irish and Anglo-Irish churchmen and laity turned, not to the established church, but to its Catholic rival. Attachment to the Catholic faith was strengthened by the influx of priests and laymen educated in the Catholic countries of mainland Europe, and by the alienation of both Anglo-Irish and native Irish from the Dublin government in the later 16th century, as policies of colonization and Anglicization displaced native inhabitants. (See COUNTER-REFORMATION.)

The consolidation of the official Reformation under James I (1603–1625)

The reign of James I has been termed the 'Second Reformation'—the period when the Church of Ireland finally established a presence throughout the whole of Ireland. Bolstered by the assertion of royal power after the defeat of Hugh *O'Neill, by the plantation of *Ulster and the influx of Protestant settlers from England and Scotland after 1607, and by the creation of the Protestant seminary of *Trinity College in 1592, the established church began to create a more clearly Protestant ministry. Yet even this Second Reformation was only partial: the new clergy were for the most part unable to speak Irish, and ministered largely to *New English and Scottish settlers and officials, while the mass of the native Irish and Anglo-Irish population remained loyal to a newly reorganized Catholic church.

In a sense the Reformation in Ireland was open ended, and it has even been suggested that it was not till the Catholic *devotional revolution of the 19th century that one can truly speak of the failure of the Protestant church in Ireland. But this is to ignore the real signs in the late 16th and early 17th centuries that a decisive change had occurred in Irish religious allegiances. What had appeared fluid, confused, and even open under Henry VIII, by the reign of James I seemed set in distinct confessional camps. The Reformation was identified as English and foreign, while Catholicism began increasingly to be identified with the native culture and people of Ireland. As William *Bedell, bishop of Kilmore, concluded in 1634, in assessing the missionary failure of the Protestant church: 'the popish clergy is double to us in number, and having the advantage of the tongue, of the love of the people, of our extortions on them, of the very inborn hatred of subdued people to their conquerors, they hold them still in blindness and superstition, ourselves being the chiefest impediments to the work that we pretend to set forward.'

Clarke, Aidan, 'Varieties of Uniformity: The First Century of the Church of Ireland', in W. J. Shiels and Diana Wood (eds.), *The Churches, Ireland and the Irish* (1989)

Ford, Alan, *The Protestant Reformation in Ireland, 1590–1641* (1987)

Murray, James, 'The Church of Ireland: A Critical Bibliography, 1536–1603', *Irish Historical Studies*, 28 (1993)

AF

reformatory. Until 1908 children under 16 years of age could be imprisoned with adults. As late as 1880 there were over 1,000 children in Irish prisons, including nearly 150 aged under 12. Reformatories for convicted children aged 12 to 16 were established from 1858, while industrial schools for convicted children under 12 and for abandoned children were introduced in 1868. By 1914 Ireland had 5 reformatories and 66 industrial schools.

ELM

Reformed Presbyterians (Covenanters). Like the *Seceders these were Scottish *Presbyterian dissenters who established a presence in Ireland in the 18th century. They are called Covenanters because of their adherence to the Scottish National Covenant of 1638 and the *Solemn League and Covenant of 1643. The latter pledged Scotland and England to extirpate prelacy and popery and reform the churches in 'these kingdoms', 'according to the Word of God and the example of the best reformed churches'. The *Williamite church settlement in Scotland in 1690, while establishing Presbyterianism there, had not implemented the Covenant in full, and this and the growing liberalism of the Scottish church led the Covenanters to secede, constituting themselves a presbytery in 1743. Their first congregation in Ulster was formed at the Vow, near Ballymoney, in 1757. Unlike the Seceders the Covenanters, who never accepted **regium donum* from an uncovenanted government, have remained outside the Irish Presbyterian church. They sing psalms exclusively without instrumental accompaniment and today have 35 congregations and 3,000 church members, six overseas missionaries, and sister churches in Britain, Australia, Canada, Japan, and the United States.

RFGH

regency crisis (1789), arising out of the mental incapacity from October 1788 of King George III. The *Whig opposition saw the prince of Wales (the future *George IV) as an ally, and pressed for a parliamentary address requesting him to assume the powers of regent. The government sought either to delay or to create a regency by act of parliament, with limited powers. While the British parliament hesitated, the Irish parliament voted (19 Feb. 1789) to ask the prince to assume the regency of Ireland. By the time a delegation had arrived in London, however, the king had recovered. The insistence of Irish parliamentarians on going their own way, on a matter touching the crown, confirmed for many British statesmen that *legislative independence had left the Anglo-Irish connection dangerously fragile. The episode also provided the impetus for the formation of a new Irish Whig Party.

Registry of Deeds, established in 1708 to permit more effective enforcement of the *penal laws against Catholic landownership. The registry contains transcripts of deeds derived from signed and witnessed copies authenticated by *justices of the peace. Deeds unlikely to be the subject of litigation were not normally registered, and few deeds involving Catholics were registered before the *Catholic Relief Act of 1778. The main categories of transaction recorded are sales, assignments, or conveyances; rent charges; leases; mortgages; marriage settlements; and wills. Deeds are arranged under date of registration, with indexes of grantors, a county index of lands, and separate indexes for cities and corporate towns.

BC

regium donum, a state grant towards the payment of *Presbyterian ministers, initiated, at £600 a year, in 1672 during Charles II's brief experiment with religious toleration (see RESTORATION). Payments were suspended under *James II, but resumed, at £1,200 per annum, under *William III. In 1714, at a time of *Tory and *high-church ascendancy, the grant was again suspended, following claims that it was being used to fund Presbyterian expansion into new areas. It was restored from 1715 and in 1718 increased to £1,600. Following the *insurrection of 1798, the government, in a conscious attempt to increase its control over the Presbyterian ministry, reorganized the *regium donum*: an increased grant was to be paid, but through an agent appointed by government rather than by the *Synod of Ulster, and ministers were to be divided into three classes, receiving £100, £70, and £50 per annum. Reluctantly accepted by the synod, the scheme lasted until 1838, when the principle of equal distribution was restored. The *regium donum* was abolished, along with all other ecclesiastical endowments, at the *disestablishment of the *Church of Ireland.

Reid, James Seaton (1798–1851), *Presbyterian historian. Reid was appointed as the *Synod of Ulster's first professor of ecclesiastical history in 1837. Four years later he moved to Glasgow University as professor of civil and ecclesiastical history. His magisterial *History of the Presbyterian Church in Ireland* (1867) was unfinished when he died suddenly, and the third volume was completed by W. D. Killen. It is an indispensable work, based on primary sources, many of which have since disappeared. RFGH

religious conflict has been a feature of Irish society since the 16th century. The *Desmond rebellions and the *Nine Years War were both, among other things, Catholic revolts against a Protestant state. The acute hostilities between Protestant settler and Catholic native created by the *Ulster plantation were bloodily revealed in the massacres that marked the outbreak of the *rising of 1641. The *Williamite War was also a religious conflict, with much of the bitterness of a civil war, though not the widespread and indiscriminate violence against non-combatants seen 40 years earlier.

After 1691, with Protestant political supremacy secured by the *penal laws and the near elimination of the Catholic landed class, open violence between Catholic and Protestant appears to have been rare. The executions of Sir James *Cotter and of Nicholas *Sheehy have been taken as evidence of the depth of underlying animosities. But apart from these isolated incidents the texture of day-to-day interaction between Catholics and Protestants remains largely undocumented. There have been suggestions that the *faction fighting between butchers and weavers in mid-18th-century Dublin had a sectarian dimension. But the feud between *Defenders and *Peep of Day Boys that began in Co. Armagh around 1784 appears to have been a new development.

This late 18th-century resurgence of sectarian animosities has traditionally been attributed to the tensions arising from growing Catholic involvement in the spinning and weaving of *linen, at a time when weavers' earnings were already under threat and population pressure was pushing up rents for farmer-weavers. More recent work, however, highlights the interaction between popular and elite politics. Plebeian Protestants sought to reassert their traditional superiority over Catholic neighbours at a time when the state and sections of the Protestant elite appeared to be abandoning the enforcement of the penal laws. The Defenders, for their part, were radicalized by the increasingly assertive tactics of the *Catholic Committee. During the 1790s localized sectarian animosities became intertwined with the developing political crisis at national level. Protestant radicals in the *United Irish movement, despite deep reservations, formed an alliance with the Defenders; upholders of the established order, in many cases suppressing their own qualms, endorsed the mobilization of Protestant loyalists through the *Orange Order and the *yeomanry. The *insurrection of 1798 was to be marked by sectarian atrocities on both sides, most notably but not exclusively in the south-east.

The animosities revealed in 1798 persisted into the early 19th century, kept alive by polemicists like *Musgrave and 'Watty' *Cox. *O'Connell's mobilization of the Catholic masses during the campaign for *Catholic emancipation brought a renewed political polarization along religious lines, reinforced by the more direct attack on Protestant privilege represented by the *Tithe War. The *Second Reformation created a further sense of Catholic grievance and suspicion, vividly revealed in the controversy over *'souperism'. By the mid-19th century there was growing segregation in *schools, *hospitals, and *philanthropy. In politics the trend towards denominational exclusiveness was resisted by *Young Ireland, the *Tenant League, and, more successfully and over a longer period, by Irish *Liberalism. By the mid-1880s, however, the *Land War and the growth of the *home rule movement had completed the polarization of politics along religious lines.

In Ulster, with its large plebeian Protestant population, the tradition of sectarian feuding established in the 1780s and 1790s was continued in episodes like the clashes between *Ribbonmen and Orangemen at *Garvagh, and the bloody affray at *Dolly's Brae. Serious religious violence also spread to the towns. In *Belfast a minor affray in 1813 was followed by more serious trouble in 1832, 1835, 1843, 1852, 1857, and 1864. In 1886, the year of the first home rule bill, at least 32 people were killed in fighting extending over several months. In part migrants from rural areas had brought their habits of sectarian confrontation with them. But the rise of urban religious violence also reflected the changing character of Ulster towns themselves. In Belfast rapid urban growth had raised the Catholic share of total population from 10 per cent or less at the start of the 19th century to perhaps more than 40 per cent in the 1840s. In *Derry, which had its first serious sectarian riots in 1870 and 1883, the Catholic population had also risen rapidly. Moreover, the development of the *railway network had transformed the annual parades of the *Apprentice Boys from local events into major and contentious gatherings.

The tensions and uncertainties associated with the third home rule crisis, the *Anglo-Irish War, and *partition brought communal violence in Ulster to new levels. Between July 1920 and July 1922 557 persons were killed in the newly established *Northern Ireland. In Belfast alone 236 were killed in the period December 1921–May 1922. Northern Irish society was to remain deeply divided, with high levels of residential segregation, denominationally based schooling, patterns of exclusive dealing in employment and commercial life, and little intermarriage. There was one major outbreak of religious violence, in 1935, when riots arising from Orange parades left eleven dead. But with this exception it was not until the rise of the *civil rights movement in the 1960s that open communal violence reappeared on a large scale (see NORTHERN IRELAND CONFLICT).

Baker, S. E., 'Orange and Green: Belfast 1832–1912', in H. J. Dyos and M. Wolff (eds.), *The Victorian City: Images and Realities* (1973)

Hepburn, A. C., 'The Belfast Riots of 1935', *Social History*, 15/1 (1990)

Rafferty, O. P., *Catholicism in Ulster 1603–1983* (1994)

religious orders. Though St *Patrick in his *Confession* mentions the presence of monks and virgins among his converts nothing is known about their lifestyle. From the 6th and 7th centuries *monasticism came to occupy a central position in the Irish church and surviving monastic rules, along with the evidence of *hagiography, give the impression of a very austere lifestyle which made few allowances for human frailty. The monastic legislation of St *Columbanus (d. 615), though intended for continental houses, particularly illustrates this. Later reformers, such as the *Céile Dé in the 8th and 9th centuries, tended to stress this ascetic dimension. This form of monasticism remained influential until the 12th century with communities lingering in some areas until the 16th.

Unlike the rest of western Europe, Ireland was relatively uninfluenced by *Benedictine monasticism and the number of Benedictine houses in medieval Ireland was small. A number of Irish Benedictine monasteries (*Schottenklöster*) were, however, established in German-speaking territories in the 11th and 12th centuries and survived until the 16th.

The *12th-century reform of the church led to the introduction of the *Cistercians and various branches of the *Augustinian canons. The presence of the Anglo-Normans after 1169 and the establishment and patronage of their own religious houses introduced the problem of the 'two nations' and racial tension was one of the chief problems of all forms of religious life in the medieval period.

In the 13th century the *Franciscan, *Dominican, *Augustinian, and *Carmelite friars were introduced. Their arrival corresponded with a period of prosperity and expansion in the Anglo-Irish colony and most of their houses were established in its towns and boroughs, though with a significant number in Gaelic areas as well. Racial antipathy also divided the friars, and their respective administrative units in Ireland remained subject to either English or Anglo-Irish superiors until the 15th and 16th centuries. The decline of the colony and the effects of the *Black Death seem to have affected Anglo-Irish communities more severely and the resurgence of religious life in the 15th century was almost exclusively a Gaelic phenomenon. Among the Cistercians and the Augustinian canons standards and numbers had reached a low ebb, though there were unsuccessful attempts to reform the former between 1435 and 1531. The mendicants were revitalized by the emergence of the *Observant reform whose structures facilitated the separatist leanings of the Gaelic friars but whose sincerity commanded the respect and support of both Anglo-Irish and Gaelic patrons.

The effects of the *Reformation and the *dissolution of the monasteries were felt unevenly in Ireland. Most of the religious houses in areas under government control were suppressed between 1536 and 1543 while the rest were nearly all suppressed during the reigns of Edward VI (1547–53) and Elizabeth I (1558–1603). In many areas stratagems were devised to allow the religious to reoccupy their old sites or others in the vicinity. The monastic orders, dependent on their lands for support, were more severely affected than the mendicants. The friars were also able to establish colleges on the Continent for the training of new members in which they were exposed to post-Tridentine Catholicism (see COUNTER-REFORMATION).

The newer orders also began to appear in Ireland in the 17th century; the *Jesuits, after an initial mission in 1542, had nineteen members by 1609, the Capuchins were established in 1615, and the Discalced Carmelites in 1625. The newer groups initially drew their recruits from the *Old English and gravitated towards the towns and there was frequent tension between them and the older orders over rights, privileges, and the occupation of sites. A short-lived attempt was made to revive Cistercian life in the first half of the century. The 17th century also saw the establishment of houses of Augustinian, Dominican, and Poor Clare *nuns in Ireland and an Irish Benedictine convent was established in Ypres in 1665.

The friars, particularly the Franciscans and Dominicans, continued to be the largest and most influential group among the regular clergy. Conditions in Ireland made it very difficult to conduct religious life along the lines approved by the post-Tridentine church and throughout the 17th and 18th centuries there were occasional complaints about the running of novitiates in Ireland. In 1751, in reaction to a number of unfavourable visitation reports, *Propaganda Fide ordered the closure of the Irish novitiates. This led to a rapid decline in numbers as only a small number of candidates could afford to enter novitiates in the continental colleges. The closure of most of these colleges by secular authorities at the end of the century excluded even this possibility and the process of decline continued until the revivals of the 19th and early 20th centuries.

Cotter, F., *The Friars Minor in Ireland* (1994)
Fenning, H., *The Undoing of the Friars in Ireland* (1972)
Gwynn, A., and Hadcock, R. N., *Medieval Religious Houses: Ireland* (repr. 1988)

CNÓC

Remonstrance, the 'loyal formulary of Irish remonstrance', a statement in the name of the Catholics of Ireland acknowledging Charles II as lawful king, to be obeyed under pain of sin, any papal claims to the contrary notwithstanding. Drafted by Richard *Bellings in December 1661, the Remonstrance was supported by leading laymen anxious to secure their position in the *Restoration land settlement, but opposed by a large majority among the clergy. *Ormond, as lord lieutenant, actively encouraged the minority of Remonstrants while harassing their opponents. In June 1666 he permitted a meeting of Catholic clergy in Dublin to consider the declaration, but rejected its offer of an alternative formula (later condemned by Rome) repudiating the pope's temporal authority. The controversy reopened the divisions on the relationship between religious and political loyalties that had arisen during the *Confederate War, the continuity being reinforced by the involvement of Peter *Walsh as a leading supporter of the Remonstrance and Edmund *O'Reilly as an opponent. As in the 1640s it was generally *Old English Catholics that were most ready to seek an accommodation with the crown, although in this case even many Old English clergy, like Oliver *Plunkett, were strongly opposed to the Remonstrance.

'Remonstrance of the Irish Princes'. This document, which survives only in Scottish manuscripts, is a manifesto sent to Pope John XXII by Donal *O'Neill (Domnall Ó Néill), king of *Cenél nEógain, probably in 1317 during Edward *Bruce's invasion of Ireland, to counteract English diplomatic activity at the papal court and to gain papal blessing for the invasion. O'Neill claims to write on behalf of the underkings, magnates, and people of Ireland, and outlines the circumstances in which, under the terms of **Laudabiliter* (a copy of which he encloses), the English came to rule Ireland; but, he argues, since they have failed to abide by its terms, they have negated their right, and he, as 'king of Ulster and true heir to all Ireland by hereditary right', has transferred Ireland to the lordship of Edward Bruce, brother of Robert, king of Scots, 'sprung from our noblest ancestors'. The document recounts well-known atrocities committed by the English, the disadvantaged position of the Irish under English *law, and the prejudices of Anglo-Irish clergy. It gives a remarkable insight into Irish national consciousness in the later medieval period and is an important statement of Irish grievances under English rule. SD

Remonstrant Synod, formed in 1830 by *Presbyterian ministers, elders, and congregations who seceded from the *Synod of Ulster when their Remonstrance against legislation affecting future students for the ministry was rejected. A Theological Examination Committee had been set up to test the orthodoxy of future ordinands and it was clear that only *evangelical and orthodox trinitarian candidates would be accepted. This marked the defeat of the liberal, New Light (see OLD LIGHT AND NEW LIGHT), non-subscribing party (see SUBSCRIPTION CONTROVERSIES) in the synod, some of whom were *Arians, and led eventually to union with other non-subscribing Presbyterians and Unitarians to form the Non-subscribing Presbyterian church in Ireland. RFGH

Renaissance, a general term for the transformation of artistic and intellectual life in Europe from the late 15th century, involving a return to classical aesthetic standards and a revival of humanist as opposed to scholastic learning. The Renaissance affected Ireland more profoundly than one might expect. As a poor peripheral region, it was not involved in artistic and architectural developments. However, Ireland did make a late contribution to Renaissance scholarship with the likes of Richard *Stanihurst, the writer and alchemist, and William Bathe (1564–1614), who developed musical notation and revolutionized the teaching of Latin.

These men worked on the Continent, whereas the leading scholars in Elizabethan Ireland were New Englishmen—translators such as Geoffrey Fenton and Ludowick Bryskett and poets such as Edmund *Spenser. Their presence and the exile of their Irish contemporaries was a consequence of the *Tudor conquest.

Ireland became a Renaissance social laboratory where classical ideas about government and colonization were applied. Humanism believed in the civilization of individuals through education and the reform of the commonwealth through princely intervention. The administrative machinery of early modern government proved incapable of achieving these reformist objectives and, by invariably resorting to force, destroyed any initial possibility of success.

In defence of its liberties, the native elite responded with the revived classical concept of **patria*. It is no surprise, perhaps, that Irish theologians, especially *Franciscans, were closely identified with scholasticism, which Renaissance humanism had sought to discredit. Maurice O'Fihely, archbishop of Tuam (d. 1513), had continued the promotion of scholasticism as a lecturer in Padua in the heart of Renaissance Italy, while Aodh Mac Aingil (archbishop of Armagh, 1626), Luke *Wadding, and others led its revival in the 17th century. HM

Renunciation Act (1783), a British act acknowledging the exclusive right of the Irish parliament and courts to make and administer laws for Ireland. It followed a campaign initiated in May 1782 by Henry *Flood, who argued that the British parliament should not simply repeal the *Declaratory Act but must formally renounce its claim to jurisdiction over Ireland. It has been suggested that Flood's campaign appealed to *Volunteers resentful of the ill-concealed anxiety of *Grattan and other *patriot leaders to see them withdraw from politics now that they had served their purpose. The agitation allowed Flood to supplant Grattan as a popular spokesman, kept political excitement at a high level despite recent constitutional concessions, and widened the division between moderates and militants in the patriot and reform movement.

repeal, shorthand for the demand for the repeal of the Act of *Union and the restoration of a separate Irish parliament. Before 1830 there were occasional demands, notably from elements within the *guilds and corporation of Dublin, for the Union to be rescinded. *O'Connell announced his commitment to repeal as soon as the *Catholic emancipation agitation concluded, and required candidates seeking his support in the general election of 1832 to take a repeal pledge. Yet he also made clear his willingness to seek an accommodation with the forces of reform in British politics. A formal parliamentary motion on repeal (30 Apr. 1834), crushingly defeated by 523 votes to 38, was a tactical dead end entered at the insistence of his followers, and from 1835 O'Connell instead accepted an alliance (the *Lichfield House compact) with the new *Whig ministry. As Whig parliamentary fortunes declined, he turned back to repeal, founding the Precursor Society (1838) and then the Loyal National Repeal Association (1840). But the initial response was muted, and O'Connell himself remained preoccupied with his duties as lord mayor of Dublin (1841–2). It was not until the end of 1842 that the repeal movement, aided by economic downturn and the propaganda of the **Nation* newspaper, gained real momentum.

The repeal movement of 1842–3 revived the techniques of mass agitation pioneered during the Catholic emancipation campaign: a network of local committees and branches, a nationwide fund-raising scheme ('the repeal rent'), effective use of newspaper reporting, and close co-operation with the Catholic bishops and clergy. A series of huge open air demonstrations ('monster meetings') commenced in spring 1843. The agitation was to climax with the election of a Council of 300, a de facto parliament that would meet in Dublin to plan a repeal bill. But when *Peel's government banned the meeting planned for 8 October at Clontarf near Dublin O'Connell complied. This surrender, followed a week later by the arrest of O'Connell and other leaders on charges of conspiracy, brought about the collapse of the agitation.

'Repeal' in theory meant the unqualified restoration of the pre-1800 Irish parliament. In practice, O'Connell must have recognized that no British government would return to a definition of the Anglo-Irish connection as loose and undefined as the *'constitution of 1782'. Instead 'repeal' was at the same time an effective slogan, the focus at popular level of extravagant and even *millenarian expectations, and an opening bid in a process of negotiation that might lead to some form of limited self-government. Attacks by *Young Ireland and others on O'Connell's willingness to abandon 'simple repeal' for negotiations with *federalists and others thus missed the point. Where O'Connell's pragmatism arguably failed him, however, was in believing that tactics of brinkmanship that had worked so well in 1828–9 would be equally successful in 1842–3. Both the government and British public opinion, deeply divided over emancipation, were largely united in their belief that repeal would fatally weaken the United Kingdom, and must be resisted at all costs.

Nowlan, K. B., *The Politics of Repeal* (1965)

Representative Church Body, see DISESTABLISHMENT.

Republican Congress, a political offshoot of the *Irish Republican Army established in 1934 in an attempt to obtain mass support for the struggle for an all-Ireland socialist republic. It was initiated by former members of *Saor Eire and supported by a large section within the IRA who were looking for a political alternative to *Fianna Fáil. It was also a response to the apparent rise of fascism in Ireland in the form of the *Blueshirts. However, the leadership of the IRA, weary of political experiments and afraid of being tainted with communism, opposed it. The proposal to form Republican Congress was narrowly defeated in the IRA Convention of 1934. A large section subsequently left the IRA and established the congress together with other radical groups.

Its objectives were set out in the Athlone manifesto. Its main contention was that a truly free republic would never be achieved except through a struggle which uprooted capitalism on its way. Its unrealistic call to all workers and small farmers from both traditions to unite on their shared class interest and to forget their 'foreign fostered' differences made it a doomed enterprise from the start. Although it initially created some enthusiasm, the organization split at its first convention in September 1934 between those who were ultimately more committed to republicanism and the more communist-minded section, and it quietly dissolved in 1935. After its demise key members played a major role in the organization of the Connolly Brigade which fought on the side of the Republican government in the *Spanish Civil War. JA

republicanism, used in relation to the 17th and 18th centuries, refers to a body of political thought, looking back to Machiavelli and beyond him to classical Rome, that emphasized civic virtue and resistance to tyranny. Concerned with citizenship rather than forms of government, republicanism in this sense was compatible with constitutional monarchy, and would include at least some Irish *patriot writing, as well as that of the 'real Whigs' or *commonwealthmen. The original programme of the *United Irishmen likewise accepted a constitutional monarch. Their later commitment to an independent republic was no doubt influenced by the new understanding of republicanism, as a principled rejection of monarchy and aristocracy, propagated by the *American and *French revolutions. But there was also a pragmatic recognition that reform on the scale they demanded could not be achieved within the existing constitutional framework.

Republicanism remained a minority current within 19th-century Irish *nationalism. In 1848 *Mitchel explicitly opposed the ideal of a republic to the *repeal movement's envisaged return to the pre-*Union constitution of king, lords, and commons. The *Fenians defined their aim as an 'independent, democratic republic', although both *Kickham and *O'Leary expressed willingness to retain a symbolic monarchy, and there was uncertainty whether the *IRB was a 'republican' or a 'revolutionary' brotherhood. Following the *rising of 1916, insistence that there could be no retreat from the republic then proclaimed as virtually established almost split the new *Sinn Féin in 1917, and provided the main basis for rejection of the *Anglo-Irish treaty. Anti-treaty forces in the *Civil War were called 'republican', although their opponents differed from them less in commitment to the republic than in their assessment of how it might be achieved. A similar narrowing of the term to denote the more intransigent or potentially violent forms of nationalism is evident in the contemporary Northern Ireland use of 'republican' to describe Sinn Féin and the IRA, as distinct from the 'nationalist' *Social Democratic and Labour Party.

Republic of Ireland. The leaders of the *rising of 1916, drawing on a long political tradition (see REPUBLICANISM), proclaimed an Irish Republic which would be a 'sovereign, independent state'. The first *Dáil constitution in 1919 did not define the state, although the Declaration of Independence and the *democratic programme both referred to the Republic.

Between 1919 and 1921 'republic' was translated in Dáil documents as 'saorstát'. When the *Irish Free State appropriated the Irish title in 1922, opponents of the *Anglo-Irish treaty reverted to the Irish word 'poblacht', which had been used in the 1916 proclamation. During the *Civil War, anti-treaty forces maintained a shadow republican government which became increasingly ineffective after the war ended and when de *Valera left *Sinn Féin in 1926.

After 1932 de Valera was pressed to declare a republic by critics from the right and the left who disliked the ambiguity of the Free State constitutional position, but refused to apply the term to one section of a partitioned Ireland. There is no reference to a republic in the 1937 *constitution although this was recommended in the 1967 review of the constitution.

After the *Second World War, there was increasing pressure to declare a republic and thus resolve Ireland's ambiguous international position. In 1948 the *interparty government passed the Republic of Ireland Act. This caused confusion because 'Republic of Ireland' was the description but not the name of the state as defined in the 1937 constitution. DMcM

resident and stipendiary magistrates. The failings of *justices of the peace during the 18th century meant that full-time, professional stipendiary magistrates had been appointed in Dublin by 1795. These men controlled the capital's *police and acted as justices of the peace in the issuing of warrants and hearing of minor cases. The practice was extended to the provinces in 1814 when 'magistrates of police' were appointed in disturbed areas. The uniquely Irish office of resident magistrate (RM), which initially attracted a salary of up to £500, was created in 1822, although the *lord lieutenant was empowered to appoint them only when requested to do so by local representatives. From 1836 legislation enabled him to appoint RMs across the country. While many were former military officers, and others were professional civil servants, RMs were increasingly required to have some relevant legal or policing experience. They were to be permanently resident in their districts, and report directly to the *chief secretary. Their professional status meant that RMs ultimately assumed responsibility for the bulk of magisterial duties, notably those of the growing petty sessions (see COURTS OF LAW). RMs also accompanied the police flying columns against the *Fenians, and coordinated the *army and police forces during the *Land War. By 1912 there were 64 RMs across Ireland. After *partition the office was replaced in the *Irish Free State by that of district justice. In *Northern Ireland it was retained and its powers enlarged. From 1935 legal qualification became for the first time a prerequisite, and RMs took over all the judicial duties of the magistracy. There are currently fifteen RMs in Northern Ireland.

NG

Restoration, the return in 1660 to the thrones of England, Ireland, and Scotland of Charles II (1630–85), exiled following the defeat of the royalists in the English civil wars (1642–6, 1648). In May 1659 English army leaders had deposed Oliver *Cromwell's son Richard, who had succeeded his father as lord protector, thus initiating a series of complex ideological and factional struggles. On 13 December Col. Theophilus Jones and other Irish officers, quickly supported by Sir Charles *Coote and Viscount Broghill (later 1st earl of *Orrery), seized *Dublin Castle, and declared their support for those in England and Scotland demanding a recall of parliament. They also began to purge the Irish army of religious and political radicals. Over the next few months support for a return to monarchy, seen as the only alternative to anarchy or military dictatorship, grew in all three kingdoms. On 15 February Coote and Broghill defeated an attempted counter-coup by Sir Hardress Waller, a Co. Limerick landholder and one of the 'regicides' who had sentenced Charles I to death. An elected *convention then awaited events in England, proclaiming Charles king on 14 May 1660, six days after London.

Irish Catholic hopes that the restored monarchy would improve their position were only partially fulfilled. Individual proprietors with a personal claim on the king's favour were restored to their estates. For others, however, the Acts of *Settlement and *Explanation modified rather than overturned the *Cromwellian land settlement. Overall Catholics were left with just over 20 per cent of Irish land, compared with 59 per cent in 1641. The Protestant landed class, a newly united blend of Cromwellian and older elements, was now dominant, enjoying an effective monopoly of public office, central and local, until the reign of *James II, when the fate of the Restoration land settlement became central to Catholic hopes and Protestant fears.

The king's personal religious sympathies remain unclear. A short period of open toleration under Baron Berkeley of Stratton, lord lieutenant 1670–2, may reflect Charles's own preferences, but might also be seen as an adjunct to the pro-French foreign policy he had embarked on at that time. The position of Catholics was further complicated during the 1660s by the *Remonstrance issue, while after 1673 and again during the *Popish Plot pressures in England led government to adopt a tougher anti-Catholic policy.

Hutton, Ronald, *Charles II* (1989)

Miller, John, *Popery and Politics in England 1660–88* (1973)

Restoration of Order in Ireland Act, in force from 9 August 1920. The act permitted government to continue, under a new label, most of the restrictions imposed under the *Defence of the Realm Acts, empowered courts martial to try a wide range of offences, and permitted military courts of inquiry to replace coroner's juries, which had produced some politically embarrassing verdicts on persons killed by crown forces. The act permitted intensified military action against the *IRA, but failed to end the damaging division between police and military authority (see ANGLO-IRISH WAR).

Resumption, Act of (1700), the concluding stage of the *Williamite confiscations. Pushed through by opposition groups in the English parliament, it cancelled the royal grants by which William III had disposed of almost nine-tenths of all lands forfeited, instead appointing trustees to supervise their sale. The trustees heard more than 3,000 cases of persons claiming an interest in confiscated properties.

They also attempted, though without success, to obtain further outlawries. The act was unpopular both as an intrusion by the English parliament into Irish affairs and because of the losses suffered by those who had bought land from the earlier grantees. An act of 1702 allowed these 'Protestant purchasers' to acquire resumed lands on favourable terms. Other lands were sold by public auction from October 1702, but poor demand led the trustees to sell over half the total to a consortium of English merchants, the Hollow Blades Company, which later disposed of it piecemeal.

Resumption, Acts of, a contentious feature of the politics of later medieval Ireland which may be set alongside *taxation and *absenteeism as an issue that helped to focus the developing political self-awareness of the English of Ireland. Royal patronage was central to political life in the lordship of Ireland, just as in England; it involved everything from the granting of minor offices for life or a term of years, through charters enlarging town privileges, to hereditary grants of lands, earldoms, or *liberty jurisdictions to magnates. In the later 15th century the revocation of earlier grants became a standard response to financial problems. It might also reflect, and cause, political instability. The Irish government was often the plaything of aristocratic *faction, which from the outbreak of the *Wars of the Roses might be aligned with the Lancastrians or Yorkists. It became common for a new governor to withdraw grants recently made, and redistribute them among his own supporters.

In the 14th century revocations had been less frequent, but were possibly more significant in political terms. The earliest was in 1331 when the government of the young Edward III, who had just shaken off the tutelage of Roger *Mortimer, extended to Ireland the cancellation of grants made during his minority (1327–30). In his efforts to assert influence in Ireland, Mortimer had been lavish, creating the earldoms of *Ormond (1328) and *Desmond (1329) with the associated liberties of Tipperary and Kerry. The threat of revocation contributed to a confrontation in 1331–2 between Edward's justiciar, Anthony *Lucy, and members of the settler aristocracy, including the 1st earl of *Desmond. More spectacularly, in 1341—when his campaigns in France had collapsed for lack of funds—Edward ordered the revocation of all gifts made since his father's accession in 1307, apparently at the suggestion of a disgruntled member of the Dublin administration. This threatened virtually the entire colonial elite, who were specially incensed since it included the rewards given to magnates and towns for services during the *Bruce invasion. There followed a general withdrawal of obedience from the Dublin government. A parliamentary assembly, meeting in the governor's absence, sent emissaries to the king loudly protesting the loyalty of the settlers; in April 1342 Edward withdrew the revocation. This episode is notable as one of the earliest instances of the English of Ireland acting collectively as a political community.

Ellis, S. G., *Reform and Revival: English Government in Ireland 1470–1534* (1986)

Frame, R., *English Lordship in Ireland 1318–1361* (1982)

RFF

revenue commissioners were first appointed in the 17th century to supervise the collection and administration of *customs and excise duties. The crown was empowered to appoint seven commissioners of customs and five of excise, but in fact only the seven customs commissioners appear to have been appointed, five of whom were then constituted commissioners for excise. By the end of the 18th century the commissioners, who were also responsible for the administration of two much smaller departments, the Quit-Rent Office and the Forfeiture Office, controlled an establishment of over 3,000 officials from their headquarters in the new Dublin *Custom House. In 1789 the number of commissioners was increased from seven to nine and the respective boards of customs and excise, though still composed of the same members, were directed to sit separately. Following the *Union the separation between the two revenue arms became more complete and in 1807 the two boards were entirely separated, seven commissioners being appointed for the management of each revenue.

Allegations of financial and administrative inefficiency had prompted a number of parliamentary investigations into the conduct of the customs and excise departments in the later part of the 18th century. Further investigation by a royal commission in 1821–2 revealed that, despite various attempts at reform, the number of officials and costs of collection remained disproportionately high. The report of the royal commission recommended the creation of two general commissions for the management of customs and excise throughout the United Kingdom. As a result the boards of Britain and Ireland were consolidated, and the control and direction of these departments conducted from London. In 1923 responsibility for the management of customs and excise, and for tax matters generally, in independent Ireland were transferred to the revenue commissioners, operating under the direction of the minister of finance, in whom were vested the powers of the commissioners of customs, the commissioners of excise, and the commissioners of inland revenue. VC

revival of 1859, one of the most controversial and dramatic events in Irish religious history. Its first manifestations occurred in the predominantly *Presbyterian villages of Kells, Connor, and Ahoghill in Co. Antrim, but within a year religious excitement had spread to most parts of eastern Ulster, including Belfast. Although the revival transcended denominational boundaries, it affected Presbyterians most and Roman Catholics hardly at all. Its notoriety stems not only from the large number of claimed converts, but also from the occurrence of unusual physical and psychological phenomena such as visions, trances, swoons, stigmata, and prophecies, especially among women and children. Supporters and opponents of the revival in Ulster and beyond used such experiences either to defend its divine origins or to attack its hysterical character. Most religious commentators found themselves somewhere in the middle, keen to defend the essentially spiritual nature of the revival, but uneasy about the raw edges of emotionalism.

The controversies generated by the revival have extended to debates about historical causation. While economic and social historians have tended to explain the revival in terms of the stresses and strains of *'modernization', particularly among female factory workers, religious historians have pointed to the impact of reports of revivalism in the United States which reached Ulster in the years 1857–9. Still others have drawn attention to an indigenous revivalistic tradition among Scots-Irish Presbyterians stemming from the long communions of the 17th and 18th centuries (see SIXMILEWATER REVIVAL). Rival interpretations are, of course, not mutually exclusive, and there is widespread agreement that the revival was promoted chiefly by the laity, not the clergy, and transcended traditional boundaries of authority, taste, and religious respectability. For good and for ill, the great folk revival of 1859 retains an almost mythical status among evangelical Protestants in Ulster. DNH

revolt of the towns, or the *recusancy revolt, a term used to refer to the re-establishment of Catholic worship in Kilkenny and the main towns of Munster between 11 April and 10 May 1603. In Cork this amounted to an armed revolt against George *Carew's *provincial presidency. *Mountjoy marched south with 5,000 men and forced the towns to submit, but refrained from retaliation. Although there were economic and political grievances incident on the *Nine Years War, the 'revolt' is generally regarded as an exasperated outburst of religious fervour born of a forlorn hope that the new king, James I, would grant religious toleration. HM

revolutionary and Napoleonic wars (1793–1802, 1803–15), fought between England and France, first under a series of regimes established following the *French Revolution, and then under Napoleon Bonaparte. High wartime prices brought prosperity to Irish agriculture, with a sharp depression following peace in 1813. The promise of French assistance inspired the *United Irish movement both before and after the *insurrection of 1798. Yet Ireland also supplied about one-third of the forces that fought against France. Wartime spending seriously weakened Irish government finances, sharply increasing taxation and hastening the merger of the British and Irish financial systems after the *Union.

revolutionary workers' groups were established in Belfast and Dublin in November 1930, replacing the Workers' Revolutionary Party as the Irish affiliate of the Comintern or third *International. Against the background of the Great Depression, members were active in a wide range of industrial disputes and popular agitations, most notably the *Outdoor Relief Protests in Belfast. In June 1933 the RWGs were superseded by a re-established Irish *Communist Party.

revolution of 1688, the replacement of *James II as king of England, Ireland and Scotland by *William III, prince of Orange and husband of James's Protestant daughter Mary (1662–94). Acting on the invitation of leading subjects hostile to James's religious policies, William landed at Torbay, Devon, with 15,000 men on 5 November. He and Mary were declared joint sovereigns on 13 February 1689. In England the revolution was largely bloodless—though troops under *Sarsfield fought a small engagement at Wincanton, Somerset, on 20 November—but in Ireland it was the prelude to the three-year long *Williamite War.

William was succeeded by Mary's sister Anne (1665–1714), but since she too had no living children the security of what was now thought of as the Protestant succession remained a central concern until James II's nearest Protestant heir George Ludwig, elector of Hanover (1660–1727), succeeded her as George I.

In later *Whig ideology 1688 was the Glorious Revolution, establishing constitutional and parliamentary monarchy. Modern accounts see the settlement as a compromise, deliberately unclear as to whether James had abdicated or been deposed, and on the nature—hereditary or parliamentary—of William and Mary's title. These ambiguities were central to the subsequent party conflict, in both Britain and Ireland, between Whig and *Tory.

Ribbonism. 'Ribbonmen' are first mentioned, as 'a new name for U[nited] Irishmen', in 1811, and the term recurs during most of the 19th century in official accounts of crime and disaffection. Such reports, often based on dubious informers' evidence and providing a convenient alibi for unsuccessful policing, cannot always be taken at face value. But there is nevertheless clear evidence, including the arrest and subsequent trial of groups of Dublin-based Ribbonmen in 1822 and again in 1839, of a well-developed underground network, secret and oath-bound, recruited from among farmers, shopkeepers, publicans, tradesmen, and wage earners. The geography of the movement, extending over the northern counties of Leinster, north Connacht, and most of Ulster, suggests a direct descent from the earlier *Defender society. There was also contact with Ribbon lodges in centres of Irish settlement in Great Britain. Like the Defenders, Ribbonism exhibited a strong Catholic sectarianism, combined with some concept of an egalitarian and independent Ireland, to be achieved by armed insurrection. But in practice its adherents seem to have devoted most of their energies to the maintenance and elaboration of rituals of secrecy, to internal feuding, and, in Ulster, to sectarian clashes with *Orange opponents. As such it can be seen as a transitional stage in the development of a popular nationalist politics.

Richard II (1367–1400), king of England (1377–99), the first English king to visit his Irish lordship since *John in 1210, and the only reigning monarch before Victoria to make more than one Irish expedition. Richard's achievements and failure have been matters of historical debate, for his involvement brought no long-term recovery. Although few records from the lordship survive, its condition was clearly known to be critical, and from 1389 a royal expedition was being considered. Such a venture had not been possible when England was at war with France. Its purpose was not only to provide immediate military support and exact submissions from Gaelic Ireland, but to reform the administration and revive the revenues. Richard's expedition in 1394–5, with a sizeable army, certainly achieved the first of these objectives. A successful campaign in Leinster and diplomatic negotiations throughout the country brought the Irish willingly to submission. Richard did not punish or exact fines from the chiefs as had been expected, but followed instead a policy of appeasement, promising them access to royal justice and arbitration on their differences with the English of Ireland. In local settlements some chiefs, such as Art *MacMurrough in Leinster, gave up lands they had seized; grants to revitalize the lordship were made to English knights. Many Irish petitioned for royal favour, but though Richard was successful in gaining oaths of homage he was unable to resolve the conflicting claims they put forward. The breakdown of peace in Ulster in 1397 was probably inevitable, given that Roger *Mortimer, 7th earl of Ulster, had been appointed king's lieutenant. The settlement's collapse was not, however, immediate, and was accelerated by a reduction in financial and military resources and by dissension within the Irish administration and the Anglo-Irish community. Richard's second expedition in 1399 was cut short by the revolt of his cousin Henry Bolingbroke. Indeed, his absence in Ireland contributed to the rapid collapse of his support in England and his deposition in late 1399.

Curtis, E., *Richard II in Ireland 1394–5* (1927)

Johnston, D., 'The Interim Years: Richard II and Ireland, 1395–99', in J. F. Lydon (ed.), *England and Ireland in the Later Middle Ages* (1981)

DBJ

Richardson, Revd John (1667–1747), rector of Belturbet, Co. Cavan, who in 1711 published an ambitious scheme to convert the Catholic masses to Protestantism by means of Irish-speaking teachers. He also published a volume of Irish sermons (1711) and an Irish-language version of the Book of *Common Prayer (1712). Despite the support of Archbishop *King and others, the plan died of quiet neglect, leaving Richardson responsible for the substantial costs incurred.

Rightboys (from the name of their mythical leader, 'Captain Right'), a movement of *agrarian protest, commencing in Co. Cork and spreading into other counties, notably Kerry, Limerick, Tipperary, Kilkenny, and Waterford, in 1785–8. The main aim was to reduce the level of *tithes. Other grievances included rents, taxes, and the financial demands of the Catholic clergy. The movement was more widespread than that of the *Whiteboys, and had a wider social base. It also had the tacit support, and in some cases active leadership, of some local gentry, who opposed the *Church of Ireland clergy either on political grounds or as competitors for a share of the tenant farmer's earnings.

ringfort, a small, roughly circular, enclosure, of between 65 and 230 feet internal diameter (averaging 130 feet), surrounded by an earthen bank with an external ditch (*rath) or by a thick stone wall (*cashel). A small proportion of ringforts have two or more concentric, close-set banks and ditches, or two or more stone walls. The typical location is well-drained, south-facing, slightly sloping land below 200 metres altitude, although in drumlin country a ringfort might crown the top of a suitable low hillock. Excavation has shown that, with the exception of a very few ringforts that date to the later part of the *Bronze Age, and some in the 'Gaelic' west that might have been built, or modified, during the *Late Medieval period, the vast majority belong to the *Early Medieval period. The Early Medieval ringfort was primarily a working farm, with an internal house and sheds, and occasionally a *souterrain. Such a ringfort was probably the habitation and farmyard of a substantial farmer, a **bó-aire*. Its defensive bank or wall was constructed simply as protection against cattle- and slave-raiding and had no military purpose. This observation is not strictly true of the minority of ringforts that are particularly strongly built, or are multivallate, or are defensively or strategically positioned. Such are likely to have been the residences of nobles or kings, and occasionally early textual evidence and excavation confirm this interpretation. It is possible that ringforts of normal appearance and location but of larger than normal diameter might have served to protect communities consisting of several families (see also MONASTIC ENCLOSURES). The original number of ringforts, estimated at over 30,000, has been drastically reduced by agricultural activity. RW

Rinuccini, Giovanni Battista (d. 1665), archbishop of the Italian diocese of Fermo. He was sent to Ireland as papal nuncio in 1645, during the *Confederate War, charged with the impossible task of achieving the public restoration of Catholicism by agreement with Charles I. When his agreement with the king's agent, the earl of Glamorgan, collapsed, the *confederate supreme council proceeded with the *Ormond peace (1646). Rinuccini had the Ormondists imprisoned, assumed interim headship of the confederate administration, and launched an offensive against Dublin. However, the campaign was crippled by conflict between *Preston and Owen Roe *O'Neill, whom the nuncio had at one point physically to prevent from coming to blows.

When the confederate assembly met in early 1647 it derided Rinuccini's proposal to sack Preston. As the military situation deteriorated sharply, it was agreed to dispatch Bishop *French and the eminent lawyer Nicholas Plunkett to Rome. The nuncio wanted money, the supreme council a statement of the minimal religious terms for an acceptable settlement. On 27 May 1648 Rinuccini excommunicated the supreme council for concluding the *Inchiquin truce. When it lodged an appeal with Rome against excommunication, Rinuccini retired to Galway. French's return from Rome, with the message that Rinuccini's actions did not have wholehearted support there, finally killed off his diminishing influence and he left Ireland in February 1649.

Rinuccini, representing the militancy of the continental *Counter-Reformation, found his main supporters among the Gaelic Irish. The *Old English deplored his unwillingness to seek a realistic accommodation with the king and his supporters, and blamed him for confederate disunity; he considered them Catholics in name only. During 1661–6 two Capuchin friars, Richard O'Ferrall and Robert O'Connell, drew on his papers to compose a comprehensive apologia, the *Commentarius Rinuccinianus*, which remains a main source for the period. HM

rising of 1641. The rising commenced in Ulster on 22 October amid a constitutional and related economic crisis convulsing Charles I's multiple monarchy. There were three plots—a conspiracy by Rory *O'More and Conor Maguire in February 1641; a conspiracy of army officers disbanded from *Wentworth's army, subsequently abandoned; and the coalescence of these earlier plots under Sir Phelim *O'Neill in August.

The insurrection has traditionally been seen as a revolt against the *Ulster plantation. However, the main conspirators were debt-ridden scions of families who were originally beneficiaries rather than victims of the plantation. Their demands were for improvements in property rights and safeguards for religious freedom, reflecting their fear of the Puritan administration that had succeeded Wentworth in Ireland and of the growing assertiveness of a virulently anti-Catholic English parliament. The successful recent revolt of the Scots Covenanters provided a model.

Although the plan to take Dublin Castle on 23 October was betrayed by Owen O'Connolly, the rising in Ulster had already begun. Co-ordinated attacks took the colony by surprise but what was conceived as an armed constitutional protest legitimized by forged royal commissions degenerated into a spate of sectarian massacres as the gentry lost control of untrained levies. At least 4,000 settlers were murdered in such incidents as the notorious drowning of a refugee convoy at Portadown. Reprisals followed against Irish living in planter-controlled districts, notably the massacre of the inhabitants of Islandmagee, Co. Antrim. From Ulster, the insurgents turned south, capturing Dundalk on 31 October and defeating a government force at Julianstown (29 Nov.). Around 3 December the *Old English gentry of the Pale, having been again denied the *Graces and fearing a government backlash against all Catholics, made a historic decision to throw in their lot with their co-religionists. Thereafter the insurrection spread nationwide, laying the basis for the *Confederate War.

Lurid propaganda produced in the aftermath of the rising, notably *Temple's *Irish Rebellion* (1646), alleging a premeditated plot to exterminate the Protestant population and wildly exaggerating the numbers killed, helped legitimize the sequestration of Catholic land in the *Adventurers' Act and *Cromwellian land settlement. Many of these accounts drew on *depositions collected from Protestant survivors. For over a century annual church services of deliverance inaugurated on 23 October 1662 alerted Irish Protestants to the fundamental disloyalty of their Catholic compatriots evidenced by the rising (see ANNIVERSARIES).

Mac Cuarta, Brian, *Ulster 1641: Aspects of the Rising* (1993)

HM

rising of 1916 (Easter Rising). The rising was planned by the military council established in May 1915 by the supreme council of the *Irish Republican Brotherhood. In this inner group Sean *MacDermott and Thomas *Clarke of the supreme council executive collaborated with *Pearse, Joseph Mary Plunkett (1887–1916), Thomas *MacDonagh, and Eamon Ceannt (1881–1916), all key figures in the *Irish Volunteers. They concealed their plans from the Volunteer commander-in-chief, Eoin *MacNeill, and to some extent from other members of the IRB. In January 1916 James *Connolly, who had been planning independent action by the *Irish Citizen Army, was admitted to the conspiracy.

The nature of the military thinking behind the rising remains unclear. The original plan envisaged a general rising, in Dublin and the provinces, with provision for a westward retreat if the capital could not be held. This was undermined by two developments. On 22 April a German steamer, the *Aud*, carrying rifles and machine guns to arm the provincial insurgents, was captured and scuttled by its captain. The same day MacNeill, who had been temporarily induced to acquiesce in the planned rising, published an order cancelling all Volunteer movements for Sunday 23rd. It was at this point that the leaders, by deciding to rise in Dublin with whatever forces they could still collect, unequivocally abandoned considerations of military feasibility. But well before that point the sketchy nature of their planning suggests that most were driven less by a real hope of victory than by the idea of reviving nationalist militancy through a bold gesture.

The rising began on Easter Monday, 24 April, when about 1,000 Volunteers and just over 200 Citizen Army seized the General Post Office and other sites in Dublin. A proclamation was read in the name of the provisional government of the Irish Republic. Fighting continued until the insurgents surrendered on 29 April. There were supporting actions in Wexford, Galway, and Co. Dublin, and an attempted mobilization in Cork (see MACCURTAIN, THOMAS). In Dublin 64 insurgents were killed, along with 132 crown forces and about 230 civilians, and extensive use of artillery devastated much of the city centre.

The government's reaction to the insurrection has been widely blamed for converting initial popular hostility to the insurgents into widespread sympathy. The murder of Francis *Sheehy Skeffington, and the apparent summary killing of civilians by soldiers during fighting in North King Street, along with widespread arrests and the continuation of *martial law, undoubtedly alienated many. Other accounts, however, suggest that the spectacle of nationalists offering a credible military challenge to crown forces had itself been sufficient to win a degree of public approval. Overall the official response was less draconian than poorly judged and unbalanced. Fifteen leaders were executed, along with Sir Roger *Casement, arrested after landing in Co. Kerry from a German submarine. Yet other participants, including such key figures as de *Valera and *Collins, not only survived, but in most cases were free within a matter of months to begin the construction of a new separatist movement.

ritualism was a development of the tractarian ('Oxford') movement. Its adherents were called 'high church' because (like the *high-church movement of an earlier generation) they emphasized the Catholic as distinct from the Protestant elements in Anglicanism, and the prerogatives of the church as against those of the state. But in common parlance the term 'high' came to denote the importance that many of this school attached to ritual in worship. The intense suspicion aroused among Protestants by anything resembling the liturgical forms of the Roman Catholic church ensured that ritualism attracted proportionately fewer adherents in Ireland than in Great Britain. But the controversy, coinciding with the disestablishment period in Ireland, nevertheless coloured the debate on Prayer Book revision (1870–8).

Thanks to leaders such as Richard Chenevix Trench, archbishop of Dublin, who attracted virulent criticism because of his 'high-church' sympathies and refusal to condemn some opinions abhorrent to anti-ritualists, the Book of Common Prayer emerged virtually unscathed from the revision process. The revised text did, however, include a new code of canons regulating public worship in a manner that reflected Protestant susceptibilities within the Church of Ireland. While these regulations were not generally challenged, infringement of them was to involve the Dublin parishes of St Bartholomew's (1892 and 1928) and St John's, Sandymount (1935 and 1937), in cases brought before the court of the General Synod.

KM

roads, in Ireland as elsewhere, began with paths or tracks created by people treading continuously along the same route. These trackways gradually became highways, where there was frequent use by mounted or carriage traffic. Although lacking the Roman legacy of road building, Ireland, according to the *annals, already had soundly constructed roads by the early Christian period. These linked palaces, monasteries, fords, harbours, towns, and villages. Five major roads or *sligthi*, wide enough to carry two passing carriages, radiated in straight lines from *Tara. They were paved with large stones and, where they crossed boglands, had foundations of oak timber. The *Slige Midluachra* ran from Tara to Grianan and Gartan in Donegal, with branches to Armagh, Downpatrick, Dunseverick, Co. Antrim, and Derry. People living along the routes had an obligation to keep them clear of brushwood, water, and weeds.

Increased commerce between the towns built in the *Viking era ensured that roads were maintained into the medieval period. From *Norman times, English legislation on roads began to be applied in Ireland. Thus the Statute of Winchester was applied, requiring that 'highways from one town to another shall be enlarged, so that there be neither dyke, tree or bush whereby man may lurk to do hurt, within two hundred feet either side'. In 1613, the Irish parliament applied the 'statute' or 'six-day' labour system, under which the parish was responsible for the roads in its area. The men of the parish did required maintenance for six days, between Easter and Midsummer Day. From this point, Irish road making was independent of England and often superior. An act of 1765 gave *grand juries power to levy money on baronies within the county for the repair of existing roads and bridges or the construction of new ones. The new roads had to be at least 21 feet wide, at least 14 feet of which was to be formed with stone or gravel. This reform was long overdue, as the parochial system was too localized, leading to a multiplicity of small roads and no standardized provision.

The new countywide system befitted a country which was now more prosperous and integrated, with many more road users drawn from an increasing *population. The grand jury road system was to last, with modifications, to 1898. Turnpike trusts, which levied a toll on users to support road maintenance, were established by an act of 1729, but were never as extensive as in England. At first subject to abuse and often short of funds, by the 1820s they compared favourably with the other road providers. An 1856 commission, however, reported that their mileage was down from 1,500 to 325 miles through competition from the *railways. The following year the remaining turnpike roads were handed over to the county surveyors, who by then were in charge of grand jury roads. In 1778, Taylor and Skinner's book of maps showed 8,000 miles of road in Ireland. The same year, Arthur *Young commented, 'everywhere I found beautiful roads without break or hindrance ... in a few years there will not be a bad piece of road except turnpikes in all Ireland.' Irish roads were better also because they were not subject to the same volume of traffic as in England.

The introduction of mail coaches in 1790 gave the Post Office an interest in the state of Irish roads. An act of 1805 granted it the right to lay down standards for road design, gradients, and widths. In 1853 these functions passed to the *Board of Works, which was also given powers of road construction. In 1853 the board, in turn, handed over its roads to the grand juries. The 1898 *Local Government Act vested responsibility for the roads in the county and rural councils. This coincided with the arrival of the *motor car, which necessitated higher standards of road building. Vehicle and driver taxation, brought in under an act of 1909, provided funds for additional construction and improvement of roads. This was needed as Irish roads had deteriorated, due to the diversion of business to the railways.

Since *partition, transport policies, in both jurisdictions, have favoured road over rail. Roads have vastly improved, due to new engineering technology and materials like asphalt, bitumen, and tarmacadam and the arrival in the 1960s and 1970s of motorways. Nevertheless many are coming to believe that the costs, in terms of pollution and environmental blight, deaths, and injuries, have outweighed the benefits of unimpeded access to the roads by motor vehicles.

Nowlan, Kevin B. (ed.), *Travel and Transport in Ireland* (2nd edn., 1993)

PC

Robinson, Richard (1709–94) 1st Baron Rokeby, *Church of Ireland archbishop of Armagh from 1765 to his death. Though noted neither for his political activity nor his theological competence, he was a conscientious prelate who promoted clerical residence and discountenanced plurality where this led to pastoral neglect. His main claim to fame is his role as improving landlord and munificent builder. The city of *Armagh owes to Robinson not only its observatory and public library but also its urban configuration. KM

Rokeby, Thomas (d. 1357), *justiciar of Ireland 1349–55 and 1356–7, praised by the Dublin *annals for his abstemiousness and for husbanding resources for soldiers' wages. He came to Ireland after long service in the *Anglo-Scottish wars; as sheriff of Yorkshire, he was one of the commanders who defeated the Scots at the battle of Neville's Cross (1346). In 1351 he held a council that issued peacekeeping ordinances foreshadowing the Statute of *Kilkenny. He led expeditions in Wicklow and organized the building of fortifications. He had close diplomatic ties with Gaelic and settler lineages in Leinster, presiding over the election of leaders of the Harolds, Archbolds, and O'Byrnes in 1350, and paying annual retainers to several Leinster chiefs. His campaign in Munster in 1352–3, when he is credited with expelling the *MacCarthys from the Lee valley, prompted the citizens of Cork to ask Edward III to reappoint him in 1355. RFF

Roman empire. Archaeological evidence for Irish contacts with the Roman empire is accumulating but its extent and effects remain controversial. Under the early empire any Romanization of western Britain was very limited: social structure and material wealth were not significantly different on either side of the Irish Sea. By the 4th century, however, Irish raids demonstrated that the Irish found western Britain sufficiently wealthy to reward the investment required to mount risky expeditions. The same impression is given by Irish settlements in western Britain; especially in the *civitates* of the Demetae and the Silures there is good evidence of the acclimatization of Irish settlers to late Roman society, once Rome's authority had vanished. In the early empire, however, the main impact may have been through trade, probably organized through designated entrepôts, perhaps protected by treaties between Irish kings and the Roman authorities. It has been claimed that surviving evidence for trade with the empire is mainly confined to the eastern part of the island, from the central plain southwards. Yet the *ogam alphabet, based on, but carefully distinguished from, a Roman model, was widely used in the south of Munster. TMC-E

Romanesque, see ARCHITECTURE.

Rothe, David (1573–1650), *Counter-Reformation bishop and apologist. Scion of a Kilkenny merchant family, he was prefect of the *Irish College at Douai and secretary to Peter *Lombard at Rome, before being sent home to Ossory in 1609, as vicar-general and, from 1620, as bishop. In brilliant polemics Rothe upheld the loyalty of Irish Catholics to King James during *Chichester's deputyship, while detailing instances of persecution and martyrdom (*Analecta sacra*, 1616–19), and defended Ireland's ecclesiastical heritage against Scottish usurpation (*Hibernia resurgens*, 1621). As Lombard's deputy, Rothe held synods in 1614, 1618, and 1624, emphasizing pastoral care, confraternities, and the creation of a mass-going public and an educated clergy subject to regular visitation. If his 1635 report is credible, he achieved success in his own diocese, despite hostility from the civil authorities and nagging disagreements with the friars. Rothe crowned his achievements by reoccupying St Canice's cathedral in Kilkenny for Rome in 1642, only to live to see *Cromwell's troops take the city and desecrate the cathedral. HM

Rotunda (Dublin Lying-in Hospital), the oldest maternity hospital in the British Isles. Opened by Bartholomew Mosse (1712–59) in a private house in 1745, it moved in 1757 into its present purpose-built premises, designed by Richard *Castle, in Great Britain (now Parnell) Street.

Like most voluntary *hospitals of the period, the Rotunda was largely dependent on fund-raising and, indeed, excelled in this activity. Pleasure gardens and a rotunda were constructed adjacent to the hospital in the 1760s, followed by assembly rooms in the 1780s. Here Dublin fashionable society could enjoy itself, in the cause of helping the hospital's impoverished patients.

Midwifery teaching for both male medical students and female midwives began in the hospital in 1774, helping make Dublin a major international centre for midwifery training (see CHILDBIRTH).

In the early years there was a high death rate among babies born in the hospital, while during the 19th century the deaths of mothers from puerperal fever was a major problem. In the 1860s death rates were so bad that the hospital had to close on several occasions. It was not until the 1880s that adequate antiseptic practices slowly brought this death rate under control. ELM

round towers (Ir. *cloigtheach*, 'bell house'). Associated principally with early Irish *monastic settlements, these tall slender beacons functioned primarily as bell towers.

Usually at least five storeys high, the towers taper inwards towards a conical roof. The top storey is pierced by four to six windows. Recent scholarship suggests that a large bell was hung in this space. The other storeys are usually lit by one window. Originally each level would have had a wooden floor, reached by a ladder.

The doorways of most towers are about 10 feet from the ground, and were commonly designed to face the principal church of the settlement. The height of the doorway was necessary to add strength to the base of the tower, as foundations were often shallow. It also provided the tower with a defensive role, as a retreat for both people and precious possessions during attack. However, the chimney-like form of the towers was not ideal for this purpose; for example the *Annals of Ulster* record that in 1097 the tower at Monasterboice was burned 'with its books and many treasures'.

The round towers appear to have been constructed during a period of roughly 300 years. The earliest annalistic reference to one is for 950, when the *Annals of Ulster* record the burning of the tower at Slane, Co. Meath. The latest is for 1238, when a tower was constructed in Annaghdown, Co. Galway. Few of the surviving towers retain material evidence through which they can be securely dated. Those at Kildare, Timahoe, and Devinish incorporate sculptural detailing which suggests a 12th-century date, but the majority of towers are plainly finished and provide no specific chronological clues.

Lalor, B., *The Irish Round Tower* (1999)
Stalley, R., *Irish Round Towers* (2000)

RM

Rowan, Archibald Hamilton (1751–1834), *United Irishman. A member of the *Volunteer Convention of 1784 and a founder member of the northern *Whig club in 1790, he joined the society of United Irishmen in 1791. Imprisoned for an allegedly seditious address to the Volunteers in 1794, he escaped after having been dangerously compromised by the Revd William *Jackson, going first to France and then to America. Disenchanted with revolutionary politics following the French Terror, he accepted a pardon in 1803 and settled on his Co. Down estate, retaining some interest in liberal politics.

Royal Dublin Society ('Royal' since 1820). Founded 1731 by fourteen members led by Thomas Prior and William Maple, it grew out of the 18th-century desire for agricultural and industrial improvement. Membership reached 300 by the 1740s, a charter being received in 1750. The society offered grants ('premiums') for land reclamation, livestock breeding, fisheries, and textiles.

In the 19th century the activities of the society underwent changes of emphasis. In 1800 it withdrew from agriculture, the domain of the newly formed Farming Society, but returned to it following the collapse of this latter body in the 1830s. The society's agricultural role was further strengthened in 1888 when it took over the almost defunct Royal Agricultural Society. Meanwhile, from 1831, an annual spring show was held at *Leinster House, the society's headquarters since 1815; and from 1838 there were exhibitions of Irish manufactures. From 1880 the society began to acquire and use land at Ballsbridge for its shows; it moved there in 1924, Leinster House having been requisitioned by the *Dáil. In addition to agricultural and other exhibitions, the present-day society organizes concerts and lectures, and possesses a fine library. Membership stands at about 7,500.

DJS

Royal Exchange (now City Hall), Dublin, built by the English architect Thomas Cooley (1740–84), who won an open competition for the design of the building in 1768. It was completed within ten years of its commission, and was one of the earliest Irish expressions of the neoclassical style. It occupied a small but well-positioned site, forming the vista for the southern end of the newly built Parliament Street. The centre of the building is filled by a large domed and colonnaded rotunda, designed as a meeting place for Dublin's merchants. In 1852 it became the headquarters of Dublin corporation.

RM

Royal Hibernian Academy, founded by royal charter in 1823 with William Ashford as its first president, followed by Francis *Johnston, who at his own expense provided the Academy with a building in Abbey Street for its exhibitions and schools. Exhibitions have been held annually from 1826 to the present. After the *Great Famine the Academy faced a financial crisis, leading to internal dissension and public controversy which resulted in a new royal charter of 1861, which enlarged the membership. The exhibitions and school prospered in the second half of the 19th century, supported by purchases by the Art Union Lottery. In the *rising of 1916 the Academy's house and possessions were destroyed and the exhibitions transferred to the National College of Art, Kildare Street, while life classes continued in rented rooms. In 1939 no. 15 Ely Place was acquired and on the site a modernist Academy building was built to the design of

Raymond McGrath, funded by Matthew Gallagher and his family. The annual exhibitions transferred there in 1985. RHA-Gallagher Gallery, supported by the Arts Council, has had a continuing programme of large loan exhibitions. The Academy has been the single most important artists' organization and exhibition body in the history of Irish art, although from the 1920s its traditionalism has been criticized by modernists. JT

Royal Irish Academy, founded in 1785 under the presidency of *Charlemont; a royal charter was granted in 1786. Membership quickly rose to 138: it comprised mostly academics, clergy, nobility, and gentry, with members of parliament and of the judiciary. The academy was accommodated in Navigation House, Grafton Street, Dublin; in 1852 it moved to its present headquarters in Dawson Street.

Although in principle the academy cultivated science, polite literature, and antiquities, in practice its interests included most fields of knowledge. By the middle of the 19th century it was the senior learned society in Ireland, much prestige deriving from the work of members such as Rowan *Hamilton, *Petrie, and *Wilde. The academy published *Transactions* (1787–1907) and *Proceedings* (1836 to the present); it also issued catalogues of libraries, exhibitions, and private papers, dictionaries of the Irish language, facsimiles and critical editions of Irish manuscripts and texts, and miscellaneous works dealing with Irish history and culture. It built up an important library and the most extensive collection of manuscripts in Ireland. By the early 1900s the academy's membership had become overwhelmingly scholarly, though without sacrificing its multidisciplinary character. In the mid-1990s membership was about 275, with 60 honorary members. DJS

Royal Irish Constabulary (RIC). The Irish Constabulary—from 1867 Royal Irish Constabulary—was created in 1836 by the consolidation of the *Peace Preservation Force (1814) and the Irish Constabulary (1822) (see POLICE). The RIC was a centrally controlled, paramilitary force: heavily armed, dressed in dark green, army-style uniforms, and subject to military drill and discipline. Its first inspector-general, a Waterloo veteran, compared it to a light infantry regiment. In this respect it differed markedly from other police forces in the United Kingdom, which were unarmed and locally controlled. The government clearly felt that policing in Ireland required military force rather than civilian regulation.

The RIC was deployed throughout the country, except for Dublin city (see DUBLIN METROPOLITAN POLICE). Small parties of young, unmarried constables lived in barracks, under the command of a chief constable (later a sergeant) who was answerable to a sub- (later district) inspector, who in turn reported to a county inspector. The constabulary office, headed by the inspector-general, was in *Dublin Castle, while the force's depot was in Phoenix Park, Dublin. In this hierarchical structure, control from the top was rigorously enforced and much paperwork was thereby generated.

Before the *Famine the constabulary was used to put down *agrarian protest, election disorders, sectarian affrays, *faction fights, drunkenness, and resistance to *evictions. The imposition of public order, rather than investigative or preventive policing, was the constabulary's main task. But in the more ordered conditions that emerged after the Famine the RIC's military character began to seem increasingly inappropriate. Constabulary duties expanded and many were civil rather than military or even criminal. Constables were used as all-purpose government officials, to collect information on and regulate everyday rural life. In these circumstances the military effectiveness of the force was gradually eroded.

By 1919, when the *Anglo-Irish War broke out, the RIC was full of long-serving, Catholic constables with little military training, a significant number of whom were nationalists. Most were ill-equipped to fight a guerrilla war and many were reluctant to do so. Even reinforced in 1920 by tough English and Scottish war veterans, in the form of the *Black and Tans and the *Auxiliaries, the RIC was not able to defeat the *IRA. In 1922 the RIC was disbanded and replaced in the north by the *Royal Ulster Constabulary and in the south by the *Gárda Síochána.

Lowe, W. J., and Malcolm, E. L., 'The Domestication of the Royal Irish Constabulary, 1836–1922', *Irish Economic and Social History*, 19 (1992)

ELM

royal schools were planned by James I as part of the plantation of *Ulster. Lands were assigned in the escheated counties of Armagh, Cavan, Coleraine (Londonderry), Donegal, and Tyrone 'for the endowment of several free schools and maintenance of schoolmasters'. Finding the settlers slow to implement his intentions, the king imposed on the respective archbishops and bishops of the *Church of Ireland the obligation to appoint the schoolmasters and endow the schools. By 1625 royal free schools had been established in Cos. Tyrone

(Dungannon), Fermanagh (Enniskillen), Cavan, Armagh, and Donegal (Raphoe). In 1629 Charles I created two further schools on royal lands in King's County (Banagher) and Wicklow (Carysfort). The institutions had many vicissitudes, and several official inquiries in the 19th century found, to quote commissioners of 1857–8, that 'no regular or systematic control or supervision' had been exercised over them. The endowed schools' commissioners reported in 1878 the existence of royal free schools at Armagh, Banagher, Carysfort, Cavan, Dungannon, Enniskillen, and Raphoe. All were grammar schools with limited numbers of free places (with the exception of Carysfort, which they designated an 'English school'). KM

Royal Ulster Constabulary (RUC). This replaced the *Royal Irish Constabulary, upon which it was modelled, in 1922 and policed *Northern Ireland until 2001, when it was succeeded by the Police Service of Northern Ireland (PSNI). In 1927 49 per cent of RUC men were former members of the *Ulster Special Constabulary, while 40 per cent had previously served in the Royal Irish Constabulary. It was originally intended that a third of the RUC should be Catholics, but the Catholic element in the force quickly declined from a peak of 21 per cent in 1923 to 17 per cent in 1927. By 1970 about 10 per cent of the RUC were Catholics. The force was therefore generally regarded by Catholics as a Protestant constabulary serving *unionist interests.

Severely criticized for its policing of *civil rights marches in 1968–9, the RUC was reformed by the 1970 Police Act. This aimed to eliminate the force's paramilitary trappings and to bring it more into line with other United Kingdom police forces. The act even provided for the disarming of the RUC, but the rise of the provisional *IRA prevented this and during the 1970s the RUC became the most heavily armed and armoured police force in the United Kingdom.

Under the policy termed 'Ulsterization', pursued by successive governments from the late 1970s, the RUC took increased responsibility from the army for the policing of the *Northern Ireland conflict. The strength of the force was trebled, but its casualty rate also increased dramatically.

The RUC was censured for its mistreatment of IRA suspects during interrogation in the mid-1970s and for its apparent adoption of a 'shoot-to-kill' policy in the early 1980s. Up to the mid-1980s Protestants strongly supported the force, while Catholic opinion remained much more divided. A poll taken early in 1985 showed that 96 per cent of Protestants thought the RUC was fair or very fair in its actions, but 53 per cent of Catholics thought the force was unfair or very unfair.

In the late 1980s the RUC was praised for its even-handed policing of Orange marches and unionist demonstrations, particularly in the wake of the *Anglo-Irish agreement. This was accompanied, however, by a marked deterioration in relations with sections of the Protestant community. Similarly, policing of the controversial Drumcree Orange parades in Portadown from the late 1990s brought the RUC into violent conflict, not only with Catholic protestors, but also with Protestant marchers.

Under the terms of the Good Friday Agreement of 1998 (see PEACE PROCESS) a commission chaired by Chris Patten, a former leading Conservative politician who had served as a minister in Northern Ireland during the 1980s, was established to formulate proposals for a reformed police force. His report, published in late 1999, recommended sweeping changes, which were largely, though not wholly, implemented by the Police (Northern Ireland) Act, 2000.

The RUC was awarded the George Medal, the UK's highest medal for civilian bravery, but shortly thereafter, in 2001, it was incorporated into the new PSNI. Under the Patten proposals, the PSNI was to be more representative than the RUC, especially by selecting half of its recruits from the Catholic community; it was to be less military in character; its new badges and symbols were to be free of any association with either the UK or the Irish Republic; it was to be regulated by a new police board; and complaints against it were to be handled by an independent police ombudsman. Sinn Féin initially refused to endorse the PSNI when not all Patten's recommendations were implemented, but it reversed this stance as part of the St Andrew's Agreement of 2006 and accepted the PSNI in early 2007.

However, investigations continued into claims of collusion during the Troubles between the RUC and loyalist paramilitary organizations. In 2003 Sir John Stevens, in his third report, concluded that collusion had occurred, while in 2007 the Northern Ireland police ombudsman identified collusion between the RUC's Special Branch and loyalists in a number of murders that took place in Belfast in 1989–2002. Controversy surrounding some of the tactics employed by the RUC during the Troubles seems set to continue, despite the force's incorporation into the PSNI.

A New Beginning: Policing in Northern Ireland. The Report of the Independent Commission on Policing for Northern Ireland (1999)

Brewer, J., et al., *The Police, Public Order and the State* (1988)

McGarry, J., and O'Leary, B., *Policing Northern Ireland: Proposals for a New Start* (1999)
Ryder, C., *The RUC: A Force under Fire* (1997)
Weitzer, R., *Policing under Fire* (1995)

ELM

Royal University, a further attempt to meet Catholic demands for *university education, the Queen's University plan (see QUEEN'S COLLEGES) having manifestly failed. The University Education (Ireland) Act of 1879 dissolved the Queen's University and replaced it with the Royal University of Ireland, an examining body whose degrees were open to all who passed its examinations. Its state-funded fellowships were divided between the Queen's Colleges, the de facto denominational Magee College, Londonderry, and the *Catholic University, the latter reconstituted under *Jesuit auspices as University College, Dublin. All degrees and prizes of the Royal University were open to women, a new departure in Irish university education. KM

rugby football was introduced to Ireland by former pupils of Rugby School and Cheltenham College who attended *Trinity College, Dublin. The university club, the first in Ireland, was founded in 1854, and rules were established by them in 1868. In the intervening period a number of other clubs had emerged, primarily in Dublin and Belfast. In 1879 the Irish Rugby Football Union (IRFU) was formed, incorporating two previous bodies, one based in Dublin, and one in Belfast. Seventy-seven clubs, most of which were linked to educational establishments, joined the new union. The first international match had taken place against England in 1875. Provincial cup competitions were established between 1882 and 1896, followed by interprovincial championships. From 1884 the Home International Championships were played annually. However, the sport did not become one of mass participation. Players were, and continue to be, drawn from the middle and upper classes. In urban areas rugby suffered from the popularity of *soccer, and in the countryside from that of *Gaelic football.

Following the *First World War, Irish rugby declined in popularity and success, though *partition and independence had no immediate effect on the game. From the 1930s rugby was increasingly taken up by the rising Catholic middle classes, and interest in the sport steadied. International success in the post-war years further raised rugby's profile. After partition international matches initially alternated between stadiums at Ravenhill Road, Belfast, and Lansdowne Road, Dublin. By the 1950s, however, the Belfast venue had become too small, and a protest in 1954 by players from the Republic about the playing of the British national anthem and the flying of the Union flag provided the occasion for confining future internationals to Dublin. Reorganization of the game and the legalisation of professionalism from 1995 have given the sport an increased level of popularity.

Diffley, S., *The Men in Green: The Story of Irish Rugby* (1973)
Van Esbyck, E., *One Hundred Years of Irish Rugby* (1974)

NG

rundale, regionally varied forms of infield-outfield *agriculture widespread in the later 18th and early 19th centuries in the north and west of Ireland, but largely disappearing after the *Famine. Practised as a form of collective farming by extended families holding land on a joint tenancy from a *landlord, rundale typically included potato gardens, permanently cultivated infields, periodically cultivated pastoral outfields, and additional summer transhumance or 'booley' pastures. Each family held a number of arable strips in the infield which were periodically reallocated according to custom or demand, sometimes under the direction of a local 'headman'. The arable was used for both subsistence (potatoes) and cash crops (oats). The associated *clachan* settlements were characteristically irregular.

Rundale is sometimes argued to have originated in pre-*Norman times, and to have survived the subsequent medieval and early modern commercialization of Irish farming as the farming system of semi-servile *betagh and, latterly, peasant groups in environmentally less favoured districts. While there is archaeological and historical evidence for the existence of early field systems which could support this interpretation, it is by no means certain that it is correct. It may be more appropriate to see rundale as the late 18th-century consequence of the interaction between existing traditions of partible inheritance, rapid *population growth, and increasing dependence on the *potato. The excessive subdivision encouraged by the system ensured that it was eventually incapable of supporting this population growth even before the Famine struck. LJP

Russell, Sean (1893–1940). As *IRA chief of staff Russell was responsible for the *bombing campaign in Great Britain in 1939–40. He was representative of those traditional republicans who believed that only physical force could bring a 32-county republic. His appointment as chief of staff was a final attempt to make the organization relevant after years of splits and inaction. As one of the last veterans of the *rising of 1916 left in the IRA he went to the USA to raise funds for the bombing campaign. He ended up in Nazi Germany to drum up support, but died aboard a German submarine on his way back to Ireland. JA

Russell, Thomas (1767–1803), radical. Born in Co. Cork, the son of an army officer, Russell served with the army in India 1783–1786/7. Back in Ireland he became a close friend of *Tone during 1790. His military duties then took him to Belfast (1790–1), where he formed links with other radicals, allowing him to play an important part in the formation of the *United Irish movement in both Belfast and Dublin. After a period as a minor legal official and justice of the peace in Co. Tyrone (1791–2), Russell became librarian of the *Linen Hall Library (1794). Throughout this period he travelled widely in north Leinster and south Ulster, playing a poorly documented but possibly important role as organizer and emissary for the United Irish movement. He was detained without trial 1796–1801, then released on condition that he left the country. In 1803 he tried unsuccessfully to organize support for Robert *Emmet's insurrection in former United Irish circles in Ulster. After Emmet's capture, Russell went to Dublin in the hope of arranging his rescue, but was himself arrested and hanged at Downpatrick.

Russell, Thomas Wallace (1841–1920), radical *Unionist politician. Russell entered politics through the *temperance movement, which provided a training in oratory and—through his work as a lobbyist—access to parliament. He became Liberal Unionist MP for South Tyrone in 1886. In 1894–5 he launched a popular campaign designed to put pressure on the Conservative and Unionist leadership to deliver land reform. In 1895 he was temporarily silenced through junior ministerial office; but in September 1900 he declared in favour of compulsory land purchase, and was dismissed. Thereafter he drifted towards an independent stand, organizing a distinctive agitation and electoral campaign between 1900 and 1906: his candidates won by-elections in East Down (Feb. 1902) and in North Fermanagh (Mar. 1903), formerly Unionist-held constituencies. This challenge was an influence behind both the *Land Act of 1903 and the local reorganization of Ulster Unionism (see ULSTER UNIONIST COUNCIL) after 1904. Russell accepted junior office from the Liberal government in 1907. He retained his South Tyrone seat until January 1910, and held North Tyrone for the Liberals between 1911 and 1918.

He was a Victorian faddist, too politically obsessive and too personally obtuse to be accommodated within a single party. His immense ability attracted the patronage of Joseph Chamberlain; but in the end Russell's unyielding approach to politics brought isolation and disappointment. AJ

Ryan, James (1891–1970), politician. A participant in the *rising of 1916, Ryan was *Sinn Féin MP for Wexford in 1918 and an *IRA commander in Wexford during the *Anglo-Irish War. As minister for agriculture 1932–47 he was responsible for implementing *Fianna Fáil's policy of promoting small-scale, tillage farming. As minister for health (1951–4) he put through a compromise Health Act (1953) which resolved the issues raised in the *Mother and Child controversy. He clashed with *Lemass in 1945 on the question of state support for small, uncommercial farms, but the two were generally allies, and Ryan was minister for finance (1957–65) in the period of the First Programme for Economic Expansion (see *ECONOMIC DEVELOPMENT*).

Ryan, W. P. (William Patrick) (1867–1942), a highly capable propagandist for the early 20th-century Irish revival, and a prominent victim of clerical censorship. Ryan was unusual in combining a commitment to the creation of a distinctive Irish culture with strong socialist convictions. Born in Co. Tipperary, he returned from a successful journalistic career in London to edit the *Irish Peasant* (1906), only to have this close down after Cardinal *Logue had condemned its alleged anticlericalism. Ryan edited his own *Irish Peasant* until 1910 then returned to London, recalling his experiences in a novel, *The Plough and the Cross* (1910), and in *The Pope's Green Island* (1912). His son **Desmond Ryan**, a pupil at *St Enda's School, later wrote extensively on the history of Irish revolutionary nationalism.

sacramental test, the requirement that persons holding offices of trust or profit under the crown should qualify themselves by taking communion in the *Church of Ireland. First introduced in England in 1673, the test was extended to Ireland by a clause added to the anti-Catholic act of 1704 (see PENAL LAWS). The aim, however, was to exclude not Catholics, already barred from office by other means, but Protestant dissenters, and especially the *Presbyterians of Ulster. Its introduction did not initiate any significant purge of salaried officials, presumably because the concentration of patronage in the hands of the overwhelmingly Anglican landed classes had already largely excluded dissenters from this area. The real impact was rather in urban local government, where the commercial wealth of Ulster Presbyterians had previously given them a strong representation. Although Presbyterians were still eligible to sit in parliament, this exclusion from the corporations that returned many borough members (see FRANCHISE) ensured that their representation there remained negligible. Attempts by *Whig ministries, in 1719 and 1733, to repeal the test by an act of the Irish parliament were defeated by large majorities. The test was removed in 1780, a by-product of the surge of reformist agitation leading to *legislative independence.

Sadleir, John (1814–56), the 'suicide banker' of popular notoriety. From a prosperous Catholic family (founders of the Tipperary Joint-Stock Bank), he qualified as a lawyer and entered the world of finance and investment, in which his interests eventually extended to Sweden, Switzerland, France, and Italy. One of the MPs pledged to *independent opposition in 1852, he nevertheless accepted office as a junior lord of the treasury. As the massive frauds underlying his investment empire were about to be exposed, he poisoned himself on Hampstead Heath in February 1856. RVC

St Enda's School (Scoil Éanna), founded in Dublin by Patrick *Pearse in 1909 to give expression to his ideals, both nationalistic and educational. He intended that the Gaelic ethos and curriculum of the school should inspire his boys to a nobility of character in which love of Ireland would be the guiding principle. Condemning contemporary intermediate education, with its rigid pedagogy, emphasis on examinations, and neglect of Irishness, as a 'murder machine', he emphasized the importance of eliciting and fostering each pupil's talent through a school regime that, while humane, yet looked to the feats of Ireland's past heroes for inspiration. KM

St Leger, Anthony, lord deputy 1540–8, 1550–1, 1553–6. With the assistance of *Cusack, St Leger supervised the establishment of the *kingdom of Ireland and the attempt to incorporate Gaelic districts by *surrender and regrant. His conciliatory policies allowed the recruitment of Irish troops for the *Boulogne expedition of 1544 and the west of Scotland expedition of 1545. The opportunity for these expansive policies was provided by St Leger's partnership with *Brabazon in widespread profiteering from dissolved monastic and confiscated rebel lands by way of speculation and undervaluation. This windfall for officials, both English and Anglo-Irish, and for local gentry, enabled St Leger to build up a personal following outside the predominant Geraldine and Butler factions. The earl of *Ormond took up the complaints of John *Alen and Robert Cowley but St Leger called their bluff at court in 1546. In his last deputyship St Leger's main task was to govern cheaply. He slashed expenditure but was unable to reduce the army much below 1,000 because of wars in Ulster and the midlands. St Leger's earlier land transactions now rebounded when William *Fitzwilliam brought widespread corruptions to light in 1556. St Leger was dismissed, tried, and surcharged £5,000. HM

St Patrick's cathedral, Dublin, the 'national' cathedral of the *Church of Ireland, originally the site of a pre-*Norman parish church immediately outside the city walls. Archbishop John *Cumin built a collegiate church here which was dedicated in 1192. In 1213, after a disagreement with the dean and chapter of *Christ Church, Archbishop *Henry of London advanced St Patrick's to cathedral status, and began to rebuild the church on a grander scale.

In 1300 rivalry between the two cathedrals was ended with a papal decree recognizing the supremacy of Christ Church. In 1320 Archbishop Alexander de Bykenore inaugurated a papal university at St Patrick's in an effort to revive its importance; this was never a success and finally ceased to exist *c*.1494. During the *Reformation St Patrick's status was further diminished to that of parish church. Its cathedral status was reinstated under Queen Mary in 1554–5 and it retained diocesan status until the *disestablishment of the Church of Ireland in 1869. Jonathan *Swift was dean there between 1713 and 1745.

Much of the fabric of the church goes back to the 13th and 14th centuries. The north-west tower was constructed under Archbishop Minot in 1362; the granite spire was added in 1749–50 to the design of the architect George Semple. In 1544 the piers and vaulting of the nave collapsed. By the early 19th century the fabric was in a poor condition and a major restoration programme, funded by Sir Benjamin Lee *Guinness, led to the reconstruction of much of the cathedral. Included in the reconstruction was the addition of the north and south porches, the west door and windows, and the nave buttresses. RM

St Patrick's Day, see CALENDAR CUSTOM.

saints, in the Christian tradition, are deceased members of the faithful believed to have already entered into heavenly glory. In the early church, saints were created by popular acclamation in response to their holiness of life, testified by martyrdom, miracles, and other forms of heroic witness to the faith. Canonization permitted the organization of a cult and the saint's inclusion in the local church's liturgical calendar. For the local Christian communities who proclaimed them, saints were both a practical moral example to follow and a bridge between themselves and the divine, available to intercede before a God who, despite the assurance of the dogma of the incarnation, could appear distant. In this sense, the saints personalized and localized the dogmas of the faith. The cults of the Virgin Mary and of such early Irish saints as *Brigid and Finian are good examples of this. Later, local bishops took control of the canonization process and it was finally reserved to the Holy See in the 12th century. Rome formalized it in the 13th century and updated it in the 1740s. In 1983 a major revision was carried out by John Paul II.

Although Irish saints crowd the local liturgical calendar, only a small number, including St *Malachy, Laurence *O'Toole, and Oliver *Plunkett, have been officially canonized by the church. The public veneration of a greater number has been papally sanctioned by the canonical process of beatification: these have included Thaddeus McCarthy (d. 1497), bishop of Ross and later Cloyne, several Reformation martyrs, and Edmund Rice (see CHRISTIAN BROTHERS). Despite the paucity of officially canonized native saints, Irish devotional practice has been marked by veneration of holy places, wells, and relics associated with both officially canonized and popularly proclaimed saints, at home and abroad. This was traditionally expressed in pilgrimages and *patterns. The neo-Tridentine church disapproved of many of these due to their semi-pagan origins and the moral licence which often accompanied them. Alternative, sanitized cults were imported, St Thérèse of Lisieux and St Maria Goretti joining a large number of earlier continental imports such as St Nicholas, St John the Baptist, and St Anne. The cult of the saints lost some of its importance with the liturgical reforms of the second *Vatican Council (1962–5), especially the renewed emphasis on the centrality of Christ and the eucharist. However, ease of travel has led to an increase in religious pilgrimages abroad, especially to Marian shrines in Europe.

Martimort, A. J., *Liturgy and Time* (1986)

TO'C

St Vincent de Paul, Society of, charitable Christian organization of Catholic tradition, founded in Paris in 1833 by Antoine Frédéric Ozanam (1813–53). He was inspired both by the example of St Vincent de Paul (1580–1660) and by 19th-century Catholic liberalism to respond to mass poverty. The society spread to Dublin in 1844 and was active in *Famine relief. By 1990 there were 980 Irish conferences with over 10,000 members. The society has been effective in evolving to meet new social needs. Basing its activity on practical work in the homes of the poor and on solid Vincentian spirituality, it remains a popular and effective charitable organization. TO'C

salt. Panning was initially the only means of obtaining this essential commodity, short of importing it from England, France, and Portugal. It was done by laying large metal pans along the shore, for the extraction of salt by the evaporation of sea water. This was a slow and painstaking process, but essential to provide salt for the preservation of meat and fish during the winter. Records of salt panning, for example by the monks of Mountcharles, Co. Donegal, date back to the 12th century, though undoubtedly it went on much earlier. By the 17th century there were many salt works, such as those at Rathalloe, on the Ards peninsula, in Co. Down, and at Ballycastle, Co. Antrim, where it continued well into the 19th century. The process was superseded by the importation of rock salt from Cheshire, where mining began in 1670. The discovery of salt deposits in Carrickfergus, Co. Antrim, in 1850, and the subsequent huge exploitation there, made mining the principal means of obtaining supplies in Ireland. Ironically, Carrickfergus was the only large coastal town in Ireland, at the beginning of the 19th century, not to have its own salt works. PC

Samhain (1 Nov.), the first day of winter and one of the four traditional 'quarter days', important in the calendar customs of Goidelic-speaking areas up to the present century. The eve of Samhain was believed to be a time of supernatural occurrences: according to medieval sources the dwellings of the fairies were revealed, and modern folklore associates the night with divination and the dead. The name appears to contain the element *sam-* 'summer', perhaps alluding to a belief in the inversion of other-worldly time. JPC

Saor Éire, a republican-socialist party set up by the *Irish Republican Army in 1931. The idea for such an organization was first aired by Peadar *O'Donnell in 1929. Despite much opposition from more military and conservative-minded IRA members, it was ultimately approved by the Army Convention in 1931. Most delegates wanted to prevent a split on the social issue and realized that a radical political alternative to *Fianna Fáil was needed. It held its first convention in September 1931, calling upon workers and small farmers to overthrow Irish capitalism and British imperialism.

Saor Éire can be seen as part of a wave of radical, often communist, organizations which developed in the late 1920s as a result of poor economic conditions. It attracted some support from other radical groups, but the aim of mobilizing independent farmers and unemployed labourers in a common movement was never realistic. The establishment of Saor Éire was seized upon by the *Cumann na nGaedheal government, for whom it provided an ideal opportunity to portray all republicans, including Fianna Fáil, as dangerous communists. To deal with this 'red scare' a *public safety bill was introduced in October 1931 which enhanced the constitutional powers of the police and declared twelve radical organizations, including Saor Éire and the IRA, illegal. In the same month the Catholic hierarchy issued a pastoral letter excommunicating all members of these organizations. Saor Éire subsequently dissolved quickly. Another organization with the same name was established in the 1960s. JA

Sarsfield, Patrick (*c.*1655–1693), earl of Lucan (1691), Jacobite military commander. The second son of a family with lands in Cos. Dublin and Kildare, Sarsfield fought in the French service *c.*1675–7 then rose rapidly in the army of *James II. In the *Williamite War he recaptured Connacht in October 1689, defeating the hitherto invincible Enniskillen Protestants. His daring raid behind Williamite lines to destroy enemy siege equipment at Ballyneety (11 Aug. 1690) contributed significantly to the failure of the first siege of Limerick and consolidated Sarsfield's reputation as the leading Irish commander on the Jacobite side. Described by a fellow Jacobite as 'a man of huge stature, without sense, very good natured and very brave', he headed the war party within the Jacobite camp, opposed to surrender and critical of *Tyrconnell. But when defeat at *Aughrim (where Sarsfield successfully defended Saint-Ruth's right) left the Jacobites confined to Limerick, he took the initiative in negotiating the treaty of *Limerick. Appointed *maréchal du camp* in the French service, he was killed at the battle of Landen, in Flanders, in 1693. Although an *Old English gentleman who had moved easily in London society, fighting two duels and taking part in two abductions, Sarsfield was also a grandson of Rory *O'More, and this mixed ancestry has been seen as important to his pre-eminence as a Jacobite hero.

Saunderson, Col. Edward (1837–1906), first leader of the Irish *unionist movement. A member of a *Whiggish landed family whose tradition of parliamentary representation began in the 17th century, Saunderson was Liberal MP for Co. Cavan 1865–74. However, the *Land War pushed him and other south Ulster landlords towards an aggressive *Orangeism (Saunderson joined the order in 1882). In 1885 he was returned for North Armagh as a Conservative, and held the seat until his death.

Saunderson sought to liberate Irish loyalism from the damaging constraints of British party politics, and was the principal force behind the new Irish Unionist parliamentary party (1885–6). He was the leading Irish unionist contributor to the debate on the first *home rule bill, and remained the principal parliamentary face of Irish loyalism until the mid-1890s. Thereafter he was diverted into a defence of the Irish landed interest. His vision of a gentry-dominated, parliamentary unionism was challenged both by T. W. *Russell and by the *Independent Orange Order, and organizational initiative within the unionist movement increasingly fell into other hands.

Saunderson was a Whig who sought to counter populist nationalism through a paternalistic and Protestant class alliance. He defined several key features of early unionist organization: a measure of independence from the British parties, a parliamentary focus, and gentry domination. His witty and emotional rhetoric provided a model for later populist unionists. But at the end of his career, faced with challenge both from nationalists and from radical unionists, he reverted to a more narrowly class-based form of politics.

Jackson, A., *Colonel Edward Saunderson: Land and Loyalty in Victorian Ireland* (1995)

AJ

Saurin, William (*c.*1757–1839), lawyer. Born in Belfast, Saurin became MP for Blessington, Co. Wicklow, in 1799 and opposed the Act of *Union. Noted for his anti-Catholic views, he served as attorney-general from 1807 until removed in 1822 at the insistence of *Wellesley.

Savage, a long-established family which came to Ulster with John de *Courcy and received large estates around Coleraine in the early 13th century. When the de Burgo (see BURKE (DE BURGH)) earldom collapsed a century later, Robert Savage was made seneschal of Ulster and later rewarded with lands in the Ards Peninsula for defending the beleaguered colonists. In the 15th century, the Savages and the other Anglo-Norman families were driven back by the *O'Neills of Clandeboye into 'the little Pale' of *Carrickfergus, the Ards, and Lecale. The last seneschal of Ulster, Rowland Savage (d. 1519), was driven out completely.

Nevertheless, the Savage family managed to remain in Ulster. The Savages of Carrickfergus, who were least subject to Gaelicization, provided five mayors and ten sheriffs of the town and its county between 1570 and 1645. Amongst the Savages of the Ards, there were branches at Portaferry and Ardkeen after primogeniture broke down. The heads of these branches Protestantized under the influence of Hugh Montgomery, Viscount Ards, in the first half of the 17th century. The exception was the Catholic cadet line of Ardkeen Savages at Ballygalget which suffered confiscation for the actions of Rowland Savage, *Jacobite army captain and MP for Newry in the *Patriot Parliament. HM

Sceilg Mhichíl (Skellig Michael), Co. Kerry, an ascetic *monastic settlement on the Great Skellig island dedicated to St Michael. The foundation date of the monastery is unknown, but records mention a *Viking attack in 823 and the deaths of monks there in 950 and 1044.

The settlement is perched roughly 550 feet above sea level. The well-preserved remains, constructed on man-made terraces, consist of six drystone huts, a boat-shaped oratory, a small church, and numerous cross-shaped slabs. On the hazardous southern peak of the island there are traces of a hermitage and the foundations of a small oratory. RM

Schomberg, Frederick Herman, duke of (1615–90), *William III's first commander in the *Williamite War. A German Protestant mercenary of international reputation, he landed at Bangor Bay, Co. Down, on 13 August 1689, with 14,500 men. He advanced south to Dundalk but declined to engage an opposing army under *James II, retiring instead to winter quarters at Blaris (Lisburn), Co. Antrim, where disease (dysentery and possibly typhus) wiped out up to half his army. His failure to make progress cost him William's favour. He was killed at the battle of the *Boyne, but his burial place in *Christ Church cathedral remained unmarked until *Swift erected a plaque there in 1731.

schools. From the early modern period, schools were a key element of state policy to spread the influence of the *Reformation. Legislation for the establishment of parish elementary schools (1537) and diocesan grammar schools (1570) proved very largely ineffectual. The *royal schools, set up as part of *plantation schemes, took root, however. The tradition of state provision as an instrument of religious and social change was continued in the 18th century by the *charter schools. There were a growing number of *charity schools, mainly in cities and towns, while elsewhere *'hedge schools' proliferated, and by the early 19th century most Irish children who received an elementary education did so outside the officially regulated, but highly inadequate, parish school system. Prosperous Catholic families continued to evade the prohibition on 'foreign education' by sending their children to colleges in France, Spain, Italy, and the Netherlands.

The *Catholic Relief Acts of 1782 and 1793 largely removed the educational constraints on Catholics, but the problem of the provision of appropriate universal education at elementary level remained to be solved.

The matter was first addressed by John *Hely-Hutchinson, provost of Trinity College, Dublin, whose ideas formed the nucleus of proposals put before the Irish House of Commons in 1787 by the *chief secretary, Thomas Orde. He described a complex educational system of restructured parish and diocesan schools, with 'great schools', one in each province, teaching 'technical arts', 'mercantile knowledge', and agriculture, and funded by diverting funds from the charter schools.

Orde left office within months of making his proposals, and nothing came of them. But the need for state-supported universal education remained. A series of commissions surveyed the scene, one of which, the Board of Education, recommended (in its influential fourteenth report of 1812–13) the setting up of a government body that would regulate and finance schools, and, by respecting denominational differences, be acceptable to all.

The *Kildare Place Society (1811), offering combined 'literary' education and Bible-reading 'without note or comment' with separate denominational education outside school hours, was successful in attracting state funding for its schools, but eventually fell foul of Catholic opinion. The reports of the Irish Education Inquiry (1825–6) endorsed the policy of 'mixed' education with denominational safeguards, and in a letter of 1831 the chief secretary Edward Stanley set out a scheme for schools regulated and financed by a government-appointed board of 'commissioners of national education'. In the event, however, pressure from all the major religious denominations ensured that both elementary education in the *national schools and *teacher-training should have a de facto denominational character.

The matter of the universal provision of intermediate (secondary) education was not to arise for more than a century. But by the late 19th century there was an awareness on the part of political and ecclesiastical leaders that existing provision was inadequate, even for the children of the middle classes for whom it was considered appropriate. Official inquiries into endowed schools began with the Wyse Committee (1837), whose findings demonstrated the patchy nature of what was available, but whose recommendations of denominationally mixed, state-funded intermediate schools were far ahead of their time. The proposals of the Kildare Commission (1857–8) were likewise left to gather dust.

The number of secondary schools grew appreciably, such Protestant endowed schools as those of Erasmus *Smith and the Incorporated Society being steadily supplemented by the activities of the Catholic religious orders: among them the *Christian Brothers, the Loreto Sisters, and the Ursulines. With the Intermediate Education (Ireland) Act of 1878, government introduced a method of providing financial support for intermediate schools without (at least in theory) infringing its self-imposed inhibition on supporting denominational education. Commissioners were appointed, and provided with £1 million from the endowments of the erstwhile established church, the proceeds of which were to be distributed to intermediate schools on the basis of the results their pupils gained in examinations conducted by the commissioners. Twenty years later the Pallas Commission (1899) endorsed the 'payment-by-results' system and further legislation (1900) widened the commissioners' powers and provided for the appointment of inspectors.

In time, a number of prestigious Catholic boys' schools had emerged (Clongowes Wood, Castleknock, Blackrock, for example). Their pupils filled many influential positions in the public service at home and throughout the British empire. Together with boys from the Christian Brothers' schools, they provided the political and administrative leadership of the newly independent Irish state, as their equivalents from *Belfast Academical Institution, Belfast Royal Academy, Campbell College, and elsewhere did in Northern Ireland. Alexandra College, Dublin, founded in 1866, pioneered access to secondary and university education for Protestant girls, its example closely followed by schools for the daughters of the Catholic middle classes. The early years of the 20th century saw a beginning made with the training of secondary teachers in the two Dublin universities and Queen's, Belfast.

The concept of state-aided but privately owned and managed secondary schools survived *partition. In Northern Ireland Lord *Londonderry's attempt to promote non-denominational primary education was abandoned in the face of concerted opposition. When compulsory education for all children between 6 and 14 years of age was introduced in 1892, the legislators had the universal provision of elementary education in mind. But the implication of raising the school-leaving age to 15 (Northern Ireland in 1957, the Republic in 1972) was that free post-primary schools would be available.

Change came first in the north. The 1947 Education Act, closely following English developments of 1944, provided for universal free secondary education. However, selection by examination for grammar or secondary modern schooling, abandoned elsewhere in the United Kingdom from the 1960s, has continued to operate. Twenty years later (1967) fees were abolished in most secondary schools in the Republic where the demand for post-primary education could only be met by widening the curriculum of the vocational (technical) schools, set up under the Vocational Education Act of 1930, and by the creation of new categories: 'comprehensive' and 'community' schools.

Technical education was even slower off the mark. The imaginative (if impracticable) proposals from Orde, the inclusion of agricultural and horticultural subjects in the national school curriculum at an early stage, and the establishment of model schools and farms by the national commissioners were not matched by any official intervention at intermediate level. Such initiatives as there were depended on the *Royal Dublin Society and the supporters of *mechanics' institutes. It was not until the setting up of the Department of *Agriculture and Technical Instruction, following legislation in 1899, that a start was made at government level, resulting in the emergence of schools specifically devoted to the teaching of technical subjects, and of financial encouragement of such teaching in intermediate schools.

See also MONASTIC SCHOOLS. KM

science. The history of Irish science begins in the 17th century with individuals such as Robert *Boyle, William *Petty, and William *Molyneux, and with the *Dublin Philosophical Society. But it was only as prosperity and population increased after 1700 that a socio-economic context favourable to sustained scientific inquiry developed. Bodies such as the *Royal Dublin Society (1731), the *Physico-Historical Society (1744), the *Royal Irish Academy (1785), and the *Belfast Natural History and Philosophical Society (1821) encouraged the application of science to agriculture and industry. The expansion of higher education helped to create a larger pool of scientific talent. *Maynooth, the *Queen's Colleges, and other university-level foundations taught scientific subjects; vocational courses were available at the Museum of Irish Industry (founded 1845, renamed 'Royal College of Science', 1867), the City of Dublin Technical School (founded 1887), and technical schools in the provinces. At Trinity College, science subjects were revised or introduced: thus, the mathematics syllabus was reformed by Bartholomew Lloyd (professor in 1813), who introduced French texts and methods, and the engineering school was established (1843) by his son Humphrey Lloyd. The social and institutional foundations of science in Ireland were further strengthened by the entry into higher education of women, who henceforth augmented the number of scientists, and the creation of more institutions of higher education in the 20th century.

Ireland's new ability to sustain scientific enterprise was seen in astronomy. Large observatories were built at Dunsink (opened in the mid-1780s) and Armagh (founded 1791). A sizeable private observatory was built at Birr (see PARSONS, WILLIAM) in 1845; others were at Markree (1831), Millbrook (1866), Daramona (1871), and Sherrington (1877). In Dublin, John Ellard Gore (from 1879) and William Stanley Monck (from 1888) also had private observatories. Irish observatories made a significant contribution to observational astronomy, and in Howard Grubb (1844–1931) Ireland had a telescope maker of international renown.

Irish scientists made important contributions to their particular disciplines. In chemistry William Higgins (1763–1825) claimed to have anticipated the atomic theory of John Dalton, and Thomas Andrews (1813–85) investigated the properties of gases. In physics, Nicolas Callan (1799–1864) and George Johnston Stoney (1826–1911) worked on electricity. Humphrey Lloyd (1800–81) was internationally known for his studies in optics and magnetism. The work of George Francis FitzGerald (1851–1901) stimulated controversies among physicists that contributed to the later emergence of the theory of relativity. John Joly (1857–1933), remembered as a geologist, also pioneered the use of radioactivity in the treatment of cancer. In atomic physics, Ernest *Walton was awarded the Nobel prize. Ireland produced fine mathematicians. In addition to William Rowan *Hamilton, other notable figures were his rival James McCullagh (1809–47), George Boole (1815–64), and John Lighton Synge (1897–1995). Other famous scientists were born or raised in Ireland, but worked elsewhere: they include the physician and natural historian Hans Sloane (1660–1753), who maintained important correspondence with French scientists, the chemist Joseph Black (1728–99), who evolved the theory of 'latent heat', John Tyndall (1820–93), for many years superintendent of the Royal Institution, and George G. Stokes (1819–1903), famed for his research in optical phenomena. In the Dublin Institute for Advanced Studies with its School of Theoretical Physics (founded 1940), Ireland was furnished with an institution capable of patronizing research at the highest level.

Some scientists have taken Ireland itself as their object of investigation. In natural history, John Templeton (1766–1825) was the first seriously to study the botany and zoology of Ireland. William Thompson (1805–52) undertook a survey of the flora and fauna of the country; he received much help from the entomologist Mary Ball (1812–98). The dominant figure in more recent times was Robert Lloyd Praeger (1865–1953), who inspired scholars such as the botanist David Charles Webb (1912–94). In geology, the Geological Society of Dublin (founded 1831) and the Geological Survey of Ireland (founded 1845) undertook surveys; they were guided by Richard *Griffith (1784–1878), whose geological map of Ireland (1839) remains a classic. Geological and Quaternary studies were further developed by William Bourke Wright (1876–1939), Anthony Farrington (1893–1973), George Francis Mitchell (1912–97), and others who continued to elucidate the natural and geological history of Ireland.

See also MEDICAL SCHOOLS.

Nudds, J. R., McMillan, N. D., Weaire, D. L., and Lawlor, S. M. P. (eds.), *Science in Ireland, 1800–1930: Tradition and Reform* (1988)

DJS

Scotland. Geographically the north of Ireland is separated from Scotland (Kintyre) by a narrow strait, 20 miles wide. Hence it is not surprising that Ulster should have been closely linked with Scotland, more so than southern Ireland, whose links were more with Wales. Colonization from northern Ireland (Dál Riata) began in the 3rd century AD. It was followed in due course by evangelization. Like other conquerors, the Irish advanced with the Bible in one hand and the sword in the other. Conquests were made at the expense of their fellow Celts, the British of Strathclyde and the Picts of eastern Scotland, and by *c.*1000 Scots-Gaelic was prevalent over much of Scotland, although it did not reach Orkney and Shetland. Irish missionaries led by *Colum Cille brought Christianity to much of Scotland and also played a key role in the Christianization of Northumbria, an area which was long regarded as being culturally and politically tied to 'the kingdom of the Scots'. Thus Ireland left a lasting mark on the history of early Christian Scotland. Fergus Mór (*c.* AD 500), ruler of Dál Riata, was seen as the founder figure of Scottish dynasties. The very name 'Scotland' means 'the Land of the Irish'. Many Scottish place names (e.g. those incorporating *sliabh*=hill, *cill*=church, *baile*=village, and *achadh*=field) have Irish origins. Early folk history, adumbrated for example in the story of Deirdre and the sons of Uisneach, implied the existence of close links between Ulster and Alba (the Gaelic name for what came to be called Scotland).

The *Viking raids (*c.*800) transformed but did not destroy the links between Ireland and Scotland. The Gaelic 'kingdom of Scots', under the McAlpine dynasty, shifted its centre of gravity from west to east under the impact of the Vikings. In the 12th century, however, a revival of Gaelic influence began under the leadership of Somerled, founder of 'the kingship of the Isles' (d. 1164). One of Somerled's sons, Donald, gave his name to the MacDonald dynasty, 'lords of the Isles' who exercised power on both sides of the sea dividing Ulster and the west of Scotland. The *MacDonnells of Antrim were key supporters of the royalist cause in the civil wars of the mid-17th century and backed Alasdair MacDonald ('Colkitto') in Montrose's campaigns in 1644–5, when Irish and Highland forces fought on behalf of Charles I.

The link between Ireland and Scotland was not confined to the lordship of the Isles. In 1315 Edward *Bruce, brother of Robert Bruce (de Brus, of Norman background), newly established 'king of Scots', came to mobilize Gaelic Ireland against English power there. After his death, however, Bruce was condemned by some as 'the common ruin of the Galls and the Gaels of Ireland'. One Irish writer, a chronicler of the O'Briens, compared the Scots to a 'black cloud with vaporous-creeping offshoots and dark mists ... [which] covered our Ireland's surface'. The result was nevertheless to undermine English influence in the north for two centuries. Ulster became a frontier region between Scotland and the English lordships in the south, where chiefs such as *O'Neill and *O'Donnell enjoyed an autonomy comparable to that of the marcher lords on the Welsh borders and the Percy family on the Anglo-Scottish borders. In maintaining their local position, Ulster chiefs routinely hired mercenaries from Scotland, the so-called *gallowglasses. It is not too much to say that during this period (1300–1500) Ireland north of the Boyne looked more to Scotland than to England.

The *Ulster plantation established links of a different kind between Ireland and Scotland. The accession of James VI of Scotland as James I of England in 1603 brought Ireland into a 'three-kingdom' political structure. The new king used his power to support colonization from the Scottish lowlands into the territories of the Gaelic chiefs O'Neill and O'Donnell. He also encouraged settlement by the Campbells in Kintyre at the expense of the MacDonalds. In the newly planted counties of Cavan, Donegal, Armagh, Coleraine (later replaced by Londonderry), Fermanagh, and Tyrone the balance on the whole favoured English settlers. In Antrim and Down, however, colonized after the purchase of the estates of Conn O'Neill, the vast majority of the new arrivals were Scottish, Lowland born and *Presbyterian in religion. They brought to Ulster a distinctive covenanting style of *Puritanism in which the papacy appeared as Antichrist. There was an inevitable and bitter clash over land and religion between the colonists and the existing Gaelic-speaking inhabitants, whose earlier cultural links were with the Highlands and the Isles, not the Lowlands. In 1641 the Ulster Catholics, led by Phelim *O'Neill, rose against a plantation in which they had lost much of their lands. A massacre of Protestants occurred which came to have the same historical resonance in Ireland as the later Scottish massacre of Glencoe in 1692 (where the Catholic MacDonalds were the victims). During the civil wars of the 1640s, in both Ulster and Scotland, clashes between Catholics and Presbyterians took on a bitterness rivalling that of the Wars of Religion in Europe.

During the 18th century, Ulster Presbyterians experienced political and religious discrimination, most notably the *sacramental test. It was such grievances which led to the disenchantment of some Presbyterians with the British government and to their involvement in a radical alliance with the Catholics—the *United Irishmen. The influence of the Scottish Enlightenment had also encouraged the growth of a more liberal and tolerant 'New Light' (see OLD LIGHT AND NEW LIGHT) movement in Presbyterian circles. It was thus not surprising that groups of Presbyterians and Catholics should have made common cause in the *insurrection of 1798 in Antrim and Down. Among the Presbyterian body as a whole, however, there was probably little sympathy with the United Irishmen and during the 19th century it was political and religious orthodoxy that was to prevail.

After the passing of the Act of *Union relations between *evangelical Anglicans and Presbyterian covenanters drew closer in the face of the threat of a resurgent Catholicism, led by *O'Connell. Economic competition for jobs in newly industrialized *Belfast added to the tensions. Belfast, once a liberal city, became a byword for sectarian violence. The liberal traditions of the Scottish Enlightenment did not disappear entirely, but they were gravely weakened.

The relationship between Ireland and Scotland underwent further changes during the *Great Famine and its aftermath. Irish refugees poured into Glasgow and its surrounding areas, where they took low-paying jobs in mining and in the cotton industry. The Irish newcomers were resented as a source of 'cheap labour', and sectarian antagonism in the Scottish Lowlands reached levels comparable to those in Belfast.

As in Northern Ireland, sectarian hostility persisted to the end of the 20th century. In Scotland, however, there has been some decline in the level of inter-ethnic bitterness and, unlike Northern Ireland, Pope John Paul II was able to pay a visit there in 1982. In recent years the problems of Northern Ireland have not seriously affected Scotland, and sectarian rivalries have largely been restricted to football grounds.

Connolly, S. J., Houston, R. A., and Morris, R. J. (eds.), *Conflict, Identity and Economic Development: Ireland and Scotland 1600–1939* (1995)

Ellis, S. G., and Barber, S. (eds.), *Conquest and Union: Fashioning a British State 1485–1725* (1995)

Kearney, H. F., *The British Isles: A History of Four Nations* (1989)

HK

Scots Irish, more usually Scotch-Irish, the latter spelling reflecting the fact that the term, probably in origin and certainly in general usage, is a North American one. 'Scotch-Irish' is widely used by scholars and commentators on the colonial, revolutionary, and early national periods of American history to denote the Irish-born section of the population and their descendants. The assumption is that these settlers were Presbyterians and that, although arriving in North America via Ireland, they, or their ancestors, had originally come from Scotland.

In the United States a self-conscious Scotch-Irish identity seems to have been at its greatest at the turn of the 19th and 20th centuries. A series of Scotch-Irish congresses were held to emphasize the key role of the group in the *American revolutionary period and, more generally, as frontier settlers and as the vital element in the founding of American Presbyterianism. These publicists for what they described as the Scotch-Irish 'race' emphasized how different they were from more recent Irish Catholic immigrants. Less obviously, they endeavoured to stress their central place in American history, which they felt had been ignored or anyway little stressed in the New England, Puritan takeover of the interpretation of the nation's past. The coincidence of this Scotch-Irish movement with the growing professionalization of the work of the historian, the promulgation by F. J. Turner of his hugely influential 'Frontier thesis', and the then intellectually fashionable Social Darwinism, help to explain the entry of the term into scholarship, particularly on the 18th century. Both at the time and more recently strong challenges to the validity and usefulness of the term have been voiced, from those who see it as misrepresenting both the religious and ethnic composition of the first Irish emigrants to America and their sense of their own identity. However, 'Scotch-Irish' continues to be a commonplace usage in writing on the period, whether in specialist or more general works. It is likely to remain so. SJSI

script, see INSULAR SCRIPT.

scullog (scológ), an Irish term used in the 17th and 18th centuries to describe a small farmer.

Scully, William (1821–1906), member of a prosperous Co. Tipperary Catholic landed family. An armed affray involving his tenants at Ballycohey in August 1868 earned him nationwide notoriety as a proprietor. Meanwhile he was speculating in American land, eventually acquiring a quarter of a million acres, mostly in Kansas and Nebraska. This he exploited in a distinctive and lucrative fashion. At his death his estate was worth at least $10 million. RVC

sculpture. Surviving sculpture from medieval Ireland includes *high crosses, figure sculpture in stone and wood, and effigies on ecclesiastical and dynastic tombs. The tradition of dynastic tombs continued into the 16th century, with the remarkable series of recumbent effigies in St Canice's cathedral, Kilkenny. The most ambitious tombs of the early 17th century are the two commemorating Richard *Boyle, 1st earl of Cork. The one at Youghal parish church, Co. Cork (1620), was ordered from London. The huge structure in *St Patrick's cathedral, Dublin (1632), of coarse workmanship, is by an Irish sculptor named Edward Tingham. More sophisticated than either is the monument to Sir Arthur *Chichester, in St Nicholas's church, Carrickfergus, Co. Antrim, with kneeling figures. The abandonment of colouring and the exquisite handling of the drapery and lettering indicate a London workshop of high quality. But Irish sculpture does not flower until the early 18th century, after the *Williamite War.

William Kidwell (1662–1736), a pupil of the outstanding English baroque sculptor Edward Pierce, came to Ireland in 1711. Of his many church monuments, the finest is that to Sir Donatus O'Brien (*c.*1717) in Kilnasoolagh, Co. Clare. John van Nost the younger (*c.*1712–80) established himself in Dublin about 1749, and all his major work was executed there. Nost's Dublin pupils included the exceptionally talented Christopher Hewetson (*c.*1739–98), who in 1765 settled for life in Rome, where he obtained the prestigious commission to sculpt Pope Clement XIV (1776). His memorial to Provost Baldwin (1784), was transported from Italy to its site in *Trinity College, Dublin. A Londoner, Simon Vierpyl (1725–1810), taken up by the earl of *Charlemont while studying in Rome, was brought to Dublin in 1756, and worked on the Marino Casino. John Hickey (1756–95) went on to London where he died young, but not before finishing his Irish masterpiece, the monument to the banker David *La Touche (1790) in Delgany, Co. Wicklow. Of Irish sculptors who did not leave, Edward Smyth (1749–1812), a pupil of Vierpyl, worked in a robust baroque style, as shown in his most celebrated works, the Riverine Heads (*c.*1781–1784) which adorn the keystones of the windows of *Gandon's *Custom House. Edward Smyth's son John Smyth (*c.*1773–1840) was a more refined neoclassical sculptor. Succeeding his father as Master in the Dublin Society's Schools in 1812, John Smyth taught Terence Farrell and John Henry Foley.

Christopher Moore (1790–1863), having probably worked for the duke of Leinster (see KILDARE), permanently settled in London by 1821 but maintained his links with Ireland. Moore's reputation has suffered by his bronze statue of the poet Thomas Moore (1857), which has never failed to provoke ridicule. His portrait busts, however, are usually of good quality. Thomas Kirk (1781–1845), a pupil of John Smyth, was as unfortunate. His most famous work, the colossal statue of Nelson for Nelson's Pillar in Dublin, commissioned in 1818, was blown up by the IRA in 1966. Kirk executed numerous church monuments throughout Ireland.

The 19th century brings the giants of Irish sculpture. Peter Turnerelli (1774–1839), born Tognarelli to Italian parents in Belfast, had a wide practice. His sitters included the royal families of Britain, France, Portugal, and Russia. Another Catholic, John Hogan (1800–58) from Cork, settled in Rome in 1823, returning to Ireland only in 1848. His *Drunken Faun* (1825–9) caused a sensation among the art community in Rome because of its original pose. Patrick MacDowell (1799–1870), from Belfast, moved to London when young. He sculpted the colossal group *Europe* (1870), one of the four continents which surround the Albert Memorial in South Kensington. McDowell's masterpiece, however, is the memorial to the young earl of Belfast, who died of scarlet fever in Naples in 1853. The Dubliner John Henry Foley (1818–74) found even higher fame in England, as he was selected to sculpt the over-life-size gilded bronze figure of Prince Albert (unveiled 1876) for the Albert Memorial. He also did the continent group *Asia* for the same memorial, and met his death from pleurisy contracted while sitting on the wet clay while modelling this group. Foley's attention to costume, both contemporary and historical, anticipates the New Sculpture of the end of the 19th century. Sir Thomas Farrell (1827–1900), one of a family of sculptors, did not leave Ireland. Nineteenth-century Ireland also produced some vigorous architectural sculptors, notably the brothers James and John O'Shea, discovered in Co. Cork by the architects *Deane & Woodward. Their inventive decorations can be seen on the Oxford University Museum (1861).

Samuel Ferres Lynn (1834–76), brother of an architect, worked mostly on architectural sculpture.

The main Irish practitioners of the so-called New Sculpture, John Hughes (1865–1941), Oliver Sheppard (1865–1941), and Albert Power (1882–1945), produced memorable images in bronze, notably Sheppard's *Fall of Cuchulainn* (1911, Dublin, GPO) which became an icon of the *rising of 1916. Their Irish-American contemporaries Augustus Saint-Gaudens (1848–1907) and Andrew O'Connor (1874–1941) obtained important Dublin commissions, such as Saint-Gaudens's monument to Charles Stewart *Parnell (1911). Of the next generation, Oisin Kelly (1915–81) was versatile in many media. The northerner F. E. McWilliam (1909–92) worked in London for most of his career, but always maintained his Ulster contacts. Ian Stuart (b. 1926) and Edward Delaney (b. 1932) moved into abstract concepts. John Behan and the Belfast-based Deborah Brown (b. 1927), after experimenting with abstraction, returned to animal sculpture in bronze. Of the internationally known modernists of Irish origin, Barry Flanagan (born 1941 to Irish parents in North Wales) is London based and makes large abstract sculpture in mild steel. John Aiken (b. 1950) now teaches sculpture at the Slade School. Michael Warren (b. 1950) works in Co. Wexford in a minimalist style in heavy timber. Dorothy Cross (b. 1956) uses diverse material such as cows' udders, wire, and glass.

Crookshank, A. O., *Irish Sculpture from 1600 to the Present Day* (1984)

MA

sea, travel and transport by. In Ireland, this dates from the arrival of the first farmers from continental Europe in *c.*3000 BC. By 2000 BC, sea traffic linked Waterford, Wicklow, and Carlingford with the Isle of *Man, Pembrokeshire, Cornwall, and Argyll. Wicklow *gold and *copper attracted many from mainland Europe. By the *Celtic era, *c.*300 BC, sea connections between Ireland, Britain, and Europe were well established. Irish attacks on post-Roman Britain culminated in the colonization of parts of Wales and the west country.

The commonest Irish craft was a variation of the *curragh, made of skins stretched over a wood frame with a single sail. Early Irish monks travelled to Britain and Europe in such craft. Irishmen sailed as far as the Adriatic and Iceland, while St Brendan is said to have reached North America. *Viking settlements in Ireland generated much traffic with Britain and Europe. The clinker-built Viking longships, which sailed both on sea and inland waterways, were adopted by their *Norman descendants and the native Irish. Norman Ireland was closely tied in, administratively, militarily, commercially, and ecclesiastically, with Britain and the Continent, and sea traffic increased vastly. These trading, ecclesiastical, and administrative links with Britain and Europe continued throughout the Middle Ages. The Irish pilgrim, cleric, or merchant was a common arrival at European ports. *Ports like *Waterford, Youghal, Kinsale, and *Galway grew on the strength of their European connections.

Until the end of the 16th century, Hebridean-style galleys were common on the north and west coasts. But from the late Middle Ages caravel-hulled vessels, mainly foreign-owned, carried most of the trade with the Continent. The presence of so many foreign-owned vessels in Irish waters, and the activities of both foreign and native *pirates, contributed to the urgency behind the drive during the 16th century to achieve more complete control of the island (see TUDOR CONQUEST). Up to the late 17th century sea travel remained small scale, haphazard, and vulnerable to wartime disruption. Thereafter, however, Irish seamen were active participants in the growing transatlantic trade with French and British colonies in the Caribbean and North America. There was also growing *emigration, mainly from Ulster, as well as the involuntary migration of *transported criminals.

After the Act of *Union, British coal and manufactured goods and Irish agricultural produce kept a large cross-channel fleet busy. Steam and iron-cladding allowed much bigger ships to be built. Steam enabled regular timetabled crossings of the Irish Sea. Two Irish Mail steamships plied the Howth–Holyhead route from 1820. In 1838 the *Sirius* made the first wholly steam-powered transatlantic crossing from Passage West to New York. In maritime competition with Britain and other large nations, Ireland was held back by under-investment. Few Irish-owned cross-channel shipping lines survived. Nevertheless, the Dublin Steam Packet Company operated the *Kingstown (Dun Laoghaire)–Holyhead mail and passenger service from 1838 until 1914. From the 1850s, many British railway companies operated cross-channel ferries. By 1900 ferries were sailing from Derry to Glasgow, Belfast to Glasgow, Barrow, Fleetwood, and Liverpool, and from Larne to Stranraer. After the *First World War, Belfast–Heysham was added to Larne–Stranraer. Major southern routes were from Dublin to Liverpool and Heysham, Kingstown to Holyhead, Rosslare to Fishguard, and Cork and Waterford to Wales. Newry, Dundalk, and Drogheda were also ferry ports.

Belfast became a major port and world-leading *shipbuilding centre, with two yards, *Harland &

Wolff specializing in ocean liners, and the smaller (though big by any other standards) *Workman Clark. The sinking in 1912 of the Belfast-built *Titanic*, on her maiden transatlantic voyage, was the greatest single maritime disaster. In both world wars, German U-boat packs menaced Irish waters. In 1941 the Free State government set up *Irish Shipping to secure wartime supplies. It formed the nucleus of the Irish merchant fleet, until its winding-up in 1984. In the 1950s and 1960s, car ferries and container traffic were introduced on the cross-channel routes. In the 1960s, in response to the holiday boom, Rosslare and Cork became important car-ferry ports, linking Ireland to the Continent.

Nowlan, Kevin B. (ed.), *Travel and Transport in Ireland* (2nd edn., 1993)

PC

seaside resorts became popular destinations for holidaymakers and day trippers with the coming of the railways. Sea-bathing, which became fashionable in England from the 1750s, does not seem to have been so popular in Ireland at this early date. Small resorts, such as Blackrock and Howth, developed from around 1820, catering almost exclusively for visiting Dubliners. By 1880 the railways carried industrial workers and the urban middle classes further afield. Dubliners now visited Skerries, Portmarnock, Dalkey, and Bray. From Belfast workers travelled to Bangor and Newcastle in Co. Down, and to Portrush in Antrim. From Derry, Portrush and Bundoran in Co. Donegal were accessible. Resorts became venues for *theatres and *sports, though the English-style pleasure pier was totally lacking. Regular ferry services encouraged visitors from Britain, but these sailings were suspended on the outbreak of war in 1914, and never re-established on the same scale. The fortunes of resorts fluctuated with the economic climate, but their heyday came in the years immediately after 1945. The population was now wealthier and more mobile, with more leisure time. Ireland's only seaside holiday camp, run by the well-established English firm of Butlins, opened at Mosney, Co. Louth, in 1948. By the late 1960s cheaper foreign holidays undermined the domestic trade of resorts. From 1969 the *Northern Ireland conflict further accentuated the decline of resorts there. In the Republic, despite some limited success with initiatives such as the staging of equestrian events, the growth of foreign tourism has done little to arrest the decline of the traditional resorts, which continue to rely on a dwindling number of domestic day trippers.

NG

seasonal migration took two main forms. Migrant labourers (called *spalpeens) travelled from poorer regions such as Kerry and west Cork, Connemara, and Donegal into richer agricultural regions during the season of peak demand for labour at harvest time. Similar but longer journeys to find temporary work in England and Scotland were common from the 18th century. The census of 1841 recorded a total of 60,000 migrant workers passing through the main ports. In the 1860s, when *railways and steam shipping had sharply reduced journey times and costs, numbers may have been as high as 100,000 annually. Earnings from seasonal migration were important in assisting the survival of subsistence farming in the west for a generation after the *Great Famine. Their decline from the late 1860s, following the widespread introduction of machinery on British farms, encouraged a sharp rise in permanent emigration from western counties in which it had previously been resisted.

Seceders, Scottish *Presbyterian dissenters who established congregations, presbyteries, and synods in Ireland in the 18th century. They had seceded from the Church of Scotland in 1733, ostensibly on the issue of lay patronage, but essentially because they were unhappy with the Williamite church settlement in Scotland and the increasingly liberal or 'Moderatist' theology of the Church of Scotland. In Ulster they provided an alternative to the non-subscribing, New Light (see OLD LIGHT AND NEW LIGHT) *Synod of Ulster and between 1746, when their first congregation was formed at Lylehill in Co. Antrim, and 1840, when they united with the Synod of Ulster to form the General Assembly of the Presbyterian Church in Ireland, they established 144 congregations. In Scotland the Seceders were divided in 1747 over the propriety of taking a burgess oath to uphold 'the true religion presently professed within this realm'. This division was reproduced in Ireland, where such oaths were unknown, but in 1818 Irish Seceders reunited to form a single Secession Synod. The withdrawal of the *Remonstrants from the Synod of Ulster in 1830 and the synod's subsequent restoration of obligatory subscription led to the union of the Synod of Ulster and the Secession Synod to form the General Assembly.

RFGH

Second Reformation, the name given to the early and mid-19th-century campaign to promote the mass conversion of the Catholic population to Protestantism. Such efforts were inspired mainly by the growth of *evangelicalism, reinforced in some cases by awareness, in the aftermath of the *insurrection of 1798 and the era of *O'Connell's dominance, of the political dangers posed by an unregenerate Catholic majority. The first major effort was by Irish *Methodists, who in 1799 dispatched three Irish-speaking missionaries to work among the Catholic population. By 1816 there were 21 missionaries, operating from fourteen stations. Other missionary bodies included the Hibernian Bible Society (1806), the Sunday School Society (1809), the Religious Tract and Book Society (1810), and the Irish Society for Promoting the Education of the Native Irish through the Medium of their Own Language (1818), all Anglican controlled, the interdenominational Irish Evangelical Society (1814), and separate *Baptist and *Presbyterian organizations.

The missionary societies offered free elementary education, at a time when demand for *literacy was rising rapidly, combined with preaching and the distribution of bibles and other devotional material in Irish. This allowed them to make impressive-looking short-term gains, especially in the west, where the Catholic church's resources were most limited and its pastoral machinery sometimes in poor condition. In Dingle and Ventry, Co. Kerry, colonies were established to protect converts, by 1845 claimed to number around 800, from intimidation and social pressure. In 1834 an Irish clergyman, Edward Nangle (1800–83), established a similar colony on Achill Island. In 1849 the Society for Irish Church Missions, founded by the English clergyman Alexander Dallas (1791–1869), taking advantage of what Dallas saw as the God-given opportunity of the *Famine, launched a more ambitious campaign to promote Protestantism throughout Connacht. By 1860, however, both the colonies and the wider missionary effort had dwindled to insignificance as the Catholic church, taking advantage of more settled economic conditions, regained lost ground through pastoral reorganization and the systematic use of *missions in affected areas. The Second Reformation nevertheless contributed significantly to *religious conflict. In particular, allegations that Famine relief had been promised or withheld to obtain conversions (*'souperism') left lasting bitterness, while the use of schools for proselytizing purposes confirmed the Catholic church in its demand for denominational education at every level.

Bowen, D., *The Protestant Crusade in Ireland 1800–70* (1978)

Second World War (1939–45). The Second World War marked a significant watershed in Irish political relationships. The *neutrality of Southern Ireland conclusively demonstrated the new state's autonomy from Great Britain and reinforced Ulster unionist alienation from 'Eire'. By contrast, Northern Ireland's role in the war effort confirmed the province's position within the United Kingdom and (in Winston *Churchill's opinion) forged unbreakable bonds between Northern Ireland and Great Britain. Many important defence facilities were located in the province. A string of airfields was built in the north-west and Londonderry became a major base for allied North Atlantic convoy escorts. Between 1942 and 1945 some 300,000 American soldiers were stationed in the province. The development of Northern Ireland agriculture, industry, and commerce to meet wartime needs brought employment and prosperity. The unemployment rate, which had stood at over 20 per cent in the mid-1930s, fell to less than 5 per cent by the end of the war.

In April–May 1941 Belfast suffered two major German air raids in which over 1,000 people perished. In all some 56,000 houses—over half the city's total housing stock—were damaged. For unionists the suffering during 'the Belfast blitz' provided a sacrifice (though nationalists suffered equally) to match and reinforce that of the Ulster Division on the Somme 25 years earlier (see FIRST WORLD WAR).

Although the Belfast cabinet on a number of occasions called on the British government to apply conscription to Northern Ireland, London refused on the grounds that the costs raised by nationalist opposition would far outweigh any manpower benefits. Recruitment in Northern Ireland was in fact rather disappointing. In all, an estimated 38,000 people (of whom 7,000 were women) joined the British forces between 1939 and 1945. A significant number—estimated at over 43,000 men and women—also enlisted from southern Ireland, whose public stance of neutrality was modified by tacit assistance provided across a wide spectrum of activities: the intelligence services of the two countries co-operated closely; weather reports from the west of Ireland were passed on to the British Air Ministry; allied servicemen who landed in southern Ireland were quickly and quietly repatriated to the United Kingdom, while Axis personnel were interned; and overflying rights in Donegal were permitted to British and American planes operating out of Co. Fermanagh.

Barton, Brian, *Northern Ireland in the Second World War* (1995)

KJ

secret ballot, see BALLOT.

seminaries. In 1562 the Council of *Trent legislated for the establishment of diocesan seminaries to provide a pastorally competent priesthood with some knowledge of theology. In Ireland Protestant opposition and lack of resources meant that ecclesiastical students had to travel abroad for seminary education. They clustered into communities which grew into the Irish colleges at Paris (1578) and Salamanca (1592). Other foundations followed at Rome, Louvain, Madrid, Lisbon, and elsewhere. All were dogged by poverty but by the end of the 18th century provided over 500 seminary places, just over half occupied by ordained students who supported themselves through their ministry. Towards the end of the 18th century domestic seminaries were established at Kilkenny (1782) and Carlow (1793). The closure of continental seminaries following the *French Revolution produced a crisis which led parliament to found *Maynooth College in 1795. Diocesan seminaries were founded at Waterford (1807), Wexford (1819), Thurles (1837), and Clonliffe (1859). The Vincentians set up All Hallows in 1842 while the *Jesuits, the Holy Ghost Fathers, and the Society of African Missions had seminaries at Milltown, Kimmage, and Dromantine respectively. Domestic missionary orders also established seminaries. After *Vatican II looser structures, secularization, increased lay involvement in the church, and a fall in student numbers put pressure on the Tridentine seminary model. TO'C

semi-state bodies, see STATE ENTERPRISE.

Senate, the upper house of the *Oireachtas.

1921–1937

Under the *Government of Ireland Act 1920, the Senate of the Southern Ireland parliament, which was based on that proposed by the 1917 *Irish Convention, consisted of nominated members representing a range of interests in Ireland, particularly business, the professions, and education. Fifteen senators nominated by the *lord lieutenant met in June 1921, but the assembly was adjourned following the truce which ended the *Anglo-Irish War and abolished in the Irish Free State (Agreement) Act 1922.

The *constitution of the *Irish Free State provided for a Senate of 60 members who had to take the oath of allegiance. Southern *Unionists were guaranteed special representation by *Cosgrave, who as *president of the executive council nominated half of the first Senate. The election process was considerably amended. Senators were elected for a twelve-year term, later reduced to nine, with one-third retiring every three years. Popular elections were abolished in 1928, when senators were elected by the *Dáil and Senate. One member of the Senate could sit on the executive council.

Although the Senate could initiate legislation, it had no authority over money bills. If the Senate rejected a bill, the Dáil could within a year pass a resolution to send it back to the Senate and within 60 days it would pass. The Senate could also suspend for 90 days any bill passed by both houses if a majority of the Senate so requested the president of the executive council.

1937–

In 1936 de *Valera abolished the Senate, which had earlier rejected the bill to abolish the *oath of allegiance and other legislation. Contrary to expectation, the 1937 *constitution of Ireland revived the concept of an upper house. There are 60 senators, 49 elected and 11 nominated by the *taoiseach. Two members of the government can be senators and ministers can attend both houses. Of the 49 elected members, 6 represent universities; the other 43 members are elected from five panels representing language and culture, agriculture, labour, industry and commerce, and public administration. The constitution also provides for direct election by vocational groups.

Under the 1947 Seanad Electoral Act, members of the Dáil and Senate and county council members constitute the electorate for these panels and this has meant that panel members, despite their ostensibly vocational character, have tended to be party politicians.

The Senate can, like its predecessor, initiate legislation but cannot amend money bills. A bill rejected by the Senate can be passed after 180 days. The Senate and the Dáil can address a joint petition to the *president requesting him or her not to sign a bill unless the 'will of the people' has been ascertained. With the Dáil, the Senate can declare a national emergency in time of war or armed rebellion.

The Senate has aways been subordinate to the Dáil and has not, until recently, actively used its revising and initiating powers. This changed with the introduction in the 1980s of more Oireachtas committees and with more crowded Dáil agendas.

Chubb, Basil, *The Government and Politics of Ireland* (3rd edn., 1992)

Kohn, Leo, *The Constitution of the Irish Free State* (1932)

DMcM

senchléithe, a term meaning 'ancient dwelling' applied to a servile tenant whose forebears of **fuidir* or **bothach* rank have occupied the same land for three generations. Unlike the *fuidir* or *bothach*, he is bound to his lord and cannot renounce his tenancy. If the land he occupies is acquired by a new owner, he and his family go with it. He is nonetheless distinguished from the slave, who is the property of his owner and has no legal rights. FK

seneschals. Originally feudal administrators of *palatinate jurisdictions and *absentee lordships, these government appointees were a destabilizing factor during the *Tudor conquest. In 1553 the crown made Francis Agard, an English military man, seneschal of the absentee lordship of Wexford. *Sussex established constables in castles in south Leinster with rule over neighbouring clans and the use of martial law; *Sidney extended the system, gave them the job of collecting crown rents, and called them seneschals. Theoretically intended to advance civil government, seneschals operated by the Gaelic methods they were supposed to suppress. HM

sept. In the Early Modern period, English and Anglo-Irish commentators used the term 'sept', probably a variant form of 'sect' (a subdivision) also used in this context, to denote the basic corporate family group within Gaelic and Gaelicized lordships. The sept was defined by patrilineal descent within one or two generations of the ruling *ceannfine*, or family head, although, theoretically, Brehon law allowed for up to four generations (the *derbfine*). The sept had military, political, and legal functions and responsibilities within the lordship. It was a distinct group from the lineage, a wider family group which in addition to known relatives, included those who claimed relationship through a common surname. FF

serfdom, a term indicating the social condition of a tenant, servile by birth. Serfdom on *manors in Ireland was neither imported nor necessarily the consequence of the depression of formerly free tenants by their conquerors. Instead the Anglo-Normans appear to have taken over the food-rendering clients (*betaghs) of former Gaelic lords. In the largely Gaelic bishopric of Cloyne a more arbitrary servile regime prevailed than in Anglo-Norman areas, where the force of custom moderated conditions. Although many small Anglo-Norman tenants probably fled serfdom in England, they were treated as free in Ireland.

As with other classes of tenants, the serf's status was determined by tenure rather than by the nature of the labour services he rendered. Free tenements, especially those held by gavillers and cottars, were burdened with labour services too. Even *burgesses were sometimes obliged to render limited services. What distinguished the free from the unfree was the liberty to plead in free courts. In theory the serf was a slave, subject to the arbitrary will of his lord, but in practice he was protected by the custom of the manor. The serf attended the manor court, where customary law, not the will of the lord, was declared by the suitors, both free and servile. The lord, as much as his servile tenants, was bound to respect that law. Moreover, if a freeman inflicted injury on a serf, he was liable to prosecution by the serf's lord; the serf thus had some protection from the free courts. In Ireland the manorial regime was fairly benign. On the manor of Lisronagh, Co. Tipperary, in 1333 serfs were required to perform basically seasonal services on the demesnes: ploughing an acre of wheat and oats; one day of reaping in the autumn; providing carriage for grain; making hay and stacking it. In certain cases they were paid for such work, and were also entitled to receive food and drink at the lord's expense. Even their animals and corn were protected: the lord and his bailiffs 'shall have the right to purchase such for money *at a reasonable estimate*'. These services were significantly lighter than those imposed on the villein in England. Serfdom disappeared in the later Middle Ages, no doubt because the commutation of services to rent had the effect of rendering serfs indistinguishable from other classes of rent-paying tenant. CAE

servants. Domestic service was always an important employer of Irish women, but particularly so from the mid-19th century, as other opportunities for women from the labouring/small farming/working class evaporated. Such women often used service as a stopgap between other jobs, or as a way of saving money for marriage. The 19th century also saw a redefinition of domestic service, with a greater emphasis on maintaining social distance between employers and servants.

Pay and conditions varied. Servants working in a 'big house' had a place within a well-defined career structure; the job of a butler, housekeeper, or cook was a highly skilled one which commanded excellent wages (particularly for men) and good working conditions. However, the majority of servants were females working on their own as 'generals', often alongside the woman of the house, or on farms, working inside and outside. From 1911 employers were obliged to pay national health insurance for their servants, but this was difficult to enforce. The *Limerick Rural Survey* carried out by Muintir na Tire (1964) revealed that up to the mid-20th century farm servants were often not even given eating utensils. Urban servants too often had to endure appalling accommodation and inferior food.

Domestic service was enthusiastically promoted by educationalists and many shades of political opinion, including middle-class *feminists, right up to the 1950s as a morally safe occupation, and a good preparation for marriage, for working-class females. By the 1940s, however, advertisements for servants in the Irish daily papers carry a note of desperation. The number of female domestic servants fell dramatically between 1946 and 1961 as expectations rose and alternative employment became more easily available. As late as 1956 the Commission on Emigration urged that middle-class families be given government grants to employ servants—a recommendation which was never acted upon. While the numbers of girls taking domestic science at school, in evening classes, and at third level remained buoyant, most now hoped to find work as professional cooks in institutions, or to have these skills when they set up house for themselves.

Hearn, Mona, *Below Stairs: Domestic Service Remembered in Dublin and beyond 1880–1922* (1993)

CC

servitors, see ULSTER PLANTATION.

Settlement, Act of (1662), passed by the Irish parliament as part of the *Restoration land settlement. Dispossessed proprietors judged by a court of claims to have been innocent of rebellion were to be restored, the grantees under the *Cromwellian land settlement being compensated ('reprised') with lands elsewhere. Fifty-six named individuals ('nominees'), 221 'ensignmen' who had served the king during his exile, and 'articlemen' who had served the *Confederate Catholics but abided by the first or second *Ormond peace were also to regain their estates. A court of claims convened in January 1663 heard 829 cases, awarding decrees of innocence to more than 550 Catholics and to about 150 Protestants. Its sittings ended on 21 August, although hundreds of cases remained unheard. Their termination is generally attributed to fear of Protestant unrest (see BLOOD'S PLOT), though it remains unclear how far Charles II or his ministers had ever envisaged the large-scale restoration of Catholic proprietors. Even as it was, a second major bill, the Act of *Explanation, was required to resolve the conflicting claims of royalists, 'innocent' Catholics, and Cromwellian grantees.

settlement patterns, the distribution of population clusters of varying sizes in a given area. The individual *settlements* which comprise these may be either urban or rural, dispersed or nucleated, and either deliberately planned or of gradual, accretive growth. Various factors may have determined the original location, morphology, and plan of individual settlements, their subsequent development, and their collective distribution. Physical attributes, such as a water supply, a defensible site, the availability of cultivable land, the presence of raw materials, or an advantageous position relative to existing settlements or communications, as well as social factors such as the pattern of land ownership, may all have helped determine the location of individual settlements in the past. Their overall numbers and subsequent development are likely to have been influenced by other factors, including population change, technological innovation, secular economic trends, and changes in prevailing social, religious, and political ideologies. Thus settlement patterns may be seen as a social artefact, mirroring changes in society and sometimes influencing these. Consequently, in countries of great cultural antiquity such as Ireland, present-day settlement patterns retain considerable evidence relating to the structure and functioning of past societies.

Urban settlement and its origins

By 1900 Ireland's settlement pattern had more or less achieved a recognizably modern form. Dominating everything were *Dublin and *Belfast, with populations of 305,000 and 387,000 respectively. Beyond these lay a landscape of dispersed farm settlement and small market towns, in which urban industrialization was centred on north-east Ulster and the Belfast hinterland. This regional industrialization was a 19th-century phenomenon, and had altered what had been a classic example of a pre-industrial primate urban hierarchy. In 1800, Dublin, with a population of *c.*200,000, had long outgrown every other centre, but by 1900, the growth of regional textile centres such as *Derry, Lurgan, and Portadown, as well as Belfast, had distorted the earlier urban rank order.

Beyond Ulster, the provincial urban network faced stagnation as the domestic market for all forms of goods and services contracted with the continuing post-*Famine decline in population. Major regional centres such as *Cork and *Galway retained their traditional service roles, but the fate of many smaller towns depended on whether they were well connected by Ireland's rapidly expanding *railway network. Those that were, such as Athlone, Mallow, or Portarlington, were more likely to prosper as market centres than places like Castlecomer or Tallow which were bypassed.

One consequence of this relative urban stagnation was the widespread survival in the late 19th century of earlier morphologies and plans, dating not merely from the wave of urban and village improvement during the 18th-century *Enlightenment, but also from the medieval and *plantation periods. Between *c.*1700 and 1845 approximately 750 towns and villages were either founded, refounded, or rebuilt at the instigation, or with the collaboration, of their *landlords (see ESTATE VILLAGES). The opportunity to do so came with the mid-18th-century expansion of the domestic market and the strengthening of Ireland's agrarian economy. Improvements were usually undertaken with the intention of enhancing local marketing, but also sometimes for social, political, or aesthetic reasons. Generally speaking, an inverse relationship existed between the size of these improved settlements and the extent of the property monopoly any one landlord enjoyed within them. The larger regional centres, such as *Kilkenny or Cahir, Co. Tipperary, were invariably among the one-third which were of medieval or plantation origin, and in which no one landlord monopolized property ownership. Consequently, in these larger towns, the opportunities for any individual landlord to impose his own idiosyncratic vision on the community were relatively limited, and improvement was invariably piecemeal. Frequently it involved nothing more than the construction of new housing or the provision of public utilities such as churches, market houses, or shambles.

This urban and village improvement was widespread throughout Ireland, but concentrated particularly in south Ulster, the midlands, east Munster, and south Leinster. In many ways it reinforced the earlier regional patterns of medieval and plantation urban and village foundation. The major plantation contribution lay in central and west Ulster, Leix and Offaly, and Cork, where towns such as Coleraine, Tullamore, and *Bandon represented a significant extension to the urban network founded by the *Anglo-Normans in Leinster and north-east Munster. Arguably both these settlement phases were colonial in character. They were designed to articulate the economic exploitation of Ireland's resources for the eventual benefit of the English crown, whose political and strategic control over the country they were also intended to facilitate.

The exact numbers of the towns and villages established during the medieval and plantation periods are hard to establish, since not all survived and some were subject to periodic refoundation. Nevertheless, of the 149 Irish towns and cities recording a population of over 1,500 in the 1971 census, 40, or just over one-quarter, were founded by the Anglo-Normans after 1169, and a further 55, or 37 per cent, during the 16th- and 17th-century plantations. In both cases, the figures under-represent the number of such urban settlements, as only the largest and historically most successful are included. Thus nearly 180 medieval settlements are known to have been granted legal status as *boroughs, normally the *sine qua non* of urban status in the Middle Ages, while a further 50 received grants of weekly markets. Relatively small by contemporary European standards, medieval Irish towns such as Kilkenny and Carrick-on-Suir, Co. Tipperary, nevertheless displayed all the physical appurtenances of urban status: formal market places, regularly laid-out burgage plots, and, among the larger towns, town *walls (particularly from the 14th century), some of which remain to the present day.

These colonial towns were not the earliest urban foundations to survive into the 19th century. Of still earlier origin were the seven or eight Norse (see VIKING) *emporia*, or ports of trade, founded in the 10th century as successors to the earlier, temporary *longphorts. Dublin, famously, figured as both, but other foundations dating from the 10th century included Arklow, Wicklow, and *Limerick. Their significance lay in their indisputable urban status. They supported a socially complex and numerous non-agrarian population through craft and commerce, and linked Ireland to a broader, European, trading system.

Rural settlement

In contrast to the gradual evolution of Irish urban settlement, contemporary farm and village settlement patterns are largely the creation of the 18th and 19th centuries. They reflect in particular the consequences of recent population growth and decline, and the uneven social distribution of agrarian wealth. Relatively few of the extensive rural settlement forms established during the Middle Ages survived to influence this later settlement, possibly because of the radical nature of the changes in landownership which had occurred during the 16th and 17th centuries. Some agricultural villages of medieval origin survived in the Leinster heartlands of the erstwhile colony, but most of the medieval defensive *tower houses and moated sites founded by both Gaelic and *Old English lords had been abandoned. Only a few, such as Moycarkey, Co. Tipperary, survived as nodes for later farm settlement.

Thus, by the 19th century, Irish rural settlement was characterized by its relative recency and its stark social contrasts. The loss of population during and after the Famine had largely eradicated the once widespread clachan settlements (see RUNDALE), save in the most marginal western districts. In their place, the reduced farming population was accommodated with holdings in severalty, and housed in scattered, individual farmsteads. The majority of these were built in one or other of the various regional vernacular styles of architecture, using locally available, and therefore relatively cheap, building materials (see HOUSING). In more prosperous regions, and with the rise in farmers' living standards generally in the 1850s and 1860s, more substantial farmhouses were erected using imported materials such as slate, and simplified 'polite' Georgian styles.

At the other end of the social spectrum, the majority of the landlord class survived the financial crises brought on by the Famine and the *Land War, and continued to inhabit the country houses and demesnes which had been a characteristic feature of rural life since the early 18th century. Some 10,000 of these existed by the 1830s, and in their design and sophistication signalled their owners' wealth and authority as a social elite. Most were built in the 18th century in the Palladian or neoclassical styles, but a significant number were either built or reconstructed in the early 19th century in one of the then fashionable 'revival' styles, Gothic, Scots-Baronial, or 'Tudorbethan' (see ARCHITECTURE). The decay of many of these houses following the transfer of landownership to the tenants under the *Land Acts of 1870–1909 aptly illustrates the importance of social contexts to the history of settlement in Ireland.

Graham, B. J., and Proudfoot, L. J. (eds.), *An Historical Geography of Ireland* (1993)

LJP

Shackleton, Abraham (1697–1771), an English-born Quaker who came to Ireland as a tutor and subsequently set up a highly regarded school at Ballitore, Co. Kildare, which was continued by his son **Richard Shackleton** (1726–92). Noted pupils included Edmund *Burke and Paul *Cullen.

shamrock. References to the wearing of shamrock on St Patrick's Day can be traced back at least to 1681. The legend that the plant derives its association with the saint from his use of its three leaves to explain the concept of the Trinity was first recorded in 1726. Shamrocks were widely used in *Volunteer *flags and other Irish military insignia during the second half of the 18th century. Like the harp, the shamrock was subsequently incorporated into the official symbolism of the United Kingdom. *George IV wore shamrock during his visit to Ireland in 1821, and it was included in the badges of the *Royal Irish Constabulary and in the flags of Irish regiments of the British *army.

Shanavests, see CARAVATS AND SHANAVESTS.

Shannon, earls of, see BOYLE.

Shaw, George Bernard (1856–1950), playwright and socialist. His upbringing in a shabby-genteel family produced lasting dislike of Dublin. Shaw moved to London in 1876 as a journalist. He became a socialist, prominent in the Fabian Society, which advocated gradual social reform through administrative professionalism. From the 1890s he achieved fame as a playwright, becoming one of the most widely read authors of the first half of the 20th century; his work was popular for its irreverent humour, though often accused of loving ideas but fearing emotion. Though he was personally generous, belief in the rational reordering of society and disgust at social chaos led Shaw to endorse eugenics and praise interwar European dictators as harsh but necessary experimenters. Shaw stressed his Irishness as a clearsighted outsider in British society, and maintained a semi-detached relationship with the Irish *literary revival; he bequeathed his fortune to the British Museum and the National Gallery of Ireland. PM

Sheehy, Revd Nicholas (1728–66), Catholic priest executed for murder at Clonmel, Co. Tipperary. His trial was one of a series launched against local Catholic clergy and gentry at a time when sectarian passions had been inflamed both by the *Whiteboy movement and by a bitterly contested by-election (1761) involving the convert *Mathew family. Sheehy, who had apparently been active in anti-*tithe protest, had surrendered himself following an initial indictment, on the understanding that he would be tried in Dublin. He was acquitted there but then returned to Clonmel, where he was convicted, along with three prominent local Catholics, on highly suspect evidence. Their judicial assassination is widely cited as evidence of the continued strength of anti-Catholicism, and the potential for arbitrary repression, at a time when enforcement of the *penal laws was apparently diminishing.

Sheehy Skeffington, Francis (1878–1916), a leading pacifist and supporter of women's emancipation, who on his marriage added his wife's name to his own original surname 'Skeffington'. He was imprisoned for campaigning against conscription during the *First World War. Arrested as he attempted to prevent looting during the *rising of 1916, he was summarily shot on the orders of Capt. J. C. Bowen-Colthurst, who was subsequently ruled to have been insane.

Sheehy Skeffington, Hanna (1877–1946). Born Hanna Sheehy, into a very nationalist middle-class family, she was educated by the Dominican nuns and at University College, Dublin, and was one of the first generation of women both to graduate from, and to teach in, a university. She married Francis Skeffington in 1903, and they took each other's surnames as a commitment to equality. Both were founder members of the Irish Women's Franchise League in 1908, and Hanna was imprisoned for suffrage militancy. She always held firm to the belief that *feminism should remain independent of other political ideologies, but she prioritized anti-imperialist activism for several years after the murder of her pacifist husband by the military during the *rising of 1916. She opposed the *Anglo-Irish treaty, and objected to Sean O'Casey's presentation of the rising in *The Plough and the Stars* (1926). She also objected to the place allocated to women in de *Valera's *constitution of 1937. CC

sheela-na-gig, a carved female figure, generally emaciated and with distorted features, standing or sitting so as to display the genitalia. Such figures date from the 13th to the 17th centuries, mainly from areas of significant *Anglo-Norman settlement. The term, first documented in the 17th century, may derive from Irish *Síle na gCíoch* ('the hag of the breasts') or *Síle-ina-Giob* ('the old woman squatting'). Sheela-na-gigs appear to have originated as symbolic representations, paralleled in Romanesque and Gothic iconography throughout Europe, of the sin of lust. Later they came to be popularly regarded, especially in Gaelic or Gaelicized areas, as protective icons, and 17th-century Catholic ecclesiastical regulations called for their removal.

sheep have been farmed in Ireland since the *neolithic period. Early medieval literature attests the use of sheep's milk, as well as mutton and *wool. As with other livestock, breeds with standardized characteristics began to be produced only during the later 18th century, but by the mid-19th century several local types were recognized. These were of two main varieties: small, hardy mountain animals, typified by the Kerry hill type, or larger lowland types, most notably the Roscommon, which became a pedigree breed with the establishment of a herd book in 1895.

Already in the 17th century, flocks of up to 20,000 sheep were recorded, and Arthur *Young described large areas of land as being set aside as sheep walks in the 1770s. However, overall numbers remained relatively low until the mid-19th century, when a massive increase began, especially in upland areas. Depopulation and a long-term swing towards livestock farming provided an incentive for many landlords to introduce large-scale, systematic sheep rearing on marginal areas. By 1900 there were 4.4 million sheep in Ireland; by the 1990s this had risen to over 9.9 million. During the last 100 years, the most popular breeds have been Scotch Blackface and Leicesters, but an increasingly wide range of modern breeds is also represented. JB

Sheil, Richard Lalor (1791–1851), politician and playwright. Born in Co. Kilkenny, the son of a merchant and landowner, he was a leading supporter of the *veto, whose reconciliation with *O'Connell in 1823 opened the way for the successful campaign for *Catholic emancipation. As MP for Co. Louth 1831–3, Co. Tipperary 1833–41, and Dungarven 1841–51, he initially pledged himself to support *repeal, but drifted into support for the *Whig Party, from which he accepted a succession of minor offices after 1837, culminating in the positions of master of the mint (1846) and ambassador to the Tuscan court (1850).

sheriff, a title derived from the Saxon *shire reeve*, the king's principal administrative and judicial representative in each shire.

The sheriff's primary responsibility was to collect the king's revenues for the *exchequer in Dublin. These included the profits of justice, the farm of the county (the annual fee he paid for holding office), rents from royal manors, and subsidies. Failure to meet the demands of the exchequer resulted in seizure of the sheriff's property. Not surprisingly, sheriffs employed high-handed methods to satisfy these demands as much as for self-enrichment. In 1295, for example, the sheriff of Kerry was accused by a grand jury of murder, dismemberment, seizing the land of Henry fitzRys for a missing syllable in a writ, falsely seizing the estates of the bishop of Ardfert because he refused to confer the precentorship on the sheriff's brother, buying up land with the king's revenues, and much else besides. His brother Adam, the subsheriff, was accused of rigging juries and extorting money from jurors anxious to avoid doing service in Dublin.

In his judicial capacity, the sheriff presided over the county court, kept watch on the king's interests by holding his tourn court in every *cantred twice a year, summoned juries, executed writs, made attachments, levied fines, and delivered prisoners.

He was frequently obliged to defend the county in time of war and, when necessary, to enforce writs by calling on the aid of the posse (Latin *posse comitatus*). CAE

Sherlock* v. *Annesley (1717–19). The right of the Irish House of Lords to act as final court of appeal had already been raised by the cases of the *Bishop of Derry* (William *King) v. *The *Irish Society* (1698–9), and *Ward* v. *The Earl of Meath* (1703–4). When the

Irish Lords accepted Hester Sherlock's appeal from the court of exchequer in a case over forfeited lands, her adversary, Maurice Annesley, appealed to the English Lords, which ruled that the Irish house had no appellate jurisdiction. The Irish Lords responded with a representation asserting Ireland's status as a distinct dominion under the crown, and imprisoned the three barons of the Irish exchequer who had fined the sheriff of Co. Kildare for refusing to give Annesley possession. These acts of defiance provoked the introduction of the *Declaratory Act.

shipbuilding. Wooden sailing ships were built at various locations around the coast of Ireland before 1800. The occupation returns of the 1841 *census indicate that, although *Belfast was by far the most important shipbuilding centre in employment terms, the industry remained relatively rural based and widely dispersed.

In the second half of the century, the more capital-intensive production techniques required for the construction of iron- and steel-hulled ships led to larger units of production, and external economies led to regional concentration. By the late 19th century most UK mercantile tonnage was launched on the Clyde, on the north-east coast of England, and on the Lagan. The industry in Ireland was concentrated in Belfast, dominated by the two shipbuilding giants of *Harland & Wolff and *Workman, Clark & Company. In the years 1906–14 Harland & Wolff and Workman Clark between them produced 10 per cent of UK output and 6 per cent of world output.

Most ports retained the capacity to construct traditional small vessels such as brigantines, schooners, and smacks. Construction of larger vessels over 200 gross tons was confined to a few locations other than Belfast. In the first half of the 19th century *Cork was an important shipbuilding centre. The Cork firm of Andrew & Michael Hennessy built the first steamship in Ireland in 1815, and Robert J. Lecky & Company launched an iron-hulled vessel in 1845. However, the industry in Cork went into decline from the mid-1860s. In the mid-century *Waterford firms such as Pope & Co., Albert White & Co., and Charles Smith established a high reputation for construction of sailing vessels. Iron steamships of up to 2,000 tons were constructed by the Neptune Iron Works in Waterford between 1847 and 1880. There was little shipbuilding in *Dublin in the 19th century. The firm of Walpole & Webb built iron ships in the 1860s; subsequently Bewley, Webb & Company undertook repair work. No large vessels were constructed in *Derry between 1846 and the foundation of the Foyle Shipyard in 1882; it went out of business in 1892.

In the 20th century, the Dublin Dockyard Company revived shipbuilding in the city in 1901; the Londonderry Shipbuilding & Engineering Company had a brief existence between 1899 and 1904; on the same site in 1912 the North of Ireland Shipbuilding and Engineering Co. Ltd. was set up. With the downturn in demand after the *First World War, shipbuilding operations in Dublin and Derry ceased in the early 1920s and the two Belfast firms encountered financial difficulties; Workman Clark ceased operations in 1935. Harland & Wolff survived the hard inter-war years and continues to be a major European shipbuilder. Belfast has retained its almost complete domination of Irish shipbuilding until the present day.

Anderson, E. B., *Sailing Ships of Ireland* (1951)

Workman Clark (1928) Ltd., *Shipbuilding at Belfast 1880–1933* (n.d.)

FG/WJ

shirt making became an important occupation in west Ulster during the 1840s. It emerged initially as a cottage industry. When elements of the industry became mechanized, part of the work was carried out in supervised workshops. In 1853 Tillie and Henderson established the Foyle Factory, *Derry, which became the largest Irish shirt making establishment, employing 1,500 hands by the 1890s. The number of factories rose from five in the 1850s to 38 by the turn of the century. At this stage total employment in the industry in Cos. Londonderry, Donegal, and Tyrone had risen to 80,000 people (including outworkers). The various parts of the shirts were generally made in factories located in the town of Derry, and to a lesser extent in Strabane, Co. Tyrone; these parts were then made up by rural outworkers. The low cost of labour was an important factor in explaining the rapid growth of shirt making in west Ulster during the second half of the 19th century. However, employment in the industry contracted significantly towards the end of the 19th century, due to foreign competition and changing fashions. AB

Short Bros., *Belfast aircraft and aerospace manufacturers. The firm, originally known as Short & Harland, was formed in 1936 as a joint company by the long-established aircraft makers Short Bros. of Rochester, Kent, and the Belfast shipbuilders *Harland & Wolff. The factory at Queen's Island, Belfast, which was built with government financial assistance, included amongst its output flying boats, a speciality of Shorts, and, with the advent of war, bombers.

In 1947 Short & Harland was merged with the parent company of Short Bros., which had been nationalized by the British government in 1943, to form Short Bros. & Harland. The new company was then based entirely at Belfast, and Harland & Wolff retained a 15 per cent holding. Although the production of bombers continued after the war, the demand for flying boats declined. The firm diversified output with parts for Fokker passenger airliners and Skyvan freighters, the success of the 1960s, and in the same decade developed guided missiles. The company, whose name had been changed to Short Bros. in 1977, was privatized in 1989 and acquired by the Canadian aerospace firm of Bombardier. FG/WJ

shrines are places associated with a holy person, or event, at which religious activities take place. The *holy well, the link between a saint and a locality, is typical. Sometimes they can be of value historically for determining the influence of particular ecclesiastical centres (e.g. dedications to *Patrick can indicate *Armagh's influence).

There is a second, more restricted, meaning of 'shrine': containers, in wood and metal, for a saint's relics. These pointed to the significance of the relics they contained; they protected the relics from the exuberance of devotees and theft; and they were made in such a way that they enabled the relics to be transported in procession or used as a focus in worship. These functions are seen in references in the *annals to such shrines being moved, stolen, or taken on circuit to establish ecclesiastical allegiance, or as a remedy against disease and *famine. Thus, in essence, the shrine was valued as the place of access to the saint. TO'L

Sidney, Sir Henry (1529–86), lord deputy 1565–7, 1568–71, 1575–8. In his first government Sidney planned colonization and centralization. He defeated Shane *O'Neill, but earned the lasting hatred of Black Tom Butler of *Ormond. Sidney's second deputyship was intended to consolidate the first. The attainder of Shane O'Neill was passed, giving the crown title to most of Ulster, but otherwise his parliament was frustrated by *Old English opposition. Meanwhile his attempts to abolish *coyne and livery, establish *provincial presidencies, and promote colonies brought widespread rebellion. The big idea of Sidney's third government was *'composition'. He achieved agreements in Connacht and Munster, but his high-handed tactics with the Palesmen saw representations to the queen which rendered him a lame duck.

Sidney's administration has been presented as representing a new departure in the government of Ireland. In fact Sidney's reputation largely rests on effective propaganda: a bombastic memoir by himself, and the brilliant series of woodcuts of his third deputyship by John *Derrick. HM

silk manufacture was introduced to *Dublin by *Huguenots in the late 17th century and by 1730 there were about 3,000 people employed in the industry in the city. The industry prospered with the support and patronage of the nobility of Dublin, employing at least 11,000 persons in and around the city in the 1760s. The weavers worked in the Coombe, Pimlico, Spitalfields, Weaver's Square, and the surrounding areas. However, decline due to foreign competition had set in by the 1780s; by 1784 the number of looms at work was less than half of what it had been in the 1760s. The industry revived somewhat during the French wars (1793–1815) but thereafter experienced a downturn, accelerated by the removal of protective duties in 1826. The trade had shrunk back to only 116 looms by 1880. A few old firms, Atkinson's, Elliot's, Pim's, and Fry's, survived and experienced a minor revival after the turn of the century, concentrating predominantly on poplin weaving and tie making; by 1913, employment in the Dublin silk industry had risen to 650 people. The poplin tie had helped to revive the industry. AB

Síl nÁedo Sláine were one of the two major southern *Uí Néill dynasties. Their eponymous forebear, Áed Sláine, was reputedly a great-great-grandson of *Niall Noígiallach, but their most famous ancestor was Áed's father *Diarmait mac Cerbaill, who was also the progenitor of the neighbouring *Clann Colmáin. The Síl nÁedo Sláine were based in modern Co. Meath with foci at Dunshaughlin, Knowth, and Oristown. They dominated the kingship of Tara (see HIGH KINGSHIP) in the second half of the 7th century, lost power to their Clann Cholmáin relatives in the later 8th, and had a brief resurgence in the mid-10th century under Congalach Cnogba (d. 956). CS

silver, see METALWORK.

silver mining. Historically, most silver in Ireland has been imported, particularly in the *Viking era. Gerard *Boate, in his *Ireland's Natural History* (1652), describes 17th-century workings of the argentiferous galena ore at Silvermines, Co. Tipperary. Some silver was mined there in the 1960s, but it was never economically viable. In Glendasan, Co. Wicklow, in the 19th century, galena ore was being raised to the extent of 30 to 40 tons per annum, yielding 8 to 10 ounces of silver to the ton. Recent prospecting in Ireland, using the most advanced technology, has yielded only disappointingly small deposits. PC

Simms & M'Intyre (1806–70), *printer, bookseller, and publisher in Belfast and London. Starting in 1847, its low cost, mass circulation, Parlour

Library series revolutionized the market for fiction in the British Isles. VK

Simnel, Lambert (b. *c.*1475), crowned 'Edward VI' in Dublin 1487. Later said to be the son of an Oxford joiner, Simnel was brought to Ireland early in 1487, apparently at the instigation of Edward IV's sister Margaret of Burgundy, and presented as Edward, earl of Warwick (1475–99), son of George, duke of Clarence, and the potential Yorkist rival (see WARS OF THE ROSES) of Henry VII. To disprove this Warwick himself, then Henry's prisoner, was paraded in London. Nevertheless, after the landing at Dublin on 5 May of 2,000 troops raised by Margaret and accompanied by her nephew John de la Pole, earl of Lincoln, Simnel was crowned in *Christ Church cathedral on 24 May. Government proceeded in his name, Gerald, 8th earl of *Kildare, acting as his lieutenant, despite initial opposition from the town of Waterford. On 4 June a Yorkist army sailed for England, but was defeated on 16 June at Stoke. Captured there, Simnel became a royal scullion. EAEM

Sinclair, Betty (1910–81), trade unionist and communist, born in Belfast to a Protestant working-class family. A linen reeler from her mid-teens, her political beliefs were partly formed by the Catholic–Protestant alliance in the *outdoor relief strike of 1932. She became a full-time Communist Party worker in 1940 and in 1947 secretary to the Belfast Trades Council. Elected chairperson of the Northern Ireland *Civil Rights Association in 1968, she disagreed with *People's Democracy's militancy, and resigned from the executive of NICRA in 1970. CC

Sinn Féin, a radical nationalist party founded by Arthur *Griffith and Bulmer Hobson in 1905. Its name roughly translates as 'ourselves', indicating its emphasis on cultural and economic independence. The party was formed in the aftermath of the enthusiasm for radical organizations generated by the *Boer War. It attracted a disparate group of *Fenians, dissatisfied *Nationalist Party members, *feminists, and pacifists, and absorbed a number of existing radical groups, including the *Dungannon clubs, the *National Council, and *Inghinidhe na hÉireann, as well as an earlier nationalist movement, Cumann na nGaedheal, founded by Griffith in 1900.

Sinn Féin's programme was broadly based on Griffith's ideas. Ireland was to become an equal partner in a dual monarchy under the English crown. The party's economic policy emphasized the development of Ireland's own resources and a reliance on the domestic market. In this way an independent Irish industry could be built up behind high protective tariffs, allowing Ireland to support itself economically and end emigration. To achieve these goals, Sinn Féin advocated passive resistance. Irish MPs should withdraw from parliament and form a national assembly in Ireland, while citizens should withdraw their co-operation from government institutions in favour of Irish ones, starting with the courts.

Sinn Féin was not successful in political terms in this period. On the one occasion it challenged the Nationalist Party in a parliamentary election, the North Leitrim by-election of February 1908, its candidate was defeated by a margin of three to one. However, it provided a focal point for fringe movements, and had a disproportionate influence on political thinking, particularly through the writings of Griffith. As such it obtained a certain notoriety as anti-British, particularly during the *First World War, when it opposed recruitment. As a result it was widely held responsible for the *rising of 1916, although Sinn Féin as an organization had not in fact taken part.

This association with the rising explains why Sinn Féin became the name of the new militant nationalist movement that took shape during 1917 and began to supplant the Nationalist Party. The new party, however, was a coalition of radical republicans, who had participated in the Easter rising, and more moderate nationalists from the original Sinn Féin. The strains inherent in this coalition became clear in the compromise wording of its objectives agreed at its first convention in October 1917: 'Sinn Féin aims at securing the international recognition of Ireland as an independent Irish Republic. Having achieved that status the Irish people may by referendum freely choose their own form of government.' At this convention Arthur Griffith stood down as president in favour of Eamon de *Valera, the only surviving commandant of the rising.

Although there was a great deal of overlap with the leadership of the *IRA, Sinn Féin was an independent and different organization. Apart from a large number of old Sinn Féin members, its success also attracted a radical element from the old home rule party into its ranks. An analysis of its leadership shows that Sinn Féin was heavily dominated by young Catholics from lower middle-class backgrounds. Its association with the rising and its opposition to conscription ensured that the organization became very popular. By December 1918 it had attracted 112,080 members. Its new-found support became apparent in the 1918 general election, when it won 73 out of 105 seats in Ireland. Republicans have always appealed to this result, representing the last time that all Irishmen voted in a free and undivided way, to legitimize their continued fight for independence. Although republicans actually took less than 48 per cent of the vote, the fact that constituencies in which there was no opposing candidate have been excluded from this count, and that northern constituencies were divided between Sinn Féin and the Irish Party, indicates that a majority of voters probably did support Sinn Féin. However, this did not necessarily constitute agreement with the means used by republicans later on. The 1918 Sinn Féin manifesto was very vague on the use of physical force and relied heavily on passive resistance and an appeal to the Versailles Peace Conference.

The image of majority support for Sinn Féin in this period is further undercut by the results of the local elections in 1920. It did particularly poorly in the urban elections of January 1920, when it received only 30 per cent of the vote. It was better organized for the rural election the following June and managed to acquire 72 per cent of votes cast. In general the Sinn Féin vote was stronger the more Catholic, rural, western, and less northern an area was. It was highest in rural Connacht, where Sinn Féin received 97 per cent of the vote, and lowest in urban Ulster, with 15 per cent.

The influence of Sinn Féin became less the more violent the *Anglo-Irish War became. Its alternative government institutions slowly crumbled under the pressure of British measures, and the *Dáil was largely unable to exert influence on the IRA. Like all other republican organizations it split over the *Anglo-Irish treaty, the name 'Sinn Féin' being retained, after some initial uncertainty, by the anti-treaty group.

Following the defeat of the republicans in the *Irish Civil War, Sinn Féin was caught in an inescapable dilemma. If it wanted to keep to its civil war principles it had to reject the existing political institutions. However, doing so would inevitably forfeit electoral support as Sinn Féin could not represent its voters. To remain a serious force it had therefore to rely on the potential threat formed by the link with the IRA. Unable to make the republic a reality by political means, Sinn Féin therefore mainly functioned as a mobilizing institution for the IRA. Attempts to represent the people quickly came up against the obstacle of republican resistance to participation in parliamentary politics. The resulting tension has continued to haunt the movement ever since the civil war, leading to a series of splits.

Sinn Féin had become dormant in 1922, and was revived only in May 1923. Rejecting the legitimacy of all institutions set up by the *Government of Ireland Act 1920 and the treaty, it continued to recognize the second Dáil, elected in May 1921, as the *de jure* government of the Irish Republic established in 1916. Sinn Féin nevertheless participated in elections in Northern Ireland and the Free State. It did indeed do quite well in the south, but less so in the north, where the Nationalists received the majority of the Catholic vote. However, it soon became clear that abstentionism was a political dead end. As a result a large section of the party led by de Valera wanted to enter the Free State Dáil and work for the republic from within. This led to a split with the IRA in 1925, and in 1926 the party itself broke in two, with the de Valera section walking out to form *Fianna Fáil.

Without the IRA connection the remainder of Sinn Féin became increasingly irrelevant. Fianna Fáil took away most of its national and international support, and it soon ran out of money, preventing it from contesting elections. The IRA provided a new lease of life in 1938, when Sean *Russell asked the movement's permission for the *bombing campaign in Great Britain. In response the second Dáil transferred its powers as government of Ireland to the IRA army council, which now felt justified in declaring war on Britain. Official links between the IRA and Sinn Féin were again established after the Second World War when the IRA realized it needed a political party to mobilize public support. Sinn Féin enjoyed some electoral success as a result of the *border campaign. It won four Dáil seats in 1957, but with the violence going nowhere it lost all of these in subsequent elections. Realizing the republican movement needed to build a mass following, it became increasingly involved in social issues during the 1960s, moving more and more to the left.

The tensions between socialists, who eventually wanted to enter the Dáil, and the militarists who believed in the armed struggle, came to the boil under pressure of the mounting violence in Northern Ireland. As a result the movement split in January 1970 into official and provisional Sinn Féin, mirroring the split within the IRA the previous month. Official Sinn Féin changed its name in 1977 to the *Workers' Party, and went on to establish itself as a minor party in parliamentary politics in the Republic.

True to its military objective Provisional Sinn Féin refused to participate in elections in Northern Ireland and functioned mainly as a propaganda machine for the Provisional IRA. However, in the late 1970s, republicans began to realize that the conflict could not be won militarily and that they were losing popular support. Although the campaign of violence was not called off, Provisional Sinn Féin again turned to abstentionist politics after the public response to the *hunger strikes in the early 1980s convinced them this could generate support. Although the fusion of military and political means (the 'bullet and the ballot-box' strategy) seemed successful, engagement in party politics slowly led towards a fuller involvement in the political system. In 1986 Provisional Sinn Féin decided to accept the Dáil as a legitimate institution; this led to the secession of Republican Sinn Féin and its military wing, the Continuity Army Council, who refused to accept any diminution of the abstentionist policy. In the last decade, Provisional Sinn Féin has been involved in creating a new political arrangement within Northern Ireland, which also provides for institutional links with the South (see PEACE PROCESS). Their full involvement in the political process in the North has been made possible by an IRA ceasefire first called in 1994 and renewed in 1996. This has again led to opposition within the movement and to the formation of the 32-County Sovereignty Committee, with a military wing, the Real IRA.

These splits in Sinn Féin and the IRA again reveal the difficulties of operating a dual strategy of political and military action. Although initially closely linked, institutionally and in personnel, the two organizations have experienced different dynamics. The logic of membership of Sinn Féin has tended to the peace process, while IRA volunteers are naturally more convinced of the potential of physical force. These pressures have inevitably led to tensions between the two organizations, each pulling in different directions. However, in recent years the republican leadership has successfully convinced most of the army's rank and file of the value of peaceful means against historical precedent. The fear of extensive splits has created a careful and slow approach to any concessions, such as decommissioning, which could be judged an acknowledgement of the failure of the use of force. The subsequent transformation of Sinn Féin to a fully political organization has enabled it to become the largest nationalist party in Northern Ireland and, potentially, a political force to be reckoned with in the south.

Davis, Arthur, *Arthur Griffith and Non-Violent Sinn Féin* (1974)

Laffan, Michael, *The Resurrection of Ireland: The Sinn Fein Party, 1916–1923* (1999)

Patterson, Henry, *The Politics of Illusion: Republicanism and Socialism in Modern Ireland* (1989)

O'Brien, Brendan, *The Long War: The IRA and Sinn Féin 1985 to Today* (1993). JA

Sirr, Maj. Henry Charles (1764–1841). After serving in the army 1778–91, Sirr settled in Dublin as a wine merchant. In 1796, however, he was appointed town major, in effect chief of *police, a post earlier held by his father Joseph Sirr. He thus became one of *Dublin Castle's leading agents in the campaign against the *United Irish movement in the city. The high points of his career were his apprehension of Lord Edward *FitzGerald and later of Robert *Emmet. The post of town major disappeared when the Dublin police was reorganized in 1808, but Sirr was permitted to keep the title, and remained in office as an assistant magistrate until his retirement in 1826. In later life he developed a strong interest in Irish language and antiquities.

Sixmilewater revival, a religious movement among the Scottish population of eastern Ulster, at that stage still nominally part of the Church of Ireland, although already exhibiting elements of what was to develop into a *Presbyterian church structure. Commencing in the area around Antrim in 1625, the revival was initially inspired by the crude, emotive preaching of Revd James Glendinning, but was quickly taken over by more sophisticated colleagues. Thousands assembled to hear sermons, attend prayer meetings, and experience a deeply emotional process of conversion. The revival continued into the early 1630s, extending into western Scotland.

Skeffington, see MASSEREENE.

Skelton, Philip (1707–87), Church of Ireland clergyman, author of a range of literary works, including defences of Christian orthodoxy against *Toland and others. He is commemorated in Samuel Burdy's *Memoirs of Rev. Philip Skelton* (1792), which paints a powerful picture of a committed clergyman and scholar, denied preferment by the ecclesiastical establishment, subsisting in poverty and obscurity in poor rural parishes in Cos. Donegal and Tyrone.

Sloan, Thomas Henry (1870–1941), populist Protestant politician. Sloan was a cementer in the *Harland & Wolff shipyard who spoke on behalf of the militant Belfast Protestant Association. He united *temperance votes with *evangelical Protestant and populist loyalist sentiment, winning the South Belfast constituency in August 1902. He was a co-founder of the *Independent Orange Order but was damaged by his association with the *Magheramorne manifesto, and fell victim to the resurgence of orthodox *Unionism in the later Edwardian period. He was defeated in South Belfast in 1910, and retired into private life. AJ

smallpox was until the 20th century one of the great scourges of Ireland. The *annals record epidemics as early as the 6th century, and in times of war or *famine, as for example during the 1640s and early 1740s, smallpox ravaged the country. Between 1661 and 1745 smallpox accounted for 20 per cent of all deaths recorded in the Dublin bills of mortality.

Inoculation against smallpox, introduced in 1723, was adopted by itinerant healers and practised in rural areas well into the 19th century, when it had long been superseded by the more reliable method of vaccination. The first vaccination occurred in Ireland in 1800 and in 1804 the Cow Pock Institution was established in Dublin to promote the practice. But smallpox mortality remained high, accounting for 5.1 per cent of all deaths in 1841, twice the rate in England. Thus to what extent the decline in deaths from smallpox contributed to the rapid growth in Irish *population in the century after the 1740s remains controversial. ELM

Smerwick, massacre of (10 Nov. 1580). Six hundred Spanish and Italian troops sent by the pope during the *Desmond revolt fortified Dún an Óir in Smerwick Bay on the Dingle Peninsula. Lord Deputy *Grey, having forced their surrender, massacred the garrison and its Irish accomplices, excepting fifteen leaders for ransom. Zealously Protestant, Grey feared the Catholic threat and intended the action as an example to future invaders and Irish allies; Queen Elizabeth I approved his actions. HM

Smith, Erasmus (1611–91), merchant and alderman of London, and *Cromwellian land speculator. In 1657 he vested a portion of his Irish estates, 12,400 out of some 46,000 acres, in trustees, who included Thomas Harrison (Henry Cromwell's chaplain), Henry Jones (vice-chancellor of *Trinity College), and several prominent *Independent clergymen. They were to found and maintain schools 'so that the poor children inhabiting any part of his lands in Ireland should be brought up in the fear of God, and good literature and to speak the English tongue'. Scholarships to Trinity College were to be available for the most able children.

Following the *Restoration, the trust was confirmed by charter of Charles II in 1669, which appointed 'Governors of the schools founded by Erasmus Smith Esq.' While including some of the original members, these now comprised also the archbishops of Armagh and Dublin, and were empowered to establish free grammar schools at Drogheda, Galway, and Tipperary. In addition to the children of tenants of Smith's estates, 20 poor children might be admitted. The scope of the endowment was extended in 1723 to allow for the founding of new 'English Schools' and also for providing fellowships and professorships in Trinity College. KM

Smith, F. E. (1872–1930), politician and lawyer. Born in Birkenhead, called to the bar in 1899, Smith entered Liverpool politics as an 'Orange Tory', and was elected to the Commons in 1906. He quickly rose to prominence. His legal career also continued, including the defence of Crippen's mistress in 1910, and, as attorney-general, the successful prosecution of Roger *Casement in 1916. Smith had already associated himself with *Carson, initially opposing *home rule, then seeking Ulster's exclusion. Appointed lord chancellor, as Lord Birkenhead, in 1919, he was eventually a key figure in the drafting of the *Anglo-Irish treaty. Up to then a nationalist bogeyman, he finally emerged as a conciliator. NG

smuggling became a serious issue in the 18th century, as government regulation of commerce, for both fiscal and economic policy purposes, increased, and as levels of consumption grew with rising prosperity. Contraband was imported directly from France, from the Isle of *Man (until the British government purchased its trading rights in 1765), and from Guernsey. The main goods smuggled were tea (up to the sharp reduction in duties in 1784), tobacco, and spirits, mainly brandy. Suppression was hindered by the connivance of merchants and landowners. Later in the century, as costs rose, large-scale criminal organization came to play a more prominent part. Contemporaries, anxious to demonstrate the damaging effects of the *Woollen Act, maintained that large quantities of wool were illegally exported from Ireland to France, but research shows that the amounts were in fact negligible.

The *revolutionary and Napoleonic wars, followed after 1800 by the growth of free trade and more effective law enforcement, ended the first great age of Irish smuggling. In the 1930s the imposition of tariffs on Irish livestock imports to the United Kingdom (see ECONOMIC WAR) created an illegal cross-border cattle trade. Across a longer period, higher tariffs and excise duties in independent Ireland encouraged smuggling of spirits, tobacco, and manufactured goods from Northern Ireland. Accession to the *European Union was eventually to undermine this traffic, while creating, through its system of subsidies, a whole range of new opportunities to profit from the clandestine movement of livestock.

soccer officially came to Ireland with an exhibition match between two Scottish sides in Belfast in 1878. However, clubs had existed in Ulster from the 1860s, and visiting seamen had played local teams.

Organization came with the founding of the Irish Football Association (IFA) in Belfast in 1880. The Irish Cup competition began in 1881. International games followed in 1882. By 1890 the sport had spread to Dublin, and the Irish League was formed. Professionalism was legalized from 1894. By 1911 teams from all four provinces had affiliated to the IFA. In 1920–1 Irish soccer split. Prompted by political developments and dissatisfaction with IFA decisions, clubs from outside Ulster withdrew from the IFA and Irish League. In 1922 the dissidents formed the Football Association of Ireland (FAI) and League of Ireland. The following year the FAI gained international recognition and changed its name to the Football Association of the Irish Free State (FAIFS). From 1924 the FAIFS fielded an international side known as the Irish Free State, while the IFA selected an all-Ireland side known as Ireland. Thus 32 players played for two international sides. From 1936 the FAIFS reverted to being the FAI, and began to call its international side Ireland. Conciliatory approaches to the IFA were rejected. The situation was clarified by decisions of the international ruling body in 1947 and 1954. Effectively Ireland was divided into two soccer jurisdictions, coincident with the border. Although a popular amateur sport, large-scale professional soccer has not developed in Ireland. This is due primarily to the attraction of top Irish players to the British game, and the rivalry of *Gaelic football.

NG

Social Democratic and Labour Party, founded in 1970, as a merger of several opposition groups in the Northern Ireland Parliament. It included independent *civil rights MPs and breakaway elements from the *Northern Ireland Labour Party, the *Nationalist Party, and the Republican Labour Party, together with the full membership of the National Democratic Party, a short-lived group of modernizing nationalists. It quickly became the main political voice of the Catholic community in *Northern Ireland. Its double-barrelled name reflects the tensions between its two leaders and main founders: Gerry Fitt, the Belfast socialist who led the party until his resignation in 1979, and his successor John Hume, the *Derry-based social democrat and supporter of business innovation.

The SDLP represented the first serious attempt since the time of *Devlin to unite Catholic political forces across the province, divided as they were between the left-wing republicanism and secularism of the small Belfast parties and the conservative and clerically influenced Nationalist Party which had long dominated Catholic politics outside the city. Teachers and other professionals became prominent in the party's membership. It was the first Catholic party in Northern Ireland to have a regular mass-party organization. It joined the European parliamentary socialist group and established a link with the British Labour Party: winning Catholics' acceptance for these mildly leftist connections in practice proved less difficult than maintaining support for constitutional politics during acute crises such as the Unionist government's introduction of *internment in 1971 and the republican *hunger strikes of 1981.

The SDLP abstained from the *Stormont parliament (1971–2) and from the failed Assembly of 1982–6; supported a province-wide rent and rates strike (1972–4); and stopped short of full endorsement of the *Royal Ulster Constabulary. But it consistently opposed violence, and worked for Irish unity 'by consent'. It differed from traditional nationalism not only in its interest in socio-economic and European issues, but also in having immediate constitutional goals as well as its long-term aspirations for Irish unity. These focused on demands for executive-level power sharing within Northern Ireland coupled with a strong 'Irish dimension', which remained fairly constant from the *Sunningdale agreement of 1973 to the Anglo-Irish agreement of 1985 and the Framework document of 1995. Electoral support for the SDLP fluctuated between 18 per cent and 28 per cent of the electorate during the period 1973–94. Thereafter, however, it lost ground to Sinn Féin, whose share of the vote rose from 18 per cent in 1998 to 26 per cent in 2007, while that of the SDLP fell from 22 to 15 per cent in the same period.

ACH

socialism, or primitive 'Celtic communism', according to James *Connolly in *Labour in Irish History* (1910), existed as 'the Gaelic principle of common ownership by the people of their sources of food and maintenance', but was suppressed by the Anglo-Norman *feudal system. Connolly described William *Thompson as 'The First Irish Socialist: A forerunner of Marx'. Other socialist pioneers included John Scott Vandeleur, founder of the *Ralahine commune, and James Fintan *Lalor and Thomas Devin Reilly, who grafted proto-socialist ideas onto *Young Ireland. There was common ground between the *Fenians and Marx and Engels, reflected in the appointment of J. P. MacDonnell as Irish secretary to the first *International. Michael *Davitt, though in a tiny minority in Ireland, was at one with the Marxists in seeing nationalization as the solution to the land question.

In 1892 the British Independent Labour Party (ILP) came to Ireland. Connolly's *Irish Socialist

Republican Party in 1896 marked the beginning of an indigenous socialist movement. In 1910 Connolly became organizer of its successor the Socialist Party of Ireland (SPI). The labour-unionist William *Walker, who narrowly failed to become Ireland's first socialist MP, conducted a defining debate with Connolly on socialism and the national question in the Glasgow socialist paper *Forward*. Connolly's Independent Labour Party of Ireland replaced the SPI in 1912. This was the heroic period of Irish socialism, with Connolly and *Larkin on centre stage. Their revolutionary programme aimed at establishing a workers' republic. Their socialism was usually described as *syndicalism or Larkinism. In 1913 they persuaded the *Irish Trade Union Congress to establish the Irish *Labour Party on socialist principles. Their removal from the scene during the *First World War left the movement under the labourist or reformist leadership of Tom *Johnson and William *O'Brien, and from then on this would be the dominant strain in Irish socialism.

Connolly's prophesy that *partition would 'usher in a carnival of reaction north and south' was fulfilled. The *Northern Ireland Labour Party (NILP) gradually dissipated itself trying to avoid offending either community. Revolutionary socialist ideas became confined to far-left sects. Larkin for a time led an embryonic *communist group. In the depressed 1930s the communist *revolutionary workers' groups emerged. In the north the RWG played a leading role in the *Outdoor Relief Protests of 1932. Left-wing *IRA, socialists, and communists came together in the *Republican Congress, which even had supporters in the Protestant Shankill Road and east Belfast. However, 'red scare' propaganda from church and state alike helped to marginalize all these groups.

After the *Second World War the level of hostility towards even moderate socialist programmes was notoriously manifested in the quashing of Dr Noel Browne's *'Mother and Child' scheme. The British Labour government's Welfare State was installed in the north, despite lukewarm Unionist attitudes. For a time, in the late 1950s and early 1960s, the NILP formed a coherent moderate socialist opposition in *Stormont.

In the late 1960s and 1970s Irish versions of the 'New Left' included the student-based *People's Democracy and the Official Republican Movement, which for a time espoused Marxism. Its contemporary successors, the *Workers' Party and Democratic Left, have become social democratic, whereas the tiny Irish Republican Socialist Party maintains extreme ideas in isolation. The Provisional Republican Movement is ostensibly committed to Connolly's goal of a socialist republic. Others on the left have challenged the republican-socialist synthesis, notably in the *two nations thesis. Socialist ideas are also manifested in the programmes of the loyalist Ulster Democratic and Popular Unionist parties. But in the worldwide retreat from socialism in the 1990s, Ireland has had a lot less distance to travel than most countries.

O'Connor, E., *A Labour History of Ireland* (1992)

PC

social welfare. From 1924 until 1947 health and social welfare in independent Ireland were the responsibility of the minister for local government, a situation which reflected the relatively low priority given to both areas. With the abolition of the *poor law, counties and county boroughs replaced poor law unions as the primary unit of welfare administration, and an attempt was made to separate welfare provision from the provision of medical services. Development of both health and welfare services was hampered by economic depression, and by the reluctance of both central and local authorities to increase levels of *taxation. The election of the first *Fianna Fáil government in 1932 saw the adoption of a more progressive approach to social welfare with improvements to old-age pensions, increased allowances for widows and orphans, and a more generous unemployment assistance regime. Official attitudes, however, continued to be predicated upon a distinction between the deserving and undeserving poor. Home assistance was administered, as outdoor relief had been, in a manner deliberately designed to discourage people from applying for it. It was not until 1977 that a right to benefit was recognized under the Supplementary Welfare Allowance Act, which introduced means-tested benefits paid weekly at a standard rate.

Increased expenditure in the 1960s permitted the extension of social insurance and the introduction of a number of new welfare allowances, including benefits for deserted wives, prisoners' wives, and unmarried mothers. The various different forms of benefit and assistance were integrated into a comprehensive social insurance scheme in the 1970s. Social insurance contributions became mandatory for most categories of employee in 1974. At the same time benefit payments were linked to salary levels. In the mid-1980s almost one-third of the adult population were receiving social welfare payments. Lower-income groups bear a disproportionate share of the cost of the present welfare system, via the taxes on expenditure which comprise a major share of total tax revenue.

In *Northern Ireland ministers were committed to attaining parity with benefit rates in Britain, but this was achieved in the decades after *partition only at the expense of other welfare services, such as the provision of health and sanitation facilities. Local authority housing remained, in many places, insufficient in quantity and substandard. Those outside the benefit system were forced, as in the past, to resort to the poor law. In the post-war period the principle of parity with Britain was endorsed by the British government. Northern Ireland thus acquired most aspects of the Beveridge welfare state, although the welfare system remained more restrictive than in Great Britain and was maintained only with the aid of substantial subsidies. By the end of the 1950s Northern Ireland had moved significantly ahead of the Republic in the provision of social services. The gap has since narrowed. Expenditure under social welfare schemes remains higher in Northern Ireland than in the Republic (amounting in 1981 to IR£546 and IR£371 per head respectively), reflecting the age structure, higher unemployment rate, and more liberal eligibility conditions found in Northern Ireland.

See also POOR RELIEF.

Breen, R., Hannan, D. F., Rottman, D. B., and Whelan, C. T., *Understanding Contemporary Ireland: State, Class and Development in the Republic of Ireland* (1990)

Harkness, David, *Northern Ireland since 1920* (1983)

VC

Society of Friends (Quakers), initially the most radical of the sects introduced into Ireland during and after the English civil wars. Their open defiance of secular authority, and their insistence on directly challenging the clergy of other denominations, provoked harsh repressive measures from both the *Cromwellian and *Restoration governments. In 1669 the society was given a more formal organizational structure by George *Fox and William *Edmundson. By 1701 there were 53 Quaker meeting houses and about 6,000 members. By this time Quakers were no longer seen as a threat to public order. An act of 1715 allowed them to compound for service in the *militia, another in 1723 to participate in most legal proceedings without taking oaths. Their refusal to pay *tithes continued to expose them to the forcible seizure of goods, but imprisonment on this score had become rare.

The first Quakers were relatively humble farmers, traders, and artisans. By the mid-19th century, however, they had evolved into a predominantly middle- and upper middle-class body, prominent in *textile manufacture, shipping, and *railway development, as well as in retailing. Leading Quaker enterprises included the engineering firm of Jacob & Grubb in Clonmel, Co. Tipperary, the Dublin biscuit makers W. & R. Jacob, and the Bewleys, initially tea and coffee merchants, who went on to found the well-known Oriental cafés in Dublin and elsewhere. Numbers remained small, with 2,731 members in 1901. The efforts of Irish and English Quakers such as Jonathan *Pim and James Hack *Tuke to organize relief works during the *Famine were widely praised.

Society of Jesus, see JESUITS.

Solemn League and Covenant (1643), an agreement between Scots and English opponents of Charles I. For the Scots the primary commitment of the Covenant was religious, to preserve and advance the Reformation in the kingdoms of the British crown; for the English it was political, to secure the rights and liberties of both parliaments. Both agreed to extirpate popery, prelacy, and heresy, and Scottish commissioners were to attend the Westminster Assembly set up to reform the church. The Scots believed that reformation 'according to the Word of God' meant the establishment of *Presbyterianism. When the English parliament, victorious over Charles, opted for Independency, the Presbytery of Ulster were among those who protested, reaffirming their adherence to the Covenant. RFGH

sole right, shorthand for the claim that parliament had 'the sole and undoubted right' to initiate financial legislation, asserted when the House of Commons in October 1692 rejected a money bill drawn up by the Irish *privy council. This unexpected self-assertion reflected the expectations created by the *revolution of 1688, and is recognized as beginning a new stage in the history of the Irish *parliament. But parliament's revolt also reflected hostility towards the administration of Viscount Sydney, lord lieutenant 1692–3, particularly over the leniency allegedly shown towards Catholics since the treaty of *Limerick. Sydney's successor Henry Capel, lord justice 1693–5, lord deputy 1695–6, sponsored the first *penal laws in 1695 and appointed Alan *Brodrick and other leading advocates of sole right to office. This smoothed the way for a compromise settlement whereby at its next meeting, in 1695, the Commons accepted a token money bill from the privy council, but brought forward its own *heads of bills to raise most of the revenue required. Thereafter financial legislation was introduced through the Commons, although amendments to such bills by the English or Irish privy council caused occasional resentment. In 1761 the British cabinet insisted, against the fears of the Irish executive, on initiating a money bill, which duly passed. But in 1769, during the campaign against *Townshend's viceroyalty, a second such bill was rejected. The same underlying issue of parliamentary control of finance, similarly exploited for political purposes, lay behind the *money bill dispute of 1753–6.

Somerville, Edith (1858–1949), and **'Ross, Martin'** (Violet Martin, 1862–1915), cousins who collaborated on stories about their fox hunting, minor gentry milieu, best known for the three-volume series commencing with *Some Experiences of an Irish R.M.* (i.e. *resident magistrate) (1899). Their novel *The Real Charlotte* (1894) is compared to Turgenev as a portrait of a gentry in decline. Both *unionists in politics (Martin's brother Robert, a professional entertainer, combined unionist propaganda with comic Irish recitations), they are sometimes accused of malevolent stage-Irishness. Both were suffragists (see FEMINISM), and their correspondence is an important source for the obstacles facing gentry women with intellectual interests. They were also spiritualists; Somerville believed their collaboration continued after Martin's death. PM

'souperism', the use of food relief ('soup') as a means of religious proselytization, especially during the *Great Famine. Contemporary allegations of widespread abuse, reflecting the intense suspicions created by the *Second Reformation, are probably exaggerated, but the existence of well-provisioned missionary settlements in such destitute areas as Dingle and Achill Island undoubtedly created great temptations for all concerned. PHG

souterrain, the archaeological term for an artificial cave constructed for defensive purposes during the *Early Medieval period. In early Irish texts the word *uam* is used for such a structure. Souterrains were usually either tunnelled or trench built, the latter type being constructed either of dry-stone (the most usually discovered form) or wood. They typically consisted of a number of chambers and tunnels separated by narrow 'creeps', often in a quite complex arrangement. The distribution of souterrains is uneven, the vast majority being found in just a few counties, especially in the north-east and the south-west. They often occur in *ringforts and *monastic enclosures and are always found, when excavated, to have been associated with houses. Souterrains are also found in Scotland, Cornwall, Brittany, and elsewhere on the Continent. Only with those of western Scotland, however, are Irish souterrains likely to have any cultural connection. RW

South Africa. The Irish and Irish-descended persons in South Africa have never been a significant proportion of the population: in 1904, for example, the Irish-born accounted for 1.6 per cent of the white population of what later became the Republic of South Africa, and in 1951 they were 0.4 per cent. Persons of Irish ethnicity (that is, the multigenerational cohort) were an estimated 3.5 per cent of the white population in 1926. The Irish-born and Irish-descended were, of course, an even smaller proportion of the entire population, although accurate censuses on the non-white majority are hard to find.

Aside from the 200 or so men who fought on the Afrikaner side in the *Boer War, the Irish in South Africa were firmly behind the British empire and, later, most were willing participants in the development of apartheid. Irish migrants to South Africa in the 20th century were unusual in being the most highly skilled and educated (as a group) of Irish migrants to any major destination. Only a minority came from the labouring or agricultural classes. DHA

sovereignty, the ultimate locus of power and fount of authority in society, is a vexed issue in Irish history. *High kings had developed a loose and contested monarchy in Ireland but, after *Henry II's assertion of lordship in 1171, the sovereignty of Ireland rested outside the island as an inalienable attribute of the English crown. This was qualified in two ways. First the *papacy, which claimed sovereignty over islands, had granted the lordship of Ireland to the English king to reform its religion under Pope Adrian's bull **Laudabiliter* of 1156. In 1317 Irish princes asked for the bull's revocation in their *remonstrance to Pope John XXII on the grounds that its provisions had not been fulfilled by the English crown; after the *Reformation this seemed an even more pregnant possibility. Secondly, Ireland was only partially conquered—indivisible sovereignty in the shape of the common law only operated in English areas whereas *brehon law functioned in Gaelic areas, Irish political succession known as *tanistry continued, and clerical appointments in *ecclesia inter hibernicos* were made by Rome. After the Tudor conquest, tanistry, the foremost example of local sovereignty, was declared illegal. The lawyer Sir John *Davies asserted that the English right to Ireland rested solely on conquest, which abrogated any Irish or papal claims to sovereignty; native writers, notably *Keating (see LITERATURE IN IRISH), by emphasizing the voluntary submission of Irish kings to Henry II, insisted that the Irish were free subjects of a Christian prince.

The sovereignty issue re-emerged in the closing phase of British rule in Ireland. *Republicanism, with its theoretical basis in popular sovereignty and citizenship, inevitably faced difficulty over the acceptance of dominion status and an *oath of allegiance in the *Anglo-Irish treaty. De *Valera's erosion of this edifice culminated in his opponents' declaration of a *Republic of Ireland in 1949. A major aspect of national sovereignty is independent control over defence and the right to decide on peace and war. Ireland achieved this by taking possession of the *treaty ports in 1938 and by *neutrality in the *Second World War. Irish nationalism has traditionally regarded the whole island of Ireland as the national territory and this was enshrined in articles 2 and 3 of the *constitution of 1937. These claims to sovereignty have never been exercised, although the 1985 *Anglo-Irish agreement gave Dublin a consultative role in the affairs of Northern Ireland. Another elusive aspect of Irish nationalist aspirations has been economic sovereignty. The doctrine of self-sufficiency was a commonplace amongst early 20th-century nationalists and in Ireland found its voice in Arthur *Griffith, founder of *Sinn Féin. However, this policy was abandoned in the late 1950s in the pursuit of economic growth. In 1965 Ireland re-established free trade with the United Kingdom (see ANGLO-IRISH FREE TRADE AGREEMENT) and in 1972 entered the European Community (see EUROPEAN UNION) with the goal of 'ever closer union'. HM

soviets, taking their name from the governing committees created at different levels following the Bolshevik revolution in Russia, were proclaimed in different parts of Ireland during and in the immediate aftermath of the *Anglo-Irish War. The most significant were in thirteen Co. Limerick creameries owned by the Cleeve Company (1920), and in the coal mines at Arigna, Co. Roscommon. Despite the hoisting of red flags and the assertion that production was now under workers' control, it remains difficult to determine how far these were genuine attempts to initiate a socialist transformation of society, as opposed to rhetorical flourishes accompanying conventional strike action. The 'Limerick soviet' of April 1919 was in reality a general strike in the city in protest against the government's security policy.

spalpeen (Ir. *spailpín*), a migrant labourer. See SEASONAL MIGRATION.

Spanish Armada (Sept.–Oct. 1588). The Spanish Armada, defeated in its attempt to invade England, had orders to sail around Scotland and the west of Ireland. In stormy weather at least 23 ships were wrecked on the Irish coast. *Fitzwilliam gave orders to execute Spaniards coming ashore, and 6,194 were reported drowned, killed, or captured. English fears that the Spaniards would join forces with the Irish proved unfounded. The main reaction of the native population was to rob both survivors and corpses. In Irish-controlled districts of the north, certain lords—O'Rourke, MacSweeney, O'Cahan, and MacDonnell—aided the escape of up to 500 survivors to Scotland. Some 2,400 survivors from various ships gathered at Killybegs and attempted to reach Scotland in the *Girona* but sank off the north Antrim coast. Some survivors wrote accounts of their adventures in Ireland, the best known being that of Captain de Cuellar. Today the archaeological legacy gives the Armada undue prominence in Irish history. The event may have heightened English fears of Spanish intervention in Ireland, and Irish hopes of such an outcome; but for most people it was an unexpected windfall of little lasting significance. HM

Spanish Civil War (1936–9), arising from a military revolt led by General Francisco Franco against the centre-left Popular Front government of the Spanish republic. The struggle in Spain divided Irish political life, causing tensions between political parties and inducing Irishmen to fight on both sides. Perceived to be part of a worldwide struggle between communism and Catholicism, the nationalist side under Franco was supported by the Catholic bishops and by most of the Irish press and political parties. However, despite much public pressure to recognize Franco's government, *Fianna Fáil took a neutral stance. Alleged republican attacks upon the Spanish church and clergy in particular aroused public opinion. Meetings organized by the Irish Christian Front, set up to aid Franco and fight against the 'threat of communism', were extremely well attended.

The hierarchy supported a national collection for Spain, and helped Eoin *O'Duffy to visit Franco. He returned to Ireland and began to organize an *Irish Brigade to fight on Franco's side. He eventually led a force of about 700 former *Blueshirts to Spain, which did not see much action and soon returned home disillusioned. One of the few organizations to support the republican side in Spain was the dormant *Republican Congress. Its leaders called upon Irishmen to help Spain in its fight against fascism. About 150–200 men, mainly former Republican Congress and some *Irish Republican Army, formed the Connolly Column of the International Brigade under Frank Ryan. They were involved in serious fighting and casualties were high, including Ryan, who was eventually captured and ended up in Nazi Germany, where he died. JA

spas, with their supposedly medically beneficial waters, became popular from the mid-18th century. The main spas were at Mallow in Cork, Swanlinbar in Cavan, Castleconnel in Limerick, Ballyspellin in Kilkenny, Lisdoonvarna in Clare, Kilmeadan in Waterford, Tralee in Kerry, Ballynahinch in Down, Leixlip in Kildare, and Lucan in Dublin. Mallow's warm springs were promoted as a cure for consumption from 1738, and led to the town being dubbed the 'Irish Bath'. Swanlinbar was 'the Harrogate of Ireland'. Assembly rooms were constructed, and spa towns became the centres of fashionable society. However, the attractions of English spas, such as Bath and Cheltenham, were always greater for those who could afford them. From 1815 the now accessible Continent offered further distractions. Though often grand, Irish spas never afforded the same palatial facilities as the larger English resorts, and the main market was domestic. Lucan and Leixlip were accessible to Dublin day trippers. Patrons continued to visit spas until the late 19th century, and Lisdoonvarna attracted some visitors as a health resort into the 1950s. Their ultimate decline as popular centres was brought about by changes in fashion, and by the growth of rival domestic attractions, including *seaside resorts. NG

speaker. With the rise in influence of the Irish *parliament from the 1690s, the position of speaker of the House of Commons became an important political office. Elected by MPs in a procedure which government could influence but not control, the speaker was not a neutral chairman but a figure of power in his own right, the principal intermediary between the legislature and the executive. Important holders of the office during the 18th century included Alan *Brodrick, Henry *Boyle, John *Ponsonby, and John *Foster.

Special Branch. From its establishment in 1925 after the amalgamation of the *Dublin Metropolitan Police and the newly formed *Gárda Síochána, the Special Branch has played a crucial role in combating political crime and in monitoring political unrest and subversion. Initially it occupied a peculiar place in the force as a plain clothes unit staffed mainly by directly recruited armed officers with no experience of ordinary police work. It gained a reputation for rough methods, though not for systematic torture or murder, from its republican opponents in the 1920s and 1930s. The Special Branch is now fully integrated into the Gárda Síochána, and is staffed by officers recruited from the uniformed branch or from ordinary detective units. Because of its continuing counter-subversion role, some of its activities inevitably cause concern about possible abuses of civil liberties and about political interference in policing. Such concerns are likely to intensify with increasing European police co-operation. EO'H

special courts. The long tradition of replacing trial by jury with specially constituted courts commenced with the provision for two magistrates (from 1807 a special session chaired by a king's counsel) to try offences under the *Insurrection Act. Various *Coercion Acts gave powers to military and other non-jury courts. Trial by court martial was permitted under the *Defence of the Realm Acts, for breaches of regulations made under the acts, and under the *Restoration of Order in Ireland Act for a range of general offences. Courts martial were also held under *martial law in 1798–1806, in 1920–1, and during the *Irish Civil War.

In independent Ireland special criminal courts composed of officers of the defence forces were authorized (though never set up) under the *Public Safety Act (1927). The military tribunal created by a further Public Safety Act in 1931 tried 58 persons during 1931–2, and 94 following its revival by de *Valera during 1933–7. During the *Second World War, there were two special courts: a military tribunal established under the *Emergency Powers Acts (1939, 1940), which sat 1940–3, and a Special Criminal Court composed of five military officers set up under the *Offences against the State Act, which sat during 1939–46 and 1961–2. The latter was re-established in May 1972, although its members now consisted of serving or retired judges.

In Northern Ireland the *Special Powers Act (1922) gave any two resident magistrates summary jurisdiction over offences under the act. However the Criminal Procedure Act (1922), providing for special courts, was never implemented, and expired in 1923. The Emergency Provisions Act (1978) provided for non-jury trial for scheduled offences and since the phasing out of *internment these 'Diplock courts' (named after the chairman of a review commission in 1972) have provided the main means of dealing with terrorist offences.

Special Powers Act, officially the Civil Authorities (Special Powers) Act, a wide-ranging emergency law of the Northern Ireland Parliament (Apr. 1922). It replaced Westminster's *Restoration of Order in Ireland Act (1920), repealed as part of the *Anglo-Irish treaty. Like similar legislation in the Irish Free State (see PUBLIC SAFETY ACTS; OFFENCES AGAINST THE STATE ACT), it was a draconian response to civil war, but it was renewed annually long after the disorder had ended, and made permanent in 1933. It gave remarkably wide powers of arrest and detention to the *Royal Ulster Constabulary as agents of the minister for home affairs, and enabled the minister to proscribe organizations and ban or reroute parades. Until the late 1960s the act was used almost exclusively against Catholics, who regarded it as a major symbol of repression. It proved unsusceptible to any legal challenge. It was the legal basis for *internment in 1971, but was repealed in 1973 and replaced by Westminster legislation, the NI Emergency Provisions Act (1973) and the Prevention of Terrorism Act (1974). ACH

Spenser, Edmund (*c*.1552–1599), celebrated English *Renaissance poet and New English planter. Spenser probably came to Ireland in 1580 as secretary to Sir Arthur Grey, lord deputy, and was later an official in the *provincial presidency. During the *Munster plantation he obtained an estate at Kilcolman, Co. Cork. His verse epic *The Faerie Queene* (1590–6) has been seen as an allegorical demand for more forceful policies in Ireland. *A View of the Present State of Ireland*, by contrast, was a direct appeal to policy-makers in the form of a prose dialogue between proponents of hard and soft policies in Ireland. Written in the early stages of the *Nine Years War, it blamed the inappropriate use of the common law in a corrupt environment (exemplified by the degeneration of the Catholic *Old English), and aimed to re-establish Grey's draconian martial law policy as the only way to complete the conquest of Ireland. Different assessments have presented him as representative of colonial policy-makers and an important forging agent of an Anglo-Irish identity in Ireland, or alternatively as an unrepresentative extremist inspired by a combination of warped humanism and Protestant fundamentalism. The latter view has been underwritten by the notion that the *View* was censored by the English authorities in the 1590s, appearing only later, in an edited form, in 1633. More recent work, however, suggests that its delayed publication was the result of a dispute between rival publishers. Spenser died in penury in London in 1599 after being driven off his Irish estates. HM

'Speranza', see WILDE, LADY JANE.

sport of various kinds has been played in Ireland since early times. For example, it is known that *hurling in some form was being played 2,000 years ago. Legislation in the 14th century sought to restrain English settlers from playing Irish games, though as with laws passed in the Interregnum and post-revolutionary years, such attempts to reform popular culture were largely unsuccessful. During the 18th century sport, already an appendage to fairs and festivals, and increasingly associated with patronage, became subject to a measure of commercialization. *Horse racing, for example, supported by the wealthy, took on a new formality; jockeys were among the first professional sportsmen. *Gambling, by way of prize moneys and side bets, was prominent in encouraging competition.

The first half of the 19th century saw a marked decline in traditional culture, reflecting the spread of new social aspirations and standards of behaviour, reinforced after 1845 by the disruption and loss of population caused by the *Famine. Traditional sports, such as hurling and local forms of football, almost totally fell into abeyance. Meanwhile changing fashions, and the influence of the large Irish garrison, made English sports more popular and widespread. By 1860 *cricket was probably the most popular sport in Ireland. The late Victorian era, in Ireland as elsewhere, was a period of rapid growth for organized sport. Games became codified and governing bodies were formed, while the emergence of the paying spectator heralded a new wave of commercialization. Many Irishmen, notably athletes, became affiliated to English organizations. But there was also disquiet at the social exclusiveness of athletics meetings, at the prevalence elsewhere of cash prizes and gambling, at the predominance of English sports such as *rugby and cricket, and at the influence of English regulating bodies. The creation and rapid growth of the *Gaelic Athletic Association (1884) was an important part of the *'new nationalism' of the period before the *First World War. It gave the choice of sports a political significance that it retains, in Northern Ireland in particular, to the present day.

The First World War disrupted Gaelic games to a lesser extent than their Anglicized rivals, although political disorder (see ANGLO-IRISH WAR) created factions in the GAA and chaos in all sporting programmes. *Partition created some confusion in Irish sport, though only a minority of sports, notably *soccer and athletics, did not continue on an all-Ireland basis.

In the *Irish Free State Gaelic sports became part of the officially sponsored culture, notably through the *Tailteann games. Other sports received little official attention, though the Catholic middle classes quickly adopted the Anglicized sports, especially rugby. The first international team to compete as the Irish Free State was the lawn tennis team which entered the Davis Cup in 1924. Though Gaelic games retained their domestic supremacy, national rugby, hockey, and soccer teams received some official recognition following international success. Although *Gaelic football is the premier spectator sport, soccer has higher levels of participation.

In Northern Ireland sport retained a sectarian bent, though national sides were selected primarily on grounds of ability. Sport could not be used as a means of consolidating the new state from 1920, mainly because of the persistence of both all-Ireland and United Kingdom teams and officiating bodies. Gaelic sports, seen as inherently Catholic and nationalist, have continued to be largely shunned by the majority Protestant population. Soccer is the most popular spectator and participation sport. Most other sports, such as horse racing and *golf, continue, though necessarily on a smaller scale than in the Republic. Renewed civil disorder from 1969 (see NORTHERN IRELAND CONFLICT) temporarily disrupted domestic sporting programmes and international fixtures, but did little lasting damage.

Large-scale professional sports have not developed in Ireland. This is due to the amateur ethos of the GAA, the attraction of leading sportsmen to established professional sports abroad, and the small potential internal market. Women's sport in Ireland has always been of limited appeal to both competitors and spectators. *Camogie attracts few participants. Hockey remains the country's major women's sport, though interestingly Ireland now has internationally recognized female cricket and rugby sides.

There is no comprehensive history of sport in Ireland. Histories of the more important individual sports are noted at the end of the relevant entries. NG

Stack, Austin (1879–1929), commandant of the Kerry Brigade of the *Irish Volunteers in 1916. Stack was responsible for making contact with the *Aud*, which contained the arms sent over from Germany, but failed to do so. He was arrested and sentenced to death but this was commuted. As minister for home affairs in the first *Dáil government he was responsible for organizing the *Dáil courts. He rejected the *Anglo-Irish treaty and fought in the *Irish Civil War. He remained a leading member of *Sinn Féin and the second Dáil until his death in 1929. JA

stage coach travel in Ireland began its golden age in the 18th century. There was a good road system and routes generally radiated to and from Dublin. By 1737 there were regular services from the capital to Drogheda, Kilkenny, Kinnegad, and Athlone. The first permanent Dublin–Belfast route, running two or three days a week, was established in 1788, bringing the number of provincial centres linked by stage to Dublin up to twelve. The Post Office, from 1789, awarded mail contracts to coaching firms. By 1834 there were 28 mail coach lines, with 40 coaches, operating out of Dublin. Fresh teams of horses were introduced at stages, usually at coaching inns. Journey times improved. In the 1840s the Dublin–Cork mail coach took eighteen hours and Dublin–Belfast twelve. A century earlier, a Dublin–Belfast winter journey took three days. Up to twelve passengers travelled inside and eight on top. Often, if the coach broke down, passengers had to walk to the next stage. Until the 1820s coaches were accompanied by military detachments and blunderbuss-wielding guards to forestall highwaymen. In 1838 a Dublin–Belfast ticket cost 27*s*. 6*d*. inside and 15*s*. outside, plus a tip for the coachman. Journeys were timetabled and advertised, with contractors' penalty clauses operating. By the 1840s the *railways had supplanted stage coaches. PC

Stanihurst, Richard (1547–1618), Ireland's closest approximation to a *Renaissance 'Magus'. Born into a prominent Dublin family, Stanihurst studied at Oxford, where he met Edmund *Campion and became interested in Neoplatonism. In Ireland he tutored the children of Gerald, the 11th earl of *Kildare. In 1577 Stanihurst contributed a large part of the Irish section of Holinshed's *Chronicles*, his version of the *Kildare rebellion landing him in trouble with the English authorities.

In 1581 he went into exile in the Spanish Netherlands amid political suspicions over his connections with Kildare and Campion. His *De rebus in Hibernia gestis* (Antwerp, 1584)—basically Ireland from an *Old English viewpoint—was later banned in Portugal after Philip *O'Sullivan Beare complained to the Inquisition. Famed in the Netherlands for his curative elixirs (possibly whiskey based), he was invited to Spain by Philip II in the early 1590s and given a laboratory in the Escorial. Despite casting aspersions on the 1593 Irish mission to the Spanish court, Stanihurst became increasingly involved in the intrigues of English and Irish exiles to secure a Spanish succession to the English throne. He spent his final years as a *Jesuit. HM

Stanley, John (d. 1414), lieutenant to Robert de *Vere, marquis of Dublin and duke of Ireland, 1386–7. As *justiciar (1389–92) Stanley faced allegations of official misconduct in 1391. An investigation was ordered, with particular reference to the revenues of the lordship, the strength of his retinue, and his actions concerning the ransoming of Niall O'Neill. He was in Ireland during *Richard II's first expedition, and served as Henry IV's lieutenant in the lordship 1399–1401. His final appointment in 1413 as lieutenant was cut short by his death in 1414. His pay was often in arrears, which may help to explain the reputation he left in Ireland for oppressive extortions. DBJ

Staples, Edward (*c.*1492–*c.*1558). Born in Lancashire and educated at Cambridge and Oxford, Staples was provided by the pope to the see of Meath on 3 September 1520, but subsequently became a strong supporter of royal supremacy (see REFORMATION). During the reign of Edward VI he was responsible for the introduction of the Book of *Common Prayer in the face of considerable opposition. With the restoration of Catholicism under Queen Mary, Staples was deprived on 29 June 1554. AF

state enterprise was long favoured by the governments of independent Ireland as a means of promoting economic development. Some state companies such as the *Electricity Supply Board, *Irish Shipping, and *Aer Lingus were established to provide public services not previously available nationally. Others such as *Bord na Móna and the Irish Sugar Company were set up to exploit domestic resources, reduce dependence on imports, and increase employment. Very few were created as a result of nationalization, and then only in cases such as the rail and bus systems where companies had been threatened with closure. Thus state enterprise has never been a significant ideological battleground, despite its recent difficulties. After the oil crisis of 1973–4 state enterprise experienced considerable problems: modernization, rationalization, and the pursuit of profits were hampered by government insistence on retaining employment levels and on fulfilling other social goals. The public financial crisis of the early 1980s, together with strengthened *European Union competition laws, progressively forced drastic change: two debt-ridden firms were allowed to collapse, some profitable enterprises have since been sold off, and others such as Aer Lingus, the ESB, and the telecommunications and postal companies are pursuing major cost and staff reductions in order to survive. EO'H

State Paper Office, see PUBLIC RECORDS.

state papers contain correspondence between the sovereign and his ministers and chief officers and between the latter and their subordinates concerning affairs of state, supplemented by reports, estimates of expenditure, accounts of moneys received, records of military affairs, proposals and plans for the government of the country, and petitions from individuals. The largest single extant collection of documents on early modern Ireland, now widely available on microfilm, the State Papers Ireland collection (SP60–SP63 and SP65) in the Public Record Office, London, are calendared and indexed in *Calendar of State Papers Relating to Ireland* (24 vols., 1860–1912) for the period 1509 to 1670. For the period 1671–1704 they are included in the *Calendar of State Papers Domestic* (81 vols., 1856–1972). BC

steam power was first reliably put to use by Thomas Newcomen in the early 1700s, in water-pumping machines. It was being used as such in the Leinster coalfields by the 1740s. In 1746 the first steam pump in the north was erected in Drumglass Colliery in Co. Tyrone. Pumping engines were also used to return water to the top of a waterwheel, where there was an insufficient water supply. This was the case in Belfast's first steam engine installed in 1790 at Springfield *cotton mill. Watt's improvement on the Newcomen design, using only a quarter of the coal, could drive rotating machinery directly. Cotton mills could now be set up on sites where water was unavailable. The virgin site of *Prosperous in Co. Kildare was one of a number of huge centres of steam-powered cotton spinning and weaving established in southern Ireland. Others were located at Cork, the Dublin liberties, Stratford-on-Slaney, Co. Wicklow, Balbriggan, and Malahide. The most successful of these enterprises, set up in 1826, in *Portlaw, Co. Waterford, by the Lurgan-born Quaker David Malcolmson, lasted for half a century. As the 19th century continued, Ireland as a whole was also affected by the transport revolution ushered in by steam-powered *railways, ships, and traction engines.

The most extensive use of steam power was, however, in Belfast, Ireland's only major centre of factory-based *manufacturing industry. From 1800 to 1812 fifteen steam engines of 212 hp were erected in the Belfast area. By the 1830s eighteen steam engines of 690 hp were used in powering *linen wet spinning in Belfast. Steam engines were used in foundries, flour mills, *paper and whiskey making, and even in grinding coffee. In 1838 there were fifty steam engines in Belfast, about a third of the total in Ireland. By the 1860s linen weaving was becoming mechanized by steam-powered looms.

The steam-powered industrial revolution radically changed the lives of thousands of workers who now became subject to the tyranny of the factory system. Belfast replaced Dublin as the centre of steam-engine making, with leading firms such as McAdam Bros., John Rowan & Sons, Victor Coates, and the Falls Foundry of Coombe Barbour & Coombe. Although Ireland had few coal resources, costs of imports from Britain were to an extent offset by low labour costs. *Water power nevertheless prevailed in many manufacturing processes until the 20th century. Many industries moved directly from water to *electric power, missing out the intermediate stage of steam power. PC

Steelboys, see HEARTS OF STEEL.

Stephens, James (1824–1901), from Kilkenny, an apprentice railway engineer before joining in the *rebellion of 1848. In exile in Paris Stephens was one of the small group among whom the formula of secret preparation for a foreign-aided insurrection was nurtured. Assured of Irish-American support he launched the society later known as the *Fenians or *Irish Republican Brotherhood in Dublin on 17 March 1858. On the strength of its early success Stephens seized nominal headship of its sister movement in the USA in early 1859. From 1861 to 1866 Stephens's influence was at its zenith. His organization flourished in Ireland, Britain, and the USA; he established a successful propagandist newspaper, the *Irish People*; he stymied the efforts of others to launch rival nationalist mobilizations; and his followers were able to spring him from a Dublin prison within weeks of his arrest in November 1865. When in December 1866 he abandoned the rising he had rashly promised by year's end, Stephens's reputation and influence suffered irreparable damage. The leaders of the rising of March 1867 and of the post-1867 IRB repudiated him. Stephens remained in exile until 1891 when he came to retire quietly in Dublin. RVC

sterling. Throughout the 18th century the Irish pound existed as a notional currency, whose value was fixed at twelve-thirteenths of a pound sterling. The first notes issued by the Bank of Ireland in 1783 could be redeemed at twelve-thirteenths of the specie value of the English pound. From 1797 the value of the Irish pound was allowed to float and it depreciated against the English pound. In 1826 both currencies were assimilated. Although the *Irish Free State issued its own currency after 1927, it was at parity with the pound sterling, with 100 per cent backing in gold, sterling, or British government securities. This remained the position until 1979 when Ireland, but not Britain, joined the European Monetary System.

See also MONEY. MED

Stewart, see LONDONDERRY (STEWART).

stock exchange. The formal origins of the Dublin Stock Exchange date from 1799 when the Irish parliament passed a bill to regulate stock brokers. The original membership stood at thirteen; before that time informal dealings had been conducted by a small number of businessmen. The foundation of the stock exchange reflects the growth of Irish government debt at the close of the 18th century and the increased volume of canal debentures held in Dublin. In 1844 there were 47 joint-stock companies listed in Ireland; however, in the 50 years following the introduction of limited liability in 1855 approximately 2,850 companies were registered under the Company Acts. Separate stock exchanges were established in *Cork in 1886 and in *Belfast in 1895. In 1971 the Cork Stock Exchange merged with all stockbrokers operating in the Irish Republic to constitute the Irish Stock Exchange. In 1973 Belfast became a unit within The Stock Exchange, a body embracing all UK stock exchanges. The Irish Stock Exchange also merged with The Stock Exchange in 1973, but became independent once again in 1996, a move which reflects the growing divergence of the British and Irish economies. MED

Stone, George (*c.*1708–1764), political prelate. A Londoner, Stone came to Ireland as chaplain to the duke of Dorset, lord lieutenant 1730–7, and rose rapidly in the Church of Ireland to become archbishop of Armagh 1747. Following the return of his patron Dorset as lord lieutenant in 1750, Stone began a power struggle with Henry *Boyle, presenting himself to English ministers as working to break the power of the *undertakers who had usurped control of Irish affairs. Temporarily isolated following the government's settlement with Boyle, Stone re-emerged from 1758 as a powerful undertaker in his own right, now willing to defy the London government when popular Irish interests were at stake.

Stormont, the site of the parliament of *Northern Ireland, on the eastern outskirts of *Belfast, frequently used as shorthand for the parliament itself. The neoclassical parliament building, located at the end of a straight, mile-long drive with a statue of Sir Edward *Carson dominating the final approach, was designed by Sir Arnold Thornely. Its opening (16 Nov. 1932), presided over by a noticeably unenthusiastic prince of Wales, was the occasion for a display of *unionist pageantry, consciously recalling the triumphant mobilization of Protestant Ulster against the third *home rule bill in 1912–14.

street lighting was undertaken originally as a deterrent to crime. Private individuals had erected lights in Irish cities prior to 1697, but it was in this year that legislation provided for Dublin and its liberties to be lit at public expense. Lamps, fuelled with tallow, were modelled on those current in London. Cork and Limerick (1719), and Waterford and Galway (1729), were later given comparable legislation. By 1720 rape or fish oil had replaced tallow. From 1759 all urban corporations and *justices of the peace were empowered to initiate lighting programmes. From 1765 *parish vestries were permitted to raise moneys and implement schemes. There were also private initiatives, such as those in Rutland (1784) and Merrion (1791) squares in Dublin. Funding and supervision were often problematic, and damage and theft common. By 1800, however, most urban centres had publicly funded street lighting. From 1820 gas lights, using locally generated coal gas, replaced earlier oil lamps. Experimentation with *electric lights began in 1889, using power generated from coal and hydroelectric power. Full electrification was achieved in the Irish Free State by the late 1930s. In Northern Ireland full conversion was not complete until after 1947. NG

Strongbow, nickname of Richard fitz Gilbert, alias Richard de Clare (d. 1176), who succeeded his father as earl of Pembroke in 1148 but was deprived of the comital title and earldom by *Henry II on his accession as king of England in 1154. Diarmait *Mac Murchada, exiled king of Leinster, recruited him in south Wales to fight on his behalf in Ireland. In August 1170 Strongbow landed with an army near Waterford, captured the city, and shortly afterwards was married to Mac Murchada's daughter *Aífe. Strongbow went on to take Dublin and fought alongside Mac Murchada until the latter's death around May 1171, when he succeeded him as lord of Leinster. King Henry II threatened to confiscate Strongbow's landholdings in his dominions unless he agreed to recognize the English king as overlord of his Irish acquisitions. In autumn 1171 Henry mounted an expedition to Ireland and reached an accommodation whereby he agreed to recognize Strongbow as lord of Leinster and earl of Strigoil (a title taken from Strongbow's castle at Chepstow), but still refused to restore to him the earldom of Pembroke. Until his death in 1176 Strongbow waged war to secure the settlement of Leinster with tenants drawn from his English and Welsh estates. By his wife Aífe he had a son, Gilbert (d. after 1185), and a daughter, Isabella. In 1189 Isabella married William *Marshal, who succeeded to the lordship of Leinster in right of his wife, and recovered the earldom of Pembroke in 1199. MTF

subscription controversies divided Irish *Presbyterianism in the 18th and early 19th centuries. In 1698 and 1705 the *Synod of Ulster followed the Church of Scotland in requiring ordinands to subscribe the confession of faith drawn up by the Westminster Assembly in the 17th century. Opposition soon came from those who disapproved of subscription to human formularies as a test of faith, some of whom also disapproved of the theology of the Confession. The Belfast Society, in which some avant-garde ministers and elders met to discuss theology, became an important influence promoting non-subscription and New Light doctrines (see OLD LIGHT AND NEW LIGHT). To meet this challenge the synod introduced a pacific pact, allowing ministers and ordinands to substitute their own words for passages in the Confession which they could not subscribe. This failed when the Revd Samuel Haliday refused to subscribe in any form at his installation in the First Belfast congregation. Another expedient, the formation of a separate non-subscribing presbytery, the Presbytery of Antrim, did not halt the advance of non-subscription in the synod, and by the end of the century more than two-thirds of its presbyteries were non-subscribing. This process was reversed in the 1820s as a result of what some have called the second subscription controversy. This was envenomed by the fact that some non-subscribers had become *Arians and also by political animosities, *Montgomery, the non-subscribing leader, being liberal in politics, and his opponent, *Cooke, conservative. It is wrong, however, to describe the controversy as a political conflict in disguise. When seventeen non-subscribers seceded in 1830 to form the *Remonstrant Synod, obligatory subscription was restored in the Synod of Ulster and remains the practice of mainstream Irish Presbyterianism.

Barkley, J. M., *The Westminster Formularies in Irish Presbyterianism* (1956)
Haire, J. L. M. (ed.), *Challenge and Conflict: Essays in Irish Presbyterian History and Doctrine* (1981)

RFGH

suburbs. Walls (see WALLED TOWNS) protected most urban dwellers for the first millennium of Irish urbanization, but even in the 12th century the Anglo-Norman capture and refortification of Hiberno-Norse centres (notably *Dublin, *Waterford, and *Cork) led to the partial or complete exclusion of the earlier citizenry beyond the walls. Other suburban settlements (the Irishtowns of *Kilkenny and *Limerick) may have developed in tandem with the Norman citadels that overshadowed them as they became centres of artisan activity. The *Franciscan and *Dominican *religious orders generally chose sites outside the walls and these often formed the nucleus for secular development. In the case of Dublin, by 1300 most of the city was located outside the walls, partly on the north side of the river. Suburban settlements there and elsewhere bore the brunt of warfare in the 14th and 15th centuries, and some disappeared at that period or were incorporated inside walled towns.

The resurgence of suburban development around 16th-century Dublin and elsewhere in the early 17th century was a measure of general urban expansion; it was also because of the clustering of craft activities not suited or not welcome in the urban core. *Liberties, notably that of St Thomas and Donore south-west of Dublin's walls, became distinctive urban communities outside the jurisdiction of their parent city. The religious purges during and after the *Confederate War either temporarily or permanently swelled the suburbs of leading corporate towns and contributed to the religious segregation evident for example in 18th-century Cork.

However, in the long cycle of city growth, sharp distinctions emerged between types of suburban settlement: old artisanal neighbourhoods (Blackpool in Cork and Ballymacarett abreast of Belfast); new areas of high-status residential development (Ballsbridge and Clontarf outside Dublin); and satellite settlements centred on specialized economic activities such as textile finishing, quarrying, or seafaring (Douglas, in the case of Cork, Palmerstown, Rathgar, and Ringsend in the case of Dublin). And by the early 19th century there was a swathe of villa residences inhabited by the well-to-do pioneering commuters around Irish cities; they in turn were serviced from the satellite villages.

*Railway construction in the 1830s and 1840s created the first commuter suburbs of Dublin (Blackrock, *Kingstown) and the pattern was repeated slightly later around Belfast and Cork. The horse omnibus, the horse tram, and towards the end of the century the electric tram articulated the process. Only in greater Dublin did independent township authorities emerge in the mid-19th century; some of these were controlled by private landowners (e.g. Pembroke), railway companies (Kilmainham), or a tight group of speculative developers (Rathmines). All but Kingstown/Dún Laoghaire were absorbed into Dublin corporation in the early 20th century.

Three processses transformed the scale of suburbanization in 20th-century Ireland: the pronounced general growth of towns since the 1920s; the huge local authority programmes for the rehousing of the inner-city working classes; and transport changes, first cheap motor-bus services and later the popularization of car ownership. Thus by the end of the century most Irish people resided in what technically were suburbs.

Graham, B. J., and Proudfoot, L. J. (eds.), *An Historical Geography of Ireland* (1993)

DD

Sullivan, Alexander Martin (1829–84), one of the foremost propagandists of Irish nationalism. As proprietor of the **Nation* 1855–74 Sullivan created a series of ancillary titles and, with his brothers Timothy Daniel and Donal, conducted a multifaceted publication enterprise with productions including *Speeches from the Dock* (1867). His *Story of Ireland* (1870) is a myth-making classic. *New Ireland* (1877) reflects the more open-minded attitude that he developed while living in London as an MP for Louth (1874–80) and Meath (1880–2). RVC

Sunday schools had their origins in English towns and cities in the 1780s in response to rapid demographic growth and fears of lower-class infidelity. They spread rapidly in Ireland in the first half of the 19th century, chiefly, but not exclusively, under the auspices of the Hibernian Sunday School Society formed in Dublin in 1809. By 1841 this interdenominational voluntary society had established over 3,000 Sunday schools, the majority of which were located in the province of Ulster. During the 19th century the original interdenominational ideal of the early Sunday schools largely collapsed under the weight of denominational competition as churches began to see their potential as recruiting agencies.

The primary aim of Sunday schools was to facilitate the reading of the scriptures and other religious literature, but they also inculcated the values of good manners, sound morals, and respectable appearance. In wider social terms they made a distinctive contribution to working-class life through their anniversary celebrations, street parades, Whitsun outings, book prizes, and benefit societies. Through its loyal band of unpaid teachers and its supply of cheap educational benefits to the poor, the Sunday school movement probably made a bigger impact on the urban working classes than any other voluntary religious institution. DNH

Sunningdale agreement (9 Dec. 1973), the first attempt to implement a comprehensive political settlement for *Northern Ireland following the closure of its parliament in 1972, concluded at a meeting attended by the heads of the British and Irish governments and the leaders of the *Unionist, *Alliance, and *Social Democratic and Labour parties. The more militant unionist parties and the republicans were not invited. The agreement included a new constitutional structure for the province, based on a power-sharing executive which would require support in the Northern Ireland Assembly (see CONSTITUTION OF NORTHERN IRELAND ACT) from major parties representative of both Catholic and Protestant communities, and on cross-border co-operation in socio-economic and security matters. This was to be organized through a *council of Ireland, with a council of ministers and an indirectly elected assembly on similar lines to the European Economic Community as it existed at that time. It quickly became clear that the Unionist leadership was unable to carry its followers with it: the power-sharing executive was briefly established, but was destroyed by the *Ulster Workers' Council action of May 1974. The agreement was never formally ratified. ACH

Supremacy, Acts of (1537, 1560), two measures passed by the Irish *parliament, each designed to assert the control of the English monarch over the Irish church. The first, Henry VIII's act authorizing the king, his heirs, and successors to be supreme head of the *Church of Ireland (28 H. VIII c. 5), marks the official beginning of the Irish *Reformation. Since Henry was more concerned with jurisdiction than theology, it was possible for clergy to remain within the established church without major changes to their beliefs or practices. The Dublin government sought to win acceptance for royal supremacy, not only within the areas it directly controlled, but also from Gaelic chieftains, as part of the programme of *surrender and regrant. The act was repealed in 1557 when Catholicism returned under Queen Mary. Royal supremacy was restored by the 1560 act, though with the less sweeping assertion that Elizabeth was 'supreme governor'. This act required that all clergy and secular officials should swear an oath accepting Elizabeth's supremacy and renouncing all foreign jurisdictions. This was subsequently used as a means of excluding Catholics from public office. Together with the Act of *Uniformity, it formed the basis of the Protestant Elizabethan settlement. AF

Supreme Court. Under the *constitution of the Irish Free State and the Courts of Justice Act 1924, the Supreme Court was solely a court of appeal. The High Court had sole jurisdiction on the constitutionality of legislation. The power of judicial review was limited because the 1922 constitution could be amended by ordinary legislation.

In the 1937 *constitution of Ireland the powers of the Supreme Court, influenced by the American model, were greatly strengthened. It is the court of final appeal and consists of at least five judges (increased to eight in 1995), including the chief justice. It has appellate jurisdiction over decisions of the other courts and its authority in cases of challenges to laws is entrenched. In cases concerning the validity of a law with reference to the constitution, only one judgment, with no assenting or dissenting opinions, can be given. This also applies to bills referred to the Supreme Court by the *president. Since the 1961 Courts Act, the Supreme Court has extended its jurisdiction to other areas, notably *habeas corpus, orders for costs, and appeals against acquittals.

After 1937, judges were initially slow to use judicial review. A more assertive stance commenced with Justice George Gavan Duffy (1882–1951) of the High Court, and with Cearbhall Ó Dálaigh, a Supreme Court judge from 1953 and chief justice 1962–73. Between 1939 and 1987, the 50th anniversary of the constitution, the number of cases per decade referred to the court more than quintupled. Since the 1960s the court has delivered landmark decisions in many areas, especially personal rights, but with Ireland's accession to the *European Union in 1973, the finality of the Supreme Court's decisions has been limited by the European Court of Justice and the European Court of Human Rights. DMcM

surnames. In Ireland a man was called by his own name and that of his father, after *mac* ('son'), or his grandfather, after *ua/ó* ('grandson'). From the mid-10th century such patronymics and 'papponymics' become fixed surnames. A child was not named directly after a patron saint but was called his 'devotee' (*maol*) or 'servant' (*giolla*). Both elements are common in surnames, e.g. Ó Maoil Eoin ('descendant of the devotee of St John'), Mac Giolla Phádraig ('son of the servant of St Patrick'). Some surnames in Mac contain not the father's name but his status, e.g. Mac an Airchinnigh ('son of the *erenach'). A handful of Gaelic names are adjectives, Cinnsealach ('Kinsella'—see UÍ CHENNSELAIG), for example. When referring to women Mac and Ó become Nic (<*iníon Mhic*, 'daughter of the son of') and Ní (<*iníon Uí*, 'daughter of the descendant of') respectively. The *Anglo-Norman conquest introduced surnames of varied origin, e.g. Fleming, Butler, Purcell<French *pourcel*, 'piglet'. Many Norman names were Gaelicized: Walsh ('Welsh')> Breatnach, Fitzgerald>Mac Gearailt.

From the 16th century onwards Gaelic and Gaelicized names were Anglicized, by transliteration (Ó Néill>O'Neill), by substitution (Ó Brolcháin>Bradley), or by translation (Ó Gabhann>Smyth). *Plantation introduced further surnames from Britain, some of which, Davis, Jones, and Wilson, are now among the commonest in the country. Plantation also brought many Scottish Gaelic surnames, e.g. MacCambridge<Mac Ambróis, and MacEllistrum <Mac Alastraim.

The Irish revival at the turn of the century re-established the use of Irish forms of names and surnames. NJAW

surrender and regrant was the principal Tudor policy to integrate Gaelic and Gaelicized lordships into a revamped Irish polity. In the Middle Ages Gaelic lords had no security of tenure and were accounted Irish enemies of the crown. In 1520 Henry VIII himself suggested in debate with *Surrey their assimilation by way of land grants. The difficulties caused by the *Geraldine League paved the way for the new conciliatory initiative under *St Leger and his local ally, Sir Thomas *Cusack. The establishment of the *kingdom of Ireland provided the constitutional framework.

St Leger had financial leeway from the proceeds from the *dissolution of the monasteries, but was not averse to using force against the Leinster Irish and against O'Neill to ensure their co-operation. The reconciliation of the earl of *Desmond, who agreed to the revival of crown government in his territories, and the attendance of Gaelic and Gaelicized lords at parliament promoted an atmosphere of compromise. The process involved three indentures. In the first the lord recognized the king as sovereign and surrendered his lands, while applying for a grant and peerage; in the second he renounced his Gaelic title and promised to assist the establishment of English law and customs, to render military service, and to pay rents to the crown, receiving in return a charter for lands and noble title; in the third the lord arbitrated internally with his vassals and kinsmen over their respective rights and duties. The final enrolment of these documents in chancery copperfastened the legality of the settlement.

By these means MacWilliam *Burke became earl of Clanricard and MacGillapatrick became baron of Upper Ossory. The greatest success was O'Neill's creation as earl of Tyrone in London amid much pomp and propaganda in 1542. It used to be argued that this initiative was achieved by bribing the Gaelic lords with freehold grants of the lands of the whole clan. This was never the crown's intention, though lords later used uncompleted agreements to claim absolute ownership. The crown wanted to stabilize all existing tenures by feudalizing them and there were definite plans to do so in the lordships of O'Neill, O'Reilly, O'Toole, and O'Brien when the policy ground to a halt in 1543. Although the establishment of primogeniture was a long-term goal, the crown was not inflexible, agreeing the succession of the tanist (see *tánaiste*) in both Tyrone and Thomond. The Gaelic lords lost their local sovereignties but their new spirit of co-operation was evident in their military contributions to the *Boulogne expedition.

Sidney revived surrender and regrant to detach *MacCarthy Mór, as earl of Clancare, from Desmond and had similar projects to detach O'Reilly and O'Donnell from Shane *O'Neill. His parliament passed an act to take surrenders and the calendar of *fiants for this period shows that the policy was continuous in the late Elizabethan period. In the 1580s *Perrot supervised another extensive round of surrenders and regrants in Ulster and north Connacht. The policy could entail confiscation for treasonable action and this occurred with the MacMahon lordship resulting in the partition of *Monaghan between the collaterals and freeholders. This use of subinfeudation to break the power of a great lordship provoked the *Nine Years War and in its aftermath legal disputes continued with Hugh *O'Neill claiming that his patent entitled him to freehold ownership. In the 17th century surrender and regrant continued under the auspices of the Commissions for *Defective Titles, though most applications were now *Old English.

Bradshaw, Brendan, *The Irish Constitutional Revolution of the Sixteenth Century* (1979)

HM

Surrey, Thomas Howard, earl of (d. 1554). Surrey's lord lieutenancy (1520–2) was an experiment in direct rule from England, presaging many problems encountered during the *Tudor conquest. His English troops proved unsuited to Irish conditions and he had to levy forces locally. Raising only £750 from the annual Irish revenues, and refused extra money by parliament, he was forced to continue *coyne and livery and to request subventions from England amounting to £18,000. Without the good offices of Gerald (Gearóid Óg) FitzGerald, earl of *Kildare (on bail in England), he had to exact submissions from O'Neill and other great lords on progresses round the country. Order was restored in the *Pale but increasing likelihood of English involvement in a European war forced him into truces with the Gaelic lords in 1521. A debate over the extension of sovereignty throughout the island was initiated. Surrey advocated the establishment of forts, towns, and plantations, with 2,500 men required over a number of years for a gradual conquest, or 6,000 men needed for a rapid one. Henry VIII and Cardinal Wolsey favoured the cheaper method of concessions to co-opt the Gaelic lords into the English system.

HM

Survey and Distribution, books of, manuscript volumes summarizing the *Cromwellian land settlement and its modification at the *Restoration. Laid out by *county, *barony, *parish, and *townland, they show the ownership of land in 1641, as set out in the *Down Survey, followed by details of subsequent confiscations and transfers of ownership. Five sets of books are known to have existed, one of which was destroyed with other *public records in 1922. Of the remainder, that in the *Royal Irish Academy, and the 'Headford set' in the National Archives, Dublin, probably date from the 1660s and 1670s. The auditor-general's set in the National Archives, and the Annesley set in the Public Record Office of Northern Ireland, appear to have been compiled in the 1680s, and the former contains annotations on changes in ownership up to 1702.

Sussex, Thomas Radcliffe, earl of (1523–83). This inflexible, military-minded chief governor (1556–64) replaced the gradualist regime of *St Leger. A courtier with little administrative experience, Sussex relied on martial law and built up the military establishment by appointing English relatives and clients as commanders and privy counsellors. He fought the O'Connors and O'Mores to consolidate the *Laois-Offaly plantation and tried unsuccessfully to evict the *MacDonnells for a similar project in Antrim. His militaristic approach, with its jobbery, related debasement of the currency, and forced billeting of troops on loyal communities (*cess) antagonized the Palesmen. Court connections helped him to fend off a protest movement headed by Archbishop George Dowdall of Armagh.

Sussex now staked all on defeating Shane *O'Neill but achieved only a number of expensive failures. The Pale opposition, this time headed by the earl of *Kildare, succeeded in having him recalled with the support of his enemy at the court, Robert Dudley. Sussex's most lasting achievement was religious not military—the re-establishment of the Church of Ireland in the 1560 parliament which reversed his own restoration of Catholicism under Mary three years earlier.

HM

Swift, Jonathan (1667–1745), clergyman, poet, satirist, and political writer. Born in Dublin, the son of an English-born lawyer, Swift spent 1691–9 in Moor Park, Surrey, as secretary to the retired diplomat Sir William Temple, with an interval as vicar of Kilroot, Co. Antrim, 1695–6. He became vicar of Laracor, Co. Meath, in 1700. *A Tale of a Tub* (1704), a religious allegory, lampooned Catholicism and dissent. In 1707 Swift returned to England to negotiate financial concessions (see FIRST FRUITS AND TWENTIETH PARTS) for the Church of Ireland. Formerly an associate of leading *Whigs, he became from 1710 a client of the *Tory leader Robert Harley, for whose administration (1710–14) he wrote highly effective propaganda, particularly against the continuation of war with France. Swift's efforts won him appointment as dean of *St Patrick's cathedral, Dublin (1713), but not the English bishopric he hoped for, and the exclusion of the Tories from power after 1714 forced him back to Ireland.

During the 1720s Swift became a fierce controversialist on Irish issues, notably with *A Proposal for the Universal Use of Irish Manufacture* (1720), advocating a boycott of English goods, and the **Drapier's Letters*. Other pamphlets attacked English misgovernment of Ireland, along with the native vices of corruption, idleness, and exploitative and absentee landlordism. *A Modest Proposal* (1729), arguing that Ireland could escape from poverty by raising children for food, has been read variously as a reflection of Swift's misanthropy, as the ultimate indictment of England's oppression of Ireland, and as a frustrated reformer's abandonment of the Irish to the consequences of their own indolence and folly. *Gulliver's Travels* (1726) is a more broadly based satire on contemporary politics, religion, and literature.

Swift's abandonment of the Whigs was due partly to their failure to uphold the established church, whose defence against irreligion and dissent remained one of his main concerns, and partly to a belief that post-revolution Whiggery had abandoned liberty for oligarchy. Much later he still insisted that he, and Harley, were 'real' Whigs (see COMMONWEALTHMEN). The same concern for constitutional rights, intermixed with bitterness at his banishment to Dublin, inspired his Irish pamphleteering. As with other *patriot writers, the liberties he defended were those of the Anglican minority, whose Englishness was throughout one of his central contentions.

Downie, J. A., *Jonathan Swift, Political Writer* (1984)

Swiney, Eugene (d. 1781), *printer, bookseller, and *newspaper proprietor in Cork. He produced a broad range of publications, including many Catholic works.

VK

syndicalism, a movement looking to the use of trade union power to achieve the restructuring of society along *socialist lines. Both *Larkin and *Connolly were influenced by French and American syndicalist ideas. A similar belief in industrial action as a direct route to the achievement of social revolution may be detected in some at least of the *soviets set up during and after the *Anglo-Irish War. The subsequent history of Irish labour politics, however, suggests that these were never more than minority tendencies in a movement most of whose members saw the assertion of trade union rights primarily as a means of preserving or improving wages and conditions within the existing industrial order.

Synod of Ulster, the supreme court of mainstream Irish *Presbyterianism until its union with the Secession Synod in 1840 to form the General Assembly. The synod grew out of the original Presbytery of Ulster, which subdivided during the 1650s. Following the *Restoration Presbyterian church courts were suppressed, but after 1690 the synod met openly and its published records are in print. *Subscription controversies divided the synod in the 18th century, enabling Scottish *Seceders and *Covenanters to establish congregations, presbyteries, and synods. The restoration of obligatory subscription in 1836 opened the way for the union of 1840. RFGH

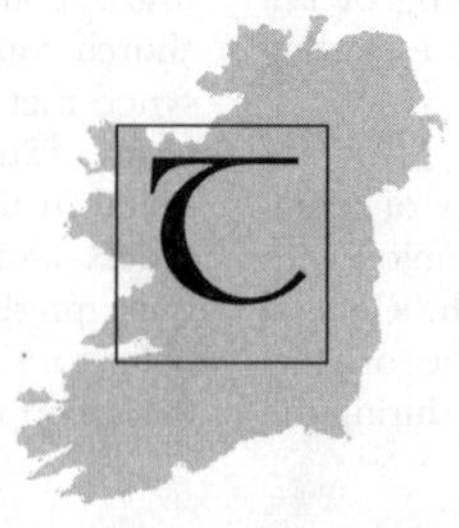

Tailteann Games, involving athletic and artistic competition, were said to have been held in pre-Christian Ireland (see ÓENACH TAILTEN), though they had been curtailed by 1169. From the 1880s their revival became an element of nationalist rhetoric. The issue was raised in the *Dáil in 1920. Official planning for the 'Irish Olympic' began in 1922. Finally held in 1924, under the control of the *Irish Free State government assisted by the *Gaelic Athletic Association, the games were a qualified success. Events as diverse as shooting and motorbike riding were included, along with Gaelic sports. Further contests in 1928 and 1932 attracted more foreign competitors. Due to financial restrictions and the waning interest of the GAA, however, the expected series did not continue.

NG

Táin Bó Cuailnge ('Cattle-Raid of Cooley'), the central tale of the Ulster Cycle (see LITERATURE IN IRISH). It depicts an invasion of Ulster by Queen Medb of Connacht in an attempt to secure a renowned brown bull. The raid is blocked by the Ulster champion Cú Chulainn until the Ulstermen arrive to defeat the invaders in a pitched battle and the Ulster bull tears apart its Connacht counterpart. Around this tale were built a series of other stories, both sequels and 'prequels'.

The tale has grown considerably in content and perhaps intention, between its earliest literary origin (*c.* 7th century) and its first appearance in Irish manuscripts of the 11th century. It has been variously seen as the product of a native pagan oral tradition, a deliberate attempt to create an early Irish literary epic, and a political commentary on dynastic disputes over episcopal succession at Armagh. JPM

Talbot, John (*c.*1387–1453), earl of Shrewsbury (from 1442) and Waterford (from 1446), chief governor 1414–16, 1416–18, 1418–19, 1425, 1446–7. Brother of Archbishop Richard *Talbot and protagonist in the *Talbot–Ormond feud, John Talbot, then Lord Furnival and claimant to the lordship of Westmeath, first arrived in Ireland as lieutenant in 1414. Despite financial difficulties, he campaigned extensively, securing many submissions and taking MacMurrough (Donnchadh Mac Murchadha) prisoner to England in 1419. In November 1418 he was ordered to report on the affair of the **Modus tenendi parliamentum*, which had embroiled his brother Thomas as deputy that year. Inheriting a further claim to the lordship of Wexford as Lord Talbot in 1421, he returned to Ireland in 1424 with Edmund, earl of March (see MORTIMER, EDMUND), and on the latter's death in January 1425 served for three months as *justiciar. Thereafter Talbot's career was spent largely in France, but his second Irish lieutenancy (1446–7) confirmed his vigour and ruthlessness in dealing with Gaelic chiefs. EAEM

Talbot, Matt (1856–1925), ascetic and figure of popular devotion. Born in Dublin, Talbot fell into alcohol abuse at an early age. In 1884, while working in the port of Dublin, he underwent a religious conversion. Taking the teetotal pledge, he committed himself to regular sacramental practice, acts of physical penance, and practical charitable activity, notably during the *Dublin lockout. Beatified in 1976, his cult is popular in places as far afield as Poland. TO'C

Talbot, Richard (d. 1449), archbishop of Dublin 1418–49. Younger brother of John *Talbot and previously dean of Chichester, Richard Talbot was more prominent in royal government in Ireland than any other late medieval archbishop of Dublin. He served three deputy lieutenancies (1419–20, 1435–7, 1447–8), five justiciarships (1420, 1422–3, 1430–1, 1437–8, 1445–6), and was twice chancellor (1423–6, 1427–31). A protagonist in the *Talbot–Ormond feud, he is best known for the charges of misgovernment he made in England against James, 4th earl of *Ormond, after the latter's third appointment as lieutenant in February 1442. Before returning to Ireland, Talbot was reappointed chancellor in August, but counter-charges in Ireland in November deprived him of office. He retaliated in 1445 by ousting Ormond's deputy.

Although twice, abortively, a candidate for the archbishopric of Armagh (1416, 1443), Talbot staunchly defended Dublin's independence of Armagh's primatial jurisdiction. His memorial in *St Patrick's cathedral commemorates his establishment of minor canons and choristers in 1432. EAEM

Talbot–Ormond feud (1414–47), a factional conflict in which the chief protagonists were John *Talbot, his brother Richard, archbishop of Dublin, and James, 4th earl of *Ormond. The feud developed from hostility between Ormond and John Talbot after the latter's first arrival in Ireland as lieutenant in 1414. In 1417 Talbot confiscated Ormond's lands in Ireland for non-payment of debts at the Dublin exchequer. On obtaining the lieutenancy himself in 1420, Ormond purged Talbot appointees from the Irish administration. Thereafter there was fierce competition to control or influence the power and patronage of the chief offices and numerous charges and counter-charges of misgovernment. Factional tension, which was reported by 1428 to have spread throughout Ireland, was punctuated by periods of quiescence, one following a temporarily successful investigation in England in 1422–3, and outbreaks of open violence, most notably in 1429. Little significant progress towards reconciliation was made until a marriage was arranged, outside Ireland, in 1444–5, between John Talbot's eldest son and Ormond's daughter Elizabeth. However, the feud did not end in Ireland until John Talbot returned as lieutenant in 1446–7.

Nationalist interpretations of the feud as a confrontation between English unionism and Anglo-Irish patriotism have been discarded. Modern interpretations stress the personal nature of the quarrel and its destructive effect on government and justice. More recent work emphasizes the way in which the feud, in offering leading figures in Ireland an incentive to take charge of the Dublin administration, stimulated a necessary exploitation of local financial resources at a time of marked reduction in English exchequer support. EAEM

tánaiste. In Gaelic Ireland the *tánaiste* was the designated successor of the king or chief, nominated during his lifetime. English observers in the 16th and 17th centuries used 'tanistry' (as in case of *tanistry) more loosely, to mean the whole system of succession in Gaelic Ireland. Under the *constitution of Ireland (1937) the *tánaiste* is the deputy prime minister.

Tandy, James Napper (*c.*1737–1803). Variously described as ironmonger and land agent, Tandy was a prominent *patriot activist in *guild and corporation politics, commander of artillery for the city's *Volunteers, and leader in 1784 of the more aggressive and plebeian campaign for *parliamentary reform, protectionism, and a limited Catholic franchise that succeeded the main Volunteer agitation. Approached by *Tone and *Russell, he convened the Dublin branch of the *United Irish movement and became its first secretary. When an attempt to establish contact with the *Defenders exposed him to capital charges, he fled to America (1793) and then France (1797), where his rivalry with Tone divided the Irish radical exiles. In 1798 he sailed as commander of the *Anacréon*, with supplies for *Humbert. On 16 September the expedition landed briefly on Rutland Island (see CONYNGHAM, WILLIAM) but withdrew on learning of Humbert's defeat. Tandy's arrest in neutral Hamburg in November provoked a diplomatic controversy. He was returned to Ireland, convicted, and sentenced to death, but deported to France in 1802.

tanistry, case of, decided by the Irish judges in King's Bench in 1608, and recorded in Sir John *Davies's *Reports* (1615). It arose from the disputed possession of the castle and lands of Dromaneen, Co. Cork. The plaintiff, Murrough MacBryan, asserted tanist right; the defendant, Cahir O'Callaghan, claimed common law inheritance. The case, referred in 1604 by the Munster *presidency court, had been argued out in King's Bench, with Davies defending, but left undecided. The parties instead made a partition between themselves in *chancery.

Afterwards the Irish judges decided to review the case and passed a special ruling abolishing tanistry, the Gaelic method of political succession, and the lands attached to the office (see *tánaiste*). This voided Irish sovereign rights, which were considered obnoxious to the crown and destabilizing to the country, by vesting the lands in the crown by conquest right, and strengthened the 1606 decision in the case of *gavelkind, where tanistry had been abolished only by implication. It also voided the 1593 *surrender and regrant of Dromaneen, thereby endangering the letters patent of other Gaelic lords whose power originated in tanistry. Davies made immediate use of this ruling to facilitate the *plantation of Ulster by quashing Gaelic freeholders' rights which he himself had previously advocated. HM

tanning was a significant industry during the 18th century; by 1796, there were 876 operative tanners in the country. New excise laws in 1798 and 1813 eliminated many smaller tanners and contributed to the concentration of the industry in bigger tanyards in the larger towns; *Cork and *Dublin were the main centres. However, decline wasevident by the

1840s; the growing export of live cattle reduced the supply of hides; the fall in population in the post-*Famine years and British penetration of the Irish market for boots, shoes, and other leather goods reduced demand. In particular imports of cheaper British sole leather and prepared uppers, produced in English yards utilizing the best technologies and chemicals to increase productivity, undermined much of the Irish tanning trade. A few large yards survived by adopting new methods; but there were only eighteen tanning firms in the whole country by 1902. *Limerick at this stage had displaced Cork as the main centre of the industry, specializing in sole and harness leather; there were others in this trade in *Derry, New Ross, and Ballitore, while centres of upper and harness leather included *Belfast, Newry, Coleraine, *Drogheda, Dunmanway, Bantry, Clonmel, Mountmellick, and Richhill. These surviving firms tended to be larger and more highly capitalized than the typical tanyard of the early 19th century, and they could compete with British imports. AB

taoiseach (prime minister), successor under the 1937 *constitution to the *president of the executive council. The offices were substantially the same but de *Valera's modifications increased the taoiseach's power. In article 28 the taoiseach is unequivocally 'the Head of Government'. He has to keep the *president 'generally informed' on domestic and international matters. The taoiseach nominates the **tánaiste* and ministers are appointed by the president on his advice, with the approval of the *Dáil. He also nominates the attorney-general and eleven members of the *Senate. Two major departures from the 1922 constitution concern dissolution and the resignation of ministers. The taoiseach (not the executive council as previously) has the right to dissolve the Dáil, unless he loses his majority. He also has the right to dismiss ministers 'for reasons which seem to him sufficient', a provision the opposition attacked in 1937, claiming that this was a decision for the government as a whole. In *interparty governments, the taoiseach's power to dismiss ministers not of his own party is in practice more circumscribed.

Constitutionally and administratively, the office of taoiseach is at the centre of government, but the emphasis on leadership and personality in Irish political life has, depending on the occupant, further increased its authority. DMcM

Tara, a prehistoric complex associated with the *high kingship of Ireland. The Hill of Tara is a low-lying ridge situated midway between Navan and Dunshaughlin in Co. Meath. The principal monuments consist of a *neolithic passage tomb, a cursus or linear earthwork, a hillfort, a stone pillar reputed to be the inauguration stone known as the *Lia Fáil*, numerous barrows, and other enclosures of uncertain date. Limited archaeological excavations were conducted in the 1950s and in 1997. The original meaning of the Irish name *Temair* is obscure. It has been explained as meaning 'a height with a view', 'a sacred space', or 'the gates to the otherworld'.

Tara has been regarded traditionally as the seat of the high kings of Ireland. A recurring theme in early Irish mythology is that of the exalted status of the kingship of Tara. The god Lug, the most potent god in the Irish pantheon, becomes the king of Tara in the tale *Cath Maige Tuired* (The Battle of Moytura). The goddesses Medb and Eithne, renowned goddesses of fertility and sovereignty, represent the female aspect of the kingship of Tara. The universal principles of kings ruling justly, peacefully, prosperously, and truthfully, summed up in the phrase *fír flathemon* ('the justice of a ruler'), govern the actions of heroic kings of Tara such as Conaire Mór mac Etarscéla and *Cormac mac Airt. The king of Tara was bound by taboos, some of which are literary fictions, but others of which are probably genuine axioms devised to safeguard this concept of *fír flathemon*.

In political terms, it is unlikely that any king had sufficient authority to dominate the whole of Ireland prior to the 9th century. However, the title *rí Temro* or *rex Temro* ('king of Tara') was always accorded a special status. Early historical references to Tara, in documents dated primarily to the 7th and 8th centuries but which reflect vaguely events of earlier centuries, describe contention for the kingship between rival dynasties from the *Laigin, the *Ulaid and the *Uí Néill. The latter attempted to dominate Tara, both politically and conceptually, from the 7th century to the 11th century. When the high kingship of Ireland became a more realistic institution in the early 11th century, control of Dublin and other coastal towns, such as Limerick or Waterford, was more important to an aspiring high king than dominance over Tara. The old capital retained its symbolic significance, however, by continuing to evoke associations of strength, nobility, and legitimacy of power.

Of the many popular tales associated with Tara, the most renowned tale is the dramatic account of St *Patrick lighting the Paschal fire on the Hill of Slane and of his confrontation with *Lóegaire, king of Tara, and his druids at Tara. It is contained in a biography of Patrick written in the 7th century by Muirchú moccu Machtheni. Tara, according to legend, was abandoned when

St Rúadán of Lorrha cursed it and its king, *Diarmait mac Cerbaill (d. *c.*565), the last king of Tara to celebrate the old fertility rite *Feis Temro. While this tale was probably composed to explain the official adoption of Christianity by the kings of Tara, archaeological evidence suggests that Tara's monuments are prehistoric in date, predominantly late neolithic and *Bronze Age, with little indication of activity taking place into the historic period.

Tara's potency as a site of symbolic importance persisted into the modern period, mainly reflected in the custom of gathering there as part of military or political campaigns. The hill was the focus of activity during the *rising of 1641 and of a skirmish during the 1798 *insurrection. It was also the scene of one of Daniel *O'Connell's 'monster meetings' held on 15 August 1843, a meeting reputedly attended by 1 million people.

Bhreathnach, E., *Tara: A Select Bibliography* (1995)
Macalister, R. A. S., *Tara: A Pagan Sanctuary of Ancient Ireland* (1931)
Newman, C., *Tara: An Archaeological Survey* (1997)
Petrie, G., 'On the History and Antiquities of Tara Hill', *Transactions of the Royal Irish Academy*, 18 (1839)

EB

taxation. In early Christian Ireland all land not specifically exempted was subject to *cís, congbáil ocus slógad* (royal tribute, lodging of royal and ecclesiastical retinues, and military service). By the early 12th century lodging duty had extended from periodic visitations or 'guesting' (*coinnmheadh*) to the regular billeting (**buannacht*) of royal mercenaries. The Anglo-Irish marcher lords were subsequently to adopt the system as suited to a subsistence economy. Like the chieftains, their exactions included 'bonaght' (*buannacht*), *'coyne (*coinnmheadh*) and livery', 'chiefry' or *tighearnus* (tribute from lands acknowledging the ruler's lordship), *'coshering' (a feast for the lord's household and followers), and 'canes' (from **cáin*), fines for law-breakers. Expenses incurred by the lord through travelling, lawsuits, or fines were levied from his subjects by assessment. In the 16th century this led to regular tallaging (literally translated as 'cutting' or *gearradh*), notoriously without the consent of the taxpayers.

Taxation in *Anglo-Norman Ireland was initially based on the liability of all *feudal tenants to contribute financially to meet the needs of their overlord, the king. In the late 13th century, the concept grew of a common necessity being dealt with by taxation granted with the free consent of the representatives of those being taxed. Grants of subsidy made in a *parliament or great council became the normal form of taxation, usually based on land and moveable goods, with the clergy contributing a separate tax based on the value of their benefices. The money received from a subsidy was applied to the costs of the Dublin administration in dealing with unrest in various parts of Ireland, though on several occasions, ending in 1335, money was raised in Ireland for the *Anglo-Scottish wars. From the mid-14th century onwards, taxes were frequently granted by local assemblies for the cost of local defence.

Taxation in early modern Ireland, growing out of these medieval foundations, comprised those taxes granted to the king by parliament at the outset of his reign, including *customs and excise duties, along with more irregular subsidies granted by parliament as required. During the 1650s the high cost of the *army in Ireland demanded more regular taxation and a monthly assessment was introduced. After 1660 this trend towards more regular taxation continued with the introduction in the parliament of 1661–6 of a continuing hearth tax and the perpetual grant to the crown of customs and excise. Up to the end of the 1680s these grants were sufficient to meet the expenses of government, and even to yield a surplus. From the 1690s, however, it became necessary to rely on the Irish parliament to pass regular money bills authorizing borrowing and permitting the levying of additional taxes. Ad hoc levies such as the poll tax were imposed in 1660 and again in the 1690s, but as emergency measures which were quickly abandoned. There were also a variety of local taxes such as the parish *cess, levied by the *parish vestry, and the county cess, levied by the *grand jury for bridge building and after 1760 for *road building.

By the end of the 18th century Ireland was paying £3.5 million annually into the exchequer, primarily in customs and excise duties. During the 19th century total annual revenue from taxes rose from just over £4 million in 1829 to almost £7 million in 1879–80. The burden of local taxation also increased. Annual receipts from county cess and *poor law rates exceeded £2 million by the 1880s. Moves to equalize taxation in Britain and Ireland, beginning with the introduction of income tax in 1853, provoked allegations that overtaxation was stifling the Irish economy. Although a government inquiry in the 1890s concluded that Ireland had been paying more than her national income warranted, historians have judged the case for overtaxation not proven.

KS/PhC/RG/VC

Taylor, Jeremy (1613–67), *Church of Ireland bishop and noted devotional writer, theologian, and preacher. Born and educated at Cambridge (BA 1631, MA 1634), Taylor was closely associated with the high church regime of Archbishop William Laud of Canterbury and with the royalist cause in the English civil wars. In 1658 he accepted a lectureship near Lisburn, Co. Antrim, and after the *Restoration was made bishop of Down and Connor (consecrated 27 Jan. 1661), to which was added the responsibility for administering the diocese of Dromore. Down and Connor were a stronghold of Irish *Presbyterianism, and Taylor repeatedly clashed with Presbyterian ministers in his efforts to impose uniformity. Unhappy in Ireland, he sought translation to England, but was unsuccessful and died at Lisburn on 13 August 1667. His main achievements were his stylish prose works, which include *A Dissuasive from Popery* (1664), *The Rule and Exercises of Holy Living* (1651), *The Rule and Exercises of Holy Dying* (1668), and *Doctor Dubitantium, or the Rule of Conscience* (1660). AF

teacher-training was only gradually accepted as essential, apprentice 'monitors' being the norm until well into the 19th century. The *Kildare Place Society was a pioneer in the field, establishing *model schools based on Joseph Lancaster's monitorial system, with residential accommodation for the candidate teachers. This was the method adopted by the commissioners for *national schools, but the commissioners' district model schools and training institution at Marlborough Street, Dublin, were declared unsuitable for Catholic teachers. It was not until 1883 that government accepted the principle of state aid for denominational training institutions, financial support being given to two Catholic colleges in Dublin (Drumcondra and Carysfort) and to the Church of Ireland Training College (Kildare Place), enabling them to extend facilities and provide two-year courses of training.

Other colleges were added to a system which remained virtually unchanged for several decades. With *partition, the existing denominational colleges in the Irish Free State continued to supply the denominationally managed national school system there, Marlborough Street being closed. In Northern Ireland, Stranmillis College was founded to supply the state sector. Women teachers for the voluntary Catholic schools attended St Mary's College, Belfast, the men attending Strawberry Hill, in London, until the foundation of St Joseph's College in Belfast. (St Mary's and St Joseph's form St Mary's University College since 1999.) KM

telegraph. The electric telegraph, invented in 1837, came to Ireland in 1866 with the establishment by the Anglo-American Telegraph Co. of a permanent cable link between Valentia Island and Newfoundland. Three stations in all were set up in Kerry, chosen as the westernmost part of Europe. In 1874 Anglo-American opened a second station at Ballinskelligs. A third was put into operation in 1885 at Waterville by the American-owned Commercial Cable Co. By the end of the century, Kerry was linked to Newfoundland, Nova Scotia, Britain, Germany, and France. In 1911 Ballinskelligs and Valentia were taken over by the Western Union Telegraph Co. of America. The Irish cable stations were now part of the worldwide communications network called the 'All Red Routes'. During the *First World War, the cable stations were subject to government censorship. The war led to a vast increase in cable traffic and staff numbers at Valentia rose to 200 working round-the-clock shifts. In 1919 the British government bought Ballinskelligs but the station was closed in 1922 and its functions moved to Penzance. Valentia and Waterville stations remained in operation until the mid-1960s, when modern advances in telecommunications rendered them obsolete. PC

telephone exchanges opened in Dublin and Belfast in 1880, only four years after Bell's first transmission. Dublin–Belfast trunk routes were installed in 1884. The first submarine telephone cable, laid from Port Patrick in Scotland to Donaghadee, Co. Down, in 1893, cost £20,000. By 1900 there were 56 exchanges in Ireland. In 1912 the Post Office took over the service. Following *partition, two separate systems emerged on the island. By 1930 only Co. Donegal and western Mayo remained unconnected. The first automatic exchange opened in Dublin in 1927, followed, in the north, by Groomsport, Co. Down, in 1929, and Belfast in 1935. During the *Second World War, both networks were urgently upgraded for security reasons. In the Irish Free State, in 1945, 107 exchanges gave continuous service to 23,700 subscribers, with a further 732 exchanges on restricted-hour service to 5,900 subscribers. The first transatlantic telephone cable was laid in 1956. In 1957–8, Subscriber Trunk Dialling began in Athlone and Cork. Belfast switched to STD in 1961. Dublin's first international telephone exchange opened in 1971. By 1977 there were 250,000 subscribers in Northern Ireland. In 1980 responsibility for the telephone service in Northern Ireland, as in the rest of the UK, was privatized and transferred to British Telecom. The following year, there was a similar transfer of the Republic's phone services to Telecom Éireann. PC

television first reached Ireland from Great Britain. By 1960 a significant proportion of homes on the east coast had aerials permitting them to receive BBC and Independent Television programmes, either from Great Britain or from Northern Ireland, where BBC television broadcasts had begun in 1955 and Ulster television in 1959.

An Irish television service was inaugurated on 31 December 1961. It was a public service broadcaster, financed by a combination of licence fees and advertising revenue, and supervised by a government appointed body, the Radio Telefís Éireann (RTE) Authority, established in 1966, replacing the Radio Éireann (see RADIO) authority. The advent of RTE, broadcasting to the whole country, greatly increased the number of potential viewers. By 1963 about one-third of Irish households had television licences, rising to more than 90 per cent by the early 1980s. However, the output of British stations continued to attract a wide Irish audience, expanded by the advent of cable, which by 1984 had given two-thirds of all households access to good-quality reception of British television stations. When a second Irish television channel, RTE2, was launched in 1978, commercial realities and consumer pressure combined to ensure that its main function was to repackage popular BBC and ITV programmes for transmission to those parts of the country where they could not be received directly. Although RTE's own output, notably in current affairs, drama (especially certain long-running serials), and light entertainment, gained a secure place in popular culture, the proportion of home-produced material shown declined from around two-thirds in the first years of the station to only 30 per cent by the 1980s. RTE2 was relaunched as Network 2 in 1988. An Irish language station, Teilifís na Gaeilge, later TG4, was launched in October 1996.

Irish television was created at the beginning of a decade of cultural transformation and political debate. In consequence its relationship with the authorities in church and state was more fraught than that of radio had ever been. The discussion programme *The Late, Late Show* (1962–) was involved in a series of controversies arising out of frivolous or iconoclastic studio discussion of previously sacrosanct personalities and doctrines. The current affairs programme *Seven Days* (1966–) regularly incurred disapproval for what were in Ireland novel techniques of investigative reporting. In 1966 the *Fianna Fáil government, objecting to reporting of its dispute with the Irish Farmers' Association, provoked controversy by its claim that RTE, as a state broadcasting service, was 'an instrument of public policy'. From 1969 the main focus of conflict has switched to reporting of the revived *Northern Ireland conflict. In 1971 the government issued an order under section 31 of the Broadcasting Act of 1960 restricting reports on the activities of illegal organizations. The following year the entire RTE authority was dismissed for having sanctioned an interview with an IRA spokesman. Restrictions were further tightened in 1976 and remained a source of controversy until their removal following the IRA ceasefire in 1994.

temperance and total abstinence. The first substantial temperance societies were established in Ireland in 1829, mainly inspired by the successes of the anti-spirits movement in the United States. The increasing consumption of whiskey, particularly illicit whiskey or poteen, among all classes had been causing considerable alarm in Ireland since the 1790s and temperance societies were seen as a way of countering this trend.

The first societies were directed against spirit drinking among the upper classes and were supported by the clergy, especially Belfast *Presbyterians, by members of the Dublin professional elite, by *Quakers, and by a handful of *evangelical landlords. In the face of serious economic dislocation and *agrarian protest after 1815, and of Daniel *O'Connell's successful campaign for *Catholic emancipation during the 1820s, temperance offered the *Protestant ascendancy a means of proving its superiority and of thereby bolstering its status during a challenging period.

Temperance did not become a major popular movement in Ireland until total abstinence was introduced from England in 1835 and Fr. Theobald Mathew (1790–1856), a Capuchin from Cork, took up the teetotal cause early in 1838. Fr. Mathew's crusade was a phenomenal success: by 1841–2 perhaps 5 million people, out of a total population of 8.2 million, had taken the teetotal pledge. The crusade was supported by the Catholic urban middle class and by radical Protestants, who saw it as a reforming and modernizing force. Yet most of its adherents were poor rural Catholics and their motives for joining are harder to unravel. A desire for economic and social betterment was certainly important, but Fr. Mathew was endowed in the popular mind with miraculous powers. The crusade was also therefore an expression of the popular religious beliefs and *millenarian fantasies that characterized Ireland in the decades before the *Famine.

O'Connell took the pledge himself in 1840 and it would seem that the startling success of Fr. Mathew's crusade served to encourage him to establish the*Repeal Association in the same year. Indeed the repeal movement benefited in a variety of ways from the crusade, making use of temperance bands and reading rooms, to say nothing of a sober population when it came to organizing the monster meetings of 1843.

Although many priests and the majority of the hierarchy supported the crusade, Fr. Mathew was a controversial figure within his own church. His interpretation of the teetotal pledge as a sacred vow, his mismanagement of crusade finances, his friendships with Protestants, and his acceptance of a government pension in 1847, all helped alienate many of his fellow clergy.

After the Famine and the swift decline of teetotalism, the Catholic church showed little enthusiasm for another such crusade. The hierarchy favoured temperance over teetotalism and it was not until the 1890s that another significant total abstinence movement emerged within the church. This was the Pioneer Total Abstinence Association of the Sacred Heart, established in Dublin in 1898–1901 by a Jesuit, Fr. James Cullen (1841–1921).

As its name implies, the Pioneer Association was an elitist devotional organization, not a populist crusade. It did not aspire to a mass following, nor did it aim to reclaim drunkards. The Pioneers were to be small bands of devoted Catholics, setting an example of piety and asceticism for others. Yet the success of the Pioneers far exceeded Cullen's expectations. By the 1920s the association had some 300,000 members and today it remains one of the largest temperance organizations in the world.

Temperance continued to be influential among Protestants after the Famine. In Ulster, Presbyterians, *Methodists, and other dissenters increasingly practised total abstinence, to the extent that wine was banished from the communion service in most churches. Protestants were also active in various temperance societies which campaigned vigorously from the 1850s onwards for anti-drink legislation. Sunday closing was introduced in the five main Irish cities in 1878, but with the rise of the *home rule party from the 1870s, strongly supported by the drink trade, the political base of the Irish temperance movement was severely eroded.

Yet temperance has remained a significant force in both Northern Ireland and the Republic. Although the Republic has long derived a substantial portion of its revenue from taxes on the country's large *brewing and *distilling industries, it was nevertheless estimated in the late 1970s that some 20 per cent of the adult population were total abstainers. Teetotalism is also strong in the north and during the *Stormont regime (1921–72) the temperance movement succeeded in achieving total Sunday closing and rigorous enforcement of the licensing laws.

Kerrigan, C., *Father Mathew and the Irish Temperance Movement, 1838–49* (1992)

Malcolm, E. L., *'Ireland Sober, Ireland Free': Drink and Temperance in Nineteenth-Century Ireland* (1986)

ELM

Temple, Sir John (1600–77), master of the rolls, author of the *History of the Irish Rebellion* (1646). He was given a seat in the English Commons after being imprisoned by the king for disagreeing with the truce with the *Confederate Catholics in 1643. His best-selling account of the *rising of 1641 with sensationalist woodcuts and exaggerated death tolls was used to promote a parliamentary reconquest of Ireland under Lord Lisle. Its frequent republication—nine times by 1812—reflected periods of Protestant anxiety. Conversely, Temple's book was loathed by Catholics and publicly burned on the orders of the *patriot parliament of 1689.

HM

Tenant League (Irish Tenant League). Formed in Dublin in August 1850, the league combined two movements prompted by the agrarian crisis of the late 1840s. In the north-east tenants were demanding legislative underpinning of customary rights (see TENANT RIGHT) under threat from landlords. In the south a number of local tenant protection societies had been endeavouring to use collective passive resistance to bargain with landlords about rents. Presbyterian ministers and Roman Catholic priests were prominent in the respective movements, as were the journalists William McKnight and Charles Gavan *Duffy. The latter was the main strategist of the League, which set out its demands in the *'three Fs'. The extension of the Irish county *franchise in 1850 to occupiers of land valued at £12 (13 & 14 Vic. c. 69) encouraged the league to put its trust in parliamentary politics, and more than 40 of the MPs returned in 1852 were committed to its support. Involvement in the contentious politics of the *Independent Opposition Party proved ruinous and the prosperity of the mid-1850s took the edge off tenant agitation. The league held its last meeting in 1858. RVC

tenant right, also known as the Ulster custom. The demand for tenant right became increasingly widespread during and after the *Great Famine. It was a primary aim of the Irish *Tenant League in the 1850s, and of the *Land League after 1879. Although little consensus existed over its meaning, tenant right was conventionally held to refer to one of the *'three Fs': a departing tenant's right to dispose of his saleable interest in his tenancy to the highest bidder, subject to the *landlord's approval of the purchaser. The nature of this interest was itself ambiguous. It was commonly thought to include not only the value of any improvements carried out by the tenant, but also the difference between the competitive market rent and the lower or 'fair' rent he actually paid. By implication, therefore, tenant right only had meaning in the context of under-renting by landlords. Its opponents argued that incoming tenants were crippled by demands that could amount to the equivalent of several years' rent. The 1870 *Land Act conceded tenant right in regions where it was customary; the 1881 Land Act conceded it throughout Ireland.

LJP

termon (O.Ir. *termonn*, from Latin *terminus*, 'a limit') referred in the later Middle Ages to church lands held by hereditary tenants known as *coarbs and *erenachs. However, in pre-*Norman Ireland the connotations of *termon* were primarily legal. It signified a defined area around a church, affording legal protection or sanctuary, breach of which entailed compensation to the church. In the 7th century *Armagh claimed a *terminus* encompassing much of east Ulster, apparently involving legal jurisdiction rather than landownership. Yet 8th-century Hiberno-Latin *canon law indicates that a surrounding *terminus* might provide pasture for a church's cattle. CE

Territorial Army (TA), a part-time, volunteer branch of the British army. Although units were first raised in Northern Ireland in the late 1930s for coast defence, a full TA organization was not established until 1946. The 'Territorials' reached a peak strength of over 7,000 men and women in 1954, falling back to some 3,000 in the 1990s. The force has never been used for any sort of internal security duties. KJ

terrorism. The literature on terrorism is dogged by the apparently insoluble problem of definition. Some commentators evade definitional problems by assuming an ideological consensus among their readers, others simply define terrorism as anti-state activity. Other approaches attempt to include state activities in the definition, by defining terrorism as involving the attempt to coerce target populations through the use of actions designed to induce extreme fear. Such general definitions, while focusing upon acts carried out against unarmed and innocent civilians, tend to blur the distinction between war and terror, since modern warfare involves the mobilization and the targeting of the civilian population.

The use of the term in the context of Irish history reflects these ambiguities. During the *Anglo-Irish War the intimidation and murder of civilians was practised by both the *IRA and the crown forces. As in all modern wars, the majority of those killed in the *Northern Ireland conflict since 1969 have been uninvolved civilians, and loyalist paramilitary groups have followed a consistent policy of killing uninvolved Catholics.

The current official definition of terrorism in *Northern Ireland comes from the Diplock Report of 1972. Diplock defines violence as the 'use or threat of violence to achieve political ends', a definition which, on the surface, could include certain state activities. Diplock, however, restricts his definition to 'those crimes which are committed at the present time by members of terrorist organisations'. This somewhat tautological approach characterizes conventional attempts to separate the usage of the term from any consideration of historical, social, or economic circumstances and fails to deal with the phenomenon as something created by human collectivities in the context of human history. JS

textiles, as one of the most basic consumer goods, play a prominent part in the history of *manufacturing industry. In Ireland records of commercial hand spinning and weaving of wool go back to the 8th century. An export trade in woollen cloth became established during the Middle Ages, and expanded rapidly in the 16th and 17th centuries until choked off by the *Woollen Act of 1699. The industry nevertheless grew during the 18th century to supply an expanding home market. In the 1830s dumping from steam-powered English concerns undermined Irish production, although the manufacture of specialized varieties, notably tweed, continued. *Silk manufacture was established in the 1690s by *Huguenot immigrants in Dublin. Poplin, a composition of wool and silk, was manufactured in the 'liberties' area of the capital, but largely perished in the 20th century due to competition from synthetic textiles. *Cotton spinning, in *steam- and *water-powered mills, grew rapidly in the late 18th century, but declined from the 1820s. Instead it was *linen, already a major household manufacture in the 18th century and successfully mechanized from the 1820s, that became Ireland's most enduring industrial success story.

*Shirt making, centred in *Derry city, Cos. Donegal and Tyrone, and *Belfast, took off after 1850, with the introduction of automated sewing and cutting machines. It declined after the *Second World War, due largely to foreign competition. Man-made fibre manufacture was introduced in Northern Ireland shortly after the war, to replace the declining linen industry. Prominent British firms, like ICI at Larne and Courtaulds at Carrickfergus, were joined by the Dutch-owned British Enkalon at Antrim and the American DuPont at Derry. Due to global pressures and domestic political conflict the synthetic textile industry declined in the 1980s and only DuPont now remains.

Ó Gráda, Cormac, *Ireland: A New Economic History 1780–1939* (1995)

PC

theatre. The earliest recorded plays in Ireland were mystery plays staged in certain towns by the medieval *guilds; these died out as a result of the *Reformation, though some attempts were made to adapt them to the new religion. An indigenous tradition of 'mumming plays' survived until recently in some areas, and has been drawn on by modern dramatists. Secular theatre first appeared in Ireland in the early 17th century under the patronage of the viceregal court. Later in the century commercial playhouses appeared in Dublin, and during the ensuing century a lively tradition of commercial theatre grew up.

While an important role in the development of Irish theatre was played by migrants from England, the 18th century saw the establishment of a lasting tendency for Irish playwrights and actors of merit to migrate to London as the centre of theatrical activity in the British Isles. (The 19th-century actor Barry Sullivan was considered unusual because he preferred to remain in Ireland.) The Irishness of London-based dramatists such as William Congreve, Charles Macklin, Oliver Goldsmith, R. B. Sheridan, the melodramatist Dion Boucicault, Oscar Wilde, and G. B. *Shaw was later to be disputed due to a growing emphasis on Gaelic and Catholic culture as the sources of 'true' Irishness, the view that national art should find its primary audience among its own people, and critical reaction against their idioms. (These writers were not all equally disparaged; all but the most fervent cultural chauvinists regarded Goldsmith as an honorary Irishman, though this was primarily due to *The Deserted Village* rather than his plays.) Recent criticism takes a broader view of Irishness and emphasizes the subversive sense of difference from the English that informs the work of these writers.

Nineteenth-century Ireland saw the further development of commercial theatre in Dublin and provincial cities. (Smaller towns were catered for by travelling repertory companies known as 'fit-'em-ups', or by local amateurs.) While it drew on the classical repertoire, commercial theatre produced little original work of any value, and its reliance on spectacle is seen as prefiguring the *cinema, which eventually superseded it. (An interesting product of this period, on political if not artistic grounds, was the patriotic melodrama focusing on nationalist heroes such as *Sarsfield and Robert *Emmet.)

The 1890s saw the appearance of an Irish version of the 'little theatre' movement, whose founders reacted against the spectacular commercial theatre of the period and wished to produce plays of a higher artistic standard. At this time the first plays in Irish were written (by authors such as Douglas *Hyde) and produced by amateur actors. Both developments were often linked to a political outlook which saw commercialism and vulgarity as English importations, and Irish patriotism, spirituality, and artistic excellence as intimately linked.

The mainstream of the 'national theatre' produced the *Abbey, some of whose founding members seceded to form the Theatre of Ireland (more nationalistic and with a greater emphasis on European drama), which survived into the 1920s. Amateur groups in imitation of the Abbey were founded in Belfast and Cork. The Ulster Literary Society (founders included Bulmer Hobson and 'Rutherford Mayne') soon lost most of its founders but survived into the 1950s. The Cork Dramatic Society (1908–14, founders included Daniel *Corkery and Terence *MacSwiney) initiated an intermittent tradition of Little Theatre in Cork, later represented by such groups as James N. Healy's Theatre of the South.

Despite the symbolist ambitions of *Yeats (shared in different forms by other pioneers of the movement), the Abbey and its regional imitators came to be dominated by naturalist drama. At its best this was inspired by a desire to make the audience see and transform the world around them but it easily degenerated into crowd-pleasing, stereotyped 'kitchen comedies' and pseudo-realist melodrama, a tendency reinforced by financial pressures.

To some extent the gap was filled by the Dublin Drama League, founded to present modern European drama (a similar group in Cork fell foul of puritanical objectors), and after 1928 by the Gate theatre, founded by Hilton Edwards and Micheal Mac Liammoir with the financial assistance of Lord Longford (1928 also saw the first permanent Irish-language theatre, An Taibhdhearc, in Galway).

Since the 1960s there has been a large-scale revival of Irish drama, linked to changes in Irish society which loosened constraints on the theatre and provided dramatists with new opportunities to explore clashing attitudes. An important role has been played by regional groups such as Druid in Galway and Field Day in Derry.

Fitz-Simon, Christopher, *The Irish Theatre* (1983)
Hogan, Robert, et al., *A History of Irish Theatre 1899–1926* (6 vols., 1975–92)
Roche, Anthony, *Contemporary Irish Drama* (1994)

PM

Theobald Walter (d. 1205), founder of the *Butler family in Ireland, who derived their name from Theobald's honorific office of butler in the household of *John, lord of Ireland, later king of England. In 1185 Theobald accompanied John to Ireland and received extensive grants of land in north Munster, and subsequently also in Leinster. His title of *pincerna* is attested in charters issued by John in Ireland in 1185. MTF

Thom, Alexander (1801–79), *printer and publisher in Dublin. He did extensive government printing, and was proprietor of *Thom's Dublin Directory*. The firm continued after his death. It was taken over by Helys in 1962, to become Hely Thom, which in turn was absorbed by the Smurfit Group in 1970. VK

Thomond, see O'BRIEN.

Thompson, William (1775–1833), of Roscarbery, Co. Cork, *socialist and *feminist writer. The son of a rich merchant, John Thompson, a former mayor of Cork, he inherited 1,400 acres and several merchant ships in 1814. Writing that he felt ashamed of living off 'the produce of the efforts of others', Thompson gave his tenants very favourable leases, attracting the ire of his own class. A leading advocate of the co-operative movement, he wrote many long treatises which were clear espousals of scientific socialism well ahead of Marx. With his lover Anna Wheeler (1785–1848), Thompson wrote the eloquently titled *An Appeal of One Half of the Human Race, Women, against the Pretensions of the Other Half, Men, to Restrain them in Political and thence in Civil and Domestic Slavery* (1825). His will, leaving everything to the co-operative movement, was overturned by relatives after a lengthy lawsuit. PC

Three Candles Press (1926–89), *printer and publisher in Dublin. It was founded by Colm Ó Lochlainn (1892–1972), who was noted for the quality of his typography. VK

'three Fs', the alliterative label widely used in post-*Famine Ireland to describe long-standing, but in reality ambiguous, tenant demands for fair rents, fixity of tenure, and free sale (another name for *tenant right). Free sale, together with fixity of tenure, was a particular demand of larger tenant farmers. Fair rents were of more importance for poorer tenants. All three rights were given legal status throughout Ireland under *Gladstone's second *Land Act of 1881. LJP

Thurles, Synod of (1850), the first formal meeting of the Irish episcopacy since 1642. Called by Archbishop Paul *Cullen it dealt with the *Queen's Colleges question and the standardization of pastoral practices. The issue of individual bishops speaking on government matters later arose. The bishops adopted the papal condemnation of the 'godless colleges' but were divided over priests accepting college positions and lay involvement. Cullen's hardline positions narrowly carried the day. The synod demonstrated the church's growing confidence. TO'C

Thurot, Commodore François (1727–60), French naval commander whose squadron of three ships anchored off *Carrickfergus on 21 February 1760. The French captured the castle after a short engagement and held the town until the arrival of reinforcements on 27 February. Thurot then put to sea but his ships were engaged and defeated, and he himself killed, the following day. The mini-invasion inspired a widespread mobilization of the Protestant population of Ulster, seen as prefiguring the later *Volunteer movement.

Tierney, Michael (1894–1975), academic and public intellectual. Son of a small farmer, he attained an academic career through a series of scholarships, becoming professor of Greek at University College, Dublin, in 1922. A separatist activist from 1913, he supported the *Anglo-Irish treaty, serving as *Cumann na nGaedheal TD (1925–7, 1927–32) and *Fine Gael senator (1938–44). In the 1930s he advocated Catholic corporatism and the *Blueshirts. Tierney exalted Gaelic and Catholic traditions, parliamentary politics, and liberal education; he detested Anglo-Irish and Protestant traditions as colonial impositions. As president of UCD 1947–64 he asserted succession from *Newman's *Catholic University. His transfer of UCD from the city centre to Belfield in south Dublin can be seen both as skilful preparation for expansion and as a high-handed attempt to distance UCD from *Trinity College. The authoritarian ethos associated with his leadership of UCD disintegrated from the late 1960s. Tierney was the son-in-law and biographer of Eoin *MacNeill, whose historical reputation he promoted. PM

tillage, the preparation of ground for crops, has been an essential *farming operation in Ireland since *neolithic times. Archaeological evidence shows that the cultivation of crops in narrow, steep-sided ridges was established by around 2,500 BC. These ridges were probably constructed using spades or simple 'ard' ploughs, which consisted of a share, beam, and handles, but lacked a coulter or mouldboard. Pieces of wood identified as parts of ploughs have been found in *Bronze Age contexts. Complete spades have survived from the early medieval period. These have wooden blades shod with metal, the blades being of both one- and two-sided types.

The development of plough design in Ireland can be paralleled in many parts of Europe. By the medieval period, large wooden ploughs with flat mouldboards and iron shares and coulters were used on *Norman manorial and monastic farms. These evolved slowly into the 'common' Irish ploughs, described by observers in the late 18th century as requiring up to three operators, and teams of between four and six *horses, or more rarely oxen. Most early 19th-century agriculturalists condemned the common ploughs, and urged Irish farmers to adopt metal swing (wheelless) ploughs, developed in Scotland by James Small and other engineers. By the 1830s, these had become the standard plough in many parts of Ireland. During the same period, wheel ploughs based on English prototypes began to be manufactured in Irish foundries such as Pierce's of Wexford. These ploughs, which could be adjusted so that the depth and width of furrow turned was fixed, were widely used on large lowland farms until the 1920s, when they began to be replaced by tractor-drawn ploughs.

During the last 250 years, hundreds of different types of spade have been used in Ireland. These were made by local blacksmiths, but also in spade mills. In the early 19th century, there were more than 70 of these mills in operation, concentrated mostly in Ulster, and around Dublin and Cork. In the 1830s, one spade mill in Co. Tyrone produced 230 different types of spade.

Spades were used in a wide range of tillage operations: turning, trenching, making *drills, and especially in constructing cultivation ridges of the type known as lazy beds. Ridge making was part of a complex system, the ridge's size and shape being adjusted in response to changes in slope, aspect, soil type, the crop grown, its place in the rotation, and the time of planting. Ridges are still made in areas of wet shallow soil, particularly in Cos. Cavan, Leitrim, and Longford. Skilled horsemen could make lazy beds using ploughs, and this skill is sometimes still used, the horse plough being pulled by a tractor. In most parts of Ireland, however, the spread of underground field drainage during the 19th century largely removed the need for ridges. Almost all field crops in modern Ireland are planted in flat ground or in drills.

Bell, J., and Watson, M., *Irish Farming* (1986)

JB

time. In Ireland, as elsewhere, the standardization of time was primarily a response to the exigencies of the *railway timetable. Before that, nearly every community had its own time. Clocks in Cork were eleven minutes behind those of Dublin, while those in Belfast were one minute and nineteen seconds ahead. The Time Act of 1880 established Greenwich Mean Time (GMT) for Britain, with Dublin Mean Time (DMT), twenty-five minutes behind GMT, for Ireland. However, although northern railway clocks had long since adopted DMT, it was not until GMT was extended to the whole of Ireland, in 1916, that the Albert Clock stopped showing Belfast Time. PC

tinkers, a vagrant population, also known as 'itinerants' or, euphemistically, as 'travellers'. Irish tinkers, unlike European gypsies, are genetically indistinguishable from the settled population. They are nevertheless defined by some observers as a separate ethnic group, characterized by a high degree of endogamy and preserving a distinctive way of life across generations. The *Poor Inquiry of the 1830s distinguished between tinkers and other types of vagrant. Their longer-term origin remains unclear, despite fanciful attempts to link them to a specialized caste of wandering metalworkers in early medieval times. 'Shelta', sometimes described as the distinctive language of tinkers, is better classified as a cant or argot, composed mainly of distorted versions of Irish words and not necessarily of antique origin. Nineteenth-century tinkers combined the manufacture and repair of tin implements with chimney sweeping, peddling, and occasional agricultural work. Their modern descendants deal mainly in scrap metal and used cars. Earnings from these sources have throughout been supplemented by begging on the part of wives and children. Initially travelling on foot and living in tents, tinkers adopted horse-drawn covered wagons early in the 20th century, increasingly replaced from the 1960s by motor-drawn caravans. In 1974 there were 9,000 tinkers in the Irish republic.

Tiptoft, John (1427–70), earl of Worcester, chief governor 1467–70. Noted for his scholarship and patronage of humanist studies, for his loyalty to Edward IV, and for his ruthlessness against traitors as constable of England (1462–7, 1470), Tiptoft was appointed chancellor of Ireland by the king in 1464 and deputy lieutenant in 1465 and 1467, but did not go to Ireland before the autumn of the latter year. His deputyship is chiefly remembered for his summary execution of Thomas, earl of *Desmond, at Drogheda on 15 February 1468, following the parliamentary attainder of the earl, together with Thomas, earl of *Kildare, and a former sheriff of Meath, Edward Plunkett, for treason. This shocked contemporary opinion in Ireland, causing widespread unrest and, in Munster, lasting damage to royal authority. On returning to England, Tiptoft was appointed lieutenant in his own right in March 1470, but was himself executed at the outset of the brief Lancastrian restoration (see WARS OF THE ROSES) later that year. EAEM

Titanic, a White Star liner, launched by *Harland & Wolff in Belfast in 1912. The largest ship in the world, she was dubbed 'virtually unsinkable' by the *Shipbuilder*. At 11.40 p.m. on 14 April, on her maiden voyage across the Atlantic, she struck a huge iceberg, tearing a 300-foot hole in her hull. At 2.20 a.m. she sank, taking with her 1,490 passengers and crew, out of a total of 2,201. The *Belfast Newsletter* expressed its readers' despair: 'her loss constitutes the most appalling shipping disaster in the history of the world.' PC

Tithe Applotment Books, see TITHE COMPOSITION ACT.

Tithe Composition Act (1823). Introduced as a conciliatory measure under *Wellesley, this did away with the contentious annual valuation of crops by permitting clergymen and parishioners to negotiate a fixed twice-yearly payment. This charge was apportioned among landholders of the parish, a process recorded in the Tithe Applotment Books (National Archives, Dublin), a major source for pre-*Famine landholding patterns as well as for family history. By including pasture as well as cultivated land, the act reversed an exemption established in 1735. By 1830 half of all parishes had compounded. An act of 1832 made composition compulsory.

tithes, a tax levied for the support of the church. Great tithes were those levied on major crops, such as wheat and oats. Small tithes were levied on minor produce, such as cheese and eggs. Personal tithes were levied on labour and the profits of trade. Monasteries in pre-Norman Ireland had collected a levy, referred to as tithes, from their clients. However, a uniform tithe system was first introduced as part of the *12th-century reform. It appears to have been more comprehensive in English areas than in Gaelic Ireland, where there are reports of resistance to the payment of tithes on anything other than major crops. In 1541, as part of the legislation comprising the Irish *Reformation, the tithe system was given the backing of statute law. By the 17th century tithes, originally conceived of as comprising 10 per cent of all produce, were generally converted into a money payment.

Although the theoretical purpose was to support the parochial clergy, the great tithes of many benefices were in practice 'appropriate', payable to a bishop, cathedral chapter, or other ecclesiastical recipient, or 'impropriate', payable to a lay owner. In 1832 £48,000 out of gross parochial revenues of £611,000 were appropriate, and £109,000 impropriate.

The requirement that Catholics (and later Protestant dissenters) should make compulsory contributions for the support of the minority *Church of Ireland inevitably caused resentment. The *patriot parliament of 1689 attempted to resolve the issue by legislation requiring members of each denomination to support their own clergy. The earliest open attack on the tithe system, however, came from the Anglican landlord class, who had their own reason to dislike tithes as competing with rents for a share of the tenant farmer's income. In 1736 the House of Commons resolved that every legal means should be used to resist the tithe of agistment, strictly speaking pasture for dry and barren cattle, although in practice taken to cover milch cows also. This resolution, although not legally binding, effectively exempted pasture from tithe, placing the whole burden on tillage farming. In Munster and parts of Leinster, tithe was also levied on *potatoes, further increasing the burden on the rural poor.

Demands for a reform of the tithe system played a part in the protests of the *Whiteboys of the 1760s, and of the *Oakboys and *Hearts of Steel movements in Ulster. The *Rightboy movement of the 1780s for the first time made tithe its main grievance. The growing prominence of the issue was due partly to the shift from pasture to tillage in the last decades of the 18th century. In addition, as rising agricultural profits made the sums at stake more significant, tithe holders had increasingly resorted to tithe farmers, who took over for a fixed price the right to collect whatever tithes they could extract. Grievances over tithes contributed to continued unrest during the 1790s and into the early decades of the 19th century. The *Tithe Composition Act converted tithe into a more predictable charge on land. Despite this, the following decade saw the most sustained and violent attack yet mounted on the system, the *Tithe War. The Tithe Rentcharge Act of 1838 converted tithe into a charge payable by landlords rather than occupiers. This largely ended direct agitation on the topic, although the anomaly of a minority church supported by a tax on the entire agricultural system remained central to the ultimately successful campaign for the *disestablishment of the Church of Ireland.

Tithe War, a widespread campaign against *tithes during 1830–3, began in October 1830 at Graiguenamanagh, Co. Kilkenny. Against a background of agricultural depression and raised Catholic expectations following the *Catholic emancipation campaign, the movement spread through Cos. Kilkenny, Carlow, Wexford, and Queen's, and subsequently into other parts of Leinster and Munster. By 1833 there were 22 counties in which half or more of tithes owed were unpaid. The campaign differed from contemporary *agrarian protest in having the active support of large farmers, who had been particularly affected by the return of tithes on pasture land under the *Tithe Composition Act 1823. It was openly supported by Archbishop *MacHale, Bishop *Doyle, and many of the Catholic parish clergy, as well as by local O'Connellite activists, although *O'Connell himself kept his distance. The movement began as one of passive resistance, but the use of *police and *yeomen to seize livestock and other goods for non-payment of tithe led to several violent affrays, notably at Newtownbarry, Co. Wexford (18 June 1831), where yeomanry were reported to have killed up to fourteen persons, and at Carrickshock, Co. Kilkenny, on 14 December, where protesters killed a process server and twelve accompanying policemen. From June 1833 government abandoned the use of soldiers and police to enforce tithe payment. Clergy in distress from non-payment received loans (eventually written off) from public funds, while the Tithe Rentcharge Act (1838) mitigated popular hostility to the system.

tobacco consumption was well established in Ireland by the early 17th century, and the word 'tobaca' occurs in a native Irish text written between 1605 and 1615. In the late 16th century some Munster settlers had considered growing tobacco on their lands but this did not prosper. Imports came mainly from England, but there were also direct shipments from the American colonies. The importance of the trade is shown by the violent reaction to the attempt by Lord Deputy *Wentworth to establish a tobacco monopoly in 1638 which affected both suppliers and retailers and became one of the complaints against him at his impeachment in 1640.

The most significant expansion of the tobacco trade came in the late 17th century. This was facilitated by growing trade with the Americas, an increase in disposable income, and a growing monetization that made luxury purchases easier. The *Navigation Acts of 1671 prohibited direct importation of tobacco into Ireland, thus marginally increasing its price, but this had little effect on consumption. Imports rose from 1.8 million pounds in 1665 to 2.4 million pounds by the end of the 1670s and to 3.3 million pounds by 1686. (By contrast the volume of trade only doubled over the entire 18th century.) So universal was smoking by the 1690s that one account of Ireland described men, women, and even children as being addicted to tobacco. It seems likely that tobacco consumption per capita varied little until the middle of the 19th century, with the sharp decline in official imports around 1815 being offset by smuggling. Post-*Famine prosperity permitted a significant increase in tobacco consumption so that by 1870 it had risen to English levels. The growth in industrial activity in Ulster during the late 19th century saw Ireland become an exporter of manufactured tobacco and by 1907 Belfast produced almost all the 5.7 million pounds of manufactured tobacco exported annually.

Smoking was an important aspect of Irish sociability at all social levels. It was usual at events such as *wakes and weddings to provide pipes for communal use. John Dunton in the 1690s described the distribution of pipes and snuff at funerals and dances where a short pipe would serve a dozen people. At upper social levels tobacco was a normal stimulant available at the Dublin coffee houses of the 18th century.

Bielenberg, A., and Johnson, D., 'The Production and Consumption of Tobacco in Ireland 1800–1914', *Irish Economic & Social History*, 25 (1998) RG

Tod, Isabella (1836–96), suffragist and campaigner for women's education. Tod was Scots-born but lived most of her life in Belfast. Her feminism, like that of many others of her era, was in part a development of a morally prescriptive philanthropy and public-spiritedness; she took part in the campaign to repeal the Contagious Diseases Acts (see PROSTITUTION), and was a lifelong *temperance advocate. Her *On The Education of Girls of the Middle Classes* (1874) called for practical education along the lines of that supplied in the Belfast Ladies' Institute, which she had set up in 1867 to enable women from this background to earn a living. It was pressure on government from Tod, among others, which led to the inclusion of girls in the Intermediate Education Act (1878). Tod actively opposed *home rule. CC

Toland, John (1670–1722), philosopher, a protégé of *Molesworth. Born into a Gaelic Irish family in Co. Donegal, he converted to *Presbyterianism but later became the period's most notorious critic of religious orthodoxy. *Christianity not Mysterious* (1696) was burnt by order of the Irish parliament and Toland was obliged to flee the kingdom. He was also interested in Gaelic antiquities, and was probably the author of an anonymous pamphlet against the *Declaratory Act.

Toler, John (1745–1831), 1st Earl Norbury. In parliament from 1776, Toler became solicitor-general in 1789 and attorney-general in 1798. Following his support for the Act of *Union he became Baron Norbury and chief justice of the common pleas. His savagery as a judge, and his known anti-Catholic bigotry, made him a favourite target for attack by *O'Connell. He was induced to resign in 1822 by the offer of an earldom and a pension.

Toleration Act (1719). Introduced by opponents of the *Presbyterians to forestall anything more generous, this exempted Protestant dissenters from the restrictions imposed by the Act of *Uniformity (1666). In fact these restrictions had long been inoperable, and dissenters remained liable to pay *tithes and subject to the authority of the ecclesiastical courts. The act thus fell far short of what Presbyterians had hoped for in the aftermath of the *revolution of 1688 and the *Whig victory in 1714.

Tone, Theobald Wolfe (1763–98), radical. Born in Dublin, the son of an initially prosperous Protestant tradesman, Tone was educated at *Trinity College and qualified as a barrister. He initially sought the favour of the Irish *Whigs, but quickly became disillusioned with their moderation. *An Argument on Behalf of the Catholics of Ireland* (1791), insisting on the common political interests uniting Protestants and Catholics, attracted much attention and led to an invitation to take part in the establishment later that year of the *United Irish movement. In July 1792 Tone became secretary to the *Catholic Committee and was one of the delegation sent to London by the *Catholic Convention. Having been compromised by the Revd *Jackson, he agreed in 1795 to go into exile in America. From there he travelled to France in February 1796 and embarked on a highly successful diplomatic mission aimed at persuading the Directory to support an Irish insurrection. Having earlier accompanied the *Hoche expedition, he sailed in September 1798 with another force, was captured off the Irish coast, and committed suicide while under sentence of death.

Tone is widely regarded as a founding father of modern Irish *republicanism. His grave at Bodenstown, Co. Kildare, is the site of annual commemorations by *Sinn Féin and others. His reputation owes much to the engaging personality revealed in his posthumously published journals and autobiography, and to his dramatic and ultimately tragic career. Modern accounts suggest that he was neither a systematic nor an original thinker. As early as 1791, in a private letter later publicized by the authorities, and subsequently much quoted, he described England as the never-failing source of all Ireland's ills. But it is suggested that this, like the indiscreet discussion of the potential for Irish revolution that led to his exile, must be placed in the context of a gradual political evolution, not complete until after his arrival in America, and moulded throughout more by pressure of circumstances than by theory for its own sake.

Elliott, M., *Wolfe Tone: Prophet of Irish Independence* (1989)

torture has been an occasional feature of the Irish legal system since the 13th century. An English statute of 1275 later extended to the lordship of Ireland authorized strict imprisonment and a diet of bread and water to bring pressure on criminal defendants who refused to plead in answer to charges made against them. This later developed (as in England) into *peine forte et dure:* the pressing of such defendants to death by loading weights on their chests. This continued until the later 18th century. In the mid-15th century the use of torture by rack and other devices began to be authorized in England, particularly but not exclusively against those suspected of political and later also of religious offences. The purpose was not to gain confessions but to acquire information about confederates. It was used for a similar purpose in Ireland in 1584 against the Catholic archbishop of Cashel, Dermot O'Hurley, with the authority of the English privy council, but seems then to have been a novelty. Flogging and other methods were widely used, though with no statutory basis, to extract information from *United Irishmen and other suspects in the period preceding the *insurrection of 1798. Some of the methods used following the introduction of *internment in Northern Ireland were found in 1978 by the European Court of Human Rights to have amounted to 'inhuman and degrading treatment' but not torture. PAB

tory has two meanings: originally a specifically Irish term for an outlaw or a bandit of the 17th and early 18th centuries, it also became the name of a major British (and Irish) political party.

The word 'tory', from the Irish *toraidhe* ('raider'), has been traced back to 1646. Later it was used largely interchangeably with 'rapparee', from Irish *rapaire*, a sort of pike. In both cases the reference was to a robber, operating either singly or as part of an outlaw band, who preyed on houses and travellers, in some cases extorting protection money from those wishing to be spared from attack. Leading tories of the period following the *Restoration included Redmond *O'Hanlon and the Brennan brothers, James, 'little James', and Patrick, who operated in Co. Kilkenny during 1683–5, before being recruited to hunt down other robbers. Tory activity remained widespread in the disturbed years immediately following the *Williamite War, but continued into the early 18th century only in south Ulster and part of the south-west, where areas of still largely impenetrable bog and mountain lay conveniently close to prosperous raiding grounds.

The original tories of the Restoration period were perceived as dispossessed Catholics waging a war of revenge against the new social order created by the land confiscations of the 1640s and 1650s. Yet it remains unclear how far all toryism, even in the Restoration period, was of this character, and how far some at least of what was so described should be seen as representing banditry of the kind found in remote and underpoliced regions throughout early modern Europe.

The use of 'Tory' in English politics goes back to the exclusion crisis of 1679–81. The *Whigs who sought to exclude the future *James II, as a Catholic, from the throne, applied the term derisively to James's supporters. After the *revolution of 1688 'Tory' re-emerged as the generally accepted name for one of the two sides in an increasingly bitter party conflict. The Tory Party that thus took shape, in both Great Britain and Ireland, included a *Jacobite minority loyal to James and his successors. The majority accepted the revolution as a regrettable necessity, but were alarmed by the Whig language of contract theory and the right of resistance. The other central Tory tenet was the defence of the established church against Protestant dissent, seen as a threat equal to or greater than that posed by the defeated Catholics. A Tory ministry held power 1710–14 but its abandonment of continental allies to make peace with France in the treaty of Utrecht (1713), along with the party's perceived ambivalence towards the revolution, led George I (1714–27) and George II (1727–60) to exclude it permanently from favour.

In Ireland the Tories formed a strong party among the clergy of the *Church of Ireland and a minority among the Protestant gentry, as well as attracting conspicuous support from surviving Catholic and recent convert interests. After 1714, however, the party declined much more quickly than its English counterpart. The loss of the 2nd duke of *Ormond was catastrophic for Tory morale. The taint of Jacobitism was also particularly damaging in an Irish context, while the discovery that most Irish Whigs had little real sympathy for *Presbyterianism made the defence of the established church less urgent.

From the 1760s the new Whig Party branded its opponents 'Tories', though many of these, including their leader, the younger William Pitt, continued to call themselves Whigs. From the mid-1830s Conservative became the usual party label, although 'Tory' is still often used, either as a synonym or to highlight the traditional aristocratic and landed (or, in Ireland, the Protestant sectarian) elements within the party.

tourism in Ireland was long undeveloped because of the poor roads and transport. The development of *canals, from the late 18th century, facilitated travel; indeed the first hotel network was built along the Grand canal. The *Bianconi system of cars and the *railways were a great spur to mainly internal tourism. Railway companies built seaside terminus hotels and promoted excursions. Cooks ran the first package tour from America to Killarney and Glengarriff in 1895. By 1900 their Irish brochure was 100 pages long. Steamer cruises on the Shannon, Corrib, and Erne lakes were popular. Edward VII's 1903 visit to Connemara set a fashion for fishing and shooting holidays for the rich.

Following *partition, the Irish Tourist Association (ITA) and the Ulster Tourist Development Association (UTDA) were both set up in 1924. Both promoted hotels and encouraged excursions from Great Britain, which was helped by the introduction of scheduled *air travel in 1936. In 1939 Bord Cuartaoichta na hÉireann replaced the ITA, with additional powers of registration and grading hotels. During the *Second World War, the UTDA promoted tourism among British and US forces stationed in Northern Ireland, which paid dividends after the war. In 1948 the Northern Ireland Tourist Board (NITB) was set up. In 1955 Bord Failte Éireann took over in the south. Transatlantic air travel, beginning in the 1960s, brought in a huge and lucrative tourist business. With extensive marketing budgets, both tourist boards opened offices all over the world, successfully portraying a welcoming people and an uncrowded, unspoilt, and beautiful environment. Irish history and culture has an appeal to the *Irish diaspora, and to the Germans, Dutch, and Scandinavians for whom *Celtic Ireland has a special fascination. The *Northern Ireland conflict has greatly affected tourism, particularly in the north. More recently, both boards have begun joint promotion of the island as a tourist entity.

PC

tours of Ireland. Descriptions of Ireland, as a recognizable literary genre, can be traced back to the 16th century. However, these first accounts, like

*Spenser's *Present State of Ireland* (1596), were generally adjuncts to a discussion of political and religious problems and their solution, or, like those of Edmund *Campion (1571) and James Perrott (*The Chronicle of Ireland 1584–1608*), were attached to chronicles of events. Description for its own sake, though still closely linked to prescriptions of policy, is more evident in the work of Fynes *Moryson. *Petty's *Political Anatomy of Ireland*, written in 1672, combines social and political comment with a pioneering venture in statistical inquiry.

Tours proper began to appear only in the more settled conditions following the end of the *Williamite War. The English bookseller John Dunton published vivid if sometimes burlesque accounts of a business trip to Ireland in 1699 and 1705. The most notable in a multiplying series during the second half of the 18th century, apart from *Young's celebrated *Tour*, were probably John Bush's *Hibernia curiosa* (1764) and Richard Twiss's *A Tour in Ireland in 1775* (1776), whose frivolous condescension caused great offence. *A Philosophical Survey of the South of Ireland* (1776), though written by an Irish clergyman, Thomas Campbell (1733–95), was presented, revealingly, as the letters of an English visitor.

The first half of the 19th century was the golden age of the Irish tour. Edward Wakefield's *Account of Ireland* (1812) continued Young's tradition of combining first-hand observation and comment with extensive statistical data. John Carr (1806), J. E. Bicheno (1830), and Henry Inglis (1835) produced substantial accounts. But improved communications by *sea and *road also encouraged such hasty and frankly commercial ventures as W. M. Thackeray's *The Irish Sketch Book* (1843). Somewhere between the two comes *Ireland: Its Scenery and Character* (1842), by the Irish-born novelist Anna Maria Hall (1800–81) and her English husband S. C. Hall (1800–89). The growing interest in Irish affairs, in particular concerning *O'Connell's experiments in popular politics, in continental Europe is evident in the unpublished account of the French political theorist Alexis de Tocqueville, in his travelling companion Gustave de Beaumont's *Ireland: Social, Political and Religious* (1839), and in the German J. G. Kohl's *Travels in Ireland* (1844).

Accounts of Ireland, both travel books and descriptions of life and conditions, continued to appear after 1850. The lengthy expedition that James *Stephens was later to present as a 3,000-mile walk round Ireland to test the political temper of the people before he founded the *Fenian movement is now thought to have been in preparation for one such intended venture. Yet even if the grim spectacle of the *Great Famine did not entirely kill off the public appetite for accounts of rural Irish quaintness, the growing Anglicization and commercialization of post-Famine popular culture meant that the island could never again be as rich a source of material for authors of all kinds, from the serious inquirer to the literary hack, as it had been in the years before 1845.

tower houses were the distinctive fortified stone dwellings built by the rising gentry and rich patricians between 1400 and 1650. Square or rectangular, with four storeys in a style known as Irish Gothic, they were commodious and ostentatious. Thick walls, machicolations, murder holes, arrow slits, and later gun loops provided defence. Up to 2,900 were built, mainly in Anglo-Irish and marcher lordships and in towns. Originally whitewashed and surrounded by *bawns in the countryside, most are now ruinous or demolished. Kilclief, Co. Down, dating from the early 15th century, is an exquisite example. HM

townland, a division of land of varying extent. The smallest, of around 1 acre, is Mill Tenement in Co. Armagh; the largest, of 7,012 acres, is Sheskin in Mayo. There are over 60,000 townlands in Ireland, constituting the smallest recognized administrative division. Their origins are various, relating to ancient clan lands, Anglo-Norman *manors, *plantation divisions, or later creations of the *Ordnance Survey. Though formerly bases for the levying of *tithes and land valuation, they no longer have any administrative significance. Despite their name, townlands do not necessarily contain urban centres. In Northern Ireland a campaign to preserve townland names in postal addresses has received official backing. NG

Townshend, George (1724–1807), 1st Marquis Townshend, *lord lieutenant 1767–72, responsible for the overthrow of the *undertaker system. By the 1760s there was growing concern at the power of these Irish managers, recently displayed in the *money bill dispute, and resentment of their increasing demands. Events in America also highlighted the need for effective control of overseas possessions. Nevertheless, it now appears that Townshend's initial instructions were only to secure an increase ('augmentation'), from 12,000 to 15,000, in the size of the Irish *army. It was the leading undertakers, John *Ponsonby and the 2nd earl of Shannon (see BOYLE), who initiated the wider conflict, by demanding too high a price for supporting the augmentation. When this was refused they organized the rejection, first of the augmentation bill, and then (21 Nov. 1769) of a money bill. In response Townshend, aided by his able *chief secretary George Macartney, initiated what was to be a new system of management, whereby a permanently resident lord lieutenant took direct responsibility for building up a 'Castle party' in the Irish parliament. The division of the *Revenue Board into separate *customs and excise divisions, implemented by king's letter after parliament had rejected the scheme, further increased the lord lieutenant's patronage, and destroyed an important independent power base. Although Townshend saw himself as overturning a system of aristocratic corruption, the pattern of parliamentary management was modified rather than reformed. In effect *Dublin Castle became the principal undertaker, continuing to offer powerful parliamentary figures (including, from 1772, a rehabilitated Shannon) favour and influence in exchange for their support. But the transition from Irish intermediaries to direct management by an English lord lieutenant and chief secretary nevertheless contributed sigificantly to the growth of *patriot sentiment evident during the 1770s.

trade unionism in Ireland may be traced back to the *guilds, but by the 18th century combinations serving the separate interests of wage earners had become common. From 1729 such combinations were forbidden by law, but many continued under the guise of *friendly or benevolent societies. Without proper channels, workplace relations were usually bad and often violent. Trade unions, in the modern sense, date from the repeal of all anti-combination legislation in 1824. However, industrial violence continued, many early trade unions borrowing the tactics of secret societies such as the *Whiteboys and *Ribbonmen.

Until the late 19th century unions were largely confined to skilled craft workers. Effective organization of unskilled workers was impeded by low morale, lack of resources, and the ease with which workers could be replaced from the large reserve of underemployed manpower available in both town and countryside. The main purposes of craft unions were to control entry into their trades, to stop masters from employing cheap or unskilled workers, to avoid wage reductions, and to look after the members' welfare. In the south, unions were mostly low membership and locally based. They campaigned for native industry and consequently opposed free trade, especially British penetration of the Irish market. They were generally nationalist in political outlook, and gave significant support to the *repeal movement (despite O'Connell's hostility to trade unionism) and later to *Parnell.

Industrialization in the north-east produced a skilled working class more like that of Britain, with comparatively high wage rates and morale. In particular artisan unions proliferated in *shipbuilding and *engineering. These favoured free trade, under which their industries prospered. From the 1880s their mainly Protestant members abandoned *Liberalism for Conservative or Liberal Unionist politics, although continued *class tensions found an outlet in the temporary successes of the *Independent Orange Order and of William *Walker's pro-union socialism. There were also skilled unions in the linen industry, such as the flaxdressers and powerloom tenters, but the mass of unskilled factory workers remained unorganized.

The 'new model unions', such as the Amalgamated Society of Engineers and the Amalgamated Society of Carpenters and Joiners, brought an increased British influence in Irish trade unionism. Some Irish unions affiliated to the British Trades Union Congress, formed in 1868, and several congresses were held in Ireland. However, mainly due to the TUC's remoteness from Ireland, an Irish Trade Union Congress (ITUC) was established in 1893 (see IRISH CONGRESS OF TRADE UNIONS).

Another British institution, trades councils, became important in Ireland in the 1880s. The Belfast and Dublin councils were more influential in the movement than the ITUC, until the years immediately before the *First World War. By then different kinds of union had evolved. 'New' general unions of unskilled workers, such as the Gasworkers' Union, the National Union of Dock Labourers, and the National Amalgamated Union of Labour, came from Britain in the late 1880s. Their leadership was politically motivated. The Irish Textile Operatives, centred on the northern linen industry, was the first union for women.

The new unionism of the unskilled suffered a setback in the depressed late 1890s, but revived with the arrival of *Larkin. He led the Belfast docks strike in 1907, one of the major events in labour history. His establishment of the *Irish Transport and General Workers' Union (ITGWU) in 1909 initiated a period of industrial and political militancy. Larkin was responsible for the radicalization of the ITUC, which turned itself into the Irish Labour Party (ITUC&LP). The *Dublin lockout, which ended in defeat, nevertheless did not end the phenomenal growth in Irish unions. Membership affiliated to the ITUC grew from 70,000 in 1910 to 189,000 in 1922. In Belfast in 1919 a strike for a 44-hour week, organized by the local Federation of Engineering and Shipbuilding Trades, brought the city to a standstill for several weeks. But all this was against the background of a political crisis that was to divide the labour movement. Initially *Johnson and other leaders sought to remain neutral in the interests of working-class unity. The 1916 Congress of ITUC paid tribute both to those killed in the *rising of 1916 and to those fighting in the First World War. In 1918, however, the ITUC and Labour Party played a major role in the anti-conscription campaign, mounting the first general strike in western Europe. Labour's decision to stand aside in the 1918 general election was based more on electoral calculations than on deference to *Sinn Féin. But over the next three years trade unionists in the south increasingly used industrial action to protest against government policy, and in doing so estranged themselves from the northern membership.

*Cosgrave's government was hostile to the union movement even though it was now led by moderates like William *O'Brien and Thomas Johnson. Larkin's return from America in 1923 threatened to usher in a period of militancy. A split within the ITGWU led to the formation of the Workers' Union of Ireland (WUI), reflecting both the right–left tension within the movement and personal rivalry between Larkin and O'Brien. The more pro-union *Fianna Fáil government, after 1932, implemented measures to help native industry (see PROTECTIONISM) which had the support of the union movement. In the north, the Unionist government's refusal to recognize the ITUC and its successors was to last until the more conciliatory regime of Terence *O'Neill.

After the *Second World War white-collar unions played a greater role in the movement. The teachers' strike in 1946 led *Lemass to set up the *Labour Court to arbitrate. Between 1945 and 1959 both trade unionism and political labour were weakened by the damaging split between the ITUC and the breakaway Congress of Irish Unions. In the 1960s, workers experienced unprecedented employment, largely due to incoming industry. However, the downturn in the early 1970s, due to soaring oil prices, took the gloss off this. The global strategies of transnational companies often led to the closure, without consultation, of their Irish subsidiaries. The unions had to learn to exist in the global economy. In the *Northern Ireland conflict the unions and their members sometimes came under violent pressure. The Northern Ireland Committee of ICTU steered a neutral path, with anti-sectarian initiatives such as the 'Better Life for All' campaign.

Rationalization has produced union mergers. The biggest was in 1990 when ITGWU and WUI became the Services, Industrial, Professional and Technical Union (SIPTU). In both jurisdictions governments appoint union membership to public bodies. The southern government also assigns ICTU a part in economic planning through the negotiation of annual 'pay rounds'. The success of trade unionism in Ireland has been in marked contrast to the failure of labour in politics.

See also LABOUR PARTY.

O'Connor, E., *A Labour History of Ireland* (1992)

PC

transplantation (to Connacht). Under the *Cromwellian land settlement, landowners who had not shown 'constant good affection' to parliament during the *Confederate War forfeited their estates. However, those not responsible for massacre or aggravated rebellion were to be removed to the counties of Galway, Roscommon, Mayo, or Clare, where they would receive, depending on their degree of 'guilt', the equivalent of two-thirds, one-third, or one-fifth of their former lands. Proposals to remove the Catholic population as a whole, leaving most of the island free for British settlement, were supported by army radicals but successfully opposed by spokesmen for the 'old Protestants' (i.e pre-1641 settlers), who recognized the economic dislocation that would result.

Transplantable landowners were required to remove themselves, with their servants and other dependants and any moveable goods, by 1 May 1654 (extended to 1 March 1655). A commission at Athlone checked levels of 'guilt' while a second, at Loughrea, allocated land. Allocations became increasingly arbitrary as the administrative resources available proved inadequate to the scale of the operation. In June 1657 the process was declared complete, even though many had got less than their entitlement and some nothing at all. Some proprietors originally deemed liable to total forfeiture had used bribes or personal influence to obtain land in Connacht; others eligible to transplant had refused to move, despite threats of punishment. Seven hundred and seventy transplantees, along with 1,130 landowners transplanted within Connacht itself, received a total of 700,000 acres.

Simington, R. C., *The Transplantation to Connacht, 1654–58* (1970)

HM

transportation. The *Cromwellian regime of the 1650s dispatched several thousand prisoners of war, priests, vagrants, and other dangerous persons to servitude in the West Indies. From the 1660s transportation both to the Caribbean and to the North American colonies began to be routinely used, first for those reprieved after sentence of death, then, from the early 18th century, for non-capital offenders. On arrival transportees were disposed of as unfree labourers, generally required to serve for periods of seven years, fourteen years, or life, the proceeds being used to defray the cost of shipping. Following the *American Revolution, new penal colonies for transported convicts were established in Australia, at Botany Bay (1788) and Van Diemen's Land (1803).

Fragmentary records for the years 1737–43 suggest that the average number of persons transported from Ireland (excluding as probably untypical the *famine years of 1741–2) was around 227 per year. Just under half of these had been convicted of criminal offences. The remainder were vagrants unable to provide security for their good behaviour, whom an act of 1707 had also made liable to transportation, although recent research indicates that many of this latter group were persons recently acquitted on criminal charges. The number of Irish convicts shipped to Australia between 1788 and the abolition of transportation in 1868 was about 40,000, around a quarter of the total so transported.

Treacy, Sean (1895–1920), leading organizer of the *Gaelic League and the *Irish Volunteers in south Tipperary. Treacy became vice-commander of the South Tipperary Brigade in 1918. Together with Seamus Robinson and Dan *Breen he was involved in the Soloheadbeg ambush, which has for a long time been seen as marking the start of the *Anglo-Irish War. They visited Dublin on many occasions and were involved in the attempt to assassinate the lord lieutenant, Viscount French, in December 1919. Treacy was killed in a shoot-out in Dublin's Talbot Street on 14 October 1920. JA

treasurer and treasury. The treasurer, the royal official responsible for receiving and disbursing the king's revenues in Ireland, is first mentioned in 1217. Appointments were usually made from England and holders of the office included bishops and members of religious orders as well as royal clerks. The treasurer was a senior member of the king's *council in Ireland and received an annual fee at the Irish *exchequer. Initially his accounts were audited in Ireland by specially appointed auditors, but following the serious allegations of fraud and malpractice brought against the treasurer Stephen de *Fulborn in 1285 and subsequently against his successor Nicholas de Clere, who had been appointed to reform Irish finances, the practice was instituted of auditing the treasurer's accounts at the English exchequer. This continued on a regular basis until the late 14th century, with the treasurer and one of the chamberlains of the exchequer bringing their records to Westminster for the audit. The regularity of audits did not prevent further instances of financial malpractice, the most notable being those involving Alexander Bicknor, treasurer from 1308 to 1314, and his successor Walter Islip. From 1379 onwards, for political and administrative reasons, treasurers were frequently exempted from accounting for their receipts and expenditure.

During the late 15th and early 16th centuries effective control of royal finances passed from the treasurer to his nominal deputy, the under-treasurer, although this process was temporarily reversed after the earl of *Kildare's restoration in 1524.

By the 18th century growing criticism of the management of government finance focused both on malpractice on the part of individual under-treasurers and, increasingly, on the relationship between the British and Irish treasuries. Issues of public money could, for example, be made, without the authorization of the Irish treasurer, on a British treasury warrant countersigned by the *chief secretary. Anxious to increase government accountability and responsibility, Irish *Whigs made reform of the treasury a central plank of their reform programme, and in 1793 succeeded in vesting the duties and powers of the high treasurer in a board of commissioners, drawn from members of the Irish parliament. Henceforth all warrants for the issue of public money were to require the signature of three treasury commissioners. Although the treasury seemed set to become the sole organ for the control of public expenditure in Ireland, this did not happen, partly because the government continued to interfere in its work, and partly because after the *Union the commissioners, who now sat in the *Westminster parliament, spent much of their time in London. The Irish treasury was fused with its British counterpart in 1817, following the consolidation of the British and Irish revenues the previous year. PhC/VC

treaty ports, harbour, aviation, and storage facilities in Berehaven, Queenstown (Cobh), Lough Swilly, Haulbowline, and Rathmullen reserved to Britain under the *Anglo-Irish treaty. Other facilities were to be granted in time of war. During the treaty debates, these provisions were particularly attacked by Erskine *Childers.

Proposals in 1927 and 1932 to return the facilities were rejected by the admiralty. In 1938, however, the chiefs of staff, citing cost and the difficulty of defending the installations against a hostile hinterland in wartime, overruled admiralty objections. When de *Valera refused to sign a defence agreement because of *partition, the ports were returned unconditionally.

DMcM

Trent, Council of (1545–63). The centrepiece of the *Counter-Reformation, the council confirmed Catholic doctrine *vis-à-vis* Protestantism, strengthened ecclesiastical discipline, and attacked superstition in popular culture. Three Irish bishops, Thomas O'Herlihy (Ross), Donal McGonigle (Raphoe), and Eugene O'Harte (Achonry), attended the final session but played no significant role in proceedings. The Tridentine decrees were promulgated in Ireland at provincial synods in Connacht in 1566 and Ulster in 1587.

Their establishment in practice depended on a preaching ministry and catechesis among a literate laity. The final session of Trent suggested diocesan seminaries as the answer to low clerical standards. Pius IV's bull *Dum exquisita* (1564) specifically lamented the low educational attainments of Irish priests. Political circumstances dictated that the *Irish colleges be founded abroad. These institutions, especially St Anthony's, Louvain, produced *catechisms, the first printed edition being Bonaventure Ó hEodhasa's *An Teagasg Críosdaithe* (1611). Mostly foreign texts adapted for an Irish audience, these reiterated dogma on the creed, sacraments, and commandments, taught correct behaviour at mass and penance, and underlined Tridentine innovations. The state's hostility towards seminary priests and the scarcity of the catechisms amid low levels of *literacy were problems, but Tridentine Catholicism made slow progress even in Catholic-controlled countries. HM

tribe. The description of the political organization of early Christian Ireland as 'tribal' arose from the equation of **tuath*, a population group or petty kingdom, with 'tribe', and to a lesser extent the translation of the very different words *cenél*, a kindred or dynasty, and *fine*, an extended family or kin-group, by the word tribe also. The practice went unchallenged until Eoin *MacNeill, in objecting to P. W. Joyce's indiscriminate use of 'tribe', pointed out the wide range of meanings attributed to the word by the *Oxford English Dictionary*. Its use was thus in effect to explain the unknown by the unknown. In particular MacNeill warned against the romantic image of the *clan chief perpetuated by Walter Scott, according to whom every subject of the chief, however poor and lowly, conceived himself or herself to be distantly related to their leader. He argued that even in the petty kingdom or *tuath*, there were marked class distinctions, and the royal family was a small, well-defined group as in kingdoms elsewhere in Europe. Subsequently D. A. Binchy was to revive the word 'tribal' as describing a primary aggregate of people under a headman or chief. This usage was hesitantly sanctioned by F. J. Byrne, to underline the fact that up to the 8th century the primary meaning of *tuath* was population group rather than territory, though not necessarily a population who believed in a shared ancestry; Byrne rejected the word as a translation of *cenél* or *fine*. As Byrne pointed out, Binchy's usage ignored five of the six definitions of tribe given by the *OED*. More recently the trend has been to translate *tuath* with the phrase 'petty kingdom' and avoid the word 'tribal' altogether.

Byrne, F. J., 'Tribes and Tribalism in Early Ireland', *Ériu*, 22 (1971)

KS

Trim Castle, Co. Meath, the largest and one of the best-preserved *Anglo-Norman castles in Ireland. Evidence from *The Song of Dermot and the Earl* (*c.*1210) suggests that the first fortification at Trim was wooden, surrounded by an earthen bank (a ringwork) built by Hugh de *Lacy *c.*1172. De Lacy probably started the erection of the stone keep and outer defences *c.*1175; its construction was continued under his son Walter. The keep is of particular interest for its unique plan, consisting of a square core with square towers centrally projecting from each side. The surrounding curtain wall, punctuated by eight towers and the gatehouse, encloses an area of roughly 3 acres. In 1254 Trim Castle was made the demesne manor of Geoffrey de *Geneville. Archaeological evidence suggests that the castle ceased to be occupied from the middle of the 14th century. RM

Trinity College, Dublin, the only college of Dublin University, was the first Irish *university established on a permanent basis. Though it had long been agreed that there was great need for a native university, shortage of funds and inability to agree on a site delayed its foundation to 1592, when Trinity College was established with the help of Dublin Corporation and Adam *Loftus, the Protestant archbishop of Dublin. Though Queen Elizabeth expressed the hope that it would provide for the education of all Irish youth, the fact that it was firmly Protestant and modelled on a Cambridge college ensured that its students were largely Protestant and *New English. Trinity's first three provosts, Walter Travers (1594–8), William Alvey (1599–1609), and William Temple (1609–26), were firmly *puritan in their outlook, and ensured that the college remained a bastion of Calvinist theology and produced a regular supply of clergy for the Church of Ireland. Provost William *Bedell (1627–9) attempted to ensure that the college was able to educate its students in the Irish language, but after his departure Trinity slipped back into its Anglocentric ways.

The appointment of William Laud as chancellor in 1633, and his subsequent imposition, with the firm support of Lord Deputy *Wentworth, of his protégé, the Arminian William Chappell, as provost, marked a serious attempt to rid the college of its puritanism and impose a firmer disciplinary regime. The statutes were extensively revised by Laud and the new code, adopted in 1637, established the basic constitutional and administrative framework of the college down to the 20th century. Hostility within the college to Chappell's reforms climaxed in 1640–1 when Wentworth's departure from Ireland and Chappell's resignation as provost was followed by a parliamentary inquiry into the university. The *rising of 1641 deprived the college of much of its revenue, and it ceased admitting students in 1645. The *Cromwellian regime revived the university, re-endowing it and seeking, unsuccessfully, to found an additional college. The Independent Samuel *Winter served as provost 1652–60 and oversaw a steady increase in student numbers before being ejected at the *Restoration.

The Restoration determined the Anglican character of Trinity for a further 300 years. The college settled down into a period of considerable academic achievement, briefly disrupted by the imposition by *James II of a Catholic provost, Michael Moore, and by the subsequent expulsion of scholars and fellows by *Jacobite forces. Distinguished late 17th-century figures included the orientalist Narcissus Marsh (1638–1713), provost 1679–83 and later archbishop of Cashel (1691–4), Dublin (1694–1703), and Armagh (1703–13), Henry Dodwell (1641–1711), a fellow 1662–6, who became Camden professor of history at Oxford (1688–91) and a leading *non-juror, and John Stearne (1624–69), professor of physic from 1662 and founder of the Irish College of Physicians.

The first half of the 18th century was less distinguished for its academic brilliance. This may have owed something to the appointment of a succession of doughty *Whig provosts such as Richard Baldwin (1717–58), committed above all to the extirpation of any remaining traces of the *Tory and *high-church reputation which the college had acquired after the Glorious *Revolution. A quickening of intellectual vigour from mid-century was accompanied by intensifying undergraduate debate. The Debating Club, founded by Edmund *Burke in 1747, and of which *Tone was auditor in 1785, provided a forum for student radicals, whose activities at the end of the century alarmed both college and state. A visitation in 1798, headed by the lord chancellor, *Fitzgibbon, led to the expulsion of several students (including Robert *Emmet) associated with the *United Irishmen.

For all this Trinity was essentially the university of the *Protestant ascendancy. Parliament showed its favourable disposition by generous support for an 18th-century building programme ('the finest ensemble of classical architecture in Ireland') that began with the magnificent library in 1712. Not until 1793 were the university and its degrees open to Catholics, and it was 1873 before all religious tests were abolished.

Against the background of 19th-century political and ecclesiastical debate on the university question (which Trinity survived intact), the professional schools of divinity, law, medicine (which contributed notably to Dublin's great age of *medicine), and engineering gained international reputations. More building took place, and Trinity produced such notable scholars as the classicist Robert Tyrrell (1844–1914), the ancient historian J. P. Mahaffy (1839–1919), and the historian J. B. Bury (1861–1927). In 1904 it was the first of the ancient universities of Great Britain and Ireland to admit women.

Social and political change accelerated after the *First World War, and with *partition Trinity withdrew into itself. It was seriously lacking in resources, and its intake of undergraduates was greatly restricted by the inhibition imposed by the Roman Catholic hierarchy on Catholics attending Trinity. Furthermore, some of its more prominent members, by showing a lack of sensitivity to nationalist culture and politics, provided ammunition for those who regarded the college as west British, even anti-national.

The tide turned mid-century with a dramatic development in government policy whereby Trinity for the first time received state funding (today the main source of income). A. J. McConnell, provost 1952–74, provided vigorous and progressive leadership, and the lifting of the Catholic hierarchy's 'ban' (1970) made the college more attactive to the population at large. Student numbers soared, with intense pressure, particularly from Dublin, for places. Seeing the provision of places for Irish students as its first duty, Trinity, with some reluctance, felt bound to restrict numbers from overseas. Considerable efforts were made to continue links with schools in Northern Ireland. Though applicants from Protestant schools in the north diminished (partly because of competition from British universities, and partly because the *Northern Ireland conflict made education in the Republic less appealing), a new source of undergraduates was found in Catholic schools there.

Growing numbers necessitated new building. The 20th-century Berkeley Library and Arts Building, along with other developments, have generally been regarded as a worthy continuation of Trinity's contribution to Dublin architecture. The university has greatly extended its role in Irish society by forming relationships with the Dublin Institute of Technology and with colleges of education of different religious traditions, while the erstwhile Anglican divinity school has developed into a non-denominational school of Hebrew, biblical, and theological studies.

McDowell, R. B., and Webb, D. A., *Trinity College, Dublin 1592–1952: An Academic History* (1982)

AF/KM

Troy, John Thomas (1739–1823), Catholic archbishop of Dublin 1786–1823. A Dublin-born *Dominican friar, Troy had taught at St Clement's in Rome, becoming prior in 1772. As bishop of Ossory 1776–86, he had strenuously opposed *Whiteboy activity. Politically conservative, he abhorred the radicalization of Irish politics in the 1790s and was especially anxious to counter the spread of revolutionary ideas, 'the French disease', among his clergy and laity. A competent political pragmatist, he attempted to retain the confidence of the ever more radical *Catholic Committee while maintaining good relations with the security-obsessed Dublin government in order to preserve the position of the emerging Catholic community within the existing political structures. Hence his loud denunciation of the 1798 *insurrection and his welcome for the Act of *Union which he saw as a stepping stone to *Catholic emancipation. Under his rule, the Catholic community in Dublin continued to build itself up institutionally, Troy working hard to impose discipline on his clergy. His support of the *Maynooth College project (1795) was probably part of this strategy. TO'C

tuarastal in the Old Irish *law tracts signified 'the evidence of an eye-witness', or 'conclusive evidence', but by the 11th century, especially in the Book of Rights (*Lebor na Cert*), it meant the ceremonial gift or retaining fee paid by an overlord to a submitting vassal-chief, or wages of any kind, especially in reward of military service. Ceremonial *tuarastal* is occasionally mentioned in the annals up to the 15th century as proof of vassalage. KS

tuath, an Old Irish word, the primary meaning of which is 'people' or 'community'. In 8th-century glosses, it is used to translate Latin *plebs*, and as a synonym for Irish *popul* (people). Such communities are led by a single leader (*tuath Dé*, 'God's people', or *tuath Barrfind*, 'Barrfind's people') and most commonly this leader is a *king (*rí*). The word also has extended meanings which give some insight into the nature of communities in pre-*Norman Irish society: territory, a band of warriors, or the institutions of the secular world as opposed to those of the church. *Tuatha* can range in size from the island of Ireland to Tuosist parish (*Tuath Ó Siosta*), Co. Kerry. Since specification of size is extremely rare, such variation makes it impossible to calculate the number of *tuatha* at any one time. Similarly, legal formulations as to the number of warriors in a *tuath* or the necessity for each to have a scholar, a poet, and a churchman should be seen as aspirational rather than prescriptive. Secondary literature occasionally uses *tuath* as a shorthand for *'tribe in archaic state of organization'. This notion originates in 19th-century historiography, but is increasingly disregarded as knowledge of Old Irish has grown. CS

tuberculosis has been known in Ireland since early times, but it became a major scourge, especially in urban areas, in the late 19th and early 20th centuries. In 1906 tuberculosis caused nearly 16 per cent of all Irish deaths. Two sanatoriums were built in the 1890s, but attempts to make tuberculosis a notifiable disease were opposed by Irish politicians and tuberculosis remained a major killer throughout the 1920s and 1930s. The Women's National Health Association, established in 1907 by Lady *Aberdeen, took the lead in attempts to combat the disease. However, it was only in the late 1940s that tuberculosis became a notifiable disease in Ireland, both north and south. At the same time a Tuberculosis Authority was established in Northern Ireland, which helped reduce the number of cases substantially during the 1950s, and Dr Noel *Browne, the Irish health minister, launched a campaign that within a matter of a few years had brought tuberculosis under control in the Republic as well. ELM

Tudor conquest, a term denoting the extension of English lordship, previously effective only in the *Pale, to full English sovereignty throughout Ireland. This was the result of a reform policy which invariably ended being applied by force. Sir John Davies's *Discovery of the True Causes* (1610), trumpeting the subsequent establishment of the common law, did not hesitate to use the term 'conquest'. The process, generally seen as getting under way in 1534 and lasting until 1603, involved conflicts of increasing scale: the *Kildare rebellion, the war of the *Geraldine League, the revolt of

Shane *O'Neill, the *Desmond and *Baltinglass revolts, and the *Nine Years War.

An important reason for the Tudor conquest was the existence of a frontier and the related problems of defence and grand strategy. The original objective in 1534 was merely the reform of the Pale under the closer direction of Whitehall. This departure coincided with England's break with Rome, which left her diplomatically isolated and strategically vulnerable. An English *lord deputy with a standing *army and little local support was always apt to take the military option. Such actions in Ireland created strategic threats where none had hitherto existed. The military activities of Lord Deputy *Grey in the 1530s resulted in the establishment of the Geraldine League with its appeals to the Scottish king. The creation of the *kingdom of Ireland (1541) necessarily entailed consideration of administrative centralization across the whole island. When the related integrative policy of *surrender and regrant faltered, the placement of garrisons in Leix and Offaly caused the O'Mores and O'Connors to appeal to France. The line of the Pale was breached, the frontier was now moving, and the process continuous. The crown became anxious to assert control for fear that foreign powers would exploit the situation. It is not unreasonable to suggest that the New English, as captains, constables, *seneschals, and *provincial presidents, deliberately provoked conflicts so as to reap rewards in the lands and offices which subsequently became available. The commissions of martial law to local commanders introduced by *Sussex in 1556 escalated the level of violence involved. A new English colonialism justified by old chauvinist ideas and new religious prejudices was generated, with land-hungry younger sons acquiring confiscated Irish estates as a means of providing an income and gentry status.

The role of lords deputy as architects of the conquest is a subject of debate. The most aggressive policies belong to Sussex, *Sidney, Grey, and *Perrot, but ironically those of the corrupt, reactive, and underfinanced *Fitzwilliam caused the most bother. Canny asserts that Sidney produced a blueprint of *plantations and provincial presidencies for the establishment of Tudor rule. Brady insists that the government's intention was always the establishment of the common law by reform not conquest, and concentrates on Sidney's alternative policy of *composition. Crawford emphasizes the role of the *privy council. This executive body had an obvious interest in making English sovereignty effective. At local level the object was shire government with sheriffs, justices of the peace, jailhouses, and visiting *assizes. Most of Ireland was shired on paper by the mid-1580s (see COUNTIES), but it was physical control of the country after 1603 that enabled the system to operate.

Military matters bulk large in any account of the Tudor conquest. The army grew to a peak of 16,000 during the Nine Years War. Expeditions into the interior against errant Gaelic lords were pointless. The only effective strategy was the establishment of garrisons followed by spoliation of the people, their crops, and their livestock, bringing starvation and eventual submission. These tactics were very expensive to maintain and were employed only in the Desmond and Nine Years wars. Massacres took place at *Rathlin, Belfast, *Mullaghmast, and *Smerwick. Hostages were frequently taken to guarantee ceasefires during wartime and to secure compliance during peacetime. Irish revenues never sustained the cost of the standing army, which had always to be subsidized from England. The Irish lords also increased and modernized their forces. They employed large numbers of *redshanks and then utilized the supply system these developed to increase local infantry recruits. *Firearms aided Irish guerrilla tactics, and assisted in victories such as *Glenmalure and the *Yellow Ford, but the infrastructure needed for siege warfare was lacking.

Brady, Ciaran, *The Chief Governors: The Rise and Fall of Reform Government in Tudor Ireland* (1994)

Canny, N., *The Elizabethan Conquest of Ireland* (1976)

Crawford, J., *Anglicizing the Government of Ireland: The Irish Privy Council and the Expansion of Tudor Rule 1556–78* (1995)

HM

Tuke, James Hack (1819–96), an English Quaker banker and philanthropist who was active in the distribution of relief in Ireland during 1847 and again in 1880. On both occasions he published widely read and influential accounts of what he had witnessed. *Irish Distress and its Remedies* (1880) advocated peasant proprietorship, the development of poorer regions by means of light railways and the promotion of local industry, and assisted emigration. During 1882–4 Tuke promoted and managed a fund, raised from private and official sources, which financed the emigration of about 9,500 persons from areas worst hit by the agrarian depression.

Tullaghoge rath, in north-east Co. Tyrone, was originally associated with the Uí Tuirtre and then between the 11th and 17th centuries with the O'Hagans. A large boulder, known as *leac na rí* or the flagstone of the kings, stood outside the rath.

At some period three slabs were placed around the boulder to resemble a chair. In the later middle ages the *O'Neills were inaugurated on it by O'Cahan and O'Hagan—one threw a shoe over the new lord's head and the other presented a rod of office. *Mountjoy destroyed the chair in August 1602, symbolically ending O'Neill's sovereignty.

HM

turf, see BOGS.

Turgesius (d. 845), a *Viking chief who, according to the account of his activities in **Cogadh Gáedhel re Gallaibh*, caused havoc throughout Ireland: on arrival in Ireland he assumed overlordship of the Vikings there, took control of *Armagh by banishing the abbot, and installed his wife Ota at *Clonmacnoise; but justice was finally seen to be done when he was drowned in Lough Owel, Co. Westmeath, by *Máel Sechnaill I (Malachy). The circumstances of his death apart, however, the account of his career given in *Cogadh Gáedhel re Gallaibh* has been described as a cleverly constructed fiction designed to highlight the remarkable nature of the Uí Briain (see DÁL CAIS) achievement in ridding Ireland of numerous such invaders.

MNíM

turnpikes, see ROADS.

twelfth-century reform, an Irish response to the ecclesiastical reform movement associated with Pope Gregory VII (1073–85). The *papacy and the archbishopric of *Canterbury complained of too many bishops in Ireland, of *divorce and other improprieties permitted by Irish *marriage law, and of various abuses. In the first documented response, the Synod of *Cashel (1101) condemned marriage with certain close relatives and lay encroachment on the church, and required that the (usually lay) ecclesiastical head or *erenach be celibate and in orders. The Synod of *Ráith Bressail (1111) traditionally is credited with first introducing territorial dioceses to an Irish church previously dominated by *monasticism, governed by abbots, and organized in dispersed filiations of monasteries. This view has been challenged recently. Dioceses apparently had developed before the 12th century and are attested, for instance, in 10th- and 11th-century annals, but without the co-ordination achieved at Ráith Bressail, which ordained a comprehensive network of 24 dioceses under two archbishops of Armagh and Cashel. At the Synod of *Kells (1152), archbishoprics of Dublin and Tuam were also sanctioned and the dioceses consequently reallocated. The reform partly succeeded in wresting control of *Armagh from a hereditary dynasty of laymen and insisted that it should be headed by a bishop. Prominent in this struggle was *Malachy, the best-known reformer. He introduced the *Cistercians, the most celebrated of the European monastic orders. Their arrival was a prominent feature of the reform, although the *Augustinian Canons Regular spread more widely. The introduction of new monastic orders and diocesan reorganization were the main innovations of the reform, which clearly separated secular and regular clergy. Many older ecclesiastical establishments lost resources and prestige, and cultivation of secular learning and letters by the church largely ceased. In other respects, notably in regard to clerical celibacy and dynastic control of church offices, the reform was less successful. A perception that further reform was needed prompted papal authorization of *Henry II's intervention in Ireland (see *laudabiliter*). This apparently was endorsed by Irish prelates at the Synod of Cashel (1172), which legislated regarding *tithes and wills and was the last of the major reforming assemblies of the 12th century.

Gwynn, Aubrey, *The Irish Church in the Eleventh and Twelfth Centuries* (1992)

Sharpe, Richard, 'Some Problems Concerning the Organization of the Church in Early Medieval Ireland', *Peritia*, 3 (1984)

Watt, J. A., *The Church and the Two Nations in Medieval Ireland* (1972)

CE

two nations theory, the argument that conflict between *nationalism and *unionism arises from the existence of two nations in Ireland, based upon distinct cultures, political allegiances, and economic histories. The thesis first emerged in the late 19th century, an example being T. MacKnight's *Ulster as It Is* (1896). Later proponents have included the human geographer M. W. Heslinga, whose *The Irish Border as a Cultural Divide* (1971) argued that the border between Northern and independent Ireland marks off two different cultures, and Peter Gibbon, whose *Origins of Ulster Unionism* (1975) saw two divergent modes of production as leading to the emergence of two distinct types of society within Ireland. Gibbon's approach is that of a Marxist concerned to explain the absence of working-class unity in the north. The same theme was taken up in the 1970s by the British and Irish Communist Organization in a series of pamphlets that gradually descended into left-wing sectarianism.

Nationalists would argue that, historically, there is one nation in Ireland, and in many cases would see differences of religion and outlook as the result of political and economic manipulation by successive British governments. A more sophisticated approach, developed by David Miller, is that Unionist loyalty to Britain is to the crown rather than the government of the day, and is conditional on the crown protecting Protestant interests.

While there is a distinct unionist cultural identity, the fragmented nature of loyalism and unionism seems to preclude the possibility of a distinct nation. On the other hand the differences are deep enough to cast doubt upon the one nation approach of nationalists. JS

Tyrconnell, Richard Talbot, 1st earl of (1630–91), Catholic leader. The youngest son of a Co. Meath *Old English family, Talbot fought with the Catholic and royalist forces in the *Confederate War, narrowly escaping death at *Drogheda, then served with the future *James II in the French and Spanish armies. Following the *Restoration he emerged as the leading Irish Catholic spokesman at court. A rake and duellist, he was noted for his violent tongue but proved himself a shrewd and subtle political manipulator. After James's accession Talbot, now earl of Tyrconnell, steadily increased his power, undermining more moderate rivals like the earl of Clarendon, lord lieutenant 1685–6, and eventually securing James's agreement not just to the creation of an almost wholly Catholic army and civil administration, but also to preparations for a parliament that would revise the Restoration land settlement.

After the *revolution of 1688 Tyrconnell apparently considered making terms with *William III, before deciding to hold Ireland for James. His advocacy of a negotiated surrender following the battle of the *Boyne brought him into conflict with the war party headed by *Sarsfield. With most native Irish among the militants, the conflict was exacerbated by Tyrconnell's narrowly Old English sympathies. After the battle of *Aughrim, by contrast, Tyrconnell favoured continued resistance, but died on 14 August 1691. His wife Frances Jennings (d. 1731) was outlawed in 1693 as a dangerous papist in her own right, but a private act in 1702, obtained through her sister Sarah, duchess of Marlborough, secured her jointure from the forfeited estate.

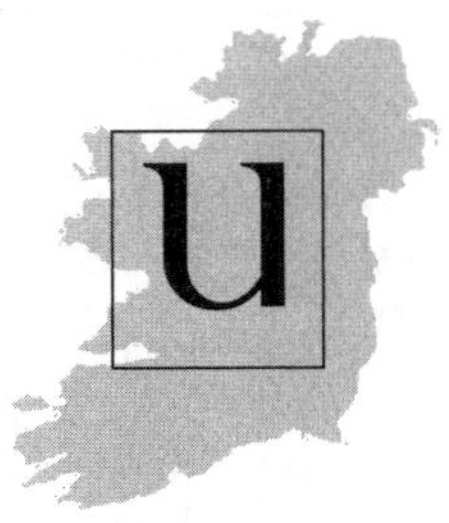

Ua Briain, Muirchertach (d. 1119), king of Munster, son of Toirdelbach *Ua Briain. An ambitious ruler, Muirchertach was arguably the most powerful king in Ireland in his day. Already politically active during the reign of his father, he assumed power on Toirdelbach's death in 1086. Connacht and *Mide proved resistant to his overlordship but he ruthlessly imposed his authority there. Attempts to extend his sway further northwards, however, were less successful, as he faced formidable opposition from the able *Cenél nEógain ruler, Domnall Mac Lochlainn. The Irish Sea region provided Muirchertach with another outlet for his political ambition and the kingdom of Man, in particular, claimed his attention. His outward-looking tendencies also brought him into contact with the church reform movement which he sought to promote at the synods of *Cashel and *Ráith Bressail in 1101 and 1111. Illness in his later years, however, led to his position being considerably weakened by the time of his death in 1119. MNíM

Ua Briain, Toirdelbach, king of Munster 1063–86. Toirrdelbach succeeded in restoring the Uí Briain (see DÁL CAIS) dynasty to the political dominance it had enjoyed during the reign of his grandfather *Brian Bóruma (Boru). Having wrested control of Munster from his uncle Donnchad, with the aid of his ally *Diarmait mac Máel na mBó, he sought to assert his authority in Leinster on Diarmait's death in 1072. Subsequently, he marched on Dublin and installed his son Muirchertach *Ua Briain as ruler there. Assertion of control in Connacht and in the midland territory of *Mide proved more difficult owing to continuous opposition on the part of the Uí Chonchobair (*O'Connors) and Uí Ruairc (*O'Rourkes). Nevertheless, for much of his reign, Toirdelbach's dominance over the southern half of Ireland was secure. Reflecting this he is termed *rí Érenn* (king of Ireland) in his death notice in the *Annals of Ulster*. MNíM

Ua Conchobair, Toirdelbach (Turlough O'Connor) (1088–1156), *high king of Ireland. Toirdelbach became king of Connacht in 1106 and rose to national importance following the fall from power of Muirchertach *Ua Briain in 1114. He spent the period to 1131 asserting power over the other provinces, then suffered setbacks, began to reassert himself in 1138, and from then until 1150, when Muirchertach *Mac Lochlainn began to challenge him for the position, was widely recognized as king of Ireland. He was an innovatory military commander and his reign is notable for the use he made of naval forces and for the construction of *castles and bridges. He deposed other provincial kings and partitioned their kingdoms, and his favourite son Conchobar (d. 1143) was appointed at various stages king of Dublin, Leinster, and Meath. He died in 1156, aged 68, at his fortress at Dunmore, Co. Galway, was buried in *Clonmacnoise, and was succeeded by his son Rory *O'Connor. SD

Ufford, Ralph (d. 1346), *justiciar of Ireland 1344–6, one of the most vigorous governors of the 14th century whose rule was denounced as oppressive by the Dublin annals. A banneret of Edward III's household, Ufford married *c.*1343 Matilda of Lancaster, widow of William de *Burgh, earl of *Ulster. He arrived in Ireland with an English retinue of 40 men-at-arms and 200 archers. Early in 1345 he entered Ulster, deposing Henry O'Neill (Éinrí Ó Néill) from kingship and replacing him with Aodh Reamhar O'Neill. Ufford's ties with *absentees and insistence on the letter of the law provoked war with the 1st earl of *Desmond. Later in 1345 he outlawed Desmond, gathered a large army, and seized his castles and lordships; he also imprisoned the earl of *Kildare, by trickery according to the Dublin annals. After his death Edward III rehabilitated the earls, employing them in the justiciarship during the 1350s. RFF

Uí Briain, see DÁL CAIS, O'BRIEN.

Uí Briúin were a *Connachta dynasty whose eponymous ancestor was Brión (Brian), son of

Eochaid Mugmedón and step-brother of *Niall Noígiallach. This reputed relationship was used in early Ireland to underpin perceived connections between the *Uí Néill and the Connachta, the two most powerful groupings in *Leth Cuinn. The Uí Briúin and their descendants, the Síl Muiredaig and the Uí Chonchobair, controlled the kingship of Connacht for most of the pre-*Norman period; within their lands was the important centre of *Crúachain (Rathcroghan), the western equivalent of *Tara. Subgroupings of the Uí Briúin include Uí Briúin Aí of central Roscommon, Uí Briúin Seóla east of Lough Corrib, Uí Briúin Umaill of Clew Bay, and Uí Briúin Bréifne in modern Leitrim and Cavan. Genealogical connections between these various groupings often depend on otherwise unattested sons of Brión, and many appear to represent falsification of pedigrees by emerging dynasties in Connacht. CS

Uí Chennselaig, a population group and ruling dynasty in Leinster claiming descent from Énna Cennselach ('the proud or domineering'). The earliest records of the Uí Chennselaig, dated to the late 6th century, indicate that they were divided into dynastic segments which shared their kingship and contended with other dynasties for the kingship of Leinster (see LAIGIN). The most renowned early Uí Chennselaig king of Leinster was Brandub mac Echach (d. 605). Brandub's centre of power was located around Ráith Bile (Rathvilly, Co. Carlow). He is depicted as a king of Leinster defending the province against incursions from the northern *Uí Néill. He is the king-hero of the Leinster saga *Bóruma Laigen* (The Cattle Tribute of the Leinstermen). While the Uí Chennselaig contended for the kingship of Leinster in the 7th century, they were excluded from the mid-8th to the 11th centuries by the north Leinster dynasty of the *Uí Dúnlainge. During that period dynastic segments of the Uí Chennselaig, some of whom were based in the monasteries of St Mullins (Co. Carlow) and Ferns (Co. Wexford), dominated the southern part of Leinster. *Diarmait mac Máel na mBó became king of Leinster in 1042, the first of the Uí Chennselaig kings to hold the kingship since the 8th century. Despite much internecine warfare and occasional intrusions from outsiders, the Uí Chennselaig held the kingship of Leinster to the late 12th century, until the death of Diarmait *Mac Murchada (d. 1171). EB

Uí Dúnlainge, a population group and ruling dynasty in Leinster claiming descent from Dúnlaing, son of Énna Nia. Fáelán mac Colmáin (d. *c.*645 or 666) was the first of the Uí Dúnlainge dynasty to seek the kingship of Leinster. He exercised influence in the monasteries of *Glendalough (Co. Wicklow) and Kildare (Co. Kildare). His brother Áed Dub mac Colmáin (d. 639) was abbot and bishop of Kildare. On the death of the king of Leinster, Cellach Cualann of the Uí Máil, in 715, Murchad mac Brain, Fáelán's great-grandson, asserted the Uí Dúnlainge claim to the kingship of Leinster. Murchad's sons, Dúnchad, Fáelán, and Muiredach, were the progenitors of three kindreds (Uí Dúnchada, Uí Fáeláin, Uí Muiredaig) who were to rotate the kingship of Leinster between them from the mid-8th to the mid-11th centuries. This period was not devoid of internecine strife or of outside interference, especially by the *Uí Néill, who often sustained Uí Dúnlainge dominance of Leinster. From the late 9th century the kings of Osraige, a territory which acted as a buffer between Leinster and Munster, contested the kingship of Leinster. Weakened by internal feuding and by intrusions from the north and from Munster, the Uí Dúnlainge lost the kingship to Donnchad mac Gilla Pátraic (Donough, son of Gilla Pátraic, later Fitzpatrick), king of Osraige (d. 1039), in 1036. Though they regained it briefly, this interlude had weakened their capacity to hold onto the kingship and it passed in 1042 to the *Uí Chennselaig contender, *Diarmait mac Máel na mBó. EB

Uí Fiachrach were a *Connachta dynasty whose eponymous ancestor, Fiachra, was the eldest son of Eochaid Mugmedón and step-brother to *Niall Noígiallach. Medieval writers claimed they provided the only two Connachta kings of *Tara in the 5th century. The Uí Fiachrach Aidne branch (in the diocese of Kilmacduagh) are said to have attained the kingship of Connacht in the early 7th century, notably under Guaire Aidne mac Colmáin (*fl.* 627–63), whose generosity was legendary. The northern Uí Fiachrach Muaide (around the river Moy) held the provincial kingship in the late 7th and 8th centuries. Other branches of the family included the Uí Fiachrach Muirsce of Tireragh barony, Co. Sligo, the Cenél Maic Ercae of Carra barony, Co. Mayo, and the Uí Amolngid of Tirawley and Erris. The northern Uí Fiachrach kings became known in the 11th century as the Uí Dubda (O'Dowds), the southern as Uí hEidin (Hynes). CS

Uí Néill claimed primacy amongst Irish kings (symbolized by the kingship of *Tara), while ruling over much of the northern half of Ireland between the 7th century and the 11th. They are some of the most extensively documented early medieval European kings, but the evidence—in contrast to that for counterparts elsewhere—is primarily found in a myriad of short texts of unknown authorship and often dubious date. Allied to the lack of research on early Irish history, this means that we know relatively little about the dynasty. They identified themselves as descendants of *Niall Noígiallach and ultimately of *Conn Cétchathach. Early texts refer to the Uí Néill as *Moccu Cuind* or *Dál Cuinn* (descendants of Conn), and undated traditions identify Niall as brother of the forebears of the *Connachta.

Their original homeland is unknown: the arguments of Eoin *MacNeill and F. J. Byrne for Connacht, possibly Sligo, are now more widely accepted than those of T. F. O'Rahilly who believed they stemmed from Goidelic invaders of Meath. The extent of Uí Néill territories is first indicated in 7th-century sources, by which stage *Lóegaire mac Néill (said to be a 5th-century figure) is claimed to have been king of Tara (see HIGH KINGSHIP), while his brothers Conall (Cremthainne) and Coirpre are associated with the area of Teltown, Co. Meath, Fíachu with Uisnech, Co. Westmeath, and Conall (Gulban) with Barnesmore Gap, Co. Donegal.

Later literary traditions state that three sons of Niall, Eógan, Conall Gulban, and Énna, conquered Donegal in the 5th century. Their descendants (*Cenél nEógain, *Cenél Conaill, Cenél nÉnnai) form the group known to modern historians as the northern Uí Néill.

More obscure sons of Niall, Coirpre, Maine, and Fíachu, are credited with conquering Westmeath and Longford from the *Laigin in the 5th century, but the later rulers of the southern Uí Néill (*Síl nÁedo Sláine in Meath, *Clann Cholmáin in Westmeath) claimed descent from *Diarmait mac Cerbaill, a great-grandson of Niall through Conall Cremthainne. In ostensibly 6th-century *annals, dated linguistically to the 9th, Diarmait is described as a king of Ireland who fought the northern Uí Néill at Cúl Dreimne (near Benbulben, Co. Sligo). This division between northern and southern Uí Néill mirrors developments from the 8th century and later, when Clann Cholmáin and Cenél nEógain each sought to dominate the *high kingship.

The lack of detailed research on the Uí Néill has fostered the convention of depicting them as a unified force. In the annals, however, attention is focused more on infighting between the various branches than on concerted action. The evidence suggests the primary goal was for regional power; Cenél nEógain dynasts fought *Ulaid, *Cruthin, and *Airgialla as well as the Cenél Conaill before seeking the Tara kingship. Similarly, Síl nÁedo Sláine and Clann Cholmáin candidates had to gain victories over Laigin, Munster kingdoms and each other. Domination of all Uí Néill territory by a single ruler was rarely if ever achieved.

Byrne, F. J., *Irish Kings and High-Kings* (1973)

CS

uirrí (Anglicized as urriogh or urriaghe), literally a sub-king, or satrap. The relationship between the overlord and his sub-king or chief was based on personal lordship, and did not confer jurisdiction over the lesser power's territory. English sources in the 16th century often confuse the term with the phonetically similar 'euragh' (also 'urraght') from the Irish *aireachta*, which by that time had the dual meaning of the lord's vassals and of his subject territory (see OIREACHT). FF

Uí Sínaich, see CLANN SÍNAICH.

Ulaid, from whom comes the name Ulster, a dynastic group who ruled, from their capital at *Emain Macha, a confederation of kingdoms once stretching as far south as the Boyne, and whose conflicts with the *Connachta form the background to *Táin Bó Cuailnge. About the mid-5th century they were ousted from Emain by the *Uí Néill or the *Airgialla, being confined thereafter roughly to the area east of the Bann. Within the overkingdom were several distinct groupings: the Dál Riata (in the Glens of Antrim), who, by the 6th century, had extended into western Scotland; Dál nAraide (in the area around Belfast Lough); Uí Echach Coba (in what became the diocese of Dromore); and Dál Fiatach (in the diocese of Down). The latter, by the 10th century, had come to monopolize the overkingship, which was ruled at the time of the *Anglo-Norman invasion by a branch of the Dál Fiatach bearing the surname Mac Duinn Sléibe (*MacDonlevy). However, the capture in 1177 of their capital, Down, by the Anglo-Norman adventurer John de *Courcy led to the demise of the Mac Duinn Sléibe family, the eventual extinction of their kingdom, and its replacement by the earldom of *Ulster. SD

Ulster, earldom of, the key unit of medieval English lordship in the north of Ireland. Its founder, John de *Courcy, never bore the title of earl, which was first given to his rival, Hugh de *Lacy II, by King *John in 1205. Lacy died without heirs in 1242, and, after a spell of royal rule, Ulster was granted to the de *Burghs in 1263. The earldom was based on de Courcy's conquest of *Ulaid, where the earls had their main castles such as *Carrickfergus, Dundrum, and Greencastle (Co. Down). Richard de *Burgh, the Red Earl (1280–1326), acquired *Derry from its bishop, and built Northburgh Castle on the Inishowen peninsula. The earldom, which had *liberty jurisdiction, was organized into administrative shires based around centres such as Antrim, Carrickfergus, and Newtownards. These areas saw settlement by gentry and traders from north-west England and southern Scotland; prominent among the former were the *Savages of the Ards, originally from Chester, who often served as seneschals of Ulster in the late Middle Ages.

At its height, the earls' power radiated into the Gaelic districts, where the *O'Neills, *O'Cahans, O'Flynns, and others owed military services and sought their patronage. This overlordship was lost as a result of the *Bruce invasion (1315–18) and the murder in 1333 of William, the last de Burgh earl, who was succeeded by *absentees. English Ulster did not collapse immediately: in the 1350s William's mother Elizabeth de Clare drew a substantial income from her manors around Coleraine. But it was gradually eroded by the Irish recovery and the intrusion of the *MacDonnells from Scotland. In the 15th century the earldom was confined to Carrickfergus and coastal enclaves in Down. The title itself passed to the crown, through the *Mortimers and Richard of *York, on the accession of Edward IV in 1461.

Duffy, S., 'The First Ulster Plantation: John de Courcy and the Men of Cumbria', in T. B. Barry, R. Frame, and K. Simms (eds.), *Colony and Frontier in Medieval Ireland* (1995)

McNeill, T. E., *Medieval Ulster: The History of an Irish Barony* (1980)

Orpen, G. H., *Ireland under the Normans 1169–1333* (1911–20)

RFF

Ulster custom, see TENANT RIGHT.

Ulster Defence Association (UDA), a loyalist paramilitary organization established in *Northern Ireland in the autumn of 1971. In its early years it was closely associated with the *Ulster Vanguard movement. During 1972 it grew to an estimated membership of 40,000, and was prominent in the mass protests against the closure of *Stormont. In the same year its threatened opposition to the British army on the streets of Belfast increased the pressure on the government to end the republican no-go areas. This reactive style soon developed a more sinister dimension as elements apparently operating within the UDA, using the title Ulster Freedom Fighters, began a campaign of assassination—sometimes of republican activists, but often of randomly selected Catholics—in response to *IRA actions.

During the mid-1970s and later, these activities played an important part, alongside republican violence, in ratcheting up the level of residential segregation in Belfast and elsewhere. The UDA operated drinking clubs and other businesses, and allegations of protection rackets and gangsterism were frequent. It also sought to improve its image by a more formal involvement in housing allocation, and its leaders were associated with Vanguard's 1975 attempt to restore devolved government to the province by establishing a 'voluntary coalition' with the *Social Democratic and Labour Party, which was thwarted by the *Ulster Unionist Party and the *Democratic Unionist Party (DUP). This combination of extreme violence and hints of political flexibility has continued to characterize the UDA during the 1980s and 1990s. It established a 'Combined Loyalist Paramilitary Command' in partnership with the rival *Ulster Volunteer Force, and an open political party, the Ulster Democratic Party, to contest local elections. Its leadership is predominantly urban working class and secular in tone: it has consistently sought to avoid domination by more conventional politicians, especially Ian Paisley and the DUP. ACH

Ulster Defence Regiment (UDR). Established in 1970, this was a full- and part-time military force, liable only for service in Northern Ireland. It was intended to replace the discredited 'B-Special' police reserve (see ULSTER SPECIAL CONSTABULARY) and provide locally raised support for the regular army. At its maximum the UDR had 9,000 soldiers, though by the mid-1980s this had been reduced to under 6,000. It had a very considerable turnover of personnel, with over 40,000 men and women serving at different times. Although the government hoped it would be a cross-community force, it quickly became almost entirely Protestant, and it was frequently characterized by nationalists as no more than a re-formed B-Specials, composed of ill-disciplined loyalist extremists. The involvement of UDR members in sectarian attacks—including murder—was adduced in support of this view. The regiment was never used for riot control, and its duties were confined to patrolling, manning vehicle check points, and static guard duties. In 1992 the government, hoping to defuse the criticisms of the UDR, merged it with the full-time, regular Royal Irish Rangers (which was 30 per cent Catholic) to form a new unit called the Royal Irish Regiment.

KJ

Ulster king of arms (established 1552), the official who oversaw *heraldry in Ireland. Ulster, assisted by deputy Ulster and the Athlone pursuivant, granted and confirmed coats of arms and ensured correct use of insignia. His initial function of checking pedigrees to ensure entitlement expanded to take in authenticating and even falsifying genealogies for Irishmen in *foreign armies in the 18th century, and dealing with the complicated claims to peerages at home in the 19th. Other duties included recording deaths of peers, overseeing protocol at their funerals, and authorizing admissions to the House of *Lords. The herald's original medieval function survived in a responsibility to organize state occasions and to make formal announcements. When de *Valera established the Genealogical Office (1943), under a chief herald of Ireland (Dr Edward MacLysaght), the Ulster king of arms was incorporated into the College of Arms, London. HM

Ulster Liberal Party, a small grouping which existed from time to time in the province between 1886, when *Gladstone's espousal of *home rule destroyed the Irish *Liberals, and the early 1970s, when it lost its remaining support to the *Alliance Party. Support from the British Liberal Party revived it briefly in 1906–14 and again in 1929. Its apparently final revival, between 1958 and 1969, when it attracted almost 4 per cent of voters, centred on the *Queen's University constituency, which included many British graduates. ACH

Ulster plantation, the British colonization of Cos. Armagh, Cavan, Donegal, Fermanagh, Londonderry, and Tyrone, escheated to the crown following the *Flight of the Earls. Lord Deputy *Chichester favoured a cautious settlement with extensive regrants to natives, even after the unexpected revolt of Sir Cahir *O'Doherty. James I, advised by Sir Francis Bacon, preferred the more radical approach advocated by Chief Justice Sir James Ley and Sir John *Davies. Their 1609 'orders and conditions' provided the framework for the plantation.

Land was divided into 'proportions' of 2,000, 1,500, and 1,000 acres, with three categories of grantee. English and Scottish chief planters (undertakers) had the heaviest responsibilities as regards fortification and settlement. Civil and military servants of the crown in Ireland (servitors) were allowed to have Irish tenants, but could have lower rents if they settled the required number of 24 adult English and Lowland Scots per 1,000 acres. Local recipients (natives) were to pay higher rents and abstain from Irish exactions and tillage methods. The plantation was delayed until Sir Josias Bodley had mapped the country, estimated its acreage, and sorted temporal from spiritual lands. On this basis 28 baronies or 'precincts' were established, eight for English undertakers, eight for Scottish ones, and twelve for servitors and natives jointly.

Successful applicants for grants came from lists drawn up in London and Edinburgh. English undertakers received 51 'proportions' of the best-quality land, or 18 per cent of the total. Some were nobles hoping to restore their fortunes; most were gentry from East Anglia and the midlands with annual incomes of about £200. Scottish undertakers, mostly from the central lowland belt, received a similar proportion of less profitable lands and being of small means (probably £150 per annum on average) were allotted smaller estates in baronies sprinkled throughout the escheated counties. A further 10 per cent went to the *Irish Society and its associated London companies for the strategic plantation of Londonderry. The servitors, including leading officials such as Chichester, Davies, and Sir William Parsons, the surveyor-general, local garrison commanders, and Palesmen in Co. Cavan, received 12 per cent. The Church of Ireland received 16 per cent, *Trinity College 3 per cent, and local schools, towns, and forts a further 3 per cent.

Native grantees received only 20 per cent of the planted counties. These individuals had assisted the state during the *Nine Years War, but even so they were given reduced holdings, often shifted to place them under servitor supervision, and forbidden to buy additional land. Some received life grants only. The promises made to Niall Garbh *O'Donnell and Donell O'Cahan, now imprisoned in the Tower of London for alleged involvement in O'Doherty's revolt, were ignored. The rights of freeholders, which the government had vigorously promoted before the Flight, were deliberately disregarded. On the eve of the plantation Sir Toby Caulfeild reported that there was 'not a more discontented people in Europe'.

In 1610 landless Irish, who were to remove themselves to servitor or church estates, were given a stay of eviction because undertakers had not yet arrived. When undertakers or their agents did appear, tenancies were parcelled out to natives, contrary to plantation rules, because they were willing to pay high rents. Chichester shipped out 6,000 *idlemen as mercenaries, but others remained in Ulster, more interested in menacing the plantation as 'woodkern' than in farming as tenants. After a further conspiracy involving O'Neills and O'Cahans in 1615, more freeholds were confiscated and a draconian security policy saw the hanging of hundreds of woodkern. Anxieties about the possible return of Hugh *O'Neill and speculation in land grants slowed progress. Government inspections, such as Pynnar's survey in 1619, found deficiencies in fortification and settlement, along with slowness in evicting the natives. New patents were eventually issued to errant undertakers in 1628 permitting them to keep native tenants on a quarter of their proportions at double the old rent. However, inability to compete with English and Scottish tenants soon forced the Irish into subsistence on marginal lands.

By 1630 about 6,500 adult British males had settled in the escheated counties. Settlers were now arriving on their own initiative, rather than being brought over from the undertaker's home region. This facilitated a process of colonial spread from ports of entry to the hinterland, and quickly became the dominant migration pattern. Internal migration also developed as tenantry pursued easier tenures and better land. The patterns of settlement were set as early as 1622 and distinct English, Scottish, and Irish localities were emerging. Sixteen new corporate towns were established, tilting the balance in favour of Protestants in the Irish *parliament. An infrastructure of roads, inns, and mills developed, and an agrarian export economy emerged strongly and then languished in the 1630s. Gaelic methods of tillage, harvesting, and threshing, which were well suited to local conditions, were slow in disappearing.

Robinson, Philip, *The Plantation of Ulster: British Settlement in an Irish Landscape 1600–1670* (1984)

HM

Ulster Scots, also known as 'Ullans', the language imported into Ulster by 17th-century Scottish immigrants. In the letters of the gentry, the only group to leave written records in this period, a distinctive Scots spelling, vocabulary, and grammar are initially strong, but by the mid-17th century have been wholly replaced by standard English forms. However Scots survived in popular speech, particularly in Cos. Antrim, Down, Londonderry, and parts of Donegal. In the late 18th and early 19th centuries, partly under the influence of Robert Burns and the Scottish literary revival, local poets like James Orr (1770–1816), of Ballycarry, Co. Antrim, published volumes of verse in Scots. In recent years *unionists in Northern Ireland, largely in response to the claims made on behalf of Irish by nationalists and republicans, have pressed, with some success, for official recognition of Ulster Scots as a minority language.

Ulster Special Constabulary (USC). During the *Anglo-Irish War the *Royal Irish Constabulary was reinforced in 1920 in the south by the *Black and Tans and *Auxiliaries and in the north by the Ulster Special Constabulary. Recruited from the revived *Ulster Volunteer Force, the new constabulary had three sections: A men were full-time, paid, and armed; B men were part-time, paid, and armed; while C men were an unpaid reserve. Until the *Royal Ulster Constabulary (RUC) was established in 1922, the USC took a leading role in countering *IRA attacks in the north. But the often brutal tactics employed by the Specials alienated the Catholic population, who regarded them as little more than Protestant vigilantes. In 1926, after the shelving of the *Boundary Commission report, the A and C Specials were disbanded, but the B Specials continued to support the RUC. In 1940–4 they were expanded into an Ulster Home Guard, while in 1968–9 they were used extensively in the policing of *civil rights marches. However, inquiries into the disorders sparked off by the marches condemned the B Specials as biased and ill-disciplined. As a result they were disbanded in 1970 and replaced by the *Ulster Defence Regiment, which many of them joined. ELM

Ulster Unionist Council, created during 1904–5 as a unifying organization for northern *unionism. After the defeat of the second *home rule bill in 1893, Ulster unionism was threatened by internal division in the form of T. W. *Russell's campaigns on the land issue, and by the widely ranging populism of the *Independent Orange Order. In an effort to regain the local initiative, and to counter the threat created by the devolution issue, younger unionist leaders such as William Moore, C. C. Craig, and John B. Lonsdale urged a reform of party organization: this pressure resulted in the creation of the Ulster Unionist Council, which was launched in Belfast on 3 March 1905.

The functions of the UUC were defined as uniting the local unionist associations, binding Ulster Unionist MPs and their constituents, contributing to the formulation of parliamentary policy, and expressing the opinions of the broader movement. Aided by the re-emergence after 1906 of the home rule threat, the UUC was able to achieve a reactivation of local unionism in Ulster. More broadly, it contributed to the localization of the Ulster unionist movement through annexing powers which had formerly been exercised by the Irish Unionist parliamentary party. The UUC, and its standing committee, were central to the successful mobilization of popular Unionism in opposition to the third home rule bill (1912–14).

Subsequent modifications to the council's structure created a more representative as well as a more diffuse institution. The UUC was enlarged in 1911, in 1918, 1921, 1929, and again in 1944. The resultant, highly unwieldy structure was reformed through the party constitution of 1946, which created, in the form of the executive committee and its attendant subcommittees, a new, high-level tier of representation. However, it is hard to escape the conclusion that—certainly for the *Stormont period—the intricate elaboration of the UUC constitution has diverted attention from its comparative insignificance. Indeed, before 1972 the presence of a cohesive body of representative unionists at Stormont undermined the essential purpose of the UUC. Since the Belfast Agreement of 1998 (see PEACE PROCESS), well-publicized debates within the council over critical leadership and policy issues have given it an apparently renewed significance.

Harbinson, John, *The Ulster Unionist Party, 1882–1973: Its Development and Organisation* (1973)

AJ

Ulster Unionist Party, the governing party of *Northern Ireland between 1921 and 1972. The party evolved in 1885–6 as a protest movement, united by a broad antipathy to *home rule but otherwise highly fissile. After 1921, and the creation of the Northern Ireland parliament, it remained a cumbersome coalition which sustained unity through a trenchant stand on the Union, an implicit anti-Catholicism, and a passive or reactive approach to most other areas of policy.

The party embraced a broad range of Ulster Protestant opinion, but was led by the commercial elite of eastern Ulster, with a notable residual landed presence. Although the influence of the landed gentry had been decisively countered in the Edwardian party, three of the six Unionist leaders of the period 1921–72 (*Brooke, *O'Neill, and Major James Chichester-Clark) were landed gentlemen. However, the Unionist parliamentary party at Stormont, both within the House of Commons and the Senate, was dominated by the Protestant professional classes. Proletarian unionism was never adequately represented within the Ulster Unionist leadership. Catholics have never been effectively courted by the party, and indeed the increasingly parochial nature of Unionism in 20th-century Ireland has tended to reinforce its anti-Catholicism.

Hampered by the fragile and diverse nature of its support, the Unionist Party never developed far from its original ideology of protest: unity has often been bought at the price of inactivity. Recurrent *IRA violence reinforced the defensive loyalism of the party: this has brought a lasting emphasis on law and order policy, from the *Special Powers Act (1922) through to the Prevention of Terrorism Act (1974). In addition, the anti-partitionism of successive Dublin administrations permitted the Unionist Party to survive on the basis of an uncomplicated appeal to British loyalty: the Irish *constitution of 1937 allowed Lord Craigavon (see CRAIG) to reunite unionism in the Stormont election of 1938, while the declaration of a *republic enabled Sir Basil Brooke to perform a similar feat in 1949. The fragile nature of the Unionist coalition, and its socially conservative leadership, has meant that broader social and welfare issues have tended to be relegated within the party's priorities. British welfare legislation, in particular the legislation of Attlee's post-war government, was duplicated by the Unionist Party, but on Unionist principles, rather than from an intrinsic commitment to reform.

The Unionist Party splintered under the impact of the *civil rights movement and the renewal of IRA violence in 1969. Liberal Unionists, dissatisfied with internal opposition to O'Neill, joined the *Alliance Party; working-class loyalists, angered by O'Neill's apparently high-handed and paternalistic leadership, joined the *Democratic Unionist Party. Militant loyalists, dissatisfied with the apparently impotent constitutionalism of the Unionist Party, turned to the *Ulster Vanguard movement or to the populist vigilante bodies later unified as the *Ulster Defence Association. Under the leadership of James Molyneaux (1979–95) some degree of consolidation was achieved: the party successfully contained the challenge of the DUP, and profited from the failure of the *Unionist Party of Northern Ireland and of Vanguard. The election of David Trimble as leader in 1995 at first seemed like an affirmation of hard-line attitudes; but his endorsement of the Belfast Agreement of 1998 (see PEACE PROCESS) and other reformist impulses provoked a degree of confusion and division among the party's supporters. In 1998, with the splintering of the Unionist vote, the party came second to the *Social Democratic and Labour Party in the elections to the Northern Ireland Assembly. It is as yet unclear whether this, and other electoral setbacks, represent more than a temporary downturn in the Ulster Unionists' fortunes.

Buckland, Patrick, *The Factory of Grievances: Devolved Government in Northern Ireland, 1921–39* (1979)
Cochrane, Feargal, *Unionist Politics and the Politics of Unionism since the Anglo-Irish Agreement* (1997)
Hume, David, *The Ulster Unionist Party 1972–1992: A Political Movement in an Era of Conflict and Change* (1996)

AJ

Ulster Vanguard, launched in early 1972 by William Craig (b. 1924), the former minister for home affairs whose handling of the *civil rights movement had led to his dismissal by Terence *O'Neill in December 1968. Vanguard was designed as a means of unifying and directing a then highly fissile loyalism. From the start it was associated with a trenchant opposition to *direct rule, and with a highly militant rhetoric: it had close connections with paramilitary loyalism, and in 1972–3 possessed its own paramilitary wing, the Vanguard Service Corps. Craig's militancy and unpredictability, and his emphasis on the possibility of independence for Northern Ireland, pushed him to the margins of unionism. The movement crystallized into a formal political party (the Vanguard Unionist Progressive Party) in March 1973, profiting briefly from the divisions within mainstream unionism. However, the VUPP itself split when Craig—in opposition to the majority of his party—supported the idea of a voluntary coalition with the SDLP. In 1977 the dissidents regrouped under Ernest Baird as the United Ulster Unionist Movement. Vanguard ceased to function as a separate party in February 1978, and reverted to its origins as a loyalist pressure group. Although Craig returned to the Ulster Unionist Party, he continued to pursue a highly individualistic agenda. His principal lieutenant, David Trimble, was more thoroughly reintegrated into the unionist mainstream, becoming leader of the Ulster Unionist Party in September 1995. AJ

Ulster Volunteer Force, created in January 1913, during the third *Home Rule crisis, to coordinate the paramilitary activities of Ulster *unionists. Volunteer activity spread among unionists in 1911–12, and was brought under the control of the Ulster Unionist leadership through the launch of the UVF. The UVF, with a membership of *c.*90,000, and led by retired officers of the British army, represented a formidable political tool. Grass-roots pressure brought the *Larne gun-running of April 1914, and the partial arming of the UVF, but its military condition remained imperfect. Nevertheless, the Volunteers made a substantial contribution to Kitchener's New Army through their role in the 36th (Ulster) Division. The UVF was revived in July 1920, in the context of the *Anglo-Irish war; but was later largely incorporated within the official *Ulster Special Constabulary.

The title 'Ulster Volunteer Force' was resurrected in 1966, and applied to a group of militant loyalists from the Shankill Road, Belfast, who were opposed to the liberal unionism of Terence *O'Neill: this organization was proscribed by O'Neill after two murders committed in June 1966. By 1972 the UVF had attained a strength of *c.*1,500. It was legalized in April 1974 in an effort to guide it towards constitutional activity, but was again banned in October 1975. Successful prosecutions, following penetration by police informants, reduced its size and effectiveness in the later 1970s and 1980s, but a ruthless and elusive core remained. Between 1969 and 1994, when its leadership signed the joint loyalist ceasefire, the UVF was the principal loyalist organization responsible for sectarian and political assassination in Northern Ireland. AJ

Ulster Workers' Council (UWC), a loyalist grouping established in *Northern Ireland early in 1974 to oppose the *Sunningdale agreement. Its leadership was associated mainly with the *Ulster Vanguard movement, but it also had low-key support from the other unionist parties opposed to Sunningdale. It drew strong grass-roots support from the paramilitary *Ulster Defence Association (UDA). In May 1974 the council called a 'constitutional stoppage' or general strike. Widespread Protestant hostility to Sunningdale, reinforced significantly by UDA intimidation and by the British government and army's apparent inability to operate the power stations, brought the province to a standstill. The crisis was ended only by the resignation of the Northern Ireland executive and the collapse of the agreement. The UWC attempted to mount a second action in 1977, but the issues were less clear-cut: only the Paisleyite (see DEMOCRATIC UNIONIST PARTY) wing of unionism supported it, and it quickly petered out. ACH

ultramontanism, a current of opinion in the Catholic church which favoured papal over national or diocesan authority. It came to prominence in the 18th century, especially after the Civil Constitution of the Clergy (1790), which had imposed explicit state control on the French church. Early 19th-century popes, fearing the opposition of national governments and local hierarchies, were reluctant to encourage ultramontanism, but it grew among laity and clergy who sought a new Catholic identity to fill the gap left by waning state support for established religion. With the failure of Catholic liberalism and the increasingly precarious position of the papal states, popes turned increasingly to ultramontanist policies of church centralization. Papal authority extended itself notably with the Syllabus of Errors (1864) and the declaration of papal infallibility (1870). Although ultramontanism in Ireland has been associated with the influence of the Rome-educated Paul *Cullen, its 19th-century success owed more to the needs of the emerging Catholic community, particularly its search for a modern, vibrant identity. Ultramontanism provided this, proving flexible enough to accommodate the late 19th-century alliance between Catholicism and Irish nationalism. It began to lose its attraction as this alliance weakened and as the church reinterpreted the notion of papal authority following the second *Vatican Council. TO'C

undertakers, see ULSTER PLANTATION.

undertakers, the name given to a succession of local power brokers who in the 18th century undertook to manage the business of government in the Irish *parliament. In return undertakers expected to be consulted regarding policy and to receive a substantial share in the patronage at government's disposal, using this, along with their personal influence, to deliver the required parliamentary majorities. Such local managers were necessary because *lords lieutenant were English politicians who served for relatively short periods and resided in Ireland only during parliamentary sessions. Up to 1714 the role was filled by the leaders of the Irish *Whig and *Tory parties. Thereafter government business was managed by William *Conolly until his death in 1729, by Sir Ralph Gore, less successfully, until he too died in 1733, and then by Henry *Boyle, until the *money bill dispute ended with a division of power between Boyle and the Ponsonby family. Each leading undertaker, from Conolly to John *Ponsonby, was *speaker of the House of Commons and held office as a *revenue commissioner, *chancellor of the exchequer or both, as well as serving as a *lord justice when the lord lieutenant was not in residence. Following Lord *Townshend's viceroyalty, reliance on undertakers gave way to direct management by a resident lord lieutenant.

Uniformity, Acts of (1560, 1666), designed to ensure that the nation followed a uniform Protestant liturgy. The 1560 Act for the Uniformity of Common Prayer and Service in the Church (2 Eliz. 1 c. 2) required all clergy in Ireland to use the English Prayer Book of 1559. Punishments were prescribed for clergy who refused to use the book, with the ultimate sanction for repeated offences being deprivation and life imprisonment. Laity who refused to attend services were subjected to a fine of 12*d*. and this was subsequently used to try to force people to attend the *Church of Ireland. By the early 17th century it was becoming clear that it would not be possible to impose uniformity by legislative fiat and the 12*d*. fine was seen more as a way of raising revenue than as a means to make people Protestant.

The passing of the English Act of 1662, establishing a slightly revised Prayer Book, was followed in Ireland by the 1666 act. This reiterated the need for conformity, but was also directed at tightening control over schoolmasters and ensuring uniformity within the established church by excluding those with *Presbyterian sympathies. Like its predecessor, however, it was 'more effective in stating the ideal of uniformity than enforcing the reality'. AF

Union, Act of (1800), in fact two identical measures passed in 1800 by the British and Irish parliaments. These created, with effect from 1 January 1801, the United Kingdom of Great Britain and Ireland. Negotiated by *Cornwallis and *Castlereagh, under the supervision of the prime minister, William Pitt, the Union provided that Ireland should be represented in the House of Lords by four bishops and 28 representative peers, and in the Commons by 100 MPs. Initially each country retained its own financial system and national debt, with Ireland meeting two-seventeenths of future expenditure. The two exchequers were united in 1817 and Irish and British *taxation gradually brought into line. Protective duties on a range of manufactured goods entering Ireland were maintained at a reduced level until 1824.

The immediate occasion for the Union was the *insurrection of 1798, seen as confirming the need for direct control of a neighbouring dependency whose instability had become a serious threat. But there had been concern, ever since 1782, at the fragility of the Anglo-Irish connection in the wake of *legislative independence. Opponents of the measure included not only the existing *Whig opposition and threatened commercial interests, particularly in the city of Dublin, but also prominent former supporters of government, such as John *Foster. These last were motivated partly by *patriot sentiment but also by the fear that direct rule from London could not be trusted to maintain Protestant supremacy. Politically conscious Catholics, by contrast, generally supported the Union, in the belief, encouraged by government, that it would be followed by rapid progress towards full *Catholic emancipation.

On 24 January 1799 the Irish Commons voted 111 to 106 to remove from an address to the *lord lieutenant a reference to possible union. But when parliament reassembled in January 1800 there was a comfortable pro-union majority. In the interval Cornwallis and Castlereagh had dismissed prominent anti-unionists like Foster, while luring potential supporters with office or the promise of future favours. They also undertook to compensate patrons of boroughs for the loss of electoral influence. Nationalist historians and polemicists were later to claim that the Union had been imposed by bribery. Modern accounts suggest that the exchange of patronage for parliamentary support remained within the limits of 18th-century convention, and emphasize the extent to which both sides engaged, through pamphleteering, petitions, and public meetings, in a competition for public opinion as well as parliamentary votes.

The Union did not succeed in making Ireland part of a unitary British state. There were suggestions, in 1800 and at intervals thereafter, that the Union had made a separate Irish executive unnecessary. But in practice Ireland's physical separateness and size (a *population in 1800 half that of England, Scotland, and Wales), as well as its problems of political disaffection, religious conflict, and economic underdevelopment, ensured that day-to-day government continued to be conducted from *Dublin Castle, under the direction of a lord lieutenant and *chief secretary. During the 19th century government came to be characterized by a high level of state intervention, in education (see SCHOOLS), public health (see HOSPITALS), and economic development, and by a degree of central control, which further highlighted Ireland's separateness from the rest of the United Kingdom.

Protestant opponents fairly quickly came to terms with the Union. The appearance from the 1820s of a politically mobilized Catholic electorate confirmed most in a belief that Ireland's continued membership of the United Kingdom represented their only security. Catholic enthusiasm for the measure, on the other hand, diminished when the declared hostility of King George III led Pitt to abandon plans for emancipation. Perceptions of the Union were also strongly influenced by the contrast between the prosperity that had apparently accompanied legislative independence and the industrial decline that followed the abolition of tariffs in 1824. In the 1840s *O'Connell built up a formidable mass agitation in support of *repeal. The 1850s and 1860, however, saw a fuller, though still incomplete, incorporation of Ireland into the politics of the United Kingdom, and it was arguably not until the rise of the *home rule movement in the 1870s that it became clear that the Union had irrevocably failed to provide a generally accepted framework for Anglo-Irish relations.

Bolton, G. C., *The Passing of the Irish Act of Union* (1966)

unionism. As a political tradition, Irish unionism can be traced back to that strand of late 17th- and early 18th-century *patriotism which held that full political integration with Great Britain was preferable to a flawed or unattainable legislative independence. By 1801, when the Act of *Union passed into law, unionism, whether in Ulster or the rest of Ireland, still lacked a significant political base. As a popular political war-cry, therefore, unionism developed only in the first half of the 19th century; Unionism as an organized movement dates from the *home rule crisis of 1885–6. Demotic unionism was thus in no sense automatic or predetermined: it was made possible by the emergence of a newly unified Protestantism and a newly distinctive British identity in 19th-century Ireland. These in turn depended on the economic development of Ulster, and—indirectly—on the political and institutional consolidation of Irish Catholicism.

Formal Irish Unionist organization emerged in 1885–6 in the wake of a revitalized *Orangeism and Conservatism which, in turn, represented a reaction to the *Land War. Electoral reform in 1884–5 (see FRANCHISE) created a more representative, and therefore a more Catholic, electorate, and threatened to annihilate a still divided loyalism. It was in response to this combined electoral and constitutional challenge that a group of Orange Conservatives, including Edward *Saunderson, sought to create a coalition stretching beyond the traditional, Tory, bounds of loyalism. In February 1885 the first, short-lived, Irish loyalist parliamentary party was created, while in the summer of 1885 a popular base was being added in both Belfast and Dublin. By March 1886, when *Gladstone introduced the home rule bill, a coherent unionist organization was in place both inside and outside the House of Commons. The strength of this organization lay in the fact that it was not merely an immediate or improvised response to Gladstone's challenge.

Southern Irish unionism was initially an important element of this political strength. Southern Irish unionists (numbering at most 250,000) were primarily landed and Anglican, and provided considerable financial and organizational direction to unionists in all parts of Ireland. In common with other economic elites, southern unionists were over-represented in both houses of the British parliament. Unionists claimed in the 1880s and 1890s to be a movement which embraced the entire island, and southern unionists, though numerically slight, were important in lending credibility to this claim.

Southern unionist decline (during and after the Edwardian period), occurred partly because of the rapid erosion of the economic and political position of Irish *landlords, and partly because of the gradual development of popular unionist organization in Ulster. In 1904–5, moved by English Conservative neglect, and by the internal challenges of T. W. *Russell and of the *Independent Orange Order, a group of young, middle-class unionists (including James *Craig) created the *Ulster Unionist Council. This spearheaded a more militant localized unionism, based in Belfast, and reflecting narrowly northern concerns. It was the UUC which directed the unionist campaign during the passage of the third home rule bill (1912–14), and which lent this campaign its popular and threatening tone.

Ulster unionist domination of the movement led to a modification of its rhetoric and strategy.

Under the charismatic Edward *Carson a unique mass mobilization of northern unionists was achieved. Potentially explosive popular emotions were cultivated by Carson and by his lieutenant Craig, and guided into the paramilitary *Ulster Volunteer Force, and into regimented protest demonstrations. Unionist claims to repudiate home rule for all of Ireland were now more qualified, while emphasis was given to the rights of the by now more coherent Protestant community in Ulster. By July 1914 Ulster unionists had abandoned the all-Ireland unionism of 1886 and 1893, and were prepared to negotiate for a partition settlement. Equally, by July 1914 Ulster unionists had abandoned the essentially constitutional strategies of 1886 and 1893, and were importing large quantities of weapons (most spectacularly in the *Larne gun-running of April 1914).

Superficially the outbreak of the *First World War in August 1914 defused the constitutional crisis, for the operation of home rule was suspended for the duration of the war. Yet the war helped to further the geographical polarization of Irish politics, indirectly promoting the division of Irish unionism, and broadening the distance between unionism and nationalism. The UVF was transformed into the 36th (Ulster) Division of the British army, and was decimated on the Somme in July 1916: this sacrifice served to reinforce a peculiarly northern sense of identity. While Ulster unionists grew more particularist, southern unionists, weakened by immense wartime losses, and horrified by the development of *Sinn Féin, grew more pragmatic: southern unionist representatives at the *Irish Convention of 1917 were prepared to endorse home rule. This apostasy helped to confirm the partitionist sympathies of Ulster unionists.

In 1920 the UUC accepted the creation, under the *Government of Ireland Act, of a six-county Northern Ireland. Unionism, which had emerged as a coalition demanding the maintenance of a united parliament in London, became the majority party in a devolved parliament, and the guarantor of a home rule and partition settlement. This rapid change of function would soon promote further ideological shifts inside unionism, turning it into a primarily devolutionist movement. By 1972, when they reacted with dismay to the reintroduction of direct rule, unionists had rediscovered the priorities of the colonial patriots, for whom a true union had been less desirable than local autonomy.

Jackson, Alvin, *The Ulster Party: Irish Unionists in the House of Commons, 1884–1911* (1989)

AJ

Unionist Party of Northern Ireland (UPNI), founded in September 1974 by Brian *Faulkner. In January 1974 Faulkner failed to persuade the majority of the *Ulster Unionist Council to accept the *Sunningdale proposals. His supporters, styling themselves 'Unionist Pro-Assembly' candidates, carried their case to the broader electorate in the Westminster election of February 1974, and—after the failure of the assembly and executive—created UPNI. The party survived, despite a very low level of electoral endorsement, until 1981. AJ

United Irish League (UIL), founded in 1898 by William *O'Brien to agitate for the redistribution of the western grass ranches to small farmers. It was instrumental in reuniting the *Nationalist Party in 1900, after which it became a constituency and fund-raising organization. O'Brien lost control of the UIL after 1903, and soon opposed it bitterly. In later years it was propped up by the *Ancient Order of Hibernians, but contracted sharply after 1916; the Dublin offices closed in 1920. In Great Britain the Irish *National League was renamed the United Irish League of Great Britain in 1900 under T. P. *O'Connor, who delivered its remaining membership to the Labour Party after 1921.

The land question was the UIL's strength and its weakness. Its inability to take up other issues was symptomatic of the Nationalist Party's failure to prevent the development of cultural nationalism into a hostile political force between 1900 and 1916. This became crucial once land tenure ceased to be a unifying issue. The UIL could still be militant in eastern Connacht, especially during 1898–1901 and 1906–9 (see RANCH WAR), where the letting of large grass ranches to graziers on short tenancies stood in contrast to the position of the established tenants, often on poorer holdings of uneconomic size. But in other parts of the country, following the 1903 *Land Act, large graziers might be active Nationalists themselves, and hold office in the league.

O'Brien intended that the UIL should reflect the voice of the grass roots, with a system of graded elections from local to national level, and a National Directory independent of the party, unlike the constituency organizations of the 1880s and 1890s. In practice the UIL soon fell under party control, with *Redmond as president from 1900, Joe *Devlin as general secretary from 1905, and party loyalists dominating the National Directory. Parliamentary candidates were selected by constituency conventions made up of clergy and local bodies, but they were chaired by a headquarters nominee who was in practice able in most cases to deliver the party's preferred candidate. After 1914 the convention system withered away, along with the party's support.

Bew, Paul, *Conflict & Conciliation in Ireland, 1890–1910* (1987)

Lyons, F. S. L. *The Irish Parliamentary Party, 1890–1910* (1951)

ACH

United Irishmen, Society of, established in Belfast (by Neilson, *Tone, and *Russell) on 18 October 1791 and in Dublin (by Tone, Russell, and *Tandy), on 9 November, with smaller clubs in other centres. The membership of the Belfast society was Presbyterian and predominantly middle class; that of the Dublin society, roughly equally divided between Protestant and Catholic, was middle class with a sprinkling of gentry and aristocracy. The society's ideology combined the new radicalism inspired by the *American and *French Revolutions with the older traditions of British advanced *Whig or *commonwealth doctrine, and Irish *patriotism. Its main aims were *parliamentary reform and the removal of English control of Irish affairs. It was not until 1794, however, that the Dublin society defined reform in terms of indirect elections by universal male suffrage, and the early United Irishmen also stopped short of overt separatism or *republicanism. The society's most distinctive commitment was to a union of Irishmen of all denominations, though here too some Protestant members were privately uneasy at the prospect of full *Catholic emancipation.

The United Irishmen initially operated as a radical club, disseminating propaganda through the **Northern Star* and other publications, and seeking to act as a radicalizing influence within larger bodies, notably the *Volunteers. During 1793 the Gunpowder Act and *Convention Act curtailed Volunteering, while prosecutions silenced leading radicals like Hamilton *Rowan. In May 1794, following the arrest of William *Jackson, the Dublin society was suppressed. United Irish leaders were later to blame these repressive measures for driving them to revolution. Recent research suggests that the effect was rather to advance a conspiratorial element already present, particularly within the Ulster movement, which now reorganized itself as a secret, oath-bound organization geared for armed insurrection. The new clandestine structures, formalized in a revised constitution adopted on 10 May 1795, were extended to Dublin from the summer of 1796 and from there to surrounding counties. Meanwhile Tone had arrived in France in February 1796 to seek military support, and the *Hoche expedition of December dramatically boosted recruitment and morale. By February 1798 the society claimed over 280,000 active members. This expansion, along with the increasingly close alliance with the *Defenders, inevitably widened the gulf between the ideas of leaders and followers, as the goal of a democratic republic was reinforced, if not displaced, by ideas of a radical social transformation, and even of a settling of accounts with 'heretic' Protestants.

During 1797 the campaign of determined counter-insurgency directed by General *Lake severely weakened the United Irish organization in its Ulster heartland. In spring 1798 the focus of repression moved to the counties round Dublin. Lord Edward *FitzGerald, Arthur *O'Connor, and other United Irish leaders advocated immediate insurrection, but were opposed by moderates led by *Emmet and W. J. MacNevin. The arrest of most members of the Leinster Directory on 12 March allowed Lord Edward, the Sheares brothers, and Neilson to frame plans for a rising. However, they too were in custody by 23 May, and it remains unclear how far the eventual insurrection of 1798 was centrally coordinated.

A new United Irish organization, more tightly knit than its predecessor, appeared quite quickly after 1798, but collapsed following Robert Emmet's insurrection of 1803, although in France United Irish representatives remained active up to the fall of Napoleon.

Curtin, Nancy, *The United Irishmen: Popular Politics in Ulster and Dublin 1791–1798* (1994)

United Nations, global intergovernmental organization established in 1945 to regulate post-war international relations on the basis of collective security. Ireland entered in 1955, when a 'package deal' which admitted a balanced group of states from east and west persuaded the Soviet Union to remove a long-standing veto.

Entering under the Fine Gael-led *interparty government, Ireland's performance in the organization was initially unremarkable. Outlining his intended approach to the *Dáil, external affairs minister Liam Cosgrave insisted that Ireland would tend naturally towards western positions on most issues. The one advance on existing practice in international organizations (principally at this time the *Council of Europe) was to be the abandonment of the incessant rehearsal of the irredentist claim to Northern Ireland—the policy of the 'sore thumb' in the expression of its most enthusiastic practitioner, Sean *MacBride.

The return to power of *Fianna Fáil in 1957 changed fundamentally Ireland's policy and image at the UN. External affairs minister Frank *Aiken embarked on a campaign of activism which placed Ireland firmly among the diplomatically forward-looking 'middle powers' of the period, such as Sweden, Norway, and Canada. This grouping was characterized by its initiatives on a range of international problems, its dominant role in the internal diplomacy of the UN, and its extensive participation in peacekeeping operations. During the 1960s and 1970s Ireland was a major contributor to the UN forces in the Congo, Cyprus, Israel's disputed borders, and Lebanon.

The prestige within the UN which this identity conferred was not always valued at home. Throughout the later 1950s and the 1960s UN policy was a frequent target of opposition criticism in the Dáil, particularly where it appeared to depart from western positions on matters such as the representation of China at the UN and advocacy of nuclear disengagement in Europe. By the later 1960s, however, the gradual radicalization of the General Assembly, a consequence of its increased Third World membership, had diminished Ireland's progressive image in the organization. And, as the prospect of membership of the European Community (see EUROPEAN UNION) changed domestic perceptions of Ireland's place in the world, the continuing primacy of the UN in Irish foreign policy was increasingly questioned.

With entry to the European Community in 1973 the middle power role at the UN was maintained, but was performed increasingly in the context of co-operation with the other smaller states of the Community. An attempt by the domestically beleaguered Fianna Fáil government of Charles Haughey in 1982 to pursue a Security Council initiative on the Falklands crisis independent of European partners was both untypical and unsuccessful. The commitment to UN peacekeeping, however, has remained as strong in the post-Cold War period as it had been in the 1960s and 1970s.

The rejection of the 'sore thumb' tactic notwithstanding, the national question inevitably found its way into UN policy with the outbreak of the *Northern Ireland conflict. The sudden upsurge of anti-Catholic violence led Jack Lynch's Fianna Fáil administration to seek Security Council discussion of a peacekeeping operation for the north. But the initiative, pre-doomed by the British veto, was not pursued with any great energy. In fact Northern Ireland rarely had a major place in Irish UN policy, and hardly featured at all after the imposition of direct rule from Westminster in 1972. Ireland's forte at the UN appeared to be intervention in the problems of others rather than the exposure of its own.

MacQueen, N., 'Ireland's Entry to the United Nations, 1945–56', in T. Gallagher and J. O'Connell (eds.), *Contemporary Irish Studies* (1983)

—— 'Frank Aiken and Irish Activism at the United Nations, 1957–61', *International History Review*, 6 (1984)

Skelly, J. M., *Irish Diplomacy at the United Nations 1945–65: National Interests and International Order* (1997)

NMacQ

United States of America. The high water marks of the impact of Irish immigrants on the United States were in the 40 years before the *American Civil War. Between 1820 and 1860 emigrants from Ireland never formed less than 35 per cent of all new immigrants, and sometimes as much as 45 per cent. By the 1880s this figure was down to 12.5 per cent, and by the turn of the century it stood at less than 4 per cent. In 1960 Irish immigrants formed less than 1 per cent of the total. These realities are central to an understanding of how the Irish American group in the USA was formed and continues to be formed. What was once the largest obvious immigrant community in America, including within it a large minority born in Ireland, has become one mature, complex, multigenerational group among many.

Estimates of the overall numbers who left Ireland to settle in the USA are difficult to formulate. The problems include the frequently ineffectual counting system at ports both of entry and departure, the ease with which, for much of its history, the US–Canadian border could be crossed and recrossed, and the fact that Irish immigrants did not necessarily arrive in America direct from their homeland. In the last case, for instance, a large minority of Irish settlers in California came via *Australia. Overall it seems that in excess of 5.5 million, but not more than 6 million, people have left Ireland for the United States since the foundation of the American Republic in 1776. Because the predominant mass of immigrants arrived before 1900, and because there were perhaps as many as 400,000 people in the USA with an Irish background at the time of the first census in 1790, the current size of the Irish multigenerational group is very large. Estimates of its late 20th-century size vary strikingly, but by some reckonings it was in excess of 40 million people. No one, whatever their method of calculation, would put it below 21 million.

Whatever the absolute numbers, there is an unusual degree of agreement that over 50 per cent of Americans of Irish descent are Protestant. To understand this superficially surprising finding, it is worth emphasizing that a study conducted in the 1970s discovered that while 41 per cent of Catholic Irish-Americans surveyed were at least fourth generation, no less than 83 per cent of Irish-American Protestants were fourth generation or more. A powerful 'accelerator factor' is at work. Further, although it is almost certain that since the 1830s the majority of Irish immigrants have been Catholic, significant Protestant immigration continued down to the *First World War. To balance, if also to complicate, this last point, there was a substantial minority of Catholics among Irish immigrants before 1830. These found themselves in an atmosphere hostile to their religion and with a skeletal church organization to receive them—quite apart from the fact that many arrived as indentured servants and were widely dispersed. Since the middle of the 19th century, an increasingly confident and well-funded Catholic church, under a mainly Irish and Irish-American leadership, has transformed this situation. But in earlier periods some Catholic emigrants conformed to the dominant Protestant culture.

Such discussion begs the question of what we mean by the term 'Irish-American'. Since the *Great Famine this has become synonymous, both inside and outside America, with Catholicism and with a commitment, whether weak or strong, to the Irish national cause variously defined over the years (see IRISH-AMERICAN NATIONALISM). The great weight of relevant scholarship has been founded on this assumption. If the focus remains exclusively on those from such a background, then the narrative is one of mounting success, and success defined in characteristically American terms. It is increasingly clear that among immigrants from Europe only Jewish-Americans rank higher on such scales as time spent in formal education and levels of home income than do Catholic Irish-Americans. By such criteria, those Protestants with an Irish heritage form a less successful group.

Taking the group as a non-sectarian whole, its political history, like its social and economic one, again fits a properly American pattern of success. At the obvious pinnacle of the White House, the list of presidents with an exclusively or predominantly Irish origin stretches from Andrew Jackson (1828–36) to John F. Kennedy (1960–3). Many who failed to gain the presidency made a powerful contribution to Washington politics, and they range from such figures as James G. Blaine in the late 19th-century Republican Party to speaker of the House Thomas P. O'Neill in the Democratic Party 100 years later. Because much that is important in the US federal system goes on in local politics, it is equally necessary to emphasize the role of Irish-Americans at this level, particularly in large urban centres. This is most obvious in the history of New York, Boston, and Chicago politics, but the list could be much extended. Any list of potent Irish-American political figures in this context would include John F. FitzGerald (1863–1950) in Boston, Richard J. Daly (1902–77) in Chicago, and Charles F. Murphy (1858–1924) in New York. Murphy was an unusually effective organizer in a long line of Irish-Americans involved with and usually dominating the political 'machine' associated with Tammany Hall, an organization which came to typify such politics in the USA. Such city power bases could be effectively linked to national politics, whether the example is Richard Daly's role in gaining John F. Kennedy the Democratic nomination, and the presidency itself, in 1960, or the way in which Alfred C. Smith emerged from Charles F. Murphy's organization first into New York state politics and then, as the Democratic candidate in 1928, to be the first Catholic to run for president.

That his religion was an important factor in Smith's defeat, and that Kennedy both suffered and gained in electoral terms because of his faith and origins, is a reminder of another kind of impact of Irish Catholic immigrants on the USA. This might be described as a negative impact. Anti-Catholic and anti-Irish feelings were frequently a force in American politics. The 'Know Nothing' movement of the 1850s, and the American Protective Association which reached its membership peak in 1895, are two examples of hostile, organized reaction to the Irish Catholic presence. The revived Ku-Klux-Klan, which reached its greatest potency in the 1920s, included anti-Catholicism in its litany of prejudices, and worked hard to block Smith's earlier attempt to secure the Democratic presidential nomination in 1924. By then Irish-Americans who were Catholic were linked to the battle to end prohibition, and so were 'Wets'. Those who were Protestant were more likely to be 'Drys', determined to make the great Protestant prohibitionist crusade a successful one.

Clearly by this time, and indeed long before it, Irish-Americans broadly defined were showing a tendency to be divided on many issues along what, in Ireland itself, would be seen as predictably antagonistic lines. The first Irish-American president, Andrew Jackson (both of whose parents were Presbyterians from Co. Antrim), was able to appeal to an undifferentiated Irish vote, confident that his own deep-seated hostility to the British crown would be attractive to the whole group. Very quickly divisions began to emerge, and by mid-century the two communities were largely, if never entirely, going their separate ways. Catholic

Irish-Americans were a vital element in Democratic Party support, while since its foundation in the decade before the Civil War Protestant Irish-Americans tended to support the Republican Party. There were, and are, of course, significant individual exceptions to this important general rule. Examples include Woodrow Wilson, the Democrat who was president 1912–20, and Adlai E. Stevenson I, Democratic vice-president 1892–6. But the political division could take extreme forms. The list of frequently sanguinary 'Orange and Green' riots in New York city stretches from the 1820s to the 1870s. There is evidence that those who led the *Scots Irish movement of the late 19th century tried to enlist support for opposition to *home rule. But such activity was trivial compared to the efforts of some Catholic Irish-Americans to activate their community in the cause of Irish nationalism.

Akenson, D. H., *The Irish Diaspora* (1993)

Doyle, D. N., 'The Irish in North America', in W. E. Vaughan (ed.), *New History of Ireland*, v: *Ireland under the Union 1801–70* (1989)

Miller, K. H., *Emigrants and Exiles* (1985)

SJSI

universities. Although there are references to attempted foundations in Dublin in 1320 and 1358, Ireland's first university was *Trinity College, Dublin (TCD), 1592. Although some of the Anglican elite continued even after its foundation to go abroad for higher education, the number was relatively small. Even in the second half of the 18th century Irish students enrolled in the universities of Oxford and Cambridge averaged only ten a year. By contrast Catholics and dissenters, formally excluded from TCD until 1793 and unwilling even after that date to submit to its Anglican ethos, were forced to look entirely outside Ireland, Catholics to the *Irish colleges of continental Europe, and *Presbyterians to the Scottish universities, especially Glasgow and Edinburgh.

From the late 18th century the demand for educational provision for Presbyterians in Ireland had led to the establishment of academies in several Ulster towns. Of these the *Belfast Academical Institution was the most distinguished, yet its ambition to become a college for Presbyterians was frustrated by government resistance to denominational universities. Magee College, founded in Derry in 1865 under the terms of the will of Martha Maria Magee, was a Presbyterian college that included faculties of arts and theology. As an approved college it shared in the fellowships of the *Royal University of Ireland, and on the dissolution of that body entered into an arrangement whereby Magee students could complete their degrees in TCD. Meanwhile the Presbyterian College, Belfast ('Assembly's College') (1853), catered for the theological training of Presbyterian students, who also followed courses in the newly established *Queen's College, Belfast. *Maynooth College, created in 1795 to provide for the training of Catholic priests in Ireland, initially included a school for the Catholic laity, but this closed in 1817.

The search for a form of university education acceptable to an increasingly assertive Catholic clergy and laity was to dominate policy-making for the next 100 years. Catholic rejection of the Queen's Colleges was followed by the attempted establishment of an autonomous *Catholic University. The Royal University of Ireland (1882) was another unsuccessful experiment, and numbers in the new colleges, apart from Belfast, remained low. Eventually the Irish Universities Act (1908) created two institutions, the Queen's University of Belfast and the *National University of Ireland (NUI), while leaving TCD untouched.

After *partition university education in Northern Ireland remained focused on Queen's. From 1945 increased funding and mandatory grants brought a considerable increase in numbers; in particular Catholic participation rose sharply, providing one seedbed for the growth of the *civil rights movement of the 1960s. Following the report of the Lockwood Committee on Higher Education (1965) a New University of Ulster, controversially located in predominantly unionist Coleraine rather than in largely nationalist Derry, was established in 1968. In 1984 it was merged with the Ulster Polytechnic (1971) and the Ulster College of Art to create the multi-campus University of Ulster.

In the Republic of Ireland higher education, though significantly less well funded, also expanded rapidly from the 1950s, the number of full-time university students rising from 6,796 in 1948–9 to 63,737 in equivalent institutions in 1998–9. Across that period the common perception of TCD and NUI as 'Protestant' and 'Catholic' institutions respectively largely disappeared. Following recommendations of the report of a Commission on Higher Education (1967), National Institutes of Higher Education were created in Limerick (1970) and Dublin (1976), both becoming universities in 1989. The NUI colleges at Dublin, Cork, and Galway and Maynooth College were granted independence in 1998; earlier, in 1968, government proposals (contrary to the commission's recommendations) for the merging of TCD and University College, Dublin, proved abortive.

KM

urban government in early modern Ireland developed in several dozen towns and proto-towns along broadly English lines. The English influence came by two routes. First, there was the small number of centres, less than twelve, where there was some measure of administrative continuity from the medieval colony. (There were of course many other boroughs with medieval charters, or the claim to medieval borough status, which lacked any tangible legacy.) Secondly, there were the entirely new plantation boroughs of late 16th- or early 17th-century creation which developed urban functions and local government relatively quickly—*Bandon, Londonderry (see DERRY), Coleraine, and *Belfast for example.

The corporate character of individual towns varied widely but actual practice was to a great extent determined by the attitude of the dominant landowner in the neighbourhood—burgesses were tenants first, freemen second. Depending on the charter, the chief officer was designated mayor, provost, sovereign, or portreeve, and municipal functions were supposedly shared with a group, usually twelve burgesses in all but the largest centres. In most cases these became a self-perpetuating group. At its simplest municipal governance was concerned with market regulation, the provision of petty justice, and the detention of malefactors, but in the larger jurisdictions the corporate framework allowed for much more diverse functions. However, even in these towns local government was rarely the exclusive concern of the municipal corporation; seigniorial manor courts and *parish vestries often assumed civic responsibilities, sometimes in the place of an active corporation.

Until the 1640s there was a sharp division between the corporations of the older towns, where there was an entrenched *Old English citizenry hostile to the state's religious policy, and those in the plantation towns where there were strongly Protestant but often quite independent civic leaders. The systematic expulsions of Catholics during or at the end of the *Confederate War opened several of the old towns to a new governing group. But *Restoration governments, confronted by religious dissent in some of these remodelled corporations, tightened their control over freeman admission and mayoral appointments, notably from 1671 (see NEW RULES). In turn *James II's government granted new charters in many cases and reopened civic office to those excluded since the 1640s. The last of the political twists came with the *sacramental test, which excluded dissenters from municipal office, permanently changing the character of local government in towns like Derry and Belfast.

In the larger Irish centres most Protestant freemen had at least nominal participation in local government through membership of chartered trade *guilds and with their civic freedom (which tended to overlap with trade freedom). In so far as all such towns were parliamentary boroughs, electoral calculation on the part of borough patrons (or aspirant patrons) overrode all other aspects of governance, and often quite distorted local constitutions. Some centres which were shackled by particularly oligarchic corporations—Belfast, Sligo, and *Limerick, for example—secured statutory 'police' commissioners or parish commissioners at the beginning of the 19th century to act in effect as a local governing trust. In the case of Dublin the powers of the aldermanic upper house had been diluted in 1760 after an effective campaign by the trade guilds, led initially by Charles *Lucas.

With the removal of statutory restrictions on Catholic civic freedom in 1793, municipal corporations had the option of formally admitting a larger share of their propertied citizenry; this in nearly all cases they declined to do. As a result Irish corporations came to be seen as bulwarks of Protestant reaction that deserved to be swept away in their entirety, this at a time when increasing numbers of the Catholic citizenry in nine of the largest towns were getting a taste for politics in so far as they were securing the parliamentary franchise as *40-shilling freeholders. The long and highly political battle over municipal reform (not of course an exclusively Irish issue) was finally settled in 1840, and even then the diminished powers of the new, more representative corporations was a major disappointment to the reformers. However, the campaign had given rise to the mammoth parliamentary report on Irish municipal corporations (1835), still the fundamental primary source for pre-reform urban history.

Urban government in independent Ireland reflects demographic and economic trends seen in many other European countries. Ever since independence there has been a drift of population from rural areas to large towns and cities. Expansion typically was accommodated by rather haphazard suburban development, which has created many serious infrastructural, social, and environmental problems. The fact that much urban growth has occurred outside the legal city limits has added to problems of co-ordination between the separate local authorities involved. Inner cities have suffered from long-term decay, traffic congestion, and population decline, although tax-aided private redevelopment schemes have wrought a partial revitalization since 1986.

Urban government has suffered from the same malaise as the rest of local government. Elected members of city councils or corporations (legally, these are termed county borough corporations) have little administrative power, while the presence of a partisan national party spirit in council chambers has tended to inhibit an effective approach to strategic issues. Urban status is prized almost solely as a matter of prestige, rather than as conferring any significant increase in practical powers.

Jupp, Peter, 'Urban Politics in Ireland 1801–31', in David Harkness and Mary O'Dowd (eds.), *The Town in Ireland* (1981)

DD/EO'H

urbanization over the last millennium has been a distinctly weaker process in Ireland than in Great Britain or elsewhere in north-western Europe. Irish towns before the 17th century were very small, and it is only since the 1960s that more than half the population on the island has lived in towns or cities. In the dominant narratives of Irish history, urban life and urban culture have played only a modest part. Towns and their creation have been characterized as alien, or at best as a conduit through which colonial and other unwelcome influences have entered.

More sympathetic studies of Irish towns and cities were for long restricted to single-case studies and biased towards the *architectural and monumental. Comparative studies of the history of Irish urbanization have been late in coming and have tended to be specific as to period. Medieval debates have centred on pre-*Norman urban origins; the nature and functions of the Anglo-Norman boroughs; the character and fortunes of the trading cities; and the almost complete absence of urbanization in Gaelic and Gaelicized areas. Early modern studies have been concerned with the fate of the *Old English urban communities; the role of towns in public and private policies of *plantation, reformation, and improvement; and the rise of *Dublin. More modern concerns include the evolution of the estate town; the rise and fall of municipal oligarchy (see URBAN GOVERNMENT); the mushrooming of the 18th-century port cities and the changing commercial hierarchy; the genesis of street architecture, planning, and property speculation; and the role of the towns in popular *politicization. From the early 19th century both the quality and range of evidence of urbanization improves dramatically: thus there is abundant documentation on the final stages of a long growth phase which in the case of most towns and cities was halted at mid-century, with urban expansion thereafter restricted to east and north Ulster and the greater Dublin conurbation. Little comparative work on this divergent experience has been done, although *Belfast's golden age of growth has attracted a considerable literature. Ironically, the urbanization of the Irish emigrant in Great Britain and North America has been far more closely studied than the domestic urban experience in the era of mass *emigration. The return of urban growth in the 1920s and its unbalanced character, the housing and transport revolutions in the following generation, and the impact of town and regional planning have been the subject of many micro-studies, but the literature remains strangely silent on the general character of this process and on the degree to which the Irish path to mass urbanization has been either innovative or unique.

Prior to 1550 three major phases of town development may be recognized. The first stirrings of town life occurred at *monasteries during the 7th century, and from *c.*900 one may talk about the existence of monastic towns. The second phase is represented by the *Vikings, who established port towns in the 9th and 10th centuries. The third phase occurred during the late 12th and 13th centuries when about 50 new towns were established by the Anglo-Normans.

Although founded primarily as hermitages, many monasteries had by the late 7th century attracted a dependent population of criminals, traders, and drifters. The description of Kildare, *c.*670, by Cogitosus emphasizes its populated nature. Ecclesiastical legislation permitted such people to live and work outside the holiest area of the monastery, i.e. outside the area which contained the church, shrines, and burial ground. Archaeological excavations at sites such as *Clonmacnoise, Co. Offaly, have located domestic occupation outside the centrally placed ecclesiastical zone; there the remains consist of round houses, boundary fences, a boat slip, and paved surfaces, as well as evidence for a range of craft working activities including bronze smithing, *gold working, *iron working, jet bracelet manufacturing, and comb making. Evidence for trade and exchange at monastic sites increases substantially after the year 900. *Fairs and markets were held; kings began to build their palaces at or beside churches; and there is increasing documentary evidence for domestic structures, for residential precincts, and for the presence of streets.

The construction, in 841, of *longphorts at Dublin and Annagassan, Co. Louth, marks the beginnings of Viking settlement. To date, nothing is known of the physical appearance of these centres but it has been speculated that they may have inspired the form and layout of the towns established in the following century. In 914 a great Scandinavian fleet landed at *Waterford, initiating a major phase of urbanization. *Cork was established *c.*915, while Dublin, abandoned in 902, was refounded in 917. Other fleets were responsible for the foundation of Wexford (*c.*921) and *Limerick (922). Archaeological excavation in Dublin, notably at *Wood Quay, has shed a great deal of light on the nature of these 10th-century towns. They were characterized by having a series of long narrow properties with houses fronting onto the streets, and were enclosed by a defensive rampart. Virtually all of the buildings were of wood with post and wattle as the most common form of construction; all were of rectangular plan with typical measurements of 25 by 18 feet. The archaeological evidence so far uncovered from Waterford dates to the 11th and 12th centuries but it parallels the Dublin record in many ways. At Cork the Scandinavians established themselves on an island in the estuary of the river Lee, immediately below the monastery of St Finbarr; by the 12th century it was defended by a stone wall with gates. Excavations at Wexford and Limerick have also uncovered buildings of Viking age date. Although claims have been made that Arklow and Wicklow were towns at this time, hard evidence is lacking.

The initial urban activity of the Anglo-Normans consisted of expanding pre-existing towns such as Dublin and Kildare. New towns, like *Drogheda, were founded before the end of the 12th century, however, and they were a common feature of 13th-century expansion and settlement. The chronology of town foundation is relatively short with Roscommon, established in 1282, as the latest example. The distribution of towns is predominantly eastern with westward extensions to Dingle, *Galway, and Sligo; this essentially reflects the areas colonized by the Anglo-Normans. The street layout was predominantly linear although more complex plans, such as the chequer patterns of Drogheda, New Ross, and Galway, also occur. Colonists were attracted by the offer of a plot of land within the town on which to build a house and by the opportunity of becoming a *burgess. The new towns normally possessed one parish church, in contrast with the older centres where many parishes are found, and all were *walled towns. The general pattern of urban development in the 13th century is one of expansion, followed by contraction in the 14th century, renewal in the 15th century, and expansion again in the 16th century. If one may generalize from the evidence at Kilkenny, Galway, and Dublin then it would seem that by the late 15th century urban government was in the hands of a self-interested local oligarchy. During the later Middle Ages a number of towns, such as Cavan, Granard, Co. Longford, and Sligo, were developed and patronized by Gaelic Irish lords.

The cycle of urban creation and large-town consolidation that occurred in the late 12th and 13th centuries may usefully be compared with the next such cycle, extending from the late 16th to the early 18th century. In both cycles there was a convergence of interest, albeit temporary and wavering, between an expansionary royal authority that saw in town foundation a means of strategic military control, and the colonial grantees and venturers for whom the attraction of settlers could best be achieved by offering them physical security and legal privilege in an urban setting. In both phases of urban growth there were many false dawns: over 330 Anglo-Norman boroughs were created by 1300 but more than two-thirds of them failed to develop identifiable urban characteristics. In the first half of the 17th century over 500 grants for the holding of markets were made, with a further 130 later in the century, some of which in both cases were revived 13th-century grants; again, a great many were stillborn. Indeed the obligation on late 16th- and early 17th-century plantation grantees to build towns and introduce 'civility' was not continued in the huge land grants of the *Cromwellian era.

At least ten of the larger medieval towns had 'Irishtowns', an indication that at critical moments in their history there had been some degree of ethnic exclusivity. By the late medieval period the provincial ports played up their allegiance to the English crown in formal contrast with the rebels at their gates, but in reality with depopulation and isolation their cultural make-up had become fairly mixed. Something similar was to occur in the larger cities in the second cycle: in nearly every case their Catholic and predominantly Old English inhabitants were expelled beyond the walls, whether by military action between 1644 and 1655 or through the enforcement of anti-Catholic legislation after 1692. Immigrants at first filled their shoes, and thus the chief ports of the south and east had a predominantly Protestant citizenry around 1700. But as these centres grew in size and complexity in the 18th century the migration field became more local and the migrants predominantly Catholic; formal blocks on trade and residence gradually broke down again.

Despite these parallels, the wave of urbanization during the 'long' 17th century also had its distinctive features. Urbanization in Ulster moved from being of marginal significance in the 13th century to centre stage, with many successful foundations, including the port town of Belfast; there were the first signs of town planning, notably in the greenfield sites at *Derry and *Bandon; and there was a sharp divergence of trend among the two dozen established trading centres: some of these marked time (for example, New Ross, the largest medieval walled town); others enjoyed a short-lived greatness (notably 17th-century Youghal); and a select few cornered the lion's share of overseas trade for a longer period and expanded beyond their old walled cores as a result (Limerick, Waterford, and Cork). Dublin was a special case: its capital status had meant relatively little before the 1590s, but the growth of the apparatus of the state and its increasing attractions as a social centre for the new gentry class propelled it far beyond the size of any Irish town. It undermined its rivals in Leinster and became the main port and market for food and fuel within the Irish Sea by 1700.

In the following century and a half the runaway growth of Dublin and Cork slackened somewhat, and many of the second-line cities and market towns displayed greater demographic dynamism. There were several reasons for this: the gradual reorientation of Irish foreign trade towards short distance Anglo-Irish exchanges gave the secondary ports a chance to compete on more equal terms; these centres developed complex service and industrial functions with the growing wealth of the consumers in their hinterlands; and with the general growth of Irish population in the later 18th century and beyond, many Irish towns developed labouring ghettos, at first on the approach roads and in the suburbs, later among the obsolescent housing stock within the urban core.

The cycle of urban creation during the 'long' 17th century also involved more modest initiatives: the establishment of *estate villages with limited commercial functions and no corporate life. It has been estimated that landlords were involved in the development of around 750 such villages between 1600 and 1850. The successful ones were a means of introducing immigrant craftsmen and of providing a market for tenants' produce, and a minority (for example, Cookstown, Co. Londonderry, Castlecomer, Co. Kilkenny, and Mitchelstown, Co. Cork) developed into major wholesale centres, even challenging existing county towns (as in the case of Tullamore in King's County and Westport, Co. Mayo). In such settlements the market place and the Church of Ireland church usually formed the key elements in the urban plan.

Most Irish urban places were in trouble by the second quarter of the 19th century: population had in many cases trebled in fifty years, and the infrastructure rarely managed to cope with the new urban poor. The startling decline of workshop industry coupled with rural economic distress was a poisonous mix. The problem was compounded by a growing hostility between those who controlled municipal government and the bulk of the governed; the constitution of Irish corporations, restricted in the 1670s (see NEW RULES), seemed increasingly inappropriate with the slippage of Protestant numbers and the continuing denial of civic freedom to Catholics even after the *Catholic Relief Act of 1793 had theoretically admitted them to participation in corporate political life. The politicization of municipally unenfranchised Catholic freeholders put town corporations on the defensive and delayed local ameliorative action.

Municipal reform when it finally came in 1840 changed the party colour of the aldermen (outside Ulster), but the social malaise of the towns was only very slowly addressed. Legislation reorganizing the *poor law, public health, and urban infrastructure drew on British precedents but enforcement followed at an embarrassing distance. The problem in most towns was a declining tax base, the result of the general fall in urban population after 1850 (to urban worlds outside Ireland) and of the specific movement of middle-class residents to suburbs outside the municipal jurisdiction (Dublin was the most extreme case of this). By contrast the tightly conservative burghers of Belfast during its period of break-neck growth were far more successful in providing an acceptable urban environment for its citizenry; but they had the financial resources so to do. A measure of their distinctive self-belief is the construction of two town halls within 40 years, the second (1906) being the most elaborate piece of civil architecture ever erected in an Irish town.

Elsewhere the increasingly democratic municipal governments were presiding over what were statistically stagnant urban communities. But Irish town life by 1900 was being transformed in a number of ways: the *railway, the omnibus, and then the tramway heightened social segregation, then allowed all the possibility of at least periodic escape to the new *seaside towns; working-class culture in city and town was being redefined by the availability of cheap newsprint, spectator *sports, *trade unions for the unskilled, and a very visible range of religious organizations seeking working-class support.

The resurgence of large towns from the 1920s and their acceleration in the 1960s reflected first industrial growth, and then the late 20th-century service revolution. However, in the case of Belfast, much of its metropolitan population moved to dormitory towns and secondary nodes in the region. In the case of Dublin, despite talk of green belts and decentralization, the conurbation doubled in population between the 1920s and the 1980s; the major population shift was first to a series of new working-class suburbs, and from the 1950s to a series of satellite 'towns' around the western perimeter of the city-region. Urban housing stock was transformed from the 1920s, first by local authority slum clearance programmes, and later by private speculative developers: in 1981 two-thirds of the houses in the Dublin region were less than 40 years old. No Irish city encouraged either a high-rise business district or (with the exception of the troubled Ballymun development north of Dublin in the 1960s) high-density public housing. The low-density character of the Irish urban environment at the end of the 20th century was a largely fortuitous bonus arising from the discontinuous pattern of Irish urbanization.

Bradley, John, *Walled Towns in Ireland* (1995)

Doherty, C., 'The Monastic Town in Early Medieval Ireland', and Bradley, J., 'Planned Anglo-Norman Towns in Ireland', in H. B. Clarke and A. Simms (eds.), *Comparative History of Urban Origins in Non-Roman Europe* (1985)

Graham, B. J., and Proudfoot, L. J. (eds.), *An Historical Geography of Ireland* (1993)

Harkness, David, and O'Dowd, Mary (eds.), *The Town in Ireland* (1981)

Wallace, P. F., 'The Archaeological Identity of the Hiberno-Norse Town', *Journal of the Royal Society of Antiquaries of Ireland*, 122 (1992)

JBr/DD

urraght, see OIREACHT.

Ussher, James (1581–1656), *Church of Ireland bishop and scholar. Born of an established Anglo-Irish family in Dublin, Ussher was educated there in the newly founded *Trinity College, staying on to become professor of theological controversies. In 1621 he was appointed to the see of Meath, two years later he was made a privy counsellor, and in 1625 King James promoted him to Armagh.

Ussher was a meticulous scholar with an international reputation in the fields of biblical chronology and early church history. Together with other Protestant and Catholic scholars such as *Ware and the Franciscan John Colgan, he made a major contribution to the study of St *Patrick and the early Irish church. At the same time he used these researches to construct a legitimate parentage for the Church of Ireland, seeking to demonstrate in his *A Discourse on the Religion Anciently Professed by the Irish and British* (1623) that it was the heir of a largely Protestant *Celtic Christianity. Theologically, Ussher was a firm Calvinist, deeply hostile both to Catholicism and to the alleged abandonment of the doctrine of predestination by a supposed 'Arminian' party within the Church of England. He devoted much of his scholarly energies to controversial theology, seeking to refute Catholic doctrine in great detail. As a churchman, though anxious whenever possible to secure time for academic research, he was a reliable administrator and responsible leader, using his position as privy counsellor to defend the church and its property. After the new lord deputy, Thomas *Wentworth, imposed the English Thirty-Nine Articles on the Church of Ireland in 1634, Ussher, always a stout defender of the independence of the Irish church, largely withdrew from public political life, leaving the task of running the Irish church to Wentworth's ally John *Bramhall. In 1640 Ussher visited England, being forced to remain there permanently by the outbreak of the *rising in 1641. He played a subsidiary role in the events leading up to the Civil War, advising the king, and ministering to Wentworth before his execution. Though a firm royalist, his tolerance of *puritans in Ireland ensured that he was respected by *Cromwell, who, when Ussher died on 21 March 1656, ordered that he be buried in Westminster abbey.

Knox, R. B., *James Ussher Archbishop of Armagh* (1967)

Trevor-Roper, Hugh, 'James Ussher, Archbishop of Armagh', in *Catholics, Anglicans and Puritans* (1989)

AF

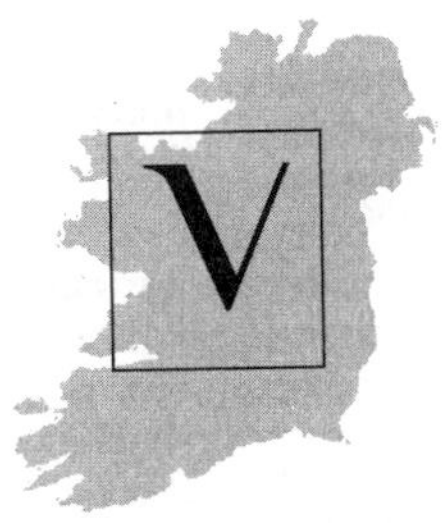

Valence, de, family. Following the death in 1245 of the last son of William *Marshal the elder, the great lordship of Leinster was partitioned between his five daughters. The second of these, Joan, wife of Warin de Munchensy, was already deceased, and thus her share went to her daughter, also Joan, who was married to William de Valence, the half-brother of Henry III. On 12 August 1247 King Henry instructed that Joan and William be given possession of their share of the estate, which consisted of the towns of Wexford, Ferns, Rosslare, Bannow, and Ferrycarrig, all in Co. Wexford, and Odagh, Co. Kilkenny. William, who was created earl of Pembroke in 1264, died in 1296, while Joan died in 1307, to be succeeded by their son Aymer de Valence. At Joan's death the Irish estate was valued at £324, but by 1324 it was worth only £214, and much of it had been repossessed by the Irish. The de Valences were almost always absentees from Ireland, and when Aymer, earl of Pembroke and lord of Wexford, died without issue on 23 June 1324, the de Valence interest in Ireland came to an end, the estate being divided between his nephew and two nieces. SD

Valera, Eamon de (1882–1975), pre-eminent leader in post-independence Ireland. Born in New York but brought up in Limerick, de Valera studied mathematics at the Royal University. In 1908 he joined the *Gaelic League and remained dedicated to the Irish language. He joined the *Irish Volunteers in 1913 and during the rebellion of 1916 commanded the 3rd Battalion at Boland's Mill. Sentenced to death, de Valera was reprieved partly because of his American birth.

On his release from prison in 1917, de Valera was elected MP for East Clare and became president of both *Sinn Féin and the Irish Volunteers. In 1918 he and other Sinn Féin leaders were arrested for complicity in an alleged German plot. He escaped from Lincoln jail in February 1919 and was elected president of the first *Dáil. In June 1919 he went to America and raised over $5 million for the republican cause but failed to obtain American recognition for the republic. His visit also led to a bitter power struggle with the leaders of the Irish-American movement, John *Devoy and Judge Cohalan.

After his return from America in December 1920, de Valera's relationship with Michael *Collins, who had effectively masterminded the *IRA campaign in his absence, came under strain as differences emerged over the conduct of the *Anglo-Irish War. These were accentuated when de Valera decided not to lead the Irish delegation that negotiated the *Anglo-Irish treaty. There have been two opposing interpretations of this decision. The more hostile view is that he allowed Collins to take the responsibility for what he knew would be a partial surrender. His own explanation was that by staying in Dublin he could better preserve national unity and ensure general acceptance of any agreement reached.

De Valera rejected the Anglo-Irish treaty and resigned as president following its acceptance by the Dáil. In the run-up to the *Civil War, he found himself sidelined by more hardline opponents of the treaty, who distrusted his alternative of *external association, while attracting fierce criticism from pro-treaty supporters for his inflammatory speeches. After civil war broke out in June 1922, his attempts to maintain a republican political organization were rebuffed by the republican military leaders, particularly Liam *Lynch. Lynch's death enabled de Valera to reassert some control and in May 1923 the war ended. In August 1923 he was arrested and spent a year in jail.

After his release, de Valera became increasingly dissatisfied with Sinn Féin's political abstention and in 1926 he formed a new party, *Fianna Fáil. In 1927 he reluctantly took the *oath of allegiance and entered the Free State Dáil. He spent much of the next five years building up the party organization to a formidable machine and establishing a newspaper, the **Irish Press*.

Fianna Fáil's election victory in 1932 marked the beginning of sixteen years in power during which de Valera was both prime minister and minister for external affairs. Policies of promoting small-scale tillage farming and industrial development behind high tariff walls, reinforced by the *Economic War, reflected the traditional nationalist goal of economic self-sufficiency. On the political front, de Valera saw off the threat from both the *Blueshirts and the IRA and in 1937 his new *constitution was enacted. In foreign affairs de Valera achieved some notable successes. The Economic War was concluded in 1938 on very favourable terms and at the *League of Nations de Valera was president of both the council and the assembly.

During the *Second World War Irish *neutrality caused friction with the allies but had overwhelming popular support. After the war, the economy and emigration were serious problems. During 1948–51 and 1954–7 Fianna Fáil lost power to *interparty governments. Fianna Fáil won the 1957 election with a big majority, and in the last two years of de Valera's political career the *First Programme for Economic Expansion was implemented. In 1959 he resigned as *taoiseach and ensured the succession for *Lemass. He served two terms as president 1959–73.

With the opening of private and public archives since the 1970s, many aspects of de Valera's complex political legacy are being reassessed. There is his role in the Civil War and his relations with the other republican leaders; the development of Fianna Fáil and his own record as a master of political tactics and strategy; his relations with his cabinets; the drafting of the 1937 constitution; church–state relations, which were often less harmonious than has been assumed; the economic and social policies pursued by his ministers, and in particular a reassessment of the 1950s as a watershed decade in post-independence Ireland; the failure to make progress towards either of his cherished aims of ending partition and restoring the Irish language.

No satisfactory biography of de Valera has yet appeared. Lord Longford and T. P. O'Neill, *Eamon de Valera* (1970) is an official biography, to be used with care. DMcM

Vallancey, Charles (*c*.1726–1812), engineer and antiquary. Born in Windsor of French stock, Vallancey arrived in Ireland in about 1750, and was employed there as a military engineer from 1760. His travels catalysed his subsequent obsession with the language and history of Ireland. Despite acquiring only a minimal knowledge of either, he published a number of works from 1772, in which he made extravagant claims for the origins and antiquity of the language. He related it variously to Algonquin, Sanskrit, and Arabic. He was a founding member of the *Royal Irish Academy, served as secretary to the Society of Antiquaries in Ireland, and in 1784 became a fellow of the Royal Society, but today is remembered more as an eccentric than as a serious scholar. NG

Vatican councils. The first Vatican Council (the 20th ecumenical council by Catholic reckoning) met in Rome under Pius IX in 1869 and was suspended due to the Franco-Prussian War in 1870. Responding to intellectual change and the declining political status of the papacy, it produced two doctrinal constitutions. *Dei Filius* (1870) treated of the relationship between faith and reason in the world while *Pastor aeternis* (1870) defined the jurisdictional primacy of the pope. The latter's elaboration divided the council fathers, a minority, including *MacHale, opposing it. Archbishop *Cullen's schema finally carried the day, providing for a moderate form of papal infallibility, restricted to those occasions when, speaking *ex cathedra*, the pope defined a doctrine regarding faith or morals. The council marks the high point of the *ultramontanist movement in the church.

The second Vatican Council (1962–5), for Roman Catholics the 21st ecumenical council, was convened by John XXIII to modernize church teaching, discipline, and organization. In Ireland implementation of the council's decrees was obedient but pragmatic and proved insufficient to the new needs of the Irish church. In fact, the almost global acceptance of the reforms and the maintenance of a high practice rate hid a gradual decline in traditional Catholicism characterized by the personalization of religious sentiment, moral individualism, and doctrinal indifferentism. TO'C

Verdon, de. The first member of this family to enter Ireland was **Bertram** (d. 1192), from Alton in Staffordshire, who took part in Prince *John's expedition of 1185 and was left as John's seneschal on his departure. About 1189 Bertram was granted by John substantial lands in Co. Louth, to hold in return for providing the service of 20 knights. These lands came to include the baronies of Lower Dundalk (the Cooley peninsula), Upper Dundalk (in which the town of Dundalk is situated and which was the caput of the de Verdon lordship until the great castle at Roche was built in the mid-13th century), and Ferrard; they also claimed lands in part of the modern Co. Armagh. After 1244 the de Verdons secured by marriage a half-share in the great lordship of Meath, thereby gaining lands in counties Meath, Westmeath, Longford, and Offaly. Several members of the family were responsible for an outbreak of disturbances in Co. Louth in 1312, but they played a prominent role in opposing the invasion of Edward *Bruce three years later. When the head of the family, **Theobald**, the great-great-great-grandson of Bertram de Verdon, died in 1316 without a male heir, the Irish estate, as well as lands in England and the Welsh marches, was partitioned among heiresses, and although cadet branches of the family survived in Ireland for centuries, their days as one of the leading Anglo-Irish aristocratic families were ended. SD

Vere, Robert de (1362–92), earl of Oxford and duke of Ireland, favourite of *Richard II. De Vere's appointments in 1385 and 1387 as marquis of Dublin and duke of Ireland should probably be understood in the light of contemporary English political affairs. The grants gave him *palatinate powers; writs ran in his name and his arms replaced the king's. He never came to Ireland, and in 1387 fled from England after the Merciless Parliament condemned him with other supporters of Richard. DBJ

Vescy, de. This family's connection with Ireland was of limited duration. Following the death without male heir of the last of the *Marshal family, their lordship of Leinster was divided between heiresses (the five daughters of William *Marshal the elder) in 1247. The fourth daughter, Sibyl, was already dead by this date, and her one-fifth of Leinster was divided in turn between her seven daughters. One of these, Agnes, was married to the important English baron William de Vescy, and she gained by the partition the castle and manor of Kildare. In time, Agnes became the sole ruler of the *liberty of Kildare (owing only money payments to her sisters), which, for administrative purposes, included not only the modern county but Laois and Offaly, whose holders, however important in their own right, owed suit at the county court of Kildare. Agnes was dead by June 1290, and was succeeded by her son William de *Vescy, who tended to exercise his authority in a high-handed and unscrupulous manner, and thereby aroused the opposition of his tenants. In 1297 he surrendered his Irish lands to the king, whereupon Kildare became a royal shire, and the de Vescy interest in Ireland came to an end. SD

Vescy, William de, justiciar of Ireland 1290–4, lord of Alnwick in Northumberland. He inherited the *liberty of Kildare in 1290 and was appointed *justiciar on 12 September. Although relations with the Irish were comparatively peaceful during his justiciarship, it was marked by a series of legal disputes and a violent disagreement with the baron of Offaly, John fitz Thomas. Various complaints were made against de Vescy in the English parliament in 1293, and at a council in Dublin in April 1294 he and fitz Thomas made mutual accusations, the latter alleging that de Vescy had slandered the king. They challenged each other to battle but de Vescy won by default when fitz Thomas failed to appear on 24 July. By then, however, he had been removed from the justiciarship. In 1297 he surrended his liberty of Kildare to the crown. SD

veto, contemporary shorthand for proposals to give the monarch power to approve or reject candidates for appointment to Catholic bishoprics in Great Britain and Ireland. The aim was to make *Catholic emancipation more acceptable, by ensuring that spiritual authority remained in loyal hands. First proposed in 1782, the veto reappeared during parliamentary debates on the Catholic petitions of 1808 and 1810 and on *Grattan's relief bill of 1813. A strong majority of Irish Catholics, led by *O'Connell, rejected any extension of state control over their church. The Catholic bishops, some of whom had earlier (1799) accepted the idea in principle, now declared it unacceptable, despite a rescript in its favour by Giovanni Quarantotti, secretary of *Propaganda. A pro-veto minority, headed by Sir Edward Bellew, Lord Trimleston, and R. L. *Sheil, seceded from the main Catholic movement in 1815. Hostility to the veto also divided Irish Catholics both from their English co-religionists and from sympathetic Protestant liberals. Catholic politics were thus radicalized, preparing the way for the militant emancipation campaign of the 1820s.

Vikings, Scandinavian adventurers, subsequently known as Ostmen (Old Norse 'men of the east') or Lochlannaigh (Irish 'people from the land of loughs'). They first appear in Irish sources as plunderers and this remains their dominant image in popular memory. In reality their involvement with Ireland lasted almost 400 years, during which time the Scandinavians were transformed into farmers, traders, colonists, and *urban developers.

The first Viking raid on Ireland occurred in 795 when Reachrainn, probably Rathlin Island (but Lambay Island has also been suggested), was attacked. During the next 25 years there was, on average, one Viking attack per year. The raids were hit-and-run affairs. *Monasteries were the prime target, not only because they possessed treasuries of precious objects but also because they were densely populated centres with substantial stores of provisions and potential slaves. Archaeologically this phase of activity has left no trace in Ireland, but about 60 metalwork objects of Irish manufacture have been discovered in graves of 9th-century date in western Norway. These artefacts are normally interpreted as the result of plundering raids, but it should be noted that most of the objects are domestic in function and may have been the result of trade or exchange.

The pattern of hit-and-run raids ceased during the 830s with the arrival of large Viking fleets on the rivers Liffey, Boyne, Shannon, and Erne. The forces transported by these fleets were substantial and, commonly, they terrorized an area for some weeks or months before returning to Scandinavia for winter. The success of these campaigns clearly gave rise to the next development, the foundation of *longphorts at *Dublin and Annagassan, Co. Louth, in 841. These were the first permanent Viking settlements in Ireland and were originally envisaged as defended bases in which the Scandinavian forces could overwinter and plan the renewal of campaigning in the spring. In the course of the 9th century Dublin developed into an important slaving centre and some of Dublin's rulers, notably Olaf the White (d. 871) and Ivar the Boneless (d. 873), campaigned extensively in Scotland and Northumbria, from where they brought valuables and slaves to the Dublin markets. While the longphorts provided the Vikings with a permanent base, they also gave the Irish kings a fixed objective to attack. In 848 the longphort at *Cork was captured, while the assault on Dublin in 902 was so successful that the Vikings abandoned the settlement and moved to northern Britain and the Isle of *Man. Archaeologically little is known about the nature of these longphorts. The cemetery of the 9th-century Dublin Vikings has been uncovered and shows, not surprisingly, that warriors formed a prominent element of the population. There are some hints of rural settlement in the immediate vicinity of Dublin at this time and there are slight indications of rural colonization in underpopulated areas such as western Connemara.

In 914 a great Scandinavian fleet, originating in northern France, landed at *Waterford, initiating a new phase of plundering activity. Munster was devastated in 915 and Dublin was re-established two years later. The Viking position was consolidated in 919 when they defeated the king of *Tara, *Niall Glúndub, in battle. Other fleets also descended on Ireland. *Limerick was founded in 922 by the leader of one such fleet and Wexford (*c.*921) by another. The kings of Dublin played an important role in Irish political life for much of the 10th century, although most of their attention was expended on controlling Northumbria and in obtaining authority over the other Viking centres in Ireland. Dublin and York were closely connected and were ruled by members of the same family until 952 when Olaf Cuarán (d. 981) was forced out of York and returned to Dublin. After their defeat at the battle of Tara (980) the role of the Scandinavians diminished and their territories were gradually integrated into the Irish political framework.

The significance of the battle of *Clontarf (1014) has been much overestimated largely due to the literary skills of the compiler of the **Cogadh Gáedhel re Gallaibh*, a 12th-century work eulogizing the Uí Briain. In more recent centuries the battle acquired mythic status in nationalist historiography as a synonym for the defeat and expulsion of invaders. In fact Limerick had been captured by the *Dál Cais in 967 and it was to be ruled by their descendants until 1197. Dublin maintained a semblance of independence until 1052 when the king of Leinster, *Diarmait mac Máel na mBó, forced the Dubliners to accept his son Murchad as their ruler. Paradoxically, however, as Dublin's political power declined its economic importance increased and from 1049 onwards any king with pretensions to the *high kingship of Ireland had to control Dublin.

It has been argued that the Vikings had a negative impact on Irish society, promoting violence, accelerating church abuses, and terminating the 'golden age' of Irish art. Modern historiography, however, has largely discredited these views and the port towns of Dublin, Wexford, Waterford, Cork, and Limerick are generally regarded as the Scandinavians' most enduring legacy. Archaeological excavations have yielded good evidence of the urban layout and building fabric of these 10th–12th-century towns but less is known about rural settlement in their vicinity. Each port had a rural hinterland (that of Dublin is referred to as Dyflinarskíri), and the archaeological evidence suggests that they were settled by a mixed community that was heavily Hibernicized. Scandinavian settlement in Ireland is unusual in its urban bias and motives more complex than the provision of pirate bases may have influenced the foundation of these towns. They were all well placed, for instance, to take advantage of trade with the interior. The colonization of large tracts of territory does not seem to have been a primary objective of the Scandinavians in Ireland and it cannot be without significance that they put so much of their resources into the development of towns. An influencing factor in this regard may have been the view that Britain, rather than Ireland, was the principal area in which to achieve conquest and colonization.

Bradley, J., 'The Interpretation of Scandinavian Settlement in Ireland', in J. Bradley (ed.), *Settlement and Society in Medieval Ireland* (1988)

Ó Corráin, D., *Ireland before the Normans* (1972)
Smyth, A. P., *Scandinavian York and Dublin* (2 vols., 1975–9)

JBr

Vinegar Hill, near Enniscorthy, the main camp of the Wexford rebels in the *insurrection of 1798, successfully stormed on 21 June by 10,000 men under General *Lake. The engagement is remembered as the decisive defeat of the Wexford rebels, although in fact reinforcements under General Francis Needham arrived too late to cut off the rebel retreat, and they lost only 500 or so men out of a total of 20,000.

Volunteers, a part-time military force raised by local initiative during 1778–9. Its original purpose was to guard against invasion and to preserve law and order, at a time when regular troops had been removed to combat the *American Revolution, and government lacked the money to revive the *militia. Numbers rose from an estimated 12,000 in spring 1779 to 40,000 by September and to over 60,000 by May 1782. Members were drawn mainly from the urban and rural middle classes; officers, though elected by the rank and file, were generally from the gentry and aristocracy. The movement soon took on a wider political importance, both as the expression of an emerging middle-class consciousness and as the basis of a new kind of organized extra-parliamentary support for popular causes. *Grattan, the duke of Leinster (see KILDARE), and other *patriots took leading positions in the Volunteers, and under their leadership the movement played a central part in the campaign during 1779 for *free trade. During 1780–2 the Volunteers gave continued support to the more militant patriots, their Convention at *Dungannon (Feb. 1782) providing the starting point for the final, successful drive for *legislative independence.

Following the *Renunciation Act controversy the Volunteers, now under the leadership of *Flood and Bishop *Hervey, took up the issue of *parliamentary reform. A Volunteer National Convention in Dublin (10 Nov.–2 Dec. 1783) drew up a detailed reform plan, but the House of Commons rejected bills based on its principles on 29 November and again on 21 March 1784. By this time the majority of the landed and parliamentary elite had reverted to open hostility towards the sort of 'out of doors' opinion represented by the Volunteers. During 1784 some Dublin radicals, notably *Tandy, sought to broaden the base of the movement, recruiting growing numbers of working-class Protestants, and also of Catholics, who had up to this point been largely excluded from the movement in deference to the continued legal prohibition on their bearing arms. However, this attempt to compensate for the loss of elite patronage by creating a mass movement proved ineffective. Meanwhile *Charlemont, alarmed by signs that government might suppress Volunteering, successfully used his influence as commander-in-chief to damp down political agitation within the movement.

Enthusiasm for Volunteering recovered after 1789, as part of the general radical revival following the *French Revolution. The early *United Irishmen in particular looked to the resurgent movement as the instrument of reform, the staging of a third Dungannon convention (15–16 Feb. 1793) testifying to their hopes of repeating the triumphs of 1779–82. During 1793, however, the Gunpowder Act, prohibiting the import of arms, and the *Convention Act effectively killed off Volunteering, while the raising of a new militia, followed by the *yeomanry, removed its ostensible justification as a voluntary defence force.

O'Connell, M. R., *Irish Politics and Social Conflict in the Age of the American Revolution* (1965)

Wadding, Luke (1588–1657), Franciscan scholar and a leading light in the *Irish college movement. Wadding founded St Isidore's for Irish Franciscans in Rome in 1625 and with the assistance of Cardinal-Protector Ludovisi attached a college for diocesan clergy next door in 1627. Under Wadding's influence Irish Franciscan colleges were established in Prague (1629), Vielun, Poland (1645), Paris (1653), and Capranica, Italy (1656). However, dissension hit the secular college at Rome, with a Gaelic Irish coterie working to oust him from the rectorship.

In 1642 Wadding secured a subsidy for Owen Roe *O'Neill to return home and was subsequently appointed Roman agent to the *Confederate Catholics. He encouraged Innocent X to send *Rinuccini but considered the nuncio's excommunication of the supreme council in 1648 a mistake. Wadding edited the works of St Francis and the medieval scholar Duns Scotus (whom he claimed as Irish), and wrote a history of the order, *Annales Minorum* (1625–54). HM

Wadding, Luke (*c.*1628–1691), Catholic ecclesiastic. Vicar-general of the south-eastern diocese of Ferns from 1668 and coadjutor (assisting) bishop from 1671, Wadding succeeded to the bishopric in 1678 but was not consecrated until 1683/4 because of the tensions associated with the *Popish Plot. Like Oliver *Plunkett he was one of a new generation of bishops appointed to resume the work of reorganizing the Irish church along *Counter-Reformation lines after the disruption of the *Cromwellian years and the uncertainties of the period immediately following the *Restoration. His *A Small Garland of Pious and Godly Songs* was published in Ghent in 1684.

wake, a festive gathering round the body of a dead person prior to burial. Relatives, neighbours, and friends gathered to spend a night in drinking, singing, dancing, story-telling, and other amusements. Similar festive gatherings have been reported in both European and non-European societies from early times. Within Ireland itself they were to be found, at least up to the early 19th century, in Protestant Ulster as well as elsewhere. The custom can be interpreted as a means of honouring the dead person by a last feast in his or her honour. Alternatively it has been seen as an assertion of continuity and vitality in the face of mortality, a perspective which helps to explain the explicit sexual content of some of the rituals and games reported at Irish wakes. From at least the early 17th century wakes were condemned by the Catholic church as occasions of drunkenness, immorality, and impiety. But the tradition of a festive gathering remained strong up to the late 19th century or beyond, giving way at length to the more decorous assembly, characterized by collective prayer and expressions of sympathy, which survives in some circles up to the present.

Wales. Ireland and Wales are frequently bracketed together as 'Celtic' countries, largely on the basis of language. The Irish and Welsh languages do indeed share similarities of structure, though this fact is outweighed by the inability of the speakers of the one to comprehend the other. The Irish are 'Q' Celts (thus *ceann* is the word for 'head'), whereas the Welsh are 'P' Celts (their word for 'head' is *pen*). These linguistic divisions, however, did not prevent political and cultural ties being forged between south-eastern Ireland and south Wales during the early Christian centuries. Clear evidence of Irish links is provided by 40 *ogam stones, most of them in south Wales, testifying to the memory of Irish rulers in that area (*Brycheiniog* or Brecon). St David, whose main associations were also with south Wales, was mentioned regularly in Irish saints' Lives. There was an Irish translation of the *Historia Brittonum*. Christianity itself may also have reached Ireland from Wales. It was not until the *Viking centuries (800–1000) that the links between the Christian communities across the Irish Sea were seriously weakened and the Welsh scribes learned to differentiate between the Viking 'Gentiles' of Dublin (*Gynhon Dulyn*) and the Irish (*Gwyddl*).

During the early Christian period, *monasticism in Wales and Ireland seems to have been organized on similar 'Celtic' lines, with bishops playing a minor role. In modern times, however, Irish and Welsh have been divided by religion. Outside Ulster the religious identity of the majority of the Irish population is Catholic. In contrast Welsh identity since the late 18th century has been largely shaped by Calvinism. In Wales as in Scotland (another 'Celtic' country) Irish immigrants after the *Great Famine were made to feel unwelcome. The Monmouth militia was termed 'the Pope's Own' because of the large number of 'papists' in its ranks. In Wales, as in Ulster, many opposed the Irish *home rule bill of 1886 on the grounds that home rule meant Rome rule. The Irish were also seen as a threat to the survival of the Welsh language, since they turned more to English than Welsh as a means of communication. A Catholic Irishman, though a Celt, might feel as unwelcome in Celtic Wales as in Saxon England.

In broad political and social terms, however, the histories of Wales and Ireland offer many parallels. In particular both countries have experienced colonization at the hand of a more populous and powerful neighbour. By the 7th century the Britons had been driven west of the Severn. Offa's Dyke became the de facto border, though the Welsh, who still saw themselves as 'Britons', dreamed of driving the Saxons east, out of their homeland. (Welsh was in fact the Saxon word for the Britons. The Welsh themselves used *Cymry*, 'fellow countrymen', cognate with 'Cumbria' and related to 'co' as in co-operative.) A second wave of colonization from the east took place after the Norman Conquest of 1066 and it is this period which offers the closest parallels with Ireland after the *Anglo-Norman invasion of 1169. As in Ireland, English and Flemish settlers colonized the most fertile areas. As in Ireland, towns became English-speaking settlements from which the natives were excluded. And as in Ireland, a Celtic resurgence took place in Wales following upon the demographic crises of the mid-14th century. There was also a strong Anglo-Norman military presence in both countries, symbolized by the stone castles and earthwork *mottes of the marcher lordships. In fact the Anglo-Norman lords who had successfully established themselves in Wales in the century after 1066 moved to Ireland as their 'next assignment'. The Fitzgeralds, who took their name from Gerald of Pembroke, were the most successful of these conquistadors, occupying the rich lands of Leinster and the Golden Vale of Limerick. Like their equivalents in Wales these marcher lords enjoyed a great deal of power at the local level.

After the extension of royal power in England from the 1530s onwards, the incorporation of both Wales and Ireland into a wider monarchical structure became possible. English common law, English-style *county administration, and a state church on English lines were introduced into both Wales and Ireland. In Wales the changes met with some resistance, but this was soon overcome. In Ireland there was little resistance at first, but religion proved to be a stumbling block. In a period of prolonged Anglo-Spanish rivalry the strategic significance of Ireland for the Tudors was immense and Ireland became the target for a new wave of colonization. Such figures as Sir Henry *Sidney, Sir John *Perrott, and Sir John *Davies, all of Welsh background, played key roles in the Elizabethan conquest and the accompanying plantations, as did Welsh settlers of more humble origins. The work of *Gerald of Wales, who had commented on Ireland and Wales in the 12th century, was referred to 500 years later by Davies in his *True Causes*.

The Welsh model of Anglicization was indeed seen as appropriate for Ireland, but whereas Wales was, on the whole, incorporated peaceably into a closer union with England, Anglo-Irish relations remained troubled during the 17th century and erupted once again during the 1790s. There was no equivalent in Wales of the *insurrection of 1798.

During the 19th century, the economies of Wales and Ireland began to diverge. Large-scale industrialization came to south Wales (and parts of the north) in the form of coal and slate mining and iron working. This was in marked contrast to Ireland, where the Lagan valley in the north-east was the only area to be industrialized. It was industrialization which enabled Wales to avoid the massive depopulation and large-scale emigration which most of Ireland experienced after the Famine. In rural Wales, however, there were obvious parallels with rural Ireland, in particular the religious tensions existing between Anglican landlords and nonconformist tenants. In the 1859 Merioneth election tenants at Bala who had opposed the wishes of their landlord were evicted. The result was to create an enduring bitterness which led eventually to the decline of the Anglo-Welsh ascendancy. The rise of the 'Young Wales' nationalist party (Cymru Fydd) in the 1880s owed a great deal to the model provided by Parnell's *Nationalist Party. Indeed Tom Ellis, leader of Cymru Fydd, was known as the 'Parnell of Wales'. Liberalism, however, linked as it was to nonconformity, proved to be more powerful than nationalism in Wales. Welsh nationalism took a cultural form in the shape of enthusiasm for the Welsh language and attendance at festivals of Welsh culture (*eisteddfodau*). Here parallels with the *Gaelic League in Ireland suggest themselves.

During the 20th century Wales and Ireland took divergent paths. Ireland was partitioned into two states, one of which became the Republic of Ireland. In Wales, political nationalism remained very much a minority movement and south Wales, at the western end of the M4 corridor, became closely tied economically with southern England. In the choice between union and independence, Wales seems to have decided that its best interests lay with the Union, provided that its own cultural identity could be maintained.

Davies, R. R., *Domination and Conquest: The Experience of Ireland, Scotland and Wales 1100–1300* (1990)

Evans, D. Simon, 'The Welsh and the Irish before the Normans: Contact or Impact?', *Proceedings of the British Academy*, 75 (1989)

Morgan, K. O., *Rebirth of a Nation: Wales 1880–1980* (1981)

HK

Walker, George (*c.*1646–1691). The rector of Donoughmore, Co. Tyrone, Walker raised a Protestant force to secure Dungannon against *Tyrconnell in 1688, was joint governor during the siege of *Derry, and was killed at the battle of the *Boyne. His *True Account of the Siege of Londonderry* (1689) was attacked by the Presbyterian minister John Mackenzie and others as an exercise in self-glorification that ignored the Presbyterian contribution to the city's defence. The controversy partly explains the negative depiction of Walker as a self-promoting meddler by writers otherwise sympathetic to the Williamite cause, most notably T. B. Macaulay in his *History of England* (1849). (The added incongruity implied in Macaulay's depiction of a septuagenarian warrior, however, arises from a confusion of Walker's birth-date with that of his father.) In Protestant tradition Walker nevertheless remains the hero of the siege. A monument erected in 1828 by the *Apprentice Boys of Derry was blown up in 1973.

Walker, John (1768–1833), the founder of the Church of God (Walkerites). Walker was born in Roscommon, the son of a Church of Ireland clergyman. He graduated from *Trinity College, Dublin, in 1790, was ordained priest in the Church of Ireland, and from 1794 to 1804 served as a chaplain in Bethesda chapel, the spiritual centre of Church of Ireland *evangelicalism. Walker was also a fellow of Trinity College, an eminent classical scholar, and a formidable theological controversialist. In the early 1800s he became steadily more critical of the Church of Ireland and of his fellow evangelicals, resulting in his secession in 1804.

Walker was an anti-establishment Calvinist who advocated separation from the world and the pursuit of the apostolic authenticity of the primitive church. Although committed to the ideal of Christian love and fellowship, he was a notoriously vigorous critic of all other forms of religion but his own. His church spread to England and Scotland, but never amounted to more than a dozen small congregations. The significance of his career lies not so much in what he founded, as in the central place he occupied within the controversial landscape of Dublin evangelicalism at the turn of the century. DNH

Walker, William (1871–1918), socialist. Born in Belfast, the son of a shipyard worker, he was apprenticed after elementary school as a joiner in *Harland & Wolff. He represented the Amalgamated Society of Carpenters and Joiners on Belfast Trades Council. A *unionist politically, he helped found the Belfast branch of the Independent Labour Party in 1893. He was elected a poor law guardian in 1899 and a city councillor in 1903. In 1904 he became president of the Irish Trade Union Congress. He was an executive member of the British Labour Party. In 1905 he narrowly failed to get elected in the North Belfast by-election, the first of several attempts at getting into parliament. His input into the *Connolly–Walker controversy on socialism and nationalism, in the socialist paper *Forward*, is a classic statement of the unionist-labour outlook subsequently known as Walkerism. In 1911, Walker became an official in the new National Insurance scheme. PC

walled towns. Town defences not only provided protection against attack, they also formed barriers which permitted control of movement to and from the town; in addition, one of the most important functions of town gates was as customs posts where tolls were collected. Archaeological excavations have shown that the Hiberno-Scandinavian (see VIKINGS) towns were defended with ramparts of timber and earth from the early 10th century; at *Dublin and *Waterford these defences were replaced, during the early or mid-12th century, with walls of stone. There are indications that some contemporary monastic towns, notably Armagh and *Glendalough, were similarly defended.

The *Anglo-Normans, however, constructed most of Ireland's walled towns. Their initial defences were earthen but from the early 13th century onwards towns began to construct walls of stone. This was achieved largely with the help of murage grants which permitted the townspeople to collect tolls on specified goods brought into the town for sale. The moneys so collected were then expended on building and maintaining the walls. Town defences continued to be built until the late 17th century. Notable surviving examples include Athenry, Fethard (Co. Tipperary), and *Derry. JBr

Walsh, Peter (*c.*1614–1688), *Franciscan friar. Walsh supported the supreme council of the *Confederate Catholics in their conflict with *Rinuccini in 1648, and became a close associate of *Ormond. He was excommunicated in 1651 after the failure of an attempt to gain control of the Franciscan order for the Ormondist faction. Allowed to remain in Ireland by the Cromwellian regime, he went to Spain in 1654, returning after a spell in prison to England. Following the *Restoration he attempted, with Ormond's energetic backing, to build up a party among the Irish Catholic clergy in favour of the *Remonstrance. From 1669 he lived mainly in London, still Ormond's protégé. He published *The History and Vindication of the Loyal Formulary of Irish Remonstrance* (1674) as well as other historical and political works.

Walsh, William Joseph (1841–1921), Catholic archbishop of Dublin from 1885. Ordained in 1866, Walsh had been a professor at *Maynooth, where he revived the *Irish Ecclesiastical Record* and became president in 1880. A nationalist, he supported the *Plan of Campaign and *home rule but opposed *Parnell over his divorce case. Hostile towards *Redmond and *Dillon, he supported *Sinn Féin, and was a firm opponent of the *Government of Ireland Act, but strongly condemned violence. He wrote in support of a state-funded Catholic university, and became first chancellor of the *National University of Ireland. TO'C

Walton, Ernest T. S. (1903–95), Nobel prizewinner in physics (1951) with John Cockroft. Born in Co. Waterford and son of a Methodist minister, Walton was educated at Methodist College, Belfast, and *Trinity College, Dublin (graduated 1926). From 1927 to 1934 he worked at the Cavendish Laboratory (Cambridge) under Rutherford, earning his doctorate in 1931; while there he collaborated with Cockroft. He returned to Trinity College (1934) and in 1946 was appointed professor of natural and experimental philosophy. By deploying a particle accelerator, Cockroft and Walton raised charged particles to high energies, these streams of particles then being used to produce transmutations in the nuclei of atoms. Their work stimulated nuclear research worldwide. DJS

Wandesford, Sir Christopher (1592–1640), lord deputy (Apr.–Dec. 1640), cousin and right-hand man of *Wentworth, whom he followed to Ireland as *master of the rolls. Wandesford's loyalty was rewarded with a grant of the O'Brennans' lands in Kilkenny (1635). Wentworth left him as lord deputy to extract newly agreed subsidies, but he lost control of parliament and failed to prevent a commons committee departing to England to complain about misgovernment. He died in office. HM

Warbeck, Perkin (d. 1499), in Ireland as the pretender 'Richard IV', 1491–2, 1495, 1497 (see WARS OF THE ROSES). Apparently the tool of an English Yorkist agent, John Taylor, Warbeck, son of a burgess from Tournai, Flanders, arrived at Cork in November 1491 and began a sustained impersonation of Edward V's brother Richard, duke of York (1473–*c.*1483). He became a considerable threat to Henry VII by attracting support not only within Ireland, but also from Charles VIII of France, Margaret of Burgundy, Emperor Maximilian I, and James IV of Scotland, who married his cousin Katherine Gordon to the pretender in 1496. In July 1495, after an abortive landing in Kent, Warbeck joined a rebellion in Ireland led by Maurice, earl of *Desmond, besieging Waterford until beaten off on 3 August by Edward *Poynings. Rebuffed on returning to Ireland in July 1497, he proceeded instead to Cornwall. Captured by Henry VII, he was hanged at Tyburn two years later, along with the former mayor of Cork, John Water. EAEM

wardship, the right of a feudal lord to retain and profit from the land a deceased tenant had held of him by *knight service, until the legal heir came of age. In the medieval period the wardship of the lands of tenants-in-chief, who held directly of the crown, was a valuable form of political patronage; such wardships, together with the *marriages of the heirs, might be awarded on easy terms to those the king favoured, or simply sold to the highest bidder. The administration of crown wardships was normally entrusted to an official known as the *escheator. Sixteenth-century wardship was administered through commissions, but reforms were introduced by the commissions of 1616–19, and in 1622 a court of wards was established. By 1628 the court yielded £7,000 a year, or one-seventh of total Irish revenue. Wards were educated in *Trinity College, Dublin, and had to take the oath of *supremacy before entering into their estates. The *Old English objected in 1613 and seven of the *Graces, which seem to have had some effect, concerned the court. The administration was tightened by *Wentworth, who tried to increase the number of landowners holding by knight service and prevent evasion by the Statute of Uses (1634). This produced little income but it was a political irritant to all groups in Ireland. The court collapsed in the 1640s and was abolished by the Feudal Tenures Abolition Act (1666). RFF/RG

Ware, Sir James (1594–1666), the major Irish antiquarian of his age. Educated at *Trinity College, Dublin, under *Ussher, Ware became auditor-general (1632) and supported *Wentworth and *Ormond. His main interest was historical research: collecting manuscripts, editing texts, and compiling seminal works on bishops, writers, and antiquities, assisted by Gaelic scribes and scholars, notably MacFirbis (see LITERATURE IN IRISH). Ware wrote in Latin and pursued objective standards, but later translators and continuators (his son Robert and his grandson-in-law Walter Harris) intruded anti-Catholic sentiments. Ware (together with Ussher) helped create an Anglo-Irish identity by revealing the ancient Irish past to the *New English Protestant ruling class. HM

warfare in Gaelic society was on a small scale. The local battles of early Christian Ireland were waged by freemen whose landownership entailed military service to their kings, and who could be reinforced by pagan warrior-bands or *fianna*. After the *Viking invasions and still more in post-*Norman times there was an increasing use of mercenary troops, the cult warbands of the *fianna* giving way to paid bands of *ceithearnaigh*, or *kerns, though the methods employed changed little before the 16th century. An anonymous writer *c.*1515 calculated that the largest chieftaincy could field no more than 2,000 men (500 mounted spearmen, 500 *gallowglasses and 1,000 kerns) besides the irregular troops of armed subjects; the norm was 200 spearmen and 600 kerns, with the smallest districts furnishing perhaps 40 spearmen and 200 or 300 kerns. This reflected not only low population levels, but lack of financial resources in a rural, subsistence economy. Large imported warhorses, for instance, were unaffordable, and Irish cavalrymen used the small domestic breed. Technology was also primitive. In particular large-scale foundries seem to have been lacking, so that home-produced armour and weapons ran to chain mail rather than plate armour, and handguns rather than cannon. Fourteenth-century statutes forbade Anglo-Irish to supply armour, weapons, or horses to the Gaelic Irish at any time, though this was often violated. At the same time the rough terrain and poor communications made the reduction of little independent chieftainships difficult for the crown forces, and the small stone *tower houses of the 15th to early 17th centuries retained their defensive function long after cannon made private castles obsolete in England.

Some major battles are recorded, as when Brian MacMahon (Mac Mathghamhna) defeated the English of Co. Louth in 1346, killing at least 300 of his enemies—a figure confirmed by the kerns' custom, inherited from the warrior cults of earlier times, of decapitating the slain and counting the heads. However, most Irish chiefs used harrying and plundering, raiding at dawn, burning houses and crops, rounding up and driving off cattle, to gain control over additional subjects, or increase their political influence. Fighting took place as the pursuing force (*tóir*) caught up with the plunderers (*creach*), when the chief himself and his relatives defended the rear, while the light-armed kerns were chiefly employed in driving cattle. If warning was received, the raiders might have to pursue a band of refugees and cattle, the *imirce*, protectively surrounded by their spearmen and gallowglasses. The booty gained in such raids was quickly shared out among military followers, with shares to the church and the poets. With the possible exception of the Irish of Wicklow, the chiefs' profit from these raids lay not in the booty itself, but rather in gaining added territory, and enforcing tribute or *black rent from victims who feared a repetition.

Bartlett, T., and Jeffery, K. (eds.), *A Military History of Ireland* (1996)

Hayes-McCoy, G. A., *Irish Battles* (1969)

Simms, K., 'Warfare in the Medieval Gaelic Lordships', *Irish Sword*, 12 (1975)

KS

War of Independence, see ANGLO-IRISH WAR.

Wars of the Roses (*c.*1455–87), modern name for the civil war between the English houses of Lancaster and York, commencing under Henry VI (1421–61, 1470–1); continuing under the Yorkist kings Edward IV (1461–70, 1471–83), Edward V (1483), and Richard III (1483–5); and petering out after the accession of Henry VII (1485–1509). Ireland's role in the wars chiefly reflected its strategic importance as a springboard for invading England. It also supplied experienced troops—English 'bills and bows' (troops armed with the battleaxe with long wooden handle, or the longbow) and Gaelic *kerns—but not in overwhelming numbers. As in other outlying regions, feuding between the lordship's leading families became aligned in the 1450s with rivalries in England. The FitzGerald earls of *Desmond and *Kildare were retainers of Richard, duke of *York, while the 5th earl of *Ormond was a leading Lancastrian. The Yorkist ascendancy in Ireland was threatened by York's death at Wakefield (1460) but confirmed by the Yorkist victory at Towton (1461). Towton also consolidated Geraldine influence but precipitated a crisis of lordship. The accession of York's heir as Edward IV meant that his Irish estates were held by a permanent absentee; and after Ormond's execution for treason, the senior Butler line disappeared from politics until 1475, when the attainder was reversed. Ireland served as a base for Yorkist invasions of England in 1460 (by York himself) and 1487 (by Lambert *Simnel). Ormond's heir, Sir John Butler, led an unsuccessful counter-invasion in 1462; and the Yorkist pretender Perkin *Warbeck tried three times in the 1490s to wrest control of Ireland from Henry VII before the wars petered out. SGE

Waterford, the commercial centre of the south-east since the 12th century. Excellent deep berthage and relatively sheltered access encouraged permanent *Viking settlement on a promontory site around Reginald's tower in the early 10th century; the present structure, however, is probably of 13th-century date. Captured by *Strongbow in 1170, Waterford flourished for over a century as chief outport for the zones most intensively colonized by the Anglo-Normans in north-east Munster and south Leinster. Excellent navigation upstream along the rivers Suir, Nore, and Barrow led to a long history of commercial rivalry with Clonmel, *Kilkenny, and especially New Ross. But as a royal borough Waterford nearly always had the upper hand, and its resolute loyalty to the English crown, particularly in the 15th and 16th centuries, earned it valuable privileges.

The rigidly Catholic deportment of Waterford's merchants, nourished by close trading and educational links with France and the Low Countries, destroyed that relationship in the early 17th century. The city became a centre of *Confederate Catholic activity throughout the 1640s. After a long siege, however, what a contemporary had described as *Roma parva* fell to Cromwell's forces in 1650 and its burgher elite were expelled.

Waterford's hinterland remained overwhelmingly Catholic in the following century; thus Protestantization of the city was incomplete. In the great cycle of commercial growth from the mid-18th to the mid-19th centuries Catholic and Quaker (see SOCIETY OF FRIENDS) merchants played the leading part in the key sectors—the *Newfoundland provisions trade and fresh food exports to Britain. One such merchant, Edmund Rice, founded the *Christian Brothers and opened what became the order's first school in 1802.

Bacon and flour were the foundations of Waterford's prosperity until the end of the 19th century, but collateral industrialization was limited; population did not exceed 25,000 until 1901. Politically Waterford was less polarized than most Irish cities, and was remarkable for resisting the *Sinn Féin tidal wave in 1918.

The city's modern growth commenced only after 1945, when old industrial traditions in iron-founding, meat processing, and glass making were reinvigorated. Of these, crystal glass manufacture has made Waterford a brand name and the centre of a multinational 'giftsware' conglomerate. Meanwhile the surge in Irish/continental trade restored the port to its medieval significance.

Clarke, Clark (ed.), *Irish Cities* (1995)

Nolan, William, and Power, T. P. (eds.), *Waterford: History and Society* (1992)

DD

water power in Ireland can be traced back to the early Christian era. Then it was employed in grinding grain for family use. Primitive mills, powered by waterwheels, were usually sited along a small mountain water course. Many monastic settlements had water-powered grain mills. The waterwheels had their paddles set horizontally to catch the flow of water. They were attached to millstones which were turned to grind the grain. Some have been dated between AD 630 and AD 926. Water power technology remained at this level until the early 17th century *plantations. Settlers brought with them new developments in water power from Great Britain and the Continent. These were introduced or adapted to tasks previously performed by humans or animals. Among these improvements was the now familiar vertical waterwheel.

Water power was vital for industrialization, in a country largely devoid of coal and iron. In 1870 it provided one-quarter of Ireland's recorded horsepower, compared to one-twentieth of Great Britain's. The drawback of water power is that its user can be at the mercy of floods and frost in winter or droughts in summer. Its use was greatest in Ulster, particularly in the development of the *linen industry, from the first quarter of the 18th century. Then water was used in flax scutching mills, and in beetling mills, wash mills, and for rubbing boards in the bleaching process. In the 19th century, mechanized spinning and powerloom weaving were driven by water as well as *steam. Many model mill villages were specifically built on sites suitable for the exploitation of their water power resource. The *Ordnance Survey maps of the 19th century show an extensive network of rural mills, of every kind, powered by water. The main types were *flour mills, threshing mills, spade mills, saw mills, and *paper mills.

The turbine, pioneered by an Ulsterman, James Thomson, brother of Lord Kelvin and professor of engineering at *Queen's University 1854–73, was a significant development, making water power much more effective and removing the need for large waterwheels. Turbines in turn made possible the generation of *electricity by hydroelectric power. This was used from the end of the 19th century to run trams from Bessbrook to Newry in Co. Down and from Portrush, Co. Antrim, to the nearby tourist attraction of the Giant's Causeway. Later the same technology became the major source of electricity in southern Ireland, through the Shannon Hydroelectric Scheme at *Ardnacrusha.

Coe, W. E., *The Engineering Industry of the North of Ireland* (1969)

PC

Wellesley, Richard Colley (1760–1842), Marquis Wellesley, elder brother of *Wellington, *lord lieutenant 1821–8, 1833–4, having earlier been governor-general of India 1798–1805. His support for *Catholic emancipation, and his marriage in 1825 to an American Catholic, made him unpopular with Protestants. On 14 December 1822, after Wellesley had prohibited 12 July and 4 November celebrations in memory of *William III, he was the target of the 'bottle riot', when a quart bottle and part of a watchman's rattle were thrown at the viceregal box during a performance in a Dublin theatre. Reappointed as lord lieutenant (1833–4) by a *Whig ministry, he was unable to respond effectively to *agrarian protest, *Tithe War, and the *repeal agitation.

Wellington, Arthur Wellesley, 1st duke of (1769–1852). Though Irish born, the third son of the earl of Mornington, Wellington spent most of his long career, beginning as Britain's leading military commander in the *revolutionary and Napoleonic wars and ending as Tory prime minister 1828–30, outside Ireland. However, he sat in the Irish parliament as MP for Trim 1790–5, when he supported the *Catholic relief bill of 1793. His refusal to relinquish his military commitments made him a partially absentee *chief secretary for Ireland 1807–9, but he nevertheless carried through a reorganization of the Dublin *police.

Wentworth, Thomas (1593–1641), created 1st earl of Strafford in 1640, and appointed *lord deputy by Charles I in 1632. Wentworth aimed at restoring church and king at the expense of *Old English recalcitrance and New English corruption by an active policy, nicknamed 'thorough', in finance, religion, land, and administration.

Irish customs revenue was boosted and a regular subsidy obtained from the Dublin parliament by playing Old English off against New over the *Graces. Wentworth subsequently created a government party of trusted officials including *Wandesford, Sir George Radcliffe, chief secretary 1633–9, and Sir Philip Mainwaring, as well as various MPs divorced from country interests.

Wentworth forced the Church of Ireland *convocation to discard its 'Calvinistic' articles of 1615 and began installing high-church bishops such as John *Bramhall in Derry. Lay impropriations were attacked to strengthen the church financially and enable it to support a well-educated clergy.

By discovering ancient royal titles, Wentworth hoped to plant a quarter of Old English-held lands. Beginning in Connacht in 1635 juries proved crown title in Mayo, Sligo, and Roscommon, and eventually, despite the activism of Patrick *Darcy and Richard Burke, earl of *Clanricard, in Galway. Parts of Clare and Tipperary were also to be planted and Wentworth himself commenced in Wicklow. The object was to increase crown revenue and to so impoverish the Catholic gentry that they could no longer maintain their clergy.

Wentworth was not uniformly successful—the king eventually exempted the Clanricard estates in Galway. Richard *Boyle and Adam *Loftus may have been humbled but *Mountnorris escaped punishment for maladministration. Indeed, Wentworth's policies and *absolutist methods, including the manipulation of *Poynings's Law and the use of *Castle Chamber, alienated all sections of Irish society.

When war broke out in Scotland (1639), Wentworth imposed the *Black Oath and returned to England as the king's chief adviser. He was created earl and promoted to lord lieutenant. The Irish army he prepared to invade Scotland frightened the English parliament, which in November 1640 commenced impeachment proceedings. A delegation of Irish parliamentarians, combining Old and New English, testified against him. Although Wentworth countered charges of subverting the fundamental laws of England and Ireland, parliament passed a bill of attainder. 'Black Tom Tyrant' was so unpopular that the king was forced to assent to his execution on 12 May 1641. Van Dyck's two portraits of Wentworth—as the energetic administrator and the military governor—are hugely symbolic.

Kearney, Hugh, *Strafford in Ireland 1633–41: A Study in Absolutism* (1959)

HM

Wesley, John (1703–91), evangelist from whose work most of the *Methodist churches across the world, including Ireland, later emerged. Wesley made the first of 21 visits to Ireland in 1747 and by his death in 1791 there were some 15,000 members enrolled in Methodist societies, with many more under the influence of Methodist preaching. Wesley's approach to Ireland was based not so much on a planned and considered evangelistic strategy as on a set of religious and social assumptions which included dislike of Calvinistic Presbyterianism and Roman Catholicism. Although he was the author of one of the most ecumenically friendly letters to Roman Catholics written by an 18th-century Protestant, Wesley was generally ill-disposed to the effects of Roman Catholicism on the Irish population. Whereas in England Wesley saw himself as having a special ministry to the poor, in Ireland his mission worked downward from the gentry class and outward from the garrison. He helped revive the flagging religious zeal of European Protestant minorities (see PALATINES) and stimulated an *evangelical movement within the clergy and laity of the *Church of Ireland. His writings on Ireland and the Irish reveal a curious mixture of affection and impatience.

DNH

Westminster, Irish representation at. Ireland was represented in the United Kingdom parliament (see UNION, ACT OF) by 100 seats, increased to 105 in 1832 and reduced to 103 in 1870.

Ireland's MPs remained for most of the 19th century highly unrepresentative of the society they nominally spoke for. Those returned in the first two decades after the Union were drawn overwhelmingly from landed families, many of which had been prominent in the Irish parliament before 1800. All, up to 1829, were Protestant. *Catholic emancipation, *parliamentary reform, and the growth of popular politics somewhat broadened the social base of Ireland's parliamentary representation. Yet the hold of the Protestant propertied classes remained strong. Almost two-thirds of Irish MPs returned between 1832 and 1885 were from landed families, and a further one-fifth from professional backgrounds; about two-thirds were Protestants, among whom *Presbyterians were heavily outnumbered by members of the Church of Ireland.

A major shift in the social composition of Ireland's parliamentary representation began only with the general election of 1874, when for the first time half of the MPs returned were Catholics, and almost half from non-landed backgrounds. By 1885 Protestant landlords as a class had been eliminated from parliamentary politics outside Ulster. In the *Nationalist Party parliamentary representation was now divided between a Catholic upper middle class of landowners, businessmen, and professionals, and a gradually increasing lower middle class dominated by farmers, traders, and the lower professions. The decline of landlord power within *unionist politics was later, but no less inexorable. In 1885 landlords and sons of landlords still accounted for more than half of all Unionist MPs. By 1918 this had fallen to only 4 per cent, with leadership passing into the hands of the Protestant professional and mercantile elite.

The Irish MPs of the first two decades of the 19th century did not for the most part play a very prominent part in parliamentary affairs. The majority were noted mainly for their mercenary willingness to support whatever ministry was in power. Later there were to be attempts to create a separate parliamentary grouping, first in *O'Connell's *repeal party, later through *independent opposition. Neither of these initiatives, however, managed wholly to escape from the role of the Irish wing of British liberalism (see POLITICAL PARTIES). It is also important to remember that the great majority of those who sat as Irish members before the 1880s defined themselves in terms of British party politics, as Liberals or Conservatives. Even after that date the Irish Unionists were a part of the British Conservative Party, while Nationalists were less formally but nevertheless closely tied to the Liberals.

Westminster, Statute of (1931). The statute, resulting from the new definitions of dominion status negotiated at the imperial conferences of 1926 and 1930 (see COMMONWEALTH), abolished the right of the British parliament to legislate for the dominions under the 1865 Colonial Laws Validity Act. It also declared that the dominions must be consulted in matters affecting the royal succession, a provision of significance during the 1936 abdication crisis. Some Conservative MPs, including Winston *Churchill, sought to exclude the *Irish Free State from the statute's operation, arguing that it would enable the Irish to repudiate the *Anglo-Irish treaty, despite Irish assurances that this would be altered only by consent. However, their objections were overruled, and the Free State was the first government to ratify the statute. De *Valera, coming to power a year later, was reluctant to acknowledge the statute as a basis for Irish legislation. But when his bill abolishing the right of appeal to the privy council was declared *ultra vires* by the Irish courts in 1934, the judicial committee of the privy council itself ruled that in British law—though not in Irish—the Statute of Westminster gave the *Oireachtas the power to amend or repeal the *constitution of the Irish Free State. DMcM

Whately, Richard (1787–1863), archbishop of Dublin 1831–63. Whately came to the *Church of Ireland from a chair of political economy at Oxford. Unfamiliarity with affairs of church and state in Ireland did not inhibit him from exercising with vigour the powers of his office to further his broad-church and liberal principles. In contrast with his contemporary at Armagh, *Beresford, he proved accommodating, though by no means subservient, where government policy was concerned, and attracted criticism for his attitude to the *Church Temporalities Act and the *tithe question. His leading role in the establishment of the *national school system (for which he wrote some controversial textbooks) earned him particular opprobrium in some church circles. His relations with Archbishop *Murray were cordial, but, though a supporter of *Catholic emancipation, he had little sympathy with Roman Catholicism, or with the tractarians in his own church. KM

Wheatley, Francis (1747–1801), painter. Born in London, he was trained at William Shipley's academy, winning prizes from the Society of Artists in the early 1760s. He made a short visit to Ireland in 1767. In 1769 he enrolled at the Royal Academy Schools. His early work comprised mainly small-scale portraits, conversation pieces, and a few landscapes. He collaborated with John Hamilton Mortimer on the decoration of a ceiling at Brocket Hall, Hertfordshire (1771–3). In 1779 he fled to Dublin to escape his creditors and immediately received commissions for small whole-length portraits. His main achievement in Ireland was to paint a number of *Volunteer subjects. In 1780 he completed *View of College Green with a Meeting of the Volunteers*, and *The Irish House of Commons*. He also painted the *Review of the Irish Volunteers in the Phoenix Park* (1781) and *Review in Belan Park, Co. Kildare*, as well as drawings of Irish country estates. In 1783 he returned to London carrying with him sketches of Irish subjects which resulted in *Donnybrook Fair* and other items exhibited in 1784. He worked for the London print publisher John Boydell, and it was the work that Boydell engraved, such as illustrations to literature and the *Cries of London*, which established Wheatley's reputation. He also painted portraits, landscapes, and history subjects. He became a member of the Royal Academy in 1791 and died in 1801 after a long illness. JT

Whigs. The English Whigs originated as opponents of the succession to the throne of the future *James II. Later they provided the most committed supporters of the *revolution of 1688. From the 1690s, however, their transformation into a party of government (after 1714 the only party of government) gave them an increasingly oligarchic character, the radical implications of the original Whig appeal to a contract between rulers and ruled being developed only by the minority of *commonwealthmen. From the late 1760s the name Whig was revived, in a new, exclusive sense, by followers of the marquis of Rockingham, who attacked what they claimed was a revival of arbitrary royal power and denounced their ministerial opponents as *Tories. This new Whig Party opposed the wars against America and revolutionary France (though the latter issue produced a conservative secession led by the duke of Portland), and developed a programme of administrative reform, *parliamentary reform, and *Catholic emancipation.

In Ireland the defenders of the *sole right and opponents of the treaty of *Limerick formed an embryonic Whig Party, but clear-cut party divisions appeared only from 1703–4. As in Britain, Whigs defended 'Revolution principles' and advocated tough measures against Catholics and *Jacobites. They also advocated tolerance for dissenters in the name of Protestant unity, although given the numerical strength of Irish *Presbyterianism, they were notably less enthusiastic than their English counterparts about the admission of dissenters to full political rights.

From 1782 the English Whig Party saw the *Ponsonbys as the potential nucleus of a sister party in Ireland. However, it was only after the *regency crisis that a Whig Party emerged in the Irish parliament, uniting *patriots like *Grattan and *Charlemont with the Ponsonbys, the earl of Shannon (see BOYLE), and other political interests now out of favour. An Irish Whig Club was established in Dublin in June 1789, followed by a Northern Whig Club in Belfast (Feb. 1790), and smaller clubs in other centres. These were generally dominated by aristocrats and landed gentry, although two, the Belfast Whig Club and the Dublin-based Whigs of the capital, were more middle class in character. Basing themselves on the constitution of 1688 'as re-established in 1782', the Whigs advocated the reduction of government patronage, the exclusion of office holders from parliament, and financial accountability by the executive to parliament. From 1793 they also advocated parliamentary reform. The parliamentary following, initially 90 or more, slumped to 14 by 1797, as the middle ground of moderate reform had been eroded by sectarian and political polarization. However, some individuals, like Grattan, carried their Whig affiliation into the united parliament after the Act of *Union, and George Ponsonby led the party in the Commons during 1808–17.

From the mid-1830s 'Whig' was replaced as a party label by *Liberal, but was still used to describe aristocratic supporters of moderate reform from above, many of whom moved over the next few decades into the *Conservative Party.

Whitby, Synod of (664), the setting for the resolution of a local flare-up of the *paschal controversy in Northumbria. Oswald, king of Northumbria (634–42), was baptized in *Iona and introduced missionaries from there to establish the church in his kingdom. His brother King Oswiu (642–70), according to *Bede, 'thought nothing could be better than Irish teaching, having been instructed and baptized by the Irish and having a complete grasp of their language'. By this time the Irish churches were themselves divided on the paschal question, and an argument erupted in England between Bishop Fínán of Lindisfarne, originally from Iona, and a southern Irishman Rónán, 'who had been instructed in Gaul and Italy in the authentic practice of the church'. Their dispute divided the king, who followed the Celtic practice, and the queen, from Kent, who followed the Roman method. At a synod in Whitby, the centre piece of Bede's *Ecclesiastical History*, the queen brought the English Bishop Wilfrid and a Frankish bishop Agilbert, trained in the south of Ireland, to dispute with Fínán's successor Colmán, and King Oswiu agreed to adopt the Roman practice. The Iona clergy left Northumbria at this point, and Bishop Wilfrid toured England to spread the Roman practice there. The notion that this synod represented the end of an entity that could be called the Celtic church, independent of Roman control, derives from a simplistic Protestant reading of Bede's work. RS

White, (Capt.) J. R. (1879–1946). Born near Ballymena, Co. Antrim, the son of Field Marshal Sir George White, VC, he was educated at Winchester and Sandhurst, and won the DSO during the *Boer War. Reacting against his background, he took labouring jobs in North America and England. An anarchist, associated with *Connolly and Larkin during the *Dublin lockout, White largely established and drilled the *Irish Citizen Army, later calling it 'the first Red Army'. He joined an ambulance unit in France in 1914. He was charged with urging Welsh miners to strike against the executions following the *rising of 1916. He was later arrested during the 1932 *Outdoor Relief Protests in Belfast. PC

Whiteboys (Ir. *buachaillí bána*), a movement of *agrarian protest, so called because of the white shirts worn over everyday clothing. Protest began in Co. Tipperary in 1761, spreading to Cos. Limerick, Waterford, Cork, and Kilkenny, and continuing to 1765. The main grievances were the *enclosure of common land, the encroachment of livestock on tillage, and *tithes, especially on potatoes. A second wave of protest, in 1769–75, affected Kilkenny, Tipperary, Queen's County (Laois), Carlow, and Wexford, with tithes on corn, rents, and evictions as the major grievances. In the early 19th century, 'Whiteboy' continued to be used as a general term for agrarian protestors. The Whiteboy Acts (1766, 1776, 1787) created numerous capital offences connected with protest.

widows and heiresses represented a major complicating factor in the combination of landownership and military service on which the *feudal system rested. In the feudal system, property was inherited by male primogeniture. The entitlement of women was limited to the right of a widow to a life interest in part of her husband's estate, and to the right of the nearest female relative or relatives to inherit in default of male heirs.

A widow was entitled to her dower, which was usually one-third of her husband's estate, unless otherwise specified at the time of the marriage, and she held it for life, irrespective of any subsequent remarriage. This contrasted with the right of a widower to a life interest in all of his wife's property, if a living child had been born of the marriage. The simultaneous existence of widows of successive holders of the same land meant the diminution of the inheritance of the eventual heir and could cause major problems relating to the defence and administration of the lands. Legally a widow could not remarry without the consent of the lord, and there were severe financial penalties for doing so. However, she could not be coerced into marriage, and might purchase the right to marry a man of her choice.

Except in cases of entailed property, such as earldoms, the lack of a direct male heir meant that the property went to the dead man's closest female relative or relatives. Unlike male descent, which went by strict primogeniture, heiresses who were in the same relationship to the deceased tenant took equal shares, which were inheritable by their heirs. The eldest co-heiress usually received the caput or chief manor of the estate as part of her share. This subdivision of estates led to problems in management and local defence, and sometimes gave rise to unrest among the junior branches of the family, who were excluded from the inheritance. In the 13th and 14th centuries, the estates of many of the original tenants-in-chief in Ireland were inherited by co-heiresses. Examples of major estates fragmented in this way include the *Marshal and de *Verdon estates and the lands of the earl of Gloucester, while the earldom of *Ulster eventually came into the possession of the crown through the marriages of a succession of heiresses.

The marriage of an heiress, like that of a male heir, belonged to the lord, and was a commodity which could be bought and sold. The lord could choose her husband, but she was protected by a provision in Magna Carta which prevented her from being married to someone inferior in rank. Many of the heiresses of estates in Ireland married husbands resident in England; this led to problems of defence and exacerbated the wider problem of *absenteeism which confronted the Dublin government during the later Middle Ages.

Otway-Ruthven, A. J., 'The Partition of the de Verdon Lands in Ireland in 1332', *Royal Irish Academy Proceedings*, 66C (1967)

PhC

Wilde, Lady Jane ('Speranza') (1821–96), poet and nationalist. In the late 1840s Jane Frances Elgee wrote patriotic verse for the **Nation* as 'Speranza'. After the 1848 rising she helped Charles Gavan *Duffy escape conviction by admitting authorship of a treasonable article attributed to him. In 1851 she married Sir William *Wilde and became a leading Dublin literary hostess. Financial problems after her husband's death sent her to London, where she lived penuriously, held salons, engaged in journalism, and wrote up some of Sir William's unpublished folkloric and antiquarian material. Her flamboyant personality and bohemian attitudes influenced her son, Oscar Wilde. PM

Wilde, Sir William (1815–76), born near Castlerea, Co. Roscommon, an internationally famous eye and ear surgeon, medical historian, statistician, and archaeologist. Wilde qualified in medicine in Dublin in 1837 and later studied in London and Vienna. After returning to Dublin, he established St Mark's eye and ear hospital in 1844, which in 1897 became the Royal Victoria eye and ear hospital. In addition to practising as a surgeon and publishing a major textbook on aural surgery (1853), Wilde also worked on both the 1841 and 1851 *censuses. His medical appendix to the 1851 census is a pioneering work in medical history and statistics. He also wrote accounts of his travels in the eastern Mediterranean (1839) and Austria (1845), and published archaeological studies of the Boyne river (1849) and Lough Corrib (1867) areas. Wilde had several illegitimate children, but in 1851 married Jane Francesca Elgee (see WILDE, LADY JANE). They had two sons, William (1852–99), a Dublin barrister, and Oscar (1854–1900), the playwright and poet. ELM

wild geese, a term applied to those leaving Ireland to serve in *foreign armies during the 18th century. It is mentioned, as a term requiring explanation and hence possibly new, in an official letter of 1726. HM

William III (1650–1702), declared joint sovereign of England, Scotland, and Ireland following the *revolution of 1688. As prince of Orange he had seized power in the Dutch Republic following a French invasion in 1672. The defence of the republic against Louis XIV's France remained his overriding concern, and it was his belief that *James II was turning England into a French satellite that led him to intervene there in 1688. He came to Ireland reluctantly in June 1690, returning after the failure of the first siege of Limerick to the continental war that remained his first priority. Personally tolerant, and unwilling to offend Catholic allies, he initially blocked proposed *penal laws, but gave way to Irish Protestant pressure. His birthday (4 Nov.) was a major state festival up to 1806, while his 'glorious and immortal memory' was a popular toast. From the 1790s Williamite celebration was appropriated by Protestant conservatives, with anti-Catholicism displacing the defeat of arbitrary government as the central theme. The equestrian statue erected in 1701 in front of *Trinity College, Dublin, was defaced by students in 1710, blown up but reassembled in 1836, and finally destroyed by another bomb in 1929.

William of Windsor, *king's lieutenant 1369–72, 1374–6, had served with *Lionel of Clarence in Ireland in the 1360s and his appointment was a continuation of the policy of military intervention in Ireland financed largely from England. However, the failure to maintain this financing at an adequate level led to a conflict between Windsor and the Irish *parliament. Discovering that military conditions in Ireland necessitated a larger force, he resorted to increasing customs duties, compelling *absentees to pay for the defence of their Irish lands, and procuring grants of taxation from the Irish parliament. His unprecedented demands aroused the antagonism of the Anglo-Irish, who complained to the king and council in England, accusing him of coercing the commons to assent to taxation. He was recalled in 1372, but no action was taken and he was reappointed in 1373. His financial problems continued, and the Irish commons opposed the granting of any further subsidy. In 1376 representatives of the commons were summoned to England in the hope of getting their assent to taxation, but the communities refused to give them power to do so. By this stage, the Anglo-Irish conflict with Windsor had become entangled with English politics. Windsor's wife Alice Perrers was the king's mistress and she and her associates came under attack from the commons in the English parliament held in 1376. Windsor was replaced as chief governor and arrested, but no further action was taken against him. PhC

Williamite confiscations, the disposal of land forfeited by supporters of *James II following the *Williamite War. Confiscation was by individual indictments for treason, leading to outlawry and forfeiture of possessions. The immunities offered by the articles of *Galway and the treaty of *Limerick were generally honoured: of 1,238 claims for protection under their terms heard before the Irish *privy council (1692–4) and a court of claims (1697–9) all but 16 were accepted. Confiscation was thus largely confined to those killed or captured, or taking protection from the Williamite authorities, during the war, along with those choosing to go to France at its conclusion. In addition relatives of forfeiting proprietors were allowed to claim a complete or partial interest under family settlements, while 24 outlawed proprietors received royal pardons. Overall just over half a million Irish acres were confiscated, reducing the Catholic share of landed property from 22 per cent in 1688 to 14 per cent by 1703. Conflict over the disposal of these confiscated lands led to the contentious Act of *Resumption. The confiscations differed from the *Cromwellian land settlement both in their limited scale and in introducing no substantial group of new proprietors, the great bulk of forfeited land being eventually acquired by existing Protestant proprietors.

Williamite War (1689–91), between supporters of *James II and *William III. Despite James's fall in England, *Tyrconnell remained in control of most of Ireland. In Munster Justin *MacCarthy suppressed Protestant resistance in Bandon (surrendered 2 Mar. 1689) and elsewhere. In eastern Ulster a Protestant association led by the earl of Mountalexander was defeated at Dromore in Co. Down (14 Mar.). However, the Protestants of north Connacht and south Ulster had assembled a formidable force commanded by Gustavus Hamilton, with headquarters at Enniskillen, and declared their allegiance to William, as, after some debate, did those of Derry. Following James's arrival on 12 March, bringing French officers and supplies, Tyrconnell's hastily expanded army was reduced from 45,000 or above to a more manageable 35,000 and placed under the command of Conrad van Rosen, a Livonian in French service. But its first major operation, the siege of *Derry (18 Apr.–31 July), ended in failure. Meanwhile the Enniskillen Protestants, led by Thomas Lloyd, nicknamed 'the little Cromwell', defeated Jacobites threatening Ballyshannon at Belleek, Co. Fermanagh (7 May), slaughtered MacCarthy's Jacobites at Newtownbutler (31 July), occupied Sligo town, and defeated another Jacobite force at Boyle, Co. Roscommon (20 Sept.). However, the major Williamite expedition under *Schomberg that landed near Belfast on 13 August failed to advance beyond Ulster, while in October *Sarsfield recaptured Sligo and drove the Enniskillen men out of Connacht. The year 1689 thus ended inconclusively.

William reluctantly came to Ireland in June 1690 to take personal charge of what was now an army of 37,000 men, made up of Dutch, *Huguenot, Danish, and English troops (the last including many Irish Protestant officers), as well as six regiments formed from Ulster Protestant forces. Meanwhile Louis XIV had sent about 6,000 troops, half French, the rest Germans and Walloons, to assist James, along with a new commander, the comte de Lauzun. Victory at the battle of the *Boyne (1 July 1690) gave the Williamites control of Dublin and eastern Ireland, but the Jacobites still held Munster and Connacht. Williamites failed to force a crossing of the Shannon at Athlone (17–24 July), and abandoned their siege of the main Jacobite stronghold at Limerick on 30 August. Just before campaigning ended for the winter, however, they gained control of south Munster, after a seaborne expedition of 5,000 men commanded by the earl of Marlborough had captured Cork (28 Sept.) and Kinsale (15 Oct.). Tyrconnell and Lauzun sailed to France around 12 September, taking with them the French troops and leaving the duke of Berwick, James II's illegitimate son, in command. A new French commander, the marquis de Saint Ruth, arrived on 9 May 1691 to take charge of a new campaigning season. However, the capture of Athlone after a bloody ten-day siege (21–30 June) allowed the Williamites to cross the Shannon. Defeat at *Aughrim (12 July), followed by the surrender of Galway and the encirclement of Limerick, completed the collapse of what had been an apparently strong Jacobite position.

William III had initially hoped to pay for the war out of forfeited Jacobite lands. Following the failure of the first siege of Limerick, he became more flexible, but remained less ready than *Ginkel to forgo the prospect of extensive forfeitures by offering the Jacobites attractive surrender terms. On the Jacobite side there were deep divisions. Surrender on terms was particularly attractive to 'new interest men', predominantly *Old English, who held property under the *Restoration settlement. Those with nothing to lose, which included most of the Gaelic Irish, were more inclined to fight on. Secret negotiations with representatives of the Jacobite peace party began in July 1690; in January 1691 Sarsfield arrested some of those involved. A Williamite proclamation on 7 July 1691 offered only limited assurances, but the articles of *Galway provided more attractive surrender terms and the conversion of Sarsfield to negotiations cleared the way for the war to end with the treaty of *Limerick.

The war was both an episode in a major European conflict and an Irish civil war. Despite the *penal laws, the main outcome was to confirm the Protestant dominance of Irish society already established at the Restoration. The *Williamite land settlement was also limited in scope. Memories of the conflict, perpetuated by regular commemoration of the victories at Derry, the Boyne, and Aughrim, nevertheless became an important part of Protestant political culture, though the precise content of the Williamite tradition was to change significantly over time.

Maguire, W. A. (ed.), *Kings in Conflict* (1990)
Simms, J. G., *Jacobite Ireland 1685–91* (1969)

Wilson, Sir Henry (1864–1922), soldier and *Unionist politician. An Irish Protestant, Wilson rose to become field marshal and chief of the imperial general staff. He gained a reputation for political intrigue, especially during the *'Curragh incident' (1914). After 1919, while deploring the excesses of the *Black and Tans, he favoured a vigorous policy of repression in Ireland. After leaving the army he was elected Unionist MP for North Down and continued to recommend stringent security measures to the Belfast government. His assassination in London, on 22 June 1922, by two *IRA men apparently acting on their own initiative, produced an ultimatum from the British to the Irish *Provisional Government that helped to precipitate the *Irish Civil War. KJ

Windsor, treaty of (6 Oct. 1175), between *Henry II and Rory *O'Connor. Rory had not made submission to Henry during his expedition to Ireland, September 1171–April 1172, and the treaty was intended to address this omission. By its terms, Henry II reserved Meath and Leinster and the cities of Dublin, Wexford, and Waterford as his sphere of lordship, confirmed Rory as king of Connacht, and ceded him overlordship of the remainder of Ireland conditional on payment of one-tenth of all cattle tribute which Rory might collect, to be paid in the form of animal hides. The treaty failed because Henry II did not prevent Anglo-Norman settlers from expanding beyond the area which he had claimed, while Rory proved unable to exert effective overlordship over the remainder of Ireland. MTF

'wings', the name given to two proposed safeguards attached to Sir Francis Burdett's unsuccessful *Catholic emancipation bill in 1825. These disenfranchised the *40-shilling freeholders, and provided for a state payment to the Catholic clergy. *O'Connell, who believed Burdett's bill had a real chance of success, agreed to both proposals, a decision for which he was later attacked. His acquiescence, only a year before the general election of 1826 demonstrated the political effectiveness of the poorer Catholic voters, confirms that O'Connell himself did not always fully comprehend the political revolution he had unleashed.

Winter, Samuel (1603–66), leader of the *Independent sect in Ireland. Winter arrived as chaplain to the 1650 parliamentary commissioners, and was made provost of *Trinity College, Dublin, in 1652. He hoped in vain that Henry *Cromwell's arrival would restore the fortunes of his church. He lost favour in 1658 and was sacked from the provostship by the *convention of 1660. HM

witchcraft can take many forms. Anthropologists distinguish between 'sorcery', the manipulation of spells and potions, and 'witchcraft', supernatural aggression based on an innate power. There is also a distinction between the belief in an ability to do harm by *magic, universal in European popular culture, and the more specific concept, developed into an elaborate mythology by church and state, of the witch whose power derived from a pact with Satan. Ireland provides, in the *Kyteler case, a particularly well-documented early example of a legal trial for witchcraft as devil worship. There are also a handful of later cases, notably those of Florence Newton, executed at Cork in 1661, and the nine people from Island Magee, Co. Antrim, imprisoned and pilloried in 1711. In general, however, Ireland, whether because of its peripheral location or the alternative outlets found for its communal tensions, largely escaped the great European witch hunts of the 16th and 17th centuries. (Bridget Cleary, burned to death by relatives in Co. Tipperary in 1895, is often referred to as a witch but was in fact attacked as a changeling, a simulacrum left behind when the real Bridget was supposedly abducted by the fairies.) Belief in witchcraft in the wider sense was common among both Catholics and Protestants. Means of inflicting harm included the evil eye, whose possessors brought bad luck on whatever they complimented, reversals of the normal procedures followed at *holy wells, and the use of charms and potions.

Wogan, John de (d. 1321), *justiciar 1295–1308, 1309–12, lord of Picton Castle near Haverfordwest in Pembrokeshire. Wogan seems to have had no connection with Ireland prior to his appointment as justiciar on 18 October 1295, though he founded a family which remained important in north Kildare until the early 18th century. Because calendared versions of the justiciary rolls survive for his period in office historians have perhaps exaggerated his importance, but he was certainly an energetic and effective justiciar, under whom the area under direct royal control was considerably increased. He also oversaw the ending of the long-running *FitzGerald–de *Burgh feud, presided over the Kilkenny parliaments of 1297 and 1310 which sought to address the growing problem of lawlessness and rebellion in Ireland, led numerous campaigns to restore order in the localities, and organized large contingents from the colony for participation in Edward I's campaigns in Scotland and Flanders. SD

Wogan, Patrick (*c.*1740–1816), principal Catholic *printer and bookseller in late 18th-century Dublin. VK

Wolff, Gustav Wilhelm (1834–1913), *Belfast *shipbuilder. Wolff was born in Hamburg and served an apprenticeship with the Manchester engineering firm of Joseph Whitworth & Company. In 1861 Wolff entered into partnership with Harland to form *Harland & Wolff. Although in the early years Wolff was responsible for managing the yard, he was later influential in securing orders from other shipping lines in Britain and in Hamburg. By the time the partnership became a limited company, in 1888, Wolff played little active part in the business, and devoted his attention instead to the management of the Belfast Ropeworks, which he had helped found in 1872–3, and which became one of the largest ropeworks in the world. Wolff was also a Belfast harbour commissioner 1887–93, and became *Unionist MP for East Belfast 1892–1910. He retired formally from Harland & Wolff in 1906. FG/WJ

wolves, though indigenous to Ireland, are now extinct. Prehistoric remains have been found, and documentation of their presence exists from the 7th century. Wolf hunting took place from at least the 16th century, and as pastoral farming grew in importance the wolf suffered both from increased persecution and from a declining habitat. During the 17th century hunting was organized by improving *landlords, encouraged by government bounties, and often stipulated in leases as a condition of tenure. The exact date of extinction is uncertain. The last known rewards for killing wolves were claimed in Cork and Kerry in 1710, but elsewhere popular traditions date the last killing as late as 1786. NG

women. *Renaissance and *Reformation brought many changes to the role of women, compounded in Ireland by conquest and colonization. The upper classes were most affected. Dynastic marriage, including *divorce and remarriage, had given women a central importance in the politics of Gaelic and Anglo-Irish lordships. In particular circumstances, women, especially those with independent military resources, political connections, or a good education, could lead a lordship and negotiate with the encroaching state. Notable examples are Agnes *Campbell, Finola *MacDonnell, Grace *O'Malley, and Eleanor, countess of *Desmond. Such women retained their own surnames and had their own lands for life within the lordship, but in the more centralized state of the 17th century any semblance of independence was lost to a more domesticated role.

The triumph of common law affected women's property rights. Under the Gaelic system women had the right to hold property independently of their husbands, though not the right to inherit or pass on land, because this belonged to the kin group. The goods women brought with them as dowries were regainable on divorce. These, usually livestock and household goods, were an insurance against penury, but Finola's dowry of mercenaries gave her political independence. Under the common law, women had no rights to property independent of their husbands, including their own dowries. The use of jointures did afford women some rights, while the court of *chancery enabled divorced women to apply for unreturned dowry goods, heiresses to make claims to family lands, and *widows to have lifetime use of their husband's property. This more impersonal system may have favoured poorer women, or at least those with less political power.

Rape, like murder, was no longer a matter of compensation, but a capital offence under English law. However, there was now greater social control exercised over aberrant women such as scolds and *witches, although the few such cases in Ireland were confined to the colonial community, reflecting an ethnically divided, sparsely populated country where informal mechanisms of community control remained dominant.

The Protestant and Catholic reformations adversely affected the religious authority of women.

Abbesses such as Mary Cusack and Alison White were pensioned off following the *dissolution of abbeys and convents. Where convents enjoyed a clandestine existence in the following century, they were now enclosed institutions. Nevertheless women remained influential in religion. Educated Paleswomen are now seen as a key element in the survival of Catholicism in the 1560s and 1570s. But these were in some respects harbingers of the new domestic role to be assigned to women of both religions, centred on catechesis or, for Protestants, Bible reading with their children. During the upheavals of the mid-17th century Quakerism (see SOCIETY OF FRIENDS) gave women a public role in religion. But even there patriarchy reasserted itself once the denomination became established, and women retired from the preaching role they had played in its evangelical phase. Women's educational opportunities lessened as convents became contemplative. However, aristocratic and patrician women often had private tutors, and some, like Catherine Boyle, Lady Ranelagh, could make a significant impact in intellectual circles.

The vast majority of women were poor, and their economic role was in childbearing, childrearing, agriculture, and textile production. All classes of women had frequently to survive independently, as widows or with husbands at war. For upper-class women this meant assuming management of large households, or even estates, as in the case of Elizabeth, wife of the duke of *Ormond, during her husband's exile.

The 19th and early 20th centuries saw a gradual improvement in the legal and political status of women, as gender-based disabilities in the fields of property, guardianship of children, education, and political participation were slowly dismantled. Piecemeal legal reforms, north and south, from the 1920s, and a spate of legislation from 1970, built on some of these earlier reforms, while also, in independent Ireland, undoing some of the attacks on women's employment and citizenship made by the new state in the 1920s and 1930s.

For upper middle-class women this entire period was characterized by opportunity and broadening horizons; even the idealization of the middle-class woman in the home, sometimes employed as an argument against female employment and political activity, was also used effectively by female philanthropists and feminists as a justification for extending women's 'morally superior' influence into the world of work, especially the 'caring' professions. Most Catholic women who were interested in philanthropy entered the ever-expanding ranks of women religious (see NUNS); Protestant women ran a wide range of philanthropic activities. A small proportion of upper middle-class women went to university from the late 19th century and the first generation of female university lecturers and professors had a high profile in political life in the first half of the 20th century. Like women working in law, medicine, and accountancy, however, female academics made up only a tiny proportion of Irish working women up to the 1970s.

For other sections of the population change was more gradual, with progress in everyday living conditions lagging well behind improvements in formal political and legal status. Housework remained, up to the 1960s at least, a crushing burden for most people; in 1946 almost half of all Irish dwellings, and 91 per cent of rural households, had no piped water. Motherhood only gradually became less dangerous and less harrowing, notably when the development of health-care services in the 1940s and 1950s brought about a steady decline in maternal and infant mortality rates. Domestic responsibilities prevented many women from engaging in paid semi-skilled or unskilled work, while from the 1920s marriage bars, in both jurisdictions, against women in the public service imposed new restrictions on access to better-paid employment.

Against this background the pattern of women's employment remained up to the 1950s fairly stable. As late as 1946 women assisting on farms—not farmers' wives, who were enumerated under a different heading—made up the largest group of women in the workforce of independent Ireland. Domestic service (see SERVANTS), shop service, office work, nursing, teaching, and factory work all employed considerable numbers. Female factory workers remained concentrated in the textile mills of Belfast, Derry, and their hinterlands, though there was also factory work for women in the other Irish cities, mostly in food processing and apparel industries.

Home-based, remunerative work for women also existed in various forms up to the 1950s and 1960s. Farm women generally controlled the poultry, eggs, and butter money. In Ulster, despite the huge loss of domestic employment opportunities caused by the transfer of linen spinning to the factories from the 1820s, other forms of home-based textile work remained an important source of income for women. Urban and non-farming women could, depending on resources, keep a shop, dress-make, take music pupils; poorer women resorted to a variety of strategies to earn income—taking in lodgers (even in one-room tenements), going out charring, and taking in washing. Women begging, especially when accompanied by children, always received more sympathy than did men, and were less likely to be sent to prison for vagrancy. Nevertheless other institutions—the workhouse, the lunatic asylum, the 'Magdalen' home—absorbed increasing numbers of destitute women.

The entire landscape of Irish women's paid work changed almost beyond recognition between 1946 and 1961, as farm work and domestic service, the two largest categories, gave way to office work, teaching, nursing, and shop work. From the mid-1940s many of the women who would previously have gone into service, or stayed at home as assisting relatives on farms, emigrated instead to Great Britain.

Emigration was not new to Irish women; Irish emigrants to North America, unusually among European emigrants in the years 1870–1930, comprised a very high proportion of young, single women facing a new life in apparent independence of older relatives. Emigration might have meant self-realization and independence for some, but for a considerable number who went in the late 19th century it represented a long-distance extension of their family responsibilities as they sent money home to support smallholdings and to bring other family members out. Going to Great Britain in the 1940s and 1950s was more likely to be a fulfilment of individual goals, as young women sought training, comparatively well-paid work, and, perhaps, marital opportunities lacking at home. Some of those who did not emigrate stayed on at school to compete later for secure white-collar and professional employment; others benefited from the commercial and industrial growth from the late 1950s which provided jobs in shops and in light industries. The expansion of health services north and south provided further new opportunities for training and work.

Apart from high-profile individuals, women's involvement in politics and in public life was low key until the late 1960s (see FEMINISM). The numbers of women in organizations of various kinds were, however, rising from the 1940s, and it would seem that the rapid changes in women's working lives—in the house and outside it—were crucial to their stepped-up participation in public life in the 1970s, 1980s, and 1990s.

Luddy, Maria, and Murphy, Cliona, *Women Surviving: Studies in Irish Women's History* (1990)

MacCurtain, Margaret, and O'Dowd, Mary, *Women in Early Modern Ireland* (1991)

—— and Ó Corráin, D. (eds.), *Women in Irish Society: The Historical Dimension* (1978)

HM/CC

women's education. Throughout the Middle Ages women were almost wholly excluded from the cultural and intellectual life of both Anglo-Irish and Gaelic Ireland. Sixteenth-century humanist influences promoted a more positive attitude to their schooling; in the 17th century, on the other hand, there are signs that opportunities narrowed again as part of a general conservative response to the weakening of traditional structures. By the mid-18th century female writers and intellectuals from a wider range of middle- and upper-class backgrounds, such as Mary Delany and the poet Mary Barber (*c.*1690–1757), had begun to make their mark.

From the late 18th century the education of poor females in virtue and industry was a dominant concern of philanthropists of all religions. In the late 19th and early 20th centuries, the right of access to the same educational facilities as men was one of the main planks of the western *feminist agenda. These two tendencies informed most developments in women's education. However, the provision of free primary education in the *national school system from 1831, which offered both sexes the same core curriculum and enabled them to win scholarships to train as teachers, must be seen, along with the enforcement of compulsory education in 1892, as the key development in women's education in the 19th century.

Up to the last quarter of the 19th century fee-paying schools, for daughters of the upper middle and upper classes, still concentrated on reading, writing, and accomplishments suitable to a 'lady'. The establishment in 1878 of a standard school-leaving examination, the Intermediate, open to both boys and girls, forced curriculum change in many girls' schools, as did the demand, from the 1880s, to prepare pupils for university matriculation. By 1892 the *Queen's Colleges in Belfast, Galway, and Cork were admitting women to all courses; the Dublin universities were slower but were admitting women by 1910. The first generation of women university lecturers and professors were prominent in political life in the first half of the 20th century. University education, however, was for many years open to only a small minority of women, owing to the cost, not only of university itself, but of the secondary schooling preceding it. It was not until the second half of the 20th century that sweeping reforms in Northern Ireland, and more gradual progress towards public funding for secondary and third-level study in independent Ireland, made equal educational opportunity for females a reality.

Cullen, Mary (ed.), *Girls Don't Do Honours* (1987)

CC

Wood Quay, archaeological site in Dublin city and focus of public controversy in the 1970s. The 4-acre site was redeveloped by Dublin corporation as its new civic offices. This necessitated the removal of archaeological layers before building work could begin. Controversy arose in 1977 when conservationists, led by Professor F. X. Martin, OSA, chairman of the Friends of Medieval Dublin, sought more time for excavation than had been allowed. Part of the site was bulldozed by the developer and irretrievably destroyed but much information was recovered by the archaeological excavations which concluded in 1981.

Archaeologically the importance of the site rested in its excellent preservation and the deep, stratified deposits ranging in date from *c.*925 to *c.*1320. The *Viking age levels consisted of fourteen house plots and a stretch of the town defences; thirteen phases of development were recognized in which houses replaced one another in rough succession between the 10th century and the 12th. During the 13th century, land was reclaimed from the river when wooden quaysides were built out into the Liffey. JB

woods and forests formed the original post-glacial natural or 'climax' vegetation over most of Ireland, but have been progressively destroyed by 5,000 years of human land use, particularly during the last 300 years. Thus despite plantings of exotic hardwoods and conifers by *landlords during the 18th and 19th centuries, and more recent state afforestation programmes in both parts of Ireland, the country remains one of the least wooded in Europe, with approximately 4 per cent of its land area forested.

None of the post-glacial climax woodlands survive in their original form, but palaeobotanical research has indicated a complex sequence of species change and colonization in response to climatic fluctuations following the retreat of the local ice caps by the end of the last, *Midlandian*, cold phase *c.*10,000 years BP (before present). Late glacial sea levels were much lower than they are today, and these species either colonized Ireland via the land bridge thus created over part of the Irish Sea, or else spread back from their refuge areas far to the south-west of modern-day Ireland.

As temperatures rose, the sub-glacial tundra was colonized by juniper, willow, and birch. These were themselves increasingly replaced by hazel and pine between 9,000 and 8,500 years BP. As climatic warming continued, oak and elm replaced hazel on the heavier soils, while alder became increasingly confined to wetland margins, pine to lighter, sandier soils, and ash to limestone. Around 7,000 years BP, Ireland's climate became wetter, and this encouraged a final sequence of species change which culminated in the creation of a climax deciduous woodland of hazel, oak, alder, and elm.

This species mix remained remarkably stable for about 2,000 years, until either climatic change, selective clearance by early farmers, or disease resulted in a dramatic fall in the numbers of elm trees, the so-called 'elm decline'. More fundamentally, from this point on, Ireland's woodlands came under progressively more sustained attack as the country's population gradually rose and land was cleared for agriculture. The process was neither simple nor linear and, during prehistoric times at least, involved the frequent abandonment of previously cleared land as part of a cycle of shifting agriculture. In turn this permitted the regrowth of secondary woodland to create a complex mosaic of farmland, virgin woodland, and secondary scrub. Clearance was progressive, however, and by the 8th century AD *Brehon *law tracts were classifying different types of tree according to their social value and specifying penalties for damaging specific varieties such as oak or ash. This suggests that by this time, some types of woodland were perceived as an increasingly scarce and important resource.

Woodland clearance continued during the Middle Ages, particularly under the aegis of the *Cistercians and as *manorialism in general encouraged commercial farming. The most rapid destruction, however, occurred during and after the *plantations. By 1600, approximately 12 per cent of Ireland's *lowlands* were still forested, but by 1800 this had dropped to around 2 per cent, as a result of accelerated clearance for industrial and agricultural as much as strategic purposes. Thus specialized 17th-century industries such as the charcoal-fired *iron smelting in Co. Cork, together with the more general demands for timber generated by coopers, *tanners, *shipbuilders, and housebuilders, contrived to turn Ireland from a net timber exporting country in the 17th century to a net importer in the 18th. Contemporary descriptions of the open or 'champion' nature of much of Ireland's landscape reflect this transformation.

Mitchell, F., *Shell Guide to Reading the Irish Landscape* (2nd edn., 1986)

LJP

Wood's Halfpence controversy (1722–5), a campaign against the patent to mint £100,800 worth of copper coin for Ireland acquired by William Wood, a Wolverhampton manufacturer. Opponents argued that the patent, allegedly purchased from George I's mistress, the duchess of Kendal, would flood Ireland with worthless coin. The scheme provoked hostile pamphlets and popular demonstrations, but the really effective opposition came from the political establishment. The House of Lords and House of Commons both passed hostile resolutions, and the *lords justices, *privy council, and *revenue commissioners resisted pressure to use the coin in official receipts and payments. Having failed to overcome opposition by reducing the proposed issue to £40,000 and replacing the ineffective duke of Grafton, *lord lieutenant 1720–4, with the astute and sociable Lord Carteret, Sir Robert Walpole's ministry cancelled the patent in September 1725.

Walpole saw resistance to the patent as revealing a desire for 'independency', and Swift's *Drapier's Letters* did in fact raise the issue of Ireland's political subordination. Most opponents, however, concentrated on the damaging consequences of the patent, rather than challenging its legality. The determined defence of Irish against English interests nevertheless gives the episode a place in the development of *patriotism. The crisis led Walpole's ministry to initiate a policy of ensuring that a proportion of key posts (including, invariably, the *lord chancellorship and the archbishopric of Armagh) were in the future held by politically reliable Englishmen. But the rejection of the patent also demonstrated that the English government could manage Ireland only with the assistance of Irish *undertakers, among whom William *Conolly now emerged, through the eclipse of his rival *Brodrick, as the undisputed chief.

Woodward, Richard (1726–94), *Church of Ireland bishop of Cloyne from 1781 to his death. The Poor Relief Act of 1772 owed much to Woodward's pamphlet on the subject, and he was a founder of the *house of industry in Dublin. While urging in parliament repeal of the *penal laws, he defended the Church of Ireland's established status. *The Present State of the Church of Ireland* (1787), written in response to the *Rightboy movement, sought to refute criticisms from Catholics and dissenters. KM

wool and woollen cloth. Although wool was worn from earliest times (see DRESS), there is no evidence of systematic large-scale production for the market prior to the arrival of the *Anglo-Normans and the development of a *manorial system of farming. Sheep farming was extensively developed on the *Cistercian monastic estates from 1142 onwards, especially in the favourable conditions of the south-east. By the 13th century many of the manors, often located on limestone areas which provided good grazing, were producing so much wool that they were major contributors to the Great Custom on wool and woolfells, first levied in 1275. Over half the total of this tax was paid by the almost contiguous ports of New Ross and *Waterford, as these were located at the estuary of the Barrow–Nore–Suir river system on which much of the wool was transported. This trade was dominated by Flemish merchants, and was financed by great Italian merchant families from cities such as Lucca and Florence. As a result the king, nobility, and religious houses were nearly always in debt to these Italian banking firms. But much of the wool must also have been produced from the smaller flocks of lesser lords and peasants, and sold to the neighbouring town.

Although Irish wool was of poorer quality than English and was used for making coarser, heavier cloth, Irish cloaks were widely exported throughout Europe. The industry expanded throughout the first half of the 14th century and skilled Irish weavers migrated to England where many of them were employed in the growing industry in the west country. In the later Middle Ages more ready-made cloaks, worsted, and serge were being made and exported, which caused a decline in raw wool exports. The main export markets in the 15th century were Flanders and the Low Countries, mainly through the port of Calais.

From *c.*1500 woollens, generally coarse frieze, were the most common cloth type made and worn in Ireland, and there was also an export trade, largely to England, in wool and frieze. Wool exports increased dramatically between the 1580s and 1640s, with the more commercialized areas of Munster dominating this trade. At this stage government regulations ensured that most Irish wool exports went to England rather than continental Europe. With favourable price trends the trade in wool had increased further by the end of the 17th century. By this time there were about 50,000 settlers engaged in woollen manufacture. The *Woollen Act (1699) ended the export trade, but the manufacture of wool for the home market remained important throughout the 18th century and beyond.

The rural cottage-based industry produced a coarse cloth range, while a more specialist craft-based industry producing finer woollens had developed in a number of towns during the 18th century. *Dublin was the largest centre, and also the most important for finishing and marketing cloth made in rural Ireland. Other urban centres included *Cork, Bandon, Blarney, Newmarket, Doneraile, Castlemartyr, *Kilkenny, Carrick-on-Suir, Maryborough, and Mountmellick. Imports of finer British woollens increased from the 1770s, when Yorkshire manufacturers began to adopt carding and spinning machinery, damaging the urban-based industry in Ireland. The domestic manufacture of coarse cloths (which most of the population wore) proved more resilient and was still expanding by the turn of the century. But as mechanization proceeded, costs could be reduced and both English and Irish factory-based producers were gradually able to gain a greater share of the Irish market for coarse cloth.

From the 1790s a number of urban manufacturers began to introduce machinery, notably in Dublin, and with protection from British competition until the removal in 1824 of the transitional protective tariffs permitted under the Act of *Union, these manufacturers of coarse cloth built up a reasonable trade. Cork was the main centre of the worsted industry, and here too a number of manufacturers had invested in machinery. However, after the removal of the protection afforded by the union duties in 1824, the precarious growth of the factory industry was thrown into reverse as British competition became more intense; the number of mills declined from 36 in 1835 to 11 by the mid-19th century. British imports also began to make inroads into parts of the domestic industry, notably in Leinster and Munster. Wool's role as a traded or bartered commodity remained significant in poorer peripheral regions, but even this experienced contraction during the second half of the 19th century.

Domestic spinning and handloom weaving nevertheless survived after the end of the 19th century in Donegal, Galway, Kerry, Mayo, and some other districts, with the help of the *Congested Districts Board, which made efforts to revive the flagging industry. Irish factory production, meanwhile, made significant progress during the second half of the 19th century competing successfully with British imports. By importing machinery from the best British machine makers and specializing in Irish cloth types (for example, Blarney tweed) Irish manufacturers were able to retain a niche in the market for machine-made fabrics, building a limited export trade. The number of mills between 1850 and 1904 rose from 11 to 100, and Cork emerged as the most important centre of the factory industry; it was here that Mahony's of Blarney (the largest and most innovative firm in the country, and the first to mechanize all aspects of the industry) were located.

Bielenberg, A., 'British Competition and the Vicissitudes of the Irish Woollen Industry 1785–1923', *Textile History*, 31 (2000)

Cullen, L., *An Economic History of Ireland since 1660* (1972)

Gillespie, R., *The Transformation of the Irish Economy 1550–1700* (1991)

TB/AB

Woollen Act (1699), an act of the English parliament banning the export of woollen goods from Ireland to any destination other than England, where they already faced prohibitive import duties. The act remained in force until the granting of *free trade in 1779. The assumption of legislative supremacy was contested by *Molyneux's **Case of Ireland*. Though later presented as part of a coherent policy of weakening Ireland's manufacturing economy, the act was in fact promoted, against the wishes of government, by MPs representing English clothing interests. The economic effects are also now seen as limited and localized: the export trade cut off was small, the woollen industry continued to thrive on the basis of an expanding home market, and the supposed increase in wool *smuggling was much exaggerated.

Workers' Party/Democratic Left. The Workers' Party had its roots in the schism within *Sinn Féin which opened at the Ard Fheis of 1970. Official Sinn Féin, which emerged from the split under the leadership of Tómas MacGiolla, was Marxist in orientation and supported the creation of a democratic socialist republic in Ireland: it was linked to the Official *IRA. In January 1977 Official Sinn Féin became 'Sinn Féin: The Workers' Party' and in 1982 (in a further effort to distance itself from paramilitarism) this title was shortened to 'the Workers' Party'. The Workers' Party fared rather better in the Republic than in Northern Ireland, where it achieved an electoral peak in the 1982 Assembly elections, with 2.7 per cent of first-preference votes. In the Republic the Workers' Party won 4.3 per cent of the vote in 1989, and returned seven TDs. In February 1992 the party split over allegations that there were residual links with the Official IRA and that financial support had been accepted from the Soviet Union: the majority of members supported the reformist leader, Proinsías De Rossa, and left the party to form New Agenda (later renamed as Democratic Left). The recusant Workers' Party lost its single member of the Dáil at the election of November 1992; but DL was able to return four deputies. De Rossa was minister for social welfare in the coalition government of 1994–7, which was supported by his party colleagues. In January 1999 DL united with the *Labour Party. Neither the DL nor the vestigial Workers' Party achieved any significant electoral showing in Northern Ireland during the 1990s. Despite this DL and the pre-1992 Workers' Party had a greater intellectual influence in debate on Northern Ireland than might have been expected. In the Republic DL has sustained an important social and constitutional critique. AJ

workhouse. The workhouse system was introduced to Ireland under the *Poor Law Act of 1838. In appearance and administration workhouses reflected the ethos of the act, being designed to deter anyone not in dire need from entering. The buildings were constructed according to standardized plans drawn up by the English architect George Wilkinson, and furniture was kept to a minimum. Families were required to enter the workhouse together, individual members being ineligible for relief. Once admitted family groups were split up, with men, women, and children over 2 years of age being assigned to separate wards. Food was limited and monotonous, consisting primarily of porridge, potatoes, and milk; discipline was strict. Inmates were required to work at breaking stones, or at manual tasks about the house. Children were required to attend workhouse schools. Many workhouses also contained hospitals in which, from 1862, the non-destitute could also receive treatment. In independent Ireland, following the abolition of the workhouse test for relief in the period after 1921, many workhouses were converted into county homes for the elderly or into hospitals; others were closed. In *Northern Ireland, although the system survived until 1946, the number of workhouses declined; 20 were converted into district hospitals during the 1920s and 1930s. VC

Workman Clark & Company, the *Belfast *shipbuilding company, was formed in 1880 by George *Clark and Francis Workman (1856–1927). Workman had established a small shipyard on the Lagan three years earlier.

Workman Clark pioneered the development of the Charles Parsons turbine engine and the construction of insulated and refrigerated fruit-carrying vessels. It specialized in medium-sized cargo boats and combined cargo and passenger vessels. Between 1905 and 1913 inclusive, annual tonnage launched placed Workman Clark among the top five UK shipbuilding firms on four occasions.

The 1920s proved a difficult decade for the shipbuilding industry. Workman Clark also encountered financial problems arising from its takeover in 1920 by the Northumberland Shipping Company. In 1927 an action for having issued a misleading and fraudulent prospectus was settled out of court, and the company was forced into temporary liquidation. Workman Clark was revived in 1928 as Workman Clark (1928) Ltd., but did not survive the world depression which began in 1929. It launched its last vessel in 1934. In 1935 Workman Clark was acquired by the National Shipbuilders Security Ltd.; its yards on the south bank of the Lagan were taken over by *Harland & Wolff and those on the north bank were closed. FG/WJ

Wyndham, George (1863–1913), scion of the English aristocracy who claimed descent from the rebel Lord Edward *FitzGerald. A colourful liberal Tory, Wyndham was *chief secretary for Ireland 1900–5, joining *Balfour's cabinet in 1902. He was an ambitious reformer, achieving success with the *Land Act of 1903. He broke with civil service convention to appoint Sir Antony *MacDonnell as under-secretary, and attempted to implement a scheme for administrative reform. Unionist opposition to this initiative brought about the *devolution crisis, and he resigned from the government in March 1905. ACH

Wyse, Sir Thomas (1791–1862). The son of a Catholic gentleman from Co. Waterford, Wyse took a leading part in the campaign for *Catholic emancipation, notably in the successful challenge to the *Beresford interest in the county in 1826. His *Historical Sketch of the Late Catholic Association of Ireland* (1829) is a vivid contemporary account. He was MP for Co. Tipperary 1830–2 and for Waterford 1835–47. Though interested in *federalism he refused to support the *repeal movement. Instead his career was that of a Catholic *Whig, holding junior ministerial office 1839–41 and 1846–9, and subsequently serving as British envoy in Athens. He was knighted in 1856.

Yeats, Jack B. (1871–1957), painter of genre scenes and subject pictures, usually regarded as the most important Irish painter of his generation. The son of the painter John Butler Yeats (1839–1922) and brother of William Butler *Yeats, he was brought up in Sligo, but educated at the South Kensington, Chiswick, and Westminster schools of art in London. In 1888, in London, he began working as an illustrator on numerous journals, but in 1897 moved to Devon and began painting in watercolours and, later, in oils. In 1905 he toured the west of Ireland gathering material for illustrations to Synge's *The Aran Islands*, and in 1910 settled permanently in Ireland. Thereafter he exhibited regularly in Dublin and occasionally in London, New York, and elsewhere. He was elected a member of the *Royal Hibernian Academy in 1916. Typically Yeats worked from what he termed 'a pool of memories', from 1915 till the early 1920s recording many of the momentous events taking place in Ireland. In the mid-1920s he turned his attention upon the inner world of thoughts and feelings, but his subject matter was still drawn from the life around him. An individualist, his work from the 1930s and later became increasingly Expressionist in technique, his imagery enigmatic in appearance but often conveying an intense humanity.

Arnold, Bruce, *Jack Yeats* (1998)

SBK

Yeats, William Butler (1865–1939), the greatest modern Anglo-Irish poet. Yeats's father was an artist and (chronically insolvent) landowner; his mother's family were Sligo merchants. He was brought up in London, Dublin, and Sligo. His first poems were published in the 1880s; thereafter he drew extensively on Gaelic literature and Sligo folklore. Yeats became active in advanced nationalist politics after the *Parnell split and tried to mobilize nationalist literary groups as the basis for a national artistic revival. This culminated in the foundation of the Irish Literary Theatre (subsequently the *Abbey). He quarrelled with clericalists, and subsequently with nationalists, over the moral and political role of theatre, and was criticized for accepting a crown pension in 1910. He served in the *Irish Free State *Senate 1922–8.

Yeats is the source of much historical controversy, due to his habit of assimilating Irish events into his personal mythology and the tendency of some admirers to adopt his perspective uncritically. (His images of the Parnell split, the relationship between the Irish *literary revival and the *rising of 1916, and the nature of the Anglo-Irish aristocracy have attracted particular attention.) Some commentators praise him as a defender of liberty, emphasizing his insistence on artistic self-determination, resistance to *censorship, and opposition to Catholic church influence over the Irish Free State; others emphasize the elitism displayed in his occult activities, his later cult of the aristocracy, and the frequently expressed admiration for fascism which led him to support the *Blueshirts in the 1930s. Yeats is perhaps best seen as part of a tradition of 'patriotic Tory' Irish Protestant intellectuals, including Isaac *Butt and Standish *O'Grady, who presented themselves as defenders of Irish agrarian and spiritual values against English *Whig materialism and Roman clerical legalism.

PM

Yellow Ford, battle of (14 Aug. 1598), the greatest single defeat suffered by English forces in 16th-century Ireland. The queen's army under Henry Bagenal, taking supplies to the beleaguered Blackwater Fort, was ambushed in difficult terrain north of Armagh by Hugh *O'Neill. Bagenal and 800 of his men were killed and the Blackwater and Armagh garrisons had to be abandoned. O'Neill gained unimpeded access to the midlands enabling in turn the overthrow of the *Munster plantation.

HM

Yelverton's Act (1782) modified *Poynings's Law by providing that all bills passed by both houses of the Irish parliament should be forwarded to England, and that only such bills, having received the royal assent under the great seal of Great Britain, could become law. The cumbersome procedure of *heads of bills thus became redundant. Both *privy councils lost their power to initiate or amend legislation, and the Irish council its power of suppression, though the English council could still refuse the royal assent. Introduced by Barry Yelverton (1736–1805), a leading *patriot, on 18 December 1781, the measure was not opposed by the executive; however Henry *Flood, anticipating his stand on the *Renunciation Act, attacked it as inadequate. Yelverton, later Lord Avonmore, became attorney-general (1782) and chief baron of the Irish exchequer (1783), and supported the Act of *Union.

yeomanry, originally a part-time local force raised in 1796 to combat the threat posed by the *revolutionary war and the *United Irish and *Defender movements. By 1797 30,000 men had been enrolled. Although some Catholics were recruited, particularly in the south, the most enthusiastic recruitment was among Protestants, often in close association with the recently formed *Orange Order, and the force quickly attracted a reputation for indiscipline and indiscriminate sectarian violence. After 1800 increased reliance on the yeomanry for the defence and security duties formerly discharged by the *militia meant that yeomen were more frequently on permanent duty, and deployed throughout the country. The force also became even more exclusively Protestant. After 1822 yeomanry ceased to be used for policing duties. A brief reactivation in 1831–4 merely confirmed their unsuitability, and later calls for the establishment of a similar volunteer force were resisted, at least up to the establishment of *Northern Ireland (see ULSTER SPECIAL CONSTABULARY).

York, Richard Plantagenet, duke of (1411–60), earl of Ulster, lord of the liberty of Meath and chief governor 1449–50, 1459–60. Descended on both sides from Edward III (through Lionel, duke of Clarence, and Edmund, duke of York), he inherited his dukedom from his paternal uncle Edward in 1415, and his Irish lands, with others in England and Wales, from his maternal uncle Edmund, earl of March, in 1425. Previously Henry VI's lieutenant in France (1436–7, 1440–6), he was appointed lieutenant of Ireland in 1447. The truth behind contemporary rumours that this was an attempt to exile York (then the king's nearest, but unacknowledged, heir) from English politics has been much debated. In fact he exercised the office mainly by deputy and found it advantageous to retain it, notwithstanding his preoccupations as leader of the Yorkist faction in the early stages of the *Wars of the Roses. Except when briefly displaced (1453–4) by James, earl of Wiltshire and 5th earl of *Ormond, he remained lieutenant until his death.

York's two personal visits to Ireland are amongst the best known of late medieval chief governorships. The appointment of such a high-ranking lieutenant was well received. After his arrival at Howth in July 1449, a minimal show of force in the north and Leinster achieved, short-lived though they proved, the most impressive series of Gaelic submissions since *Richard II's expedition of 1394–5. Financial difficulties and news of political crisis in England prompted his departure at the end of August 1450, but the strength of the support York won in Ireland was proved in 1459, when he took refuge there after fleeing on 12 October from a prospective battle against a royal army near Ludlow, Shropshire. Despite his attainder for treason in England in November, a parliament at Drogheda confirmed York as lieutenant, protected him from English jurisdiction by the *declaration of 1460, and created a separate Irish coinage. The successful Yorkist invasion of England that summer was planned in Ireland.

Although York was killed in a battle at Wakefield, Yorkshire, on 30 December, the lasting sympathy in Ireland for his cause was demonstrated by the support later given to Lambert *Simnel and Perkin *Warbeck.

Johnson, P. A., *Duke Richard of York, 1411–1460* (1988)

EAEM

Young, Arthur (1741–1820), agriculturalist and writer. Born in London, the son of a clergyman, he began his writing career in 1758, producing a variety of political pamphlets and novels. In 1763 he briefly took up farming, and in 1767 published the first of many agricultural pamphlets. In 1776, following the success of published accounts of his tours in England, he visited Ireland. The following year he returned to Mitchelstown, Co. Cork, as the agent of Lord Kingsborough. He stayed for two years, during which time he toured Ireland extensively, and collected material for *A Tour in Ireland* (1780). Described by Maria *Edgeworth as the most reliable portrait of the Irish peasantry ever printed, it remains the most widely quoted source for the social history of 18th-century Ireland. NG

Young Ireland, a romantic nationalist group active 1842–8. Initially led by Thomas *Davis, Charles Gavan *Duffy, and John Blake *Dillon, and focused on the **Nation* newspaper, the group comprised mainly middle-class graduates, from both Catholic and Protestant backgrounds, of *Trinity College, Dublin. It sought to create a non-sectarian public opinion in Ireland infused with a sense of cultural nationality, and believed it necessary to promote a national literature and to revive the *Irish language, although few practical steps were taken towards the latter objective. The group was fully involved in the *repeal campaign, but rejected Daniel *O'Connell's pragmatic overtures towards *federalists in 1844, and clashed with him over the *Queen's Colleges bill in May 1845. Davis, a convinced advocate of mixed education and a fierce critic of sectarianism within the repeal movement, failed to grasp Catholic sensitivities on this subject, while O'Connell's son John saw the group as potential rivals for the leadership of the movement.

The *Nation* group were first labelled Young Ireland in late 1844 by observers who noted similarities with romantic nationalist groups on the Continent, but the term was used pejoratively from 1845 to distinguish them from the Old Irelanders around the O'Connells. In 1846 O'Connell responded to Young Ireland criticisms of his negotiations for a new *Whig alliance by requiring members of the Repeal Association to renounce the use of force. Although Young Ireland had no plans for rebellion, they refused to accept these peace resolutions, and, with William Smith *O'Brien, they withdrew from the association on 28 July. The split was formalized with the establishment of the *Irish Confederation.

Young Ireland had little popular support outside Dublin or amongst the Catholic clergy, and was divided over its political strategy. O'Brien and Duffy hoped to attract the support of the patriotic gentry to a broad campaign against the government's famine policy, while the militants, led by John *Mitchel and inspired by James Fintan *Lalor, looked to a spontaneous peasant-led social revolution. News of the revolution in France in February 1848 helped restore some degree of unity, but the *rebellion of 1848 was an abject failure and the movement's leaders fled abroad or were *transported. Their legacy lay not in the insurrectionary fiasco of 1848, but with their success in inculcating a romantic sense of nationality into subsequent generations of Irish nationalists.

Davis, R., *The Young Ireland Movement* (1987)

PG

Zoological Gardens. In 1831 the Zoological Society of Ireland (founded 1830) opened its zoo in Dublin; the aim was to advance scientific research as well as inform and divert the public. Belfast (1934) was the first municipal zoo in the United Kingdom; it too had both scientific and leisure purposes. Belfast in the 1980s and Dublin in the 1990s reorganized, placing a stronger emphasis on conservation (especially of endangered species) and education. The Causeway Safari Park, Co. Antrim (1970–97), and the Fota Wildlife Park, Co. Cork (founded 1983), adopted a somewhat different policy by emphasizing the liberty of movement of stock. DJS

Maps

Maps

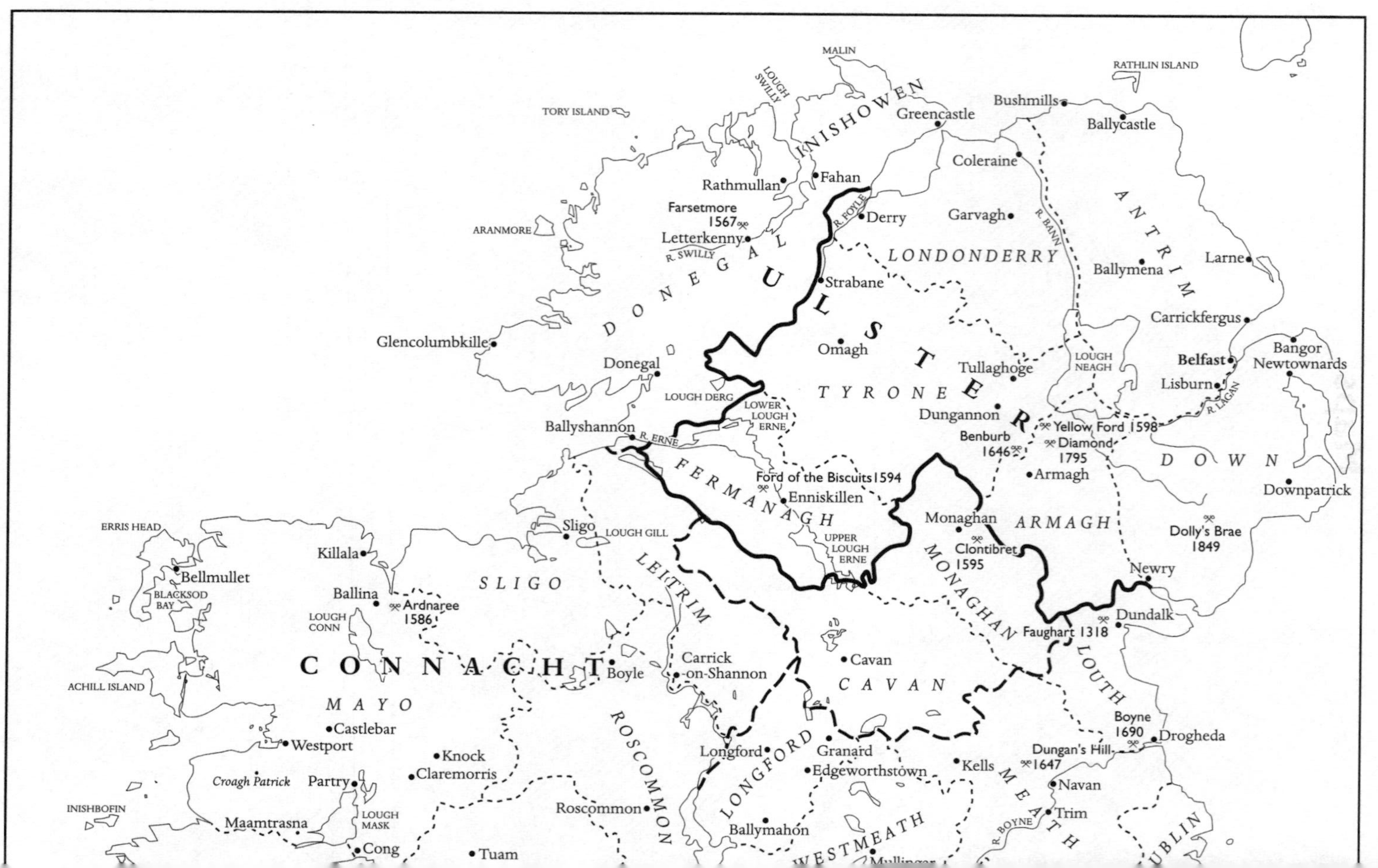

MALIN
LOUGH SWILLY
INISHOWEN
RATHLIN ISLAND
TORY ISLAND
Bushmills
Ballycastle
Greencastle
Coleraine
Fahan
Rathmullan
Farsetmore 1567
Letterkenny
R. SWILLY
ARANMORE
R. FOYLE
Derry
Garvagh
R. BANN
ANTRIM
Larne
Ballymena
LONDONDERRY
DONEGAL
ULSTER
Strabane
Carrickfergus
Glencolumbkille
Omagh
Bangor
Newtownards
Belfast
Lisburn
R. LAGAN
LOUGH NEAGH
Tullaghoge
Donegal
TYRONE
LOUGH DERG
LOWER LOUGH ERNE
Dungannon
Yellow Ford 1598
Diamond 1795
Benburb 1646
Ballyshannon
R. ERNE
DOWN
Downpatrick
FERMANAGH
Ford of the Biscuits 1594
Enniskillen
Armagh
Monaghan
ARMAGH
Dolly's Brae 1849
ERRIS HEAD
Sligo
LOUGH GILL
UPPER LOUGH ERNE
Clontibret 1595
Killala
Bellmullet
LEITRIM
Newry
SLIGO
BLACKSOD BAY
Ballina
Ardnaree 1586
MONAGHAN
Dundalk
LOUGH CONN
Faughart 1318
Carrick -on-Shannon
Cavan
CONNACHT
Boyle
ACHILL ISLAND
CAVAN
LOUTH
MAYO
Castlebar
ROSCOMMON
Boyne 1690
Drogheda
Westport
Knock
Claremorris
Longford
LONGFORD
Granard
Edgeworthstown
Kells
Dungan's Hill 1647
MEATH
Navan
Croagh Patrick
Partry
INISHBOFIN
LOUGH MASK
Roscommon
Trim
R. BOYNE
Maamtrasna
Ballymahon
WESTMEATH
DUBLIN
Cong
Tuam

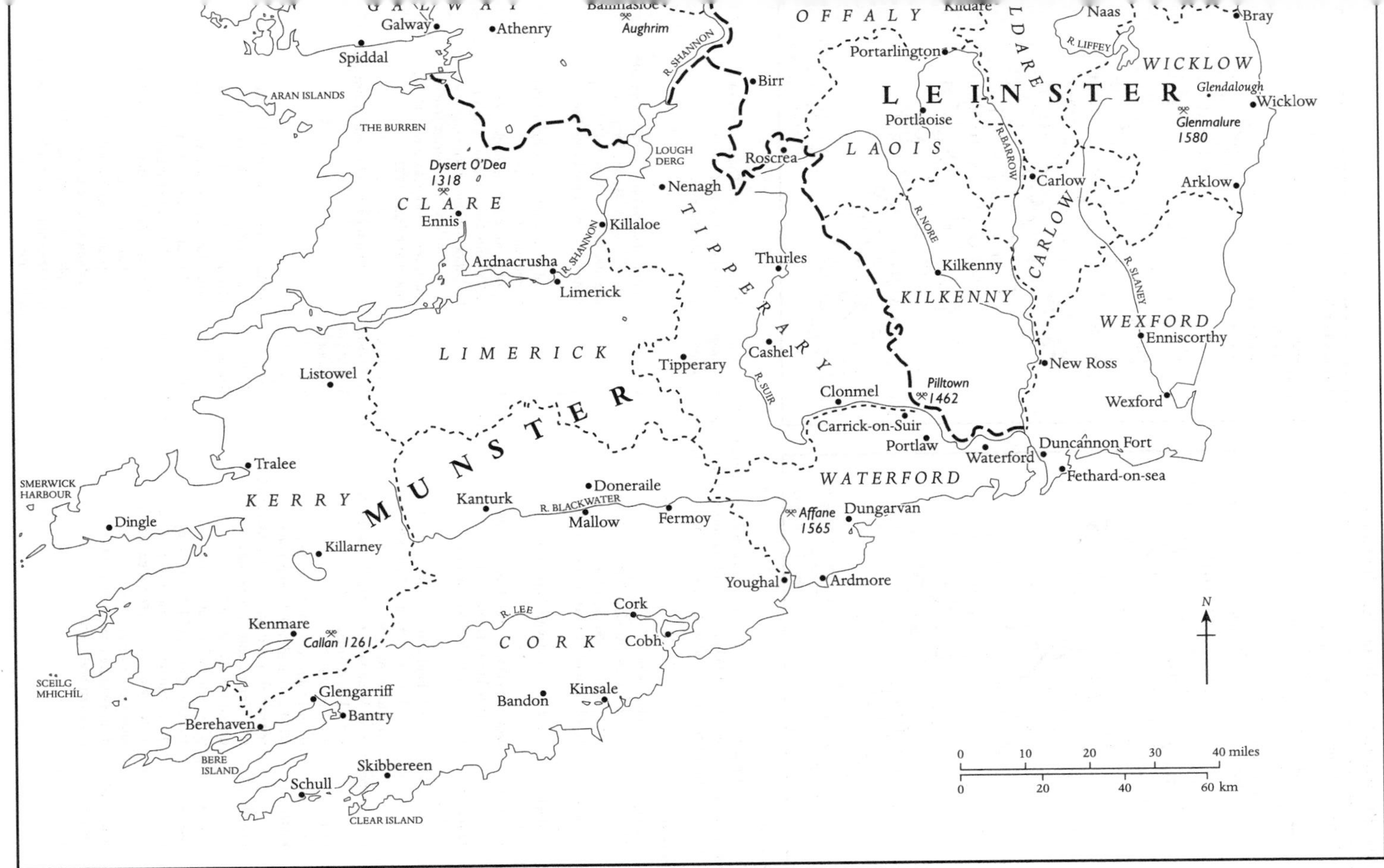

Modern Ireland, showing provinces, counties, principal towns, and other places mentioned in the text

Maps

Post-Reformation ecclesiastical divisions

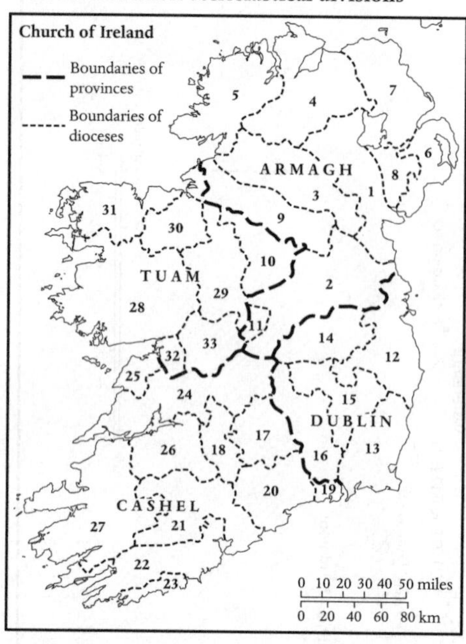

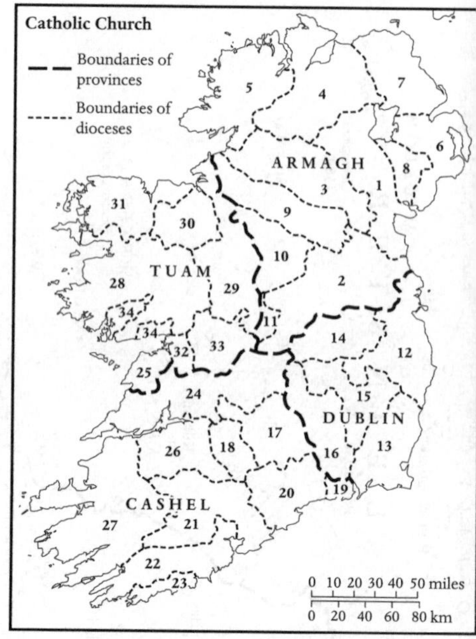

Provinces

The Church of Ireland provinces of Tuam and Cashel were abolished by the *Church Temporalities Act. The dioceses of the latter became part of the province of Dublin; those of the former became part of Armagh, with the exception of Clonfer which by this time had been united with the Cashel diocese of Killaloe, and so became part of Dublin province.

Dioceses

1	Armagh	archbishopric
2	Meath	(C of I): transferred to Dublin province, and joined to Kildare, 1976
3	Clogher	(C of I): united to Armagh 1850–86
4	Derry	
5	Raphoe	(C of I): united with Derry 1834
6	Down	
7	Connor	united to Down 1453. C of I diocese separated from Down 1944
8	Dromore	(C of I): united with Down 1842
9	Kilmore	
10	Ardagh	(C of I): held with Kilmore 1604–33, 1661–1742, with Tuam 1742–1839, united with Kilmore 1839
11	Clonmacnoise	(C of I): united with Meath 1569; (RC): united with Ardagh 1756
12	Dublin	archbishopric
13	Ferns	(C of I): united with Ossory 1835
14	Kildare	(C of I): united with Dublin 1846; separated from it and joined to Meath 1976
15	Leighlin	(RC): united with Kildare 1694; (C of I): united with Ferns 1597
16	Ossory	(C of I): joined to Cashel 1976
17	Cashel	archbishopric (C of I: to 1838 only)
18	Emly	(RC): united with Cashel 1718; (C of I): united with Cashel 1569; separated and joined to Limerick 1976
19	Waterford	(C of I): united with Cashel 1833
20	Lismore	united to Waterford 1363
21	Cloyne	united to Cork 1429; (C of I): separated from Cork 1638–52 and from 1679; reunited with Cork 1835; (RC): separated from Cork and united with Ross 1747
22	Cork	
23	Ross	(C of I): held with Cork from 1583; (RC): united with Cloyne 1747
24	Killaloe	(C of I): joined to Limerick 1976
25	Kilfenora	(RC): united with Kilmacduagh 1750 and both dioceses united with Galway 1883; (C of I): held with Limerick 1606–17, Tuam 1661–1741, Clonfert 1742–52; united to Killaloe 1752
26	Limerick	
27	Kerry (RC) Ardfert and Aghadoe (C of I)	(C of I): united with Limerick from 1661
28	Tuam	archbishopric (C of I: to 1839 only)
29	Elphin	(C of I): united with Kilmore 1841
30	Achonry	(C of I): held with Killala 1591–1607, with Cashel 1607–22, united with Killala from 1622
31	Killala	(C of I): united with Tuam 1834
32	Kilmacduagh	(C of I): held with Clonfert from 1625; (RC): united with Kilfenora 1750; both united to Galway from 1883
33	Clonfert	(C of I): united with Killaloe 1834
34	Galway	A Catholic diocese only, created in 1831 to replace the *wardenship of Galway, from 1883 united with Kilmacduagh and Kilfenora

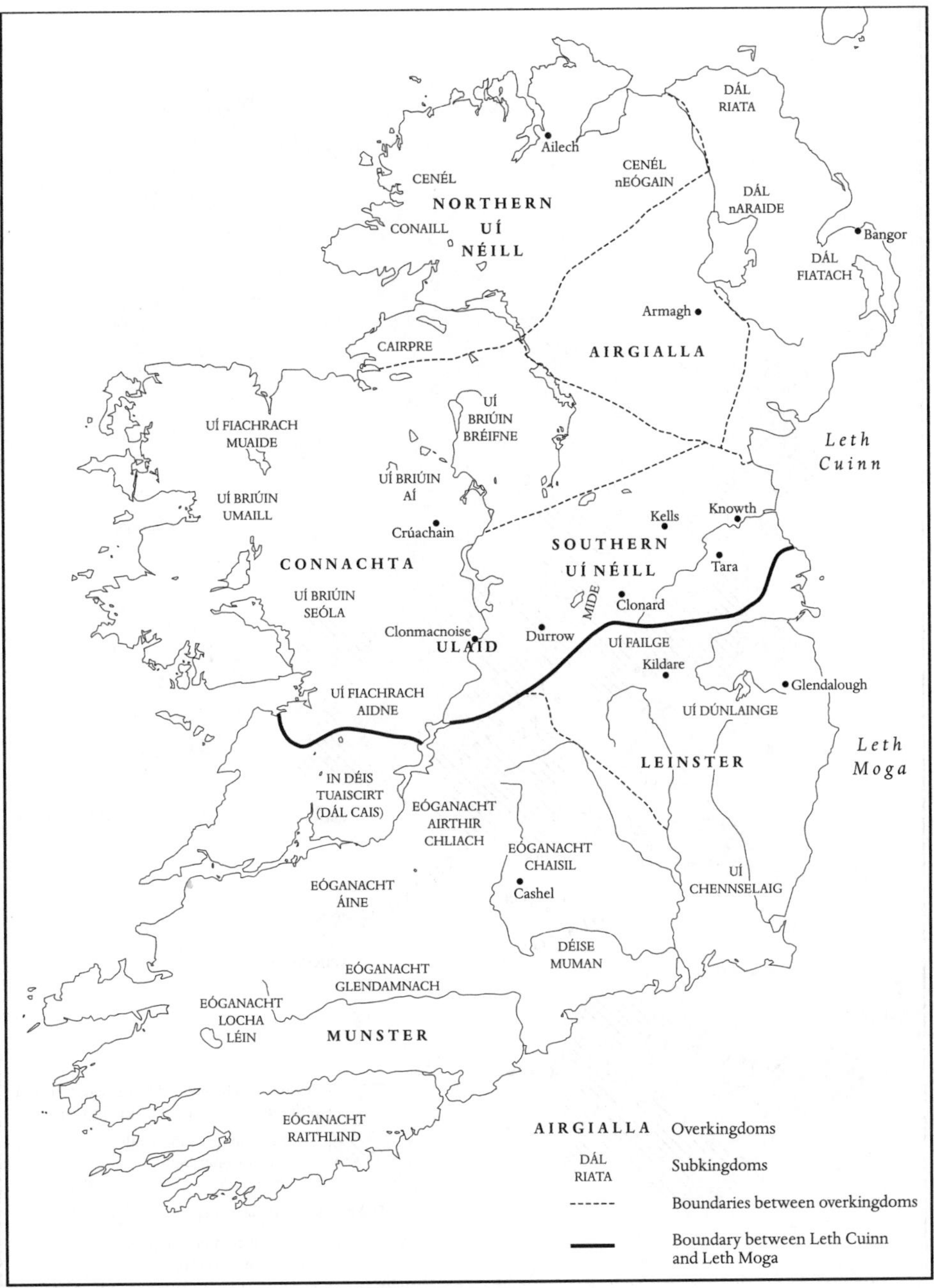
DÁL RIATA
Ailech
CENÉL nEÓGAIN
CENÉL
NORTHERN
UÍ
NÉILL
CONAILL
DÁL nARAIDE
Bangor
DÁL FIATACH
Armagh
CAIRPRE
AIRGIALLA
UÍ BRIÚIN BRÉIFNE
UÍ FIACHRACH MUAIDE
Leth Cuinn
UÍ BRIÚIN AÍ
UÍ BRIÚIN UMAILL
Crúachain
Kells
Knowth
SOUTHERN
UÍ NÉILL
Tara
CONNACHTA
UÍ BRIÚIN SEÓLA
MIDE
Clonard
Clonmacnoise
ULAID
Durrow
UÍ FAILGE
Kildare
Glendalough
UÍ FIACHRACH AIDNE
UÍ DÚNLAINGE
Leth Moga
LEINSTER
IN DÉIS TUAISCIRT (DÁL CAIS)
EÓGANACHT AIRTHIR CHLIACH
EÓGANACHT CHAISIL
Cashel
EÓGANACHT ÁINE
UÍ CHENNSELAIG
DÉISE MUMAN
EÓGANACHT GLENDAMNACH
EÓGANACHT LOCHA LÉIN
MUNSTER
EÓGANACHT RAITHLIND
AIRGIALLA Overkingdoms
DÁL RIATA Subkingdoms
Boundaries between overkingdoms
Boundary between Leth Cuinn and Leth Moga

Political divisions *c.* 800, with selected sites mentioned in text

Maps

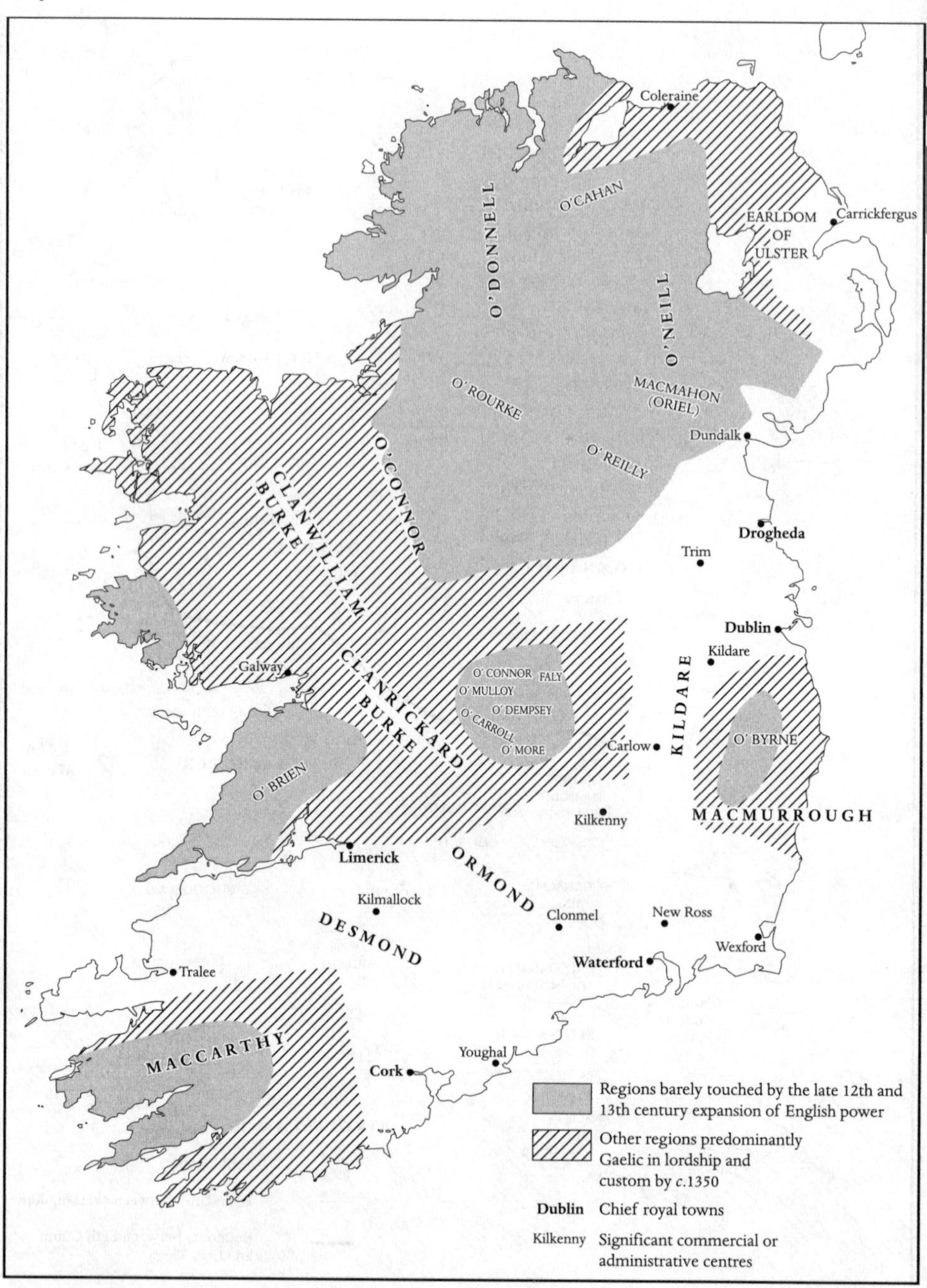

Coleraine
Carrickfergus
EARLDOM OF ULSTER
O'CAHAN
O'DONNELL
O'NEILL
MACMAHON (ORIEL)
O'ROURKE
O'REILLY
Dundalk
Drogheda
Trim
O'CONNOR
CLANWILLIAM BURKE
Dublin
Kildare
KILDARE
Galway
CLANRICKARD BURKE
O' CONNOR FALY
O' MULLOY
O' DEMPSEY
O' CARROLL
O' MORE
Carlow
O' BYRNE
O' BRIEN
Kilkenny
MACMURROUGH
Limerick
ORMOND
Kilmallock
DESMOND
Clonmel
New Ross
Wexford
Waterford
Tralee
MACCARTHY
Youghal
Cork
Regions barely touched by the late 12th and 13th century expansion of English power
Other regions predominantly Gaelic in lordship and custom by c.1350
Dublin Chief royal towns
Kilkenny Significant commercial or administrative centres

Ireland *c.* 1350

Boundaries of counties and lordships
Boundaries of lesser lordships
Boundary of Pale in statute of 1488
THE SCOTS OF THE GLENS
MACQUILLAN OF THE ROUTE
O'CAHAN
O'NEILL OF CLANDEBOYE
Carrickfergus
O'DONNELL
L. Neagh
THE GREAT O'NEILL
MAGENNIS
O'NEILL OF THE FEWS
THE ENGLISH OF ULSTER
MAGUIRE
O'ROURKE
MAGAURAN
MACMAHON
O' CONNOR OF SLIGO
MACRANNELL
O'REILLY
CO. LOUTH
MACWILLIAM BURKE OF MAYO
MACDERMOT
O' CONOR DON AND O'CONOR RUA
O'FERRALL
CO. MEATH
O' MALLEY
ENGLISH OF WESTMEATH
O'FLAHERTY
O'KELLY
IRISH OF WESTMEATH
O' CONNOR FALY
CO. KILDARE
CO. DUBLIN
O' MADDEN
O' TOOLE
CLANRICARD BURKE
O' MORE OF LEIX
O' BYRNE
CARLOW
O' BRIEN
THE IRISH OF ORMOND
ORMOND
MACMURROUGH
EARLDOM AND SUPREMACY OF ORMOND
CLANWILLIAM BURKE
O' MORCHOE
O' CONNOR KERRY
CO. WEXFORD
POERS
EARLDOM AND SUPREMACY OF DESMOND
MACCARTHY
MACCARTHY
O' SULLIVAN MÓR
O' SULLIVAN BEARE
0 10 20 30 40 50 miles
0 20 40 60 80 km

Ireland in the later 15th century showing boundaries of lordships

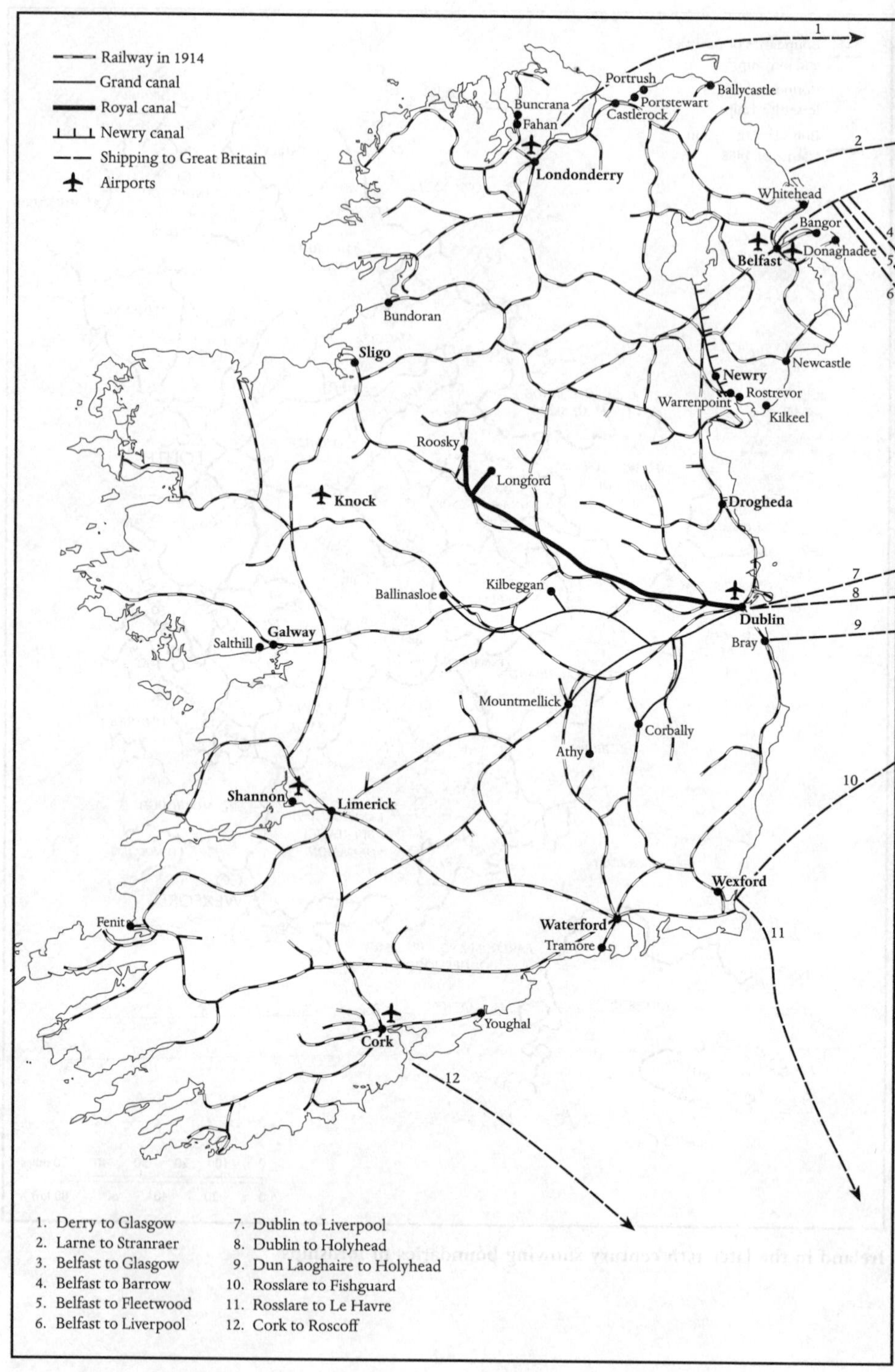

Transport and communications

Subject Index

These references are to **headwords**. General entries are followed by more specific ones, then by names of relevant individuals.